KU-444-026

C · H · I · L · D
DEVELOPMENT

Sixth Edition

C · H · I · L · D
DEVELOPMENT

John W. Santrock
University of Texas, Dallas

WCB Brown & Benchmark
PUBLISHERS

Madison, Wisconsin · Dubuque, Iowa

Book Team

Editor *Michael Lange*
Developmental Editor *Sheralee Connors*
Production Editor *Jayne Klein*
Designers *K. Wayne Harms/Gail Ryan*
Art Editor *Rachel Imsland*
Photo Editor *Carol A. Judge*
Permissions Coordinator *Karen L. Storlie*
Visuals/Design Developmental Consultant *Marilyn A. Phelps*
Visuals/Design Freelance Specialist *Mary L. Christianson*
Publishing Services Specialist *Sherry Padden*
Marketing Manager *Steven Yetter*
Advertising Manager *Brett Apold*

WCB Brown & Benchmark

A Division of Wm. C. Brown Communications, Inc.

Executive Vice President/General Manager *Thomas E. Doran*
Vice President/Editor in Chief *Edgar J. Laube*
Vice President/Sales and Marketing *Eric Ziegler*
Director of Production *Vickie Putman Caughron*
Director of Custom and Electronic Publishing *Chris Rogers*

Wm. C. Brown Communications, Inc.

President and Chief Executive Officer *G. Franklin Lewis*
Corporate Senior Vice President and Chief Financial Officer *Robert Chesterman*
Corporate Senior Vice President and President of Manufacturing *Roger Meyer*

Cover Credit © Tom Rosenthal/Superstock
Copyedited by Marilyn Frey

The credits section for this book begins on page 583 and is considered an extension of the copyright page.

Copyright © 1978, 1982, 1987, 1989, 1992, 1994 by Wm. C. Brown Communications, Inc. All rights reserved

A Times Mirror Company

Library of Congress Catalog Card Number: 93–71123

ISBN 0–697–14512–3 (paper)
      0–697–14511–5 (casebound)

No part of this publication may be reproduced, stored in a retrieval system, or transmitted, in any form or by any means, electronic, mechanical, photocopying, recording, or otherwise, without the prior written permission of the publisher.

Printed in the United States of America by Wm. C. Brown Communications, Inc., 2460 Kerper Boulevard, Dubuque, IA 52001

10 9 8 7 6 5 4 3 2

With special appreciation to my wife Mary Jo, my children Tracy and Jennifer, and my granddaughter Jordan.

BRIEF CONTENTS

CONTENTS

SECTION ONE

The Nature of Child Development 3

CHAPTER 1

Introduction 5

We reach backward to our parents and forward to our children and through their children to a future we will never see, but about which we need to care.

—Carl Jung

PERSPECTIVES ON PARENTING AND EDUCATION

Thinking about Your Future as a Parent and the Education of Your Children 27

CHAPTER 2

The Science of Child Development 33

There is nothing quite so practical as a good theory.

—Kurt Lewin, Psychologist, 1890–1947

PERSPECTIVES ON PARENTING AND EDUCATION

*An Important Mesosystem Connection:
Family and School 63*

SECTION TWO

*Biological Processes, Physical Development,
and Perceptual Development 71*

CHAPTER 3

Biological Beginnings 73

There are one hundred and ninety-three living species of
monkeys and apes. One hundred and ninety-two of them
are covered with hair. The exception is the naked ape self-
named, Homo sapiens.

—Desmond Morris

PERSPECTIVES ON PARENTING AND EDUCATION

The Effects of Early Intervention on Intelligence 94

CHAPTER 4

Prenatal Development and Birth 99

The history of man for nine months preceding his birth
would, probably, be far more interesting, and contain
events of greater moment than all three score and ten
years that follow it.

—Samuel Taylor Coleridge

CHAPTER 12

The Self and Identity 351

*Explore thyself. Herein are demanded the eye and the
nerve.*

—Henry David Thoreau

CHAPTER 13

Gender 375

*It is fatal to be man or woman pure and simple; one must
be woman-manly or man-womanly.*

—Virginia Woolf

CHAPTER 14

Moral Development 401

*It is one of the beautiful
compensations of this life that no
one can sincerely try to help
another without helping himself.*

—Charles Dudley Warner, 1873

PERSPECTIVES ON PARENTING AND EDUCATION

A Comprehensive Approach to Moral Education 426

SECTION FIVE

Social Contexts of Development 431

CHAPTER 15

Families 433

There's no vocabulary for love within a family,
love that's lived in but not looked at,
love within the light of which all else is seen,
the love within which all other love finds speech.
This love is silent.

—T. S. Eliot

PERSPECTIVES ON PARENTING AND EDUCATION

The Goals of Caregiving 461

CHAPTER 16

Peers, Play, and the Media 467

The little ones leaped, and shouted, and
Laugh'd and all the hills echoed.

—William Blake

CHAPTER 17

Schools 495

The world rests on the breath of the children in the schoolhouse.

—The *Talmud*

PERSPECTIVES ON PARENTING AND EDUCATION

*The Role of Parenting in Young Children's Learning
and Education 517*

CONCEPT TABLES

EXPLORATIONS IN CHILD DEVELOPMENT

SOCIOCULTURAL WORLDS OF CHILDREN

PERSPECTIVES ON PARENTING AND EDUCATION

PREFACE

This book is the sixth edition of *Child Development*. The six editions span almost two decades. The journey through childhood, if anything, grows in fascination for me. It is an exciting time to study and write about children's development. Scholars around the world are making new discoveries and developing new insights about virtually every domain of child development at a much faster pace than in previous decades. The field of child development is also maturing to the point at which the knowledge that is being gained can be applied to children's lives to improve their adaptation, health, and well-being.

The sixth edition of *Child Development* continues to follow a topical format. The core knowledge of the field has been retained, but, as in the fifth edition, I carefully added to, subtracted from, integrated, and simplified the material for this sixth edition of the book. The significant changes involve updating the research knowledge base that is the foundation of what we know about children's development and considerably expanding the applications of what we know about child development to the real lives of children.

SECTION AND CHAPTER CHANGES IN THE SIXTH EDITION OF *CHILD DEVELOPMENT*

One important change in the organization of the sixth edition of *Child Development* is the division of social and personality development (Section Four in the fifth edition) into two sections. In the sixth edition, Section Four is now Socioemotional Development and the Self with chapters on attachment, temperament, and emotional development; the self and identity; gender; and moral development. Section Five in the sixth edition is Social Contexts of Development with chapters on families; peers, play, and the media; and schools. This change was necessitated by the increased interest in children's emotional development and family processes, both of which receive expanded coverage in the sixth edition with this new format.

Also, in the fifth edition, temperament was presented in chapter 3 (Biological Beginnings). In the sixth edition, temperament is discussed in chapter 11 (Attachment, Temperament, and Emotional Development). This change allows for greater coverage of genetic issues in chapter 3 of the sixth edition.

Another change involves the movement of methods to chapter 2 and a more streamlined presentation of theories in that chapter to accommodate the methods discussion. This allows expanded coverage of contemporary and developmental issues in chapter 1. It also provides a more cohesive, integrated portrayal of the main themes of a science of child development—theories and methods—in a single chapter.

The epilogue in the sixth edition has been greatly expanded. It now includes two main parts: 1) Themes in Children's Development (an overview of main topics and issues in the book); and 2) The Journey of Childhood (a photojournalistic essay that conveys the power, beauty, and complexity of children's development).

Other highlights and changes in the sixth edition of *Child Development* include increased and updated coverage of culture, ethnicity, and gender; families and parenting; health and well-being; and many other content areas.

Another change in the book's sixth edition is the replacement of the summary outline at the end of each chapter with a section called Conclusions. The Conclusions section briefly highlights the main topics that have been covered in the chapter and reminds students to again read the concept tables for an overall summary of the chapter. This change eliminates the redundancy of information that appeared in the book's fifth edition—an almost exact repetition of the second concept table and the second half of the summary.

SCIENCE AND RESEARCH

Above all else, the sixth edition of *Child Development* is an extremely up-to-date presentation of research in the three primary domains of child development: Biological processes, cognitive processes, and socioemotional processes. Research on biological, cognitive, and socioemotional development continues to represent the core of the book. This core includes classic and leading-edge research. Approximately 30% of the references in the sixth edition of *Child Development* are new. More than 250 come from 1993, 1994, and in-press sources.

APPLICATIONS

I hope that students not only have a much better understanding of the scientific basis of child development when they complete this book, but also increase their wisdom about practical applications to the real lives of children. The increased emphasis on applications appears throughout the book. It also is present in a new feature that appears at the end of every chapter: *Perspectives on Parenting and Education.*

WRITING AND PEDAGOGY

I continue to strive to make this book more student-friendly. I have explored alternative ways of presenting ideas and continue to ask college students of all ages to give me feedback on which strategies are most effective. Covering all of child development's many topics in one book and in one course is a challenging task. To incorporate the basic core knowledge of the field of child development, present the latest advancements on the scientific front, and describe practical applications in different domains of children's lives require very careful evaluation of what to include in a book of this nature (as well as what to exclude), and how to include it.

This challenging task requires clear writing and a very usable pedagogical system. In writing both the fifth and the sixth editions of *Child Development*, I rewrote virtually every paragraph and section—adding, subtracting, integrating, and simplifying. This book also has an extensive, very effective pedagogical system that will improve student learning. The key features of this learning system will be presented shortly in a "visual" preface for students.

MOTIVATION

Students learn best when they are highly motivated and interested in what they are reading and experiencing. It is important to be motivated right from the start, so each chapter of the book begins with a high-interest piece called *Images of Children* that should motivate students to read the chapters. For example, the images introduction for chapter 13, Gender, focuses on tomorrow's gender worlds for today's children. The increased applications to the real lives of children in the sixth edition should also motivate student interest. I also tried to communicate the discoveries in the field of child development with energy and enthusiasm. And when I introduced a concept, I tried to provide lively examples of it. I also personally chose virtually every photograph in this book because I believe the combination of the right photograph with the right words helps to improve student motivation and learning. I also extensively participated in the design of this book and created a number of visual figures that combine photographs with figure information or summaries of concepts because I also believe these enhance student learning and motivation. We also know that learning is facilitated when the learner is in a good mood—to that end, cartoons appear where appropriate in every chapter.

In summary, I have tried to convey the complex *and* exciting story of how children develop and how they become who they are in a manner that is both informative and enjoyable. If students are bored with this book, and don't feel they have con-

siderably more knowledge about both the scientific and applied worlds of children's development upon finishing it, then I will have not reached the goals I set for the sixth edition of this book.

OTHER HIGHLIGHTS AND CHANGES IN THE SIXTH EDITION

Other highlights and changes in the sixth edition of *Child Development* include increased and updated coverage of culture, ethnicity, and gender; health and well-being; families and parenting; and many other content areas. I also moved the discussion of methods to chapter 2 and streamlined the presentation of theories in that chapter to accommodate the methods discussion. This allowed me to expand the discussion of contemporary and developmental issues in chapter 1. It also provides a cohesive, integrated presentation of the main themes of a science of child development—theories and methods—in a single chapter. The epilogue—Children: The Future of Society—has been greatly expanded. It now includes two main parts: 1) Themes in Children's Development (an overview of main themes and issues in the book); and 2) The Journey of Childhood (a photojournalistic essay that conveys the power, beauty, and complexity of children's development). Another change in the book's sixth edition is the replacement of the summary outline at the end of the chapter with a section called Conclusions. The Conclusions section briefly highlights the main topics that have been covered in the chapter and reminds students to again read the concept tables for an overall summary of the chapter.

SUPPLEMENTARY MATERIALS

The publisher and ancillary team have worked together to produce an outstanding integrated teaching package to accompany *Child Development*. The authors of the ancillaries are all experienced teachers of the child development course. The ancillaries have been designed to make it as easy as possible to customize the entire package to meet the unique needs of professors and students.

The key to this teaching package, the *Instructor's Course Planner*, was created by Janet A. Simons of the University of Iowa. This flexible planner provides a variety of useful tools to enhance teaching efforts, reduce workload, and increase enjoyment. For each chapter of the text, the planner provides a summary outline, learning objectives, key terms, research projects, classroom activities, discussion topics, mini-lecture topics, essay questions, and a transparency guide. The planner also contains a section on "Ethical Practices in Research with Human Subjects" and a chapter-by-chapter film and videotape list. The *Instructor's Course Planner* is conveniently housed within an attractive 11″ × 13″ × 9″ carrying case. This case is designed to accommodate the complete ancillary package by containing each chapter's material within a separate hanging file, allowing instructors to keep all their class materials organized at their fingertips.

The *Test Item File* was constructed by Grace Galliano of Kennesaw State College. Grace is an experienced, award-winning teacher who has offered workshops on test item construction at teaching conferences across the country. This comprehensive test book includes over 1,700 new multiple-choice test questions that are keyed to the text and learning objectives. Each item is also designated as factual, conceptual, or applied based upon the first three levels of Bloom's *Taxonomy of Educational Objectives.*

The *Student Study Guide* was also prepared by Janet Simons of the University of Iowa. For each chapter of the text, students are provided a summary outline, learning objectives, a fill-in-the-blank guided review, key terms, a "This 'N That" section consisting of crossword puzzles and anagrams, two sets of 20 multiple-choice items for self-testing, and questions to encourage critical thinking. The guide also contains a section on "How to Study Effectively and Efficiently" and another on "Ethical Practices in Research with Human Subjects." The students are also provided the list of research projects that appears in the *Instructor's Course Planner.*

The *Brown & Benchmark Developmental Psychology Transparency/Slide Set* consists of 100 acetate transparencies or slides. These full-color illustrations include graphics from various outside sources. Created by Lynne Blesz Vestal, these transparencies were expressly designed to provide comprehensive coverage of all major topic areas generally covered in developmental psychology. A comprehensive annotated guide provides a brief description for each transparency and helpful suggestions for use in the classroom.

The *Brown & Benchmark Customized Reader* allows instructors to select from a menu of over 100 journal or magazine articles provided by Brown & Benchmark sales representatives. These readings will be custom printed for students and bound into an attractive 8 ¼″ × 11″ book, giving instructors the opportunity to create their own student reader.

The questions in the *Test Item File* are available on *MicroTest III*, a powerful but easy-to-use test generating program by Chariot Software Group. MicroTest is available for DOS, Windows, and Macintosh personal computers. With MicroTest, an instructor can easily view and select the *Test Item File* questions, then print a test and answer key. You can customize questions, headings, and instructions; you can add or import questions of your own; and you can print your test in a choice of fonts if your printer supports them. Diskettes are available through a local Brown & Benchmark sales representative or by phoning Educational Resources. The package contains complete instructions for making up an exam.

Selections from the *Brown & Benchmark Psychology Videotape Library* are available free to adopters of Brown & Benchmark texts. Video policies vary between texts and depend on the number of texts adopted. Please contact your Brown & Benchmark sales representative to determine the policy for your adoption situation.

ACKNOWLEDGMENTS

The sixth edition of this book has benefited from a carefully selected board of reviewers, who provided in-depth reviews based on their experience as instructors of child development courses. For their generous help and countless good ideas, I would like to thank:

William H. Barber, *Midwestern State University*

Kathryn Norcross Black, *Purdue University*

Beverly B. Dupré, *Southern University at New Orleans*

L. Sidney Fox, *California State University–Long Beach*

Sheryll Mennicke, *Concordia College, St. Paul*

Dorothy Justus Sluss, *Virginia Polytechnic Institute and State University*

Kimberlee L. Whaley, *Ohio State University*

Belinda M. Wholeben, *Northern Illinois University*

I also remain indebted to the following individuals, who reviewed previous editions and whose helpful guidance has been carried forward into the current edition of this text:

Ruth L. Ault, *Davidson College*

Michael Bergmire, *Jefferson College*

David Bernhardt, *Carleton University*

Elaine Blakemore, *Indiana University*

Susan Bland, *Niagara County Community College*

Maureen Callahan, *Webster University*

Theodore Chandler, *Kent State University*

Audrey E. Clark, *California State University, Northridge*

Debra E. Clark, *SUNY–Cortland*

Robert C. Coon, *Louisiana State University*

Roger W. Coulson, *Iowa State University*

Denise M. DeZolt, *Kent State University*

Daniel R. DiSalvi, *Kean College*

Diane C. Draper, *Iowa State University*

Claire Etaugh, *Bradley University*

Dennis T. Farrell, *Luzerne County Community College*

Saul Feinman, *University of Wyoming*

Jane Goins Flanagan, *Lamar University*

Janet Fuller, *Mansfield University*

Irma Galejs, *Iowa State University*

Colleen Gift, *Highland Community College*

Margaret S. Gill, *Kutztown State College*

Donald E. Guenther, *Kent State University*

Robert A. Haaf, *University of Toledo*

Elizabeth Hasson, *Westchester University*

Rebecca Heikkinen, *Kent State University*

Stanley Hensen, *Arkansas Technical University*

Seth Kalichman, *Loyola University*

Kenneth Kallio, *SUNY–Geneseo*

Daniel W. Kee, *California State University, Fullerton*

Melvyn B. King, *SUNY–Cortland*

John W. Kulig, *Northern Illinois University*

Daniel K. Lapsley, *University of Notre Dame*

Dottie McCrossen, *University of Ottawa*

Carolyn Meyer, *Lake Sumter Community College*

Dalton Miller-Jones, *NE Foundation for Children*

Jose E. Nanes, *University of Minnesota*

Sherry J. Neal, *Oklahoma City Community College*

Daniel J. O'Neill, *Bristol Community College*

Robert Pasnak, *George Mason University*

Cosby Steele Rogers, *Virginia Polytechnic Institute & State University*

Douglas B. Sawin, *University of Texas, Austin*

Ed Scholwinski, *Southwest Texas State University*

Bill M. Seay, *Louisiana State University*

Matthew J. Sharps, *University of Colorado*

Marilyn Shea, *University of Maine, Farmington*

Mark S. Strauss, *University of Pittsburgh*

Cherie Valeithian, *Kent State University*

The quality of this text is greatly due to the ideas and insights of many other colleagues. I would like to thank the following individuals for sharing their thoughts and beneficial suggestions for improving *Child Development:*

Stewart R. Beasley, *Central State University*
Phil Brown, *College of Eastern Utah*
William J. Cumes, *University of Calgary*
Philip S. Dale, *University of Washington*
Coralie Dietrich, *University of Wisconsin*
John Durkin, *University of Victoria*
Francene Evans, *Worthington Community College*
Nancie Lobb, *Alvin Community College*
Daniel Lynch, *University of Wisconsin*
Chloe Merrill, *Weber State College*
Elizabeth Pemberton, *University of Iowa*
Bridgett Perry, *Framingham State College*
Ann A. Rhodes, *Arkansas College*
Amy Tolson, *Delta College*
Hope Underwood, *University of Wisconsin*
Marcia Weinstein, *Salem State College*
Eileen Wood, *Wilfrid Laurier University*

A final note of thanks goes to my family. Mary Jo Santrock has lived through sixth editions of *Child Development,* and I appreciate the support and encouragement she has given to my writing. My daughters have provided me with firsthand experience at watching children develop. Tracy was 7 and Jennifer was 5 when the first edition of *Child Development* was published. Now Tracy is 27 and Jennifer is 24. Through these years, they have helped me render a treatment of children's development that captures its complexity, its subtlety, and its humanity.

TO THE STUDENT

HOW THE LEARNING SYSTEM WORKS

This book contains a number of learning devices, each of which presents the field of child development in a meaningful way. The learning devices in *Child Development* will help you learn the material more effectively.

Chapter Outlines

Each chapter begins with an outline, showing the organization of topics by heading levels. The outline functions as an overview to the arrangement and structure of the chapter.

Images of Children

Opening each chapter is an imaginative, high-interest piece, focusing on a topic related to the chapter's content.

Preview

This brief section describes the chapter's main points.

Visual Figures and Tables

These include both a description of important content information and photographs that illustrate the content. They review and summarize important theories and ideas contained in the text.

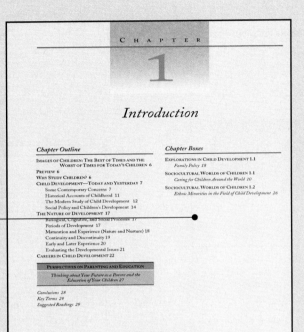

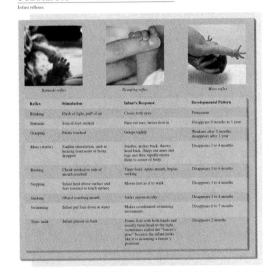

Critical Thinking Questions

Critical Thinking Questions appear three or more times in every chapter. These questions will challenge you to think more deeply about the contents of the chapters.

Concept Tables

Two times in each chapter we review what has been discussed so far in that chapter by displaying the information in concept tables. This learning device helps you get a handle on material several times a chapter so you don't wait until the end of the chapter and have too much information to digest.

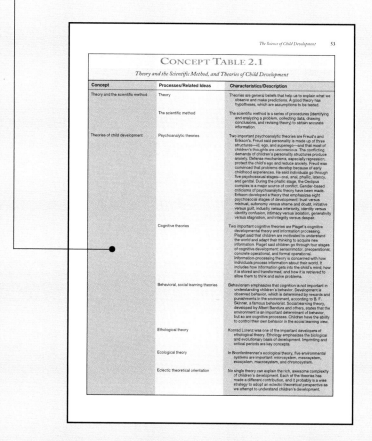

Photographs and Legends

Special attention was given to the selection of photographs for *Child Development*. In a number of places, experts on child development sent photographs to be included in the text. Legends were carefully written to clarify and elaborate concepts.

Sociocultural Worlds of Children Boxes

Child Development gives special attention to the cultural, ethnic, and gender worlds of children. Each chapter has one or more boxed inserts that highlight the sociocultural dimensions of life-span development.

Perspectives on Parenting and Education

This chapter endpiece highlights applications to parenting and education that encourages critical thinking about ways to improve children's well-being.

Explorations in Child Development Boxes

Explorations in Child Development boxes provide additional coverage of a wide variety of topics and issues related to children's development. Each chapter has one or more boxed inserts.

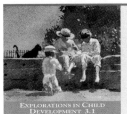

Conclusions

At the end of each chapter, a section called Conclusions helps you to review the main ideas of the entire chapter.

Key Term Definitions

Key terms appear in boldface type with their definitions immediately following in italic type. This provides you with a clear understanding of important concepts.

Key Terms

Listed at the end of each chapter are key terms that are defined throughout the chapter. They are listed and defined again here and in a glossary at the end of the book.

Suggested Readings

At the end of each chapter, suggested further readings are briefly described. Special attention was given to selecting both research and applied practical readings.

Life for My Child Is Simple, and Is Good

Life for my child is simple, and is good.

He knows his wish. Yes, but that is not all.

Because I know mine too.

And we both want joy of undeep and unabiding things,

Like kicking over a chair or throwing blocks out of a window

Or tipping over an icebox pan

Or snatching down curtains or fingering an electric outlet

Or a journey or a friend or an illegal kiss.

No. There is more to it than that.

It is that he has never been afraid.

Rather, he reaches out and lo the chair falls with a beautiful crash,

And the blocks fall, down on the people's heads,

And the water comes slooshing sloppily out across the floor.

And so forth.

Not that success, for him, is sure, infallible.

But never has he been afraid to reach.

His lesions are legion.

But reaching is his rule.

—Gwendolyn Brooks

Gwendolyn Brooks (1917–) is a Pulitzer prize-winning poet and novelist. One of the most respected of contemporary poets, she is rooted in the Black experience and her childhood in Chicago, but her appeal, as this poem reveals, stretches across the full range of human experience.

The Nature of Child Development

In every child who is born, under no matter what circumstances, and of no matter what parents, the potentiality of the human race is born again.

—James Agee

Examining the shape of childhood allows us to understand it better. Every childhood is distinct, the first chapter of a new biography in the world. This book is about children's development—its universal features, its individual variations, its nature as we move ever closer to the twenty-first century. *Child Development* is about the rhythm and meaning of children's lives, about turning mystery into understanding, and about weaving together a portrait of who each of us was, is, and will be. In Section One you will read two chapters: Introduction (chapter 1) and The Science of Child Development (chapter 2).

Girl with a Dove, Pablo
Picasso (Detail)

1

Introduction

Chapter Outline

PERSPECTIVES ON PARENTING AND EDUCATION

Chapter Boxes

*We reach backward to our parents and
forward to our children and through
their children to a future we will never
see, but about which we need to care.*
—Carl Jung

Children are on a different plane. They belong to a generation and way of feeling properly their own.

—George Santayana

IMAGES OF CHILDREN

The Best of Times and the Worst of Times for Today's Children

It is both the best of times and the worst of times for today's children. Their world possesses powers and perspectives inconceivable 50 years ago: computers, longer life expectancies, the ability to reach out to the entire planet through television, satellites, air travel. So much knowledge, though, can be chaotic, even dangerous. School curricula have been adapted to teach students new topics—AIDS, suicide, drug and alcohol abuse, incest. Children want to trust, but the world has become an untrustworthy place. The sometimes-fatal temptations of the adult world sometimes descend upon children so early that their ideals become tarnished. Crack cocaine is a far more addictive and deadly substance than marijuana, the drug of an earlier generation. Strange depictions of violence and sex come flashing out of the television set and lodge in the minds of children. The messages are powerful and contradictory: Rock videos suggest orgiastic sex. Public health officials counsel safe sex. Oprah Winfrey and Phil Donahue conduct seminars on lesbian nuns, exotic drugs, transsexual surgery, serial murders. Television pours a bizarre version of reality into children's imaginations. In New York City, two 5-year-olds argue about whether there is a Santa Claus and what Liberace died of. In New Orleans, a first-grader shaves a piece of chalk and passes the dust around the classroom, acting as if it is cocaine.

Every stable society transmits values from one generation to the next. That is civilization's work. In today's world, the transmission of values is not easy. Parents are raising children in a world far removed from Ozzie and Harriet's era of the 1950s, when two of three American families consisted of a breadwinner (the father), a caregiver (the mother), and the children they were raising. Today fewer than one in five families fits that description. Phrases like "quality time" have found their way into the American vocabulary. A motif of absence plays in the lives of many children. It may be an absence of authority and limits or an absence of emotional commitment (Morrow, 1988).

PREVIEW

By examining the shape of childhood, we can understand it better. This book is a window into the nature of children's development—your own and every other child of the human species. In this first chapter, you will be introduced to some ideas about why we should study children, contemporary concerns about child development, and a historical perspective on children's development. You will learn what development is and what issues are raised by a developmental perspective on children.

WHY STUDY CHILDREN?

Why study children? Perhaps you are or will be a parent or teacher. Responsibility for children is or will be a part of your everyday life. The more you learn about children, the better you can deal with them. Perhaps you hope to gain some insight into your own history—as an infant, as a child, and as an adolescent. Perhaps you just stumbled onto this course thinking that it sounded interesting and that the topic of child development would raise some provocative and intriguing issues about how human beings grow and develop. Whatever your reasons, you will discover that the study of child development *is* provocative, *is* intriguing, and *is* filled with information about who we are and how we grew to be this way.

As you might imagine, understanding children's development, and our own personal journey through childhood, is a rich and complicated undertaking. You will discover that various experts approach the study of children in many different ways and ask many different questions. Amid this richness and complexity we seek a simple answer: to understand how children change as they grow up and the forces that contribute to this change.

What are some of these changes? Children grow in size and weight. They learn to stand, walk, and run. They learn to read, to write, and to solve math problems. They learn behaviors and roles that society considers acceptable for "girls," "boys," "women," and, "men." They learn the necessity of curbing their will and develop an understanding of what is morally acceptable or unacceptable. They learn how to communicate and to get along with many different people. Their families—parents and siblings—are very important influences in their lives, but their growth also is shaped by successive choirs of friends, teachers, and strangers. In their most pimply and awkward moments as adolescents, they become acquainted with sex and try on one face after another, searching for an identity they can call their own. These are but a few of the fascinating changes that take place as children develop—many more await you in this text.

In a sense, then, the modern study of child development is concerned with the same matters that we, as ordinary people, might want to understand if and when we raise our own sons and daughters; teach children in school; or try to get along with children as brothers or sisters, aunts or uncles. Whatever the context, though, it will help us immensely to understand precisely how children change.

CHILD DEVELOPMENT— TODAY AND YESTERDAY

Everywhere an individual turns in contemporary society, the development and well-being of children capture public attention, the interest of scientists, and the concern of policymakers. Through history, though, interest in the development of children has been uneven.

Some Contemporary Concerns

Consider some of the topics you read about in the newspapers and magazines every day: contemporary changes in the family, educational reform, sociocultural issues such as the changing status of ethnic minority groups and gender roles. What the experts are discovering is that each of these areas has direct and significant consequences for understanding children and for our decisions as a society on how children should be treated. An important theme of this textbook is to provide detailed, up-to-date coverage of the roles that family processes, education, and sociocultural contexts play in children's development. These topics are integrated into discussions throughout the book, and at the end of each chapter you will read a section titled "Perspectives on Parenting and Education." Every chapter also includes one or more "Sociocultural Worlds of Children" boxes that explore how culture, ethnicity, and gender impact children's lives.

Family Issues

We hear a great deal from experts and popular writers about pressures on contemporary families. The number of families in which both parents work is increasing; at the same time, the number of one-parent families has risen over the past two decades as a result of a climbing divorce rate. With more children being raised by single parents or by parents who are both working, the time parents have to spend with their children is being squeezed and the quality of child care is of concern to many (Burgess, 1993). Are working parents better using the decreased time with their children? Do day-care arrangements provide high-quality alternatives for parents? How troubled should we be about the increasing number of latchkey children—those at home alone after school, waiting for their parents to return from work? Answers to these questions can be formed by several different kinds of information obtained by experts in child development. This information comes from studies of the way working parents use the time with their children and the nature of their parenting approaches and behaviors, studies of the way various day-care arrangements influence children's social and intellectual growth in relation to home-care arrangements, and examination of the consequences of a child being without adult supervision for hours every day after school (Davies, 1993; Kontos & Dunn, 1993; Field, in press; McCartney & others, 1993).

Education

During the past several years, the American educational system has come under attack (Holtzman, 1992). A national commission appointed by the Office of Education concluded that our children are poorly prepared for the increasingly complex future they will be asked to face in our society. The problems are legion—declining skills of those entering the teaching profession, adolescents graduating from high school with primary-grade-level reading and mathematics skills, a shortage of qualified mathematics and science teachers, less time being spent by students in engaging academic work in their classrooms, an absence of any real signs of challenge and thinking required by school curricula, and a high dropout rate over the four years of high school. Solutions to these problems are not easy. However, in searching for solutions, policymakers repeatedly turn to experts in the field of child development because, to design an engaging curriculum, a planner must know what engages and motivates children (Gardner, 1993). To improve our national effort in teaching thinking skills, planners must understand what thinking is and how it changes across the school years (Kuhn, 1991). To understand the roots of the social difficulties encountered by so many of today's adolescents—difficulties that lead them to drop out of school in droves—planners need to understand the nature of the socialization processes involved in the transition to adolescence

FIGURE 1.1

Ethnic minority population increases in the United States. The percentage of Black American, Hispanic American, and Asian American individuals increased far more from 1980 to 1988 than did the percentage of Whites. Shown here are two Korean-born children on the day they became United States citizens. Asian American children are the fastest-growing group of ethnic minority children.

and the ways in which schools fail to address them (Entwisle & Alexander, 1992; Kuhn, 1993; Linney, 1993; Resnick, 1993; Seidman & Feinman, 1993).

Sociocultural Contexts

The tapestry of American culture has changed dramatically in recent years. Nowhere is the change more noticeable than in the increasing ethnic diversity of America's citizens (see figure 1.1). Ethnic minority groups—Black American, Hispanic

American, Native American (American Indian), and Asian, for example—made up 20 percent of all children and adolescents under the age of 17 in 1989. Projections indicate that, by the year 2000, one-third of all school-aged children will fall into this category. This changing demographic tapestry promises not only the richness that diversity produces but also difficult challenges in extending the American dream to individuals of all ethnic groups. Historically, ethnic minorities have found themselves at the bottom of the economic and social order.

They have been disproportionately represented among the poor and the inadequately educated. Half of all Black American children and one-third of all Hispanic American children live in poverty. School dropout rates for minority youth reach the alarming rate of 60 percent in some urban areas. These population trends and our nation's inability to prepare ethnic minority individuals for full participation in American life have produced an imperative for the social institutions that serve ethnic minorities (Allen & Santrock, 1993; Anderson, 1993; Comer, 1993; Ho, 1992; Marín & Marín, 1991; Padilla, 1993; Sue, 1992). Schools, social services, health and mental health agencies, juvenile probation services, and other programs need to become more sensitive to ethnic issues and to provide improved services to ethnic and minority and low-income individuals.

An especially important idea in considering the nature of ethnic minority groups is that not only is there ethnic diversity within a culture such as the United States, but there is also considerable diversity within each ethnic group (McAdoo, 1993; Trawick-Smith, 1993). All Black American children do not come from low-income families. All Hispanic American children are not members of the Catholic church. All Asian American children are not geniuses. All Native American children do not drop out of school. It is easy to make the mistake of thinking about an ethnic minority group and stereotyping its members as all being the same. Keep in mind that as we describe children from ethnic groups, each group is heterogeneous.

Sociocultural contexts of development include four important concepts: contexts, culture, ethnicity, and gender. These concepts are central to our discussion of children's development in this book so we need to clearly define them. **Context** *refers to the setting in which development occurs, a setting that is influenced by historical, economic, social, and cultural factors.* To sense how important context is in understanding children's development, consider a researcher who wants to discover whether today's children are more racially tolerant than they were a decade ago. Without reference to the historical, economic, social, and cultural aspects of race relations, the students' racial tolerance cannot be fully understood. Every child's development occurs against a cultural backdrop of contexts. These contexts or settings include homes, school, peer groups, churches, cities, neighborhoods, communities, university laboratories, the United States, China, Mexico, Japan, Egypt, and many others—each with meaningful historical, economic, social, and cultural legacies.

Three sociocultural contexts that many child development researchers believe merit special attention are culture, ethnicity, and gender. **Culture** *refers to the behavior patterns, beliefs, and all other products of a particular group of people that are passed on from generation to generation.* The products result from the interaction between groups of people and their environment over many years. A cultural group can be as large as the United States, or as small as an African hunter-gatherer group. Whatever its size, the group's culture influences the identity, learning, and social behavior of its members (Bidell, 1993; Bloom, 1992; Brislin, 1993; Cole, 1993; Lee, 1992). For example, the United States is an achievement-oriented culture

with a strong work ethic, but recent comparisons of American and Japanese children revealed that the Japanese were better at math, spent more time working on math in school, and spent more time doing homework than Americans (Stevenson, 1991, 1993).

Cross-cultural studies—*the comparison of a culture with one or more other cultures—provide information about the degree to which children's development is similar, or universal, across cultures, or to what degree it is culture-specific.* A special concern in comparing the United States with other cultures is our nation's unsatisfactory record in caring for its children. To read more about cross-cultural comparisons in caring for children turn to Sociocultural Worlds of Children 1.1.

Ethnicity *(the word "ethnic" comes from the Greek word for "nation")* is based on cultural heritage, nationality characteristics, race, religion, and language. Ethnicity is central to the development of an **ethnic identity,** *which is a sense of membership based upon the shared language, religion, customs, values, history, and race of an ethnic group.* Each of you is a member of one or more ethnic groups. Your ethnic identity reflects your deliberate decision to identify with an ancestor or ancestral group. If you are of Native American and African slave ancestry, you might choose to align yourself with the traditions and history of Native Americans, although an outsider might believe that your identity is African American.

Recently, some individuals have voiced dissatisfaction with the use of the term *minority* within the phrase *ethnic minority group.* Some individuals have also raised objections about using the term *Blacks* or *Black Americans,* preferring instead the term *African Americans* to emphasize their ancestry. What is the nature of such dissatisfaction and objections? The term *minority* has traditionally been associated with inferiority and deficits. Further, the concept of minority implies that there is a majority. Indeed, it can be argued that there really is no majority in the United States because Whites are actually composed of many different ethnic groups, and Whites are not a majority in the world. When we use the term *ethnic minority* in this text the use is intentional. Rather than implying that ethnic minority children should be viewed as inferior or deficient in some way, we want to convey the impact that minority status has had on many ethnic minority children. The circumstances of each ethnic group are not solely a function of its own culture. Rather, many ethnic groups have experienced considerable discrimination and prejudice. For example, patterns of alcohol abuse among Native American adolescents cannot be fully understood unless the exploitation that has accompanied Native Americans' history is also considered (Sue, 1990).

Our most basic link is that we all inhabit the same planet. We all breathe the same air. We all cherish our children's future.

—John F. Kennedy

A third very important aspect of sociocultural contexts that is receiving increased attention is gender (Denmark, 1993; Golombok & Fivush, 1994; Matlin, 1993; Spence, 1992;

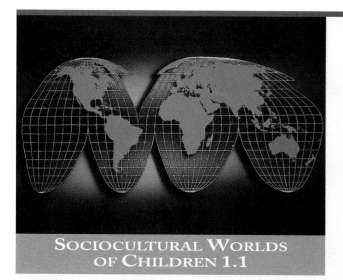

SOCIOCULTURAL WORLDS OF CHILDREN 1.1

Caring for Children Around the World

According to a report by the Children's Defense Fund (1990), the United States does not fare well in caring for children when compared with other nations. In this report, the Children's Defense Fund gave the United States an "A" for capacity to care for children but an "F" for performance on many key markers of children's well-being. Consider the following cross-cultural comparisons:

- United States 1-year-olds have lower immunization rates against polio than 1-year-olds in 14 other countries. Polio immunization rates for non-White

infants in the United States rank behind 48 other countries, including Albania, Colombia, and Jamaica.
- The United States' overall infant mortality rate lags behind 18 other countries. Our non-White infant mortality rate ranks 13th compared to other nations' overall rates. A Black American child born in inner-city Boston has less chance of surviving the first year of life than a child born in Panama, North or South Korea, or Uruguay.
- In a study of 8 industrialized nations (the United States, Switzerland, Sweden, Norway, former West Germany, Canada, England, and Australia), the United States had the highest poverty rate.
- The United States has the highest adolescent pregnancy rate of any industrialized Western nation.
- The United States and South Africa are the only industrialized countries that do not provide universal health coverage to families and child care.
- American school children know less geography than school children in Iran, less math than school children in Japan, and less science information than school children in Spain.
- The United States invests a smaller portion of its gross national product (GNP) in child health than 18 other industrialized nations. It invests a smaller portion of its GNP in education than 6 other industrialized countries.

In sum, the United States needs to devote more attention to caring for its children. Too many American children from every socioeconomic and ethnic group are neglected and are not given the opportunity to reach their full potential.

The United States does not fare well in caring for children when compared to other nations. The United States' overall infant mortality rate lags behind eighteen other countries. A Black American child born in inner-city Boston has less chance of surviving the first year of life than a child born in Panama, North or South Korea, or Uruguay. American school children know less science information than their counterparts in Spain.

Psychologist Rhoda Unger, here talking with students, urges psychologists to use the word sex *only when referring to biological mechanisms (such as sex chromosomes or sexual anatomy) and to use the word gender only when describing the social, cultural, and psychological aspects of being male or female. Like Unger, psychologist Carolyn Sherif noted some of the problems the word* sex *has brought to the study of gender. Sherif argued that the term* sex *roles uncritically couples a biological concept (sex) with a sociocultural, psychological concept (gender). Sherif stressed that through this coupling many myths about sex may be smuggled into the concept of sociocultural aspects of male and female roles, causing confusion and possible stereotyping.*

Unger, 1993). **Gender** *is the sociocultural dimension of female and male.* Sex refers to the biological dimension of being female or male. Few aspects of children's development are more central to their identity and to their social relationships than their sex or gender. Society's gender attitudes are changing. But how much? Is there a limit to how much society can determine what is appropriate behavior for male and female? These are among the provocative questions about gender we explore in *Child Development*.

Critical Thinking

Family issues, educational reform, and sociocultural issues involving culture, ethnicity, and gender are concerns in children's development. What other contemporary concerns related to children's development can you generate?

Historical Accounts of Childhood

Childhood has become such a distinct period that it is hard to imagine that it was not always thought of in that way. However, in medieval times, laws generally did not distinguish between childhood and adult offenses. After analyzing samples of art along with available publications, historian Philippe Ariès

FIGURE 1.2

These artistic impressions show how children were viewed as miniature adults earlier in history. Artists' renditions of children as miniature adults may have been too stereotypical.

(1962) concluded that European societies did not accord any special status to children prior to 1600. In the paintings, children were often dressed in smaller versions of adultlike clothing (see figure 1.2).

Were children actually treated as miniature adults with no special status in medieval Europe? Ariès' interpretation has been criticized. He primarily sampled aristocratic, idealized subjects, which led to the overdrawn conclusion that children were treated as miniature adults and not accorded any special status. In medieval times, children did often work and their emotional bond with parents may not have been as strong as it is for many children today. However, in medieval times, childhood probably was recognized as a distinct phase of life more than Ariès believed. Also, we know that, in ancient Egypt, Greece, and Rome, rich conceptions of children's development were held.

Through history, philosophers have speculated at length about the nature of children and how they should be reared. Three such philosophical views are original sin, *tabula rasa*, and innate goodness. In the **original sin view,** *especially advocated during the Middle Ages, children were perceived as basically bad, being born into the world as evil beings.* The goal of childrearing was to provide salvation, to remove sin from the child's life. Toward the end of the seventeenth century, the **tabula rasa view** *was proposed by English philosopher John Locke. He argued that children are not innately bad but instead are like a "blank tablet,"* a tabula rasa. Locke believed that childhood experiences are important in determining adult characteristics. He advised parents to spend time with their children and to help them become contributing members of society. In the eighteenth century, the **innate goodness view** *was presented by Swiss-born philosopher Jean-Jacques Rousseau, who stressed that children are inherently good.* Because children are basically good, said Rousseau, they should be permitted to grow naturally, with little parental monitoring or constraint.

In the past century and a half, our view of children has changed dramatically. We now conceive of childhood as a highly eventful and unique period of life that lays an important foundation for the adult years and is highly differentiated from them. In most approaches to childhood, distinct periods are identified, in which children master special skills and confront new life tasks. Childhood is no longer seen as an inconvenient "waiting" period during which adults must suffer the incompetencies of the young. We now value childhood as a special time of growth and change, and we invest great resources in caring for and educating our children. We protect them from the excesses of the adult work world through tough child labor laws; we treat their crimes against society under a special system of juvenile justice; and we have governmental provisions for helping children when ordinary family support systems fail or when families seriously interfere with children's well-being.

The Modern Study of Child Development

The modern era of studying children has a history that spans only a little more than a century (Cairns, 1983). This era began with some important developments in the late 1800s and extends to the current period of the 1990s. Why is this past century so special? During the past 100 years, the study of child development has evolved into a sophisticated science. A number of major theories, along with elegant techniques and methods of study, help organize our thinking about children's development. New knowledge about children—based on direct observation and testing—is accumulating at a breathtaking pace.

During the last quarter of the nineteenth century, a major shift took place—from viewing human psychology from a strictly philosophical perspective to one that includes direct observation and experimentation. Most of the influential early psychologists were trained either in the natural sciences (such as biology or medicine) or in philosophy. In the field of child development, this was true of such influential thinkers as Charles Darwin, G. Stanley Hall, James Mark Baldwin, and Sigmund Freud. The natural scientists, even then, underscored the importance of conducting experiments and collecting reliable observations of what they studied. This approach had advanced the state of knowledge in physics, chemistry, and biology; however, these scientists were not at all sure that people, much less children or infants, could be profitably studied in this way. Their hesitation was due, in part, to a lack of examples to follow in studying children. In addition, philosophers of the time debated, on both intellectual and ethical grounds, whether the methods of science were appropriate for studying people.

The deadlock was broken when some daring and entrepreneurial thinkers began to study infants, children, and adolescents, trying new methods of study. For example, near the turn of the century, French psychologist Alfred Binet invented many tasks to study attention and memory (Siegler, 1992). He used them to study his own daughters, normal children, retarded children, extremely gifted children, and adults. Eventually, he collaborated in the development of the first modern test of intelligence, which is named after him (the Binet). At about the same time, G. Stanley Hall pioneered the use of questionnaires with large groups of children and popularized the findings of earlier psychologists, whom he encouraged to do likewise. In one investigation, Hall tested 400 children in the Boston schools to find out how much they "knew" about themselves and the world, asking them such questions as "Where are your ribs?"

Later, during the 1920s, a large number of child development research centers were created (Cairns, 1983; Senn, 1975), and their professional staffs began to observe and chart a myriad of behaviors in infants and children. The centers at the Universities of Minnesota, Iowa, California at Berkeley, Columbia, and Toronto became famous for their investigations of children's play, friendship patterns, fears, aggression and conflict, and sociability. This work became closely associated with the so-called child study movement, and a new organization, The Society for Research in Child Development, was formed at about the same time.

Another ardent observer of children was Arnold Gesell. With his photographic dome, Gesell (1928) could systematically observe children's behavior without interrupting them (see figure 1.3). The direct study of children, in which investigators directly observe children's behavior, conduct experiments, or obtain information about children by questioning their parents and teachers, had an auspicious start in the work of these child study experts. The flow of information about children, based on direct study, has not slowed since that time.

Gesell not only developed sophisticated observational strategies for studying children, but he also had some provocative views on the nature of children's development. He theorized that certain characteristics of children simply "bloom" with age because of a biological, maturational blueprint. Gesell strived for precision in charting what a child is like at a specific age. Gesell's views, as well as G. Stanley Hall's, were strongly influenced by Charles Darwin's evolutionary theory (Darwin had made the scientific study of children respectable when he developed a baby journal for recording systematic observations of children). Hall (1904) believed that child development follows a natural evolutionary course that can be revealed by child study. He also theorized that child development unfolds in a stagelike fashion, with distinct motives and capabilities at each stage. Hall had much to say about adolescence, arguing that it is full of "storm and stress."

Sigmund Freud's psychoanalytic theory was prominent in the early part of the twentieth century. Freud believed that children are rarely aware of the motives and reasons for their behavior and that the bulk of their mental life is unconscious. His ideas were compatible with Hall's, emphasizing conflict and biological influences on development, although Freud did stress that a child's experiences with parents in the first 5 years of life are important determinants of later personality development.

FIGURE 1.3

Gesell's Photographic Dome. Gesell is shown inside his photographic dome with an infant. Cameras rode on metal tracks at the top of the dome and were moved as needed to record the child's activities. Others could observe from outside the dome without being seen by the child.

Freud envisioned the child moving through a series of psycho-sexual stages, filled with conflict between biological urges and the environmental demands placed on the child by society. Freud's theory has had a profound influence on the study of children's personality development and socialization, especially in the areas of gender, morality, family processes, and problems and disturbances.

During the 1920s and 1930s, John Watson's (1928) theory of behaviorism influenced thinking about children. Watson proposed a view of children very different from Freud's, arguing that children can be shaped into whatever society wishes by examining and changing the environment. One element of Watson's view, and behaviorism in general, was a strong belief in the systematic observation of children's behavior under controlled conditions. Watson had some provocative views about childrearing as well. He stressed that parents are too soft on children; quit cuddling and smiling at babies so much, he told parents.

Whereas John Watson was observing the environment's influence on children's behavior and Sigmund Freud was probing the depths of the unconscious mind to discover clues about our early experiences with our parents, others were more concerned about the development of children's conscious thoughts—that is, the thoughts of which they are aware. James Mark Baldwin was a pioneer in the study of children's thought (Cairns, 1992). **Genetic epistemology** *was the term Baldwin gave to the study of how children's knowledge changes over the course of their development.* (The term "genetic" at that time was a synonym for "development," and the term "epistemology" means the nature or study of knowledge.) Baldwin's ideas were initially proposed in the 1880s. Later, in the twentieth century, Swiss psychologist Jean Piaget adopted and elaborated on many of Baldwin's themes, keenly observing the development of thoughts in his own children and devising clever experiments to investigate how children think. Piaget became a giant in developmental psychology. Many of you, perhaps, are already familiar with his view that children pass through a series of cognitive, or thought, stages from infancy through adolescence. According to Piaget, children think in a qualitatively different manner than do adults.

Our introduction to several influential and diverse theories of children's development has been brief, designed to give you a glimpse of some of the different ways children have been viewed as the study of child development unfolded. You will read more about theoretical perspectives later in the text.

Social Policy and Children's Development

Social policy *is a national government's course of action designed to influence the welfare of its citizens.* A current trend is to conduct child development research that produces knowledge that will lead to wise and effective decision making in the area of social policy (Duncan, 1993; McLoyd, 1993). When more than 20 percent of all children and more than half of all ethnic minority children are being raised in poverty, when between 40 and 50 percent of all children born in a particular era can expect to spend at least five years in a single-parent home, when children and young adolescents are giving birth, when the use and abuse of drugs is widespread, and when the specter and spread of AIDS is present, our nation needs revised social policy related to children (Horowitz & O'Brien, 1989). Figure 1.4 vividly portrays one day in the lives of children in the United States.

The shape and scope of social policy related to children is heavily influenced by our political system, which is based on negotiation and compromise (Garwood & others, 1989). The values held by individual lawmakers, the nation's economic strengths and weaknesses, and partisan politics all influence the policy agenda and whether the welfare of children will be improved. Periods of comprehensive social policy are often the outgrowth of concern over broad social issues. Child labor laws protected children and jobs for adults as well; federal day-care funding during World War II was justified by the need for women laborers in factories; and Head Start and the other War on Poverty programs in the 1960s were implemented to decrease intergenerational poverty (McLoyd, 1990; Zigler & Muenchow, 1992).

Among the groups that have worked to improve the lives of the world's children are UNICEF in New York and the Children's Defense Fund in Washington, D.C. (Albee, Bond, & Monsey, 1992; Edelman, 1992). At a recent United Nations convention, a number of children's rights were declared; a sampling of these rights appears in table 1.1. Marian Wright Edelman, president of the Children's Defense Fund, has been a tireless advocate of children's rights and has been instrumental in calling attention to the needs of children. Especially troubling to Edelman (1992) are the indicators of societal neglect that place the United States at or near the bottom of industrialized nations in the treatment of children. Edelman says that parenting and nurturing the next generation of children is our society's most important function and that we need to take it more seriously than we have in the past. She points out that we hear a lot from politicians these days about the importance of "family values," but that when we examine our nation's policies for families, they don't reflect the politicians' words.

Edward Zigler has also worked extensively as a champion of children's rights, initially to urge government funding of Project Head Start and to improve the lives of mentally retarded

Marian Wright Edelman, president of the Children's Defense Fund (shown here interacting with a young child), has been a tireless advocate of children's rights and has been instrumental in calling attention to the needs of children.

FIGURE 1.4

One day in the lives of children in the United States.

17,051 women get pregnant.	6 teenagers commit suicide.
2,795 of them are teenagers.	135,000 children bring a gun to school.
1,106 teenagers have abortions.	7,742 teens become sexually active.
372 teenagers miscarry.	623 teenagers get syphilis or gonorrhea.
1,295 teenagers give birth.	211 children are arrested for drug abuse.
689 babies are born to women who have had inadequate prenatal care.	437 children are arrested for drinking or drunken driving.
719 babies are born at low birthweight.	1,512 teenagers drop out of school.
129 babies are born at very low birthweight.	1,849 children are abused or neglected.
67 babies die before one month of life.	3,288 children run away from home.
105 babies die before their first birthday.	1,629 children are in adult jails.
27 children die from poverty.	2,556 children are born out of wedlock.
10 children die from guns.	2,989 see their parents divorced.
30 children are wounded by guns.	34,285 people lose jobs.

TABLE 1.1

A Partial Listing of the Declaration of Children's Rights Presented to the United Nations

Abuse and neglect
The need to protect children from all forms of maltreatment by parents and others: In cases of abuse and neglect, the government is obligated to undertake preventive and treatment programs

Best interests of the child
The need for the best interests of children to prevail in all legal and administrative decisions, taking into account children's opinions

Child labor
The need to protect children from economic exploitation and from engaging in work that is a threat to their health, education, and development

Children of ethnic minorities
The right of children from ethnic minority backgrounds to enjoy their own culture and to practice their own religion and language

Children without families
The right to receive special protection and assistance from the government when deprived of family support and to be provided with alternative care

Drug abuse
The need of children to be protected from illegal drugs, including their production or distribution

Education
The right to education: The government should be obligated to provide free and compulsory education and to ensure that school discipline reflects children's human dignity

Aims of education
Education that develops a child's personality and talents and fosters respect for human rights and for children's and others' cultural and national value

Sexual exploitation
The right of children to be protected from sexual exploitation and abuse, including prostitution and pornography

Freedom from discrimination
The need to protect children without exception from any form of discrimination

Handicapped children
The right of handicapped children to special care and training designed to help them achieve self-reliance and a full, active life in society

Health and health services
The right to the highest standard of health and access to medical services: The government should be obligated to ensure preventive health care, health care for expectant mothers, health education, and the reduction of infant and child mortality

Leisure and recreation
The right to leisure, play, and participation in cultural and artistic activities

Standard of living
The right to an adequate standard of living: The government should have a responsibility to assist parents who cannot meet this responsibility

children, and more recently to encourage the formation of a national policy on day care. Several comprehensive child-care bills have recently been proposed in Congress but have not yet been made law. One proposal places public schools at the hub of a new national system of child-care services. Before-school and after-school programs would be housed in available classrooms, with a network of family day-care providers caring for younger children. Traditional child-care services would be augmented by a home visitation program for new parents, parent education, and training for child-care staff. Another proposal, the Comprehensive Child Care bill, addresses issues that range from the licensing standards of child-care services to the upgrading of the quality and status of child-care providers.

We may be facing a new era of comprehensive change in federal child-care policy. Public concern over the provision of day care is mounting as an increasing number of women enter the work force. In one poll, 34 percent of the respondents said they would support higher taxes to fund better early childhood education programs and to improve programs that affect children's health (Hart, 1987). Seventy percent of the respondents said the next president of the United States should give children's health issues more attention, and 52 percent said preschool education deserves more presidential attention. Similarly, the Committee for Economic Development (1987), a nonprofit organization of business leaders and higher education officials, underscored the need for comprehensive reform in several areas of child care, including early childhood education aimed at disadvantaged young children.

Child developmentalists can play an important role in social policy related to children by helping develop more positive public opinion for comprehensive child welfare legislation, by contributing to and promoting research that will benefit children's welfare, and by helping provide legislators with information that will influence their support of comprehensive child welfare legislation.

An important dimension of social policy is family policy. To read about the nature of family policy, turn to Explorations in Child Development 1.1.

As the twenty-first century approaches, the well-being of children is one of America's foremost concerns. We all cherish the future of our children, because they are the future of any society. Children who do not reach their potential, who are destined to make fewer contributions to society than it needs, and who do not take their place as productive adults diminish the power of society's future (Horowitz & O'Brien, 1989; Huston, 1991).

A summary of the main ideas we have discussed so far is presented in Concept Table 1.1. Next, we explore some important developmental issues in the study of children.

Critical Thinking

What do you believe is the most important social policy issue involving children today? How would you persuade the government to improve children's lives related to this particular issue?

CONCEPT TABLE 1.1

The Reasons for Studying Children and the History of Studying Children

Concept	Processes/Related Ideas	Characteristics/Description
Why study children?	Explanations	Responsibility for children is or will be a part of our everyday lives. The more we learn about children, the more we can better deal with them and assist them in becoming competent human beings.
Child-development— today and yesterday	Contemporary concerns	Today, the well-being of children is a prominent concern in our culture—such concerns include family processes, education, and sociocultural issues.
	Sociocultural contexts	Sociocultural contexts include the important concepts of context, culture, ethnicity, and gender. Context refers to the setting in which development occurs, a setting that is influenced by historical, economic, social, and cultural factors. Culture refers to the behavior patterns, beliefs, and all other products of a particular group of people that are passed on from generation to generation. Ethnicity is based on cultural heritage, nationality characteristics, race, religion, and language. Gender is the sociocultural definition of male or female.
	Child development and history	The history of interest in children is long and rich. In the Renaissance, philosophical views were important, including original sin, *tabula rasa,* and innate goodness. We now conceive of childhood as highly eventful. The modern era of studying children spans a little more than a century, an era in which the study of child development has developed into a sophisticated science. Methodological advances in observation and theoretical views—among them psychoanalytic, behavioral, and cognitive-developmental—characterized this scientific theme.
	Social policy research	A current trend is to conduct child development research that is relevant to the welfare of children. The shape and scope of social policy are influenced by our political system. Child developmentalists can play an important role in social policy. Improved social policy related to children is needed to help all children reach their potential.

THE NATURE OF DEVELOPMENT

Each of us develops in certain ways like all other individuals, like some other individuals, and like no other individuals. Most of the time, our attention is directed to a person's uniqueness, but psychologists who study development are drawn to our shared as well as our unique characteristics. As humans, each of us has traveled some common paths. Each of us—Leonardo da Vinci, Joan of Arc, George Washington, Martin Luther King, Jr., and you—walked at about the age of 1, talked at about the age of 2, engaged in fantasy play as a young child, and became more independent as a youth.

What do psychologists mean when they speak of an individual's development? **Development** *is the pattern of movement or change that begins at conception and continues through the life cycle.* Most development involves growth, although it includes decay (as in death and dying). The pattern of movement is complex because it is the product of several processes—biological, cognitive, and social.

Biological, Cognitive, and Social Processes

Biological processes *involve changes in an individual's physical nature.* Genes inherited from parents, the development of the brain, height and weight gains, motor skills, and the hormonal changes of puberty all reflect the role of biological processes in development.

Cognitive processes *involve changes in an individual's thought, intelligence, and language.* The tasks of watching a colorful mobile swinging above a crib, putting together a two-word sentence, memorizing a poem, solving a math problem, and imagining what it would be like to be a movie star all reflect the role of cognitive processes in children's development.

EXPLORATIONS IN CHILD DEVELOPMENT 1.1

Family Policy

The last decade has been one of extremes with respect to family policy in the United States, ranging from efforts to dismantle welfare programs to modest efforts at reform (Berardo, 1990). Controversy has focused on the ability of government intervention to reduce poverty and promote family well-being. The Family Support Act was passed in 1988, linking family welfare payments to job training or work obligations and strengthening child support enforcement strategies, so that families would ultimately become economically independent.

Another family policy debate involves whether government programs have improved the situation of the elderly at the expense of younger individuals, especially children. The con-

cept of *generational inequity* states that an aging society is being unfair to its younger members because older adults pile up advantages by receiving inequitably large allocations of resources. Some authors argue that generational inequity produces intergenerational conflict and divisiveness in the society at large (Longman, 1987). A special concern involves disadvantaged children. Possibly older adults are advantaged because they have publicly provided pensions, health care, food stamps, housing subsidies, tax breaks, and other benefits that younger individuals do not have. While there has been a trend toward greater services for the elderly, the percentage of children in poverty has been increasing. Distinguished developmentalist Bernice Neugarten (1988) says it is undeniable that the large numbers of poor children are a disgrace to an affluent society like the United States. However, she stresses that the problem should not be viewed as one of generational inequity, but rather as a major shortcoming of our economic and social policies.

Much of the controversy surrounding family policy involves a lack of agreement on objectives. A major barrier to sound family policy is its emotional nature, often visible in the actions and statements of highly vocal pressure groups. Policy makers often become enmeshed in hotly debated ideological and moral issues, such as family planning and abortion, or child care and parental leave legislation. At this point, there is no clear indication that sharp differences over the role of families and government will be resolved in favor of rational solutions in the near future (Berardo, 1990).

According to social commentator Richard Louv (1990), a successful family policy will not be shaped primarily by committees and lobbyists in Washington, D.C., but by parents themselves, when they come to understand their need for each other and the interconnectedness of families, schools, and communities.

The chess-board is the world. The pieces are the phenomena of the universe. The rules of the game are what we call laws of nature.

—Thomas Henry Huxley

I think, therefore I am.

—René Descartes

Man is by nature a social animal.

—Aristotle

Socioemotional processes *involve changes in an individual's relationships with other people, changes in emotions, and changes in personality.* An infant's smile in response to her mother's touch, a young boy's aggressive attack on a playmate, a girl's development of assertiveness, and an adolescent's joy at the senior prom all reflect the role of social processes in children's development.

Remember as you read about biological, cognitive, and socioemotional processes that they are intricately interwoven. You will read about how socioemotional processes shape cognitive processes, how cognitive processes promote or restrict socioemotional processes, and how biological processes influence cognitive processes. Although it is helpful to study the various processes involved in children's development in separate sections of the book, keep in mind that you are studying the development of an integrated human child who has only one interdependent mind and body (see figure 1.5).

Periods of Development

For the purposes of organization and understanding, we commonly describe development in terms of periods. The most widely used classification of developmental periods involves the following sequence: the prenatal period, infancy, early childhood, middle and late childhood, and adolescence. Approximate age bands are placed on the periods to provide a general idea of when a period first appears and when it ends.

Family policies can be divided into those that help parents in their "breadwinning" roles and those that concentrate on their nurturing and caregiving roles (Kamerman & Kahn, 1978). Breadwinning family policy supports the family as a viable economic unit, either by maintaining a certain minimal family income or by providing for the care of children while parents work. Nurturing and caregiving family policy focuses on the internal life of the family by promoting positive family functioning and the development and well-being of individual family members.

Consider the plight of the homeless (Jacobs & Davies, 1991). Some people maintain that homeless families only need housing. Others argue that homeless families need a broader economic package of affordable housing, decent jobs, child care, and health care. And yet others stress that homeless families need more than economic assistance, that the factors that precipitated their plight and the harmful effects of being homeless call for additional support—a "caregiving package" that includes services such as home management training, parental support groups, and parent education (Bassuk, Carman, & Weinreb, 1990; Jacobs, Little, & Almeida, 1993; Little, in press). In the last decade, public support for caregiving and nurturing policies has increased, but less so than support for economic assistance.

The family policies of the United States are overwhelmingly treatment-oriented, with only those families and individuals already having problems being eligible; few preventive programs are available on any widespread basis. For example, families on the verge of having their children placed in foster care are eligible, and often required, to receive counseling; families in which problems are brewing but are not yet full blown, usually cannot qualify for public services (Jacobs & Davies, 1991). Most experts on family policy believe more attention should be given to preventing family problems.

What are some family policy issues that are involved in helping the homeless?

The **prenatal period** *is the time from conception to birth.* It is a time of tremendous growth—from a single cell to an organism complete with a brain and behavioral capabilities, produced in approximately a nine-month period.

Infancy *is the developmental period that extends from birth to 18 or 24 months.* Infancy is a time of extreme dependence on adults. Many psychological activities are just beginning—language, symbolic thought, sensorimotor coordination, and social learning, for example.

Early childhood *is the developmental period that extends from the end of infancy to about 5 or 6 years; sometimes the period is called the preschool years.* During this time, young children learn to become more self-sufficient and to care for themselves, develop school readiness skills (following instructions, identifying letters), and spend many hours in play and with peers. First grade typically marks the end of this period.

Middle and late childhood *is the developmental period that extends from about 6 to 11 years of age, approximately corresponding to the elementary school years; sometimes the period is called the elementary school years.* Children master the fundamental skills of reading, writing, and arithmetic, and they are formally exposed to the larger world and its culture. Achievement becomes a more central theme of the child's world, and self-control increases.

Adolescence *is the developmental period of transition from childhood to early adulthood, entered approximately at 10 to 12 years of age and ending at 18 to 22 years of age.* Adolescence begins with rapid physical changes—dramatic gains in height and weight; changes in body contour; and the development of sexual characteristics such as enlargement of the breasts, development of pubic and facial hair, and deepening of the voice. At this point in development, the pursuit of independence and an identity are prominent. Thought is more logical, abstract, and idealistic. More and more time is spent outside the family during this period.

FIGURE 1.5

Changes in development are the result of biological, cognitive, and socioemotional processes. These processes are interwoven as the child develops.

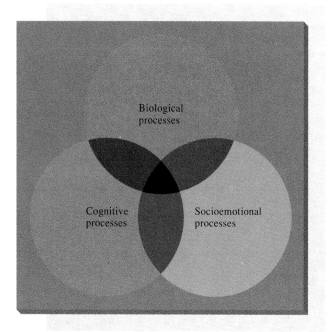

Today, developmentalists do not believe that change ends with adolescence (Hetherington & Baltes, 1989; Santrock, 1994). They describe development as a life-long process. However, the purpose of this text is to describe the changes in development that take place from conception through adolescence.

The periods of development from conception through adolescence are shown in figure 1.6, along with the processes of development—biological, cognitive, and socioemotional. The interplay of biological, cognitive, and socioemotional processes produces the periods of development. A number of issues generate spirited debate among developmentalists: To what extent is development influenced by maturation and experience (nature and nurture)? To what extent is it characterized by continuity and discontinuity? To what degree does it involve early versus later experiences?

Maturation and Experience (Nature and Nurture)

We can think of development as produced not only by the interplay of biological, cognitive, and social processes but also by the interplay of maturation and experience. **Maturation** *is the orderly sequence of changes dictated by the genetic blueprint we each have.* Just as a sunflower grows in an orderly way—unless flattened by an unfriendly environment—so does a human being grow in an orderly way, according to the maturational view. The range of environments can be vast, but the maturational approach argues that the genetic blueprint produces communalities in our growth and development. We walk before we talk, speak one word before two words, grow rapidly in infancy and less so in early childhood, experience a rush of sexual

hormones in puberty after a lull in childhood, reach the peak of our physical strength in late adolescence and early adulthood and then decline, and so on. The maturationists acknowledge that extreme environments—those that are psychologically barren or hostile—can depress development, but they believe that basic growth tendencies are genetically wired into human beings.

By contrast, other psychologists emphasize the importance of experiences in child development. Experiences run the gamut from individuals' biological environment—nutrition, medical care, drugs, and physical accidents—to their social environment—family, peers, schools, community, media, and culture.

The debate about whether development is primarily influenced by maturation or by experience has been a part of psychology since its beginning. This debate is often referred to as the **nature-nurture controversy.** *"Nature" refers to an organism's biological inheritance, "nurture" to environmental experiences. The "nature" proponents claim biological inheritance is the most important influence on development, the "nurture" proponents that environmental experiences are the most important.*

Ideas about development have been like a pendulum, swinging between nature and nurture. In the 1980s, we witnessed a surge of interest in the biological underpinnings of development, probably because the pendulum previously had swung too far in the direction of thinking that development was exclusively due to environmental experiences. As we entered the 1990s, a heightened interest in sociocultural influences on development was emerging, again probably because the pendulum in the 1980s had swung so strongly toward the biological side.

Continuity and Discontinuity

Think about your development for a moment. Did you gradually grow to become the person you are, like the slow, cumulative growth of a seedling into a giant oak, or did you experience sudden, distinct changes in your growth, like the way a caterpillar changes into a butterfly? (See figure 1.7.) For the most part, developmentalists who emphasize experience have described development as a gradual, continuous process; those who emphasize maturation have described development as a series of distinct stages.

Some developmentalists emphasize the **continuity of development,** *the view that development involves gradual, cumulative change from conception to death.* A child's first word, while seemingly an abrupt, discontinuous event, is actually the result of months of growth and practice. Puberty, while also seemingly an abrupt, discontinuous occurrence, is actually a gradual process occurring over several years.

Other developmentalists focus on the **discontinuity of development,** *the view that development involves distinct stages in the life span.* Each of us is described as passing through a sequence of stages in which change is qualitatively rather than quantitatively different. As an oak moves from seedling to giant tree, it becomes *more* oak—its development is continuous. As a caterpillar changes into a butterfly, it becomes not just more caterpillar but a *different kind* of organism—its development is

FIGURE 1.6

Processes and periods of development. Development moves through the prenatal, infancy, early childhood, middle and late childhood, and adolescence periods. These periods of development are the result of biological, cognitive, and social processes. Development is the creation of increasingly complex forms.

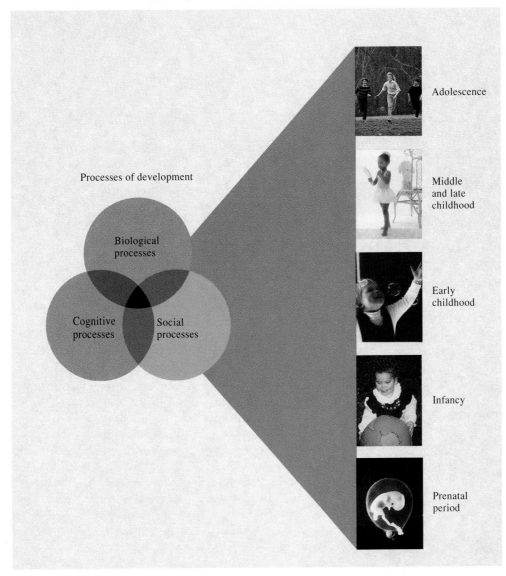

discontinuous. For example, at a certain point, a child moves from not being able to think abstractly about the world to being able to do so. This is a qualitative, discontinuous change in development, not a quantitative, continuous change.

Early and Later Experience

Another important developmental topic is the **early-later experience issue,** *which focuses on the degree to which early experiences (especially in infancy) or later experiences are the key determinants of the child's development.* That is, if infants experience negative, stressful circumstances in their lives, can those experiences be overcome by later, more positive experiences? Or, are the early experiences so critical, possibly because they are

the infant's first, prototypical experiences, that they cannot be overridden by a later, more enriched environment?

The early-later experience issue has a long history and continues to be hotly debated among developmentalists. Some believe that unless infants experience warm, nurturant caregiving in the first year or so of life, their development will never be optimal (Bowlby, 1989; Bretherton, 1993; Sroufe, in press). Plato was sure that infants who were rocked frequently became better athletes. Nineteenth-century New England ministers told parents in Sunday sermons that the way they handled their infants would determine their children's future character. The emphasis on the importance of early experience rests on the belief that each life is an unbroken trail on which a psychological quality can be traced back to its origin (Kagan, 1984, 1992).

FIGURE 1.7

Continuity and discontinuity in development. Is development like a seedling gradually growing into a giant oak? Or is it more like a caterpillar suddenly becoming a butterfly?

"If you ask me, he's come too far too fast."
Drawing by Lorenz; © 1988 The New Yorker Magazine, Inc.

How important are early experiences in development?

The early experience doctrine contrasts with the later experience view that, rather than statuelike permanence after change in infancy, development continues to be like the ebb and flow of a river. The later experience advocates argue that children are malleable throughout development and that later sensitive caregiving is just as important as earlier sensitive caregiving. A number of life-span developmentalists, who focus on the entire life span rather than only on child development, stress that too little attention has been given to later experiences in development (Baltes, 1987; Helson, 1993). They accept that early experiences are important contributors to development, but no more important than later experiences. Jerome Kagan (1992) points out that even children who show the qualities of an inhibited temperament, which is linked to heredity, have the capacity to change their behavior. In his research, almost one-third of a group of children who had an inhibited temperament at 2 years of age were not unusually shy or fearful when they were 4 years of age (Kagan & Snidman, 1991).

People in Western cultures, especially those steeped in the Freudian belief that the key experiences in development are children's relationships with their parents in the first five years of life, have tended to support the idea that early experiences are more important than later experiences (Chan, 1963; Lamb, & Sternberg, 1992). By contrast, the majority of people in the world do not share this belief. For example, people in many Asian countries believe that experiences occurring after about 6 to 7 years of age are more important aspects of development than earlier experiences. This stance stems from the long-standing belief in Eastern cultures, that children's reasoning skills begin to develop in important ways in the middle childhood years.

Evaluating the Developmental Issues

As we consider further these three salient developmental issues—nature and nurture, continuity and discontinuity, and stability and change—it is important to realize that most developmentalists recognize that it is unwise to take an extreme position on these issues. Development is not all nature or all nurture, not all continuity or all discontinuity, and not all stability or all change. Nature and nurture, continuity and discontinuity, and early and later experience characterize our development through the human life cycle. For example, in considering the nature-nurture issue, the key to development is the *interaction* of nature and nurture rather than either factor alone (Loehlin, 1992; Plomin, 1993). For example, an individual's cognitive development is the result of heredity-environment interaction, not heredity or environment alone. Much more about the role of heredity-environment interaction appears in chapter 3.

Nonetheless, although most developmentalists do not take extreme positions on these three important issues, this consensus has not meant the absence of spirited debate about how strongly development is influenced by each of these factors. Are girls less likely to do well in math because of their "feminine" nature or because of society's masculine bias? If, as children, adolescents experienced a world of poverty, neglect by parents, and poor schooling, can enriched experiences in adolescence remove the "deficits" they encountered earlier in their development? The answers developmentalists give to such questions depends on their stance on the issues of nature and nurture, continuity and discontinuity, and early and later experience. The answers to these questions also influence public policy decisions about children, and they influence how each of us lives through the human life cycle.

CAREERS IN CHILD DEVELOPMENT

A career in child development is one of the most rewarding vocational opportunities people can pursue. By choosing a career in child development, you will be able to help children who might not reach their potential as productive contributors to society develop into physically, cognitively, and socially mature individuals. Adults who work professionally with children invariably feel a sense of pride in their ability to contribute in meaningful ways to the next generation of human beings.

If you decide to pursue a career related to children's development, a number of options are available to you. College and university professors teach courses in child development, education, family development, and nursing; counselors, clinical psychologists, pediatricians, psychiatrists, school psychologists, pediatric nurses, psychiatric nurses, and social workers see children with problems and disturbances or illnesses; teachers instruct children in kindergartens, elementary schools, and secondary schools. In pursuing a career related to child development, you can expand your opportunities (and income) considerably by obtaining a graduate degree, although an advanced degree is not absolutely necessary.

Most college professors in child development and its related areas of psychology, education, home economics, nursing, and social work have a master's degree and/or doctorate degree that required two to five years of academic work beyond their undergraduate degree. Becoming a child clinical psychologist or counseling psychologist requires five to six years of graduate work to obtain the necessary Ph.D.; this includes both clinical and research training. School and career counselors pursue a master's or doctorate degree in counseling, often in graduate programs in education departments; these degrees require two to six years to complete. Becoming a pediatrician or psychiatrist requires four years of medical school, plus an internship and a residency in pediatrics or psychiatry, respectively; this career path takes seven to nine years beyond a bachelor's degree. School psychologists obtain either a master's degree (approximately two years) or a D.Ed. degree (approximately four to five years) in school psychology. School psychologists counsel children and parents when children have problems in school, often giving psychological tests to assess children's personality and intelligence. Social work positions may be obtained with an undergraduate degree in social work or related fields, but opportunities are expanded with an M.S.W. (master's of social work) or Ph.D., which require two and four to five years, respectively. Pediatric and psychiatric nursing positions can also be attained with an undergraduate R.N. degree; M.A. and Ph.D. degrees in nursing, which require two and four to five years of graduate training, respectively, are also available. To read further about jobs and careers that involve working with children, turn to table 1.2. This list is not exhaustive but rather is meant to give you an idea of the many opportunities to pursue a rewarding career in child development and its related fields. Also keep in mind that majoring in child development or a related field can provide sound preparation for adult life.

One of our major concerns is the underrepresentation of ethnic minority individuals, not only as research subjects and the focus of developmental inquiry, but also as child developmentalists. To read about the history of ethnic minority individuals in child development and their current representation in the field of child development, turn to Sociocultural Worlds of Children 1.2.

At this point we have studied a number of ideas about the nature of development, developmental issues, and careers in child development. A summary of these ideas is presented in Concept Table 1.2. Next, to end the chapter, we encourage you to think about the importance of parenting and education in children's development.

TABLE 1.2

Jobs and Careers in Child Development and Related Fields

Jobs/Careers	Degree	Education Required
Child clinical psychologist or counseling psychologist	Ph.D.	5–7 years postundergraduate
Child life specialist	Undergraduate degree	4 years of undergraduate study
Child psychiatrist	M.D.	7–9 years postundergraduate
Child welfare worker	Undergraduate degree is minimum	4 years minimum
College/university professor in child development, education, family development, nursing, social work	Ph.D. or master's degree	5–6 years for Ph.D. (or D.Ed.) postundergraduate; 2 years for master's degree postundergraduate
Day-care supervisor	Varies by state	Varies by state
Early childhood educator	Master's degree (minimum)	2 years of graduate work (minimum)
Elementary or secondary school teacher	Undergraduate degree (minimum)	4 years
Exceptional children teacher (special education teacher)	Undergraduate degree (minimum)	4 years or more (some states require a master's degree or passing a standardized exam to obtain a license to work with exceptional children)
Guidance counselor	Undergraduate degree (minimum); many have master's degree	4 years undergraduate; 2 years graduate
Pediatrician	M.D.	7–9 years of medical school
Pediatric nurse	R.N.	2–5 years
Preschool/kindergarten teacher	Usually undergraduate degree	4 years
Psychiatric nurse	R.N.	2–5 years
School psychologist	Master's or Ph.D.	5–6 years of graduate work for Ph.D. or D.Ed.; 2 years for master's degree

Nature of Training	Description of Work
Includes both clinical and research training; involves a one-year internship in a psychiatric hospital or mental health facility.	Child clinical psychologists or counseling psychologists diagnose children's problems and disorders, administer psychological test, and conduct psychotherapy sessions. Some work at colleges and universities where they do any combination of teaching, therapy, and research.
Many child life specialists have been trained in child development or education but undergo additional training in child life programs that includes parent education, developmental assessment, and supervised work with children and parents.	Child life specialists are employed by hospitals and work with children and their families before and after the children are admitted to the hospital. They often develop and monitor developmentally appropriate activities for child patients. They also help children adapt to their medical experiences and their stay at the hospital. Child life specialists coordinate their efforts with physicians and nurses.
Four years of medical school, plus an internship and residency in child psychiatry are required.	The role of the child psychiatrist is similar to the child clinical psychologist, but the psychiatrist can conduct biomedical therapy (for example, such as using drugs to treat clients); the child clinical or counseling psychologist cannot.
Coursework and training in social work or human services.	Child welfare workers are employed by the Child Protective Services Unit of each state to protect children's rights. They especially monitor cases of child maltreatment and abuse, and make decisions about what needs to be done to help protect the abused child from further harm and effectively cope with their prior abuse.
Take graduate courses, learn how to conduct research, attend and present papers at professional meetings.	College and university professors teach courses in child development, family development, education, or nursing; conduct research; present papers at professional meetings; write and publish articles and books; and train undergraduate and graduate students for careers in these fields.
The Department of Public Welfare in many states publishes a booklet with the requirements for a day-care supervisor.	Day-care supervisors direct day-care or preschool programs, being responsible for the operation of the center. They often make decisions about the nature of the center's curriculum, may teach in the center themselves, work with and consult with parents, and conduct workshops for staff or parents.
Coursework in early childhood education and practice in day-care or early childhood centers with supervised training.	Early childhood educators usually teach in community colleges that award associate or bachelor's degrees in early childhood education with specialization in day care. They train individuals for careers in the field of day care.
Wide range of courses with a major or concentration in education.	Elementary and secondary teachers teach one or more subjects; prepare the curriculum; give tests, assign grades, and monitor students' progress; interact with parents and school administrators; attend lectures and workshops involving curriculum planning or help on special issues, and direct extracurricular programs.
Coursework in education with a concentration in special education.	Exceptional children teachers (also called special education teachers) work with children who are educationally handicapped (those who are mentally retarded, have a physical handicap, have a learning disability, or have a behavioral disorder) or who are gifted. They develop special curricula for the exceptional children and help them to adapt to their exceptional circumstances. Special education teachers work with other school personnel and with parents to improve the adjustment of exceptional children.
Coursework in education and counseling in a school of education; counselor training practice.	The majority of guidance counselors work with secondary school students, assisting them in educational and career planning. They often give students aptitude tests and evaluate their interests, as well as their abilities. Guidance counselors also see students who are having school-related problems, including emotional problems, referring them to other professionals such as school psychologists or clinical psychologists when necessary.
Four years of medical school, plus an internship and residency in pediatrics.	Pediatricians monitor infants' and children's health and treat their diseases. They advise parents about infant and child development and the appropriate ways to deal with children.
Courses in biological sciences, nursing care, and pediatrics (often in a school of nursing); supervised clinical experiences in medical settings.	Pediatric nurses promote health in infants and children, working to prevent disease or injury, assisting children with handicaps or health problems so they can achieve optimal health, and treating children with health deviations. Some pediatric nurses specialize in certain areas (for example, the neonatal intensive care unit clinician cares exclusively for newborns; the new-parent educator helps the parents of newborns develop better parenting skills). Pediatric nurses work in a variety of medical settings.
Coursework in education with a specialization in early childhood education; state certification usually required.	Preschool teachers direct the activities of prekindergarten children, many of whom are 4-year-olds. They develop an appropriate curriculum for the age of the children that promotes their physical, cognitive, and social development in a positive atmosphere. The number of days per week and hours per day varies from one program to another. Kindergarten teachers work with young children who are between the age of preschool programs and the first year of elementary school; they primarily develop appropriate activities and curricula for 5-year-old children.
Courses in biological sciences, nursing care, and mental health in a school of nursing; supervised clinical training in child psychiatric settings.	Psychiatric nurses promote the mental health of individuals; some specialize in helping children with mental health problems and work closely with child psychiatrists to improve these children's adjustment.
Includes coursework and supervised training in school settings, usually in a department of educational psychology.	School psychologists evaluate and treat a wide range of normal and exceptional children who have school-related problems; work in a school system and see children from a number of schools; administer tests, interview and observe children, and consult with teachers, parents, and school administrators; and design programs to reduce the child's problem behavior.

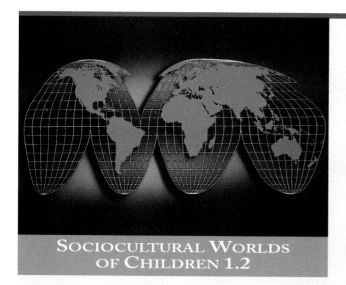

SOCIOCULTURAL WORLDS OF CHILDREN 1.2

Ethnic Minorities in the Field of Child Development

Barriers have prevented the entry of Black Americans, Hispanic Americans, Asian Americans, and Native Americans into the field of child development throughout most of its history. Ethnic minority individuals who obtained doctoral degrees were very dedicated and overcame extensive bias against their ethnic group. One pioneering Black American psychologist was Kenneth Clark, who with his wife Mamie, conducted research on Black American children's self-conceptions and identity (Clark & Clark, 1939). In 1971, Kenneth Clark became the first Black American president of the American Psychological Association. In 1932, Hispanic American psychologist George Sanchez conducted research that demonstrated the cultural bias of intelligence tests for ethnic minority children.

In the past 25 years, important movements calling for recognition of the rights and needs of ethnic minorities in higher education have surfaced (Bronstein & Quina, 1988; Stricker & others, 1990). The civil rights movement has led to social change, stimulating developmentalists—especially those who also are members of ethnic minority groups—to reexamine the existing body of knowledge about children's development and to question to what degree it is relevant to ethnic minority children. This questioning has formed the basis of new areas of developmental inquiry, focusing on populations who previously were omitted from subject pools of developmental research and from the theoretical ideas of mainstream child development.

Recognizing the underrepresentation of ethnic minority individuals in psychology, the American Psychological Association (APA)—the main organization of psychologists in the United States—has formed the Board of Ethnic Minority Affairs to represent the ethnic group concerns of its members. In one survey, only 5 percent of doctoral psychologists in the developmental area, 4.7 percent in the clinical, counseling, and school areas, and 7.5 percent in the educational area were members of ethnic minority groups (Stapp, Tucker, & VandenBos, 1985). The percentage of Hispanic American and Native American individuals with doctorates in these areas is especially low. And in nursing, the percentage of those with master's and doctoral degrees who represent ethnic minorities is equally low (for example, Black Americans—5 percent; Asian Americans—2 percent; Hispanic Americans—1 percent; and Native Americans—.2 percent).

Job opportunities are increasingly available to qualified applicants from every ethnic group. We need more qualified ethnic minority individuals in the field of child development.

George Sanchez

Mamie and Kenneth Clark conducted pioneering research on Black children's self-conceptions and identity.

CONCEPT TABLE 1.2

The Nature of Development, Developmental Issues, and Careers in Child Development

Concept	Processes/Related Ideas	Characteristics/Description
The nature of development	What is development?	Development is the pattern of movement or change that occurs throughout the life span.
	Biological, cognitive, and social processes	Development is influenced by an interplay of biological, cognitive, and social processes.
	Periods of development	Development is commonly divided into the following periods from conception through adolescence: the prenatal period, infancy, early childhood, middle and late childhood, and adolescence.
Developmental issues	Maturation and experience (nature and nurture)	The debate over whether development is due primarily to maturation or to experience is another version of the nature-nurture controversy.
	Continuity and discontinuity	Some developmentalists describe development as continuous (gradual, cumulative change), others as discontinuous (abrupt, sequence of stages).
	Early and later experiences	This hotly debated issue focuses on whether early experiences (especially in infancy) are more important in development than later experiences.
	Evaluating the developmental issues	Most developmentalists recognize that extreme positions on the nature-nurture, continuity-discontinuity, and stability-change issues are unwise. Despite this consensus, spirited debate still occurs on these issues.
Careers in child development	Their nature	A wide range of opportunities are available to individuals who want to pursue a career related to child development. These opportunities include jobs in college and university teaching, child clinical psychology and counseling, school teaching and school psychology, nursing, pediatrics, psychiatry, and social work. A special interest is the history of ethnic minority individuals in the field of child development, and the current educational status of ethnic minority individuals.

PERSPECTIVES ON PARENTING AND EDUCATION

Thinking about Your Future as a Parent and the Education of Your Children

Famous playwright George Bernard Shaw once commented that while parenting is a very important profession, no test of fitness for it is ever imposed. If a test were imposed, some parents would turn out to be more fit than others. Most parents do want their children to grow into socially mature individuals, but they often are not sure about what to do as a parent to help their children reach this goal. One reason for the frustration of parents is that they often get conflicting messages about how to deal with their children. One "expert" may urge them to be more permissive with their children, another may tell them to place stricter controls on them or they will grow up to be spoiled brats.

Most of you taking this course will be a parent someday; some of you already are. I hope that each of you will take seriously the importance of rearing your children because they are the future of our society. Good parenting takes a considerable amount of time. If you choose to become a parent, you should be willing to commit yourself, day after day, week after week, month after month, and year after year, to providing your children with a warm, supportive, safe, and stimulating environment that will make them feel secure and allow them to reach their full potential as human beings.

Understanding the nature of children's development can help you to become a better parent. Many parents learn parenting practices and how to care for their children from their parents—some they usually accept, some they discard. Unfortunately, when parenting practices and child care strategies are passed on from one generation to the next, both desirable and undesirable ones are perpetuated. This book and your instructor's lectures in this course can help you become much more knowledgeable about the nature of children's development and to sort through which practices in your own upbringing you would like to continue with your own children and which you would like to abandon.

Like parenting, education is an extremely important dimension of children's lives. When we think of education we usually associate it with schools. Schools are an extremely important aspect of education, but education also occurs in contexts other than schools. Children learn from their parents, from their siblings, from their peers, from books, from watching television, and from computers as well.

You can probably look back on your own education and think of ways it could

have been a lot better. Some, or even most, of your school years may have been spent in classrooms in which learning was not enjoyable but boring, stressful, and rigid. Some of your teachers may have not adequately considered your own unique needs and skills. On the other hand, you probably can remember some classrooms and teachers that made learning exciting, something you looked forward to each morning you got up. You liked the teacher and the subject, and you learned.

There is widespread agreement that something needs to be done to improve the education our nation's children are receiving. What would you do to make the education of children more effective? What would you do to make schools more productive and enjoyable contexts for children's development? Would you make the school days longer or shorter? The school year longer or shorter? Or keep it the same and focus more on changing the curriculum itself? Would you emphasize less memorization and give more attention to the development of children's ability to process informa-

tion more efficiently? Have schools become too soft and watered-down, or should they make more demands and have higher expectations of children? Should schools focus only on developing the child's knowledge and cognitive skills, or should they pay more attention to the whole child and consider the child's socioemotional and physical development as well? Should more tax dollars be spent on schools and should teachers be paid more to educate our nation's children? Should schools be dramatically changed so that they serve as a locus for a wide range of services, such as primary health care, child care, preschool education, parent education, recreation, and family counseling, as well as the traditional educational activity of learning in the classroom?

These are provocative questions, and how they are answered will influence the future of your children. We will discuss a number of these issues later in the text in much greater detail. Good parenting and good education serve as important bases for the development of competent children. ■

CONCLUSIONS

Children should have a special place in any society for they are the society's future. An important concern is that too many children today will not reach their full potential because of inadequate rearing conditions. Far too many children live in poverty, have parents who do not adequately care for them, and go to schools where learning conditions are far from optimal.

In this chapter, you were introduced to the field of child development. You read about how today is both the best of

times and the worst of times for children and why it is important to study children. You learned about the nature of child development through history, some contemporary concerns, the modern study of child development, and social policy issues. You also studied the nature of development by exploring biological, cognitive, and social processes; periods of development; maturation and experience (nature and nurture); continuity and discontinuity; and early and later experiences. You read about a number of

careers in child development and thought about your future as a parent and the education of your children. To obtain a summary of the chapter, go back and again read the two concept tables on pages 17 and 27.

In the next chapter, we turn our attention to the field of child development as a science. You will learn abut the importance of the scientific method, theories, and methods in studying children.

KEY TERMS

context   Development occurs in settings that are called contexts. These settings are influenced by historical, economic, social, and cultural factors. (9)

culture   The behavior patterns, beliefs, and all other products of a group that are passed from generation to generation. (9)

cross-cultural studies   Studies of this type compare a culture with one or more other cultures. Such studies provide information about the degree to which children's development is similar, or universal, across cultures, or to the degree to which it is culture-specific. (9)

ethnicity   A dimension of culture based on cultural heritage, nationality characteristics, race, religion, and language. (9)

ethnic identity   An individual develops a sense of membership based upon the shared language, religion, customs, values, history, and race of an ethnic group. (9)

gender   The sociocultural dimension of being male or female. (11)

original sin view   The idea, especially advocated during the Middle Ages, that children are basically born bad and born into the world as evil beings. (11)

tabula rasa view   The idea, proposed by John Locke, that children are not innately bad but instead are like a "blank tablet." (11)

innate goodness view   The idea, presented by Swiss-born philosopher Jean-Jacques Rousseau, that children are inherently good. (12)

genetic epistemology   The study of how children's knowledge changes over the course of their development. (13)

social policy   A national government's course of action designed to influence the welfare of its citizens. (14)

development   The pattern of movement or change that begins at conception and continues through the life cycle. (17)

biological processes   Changes in an individual's physical nature. (17)

cognitive processes   Changes in an individual's thought, intelligence, and language. (17)

socioemotional processes   Changes in an individual's relationships with other people, emotions, and personality. (18)

prenatal period   The time from conception to birth. (19)

infancy   The developmental period that extends from birth to 18 or 24 months. (19)

early childhood   The developmental period that extends from the end of infancy to about 5 or 6 years of age; sometimes called the preschool years. (19)

middle and late childhood   The developmental period that extends from about 6 to 11 years of age, approximately corresponding to the elementary school years; sometimes called the elementary school years. (19)

adolescence   The developmental period of transition from childhood to early adulthood, entered at approximately 10 to 12 years of age and ending at 18 to 22 years of age. (19)

maturation   The orderly sequence of changes dictated by a genetic blueprint. (20)

nature-nurture controversy   "Nature" refers to an organism's biological inheritance, "nurture" to environmental experiences. The "nature" proponents claim biological inheritance is the most important influence on development; the "nurture" proponents claim that environmental experiences are the most important. (20)

continuity of development   The view that development involves gradual, cumulative change from conception to death. (20)

discontinuity of development   The view that development involves distinct stages in the life span. (20)

early-later experience issue   This issue focuses on the degree to which early experiences (especially in infancy) or later experiences are the key determinants of the child's development. (21)

SUGGESTED READINGS

Borstelmann, L. J. (1983). Children before psychology: Ideas about children from antiquity to the late 1800s. In P. H. Mussen (Ed.), *Handbook of child psychology* (4th ed., Vol. 1). New York: Wiley. This is a comprehensive treatment of the historical perception of children from ancient times to the twentieth century.

Child Development and *Developmental Psychology*. These are two of the leading research journals in the field of children's development. Go to your library and leaf through issues from the past several years to get a feel for the research interests of developmentalists.

Children's Defense Fund (1993). *Children 1993*. Washington, DC: Children's Defense Fund. The Children's Defense Fund is an important advocate of children's rights. This book charts how our nation's social policy toward children does not provide adequate care for them.

Louv, R. (1990). *Childhood's future.*
Boston: Houghton Mifflin. Social
commentator Richard Louv criss-
crossed the United States for three
years and conducted interviews with
parents and children. Louv describes
the vast reduction in family time,
the growing conflict between home
and work, and a pervasive concern
about how our culture is reshaping
childhood. He then describes how
families can face these challenges.

Time, October 8, 1990. Suffer the little
children: Shameful bequests to the
next generation. This article delves
into how America has not
adequately cared for its children.
Arguments are made for spending
more government money on
prevention, including prenatal care,
sex education, and social services.

Hayward L. Oubre,
Pensive Family (Detail)

The Science of Child Development

*There is nothing quite so practical as a
good theory.*
    —Kurt Lewin, Psychologist, 1890–1947

The childhood shows the man, as morning shows the day

—Milton

IMAGES OF CHILDREN

Erikson and Piaget as Children

Imagine that you have developed a major theory of child development. What would influence someone like you to construct this theory? A person interested in developing such a theory usually goes through a long university training program that culminates in a doctoral degree. As part of the training, the future theorist is exposed to many ideas about a particular area of child development, such as biological, cognitive, or socioemotional development. Another factor that could explain why someone develops a particular theory is that person's life experiences. Two important developmental theorists, whose views we will describe later in the chapter, are Erik Erikson and Jean Piaget. Let's examine a portion of their lives as they were growing up to discover how their experiences might have contributed to the theories they developed.

Erik Homberger Erikson was born in 1902 near Frankfort, Germany, to Danish parents. Before Erik was born, his parents separated and his mother left Denmark to live in Germany. At age 3, Erik became ill, and his mother took him to see a pediatrician named Homberger. Young Erik's mother fell in love with the pediatrician, married him, and named Erik after his new stepfather.

Erik attended primary school from the ages of 6 to 10 and then the gymnasium (high school) from 11 to 18. He studied art and a number of languages rather than science courses such as biol-

ogy and chemistry. Erik did not like the atmosphere of formal schooling, and this was reflected in his grades. Rather than go to college at age 18, the adolescent Erikson wandered around Europe, keeping a diary about his experiences. After a year of travel through Europe, he returned to Germany and enrolled in art school, became dissatisfied, and enrolled in another. Later he traveled to Florence, Italy. Psychiatrist Robert Coles described Erikson at this time:

> To the Italians he was . . .
> the young, tall, thin Nordic
> expatriate with long, blond
> hair. He wore a corduroy suit
> and was seen by his family and
> friends as not odd or "sick"
> but as a wandering artist who
> was trying to come to grips
> with himself, a not unnatural
> or unusual struggle. (Coles,
> 1970, p. 15)

The second major theorist whose life we will examine is Jean Piaget. Piaget (1896–1980) was born in Neuchâtel, Switzerland. Jean's father was an intellectual who taught young Jean to think systematically. Jean's mother was also very bright. His father had an air of detachment from his mother, whom Piaget described as prone to frequent outbursts of neurotic behavior.

In his autobiography, Piaget detailed why he chose to study cognitive de-

velopment rather than social or abnormal development:

> I started to forego playing for
> serious work very early.
> Indeed, I have always detested
> any departure from reality, an
> attitude which I relate to . . .
> my mother's poor health. It
> was this disturbing factor
> which at the beginning of my
> studies in psychology made
> me keenly interested in
> psychoanalytic and
> pathological psychology.
> Though this interest helped
> me to achieve independence
> and widen my cultural
> background, I have never
> since felt any desire to involve
> myself deeper in that
> particular direction, always
> much preferring the study of
> normalcy and of the workings
> of the intellect to that of the
> tricks of the unconscious.
> (Piaget, 1952a, p. 238)

These excerpts from Erikson's and Piaget's lives illustrate how personal experiences might influence the direction in which a particular theorist goes. Erikson's own wanderings and search for self contributed to his theory of identity development, and perhaps Piaget's intellectual experiences with his parents and schooling contributed to his emphasis on cognitive development.

PREVIEW

Some individuals have difficulty thinking of child development as a science in the same way physics, chemistry, and biology are sciences. Can a discipline that studies how babies develop, how parents nurture children, how peers interact, and how children think be equated with disciplines that investigate how gravity works and the molecular structure of a compound? Science is not defined by *what* it investigates but by *how* it investigates. Whether you are studying photosynthesis, butterflies, Saturn's moons, or human development, it is the *way* you study that makes the approach scientific or not.

In this chapter, we will study three key ingredients of child development as a science—the scientific method, theories, and methods. You also will learn about how to be a wise consumer of information about children's development.

THEORY AND THE SCIENTIFIC METHOD

According to nineteenth-century French mathematician Henri Poincaré, "Science is built of facts the way a house is built of bricks, but an accumulation of facts is no more science than a pile of bricks a house." Science *does* depend on the raw material of facts or data, but, as Poincaré indicated, child development's theories are more than just facts.

A **theory** *is a coherent set of ideas that help explain data and make predictions.* A theory contains **hypotheses,** *assumptions that can be tested to determine their accuracy.* For example, a theory about children's aggression would explain our observations of aggressive children and predict why children become aggressive. We might predict that children become aggressive because of the coercive interchanges they experience and observe in their families. This prediction would help direct our observations by telling us to look for coercive interchanges in families.

Critical Thinking

Theories help us make predictions about how we develop and how we behave. Do you believe we can predict an individual's behavior and development? Explain your answer.

The **scientific method** *is an approach that can be used to discover accurate information about behavior and development which includes the following steps: identify and analyze the problem, collect data, draw conclusions, and revise theories.* For example, you decide that you want to help aggressive children control their

aggression. You *identify a problem*, which does not seem like a difficult task. However, as part of the first step, you need to go beyond a general description of the problem by isolating, analyzing, narrowing, and focusing on what you hope to investigate. What specific strategies do you want to use to reduce children's aggression? Do you want to look at only one strategy, or several strategies? What aspect of aggression do you want to study—its biological, cognitive, or social characteristics? Gerald Patterson and his colleagues (Dishion & others, 1992; Patterson, 1991; Patterson, Capaldi, & Bank, 1991) argue that parents' failure to teach reasonable levels of compliance sets in motion coercive interchanges with family members. In this first step in the scientific method, a problem is identified and analyzed.

After you have identified and analyzed the problem, the next step is to *collect information (data)*. Psychologists observe behavior and draw inferences about thoughts and emotions. For example, in the investigation of children's aggression, we might observe how effectively parents teach reasonable compliance levels to their children and the extent to which coercive exchanges take place among family members.

> *Truth is arrived at by the painstaking process of eliminating the untrue.*
> —Arthur Conan Doyle

Once data have been collected, psychologists use *statistical procedures* to understand the meaning of quantitative data. They then try to *draw conclusions*. In the investigation of children's

Researchers use the scientific method to obtain accurate information about children's behavior and development. Data collection is part of the scientific method, demonstrated here by a researcher conducting a study of infant development.

aggression, statistics would help us determine whether or not our observations were due to chance. After data have been collected, psychologists compare their findings with what others have discovered about the same issue.

The final step in the scientific method is *revising theory.* Psychologists have generated a number of theories about children's development; they also have theorized about why children become aggressive. Data such as those collected by Patterson and his colleagues force us to study existing theories of aggression to see if they are accurate. Over the years, some theories of children's development have been discarded and others revised. Theories are an integral part of understanding the nature of children's development. They will be weaved through our discussion of children's development throughout the remainder of the text.

THEORIES OF CHILD DEVELOPMENT

We will briefly explore five major theoretical perspectives on child development: psychoanalytic, cognitive, behavioral/social learning, ethological, and ecological. You will read more in-depth portrayals of these theories at different points in later chapters in the book.

The diversity of theories makes understanding children's development a challenging undertaking. Just when you think one theory correctly explains children's development, another theory crops up and makes you rethink your earlier conclusion. To keep from getting frustrated, remember that children's development is a complex, multifaceted topic, and no single theory has been able to account for all its aspects. Each theory has contributed an important piece to the child development puzzle. Although the theories sometimes disagree about certain aspects of children's development, much of their information is *complementary* rather than contradictory. Together the various theories let us see the total landscape of children's development in all its richness.

Psychoanalytic Theories

For psychoanalytic theorists, development is primarily unconscious—that is, beyond awareness—and is heavily colored by emotion. Psychoanalytic theorists believe that behavior is merely a surface characteristic and that to truly understand development, we have to analyze the symbolic meanings of behavior and the deep inner workings of the mind. Psychoanalytic theorists also stress that early experiences with parents extensively shape our development. These characteristics are highlighted in the main psychoanalytic theory, that of Sigmund Freud.

The passions are at once tempters and chastisers. As
tempters, they come with garlands of flowers on the brows
of youth; as chastisers, they appear with wreaths of snakes
on the forehead of deformity. They are angels of light in
their delusion; they are fiends of torment in their
inflictions.

—Henry Giles

Freud's Theory

Freud (1856–1939) developed his ideas about psychoanalytic
theory from work with mental patients. He was a medical doctor who specialized in neurology. He spent most of his years in
Vienna, though he moved to London near the end of his career
because of the Nazis' antisemitism.

Freud (1917) believed that personality has three structures:
the id, the ego, and the superego. The **id** *is the Freudian structure of personality that consists of instincts, which are an individual's reservoir of psychic energy.* In Freud's view, the id is totally
unconscious; it has no contact with reality. As children experience the demands and constraints of reality, a new structure of
personality emerges—the **ego,** *the Freudian structure of personality that deals with the demands of reality.* The ego is called the
executive branch of personality because it makes rational decisions. The id and the ego have no morality. They do not take
into account whether something is right or wrong. The **superego** *is the Freudian structure of personality that is the moral branch*

Sigmund Freud, the pioneering architect of psychoanalytic theory.

of personality. The superego takes into account whether something is right or wrong. Think of the superego as what we often
refer to as our "conscience." You probably are beginning to
sense that both the id and the superego make life rough for the
ego. Your ego might say, "I will have sex only occasionally and
be sure to take the proper precautions because I don't want the
intrusion of a child in the development of my career." However,
your id is saying, "I want to be satisfied; sex is pleasurable." Your
superego is at work too: "I feel guilty about having sex."

Remember that Freud considered personality to be like an
iceberg; most of personality exists below our level of awareness,
just as the massive part of an iceberg is beneath the surface of
the water. Figure 2.1 illustrates this analogy.

How does the ego resolve the conflict between its demands
for reality, the wishes of the id, and constraints of the superego?
Through **defense mechanisms,** *the psychoanalytic term for unconscious methods, the ego distorts reality, thereby protecting it from
anxiety.* In Freud's view, the conflicting demands of the personality structures produce anxiety. For example, when the ego
blocks the pleasurable pursuits of the id, inner anxiety is felt.
This diffuse, distressed state develops when the ego senses
that the id is going to cause harm to the individual. The anxiety alerts the ego to resolve the conflict by means of defense
mechanisms.

FIGURE 2.1

Conscious and unconscious processes: the iceberg analogy. This
rather odd-looking diagram illustrates Freud's belief that most of
the important personality processes occur below the level of
conscious awareness. In examining people's conscious thoughts
and their behaviors, we can see some reflections of the ego and
the superego. Whereas the ego and superego are partly conscious
and partly unconscious, the primitive id is the unconscious,
totally submerged part of the iceberg.

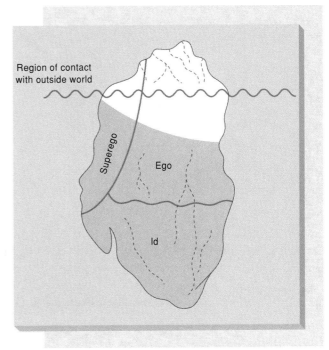

Repression *is the most powerful and pervasive defense mechanism, according to Freud; it works to push unacceptable id impulses out of awareness and back into the unconscious mind.* Repression is the foundation from which all other defense mechanisms work; the goal of every defense mechanism is to *repress* or push threatening impulses out of awareness. Freud said that our early childhood experiences, many of which he believed were sexually laden, are too threatening and stressful for us to deal with consciously. We reduce the anxiety of this conflict through the defense mechanism of repression.

They cannot scare me with their empty spaces
Between stars—on stars where no human race is.
I have it in me so much nearer home
To scare myself with my own desert places.

—Robert Frost

As Freud listened to, probed, and analyzed his patients, he became convinced that their problems were the result of experiences early in life. Freud believed that we go through five stages of psychosexual development and that, at each stage of development, we experience pleasure in one part of the body more than in others. **Erogenous zones** *refer to Freud's concept of the parts of the body that have especially strong pleasure-giving qualities at each stage of development.*

THE FAR SIDE   By GARY LARSON

"So, Mr. Fenton . . . Let's begin with your mother."

THE FAR SIDE cartoon by Gary Larson is reprinted by permission of Chronicle Features, San Francisco, CA. All rights reserved.

Freud thought that the adult personality is determined by the way conflicts between the early sources of pleasure—the mouth, the anus, and then the genitals—and the demands of reality are resolved. When these conflicts are not resolved, the individual may become fixated at a particular stage of development.

For example, a parent may wean a child too early, be too strict in toilet training, punish the child for masturbation, or smother the child with warmth. We will return to the idea of fixation and how it may show up in an adult's personality, but first we need to learn more about the early stages of personality development.

The **oral stage** *is the first Freudian stage of development, occurring during the first 18 months of life, in which the infant's pleasure centers around the mouth.* Chewing, sucking, and biting are the chief sources of pleasure. These actions reduce tension in the infant.

The **anal stage** *is the second Freudian stage of development, occurring between 1½ and 3 years of age, in which the child's greatest pleasure involves the anus or the eliminative functions associated with it.* In Freud's view, the exercise of anal muscles reduces tension.

The **phallic stage** *is the third Freudian stage of development, which occurs between the ages of 3 and 6; its name comes from the Latin word* phallus, *which means "penis."* During the phallic stage, pleasure focuses on the genitals as the child discovers that self-manipulation is enjoyable.

In Freud's view, the phallic stage has a special importance in personality development because it is during this period that the Oedipus complex appears. This name comes from Greek mythology, in which Oedipus, the son of the King of Thebes, unwittingly kills his father and marries his mother. The **Oedipus complex** *is the Freudian concept in which the young child develops an intense desire to replace the parent of the same sex and enjoy the affections of the opposite-sex parent.* Freud's concept of the Oedipus complex has been criticized by some psychoanalysts and writers. To learn more about cultural- and gender-based criticisms of Freud's theory, turn to Sociocultural Worlds of Children 2.1.

How is the Oedipus complex resolved? At about 5 to 6 years of age, children recognize that their same-sex parent might punish them for their incestuous wishes. To reduce this conflict, the child identifies with the same-sex parent, striving to be like him or her. If the conflict is not resolved, though, the individual may become fixated at the phallic stage.

The **latency stage** *is the fourth Freudian stage of development, which occurs between approximately 6 years of age and puberty; the child represses all interest in sexuality and develops social and intellectual skills.* This activity channels much of the child's energy into emotionally safe areas and helps the child forget the highly stressful conflicts of the phallic stage.

The **genital stage** *is the fifth and final Freudian stage of development, occurring from puberty on. The genital stage is a time of sexual reawakening; the source of sexual pleasure now becomes someone outside of the family.* Freud believed that unresolved conflicts with parents reemerge during adolescence. When resolved, the individual is capable of developing a mature love relationship and functioning independently as an adult.

Erik Erikson with his wife, Joan, who is an artist. Erikson generated one of the most important developmental theories of the twentieth century.

Freud's theory has undergone significant revisions by a number of psychoanalytic theorists. Many contemporary psychoanalytic theorists place less emphasis on sexual instincts and more emphasis on cultural experiences as determinants of an individual's development. Unconscious thought remains a central theme, but most contemporary psychoanalysts believe that conscious thought makes up more of the iceberg than Freud envisioned. Next, we explore the ideas of an important revisionist of Freud's ideas—Erik Erikson.

Erikson's Theory

Erik Erikson (1902–   ) recognized Freud's contributions but believed that Freud misjudged some important dimensions of human development. For one, Erikson (1950, 1968) says we develop in *psychosocial stages,* in contrast to Freud's psychosexual stages. For another, Erikson emphasizes developmental change throughout the human life cycle, whereas Freud argued that our basic personality is shaped in the first five years of life. In Erikson's theory, eight stages of development unfold as we go through the life cycle. Each stage consists of a unique developmental task that confronts individuals with a crisis that must be faced. For Erikson, this crisis is not a catastrophe but a turning point of increased vulnerability and enhanced potential. The more an individual resolves the crises successfully the healthier development will be.

Trust versus mistrust *is Erikson's first psychosocial stage, which is experienced in the first year of life. A sense of trust requires a feeling of physical comfort and a minimal amount of fear and apprehension about the future.* Trust in infancy sets the stage for a lifelong expectation that the world will be a good and pleasant place to live.

Autonomy versus shame and doubt *is Erikson's second stage of development, occurring in late infancy and toddlerhood (1–3 years).* After gaining trust in a caregiver(s), infants begin to discover that their behavior is their own. They start to assert their sense of independence or autonomy. They realize their *will.* If infants are restrained too much or punished too harshly, they are likely to develop a sense of shame and doubt.

Initiative versus guilt *is Erikson's third stage of development, occurring during the preschool years.* As preschool children encounter a widening social world, they are challenged more than when they were infants. Active, purposeful behavior is needed to cope with these challenges. Children are asked to assume responsibility for their bodies, their behavior, their toys, and their pets. Developing a sense of responsibility increases initiative. Uncomfortable guilt feelings may arise, though, if the child is irresponsible and is made to feel too anxious. Erikson has a positive outlook on this stage. He believes that most guilt is quickly compensated for by a sense of accomplishment.

Industry versus inferiority *is Erikson's fourth developmental stage, occurring approximately in the elementary school years.* Children's initiative brings them in contact with a wealth of new experiences. As they move into middle and late childhood, they direct their energy toward mastering knowledge and intellectual skills. At no other time is the child more enthusiastic about learning than at the end of early childhood's expansive imagination. The danger in the elementary school years is the development of a sense of inferiority—of feeling incompetent and unproductive. Erikson believes that teachers have a special responsibility for children's development of industry. Teachers should mildly but firmly coerce children into the adventure of finding out that one can learn to accomplish things which one would never have thought of by oneself " (Erikson, 1968, p. 127).

Identity versus identity confusion *is Erikson's fifth developmental stage, which individuals experience during the adolescent years. At this time individuals are faced with finding out who they are, what they are all about, and where they are going in life.* Adolescents are confronted with many new roles and adult statuses—vocational and romantic, for example. Parents need to allow adolescents to explore many different roles and different paths within a particular role. If the adolescent explores such roles in a healthy manner and arrives at a positive path to follow in life, then a positive identity will be achieved. If an identity is pushed on the adolescent by parents, if the adolescent does not adequately explore many roles, and if a positive future path is not defined, then identity confusion reigns.

Intimacy versus isolation *is Erikson's sixth developmental stage, which individuals experience during the early adulthood years. At this time, individuals face the developmental task of forming intimate relationships with others.* Erikson describes intimacy as finding oneself yet losing oneself in another. If the young adult forms healthy friendships and an intimate close relationship with another individual, intimacy will be achieved; if not, isolation will result.

Generativity versus stagnation *is Erikson's seventh development stage, which individuals experience during middle adulthood.* A chief concern is to assist the younger generation in

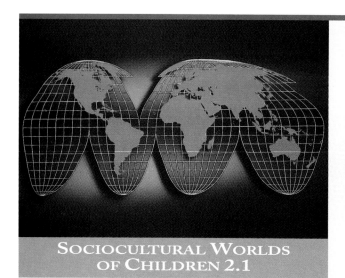

SOCIOCULTURAL WORLDS OF CHILDREN 2.1

Bwaitalu village carvers in the Trobriand islands of New Guinea with children. In the Trobriand islands, the authoritarian figure in the young boy's life is the maternal uncle, not the father. The young boys in this culture fear the maternal uncle, not the father. Thus, it is not sexual relations in a family that create conflict and fear for a child, a damaging finding for Freud's Oedipus complex theory.

Gender-Based Criticisms of Freud's Theory

The Oedipus complex was one of Freud's most influential concepts pertaining to the importance of early psychosexual relationships for later personality development. Freud's theory was developed during the Victorian era of the late nineteenth century when the male was dominant and the female was passive, and when sexual interests, especially the female's, were repressed. According to Freud, the sequence of events in the phallic stage for the girl begins when she realizes that she has no penis. According to Freud, she recognizes that the penis is superior to her own anatomy, and thus develops *penis envy*. Since her desire for having a penis can never be satisfied directly, Freud said that the young girl develops a wish to become impregnated by her father. Holding her mother responsible for her lack of a penis, she renounces her love for her mother and becomes

intensely attached to her father, thus forming her own version of the Oedipus complex, sometimes referred to as the Electra complex. Thus the sequence of events becomes reversed: for the boy, the Oedipal complex produces castration anxiety; whereas for the girl, penis envy—the parallel to castration anxiety—occurs first and leads to the formation of the Oedipus complex (Hyde, 1985).

Many psychologists believe Freud overemphasized behavior's biological determinants and did not give adequate attention to sociocultural influences and learning. In particular, his view on the differences between males and females, including their personality development, has a strong biological flavor, relying mainly on anatomical differences. That is, because

---

developing and leading useful lives—this is what Erikson means by *generativity*. The feeling of having done nothing to help the next generation is *stagnation*.

Integrity versus despair *is Erikson's eighth and final developmental stage, which individuals experience during late adulthood.* In the later years of life, we look back and evaluate what we have done with our lives. Through many different routes, the older person may have developed a positive outlook in most or all of the previous stages of development. If so, the retrospective glances will reveal a picture of a life well spent, and the person will feel a sense of satisfaction—integrity will be achieved. If the older adult resolved many of the earlier stages negatively, the retrospective glances likely will yield doubt or gloom—the despair Erikson talks about.

Each of us stands at the heart of the earth pierced through by a ray of sunlight: and suddenly it is evening.

—Salvatore Quasimodo

Erikson does not believe the proper solution to a stage crisis is always completely positive in nature. Some exposure or commitment to the negative end of the person's bipolar conflict is sometimes inevitable—you cannot trust all people under all circumstances and survive, for example. Nonetheless, in the healthy solution to a stage crisis, the positive resolution dominates. A summary of Erikson's stages is presented in figure 2.2.

they have a penis, boys are likely to develop a dominant, powerful personality, girls a submissive, weak personality. In basing his view of male/female differences in personality development on anatomical differences, Freud ignored the enormous impact of culture and experience in determining the personalities of the male and the female.

More than half a century ago, English anthropologist Bronislaw Malinowski (1927) observed the behavior of the Trobriand islanders of the Western Pacific. He found that the Oedipus complex is not universal but depends on cultural variations in families. The family pattern of the Trobriand islanders is different than found in many cultures. In the Trobriand islands, the biological father is not the head of the household, a role reserved for the mother's brother, who acts as a disciplinarian. Thus, the Trobriand islanders tease apart the roles played by the same person in Freud's Vienna and in many other cultures. In Freud's view, this different family constellation should make no difference: the Oedipal complex should still emerge, in which the father is the young boy's hated rival for the mother's love. However, Malinowski found no indication of conflict between fathers and sons in the Trobriand islanders, though he did observe some negative feelings directed by the boy toward the maternal uncle. Thus, the young boy feared the man who was the authoritarian figure in his life, which in the Trobriand island culture was the maternal uncle, not the father. In sum, Malinowski's study documented that it was not the sexual relations within the family that created conflict and fear for a child, a damaging finding for Freud's Oedipal complex theory.

Karen Horney developed the first feminist-based criticism of Freud's theory. Horney's model emphasizes women's positive qualities and self-evaluation.

Nancy Chodorow has developed an important contemporary feminist revision of psychoanalytic theory that emphasizes the meaningfulness of emotions for women.

The first feminist-based criticism of Freud's theory was proposed by psychoanalytic theorist Karen Horney (1967). She developed a model of women with positive feminine qualities and self-evaluation. Her critique of Freud's theory included reference to a male-dominant society and culture. Rectification of the male bias in psychoanalytic theory continues today. For example, Nancy Chodorow (1978, 1989) emphasizes that many more women than men define themselves in terms of their relationships and connections to others. Her feminist revision of psychoanalytic theory also emphasizes the meaningfulness of emotions for women, as well as the belief that many men use the defense mechanism of denial in self-other connections.

Cognitive Theories

Whereas psychoanalytic theories stress the importance of children's unconscious thoughts, cognitive theories emphasize their conscious thoughts. Two important cognitive theories are Piaget's cognitive development theory and information processing.

Piaget's Theory

The famous Swiss psychologist Jean Piaget (1896–1980) stressed that children actively construct their own cognitive worlds; information is not just poured into their mind from the environment. Piaget believes that children adapt their thinking to include new ideas because additional information furthers understanding.

Piaget also believed that we go through four stages in understanding the world. Each of the stages is age-related and consists of distinct ways of thinking. Remember, it is the *different* way of understanding the world that makes one stage more advanced than another; knowing *more* information does not make a child's thinking more advanced in the Piagetian view. This is what Piaget meant when he said a child's cognition is *qualitatively* different in one stage compared with another. What are Piaget's four stages of cognitive development like?

The **sensorimotor stage,** *which lasts from birth to about 2 years of age, is the first Piagetian stage. In this stage, infants construct an understanding of the world by coordinating sensory experiences (such as seeing and hearing) with physical, motoric actions—hence the term* sensorimotor. At the beginning of this stage, newborns have little more than reflexive patterns with

FIGURE 2.2

Erikson's eight stages of human development.

Erikson's stages	Developmental period	Characteristics
Trust versus mistrust	Infancy (first year)	A sense of trust requires a feeling of physical comfort and a minimal amount of fear about the future. Infants' basic needs are met by responsive, sensitive caregivers.
Autonomy versus shame and doubt	Infancy (second year)	After gaining trust in a caregiver(s), infants start to discover that they have a will of their own. They assert their sense of autonomy, or independence. They realize their will. If infants are restrained too much or punished too harshly, they are likely to develop a sense of shame and doubt.
Initiative versus guilt	Early childhood (preschool years, ages 3–5)	As preschool children encounter a widening social world, they are challenged more and need to develop more purposeful behavior to cope with these challenges. Children are now asked to assume more responsibility. Uncomfortable guilt feelings may arise, though, if the children are irresponsible and are made to feel too anxious.
Industry versus inferiority	Middle and late childhood (elementary school years, 6 years–puberty)	At no other time are children more enthusiastic than at the end of early childhood's expansive imagination. As children move into the elementary school years, they direct their energy toward mastering knowledge and intellectual skills. The danger at this stage involves feeling incompetent and unproductive.

Erikson's stages	Developmental period	Characteristics	
Identity versus identity confusion	Adolescence (10 to 20 years)	Individuals are faced with finding out who they are, what they are all about, and where they are going in life. An important dimension is the exploration of alternative solutions to roles. Career exploration is important.	
Intimacy versus isolation	Early adulthood (20s, 30s)	Individuals face the developmental task of forming intimate relationships with others. Erikson described intimacy as finding oneself yet losing oneself in another person.	
Generativity versus stagnation	Middle adulthood (40s, 50s)	A chief concern is to assist the younger generation in developing and leading useful lives.	
Integrity versus despair	Late adulthood (60s –)	Individuals look back and evaluate what they have done with their lives. The retrospective glances can either be positive (integrity) or negative (despair).	

which to work. At the end of the stage, 2-year-olds have complex sensorimotor patterns and are beginning to operate with primitive symbols.

The **preoperational stage,** *which lasts from approximately 2 to 7 years of age, is the second Piagetian stage. In this stage, children begin to represent the world with words, images, and drawings.* Symbolic thought goes beyond simple connections of sensory information and physical action. However, although preschool children can symbolically represent the world, according to Piaget, they still lack the ability to perform operations, the Piagetian term for internalized mental actions that allow children to do mentally what they previously did physically.

The **concrete operational stage,** *which lasts from approximately 7 to 11 years of age, is the third Piagetian stage. In this stage, children can perform operations, and logical reasoning replaces intuitive thought as long as reasoning can be applied to specific or concrete examples.* For instance, concrete operational thinkers cannot imagine the steps necessary to complete an algebraic equation, which is too abstract for thinking at this stage of development.

The **formal operational stage,** *which appears between the ages of 11 and 15, is the fourth and final Piagetian stage. In this stage, individuals move beyond the world of actual, concrete experiences and think in abstract and more logical terms.* As part of thinking more abstractly, adolescents develop images of ideal circumstances. They may think about what an ideal parent is like and compare their parents with this ideal standard. They begin to entertain possibilities for the future and are fascinated with what they can be. In solving problems, formal operational thinkers are more systematic, developing hypotheses about why something is happening the way it is, then testing these hypotheses in a deductive fashion. Piaget's stages are summarized in table 2.1.

Information Processing

Information processing *is concerned with how individuals process information about their world—how information enters the mind, how it is stored and transformed, and how it is retrieved to perform such complex activities as problem solving and reasoning.* A simple model of cognition is shown in figure 2.3.

Cognition begins when children detect information from the world through their sensory and perceptual processes. Then children store, transform, and retrieve the information through the processes of memory. Notice in our model that information can flow back and forth between memory and perceptual processes. For example, children are good at remembering the faces they see, yet their memory of a person's face may differ from the way the person actually looks. Keep in mind that our information processing model is a simple one, designed to illustrate the main cognitive processes and their interrelations. We could have drawn other arrows—between memory and language, between thinking and sensory and perceptual processes, and between language and sensory and perceptual processes, for example. Also, it is important to know that the boxes in fig-

Jean Piaget, the famous Swiss developmental psychologist, changed the way we think about the development of children's minds. For Piaget, a child's mental development is a continuous creation of increasingly complex forms.

ure 2.3 do not represent sharp, distinct stages in processing information. There is continuity and flow between the cognitive processes, as well as overlap.

Behavioral, Social Learning Theories

Behaviorists believe we should examine only what can be directly observed and measured. At approximately the same time that Freud was interpreting his patients' unconscious minds through early childhood experiences, behaviorists such as Ivan Pavlov and John B. Watson were conducting detailed observations of behavior in controlled laboratory circumstances. Out of the behavioral tradition grew the belief that development is observable behavior, learned through experience with the environment. The two versions of the behavioral approach that are prominent today are the view of B. F. Skinner and social learning theory.

Skinner's Behaviorism

Behaviorism *emphasizes the scientific study of observable behavioral responses and their environmental determinants.* In Skinner's behaviorism, the mind, conscious or unconscious, is not needed to explain behavior and development. For him, development is behavior. For example, observations of Sam reveal that his behavior is shy, achievement-oriented, and caring. Why is Sam's behavior this way? For Skinner, rewards and punishments in Sam's environment have shaped him into a shy, achievement-oriented, and caring person. Because of interactions with family members, friends, teachers, and others, Sam has *learned* to behave in this fashion.

TABLE 2.1

Piaget's Four Stages of Cognitive Development

Stage	Description	Age range
Sensorimotor	An infant progresses from reflexive, instinctual action at birth to the beginning of symbolic thought. The infant constructs an understanding of the world by coordinating sensory experiences with physical actions.	Birth to 2 years
Preoperational	The child begins to represent the world with words and images; these words and images reflect increased symbolic thinking and go beyond the connection of sensory information and physical action.	2 to 7 years
Concrete operational	The child can now reason logically about concrete events and classify objects into different sets.	7 to 11 years
Formal operational	The adolescent reasons in more abstract and logical ways. Thought is more idealistic.	11 to 15 years

FIGURE 2.3

A model of cognition.

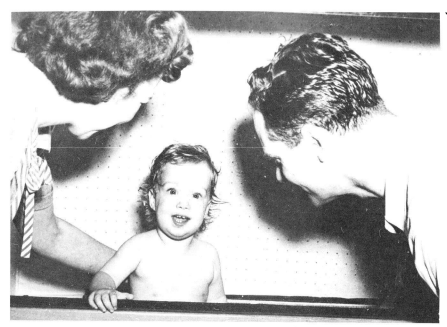

B. F. Skinner was a tinkerer who liked to make new gadgets. The younger of his two daughters, Deborah, was raised in Skinner's enclosed Air-Crib, which he invented because he wanted to control her environment completely. The Air-Crib was soundproofed and temperature controlled. Some critics accused Skinner of monstrous experimentation with his children; however, the early controlled environment has not had any noticeable harmful effects. Debbie, shown here as a child with her parents, is currently a successful artist, is married, and lives in London (Leo, 1983).

Bandura's research program has focused heavily on observational learning, learning that occurs through observing what others do. Observational learning is also referred to as imitation or modeling. What is *cognitive* about observational learning in Bandura's view? Bandura (1925–   ) believes that people cognitively represent the behavior of others and then sometimes adopt this behavior themselves. For example, a young boy may observe his father's aggressive outbursts and hostile interchanges with people; when observed with his peers, the young boy's style of interaction is highly aggressive, showing the same characteristics as his father's behavior. A girl may adopt the dominant and sarcastic style of her teacher. When observed interacting with her younger brother, she says, "You are so slow. How can you do this work so slow?" Social learning theorists believe that children acquire a wide range of such behaviors, thoughts, and feelings through observing others' behavior. These observations form an important part of children's development.

Social learning theories also differ from Skinner's behavioral view by emphasizing that children can regulate and control their own behavior. For example, another girl who observes her teacher behaving in a dominant and sarcastic way toward her students finds the behavior distasteful and goes out of her

Since behaviorists believe that development is learned and often changes according to environmental experiences, it follows that rearranging experiences can change development. For behaviorists, shy behavior can be transformed into outgoing behavior; aggressive behavior can be shaped into docile behavior; lethargic, boring behavior can be turned into enthusiastic, interesting behavior.

Social Learning Theory

Some psychologists believe that the behaviorists basically are right when they say development is learned and is influenced strongly by environmental experiences. However, they believe that Skinner went too far in declaring that cognition is unimportant in understanding development. **Social learning theory** *is the view of psychologists who emphasize behavior, environment, and cognition as the key factors in development.*

The social learning theorists say we are not like mindless robots, responding mechanically to others in our environment. Neither are we like weathervanes, behaving like a Communist in the presence of a Communist or like a John Bircher in the presence of a John Bircher. Rather, we think, reason, imagine, plan, expect, interpret, believe, value, and compare. When others try to control us, our values and beliefs allow us to resist their control.

American psychologists Albert Bandura (1977, 1986, 1989, 1991) and Walter Mischel (1973, 1984, 1993) are the main architects of social learning theory's contemporary version, which Mischel (1973) labeled *cognitive* social learning theory. Both Bandura and Mischel believe that cognitive processes are important mediators of environment-behavior connections.

Albert Bandura has been one of the leading architects of the contemporary version of social learning theory—cognitive social learning theory.

way to be encouraging and supportive toward her younger brother. Someone tries to persuade an adolescent to join a particular club at school. The adolescent thinks about the offer to join the club, considers her own interests and beliefs, and makes the decision not to join. The adolescent's *cognition* (thoughts) led her to control her own behavior and resist environmental influence in this instance.

Like the behavioral approach of Skinner, the social learning approach emphasizes the importance of empirical research in studying children's development. This research focuses on the processes that explain children's development—the social and cognitive factors that influence what children are like.

Ethological Theories

Sensitivity to different kinds of experience varies over the life cycle. The presence or absence of certain experiences at particular times in the life span influences individuals well beyond the time they first occur. Ethologists believe that most psychologists underestimate the importance of these special time frames in early development and the powerful roles that evolution and biological foundations play in development (Charlesworth, 1992; Hinde, 1992a).

Ethology emerged as an important view because of the work of European zoologists, especially Konrad Lorenz, (1903–1989). **Ethology** *stresses that behavior is strongly influenced by biology, is tied to evolution, and is characterized by critical or sensitive periods.*

Working mostly with greylag geese, Lorenz (1965) studied a behavior pattern that was considered to be programmed within the birds' genes. A newly hatched gosling seemed to be born with the instinct to follow its mother. Observations showed that the gosling was capable of such behavior as soon as it hatched. Lorenz proved that it was incorrect to assume that such behavior was programmed in the animal. In a remarkable set of experiments, Lorenz separated the eggs laid by

one goose into two groups. One group he returned to the goose to be hatched by her; the other group was hatched in an incubator. The goslings in the first group performed as predicted; they followed their mother as soon as they hatched. However, those in the second group, which saw Lorenz when they first hatched, followed him everywhere, as though he were their mother. Lorenz marked the goslings and then placed both groups under a box. Mother goose and "mother" Lorenz stood aside as the box lifted. Each group of goslings went directly to its "mother" (see figure 2.4). Lorenz called this process **imprinting,** *the ethological concept of rapid, innate learning within a limited critical period of time that involves attachment to the first moving object seen.*

The ethological view of Lorenz and the European zoologists forced American developmental psychologists to recognize the importance of the biological basis of behavior. However, the research and theorizing of ethology still seemed to lack some ingredients that would elevate it to the ranks of the other theories discussed so far in this chapter. In particular, there was little or nothing in the classical ethological view about the nature of social relationships across the human life cycle, something that any major theory of development must explain. Also, its concept of **critical period,** *a fixed time period very early in development during which certain behaviors optimally emerge,* seemed to be overdrawn. Classical ethological theory was weak in stimulating studies with humans. Recent expansion of the ethological view has improved its status as a viable developmental perspective.

Like behaviorists, ethologists are careful observers of behavior. Unlike behaviorists, ethologists believe that laboratories are not good settings for observing behavior; rather, they

FIGURE 2.4

Konrad Lorenz, a pioneering student of animal behavior, is followed through the water by three imprinted greylag geese. Lorenz described imprinting as rapid, innate learning within a critical period that involves attachment to the first moving object seen. For goslings, the critical period is the first 36 hours after birth.

When imprinting studies go awry . . .

"THE FAR SIDE" cartoon by Gary Larson is reprinted by permission of Chronicle Features, San Francisco, CA. All rights reserved.

Urie Bronfenbrenner (above with his grandson) has developed ecological theory, a perspective that is receiving increased attention. His theory emphasizes the importance of both micro and macro dimensions of the environment in which the child lives.

meticulously observe behavior in its natural surroundings, in homes, playgrounds, neighborhoods, schools, hospitals, and so on (Hinde, 1992b).

Ecological Theory

Ethological theory places a strong emphasis on the biological foundations of children's development. In contrast to ethological theory, Urie Bronfenbrenner (1917–   ) has proposed a strong environmental view of children's development that is receiving increased attention. **Ecological theory** *is Bronfenbrenner's sociocultural view of development, which consists of five environmental systems ranging from the fine-grained inputs of direct interactions with social agents to the broad-based inputs of culture. The five systems in Bronfenbrenner's ecological theory are the microsystem, mesosystem, exosystem, macrosystem, and chronosystem.* We will consider each in turn. Bronfenbrenner's (1979, 1986, 1989, 1993) ecological model is shown in figure 2.5.

The **microsystem** *in Bronfenbrenner's ecological theory is the setting in which an individual lives. This context includes the person's family, peers, school, and neighborhood.* It is in the microsystem that most of the direct interactions with social agents take place—with parents, peers, and teachers, for example. The in-

dividual is not viewed as a passive recipient of experiences in these settings, but as someone who helps construct the settings. Bronfenbrenner points out that most of the research on sociocultural influences has focused on microsystems.

The **mesosystem** *in Bronfenbrenner's ecological theory involves relations between microsystems or connections between contexts.* Examples are the relation of family experiences to school experiences, school experiences to church experiences, and family experiences to peer experiences. For instance, a child whose parents have rejected him may have difficulty developing positive relations with teachers. Developmentalists increasingly believe it is important to observe behavior in multiple settings—such as in family, peer, and school contexts—to obtain a more complete picture of an individual's development.

The **exosystem** *in Bronfenbrenner's ecological theory is involved when experiences in a social setting in which an individual does not have an active role influence what that person experiences in an immediate context.* For example, work experiences may affect a woman's relationship with her husband and their adolescent. The woman may receive a promotion that requires more travel, which might increase marital conflict and change patterns of parent-adolescent interaction. Another example of an

FIGURE 2.5

Bronfenbrenner's ecological theory of development. Bronfenbrenner's ecological theory consists of five environmental systems: microsystem, mesosystem, exosystem, macrosystem, and chronosystem.

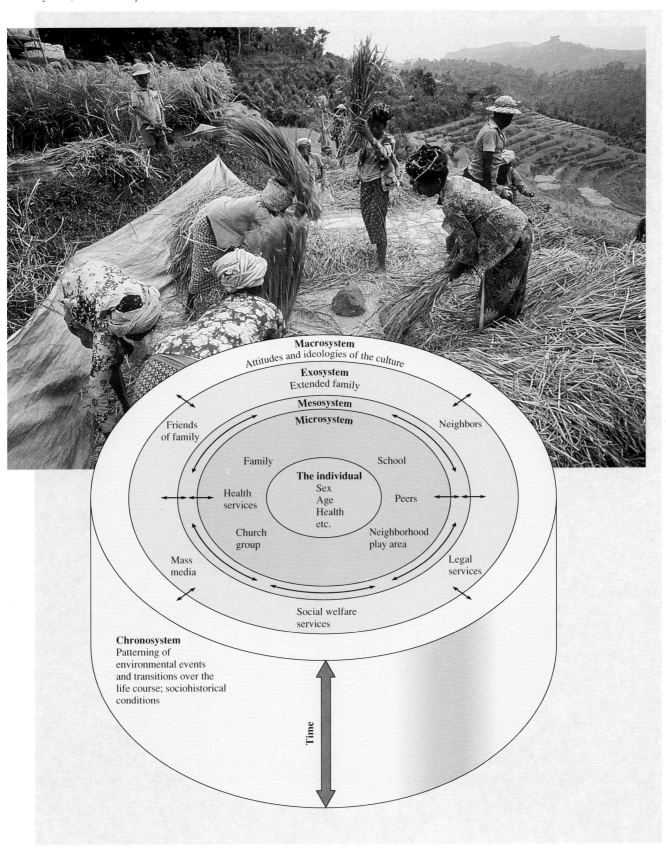

SOCIOCULTURAL WORLDS OF CHILDREN 2.2

Culture and Personality: Individualistic and Collectivistic Orientations

Because the concept of personality, or self—like other concepts—is socially constructed, it is likely to involve at least some cross-cultural variation (Kagitcibasi & Berry, 1989). Many of the assumptions about personality have been developed in Western cultures, which emphasize the individual, or self. Self-oriented terms dominate thinking about personality in such Western cultures as that of the United States—self-actualization, self-awareness, self-concept, self-efficacy, self-reinforcement, self-criticism, self-serving, selfishness, self-doubt, and so on (Lonner, 1988).

Many non-Western cultures, including Russia and Eastern countries such as Japan, China, and India, are collectivistic rather than individualistic (Hui & Villareal, 1989; Kagitcibasi, 1988; Triandis, 1985). *Individualistic* describes an individual, or self, orientation that involves separating the self from others. *Collectivistic* refers to a group orientation that involves relating the self to others. In one investigation of 40 nations, an individualistic versus collectivistic orientation was found to be a basic dimension of nation culture (Hofstede, 1980).

The individualistic/collectivistic dichotomy has not gone uncriticized. Describing entire nations of children and adults as having a basic personality obscures the extensive diversity and individual variation that characterizes a nation's people. Critics of the individualistic, self-orientation of Western personality conceptions point out that human beings have always lived in groups, communities, and societies, mutually needing one another. However, the individualistic orientation of many Western cultures, especially of the United States, may undermine our species' basic need for relatedness (Kagitcibasi, 1988). Some social scientists believe that many of our problems, such as anxiety, depression, and shyness, would not be as intense if the American cultural emphasis on the self and independence were not so strong (Munroe & Munroe, 1975). The pendulum may have swung too far in the individualistic direction in Western cultures. To develop a healthy, optimal personality, all people in all cultures need to develop a positive sense of self *and* a positive connectedness with others.

For American children, the development of autonomy, or independence, is believed to be a prerequisite for an ideal personality. Many American parents train their children to be self-sufficient at an early age. In many non-Western cultures, however, parents and other adults train children to be more other- or group-oriented. These non-Western cultures include Russia, China, Japan, and Israel. In North America, many Mexican parents also train their children to be more group-oriented than do American parents (Holtzmann, 1982).

In Japan, beginning in kindergarten, children wear the same type of uniform, including caps of different colors to indicate the classrooms to which the children belong. The students have identical sets of equipment kept in identical drawers and shelves. This is not intended to turn the Japanese children into robots, as some Americans have observed, but to impress on them that other people just like them have needs and rights that are equally as important as their own (Hendry, 1986). In sum, our American culture needs to emphasize a stronger sense of connectedness in addition to a positive development of self.

In Japan, schools emphasize a group orientation and connectedness to others rather than individualism.

exosystem is a city government, which is responsible for the quality of parks, recreation centers, and library facilities for children and adolescents.

The **macrosystem** *in Bronfenbrenner's ecological theory involves the culture in which individuals live.* Remember from chapter 1 that *culture* refers to the behavior patterns, beliefs, and all other products of a group of people that are passed on from generation to generation. Remember also that *cross-*

cultural studies—the comparison of one culture with one or more other cultures—provide information about the generality of children's development. To read further about culture's role in children's development, turn to Sociocultural Worlds of Children 2.2.

The **chronosystem** *in Bronfenbrenner's ecological theory involves the patterning of environmental events and transitions over the life course and sociohistorical circumstances.* For example, in studying the effects of divorce on children, researchers have found that the negative effects often peak in the first year after the divorce and the effects are more negative for sons than for daughters (Hetherington, 1989; Hetherington, Cox, & Cox, 1982). By two years after the divorce, family interaction is less chaotic and more stable. With regard to sociocultural circumstances, girls today are much more likely to be encouraged to pursue a career than they were 20 to 30 years ago. In ways such as these, the chronosystem has a powerful impact on children's lives.

An Eclectic Theoretical Orientation

An **eclectic theoretical orientation** *does not follow any one theoretical approach, but rather selects and uses whatever is considered the best in all theories.* No single theory described in this chapter is indomitable or capable of explaining entirely the rich complexity of child development. Each of the theories has made important contributions to our understanding of children's development, but none provides a complete description and explanation. Psychoanalytic theory best explains the unconscious mind. Erikson's theory best describes the changes that occur in adult development. Piaget's theory is the most complete description of children's cognitive development. The behavioral and social learning and ecological theories have been the most adept at examining the environmental determinants of development. The ethological theories have made us aware of biology's role and the importance of sensitive periods in development. It is important to recognize that, although theories are helpful guides, relying on a single theory to explain children's development is probably a mistake.

An attempt was made in this chapter to present five theoretical perspectives objectively. The same eclectic orientation will be maintained throughout the book. In this way, you can view the study of children's development as it actually exists—with different theorists making different assumptions, stressing different empirical problems, and using different strategies to discover information.

Critical Thinking

What personal experiences in your own life might influence the kind of developmental theory you would construct?

These theoretical perspectives, along with research issues that were discussed in chapter 1 and methods that will be described shortly, provide a sense of development's scientific nature. Table 2.2 compares the main theoretical perspectives in terms of how they view important developmental issues and the methods they prefer to use when they study children.

At this point we have discussed a number of ideas about the scientific method and theories of child development. A summary of these ideas is presented in Concept Table 2.1. Next, we explore the methods child developmentalists use to study children, beginning with the measures they use.

MEASURES

Systematic observations can be conducted in a number of ways. For example, we can watch behavior in a laboratory or in a more natural setting such as a school, home, or neighborhood playground. We can question children using interviews and surveys, develop and administer standardized tests, conduct case studies, examine behavior cross-culturally, or carry out physiological research. To help you understand how developmentalists use these methods, we will continue to draw examples from the study of children's aggression.

Observation

Sherlock Holmes chided Watson, "You see but you do not observe." We look at things all the time; however, casually watching a mother and her infant is not scientific observation. Unless you are a trained observer and practice your skills regularly, you may not know what to look for, you may not remember what you saw, what you are looking for may change from one moment to the next, and you may not communicate your observations effectively.

For observations to be effective, we have to know what we are looking for, who we are observing, when and where we will observe, how the observations will be made, and in what form they will be recorded. That is, our observations have to be made in a *systematic* way. Consider aggression. Do we want to study verbal or physical aggression, or both? Do we want to study younger or older children, or both? Do we want to evaluate them in a university laboratory, at school, at home, at a playground, or at all of these locations? A common way to record observations is to write them down, using shorthand or symbols.

Observation is an extremely valuable method for obtaining information about children's development. Here a researcher observes the social interaction of young children using a one-way mirror through which the observer can see the children, but the children cannot see the observer.

ABLE 2.2

A Comparison of Theories and the Issues and Methods in Child Development

Theory	Issues and Methods			
	Continuity/discontinuity, early versus later experiences	Biological and environmental factors	Importance of cognition	Research methods
Psychoanalytic	Discontinuity between stages—continuity between early experiences and later development; early experiences very important; later changes in development emphasized in Erikson's theory	Freud's biological determination interacting with early family experiences; Erikson's more balanced biological-cultural interaction perspective	Emphasized, but in the form of unconscious thought	Clinical interviews, unstructured personality tests, psychohistorical analyses of lives
Cognitive	Discontinuity between stages—continuity between early experiences and later development in Piaget's theory; has not been important to information-processing psychologists	Piaget's emphasis on interaction and adaptation; environment provides the setting for cognitive structures to develop; information-processing view has not addressed this issue extensively, but mainly emphasizes biological-environmental interaction	The primary determinant of behavior	Interviews and observations
Behavioral and social learning	Continuity (no stages); experience at all points of development important	Environment viewed as the cause of behavior in both views	Strongly deemphasized in the behavioral approach but an important mediator in social learning	Observation, especially laboratory observation
Ethological	Discontinuity but no stages; critical or sensitive periods emphasized: early experiences very important	Strong biological view	Not emphasized	Observation in natural settings
Ecological	Little attention to continuity/discontinuity; change emphasized more than stability	Strong environmental view	Not emphasized	Varied methods; especially stresses importance of collecting data in different social contexts

However, tape recorders, video cameras, special coding sheets, one-way mirrors, and computers are increasingly used to make observations more efficient (Roberts, 1993).

Frequently, when we observe, it is necessary to control certain factors that determine behavior but that are not the focus of our inquiry. For this reason, much psychological research is conducted in a **laboratory,** *a controlled setting in which many of the complex factors of the "real world" are removed.* For example, Albert Bandura (1965) brought children into a laboratory and had them observe an adult repeatedly hit an inflated plastic

Bobo doll about 3 feet tall. Bandura wondered to what extent the children would copy the adult's behavior. After the children saw the adult attack the Bobo doll, they, too, aggressively hit the inflated toy. By conducting his experiment in a laboratory with adults the children did not know as models, Bandura had complete control over when the children witnessed aggression, how much aggression the children saw, and what form the aggression took. Bandura could not have had as much control in his experiment if other factors, such as parents, siblings, friends, television, and a familiar room, had been present.

CONCEPT TABLE 2.1

Theory and the Scientific Method, and Theories of Child Development

Concept	Processes/Related Ideas	Characteristics/Description
Theory and the scientific method	Theory	Theories are general beliefs that help us to explain what we observe and make predictions. A good theory has hypotheses, which are assumptions to be tested.
	The scientific method	The scientific method is a series of procedures (identifying and analyzing a problem, collecting data, drawing conclusions, and revising theory) to obtain accurate information.
Theories of child development	Psychoanalytic theories	Two important psychoanalytic theories are Freud's and Erikson's. Freud said personality is made up of three structures—id, ego, and superego—and that most of children's thoughts are unconscious. The conflicting demands of children's personality structures produce anxiety. Defense mechanisms, especially repression, protect the child's ego and reduce anxiety. Freud was convinced that problems develop because of early childhood experiences. He said individuals go through five psychosexual stages—oral, anal, phallic, latency, and genital. During the phallic stage, the Oedipus complex is a major source of conflict. Gender-based criticisms of psychoanalytic theory have been made. Erikson developed a theory that emphasizes eight psychosocial stages of development: trust versus mistrust, autonomy versus shame and doubt, initiative versus guilt, industry versus inferiority, identity versus identity confusion, intimacy versus isolation, generativity versus stagnation, and integrity versus despair.
	Cognitive theories	Two important cognitive theories are Piaget's cognitive developmental theory and information processing. Piaget said that children are motivated to understand the world and adapt their thinking to acquire new information. Piaget said children go through four stages of cognitive development: sensorimotor, preoperational, concrete operational, and formal operational. Information-processing theory is concerned with how individuals process information about their world. It includes how information gets into the child's mind, how it is stored and transformed, and how it is retrieved to allow them to think and solve problems.
	Behavioral, social learning theories	Behaviorism emphasizes that cognition is not important in understanding children's behavior. Development is observed behavior, which is determined by rewards and punishments in the environment, according to B. F. Skinner, a famous behaviorist. Social learning theory, developed by Albert Bandura and others, states that the environment is an important determinant of behavior, but so are cognitive processes. Children have the ability to control their own behavior in the social learning view.
	Ethological theory	Konrad Lorenz was one of the important developers of ethological theory. Ethology emphasizes the biological and evolutionary basis of development. Imprinting and critical periods are key concepts.
	Ecological theory	In Bronfenbrenner's ecological theory, five environmental systems are important: microsystem, mesosystem, exosystem, macrosystem, and chronosystem.
	Eclectic theoretical orientation	No single theory can explain the rich, awesome complexity of children's development. Each of the theories has made a different contribution, and it probably is a wise strategy to adopt an eclectic theoretical perspective as we attempt to understand children's development.

Laboratory research, however, has some drawbacks. First, it is almost impossible to conduct the research without the participants knowing they are being studied. Second, the laboratory setting may be *unnatural* and, therefore, elicit unnatural behavior from the participants. Subjects usually show less aggressive behavior in a laboratory than in a more familiar natural setting, such as in a park or at home. They also show less aggression when they are unaware they are being observed than when they are aware that an observer is studying them. Third, some aspects of child development are difficult if not impossible to examine in a laboratory. Certain types of stress are difficult (and unethical) to study in the laboratory, such as recreating the circumstances that stimulate family conflict.

Although laboratory research is a valuable tool for developmentalists, naturalistic observation provides insight we sometimes cannot achieve in a laboratory. In **naturalistic observation,** *scientists observe behavior in real-world settings and make no effort to manipulate or control the situation.* Developmentalists conduct naturalistic observations at day-care centers, hospitals, schools, parks, homes, malls, dances, and other places where people live and frequent. In contrast to Bandura's observations of aggression in a laboratory, developmentalists observe the aggression of children in nursery schools, of adolescents on street corners, and of marital partners at home (Bronfenbrenner, 1989).

Interviews and Questionnaires

Sometimes the best and quickest way to get information from children is to ask them for it. Psychologists use interviews and questionnaires to find out about children's experiences and attitudes. Most interviews occur face-to-face, although they can take place over the telephone.

The types of interviews range from highly unstructured to highly structured. Examples of unstructured interview questions include: How aggressive do you see yourself? and How aggressive is your child? Examples of structured interview questions include: In the last week how often did you yell at your spouse? and How often in the last year was your child involved in fights at school? Structure is imposed by the questions themselves, or the interviewer can categorize answers by asking respondents to choose from several options. For example, in the question about your level of aggressiveness, you might be asked to choose from "highly aggressive," "moderately aggressive," "moderately unaggressive," and "highly unaggressive." In the question about how often you yelled at your spouse in the last week, you might be asked to choose "0," "1–2," "3–5," "6–10," or "more than 10 times."

Child developmentalists also question children and adults using questionnaires or surveys. A **questionnaire** *is similar to a highly structured interview except that respondents read the questions and mark their answers on paper rather than respond verbally to the interviewer.* One major advantage of surveys and questionnaires is that they can be given to a large number of people easily. Good surveys have concrete, specific, and unambiguous questions and assessment of the authenticity of the replies.

Case Studies

A **case study** *is an in-depth look at an individual; it is used mainly by clinical psychologists when the unique aspects of a person's life can-*

not be duplicated, either for practical or ethical reasons. A case study provides information about an individual's fears, hopes, fantasies, traumatic experiences, upbringing, family relationships, health, or anything that helps a psychologist understand that person's development. Some vivid case studies appear at different points in this text, among them one about a modern-day wild child named Genie, who lived in near isolation during her childhood (chapter 10).

Although case studies provide dramatic, in-depth portrayals of people's lives, we need to exercise caution when generalizing from this information. The subject of a case study is unique, with a genetic makeup and experiences no one else shares. In addition, case studies involve judgments of unknown reliability, in that usually no check is made to see if other psychologists agree with the observations.

Standardized Tests

Standardized tests *require people to answer a series of written or oral questions. They have two distinct features. First, psychologists usually total an individual's score to yield a single score, or set of scores, that reflects something about the individual. Second, psychologists compare the individual's score to the scores of a large group of similar people to determine how the individual responded relative to others.* Scores are often described in percentiles. For example, perhaps a child scored in the 92nd percentile of the Stanford-Binet Intelligence Test. This method informs us how much lower or higher the child scored than the large group of children who had taken the test previously.

To continue our look at how different measures are used to evaluate aggression, consider the Minnesota Multiphasic Personality Inventory (MMPI), which includes a scale to assess delinquency or antisocial tendencies. The items on this scale ask you to respond whether or not you are rebellious, impulsive, and have trouble with authority figures. This part of the MMPI might be given to adolescents to determine their delinquent and antisocial tendencies.

Cross-Cultural Research and Research with Ethnic Minority Groups

When researchers examine the behavior and mental processes of children in different cultures and different ethnic minority groups, they must follow certain strategies. When measures are used with cultural and ethnic groups with whom the researchers are unfamiliar, it is vital that they construct the measures so that they are meaningful for all of the cultural or ethnic minority groups being studied. To accomplish this objective, cross-cultural researchers do not use one culture as the sole source for developing a measure. Rather, informants from all cultures in the investigation provide information to the researchers so they can develop a meaningful measure (Berry & others, in press).

In keeping with our theme of applying different ways of obtaining information about children to aggression, what have cross-cultural psychologists discovered about aggression in different cultures? They have found that aggression is a cultural universal, appearing in all cultures studied; however, the ways in which aggression is expressed may be culture-specific. For example, in the !Kung culture of southern Africa, the members

Systematic observations in natural settings provide valuable information about behavior across cultures. For example, in one investigation, observations in different cultures revealed that American children often engage in less work and more play than children in many other cultures (Whiting & Whiting, 1975). However, conducting cross-cultural research using such methods as systematic observation in natural settings is difficult and requires attention to a number of methodological issues.

actively try to dissuade individuals from behaving aggressively, whereas, in the Yanamamo Indian culture of South America, the members promote aggression. Yanamamo youth are told that they cannot achieve adult status unless they are capable of killing, fighting, and pummeling others.

In conducting research on cultural and ethnic minority issues, investigators distinguish between the emic approach and the etic approach (Brislin, 1993; Harkness, 1992). In the **emic approach,** *the goal is to describe behavior in one culture or ethnic group in terms that are meaningful and important to the people in that culture or ethnic group, without regard to other cultures or ethnic groups.* In the **etic approach,** *the goal is to describe behavior so that generalizations can be made across cultures.* That is, the emic approach is culture specific; the etic approach is culture universal. If researchers construct a questionnaire in an emic fashion, their concern is only that the questions are meaningful to the particular culture or ethnic group being studied. If, however, the researchers construct a questionnaire in an etic fashion, they want to include questions that reflect concepts familiar to all cultures involved.

How might the emic and etic approaches be reflected in the study of family processes? In the emic approach, the researchers might choose to focus only on middle-class White families, without regard for whether the information obtained

in the study can be generalized or is appropriate for ethnic minority groups. In a subsequent study, the researchers may decide to adopt an etic approach by studying not only middle-class White families, but also lower-income White families, Black American families, Hispanic American families, and Asian American families. In studying ethnic minority families, the researchers would likely discover that the extended family is more frequently a support system in ethnic minority families than in White American families. If so, the emic approach would reveal a different pattern of family interaction than would the etic approach, documenting that research with middle-class White families cannot always be generalized to all ethnic groups.

In a recent symposium on racism in developmental research (Bloom, 1992; Lee, 1992; Padilla & Lindholm, 1992), the participants concluded that we need to include more ethnic minority children in our research. Historically, ethnic minority children have essentially been discounted from research and viewed simply as variations from the norm or average. The development of nonmainstream children has been viewed as "confounds" or "noise" in data, and consequently, researchers have deliberately excluded such children from the samples they have selected. Because ethnic minority children have been excluded from research for so long, there likely is more variation in children's real lives than our research data have indicated in the past.

Cross-cultural psychologist Joseph Trimble (1989) is especially concerned about researchers' tendencies to use ethnic gloss when they select and describe ethnic groups. By **ethnic gloss,** Trimble means *using an ethnic label, such as Black, Hispanic, Asian, or Native American, in a superficial way that makes an ethnic group seem more homogeneous than it actually is.* For example, the following is an unsuitable description of a research sample, according to Trimble: "The subjects included 28 Blacks, 22 Hispanics, and 24 Whites." An acceptable description of each of the groups requires much more detail about the participants' country of origin, socioeconomic status, language, and ethnic self-identification, such as this: "The 22 subjects were Mexican Americans from low-income neighborhoods in the southwestern area of Los Angeles. Twelve spoke Spanish in the home, while 10 spoke English; 11 were born in the United States, 11 were born in Mexico; 16 described themselves as Mexican, 3 as Chicano, 2 as American, and 1 as Latino." Trimble believes that ethnic gloss can cause researchers to obtain samples of ethnic groups and cultures that are not representative of their ethnic and cultural diversity, leading to overgeneralizations and stereotypes.

Physiological Research and Research with Animals

Two additional methods that psychologists use to gather data are physiological research and research with animals. Research on the biological basis of behavior and technological advances continue to produce remarkable insights about mind and behavior. For example, researchers have found that the electrical stimulation of certain areas of the brain turn docile, mild-mannered people into hostile, vicious attackers, and higher concentrations of some hormones have been associated with anger in adolescents (Susman & Dorn, 1991).

FIGURE 2.6

Possible explanations of correlational data. An observed correlation between two events cannot be used to conclude that one event causes a second event. Other possibilities are that the second event causes the first event or that a third, unknown event causes the correlation between the first two events.

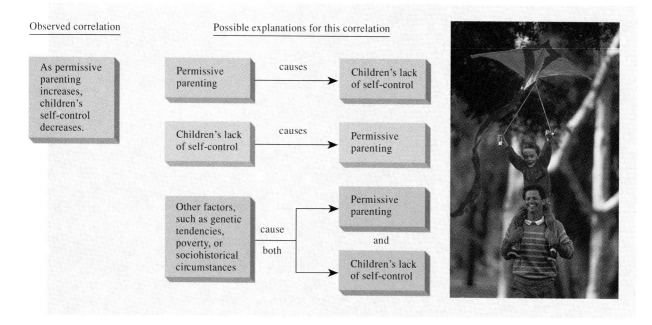

Since much physiological research cannot be carried out with humans, psychologists sometimes use animals. Animal studies permit researchers to control their subjects' genetic background, diet, experiences during infancy, and many other factors. In studying humans, psychologists treat these factors as random variation, or "noise," that may interfere with accurate results. In addition, animal researchers can investigate the effects of treatments (brain implants, for example) that would be unethical with humans. Moreover, it is possible to track the entire life cycle of some animals over a relatively short period of time. Laboratory mice, for instance, have a life span of approximately 1 year.

Multimeasure, Multisource, Multicontext Approach

The various methods have their strengths and weaknesses. Direct observations are extremely valuable tools for obtaining information about children, but there are some things we cannot observe in children—their moral thoughts, their inner feelings, the arguments of their parents, how they acquire information about sex, and so on. In such instances, other measures, such as interviews, questionnaires, and case studies may be valuable. Because virtually every method has limitations, many investigators use multiple measures in assessing children's development. For example, a researcher might ask children about their aggressive behavior, check with their friends, observe them carefully at home and in their neighborhood, interview their parents, observe the children at school during recess, and ask teachers to rate the children's aggression. Researchers hope that the convergence of multimeasure, multisource, and multicontext information provides a more comprehensive and valid assessment of children's development.

STRATEGIES FOR SETTING UP RESEARCH STUDIES

How can we determine if a pregnant woman's cigarette smoking affects her offspring's attentional skills? How can we determine if responding nurturantly to an infant's cries increases attachment to the caregiver? How can we determine if day care is damaging to a child's development? How can we determine if listening to rock music lowers an adolescent's grades in school? When designing a research study to answer such questions, investigators must decide whether to use a correlational or an experimental strategy.

Correlational Strategy

In the **correlational strategy,** *the goal is to describe the strength of the relation between two or more events or characteristics. This is a useful strategy because, the more strongly events are correlated (related, or associated), the more we can predict one from the other.* For example, if we find that as parents use more permissive ways to deal with their children the children's self-control decreases, this does not mean that the parenting style caused the lack of self-control. It could mean that, but it could also mean that the children's lack of self-control stimulated the parents to simply throw up their arms in despair and give up trying to control the obstreperous children's behavior, or it could mean that other factors might cause this correlation, such as genetic background, poverty, and sociohistorical conditions. (Several decades ago a permissive parenting strategy was widely advocated but today it no longer is in vogue.) Figure 2.6 portrays these possible interpretations of correlational data.

The **correlational coefficient** *is a number based on statistical analysis that is used to describe the degree of association between two variables. The correlation coefficient ranges from −1.00 to +1.00.* A negative number means an inverse relation. For example, today we often find a *negative* correlation between permissive parenting and children's self-control, and we often find a *positive* correlation between a parent's involvement in and monitoring of a child's life and the child's self-control. The higher the correlation coefficient (whether positive or negative), the stronger the association between the two variables. A correlation of 0 means that there is no association between the two variables. A correlation of −.40 is a stronger correlation than +.20 because we disregard the negative or positive nature of the correlation in determining the correlation's magnitude.

Experimental Strategy

Whereas the correlational strategy allows us to say only that two events are related, the **experimental strategy** *allows us to precisely determine behavior's causes. Developmentalists accomplish this task by performing an experiment, which is a study done in a carefully regulated setting in which one or more of the factors believed to influence the behavior being studied is manipulated and all others are held constant.* If the behavior under study changes when a factor is manipulated, we say that the manipulated factor causes the behavior to change. Experiments establish cause and effect between events, something correlational studies cannot do. *Cause* is the event being manipulated and *effect* is the behavior that changes because of the manipulation. Remember that, in testing correlation, nothing is manipulated; in an experiment, a researcher actively changes an event to see its effect on behavior.

The following example illustrates the nature of an experiment. The problem to be studied is whether aerobic exercise during pregnancy affects the development of infants. We need to have one group of pregnant women engage in aerobic exercise and the other not engage in aerobic exercise. We randomly assign our subjects to these two groups. **Random assignment** *occurs when researchers assign subjects to experimental and control conditions by chance, thus reducing the likelihood the results of the experiment will be due to preexisting differences in the two groups.* For example, random assignment greatly reduces the probability the two groups will differ on such factors as age, social class, prior aerobic exercise, intelligence, health problems, alertness, and so on.

The **independent variable** *is the manipulated, influential, experimental factor in an experiment. The label* independent *is used because this variable can be changed independently of other factors.* In the aerobic exercise experiment, the amount of aerobic exercise is the independent variable. We manipulate the amount of the aerobic exercise by having the pregnant women exercise four times a week under the direction of a trained instructor. The **dependent variable** *is the factor that is measured in an experiment; it may change because of the manipulation of the independent variable. The label* dependent *is used because this variable depends on what happens to the subjects in the experiment.* In the aerobic exercise experiment, the dependent variable is represented by two infant measures—breathing and sleeping pat-

FIGURE 2.7

Principles of experimental strategy. The effects of aerobic exercise by pregnant women on their newborns' breathing and sleeping patterns.

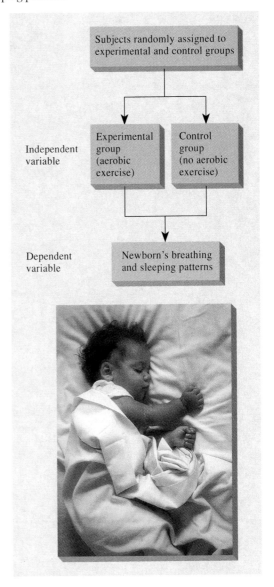

terns. The subjects' responses on these measures depend on the influence of the independent variable (whether or not pregnant women engaged in aerobic exercise). An illustration of the nature of the experimental strategy, applied to the aerobic exercise study, is presented in figure 2.7. In our experiment, we test the two sets of offspring in the first week of life. We find that the experimental group infants have more regular breathing and sleeping patterns than their control group counterparts; thus, we conclude that aerobic exercise by pregnant women promotes more regular breathing and sleeping patterns in newborn infants.

It might seem as if we should always choose an experimental strategy over a correlational strategy, since the experimental strategy gives us a better sense of the influence of one variable on another. Are there instances when a correlational strategy might be preferred? Three such instances are (1) when

FIGURE 2.8

A comparison of cross-sectional and longitudinal approaches.

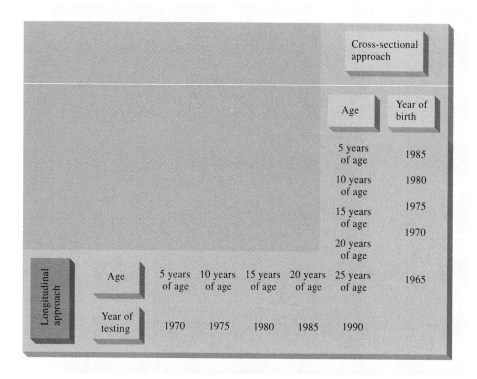

the focus of the investigation is so new that we have little knowledge of which variables to manipulate (as when AIDS first appeared), (2) when it is physically impossible to manipulate the variables (such as factors involved in suicide), and (3) when it is unethical to manipulate the variables (for example, in determining the association between illness and exposure to dangerous chemicals).

TIME SPAN OF INQUIRY

A special concern of developmentalists is the time span of a research investigation. Studies that focus on the relation of age to another variable are common in the field of child development. We have several options—we can study different children of different ages and compare them, or we can study the same individuals as they grow older.

Cross-Sectional Approach

The **cross-sectional approach** *is a research strategy in which individuals of different ages are compared all at one time.* A typical cross-sectional study might include a group of 5-year-olds, 8-year-olds, and 11-year-olds. The different groups can be compared with respect to a variety of dependent variables—IQ, memory, peer relations, attachment to parents, hormonal changes, and so on. All of this can be accomplished in a short time. In some studies, data are collected in a single day. Even large-scale cross-sectional studies with hundreds of subjects

usually do not take longer than several months to complete data collection.

The main advantage of a cross-sectional study is that researchers do not have to wait for subjects to grow up. Despite its time efficiency, the cross-sectional approach has its drawbacks: It gives no information about how individuals change or about the stability of their characteristics. The increases and decreases—the hills and valleys—of growth and development can become obscured in the cross-sectional approach. Also, because the children studied are of different ages and different groups, they were born at different times; they may have experienced different types of parenting and schooling; and they may have been influenced by different trends in dress, television, and play materials.

Longitudinal Approach

The **longitudinal approach** *is a research strategy in which the same individuals are studied over a period of time, usually several years or more.* In a typical longitudinal study of the same topics we discussed with the cross-sectional approach, we might structure a test to administer to children once a year when they are 4, 8, and 12 years old. In this example, the same children would be studied over an 8-year time span, allowing us to examine patterns of change within each child. One of the great values of the longitudinal approach is that we can evaluate how individual children change as they grow up.

Fewer longitudinal than cross-sectional studies are conducted because they are time consuming and costly. A close examination of the longitudinal approach reveals some additional problems: (1) When children are examined over a long period of time, some drop out because they lose interest or move away and cannot be recontacted by the investigator. A fairly common finding is that the remaining children represent a slightly biased sample, in that they tend to be psychologically superior to those who dropped out on almost every dimension (intelligence, motivation, and cooperativeness, for example) that the investigator checks. (2) With repeated testing, some children may become more "testwise," which may increase their ability to perform "better" or "more maturely" the next time the investigator interacts with them. For a comparison of longitudinal and cross-sectional research designs, see figure 2.8.

"That's my dad when he was 10 . . . . He was in some sort of cult."
© 1986; Reprinted courtesy of Bill Hoest and Parade Magazine.

Cohort Effects

Cohort effects *are those due to a subject's time of birth or generation but not actually to age.* Today's children are living a childhood of firsts (Louv, 1990). They are the first day-care generation; the first truly multicultural generation; the first generation to grow up in the electronic bubble of an environment defined by computers and new forms of media; the first post-sexual revolution generation; the first generation to grow up in new kinds of dispersed, deconcentrated cities, not quite urban, rural, or suburban.

> *The mark of the historic is the nonchalance with which it picks up an individual and deposits him in a trend, like a house playfully moved in a tornado.*
>
> —Mary McCarthy

Cohort effects are important because they can powerfully affect the dependent measures in a study ostensibly concerned with age. Researchers have shown that cohort effects are especially important to investigate in the assessment of intelligence (Willis & Schaie, 1986). For example, individuals born at different points in time—such as 1920, 1940, and 1960—have had varying opportunities for education, with the individuals born in earlier years having less access. Explorations in Child Development 2.1 provides further information about the role of cohort effects in children's development.

Now that we have considered the main ways that child developmentalists conduct research, it is also important to examine how child development research can become less sexist and some ethical considerations in child development research.

REDUCING SEXIST RESEARCH

Traditional science is presented as being value free and, thus, a valid way of studying mental processes and behavior. However, there is a growing consensus that science in general

Florence Denmark (shown here talking with a group of students) has developed a number of guidelines for nonsexist research. Denmark and others believe that psychology needs to be challenged to examine the world in a new way, one that incorporates girls' and women's perspectives.

and psychology in particular are not value free (Doyle & Paludi, 1991). A special concern is that the vast majority of psychological research has been male oriented and male dominated. Some researchers believe that male-dominated sciences, such as psychology, need to be challenged to examine the world in a new way, one that incorporates girls' and women's perspectives and respects their ethnicity, sexual orientation, age, and socioeconomic status. For example, Florence Denmark and her colleagues (1988) provided the following three recommendations as guidelines for nonsexist research:

1. Research methods

   Problem: The selection of research participants is based on stereotypic assumptions and does not allow for generalizations to other groups.

   Example: On the basis of stereotypes about who should be responsible for contraception, only females are studied.

   Correction: Both sexes should be studied before conclusions are drawn about the factors that determine contraception use.

2. Data analysis

   Problem: Gender differences are inaccurately magnified.

   Example: Whereas only 24 percent of the girls were found to . . . fully 28 percent of the boys were . . .

   Correction: The results should include extensive descriptions of the data so that differences are not exaggerated.

3. Conclusions

   Problem: The title or abstract (summary) of an article makes no reference to the limitations of the study participants and implies a broader scope of the study than is warranted.

EXPLORATIONS IN CHILD DEVELOPMENT 2.1

Cohort Effects and Children's Computer Skills

For some time, educators have been interested in teaching school-age children basic information about computers. The programming language BASIC, which was invented in the 1960s, is one of the tools many experts feel they can teach young children. Imagine a study of a group of elementary school children, designed to determine just how much of this language children can learn. Following is a brief summary of this hypothetical investigation.

FIGURE 2.A

Children's knowledge of BASIC.

			Grade		
	1	*2*	*3*	*4*	*5*
Correct answers, 1975	5.5	5.3	6.8	7.0	8.8
Correct answers, 1990	12.5	13.0	15.2	18.5	20.0

Example: A study purporting to be about "perceptions of the disabled" examines only blind White boys.

Correction: Use more precise titles and clearly describe the sample and its selection criteria in the abstract or summary.

ETHICS IN RESEARCH ON CHILD DEVELOPMENT

Increasingly, child developmentalists recognize that considerable caution must be taken to ensure the well-being of children when they are involved in a research study. Today, colleges and universities have review boards that evaluate the ethical nature of research conducted at their institutions. Proposed research plans must pass the scrutiny of an ethics research committee before the research can be initiated. In addition, the American Psychological Association (APA) has developed guidelines for its members' ethics.

The code of ethics adopted by the APA instructs researchers to protect their subjects from mental and physical harm. The best interests of the subjects must be kept foremost in the researcher's mind. All subjects, if they are old enough, must give their informed consent to participate in a research study. This requires that subjects know what their participation will entail and any risks that might develop. For example, subjects in an investigation of the effects of divorce on children should be told beforehand that interview questions might stimulate thought about issues they might not anticipate. The subjects should also be informed that in some instances a discussion of the family's experiences might improve family relationships, but in other instances it might bring up issues that bring the children unwanted stress. After informed consent is given, the subjects reserve the right to withdraw from the study at any time.

Special ethical concerns govern the conduct of research with children. First, if children are to be studied, informed consent from their parents or legal guardians must be obtained. Parents have the right to a complete and accurate description of what will be done with their children and may refuse to let them participate. Second, children have rights too. Psychologists are obliged to explain precisely what the children will experience. The children may refuse to participate, even after parental permission has been given. Also, if a child becomes upset during the research study, it is the psychologists's obligation to calm the child. Third, psychologists must always weigh the potential for

In 1975, a large group of children in grades one through five (roughly 6 to 10 years of age) is randomly selected from two schools in the same school district of a small city. The children are given 10 hours of instruction about the BASIC programming language, including the definition and usage rules of elementary programming commands (such as PRINT, HOME, REMARK, =, LET, FOR, NEXT, ":", GO TO, and END) and the rules for writing and sequencing simple lines of code, such as:

10 PRINT "HELLO, STUDENTS"

20 PRINT "DO YOU LIKE THIS CLASS"

30 END

At the end of their instruction, they are given a standard test to determine how many commands they know and how well they can correct errors in simple programs. Figure 2.A shows how many of 30 questions children at each grade correctly answer.

Fifteen years later, in 1990, the same instructional study is repeated with children randomly sampled from the same schools. The researchers check the backgrounds of this new sample of children and discover that they are equivalent to the 1975 sample in terms of their average ability levels, their achievement in school, and their socioeconomic backgrounds. Figure 2.A shows how this new sample of children performs on the same test given to the children in 1975. Take a careful look at the results for these two samples. What do you see?

In 1975, the youngest children were able to correctly answer five to six questions, with a modest increase in average performance of fifth graders to eight to nine correct answers. In 1990, however, the youngest children correctly answered more than twice as many questions as their earlier counterparts and actually outperformed the fifth graders tested a decade and a half earlier. Again, in 1990, we see an increase in children's average level of performance across the elementary school grades.

This hypothetical study is a classic example of a cohort effect. Children born in one era perform differently than do children born in another era. It does not take much imagination to arrive at a plausible explanation of the cohort effect. An elementary analysis of major historical events between 1975 and 1990 would show that millions of homeowners purchased computers during this time. Most of those homeowners used their computers for word processing and for playing skill and adventure games. They also made modest efforts to learn simple programming with the BASIC language.

The children tested in 1990 were not necessarily better learners than those tested in 1975. They simply knew more to begin with—before instruction began—than the children from a decade and a half earlier. We are not aware of any investigation of children's development that documents such a dramatic cohort effect, although, if someone had had the foresight to envision the modern computer revolution, results such as these would be easily found.

harming children against the prospects of contributing some clear benefits to them. If there is the chance of harm—as when drugs are used, social deception takes place, or children are treated aversively (that is, punished or reprimanded)—psychologists must convince a group of peers that the benefits of the experience clearly outweigh any chance of harm. Fourth, since children are in a vulnerable position and lack power and control when facing adults, psychologists should always strive to make a professional encounter a positive and supportive experience.

BEING A WISE CONSUMER OF INFORMATION ABOUT CHILDREN'S DEVELOPMENT

We live in an information society in which there is a vast amount of information about children's development available for public consumption. The information varies greatly in quality. How can you become a wise consumer of information about children's development?

Be Cautious about What Is Reported in the Media

Research and clinical findings about children's development are increasingly talked about in the media. Television, radio, newspapers, and magazines all make it a frequent practice to report on research and clinical findings involving children that are likely to be of interest to the general public. Many professional and mental health and psychological organizations regularly supply the media with information about research and clinical findings. In many cases, this information has been published in professional journals or presented at national meetings. And most major colleges and universities have a media relations department that contacts the press about current research by their faculty.

Not all psychological and mental health information involving children that is presented for public consumption comes from professionals with excellent credentials and reputations at colleges, universities, and in applied mental health settings. Journalists, television reporters, and other media personnel are not scientifically and clinically trained. It is not an easy task for them to sort through the widely varying material they come across and make a sound decision about which research and clinical information that involves children should be presented to the public.

Unfortunately, the media often focus on sensational and dramatic psychological findings. They want you to read what they have written or stay tuned and not flip to another channel. They can capture your attention and keep it by presenting dramatic, sensational, and surprising information. As a consequence, media presentations of information about children tend to go beyond what actual research articles and clinical findings really say.

Even when excellent research and clinical findings are presented to the public, it is difficult for media personnel to adequately inform people about what has been found and the implications for their lives. For example, throughout this text, you will be introduced to an entirely new vocabulary. Each time we present a new concept we precisely define it and give examples of it as well. We have an entire book to carry out our task of carefully introducing, defining, and elaborating on key concepts and issues, research, and clinical findings about children's development. However, the media do not have the luxury of time and space to go into considerable detail and specify the limitations and qualifications of research and clinical findings. They often have only a few minutes or few lines to summarize the best they can the complex findings of a study about children's development.

Among the other ways that you can think critically about the psychological information you see, hear, or read are to understand the distinction between nomothetic research and idiographic needs, to be aware of the tendency to overgeneralize from a small sample or a unique clinical sample, to know that a single study is often not the final and definitive word about an issue or topic, to be sure you understand why causal conclusions cannot be drawn from a correlational study, and to always consider the source of the information about children and evaluate its credibility.

Know How to Make a Distinction between Nomothetic Research and Idiographic Needs

In being a wise consumer of information about children it is important to understand the difference between nomothetic research and idiographic needs. **Nomothetic research** *is conducted at the level of the group.* Most research on children's development is nomothetic research. Individual variations in how children respond is often not a major focus of the research. For example, if researchers are interested in the effects of divorce on children's ability to cope with stress, they might conduct a study of 50 children from divorced families and 50 children from intact, never divorced families. They might find that divorced children, as a group, cope more poorly with stress than children from intact families. That is a nomothetic finding that applies to divorced children as a group. And that is what commonly is reported in the media. In this particular study, it likely was the case that some of the divorced children were coping better with stress than some of the children from intact families—not as

many, but some. Indeed, it is entirely possible that of the 100 children in the study, the 2 or 3 children who were coping the very best with stress might have been children from divorced families and the findings still be reported that children from divorced families (as a group) cope more poorly with stress than children from intact families do.

As a consumer of information, you want to know what the information means for you *individually,* not necessarily a group of people. **Idiographic needs** *refer to what is important for the individual, not the group.* The failure of the media to inadequately distinguish between nomothetic research and idiographic needs is not entirely their fault. Researchers have not adequately done this either. The research they conduct too often fails to examine the overlap between groups and tends to present only the differences that are found. And when those differences are reported, too often they are reported as if there is no overlap between the groups being compared (in our example, children from divorced families and children from intact families) when in reality there is substantial overlap. If you read a study in a research journal or a media report of a study which states that children from divorced families coped more poorly with stress than children from intact families, it does not mean that all children from divorced families coped more poorly than all children from intact families. It simply means that as a group intact family children coped better.

Recognize How It Is Easy to Overgeneralize from a Small or Clinical Sample

There often isn't space or time in media presentations of information about children to go into details about the nature of the sample. Sometimes you will get basic information about the sample's size—whether it is based on 10 subjects, 50 subjects, or 200 subjects, for example. In many cases, small or very small samples require that care be exercised in generalizing to a larger population of individuals. For example, if a study of divorced children is based on only 10 or 20 divorced children, what is found in the study may not generalize to all divorced children because the sample investigated may have some unique characteristics. The sample might come from families who have substantial economic resources, are White American, live in a suburb of a small Southern town, and are all undergoing psychotherapy. In this study, then, we clearly would be making unwarranted generalizations if we thought the findings also characterize divorced children from families who have moderate to low incomes, are from other ethnic backgrounds, live in different locations, and are not undergoing psychotherapy.

Be Aware that a Single Study Is Usually Not the Defining Word about Some Aspect of Children's Development

The media may identify an interesting piece of research or a clinical finding and claim that it is something phenomenal with far-reaching implications. While such studies and findings do occur, it is rare for a single study to provide earth-shattering and conclusive answers, especially answers that apply to all children. In fact, in most domains of children's development, where there are a large number of investigations, it is not unusual to find conflicting results about a particular topic or issue. Answers to questions about children's development usually emerge after many scientists and/or clinicians have conducted similar investigations or therapy has been practiced by a number of mental health professionals who have drawn similar conclusions. Thus, a report of one study or clinical observations by only one or two therapists should not be taken as the absolute, final answer to a problem.

In our example of divorce, if one study reports that a particular therapy conducted by a therapist has been especially effective with divorced children, we should not conclude that the therapy will work as effectively with all divorced children and with other therapists until more studies are conducted.

Remember that Causal Conclusions Cannot Be Made from Correlational Studies

Drawing causal conclusions from correlational studies is one of the most common mistakes made by the media. In studies in which an experiment has not been conducted (remember that in an experiment, subjects are randomly assigned to treatments or experiences), two variables or factors may be related to each other. However, causal interpretations cannot be made when two or more factors are simply correlated or related to each other. We cannot say that one causes the other. In the case of divorce, a headline might read "Divorce causes children to have problems in school." We read the article and find out the headline was derived from the results of a research study. Since we obviously cannot, for ethical or practical purposes, randomly assign children to families that will become divorced or stay intact, this headline is based on a correlational study and such causal statements cannot be accurately made. At least some of the children's problems in school probably occurred prior to the divorce of their parents. Other factors, such as poor parenting practices, low socioeconomic status, a difficult temperament, and low intelligence, may also contribute to children's problems in schools and not be a direct consequence of divorce itself. What we can say in such studies, if the data warrant it, is that divorce is related to or associated with problems in school. What we cannot legitimately say in such studies is that divorce causes problems in school.

Always Consider the Source of the Information and Evaluate Its Credibility

Studies are not automatically accepted by the research community. Researchers usually have to submit their findings to a research journal where it is reviewed by their colleagues, who make a decision about whether to publish the paper or not. While quality of research in journals is not uniform, in most cases the research has undergone far greater scrutiny and careful consideration of the quality of the work than is the case for research or any other information that has not gone through the journal process. And within the media, we can distinguish between what is presented in respected newspapers, such as *The New York Times* and *Washington Post*, as well as credible magazines, such as *Time* and *Newsweek*, and much less respected and less credible tabloids, such as *The National Enquirer* and *Star*.

Since our last review, we have discussed a number of ideas about methods and how to be a wise consumer of information about children's development. A summary of these ideas is presented in Concept Table 2.2.

PERSPECTIVES ON PARENTING AND EDUCATION

An Important Mesosystem Connection: Family and School

In Bronfenbrenner's ecological theory, the mesosystem refers to connections between microsystems or social contexts. An important mesosystem connection is between families and schools. Researchers have consistently found that successful students often receive long-term support from parents or other adults at home, as well as strong support from teachers and others at school. Involving parents in learning activities with their children at home is one kind of parental involvement that many educators believe is an important aspect of the child's learning. Family researcher and educator Ira Gordon (1978) concluded that parents of students in the early grades can play six key roles: volunteer, paid employee, teacher at home, audience, decision maker, and adult learner. These roles likely influence not only parents' behavior and their children's schoolwork, but also the quality of schools and communities.

Today, after many decades of limited success, schools are beginning to put more thought into their communication with parents, recognizing that the initial contacts can make or break relationships and that first contacts affect later communication (Epstein, 1990, 1992). Recognizing the importance of parental involvement in education, a number of programs are being developed to enhance communication between schools and families.

Three types of school/family programs are: face-to-face, technological, and written communication (D'Angelo & Adler, 1991). In Lima, Ohio, the main goal is for each school to establish a personal relationship with every parent.

CONCEPT TABLE 2.2

Methods and How to Be a Wise Consumer of Information about Children's Development

Concept	Processes/Related Ideas	Characteristics/Description
Ways of collecting information—measures	Observation	It is a key ingredient in research that includes laboratory and naturalistic observation.
	Interviews and questionnaires	They are used to assess perceptions and attitudes. Social desirability and lying are problems with their use.
	Case studies	They provide an in-depth look at an individual. Caution in generalizing is warranted.
	Standardized tests	They are designed to assess an individual's characteristics relative to those of a large group of similar individuals.
	Cross-cultural research and research with ethnic minority groups	This research focuses on the culture-universal (etic approach) and culture-specific (emic approach) nature of mind and behavior. A special concern in research with ethnic minority groups is ethnic gloss. In the past, ethnic minority children have often been excluded from research because researchers wanted to reduce variation in their data. We need to include more ethnic minority children in research.
	Physiological research and research with animals	Physiological research provides information about the biological basis of behavior. Since much physiological research cannot be carried out with humans, psychologists sometimes use animals. Animal studies permit researchers to control genetic background, diet, experiences in infancy, and countless other factors. One issue is the extent research with animals can be generalized to humans.
	Multiple measures, sources, and contexts	Researchers are increasingly adopting a multimeasure, multisource, multicontext approach.
Strategies for setting up research studies	Correlational strategy	It describes how strongly two or more events or characteristics are related. It does not allow causal statements.
	Experimental strategy	It involves manipulation of influential factors—independent variables—and measurement of their effect on the dependent variables. Subjects are randomly assigned to experimental and control groups in many studies. The experimental strategy can reveal the causes of behavior and tell us how one event influenced another.

At an initial parent/teacher conference, parents are given a packet that is designed to increase their likelihood of engaging in learning activities with their children at home. Conferences, regular phone calls, and home visits establish an atmosphere of mutual understanding that makes other kinds of communication (progress reports, report cards, activity calendars, or discussions about problems that arise during the year) more welcome and successful.

Many programs are discovering new ways to use electronic communication to establish contact with a wider range of parents. In McAllen, Texas, the school district has developed a community

An important dimension of effective schooling is the role of families in children's education. Shown here is a parent–teacher conference in Lima, Ohio, where a systematic effort has been made to more extensively involve parents in children's education.

Concept	Processes/Related Ideas	Characteristics/Description
Time span of inquiry	Cross-sectional approach	Individuals of different ages are compared all at one time.
	Longitudinal approach	The same individuals are studied over a period of time, usually several years or more.
	Cohort effects	Cohort effects are due to a subject's time of birth or generation but not actually to age. The study of cohort effects underscores the importance of considering the historical dimensions of development.
Reducing sexism	Its nature	A special concern is that the vast majority of psychological research has been male oriented and male dominated. Some researchers believe that developmentalists need to be challenged to examine children's worlds in a new way, one that incorporates girls' and women's perspectives. Recommendations have been made for conducting nonsexist research.
Ethics in research on child development	Their nature	Researchers must ensure the well-being of subjects in research. The risk of mental and physical harm must be reduced, and informal consent should be obtained. Special ethical considerations are involved when children are research subjects.
Being a wise consumer of information about children's development	Its nature	In many instances the quality of information you read about children's development, especially in the media, varies greatly. Being a wise consumer involves understanding the distinction between nomothetic research and idiographic needs, being aware of the tendency to overgeneralize from a small sample or a unique sample, knowing that a single study is often not the defining word about an issue or problem, understanding why causal conclusions cannot be drawn from a correlational study, and always considering the source of the information and evaluating its credibility.

partnership with local radio stations, and it sponsors "Discusiones Escolares," a weekly program in Spanish that encourages parents to become more involved in their children's education. Family and school relationships, parent involvement at school, preventing school dropouts, creating a learning atmosphere at home, and communicating with adolescents are some of the topics the radio programs have addressed. Parents and others in the communities may check out copies of the script or a cassette tape of each program from the parent coordinators at their schools.

In Omaha, Nebraska, a monthly newsletter is sent to parents that highlights home activities that are coordinated with classroom activities. Each month's issue reports on the meeting of the parent advisory council and gives information about how parents can become more involved in their children's education. The monthly newsletters also focus on classroom themes. In addition to the newsletter, a calendar is published each year, and families are offered many opportunities for added learning. For example, during school vacations, students receive "The Sizzler"—a packet of learning materials for the entire family to use at home.

In sum, extra care in developing and maintaining channels of communication between schools and families is an important aspect of children's development. ■

CONCLUSIONS

A discipline that studies how babies develop, how parents nurture children, how peers interact, and how children think can be a science just as much as disciplines that investigate how gravity works and the molecular structure of a compound. That is because science is not determined by what it investigates but by how it investigates.

We began the study of child development as a science by examining the nature of theory and the scientific method. Then we evaluated five main theories—psychoanalytic (Freud and Erikson), cognitive (Piaget and information processing), behavioral/social

learning (Skinner and Bandura), ethological (Lorenz) and ecological (Bronfenbrenner)—as well as an eclectic theoretical orientation. We studied a variety of measures that can be used to collect information about children such as observations, interviews and questionnaires, case studies, standardized tests, cross-cultural research and research with ethnic minority individuals, physiological research and research with animals, and the importance of a multimethod, multisource, multicontext approach. We also examined strategies for setting up research studies, the time span of inquiry, reducing sexism in research, ethics in re-

search on children, and how to be a wise consumer of information about children. You also read about the important mesosystem connection between families and schools. Don't forget to again read the two concept tables on pages 53 and 64 that together will provide you with a summary of the chapter's main contents.

This concludes Section One of the book. In Section Two, we will explore the biological basis of children's development, their physical growth, and their perceptual development, beginning with chapter 3, Biological Beginnings.

KEY TERMS

theory   A coherent set of ideas that helps explain data and make predictions. (35)

hypotheses   Assumptions that can be tested to determine their accuracy. (35)

scientific method   An approach that can be used to discover accurate information about behavior and development and that includes the following steps: identify and analyze the problem, collect data, draw conclusions, and revise theories. (35)

id   The Freudian structure of personality that consists of instincts, which are an individual's reservoir of psychic energy. (37)

ego   The Freudian structure of personality that deals with the demands of reality. (37)

superego   The Freudian structure of personality that is the moral branch. The branch that takes into account whether something is right or wrong. (37)

defense mechanisms   The psychoanalytic term for unconscious methods used by the ego to distort reality in order to protect itself from anxiety. (37)

repression   The most powerful and pervasive defense mechanism. It pushes unacceptable id impulses out of awareness and back into the unconscious mind. (38)

erogenous zones   Freud's concept of the parts of the body that have especially strong pleasure-giving qualities at each stage of development. (38)

oral stage   The first Freudian stage of development, occurring during the first 18 months of life, in which the infant's pleasure centers around the mouth. (38)

anal stage   The second Freudian stage of development, occurring between 1½ and 3 years of age, in which the child's greatest pleasure involves the anus or the eliminative functions associated with it. (38)

phallic stage   The third Freudian stage of development, which occurs between the ages of 3 and 6; its name comes from the Latin word *phallus,* which means "penis." During this stage, the child's pleasure focuses on the genitals, and the child discovers that self-manipulation is enjoyable. (38)

Oedipus complex   The Freudian concept that young children develop an intense desire to replace the parent of the same sex and enjoy the affections of the opposite-sex parent. (38)

latency stage   The fourth Freudian stage, which occurs between approximately 6 years of age and puberty; the child represses all interest in sexuality and develops social and intellectual skills. (38)

genital stage   The fifth and final Freudian stage of development, occurring from puberty on. This stage is one of sexual reawakening; the source of sexual pleasure now becomes someone outside of the family. (38)

trust versus mistrust   Erikson's first psychosocial stage, which is experienced in the first year of life. A sense of trust requires a feeling of physical comfort and a minimal amount of fear and apprehension about the future. (39)

autonomy versus shame and doubt   Erikson's second stage of development, occurring in late infancy and toddlerhood (1–3 years). (39)

initiative versus guilt Erikson's third stage of development, occurring during the preschool years. (39)

industry versus inferiority Erikson's fourth developmental stage, occurring approximately in the elementary school years. (39)

identity versus identity confusion Erikson's fifth developmental stage, which individuals experience during the adolescent years. At this time, individuals are faced with finding out who they are, what they are all about, and where they are going in life. (39)

intimacy versus isolation Erikson's sixth developmental stage, which individuals experience during the early adulthood years. At this time, individuals face the developmental task of forming intimate relationships with others. (39)

generativity versus stagnation Erikson's seventh developmental stage, which individuals experience in middle adulthood. (39)

integrity versus despair Erikson's eighth and final developmental stage, which individuals experience during late adulthood. (40)

sensorimotor stage The first of Piaget's developmental stages, which lasts from birth to about 2 years of age. Infants construct an understanding of the world by coordinating sensory experiences (such as seeing and hearing) with motoric actions. (41)

preoperational stage The second Piagetian developmental stage, which lasts from about 2 to 7 years of age. Children begin to represent the world with words, images, and drawings. (44)

concrete operational stage Piaget's third developmental stage lasts from approximately 7 to 11 years of age. Children can perform operations, and logical reasoning replaces intuitive thought as long as the reasoning can be applied to specific concrete examples. (44)

formal operational stage Piaget's fourth and final developmental stage appears between the ages of 11 and 15. Individuals move beyond the world of actual, concrete experiences and think in more abstract and more logical ways. (44)

information processing A model of cognition concerned with how individuals process information about their world—how information enters the mind, how it is stored and transformed, and how it is retrieved to perform such complex activities as problem solving and reasoning. (44)

behaviorism The theory that emphasizes the scientific study of observable behavioral responses and their environmental determinants. (44)

social learning theory The view of psychologists who emphasize a combination of behavior, environment, and cognition as the key factors in development. (46)

ethology The theory that behavior is strongly influenced by biology, is tied to evolution, and is characterized by critical or sensitive periods. (47)

imprinting The ethological concept of rapid, innate learning within a limited critical period of time, which involves attachment to the first moving object seen. (47)

critical period A fixed time period very early in development during which certain behaviors optimally emerge. (47)

ecological theory Emphasis is given to the role of social contexts in development. (48)

microsystem In Bronfenbrenner's ecology theory, this system is the setting or context in which an individual lives. This system includes the person's family, peers, school, and neighborhood. The most direct interactions with social agents occur in the microsystem. (48)

mesosystem This system involves relationships between microsystems or connections between contexts such as the family experience to the school experience. (48)

exosystem This system is involved when experiences in another social setting—in which the individual does not have an active role—influence what the individual experiences in an immediate context. (48)

macrosystem This system involves the culture in which individuals live. Culture refers to behavior patterns, beliefs, and all other products of a particular group of people that are passed on from generation to generation. (50)

chronosystem This system involves the patterning of environmental events and transitions over the life course and their sociohistorical contexts. (50)

eclectic theoretical orientation Uses whatever is considered the best in all theories. (51)

laboratory This is a controlled setting in which many of the complex factors of the "real world" are removed. (52)

naturalistic observation This is a method in which scientists observe behavior in real-world settings and make no effort to manipulate or control the situation. (54)

questionnaire This is similar to a highly structured interview except that respondents read the questions and mark their answers on paper, rather than responding verbally to an interviewer. (54)

case study This is an in-depth look at an individual; it is used mainly by clinical psychologists when the unique aspects of a person's life cannot be duplicated, either for practical or ethical reasons. (54)

standardized tests These require an individual to answer a series of written or oral questions. They have two distinct features. First, psychologists usually total an individual's score to yield a single score, or set of scores, that reflects something about the individual. Second, psychologists compare the individual's score with the scores of a large group of persons to determine how the individual responded relative to others. (54)

emic approach In this approach, the goal is to describe behavior in one culture or ethnic group in terms that are meaningful and important to the people in that group, without regard to other cultures or ethnic groups; culture-specific. (55)

etic approach   The goal in this approach is to describe behaviors so that generalizations can be made across cultures; culture-universal. (55)

ethnic gloss   Using an ethnic label, such as Black, Hispanic, Asian, or Native American, in a superficial way that makes an ethnic group seem more homogeneous than it actually is. (55)

correlational strategy   The goal in this strategy is to describe the strength of the relation between two or more events or characteristics. (56)

correlational coefficient   A number based on statistical analysis used to describe the degree of association between two variables. (57)

experimental strategy   This strategy allows investigators to precisely determine behavior's causes by performing an experiment which is a precisely regulated setting in which one or more of the factors believed to influence the behavior being studied are manipulated and all others are held constant. (57)

random assignment   This occurs when researchers assign subjects to experimental and control conditions by chance, thus reducing the likelihood that the results of the experiment will be due to preexisting differences in the two groups. (57)

independent variable   This is the manipulated, influential, experimental factor in the experiment. (57)

dependent variable   This is the factor that is measured in an experiment; it may change because of the

manipulation of the independent variable. (57)

cross-sectional approach   This is a research strategy in which individuals of different ages are compared all at one time. (58)

longitudinal approach   This is a research strategy in which the same individuals are studied over a period of time, usually several years or more. (58)

cohort effects   Effects may occur due to an individual's time of birth or generation that have nothing to do with the individual's actual age. (59)

nomothetic research   Research that is conducted at the group level in which individual variation is not a major focus. (62)

idiographic needs   This refers to what is important to the individual, not the group. (62)

SUGGESTED READINGS

Bronfenbrenner, U. (1986). Ecology of the family as a context for human development: Research perspectives. *Developmental Psychology, 22,* 723–742. In this article, Bronfenbrenner adds the chronosystem to his other four environmental systems. It includes a discussion of a number of research studies involving various environmental systems.

Cowan, P. (1978). *Piaget with feeling.* New York: Holt, Rinehart & Winston. This text provides a well-written overview of Piaget's theory and draws implications for understanding children's emotional development.

Erikson, E. H. (1968). *Identity: Youth and crisis.* New York: W. W. Norton. Erikson's book is must reading for anyone interested in developmental psychology. Erikson outlines his eight stages of the life

cycle and talks extensively about identity.

Miller, P. H. (1993). *Theories of developmental psychology* (3rd ed.). New York: W. H. Freeman. An excellent presentation and evaluation of a number of the developmental theories discussed in this chapter are presented in this book.

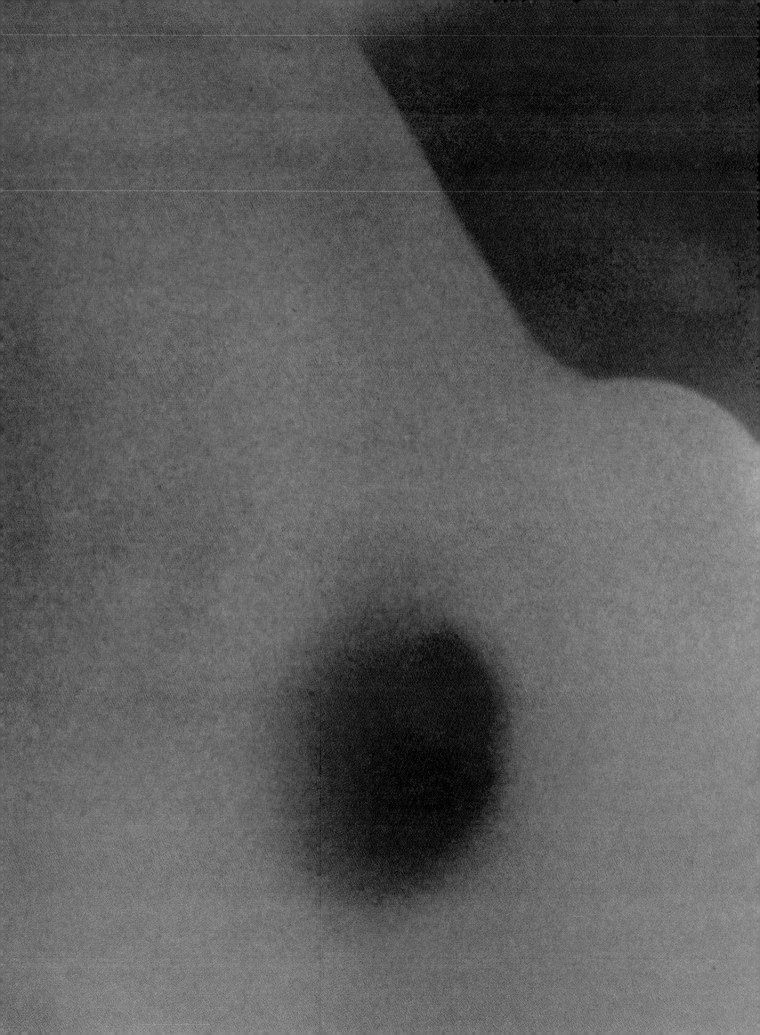

Biological Processes, Physical Development, and Perceptual Development

What endless questions vex the thought, of whence and whither, when and how.

—Sir Richard Burton, *Kasidah*

The rhythm and meaning of life involve beginnings. Questions are raised about how from so simple a beginning endless forms develop and grow and mature. What was this organism, what is this organism, what will this organism be? In Section Two you will read four chapters: Biological Beginnings (chapter 3), Prenatal Development and Birth (chapter 4), Physical, Motor, and Perceptual Development in Infancy (chapter 5), and Physical Development in Childhood and Puberty (chapter 6).

Boys and Kitten, 1873, Winslow Homer
1836–1910 (Detail)

Biological Beginnings

There are one hundred and ninety-three living species of monkeys and apes. One hundred and ninety-two of them are covered with hair. The exception is the naked ape self-named, Homo sapiens.

—Desmond Morris

> *The frightening part about heredity and environment is that we parents provide both.*
>
> —Notebook of a Printer

IMAGES OF CHILDREN

The Jim and Jim Twins

Jim Springer and Jim Lewis are identical twins. They were separated at 4 weeks of age and did not see each other again until they were 39 years old. Both worked as part-time deputy sheriffs, vacationed in Florida, drove Chevrolets, had dogs named Toy, and married and divorced women named Betty. One twin named his son James Allan, and the other named his son James Alan. Both liked math but not spelling, enjoyed carpentry and mechanical drawing, chewed their fingernails down to the nubs, had almost identical drinking and smoking habits, had hemorrhoids, put on 10 pounds at about the same point in development, first suffered headaches at the age of 18, and had similar sleep patterns.

But Jim and Jim had some differences. One wore his hair over his forehead, the other slicked it back and had sideburns. One expressed himself best orally, the other was more proficient in writing. But for the most part, their profiles were remarkably similar.

Another pair, Daphne and Barbara, were called the "giggle sisters" because they were always making each other laugh. A thorough search of their adoptive families' histories revealed no gigglers. And the identical sisters handled stress by ignoring it, avoided conflict and controversy whenever possible, and showed no interest in politics.

Two other female identical twin sisters were separated at 6 weeks and reunited in their fifties. Both had nightmares, which they describe in hauntingly similar ways: Both dreamed of doorknobs and fishhooks in their mouths as they smothered to death! The nightmares began during early adolescence and had stopped in the last 10 to 12 years. Both women were bed wetters until about 12 or 13 years of age, and they

Jim Lewis (left) and Jim Springer (right).

reported educational and marital histories that were remarkably similar.

These sets of twins are part of the Minnesota Study of Twins Reared Apart, directed by Thomas Bouchard and his colleagues. They bring identical twins (identical genetically because they come from the same egg) and fraternal twins (dissimilar genetically because they come from two eggs) from all over the world to Minneapolis to investigate their

lives. The twins are given a number of personality tests, and detailed medical histories are obtained, including information about diet, smoking, exercise habits, chest X-rays, heart stress tests, and EEGs (brain-wave tests). The twins are interviewed and asked more than 15,000 questions about their family and childhood environment, personal interests, vocational orientation, values, and aesthetic judgments. They also are given ability and intelligence tests (Bouchard & others, 1981; Bouchard & others, 1990).

Critics of the Minnesota identical twins study point out that some of the separated twins were together several months prior to their adoption, that some of the twins had been reunited prior to their testing (in some cases, a number of years earlier), that adoption agencies often place twins in similar homes, and that even strangers who spend several hours together and start comparing their lives are likely to come up with some coincidental similarities (Adler, 1991). Still, even in the face of such criticism, the Minnesota study of identical twins indicates how scientists have recently shown an increased interest in the genetic basis of human development, and that we need further research on genetic and environmental factors.

PREVIEW

The examples of Jim and Jim, the giggle sisters, and the identical twins who had the same nightmares stimulate us to think about our genetic heritage and the biological foundations of our existence. Organisms are not like billiard balls, moved by simple, external forces to predictable positions on life's pool table. Environmental experiences and biological foundations work together to make us who we are. Our coverage of life's biological beginnings focuses on evolution, genetics, heredity's influence on development, and the interaction of heredity and environment.

THE EVOLUTIONARY PERSPECTIVE

In evolutionary time, humans are relative newcomers to Earth, yet we have established ourselves as the most successful and dominant species. If we consider evolutionary time in terms of a calendar year, humans arrived here late in December (Sagan, 1977). As our earliest ancestors left the forest to feed on the savannahs, and finally to form hunting societies on the open plains, their minds and behaviors changed. How did this evolution come about?

Natural Selection

Natural selection *is the evolutionary process that favors individuals of a species that are best adapted to survive and reproduce.* To understand natural selection, let's return to the middle of the nineteenth century, when Charles Darwin was traveling around the world observing many different species of animals in their natural surroundings. Darwin (1859), who published his observations and thoughts in *On the Origin of Species,* observed that most organisms reproduced at rates that would cause enormous increases in the population of most species, yet populations remained nearly constant. He reasoned that an intense, constant struggle for food, water, and resources must occur among the many young born each generation, because many of the young do not survive. Those that do survive pass their genes on to the next generation. Darwin believed that those who do survive to reproduce are probably superior in a number of ways to those who do not. In other words, the survivors are better adapted to their world than the nonsurvivors. Over the course of many generations, organisms with the characteristics needed for survival would comprise a larger percentage of the population. Over many, many generations, this could produce a gradual modification of the whole population. If environmental conditions change, however, other characteristics might develop, moving the process in a different direction.

What seest thou else in the dark backward and abysm of time.

—William Shakespeare

I am a brother to dragons, and a companion to owls.

—Job 30.29

Over a million species have been classified, from bacteria to blue whales, with many varieties of beetles in between. The work of natural selection produced the disappearing acts of moths and the quills of porcupines. And the effects of evolution produced the technological advances, intelligence, and longer parental care of human beings (see figure 3.1).

FIGURE 3.1

The better an animal is adapted, the more successful it becomes. Humans, more than any other mammal, adapt to and control most types of environments. Because of longer parental care, humans learn more complex behavior patterns, which contribute to adaptation.

SOCIOCULTURAL WORLDS OF CHILDREN 3.1

The Human Species Is a Culture-Making Species

Unlike all other animal species, which evolve mainly in response to random changes in their environment, humans have more control over their own evolution. This change occurs through *cultural evolution.* For example, we've made astonishing accomplishments in the past 10,000 years or so, ever since we developed language. Biological (Darwinian) evolution continues in our species, but its rate, compared with cultural evolution, is so slow that its impact seems almost negligible. There is no evidence, for example, that brain size or structure has changed since *Homo sapiens* appeared on the fossil record about 50,000 years ago.

As humans evolved, we acquired knowledge and passed it on from generation to generation. This knowledge, which originally instructed us how to hunt, make tools, and communicate, became our culture. The accumulation of knowledge has

gathered speed—from a slow swell to a meteoric rise. Hunter-gatherer tribes, characteristic of early human society, changed over thousands of years into small agricultural communities. With people rooted in one place, cities grew and flourished. Life within those cities remained relatively unchanged for generations. Then industrialization put a dizzying speed on cultural change. Now technological advances in communication and transportation—computers, FAX machines, the SST—transform everyday life at a staggering pace.

Whatever one generation learns, it can pass to the next through writing, word of mouth, ritual, tradition, and a host of other methods humans have developed to assure their culture's continuity (Gould, 1981). By creating cultures, humans have built, shaped, and carved out their own environments. The human species is no longer primarily at nature's mercy. Rather, humans are capable of changing their environment to fit their needs (McCandless & Trotter, 1977).

More than 99 percent of all humans now live in a different kind of environment from that in which the species evolved. By creating cultures, humans have, in effect, built, shaped, and carved out their own environments.

Generally, evolution proceeds at a very slow pace. The lines that led to the emergence of human beings and the great apes diverged about 14 millions years ago! Modern humans, *Homo sapiens,* came into existence only about 50,000 years ago. And the beginning of civilization as we know it began about 10,000 years ago. No sweeping evolutionary changes in humans occurred since then—for example, our brain is not ten times as big, we do not have a third eye in the back of our head, and we haven't learned to fly.

While no dramatic evolutionary changes have occurred since *Homo sapiens* appeared on the fossil record 50,000 years ago, there have been sweeping cultural changes. Biological evolution shaped human beings into a culture-making species. More information about the human species as a culture-making species appears in Sociocultural Worlds of Children 3.1.

Sociobiology

Sociobiology *is a contemporary evolutionary view that emphasizes the power of genes in determining behavior and explains com-*

plex social interactions that natural selection cannot. It states that all behavior is motivated by the desire to contribute one's genetic heritage to the greatest number of descendants. That is, sociobiologists believe that an organism is motivated by a desire to dominate the gene pool (Wilson, 1975).

Even complex social behaviors, such as altruism, aggression, and socialization, have been explained as the urge to propagate our own genes. Take altruism, for example. Parents are likely to risk their own lives to save their children from a blazing fire. Although the parents may die, their children's genes survive, increasing the probability that their genes will dominate the gene pool. Similarly, males have been said to be more aggressive than females because the males' former role as a hunter required them to be aggressive if they were to be successful.

Since evolution's imperative, according to sociobiologists, is to spread our genes, men and women have evolved different strategies for doing so. Sperm is abundant; men produce billions in a lifetime. However, women have a limited number of eggs, only about 400 in a lifetime. Men have the potential, then, to produce many more offspring than do women. To ensure that they spread their genes, it is to a male's advantage to impregnate as many females as possible. Given that women have few eggs and gestation takes a long time, it is to a woman's advantage to choose a mate who will protect her. This, say some sociobiologists, explains why women tend to be monogamous and men do not.

Sociobiologists point to animal models to support their theories. For example, the males of most species initiate sexual behavior more frequently than females. In some species, such as seals, cattle, and elephants, the male maintains a large harem of females to inseminate and protect. Some human societies incorporate this reproductive strategy into their culture (Hinde, 1984). Sociobiologists also contend that the universality of certain behaviors, such as incest taboos and religious laws, are proof that such behaviors are genetic.

Sociobiology is controversial. Critics argue that sociobiology does not adequately consider human adaptability and experience and that it reduces human beings to mere automatons caught in the thrall of their genes. They point out that sociobiologists explain things only after the fact, with no evidence of predictive ability, which would characterize a good theory. Male aggression is said to be a sociobiological imperative, but only after sociobiologists have seen that males do indeed behave more aggressively than females. Much of the evidence to support sociobiology is based on animal research. Critics assert that findings from animal research cannot always be generalized to humans. Further, some critics see sociobiology as little more than a justification to discriminate against women and minorities under a scientific umbrella, using genetic determinism as an excuse for ignoring the social injustice and discrimination that contribute to inequality (Paludi, 1992).

Race and Ethnicity

In keeping with one of the main themes of this text—exploration of sociocultural issues—let's examine the biological concept of race and see how it has taken on elaborate, often unfortunate, social meanings. **Race** *originated as a biological concept. It refers to a system for classifying plants and animals into subcategories according to a specific physical and structural characteristics.* Race is one of the most misused and misunderstood words in the English language (Atkinson, Morten, & Sue, 1993; Mays, 1991, 1993). Loosely, it has come to mean everything from a person's religion to skin color.

The three main classifications of the human race are Mongoloid, or Asian; Caucasoid, or European; and Negroid, or African. Skin color, head shape, facial features, stature, and the color and texture of body hair are the physical characteristics most widely used to determine race.

These racial classifications presumably were created to define and clarify the differences among groups of people; however, they have not been very useful. Today many people define races as groups that are socially constructed on the basis of physical differences because race is a social construction and no longer a biological fact (Van den Berghe, 1978). For example, some groups, such as Native Americans, Australians, and Polynesians, do not fit into any of the three main racial categories. Also, obvious differences *within* groups are not adequately accounted for. Arabs, Hindus, and Europeans, for instance, are physically different, yet they are all called Caucasians. Although there are some physical characteristics that distinguish "racial" groups, there are, in fact, more similarities than differences.

Too often we are socialized to accept as facts many myths and stereotypes about people whose skin color, facial features, and hair texture differ from ours. For example, some people still believe that Asians are inscrutable, Jews are acquisitive, and Hispanics are lazy. What people believe about race has profound social consequences. Until recently, for instance, Black Americans were denied access to schools, hospitals, churches, and other social institutions attended by Whites.

Although scientists are supposed to be a fair-minded lot, some also have used racial distinctions to further their own biases. Some even claim that one racial group has a biological inheritance that gives it an adaptive advantage over other racial groups. Nineteenth-century biologist Louis Agassiz, for example, asserted that God had created Blacks and Whites as separate species. Also, in Nazi Germany, where science and death made their grisliest alliance, Jews and other "undesirables" were attributed with whatever characteristics were necessary to reinforce the conclusion that "survival of the fittest" demanded their elimination.

Unfortunately, racism cloaked in science still finds champions. Recently psychologist Philipe Rushton (1985, 1988) argued that evolution accounts for racial differences in sexual practices, fertility, intelligence, and criminality. Using these traits, he ranks Asians as superior, followed by Caucasians and people of African descent. Asians, Rushton claims, are the most intelligent, most sexually restrained, most altruistic, and least criminal of the races. Rushton ascribes a similar order to social classes: those who are impoverished resemble Blacks; those who earn high incomes resemble Asians and Whites. Rushton's theory, according to his critics, is full of "familiar vulgar stereotypes" (Weizmann & others, 1990). His notions are stitched together with frequent misinterpretations and overgeneralizations about racial differences and evolutionary history, and the data are tailored to fit his bias. Regrettably, even flimsy theories such as Rushton's provide whole cloth for anyone intent on justifying racism.

Remember that, although race is primarily a *biological* concept, ethnicity is primarily a *sociocultural* concept (Brislin, 1993). In chapter 1, you read that cultural heritage, national characteristics, religion, language, *and* race constitute *ethnicity*. Race is just one component. However, the term *race* is often mistakenly used to refer to ethnicity. Jews, for example, are thought of as a race. Most are Caucasian, but they are too diverse to group into one racial subcategory. They also share too many anatomical similarities with other Caucasians to separate them as a distinct race (Thompson & Hughes, 1958). If we think of ethnicity predominately in terms of social and cultural heritage, then Jews constitute an ethnic group.

Although we distinguish between race and ethnicity in this book, society usually does not. Race is used in a much broader way than many sociocultural psychologists recommend (Brislin,

Race originated as a biological concept but has unfortunately taken on a number of negative social meanings. Ethnicity is a sociocultural concept.

Drawing by Ziegler; © 1985 The New Yorker Magazine, Inc.

1987, 1993). Social psychologist James Jones (1990, 1993) points out that thinking in racial terms has become embedded in cultures as an important factor in human interactions. For example, people often consider what race they will associate with when they decide on such things as where to live, who will make a suitable spouse, where to go to school, and what kind of job they want. Similarly, people often use race to judge whether or not another person is intelligent, competent, responsible, or socially acceptable. Children tend to adopt their parents' attitudes about race as they grow up, often perpetuating stereotypes and prejudice.

HEREDITY

Every species must have a mechanism for transmitting characteristics from one generation to the next. This mechanism is explained by the principles of genetics. Each of us carries a genetic code that we inherited from our parents. This code is located within every cell in our bodies. Our genetic codes are alike in one important way—they all contain the human genetic code. Because of the human genetic code, a fertilized human egg cannot grow into an egret, eagle, or elephant.

What Are Genes?

Each of us began life as a single cell weighing about one twenty-millionth of an ounce! This tiny piece of matter housed our entire genetic code—the information about who we would become. These instructions orchestrated growth from that single cell to a person made of trillions of cells, each containing a perfect replica of the original genetic code.

FIGURE 3.2

The remarkable substance known as DNA. Notice that a DNA molecule is shaped like a spiral staircase. Genes are short segments of the DNA molecule. The horizontal bars that look like the rungs of a ladder play a key role in locating the identity of a gene.

The turtle lives twixt plated decks
Which practically conceal its sex.
I think it clever of the turtle
In such a fix to be so fertile.

—Ogden Nash

The nucleus of each human cell contains 46 **chromosomes,** *which are threadlike structures that come in 23 pairs, one member of each pair coming from each parent. Chromosomes contain the remarkable genetic substance deoxyribonucleic acid, or DNA.* **DNA** *is a complex molecule that contains genetic information.* DNA's "double helix" shape looks like a spiral staircase (see figure 3.2). **Genes,** *the units of hereditary information, are short segments of the DNA "staircase." Genes act as a blueprint for cells to reproduce themselves and manufacture the proteins that maintain life.* Chromosomes, DNA, and genes can be mysterious. To help you turn mystery into understanding, refer to figure 3.3.

Gametes *are human reproduction cells, which are created in the testes of males and the ovaries of females.* **Meiosis** *is the process of cell division in which each pair of chromosomes in the cell separates, with one member of each pair going into each gamete, or daughter cell.* Thus, each human gamete has 23 unpaired chromosomes. **Reproduction** *takes place when a female gamete (ovum) is fertilized by a male gamete (sperm)* (see figure 3.4). A **zygote** *is a single cell formed through fertilization.* In the zygote, two sets of unpaired chromosomes combine to form one set of paired chromosomes—one member of each pair from the mother and the other member from the father. In this manner, each parent contributes 50 percent of the offspring's heredity.

Reproduction

The ovum is about 90,000 times as large as a sperm. Thousands of sperm must combine to break down the ovum's membrane barrier to allow even a single sperm to penetrate the membrane

FIGURE 3.3

Facts about chromosomes, DNA, and genes. (*a*) The body contains billions of cells that are organized into tissue and organs. (*b*) Each cell contains a central structure, the nucleus, which controls reproduction. (*c*) Chromosomes reside in the nucleus of each cell. The male's sperm and the female's egg are specialized reproductive cells that contain chromosomes. (*d*) At conception the offspring receives matching chromosomes from the mother's egg and the father's sperm. (*e*) The chromosomes contain DNA, a chemical substance. Genes are short segments of the DNA molecule. They are the units of hereditary information that act as a blueprint for cells to reproduce themselves and manufacture the proteins that sustain life. The rungs in the DNA ladder are an important location of genes.

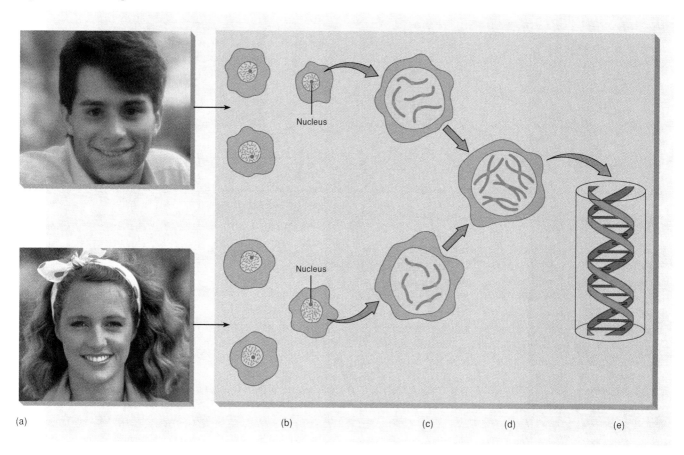

(a)   (b)   (c)   (d)   (e)

FIGURE 3.4

Union of sperm and egg.

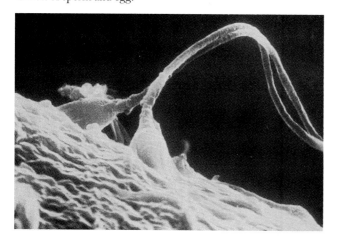

barrier. Ordinarily, females have two X chromosomes and males have one X and one Y chromosome. Because the Y chromosome is smaller and lighter than the X chromosome, Y-bearing sperm can be separated from X-bearing sperm in a centrifuge. This raises the possibility that the offspring's sex can be controlled. Not only are the Y-bearing sperm lighter, but they are more likely than the X-bearing sperm to coat the ovum. This results in the conception of 120 to 150 males for every 100 females. But males are more likely to die (spontaneously abort) at every stage of prenatal development, so only about 106 are born for every 100 females.

Reproduction's fascinating moments have been made even more intriguing in recent years. **In vitro fertilization** *is conception outside the body.* Consider the following situation. The year is 1978. One of the most dazzling occurrences of the 1970s is about to unfold. Mrs. Brown is infertile, but her physician informs her of a new procedure that could enable her to have a baby. The procedure involves removing the mother's ovum surgically,

FIGURE 3.5

In vitro fertilization. Egg meets sperm in a laboratory dish.

fertilizing it in a laboratory medium with live sperm cells obtained from the father or another male donor (see figure 3.5), storing the fertilized egg in a laboratory solution that substitutes for the uterine environment, and finally implanting the egg in the mother's uterus. For Mrs. Brown, the procedure was successful, and nine months later her daughter Louise was born.

Since the first in vitro fertilization in the 1970s, variations of the procedure have brought hope to childless couples. A woman's egg can be fertilized with the husband's sperm, or the husband and wife may contribute their sperm and egg with the resulting embryo carried by a third party, who essentially is donating her womb. Researchers have not found any developmental deficiencies in children born through in vitro fertilization.

Approximately 10 to 15 percent of couples in the United States are estimated to experience infertility, which is defined as the inability to conceive a child after 12 months of regular intercourse without contraception. The cause of infertility may rest with the woman or the man. The woman may not be ovulating, she may be producing abnormal ova, her fallopian tubes may be blocked, or she may have a disease that prevents implantation of the ova. The man may produce too few sperm, the sperm may lack motility (the ability to move adequately), or he may have a blocked passageway. In one recent investigation, long-term use of cocaine by men was related to low sperm count, low motility, and a high number of abnormally formed sperm (Bracken & others, 1990). Cocaine-related infertility appears to be reversible if users stop taking the drug for at least one year. In some cases of infertility, surgery may correct the problem, in others hormonal-based drugs may improve the probability of having a child. However, in some instances, fertility drugs have caused superovulation, producing as many as three or more babies at a time. A summary of some of infertility's causes and solutions is presented in table 3.1.

While surgery and fertility drugs can solve the infertility problem in some cases, another choice is to adopt a child. At the time of the adoption, most adoptive parents receive little information about the child's family history, and in turn, the child's biological parents are given little information about the adoptive parents. While this policy has been followed by most adoption agencies as being in the child's best interests, it is currently being challenged by a number of activist groups who argue that to seal records at the time of adoption violates the basic rights of persons to know about themselves (Nickman, 1992). Researchers have found that adopted children are often more at risk for psychological and school-related problems than nonadopted children (Brodzinky & others, 1984), although some adopted children adapt well to their circumstances (Marquis & Detweiler, 1985). Adolescence is a time when some adopted children show difficulties when, as part of their search for identity, they feel a void and incompleteness because they do not know their biological family's history.

A question that virtually every adoptive parent wants answered is "Should I tell my adopted child that he or she is adopted? If so, when?" Most psychologists believe that adopted children should be told that they are adopted, because they will eventually find out anyway. Many children begin to ask where they came from when they are approximately 4 to 6 years of age. This is a natural time to begin to respond in simple ways to children about their adopted status. Clinical psychologists report that one problem that sometimes surfaces is the desire of adoptive parents to make life too perfect for the adoptive child and to present a perfect image of themselves to the child. The result too often is that adopted children feel that they cannot release any angry feelings and openly discuss problems in this climate of perfection (Warshak, 1993).

TABLE 3.1

Fertility Problems and Solutions

Females

Problem	Solution
Damaged fallopian tubes	Surgery, in vitro fertilization
Abnormal ovulation	Hormone therapy, antibiotics, in vitro fertilization
Pelvic Inflammatory Disease (PID)	Antibiotics, surgery, change in birth control methods
Endometriosis*	Antibiotics, hormone therapy, surgery, artificial insemination
Damaged ovaries	Surgery, antibiotics, hormone therapy
Hostile cervical mucus	Antibiotics, artificial insemination, hormone therapy
Fibroid tumor	Surgery, antibiotics

Males

Problem	Solution
Low sperm count	Antibiotics, hormone therapy, artificial insemination, lowered testicular temperature
Dilated veins around testicle	Surgery, lowered testicular temperature, antibiotics
Damaged sperm ducts	Surgery, antibiotics
Hormone deficiency	Hormone therapy
Sperm antibodies	Antibiotics, in vitro fertilization

*Endometriosis occurs when the uterine lining grows outside of the uterus and causes bleeding, blocking, or scarring that can interfere with conception or pregnancy.

Source: Data from *The Fertility Solution,* 1991.

Abnormalities in Genes and Chromosomes

What are some abnormalities in genes and chromosomes? What tests can be used to determine the presence of these abnormalities?

Abnormalities

Geneticists and developmentalists have identified a range of problems caused by some major gene or chromosome defect (Holmes, 1992; Miller, 1992). **Phenylketonuria (PKU)** *is a genetic disorder in which the individual cannot properly metabolize protein. Phenylketonuria is now easily detected, but if left untreated, mental retardation and hyperactivity result.* When detected, the disorder is treated by diet to keep a poisonous substance from entering the nervous system. Phenylketonuria involves a recessive gene and occurs about once in every 10,000 to 20,000 live births. Phenylketonuria accounts for about 1 percent of institutionalized mentally retarded individuals and it occurs primarily in Whites.

Down syndrome, *the most common genetically transmitted form of mental retardation, is caused by the presence of an extra (47th) chromosome.* An individual with Down syndrome has a round face, a flattened skull, an extra fold of skin over the eyelids, a protruding tongue, short limbs, and retardation of motor and mental abilities. It is not known why the extra chromosome is present, but the health of the male sperm or female ovum may be involved (Vining, 1992). Women between the ages of 18 and 38 are less likely to give birth to a Down syndrome child than are younger or older women. Down syndrome appears approximately once in every 700 live births. Black children are rarely born with Down syndrome.

Sickle-cell anemia, *which occurs most often in Blacks, is a genetic disorder affecting the red blood cells.* A red blood cell is usually shaped like a disk, but in sickle-cell anemia, a change in a recessive gene modifies its shape to a hook-shaped "sickle." These cells die quickly, causing anemia and early death of the individual because of their failure to carry oxygen to the body's cells. About 1 in 400 Black babies is affected. One in 10 Black Americans is a carrier, as is 1 in 20 Latin Americans (Whaley & Wong, 1988).

Other disorders are associated with sex-chromosome abnormalities. Remember that normal males have an X chromosome and a Y chromosome, and normal females have two X chromosomes. **Klinefelter syndrome** *is a genetic disorder in which males have an extra X chromosome, making them XXY instead of XY.* Males with this disorder have undeveloped testes, and they usually have enlarged breasts and become tall. Klinefelter syndrome occurs approximately once in every 800 live male births.

Turner syndrome *is a genetic disorder in which females are missing an X chromosome, making them XO instead of XX.* These females are short in stature and have a webbed neck. They may be mentally retarded and sexually underdeveloped. Turner syndrome occurs approximately once in every 3,000 live female births.

The **XYY syndrome** *is a genetic disorder in which the male has an extra Y chromosome. Early interest in this syndrome involved the belief that the Y chromosome found in males contributed to male aggression and violence.* It was then reasoned that if a male had an extra Y chromosome he would likely be extremely aggressive and possibly develop a violent personality. However, researchers subsequently found that XYY males were no more likely to commit crimes than XY males (Witkin & others, 1976).

TABLE 3.2

Genetic Disorders and Conditions

Name	Description	Treatment	Incidence	Prenatal Detection	Carrier Detection
Anencephaly	Neural tube disorder that causes brain and skull malformations; most children die at birth.	Surgery	1 in 1,000	Ultrasound, amniocentesis	None
Cystic fibrosis	Glandular dysfunction that interferes with mucus production; breathing and digestion are hampered, resulting in a shortened life span.	Physical and oxygen therapy, synthetic enzymes, and antibiotics	1 in 2,000	Amniocentesis	Family history, DNA analysis
Down syndrome	Extra or altered 21st chromosome causes mild to severe retardation and physical abnormalities.	Surgery, early intervention, infant stimulation, and special learning programs	1 in 800 women; 1 in 350 women over 35	AFP, CVS, amniocentesis	Family history chromosomal analysis
Hemophilia	Lack of the clotting factor causes excessive internal and external bleeding.	Blood transfusions and/or injections of the clotting factor	1 in 10,000 males	CVS, amniocentesis	Family history, DNA analysis
Klinefelter syndrome	An extra X chromosome causes physical abnormalities.	Hormone therapy	1 in 800 males	CVS, amniocentesis	None
Phenylketonuria (PKU)	Metabolic disorder that, left untreated, causes mental retardation.	Special diet	1 in 14,000	CVS, amniocentesis	Family history, blood test
Pyloric stenosis	Excess muscle in upper intestine causes severe vomiting and death if not treated.	Surgery	1 male in 200; 1 female in 1,000	None	None
Sickle-cell anemia	Blood disorder that limits the body's oxygen supply. It can cause joint swelling, sickle-cell crises, heart and kidney failure.	Penicillin, medication for pain, antibiotics, and blood transfusions	1 in 400 Black children (lower among other groups)	CVS, amniocentesis	Blood test
Spina bifida	Neural tube disorder that causes brain and spine abnormalities.	Corrective surgery at birth, orthopedic devices, and physical/medical therapy	2 in 1,000	AFP, ultrasound, amniocentesis	None
Tay-Sachs disease	Deceleration of mental and physical development caused by an accumulation of lipids in the nervous system; few children live to age 5.	Medication and special diet	1 in 30 American Jews is a carrier	CVS, amniocentesis	Blood test
Thalassemia	Group of inherited blood disorders that causes anemic symptoms ranging from fatigue and weakness to liver failure.	Blood transfusions and antibiotics	1 in 400 children of Mediterranean descent	CVS, amniocentesis	Blood test
Turner syndrome	A missing or altered X chromosome may cause mental retardation and/or physical abnormalities.	Hormone therapy	1 in 3,000 females	None	Blood test

We have discussed six genetic disorders—phenylketonuria, Down syndrome, sickle-cell anemia, Klinefelter syndrome, Turner syndrome, and the XYY syndrome. A summary of these genetic disorders, as well as some other common ones, appears in table 3.2.

Each year in the United States, approximately 100,000 to 150,000 infants are born with a genetic disorder or malformation. These infants comprise about 3 to 5 percent of the 3 million births and account for at least 20 percent of infant deaths. Prospective parents increasingly are turning to genetic counseling for assistance, wanting to know their risk of having a child born with a genetic defect or malformation (Bernhardt & Pyeritz, 1992; Carey, 1992; Hirschhorn, 1992; Langlois, 1992). To read further about genetic counseling, turn to Explorations in Child Development 3.1.

EXPLORATIONS IN CHILD DEVELOPMENT 3.1

Genetic Counseling

Bob and Mary Sims have been married for several years. They would like to start a family, but they are frightened. The newspapers and popular magazines are full of stories about infants who are born prematurely and don't survive, infants with debilitating physical defects, and babies found to have congenital mental retardation. The Simses feel that to have such a child would create a social, economic, and psychological strain on them and on society.

Accordingly, the Simses turn to a genetic counselor for help. Genetic counselors are usually physicians or biologists who are well versed in the field of medical genetics. They are

familiar with the kinds of problems that can be inherited, the odds for encountering them, and helpful measures for offsetting some of their effects. The Simses tell their counselor that there has been a history of mental retardation in Bob's family. Bob's younger sister was born with Down syndrome, a form of mental retardation. Mary's older brother has hemophilia, a condition in which bleeding is difficult to stop. They wonder what the chances are that a child of theirs might also be retarded or have hemophilia and what measures they can take to reduce their chances of having a mentally or physically defective child.

The counselor probes more deeply, because she understands that these facts in isolation do not give her a complete picture of the possibilities. She learns that no other relatives in Bob's family are retarded and that Bob's mother was in her late forties when his younger sister was born. She concludes that the retardation was due to the age of Bob's mother and not to some general tendency for members of his family to inherit retardation. It is well known that women over 40 have a much higher probability of giving birth to retarded children than younger women. Apparently, in women over 40, the ova (egg cells) are not as healthy as in women under 40.

In Mary's case the counselor determines that there is a small but clear possibility that Mary may be a carrier of hemophilia and may transmit that condition to a son. Otherwise, the counselor can find no evidence from the family history to indicate genetic problems.

The decision is then up to the Simses. In this case, the genetic problem will probably not occur, so the choice is fairly easy. But what should parents do if they face the strong probability of having a child with a major birth defect? Ultimately, the decision depends on the couple's ethical and religious beliefs.

Tests to Determine Abnormalities

Scientists have developed a number of tests to determine whether the fetus is developing normally, among them amniocentesis, ultrasound sonography, the chorionic villus test, and the maternal blood test, each of which we discuss in turn.

Critical Thinking

Imagine that you want to start a family. Probe your family background. What questions would you want to ask a genetic counselor?

Amniocentesis *is a prenatal medical procedure in which a sample of amniotic fluid is withdrawn by syringe and tested to discover if the fetus is suffering from any chromosomal or metabolic disorders. Amniocentesis is performed between the 12th and 16th weeks of pregnancy.* The later amniocentesis is performed, the better the diagnostic potential. The earlier it is performed, the more useful it is in deciding whether a pregnancy should be terminated (see figure 3.6).

FIGURE 3.6

Amniocentesis being performed on a pregnant woman.

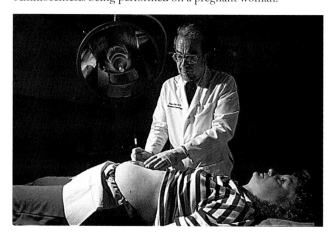

FIGURE 3.7

A 6-month-old infant poses with the ultrasound sonography record taken four months into the baby's prenatal development.

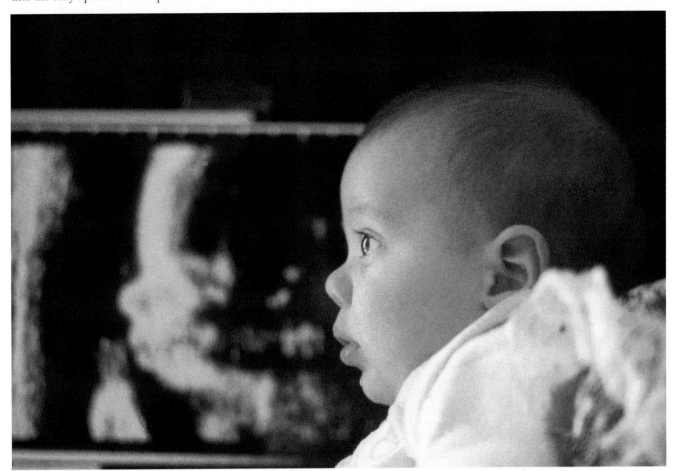

Ultrasound sonography *is a prenatal medical procedure in which high-frequency sound waves are directed into the pregnant woman's abdomen.* The echo from the sounds is transformed into a visual representation of the fetus's inner structures. This technique has been able to detect such disorders as microencephaly, a form of mental retardation involving an abnormally small brain. Ultrasound sonography is often used in conjunction with amniocentesis to determine the precise location of the fetus in the mother's abdomen (see figure 3.7).

As scientists have searched for more accurate, safe assessments of high-risk prenatal conditions, they have developed a new test. The **chorionic villus test** *is a prenatal medical procedure in which a small sample of the placenta is removed at some point between the 8th and 11th weeks of pregnancy.* Diagnosis takes approximately 10 days. The chorionic villus tests allows a decision about abortion to be made near the end of the first trimester of pregnancy, a point when abortion is safer and less traumatic than after amniocentesis in the second trimester. These techniques provide valuable information about the presence of birth defects, but they also raise issues pertaining to whether an abortion should be obtained if birth defects are present.

The **maternal blood test** *(alpha-fetoprotein—AFP) is a prenatal diagnostic technique that is used to assess blood alphaprotein level, which is associated with neural tube defects.* This test is administered to women 14 to 20 weeks into pregnancy only when they are at risk for bearing a child with defects in the formation of the brain and spinal cord.

So far in this chapter, we have discussed the evolutionary perspective, genes, chromosomes, and reproduction, and abnormalities in genes and chromosomes. A summary of these ideas is outlined in Concept Table 3.1.

GENETIC PRINCIPLES AND METHODS

What are some basic genetic principles that affect children's development? What methods do behavior geneticists use to study heredity's influence? How does heredity influence such aspects of children's development as their intelligence? And how do heredity and environment interact to produce children's development?

CONCEPT TABLE 3.1

The Evolutionary Perspective and Genetics

Concept	Processes/Related Ideas	Characteristics/Description
The evolutionary perspective	Natural selection	Natural selection is the process that favors individuals of a species that are best adapted to survive and produce. This concept was originally proposed by Charles Darwin. While no dramatic evolutionary changes have occurred since *Homo sapiens* appeared on the fossil record 50,000 years ago, there have been sweeping cultural changes. Biological evolution shaped human beings into a culture-making species.
	Sociobiology	Sociobiology argues that all behavior is motivated by a desire to dominate the gene pool. Critics say that sociobiology ignores the environmental determinants of behavior and is biased against females.
	Race and ethnicity	Race is a biological concept; ethnicity is a sociocultural concept. The concept of race has taken on a number of social meanings, some of which have resulted in discrimination and prejudice. Race continues to be a misunderstood and abused concept.
Genes, chromosomes, and reproduction	Genes and chromosomes	The nucleus of each human cell contains 46 chromosomes, which are composed of DNA. Genes are short segments of DNA and act as a blueprint for cells to reproduce and manufacture proteins that maintain life.
	Reproduction	Genes are transmitted from parents to offspring by gametes, or sex cells. Gametes are formed by the splitting of cells, a process called meiosis. Reproduction takes place when a female gamete (ovum) is fertilized by a male gamete (sperm) to create a single-celled ovum. In vitro fertilization has helped solve some infertility problems. Approximately 10 to 15 percent of couples in the United States experience infertility problems, some of which can be corrected through surgery or fertility drugs. Another choice for infertile couples is adoption.
Abnormalities in genes and chromosomes	The range of problems	A range of problems is caused by major gene or chromosome defects, among them PKU, Down syndrome, sickle-cell anemia, Klinefelter syndrome, Turner syndrome, and the XYY syndrome.
	Genetic counseling and tests	Genetic counseling has increased in popularity as couples desire information about their risk of having a defective child. Amniocentesis, ultrasound sonography, the chorionic villus test, and the maternal blood test are used to determine the presence of defects after pregnancy has begun.

Some Genetic Principles

Genetic determination is a complex affair, and much is unknown about the way genes work. But a number of genetic principles have been discovered, among them dominant-recessive genes, sex-linked genes, polygenically inherited characteristics, reaction range, and canalization.

According to the **dominant-recessive genes principle,** *if one gene of the pair is dominant and one is recessive (goes back or recedes), the dominant gene exerts its effect, overriding the potential influence of the other, recessive gene. A recessive gene exerts its influence only if the two genes of a pair are both recessive.* If you inherit a recessive gene for a trait from both of your parents, you will show the trait. If you inherit a recessive gene from only one parent, you may never know you carry the gene. Brown eyes, farsightedness, and dimples rule over blue eyes, nearsightedness, and freckles in the world of dominant-recessive genes. Can two brown-eyed parents have a blue-eyed child? Yes, they can. In each parent, the gene pair that governs eye color includes a dominant gene for brown eyes, and a recessive gene for blue eyes. Since dominant genes override recessive genes, the parents have brown eyes. But both may be carriers of blueness and pass on their recessive genes for blue eyes. With no dominant gene to override them, the recessive genes can make the child's eyes blue. Figure 3.8 illustrates the dominant-recessive genes principles.

FIGURE 3.8

How brown-eyed parents can have a blue-eyed child. Although both parents have brown eyes, each parent can have a recessive gene for blue eyes. In this example both parents have brown eyes, but each parent carries the recessive gene for blue eyes. Therefore, the odds of their child having blue eyes is one in four—the probability the child will receive a recessive gene (b) from each parent.

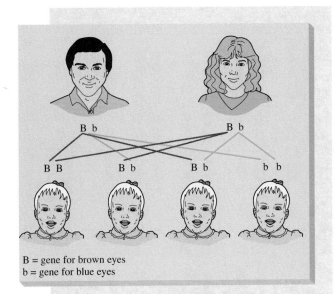

B = gene for brown eyes
b = gene for blue eyes

For thousands of years, people wondered what determined whether we become male or female. Aristotle believed that the father's arousal during intercourse determined the offspring's sex. The more excited the father was, the more likely it would be a son, he reasoned. Of course, he was wrong, but it was not until the 1920s that researchers confirmed the existence of human sex chromosomes, 2 of the 46 chromosomes human beings normally carry. As we saw earlier, ordinarily females have two X chromosomes and males have an X and a Y. (Figure 3.9 shows the chromosome makeup of a male and a female.)

Genetic transmission is usually more complex than the simple examples we have examined thus far. **Polygenic inheritance** *is a genetic principle describing the interaction of many genes to produce a particular characteristic.* Few psychological characteristics are the result of single pairs. Most are determined by the interaction of many different genes. There are as many as 50,000 or more genes, so you can imagine that possible combinations of these are staggering in number. Traits produced by this mixing of genes are said to be polygenically determined.

No one possesses all the characteristics that our genetic structure makes possible. **Genotype** *is the person's genetic heritage, the actual genetic material.* However, not all of this genetic material is apparent in our observed and measurable characteristics. **Phenotype** *is the way an individual's genotype is expressed in observed and measurable characteristics.* Phenotypes include physical traits—such as height, weight, eye color, and skin pigmentation, and psychological characteristics—such as intelligence, creativity, personality, and social tendencies.

> *That which comes of a cat will catch mice.*
>
> —English proverb

For each genotype, a range of phenotypes can be expressed. Imagine that we could identify all of the genes that would make a person introverted or extraverted. Would measured introversion-extraversion be predictable from knowledge of the specific genes? The answer is no, because even if our genetic model was adequate, introversion-extraversion is a characteristic shaped by experience throughout life. For example, parents may push an introverted child into social situations and encourage the child to become more gregarious.

To understand how introverted a person is, think about a series of genetic codes that predispose the child to develop in a particular way, and imagine environments that are responsive or unresponsive to this development. For example, the genotype of some persons may predispose them to be introverted in an environment that promotes a turning inward of personality, yet in an environment that encourages social interaction and outgoingness, these individuals may become more extraverted. However, it would be unlikely for the individual with this introverted genotype to become a strong extravert. The term **reaction range** *is used to describe the range of phenotypes for each genotype, suggesting the importance of an environment's restrictiveness or enrichment* (see figure 3.10).

Sandra Scarr (1984) explains reaction range this way: Each of us has a range of potential. For example, an individual with "medium-tall" genes for height who grows up in a poor environment may be shorter than average. But in an excellent nutritional environment, the individual may grow up taller than average. However, no matter how well fed the person is, someone with "short" genes will never be taller than average. Scarr believes that characteristics such as intelligence and introversion work the same way. That is, there is a range within which the environment can modify intelligence, but intelligence is not completely malleable. Reaction range gives us an estimate of how modifiable intelligence is.

Genotypes, in addition to producing many phenotypes, may show the opposite track for some characteristics—those that are somewhat immune to extensive changes in the environment.

FIGURE 3.9

The genetic difference between males and females. Set (*a*) shows the chromosome structure of a male, and set (*b*) shows the chromosome structure of a female. The last pair of 23 pairs of chromosomes is in the bottom right box of each set. Notice that the Y chromosome of the male is smaller than that of the female. To obtain this kind of chromosomal picture, a cell is removed from a person's body, usually from the inside of the mouth. The chromosomes are magnified extensively and then photographed.

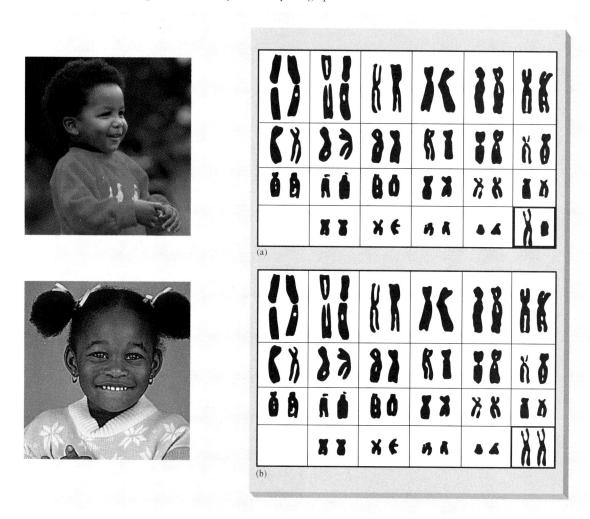

These characteristics seem to stay on a particular developmental course regardless of the environmental assaults on them (Waddington, 1957). **Canalization** *is the term chosen to describe the narrow path or developmental course that certain characteristics take. Apparently, preservative forces help to protect or buffer a person from environmental extremes.* For example, American developmental psychologist Jerome Kagan (1984) points to his research on Guatemalan infants who had experienced extreme malnutrition as infants yet showed normal social and cognitive development later in childhood. And some abused children do not grow up to be abusers themselves.

However, it is important to recognize that while the genetic influence of canalization exerts its power by keeping organisms on a particular developmental path, genes alone do not directly determine human behavior (Cairns, 1991; Gottlieb, 1991 a, b; Lerner, 1991). Developmentalist Gilbert Gottlieb (1991a) points out that genes are an integral part of the organism, but that their activity (genetic expression) can be affected by the organism's environment. For example, hormones that circulate in the blood make their way into the cell, where they influence the cell's activity. The flow of hormones themselves can be affected by environmental events such as light, day length, nutrition, and behavior.

FIGURE 3.10

Although each genotype responds favorably to improved environments, some are more responsive to environmental deprivation and enrichment than are others.

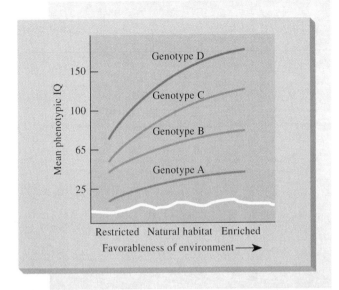

Identical twins develop from a single fertilized egg that splits into two genetically identical organisms. Twin studies compare identical twins with fraternal twins. Fraternal twins develop from separate eggs, making them genetically less similar than identical twins.

Methods Used by Behavior Geneticists

Behavior genetics *is concerned with the degree and nature of behavior's hereditary basis.* Behavior geneticists assume that behaviors are jointly determined by the interaction of heredity and environment. To study heredity's influence on behavior, behavior geneticists often use either twin studies or adoption studies.

In a **twin study,** *the behavior of identical twins is compared with the behavior of fraternal twins.* **Identical twins** *(called monozygotic twins) develop from a single fertilized egg that splits into two genetically identical replicas, each of which becomes a person.* **Fraternal twins** *(called dizygotic twins) develop from separate eggs, making them genetically less similar than identical twins.* Although fraternal twins share the same womb, they are no more alike genetically than are nontwin brothers and sisters, and they may be of different sexes. By comparing groups of identical and fraternal twins, behavior geneticists capitalize on the basic knowledge that identical twins are more similar genetically than are fraternal twins. In one twin study, 7,000 pairs of Finnish identical and fraternal twins were compared on the personality traits of extraversion (outgoingness) and neuroticism (psychological instability) (Rose & others, 1988). On both of these personality traits, identical twins were much more similar than fraternal twins, suggesting the role of heredity in both traits. However, several issues crop up as a result of twin studies. Adults may stress the similarities of identical twins more than those of fraternal twins, and identical twins may perceive themselves as a "set" and play together more than fraternal twins. If so, observed similarities in identical twins could be environmentally influenced.

In an **adoption study,** *investigators seek to discover whether the behavior and psychological characteristics of adopted children are more like their adoptive parents, who provided a home environment, or their biological parents, who contributed their heredity.* In one investigation, the educational levels attained by biological parents were better predictors of adopted children's IQ scores than were the IQs of the children's adopted parents (Scarr & Weinberg, 1983). Because of the genetic relation between the adopted children and their biological parents, the implication is that heredity influences children's IQ scores.

Heredity's Influence on Development

What aspects of development are influenced by genetic factors? They all are. However, behavior geneticists are interested in more precise estimates of a characteristic's variation that can be accounted for by genetic factors. Intelligence and temperament are among the most widely investigated aspects of heredity's influence on development.

Arthur Jensen (1969) sparked a lively and, at times, hostile debate when he presented his thesis that intelligence is

THE WIZARD OF ID

By permission of Johnny Hart and Creators Syndicate, Inc.

primarily inherited. Jensen believes that environment and culture play only a minimal role in intelligence. He examined several studies of intelligence, some of which involved comparisons of identical and fraternal twins. Remember that identical twins have identical genetic endowments, so their IQs should be similar. Fraternal twins and ordinary siblings are less similar genetically, so their IQs should be less similar. Jensen found support for his argument in these studies. Studies with identical twins produced an average correlation of .82; studies with ordinary siblings produced an average correlation of .50. Note the difference of .32. To show that genetic factors are more important than environmental factors, Jensen compared identical twins reared together with those reared apart; the correlation for those reared together was .89 and for those reared apart was .78 (a differences of .11). Jensen argued that, if environmental influences were more important than genetic influences, then siblings reared apart, who experienced different environments, should have IQs much further apart.

Many scholars have criticized Jensen's work. One criticism concerns the definition of intelligence itself. Jensen believes that IQ as measured by standardized intelligence tests is a good indicator of intelligence. Critics argue that IQ tests tap only a narrow range of intelligence. Everyday problem solving, work, and social adaptability, say the critics, are important aspects of intelligence not measured by the traditional intelligence tests used in Jensen's sources. A second criticism is that most investigations of heredity and environment do not include environments that differ radically. Thus, it is not surprising that many genetic studies show environment to be a fairly weak influence of intelligence.

Intelligence is influenced by heredity, but most developmentalists have not found as strong a relationship as Jensen found in his work. Other experts estimate heredity's influence on intelligence to be in the 50 percent range. (Plomin, DeFries & McClearn, 1990). Jensen is such a strong advocate of genetic influence that he believes we can breed for intelligence. Just such an effort—the Repository for Germinal Choice—is in progress, as we see next.

Doran (a name from the Greek word meaning "gift") learned all the elements of speech by 2 years of age. An intelli-

Robert Graham, founder of the Repository for Germinal Choice, holds a container of frozen sperm. Doran (insert), one of the offspring born through the Repository for Germinal Choice.

gence test showed that, at the age of 1, his mental age was 4. Doran was the second child born through the Nobel Prize sperm bank, which came into existence in 1980. The sperm bank was founded by Robert Graham in Escondido, California, with the intent of producing geniuses. Graham collected the sperm of Nobel Prize-winning scientists and offered it free of charge to intelligent women of good stock whose husbands were infertile.

One of the contributors to the sperm bank is physicist William Shockley, who shared the Nobel Prize in 1956 for inventing the transistor. Shockley has received his share of criticism for preaching the genetic basis of intelligence. Two other Nobel Prize winners have donated their sperm to the bank, but Shockley is the only one who has been identified.

More than 20 children have been sired through the sperm bank. Are the progeny prodigies? It may be too early to tell. Except for Doran, little has been revealed about the children. Doran's genetic father was labeled "28 Red" in the sperm bank (the color apparently has no meaning). He is listed in the sperm bank's catalog as handsome, blond, and athletic, with a math SAT score of 800 and several prizes for his classical music performances. One of his few drawbacks is that he passed along to Doran an almost one-in-three chance of developing hemorrhoids. Doran's mother says that her genetic contribution goes back to the royal court of Norway and to poet William Blake.

The odds are not high that a sperm bank will yield that special combination of factors required to produce a creative genius. George Bernard Shaw, who believed that heredity's influence on intelligence is strong, once told a story about a beautiful woman who wrote to him, that, with her body and his brain, they could produce marvelous offspring. Shaw responded that, unfortunately, the offspring might get his body and her brain!

Not surprisingly, the Nobel Prize sperm bank is heavily criticized. Some say that brighter does not mean better. They also say that IQ is not a good indicator of social competence or human contribution to the world. Other critics say that intelligence is an elusive concept to measure and that it cannot reliably be reproduced, as the sperm bank is trying to do. Visions of the German gene program of the 1930s and 1940s are created. The German Nazis believed that certain traits are superior; they tried to breed children with such traits and killed people without them.

Although Graham's Repository for Germinal Choice (as the Nobel Prize sperm bank is formally called) is strongly criticized, consider its possible contributions. The repository provides a social service for couples who cannot conceive a child, and individuals who go the sperm bank probably provide an enriched environment for the offspring. To once childless parents, the offspring produced by the sperm bank, or any of the other new methods of conception available, are invariably described as miracles (Garelik, 1985).

HEREDITY-ENVIRONMENT INTERACTION AND CHILDREN'S DEVELOPMENT

A common misconception is that behavior geneticists only analyze the effects of heredity on development. While they believe heredity plays an important role in children's development, they also carve up the environment's contribution to heredity-environment interaction.

Sandra Scarr has developed a number of important theoretical ideas and conducted a number of research investigations on the roles of heredity and environment in children's development. She believes that the environments parents select for their children depend to some degree on the parents' own genotype.

Passive Genotype/Environment, Evocative Genotype/Environment, and Active Genotype/Environment Interactions

Parents not only provide the genes for the child's biological blueprint for development, but they also play important roles in determining the types of environments their children will encounter. Behavior geneticist Sandra Scarr (1992; Scarr & McCartney, 1983; Scarr & Riccivti, in press) believes that the environments parents select for their children depend to some degree on the parents' own genotypes. Three ways behavior geneticists believe heredity and environment interact in this manner are passively, evocatively, and actively. **Passive genotype/environment interactions** *occur when parents, who are genetically related to the child, provide a rearing environment for the child.* For example, parents may have a genetic predisposition to be intelligent and read skillfully. Because they read well and enjoy reading, they provide their child with books to read, with the likely outcome that their children will become skilled readers who enjoy reading.

Evocative genotype/environment interactions *occur because a child's genotype elicits certain types of physical and social environments.* For example, active, smiling babies receive more social stimulation than passive, quiet babies. Cooperative, attentive children evoke more pleasant and instructional responses from the adults around them than uncooperative, distractible children.

Active (niche-picking) genotype/environment interactions *occur when children seek out environments they find compatible and stimulating. Niche-picking refers to finding a niche or setting that is especially suited to the child's abilities.* Children select from their surrounding environment some aspects to which they respond, learn about, or ignore. Their active selections of certain environments are related to their particular genotype. Some children, because of their genotype, have the sensorimotor skills to perform well at sports. Others, because of their genotype, may have more ability in music. Children who are athletically inclined are more likely to actively seek out sports environments in which they can perform well, while children who are musically inclined are more likely to spend time in musical environments in which they can successfully perform their skills.

Scarr (1992; Scarr & McCartney, 1983) believes that the relative importance of the three genotype/environment interactions changes as children develop from infancy through adolescence. In infancy, much of the environment that children experience is provided by adults. When those adults are genetically related to the child, the environment they provide is related to their own characteristics and genotypes. Although infants are active in structuring their experiences by actively attending to what is available to them, they cannot seek out and build their own environmental niches as much as older children can. Therefore, passive genotype/environment interactions are more common in the lives of infants and young children than they are for older children, who can extend their experiences beyond the family's influences and create their environments to a greater degree.

Shared and Nonshared Environmental Influences

Behavior geneticists also believe that another way the environment's role in heredity-environment interaction can be carved up is to consider the experiences that children have in families that are common with other children living in the same home and those that are not common or shared. Behavior geneticist Robert Plomin (1991, 1993; Plomin & Daniels, 1987) believes that common rearing, or shared environment, accounts for little of the variation in children's personality or interests. In other words, even though two children live under the same roof with the same parents, their personalities are often very different.

Shared environmental experiences *are children's common experiences, such as their parents' personalities and intellectual orientation, the family's social class, and the neighborhood in which they live.* By contrast, **nonshared environmental experiences** *refer to a child's own unique experiences, both within the family and outside the family, that are not shared with another sibling.* Parents often do interact differently with each sibling, and siblings interact differently with parents. Siblings often have different peer groups, different friends, and different teachers at school.

Not all developmentalists share the behavior genetics view. Parenting expert Eleanor Maccoby (1992) argues that there are a number of important aspects of family contexts that are shared by all family members. After all, children observe how parents are treating their siblings, and they learn from what they observe as well as what they experience directly. And, atmospheres and moods tend to be spread to whoever is in the room.

Conclusions

In sum, both genes and environment are necessary for a child to even exist. Heredity and environment operate together—or cooperate—to produce a child's intelligence, temperament, height, weight, ability to pitch a baseball, reading talents, and so on (Loehlin, 1992; Plomin, 1993; Rowe, in press; Scarr, 1992; Scarr & Waldman, 1993). Without genes, there is no child; without environment, there is no child (Scarr & Weinberg, 1980). If an attractive, popular, intelligent girl is elected president of her senior class in high school, should we conclude that her success is due to heredity or to environment? Of course, the answer is both. Because the environment's influence depends on genetically-endowed characteristics, we say the two factors *interact.*

Critical Thinking

Beyond the fact that heredity and environment always interact to produce development, first argue for heredity's dominance in this interaction, and, second, argue for environment's dominance.

A summary of the main ideas in our discussion of genetic principles and methods, heredity's influence on children's development, and how heredity and environment interact to produce development is presented in Concept Table 3.2. In the next chapter, we will continue to discuss biological beginnings, turning to the nature of prenatal development and birth.

CONCEPT TABLE 3.2

Genetic Principles and Methods, Heredity, and Heredity–Environment Interaction

Concept	Processes/Related Ideas	Characteristics/Description
Genetic principles and methods	Genetic principles	Genetic transmission is complex, but some principles have been worked out, among them dominant-recessive genes, sex-linked genes, polygenic inheritance, genotype-phenotype distinction, reaction range, and canalization.
	Methods used by behavior geneticists	Behavior genetics is the field concerned with the degree and nature of behavior's hereditary basis. Among the most important methods used by behavior geneticists are twin studies and adoption studies.
Heredity's influence on development	Its scope	All aspects of development are influenced by heredity.
	Intelligence	Jensen's argument that intelligence is due primarily to heredity sparked a lively and, at times, bitter debate. Intelligence is influenced by heredity, but not as strongly as Jensen envisioned.
Heredity-environment interaction and development	Passive genotype/environment, evocative genotype/environment, and active genotype/environment interactions	Scarr believes that the environments parents select for their own children depend to some degree on the parents' genotypes. Three ways behavior geneticists believe heredity and environment interact in this manner are passively, evocatively, and actively. Passive genotype/environment interactions occur when parents, who are genetically related to the child, provide a rearing environment for the child. Evocative genotype/environment interactions occur because a child's genotype elicits certain types of physical and social environments. Active (niche-picking) genotype/environment interactions occur when children seek out environments they find compatible and stimulating. Scarr believes the relative importance of these three forms of genotype/environment interactions changes as children develop.
	Shared and nonshared environments	Shared environmental experiences are children's common experiences, such as their parents' personalities and intellectual orientation, the family's social class, and the neighborhood in which they live. Nonshared environmental experiences refer to the child's own unique experiences, both within a family and outside the family, that are not shared by another sibling. Plomin argues that it is nonshared environmental experiences that primarily make up the environment's contribution to why one sibling's personality is different from another's.
	Conclusions	Without genes, there is no organism; without environment, there is no organism. Because the environment's influence depends on genetically endowed characteristics, we say that the two factors interact.

PERSPECTIVES ON PARENTING AND EDUCATION

The Effects of Early Intervention on Intelligence

Researchers are increasingly interested in manipulating the environment early in children's lives when they are perceived to be at risk for impoverished intelligence (Burchinal, 1993; Campbell & Ramey, 1993). In a program conducted in North Carolina by Craig Ramey and his associates (1988), pregnant women with IQs averaging 80 were recruited for a study. After their babies were born, half of the infants were cared for during the day at an educational day-care center and half were reared at home by their mothers. Both groups of children were given medical care and dietary supplements, and their families were given social services if they requested them.

At the age of 3, the children who attended the educational day-care center had significantly higher IQs than the home-reared children. This difference was likely due to the decline in the IQs of the home-reared children during the period from 12 to 18 months of age. By the time the children were 5 years old, 39 percent of the home-reared children had IQs below 85 but only 11 percent of the educational day-care children had IQs this low.

Some parents, such as those in Ramey's study, have difficulty providing an adequate environment for the intellectual needs of their infants. Once these difficulties are a repetitive part of the family system, then change efforts probably will be more difficult and costly. Early intervention in the family system is directed at changing parental adaptive and responsive functioning so that permanent negative effects are minimized (Heinicke, Beckwith, & Thompson, 1988).

A second example of a successful early intervention program was conducted in Houston, Texas, with low-income Mexican American families (Johnson & McGowan, 1984). The Mexican American children were 1 year

Craig Ramey's research has documented that high quality early educational day care can significantly raise the intelligence of young children from impoverished environments.

old at the beginning of the intervention, which lasted for two years. A family educator visited each home twice a week during the first year of the program to encourage parents to teach their infants and to be sensitive to their developmental needs. On weekends, the whole family participated in groups to discuss ways to improve family communication. In the program's second year, toddlers went to an educational day-care center four mornings each week while their mothers participated in group discussion sessions focused on family issues and parenting.

In this study, the families who experienced the intervention were compared with a control group of families from similar backgrounds who did not receive parent education, educational day care, or any other services. The intervention program was successful. Mothers in

the intervention program created a more stimulating home environment for their children, gave them more affection, and encouraged them to talk more than the control group mothers did. And, at both 2 and 3 years of age, the intervention children had higher IQs than the control group children.

In another investigation, the Infant Health and Development Program, early intervention with low birth weight children revealed that both home visitation and an educational child curriculum improved the children's IQ, decreased behavior problems, and improved home environment (Infant Health and Development Program Staff, 1990; Liaw, 1993; Liaw, Meisels, & Brooks-Gunn, 1994). The intervention was more effective with mothers with low educational attainment than those with high educational attainment, more effective for Black than White children, and effective for most at-risk children (Brooks-Gunn & others, in press; Brooks-Gunn & others, 1992).

Intervention programs have the most positive effects on children's well-being when they: (a) begin as early as possible, (b) provide services to parents as well as to the child, (c) have a low child-teacher ratio, (d) have high parental involvement, and (e) have frequent contacts (Bronfenbrenner, 1974; Bryant & Ramey, 1987; McKey & others, 1985; Innocenti & Huh, 1993; Lazar & Darlington, 1982; Schorr, 1988; Taylor & Machida, 1993). In one review of family intervention studies, intervention was more effective when there were 11 or more contacts between the intervenor and the family (Heinicke, Beckwith, & Thompson, 1988). While 11 sessions is a somewhat arbitrary number, it does indicate that a certain duration of contact is necessary for intervention success. ■

CONCLUSIONS

Biological beginnings raise questions of how we as a species came to be, how parents' genes are shuffled to produce a particular child, and how much experience can go against the grain of heredity.

In this chapter, we studied the Jim and Jim twins; the evolutionary perspective, in which we discussed natural selection, sociobiology, and race and ethnicity; the nature of heredity; what genes are; how reproduction takes place; some abnormalities in genes and chromosomes; genetic principles; methods used by behavior geneticists; heredity's influence on development; and what heredity—environment interaction is like. With regard to heredity—environment interaction, behavior geneticists believe that it is important to consider passive/genotype environment, evocative genotype/environment, and active genotype/environment interactions, as well as shared and nonshared environmental experiences. You also read about the effects of early intervention on intelligence. Remember that you can obtain a summary of the main ideas in the entire chapter by again reading the two concept tables on pages 86 and 93.

In the next chapter, we continue our exploration of children's biological beginnings by discussing the dramatic unfolding of prenatal development and the birth process.

KEY TERMS

natural selection   The evolutionary process that favors individuals within a species that are best adapted to survive and reproduce. (75)

sociobiology   This is a contemporary evolutionary view in psychology that states that all behavior is motivated by the desire to contribute one's genetic heritage to the greatest number of descendants. (76)

race   This term refers to a system for classifying plants and animals into subcategories according to specific physical and structural characteristics. (77)

chromosomes   Threadlike structures that come in 23 pairs, one member of each pair coming from each parent. Chromosomes contain the genetic substance DNA. (79)

DNA   A complex molecule that contains genetic information. (79)

genes   Units of hereditary information on the DNA "staircase." Genes act like a blueprint for cells to reproduce themselves and manufacture the proteins that maintain life. (79)

gametes   Human reproduction cells created in the testes of males and the ovaries of females. (79)

meiosis   The process of cell division in which each pair of chromosomes in a cell separates, with one member of each pair going into each gamete. (79)

reproduction   The process that occurs when a female gamete (ovum) is fertilized by a male gamete (sperm). (79)

zygote   A single cell formed through fertilization. (79)

in vitro fertilization   Conception outside the body. (80)

phenylketonuria (PKU)   A genetic disorder in which an individual cannot properly metabolize protein. PKU is now easily detected but, if left untreated, results in mental retardation and hyperactivity. (82)

Down syndrome   The most common genetically transmitted form of mental retardation, which is caused by the presence of an extra (47th) chromosome. (82)

sickle-cell anemia   A genetic disorder that affects the red blood cells and occurs most often in Black individuals. (82)

Klinefelter syndrome   A genetic disorder in which males have an extra X chromosome, making them XXY instead of just XY. (82)

Turner syndrome   A genetic disorder in which females are missing an X chromosome, making them XO instead of XX. (82)

XYY syndrome   A genetic disorder in which males have an extra Y chromosome. (82)

amniocentesis   A prenatal medical procedure in which a sample of amniotic fluid is withdrawn by syringe and tested to discover if the fetus is suffering from any chromosomal or metabolic disorders. It is performed in the 12th to 16th week of pregnancy. (84)

ultrasound sonography   A medical procedure in which high-frequency sound waves are directed into a woman's abdomen. (85)

chorionic villus test   A prenatal medical procedure in which a small sample of the placenta is removed at a certain point in the pregnancy from the 8th through the 11th week. (85)

maternal blood test   A prenatal diagnostic technique that is used to assess blood alphaprotein level, which is associated with neural tube defects. This technique is also called alpha-fetoprotein test-AFP. (85)

dominant-recessive genes principle   If one gene of a pair is dominant and one is recessive (goes back or recedes), the dominant gene exerts its effect, overriding the potential influence of the recessive gene. A recessive gene exerts its influence only if both genes in a pair are recessive. (86)

polygenic inheritance   A genetic principle that describes the interaction of many genes to produce a particular characteristic. (87)

genotype   A person's genetic heritage; the actual genetic material. (87)

phenotype   The way an individual's genotype is expressed in observed and measurable characteristics. (87)

reaction range   The range of phenotypes for each genotype, suggesting the importance of the environment's restrictiveness or enrichment. (87)

canalization   The process by which characteristics take a narrow path or developmental course. Apparently, preservative forces help protect a person from environmental extremes. (88)

behavior genetics   The degree and nature of behavior's hereditary basis. (89)

twin study   A study in which the behavior of identical twins is compared to the behavior of fraternal twins. (89)

identical twins   Twins who develop from a single fertilized egg, which splits into two genetically identical replicas, each of which becomes a person. (89)

fraternal twins   Twins who develop from separate eggs, making them genetically less similar than identical twins. (89)

adoption study   A study in which investigators seek to discover whether the behavior and psychological characteristics of adopted children are more like their adoptive parents, who provide a

home environment, or their biological parents, who contributed their heredity. (89)

passive genotype/environment interactions   The type of interactions that occur when parents, who are genetically related to the child, provide the rearing environment for the child. (91)

evocative genotype/environmental interactions   The type of interactions that occur when the child's genotype elicits certain types of physical and social environments. (92)

active (niche-picking) genotype/environment interactions   The type of interactions that occur when children seek out environments they find companionable and stimulating. (92)

shared environmental experiences   Children's common environmental experiences that are shared with their siblings, such as their parents' personalities and intellectual orientation, the family's social class, and the neighborhood in which they live. (92)

nonshared environmental experiences   The child's own unique experiences, both within a family and outside the family, that are not shared by another sibling. (92)

SUGGESTED READINGS

Cowley, G. (1990, Winter/Spring). Made to order babies. *Newsweek.* The increasing possibility that in the future parents might be able to pick the child they want on the basis of different types of characteristics such as hair color, intelligence, personality, body type, and so on, is explored.

Gould, S. (1983). *Hen's teeth and horse's toes: Reflections on natural history.* New York: W. W. Norton. This book is a collection of fascinating articles by a biologist interested in

evolution. The essays originally were published in the magazine *Natural History.*

Merewood, A. (1991, April). Sperm under siege. *Health.* This article examines how the male's sperm may be affected more by such factors as drugs, alcohol, radiation, and chemical exposure than previously thought. These changes in sperm may be transmitted to the offspring and influence whether the baby is healthy or not.

Toth, A. (1991). *Fertility Solution.*

New York: Atlantic Monthly Press. The author argues that up to 50 percent of infertility cases are caused by bacterial infections and can be cured by antibiotics.

Watson, J. D. (1968). *The double helix.* New York: New American Library. This is a personalized account of the research leading up to one of the most provocative discoveries of the twentieth century—the DNA molecule. Reading like a mystery novel, it illustrates the exciting discovery process in science.

Morisot, Berthe:
The Cradle (Detail)

Prenatal Development and Birth

*The history of man for nine months
preceding his birth would, probably, be
far more interesting, and contain events
of greater moment than all three score
and ten years that follow it.*

—Samuel Taylor Coleridge

What web is this
Of will be, is, and was?

—Jorge Luis Borges

IMAGES OF CHILDREN

Jim and Sara, an Expectant Couple

Although Jim and Sara did not plan to have a baby, they did not take precautions to prevent it, and it was not long before Sara was pregnant (Colt, 1991). Jim and Sara read the popular pregnancy book, *What to Expect When You're Expecting* (Eisenberg, Murkoff, & Hathaway, 1988). They found a nurse-midwife they liked and invented a pet name—Bibinello—for the fetus. They signed up for birth preparation classes, and each Friday night for eight weeks they faithfully practiced simulated contractions.

They drew up a birth plan that included their decisions about such matters as the type of care provider they wanted to use, the birth setting they wanted, and various aspects of labor and birth. They moved into a larger apartment so the baby could have its own room and spent weekends browsing through garage sales and secondhand stores to find good prices on baby furniture—a crib, a high chair, a stroller, a changing table, a crib mobile, a swing, a car seat.

Jim and Sara also spent a lot of time talking about Sara's pregnancy, what kind of parents they wanted to be, and what their child might be like. They also discussed what changes in their lives the baby would make. One of their concerns was that Sara's maternity leave would only last six weeks. If she wanted to stay home longer she would have to quit her job, something she and Jim were not sure they could afford. These are among the many questions that expectant couples face.

PREVIEW

This chapter includes further information about expectant parents and chronicles the truly remarkable developments from conception through birth. Imagine . . . at one time you were an organism floating around in a sea of fluid in your mother's womb. Let's now explore what development is like from the time you were conceived through the time you were born.

PRENATAL DEVELOPMENT

Imagine how you came to be. Out of thousands of eggs and millions of sperm, one egg and one sperm united to produce you. Had the union of sperm and egg come a day or even an hour earlier or later, you might have been very different—maybe even of the opposite sex. Remember from chapter 3 that conception occurs when a single sperm cell from the male unites with an ovum (egg) in the female's fallopian tube in a process called fertilization. Remember also that the fertilized egg is called a zygote. By the time the zygote ends its three- to four-day journey through the fallopian tube and reaches the uterus, it has divided into approximately 12 to 16 cells.

The Course of Prenatal Development

Prenatal development is commonly divided into three main periods: germinal, embryonic, and fetal.

Germinal

The **germinal period** *is the period of prenatal development that takes place in the first two weeks after conception. It includes the creation of the zygote, continued cell division, and the attachment of the zygote to the uterine wall.* By approximately one week after conception, the zygote is composed of 100 to 150 cells. The differentiation of cells has already commenced as inner and outer layers of the organism are formed. The **blastocyst** *is the inner*

FIGURE 4.1

Significant developments in the germinal period.

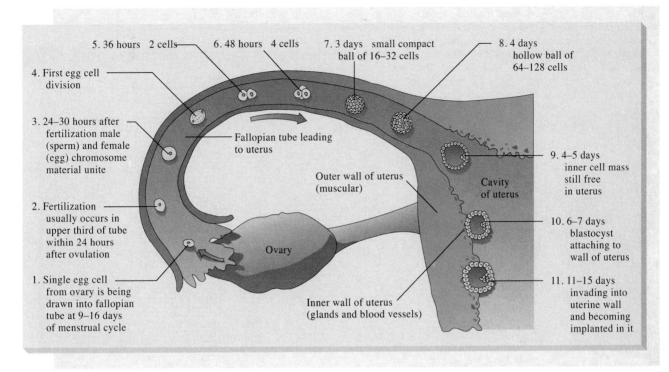

4. First egg cell division

5. 36 hours 2 cells

6. 48 hours 4 cells

7. 3 days small compact ball of 16–32 cells

8. 4 days hollow ball of 64–128 cells

3. 24–30 hours after fertilization male (sperm) and female (egg) chromosome material unite

Fallopian tube leading to uterus

Outer wall of uterus (muscular)

Cavity of uterus

9. 4–5 days inner cell mass still free in uterus

2. Fertilization usually occurs in upper third of tube within 24 hours after ovulation

Ovary

10. 6–7 days blastocyst attaching to wall of uterus

1. Single egg cell from ovary is being drawn into fallopian tube at 9–16 days of menstrual cycle

Inner wall of uterus (glands and blood vessels)

11. 11–15 days invading into uterine wall and becoming implanted in it

layer of cells that develops during the germinal period. These cells later develop into the embryo. The **trophoblast** *is the outer layer of cells that develops during the germinal period. It later provides nutrition and support for the embryo.* **Implantation,** *the attachment of the zygote to the uterine wall, takes place about 10 days after conception.* Figure 4.1 illustrates some of the most significant developments during the germinal period.

The Embryonic Period

The **embryonic period** *is the period of prenatal development that occurs from two to eight weeks after conception. During the embryonic period, the rate of cell differentiation intensifies, support systems for the cells form, and organs appear.* As the zygote attaches to the uterine wall, its cells form two layers. At this time, the name of the mass of cells changes from *zygote* to *embryo.* The embryo's **endoderm** *is the inner layer of cells, which will develop into the digestive and respiratory systems.* The outer layer of cells is divided into two parts. The **ectoderm** *is the outermost layer, which will become the nervous system, sensory receptors (ear, nose, and eyes, for example), and skin parts (hair and nails, for example).* The **mesoderm** *is the middle layer, which will become the circulatory system, bones, muscle, excretory system, and reproductive system.* Every body part eventually develops from these three layers. The endoderm primarily produces internal body parts, the mesoderm primarily produces parts that surround the internal areas, and the ectoderm primarily produces surface parts.

If I could have watched you grow
As a magical mother might.
If I could have seen through my magical transparent belly,
There would have been such ripening within . . .

—Anne Sexton, *Little Girl,*
My String Bean, My Lovely Woman

As the embryo's three layers form, life-support systems for the embryo mature and develop rapidly. These life-support systems include the placenta, the umbilical cord, and the amnion. The **placenta** *is a life-support system that consists of a disk-shaped group of tissues in which small blood vessels from the mother and the offspring intertwine but do not join.* The **umbilical cord** *is a life-support system, containing two arteries and one vein, that connects the baby to the placenta.* Very small molecules—oxygen, water, salt, food from the mother's blood, and carbon dioxide and digestive wastes from the embryo's blood—pass back and forth between the mother and infant. Large molecules cannot pass through the placental wall; these include red blood cells and harmful substances such as most bacteria, maternal wastes, and hormones. The mechanisms that govern the transfer of substances across the placental barrier are complex and are still not entirely understood (Rosenblith and Sims-Knight, 1992). Figure 4.2 provides an illustration of the placenta, the umbilical cord, and the nature of blood flow in the expectant mother

FIGURE 4.2

The placenta and the umbilical cord. Maternal blood flows through the uterine arteries to the spaces housing the placenta and returns through the uterine veins to maternal circulation. Fetal blood flows through the umbilical arteries into the capillaries of the placenta and returns through the umbilical veins to the fetal circulation. The exchange of materials takes place across the layer separating the maternal and fetal blood supplies, so the bloods never come into contact. *Note:* The area bound by the square is enlarged in the right half of the illustration. Arrows indicate the direction of blood flow.

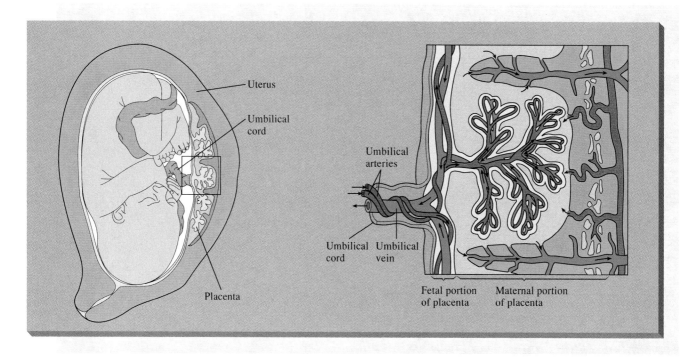

DENNIS THE MENACE

"My Mom says I come from Heaven. My Dad says he can't remember an' Mr. Wilson is POSITIVE I came from Mars!"

DENNIS THE MENACE® used by permission of Hank Ketcham and © by North America Syndicate.

and developing child in the uterus. The **amnion,** *a bag or envelope that contains a clear fluid in which the developing embryo floats, is another important life-support system.* Like the placenta and umbilical cord, the amnion develops from the fertilized egg, not from the mother's own body. At approximately 16 weeks, the kidneys of the fetus begin to produce urine. This fetal urine remains the main source of the amniotic fluid until the third trimester, when some of the fluid is excreted from the lungs of the growing fetus. Although the volume of the amniotic fluid increases tenfold from the 12th to the 40th week of pregnancy, it is also removed in various ways. Some is swallowed by the fetus and some is absorbed through the umbilical cord and the membranes covering the placenta. The amniotic fluid is important in providing an environment that is temperature and humidity controlled, as well as shockproof.

Before most women even know they are pregnant, some important embryonic developments take place. In the third week, the neural tube that eventually becomes the spinal cord forms. At about 21 days, eyes begin to appear and, at 24 days, the cells for the heart begin to differentiate. During the fourth week, the first appearance of the urogenital system is apparent, and arm and leg buds emerge. Four chambers of the heart take shape, and blood vessels surface. From the fifth to the eighth week, arms and legs differentiate further; at this time, the face starts to form but still is not very recognizable. The intestinal tract develops and the facial structures fuse. At 8 weeks, the

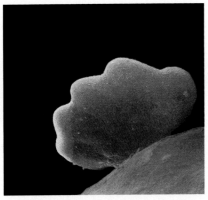
The hand of an embryo at 6 weeks.

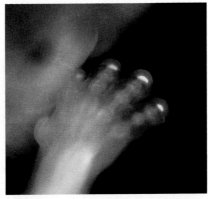
Fingers and thumb with pads seen at 8 weeks.

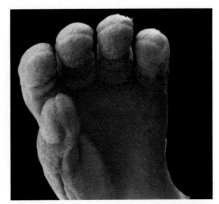
The finger pads have regressed by 13 weeks.

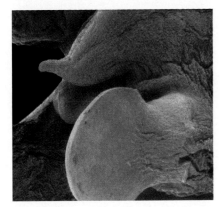
Toe ridges emerge after 7 weeks.

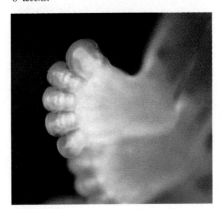
Toe pads and the emerging heel are visible by 9 weeks.

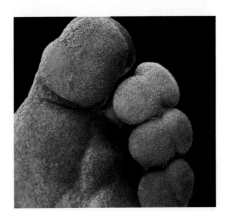
The toe pads have regressed by 13 weeks.

The fingers and toes form rapidly during the first trimester. After 13 weeks of pregnancy, the hands and feet already look remarkably similar to those of a mature human although they are still smaller than an adult's fingernail.

developing organism weighs about one-thirtieth of an ounce and is less than 1 inch long. **Organogenesis** *is the process of organ formation that takes place during the first two months of prenatal development.* When organs are being formed, they are especially vulnerable to environmental changes. Later in the chapter, we will describe the environmental hazards that are harmful during organogenesis.

The Fetal Period

The **fetal period** *is the prenatal period of development that begins two months after conception and lasts for seven months on the average.* Growth and development continue their dramatic course during this time. Three months after conception, the fetus is about 3 inches long and weighs about 1 ounce. It has become active, moving its arms and legs, opening and closing its mouth, and moving its head. The face, forehead, eyelids, nose, and chin are distinguishable, as are the upper arms, lower arms, hands, and lower limbs, and the genitals can be identified as male or female. By the end of the fourth month, the fetus has grown to about 5½ inches in length and weighs about 4 ounces. At this time, a growth spurt occurs in the body's lower parts. Prenatal reflexes are stronger; arm and leg movements can be felt for the first time by the mother.

By the end of the fifth month, the fetus is about 10 to 12 inches long and weighs ½ to 1 pound. Structures of the skin have formed—toenails and fingernails, for example. The fetus is more active, showing a preference for a particular position in the womb. By the end of the sixth month, the fetus is 11 to 14 inches long and already has gained another half pound to a pound. The eyes and eyelids are completely formed, and a fine layer of hair covers the head. A grasping reflex is present and irregular breathing occurs. By the end of the seventh month, the fetus is 14 to 17 inches long and has gained another pound, now weighing about 2½ to 3 pounds. During the eighth and ninth months, the fetus grows longer and gains substantial weight—about another 4 pounds. At birth, the average American baby weighs 7 to 7½ pounds and is about 20 inches long. In these last two months, fatty tissues develop and the functioning of various organ systems—heart and kidneys, for example—steps up.

We have described a number of developments in the germinal, embryonic, and fetal periods. An overview of some of the main developments we have discussed and some more specific changes in prenatal development are presented in figure 4.3.

So the riders of the darkness pass on their circuits: the luminous island of the self trembles and waits, waits for us all my friends, where the sea's big brush recolors the dying lives, and the unborn smiles.

—Lawrence Durrell

FIGURE 4.3

The three trimesters of prenatal development.

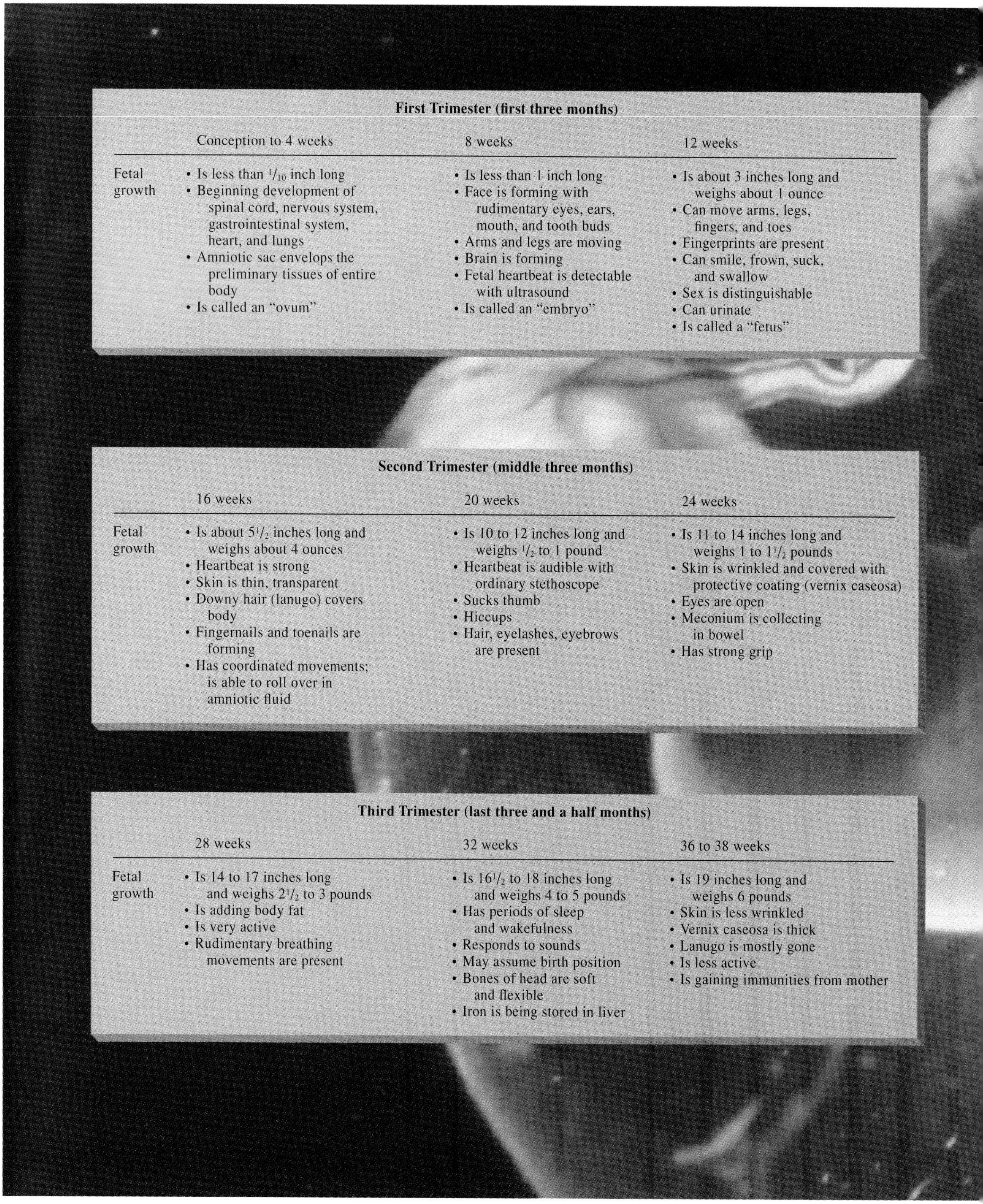

First Trimester (first three months)

	Conception to 4 weeks	8 weeks	12 weeks
Fetal growth	• Is less than $1/10$ inch long • Beginning development of spinal cord, nervous system, gastrointestinal system, heart, and lungs • Amniotic sac envelops the preliminary tissues of entire body • Is called an "ovum"	• Is less than 1 inch long • Face is forming with rudimentary eyes, ears, mouth, and tooth buds • Arms and legs are moving • Brain is forming • Fetal heartbeat is detectable with ultrasound • Is called an "embryo"	• Is about 3 inches long and weighs about 1 ounce • Can move arms, legs, fingers, and toes • Fingerprints are present • Can smile, frown, suck, and swallow • Sex is distinguishable • Can urinate • Is called a "fetus"

Second Trimester (middle three months)

	16 weeks	20 weeks	24 weeks
Fetal growth	• Is about $5\frac{1}{2}$ inches long and weighs about 4 ounces • Heartbeat is strong • Skin is thin, transparent • Downy hair (lanugo) covers body • Fingernails and toenails are forming • Has coordinated movements; is able to roll over in amniotic fluid	• Is 10 to 12 inches long and weighs $1/2$ to 1 pound • Heartbeat is audible with ordinary stethoscope • Sucks thumb • Hiccups • Hair, eyelashes, eyebrows are present	• Is 11 to 14 inches long and weighs 1 to $1\frac{1}{2}$ pounds • Skin is wrinkled and covered with protective coating (vernix caseosa) • Eyes are open • Meconium is collecting in bowel • Has strong grip

Third Trimester (last three and a half months)

	28 weeks	32 weeks	36 to 38 weeks
Fetal growth	• Is 14 to 17 inches long and weighs $2\frac{1}{2}$ to 3 pounds • Is adding body fat • Is very active • Rudimentary breathing movements are present	• Is $16\frac{1}{2}$ to 18 inches long and weighs 4 to 5 pounds • Has periods of sleep and wakefulness • Responds to sounds • May assume birth position • Bones of head are soft and flexible • Iron is being stored in liver	• Is 19 inches long and weighs 6 pounds • Skin is less wrinkled • Vernix caseosa is thick • Lanugo is mostly gone • Is less active • Is gaining immunities from mother

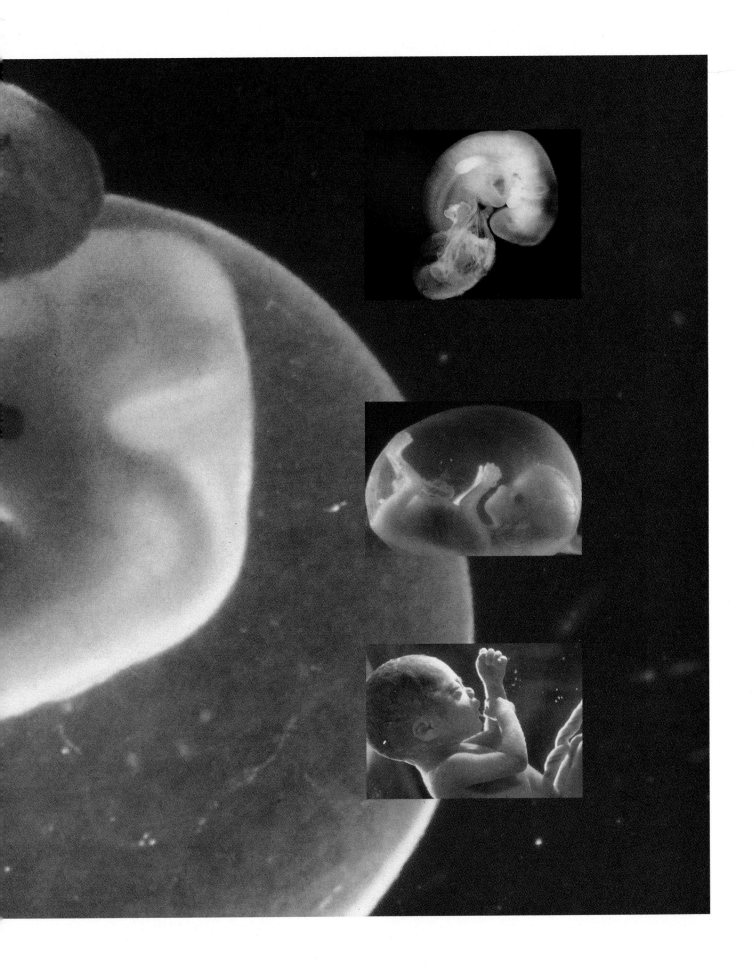

Miscarriage and Abortion

A miscarriage, or spontaneous abortion, happens when pregnancy ends before the developing organism is mature enough to survive outside the womb. The embryo separates from the uterine wall and is expelled by the uterus. About 15 to 20 percent of all pregnancies end in a spontaneous abortion, most in the first two to three months. Many spontaneous abortions occur without the mother's knowledge, and many involve an embryo or fetus that was not developing normally.

Early in history, it was believed that a woman could be frightened into a miscarriage by loud thunder or a jolt in a carriage. Today, we recognize that this occurrence is highly unlikely; the developing organism is well protected. Abnormalities of the reproductive tract and viral or bacterial infections are more likely to cause spontaneous abortions. In some cases, severe traumas may be at fault.

Deliberate termination of pregnancy is a complex issue, medically, psychologically, socially, and legally (Schaff, 1992). Carrying a baby to term may affect a woman's health, the woman's pregnancy may have resulted from rape or incest, the woman may not be married, or perhaps she is poor and wants to continue her education. Abortion is legal in the United States; in 1973, the Supreme Court ruled that any woman can obtain an abortion during the first six months of pregnancy, a decision that continues to generate ethical objections from antiabortion forces. The Supreme Court also has ruled that abortion in the first trimester is solely the decision of the mother and her doctor. Court cases also have added the point that the baby's father and the parents of minor girls do not have any say during this time frame. In the second trimester, states can legislate the time and method of abortion for protection of the mother's health. In the third trimester, the fetus' right to live is the primary concern.

What are the psychological effects of having an abortion? In 1989, a research review panel appointed by the American Psychological Association examined more than 100 investigations of the psychological effects of abortion. The panel's conclusions follow. Unwanted pregnancies are stressful for most women. However, it is common for women to report feelings of relief as well as feelings of guilt after an abortion. These feelings are usually mild and tend to diminish rapidly over time without adversely affecting the woman's ability to function. Abortion is more stressful for women who have a history of serious emotional problems and who are not given support by family or friends. According to the American Psychological Association report, only a small percentage of women fall into these high-risk categories. If an abortion is performed, it should not only involve competent medical care but the woman's psychological needs as well.

Critical Thinking

What are the arguments for and against abortion? Where do you stand on this sensitive ethical issue? Why?

Teratology and Hazards to Prenatal Development

Some expectant mothers carefully tiptoe about in the belief that everything they do and feel has a direct effect on their unborn child. Others behave casually, assuming that their experiences will have little effect. The truth lies somewhere between these two extremes. Although living in a protected, comfortable environment, the fetus is not totally immune to the larger world surrounding the mother. The environment can affect the child in many well-documented ways. Thousands of babies born deformed or mentally retarded every year are the result of events that occurred in the mother's life, as early as one or two months before conception.

Teratology

A **teratogen,** *which comes from the Greek word* tera *meaning "monster," is any agent that causes a birth defect. The field of study that investigates the causes of birth defects is called teratology.* A specific teratogen (such as a drug) usually does not cause a specific birth defect (such as malformation of the legs). So many teratogens exist that practically every fetus is exposed to at least some teratogens. For this reason, it is difficult to determine which teratogen causes which birth defect. In addition, it may take a long time for the effects of a teratogen to show up; only about half of all potential effects appear at birth.

Despite the many unknowns about teratogens, scientists have discovered the identity of some of these hazards to prenatal development and the particular point of fetal development at which they do their greatest damage (Little, 1992). As figure 4.4 shows, sensitivity to teratogens begins about three weeks after conception. The probability of a structural defect is greatest early in the embryonic period, because this is when organs are being formed. After organogenesis is complete, teratogens are less likely to cause anatomical defects. Exposure later, during the fetal period, is more likely to stunt growth or to create problems in the way organs function. The precision of organogenesis is evident; teratologists point out that vulnerability of the brain is greatest at 15 to 25 days after conception, the eye at 24 to 40 days, the heart at 20 to 40 days, and the legs at 24 to 36 days.

In the following sections, we will explore how certain environmental agents influence prenatal development. That is, we will examine how maternal diseases and conditions, the mother's age, nutrition, emotional states and stress, drugs, and environmental hazards can influence prenatal development.

Maternal Diseases and Conditions

Maternal diseases or infections can produce defects by crossing the placental barrier, or they can cause damage during the birth process itself. Rubella (German measles) is a maternal disease that can damage prenatal development. A rubella outbreak in 1964–1965 resulted in 30,000 prenatal and neonatal (newborn) deaths, and more than 20,000 infants were born with malformations, including mental retardation, blindness, deafness, and heart problems. The greatest damage occurs when mothers

FIGURE 4.4

Teratogens and the timing of their effects on prenatal development. The danger of structural defects caused by teratogens is greatest early in embryonic development. This is the period of organogenesis, and it lasts for several months. Damage caused by teratogens during this period is represented by the dark-colored bars. Later assaults by teratogens typically occur during the fetal period and, instead of structural damage, are more likely to stunt growth or cause problems of organ function.

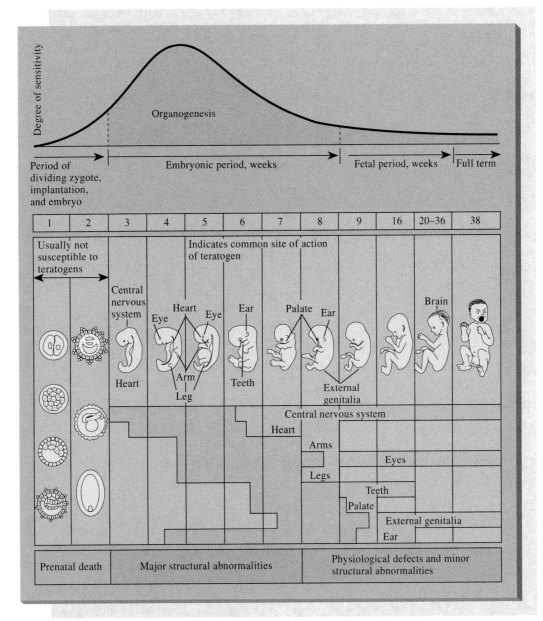

contract rubella in the third and fourth weeks of pregnancy, although infection during the second month is also damaging. Elaborate preventive efforts ensure that rubella will never again have the disastrous effects it had in the mid-1960s. A vaccine that prevents German measles is routinely administered to children, and women who plan to have children should have a blood test before they become pregnant to determine if they are immune to the disease.

Syphilis (a sexually transmitted disease) is more damaging later in prenatal development—four months or more after conception. Rather than affecting organogenesis, as rubella does, syphilis damages organs after they have formed. Damage includes eye lesions, which can cause blindness, and skin lesions.

When syphilis is present at birth, other problems involving the central nervous system and gastrointestinal tract can develop. Most states require that pregnant women be given a blood test to detect the presence of syphilis.

Another infection that has received widespread attention recently is genital herpes. Newborns contract this virus when they are delivered through the birth canal of a mother with genital herpes. About one-third of babies delivered through an infected birth canal die; another one-fourth become brain damaged. If a pregnant woman detects an active case of genital herpes close to her delivery date, a cesarean section can be performed (in which the infant is delivered through the mother's abdomen) to keep the virus from infecting the newborn (Byer & Shainberg, 1991).

The importance of women's health to the health of their offspring is nowhere better exemplified than when the mother has acquired immune deficiency syndrome (AIDS). As the number of women with HIV grows, more children are born exposed and infected with AIDS (The Health of America's Children, 1992).

AIDS was the eighth leading cause of death among children ages 1 to 4 in 1989. Through the end of 1991, 3,123 children younger than 13 had been diagnosed with AIDS. The number of pediatric AIDS cases does not include as many as 10,000 children infected with HIV who have not yet suffered the full effects of AIDS. Black and Latino children make up 83 percent of all pediatric AIDS cases. The majority of mothers who transmit HIV to their offspring were infected through intravenous drug use or heterosexual contact with injecting drug users.

There are three ways a mother with AIDS can infect her offspring: 1) during gestation across the placenta, 2) during delivery through contact with maternal blood or fluids, and 3) postpartum through breast feeding. Approximately one-third of infants born to infected mothers will ultimately become infected with the HIV virus themselves (Caldwell & Rogers, 1992). Babies born to AIDS-infected mothers can be: 1)infected and symptomatic (show AIDS symptoms), 2)infected but asymptomatic (not show AIDS symptoms), and 3) not be infected at all. An infant who is infected and asymptomatic may still develop HIV symptoms up until 15 months of age. At present there has been no documentation of an infant born to an HIV-infected mother developing HIV symptoms for the first time after 15 months of age.

The Mother's Age

When the mother's age is considered in terms of possible harmful effects on the fetus and infant, two time periods are of special interest: adolescence and the thirties and beyond. Approximately one of every five births is to an adolescent; in some urban areas, the figure reaches as high as one in every two births. Infants born to adolescents are often premature. The mortality rate of infants born to adolescent mothers is double that of infants born to mothers in their twenties. Although such figures probably reflect the mother's immature reproductive system, they also may involve poor nutrition, lack of prenatal care, and low socioeconomic status. Prenatal care decreases the probability that a child born to an adolescent girl will have physical problems. However, adolescents are the least likely of women in all age groups to obtain prenatal assistance from clinics, pediatricians, and health services.

Increasingly, women are seeking to establish their careers before beginning a family, delaying childbearing until their thirties. Down syndrome, a form of mental retardation, is related to the mother's age. A baby with Down syndrome rarely is born to a mother under the age of 30, but the risk increases after the mother reaches 30. By age 40, the probability is slightly over 1 in 100 and, by age 50, it is almost 1 in 10. The risk is also higher before age 18.

Women also have more difficulty becoming pregnant after the age of 30 (Toth, 1991). In one investigation, the clients of a French fertility clinic all had husbands who were sterile (Schwartz & Mayaux, 1982). To increase their chances of having a child, they were artificially inseminated once a month for one year. Each woman had 12 chances to become pregnant. Seventy-five percent of the women in their twenties became pregnant, 62 percent of the women 31 to 35 years old became pregnant, and only 54 percent of the women over 35 years old became pregnant.

We still have much to learn about the role of the mother's age in pregnancy and childbirth. As women remain active, exercise regularly, and are careful about their nutrition, their reproductive systems may remain healthier at older ages than was thought possible in the past. Indeed, as we will see next, the mother's nutrition influences prenatal development.

Nutrition

A developing fetus depends completely on its mother for nutrition, which comes from the mother's blood. Nutritional status is not determined by any specific aspect of diet; among the important factors are the total number of calories and the appropriate levels of protein, vitamins, and minerals. The mother's nutrition even influences her ability to reproduce. In extreme instances of malnutrition, women stop menstruating, thus precluding conception, and children born to malnourished mothers are more likely to be malformed (Rosso, 1992).

One investigation of Iowa mothers documents the important role of nutrition in prenatal development and birth (Jeans, Smith, & Stearns, 1955). The diets of 400 pregnant women were studied and the status of their newborns was assessed. The mothers with the poorest diets were more likely to have offspring who weighed the least, had the least vitality, were born prematurely, or died. In another investigation, diet supplements given to malnourished mothers during pregnancy improved the performance of their offspring during the first three years of life (Werner, 1979).

Emotional States and Stress

Tales abound about the way a mother's emotional state affects the fetus. For centuries, it was thought that frightening experiences—a severe thunderstorm or a family member's death—would leave birthmarks on the child or affect the child in more serious ways. Today, we believe that the mother's stress can be transmitted to the fetus, but we have gone beyond thinking that these happenings are somehow magically produced (Parker & Barrett, 1992). We now know that when a pregnant woman experiences intense fears, anxieties, and other emotions, physiological changes occur—among them, respiration, and glandular secretions. For example, producing adrenaline in response to fear restricts blood flow to the uterine area and may deprive the fetus of adequate oxygen.

The mother's emotional state during pregnancy can influence the birth process too. An emotionally distraught mother might have irregular contractions and a more difficult labor, which can cause irregularities in the baby's oxygen supply or tend to produce irregularities after birth. Babies born after extended labor also may adjust more slowly to their world and be more irritable. One investigation revealed a connection between the mother's anxiety during pregnancy and the newborn's condition (Ottinger & Simmons, 1964). In this study, mothers answered a questionnaire about their anxiety every three months during pregnancy. When the babies were born, the babies' weights, activity levels, and crying were assessed. The babies of the more anxious mothers cried more before feedings and were more active than the babies born to the less anxious mothers.

Drugs

How do drugs affect prenatal development? Some pregnant women take drugs, smoke tobacco, and drink alcohol without thinking about the possible effects on the fetus. Occasionally, a rash of deformed babies are born, bringing to light the damage drugs can have on a developing fetus. This happened in 1961, when many pregnant women took a popular tranquilizer, called thalidomide, to alleviate their morning sickness. In adults, the effects of thalidomide are mild; in embryos, however, they are devastating. Not all infants were affected in the same way. If the mother took thalidomide on day 26 (probably before she knew she was pregnant), an arm might not grow. If she took the drug two days later, the arm might not grow past the elbow. The thalidomide tragedy shocked the medical community and parents into the stark realization that the mother does not have to be a chronic drug user for the fetus to be harmed. Taking the wrong drug at the wrong time is enough to physically handicap the offspring for life.

Heavy drinking by pregnant women can also be devastating to offspring (Coles, Platzman, & Smith, 1991; Janzen & Nanson, 1993; Olson, Burgess, & Streissguth, 1992). **Fetal alcohol syndrome (FAS)** *is a cluster of abnormalities that appear in the offspring of mothers who drink alcohol heavily during pregnancy.* The abnormalities include facial deformities and defective limbs, face, and heart. Most of these children are below average in intelligence and some are mentally retarded. Although no serious malformations such as those produced by FAS are found in infants born to mothers who are moderate drinkers, in one investigation, infants whose mothers drank moderately during pregnancy (for example, one to two drinks a day) were less attentive and alert, with the effects still present at 4 years of age (Streissguth & others, 1984).

Expectant mothers are becoming more aware that alcohol and pregnancy do not mix. In a recent study of 1,712 pregnant women in 21 states, the prevalence of alcohol consumption by pregnant women declined from 32 percent in 1985 to 20 percent in 1988 (Serdula & others, 1991). The declines in drinking were greatest among the oldest and most educated pregnant women—19 percent of pregnant college graduates drank in 1988, a decline from the 41 percent rate in 1985. However, no decline in drinking was found among the least educated and youngest pregnant women. The proportion of drinkers among pregnant women with only a high school education stayed at 23 percent from 1985 to 1988.

Cigarette smoking by pregnant women can also adversely influence prenatal development, birth, and postnatal development (Block, 1992; Chasnoff, 1991; Fried & O'Connell, 1991;

Johnson & others, 1993; Streissguth & others, 1991). Fetal and neonatal deaths are higher among smoking mothers; also prevalent are a higher incidence of preterm births and lower birthweights (see figure 4.5). In one recent investigation, prenatal exposure to cigarette smoking was related to poorer language and cognitive development at 4 years of age (Fried & Watkinson, 1990). In another study, mothers who smoked during pregnancy had infants who were awake more on a consistent basis—a finding one might expect, since the active ingredient in cigarettes is the stimulant nicotine (Landesman-Dwyer & Sackett, 1983). Respiratory problems and sudden infant death syndrome (also known as crib death) are also more common among the offspring of mothers who smoked during pregnancy (Schoendorf & Kiely, 1992). Intervention programs designed to get pregnant women to stop smoking are successful in reducing some of smoking's negative effects on offspring, especially in raising their birthweights (Sexton & Hebel, 1984; Vorhees & Mollnow, 1987).

Marijuana use by pregnant women also has detrimental effects on a developing child (Day, 1991). Marijuana use by pregnant mothers is associated with increased tremors and startles among newborns (Fried, Watkinson, & Dillon, 1987) and poorer verbal and memory development at 4 years of age (Fried & Watkinson, 1990).

Critical Thinking

How can we reduce the number of offspring born to drug dependent mothers? If you had 100 million dollars to spend to help remedy this problem, what would you do?

It is well documented that infants whose mothers are addicted to heroin show several behavioral difficulties (Hans, 1989; Hutchings & Fifer, 1986). The young infants of these mothers are addicted and show withdrawal symptoms characteristic of opiate abstinence, such as tremors, irritability, abnormal crying, disturbed sleep, and impaired motor control. Behavioral problems are still often present at the first birthday, and attention deficits may appear later in the child's development.

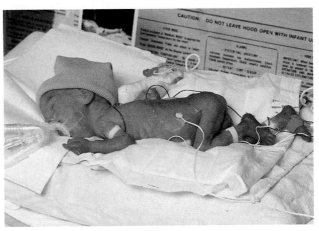

This baby was born addicted to cocaine because its mother was a cocaine addict. Researchers have found that the offspring of women who use cocaine during pregnancy often have hypertension and heart damage. Many of these infants face a childhood full of medical problems.

FIGURE 4.5

The effects of smoking by expectant mothers on fetal weight. Throughout prenatal development, the fetuses of expectant mothers who smoke weigh less than the fetuses of expectant mothers who do not smoke.

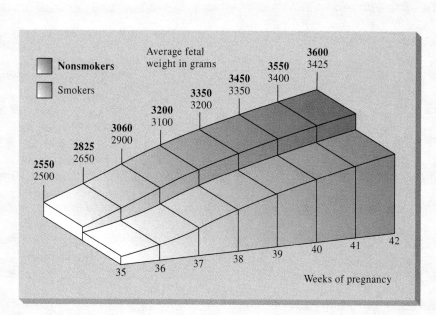

With the increased use of cocaine in the United States, there is growing concern about its effects on the embryos, fetuses, and infants of pregnant cocaine users (Ahl, 1993; Arendt, Singer, & Minnes, 1993; Davis & Mercier, 1992; Hawley, 1993; Scafidi & Wheeden, 1993). Cocaine use during pregnancy has recently attracted considerable attention because of concerns about possible harm to the developing embryo and fetus (Behnke & Eyler, 1991; Chasnoff & others, 1992; Dixon, 1991; Lester, 1991; Myers, Olson & Kaltenbach, 1992). The most consistent finding is that infants born to cocaine abusers have reduced birthweight and length (Chasnoff & others, 1989). There are increased frequencies of congenital abnormalities in the offspring of cocaine users during pregnancy, but other factors in the drug addict's life-style, such as malnutrition and other substance abuse, may be responsible for the congenital abnormalities (Eyler, Behnke, & Stewart, 1990). For example, cocaine users are more likely to smoke cigarettes and marijuana, drink alcohol, and take amphetamines than are cocaine nonusers (Little & others, 1989). Teasing apart these potential influences from the effects of cocaine use itself has not yet been adequately accomplished. Obtaining valid information about the frequency and type of drug use by mothers is also complicated since many mothers fear prosecution or loss of custody because of their drug use. A list of the effects of cocaine, and of various other drugs, on offspring and some guidelines for safe use of the drugs are presented in table 4.1.

Environmental Hazards

Radiation, chemicals, and other hazards in our modern industrial world can endanger the fetus. For instance, radiation can cause a gene mutation, an abrupt but permanent change in genetic material. Chromosomal abnormalities are higher among the offspring of fathers exposed to high levels of radiation in their occupations (Schrag & Dixon, 1985). Radiation from X rays also can affect the developing embryo and fetus, with the most dangerous time being the first several weeks after conception, when women do not yet know they are pregnant. It is important for women and their physicians to weigh the risk of an X ray when an actual or potential pregnancy is involved.

Environmental pollutants and toxic wastes are also sources of danger to unborn children. Researchers have found that various hazardous wastes and pesticides cause defects in animals exposed to high doses. Among the dangerous pollutants and wastes are carbon monoxide, mercury, and lead. Some children are exposed to lead because they live in houses where lead-based paint flakes off the walls or near busy highways, where there are heavy automobile emissions from leaded gasoline. Researchers believe that early exposure to lead affects children's mental development. For example, in one investigation, 2-year-old infants who prenatally had high levels of lead in their umbilical cord blood performed poorly on a test of mental development (Bellinger & others, 1987).

TABLE 4.1

Drug Use During Pregnancy

Drug	Effects on Fetus and Offspring	Safe Use of the Drug
Alcohol	Small amounts increase risk of spontaneous abortion. Moderate amounts (1–2 drinks a day) are associated with poor attention in infancy. Heavy drinking can lead to fetal alcohol syndrome. Some experts believe that even low-to-moderate amounts, especially in the first three months of pregnancy, increase the risk of FAS.	Avoid use.
Nicotine	Heavy smoking is associated with low-birthweight babies, which means the babies may have more health problems than other infants. Smoking may be especially harmful in the second half of pregnancy.	Avoid use.
Tranquilizers	Taken during the first three months of pregnancy, they may cause cleft palate or other congenital malformations.	Avoid use if you might become pregnant and during early pregnancy. Use only under a doctor's supervision.
Barbiturates	Mothers who take large doses may have babies who are addicted. Babies may have tremors, restlessness, and irritability.	Use only under a doctor's supervision.
Amphetamines	They may cause birth defects.	Use only under a doctor's supervision.
Cocaine	Cocaine may cause drug dependency and withdrawal symptoms at birth, as well as physical and mental problems, especially if the mother uses cocaine in the first three months of pregnancy. There is a higher risk of hypertension, heart problems, developmental retardation, and learning difficulties.	Avoid use.
Marijuana	It may cause a variety of birth defects and is associated with low birth-weight and height.	Avoid use.

Source: Modified from the National Institute on Drug Abuse.

Researchers also have found that the manufacturing chemicals known as PCBs are harmful to prenatal development. In one investigation, the extent to which pregnant women ate PCB-polluted fish from Lake Michigan was examined, and subsequently their newborns were observed (Jacobson & others, 1984). Women who had eaten more PCB-polluted fish were more likely to have smaller, preterm infants, who were more likely to react slowly to stimuli. And in one recent study, prenatal exposure to PCBs was associated with problems in visual discrimination and short-term memory in 4-year-old children (Jacobson & others, 1992).

A recent environmental concern involves women who spend long hours in front of a video display terminal. The fear is that low levels of electromagnetic radiation from the video display terminal adversely affect their offspring. In one recent investigation, 2,430 telephone operators were studied (Schnorr & others, 1991). Half of the women worked at video display terminals, half did not. During the four years of the study, 730 women became pregnant, some more than once, for a total of 876 pregnancies. Over the four years, there was no significant difference in miscarriage rates between the two groups. The researchers concluded that working at a video display terminal does not increase miscarriage risk. Critics point out that there was no check for early fetal loss and that all of the women were younger than 34 years of age, so whether the findings hold for early fetal loss and older women will have to await further research. In this study, miscarriages were higher among women who had more than eight alcoholic drinks per month or smoked more than 20 cigarettes a day. While video display terminals may not be related to miscarriage, they are associated with an increase in a variety of problems involving eye strain and the musculoskeletal system of female workers.

Critical Thinking

Where do you stand on the issue of the fertile woman's right to work at jobs that may have detrimental effects on her health and the health of the fetus? Defend your argument.

Another environmental concern is **toxoplasmosis,** *a mild infection that causes coldlike symptoms or no apparent illness in adults. However, toxoplasmosis can be a teratogen for the unborn baby, causing possible eye defects, brain defects, and premature birth.* Cats are common carriers of toxoplasmosis, especially outdoor cats who eat raw meat, such as rats and mice. The toxoplasmosis organism passes from the cat in its feces and lives up to one year. The expectant mother may pick up these organisms by handling cats or cat litter boxes, or by working in soil where cats have buried their feces. Eating raw or uncooked meat is another way of acquiring the disease. To avoid getting toxoplasmosis, expectant mothers need to wash their hands after handling cats, litter boxes, and raw meat. In addition, pregnant women should make sure that all meats are thoroughly cooked before eating them.

Yet another recent environmental concern for expectant mothers is prolonged exposure to heat in saunas or hot tubs that may raise the mother's body temperature, creating a fever that endangers the fetus. The high temperature of a fever may interfere with cell division and may cause birth defects or even fetal death if the fever occurs repeatedly for prolonged periods of time. If the expectant mother wants to take a sauna or bathe in a hot tub, prenatal experts recommend that she take her oral temperature while she is exposed to the heat. When the expectant mother's body temperature rises a degree or more, she should get out and cool down. Ten minutes is a reasonable length of time for expectant mothers to spend in a sauna or a hot tub, since the body temperature does not usually rise in this length of time. If the expectant mother feels uncomfortably hot in a sauna or a hot tub, she should get out even if she has only been there for a short time.

At this point we have discussed a number of ideas about the cause of prenatal development, miscarriage and abortion, and teratology and hazards to prenatal development. A summary of these ideas is presented in Concept Table 4.1.

BIRTH

After the long journey of prenatal development, birth takes place. Among the important topics related to birth that we explore are: stages of birth, delivery complications, and the use of drugs during childbirth; preterm infants; and measures of neonatal health and responsiveness.

Stages of Birth

The birth process occurs in three stages. For a woman having her first child, the first stage lasts an average of 12 to 24 hours; it is the longest of the three stages. In the first stage, uterine contractions are 15 to 20 minutes apart at the beginning and last up to a minute. These contractions cause the woman's cervix to stretch and open. As the first stage progresses, the contractions come closer together, appearing every 2 to 5 minutes. Their intensity increases too. By the end of the first birth stage, contractions dilate the cervix to an opening of about 4 inches so that the baby can move from the uterus to the birth canal.

Children sweeten labors . . .

—Frances Bacon, *Essays,* 1625.

The second birth stage begins when the baby's head starts to move through the cervix and the birth canal. It terminates when the baby completely emerges from the mother's body. This stage lasts approximately 1½ hours. With each contraction, the mother bears down hard to push the baby out of her

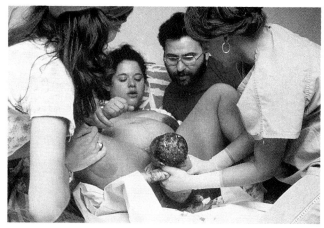

After the long journey of prenatal development, birth takes place, at which time the baby is on a threshold, between two worlds.

body. By the time the baby's head is out of the mother's body, the contractions come almost every minute and last for about a minute.

Afterbirth *is the third stage, at which time the placenta, umbilical cord, and other membranes are detached and expelled.* This final stage is the shortest of the three birth stages, lasting only minutes.

Delivery Complications

Complications can accompany the baby's delivery. **Precipitate** *is a form of delivery that takes place too rapidly. A precipitate delivery is one in which the baby takes less than 10 minutes to be squeezed through the birth canal.* This deviation in delivery can disturb the infant's normal flow of blood, and the pressure on the infant's head can cause hemorrhaging. On the other hand, **anoxia,** *the insufficient supply of oxygen to the infant,* can develop if the delivery takes too long. Anoxia can cause brain damage.

The **breech position** *is the baby's position in the uterus that causes the buttocks to be the first part to emerge from the vagina.* Normally, the crown of the baby's head comes through the vagina first, but in 1 of every 25 babies, the head does not come through first. Breech babies' heads are still in the uterus when the rest of their bodies are out, which can cause respiratory problems. Some breech babies cannot be passed through the cervix and must be delivered by cesarean section.

A **cesarean section** *is the surgical removal of the baby from the uterus.* A cesarean section is usually performed if the baby is in a breech position, if it is lying crosswise in the uterus, if the baby's head is too large to pass through the mother's pelvis, if the baby develops complications, or if the mother is bleeding vaginally. The benefits and risks of cesarean section delivery are debated. Cesarean section deliveries are safer than breech deliveries, but a higher infection rate, a longer hospital stay, greater expense, and the stress that accompanies any surgery characterize cesarean section deliveries. Some critics believe that, in the United States, too many babies are delivered by cesarean

CONCEPT TABLE 4.1

The Course of Prenatal Development, Miscarriage and Abortion, and Teratology and Hazards to Prenatal Development

Concept	Processes/Related Ideas	Characteristics/Description
The course of prenatal development	Germinal period	This period is from conception to about 10 to 14 days later. A fertilized egg is called a zygote. The period ends when the zygote attaches to the uterine wall.
	Embryonic period	The embryonic period lasts from about two to eight weeks after conception. The embryo differentiates into three layers, life-support systems develop, and organ systems form (organogenesis).
	Fetal period	The fetal period lasts from about two months after conception until nine months or when the infant is born. Growth and development continue their dramatic course and organ systems mature to the point where life can be sustained outside the womb.
Miscarriage and abortion	Their nature and ethical issues	A miscarriage, or spontaneous abortion, happens when pregnancy ends before the developing organism is mature enough to survive outside the womb. Estimates indicate that about 15 to 20 percent of all pregnancies end this way, many without the mother's knowledge. Induced abortion is a complex issue—medically, psychologically, socially, and legally. An unwanted pregnancy is stressful for the woman regardless of how it is resolved. A recent ethical issue focuses on the use of fetal tissue in transplant operations.
Teratology and hazards to prenatal development	Teratology	This field investigates the causes of congenital (birth) defects. Any agent that causes birth defects is called a teratogen.
	Maternal diseases and conditions	Maternal diseases and infections can cause damage by crossing the placental barrier, or they can be destructive during the birth process. Among the maternal diseases and conditions believed to be involved in possible birth defects are rubella, syphilis, genital herpes, AIDS, the mother's age, nutrition, and emotional state and stress. An ectopic pregnancy is the presence of a developing embryo or fetus outside the normal location in the uterus.
	Drugs	Thalidomide was a tranquilizer given to pregnant women to alleviate their morning sickness. In the early 1960s, thousands of babies were malformed as a consequence of their mother having taken this drug. Alcohol, tobacco, marijuana, heroin, and cocaine are other drugs that can adversely affect prenatal and infant development.
	Environmental hazards	Among the environmental hazards that can endanger the fetus are radiation in occupations and X rays, environmental pollutants, toxic wastes, toxoplasmosis, and prolonged exposure to heat in saunas and hot tubs.

section. More cesarean sections are performed in the United States than in any other industrialized nation. From 1979 to 1987, the cesarean section rate increased almost 50 percent in the United States alone, to an annual rate of 24 percent (Marieskind, 1989). However, a growing use of vaginal birth after a previous cesarean, greater public awareness, and peer pressure in the medical community are beginning to slow the rate of increase (Enkin, 1989; Marieskind, 1989).

The Use of Drugs during Childbirth

Drugs can be used to relieve pain and anxiety and to speed delivery during the birth process. The widest use of drugs during delivery is to relieve the expectant mother's pain or anxiety. A wide variety of tranquilizers, sedatives, and analgesics are used for this purpose (Nelson, 1992). Researchers are interested in the effects of these drugs because they can cross the placental barrier, and because their use is so widespread. One survey of hospitals found that only 5 percent of deliveries involve no anesthesia (Brackbill, 1979).

Oxytocin, *a hormone that stimulates and regulates the rhythmicity of uterine contractions, has been widely used as a drug to speed delivery. Controversy surrounds the use of this drug.* Some physicians argue that it can save the mother's life or keep the infant from being damaged. They also stress that using the drug allows the mother to be well rested and prepared for the birth process. Critics argue that babies born to mothers who have taken oxytocin are more likely to have jaundice; that induced labor requires more painkilling drugs; and that greater medical care is required after the birth, resulting in the separation of the infant and mother.

The following conclusions can be reached, based on research about the influence of drugs during delivery (Rosenblith & Sims-Knight, 1992):

1. Few research studies have been done, and many that have been completed have had methodological problems. However, not all drugs have similar effects. Some—tranquilizers, sedatives, and analgesics, for example—do not seem to have long-term effects. Other drugs—oxytocin, for example—are suspected of having long-term effects.
2. The degree to which a drug influences the infant is usually small. Birth weight and social class, for instance, are more powerful predictors of infant difficulties than are drugs.
3. A specific drug may affect some infants but not others. In some cases, the drug may have a beneficial effect, whereas in others, it may be harmful.
4. The overall amount of medication may be an important factor in understanding drug effects on delivery.

Critical Thinking

After reading the information on the use of drugs during childbirth, what considerations would be foremost in your mind if your offspring was about to be born? What questions about the use of drugs during delivery would you want to ask the individuals responsible for delivering the baby?

Next, we discuss a number of the increasing variety of childbirth strategies. In the last several decades, an increasing number of expectant mothers have chosen to have a prepared, or natural, childbirth. One aspect of prepared childbirth is an attempt to minimize the use of medication.

Childbirth Strategies

In the past two decades, the nature of childbirth has changed considerably. Where heavy medication was once the norm, now natural, or prepared, childbirth has become increasingly popular. Today, husbands much more frequently participate in childbirth. Alternative birthing centers and birthing rooms have become standard in many maternity units, and the acceptance of midwives has increased. Before we examine some of these contemporary trends in childbirth strategies, let's examine the nature of standard childbirth.

Standard Childbirth

In the standard childbirth procedure that has been practiced for many years—and the way you probably were delivered—the expectant mother is taken to a hospital, where a doctor is responsible for the baby's delivery. The pregnant woman is prepared for labor by having her pubic hair shaved and by having an enema. She then is placed in a labor room often filled with other pregnant women, some of whom are screaming. When she is ready to deliver, she is taken to the delivery room, which looks like an operating room. She is laid on the table with her legs in the air, and the physician, along with an anesthetist and a nurse, delivers the baby.

What could be wrong with this procedure? Critics list three things: (1) Important individuals related to the mother are excluded from the birth process. (2) The mother is separated from her infant in the first minutes and hours after birth. (3) Giving birth is treated like a disease, and a woman is thought of as a sick patient (Rosenblith, 1992). As we will see next, some alternatives differ radically from this standard procedure.

The Leboyer Method

The **Leboyer method,** *developed by French obstetrician Frederick Leboyer, intends to make the birth process less stressful for infants. Leboyer's procedure is referred to as "birth without violence."* He describes standard childbirth as torture (Leboyer, 1975). He vehemently objects to holding newborns upside down and slapping or spanking them, putting silver nitrite into their eyes, separating them immediately from their mothers, and scaring them with bright lights and harsh noises in the delivery room. Leboyer also criticizes the traditional habit of cutting the umbilical cord as soon as the infant is born, a situation that forces the infant to immediately take in oxygen from the air to breathe. Leboyer believes that the umbilical cord should be left intact for several minutes to allow the newborn a chance to adjust to a world of breathing air. In the Leboyer method, the baby is placed on the mother's stomach immediately after birth so the mother can caress the infant. Then the infant is placed in a bath of warm water to relax. Although most hospitals do not use the soft lights and warm baths that Leboyer suggests, they sometimes do place the newborn on the mother's stomach immediately after birth, believing that it will stimulate mother-infant bonding.

We must respect this instant of birth, this fragile moment. The baby is between two worlds, on a threshold, hesitating, . . .

—Frederick Leboyer
Birth Without Violence

Prepared, or Natural, Childbirth

Prepared, or natural, childbirth, *includes being informed about what will happen during the procedure, knowing about comfort measures for childbirth, anticipating that little or no medication will be used, and if complications arise, expecting to participate in decisions made to resolve the problems* (Bean, 1990). Medical treatment is used when there is a reason, but it should always be done with care and concern for the expectant mother and the offspring. Prepared childbirth assumes the presence and support of a partner or friend, and in some cases, a labor-support person identified through local childbirth education groups. At least two persons, including the laboring woman, are needed to work with each contraction.

Prepared childbirth includes a number of variations. Consider the following three instances of prepared childbirth. The first woman in labor lies awake under light medication with an intravenous needle in her arm into which a nearby pump introduces a labor stimulant. She is attached to electronic monitoring devices and confined to the bed. A second woman is wearing her own clothes, sitting in a rocking chair in a birthing room, relaxing, attending to her breathing, and sipping a glass of cider with none of the above medications or equipment being used. At her infant's birth there will be no gowns or masks and she will give birth in the birthing room instead of being moved to the delivery room. An older child who has learned about childbirth may even be in the room, preparing to welcome the new sibling. The third woman and her husband are "prepared" parents, who may or may not have attended cesarean preparation classes, but agree that cesarean birth is required. Both parents are in the delivery room and she is awake. Despite obvious involvement of the couple in the decision to have the cesarean birth, no one has yet described a cesarean birth as a natural one.

A basic philosophy of prepared childbirth is that information and teaching methods should support parent confidence, provide the knowledge required to carry out normal childbirth, and explain how the medical system functions in childbirth. Professional disciplines involved in childbirth now go beyond obstetrics (with its main emphasis on pathology rather than normal birth) and also include nursing, public health, education, physical therapy, psychology, sociology, and physiology. Each of these areas has contributed to teaching programs and provided increased knowledge about childbirth. But never to be overlooked, is the input to health professionals from parents themselves.

The **Lamaze method** *has become a widely used childbirth strategy; it is a form of prepared or natural childbirth developed by Fernand Lamaze, a pioneering French obstetrician.* It has become widely accepted by the medical profession and involves helping the expectant mother to cope actively with the pain of childbirth and to avoid or reduce medication. Lamaze training for parents is available on a widespread basis in the United States and usually consists of six weekly classes. In these classes, the pregnant woman learns about the birth process and is trained in breathing and relaxation exercises. As the Lamaze method has grown in popularity, it has become more common for the father to participate in the exercises and to assist in the birth process.

Lamaze exercises and breathing have much in common with the other methods of prepared childbirth, with the exception that breathing techniques are more central to the method; Lamaze breathing is very active. Whatever the method of prepared childbirth that expectant couples choose, each will provide information about birth, ways of relaxing and releasing muscle tension, breathing patterns to relieve anxiety and bring adequate oxygen to the contracting uterine muscle, ways to avoid hyperventilation (overbreathing), and basic physical conditioning exercises.

New for the Nineties

Among the current changes in childbirth are shifts in emphases, new choices, and an understanding of obstetrical terminology. And an increasing number of instructors report that they are now using a more eclectic approach to childbirth, drawing information from several different methods (Bean, 1990). Let's examine some of these trends in more detail:

- Breathing methods continue to be important but are more flexible in accord with the individual needs of the expectant mother. In general, breathing is becoming less active and less vigorous, with more attention given to other methods of providing comfort. However, some prepared childbirth instructors believe that the importance of breathing should not be downplayed too much.

- New ways of teaching relaxation are offered, including guided mental imagery, massage, and meditation.

- The use of warm water for comfort is recognized and many hospitals have showers in their labor and delivery areas. Some hospitals have introduced Jacuzzis.

- A more homelike institutional environment is believed to be important.

- Stress from intense lighting and an intrusive environment can inhibit uterine contraction, possibly slowing labor and even making the introduction of medication necessary. Hospitals are moving in the direction of having most nonsurgical births, including anesthetized births, in homelike birthing rooms that are quiet, peaceful, and less intensely lit.

- Walking during labor and the use of varied body positions during labor and birth are encouraged. For many women, the squatting position is the most comfortable and effective position.

- The "nothing by mouth" policy during labor is being seriously questioned and reexamined. Light food was initially introduced in home birth and freestanding birthing centers. It is now beginning to be offered in some hospitals.

- The use of midwife-assisted birth is becoming more widespread, allowing longer and more informative prenatal visits, labor support, and less use of medication.

- Parent-infant bonding, which we will discuss later in the chapter, is widely available and encouraged. Even if the baby is premature or ill, parents go to the intensive care nursery to see, touch, and talk to their newborn.

- Siblings and grandparents are welcome to touch and hold the baby in the hospital.

- Hospital stays have been shortened to three days or less, mainly because of recent government reimbursement regulations. Approximately five days are allowed for cesarean births.

- Increased amounts of time are spent discussing the pros and cons of various obstetrical and birthing options.

The strongest principle of human growth lies in human choice.

—Alexander Chase, *Perspectives*, 1966.

The Father's Participation

In the past several decades, fathers increasingly have participated in childbirth. Fathers-to-be are now more likely to go to at least one meeting with the obstetrician or caregiver during the pregnancy, attend childbirth preparation classes, learn about labor and birth, and be more involved in the care of the young infant (Coleman & Coleman, 1991). The change is consistent with our culture's movement toward less rigid concepts of "masculine" and "feminine."

For many expectant couples today, the father is trained to be the expectant mother's coach during labor, helping her to learn relaxation methods and special breathing techniques for labor and birth. Most health professionals now believe that, just as with pregnancy, childbirth should be an intimate, shared moment between a man and a woman who are creating a new life together. Nonetheless, some men do not want to participate in prepared childbirth, and some women also still prefer that they not have a very active role. In such cases, other people can provide support for childbirth—mother, sister, friend, midwife, or physician, for example.

Husbands who are motivated to participate in childbirth have an important role at their wives' side. In the long stretches when there is no staff attendant present, a husband can provide companionship, support, and encouragement. In difficult moments of examination or medication, he can be comforting. Initially, he may feel embarrassed to use the breathing techniques he learned in preparation classes, but he usually begins to feel more at home when he realizes he is performing a necessary function for his wife during each contraction.

Critical Thinking

How actively should the husband be involved in childbirth? Why?

Some individuals question whether the father is the best coach during labor. He may be nervous and feel uncomfortable in the hospital, and, never having gone through labor himself, he might not understand the expectant mother's needs as well as another woman. There is no universal answer to this issue. Some laboring women want to depend on another woman, someone who has been through labor herself; others want their husband to intimately share the childbirth experience. Many cultures exclude men from births, just as the American culture did until the last several decades. In some cultures, the woman's mother, or occasionally a daughter, serves as her assistant.

Siblings

If parents have a child and are expecting another, it is important for them to prepare the older child for the birth of a sibling (Simkin, Whalley, & Keppler, 1984). Sibling preparation includes providing the child with information about pregnancy, birth, and life with a newborn that is realistic and appropriate for the child's age.

Parents can prepare their older child for the approaching birth at any time during pregnancy. The expectant mother might announce the pregnancy early to explain her tiredness and vomiting. If the child is young and unable to understand waiting, parents may want to delay announcing the pregnancy until later, when the expectant mother's pregnancy becomes obvious and she begins to look "fat" to the child.

Parents may want to consider having the child present at the birth. Many family-centered hospitals, birth centers, and homebirths make this option available. Some parents wish to minimize or avoid separation from the older child, so they choose to give birth where sibling involvement is possible. These parents feel that if there is no separation, the child will not develop separation anxiety and will not see the new baby as someone who took the mother away. Sibling involvement in the childbirth may enhance the attachment between the older child and the new baby.

To help the child cope with the arrival of the new baby, parents can:

- Before and after the birth, read books to the child about living with a new baby.

- Plan for time alone with the older child and do what he or she wants to do.

- Use the time when the baby is asleep and the parent is rested to give special attention to the older child.

- Give a gift to the older child in the hospital or at home.

- "Tell" the baby about his or her special older brother or sister when the older sibling is listening.

When parents have a child and are expecting another, they can provide the child with information about pregnancy, birth, and life with a newborn that is realistic and appropriate for the child's age. This information helps the child cope with the birth of a sibling. As part of the sibling preparation process, some parents choose to have the child present at the sibling's birth.

Preterm Infants and Age-Weight Considerations

How can we distinguish between a preterm infant and a low-birthweight infant? What are the developmental outcomes for low-birthweight infants? Do preterm infants have a different profile than that of full-term infants? What conclusions can we reach about preterm infants?

Preterm and Low-Birthweight Infants

An infant is full term when it has grown in the womb for the full 38 to 42 weeks between conception and delivery. A **preterm infant** *(also called a premature infant) is one who is born prior to 38 weeks after conception.* **Low-birthweight infants** *are infants born after a regular gestation period (the length of time between conception and birth) of 38 to 42 weeks, but who weigh less than 5 1/2 pounds.* Both preterm and low-birthweight infants are considered high-risk infants (Crisafi & Driscoll, 1991; Dedrick & others, 1991; Holmes, Reich, & Gyurke, 1989; Hunt & Cooper, 1989).

In one recent study, an intervention program was implemented to improve the developmental outcomes of low-birthweight infants (Achenbach & others, 1990). The program was designed to enhance the mother's adjustment to the care of a low-birthweight infant by (a) enabling the mother to appreciate her baby's specific behavioral and temperamental characteristics; (b) sensitizing her to the baby's cues, especially those that signal stimulus overload, distress, and readiness for interaction; and (c) teaching her to respond appropriately to those cues to facilitate mutually satisfying interactions. The intervention involved seven hospital sessions and four home sessions in which a nurse helped mothers adapt to their low-birthweight babies. At age 7, the low-birthweight babies whose mothers had participated in the intervention program scored higher than a control group of low-birthweight babies on information processing measures. The researchers commented that the intervention prevented cognitive lags among low-birthweight children and that long-term follow-ups are needed to overcome major biological and environmental risks.

A short gestation period does not necessarily harm an infant. It is distinguished from retarded prenatal growth, in which the fetus has been damaged (Kopp, 1983). The neurological development of a short-gestation infant continues after birth on approximately the same timetable as if the infant still were in the womb. For example, consider an infant born after a gestation period of 30 weeks. At 38 weeks, approximately 2 months after birth, this infant shows the same level of brain development as a 38-week fetus who is yet to be born.

Some infants are born very early and have a precariously low birthweight (Friedman & Caron, 1991; Thompson & Oehler, 1991). "Kilogram kids" weigh less than 2.3 pounds (which is 1 kilogram, or 1,000 grams) and are very premature. The task of saving such a baby is not easy. At the Stanford University Medical Center in Palo Alto, California, 98 percent of the preterm babies survive; however, 32 percent of those between 750 and 1,000 grams do not, and 76 percent of those below 750 grams do not. Approximately 250,000 preterm babies are born in the United States each year and more than 15,000 of these weigh less than 1,000 grams.

Preterm infants have a different profile from that of full-term infants. For instance, Tiffany Field (1979) found that 4-month-old preterm infants vocalize less, fuss more, and avoid eye contact more than their full-term counterparts. Other researchers have found differences in the information processing skills of preterm and full-term infants. In one investigation, Susan Rose and her colleagues (1988) found that 7-month-old high-risk preterm infants are less visually attentive to novelty and show deficits in visual recognition memory when compared with full-term infants.

Stimulation of Preterm Infants

Just three decades ago, preterm infants were perceived to be too fragile to cope well with environmental stimulation, and the recommendation was to handle such infants as little as possible. The climate of opinion changed when the adverse effects of maternal deprivation (mothers' neglect of their infants) became known and was interpreted to include a lack of stimulation. A number of research studies followed that indicated a "more is better" approach in the stimulation of preterm infants. Today, however, experts on infant development argue that preterm infant care is far too complex to be described only in terms of amount of stimulation (Field, 1990; Lester & Tronick, 1990b; Thoman, 1992).

Recently, experts on the stimulation of preterm infants held a roundtable discussion and offered the following recommendations (Lester & Tronick, 1990a):

1. Preterm infants' responses to stimulation vary with their conceptual age, illness, and individual makeup. The immature brain of the preterm infant may be more vulnerable to excessive, inappropriate, or mistimed stimulation. The very immature infant should probably be protected from stimulation that could destabilize its homeostatic condition.
2. As the healthy preterm infant becomes less fragile and approaches term, the issue of what is appropriate stimulation should be considered. Infants' behavioral

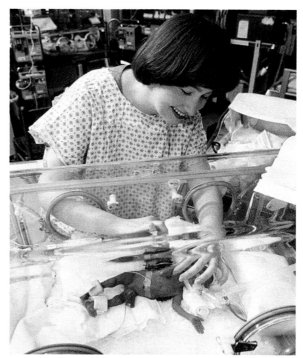

A "kilogram kid" weighing less than 2.3 pounds at birth. In the neonatal intensive care unit, banks of flashing lights, blinking numbers, and beeping alarms stand guard over kilogram kids, who are extreme preterm infants. They often lie on a water bed that gently undulates; the water bed is in an incubator that is controlled for temperature and humidity by the baby's own body. Such vital signs as brain waves, heartbeat, blood gases, and respiratory rate are constantly monitored. All of this care can be very expensive. Though the cost can usually be kept within five figures, five or six months of neonatal intensive care can result in expenses of as much as $200,000 or more.

cues can be used to determine appropriate interventions. An infant's signs of stress or avoidance behaviors indicate that stimulation should be terminated. Positive behaviors indicate that stimulation is appropriate.

One stimulation strategy that is increasingly used with preterm infants is massage. To read about the power of touch and massage in development, turn to Explorations in Child Development 4.1.

3. Intervention with the preterm infant should be organized in the form of an individualized developmental plan. This plan should be constructed as a psychosocial intervention to include the parents and other immediate family members and to acknowledge the socioeconomic, cultural, and home environmental factors that will determine the social context in which the infant will be reared. The developmental plan should also include assessing the infant's behavior, working with the parents to help them understand the infant's medical and behavioral status, and helping the parents deal with their own feelings.

EXPLORATIONS IN CHILD DEVELOPMENT 4.1

The Power of Touch and Massage in Development

There has been a surge of recent interest in the roles of touch and massage in improving the growth, health, and well-being of infants and children. The interest has especially been stimulated by a number of research investigations by Tiffany Field, director of the Touch Research Institute at the University of Miami School of Medicine. In one investigation, 40 preterm infants who had just been released from an intensive care unit and placed in a transitional nursery were studied (Field, Scafidi, & Schanberg, 1987). Twenty of the preterm babies were given special stimulation with massage and exercise for three 15-minute periods at the beginning of three consecutive hours every morning for 10 weekdays. For example, each infant was placed on its stomach and gently stroked. The massage began with the head and neck and moved downward to the feet. It also moved from the shoulders down to the hands. The infant was then rolled over. Each arm and leg was flexed and extended; then both legs were flexed and extended. Next, the massage was repeated.

The massaged and exercised preterm babies gained 47 percent more weight than their preterm counterparts who were not massaged and exercised, even though both groups had the same number of feedings per day and averaged the same intake of formula. The increased activity of the massaged, exercised infants would seem to work against weight gain. However, similar findings have been discovered with animals. The increased activity may increase gastrointestinal and metabolic efficiency. The massaged infants were more active and alert, and they performed better on developmental tests. Also, their hospital stay was about six days shorter than that of the nonmassaged, nonexercised group, which saved about $3,000 per preterm infant. Field (1992) has recently replicated these findings with preterm infants in another study.

In a more recent study, Field (1992) gave the same kind of massage (firm stroking with the palms of the hands) to preterm infants who were exposed to cocaine in utero. The infants also showed significant weight gain and improved scores on developmental tests. Currently, Field is using massage therapy with HIV-exposed preterm infants with the hope that their immune system functioning will be improved. Others she has targeted include infants of depressed mothers, infants with colic, infants and children with sleep problems, as well as children who have diabetes, asthma, and juvenile arthritis.

Field (1992) also reports that touch has been helpful with children and adolescents who have touch aversions, such as children who have been sexually abused, autistic children, and adolescents with eating disorders. Field also is studying the amount of touch a child normally receives during school activities. She hopes that positive forms of touch will return to school systems where touching has been outlawed because of potential sex abuse lawsuits.

Shown here is Dr. Tiffany Field massaging a newborn infant. Dr. Field's research has clearly demonstrated the power of massage in improving the developmental outcome of at-risk infants. Under her direction The Touch Research Institute in Miami, Florida, was recently developed to investigate the role of touch in a number of domains of health and well-being.

FIGURE 4.6

The Apgar scale.

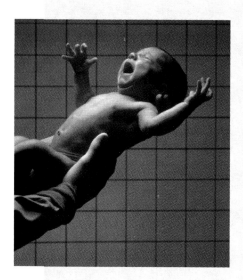

	0	1	2
Heart rate	Absent	Slow—less than 100 beats per minute	Fast—100–140 beats per minute
Respiratory effort	No breathing for more than one minute	Irregular and slow	Good breathing with normal crying
Muscle tone	Limp and flaccid	Weak, inactive, but some flexion of extremities	Strong, active motion
Body color	Blue and pale	Body pink, but extremities blue	Entire body pink
Reflex irritability	No response	Grimace	Coughing, sneezing, and crying

Some Conclusions about Preterm Infants

What conclusions can we draw from the results of research about preterm infants? Three such conclusions seem appropriate (Kopp, 1983, 1992; Kopp & Kaler, 1989):

1. As intensive care technology has improved, there have been fewer serious consequences of preterm births. For instance, from 1961 to 1965, the manner of feeding preterm infants changed and intravenous fluid therapy came into use. From 1966 to 1968, better control of hypoxemia (oxygen deficiency) was gained. In 1971, artificial ventilation was introduced. In the mid-1970s, neonatal support systems became less intrusive and damaging to infants.

2. Infants born with a problem that is identifiable at birth are likely to have a poorer developmental future than infants born without a recognizable problem. For instance, extremely sick or extremely tiny babies are less likely to survive than healthy or normal-weight babies.

3. Social class differences are associated with preterm infants' development. The higher the socioeconomic status, the more favorable is the developmental outcome for a newborn. Social class differences also are tied to many other differences. For example, the quality of the environment, cigarette and alcohol consumption, IQ, and knowledge of competent parenting strategies are associated with social class; less positive characteristics are associated with lower-class families.

Despite the advances made in prenatal care and technology in the United States, the availability of high-quality medical and educational services still needs much improvement (Brooks-Gunn, McCarton, & Tonascia, 1992). In some countries, especially in Scandinavia and western Europe, more consistent, higher-quality prenatal care is provided than in the United States. To read further about the nature of prenatal care in different countries, turn to Sociocultural Worlds of Children 4.1.

Measures of Neonatal Health and Responsiveness

The **Apgar scale** *is a method widely used to assess the health of newborns at 1 and 5 minutes after birth. The Apgar scale evaluates infants' heart rate, respiratory effort, muscle tone, body color, and reflex irritability.* An obstetrician or nurse does the evaluation and gives the newborn a score, or reading, of 0, 1, or 2 on each of these five health signs (see figure 4.6). A total score of 7 to 10 indicates that the newborn's condition is good, a score of 5 indicates there may be developmental difficulties, and a score of 3 or below signals an emergency and indicates that the baby's survival may be in doubt.

Whereas the Apgar scale is used immediately after birth to identify high-risk infants who need resuscitation, the **Brazelton Neonatal Behavioral Assessment Scale** *is given several days after birth to assess the newborn's neurological development, reflexes, and reactions to people* (Brazelton, 1973; Brazelton, Nugent, & Lester, 1987). The Brazelton scale is usually given on the third day of life and then repeated several days later. Twenty reflexes are assessed, along with reactions to circumstances such as the

SOCIOCULTURAL WORLDS OF CHILDREN 4.1

Prenatal Care in the United States and Around the World

As advanced a nation as the United States has become economically and technologically, it still has more low-birthweight infants than a number of other countries (Grant, 1986). As indicated in table 4.A, only 4 percent of the infants born in Sweden, Finland, the Netherlands, and Norway are low-birthweight, and only 5 percent of those born in New Zealand, Australia, France, and Japan are low-birthweight. Also, as indicated in table 4.A, in some developing countries, such as Bangladesh, where poverty is rampant and the health and nutrition of mothers is poor, the percentage of low-birthweight infants reaches as high as 50 percent of all infants.

In the United States, there also are discrepancies between the nature of prenatal development and the birth of Black infants and White infants. Black infants are twice as likely to: be born prematurely, have low birthweight, and have mothers who received late or no prenatal care; are three times as likely to have their mothers die in childbirth; and are five times as likely to be born to unmarried teenage mothers (Edelman, 1992).

In many of the countries with a lower percentage of low-birthweight infants than the United State, either free or very low-cost prenatal and postnatal care is available to mothers. This care includes paid maternity leave from work that ranges from 9 to 40 weeks (Miller, 1987). In Norway and the Netherlands, prenatal care is coordinated with a general practitioner, an obstetrician, and a midwife.

Pregnant women in the United States do not receive the uniform prenatal care that women in many Scandinavian and western European countries receive. The United States does not have a national policy of health care that assures high-quality assistance for pregnant women. The cost of giving birth is approximately $4,000 in the United States (more than $5,000 for a cesarean birth), and more than 25 percent of all American women of prime childbearing age do not have insurance that will pay for hospital costs. More than one-fifth of all White mothers and one-third of all Black mothers do not receive prenatal care in the first trimester of their pregnancy. Five percent of White mothers and 10 percent of Black mothers receive no prenatal care at all. Many infant-development researchers believe that the United States needs more comprehensive medical and educational services to improve the quality of prenatal care and reduce the percentage of low-birthweight infants.

TABLE 4.A
Percentage of Low-Birthweight Infants

Country	Low-Birthweight Infants (Percentage)
Bangladesh	50
India	30
Guatemala	18
Iran	14
Mexico	12
USSR	9
United States, Great Britain, Israel, Egypt	7
Canada, China	6
New Zealand, Australia, France, Japan	5
Sweden, Finland, the Netherlands, Norway	4

Source: Data from J. Grant, *State of the World's Children*, 1986.

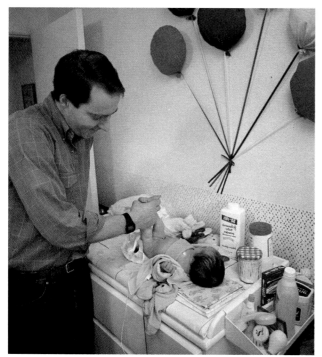

The postpartal period is a time of considerable adjustment and adaptation for both the mother and the father. Fathers can provide an important support system for mothers, especially in helping mothers care for young infants.

infant's reaction to a rattle. The examiner rates the newborn, or neonate, on each of 27 categories (table 4.2). As an indication of how detailed the ratings are, consider item 15: "cuddliness." Nine categories are involved in assessing this item, with infant behavior scored on a continuum that ranges from the infant being very resistant to being held to the infant being extremely cuddly and clinging. The Brazelton scale not only is used as a sensitive index of neurological competence in the week after birth, but it also is used widely as a measure in many research studies on infant development. In recent versions of scoring the Brazelton scale, Brazelton and his colleagues (1987) categorize the 27 items into four categories—physiological, motoric, state, and interaction. They also classify the baby in global terms, such as "worrisome," "normal," or "superior," based on these categories.

A very low Brazelton score can indicate brain damage. However, if an infant merely seems sluggish in responding to social circumstances, parents are encouraged to give the infant attention and become more sensitive to the infant's needs (Brazelton, 1990). Parents are shown how the newborn can respond to people and how to stimulate such responses. Researchers have found that the social interaction skills of both high-risk infants and healthy, responsive infants can be improved through such communication with parents (Widmayer & Field, 1980; Worobey & Belsky, 1982).

THE POSTPARTAL PERIOD

Many health professionals believe that the best postpartal care is family centered, using the family's resources to support an early and smooth adjustment to the newborn by all family members. What is the postpartal period? What physical changes does it involve? What emotional and psychological changes are encountered?

The Nature of the Postpartal Period

The **postpartal period** *(also called postpartum period) is the period after childbirth or delivery. It is a time when the woman's body adjusts, both physically and psychologically, to the process of childbearing. It lasts for about six weeks or until the body has completed its adjustment and has returned to a near prepregnant state* (Olds, London, & Ladewig, 1988). Some health professionals refer to the postpartal period as the "fourth trimester." While the time span of the postpartal period does not necessarily cover three months, the terminology of "fourth trimester" demonstrates the idea of continuity and the importance of the first several months after birth for the mother.

The postpartal period is influenced by what preceded it. During pregnancy the woman's body gradually adjusted to physical changes, but now it is forced to respond quickly. The method of delivery and circumstances surrounding the delivery affect the speed with which the woman's body readjusts during the postpartal period.

The postpartal period involves a great deal of adjustment and adaptation (Coleman & Coleman, 1991). The baby has to be cared for; the mother has to recover from childbirth; the mother has to learn how to take care of the baby; the mother needs to learn to feel good about herself as a mother; the father needs to learn how to take care of his recovering wife; and the father needs to learn how to feel good about himself as a father.

Physical Adjustments

The woman's body makes numerous physical adjustments in the first days and weeks after childbirth (Simkin, Whalley, & Keppler, 1984). She may have a great deal of energy or feel exhausted and let down. Most new mothers feel tired and need rest. While these changes are normal, the fatigue can undermine the new mother's sense of well-being and confidence in her ability to cope with a new baby and a new family life.

Involution *is the process by which the uterus returns to its prepregnant size 5 or 6 weeks after birth.* Immediately following birth, the uterus weighs 2 to 3 pounds and the fundus can be felt midway between the naval and the pubic bone. By the end of 5 or 6 weeks, the uterus weighs 2 to 3½ ounces and it has returned to its prepregnancy size. Nursing the baby helps to contract the uterus at a rapid rate.

After delivery, a woman's body undergoes sudden and dramatic changes in hormone production. When the placenta is delivered, estrogen and progesterone levels drop steeply and

TABLE 4.2

The 27 Categories on the Brazelton Neonatal Behavioral Assessment Scale (NBAS)

1. Response decrement to repeated visual stimuli
2. Response decrement to rattle
3. Response decrement to bell

4. Response decrement to pinprick
5. Orienting response to inanimate visual stimuli
6. Orienting response to inanimate auditory stimuli

7. Orienting response to inanimate visual and auditory stimuli
8. Orienting response to animate visual stimuli—examiner's face
9. Orienting response to animate auditory stimuli—examiner's voice

10. Orienting response to animate visual and auditory stimuli
11. Quality and duration of alert periods
12. General muscle tone—in resting and in response to being handled, passive, and active

13. Motor activity
14. Traction responses as the infant is pulled to sit
15. Cuddliness—responses to being cuddled by examiner

16. Defensive movements—reactions to a cloth over the infant's face
17. Consolability with intervention by examiner
18. Peak of excitement and capacity to control self

19. Rapidity of buildup to crying state
20. Irritability during the examination
21. General assessment of kind and degree of activity

22. Tremulousness
23. Amount of startling
24. Lability of skin color—measuring autonomic lability

25. Lability of states during entire examination
26. Self-quieting activity—attempts to console self and control state
27. Hand-to-mouth activity

Adapted from *Cultural Perspectives on Child Development* by Daniel Wagner and Harold W. Stevenson. Copyright © 1982 by W. H. Freeman and Company. Reprinted by permission.

remain low until the ovaries start producing hormones again. The woman will probably begin menstruating again in 4 to 8 weeks if she is not breast-feeding. If she is breast-feeding, she may not menstruate for several months, though ovulation can occur during this time. The first several menstrual periods following delivery may be heavier than usual, but soon return to normal.

Some women and men want to resume sexual intercourse as soon as possible after the birth. Others feel constrained or afraid. A sore perineum (the area between the anus and vagina in the female), a demanding baby, lack of help, and extreme fatigue affect a woman's ability to relax and to enjoy making love. Physicians often recommend that women refrain from having sexual intercourse for approximately six weeks following the birth of the baby. However, it is probably safe to have sexual intercourse when the stitches heal, vaginal discharge stops, and the woman feels like it.

If the woman regularly engaged in conditioning exercises during pregnancy, exercise will help her to recover her former body contour and strength during the postpartal period. With a caregiver's approval, the woman can begin some exercises as soon as one hour after delivery. In addition to recommending exercise in the postpartal period for women, health professionals also increasingly recommend that women practice the relaxation techniques they used during pregnancy and childbirth. Five minutes of slow breathing on a stressful day in the postpartal period can relax and refresh the new mother as well as the new baby.

Emotional and Psychological Adjustments

Emotional fluctuations are common on the part of the mother in the postpartal period. These emotional fluctuations may be due to any of a number of factors: hormonal changes, fatigue, inexperience or lack of confidence with newborn babies, or the extensive time and demands involved in caring for a newborn. For some women, the emotional fluctuations decrease within several weeks after the delivery and are a minor aspect of their motherhood. For others, they are more long-lasting and may produce feelings of anxiety, depression, and difficulty in coping with stress. Mothers who have such feelings, even when they are getting adequate rest, may benefit from professional help in dealing with their problems. Following are some of the signs that may indicate a need for professional counseling about postpartal adaptation (Simkin, Whalley, & Keppler, 1984):

- Excessive worrying
- Depression
- Extreme changes in appetite
- Crying spells
- Inability to sleep

Another adjustment for the mother and for the father is the time and thought that go into being a competent parent of a young infant. It is important for both the mother and the father to become aware of the young infant's developmental needs—physically, psychologically, and emotionally. Both the mother and the father need to develop a comfortable relationship with the young infant.

A special interest in the parent-infant relationships is **bonding,** *the occurrence of close contact, especially physical, between parents and newborn in the period shortly after birth.* Some physicians believe that this period shortly after birth is critical in development; during this time, the parents and child need to form an important emotional attachment that provides a foundation for optimal development in years to come. Special interest in bonding came about when some pediatricians argued that the circumstances surrounding delivery often separate mothers and their infants, preventing or making difficult the development of a bond. The pediatricians further argued that giving the mother drugs to make her delivery less painful may contribute to the lack of bonding. The drugs may make the mother drowsy, thus interfering with her ability to respond to and stimulate the newborn. Advocates of bonding also assert that preterm infants are isolated from their mothers to an even greater degree than fullterm infants, thereby increasing their difficulty in bonding.

Is there evidence that such close contact between mothers and newborns is absolutely critical for optimal development later in life? Although some research supports the bonding hypothesis (Klaus & Kennell, 1976), a growing body of research challenges the significance of the first few days of life as a critical period (Bakeman & Brown, 1980; Rode & others, 1981). Indeed, the extreme form of the bonding hypothesis—that the newborn must have close contact with the mother in the first few days of life to develop optimally—simply in not true.

Nonetheless, the weakness of the maternal-infant bonding research should not be used as an excuse to keep motivated mothers from interacting with their infants in the postpartum period, because such contact brings pleasure to many mothers. In some mother-infant pairs—including preterm infants, adolescent mothers, or mothers from disadvantaged circumstances—the practice of bonding may set in motion a climate for improved interaction after the mother and infant leave the hospital (Maccoby & Martin, 1983).

The new baby also changes a mother's and father's relationship with each other. Among the questions that have to be dealt with are: How will we share the housework and baby care? How can we find enough time for each other when the baby takes up so much of our time? How can we arrange to get out of the house so we can enjoy some of the things we did before the baby came? At some point, new parents have to figure out which of their commitments are the most important, and which have to get less time, or be dropped. Support from relatives, friends, and babysitters can help new parents find time to renew some of these activities they enjoyed earlier.

A special concern of many new mothers is whether they should stay home with the baby or go back to work. Some mothers want to return to work as soon as possible after the infant is born, others want to stay home with the infant for several months, then return to work, others want to stay home for a year before they return to work, and yet others, of course, did not work prior to the baby's arrival and do not plan to do so in the future.

Critical Thinking

If you are a female, what would be the key factors for you in deciding whether to work or to stay home with the baby? If you are a male, what would you want your wife to do—work or stay home with the baby? What key factors underlie your preference?

Many women, because of a variety of pressures—societal, career, financial—do not have the option of staying home after their babies are born (Eisenberg, Murkoff, & Hathaway, 1989). However, for women who have to make the choice, the process of decision making is often difficult and agonizing. By turning to Explorations in Child Development 4.2, you can read about some of the questions women can ask themselves when they face the issue of whether they should stay home with the baby or return to work.

At this point we have discussed a number of ideas about birth and the postpartal period. A summary of these ideas is presented in Concept Table 4.2.

EXPLORATIONS IN CHILD DEVELOPMENT 4.2

To Work or Not to Work

If a mother of a newborn is pondering the question of whether to work or not to work, asking herself the following questions may help her sort out which choice to make (Eisenberg, Murkoff, & Hathaway, 1989):

What are my priorities? The new mother can carefully consider what is most important in her life and rank order these on paper. Priorities might include her baby, her family, her career, financial security, and luxuries of life (such as vacations and entertainment). Her list may be different than those of a woman next door or a woman at the next desk. After charting her priorities, she can consider whether returning to employment or staying at home will best meet the most important of them.

Which full-time role suits my personality best? The woman might ask herself whether she is at her best at home with the baby or whether staying at home would make her feel impatient and tense. Will she be able to leave worries about her baby at home when she goes to her work? Will she worry about not being employed when she stays home with the baby? Or will an inability to compartmentalize her life keep her from doing her best at either job?

Would I feel comfortable having someone else take care of my baby? Does she feel no one else can do the job of caring for the baby as well as she can herself? Or does she feel secure that she can find (or has found) a person (or small group situation) that can substitute well for her during the hours she is away from home?

How much energy do I have? Considerable physical and emotional stamina are needed to rise with a baby, get ready for work, put in a full day on the job, then return to the demands of the baby, home, and husband. What often

suffers most when energy is lacking in the two-paycheck family with infants is the husband-wife relationship.

How do I feel about missing my baby's milestones? Will the mother mind hearing about some of the baby's milestones secondhand—the first time the baby laughs, sits alone, crawls, or walks? Will the mother feel hurt if the baby runs to the sitter instead of her when the baby is frightened or hurt? Does the mother feel that she can be synchronized with the baby's needs by just spending evenings and weekends together?

How stressful is the combination of my employment and the baby? If the mother's employment involves little stress and her baby is an easy baby to care for, then the employment may not present much of a problem. But if the mother's job is very stressful and her baby is difficult to care for (has physical problems, cries a lot, and so on), then she may have difficulty coping with both the job and the baby.

If I return to work, will I get adequate support from my husband or from some other source? Even a superwoman can't, and should not be expected to, do everything alone. Will her husband be willing to do his share of babysitting, shopping, cooking, cleaning, and laundry? Is the couple able to afford outside help?

What is our financial situation? If she decides not to work, will it threaten the family's economic survival or just mean cutting down on some extras the couple has been enjoying? Are there ways of cutting back so that the mother's lack of income won't hurt so much? If the mother does go back to work, how much of a dent in her income will job-related costs such as clothes, travel, and child care make?

How flexible is my job? Will the mother be able to take time off if her baby or her sitter becomes sick? Will she be able to come in late or leave early if there is an emergency at home? Does her job require long hours, weekends, or travel? Is the mother willing to spend extended time away from the baby?

If I don't return to my job, how will it influence my career? Putting a career on hold can sometimes set the woman back when she eventually does return to employment. If the mother suspects this may happen, is she willing to make this sacrifice? Are there ways to keep in touch professionally during her at-home months (or years) without making a full-time commitment?

Whatever choice the woman makes, it is likely to require some sacrifices and misgivings. Such sacrifices and misgivings are normal; since we do not live in a perfect world, we have to learn to live and cope with some of them. However, if they begin to multiply and the mother finds her dissatisfaction outweighing her satisfaction, she may want to reassess the choice she made. A choice that seemed right in theory may not work out in practice.

CONCEPT TABLE 4.2

Birth and the Postpartal Period

Concept	Processes/Related Ideas	Characteristics/Description
Birth	Stages of birth	Three stages of birth have been defined. The first lasts about 12 to 24 hours for a woman having her first child. The cervix dilates to about 4 inches. The second stage begins when the baby's head moves through the cervix and ends with the baby's complete emergence. The third stage is afterbirth.
	Delivery complications	A baby can move through the birth canal too rapidly or too slowly. A delivery that is too fast is called precipitate; when delivery is too slow, anoxia may result. A cesarean section is the surgical removal of the baby from the uterus.
	The use of drugs during childbirth	A wide variety of tranquilizers, sedatives, and analgesics are used to relieve the expectant mother's pain and anxiety, and oxytocin is used to speed delivery. Birthweight and social class are more powerful predictors of problems than are drugs. A drug can have mixed effects and the overall amount of medication needs to be considered.
	Childbirth strategies	In standard childbirth, the expectant mother is taken to the hospital, where a doctor is responsible for the baby's delivery. The birth takes place in a delivery room, which looks like an operating room, and medication is used in the procedure. Criticisms of the standard childbirth procedure have been made.
		The Leboyer method and prepared, or natural, childbirth are alternatives to standard childbirth. A widely practiced form of natural childbirth is the Lamaze method. Among the current changes in childbirth are shifts in emphases, new choices, and an understanding of obstetrical terminology. In the past several decades, fathers have increasingly participated in childbirth. Another special concern is the sibling's role in childbirth.
	Preterm infants and age-weight considerations	Preterm infants are those born after an abnormally short time period in the womb. Infants who are born after a regular gestation period of 38 to 42 weeks but who weigh less than 5 1/2 pounds are called low-birthweight infants. Preterm infant care is much too complex to be described only in terms of amount of stimulation. Preterm infants' responses vary according to their conceptual age, illness, and individual makeup. Infant behavioral cues can be used to indicate the appropriate stimulation. Intervention should be organized in the form of an individualized developmental plan.

Concept	Processes/Related Ideas	Characteristics/Description
		As intensive care technology has improved, preterm babies have benefited considerably. Infants born with an identifiable problem have a poorer developmental future than those born without a recognizable problem. Social class differences are associated with development.
	Measures of neonatal health and responsiveness	For many years the Apgar scale has been used to assess the newborn's health. A more recently developed test—the Brazelton Neonatal Behavioral Assessment Scale—is used for long-term neurological assessment. It assesses not only the newborn's neurological integrity but also social responsiveness.
The postpartal period	Its nature	The postpartal period (also called postpartum period) is the period after childbirth or delivery. It is a time when the woman's body adjusts, both physically and psychologically, to the process of childbearing. It lasts for about six weeks or until the body has completed its adjustment.
	Physical adjustments	These include fatigue, involution (the process by which the uterus returns to its prepregnant size five or six weeks after birth), hormone changes that include a dramatic drop in estrogen and progesterone, consideration of when to resume sexual intercourse, and participation in exercises to recover former body contour and strength.
	Emotional and psychological adjustments	Emotional fluctuations on the part of the mother are common in the postpartal period. They may be due to hormonal changes, fatigue, inexperience or lack of confidence with newborn babies, or the extensive time and other demands involved in caring for a newborn. For some, the emotional fluctuations are minimal and disappear in several weeks; for others, they are more long-lasting. Another adjustment for both the mother and the father is the time and thought that go into being a competent parent of a young infant. A special interest in parent-infant relationships is bonding, which has not been found to be critical in the development of a competent infant or child, but which may stimulate positive interaction between some mother-infant pairs. The new baby also changes the mother's and father's relationship with each other. A special concern of many new mothers is whether they should go back to work, or whether they should stay home with the infant.

PERSPECTIVES ON PARENTING AND EDUCATION

Becoming Knowledgeable about Pregnancy, Prenatal Development, and Childbirth Strategies

Two important aspects of parenting and education for expectant parents are, first, becoming knowledgeable about pregnancy and prenatal development, and, second, learning about different childbirth strategies and considering childbirth classes.

Early prenatal classes may include both couples in early pregnancy and prepregnancy (Olds, London, & Ladewig, 1988). The classes often focus on such topics as:

- Changes in the development of the embryo and the fetus
- Self-care during pregnancy
- Fetal development concerns and environmental dangers for the fetus
- Sexuality during pregnancy
- Birth settings and types of care providers

Early prenatal education classes focus on such topics as changes in the development of the fetus, while later classes often focus on preparation for the birth and care of the newborn.

- Nutrition, rest, and exercise
- Common discomforts of pregnancy and relief measures
- Psychological changes in both the expectant mother and her partner
- Information needed to get the pregnancy off to a good start

Early classes also may include information about factors that place the expectant mother at risk for preterm labor and recognition of the possible signs and symptoms of preterm labor. And prenatal education classes may include information on the advantages and disadvantages of breast- and bottle-feeding (we will discuss this issue in chapter 5). Researchers have found that the majority of expectant mothers (50 to 80 percent) have made this infant feeding decision prior to the sixth month of pregnancy. Therefore, information about the issues involved in breast- versus bottle-feeding in an early prenatal education class is helpful (Aberman & Kirchoff, 1985).

So far, the prenatal education classes we have described focus on expectant couples in the first trimester of pregnancy. The later classes—those when the expectant mother is in the second or third trimester of pregnancy—often focus on preparation for the birth, infant care and feeding, postpartum self-care, and birth choices. Much more about these topics appears in the next chapter.

What happens in childbirth classes? The format is often a six-part, two-hour session with one hour of discussion and one hour of practicing techniques and exercises. Instructors, working with each couple in turn, teach fathers or other partners (often called coaches) how to assist the woman in labor. One or more couples from previous classes may return for a visit, with

At the Maternity Center in New York City, the Birth Atlas is being used in a childbirth class. The purpose of the Birth Atlas is to show in precise detail how birth takes place and to help demystify birth.

their babies, to describe their childbirth experiences. This provides a valuable and interesting opportunity for expectant parents. Birth slides and films help make childbirth more real and less frightening. The Birth Atlas, a series of detailed, life-sized photographs of pregnancy, labor, and delivery from Maternity Center in New York City, is another educational tool widely used in childbirth classes throughout the United States. The purpose of the Birth Atlas is to show in precise detail how birth takes place and to help demystify birth.

The International Childbirth Education Association guide for childbirth educators endorses the concept of a health care *circle* rather than a health care *team*. The key person in the center of the health care circle is the person seeking care, in this case the expectant mother. She selects the people around her for advice, information, care, and support. The circle may include family, friends, other expectant couples, obstetrician, midwife, nurse, or others. Communication, shared decision making, and her right to make informed choices are central to effective childbirth education. ■

CONCLUSIONS

When a species reproduces itself, life comes from life. Much of this chapter was about becoming. Pregnancy is a state of becoming. An unborn baby is becoming a person capable of life outside the mother's body, and a man and a woman are becoming parents.

In this chapter, you read about the course of prenatal development and its three main periods—germinal, embryonic, and fetal, as well as about miscarriage and abortion, teratology, and hazards to prenatal development such as the mother's use of drugs. You also read about birth, including childbirth strategies, preterm infants, and age-weight considerations. And you studied the postpartal period and its physical and psychological adjustments. Don't forget that you can obtain a summary of the entire chapter by again reading the two concept tables on pages 113 and 126.

In the next chapter, we continue to examine the early aspects of the child's development, focusing on physical, motor, and perceptual development in infancy.

KEY TERMS

germinal period The period of prenatal development that takes place in the first two weeks after conception. It includes the creation of the zygote, continued cell division, and the attachment of the zygote to the uterine wall. (100)

blastocyst The inner layer of cells that develops during the germinal period. These cells later develop into the embryo. (100)

trophoblast The outer layer of cells that develops in the germinal period. These cells provide nutrition and support for the embryo. (101)

implantation The attachment of the zygote to the uterine wall, which takes place about 10 days after conception. (101)

embryonic period The period of prenatal development that occurs 2 to 8 weeks after conception. During the embryonic period, the rate of cell differentiation intensifies, support systems for the cells form, and organs appear. (101)

endoderm The inner layer of cells that develops into digestive and respiratory systems. (101)

ectoderm The inner layer of cells, which becomes the nervous system, sensory receptors (ear, nose, and eyes, for example), and skin parts (hair and nails, for example). (101)

mesoderm The middle layer of cells, which becomes the circulatory system, bones, muscles, excretory system, and reproductive system. (101)

placenta A life-support system that consists of a disk-shaped group of tissues in which small blood vessels from the mother and offspring intertwine to join. (101)

umbilical cord A life-support system containing two arteries and one vein, that connects the baby to the placenta. (101)

amnion A bag or envelope that contains a clear fluid in which the developing embryo floats. The amnion is an important life-support system. It provides an environment that is temperature and humidity controlled, as well as shockproof. (102)

organogenesis The process of organ formation that takes place during the first 2 months of prenatal development. (103)

fetal period The prenatal period of development that begins 2 months after conception and lasts for 7 months on the average. (103)

teratogen From the Greek word *tera*, meaning "monster," any agent that causes a birth defect. The field of study that investigates the causes of birth defects is called teratology. (106)

fetal alcohol syndrome (FAS) A cluster of abnormalities that appears in the offspring of mothers who drink alcohol heavily during pregnancy. (109)

toxoplasmosis A mild infection that causes coldlike symptoms or no apparent illness in adults. However, toxoplasmosis can be a teratogen for the unborn baby, causing possible eye defects, brain defects, and premature birth. (111)

afterbirth The third birth stage, when the placenta, umbilical cord, and other membranes are detached and expelled. (112)

precipitate A form of delivery that takes place too rapidly; the baby squeezes through the birth canal in less than 10 minutes. (112)

anoxia The insufficient availability of oxygen to the infant. (112)

breech position The baby's position in the uterus that causes the buttocks to be the first part to emerge from the vagina. (112)

cesarean section The surgical removal of the baby from the uterus. (112)

oxytocin A hormone that stimulates and regulates the rhythmicity of uterine contractions. It has been widely used as a drug to speed delivery. Controversy surrounds its use. (114)

Leboyer method A birth process developed by French obstetrician, Fredrick Leboyer, that tends to make birth less stressful for infants. The procedure is referred to as "birth without violence." (114)

prepared, or natural, childbirth A childbirth strategy that includes being informed about what will happen during the procedure, knowing about comfort measures for childbirth, anticipating that little or no medication will be used, and if complications arise, expecting to participate in decisions made to resolve the problems. (115)

Lamaze method   A form of prepared childbirth developed by Fernand Lamaze, a pioneering French obstetrician. Widely accepted in the medical profession, it involves helping pregnant women cope actively with the pain of childbirth to avoid or reduce medication. (115)

preterm infant   An infant born prior to 38 weeks after conception. (117)

low-birthweight infants   Infants born after a regular period of gestation (the length of time between conception and birth) of 38 to 42 weeks but who weigh less than 5½ pounds. (117)

Apgar scale   A widely used method to assess the health of newborns at 1 to 5 minutes after birth. The Apgar scale evaluates infants' heart rate, respiratory effort, muscle tone, body color, and reflex irritability. (120)

Brazelton Neonatal Behavioral Assessment Scale   A test, given several days after birth, to assess newborns' neurological development, reflexes, and reactions to people. (120)

postpartal period   The period after childbirth or delivery. It is a time when the woman's body adjusts, both physically and psychologically, to the process of childbearing. It lasts for about 6 weeks or until the body has completed its adjustment and has returned to a near prepregnant state. (122)

involution   The process by which the uterus returns to its prepregnant size 5 or 6 weeks after birth. (122)

bonding   Close contact, especially physical, between parents and their newborn in the period shortly after birth. (124)

SUGGESTED READINGS

Coleman, L. L., & Coleman, A. D. (1991). *Pregnancy: The psychological experience* (rev. ed.). New York: The Noonday Press. This is an excellent book for expectant couples that provides especially good information about the mother's role, the father's role, and communication between couples during pregnancy.

Eisenberg, A., Murkoff, H. E., & Hathaway, S. E. (1988). *What to expect when you're expecting*. New York: Workman Publishing. This book has become the most recommended book for prospective parents by physicians and caregivers. It contains detailed advice about many different areas of prenatal development and about issues of concern to expectant couples.

Nilsson, L. (1990). *A child is born* (rev. ed.). New York: Delacourt. An abundance of breathtaking photographs take you inside the womb to see the developmental unfolding of the zygote, embryo, and fetus.

Olds, S. B., London, M. L., & Ladewig, P. A. (1988). *Maternal newborn nursing: A family-centered approach*. Menlo Park, CA: Addison-Wesley. This is virtually an encyclopedia of information about prenatal development with extensive tables about various dimensions of pregnancy and prenatal growth.

Simkin, P., Whalley, J., & Keppler, A. (1984). *Pregnancy, childbirth, and the newborn: A complete guide for expectant parents*. New York: Simon and Schuster. This book is very well-written and is a concise overview of good advice for expectant couples.

Baby at Play, 1876,
Thomas Eakins (Detail)

Physical, Motor, and Perceptual Development in Infancy

Systematic reasoning is something we could not, as a species of individuals, do without. But neither, if we are to remain sane, can we do without direct perception . . . of the inner and outer world into which we have been born.

—Aldous Huxley

A baby is the most complicated object made by unskilled labor.

—Anonymous

IMAGES OF CHILDREN

Studying Newborns

The creature has poor motor coordination and can move itself only with great difficulty. Its general behavior appears to be disorganized, and, although it cries when uncomfortable, it uses few other vocalizations. In fact, it sleeps most of the time, about 16 to 17 hours a day. You are curious about this creature and want to know more about what it can do. You think to yourself, "I wonder if it can see. How could I find out?"

You obviously have a communication problem with the creature. You must devise a way that will allow the creature to "tell" you that it can see. While examining the creature one day, you make an interesting discovery. When you move a large object toward it, it moves its head backward, as if to avoid a collision with the object. The creature's head movement suggests that it has at least some vision.

In case you haven't already guessed, the creature you have been reading about is the human infant, and the role you played is that of a developmentalist interested in devising techniques to learn about the infant's visual perception. After years of work, scientists have developed research tools and methods sophisticated enough to examine the subtle abilities of infants and to interpret their complex actions. Videotape equipment allows researchers to investigate elusive behaviors, and high-speed computers make it possible to perform complex data analysis in minutes instead of months and years. Other sophisticated equipment is used to closely monitor respiration, heart rate, body movement, visual fixation, and sucking behavior, which provide clues to what is going on inside the infant.

PREVIEW

Among the first things developmentalists were able to demonstrate was that infants have highly developed perceptual motor systems. Until recently, even some nurses in maternity hospitals believed that newborns are blind at birth, and they told this to mothers. Most parents were also told that their newborns could not taste, smell, or feel pain. As you will discover later in this chapter, we now know that newborns can see (albeit fuzzily), taste, smell, and feel pain. Before we turn to the fascinating world of the infant's perception, we will discuss a number of ideas about infants' and toddlers' physical development.

PHYSICAL GROWTH AND DEVELOPMENT IN INFANCY

Infants' physical development in the first two years of life is extensive. At birth, neonates have a gigantic head (relative to the rest of the body) that flops around in an uncontrollable fashion; they also possess reflexes that are dominated by evolutionary movements. In the span of 12 months, infants become capable of sitting anywhere, standing, stooping, climbing, and usually walking. During the second year, growth decelerates, but rapid increases in such activities as running and climbing take place. Let's now examine in greater detail the sequence of physical development in infancy by studying the infant's reflexes, cephalocaudal and proximodistal sequences, height and weight, gross and fine motor skills, the brain, infant states, nutrition, toilet training, and health.

Reflexes

What is the nature of the infant's reflexes? The newborn is not an empty-headed organism. Among other things, it has some basic reflexes that are genetically carried survival mechanisms. For example, the newborn has no fear of water; it will naturally hold its breath and contract its throat to keep water out.

Reflexes govern the newborn's movements, which are automatic and beyond the newborn's control. They are built-in reactions to certain stimuli. They provide young infants with adaptive responses to their environment before they have had the opportunity to learn. The **sucking reflex** *occurs when newborns automatically suck an object placed in their mouth. The sucking reflex enables newborns to get nourishment before they have associated a nipple with food.* The sucking reflex is an example of a reflex that is present at birth but later disappears. The **rooting reflex** *occurs when the infant's cheek is stroked or the side of the mouth is touched. In response, the infant turns its head toward the side that was touched in an apparent effort to find something to suck.* The sucking and rooting reflexes disappear when the infant is about 3 to 4 months old. They are replaced by the infant's voluntary eating. The sucking and rooting reflexes have survival value for newborn mammals, who must find the mother's breast to obtain nourishment.

The **Moro reflex** *is a neonatal startle response that occurs in response to a sudden, intense noise or movement. When startled, the newborn arches its back, throws its head back, and flings out its arms and legs. Then the newborn rapidly closes its arms and legs to the center of the body.* The Moro reflex is a vestige from our primate ancestry and it too has survival value. This reflex, which is normal in all newborns, also tends to disappear at 3 to 4 months of age. Steady pressure on any part of the infant's body calms the infant after it has been startled. Holding the infant's arm flexed at the shoulder will quiet the infant.

Some reflexes present in the newborn—coughing, blinking, and yawning, for example—persist throughout life. They are as important for the adult as they are for the infant. Other reflexes, though, disappear several months following birth as the infant's brain functions mature, and voluntary control over many behaviors develops. The movements of some reflexes eventually become incorporated into more complex, voluntary actions. One important example is the **grasping reflex,** *which occurs when something touches the infant's palms. The infant responds by grasping tightly.* By the end of the third month, the grasping reflex diminishes and the infant shows a more voluntary grasp, which is often produced by visual stimuli. For example, when an infant sees a mobile whirling above its crib, it may reach out and try to grasp it. As its motor development becomes smoother, the infant will grasp objects, carefully manipulate them, and explore their qualities.

> *The experiences of the first three years of life are almost entirely lost to us, and when we attempt to enter into a small child's world, we come as foreigners who have forgotten the landscape and no longer speak the native tongue.*
>
> —Selma Fraiberg

An overview of the main reflexes we have discussed, along with others, is given in figure 5.1.

Sucking is an especially important reflex: It is the infant's route to nourishment. The sucking capabilities of newborns vary considerably. Some newborns are efficient at forceful sucking and obtaining milk; others are not so adept and get tired before they are full. Most newborns take several weeks to establish a sucking style that is coordinated with the way the mother is holding the infant, the way milk is coming out of the bottle or breast, and the infant's sucking speed and temperament.

An investigation by pediatrician T. Berry Brazelton (1956) involved observations of infants for more than a year to determine the incidence of their sucking when they were nursing and how their sucking changed as they grew older. More than 85 percent of the infants engaged in considerable sucking behavior unrelated to feeding. They sucked their fingers, their fists, and pacifiers. By the age of 1 year, most had stopped the sucking behavior.

Parents should not worry when infants suck their thumbs, fist, or even a pacifier. Many parents, though, do begin to worry when thumb sucking persists into the preschool and elementary school years. As many as 40 percent of children continue to suck their thumbs after they have started school (Kessen, Haith, & Salapatek, 1970).

Most developmentalists do not attach a great deal of significance to this behavior and are not aware of parenting strategies that might contribute to it. Individual differences in children's biological makeup may be involved to some degree in the continuation of sucking behavior.

Nonnutritive sucking, *sucking behavior unrelated to the infant's feeding,* is used as a measure in a large number of research studies with young infants because young infants quit sucking when they attend to something, such as a picture or a vocalization. Nonnutritive sucking, then, is one of the ingenious ways developmentalists study the young infant's attention and learning.

Cephalocaudal and Proximodistal Sequences

The **cephalocaudal pattern** *is the sequence in which the greatest growth always occurs at the top—the head—with physical growth in size, weight, and feature differentiation gradually working its way down from top to bottom (for example, neck, shoulders, middle trunk, and so on).* This same pattern occurs in the head area because the top parts of the head—the eyes and brain—grow faster than the lower parts—such as the jaw. An extraordinary proportion of the total body is occupied by the head during prenatal development and early infancy (see figure 5.2).

The **proximodistal pattern** *is the sequence in which growth starts at the center of the body and moves toward the extremities.* An example of this is the early maturation of muscular control of the trunk and arms as compared with that of the hands and fingers.

Height and Weight

The average North American newborn is 20 inches long and weighs 7½ pounds. Ninety-five percent of full-term newborns are 18 to 22 inches long and weigh between 5½ and 10 pounds. In the first several days of life, most newborns lose 5 to 7 percent of their body weight before they learn to adjust to neonatal feeding. Once infants adjust to sucking, swallowing, and digesting they grow rapidly, gaining an average of 5 to 6 ounces per week during the first month. By four months, they have doubled their birth weight and nearly tripled it by their

FIGURE 5.1

Infant reflexes.

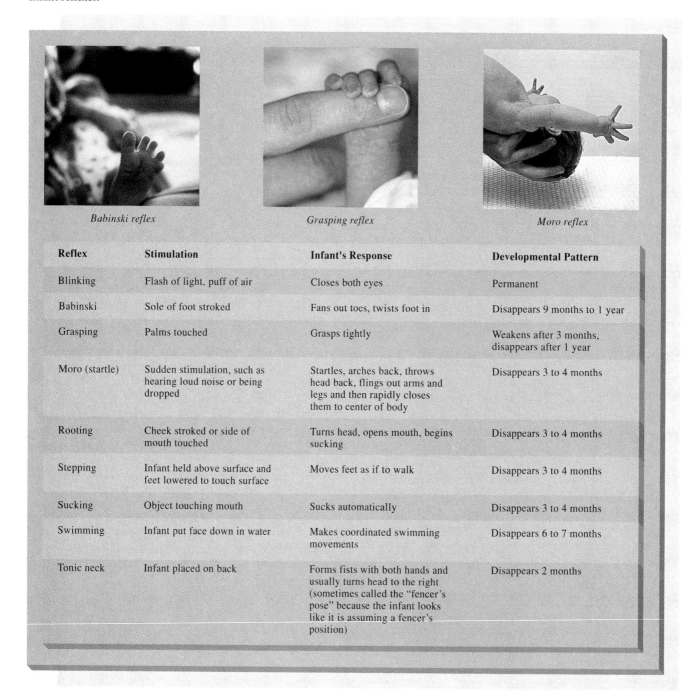

Reflex	Stimulation	Infant's Response	Developmental Pattern
Blinking	Flash of light, puff of air	Closes both eyes	Permanent
Babinski	Sole of foot stroked	Fans out toes, twists foot in	Disappears 9 months to 1 year
Grasping	Palms touched	Grasps tightly	Weakens after 3 months, disappears after 1 year
Moro (startle)	Sudden stimulation, such as hearing loud noise or being dropped	Startles, arches back, throws head back, flings out arms and legs and then rapidly closes them to center of body	Disappears 3 to 4 months
Rooting	Cheek stroked or side of mouth touched	Turns head, opens mouth, begins sucking	Disappears 3 to 4 months
Stepping	Infant held above surface and feet lowered to touch surface	Moves feet as if to walk	Disappears 3 to 4 months
Sucking	Object touching mouth	Sucks automatically	Disappears 3 to 4 months
Swimming	Infant put face down in water	Makes coordinated swimming movements	Disappears 6 to 7 months
Tonic neck	Infant placed on back	Forms fists with both hands and usually turns head to the right (sometimes called the "fencer's pose" because the infant looks like it is assuming a fencer's position)	Disappears 2 months

first birthday. Infants grow about 1 inch per month during the first year, reaching approximately 1½ times their birth length by their first birthday.

A baby is an angel whose wings decrease as his legs increase.

—French proverb

Infants' rate of growth is considerably slower in the second year of life. By 2 years of age, infants weigh approximately 26 to 32 pounds, having gained a quarter to half a pound per month during the second year; now they have reached about one-fifth of their adult weight. At 2 years of age, the average infant is 32 to 35 inches in height, which is nearly one-half of their adult height. A summary of changes in height and weight during the first 18 months of life is shown in figure 5.3.

FIGURE 5.2

Changes in body form and proportion during prenatal and postnatal growth. Note the changes in body proportions from 2 months into fetal development to 25 years of age and the "large" head of the newborn.

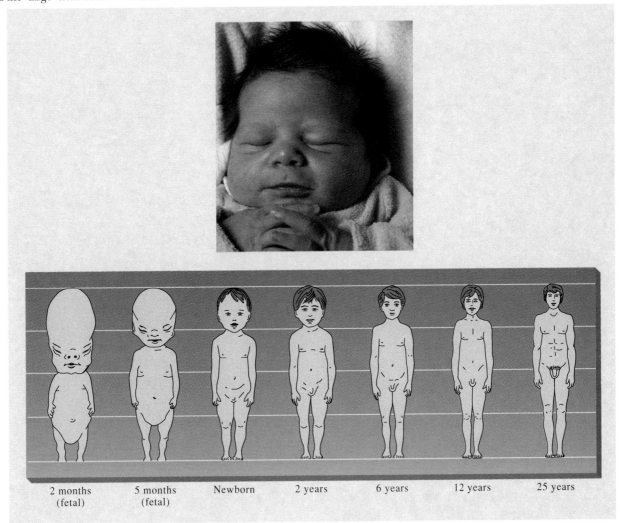

| 2 months (fetal) | 5 months (fetal) | Newborn | 2 years | 6 years | 12 years | 25 years |

Gross and Fine Motor Skills

Gross motor skills *involve large muscle activities such as moving one's arms and walking.* **Fine motor skills** *involve more finely tuned movements, such as finger dexterity.* Let's examine the changes in gross and fine motor skills in the first two years of life.

Gross Motor Skills

At birth, the infant has no appreciable coordination of the chest or arms, but in the first month the infant can lift its head from a prone position. At about 3 months, the infant can hold its chest up and use its arms for support after being in a prone position. At 3 to 4 months, infants can roll over, and at 4 to 5 months they can support some weight with their legs. At about 6 months, infants can sit without support, and by 7 to 8 months they can crawl and stand without support. At approximately 8 months, infants can pull themselves up to a standing position, at 10 to 11 months they can walk using furniture for support

(called cruising), and at 12 to 13 months the average infant can walk without assistance. A summary of the developmental accomplishments in gross motor skills during the first year is shown in figure 5.4. The actual month at which the milestones occur varies by as much as 2 to 4 months, especially among older infants. What remains fairly uniform, however, is the sequence of accomplishments. An important implication of these infant motor accomplishments is the increasing degree of independence they bring. Older infants can explore their environment more extensively and initiate social interaction with caregivers and peers more readily than when they were younger.

In the second year of life, toddlers become more motorically skilled and mobile. They are no longer content with being in a playpen and want to move all over the place. Child development experts believe that motor activity during the second year is vital to the child's competent development and that few restrictions, except for safety purposes, should be placed on their motoric adventures (Fraiberg, 1959).

FIGURE 5.3

Developmental changes in height and weight from birth to 18 months. The numbers on the colored lines in the charts refer to the percentiles for infants' height and weight at different months of age compared with other infants of the same age. The 50th percentile indicates that half of the infants of a particular age are taller and half are shorter. The 10th percentile tells us that 10 percent of the infants of that age are shorter and 90 percent are taller.

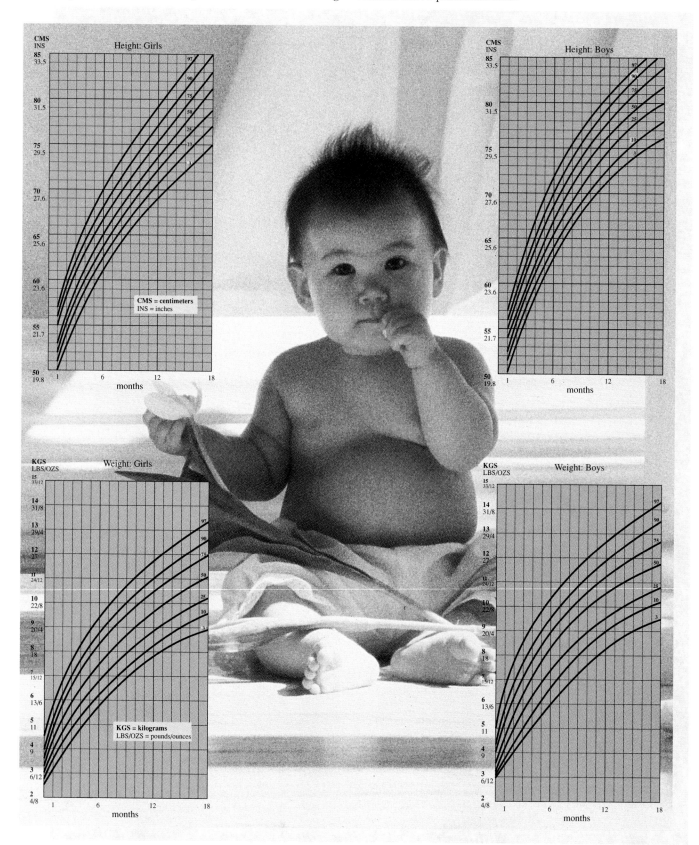

FIGURE 5.4

Developmental milestones in gross motor development.

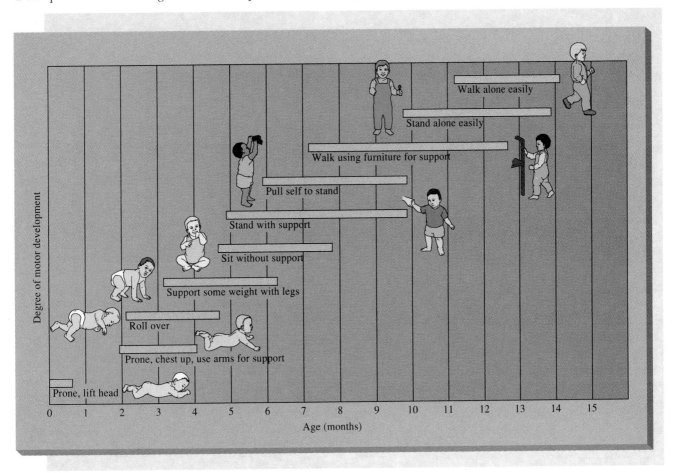

By 13 to 18 months, toddlers can pull a toy attached to a string, use their hands and legs to climb up a number of steps, and ride four-wheel wagons (White, 1988). By 18 to 24 months, toddlers can walk fast or run stiffly for a short distance, balance on their feet in a squat position while playing with objects on the floor, walk backward without losing their balance, stand and kick a ball without falling, stand and throw a ball, and jump in place (Schirmer, 1974).

Not content with their infants reaching the motor development milestones at an average rate, many American parents want to accelerate their infant's physical skills. Is this a wise practice? To learn more about this intriguing question, turn to Explorations in Child Development 5.1.

Fine Motor Skills

Infants have hardly any control over fine motor skills at birth although they have many components of what later become finely coordinated arm, hand, and finger movements (Rosenblith, 1992). The development of such behaviors as reaching and grasping become increasingly more refined during the first two years of life. Initially, infants show only crude shoulder and elbow movements, but later show wrist movements, hand rotation, and coordination of the thumb and forefinger. The maturation of hand-eye coordination over the first two years of life is reflected in the improvement of fine motor skills. Figure 5.5 provides a detailed chronological unfolding of fine motor skills in the first two years of life.

The Brain

As an infant walks, talks, runs, shakes a rattle, smiles, and frowns, changes in its brain are occurring. Consider that the infant began life as a single cell and, in 9 months, was born with a brain and nervous system that contained approximately 100 billion nerve cells. Indeed, at birth, the infant probably had all of the nerve cells (called neurons) it is going to have in its entire life. However, at birth and in early infancy, the connectedness of these neurons is impoverished. As the infant ages from birth to 2 years, the interconnection of neurons increases dramatically as the dendrites (the receiving part) of the neuron branch out (see figure 5.6).

At birth, the newborn's brain is about 25 percent of its adult weight, and by the second birthday it is about 75 percent of its adult weight.

EXPLORATIONS IN CHILD DEVELOPMENT 5.1

Babies Don't Need Exercise Classes

Six-month-old Andrew doesn't walk yet, but his mother wants him to develop his physical skills optimally. Three times a week, she takes him to a recreation center, where he participates with other infants in swimming and gymnastics classes. With the increased interest of today's adults in aerobic exercise and fitness, some parents have tried to give their infants a head start on becoming physically fit and physically talented. However, the American Academy of Pediatricians recently issued a statement that recommends against structured exercise classes for babies. Pediatricians are seeing more bone fractures and dislocations and more muscle strains in babies now than in the past. They point out that, when an adult is stretching and moving an infant's limbs, it is easy to go beyond the infant's physical limits without knowing it.

The physical fitness classes for infants range from passive fare—with adults putting infants through the paces—to programs called "aerobic" because they demand crawling, tumbling, and ball skills. However, exercise for infants is not aerobic. They cannot adequately stretch their bodies to achieve aerobic benefits.

Swimming classes before early childhood also have a downside. No one would disagree with the desire of parents that their infants learn to swim so they will not drown. However, some infants who take swimming lessons develop "infant water intoxification" by swallowing too much water (White, 1990). Water intoxification occurs when an individual swallows enough water to lower the sodium (salt) content of the blood, which makes the brain swell and can lead to a stupor, coma, or seizure. Because of the potential danger of infant water intoxification, the YMCA and the Council for National Co-operation in Aquatics state that children under age 3 should not be involved in organized swimming instruction classes. Also, children cannot cognitively learn to swim until they are 3 to 4 years of age. It is not uncommon for 4-year-olds who have had swim classes since infancy to become suddenly terrified of the water because, for the first time, they understand that they could drown.

For optimal physical development, babies simply need touch, face-to-face contact, and brightly colored toys they can manipulate. If infants are not couch potatoes who are babysat extensively by a television set, their normal play will provide them with all the fitness training they need.

What types of exercise activities and toys are developmentally appropriate for infants in the first year of life? Among the recommended activities are (Whaley & Wong, 1988):

- Birth–1 month: Rock infant, place in cradle. Use carriage for walks.
- 2–3 months: Use cradle gym. Take infant for rides in car. Exercise body by gently moving infant's extremities.
- 4–6 months: Use stroller. Bounce infant on lap while holding infant in standing position. Help infant roll over. Support infant in sitting position, let infant lean forward to gain balance.

In the first six months, suggested toys designed to give the infant developmentally appropriate exercise are: crib exerciser, crib gym, rocking crib or cradle, and weighted or suction toys.

- 6–9 months: Place infant on the floor to crawl, roll over, sit. Hold upright to bear weight and bounce. Pick up—say "up." Put down—say "down." Place toys out of reach; encourage infant to get them. Play pat-a-cake.
- 9–12 months: Give large push-pull toys to encourage walking. Place furniture in a circle to encourage cruising.

In the second half of the first year, suggested toys designed to give the infant developmentally appropriate exercise are: exercise crib toy, activity box for crib, push-pull toys, and swing.

Mothers and their babies in a swimming class. Pediatricians and child psychologists recommend that exercise classes, even swimming classes, for infants are unnecessary—and possibly produce more negative than positive outcomes.

FIGURE 5.5

The development of fine motor skills in infancy.

Birth to 6 months

2 mo.	Holds rattle briefly
2 1/2 mo.	Glances from one object to another
3–4 mo.	Plays in simple way with rattle; inspects fingers; reaches for dangling ring; visually follows ball across table
4 mo.	Carries object to mouth
4–5 mo.	Recovers rattle from chest; holds two objects
5 mo.	Transfers object from hand to hand
5–6 mo.	Bangs in play; looks for object while sitting

6–12 months

6 mo.	Secures cube on sight; follows adult's movements across room; immediately fixates on small objects and stretches out to grasp them; retains rattle
6 1/2 mo.	Manipulates and examines an object; reaches for, grabs, and retains rattle
7 mo.	Pulls string to obtain an object
7 1/2–8 1/2 mo.	Grasps with thumb and finger
8–9 mo.	Persists in reaching for toy out of reach on table; shows hand preference, bangs spoon; searches in correct place for toys dropped within reach of hands; may find toy hidden under cup
10 mo.	Hits cup with spoon; crude release of object
10 1/2–11 mo.	Picks up raisin with thumb and forefinger; pincer grasp; pushes car along
11–12 mo.	Puts three or more objects in a container

12–18 months

Places one 2-inch block on top of another 2-inch block (in imitation)

Scribbles with a large crayon on large piece of paper

Turns 2-3 pages in a large book with cardboard pages while sitting in an adult's lap

Places three 1-inch cube blocks in a 6-inch diameter cup (in imitation)

Holds a pencil and makes a mark on a sheet of paper

Builds a 4-block tower with 2-inch cube blocks (in imitation)

18–24 months

Draws an arc on piece of unlined paper with a pencil after being shown how

Turns a doorknob that is within reach using both hands

Unscrews a lid put loosely on a small jar after being shown how

Places large pegs in a pegboard

Connects and takes apart a pop bead string of five beads

Zips and unzips a large-sized zipper after being shown how

FIGURE 5.6

The development of dendritic spreading. Note the increase in connectedness between neurons over the course of the first two years of life.

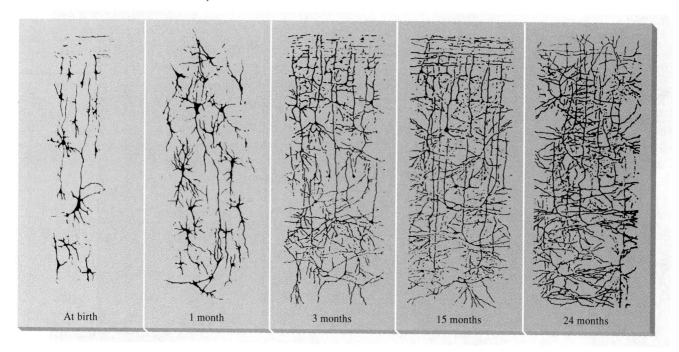

| At birth | 1 month | 3 months | 15 months | 24 months |

Infant States

To chart and understand the infant's development, developmentalists have constructed classifications of infants' states (Berg & Berg, 1987; Brown, 1964; Colombo, Moss, & Horowitz, 1989). "States" is an abbreviated term for states of consciousness, which refer to the level of awareness that characterizes the individual. One classification scheme describes seven infant states (Brown, 1964):

1. *Deep sleep.* The infant lies motionless with eyes closed, has regular breathing, makes no vocalization, and does not respond to outside stimulation.

2. *Regular sleep.* The infant moves very little, breathing might be raspy or involve wheezing, and respirations may be normal or move from normal to irregular.

3. *Disturbed sleep.* There is a variable amount of movement; the infant's eyelids are closed but might flutter; breathing is irregular; and there may be some squawks, sobs, and sighs.

4. *Drowsy.* The infant's eyes are open or partly open and appear glassy, there is little movement (although startles and free movement may occur), vocalizations are more regular than in disturbed sleep and some transitional sounds may be made.

5. *Alert activity.* This is the state most often viewed by parents as being awake. The infant's eyes are open and bright, a variety of free movements are shown, fretting may occur, skin may redden, and there may be irregular breathing when the infant feels tension.

6. *Alert and focused.* This kind of attention is often seen in older children but is unusual in the neonate. The child's eyes are open and bright. Some motor activity may occur, but it is integrated around a specific activity. This state may occur when focusing on a sound or visual stimulus.

7. *Inflexibly focused.* In this state, the infant is awake but does not react to external stimuli; two examples are sucking and wild crying. During wild crying, the infant may thrash about, but the eyes are closed as screams pour out.

Using classification schemes such as the one just described, researchers have identified many different aspects of infant development. One such aspect is the sleeping-waking cycle. When we were infants, sleep consumed more of our time than it does now. Newborns sleep for 16 to 17 hours a day, although some sleep more and others less. The range is from a low of about 10 hours to a high of about 21 hours (Parmalee, Wenner, & Schulz, 1964). The longest period of sleep is not always between 11 P.M. and 7 A.M. Although total sleep remains somewhat consistent for young infants, their sleep during the day does not always follow a rhythmic pattern. An infant might change from sleeping several long bouts of 7 or 8 hours to three or four shorter sessions only several hours in duration. By about 1 month of age, most infants have begun to sleep longer at night, and, by about 4 months of age, they usually have moved closer to adultlike sleep patterns, spending their longest span of sleep at night and their longest span of waking during the day (Coons & Guilleminault, 1984).

> *Sleep that knits up the ravelled sleave of care. . . .*
> *Balm of hurt minds, nature's second course.*
> *Chief nourisher in life's feast.*
>
> —William Shakespeare

Researchers are intrigued by the various forms of infant sleep. They are especially interested in **REM (rapid eye movement) sleep,** *a recurring sleep stage during which vivid dreams commonly occur among children and adults.* Most adults spend about one-fifth of their night in REM sleep, and REM sleep usually appears about 1 hour after non-REM sleep. However, about one-half of an infant's sleep is REM sleep, and infants often begin their sleep cycle with REM sleep rather than non-REM sleep. By the time infants reach 3 months of age, the percentage of time spent in REM sleep falls to about 40 percent and no longer does REM sleep begin the sleep cycle. The large amount of REM sleep may provide infants with added self-stimulation, since they spend less time awake than do older children. REM sleep also may promote the brain's development.

A special concern about infant sleep is **sudden infant death syndrome (SIDS),** *a condition that occurs when an infant stops breathing, usually during the night, and suddenly dies without apparent cause.* Approximately 13 percent of infant deaths are due to SIDS; between 10 days after birth and 1 year of age, SIDS results in more deaths than any other factor. While we do not know exactly what causes SIDS, infants who die from the condition reveal biological vulnerabilities early in their development, including a greater incidence of prematurity, low-birthweight, low Apgar scores, and respiratory problems (Barness & Gilbert-Barness, 1992; Buck & others, 1989; Woolsey, 1992).

Nutrition

Four-month-old Robert lives in Bloomington, Indiana, with his middle-class parents. He is well nourished and healthy. By contrast, 4-month-old Nikita lives in Ethiopia. Nikita and his parents live in impoverished conditions. Nikita is so poorly nourished that he has become emaciated and lies near death. The lives of Robert and Nikita reveal the vast diversity of nutritional status among today's children. Our coverage of infant nutrition begins with information about nutritional needs and eating behavior, then turns to the issue of breast- versus bottle-feeding, and concludes with an overview of malnutrition.

Nutritional Needs and Eating Behavior

The importance of adequate energy and nutrient intake consumed in a loving and supportive environment during the infant years cannot be overstated (Braithwaite, 1993; Pipes, 1988; Pridham & Van Riper, 1993). From birth to 1 year of age, human infants triple their weight and increase their length by 50 percent. Individual differences among infants in terms of their nutrient reserves, body composition, growth rates, and activity patterns make defining actual nutrient needs difficult. However, because parents need guidelines, nutritionists recommend that infants consume approximately 50 calories per day for each pound they weigh—more than twice an adult's requirement per pound.

Parents often want to know when to introduce new types of food. In the second half of the first year, human milk or formula continues to be the infant's primary nutritional source. The major change in feeding habits is the addition of solid foods to the infant's diet (Whaley & Wong, 1988). The one generally accepted rule is to introduce infant cereal as the first food because of its high iron content. Because of its benefit as a source of iron, infant cereal should be continued until the infant is about 18 months of age. The addition of other foods is arbitrary. A common sequence is strained fruits, followed by vegetables, and finally meats. At 6 months, foods such as a cracker or zwieback can be offered as a type of finger and teething food.

Weaning—the process of giving up one method of feeding for another—usually refers to relinquishing the breast or bottle for a cup. In Western cultures, this is often regarded as an important task for infants, being psychologically significant because the infant has to give up a major source of oral pleasure. There is no one time for weaning that is best for every infant, but most infants show signs of being ready for weaning in the second half of the first year. Weaning should be gradual by replacing one bottle- or breast-feeding at a time.

Some years ago, controversy surrounded the issue of whether a baby should be fed on demand or on a regular schedule. The famous behaviorist John Watson (1928) argued that scheduled feeding was superior because it increased the child's orderliness. An example of a recommended schedule for newborns was 4 ounces of formula every 6 hours. In recent years, demand feeding—in which the timing and amount of feeding are determined by the infant—has become more popular.

In the 1990s, we have become extremely nutrition conscious. Does the same type of nutrition that makes us healthy adults also make young infants healthy? For the answer to this question, turn to Explorations in Child Development 5.2.

Breast- Versus Bottle-Feeding

Human milk, or an alternative formula, is the baby's source of nutrients and energy for the first 4 to 6 months. For years, developmentalists and nutritionists have debated whether breast-feeding of an infant has substantial benefits over bottle-feeding. The growing consensus is that breast-feeding is better for the baby's health (Eiger, 1992; Worthington-Roberts, 1988). Breast-feeding provides milk that is clean and digestible and helps immunize the newborn from disease. Breastfed babies gain weight more rapidly than do bottle-fed babies. However, only about one-half of mothers nurse newborns, and even fewer continue to nurse their infants after several months. Mothers who work outside the home find it impossible to breastfeed their young infants for many months. Even though breast-feeding provides more ideal nutrition, some researchers argue that there is no long-term evidence of physiological or psychological harm to American infants when they are bottle-fed (Caldwell, 1964; Ferguson, Harwood, & Shannon, 1987; Forsyth, Leventhal, & McCarthy, 1985). Despite these researchers' claims that no long-term negative consequences of bottle-feeding have been documented in American children, the American Academy of Pediatrics, the majority of physicians and nurses, and two leading publications for parents—the *Infant Care Manual* and *Parents* magazine—endorse breast-feeding as having physiological and psychological benefits (Young, 1990).

EXPLORATIONS IN CHILD DEVELOPMENT 5.2

What's Good Food for an Adult Can Be Bad Food for a Baby

Some yuppie parents may not know the recipe for a healthy baby: whole milk and an occasional cookie, along with fruits, vegetables, and other foods. Some affluent, well-educated parents almost starve their babies by feeding them the lowfat, low-calorie diet they eat themselves. Diets designed for adult weight loss and prevention of heart disease may actually retard growth and development in babies. Fat is very important for babies. Nature's food—the mother's breast milk—is not low in fat or calories. No child under the age of 2 should be consuming skim milk.

In one investigation, seven cases were documented in which babies 7 to 22 months of age were unwittingly under-

What hazards might the current trends in diet foods and health preoccupation on the part of parents have when it comes to choosing foods for their infants?

nourished by their health-conscious parents (Lifshitz & others, 1987). In some instances, the parents had been fat themselves and were determined that their child was not going to be. The well-meaning parents substituted vegetables, skim milk, and other lowfat foods for what they called junk food. However, for infants, broccoli is not always a good substitute for a cookie. For growing infants, high-calorie, high-energy foods are part of a balanced diet.

Human milk, or an alternative formula, is a baby's source of nutrients for the first four to six months. The growing consensus is that breast-feeding is better for the baby's health, although controversy still swirls about the issue of breast- versus bottle-feeding.

There is a consensus among experts that breast-feeding is the preferred practice, especially in developing countries where inadequate nutrition and poverty are common. In 1991, the Institute of Medicine, part of the National Academy of Sciences, issued a report that women should be encouraged to breast-feed their infants exclusively for the first 4 to 6 months of life. According to the report, the benefits of breast-feeding are: protection against some gastrointestinal infections and food allergies for infants, and possible reduction of osteoporosis and breast cancer for mothers. Nonetheless, while the majority of experts recommend breast-feeding, the issue of breast-versus bottle-feeding continues to be hotly debated. Many parents, especially working mothers, are now following a sequence of breast-feeding in the first several months and bottle-feeding thereafter. This strategy allows the mother's natural milk to provide nutritional benefits to the infant early in development and permits mothers to return to work after several months. Working mothers are also increasingly using "pumping," in which they use a pump to extract breast milk that can be stored for later feeding of the infant when the mother is not present.

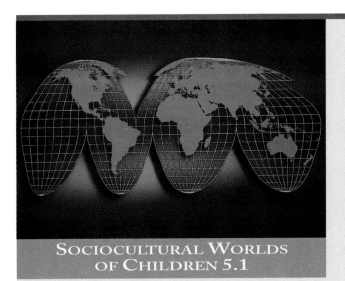

SOCIOCULTURAL WORLDS OF CHILDREN 5.1

Children Living Hungry in America

Harlingen, Texas, is a heavily Chicano city of approximately 40,000 near the Rio Grande. At Su Clinica ("Your Clinic"), which serves many Chicano residents, poverty and unemployment are evident in the waiting list of 800 families needing low-cost care. Many of the Chicanos working in Texas agriculture receive no health care benefits, and few make even the minimum wage. Farm workers usually get less than $1.50 an hour for working long days in the pesticide-infected fields. The infant mortality rate for the region is listed as good by the U.S. government, but this description is wrong. Many of the deaths

Many locations in the United States have impoverished families that have difficulty making ends meet and putting food on the table, including the ghettos of many large American cities.

are not counted. A baby dies and is buried. People outside the family seldom know. Many infants and young children experience growth problems because they do not get enough to eat. This is not unique to Harlingen, Texas; many other locations in the United States have their share of impoverished families who have difficulty making ends meet and putting food on the table. Hunger and poverty are seen in the children of poor Mississippi tenant farmers, in the children of laid-off coal miners in West Virginia, in neglected children in the ghettos of New York and Chicago, and in the increasing number of homeless families across the nation. In many instances, these children are the victims of silent undernutrition, less dramatic than in Africa or Bangladesh, but no less real (Brown & Pizer, 1987).

Critical Thinking

If and when you become a parent, what considerations would you have about the nutrition your infant gets? How important do you believe breast-feeding is for infant development? Explain.

Malnutrition in Infancy

Marasmus *is a wasting away of body tissues in the infant's first year, caused by severe protein-calorie deficiency.* The infant becomes grossly underweight and its muscles atrophy. The main cause of marasmus is early weaning from breast milk to inadequate nutrients such as unsuitable and unsanitary cow's milk formula. Something that looks like milk, but is not, usually a form of tapioca or rice, also may be used. In many of the world's developing countries, mothers used to breast-feed their infants for at least two years. To become more modern, they stopped breast-feeding much earlier and replaced it with bottle-feeding. Comparisons of breast-fed and bottle-fed infants in such countries as Afghanistan, Haiti, Ghana, and Chile document that the rate of infant death is much greater among bottle-fed than breast-fed infants, with bottle-fed infants sometimes dying at a rate five times higher than breast-fed infants (Grant, 1992).

Even if not fatal, severe and lengthy malnutrition is detrimental to physical, cognitive, and social development (Mortimer, 1992; Super, Herrera, & Mora, 1990). In some cases, even moderate malnutrition can produce subtle difficulties in development.

In one investigation, two groups of extremely malnourished 1-year-old South African infants were studied (Bayley, 1970). The children in one group were given adequate nourishment during the next six years; no intervention took place in the lives of the other group. After the seventh year, the poorly nourished group of children performed much worse on tests of intelligence than did the adequately nourished group. In yet another investigation, the diets of rural Guatemalan infants were associated with their social development at the time they entered elementary school (Barrett, Radke-Yarrow, & Klein, 1982). Children whose mothers had been given nutritious supplements during pregnancy and who themselves had been given more nutritious, high-calorie foods in their first two years of life were more active, more involved, more helpful with their peers, less anxious, and happier than their counterparts, who were not given nutritional supplements. The undernourished Guatemalan infants were only mildly undernourished in infancy, suggesting how important it is for parents to be attentive to the nutritional needs of their infants. Recently, other researchers have demonstrated that nutritional supplements early in development can improve the cognitive development of malnourished children (Engle, 1991; Super, Herrera, & Mora, 1991). Much of our discussion of malnutrition has focused on developing countries, but hunger is also a problem in some areas of the United States. To read about children living hungry in America, turn to Sociocultural Worlds of Children 5.1.

CONCEPT TABLE 5.1

Physical Growth and Development in Infancy

Concept	Processes/Related Ideas	Characteristics/Description
Reflexes	Their nature	The newborn is no longer viewed as a passive, empty-headed organism. Newborns are limited physically, though, and reflexes—automatic movements—govern the newborn's behavior.
	Sucking	For infants, sucking is an important means of obtaining nutrition, as well as a pleasurable, soothing activity. Nonnutritive sucking is of interest to researchers because it provides a means of evaluating attention.
Cephalocaudal and proximodistal patterns	Their nature	The cephalocaudal pattern is growth from the top down; the proximodistal pattern is growth from the center out.
Height and weight	Their nature	The average North American newborn is 20 inches long and weighs 7 1/2 pounds. Infants grow about 1 inch per month during the first year and nearly triple their weight by their first birthday. Infants' rate of growth is slower in the second year.
Gross and fine motor skills	Gross motor skills	Gross motor skills involve large muscle activities such as moving one's arms and walking. A number of gross motor milestones occur in infancy, among them walking at an average of 12 to 13 months.
	Fine motor skills	Fine motor skills involve more finely tuned movements than gross motor skills, and include such skills as finger dexterity. A number of fine motor milestones occur in infancy, among them the development of reaching and grasping skills.
States	Classification	Researchers have put together different classification systems; one involved seven infant state categories, including deep sleep, drowsy, alert and focused, and inflexibly focused.

Toilet Training

Being toilet trained is a physical and motor skill that is expected in the North American culture to be attained by 3 years of age (Charlesworth, 1987). By the age of 3, 84 percent of children are dry throughout the day and 66 percent are dry throughout the night. The ability to control elimination depends both on muscular maturation and on motivation. Children must be able to control their muscles to eliminate at the appropriate time and they must also want to eliminate in the toilet or potty rather than in their pants.

Currently, there is a trend toward beginning toilet training later than in the past. Many of today's parents begin the toilet training of their toddlers at about 20 months to 2 years. Developmentalists now realize that cognitive maturity needs to be added to muscular maturation and motivation for appropriate toilet training to take place. Toddlers need to be able to understand instructions and the need for accomplishing the

task. Developmentalists also recommend that toilet training be accomplished in a warm, relaxed, supportive manner.

At this point we have discussed a number of ideas about infants' reflexes, cephalocaudal and proximodistal sequences, height and weight, gross and fine motor skills, the brain, infant states, nutrition, and health. A summary of these ideas is presented in Concept Table 5.1. Next, we turn our attention to the fascinating sensory and perceptual worlds of infants.

SENSORY AND PERCEPTUAL DEVELOPMENT

At the beginning of this chapter, you read about how newborns come into the world equipped with sensory capacities. What are sensation and perception? Can a newborn see, and, if so, what can it perceive? What about the other senses—hearing, smell, taste, touch, and pain? What are they like in the newborn and

Concept	Processes/Related Ideas	Characteristics/Description
	The sleeping-waking cycle	Newborns usually sleep 16 to 17 hours a day. By 4 months, they approach adultlike sleeping patterns. REM sleep, during which children and adults are most likely to dream, occurs much more in early infancy than in childhood and adulthood. The high percentage of REM sleep—about half of neonatal sleep—may be a self-stimulatory device, or it may promote brain development. Sudden infant death syndrome (SIDS) is a condition that occurs when an infant stops breathing and suddenly dies without apparent cause.
Nutrition	Nutritional needs and eating behavior	Infants need to consume approximately 50 calories per day for each pound they weigh. A major change in the second half of the first year is the introduction of solid foods; in the first 6 months, human milk, or an alternative formula, is the baby's source of nutrition.
	Breast- versus bottle-feeding	The growing consensus is that breast-feeding is superior to bottle-feeding, but the increase in working mothers has meant fewer breast-fed babies. A current trend is for working mothers to breast-feed infants in the first several months to build up the infant's immune system, then bottle-feed after they have returned to work.
	Malnutrition	Severe infant malnutrition is still prevalent in many parts of the world. Severe protein-calorie deficiency can cause marasmus, a wasting away of body tissues. It is mainly caused by early weaning from breast milk. Even if not fatal, severe and lengthy malnutrition is detrimental to physical, cognitive, and social development.
Toilet training	Its nature	Being toilet trained is a physical and motor skill that is expected to be attained by 3 years of age in the North American culture. Currently, there is a trend toward beginning toilet training later than in the past; many of today's parents begin toilet training their toddlers at about 20 months to 2 years.

how do they develop in infancy? What kind of visual, auditory, and tactile stimulation is appropriate for infants? These are among the intriguing questions we will now explore.

What Are Sensation and Perception?

How does a newborn know that her mother's skin is soft rather than rough? How does a 5-year-old know what color his hair is? How does an 8-year-old know that summer is warmer than winter? How does a 10-year-old know that a firecracker is louder than a cat's meow? Infants and children "know" these things because of their senses. All information comes to the infant through the senses. Without vision, hearing, touch, taste, smell, and other senses, the infant's brain would be isolated from the world; the infant would live in dark silence, a tasteless, colorless, feelingless void.

Sensation *occurs when information contacts sensory receptors—the eyes, ears, tongue, nostrils, and skin.* The sensation of hearing occurs when waves of pulsating air are collected by the outer ear and transmitted through the bones of the inner ear to the auditory nerve. The sensation of vision occurs as rays of light contact the two eyes and become focused on the retina. **Perception** *is the interpretation of what is sensed.* The information about physical events that contacts the ears may be interpreted as musical sounds, for example. The physical energy transmitted to the retina may be interpreted as a particular color, pattern, or shape.

Visual Perception

How do we see? Anyone who has ever taken pictures while on vacation appreciates the miracle of perception. The camera is no match for it. Consider a favorite scenic spot that you visited and photographed some time in the past. Compare your memory of this spot to your snapshot. Although your memory may be faulty, there is little doubt that the richness of your perceptual experience is not captured in the picture. The sense of depth that you felt at this spot probably is not conveyed by the

FIGURE 5.7

Fantz's experiment on infants' visual perception. (*a*) Infants 2 to 3 months old preferred to look at some stimuli more than others. In Fantz's experiment, infants preferred to look at patterns rather than at color or brightness. For example, they looked longer at a face, a piece of printed matter, or a bull's eye than at red, yellow, or white discs. (*b*) Fantz used a "looking chamber" to study infants' perception of stimuli.

(*a*) Adapted from "The Origin of Form Perception" by R. L. Fantz. Copyright © 1961 by Scientific American, Inc. All rights reserved.

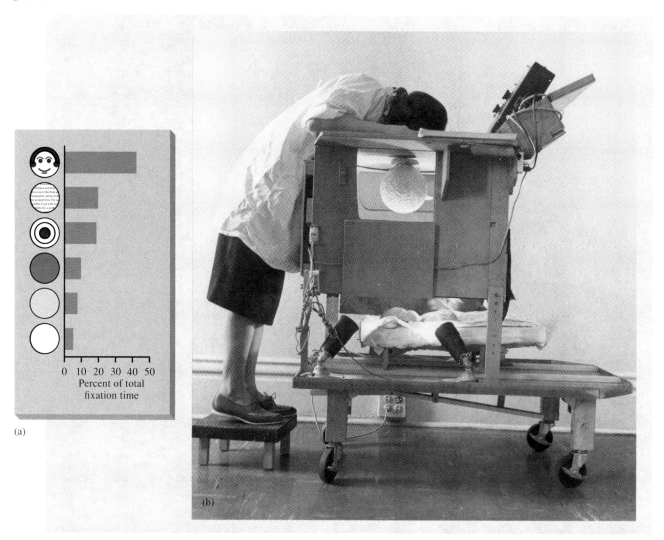

(a)

(b)

snapshot. Neither is the subtlety of the colors you perceived nor the intricacies of textures and shapes. Human vision is complex, and its development is complex too.

The Newborn's Vision

Psychologist William James (1890) called the newborn's perceptual world a blooming, buzzing confusion. Was James right? A century later we can safely say that he was wrong. Infant's perception of visual information is *much* more advanced than previously thought (Bahrick, 1992; Bower, 1989, 1993).

Our tour of visual perception begins with the pioneering work of Robert Fantz (1963). Fantz placed infants in a "looking chamber," which has two visual displays on the ceiling above the infant's head. An experimenter viewed the infant's eyes by looking through a peephole. If the infant was fixating on one of

the displays, the experimenter could see the display's reflection in the infant's eyes. This allowed the experimenter to determine how long the infant looked at each display. In figure 5.7, you can see Fantz's looking chamber and the results of his experiment. The infants preferred to look at patterns rather than at color or brightness. For example, they preferred to look at a face, a piece of printed matter, or a bull's eye longer than at red, yellow, or white discs. In another experiment, Fantz found that younger infants—only 2 days old—looked longer at patterned stimuli, such as faces and concentric circles, than at red, white, or yellow discs. Based on these results, pattern perception likely has an innate basis, or at least is acquired after only minimal environmental experience. The newborn's visual world is not the blooming, buzzing confusion William James imagined.

Critical Thinking

Other than moving a large object toward a newborn's head to see if the newborn responds to it, can you think of other techniques that could be used to determine whether a newborn can see?

Just how well can infants see? The newborn's vision is estimated to be 20/200 to 20/600 on the well-known Snellen chart that you are tested with when you have your eyes examined (Haith, 1991). This is about 10 to 30 times lower than normal adult vision (20/20). By 6 months of age, however, vision is 20/100 or better (Banks & Salapatek, 1983).

Infants' Perception of Faces

The human face is perhaps the most important visual pattern for the newborn to perceive. The infant masters a sequence of steps in progressing toward full perceptual appreciation of the face (Gibson, 1969). At about 3½ weeks, the infant is fascinated with the eyes, perhaps because the infant notices simple perceptual features such as dots, angles, and circles. At 1 to 2 months of age, the infant notices and perceives contour. At 2 months and older, the infant begins to differentiate facial features; the eyes are distinguished from other parts of the face, the mouth is noticed, and movements of the mouth draw attention to it. By 5 months of age, the infant has detected other facial features—its plasticity, its solid, three-dimensional surface, the oval shape of the head, and the orientation of the eyes and the mouth. Beyond 6 months of age, the infant distinguishes familiar faces from unfamiliar faces—mother from stranger, masks from real faces, and so on.

Depth Perception

How early can infants perceive depth? To investigate this question, infant perception researchers Eleanor Gibson and Richard Walk (1960) conducted a classic experiment. They constructed a miniature cliff with a drop-off covered by glass. The motivation for this experiment happened when Gibson was eating a picnic lunch on the edge of the Grand Canyon. She wondered whether an infant looking over the canyon's rim would perceive the dangerous drop-off and back up. In their laboratory, Gibson and Walk placed infants on the edge of a visual cliff and had their mothers coax them to crawl onto the glass (see figure 5.8). Most infants would not crawl out on the glass, choosing instead to remain on the shallow side, indicating that they could perceive depth. However, because the 6- to 14-month-old infants had extensive visual experience, this research did not answer the question of whether depth perception is innate.

Exactly how early in life does depth perception develop? Since younger infants do not crawl, this question is difficult to answer. Research with 2- to 4-month-old infants shows differences in heart rate when they are placed directly on the deep side of the visual cliff instead of on the shallow side (Campos, Langer, & Krowitz, 1970). However, an alternative

FIGURE 5.8

Examining infants' depth perception on the visual cliff. The apparatus consists of a board laid across a sheet of heavy glass, with a patterned material directly beneath the glass on one side and several feet below it on the other. Placed on the center board, the child crawls to its mother across the "shallow" side. Called from the "deep" side, the child pats the glass but, despite this tactual evidence that the cliff is a solid surface, the child refuses to cross over to the mother.

interpretation is that young infants respond to differences in some visual characteristics of the deep and shallow cliffs, with no actual knowledge of depth.

Hearing

What is the nature of hearing in newborns? Can the fetus hear? What types of auditory stimulation should be used with infants at different points in the first year? We examine each of these questions.

Immediately after birth, infants can hear, although their sensory thresholds are somewhat higher than those of adults (Trehub & others, 1991). That is, a stimulus must be louder to be heard by a newborn than by an adult. Also, in one recent study, as infants aged from 8 to 28 weeks, they became more

FIGURE 5.9

(*a*) Pregnant mothers read *The Cat in the Hat* to their fetuses during the last few months of pregnancy. (*b*) When the babies were born, they preferred listening to a recording of their mothers reading *The Cat in the Hat*, as evidenced by their sucking on a nipple that produced this recording.

(a)

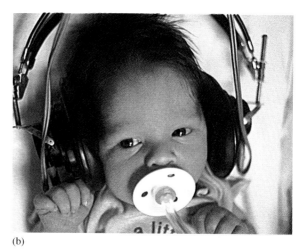

(b)

proficient at localizing sounds (Morrongiello, Fenwick, & Chance, 1990). Not only can newborns hear, but the possibility has been raised that the fetus can hear as it nestles within its mother's womb. Let's examine this possibility further.

The fetus can hear sounds in the last few months of pregnancy: the mother's voice, music, and so on. Given that the fetus can hear sounds, two psychologists wanted to find out if listening to Dr. Seuss' classic story *The Cat in the Hat*, while still in the mother's womb, would produce a preference for hearing the story after birth (DeCasper & Spence, 1986). Sixteen pregnant women read *The Cat in the Hat* or a story with a different rhyme and pace, *The King, the Mice, and the Cheese*, to their fetuses twice a day over the last 6 weeks of their pregnancies. When the babies were born, they were given a choice of listening to each story by varying their sucking rate. Sucking at one rate (slowly, for example) resulted in their hearing a recording of one story. Sucking at another rate resulted in a recording of the other story. The newborns preferred listening to *The Cat in the Hat*, which they had heard frequently as a fetus (see figure 5.9).

Two important conclusions can be drawn from this investigation. First, it reveals how ingenious scientists have become at assessing the development not only of infants but of fetuses as well, in this case discovering a way to "interview" newborn babies who cannot yet talk. Second, it reveals the remarkable ability of an infant's brain to learn even before birth.

Touch and Pain

Do newborns respond to touch? What activities can adults engage in that involve tactile (touch) stimulation at various points in the infant's development? Can newborns feel pain?

Touch in the Newborn

Newborns do respond to touch. A touch to the cheek produces a turning of the head, whereas a touch to the lips produces sucking movements. An important ability that develops in infancy is to connect information about vision with information about touch. One-year-olds clearly can do this and it appears that 6-month-olds can too (Acredolo & Hake, 1982). Whether still younger infants can coordinate vision and touch is yet to be determined.

Pain

If and when you have a son and need to consider whether he should be circumcised, the issue of an infant's pain perception probably will become important to you. Circumcision is usually performed on young boys about the third day after birth. Will your young son experience pain if he is circumcised when he is 3 days old? Increased crying and fussing occur during the circumcision procedure, suggesting that 3-day-old infants experience pain (Gunnar, Malone, & Fisch, 1987; Porter, Porges, & Marshall, 1988).

In the investigation by Megan Gunnar and her colleagues (1987), the healthy newborn's ability to cope with stress was evaluated. The newborn infant males cried intensely during the circumcision, indicating that it was stressful. The researchers pointed out that it is rather remarkable that the newborn infant does not suffer serious consequences from the surgery. Rather, the circumcised infant displays amazing resiliency and ability to cope. Within several minutes after the surgery, the infant can nurse and interact in a normal manner with his mother. And, if allowed, the newly circumcised newborn drifts into a deep sleep that seems to serve as a coping mechanism. In this experiment, the time spent in deep sleep was greater in the 60 to 240 minutes after the circumcision than before it.

FIGURE 5.10

Newborns' preference for the smell of their mother's breast pad. In the experiment by MacFarlane (1975), 6-day-old infants preferred to smell their mother's breast pad over a clean one that had never been used, but 2-day-old infants did not show this preference, indicating that this odor preference requires several days of experience to develop.

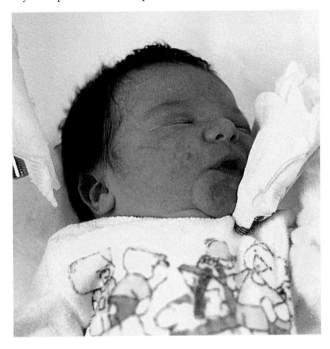

For many years, doctors have performed operations on newborns without anesthesia. The accepted medical practice was followed because of the dangers of anesthesia and the supposition that newborns do not feel pain. Recently, as researchers have convincingly demonstrated that newborns can feel pain, the longstanding practice of operating on newborns without anesthesia is being challenged.

Smell

Newborn infants can differentiate odors. For example, by the expressions on their faces, they seem to indicate that they like the way vanilla and strawberry smell but do not like the way rotten eggs and fish smell (Steiner, 1979). In one investigation, young infants who were breast-fed showed a clear preference for smelling their mother's breast pad when they were 6 days old (MacFarlane, 1975) (see figure 5.10). However, when they were 2 years old, they did not show this preference (compared to a clean breast pad), indicating that they require several days of experience to recognize this odor.

Taste

Sensitivity to taste may be present before birth. When saccharin was added to the amniotic fluid of a near-term fetus, increased swallowing was observed (Windle, 1940). Sensitivity to sweetness is clearly present in the newborn. When sucks on a nipple are rewarded with a sweetened solution, the amount of sucking increases (Lipsitt & others, 1976). In another

investigation, newborns showed a smilelike expression after being given a sweetened solution but pursed their lips after being given a sour solution (Steiner, 1979). And in one recent study 1- to 3-day-old infants cried much less when they were given sucrose through a pacifier (Smith, Fillion, & Blass, 1990).

Intermodal Perception

Are young infants so competent that they can relate and integrate information through several senses? **Intermodal perception** *is the ability to relate and integrate information about two or more sensory modalities, such as vision and hearing.* An increasing number of developmentalists believe that young infants experience related visual and auditory worlds (Bahrick, 1988, 1993; Gibson & Spelke, 1983; Rose & Ruff, 1987). To learn more about intermodal perception, turn to Explorations in Child Development 5.3. Keep in mind, though, that intermodal perception in young infants remains a controversial concept. For example, in one recent investigation of 6-month-old infants, the auditory sense dominated the visual sense, restricting intermodal perception (Lewkowicz, 1988).

The claim that the young infant can relate information from several senses has been addressed by two important theoretical perspectives. The **direct perception view** *states that infants are born with intermodal perception abilities that enable them to display intermodal perception early in infancy.* In this view, infants only have to attend to the appropriate sensory information; they do not have to build up an internal representation of the information through months of sensorimotor experiences. In contrast, the **constructivist view** *advocated by Piaget states that the main perceptual abilities—visual, auditory, and tactile, for example—are completely uncoordinated at birth and that young infants do not have intermodal perception.* According to Piaget, only through months of sensorimotor interaction with the world is intermodal perception possible. For Piaget, infant perception involves a representation of the world that builds up as the infant constructs an image of experiences.

Although the intermodal perception and direct perception/constructivist arguments have not completely been settled, we now know that young infants know a lot more than we used to think they did (Bertenthal, 1993; Bower, 1989, 1993; Kaye, 1993; Lewkowicz, 1993; Mandler, 1990, in press, a, b). They see and hear more than we used to think was possible.

Critical Thinking

Increasingly, developmentalists have been surprised by the early competencies of newborns and young infants. Are we going too far in believing that newborns and young infants are competent in dealing with their world, or are they really as sophisticated as the new wave of research seems to suggest?

At this point, we have discussed a number of ideas about perceptual development in infancy. A summary of these ideas is presented in Concept Table 5.2. In the next chapter, we will discuss the nature of physical development in childhood and puberty.

EXPLORATIONS IN CHILD DEVELOPMENT 5.3

Yellow Kangaroos, Gray Donkeys, Thumps, Gongs, and 4–Month–Old Infants

Imagine yourself playing basketball or tennis. There are obviously many visual inputs: the ball coming and going, other players moving around, and so on. However, there also are many auditory inputs: the sound of the ball bouncing or being hit, and the grunts, groans, and curses emitted by you and others. There is also good correspondence between much of the visual and auditory information:

When you see the ball bounce, you hear a bouncing sound; when a player leaps, you hear a groan.

We live in a world of objects and events that can be seen, heard, and felt. When mature observers look at and listen to an event simultaneously, they experience a unitary episode. All of this is so commonplace that it scarcely seems worth mentioning, but consider the task of a very young infant with little practice at perceiving. Can she put vision and sound together as precisely as adults?

To test intermodal perception, Elizabeth Spelke (1979) performed three experiments with the following structure. Two simple films were shown side-by-side in front of a 4-month-old infant. One film showed a yellow kangaroo bouncing up and down, and the other showed a gray donkey bouncing up and down. There also was an auditory sound track—a repeating thump or gong sound. A number of measures assessed the infant's tendency to look at one film instead of the other.

In Experiment 1, the animal in one of the films bounced at a slower rate than the animal in the other. The sound track was synchronized either with the film of the slow-bouncing animal or with the film of the fast-bouncing animal. Infants' first looks were toward the film that was specified by the sound track. Experiments 2 and 3 explored two components of the relation between the sound track and the matching film: common tempo and simultaneity of sounds and bounces. The findings indicated that the infants were sensitive to both of these components.

Spelke's clever demonstration suggests that infants only 4 months old do not experience a world of unrelated visual and auditory dimensions; they can perceive them as unified.

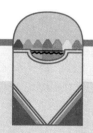

PERSPECTIVES ON PARENTING AND EDUCATION

The Right Stimulation and Suggested Activities for Visual and Tactile Stimulation of Infants

Some parents don't interact with their infants often enough and don't provide them with adequate experiences to stimulate their senses. Other well-meaning parents may actually overstimulate their baby.

Infants do need a certain amount of stimulation to develop their perceptual skills. Infants should not be unattended for long stretches of time in barren environments. Many babies born into impoverished families, as well as babies in

day care centers that are like "warehouses" where there are many babies per caregiver and an absence of appropriate stimuli and toys, are at risk for receiving inadequate sensory stimulation.

Caregivers should play with infants, give them toys, and periodically provide them with undivided attention during the course of a day. Some infant experts, however, worry that parents who want to have a "superbaby" may give their infant too much stimulation, which can cause

the infant to become confused, irritated, or withdraw (Bower, 1977; White & Held, 1966). Such parents likely place too much pressure on the infant's developing sensory systems and cause more damage than good.

In thinking about the "right" amount and type of stimulation, it is important to recognize that what is "right" may differ from one baby to another. Some infants have a low threshold for sensory stimulation—that is, they can't

CONCEPT TABLE 5.2

Sensory and Perceptual Development in Infancy

Concept	Processes/Related Ideas	Characteristics/Description
What are sensation and perception?	Sensation	When information contacts sensory receptors—eyes, ears, tongue, nostrils, and skin—sensation occurs.
	Perception	Perception is the interpretation of what is sensed.
Visual perception	The newborn's visual world	William James said it is a blooming, buzzing confusion; he was wrong. The newborn's perception is more advanced than we previously thought.
	Visual preferences	Fantz's research—showing how infants prefer striped to solid patches—demonstrated that newborns can see.
	Quality of vision	The newborn is about 20/600 on the Snellen chart; by 6 months, vision has improved to at least 20/100.
	The human face	It is an important visual pattern for the newborn. The infant gradually masters a sequence of steps in perceiving the human face.
	Depth perception	A classic study by Gibson and Walk (1960) demonstrated, through the use of a visual cliff, that 6-month-old infants can perceive depth.
Hearing	Hearing in the fetus and newborn	The fetus can hear several weeks before birth; immediately after birth, newborns can hear, although their sensory threshold is higher than adults.
Touch and pain	Touch in the newborn	Newborns do respond to touch.
	Pain	Newborns can feel pain. Research on circumcision shows that 3-day-old males experience pain and can adapt to stress.
Smell and taste	Their nature	Both of these senses are present in the newborn.
Intermodal perception	Its nature	Considerable interest focuses on the infant's ability to relate information across perceptual modalities; the coordination and integration of perceptual information across two or more modalities—such as the visual and auditory senses—is called intermodal perception. Research indicates that infants as young as 4 months of age have intermodal perception. The direct perception and constructivist views are two important views of perception that make predictions about intermodal perception.

handle a heavy load of stimulation. They become overwhelmed and cry and fuss when they are frequently exposed to sensory stimulation. Other infants have a high threshold for sensory stimulation—that is, they like a lot of sensory stimulation and can benefit from it (Korner, 1971; Zuckerman, 1979).

In sum, it is important for parents to be sensitive to their infant's stimulation needs and monitor when the infant "senses" too little or too much stimulation. Following are some suggested activities for visual and tactile stimulation of infants at different developmental levels (Whaley & Wong, 1988):

Suggested Visual Stimulation Activities

Following are appropriate activities for adults to engage in that involve the visual stimulation of infants at various points during the first year:

Birth–1 month: Look at infant within close range.

Hang bright, shiny object within 8 to 10 inches of infant's face and in midline.

2–3 months: Provide bright objects.

Make room bright with pictures or mirrors on wall.

Take infant to different rooms while doing chores.

Place infant in infant seat for vertical view of environment.

4–6 months: Position infant to see in mirror.

Give brightly colored toys to infant to grasp (toys that are small enough to grasp).

6–9 months: Give infant large toys with bright colors, movable parts, and noisemakers.

Place infant in front of mirror; infant enjoys patting mirror, making sounds at image.

Infant enjoys peekaboo, especially hiding face in towel.

Make funny faces to encourage imitation.

Give infant paper to tear and crumble.

Give infant ball of yarn or string to pull apart.

9–12 months: Show infant large pictures in books.

Take infant to places where there are animals, many people, different objects (for example, a shopping center).

Demonstrate building a two-block tower.

Suggested Tactile Stimulation Activities

Following are appropriate activities for adults to engage in that involve the infant's sense of touch:

Birth–1 month: Hold, caress, and cuddle the infant.

Keep the infant warm.

The infant may like to be swaddled.

At 4–6 months, infants can be positioned to see in a mirror and they can be given brightly colored toys to grasp (toys that are small enough to grasp).

2–3 months: Caress the infant while bathing and at diaper change.

Comb the infant's hair with a soft brush.

4–6 months: Give the infant soft squeeze toys of various textures.

Allow the infant to splash in bath.

Place the infant nude on a soft furry rug and move extremities.

6–9 months: Let the infant play with various textures of fabric.

Have a bowl with foods of different size (at least one inch in diameter) and texture to feel.

Let the infant "catch" running water.

Give wad of sticky tape to manipulate.

9–12 months: Give the infant finger foods of different textures that are at least one inch in diameter.

Let the infant mess and squash food.

Let the infant feel cold (ice cube) or warm objects, and tell the infant the temperature of each.

Let the infant feel a breeze blowing (such as from a fan). ■

CONCLUSIONS

It once was believed that the newborn infant was virtually an empty-headed organism that experienced the world as blooming, buzzing confusion. Today, child developmentalists believe the young infant has far more advanced capabilities.

In this chapter, you initially learned how newborns can be studied, and then read about physical growth and development in infancy. Among the topics you studied were the nature of the infant's reflexes, cephalocaudal and proximodistal sequences, height and weight gains, gross and fine motor skills, the development of the brain, infant states, nutrition, including the controversial issue of breast- versus bottle-feeding, and toilet training. Then, you learned about the nature of sensation and perception, how the infant's visual perception changes, as well as what the infant's hearing, touch and pain, smell, and taste are like. You also read about the infant's intermodal perception abilities, as well as the right stimulation for infants. Remember that you can obtain a summary of the entire chapter by again reading the two concept tables on pages 146 and 153.

Physical development, of course, is not just confined to infancy. In the next chapter, we explore physical development in childhood and adolescence.

KEY TERMS

sucking reflex   Newborns' built-in reaction of automatically sucking an object placed in the mouth. The sucking reflex enables them to get nourishment before they have associated a nipple with food. (135)

rooting reflex   A newborn's built-in reaction that occurs when the infant's cheek is stroked or the side of the mouth is touched. In response, the infant turns its head toward the side that was touched in an apparent effort to find something to suck. (135)

Moro reflex   A neonatal startle response that occurs in reaction to a sudden, intense noise or movement. When startled, the newborn arches its back, throws its head back, and flings out its arms and legs. Then the newborn rapidly closes its arms and legs to the center of its body. (135)

grasping reflex   A neonatal reflex that occurs when something touches an infant's palms. The infant responds by grasping tightly. (135)

nonnutritive sucking   Sucking behavior unrelated to the infant's feeding. (135)

cephalocaudal pattern   The sequence in which the greatest growth occurs at the top—the head—with growth in size, weight, and feature differentiation gradually working from top to bottom. (135)

proximodistal pattern   The sequence in which growth starts at the center of the body and moves toward the extremities. (135)

gross motor skills   Motor skills that involve large muscle activities, such as walking. (137)

fine motor skills   Motor skills that involve more finely tuned movements, such as finger dexterity. (137)

REM (rapid eye movement) sleep   A recurring sleep stage during which vivid dreams commonly occur among children and adults. (143)

sudden infant death syndrome (SIDS)   A condition that occurs when an infant stops breathing, usually during the night, and suddenly dies without apparent cause. (143)

marasmus   A wasting away of body tissues in an infant's first year, caused by a severe protein-calorie deficiency. (145)

sensation   Information that contacts the sensory receptors (eyes, ears, tongue, nostrils, and skin). (147)

perception   The interpretation of what is sensed. (147)

intermodal perception   The ability to relate and integrate information about two or more sensory modalities, such as vision and hearing. (151)

direct perception view   The view that infants are born with intermodal perception abilities that enable them to display intermodal perception early in infancy. Infants have to attend only to the appropriate sensory information; they do not have to build up an internal representation of the information through months of sensory experiences. (151)

constructivist view   Piaget's view that the main perceptual abilities are completely uncoordinated at birth and that infants do not have intermodal perception. Infant perception involves a representation of the world that builds up as the infant constructs an image of experience. (151)

SUGGESTED READINGS

Allen, K. E., & Marotz, L. (1989). *Developmental profiles. Birth-to-Six.* Albany, NY: Delmar. This handbook provides a brief, but comprehensive guide to the development of young children from birth to 6 years of age.

Brazelton, T. B. (1992). *Touchstones.* America's baby doctor of the 1990s, T. Berry Brazelton, describes the power of touch with babies and provides many helpful suggestions for parents.

Caplan, F. (1981). *The first twelve months of life.* New York: Bantam. This easy-to-read, well-written account of each of the first 12 months of life includes extensive information about motor milestones.

Leach, P. (1989). *Your baby and child: From birth to age five.* New York: Knopf. A classic guide to child care and development from birth to age 5, with more than 625 illustrations; includes many details about the physical development of infants.

Four Dancers, 1899,
Edgar Degas (Detail)

6

Physical Development in Childhood and Puberty

That energy which makes a child hard to manage is the energy which afterward makes him a manager of life.

—Henry Ward Beecher, Proverbs from Plymouth Pulpit, 1887

Only child life is real life.

—George Orwell

IMAGES OF CHILDREN

Training Children for the Olympics in China

Standing on the balance beam at a sports school in Beijing, China, 6-year-old Zhang Liyin stretches her arms outward as she gets ready to perform a backflip. She wears the bright-red gymnastic suit of the elite—a suit given to only the best ten girls in her class of 6- to 8-year-olds. But her face wears a dreadful expression; she can't drum up enough confidence to do the flip. Maybe it is because she has had a rough week; a purple bruise decorates one leg, and a nasty gash disfigures the other. Her coach, a woman in her twenties, makes Zhang jump from the beam and escorts her to the high bar, where she is instructed to hang for three minutes. If Zhang falls, she must pick herself up and try again. But she does not fall, and she is escorted back to the beam, where her coach puts her through another tedious routine.

Zhang attends the sports school in the afternoon. The sports school is a privilege given to only 260,000 of China's 200 million students of elementary to college age. The Communist party has decided that sports is one avenue China can pursue to prove that China has arrived in the modern world. The sports schools designed to produce Olympic champions were the reason for China's success in recent Olympics. These schools are the only road to Olympic stardom in China. There are precious few neighborhood playgrounds. And for every 3.5 million people, there is only one gymnasium.

Many of the students who attend the sports schools in the afternoon live and study at the schools as well. Only a few attend a normal school and then come to a sports school in the afternoon. Because of her young age, Zhang stays at

home during the mornings and goes to the sports school from noon until 6 P.M. A part-timer like Zhang can stay enrolled until she no longer shows potential to move up to the next step. Any child who seems to lack potential is asked to leave.

Zhang was playing in a kindergarten class when a coach from a sports school spotted her. She was selected because of her broad shoulders, narrow hips, straight legs, symmetrical limbs, open-minded attitude, vivaciousness, and outgoing personality. If Zhang continues to show progress, she could be asked to move to full-time next year. At age 7, she would then go to school there and live in a dorm six days a week. If she becomes extremely competent at gymnastics, Zhang could be moved to Shishahai, where the elite gymnasts train and compete (Reilly, 1988).

The training of future Olympians in the sports schools of China. Six-year-old Zhang Liyin (third from the left) *hopes someday to become an Olympic gymnastics champion. Attending the sports school is considered an outstanding privilege; only 260,000 of China's 200 million children are given this opportunity.*

PREVIEW

Later in the chapter, we will discuss further information about children's sports and physical fitness in middle and late childhood. Our coverage of children's development in this chapter will also focus on physical development in early childhood; physical development in middle and late childhood; children's health, nutrition, and exercise; puberty; adolescent sexuality; and some adolescent problems and disorders.

PHYSICAL DEVELOPMENT IN EARLY CHILDHOOD

Remember from chapter 5 that an infant's growth in the first year is extremely rapid and follows cephalocaudal and proximodistal patterns. At a point around their first birthday, most infants begin to walk. During an infant's second year, the growth rate begins to slow down, but both gross and fine motor skills progress rapidly. The infant develops a sense of mastery through increased proficiency in walking and running. Improvement in fine motor skills—such as being able to turn the pages of a book one at a time—also contributes to the infant's sense of mastery in the second year. The growth rate continues to slow down in early childhood; otherwise, we would be a species of giants.

Height and Weight

The average child grows 2½ inches in height and gains between 5 and 7 pounds a year during early childhood. As the preschool child grows older, the percentage of increase in height and weight decreases with each additional year. Figure 6.1 shows the average height and weight of children as they age from 2 to 6 years. Girls are only slightly smaller and lighter than boys during these years, a difference that continues until puberty. During the preschool years, both boys and girls slim down as the trunk of their bodies lengthens. Although their heads are still somewhat large for their bodies, by the end of the preschool years, most children have lost their top-heavy look. Body fat also shows a slow, steady decline during the preschool years, so that the chubby baby often looks much leaner by the end of early childhood. Girls have more fatty tissue than boys, and boys have more muscle tissue.

Growth patterns vary individually. Think back to your preschool years. This was probably the first time you noticed that some children were taller than you, some shorter; that some were fatter, some thinner; that some were stronger, some weaker. Much of the variation is due to heredity, but environmental experiences are involved to some extent. A review of the heights and weights of children around the world concluded that the two most important contributors to height differences are ethnic origin and nutrition (Meredith, 1978). Urban, middle-class, and firstborn children were taller than rural, lower-class, and later-born children. Children whose mothers smoked during pregnancy were half an inch shorter than children whose mothers did not smoke during pregnancy. In the United States, Black children are taller than White children.

Why are some children unusually short? The culprits are congenital factors (genetic or prenatal problems), a physical problem that develops in childhood, or an emotional difficulty. In many cases, children with congenital growth problems can be treated with hormones. Usually, this treatment is directed at the pituitary, the body's master gland, located at the base of the brain. This gland secretes growth-related hormones. With regard to physical problems that develop during childhood, malnutrition and chronic infections can stunt growth, although if the problems are properly treated, normal growth usually is attained. **Deprivation dwarfism** *is a type of growth retardation caused by emotional deprivation; children are deprived of affection, which causes stress and alters the release of hormones by the pituitary gland.* Some children who are not dwarfs may also show the effects of an impoverished emotional environment, although most parents of these children say they are small and weak because they have a poor body structure or constitution (Gardner, 1972).

The Brain

One of the most important physical developments during early childhood is the continuing development of the brain and nervous system. While the brain continues to grow in early childhood, it does not grow as rapidly as in infancy. By the time children have reached 3 years of age, the brain is three-quarters of its adult size. By age 5, the brain has reached about nine-tenths its adult size.

The brain and the head grow more rapidly than any other part of the body. The top parts of the head, the eyes, and the brain grow faster than the lower portions, such as the jaw. Figure 6.2 reveals how the growth curve for the head and brain advances more rapidly than the growth curve for height and weight. At 5 years of age, when the brain has attained approximately 90 percent of its adult weight, the 5-year-old's total body weight is only about one-third of what it will be when the child reaches adulthood.

FIGURE 6.1

Average height and weight of girls and boys from 2–6 years of age.

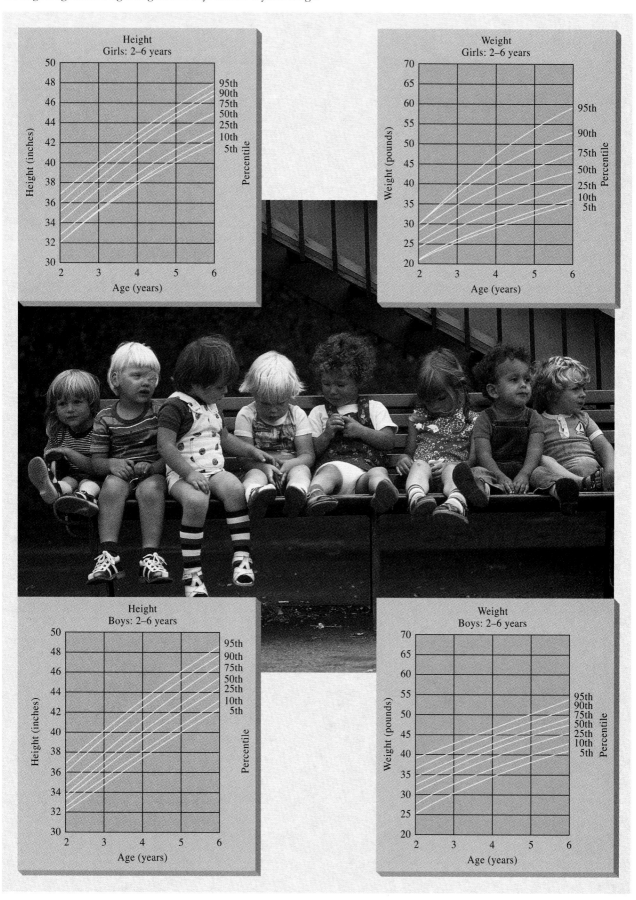

FIGURE 6.2

Growth curves for the head and brain and for height and weight. The more rapid growth of the brain and head can be easily seen. Height and weight advance more gradually over the first two decades of life.

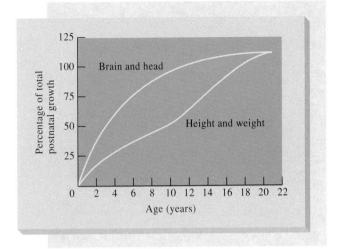

Some of the brain's increase in size is due to the increase in the number and size of nerve endings within and between areas of the brain. These nerve endings continue to grow at least until adolescence. Some of the brain's increase in size also is due to the increase in **myelination,** *a process in which nerve cells are covered and insulated with a layer of fat cells. This process has the effect of increasing the speed of information traveling through the nervous system.* Some developmentalists believe myelination is important in the maturation of a number of children's abilities. For example, myelination in the areas of the brain related to hand-eye coordination is not complete until about 4 years of age. Myelination in the areas of the brain related to focusing attention is not complete until the end of middle and late childhood (Tanner, 1978).

The increasing maturation of the brain, combined with opportunities to experience a widening world, contribute enormously to children's emerging cognitive abilities. Consider a child who is learning to read and is asked by the teacher to read aloud to the class. Input from the child's eyes is transmitted to the child's brain, then passed through many brain systems, which translate (process) the patterns of black and white into codes for letters, words, and associations. The output occurs in the form of messages to the child's lips and tongue. The child's own gift of speech is possible because brain systems are organized in ways that permit language processing.

> *Swiftly the brain becomes an enchanted loom, where millions of flashing shuttles weave a dissolving pattern— always a meaningful pattern—though never an abiding one.*
>
> —Sir Charles Sherrington, 1906

Motor Development

Running as fast as you can, falling down, getting right back up and running just as fast as you can . . . building towers with blocks . . . scribbling, scribbling, and more scribbling . . . cutting paper with scissors. During your preschool years you probably developed the ability to perform all of these activities.

Gross Motor Skills

The preschool child no longer has to make an effort simply to stay upright and to move around. As children move their legs with more confidence and carry themselves more purposefully, the process of moving around in the environment becomes more automatic (Poest & others, 1990).

At 3 years of age, children are still enjoying simple movements such as hopping, jumping, and running back and forth, just for the sheer delight of performing these activities. They take considerable pride in showing how they can run across a room and jump all of six inches. The run-and-jump will win no Olympic gold medals, but for the 3-year-old the activity is a source of considerable pride and accomplishment.

By 4 years of age, children are still enjoying the same kind of activities, but they have become more adventurous. They scramble over low jungle gyms as they display their athletic prowess. Although they have been able to climb stairs with one foot on each step for some time now, they are just beginning to be able to come down the same way. They still often revert to marking time on each step.

By 5 years of age, children are even more adventuresome than when they were 4. Five-year-olds run hard and enjoy races with each other and their parents. A summary of development in gross motor skills during early childhood is shown in figure 6.3.

You probably have arrived at one important conclusion about preschool children: They are very, very active. Indeed, researchers have found that 3-year-old children have the highest activity level of any age in the entire human life span. They fidget when they watch television. They fidget when they sit at the dinner table. Even when they sleep, they move around quite a bit. Because of their activity level and the development of large muscles, especially in the arms and legs, preschool children need daily exercise.

Fine Motor Skills

At 3 years of age, children are still emerging from the infant ability to place and handle things. Although they have had the ability to pick up the tiniest objects between their thumb and forefinger for some time now, they are still somewhat clumsy at it. Three-year-olds can build surprisingly high block towers, each block being placed with intense concentration but often not in a completely straight line. When 3-year-olds play with a form board or a simple jigsaw puzzle, they are rather rough in placing the pieces. Even when they recognize the hole a piece fits into, they are not very precise in positioning the piece. They often try to force the piece in the hole or pat it vigorously.

At 4 years of age, children's fine motor coordination has improved substantially and become much more precise. Sometimes 4-year-old children have trouble building high towers with

FIGURE 6.3

The development of gross motor skills in early childhood.

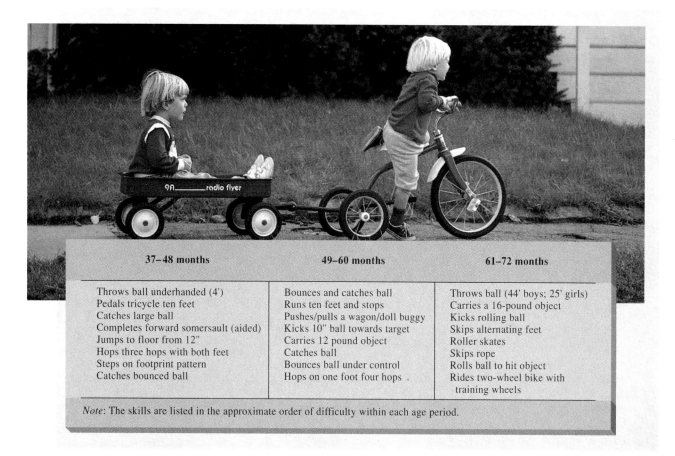

37–48 months	49–60 months	61–72 months
Throws ball underhanded (4')	Bounces and catches ball	Throws ball (44' boys; 25' girls)
Pedals tricycle ten feet	Runs ten feet and stops	Carries a 16-pound object
Catches large ball	Pushes/pulls a wagon/doll buggy	Kicks rolling ball
Completes forward somersault (aided)	Kicks 10" ball towards target	Skips alternating feet
Jumps to floor from 12"	Carries 12 pound object	Roller skates
Hops three hops with both feet	Catches ball	Skips rope
Steps on footprint pattern	Bounces ball under control	Rolls ball to hit object
Catches bounced ball	Hops on one foot four hops	Rides two-wheel bike with training wheels

Note: The skills are listed in the approximate order of difficulty within each age period.

blocks because in their desire to place each of the blocks perfectly they may upset those already stacked. By age 5, children's fine motor coordination has improved further. Hand, arm, and body all move together under better command of the eye. Mere towers no longer interest the 5-year-old, who now wants to build a house or a church complete with steeple, though adults may still need to be told what each finished project is meant to be. A summary of the development of fine motor skills in early childhood is shown in figure 6.4.

Handedness

For centuries left-handers have suffered unfair discrimination in a world designed for the right-hander. Even the devil himself was portrayed as a left-hander. For many years, teachers forced all children to write with their right hand even if they had a left-hand tendency. Fortunately, today most teachers let children write with the hand they favor.

Some children are still discouraged from using their left hand, even though many left-handed individuals have become very successful. Their ranks include Leonardo da Vinci, Benjamin Franklin, and Pablo Picasso. Each of these famous men was known for his imagination of spatial layouts, which

Today, most teachers let children write with the hand they favor.

may be stronger in left-handed individuals. Left-handed athletes also are often successful; since there are fewer left-handed athletes, the opposition is not as accustomed to the style and approach of "lefties." Their serve in tennis spins in the opposite direction, their curve ball in baseball swerves the opposite way,

FIGURE 6.4

The development of fine motor skills in early childhood.

37–48 months

Approximates circle
Cuts paper
Pastes using pointer finger
Builds three-block bridge
Builds eight-block tower
Draws *0* and +
Dresses and undresses doll
Pours from pitcher without spilling

49–60 months

Strings and laces shoelace
Cuts following line
Strings ten beads
Copies figure *X*
Opens and places clothespins
 (one handed)
Builds a five-block bridge
Pours from various containers
Prints first name

61–72 months

Folds paper into halves and quarters
Traces around hand
Draws rectangle, circle, square, and
 triangle
Cuts interior piece from paper
Uses crayons appropriately
Makes clay object with two small parts
Reproduces letters
Copies two short words

Note: The skills are listed in the
approximate order of difficulty within
each age period.

Petrinovich, 1977). Many preschool children, though, use both hands, with a clear hand preference not completely distinguished until later in development. Some children use one hand for writing and drawing, and the other hand for throwing a ball. My oldest daughter, Tracy, confuses the issue even further. She writes left-handed and plays tennis left-handed, but she plays golf right-handed. During her early childhood, her handedness was still somewhat in doubt. My youngest daughter, Jennifer, was left-handed from early in infancy. Their left-handed orientation has not handicapped them in their athletic and academic pursuits, although Tracy once asked me if I would buy her a pair of left-handed scissors.

PHYSICAL DEVELOPMENT IN MIDDLE AND LATE CHILDHOOD

The period of middle and late childhood involves slow, consistent growth. This is a period of calm before the rapid growth spurt of adolescence. Among the important aspects of body change in this developmental period are those involving the skeletal system, the muscular system, and motor skills.

The Skeletal and Muscular Systems

During the elementary school years, children grow an average of 2 to 3 inches a year until, at the age of 11, the average girl is 4 feet, 10¾ inches tall and the average boy is 4 feet, 9 inches tall. Children's legs become longer and their trunks slimmer. During the middle and late childhood years, children gain about 5 to 7 pounds a year. The weight increase is due mainly to increases in the size of the skeleton and muscular systems, as well as the size of some body organs. Muscle mass and strength gradually increase as "baby fat" decreases. The loose movements and knock-knees of early childhood give way to improved muscle tone. The increase in muscular strength is due to heredity and to exercise. Children double their strength capabilities during these years. Because of their greater number of muscle cells, boys are usually stronger than girls (Whaley & Wong, 1988). A summary of changes in height and weight in middle and late childhood appears in table 6.1.

Motor Skills

During middle and late childhood, children's motor development becomes much smoother and more coordinated than it was in early childhood. For example, only one child in a thousand can hit a tennis ball over the net at the age of 3, yet by the age of 10 or 11, most children can learn to play the sport. Running, climbing, skipping rope, swimming, bicycle riding, and skating are just a few of the many physical skills elementary schoolchildren can master. And when mastered, these physical

and their left foot in soccer is not the one children are used to defending against. Left-handed individuals also do well intellectually. In an analysis of the Scholastic Aptitude Test (SAT) scores of more than 100,000 students, 20 percent of the top scoring group was left-handed, which is twice the rate of left-handedness found in the general population (Bower, 1985). Quite clearly, many left-handed people are competent in a wide variety of human activities ranging from athletic skills to intellectual accomplishments.

When does hand preference develop? Adults usually notice a child's hand preference during early childhood, but researchers have found handedness tendencies in the infant years. Even newborns have some preference for one side of their body over the other. In one research investigation, 65 percent of infants turned their head to the right when they were lying on their stomachs in the crib. Fifteen percent preferred to face toward the left. These preferences for the right or left were related to later handedness (Michel, 1981). By about 7 months of age, infants prefer grabbing with one hand or the other, and this is also related to later handedness (Ramsay, 1980). By 2 years of age, about 10 percent of children favor their left hand (Hardyck &

TABLE 6.1

Changes in Height and Weight in Middle and Late Childhood

| | Height (inches) | | | | | |
| | Female Percentiles | | | Male Percentiles | | |
Age	25th	50th	75th	25th	50th	75th
6	43.75	45	46.50	44.25	45.75	47
7	46	47.50	49	46.25	48	49.25
8	48	49.75	51.50	48.50	50	51.50
9	50.25	53	53.75	50.50	52	53.50
10	52.50	54.50	56.25	52.50	54.25	55.75
11	55	57	58.75	54.50	55.75	57.25
	Weight (pounds)					
6	39.25	43	47.25	42	45.50	49.50
7	43.50	48.50	53.25	46.25	50.25	55
8	49	54.75	61.50	51	55.75	61.50
9	55.75	62.75	71.50	56	62	69.25
10	63.25	71.75	82.75	62	69.25	78.50
11	71.75	81.25	94.25	69	77.75	89

Note: The percentile tells how the child compares to other children of the same age. The 50th percentile tells us that half of the children of a particular age are taller (heavier) or shorter (lighter). The 25th percentile tells us that 25 percent of the children of that age are shorter (lighter) and 75 percent are taller (heavier).

Source: Data from R. E. Behrman and V. C. Vaughan (eds.), *Nelson Textbook of Pediatrics.* W. B. Saunders, Philadelphia, PA, 1987.

skills are a source of great pleasure and accomplishment for children. In gross motor skills involving large muscle activity, boys usually outperform girls rather handily.

As children move through the elementary school years, they gain greater control over their bodies and can sit and attend for longer periods of time. However, elementary schoolchildren are far from having physical maturity, and they need to be active. Elementary schoolchildren become more fatigued by long periods of sitting than by running, jumping, or bicycling. Physical action is essential for these children to refine their developing skills, such as batting a ball, skipping rope, or balancing on a beam. An important principle of practice for elementary schoolchildren, therefore, is that they should be engaged in *active,* rather than passive, activities (Katz & Chard, 1989).

Increased myelinization of the central nervous system is reflected in the improvement of fine motor skills during middle and late childhood. Children's hands are used more adroitly as tools. Six-year-olds can hammer, paste, tie shoes, and fasten clothes. By 7 years of age, children's hands become steadier. At this age, children prefer a pencil to a crayon for printing, and reversal of letters is less common. Printing becomes smaller. Between 8 to 10 years of age, the hands can be used independently with more ease and precision. Fine motor coordination develops to the point where children can write rather than print words. Letter size becomes smaller and more even. By 10 to 12 years of age, children begin to show manipulative skills similar to the abilities of adults. The complex, intricate, and rapid movements needed to produce fine-quality crafts or play a dif-

ficult piece on a musical instrument can be mastered. Figure 6.5 reflects the improvement in children's fine motor skills as they move through the elementary school years. One final point: Girls usually outperform boys in fine motor skills.

HEALTH, NUTRITION, AND EXERCISE

Although we have become a health-conscious nation, aware of the importance of nutrition and exercise in our lives, many of us still eat junk food, have extra flab hanging around our middles, and spend too much time as couch potatoes. All too often, this description fits children as well as adults.

A Developmental Perspective on Children's Health

Although there has been great national interest in the psychological aspects of adult health, only recently has a developmental perspective on the psychological aspects of children's health been proposed (Tinsley, 1992). The uniqueness of young children's health care needs is evident when we consider their motor, cognitive, and social development (Maddux & others, 1986). For example, think about the infant's and preschool child's motor development—it is inadequate to ensure personal safety while riding in an automobile. Adults must take preventive measures to restrain infants and young children in car seats. Young children may lack the intellectual skills—including reading ability—to discriminate between safe and unsafe

FIGURE 6.5

Improvement of fine motor control is evidenced by changes in handwriting. These children were asked to write their names on a blank piece of paper. As the children increase in age, their writing becomes smaller, and the evenness and the uniformity of letter configurations improve. Females generally exhibit more highly developed fine motor skills during these years because of advanced neurological development. Note the immaturity in discrimination as well as coordination of the 4-year-olds; the reversal of letters of a 6-year-old (Bridget); the mixture of upper- and lowercase letters of the 6-year-olds; and the letter dropping of the 8-year-old. All are common for the ages of the children.

As children move through the elementary school years, they gain greater control over their bodies. Physical action is essential for them to refine their developing skills.

to help children identify appropriate sources of assistance for health-related problems, and (3) to help children independently initiate the use of sources of assistance for health problems.

Caregivers have an important health role for young children (Farmer, Peterson, & Kashani, 1989). For example, by controlling the speed of the vehicles they drive, by decreasing their drinking, and by not smoking around children, caregivers enhance children's health. In one recent investigation, it was found that, if a mother smokes, her children are twice as likely to have respiratory ailments (Etzel, 1988). The young children of single, unemployed, smoking mothers are also three times more likely to be injured. Smoking may serve as a marker to identify mothers less able to supervise young children. In sum, caregivers can actively affect young children's health and safety by training them and monitoring their recreational safety, self-protection skills, proper nutrition, and dental hygiene.

Illnesses, especially those that are not life threatening, provide an excellent opportunity for young children to expand their development. The preschool period is a peak time for such illnesses as respiratory infections (colds, flu) and gastrointestinal upsets (nausea, diarrhea). The illnesses usually are of short duration and are often handled outside the medical community, through the family, day care, or school. Such minor illnesses can increase the young child's knowledge of health and illness and sense of empathy (Parmalee, 1986). Young children may confuse such terms as "feel bad" with bad behavior and "feel good" with good behavior. Examples include:

"I feel bad. I want aspirin."

"I feel bad. My tummy hurts."

"Bobby hurt me."

"I bad girl. I wet my pants."

"Me can do it. Me good girl."

"I'm hurting your feeling, 'cause I was mean to you."

"Stop; it doesn't feel good."

household substances, and they may lack the impulse control to keep them from running out into a busy street while chasing after a ball or toy.

Playgrounds for young children need to be designed with their safety in mind (Frost & Wortham, 1988). The initial steps in ensuring children's safety is to walk with children through the existing playground or the site where the playground is to be developed, talking with them about possible safety hazards, letting them assist in identifying hazards, and indicating how they can use the playground safely. The outdoor play environment should enhance children's motor, cognitive, and social development.

Health education programs for preschool children need to be cognitively simple. There are three simple but important goals for health education programs for preschool children (Parcel & others, 1979): (1) to help children identify feelings of wellness and illness and be able to express them to adults, (2)

Young children often attribute their illness to what they view as a transgression, such as having eaten the wrong food or playing outdoors in the cold when told not to. In illness and wellness situations, adults have the potential to help children sort out distressed feelings resulting from emotional upsets from those caused by physical illness. For example, a mother might say to her young daughter, "I know you feel bad because you are sick like your sister was last week, but you will be well soon, just as she is now," or a father might comment, "I know you feel bad because I am going on a trip and I can't take you with me, but I will be back in a few days" (Parmalee, 1986).

The State of Illness and Health in the World's Children

A special concern is the state of children's illness and health in developing countries around the world. One death of every three in the world is the death of a child under the age of 5 (Grant, 1992). Every week, more than a quarter of a million children die in developing countries in a quiet carnage of infection and undernutrition. The leading cause of childhood death in the world is dehydration and malnutrition as a result of diarrhea. Approximately 70 percent of the more than 40 million children killed by diarrhea in 1989 could have been saved if parents had available a low-cost breakthrough known as **oral rehydration therapy (ORT)**, *a treatment involving a range of techniques designed to prevent dehydration during episodes of diarrhea by giving the child fluids by mouth.*

Most child malnutrition and deaths could now be prevented by parental actions that are almost universally affordable and based on knowledge that is already available. Making sure that parents know they can improve their children's health by adequate birth spacing, care during pregnancy, breast-feeding, immunization, special feeding before and after illness, and regular check-ups of the children's weight can overcome many causes of malnutrition and poor growth.

A simple child,
That lightly draws its breath,
What should it know of death?

—William Wordsworth

Among the nations with the highest mortality rate under age 5 are Asian nations, such as Afghanistan, and African nations, such as Ethiopia (Grant, 1992). In Afghanistan, in 1986, for every 1,000 children born alive, 325 died before the age of 5; in Ethiopia, the figure was 255 per 1,000. Among the countries with the lowest mortality rate under age 5 are Scandinavian countries, such as Sweden and Finland, where only 7 of every 1,000 children born died before the age of 5 in 1986. The United States mortality rate under age 5 is better than that of most countries, but, of 131 countries for which figures were available in 1986, 20 countries had better rates than the United States. In 1986, for every 1,000 children born alive in the United States, 13 died before the age of 5.

What responsibility do the wealthier nations of the world have for fostering and financially supporting health and nutrition services for children in developing countries? Explain.

Nutrition and Children's Obesity

In the middle and late childhood years, children's average body weight doubles. And children exert considerable energy as they engage in many different motor activities. To support their growth and active lives, children need to consume more food than they did in the early childhood years. From 1 to 3 years of age, infants and toddlers only need to consume 1,300 calories per day on the average and only 1,700 calories per day at 4 to 6 years of age. However, at 7 to 10 years of age, children need to consume 2,400 calories per day on the average (the range being 1,650 to 3,300 depending on the child's size) (Pipes, 1988).

A special concern during middle and late childhood is the development of **obesity,** *weighing 20 percent or more above the ideal weight for a particular age taking both age and sex into account.* Some obese children do not become obese adolescents and adults, but approximately 40 percent of children who are obese at age 7 also are obese as adults. Understanding why children become obese is complex, involving genetic inheritance, physiological mechanisms, cognitive factors, and environmental influences (Brownell, 1990; Muecke & others, 1992). Some children inherit a tendency to be overweight. Only 10 percent of children who do not have obese parents become overweight themselves, whereas 40 percent of children who have one obese parent become obese, and 70 percent of children who have two obese parents become obese. The extent to which this is due to genes or experience with parents cannot be determined in research with humans, but animals can be bred to have a propensity for fatness.

Another factor in the weight of children is **set point,** *the weight maintained when no effort is made to gain or lose weight.* Exercise can lower the body's set point for weight, making it much easier to maintain a lower weight (Bennett & Gurin, 1982). Indeed, exercise is an important aspect of helping overweight children lose weight and maintain weight loss.

A child's insulin level is another important factor in eating behavior and obesity. American health psychology researcher Judy Rodin (1984, 1992) argues that what children eat influences their insulin levels. When children eat complex carbohydrates like cereals, bread, and pasta, insulin levels go up and fall off gradually. When children consume simple sugars like candy bars and Cokes, insulin levels rise and then fall sharply—producing the sugar low with which many of us are all too familiar. Glucose levels in the blood are affected by these complex carbohydrates and simple sugars. Children are more likely to eat within the next several hours after eating simple sugars than after eating complex carbohydrates. And the food children eat at one meal influences what they will eat at the next meal. So

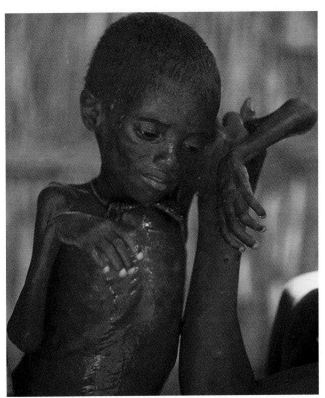

The recent crisis in Somalia brought to light how extensive malnutrition is in some developing countries.

Exercise is an important component of children's lives. Everything we know about children's development suggests that children's lives should be active and involve a number of physical activities.

consuming doughnuts and candy bars, in addition to providing minimal nutritional value, sets up an ongoing sequence of what and how much children crave the next time they eat.

Obesity is related to children's self-esteem. In one study, obese children in the third, fourth, and fifth grades had more negative self-concepts than average-weight children (Sallade, 1973).

What can parents do if their child is obese? A medical checkup is the first step to determine if the child has a metabolic disorder. If a metabolic disorder is present, the physician may be able to effectively treat the disorder with a revised diet or drugs. Next, parents need to ensure that the child is getting a well-balanced diet that especially includes complex carbohydrates, such as pasta, potatoes, and cereals. A regular program of physical exercise should be part of the weight loss plan. And every effort should be made to encourage the children's motivation to lose weight so that they feel they are responsible for their weight loss rather than that the parents have imposed the weight loss program on them and are controlling their activity.

Exercise

Many of our patterns of health and illness are longstanding. Our experiences as children contribute to our health practices as adults. Did your parents seek medical help at your first sniffle, or did they wait until your temperature reached 104 degrees? Did they feed you heavy doses of red meat and sugar or a more rounded diet with vegetables and fruit? Did they get you involved in sports or exercise programs, or did you lie around watching television all the time?

Are children getting enough exercise? The 1985 School Fitness Survey tested 18,857 children aged 6 to 17 on nine fitness tasks. Compared to a similar survey in 1975, there was virtually no improvement on the tasks. For example, 40 percent of the boys 6 to 12 years of age could not do more than one pull-up, and a full 25 percent could not do any. Fifty percent of the girls aged 6 to 17 and 30 percent of the boys aged 6 to 12 could not run a mile in less than 10 minutes. In the 50-yard dash, the adolescent girls in 1975 were faster than the adolescent girls in 1985.

The quality of life is determined by its activities.
—Aristotle, 4th century B.C.

Some experts suggest that television is at least partially to blame for the poor physical condition of our nation's children. In one investigation, children who watched little television were significantly more physically fit than their heavy-television-viewing counterparts (Tucker, 1987). The more children watch television, the more they are likely to be overweight. No one is quite sure whether this is because children spend their leisure time in front of the television set instead of chasing each other around the neighborhood or whether they tend to eat a lot of junk food they see advertised on television.

EXPLORATIONS IN CHILD
DEVELOPMENT 6.1

Parents and Children's Sports

Children's participation in sports can have both positive and negative consequences. On the positive side, sports can provide children with exercise, opportunities to learn how to compete, increased self-esteem, and a setting for developing peer relations and friendships. However, on the negative side, sports sometimes involves too much pressure to achieve and win, physical injuries, distractions from academic work, and unrealistic expectations for success as an athlete.

Most sports psychologists believe it is important for parents to show an interest in their children's sports participation. Most children want their parents to watch them perform in sports. Many children whose parents do not come to watch them play in sporting events feel that their parents do not adequately support them. However, some children become extremely nervous when their parents watch them perform, or get embarrassed when their parents cheer too loudly or make a fuss. If children request that their parents not watch them perform, parents should respect their children's wishes (Schreiber, 1990).

Parents should compliment their children for their sports performance. In the course of a game there are dozens of cir-

cumstances when the child has done something positive—parents should stress a child's good performance, even if the child has limited abilities. Parents can tell their children how much the children hustled in the game and how enthusiastically they played. Even if the child strikes out in a baseball game, a parent can say, "That was a nice swing."

One of the hardest things for parents to do is to watch their children practicing or performing at a sport without helping them, to let their children make mistakes without interfering. Former Olympic swimmer Donna deVarona commented that the best way parents can help children in sports is to let them get to know themselves, and the only way they can do this is by having experiences in life. Naturally parents want

Some of the blame also falls on the nation's schools, many of which fail to provide physical education classes on a daily basis. In the 1985 School Fitness Survey, 37 percent of the children in the first through the fourth grades took gym classes only once or twice a week. The investigation also revealed that parents are poor role models when it comes to physical fitness. Less than 30 percent of the parents of children in grades 1 through 4 exercised three days a week. Roughly half said they never get any vigorous exercise. In another study, observations of children's behavior in physical education classes at four elementary schools revealed how little vigorous exercise is done in these classes (Parcel & others, 1987). Children moved through space only 50 percent of the time they were in the class, and they moved continuously an average of only 2.2 minutes. In summary, not only do children's school weeks not include adequate physical education classes, but the majority of children do not exercise vigorously even when they are in such classes. Furthermore, most children's parents are poor role models for vigorous physical exercise.

Does it make a difference if we push children to exercise more vigorously in elementary school? One investigation says yes (Tuckman & Hinkle, 1988). One hundred fifty-four elementary school children were randomly assigned either to three 30-minute running programs per week or to regular attendance in physical education classes. Although the results sometimes varied according to sex, for the most part, the cardiovascular health as well as the creativity of children in the running program were enhanced. For example, the boys in this program had less body fat and the girls had more creative involvement in their classrooms.

Critical Thinking

Imagine that you are the physical education coordinator for the elementary schools in a large city. Describe the ideal program you would want to implement to improve children's physical fitness.

to provide their children with support and encouragement, but there is a point at which parental involvement becomes overinvolvement.

I (your author) have coached a number of young tennis players and seen many parents who handled their role as a nurturant, considerate parent well, but observed others who became overinvolved in their children's sport. Some parents were aware of their tendency to become overinvolved and backed off from pushing their children too intensely. However, some were not aware of their overintrusiveness and did not back off. The worst parent I had to deal with had a daughter who, at the age of 9, was already nationally ranked and showed great promise. Her father went to every lesson, every practice session, every tournament. Her tennis began to consume *his* life. At one tournament, he stormed onto the court during one of her matches and accused his daughter's 10-year-old opponent of cheating, embarrassing his daughter and himself. I called him the next day, told him I no longer could coach his daughter because of his behavior, and recommended that he seek counseling or not go to any more of her matches.

If parents do not become overinvolved, they can help their children build their physical skills and help them emotionally—discussing with them how to deal with a difficult coach, how to cope with a tough loss, and how to put in perspective a poorly played game. Parents need to carefully monitor their children as they participate in sports for signs of developing stress. If the problems appear to be beyond the intuitive skills of a volunteer coach or a parent, a consultation with a counselor or clinician may be needed. Also, the parent needs to be sensitive to whether the sport in which the child is participating is the best one for the child and whether the child can handle its competitive pressures.

Some guidelines provided by the Women's Sports Foundation in its booklet, *Parent's Guide to Girls' Sports,* can benefit both parents and coaches of all children in sports:

The Dos:

Make sports fun; the more children enjoy sports, the more they will want to play.

Remember that it is OK for children to make mistakes; it means they are trying.

Allow children to ask questions about the sport and discuss the sport in a calm, supportive manner.

Show respect for the child's sports participation.

Be positive and convince the child that he or she is making a good effort.

Be a positive role model for the child in sports.

The Don'ts:

Yell or scream at the child.

Condemn the child for poor play or continue to bring up failures long after they happen.

Point out the child's errors in front of others.

Expect the child to learn something immediately.

Expect the child to become a pro.

Ridicule or make fun of the child.

Compare the child to siblings or to more talented children.

Make sports all work and no fun.

In addition to the school, the family plays an important role in a child's exercise program. A wise strategy is for the family to take up activities involving vigorous physical exercise that parents and children can enjoy together. Running, swimming, cycling, and hiking are especially recommended. In encouraging children to exercise more, parents should not push them beyond their physical limits or expose them to competitive pressures that take the fun out of sports and exercise. For example, long-distance running may be too strenuous for young children and could result in bone injuries. Recently, there has been an increase in the number of children competing in strenuous athletic events such as marathons and triathalons. Doctors are beginning to see some injuries in children that they previously saw only in adults. Some injuries, such as stress fractures and tendonitis, stem from the overuse of young, still-growing bodies. If left to their own devices, how many 8-year-old children would want to prepare for a marathon? It is recommended that parents downplay cutthroat striving and encourage healthy sports that children can enjoy, a topic we discuss further in our examination of children's competitive sports.

> *We are underexercised as a nation. We look instead of play. We ride instead of walk. Our existence deprives us of the minimum of physical activity essential for healthy living.*
> —John F. Kennedy, 1961

Sports

Sports have become an increasingly integral part of American culture. Thus, it is not surprising that more and more children become involved in sports every year. Both in public schools and in community agencies, children's sports programs that involve baseball, soccer, football, basketball, swimming, gymnastics, and other activities have grown to the extent that they have changed the shape of many children's lives. (See Explorations in Child Development 6.1.)

Participation in sports can have both positive and negative consequences for children. Children's participation in sports can provide exercise, opportunities to learn how to compete, increased self-esteem, and a setting for developing peer relations

Little League baseball, basketball, soccer, tennis, dance—as children's motor development becomes smoother and more coordinated, they are able to master these activities more competently in middle and late childhood than in early childhood.

Puberty involves a dramatic upheaval in bodily change. Young adolescents develop an acute concern about their bodies. Columnist Bob Greene (1988) dialed a party line in Chicago, called Connections, to discover what young adolescents were saying to each other. The first things the boys and girls asked for—after first names—were physical descriptions. The idealism of the callers was apparent. Most of the girls described themselves as having long blond hair, being 5 feet 5 inches tall, and weighing about 110 pounds. Most of the boys said they had brown hair, lifted weights, were 6 feet tall, and weighed about 170 pounds.

and friendships. However, sports also can have negative outcomes for children: Too much pressure to achieve and win, physical injuries, a distraction from academic work, and unrealistic expectations for success as an athlete. Few people challenge the value of sports for children when conducted as part of a school physical education or intramural program, but some question the appropriateness of highly competitive, win-oriented sports teams in schools and community agencies.

There is a special concern for children in "high pressure" sports settings involving championship play with accompanying media publicity. Some clinicians and child developmentalists believe such activities not only put undue stress on the participants, but also teach children the wrong values, namely a "win-at-all-costs" philosophy. The possibility of exploiting children through highly organized, win-oriented sports programs is an ever present danger. Overly ambitious parents, coaches, and community boosters can unintentionally create a highly stressful atmosphere in children's sports. When parental,

agency, or community prestige becomes the central focus of the child's participation in sports, the danger of exploitation is clearly present. Programs oriented toward such purposes often require long and arduous training sessions over many months and years, frequently leading to sports specialization at too early an age. In such circumstances, adults often transmit a distorted view of the role of the sport in the child's life, communicating to the child that the sport is the most important aspect of the child's existence.

At this point, we have discussed a number of ideas about children's physical growth, health, nutrition, and exercise. A summary of these ideas is presented in Concept Table 6.1. Now we will turn our attention to the nature of pubertal changes.

PUBERTY

Imagine a toddler displaying all features of puberty. Think about a 3-year-old girl with fully developed breasts or a boy just slightly older with a deep male voice. That is what we would see by the year 2250 if the age at which puberty arrives were to continue to decrease at its present pace (Petersen, 1979).

In Norway, **menarche,** *first menstruation,* occurs at just over 13 years of age, as opposed to 17 years of age in the 1840s. In the United States—where children mature up to a year earlier than children in European countries—the average age of

FIGURE 6.6

Median ages at menarche in selected northern European countries and the United States from 1845 to 1969. Notice the steep decline in the age at which girls experienced menarche in five different countries. Recently the age at which girls experience menarche has been leveling off.

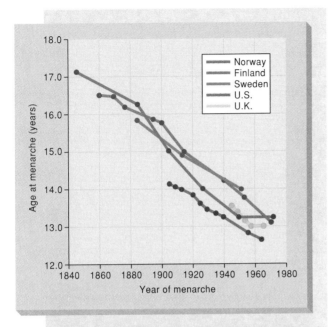

menarche has declined from 14.2 in 1900 to about 12.45 today. The age of menarche has been declining at an average of about 4 months per decade for the past century (see figure 6.6).

Fortunately, however, we are unlikely to see pubescent toddlers, since what has characterized the past century is special—most likely, a higher level of nutrition and health. The available information suggests that menarche began to occur earlier at about the time of the Industrial Revolution, a period associated with increased standards of living and advances in medical science.

Menarche is one event that characterizes puberty, but there are others. What are puberty's markers? What are the psychological accompaniments of puberty's changes? What health care issues are raised by early and late maturation?

Pubertal Change

Puberty *is a period of rapid skeletal and sexual maturation that occurs mainly in early adolescence.* However, puberty is not a single, sudden event. It is part of a gradual process. We know when a young person is going through puberty, but pinpointing its beginning and its end is difficult. Except for menarche, which occurs rather late in puberty, no single marker heralds puberty (Brooks-Gunn, 1991). For boys, the first whisker or first wet dream are events that could mark its appearance, but both may go unnoticed.

Behind the first whisker in boys and widening of hips in girls is a flood of hormones, powerful chemical substances secreted by the endocrine glands and carried through the body by the bloodstream (Dyk, 1993; Kulin, 1991). The concentrations of certain hormones increase dramatically during adolescence. **Testosterone** *is a hormone associated with the development of genitals, an increase in height, and a change in voice in boys.* **Estradiol** *is a hormone associated with breast, uterine, and skeletal development in girls.* In one investigation, testosterone levels increased 18-fold in boys but only 2-fold in girls during puberty; estradiol increased 8-fold in girls but only 2-fold in boys (Nottelmann & others, 1987).

The same influx of hormones that puts hair on a male's chest and imparts curvature to a female's breast may contribute to psychological development in adolescence (Halpern & others, 1992; Susman & Dorn, 1991). In one study of 108 normal boys and girls ranging in age from 9 to 14, a higher concentration of testosterone was present in boys who rated themselves more socially competent (Nottelmann & others, 1987). In another investigation of 60 normal boys and girls in the same age range, girls with higher estradiol levels expressed more anger and aggression (Inoff-Germain & others, 1988). However, hormonal effects by themselves may account for only a small portion of the variance in adolescent development. For example, in one recent study, social factors accounted for two to four times as much variance as hormonal factors in young adolescent girls' depression and anger (Brooks-Gunn & Warren, 1989a).

What is formed for long duration arrives slowly to its maturity.

—Samuel Johnson, *The Rambler*, 1750

CONCEPT TABLE 6.1

Physical Development in Early and Middle and Late Childhood, Health, Nutrition, and Exercise

Concept	Processes/Related Ideas	Characteristics/Description
Physical development in early childhood	Height and weight	The average child grows 2½ inches in height and gains between 5 and 7 pounds a year during early childhood. Growth patterns vary individually, though. Some children are unusually short because of congenital problems, a physical problem that develops in childhood, or emotional problems.
	The brain	The brain is a key aspect of growth. By age 5, the brain has reached nine-tenths of its adult size. Some of its increase in size is due to increases in the number and size of nerve endings, some to myelination. Increasing brain maturation contributes to improved cognitive abilities.
	Gross motor skills	They increase dramatically during early childhood. Children become increasingly adventuresome as their gross motor skills improve. Young children's lives are extremely active, more active than at any other point in the life cycle. Rough-and-tumble play often occurs, especially in boys, and it can serve positive educational and developmental functions. It is important for preschool and kindergarten teachers to design and implement developmentally appropriate activities for young children's gross motor skills. Such activities include fundamental movement, daily fitness, and perceptual-motor opportunities.
	Fine motor skills	They also improve substantially during early childhood. The Denver Developmental Screening Test is one widely used measure of gross and fine motor skills.
	Handedness	At one point, all children were taught to be right-handed. In today's world, the strategy is to allow children to use the hand they favor. Left-handed children are as competent in motor skills and intellect as right-handed children. Both genetic and environmental explanations of handedness have been given.
Physical development in middle and late childhood	The skeletal and muscular systems	During the elementary school years, children grow an average of 2 to 3 inches a year. Muscle mass and strength gradually increase. Legs lengthen and trunks slim down as "baby fat" decreases. Growth is slow and consistent.
	Motor skills	During the middle and late childhood years, children's motor development becomes much smoother and more coordinated. Children gain greater control over their

These hormonal and body changes occur, on the average, about two years earlier in females (10½ years of age) than in males (12½ years of age) (see figure 6.7). Four of the most noticeable areas of body change in females are height spurt, menarche, breast growth, and growth of pubic hair; four of the most noticeable areas of body change in males are height spurt, penile growth, testes growth, and growth of pubic hair (Malina, 1991; Tanner, 1991). The normal range and average age of these characteristics are shown in figures 6.8 and 6.9. Among the most remarkable normal variations is that two boys (or two girls) may be the same chronological age, yet one may complete the pubertal sequence before the other has begun it. For most girls, the first menstrual period may occur as early as the age of 10 or as late as the age of 15½ and still be considered normal, for example (Hood, 1991; Paikoff, Buchanon, & Brooks-Gunn, 1991).

Concept	Processes/Related Ideas	Characteristics/Description
Health, nutrition and obesity, and exercise		bodies and can sit and attend for longer frames of time. However, their lives should be activity oriented and very active. Increased myelinization of the central nervous system is reflected in improved fine motor skills. Improved fine motor development is reflected in children's handwriting skills over the course of middle and late childhood. Boys are usually better at gross motor skills, girls at fine motor skills.
	A developmental perspective on children's health	Only recently have researchers applied a developmental perspective to children's health. Children's health care needs involve their motor, cognitive, and social development.
	The state of illness and health in the world's children	One death of every three in the world is the death of a child under age 5. Every week, more than a quarter of a million children die in developing countries. The main causes of death and child malnutrition in the world are diarrhea, measles, tetanus, whooping cough, acute respiratory infections (mainly pneumonias), and undernutrition. Contributing factors include the timing of births and hygiene. Most child malnutrition and child deaths could be prevented by parental actions that are affordable and based on knowledge that is available today. The United States has a relatively low rate of child deaths compared to other countries, although the Scandinavian countries have the lowest rate.
	Nutrition and children's obesity	In the middle and late childhood years, children's average body weight doubles. And children exert considerable energy as they engage in different motor activities. To support their growth and active lives, children need to consume more food than they did in the early childhood years. However, a special concern during the middle and late childhood years is the development of obesity. Why children become obese is complex, involving genetic inheritance, physiological mechanisms, cognitive factors, and environmental influences.
	Exercise and sports	Every indication suggests that our nation's children are not getting enough exercise. Television viewing, parents being poor role models for exercise, and the lack of adequate physical education classes in schools may be the culprits. Children's participation in sports can have both positive and negative consequences.

Puberty is not simply an environmental accident; genetic factors are also involved. As indicated earlier, although nutrition, health, and other factors affect puberty's timing and variations in its makeup, the basic genetic program is wired into the nature of the species (Scarr & Kidd, 1983).

Another key factor in puberty's occurrence is body mass. For example, menarche occurs at a relatively consistent weight in girls. A body weight of approximately 103 to 109 pounds signals menarche and the end of the adolescent growth spurt. For menarche to begin and continue, fat must make up 17 percent of a girl's total body weight.

FIGURE 6.7

Pubertal growth spurt. On the average, the growth spurt that characterizes pubertal change occurs 2 years earlier for girls (10½) than for boys (12½).

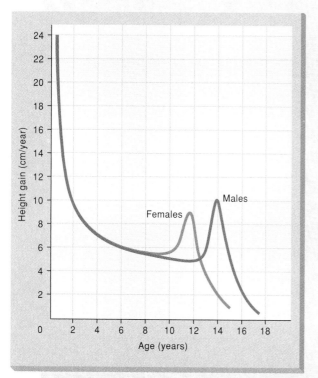

Psychological Accompaniments of Pubertal Change

A host of psychological changes accompanies an adolescent's physical development. Imagine yourself as you were beginning puberty. Not only did you probably think about yourself differently, but your parents and peers probably began acting differently toward you. Maybe you were proud of your changing body even though you were perplexed about what was happening. Perhaps your parents no longer perceived you as someone with whom they could sit in bed and watch television or as someone who should be kissed goodnight.

FIGURE 6.8

Normal range and average age of male sexual development.
Adapted from "Growing Up" by J. M. Tanner. Copyright © 1973 by Scientific American, Inc. All rights reserved.

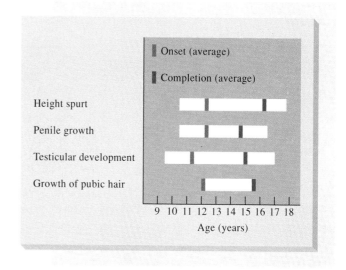

FIGURE 6.9

Normal range and average age of female sexual development.
Adapted from "Growing Up" by J. M. Tanner. Copyright © 1973 by Scientific American, Inc. All rights reserved.

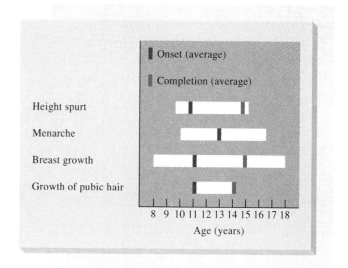

One thing is certain about the psychological aspects of physical change in adolescence: Adolescents are preoccupied with their bodies and develop individual images of what their bodies are like (Adams, 1991; Koff & Riordan, 1991). Perhaps you looked in the mirror daily or even hourly to see if you could detect anything different about your changing body. Preoccupation with one's body image is strong throughout adolescence, but it is especially acute during puberty, a time when adolescents are more dissatisfied with their bodies than in late adolescence.

Being physically attractive and having a positive body image are associated with an overall positive conception of one's self. In one investigation, girls who were judged as being physically attractive and who generally had a positive body image had higher opinions of themselves in general (Lerner & Karabenick, 1974). In another investigation, breast growth in girls 9 to 11 years old was associated with a positive body image, positive peer relationships, and superior adjustment (Brooks-Gunn & Warren, 1989b).

Some of you entered puberty early, others late, and yet others on time. When adolescents mature earlier or later than their peers, might they perceive themselves differently? Some years ago, in the California Longitudinal Study, early-maturing boys perceived themselves more positively and had more successful peer relations than did their late-maturing counterparts (Jones, 1965). The findings for early-maturing girls were similar but not as strong as for boys. When the late-maturing boys were in their thirties, however, they had developed a stronger sense of identity than the early-maturing boys (Peskin, 1967). Possibly this occurred because the late-maturing boys had more time to explore life's options or because the early-maturing boys continued to focus on their advantageous physical status instead of on career development and achievement.

More recent research confirms, though, that at least during adolescence it is advantageous to be an early-maturing rather than a late-maturing boy (Blyth, Bulcroft, & Simmons, 1981; Simmons & Blyth, 1987). The more recent findings for girls suggest that early maturation is a mixed blessing: These girls experience more problems in school but also more independence and popularity with boys. The time that maturation is assessed also is a factor. In the sixth grade, early-maturing girls showed greater satisfaction with their figures than late-maturing girls, but, by the tenth grade, late-maturing girls were more satisfied (see figure 6.10). The reason for this is that, by late adolescence, early-maturing girls are shorter and stockier, whereas late-maturing girls are taller and thinner. Late-maturing girls in late adolescence have bodies that more closely approximate the current American ideal of feminine beauty—tall and thin.

FIGURE 6.10

Early- and late-maturing adolescent girls' perceptions of body image in early and late adolescence.

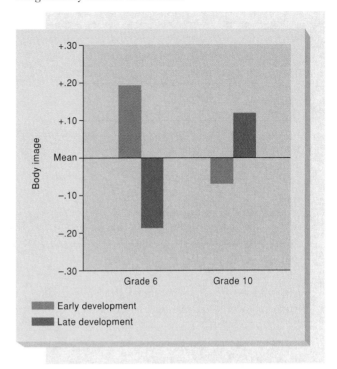

Some researchers now question whether the effects of puberty are as strong as once believed (Lerner, Peterson, & Brooks-Gunn, 1991; Montemayor, Adams, & Gullotta, 1990). Puberty affects some adolescents more strongly than others and some behaviors more strongly than others. Body image, dating interest, and sexual behavior are affected by pubertal change. The recent questioning of puberty's effects suggests that, if we look at overall development and adjustment in the human life cycle, pubertal variations (such as early and late maturation) are less dramatic than is commonly thought. In thinking about puberty's effects, keep in mind that an adolescent's world involves

Copyright © 1985, Washington Post Writers Group. Reprinted with permission.

cognitive and social changes as well as physical changes. As with all periods of development, these processes work in concert to produce who we are in adolescence (Block, 1992; Eccles & Buchanan, 1992).

Critical Thinking

Do you think puberty's effects are exaggerated? Has too much credit been given to early and late maturation? Do these changes possibly balance out over the long course of life's development?

SEXUALITY

I am 16 years old and I really like this one girl. She wants to be a virgin until she marries. We went out last night and she let me go pretty far, but not all the way. I know she really likes me too, but she always stops me when things start getting hot and heavy. It is getting hard for me to handle. She doesn't know it but I'm a virgin too. I feel I am ready to have sex. I have to admit I think about having sex with other girls too. Maybe I should be dating other girls.

—Frank C.

I'm 14 years old. I have a lot of sexy thoughts. Sometimes just before I drift off to sleep at night I think about this hunk who is 16 years old and plays on the football team. He is so gorgeous and I can feel him holding me in his arms and kissing and hugging me. When I'm walking down the hall between classes at school, I sometimes start daydreaming about guys I have met, and wonder what it would be like to have sex with them. Last year I had this crush on the men's track coach. I'm on the girls' track team so I saw him a lot during the year. He hardly knew I thought about him the way I did, although I tried to flirt with him several times.

—Amy S.

During adolescence, the lives of males and females become wrapped in sexuality. Adolescence is a time of sexual exploration and experimentation, of sexual fantasies and sexual realities, of incorporating sexuality into one's identity. At a time when sexual identity is an important developmental task of adolescence, the adolescent is confronted with conflicting sexual values and messages. The majority of adolescents eventually manage to develop a mature sexual identity, but most have periods of vulnerability and confusion along life's sexual journey (Blau & Gullotta, 1993; Kilpatrick, 1992; Miller, Christopherson, & King, 1993). Our coverage of adolescent sexuality focuses on sexual attitudes and behavior, sexually transmitted diseases, and adolescent pregnancy.

If we listen to boys and girls at the very moment they seem most pimply, awkward and disagreeable, we can partly penetrate a mystery most of us once felt heavily within us, and have now forgotten. This mystery is the very process of creation of man and woman.

—Colin Macinnes. *The World of Children*

Sexual Attitudes and Behavior

How extensively have heterosexual attitudes and behaviors changed in the twentieth century? What sexual scripts do adolescents follow? How extensive is homosexual behavior in adolescence? We will consider each of these questions in turn.

Adolescent Heterosexual Behavior— Trends and Incidence

Had you been in high school or college in 1940, you probably would have had a different attitude toward many aspects of sexuality than you do today, especially if you are a female. A review of students' sexual practices and attitudes from 1900 to 1980 revealed two important trends (Darling, Kallen, & VanDusen, 1984). First, the percentage of youth reporting that they had had sexual intercourse increased dramatically. Second, the percentage of females reporting that they had had sexual intercourse increased more rapidly than for males, although the initial base for males was greater. These changes suggest movement away from a double standard that says it is more appropriate for males than females to have sexual intercourse.

Large numbers of American adolescents are sexually active (Eager, 1992). Figure 6.11 reveals that by age 17, 66 percent of males and 50 percent of females have had sexual intercourse; by age 19, 86 percent of males and 75 percent of females have had sexual intercourse (Alan Guttmacher Institute, 1990). According to the Alan Guttmacher Institute, which periodically surveys adolescent sexual behavior, sexual intercourse among adolescents is increasing with fewer youth saving sex for adulthood, much less marriage. Among the other findings recently reported by the Institute:

- Both males and females report dramatic increases in condom use, undoubtedly due to AIDS education. However, only one-third of male adolescents use condoms all of the time.

- Nearly two-thirds of the sexually experienced girls have had at least two partners; the average, sexually active 17- to 19-year-old urban male claims he has had six partners.

- An adolescent girl having sex in 1988 was less likely to get pregnant than one having sex in 1982, probably due to increased use of contraceptives. However, because a larger number of girls had sex in 1988, overall pregnancy rates remained constant at 127 per 1,000 girls each year—a level far above that of other industrialized countries.

FIGURE 6.11

Percentage of U.S. adolescents (by sex and age) who say they have had sexual intercourse.

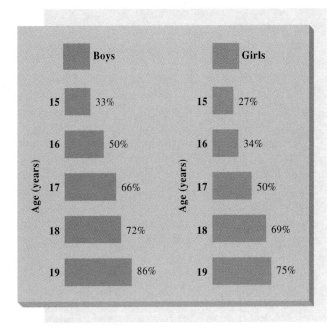

Recent data indicate that, in some areas of the country, sexual experiences of young adolescents may be even greater than these figures suggest (Forrest, 1990). In inner-city Baltimore, 81 percent of 14-year-old males said they had already engaged in sexual intercourse. Other surveys in inner-city, low-income areas also reveal a high incidence of early sexual intercourse (Clark, Zabin, & Hardy, 1984).

Adolescent Sexual Scripts

As adolescents explore their sexual identities, they engage in sexual scripts (Bancroft, 1990; Gordon & Gilgun, 1987). A **sexual script** *is a stereotyped pattern of role prescriptions for how individuals should behave sexually.* Differences in the way females and males are socialized are wrapped up in the sexual scripts adolescents follow. Discrepancies in male/female scripting can cause problems and confusion for adolescents as they work out their sexual identities. Adolescent girls have learned to link sexual intercourse with love. Female adolescents often rationalize their sexual behavior by telling themselves that they were swept away by love. A number of investigators have reported that adolescent females, more than adolescent males, report being in love as the main reason for being sexually active (Cassell, 1984). Far more females than males have intercourse with partners they love and would like to marry. Other reasons for females having sexual intercourse include giving in to male pressure, gambling that sex is a way to get a boyfriend, curiosity, and sexual desire unrelated to loving and caring. Adolescent males may be aware that their female counterparts have been socialized into a love ethic. They also may understand the pressure many

of them feel to have a boyfriend. A classic male line shows how males understand female thinking about sex and love: "If you really loved me, you would have sex with me." The female adolescent who says, "If you really loved me, you would not put so much pressure on me," reflects her insight about male sexual motivation.

Some experts on adolescent sexuality believe that we are moving toward a new norm suggesting that sexual intercourse is acceptable, but mainly within the boundary of a loving and affectionate relationship (Dreyer, 1982). As part of this new norm, promiscuity, exploitation, and unprotected sexual intercourse are more often perceived as unacceptable by adolescents. One variation of the new norm is that intercourse is acceptable in a nonlove relationship, but physical or emotional exploitation of the partner is not (Cassell, 1984). The new norm suggests that the double standard that previously existed does not operate as it once did. That is, physical and emotional exploitation of adolescent females by males is not as predominant today as in prior decades.

Other experts on adolescent sexuality are not so sure that the new norm has arrived (Gordon & Gilgun, 1987; Morrison, 1985). They argue that remnants of the double standard are still flourishing. In most investigations, about twice as many boys as girls report having positive feelings about sexual intercourse. Females are more likely to report guilt, fear, and hurt. Adolescent males feel considerable pressure from their peers to have experienced sexual intercourse and to be sexually active. As one young adolescent recently remarked, "Look, I feel a lot of pressure from my buddies to go for the score." Further evidence for males' physical and emotional exploitation of females was found in a survey of 432 14- to 18-years-olds (Goodchilds & Zellman, 1984). Both male and female adolescents accepted the right of the male adolescent to be sexually aggressive but left matters up to the female to set the limits for the male's sexual overtures. Another attitude related to the double standard was the belief that females should not plan ahead to have sexual intercourse but should be swept up in the passion of the moment, not taking contraceptive precautions. Unfortunately, although we may have chipped away at some parts of the sexual double standard, other aspects still remain.

Homosexual Attitudes and Behavior

Both the early (Kinsey) and more recent (Hunt) surveys indicate that about 4 percent of males and 3 percent of females are exclusively homosexual (Hunt, 1974; Kinsey, Pomeroy, & Martin, 1948). Although the incidence of homosexual behavior does not seem to have increased, attitudes toward homosexuality were becoming more permissive, at least until recently. In 1986, the Gallup poll began to detect a shift in attitudes brought about by public awareness of AIDS (acquired immune deficiency syndrome). For example, in 1985, slightly more than 40 percent of Americans believed that "homosexual relations between consenting adults should be legal"; by 1986, the figure had dropped to just above 30 percent (Gallup Report, 1987). Individuals who have negative attitudes about homosexuals also are likely to favor severe controls for AIDS, such as excluding AIDS carriers from the workplace and schools (Pryor & others, 1989).

Why are some individuals homosexual whereas others are heterosexual? Speculation about this question has been extensive, but no firm answers are available. Homosexual and heterosexual males and females have similar physiological responses during sexual arousal and seem to be aroused by the same types of tactile stimulation. Investigators find that, in terms of a wide range of attitudes, behaviors, and adjustments, no differences between homosexuals and heterosexuals are present (Bell, Weinberg, & Mammersmith, 1981). Recognizing that homosexuality is not a form of mental illness, the American Psychiatric Association discontinued its classification of homosexuality as a disorder, except in those cases where the individuals themselves consider the sexual orientation to be abnormal.

An individual's sexual orientation—heterosexual or homosexual—is most likely determined by a combination of genetic, hormonal, and environmental factors (McWhirter, Reinisch, & Sanders, 1990; Money, 1987; Rowlett, Patel, & Greydanus, 1992; Savin-Williams & Rodriguez, 1993). Most experts on homosexuality believe that no one factor alone causes homosexuality and that the relative weight of each factor may vary from one individual to the next. In truth, no one knows *exactly* what causes an individual to become a homosexual. Scientists have a clearer picture of what does *not* cause homosexuality. For example, children raised by gay or lesbian parents or couples are no more likely to be homosexual than are children raised by heterosexual parents (Patterson, 1992). There also is no evidence that male homosexuality is caused by a dominant mother or a weak father, or that female homosexuality is caused by girls choosing male role models. Among the biological factors believed to be involved in homosexuality are prenatal hormone conditions (Ellis & Ames, 1987). In the second to fifth months after conception, exposure to hormone levels characteristic of females is speculated to cause an individual (male or female) to become attracted to males. If this "prenatal critical period hypothesis" turns out to be correct, it would explain why researchers and clinicians have found it difficult to modify a homosexual orientation.

Adolescence may play an important role in the development of homosexuality. In one investigation, participation in homosexual behavior and sexual arousal by same-sex peers in adolescence was strongly related to an adult homosexual orientation (Bell & others, 1981). When interest in the same sex is intense and compelling, an adolescent often experiences severe conflict (Boxer, 1988; Irvin, 1988). The American culture stigmatizes homosexuality; negative labels, such as "fag" and "queer," are given to male homosexuals, and "lessie" and "dyke" to female homosexuals. The sexual socialization of adolescent homosexuals becomes a process of learning to hide (Herdt,

1988). Some gay males wait out their entire adolescence, hoping that heterosexual feelings will develop. Many female adolescent homosexuals have similar experiences. Many adult females who identify themselves as homosexuals considered themselves predominantly heterosexual during adolescence (Bell & others, 1981).

Sexually Transmitted Diseases

Tammy, age 15, has just finished listening to a lecture in her health class. We overhear her talking to one of her girlfriends as she walks down the school corridor. "That was a disgusting lecture. I can't believe all the diseases you can get by having sex. I think she was probably trying to scare us. She spent a lot of time talking about AIDS, which I've heard that normal people don't get. Right? I've heard that only homosexuals and drug addicts get AIDS, and I've also heard that gonorrhea and most other sexual diseases can be cured, so what's the big deal if you get something like that?" Tammy's view of sexually transmitted diseases (formerly called venereal disease, or VD) is common among adolescents. Teenagers tend to believe that sexually transmitted diseases always happen to someone else, can be easily cured without any harm done, and are too disgusting for a nice young person to even hear about, let alone get. This view is wrong. Adolescents who are having sex *do* run a risk of getting sexually transmitted diseases. Sexually transmitted diseases are fairly common among today's adolescents (Leukefeld & Haverkos, 1993).

Chlamydia

Sexually transmitted diseases are primarily transmitted through sexual intercourse, although they can be transmitted orally. **Chlamydia** *is as sexually transmitted disease named for the bacteria that cause it.* Chlamydia affects as many as 10 percent of all college males and females. Males experience a burning sensation during urination and a mucoid discharge. Females experience painful urination or a vaginal discharge. These signs often mimic gonorrhea. However, when penicillin is prescribed for gonorrhealike symptoms, the problem does not go away as it would if gonorrhea were the culprit. If left untreated, the disease can affect the entire reproductive tract. This can lead to problems left by scar tissue, which can prevent the female from becoming pregnant. Effective drugs are available to treat this common sexually transmitted disease.

Herpes Simplex Virus II

An alarming increase in another sexually transmitted disease, herpes simplex virus II, has occurred in recent years. **Herpes simplex virus II** *is a sexually transmitted disease whose symptoms include irregular cycles of sores and blisters in the genital area.* Although this disease is more common among young adults (estimates range as high as 1 in 5 sexually active adults), as many as 1 in 35 adolescents have genital herpes (Oppenheimer, 1982). The herpes virus is potentially dangerous. If babies are exposed to the active virus during birth, they are vulnerable to brain damage or even death, and women with herpes are eight times more likely than unaffected women to develop cervical cancer. At present, herpes is incurable.

Syphilis

Sexual problems have plagued human beings throughout history. Hippocrates wrote about syphilis in 460 B.C. The first major recorded epidemic of syphilis appeared in Naples, Italy, two years after Columbus's first return. It is believed that millions of people died of the disease, which is sexually transmitted through intercourse, kissing, or intimate body contact. The cause of syphilis is a tiny bacterium that requires warm, moist surfaces to penetrate the body. It was not until 400 years after the Italian outbreak that penicillin, a successful treatment for syphilis, was discovered.

AIDS

Today, we harbor the same fear of sexually transmitted disease as in Columbus's time, but, instead of syphilis it is AIDS, a major sexually related problem, that has generated considerable fear in today's world (Ahlstrom & others, 1992; Boyer & Hein, 1991; D'Augelli & Bingham, 1993). **AIDS (acquired immune deficiency syndrome)** *is a virus that destroys the body's immune system. Consequently, many germs that usually do not harm someone with a normal immune system produce devastating results and even death.*

In 1981, when AIDS was first recognized in the United States, there were fewer than 60 reported cases. Beginning in 1990, according to Dr. Frank Press, president of the National Academy of Sciences, we began losing as many Americans each year to AIDS as died in the Vietnam War, almost 60,000 people. According to federal health officials, 1 to 1½ million Americans are now asymptomatic carriers of AIDS—those who are infected with the virus and presumably capable of infecting others but who show no clinical symptoms of AIDS. In 1989, the first attempt to assess AIDS among college students was made. Testing of 16,861 students found 30 students infected with the virus (American College Health Association, 1989). If the 12.5 million students attending college were infected at the same rate, 25,000 students would have the AIDS virus.

Experts say that AIDS can be transmitted only through sexual contact, shared needles, or blood transfusion. Although 90 percent of all AIDS cases continue to occur among homosexual males and intravenous drug users, a disproportionate increase among females who are heterosexual partners of bisexual males or of intravenous drug users has been recently noted: This increase suggests the risk of AIDS may be increasing among

The AIDS advertisement indicates how vulnerable our nation's population is to the epidemic of AIDS, and the disease's lethal consequences.

heterosexual individuals who have multiple sexual partners. Table 6.2 describes what's risky and what's not regarding AIDS.

Evidence that the AIDS epidemic has begun to reduce promiscuous behavior in both homosexual and heterosexual individuals is appearing. In one investigation, it was found that single heterosexual males decreased their number of sexual partners from 2.8 to 1.8 from 1984 to 1986 (Winkelstein & others, 1987). In an investigation of 5,000 homosexual males, the percentage who said they were either celibate or monogamous increased from 14 to 39 percent between 1984 and 1986 (Fineberg, 1988). Although these figures in the latter study are encouraging, virtually all of the homosexual males knew that condoms reduce the risk of contracting AIDS, yet 60 percent did not use them.

If you or someone you know would like more information about AIDS, you can call the National AIDS Hot Line at 1–800–342–7432, 8 A.M.–2 A.M. EST, 7 days a week.

Adolescent Pregnancy

Angela is 15 years old and pregnant. She reflects, "I'm 3 months pregnant. This could ruin my whole life. I've made all of these plans for the future and now they are down the drain. I don't have anybody to talk to about my problem. I can't talk to my parents. There is no way they can understand." Pregnant adolescents were once practically invisible and unmentionable, but yesterday's secret has become today's national dilemma.

They are of different ethnic groups and from different places, but their circumstances have a distressing sameness. Each year more than 1 million American teenagers become pregnant, 4 out of 5 of them unmarried. Like Angela, many become pregnant in their early or middle adolescent years,

TABLE 6.2

Understanding AIDS: What's Risky, What's Not

The AIDS virus is not transmitted like colds or the flu, but by an exchange of infected blood, semen, or vaginal fluids. This usually occurs during sexual intercourse, in sharing drug needles, or to babies infected before or during birth.

You Won't Get AIDS from:
- Everyday contact with individuals around you in school, stores, or the workplace or at parties or child-care centers.
- Swimming in a pool, even if someone in the pool has the AIDS virus.
- A mosquito bite, bedbugs, lice, flies, or other insects.
- Saliva, sweat, tears, urine, or a bowel movement.
- A kiss.
- Clothes, telephones, or toilet seats.
- Using a glass or eating utensils that someone else has used.
- Being on a bus, train, or crowded elevator with an individual who is infected with the virus, or who has AIDS.

Blood Donations and Transfusions:
- You will not come into contact with the AIDS virus by donating blood at a blood bank.
- The risk of getting AIDS from a blood transfusion has been greatly reduced. Donors are screened for risk factors and donated blood is tested.

Risky Behavior:
- Having a number of sex partners.
- Sharing drug needles and syringes.
- Engaging in anal sex with or without a condom.
- Performing vaginal or oral sex with someone who shoots drugs or engages in anal sex.
- Engaging in sex with someone you don't know well or with someone who has several sex partners.
- Engaging in unprotected sex (without a condom) with an infected individual.

Safe Behavior:
- Not having sex.
- Having sex with one mutually faithful, uninfected partner.
- Not shooting drugs.

Source: *America Responds to AIDS*, U.S. government educational pamphlet, 1988.

30,000 of them under the age of 15. In all, this means that 1 of every 10 adolescent females in the United States becomes pregnant each year, with 8 of the 10 pregnancies unintended (National Research Council, 1987). As one 17-year-old Los Angeles mother of a 1-year-old boy said, "We are children having children." The only bright spot in the adolescent pregnancy statistics is that the adolescent pregnancy rate, after increasing during the 1970s, has leveled off and may even be beginning to decline (National Research Council, 1987).

The adolescent pregnancy rate in the United States is the highest of any in the Western world. It is more than twice the rate in England, France, or Canada; almost three times the rate in Sweden; and seven times the rate in the Netherlands (Alan Guttmacher Institute, 1981; Jones & others, 1985). Although

American adolescents are no more sexually active than their counterparts in these other nations, they are many times more likely to become pregnant.

Adolescent pregnancy is a complex American problem, one that strikes many nerves. The subject of adolescent pregnancy touches on many explosive social issues: the battle over abortion rights, contraceptives and the delicate question of whether adolescents should have easy access to them, and the perennially touchy subject of sex education in the public schools (Hofferth, 1990; Stevens-Simon & McAnarney, 1992).

Dramatic changes involving sexual attitudes and social morals have swept through the American culture in the last three decades. Adolescents actually gave birth at a higher rate in 1957 than they do today, but that was a time of early marriage, when almost 25 percent of 18- and 19-year-olds were married. The overwhelming majority of births to adolescent mothers in the 1950s occurred within a marriage and mainly involved females 17 years of age and older. Two or three decades ago, if an unwed adolescent girl became pregnant, in most instances her parents swiftly married her off in a shotgun wedding. If marriage was impractical, the girl would discreetly disappear, the child would be put up for adoption, and the predicament would never be discussed again. Abortion was not an option for most adolescent females until 1973, when the Supreme Court ruled it could not be outlawed.

In today's world of adolescent pregnancies, a different scenario unfolds. If the girl does not choose to have an abortion (45 percent of pregnant adolescent girls do), she usually keeps the baby and raises it without the traditional involvement of marriage. With the stigma of illegitimacy largely absent, girls are less likely to give up their babies for adoption. Fewer than 5 percent do, compared with about 35 percent in the early 1960s. However, although the stigma of illegitimacy has waned, the lives of most pregnant teenagers are anything but rosy.

The consequences of our nation's high adolescent pregnancy rate are of great concern (Brown, James, & Schlosser, 1993; Dean, 1993; Jorgensen, 1993; Ducey, 1993; Goldstein & Medora, 1993; Malik, 1993). Pregnancy in adolescence increases the health risks of both the child and the mother (Dryfoos, 1990; Osofsky, 1990). Infants born to adolescent mothers are more likely to have low birthweights (a prominent cause of infant mortality), as well as neurological problems and childhood illnesses (Furstenberg, Brooks-Gunn, & Chase-Lansdale, 1989). Adolescent mothers often drop out of school, fail to gain employment, and become dependent on welfare. Although many adolescent mothers resume their education later in life, they generally do not catch up with women who postpone childbearing. In the National Longitudinal Survey of Work Experience of Youth, it was found that only half of the women 20 to 26 years old who first gave birth at age 17 had completed high school by their twenties. The percentage was even lower for those who gave birth at a younger age (Mott & Marsiglio, 1985). By contrast, among females who waited until age 20 to have a baby, more than 90 percent had obtained a high school education. Among the younger adolescent mothers,

Serious, extensive efforts need to be developed to help pregnant adolescents and young mothers enhance their educational and occupational opportunities. Adolescent mothers also need extensive help in obtaining competent day care and in planning for the future (Barnet & others, 1992; Furstenberg, 1991). Experts recommend that, to reduce the high rate of teen pregnancy, adolescents need improved sex-education and family-planning information, greater access to contraception, and broad community involvement and support (Conger, 1988; Crockett & Chopak, 1993; Potthof, 1992; Treboux & Busch-Rossnagel, 1991). Another very important consideration, especially for young adolescents, is abstinence, which is increasingly being included as a theme in sex-education classes.

As indicated earlier, adolescent pregnancy is not a major problem in many European countries, especially Holland and the Scandinavian countries. To learn more about adolescent sexuality in Holland and Sweden, turn to Sociocultural Worlds of Children 6.1.

SOME ADOLESCENT PROBLEMS AND DISORDERS

In addition to the increase in adolescent pregnancy, other problems that may arise in adolescence are drug abuse, juvenile delinquency, suicide, and eating disorders, each of which we will discuss in turn.

Drugs

The 1960s and 1970s were a time of marked increases in the use of illicit drugs. During the social and political unrest of those years, many youth turned to marijuana, stimulants, and hallucinogens. Increases in alcohol consumption by adolescents also were noted (Robinson & Greene, 1988). More precise data about drug use by adolescents have been collected in recent years. Each year since 1975, Lloyd Johnston, Patrick O'Malley, and Gerald Bachman (1992, 1993), working at the Institute of Social Research at the University of Michigan, have carefully monitored drug use by America's high school seniors in a wide range of public and private high schools. From time to time, they also sample the drug use of younger adolescents and adults as well.

An encouraging finding from the two most recent surveys (conducted in 1991 and 1992) is the continued gradual decrease in the use of illicit drugs by high school seniors (Johnston, O'Malley, & Bachman, 1992, 1993). However, a special concern surfaced in the survey of 8th graders conducted in 1992. They increased their use of marijuana, cocaine, crack, LSD, other hallucinogens, stimulants, and inhalants. In addition, the United States has the highest rate of drug use by adolescents among the world's industrialized nations. In 1992, 27 percent of the nation's high school seniors tried an illicit drug.

Our society has not handled adolescent sex very effectively. We tell adolescents that sex is fun, harmless, adult, and forbidden. Adolescents 13 years old going on 21 want to try out new things and take risks. They see themselves as unique and indestructible—pregnancy couldn't happen to them, they think. Add to this the adolescent's increasing need for love and commitment, and the result all too often is social dynamite.

almost half had obtained a general equivalency diploma (GED), which does not often open up good employment opportunities.

These educational deficits have negative consequences for the young women themselves and for their children (Scott-Jones & White, 1990). Adolescent parents are more likely than those who delay childbearing to have low-paying, low-status jobs or to be unemployed. The mean family income of White females who give birth before age 17 is approximately half that of families in which the mother delays birth until her mid- or late twenties.

Critical Thinking

You have been asked to design a community program to reduce the rate of adolescent pregnancy in your community. What would the program be like?

SOCIOCULTURAL WORLDS OF CHILDREN 6.1

Sex Education and Attitudes among Adolescents in Holland and Sweden

Sex is much more demystified and dedramatized in Sweden than in the United States, and adolescent pregnancy rates are much lower in Sweden than in the United States.

In Holland and Sweden, sex does not carry the mystery and conflict it does in American society. Holland does not have a mandated sex education program, but adolescents can obtain contraceptive counseling at government-sponsored clinics for a small fee. The Dutch media also have played an important role in educating the public about sex through frequent broadcasts focused on birth control, abortion, and related matters. Most Dutch adolescents do not consider having sex without birth control.

Swedish adolescents are sexually active at an earlier age than are American adolescents, and they are exposed to even more explicit sex on television. However, the Swedish National Board of Education has developed a curriculum that ensures that every child in the country, beginning at age 7, will experience a thorough grounding in reproductive biology and, by the age of 10 or 12, will have been introduced to information about various forms of contraception. Teachers are expected to handle the subject of sex whenever it becomes relevant, regardless of the subject they are teaching. The idea is to dedramatize and demystify sex so that familiarity will make students less vulnerable to unwanted pregnancy and sexually transmitted diseases. American society is not nearly so open about sex education.

According to Lloyd Johnston and his colleagues (1993), considerable progress has been made over the last 10–15 years in reducing the number of adolescents who use drugs—in particular marijuana and cocaine. However, we may now be in danger of losing some of the hard-won ground as a new, more naive generation of children enter adolescence and as society decreases its communication to adolescents about the danger of drugs.

Alcohol

Some mornings, 15-year-old Annie was too drunk to go to school. Other days, she'd stop for a couple of beers or a screwdriver on the way to school. She was tall, blonde, and good looking, and no one who sold her liquor, even at 8:00 in the morning, questioned her age. Where did she get her money? She got it from baby-sitting and from what her mother gave her to buy lunch. Annie used to be a cheerleader, but no longer; she was kicked off the squad for missing practice so often. Soon, she and several of her peers were drinking almost every morning. Sometimes, they skipped school and went to the woods to drink. Annie's whole life began to revolve around her drinking. This routine went on for two years. After a while, Annie's par-

ents discovered her problem. Even though they punished her, it did not stop her drinking. Finally, this year, Annie started dating a boy she really liked and who would not put up with her drinking. She agreed to go to Alcoholics Anonymous and has just successfully completed treatment. She has stopped drinking for four consecutive months now, and she hopes that her abstinence will continue.

Alcohol is the drug most widely used by adolescents in our society. For them, it has produced many enjoyable moments and many sad ones as well. Alcoholism is the third-leading killer in the United States, with more than 13 million people classified as alcoholics, many of whom established their drinking habits during adolescence. Each year, approximately 25,000 people are killed and 1.5 million injured by drunk drivers. In 65 percent of the aggressive male acts against females, the offender is under the influence of alcohol (Goodman & others, 1986). In numerous instances of drunken driving and assaults on females, the offenders are adolescents.

How extensive is alcohol use by adolescents? Although the use of marijuana and other drugs among adolescents has declined recently, adolescents do not seem to be drinking more to offset their reduced intake of other drugs. Alcohol use by high

What is the pattern of alcohol consumption among adolescents?

school seniors has gradually declined. Monthly use declined from 72 percent in 1980 to 51 percent in 1992. The prevalence of drinking five or more drinks in a row in a two-week interval fell from 41 percent in 1980 to 28 percent in 1992. There remains a substantial gender difference in heavy adolescent drinking: 28 percent for females versus 46 percent for males in 1986, although this difference diminished gradually during the 1980s. However, data from college students show little drop in alcohol use and an increase in heavy drinking: 45 percent in 1986, up 2 percent from the previous year. Heavy drinking at parties among college males is common and is becoming more common (Johnston, O'Malley, & Bachman, 1993).

Critical Thinking

Why do you think alcohol use has remained so high during adolescence?

Cocaine

Did you know that cocaine was once an ingredient in Coca-Cola? Of course, it has long since been removed from the soft drink. Cocaine comes from the coca plant, native to Bolivia and Peru. For many years, Bolivians and Peruvians chewed the plant to increase their stamina. Today, cocaine is usually snorted, smoked, or injected in the form of crystals or powder. The effect is a rush of euphoric feelings, which eventually wear off, followed by depressive feelings, lethargy, insomnia, and irritability.

Cocaine is a highly controversial drug. Users claim it is exciting, makes them feel good, and increases their confidence. It is clear, however, that cocaine has potent cardiovascular effects and is potentially addictive. The death of sports star Len Bias demonstrates how lethal cocaine can be. When the drug's effects are extreme, it can produce a heart attack, stroke, or brain seizure. The increase in cocaine-related deaths is traced to very pure or tainted forms of the drug.

Cocaine use, which remained at peak levels throughout much of the 1980s, began an important decline in 1987 that continued through 1992 in high school and college students (Johnston, O'Malley, & Bachman, 1993). Among high school seniors, the proportion of cocaine users fell considerably from 1986 to 1991, from 6.2 percent to 1.3 percent in the previous month. A growing proportion of high school seniors are reaching the conclusion that cocaine use holds considerable, unpredictable risk. However, cocaine use among eight graders increased in 1992 (1.5 percent versus 1.1 percent in 1991).

Suicide

Suicide is a common problem in our society. Its rate has tripled in the past 30 years in the United States; each year, about 25,000 people take their own lives. Beginning at about the age of 15, the rate of suicide begins to rise rapidly. Suicide accounts for about 12 percent of the mortality in the adolescent and young adult age group (Brent, 1989). Males are about three times as likely to commit suicide as females; this may be because of their more active methods for attempting suicide—shooting, for example. By contrast, females are more likely to use passive methods, such as sleeping pills, which are less likely to produce death. Although males commit suicide more frequently, females attempt it more frequently (Maltsberger, 1988).

Estimates indicate that, for every successful suicide in the general population, 6 to 10 attempts are made. For adolescents, the figure is as high as 50 attempts for every life taken. As many as two in every three college students has thought about suicide on at least one occasion; their methods range from overdosing on drugs to crashing into the White House in an airplane.

Why do adolescents attempt suicide? There is no simple answer to this important question (Cole, 1991). It is helpful to think of suicide in terms of proximal and distal factors. Proximal, or immediate, factors can trigger a suicide attempt. Highly stressful circumstances, such as the loss of a boyfriend or girlfriend, poor grades at school, or an unwanted pregnancy, can trigger a suicide attempt. Drugs also have been involved more often in recent suicide attempts than in attempts in the past (Rich, Young, & Fowler, 1986; Wagner, Cole, & Schwartzman, 1993).

Distal, or earlier, experiences often are involved in suicide attempts as well. A longstanding history of family instability and unhappiness may be present (Hodgmann, 1992; Tishler, 1992). Just as a lack of affection and emotional support, high control, and pressure for achievement by parents during childhood are related to adolescent depression, so are such combinations of family experiences likely to show up as distal factors in suicide attempts. Lack of supportive friendships also may be present (Rubenstein & others, 1989). In an investigation of suicide among gifted women, previous suicide attempts, anxiety,

TABLE 6.3

What to Do and What Not to Do When You Suspect Someone Is Likely to Commit Suicide

What to Do

1. Ask direct, straightforward questions in a calm manner: "Are you thinking about hurting yourself?"
2. Assess the seriousness of the suicidal intent by asking questions about feelings, important relationships, who else the person has talked with, and the amount of thought given to the means to be used. If a gun, pills, rope, or other means has been obtained and a precise plan developed, clearly the situation is dangerous. Stay with the person until help arrives.
3. Be a good listener and be very supportive without being falsely reassuring.
4. Try to persuade the person to obtain professional help and assist him or her in getting this help.

What Not to Do

1. Do not ignore the warning signs.
2. Do not refuse to talk about suicide if a person approaches you about it.
3. Do not react with horror, disapproval, or repulsion.
4. Do not give false reassurances by saying such things as "Everything is going to be OK." Also do not give out simple answers or platitude, such as "You have everything to be thankful for."
5. Do not abandon the individual after the crisis has passed or after professional help has commenced.

From Gayle Dorman, et al., *Living with 10- to 15-Year-Olds: A Parent Education Curriculum.* Copyright © 1982 Center for Adolescence, Carrboro, NC. Reprinted by permission.

Anorexia nervosa has become a prominent position in adolescent females.

conspicuous instability in work and in relationships, depression, or alcoholism also were present in the women's lives (Tomlinson-Keasey, Warren, & Elliot, 1986). These factors are similar to those found to predict suicide among gifted men (Shneidman, 1971).

Just as genetic factors are associated with depression, so are they associated with suicide. The closer the genetic relationship a person has to someone who has committed suicide, the more likely that person is to commit suicide (Wender & others, 1986). Table 6.3 provides valuable information about what to do and what not to do when you suspect someone is contemplating suicide.

Eating Disorders

Fifteen-year-old Jane gradually eliminated foods from her diet to the point where she subsisted by eating *only* applesauce and eggnog. She spent hours observing her own body, wrapping her fingers around her waist to see if it was getting any thinner. She fantasized about becoming a beautiful fashion model who would wear designer bathing suits. Even when she reached 85 pounds, Jane still felt fat. She continued to lose weight, eventually emaciating herself. She was hospitalized and treated for **anorexia nervosa,** *an eating disorder that involves the relentless*

pursuit of thinness through starvation. Eventually, anorexia nervosa can lead to death, as it did for popular singer Karen Carpenter.

Anorexia nervosa afflicts primarily females during adolescence and early adulthood (only about 5 percent of anorexics are male). Most individuals with this disorder are White and from well-educated, middle- and upper-income families. Although anorexics avoid eating, they have an intense interest in food; they cook for others, they talk about food, and they insist on watching others eat. Anorexics have a distorted body image, perceiving that they will look better even if they become skeletal. As self-starvation continues and the fat content of the body drops to a bare minimum, menstruation usually stops and behavior often becomes hyperactive (Polivy & Thomsen, 1987).

Numerous causes of anorexia nervosa have been proposed. They include societal, psychological, and physiological factors (Brooks-Gunn, 1993; Fisher & Brone, 1991; Litt, 1991; Sigman & Flanery, 1992; Striegel-Moore & others, 1993). The societal factor most often held responsible is the current fashion of thinness. Psychological factors include a motivation for attention, a desire for individuality, a denial of sexuality, and a way of coping with overcontrolling parents. Anorexics sometimes have families that place high demands for achievement on them. Unable to meet their parents' high standards, anorexics feel unable to control their own lives. By limiting their food intake, anorexics gain a sense of self-control. Physiological causes focus on the hypothalamus, which becomes abnormal in a number of ways when an individual becomes anorexic. At this time, however, we are not exactly certain what causes anorexia nervosa.

Bulimia *is an eating disorder that involves a binge-and-purge sequence on a regular basis.* Bulimics binge on large amounts of food and then purge by self-induced vomiting or the use of a laxative. The binges sometimes alternate with fasting; at other times, they alternate with normal eating behavior. Like anorexia nervosa, bulimia is primarily a female disorder, and it has become prevalent among college women. Some estimates suggest that one in two college women binge and purge at least some of the time. However, recent estimates suggest that true bulimics—those who binge and purge on a regular basis—make up less than 2 percent of the college female population (Stunkard, 1987). Whereas anorexics can control their eating, bulimics cannot. Depression is a common characteristic of bulimics (Levy, Dixon, & Stern, 1989). Many of the same causes proposed for anorexia nervosa are offered for bulimia.

The Interrelation of Problems and Programs that Prevent or Reduce Adolescent Problems

So far we have described some of the major problems adolescents are at risk for developing. In the next chapter, we will discuss another major problem in adolescence—school dropouts. In many instances, adolescents have more than one problem. Researchers are increasingly finding that problem behaviors in adolescence are interrelated. For example, heavy substance abuse is related to early sexual activity, lower grades, dropping out of school, and delinquency. Early initiation of sexual activity is associated with the use of cigarettes and alcohol, use of marijuana and other illicit drugs, lower grades, dropping out of school and delinquency. Delinquency is related to early sexual activity, early pregnancy, substance abuse, and dropping out of school. As many as 10 percent of the adolescent population in the United States have serious multiple-problem behaviors (adolescents who have dropped out of school or are behind in their grade level, are users of heavy drugs, regularly use cigarettes and marijuana, and are sexually active but do not use contraception). Many, but not all, of these very high-risk youth "do it all." Another 15 percent of adolescents participate in many of these same behaviors but with slightly lower frequency and less deleterious consequences. This group of high-risk youth often engage in two- or three-problem behaviors (Barnes, Welte, & Dintcheff, 1992; Dryfoos, 1990, 1992; Scales, 1990).

> *There is no easy path leading out of life, and few are the easy ones that lie within it.*
> —Walter Savage Landor, *Imaginary Conversations,* 1824

In addition to understanding that many adolescents engage in multiple-problem behaviors, it also is important to develop programs that reduce adolescent problems. In a recent review of the programs that have been successful in preventing or reducing adolescent problems, adolescent researcher Joy Dryfoos (1990, 1992) described the common components of these successful programs. The common components include:

1. *Intensive individualized attention.* In successful programs, high-risk children are attached to a responsible adult who gives the child attention and deals with the child's specific needs. This theme occurred in a number of different programs. In a successful substance abuse program, a student assistance counselor was available full-time for individual counseling and referral for treatment.

2. *Communitywide multiagency collaborative approaches.* The basic philosophy of communitywide programs is that a number of different programs and services have to be in place (Dryfoos, 1992). In one successful substance abuse program a communitywide health promotion campaign was implemented that used local media and community education in concert with a substance abuse curriculum in the schools.

3. *Early identification and intervention.* Reaching children and their families before children develop problems, or at the beginning of their problems, is a successful strategy. One preschool program serves as an excellent model for the prevention of delinquency, pregnancy, substance abuse, and dropping out of school. Operated by the High Scope Foundation in Ypsilanti, Michigan, the Perry Preschool has had a long-term positive impact on its students (Berrueta-Clement & others, 1986). This enrichment program, directed by David Weikart, services disadvantaged Black American children. They attend a high-quality, two-year preschool program and receive weekly home visits from program personnel. Based on official police records, by age 19 individuals who had attended the Perry Preschool program were less likely to have been arrested and reported fewer adult offenses than a control group. The Perry Preschool students also were less likely to drop out of school and teachers rated their social behavior as more competent than that of a control group who did not receive the enriched preschool experience.

At this point we have discussed a number of ideas about adolescent sexuality and the problems and disturbances associated with adolescence. A summary of these ideas is presented in Concept Table 6.2. In the next section of the book, we will turn our attention to children's cognition, learning, information processing, and language development. We begin by exploring children's cognitive development in chapter 7.

CONCEPT TABLE 6.2

Puberty, Sexuality, and Some Adolescent Problems and Disorders

Concept	Processes/Related Ideas	Characteristics/Description
Puberty	Pubertal change	Puberty is a period of rapid skeletal and sexual maturation that occurs mainly in early adolescence. Testosterone plays an important role in male pubertal development, estradiol in female pubertal development. The growth spurt occurs about two years later for boys than for girls; 12 1/2 is the average age of onset for boys, 10 1/2 for girls. Individual maturation in pubertal change is extensive.
	Psychological accompaniments of physical change	Adolescents show a heightened interest in their body image. Early maturation favors boys, at least during adolescence. As adults, though, late-maturing boys achieve more stable identities than early-maturing boys. The results are more mixed for girls. Some researchers now question whether puberty's effects are as strong as once believed.
	Pubertal timing and health care	Most early- and late-maturing adolescents weather puberty's challenges competently. For those who do not, discussions with sensitive and knowledgeable health care providers and parents can improve the off-time maturing adolescent's coping abilities.
Sexuality	Heterosexual attitudes and behavior	In the twentieth century, there has been a major increase in the number of adolescents reporting intercourse. The number of females reporting intercourse has increased more rapidly than the proportion of males. National data indicate that, by age 17, 66 percent of males and 50 percent of females have had sexual intercourse. Inner-city adolescents have even higher incidences. As we develop our sexual attitudes, we follow certain sexual scripts, which often are different for females and males.
	Homosexual attitudes and behavior	Rates of homosexuality have remained constant in the twentieth century. Homosexuality is no longer classified as a disorder. Until recently, acceptance of homosexuality was increasing but, in concert with the AIDS epidemic, acceptance of homosexuality has decreased. No definitive conclusions about the causes of homosexuality have been reached.
	Sexually transmitted diseases	Any adolescent who has sex runs the risk of getting a sexually transmitted disease, formerly called venereal disease, although many adolescents underestimate their own risk. Among the sexually transmitted diseases adolescents may get are chlamydia, herpes simplex virus II, syphilis, and AIDS.
	AIDS	Acquired immune deficiency syndrome is caused by a virus that destroys the body's immune system. AIDS can only be transmitted through sexual contact, shared needles, or blood transfusion.

Concept	Processes/Related Ideas	Characteristics/Description
Adolescent problems and disorders	Adolescent pregnancy	More than 1 million American adolescents become pregnant each year. Eight of 10 adolescent pregnancies are unintended. Our nation's adolescent pregnancy rate is the highest in the Western world. Dramatic changes have swept through the American culture in the past three decades regarding adolescent sexuality and pregnancy. The consequences of adolescent pregnancy include health risks for the mother and the offspring. Adolescent mothers often drop out of school, fail to gain employment, and become dependent on welfare. Experts are calling for increased sex education and family planning, access to contraceptive methods, and broad community involvement and support. Abstention is also an important consideration.
	Drugs and alcohol	The United States has the highest adolescent drug use rate of any industrialized nation. The 1960s and 1970s were times of marked increase in adolescent drug use. Since the mid-1980s, there has been a slight overall downturn in drug use among adolescents. Alcohol is the drug most widely used by adolescents; alcohol abuse by adolescents is a major problem. Heavy drinking is common. Cocaine is a highly controversial drug. Its use by high school seniors dropped off for the first time in eight years in 1987, a trend that has continued.
	Suicide	The rate of suicide has increased. The suicide rate increases dramatically at about the age of 15. Both proximal and distal factors are involved in suicide's causes.
	Eating disorders	Anorexia nervosa and bulimia increasingly have become problems for adolescent females. Societal, psychological, and physiological causes of these disorders have been proposed.
	Interrelation of problems and programs that prevent or reduce adolescent problems	Very high-risk youth have multiple problem behaviors—they make up as many as 10 percent of adolescents. They include adolescents who have been arrested or have committed serious offenses, have dropped out of school or are behind their normal grade level, are users of heavy drugs, drink heavily, regularly use cigarettes and marijuana, and are sexually active but do not use contraception. High-risk youth include as many as 15 percent of adolescents who participate in these same behaviors but with slightly lower frequency and less deleterious consequences. Researchers are increasingly finding that problem behaviors in adolescence are interrelated. Dryfoos found a number of common components in programs designed to prevent or reduce adolescent problems; they include the importance of providing individual attention to high-risk children, the need to develop communitywide intervention, and early identification and intervention.

PERSPECTIVES ON PARENTING AND EDUCATION

Parenting, Education, and Drug Use

Parents, peers, and social support play important roles in preventing adolescent drug abuse (Cohen, Brook, & Kandel, 1991; Conger, Conger, & Simons, 1992; Dishion, 1992; Kandel, 1991). A developmental model of adolescent drug abuse has been proposed by Judith Brook and her colleagues (Brook & Brook, in press; Brook & others, 1990). They believe that the initial step in adolescent drug abuse is laid down in the childhood years, when children fail to receive nurturance from their parents and grow up in conflict-ridden families. These children fail to internalize their parents' personality, attitudes, and behavior, and later carry this absence of parental ties into adolescence. Adolescent characteristics, such as lack of a conventional orientation and inability to control emotions, are then expressed in affiliations with peers who take drugs, which, in turn, leads to drug use. In recent studies, Brook and her colleagues have found support for their model (Brook & others, 1990).

Positive relationships with parents and others are important in reducing adolescents' drug use (Hughes, Power, & Francis, 1992). In one study, social support (which consisted of good relationships with parents, siblings, adults, and peers) during adolescence substantially reduced drug abuse (Newcomb & Bentler, 1988). In another study, adolescents were most likely to take drugs when both their parents took drugs (such as tranquilizers, amphetamines, alcohol, or nicotine) and their peers took drugs (Kandel, 1974).

In a recent review of the role that schools can play in the prevention of drug abuse, Joy Dryfoos (1990) concluded that a consensus is beginning to be reached:

1. Early intervention in schools is believed to be more effective than later intervention. This intervention works best when implemented before the onset of drug use. Middle school is often mentioned as an excellent time for the inclusion of drug abuse programs in schools.
2. Nonetheless, school-based drug abuse prevention requires a kindergarten through twelfth-grade approach, with age-appropriate components available. When school prevention programs are provided, the students need follow-up and continuous attention. Counseling about drug abuse should be available throughout the school years.
3. Teacher training is an important element in school-based programs. The best-designed drug abuse curriculum is ineffective in the hands of an inadequately prepared teacher. School systems need to provide time and resources for in-service training and supervision.
4. School skills training, especially focused on coping skills and resistance to peer pressure, is the most promising of the new wave of school-based curricula. However, the effectiveness of

"Just tell me where you kids get the idea to take so many drugs."
© 1990 by Sidney Harris.

these social skills training programs over the long term and whether or not they are as effective with high-risk youth as with others are not known.
5. Peer-led programs are often more effective than teacher-led or counselor-led programs, especially when older students (senior high) are the leaders and role models for younger students (junior high and middle school).
6. Most of the school-based programs have been general programs directed at all students, rather than specific programs targeted at high-risk adolescents. More programs aimed at the high-risk group are needed.
7. The most effective school-based programs are often part of communitywide prevention efforts that involve parents, peers, role models, media, police, courts, businesses, youth-serving agencies, as well as schools. ■

CONCLUSIONS

Growth in childhood slows down from its rapid rate in infancy, otherwise we would be a species of giants. After its slow growth in childhood, however, the rapid maturational changes of puberty arrive.

In this chapter, we began by discussing physical development in early childhood and in middle and late childhood, evaluating changes in a number of areas such as gross and fine motor skills. Then, we studied children's health, nu-

trition, and exercise. The last half of the chapter was devoted to pubertal change, including its psychological accompaniments, sexuality, and the adolescent problems of drug use, suicide, and eating disorders. We also discussed the interrelation of problems, programs that prevent or reduce adolescent problems, and the roles of parents and education in drug use. Don't forget to again read the two concept tables on pages 174 and 188,

which together will provide you with a summary of the chapter's contents.

This concludes Section Two (Biological Processes, Physical Development, and Perceptual Development) of the book. In Section Three, we will study the nature of children's cognition, learning, information processing, and language development, beginning with chapter 7, Cognitive Development and Piaget's Theory.

KEY TERMS

deprivation dwarfism   A type of growth retardation caused by emotional deprivation; children are deprived of affection, which causes stress and alters the release of hormones by the pituitary gland. (161)

myelination   A process in which nerve cells are insulated with a layer of fat cells, which increases the speed at which information travels through the nervous system. (163)

oral rehydration therapy (ORT)   A treatment involving a range of techniques designed to prevent dehydration during episodes of diarrhea by giving children fluids by mouth. (168)

obesity   Weighing 20 percent or more above the ideal weight for a particular age; taking both age and sex into account. (168)

set point   This term refers to the weight maintained when no effort is made to gain or lose weight. (168)

menarche   First menstruation. (172)

puberty   A period of rapid skeletal and sexual maturation that occurs mainly in early adolescence. (173)

testosterone   A hormone associated with the development of genitals, an increase in height, and a change in voice in boys. (173)

estradiol   A hormone associated with breast, uterine, and skeletal development in girls. (173)

sexual script   A stereotyped pattern of role prescriptions for how individuals should behave sexually. (179)

chlamydia   A sexually transmitted disease named for the bacteria that cause it. (180)

herpes simplex virus II   A virus that causes a sexually transmitted disease whose symptoms include irregular cycles of sores and blisters in the genital area. (180)

AIDS (acquired immune deficiency syndrome)   A virus that destroys the body's immune system. Consequently, germs that usually do not harm someone with a normal immune system produce devastating results and death. (181)

anorexia nervosa   An eating disorder that involves the relentless pursuit of thinness through starvation. (186)

bulimia   An eating disorder that involves a binge-and-purge sequence on a regular basis. (187)

SUGGESTED READINGS

Dryfoos, J. G. (1990). *Adolescents at risk: Prevalence and prevention.* New York: Oxford University Press. This excellent book provides a broad overview of at-risk youth and programs to improve their lives.

Family Planning Perspectives. This journal includes research articles on adolescent pregnancy and contraceptive use. Leaf through the issues of the last several years to discover the nature of research in this field and to read about current ideas on adolescent sexuality.

Grant, J. P. (1993). *The state of the world's children.* New York: UNICEF and Oxford University Press. This book provides an analysis of children's illness, health, and death in more than 100 countries around the world. Detailed charts and tables about death rates and nutrition are included, as are ways to reduce the child death rate and malnutrition.

Steinberg, L., & Levine, A. (1990). *You and your adolescent.* New York: Harper Collins. An excellent book written for parents of adolescents that will help parents understand the adolescent's development.

Cognition, Learning, Information Processing, and Language Development

Learning is an Ornament in Prosperity, a Refuge in Diversity.

—Aristotle

Children thirst to know and understand. In their effort to know and understand, they construct their own ideas about the world around them. They are remarkable for their curiosity and their intelligence. In Section Three, you will read four chapters: Cognitive Development and Piaget's Theory (7), Learning and Information Processing (8), Intelligence (9), and Language Development (10).

The Gifted Boy, Paul Klee,
1879–1949 (Detail)

7

Cognitive Development and Piaget's Theory

PERSPECTIVES ON PARENTING AND EDUCATION

Apprenticeship Training 224

Chapter Boxes

We are born capable of learning.
    —Jean-Jacques Rousseau

> *I wish I could travel by the road that crosses baby's mind, and out beyond all bounds; where messengers run errands for no cause between the kingdoms of kings of no history; where Reason makes kites of her laws and flies them, and Truth sets Fact free from its fetters.*
>
> —Rabindranoth Tagore, 1913

IMAGES OF CHILDREN

The Doman Better Baby Institute and What Is Wrong with It

Matthew is 1 year old. He has already seen over 1,000 flash cards with pictures of shells, flowers, insects, flags, countries, and words on them. His mother, Billie, has made almost 10,000 of the 11-inch-square cards for Matthew and his 4-year-old brother, Mark. Billie has religiously followed the regimen recommended by Glenn Doman, the director of the Philadelphia Institute for the Achievement of Human Potential and the author of *How to Teach Your Baby to Read.* Using his methods, learned in a course called "How to Multiply Your Baby's Intelligence," Billie is teaching Matthew Japanese and even a little math. Mark is learning geography, natural science, engineering, and fine arts, as well.

Parents using the card approach print one word on each card using a bright red felt-tipped pen. The parent repeatedly shows the card to the infant while saying the word aloud. The first word is usually *mommy,* then comes *daddy,* the baby's name, parts of the body, and all the things the infant can touch. Infants are lavishly praised when they recognize the word. The idea is to imprint the large red words in the infant's memory, so that in time the baby accumulates an impressive vocabulary and begins to read. The parent continues to feed the infant with all manner of information in small, assimilable bits, just as Billie Rash has done with her two boys.

Using this method, the child should be reading by 2 years of age, and by 4 or 5 should have begun mastering some math and be able to play the violin, not to mention the vast knowledge of the world he should be able to display because of a

These infants and toddlers are being taught in the manner recommended by Glenn Doman which emphasizes the acceleration of learning to read by intensely exposing children to flash cards with many different words on them. Most developmental psychologists believe there is something fundamentally wrong with Doman's approach. They believe that, rather than pouring information into children's minds in the way Doman advises, children should be permitted to explore their environment spontaneously and to construct their knowledge independently.

monumental vocabulary. Maybe the SAT or ACT test you labored through on your way to college might have been conquered at the age of 6 if your parents had only been enrolled in "How to Multiply Your Baby's Intelligence" course and made 10,000 flash cards for you.

Is this the best way for an infant to learn? A number of developmentalists believe Doman's "better baby institute" is a money-making scheme and is not based on sound scientific evidence. They believe that we should not be trying to accelerate the infant's learning so dra-

matically. Rather than have information poured into infants' minds, infants should be permitted more time to spontaneously explore the environment and construct their knowledge. Jean Piaget called "What should we do to foster cognitive development?" the American question, because it was asked of him so often when he lectured to American audiences. Developmentalists worry that children exposed to Doman's methods will burn out on learning. What is probably more important is providing a rich and emotionally supportive atmosphere for learning.

PREVIEW

We will spend most of this chapter examining Piaget's theory of cognitive development. Piaget's four main stages of cognitive development will be examined in depth, applications of his theory to education will be presented, and contributions and criticisms of his theory will be outlined. Then we will consider a provocative theory of children's cognitive development that has recently been given a great deal of attention, that of Russian psychologist Lev Vygotsky.

PIAGET'S COGNITIVE DEVELOPMENTAL THEORY

What is Piaget's place in developmental psychology? What is the basic nature of his theory?

Jean Piaget and His Place in Developmental Psychology

In discussing Sigmund Feud's contribution to psychology, Edwin Boring (1950) remarked that it is not likely the history of experimental psychology can be written in the next three centuries without mention of Freud's name and still claim to be a general history of psychology. Indeed, the best criterion of greatness may be posthumous fame. Four decades after Boring published his book, it seems likely that his judgment was accurate—Freud is still a dominating presence in psychology. However, Jean Piaget's contribution to developmental psychology may be as important as Freud's contribution to personality and abnormal behavior. Piaget's death was a rather recent event (he died in 1980), so it may be too early to judge, but Piaget's contributions will be strongly felt for the foreseeable future. He truly is a giant in the field of developmental psychology.

Shortly after Piaget's death, John Flavell (1980), a leading Piagetian scholar, described what we owe Piaget:

> First, we owe him a host of insightful concepts of enduring power and fascination . . . concepts of object permanence, conservation, assimilation, accommodation, and decentration, for example. Second, we owe him a vast conceptual framework that has highlighted key issues and problems in human cognitive development. This framework is the now-familiar vision of the developing child, who, through its own active and creative commerce with its environment, builds an orderly succession of cognitive structures enroute to intellectual maturity. These two debts add up to a third, more general one: We owe him the present field of cognitive development. . . . Our task is now to extend and go beyond what he began so well. (p. 1)

Cognitive Developmental Theory and Processes

What is the basic nature of cognitive developmental theory? What cognitive processes are responsible for changes in a child's development?

Jean Piaget, the famous Swiss developmental psychologist, who changed forever the way we think of children's cognitive development.

Piaget stressed that children actively construct their own cognitive worlds; information is not just poured into their minds from the environment. Two processes underlie an individual's construction of the world: organization and adaptation. To make sense of our world, we organize our experiences. For example, we separate important ideas from less important ideas. We connect one idea to another. We not only organize our observations and experiences, however; we also *adapt* our thinking to include new ideas because additional information furthers understanding. Piaget (1954) believed that we adapt in two ways: assimilation and accommodation.

Assimilation *occurs when children incorporate new information into their existing knowledge.* **Accommodation** *occurs when children adjust to new information.* Consider a circumstance in which a 5-year-old girl is given a hammer and nails to hang a picture on the wall. She has never used a hammer, but from experience and observation she realizes that a hammer is an object to be held, that it is swung by the handle to hit the nail, and that it is usually swung a number of times. Recognizing each of these things, she fits her behavior into information she already has (assimilation). However, the hammer is heavy, so she holds it near the top. She swings too hard and the nail bends, so she adjusts the pressure of her strikes. These adjustments reveal her ability to alter her conception of the world slightly (accommodation).

Piaget thought that assimilation and accommodation operate even in a very young infant's life. Newborns reflexively suck everything that touches their lips (assimilation), but, after several months of experience, they construct their understanding of the world differently. Some objects, such as fingers and the mother's breast, can be sucked, and others, such as fuzzy blankets, should not be sucked (accommodation).

Piaget also emphasized that, to make sense out of their world, children cognitively organize their experiences. **Organization** *is Piaget's concept of grouping isolated behaviors into a higher-order, more smoothly functioning cognitive system. Every level of thought is organized.* Continual refinement of this organization is an inherent part of development. A boy who has only a vague idea about how to use a hammer may also have a vague idea about how to use other tools. After learning how to use each one, he must interrelate these uses, or organize his knowledge, if he is to become skilled in using tools. In the same way, children continually integrate and coordinate the many other branches of knowledge that often develop independently. Organization occurs within stages of development as well as across them.

Equilibration *is a mechanism in Piaget's theory invoked to explain how children shift from one stage of thought to the next. The shift occurs as children experience cognitive conflict or a disequilibrium in trying to understand the world. Eventually, the child resolves the conflict and reaches a balance, or equilibrium, of thought.* Piaget believed there is considerable movement between states of cognitive equilibrium and disequilibrium as assimilation and accommodation work in concert to produce cognitive change. For example, if a child believes that an amount of liquid changes simply because it is poured into a container with a different shape, she might be puzzled by such issues as where the "extra" liquid came from and whether there is actually more liquid to drink. The child will eventually resolve these puzzles as her thought becomes more advanced. In the everyday world, the child is constantly faced with such counter examples and inconsistencies. Let's now look in a detailed way at Piaget's stages of thought.

Piaget also believed that we go through four stages in understanding the world. Each of the stages is age-related and consists of distinct ways of thinking. Remember, it is the *different* way of understanding the world that makes one stage more advanced than another; knowing *more* information does not make a child's thinking more advanced in the Piagetian view. This is what Piaget meant when he said a child's cognition is *qualitatively* different in one stage compared with another. Let's now examine Piaget's first stage of cognitive development.

SENSORIMOTOR THOUGHT

Poet Nora Perry asked, "Who knows the thoughts of the child?" As much as anyone, Piaget knew. Through careful, inquisitive interviews and observations of his own three children—Laurent, Lucienne, and Jacqueline—Piaget changed our perceptions of the way infants think about their world. Two of the most important features of sensorimotor thought involve the child's coordination of sensation and action and the nonsymbolic aspects of the period.

The sensorimotor stage lasts from birth to about 2 years of age, corresponding to the period known as infancy. During this time, infants develop the ability to organize and coordinate their sensations and perceptions with their physical movements and actions. This coordination of sensation with action is the source of the term *sensorimotor*. The stage begins with the newborn, who has little more than reflexes to coordinate senses with actions. The stage ends with the 2-year-old, who has complex sensorimotor patterns and is beginning to adopt a primitive symbol system. For example, a 2-year-old can imagine looking at a toy and manipulating it with her hands before she actually does so. The child can also use simple sentences—for example, "Mommy, jump"—to represent a sensorimotor event that has just occurred.

Think about your dog or cat and the kind of intelligence the animal possesses. Although many of us brag about the intelligence of our pets, realistically we know that their cognitive abilities are limited. Piaget would argue that their abilities are limited in a specific way: They are bound up with the animal's behavior. They are not reflective or contemplative abilities, and they do not provide for conscious thinking about things that are not perceptually available. In a word, these abilities are not symbolic.

Think about your own cognition when you are engaged in behavior that is well practiced—such as driving home from work or mowing your lawn. There is a kind of intelligence in such behavior. You show tremendous physical coordination and timing and must continuously monitor perceptual information. You also must make many small adjustments and compensations, even some low-level decisions (for example, to change lanes in preparation for an upcoming turn or to stop when the light turns yellow). Yet, while accomplishing all of these complex behaviors, you may have been thinking about entirely different things (problems at work or with a personal relationship), and your subsequent ability to remember these behaviors probably is quite meager. Piaget would argue that the intelligence you use in such well-practiced behaviors is similar to that of your dog or cat—it is a nonsymbolic sensorimotor intelligence. Nonsymbolic, sensorimotor intelligence is what Piaget claimed for the very young infant, up until about 1½ years or so. Thus, the most critical aspect of Piaget's sensorimotor stage is that it is nonsymbolic throughout most of its duration (Flavell, Miller, & Miller, 1993; Piaget, 1970).

Additional arguments for the nonsymbolic nature of thought in early infancy concern the solving of problems through internal reflection or insight. Problem solving occurs quite early in life, perhaps by 12 months of age; however, Piaget claimed that, until about 1½ to 2 years of age, this problem solving is of the trial-and-error variety, devoid of an internal, symbolic component. For example, one of Piaget's daughters insightfully discovered how to get a matchbox open; looking at the slightly open matchbox, she began opening and closing her mouth. Only after making a few such movements did she reach for the matchbox and pull out its drawer with her hands. Piaget interpreted the moving-mouth behavior as reflecting internal, symbolic operations, which emerge only at the end of the sensorimotor stage.

The Substages of Sensorimotor Thought

The sensorimotor stage is divided into six substages, which describe qualitative changes in sensorimotor organization. Within a given substage, there may be different schemes—sucking, rooting, and blinking in Substage 1, for example. The term **scheme** *refers to the basic unit of an organized pattern of sensorimotor functioning.* In Substage 1, schemes are basically reflexive. From substage to substage, the organization of the schemes changes. The six substages of sensorimotor development are (1) simple reflexes; (2) first habits and primary circular reactions; (3) secondary circular reactions; (4) coordination of secondary, circular reactions; (5) tertiary circular reactions, novelty, and curiosity; and (6) internalization of schemes.

Simple reflexes *is Piaget's first sensorimotor substage, which corresponds to the first month after birth. In this substage, the basic means of coordinating sensation and action is through reflexive behaviors, such as rooting and sucking, which the infant has at birth.* In Substage 1, the infant exercises these reflexes. More important, the infant develops an ability to produce behaviors that resemble reflexes in the absence of obvious reflexive stimuli. A newborn may suck when a bottle or nipple is only nearby, for example. When the baby was just born, the bottle or nipple would have produced the sucking pattern only when placed directly in the newborn's mouth or touched to the lips. Reflexlike actions in the absence of a triggering stimulus is evidence that the infant is initiating action and is actively structuring experiences in the first month of life.

First habits and primary circular reactions *is Piaget's second sensorimotor substage, which develops between 1 and 4 months of age. In this substage, infants learn to coordinate sensation and types of schemes or structures—that is, habits and primary circular reactions.* A *habit* is a scheme based on a simple reflex, such as sucking, that has become completely divorced from its eliciting stimulus. For example, an infant in Substage 1 might suck when orally stimulated by a bottle or when visually shown the bottle, but an infant in Substage 2 might exercise the sucking scheme even when no bottle is present.

Primary circular reactions *are schemes based on the infant's attempt to reproduce an interesting or pleasurable event that initially occurred by chance.* In a popular Piagetian example, a child accidentally sucks his fingers when they are placed near his mouth; later, he searches for his fingers to suck them again, but the fingers do not cooperate in the search because the infant cannot coordinate visual and manual actions. Habits and circular reactions are stereotyped in that the infant repeats them the same way each time. The infant's own body remains the center of attention; there is no outward pull by environmental events.

Secondary circular reactions *is Piaget's third sensorimotor substage, which develops between 4 and 8 months of age. In this substage, infants become more object oriented or focused on the world, moving beyond preoccupation with the self in sensorimotor interactions.* The chance shaking of a rattle, for example, may fascinate the infant, and the infant will repeat this action for the sake of experiencing fascination. The infant imitates some simple actions of others, such as the baby talk or burbling of adults, and some physical gestures. However, these imitations are limited to actions the infant is already able to produce. Although directed toward objects in the world, the infant's schemes lack an intentional, goal-directed quality.

Coordination of secondary circular reactions *is Piaget's fourth sensorimotor substage, which develops between 8 and 12 months of age. In this substage, several significant changes take place involving the coordination of schemes and intentionality.* Infants readily combine and recombine previously learned schemes in a *coordinated* way. They may look at an object and grasp it simultaneously or visually inspect a toy, such as a rattle, and finger it simultaneously in obvious tactile exploration. Actions are even more outwardly directed than before. Related to this coordination is the second achievement—the development of *intentionality*, the separation of means and goals in accomplishing simple feats. For example, infants might manipulate a stick (the means) to bring a desired toy within reach (the goal). They may knock over one block in order to reach another to play with.

Tertiary circular reactions, novelty, and curiosity *is Piaget's fifth sensorimotor substage, which develops between 12 and 18 months of age. In this substage, infants become intrigued by the variety of properties that objects possess and by the multiplicity of things they can make happen to objects.* A block can be made to fall, spin, hit another object, slide across the ground, and so on. **Tertiary circular reactions** *are schemes in which the infant purposely explores new possibilities with objects, continually changing what is done to them and exploring the results.* Piaget said that this stage marks the developmental starting point for human curiosity and interest in novelty. Previous circular reactions have been devoted exclusively to reproducing former events, with the exception of imitation of novel acts, which occurs as early as Substage 4. The tertiary circular act is the first to be concerned with novelty.

Internalization of schemes *is Piaget's sixth sensorimotor substage, which develops between 18 and 24 months of age. In this substage, infants' mental functioning shifts from a purely sensorimotor plane to a symbolic plane, and they develop the ability to use primitive symbols.* According to Piaget, a *symbol* is an internalized sensory image or word that represents an event. Primitive symbols permit the infant to think about concrete events without directly acting them out or perceiving them. Moreover, symbols allow the infant to manipulate and transform the represented events in simple ways. In the Piagetian example mentioned earlier, Piaget's young daughter saw a matchbox being opened and closed; sometime later, she mimicked the event by opening and closing her mouth. This was an obvious expression of her image of the event. In another example, a child opened a door slowly to avoid disturbing a piece of paper lying on the floor on the other side. The child had an image of the unseen paper and what would happen to it if the door opened quickly. Developmentalists have debated whether 2-year-olds really have such representations of action sequences at their command, however (Corrigan, 1981).

Read further about Piaget's six substages of infant cognitive development in Explorations in Child Development 7.1, where you will find suggestions for a day-care curriculum based on those substages.

Object Permanence

Imagine what thought would be like if you could not distinguish between yourself and your world. Your thought would be chaotic, disorganized, and unpredictable. This is what the mental life of the newborn is like, according to Piaget. There is no self-world differentiation and no sense of object permanence (Piaget, 1952). By the end of the sensorimotor period, however, both are present.

Object permanence *is the Piagetian term for one of an infant's most important accomplishments: understanding that objects and events continue to exist even when they cannot directly be seen, heard, or touched.*

The principal way that object permanence is studied is by watching infants' reactions when an attractive object or event disappears (see figure 7.1). If they show no reaction, it is assumed they believe the object no longer exists. By contrast, if they are surprised at the disappearance and search for the object, it is assumed they believe it continues to exist. According to Piaget, object permanence develops in a series of substages that corresponds to the six substages of sensorimotor development. Table 7.1 shows how the six substages of object permanence reflect Piaget's substages of sensorimotor development.

Although Piaget's stage sequence is the best summary of what might happen as an infant fathoms the permanence of things in the world, some contradictory findings have emerged (Baillargeon, 1991, in press; Spelke, 1991). Piaget's stages

FIGURE 7.1

Object permanence. Piaget thought that object permanence was one of infancy's landmark cognitive accomplishments. For this 5-month-old boy, "out-of-sight" is literally out of mind. The infant looks at the toy monkey (top), but, when his view of the toy is blocked (bottom), he does not search for it. Eventually, he will search for the hidden toy monkey, reflecting the presence of object permanence.

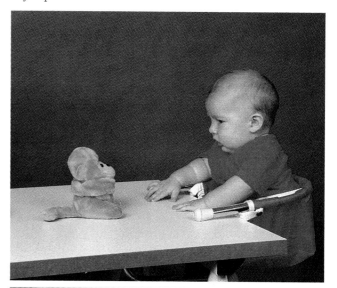

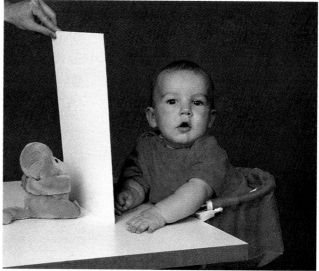

broadly describe the interesting changes reasonably well, but an infant's life is not neatly packaged into distinct organizations, as Piaget believed. Some of Piaget's explanations for the causes of change are debated.

For example, Piaget claimed that certain processes are crucial in stage transitions. The data do not always support his explanations, however. According to Piaget, the critical requirement for an infant to progress into sensorimotor Substage 4 is the coordination of vision and the sense of touch, or hand-eye coordination. Another important feature in the progress into Substage 4 is an infant's inclination to search for an object hidden in a familiar location rather than looking for the object in a new location. The **AB̄ error** *is the Piagetian object permanence concept in which an infant progressing into Substage*

TABLE 7.1

The Six Substages of Object Permanence

Sensorimotor Stage	Behavior
Substage 1	There is no apparent object permanence. When a spot of light moves across the visual field, an infant follows it but quickly ignores its disappearance.
Substage 2	A primitive form of object permanence develops. Given the same experience, the infant looks briefly at the spot where the light disappeared, with an expression of passive expectancy.
Substage 3	The infant's sense of object permanence undergoes further development. With the newfound ability to coordinate simple schemes, the infant shows clear patterns of searching for a missing object, with sustained visual and manual examination of the spot where the object apparently disappeared.
Substage 4	The infant actively searches for a missing object in the spot where it disappeared, with new actions to achieve the goal of searching effectively. For example, if an attractive toy has been hidden behind a screen, the child may look at the screen and try to push it away with a hand. If the screen is too heavy to move or is permanently fixed, the child readily substitutes a secondary scheme—for example, crawling around it or kicking it. These new actions signal that the infant's belief in the continued existence of the missing object is strengthening.
Substage 5	The infant now is able to track an object that disappears and reappears in several locations in rapid succession. For example, a toy may be hidden under different boxes in succession in front of the infant, who succeeds in finding it. The infant is apparently able to hold an image of the missing object in mind longer than before.
Substage 6	The infant can search for a missing object that disappeared and reappeared in several locations in succession, as before. In addition, the infant searches in the appropriate place even when the object has been hidden from view as it is being moved. This activity indicates that the infant is able to "imagine" the missing object and to follow the image from one location to the next.

4 makes frequent mistakes, selecting the familiar hiding place (A) rather than new hiding places (B̄). Researchers have found, however, that the AB̄ error does not show up consistently (Corrigan, 1981; Sophian, 1985). There is also accumulating evidence that AB̄ errors are sensitive to the delay between hid-

FIGURE 7.2

Piaget's description of the main characteristics of sensorimotor thought.

ing an object at B̄ and the infant's attempt to find it (Diamond, 1985). Thus, the AB̄ error might be partly due to the failure of memory.

> *There was a child who went forth every day. And the first object he looked upon, that object he became. And that object became part of him for the day, or a certain part of the day, or for many years, or stretching cycles of years.*
>
> —Walt Whitman

At this point, we have discussed a number of characteristics of Piaget's stage of sensorimotor thought. To help you remember Piaget's description of the main characteristics of sensorimotor thought, turn to figure 7.2.

A New Perspective on Cognitive Development in Infancy

In the past decade, a new understanding of infant's cognitive development has been taking place. For many years, Piaget's ideas were so widely known and respected that, to many psychologists, one aspect of development seemed certain: Human

EXPLORATIONS IN CHILD DEVELOPMENT 7.1

Suggestions for a Day–Care Curriculum Based on Piaget's Substages of Infant Cognitive Development

As more infants spend much of their day in day-care centers, it is important for the caregivers to interact in effective ways with the infants and for the day-care center to develop a curriculum that is appropriate for infant cognitive development. Following is a developmentally appropriate curriculum for infant cognitive development that was proposed by educator and developmentalist LaVisa Wilson (1990).

Piagetian Substage	Materials	Examples of Caregiver Strategies
Substage 1: Simple reflexes (birth–1 month)	Visually attractive crib and walls next to crib, objects near crib; occasional music, singing, talking, chimes	Provide nonrestrictive clothes, uncluttered crib, to allow freedom of movement; provide environment that commands attention during the infant's periods of alertness.
Substage 2: First habits and primary circular reactions (1–4 months)	Face and voice, musical toys, musical mobile, rattle; objects infant can grasp and are safe to go in the infant's mouth; objects the infant can grasp and lift	Provide change in infant's environment; carry infant around, hold infant, place infant in crib; observe, discuss, record changes in the infant; turn on musical toys and place where the infant can see them; place objects in the infant's hands or within the infant's reach; provide clothes that allow freedom of movement; provide time and space for repetition of behaviors.

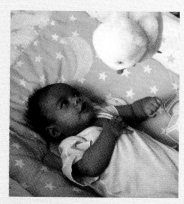

Piagetian Substage	Materials	Examples of Caregiver Strategies	
Substage 3: Secondary circular reactions (4–8 months)	Objects that attract attention (of contrasting colors, that change in sounds, have a variety of textures or designs); toys; balls	Watch movements the infant repeats, as when a waving arm hits the crib gym and then this action is repeated; provide materials that facilitate such repetitions (new items on the crib gym, for example); place blocks, dolls, ball, and other toys near the infant so they can be reached; initiate action, wait for the infant to imitate it, then repeat the action (smile, open mouth, for example).	
Substage 4: Coordination of secondary circular reactions (8–12 months)	Toys, visually attractive objects	Place objects near the infant; play hide-the-doll-under-the-blanket; place the block behind you; verbalize your own actions, such as "I put the ball behind me"; introduce new copy games; allow time and space for the infant to play.	
Substage 5: Tertiary circular reactions, novelty, and curiosity (12–18 months)	Blanket, paper, toys, dolls, spoon, interesting objects; water toys, water basin; narrow-neck milk carton and different sizes and shapes of objects	Play game of hide-the-object with infant—hide the object while the infant watches, let infant watch you move the object to a different place under the blanket, and ask, "Where is it?" "Can you find it?"; observe and allow infant to find the object, praise infant for good watching and thinking; allow infant to play with water and toys to discover different actions of water and of the objects in the water; provide time and materials that stimulate infant to think and try out new ideas; ask questions but do not tell answers or show infant; encourage infant to pretend—to drink from a pretend bottle like baby Gwen, to march like Pearl, to pick up toys; allow infant to repeat own play and develop own preferences.	
Substage 6: Internalization of schemes (18–24 months)		Allow toddler time to figure out solutions; allow toddler time to think and search for objects; observe toddler's representations and identify the ideas that seem important to the toddler; allow the toddler to act out conflict in play with toys and materials; observe toddlers play and identify consistent themes; provide clothes and materials that help the toddler pretend to be someone else.	

infants go through a long, protracted period during which they cannot think (Mandler, 1990). They can learn to recognize things and smile at them, to crawl, and to manipulate objects, but they do not yet have concepts and ideas. Piaget believed that only near the end of the sensorimotor stage of development, at about 1½ to 2 years of age, do infants learn how to represent the world in a symbolic, conceptual manner.

Piaget constructed his view of infancy mainly by observing the development of his own three children. Very few laboratory techniques were available at the time. Recently, however, sophisticated experimental techniques have been devised to study infants, and a large number of research studies on infant cognitive development have accumulated. Much of the new research suggests that Piaget's theory of sensorimotor development will have to be modified substantially.

Piaget's theory of sensorimotor development has been attacked from two sources. First, extensive research in the area of infant perceptual development suggests that a stable and differentiated perceptual world is established much earlier in infancy than Piaget envisioned. Second, researchers recently have found that memory and other forms of symbolic activity occur by at least the second half of the first year.

Perceptual Development

In chapter 5, we described research on infants' perceptual development, indicating that a number of theorists, such as Eleanor Gibson (1989), Elizabeth Spelke (1988, 1991), and Tom Bower (1989, 1993), believe that infants' perceptual abilities are highly developed very early in development. For example, Spelke has demonstrated that infants as young as 4 months of age have intermodal perception—the ability to coordinate information from two or more sensory modalities, such as vision and audition. Other research by Spelke (1988) and by Renée Baillargeon (1987, 1991) document that infants as young as 4 months expect objects to be substantial—in the sense that the objects cannot move through other objects; neither can other objects move through them—and permanent, in the sense that the objects are assumed to continue to exist when hidden. In sum, the perceptual development researchers believe that infants see objects as bounded, unitary, solid, and separate from their background, possibly at birth or shortly thereafter, but definitely by 3 to 4 months of age. Young infants still have much to learn about objects, but the world appears both stable and orderly to them and, thus, capable of being conceptualized.

Conceptual Development

It is more difficult to study what infants are thinking about than what they see. Still, researchers have devised ways to assess whether or not infants are thinking. One strategy is to look for symbolic activity, such as using a gesture to refer to something. Piaget (1952) used this strategy to document infants' motor recognition. For example, he observed his 6-month-old daughter make a gesture when she saw a familiar toy in a new location. She was used to kicking at the toy in her crib. When she saw it across the room, she made a brief kicking motion. However, Piaget did not consider this to be true symbolic activity because it was a motor movement, not a purely mental

act. Nonetheless, Piaget suggested that his daughter was referring to, or classifying, the toy through her actions (Mandler, 1990). In a similar way, infants whose parents use sign language have been observed to start using conventional signs at about 6 to 7 months of age (Bonvillian, Orlansky, & Novack, 1983).

Another type of evidence for conceptual functioning is the recall of absent objects or events. Piaget considered recall to be evidence of conceptual representation. Imagery or other symbolic means must be involved. We usually associate recall with the verbal re-creation of the past, and, as Piaget observed, this does not usually take place until about 18 months of age or older. However, recall does not have to be verbal, as we will see next.

To demonstrate recall, a researcher needs to see a baby do something such as find a hidden object after a delay or imitate a previously observed event. Andrew Meltzoff (1988) showed that 9-month-old infants can imitate actions they saw performed 24 hours earlier. This is approximately 9 months earlier than Piaget believed possible. In another recent experiment, by Baillargeon and others (1989), 8-month-olds searched for an object behind a screen 70 seconds after the object was hidden. In yet another experiment, 4-to-5-month-olds recalled an object's location 8 to 12 seconds later (Baillargeon, DeVos, & Graber, 1989). These performances of infants 9 months of age and younger reflect a representational ability that cannot be attributed to sensorimotor schemes.

In summary, the recent research on infants' perceptual and conceptual development suggests that infants have more sophisticated perceptual abilities and can begin to think earlier than Piaget envisioned. These researchers believe that infants either are born with or acquire these abilities early in their development (Mandler, 1990, 1992, in press a, b).

PREOPERATIONAL THOUGHT

The cognitive world of the preschool child is creative, free, and fanciful. In their art, suns sometimes show up as green and skies as yellow. Cars float on clouds, pelicans kiss seals, and people look like tadpoles. The imagination of preschool children works overtime and their mental grasp of the world improves. When Piaget described the preschool child's cognition as *preoperational* what did he mean?

The Nature of Preoperational Thought

Since this stage of thought is called *preoperational,* it would seem that not much of importance occurs until full-fledged operational thought appears. Not so. The preoperational stage stretches from approximately the age of 2 to the age of 7. It is a time when stable concepts are formed, mental reasoning emerges, egocentrism begins strongly and then weakens, and magical beliefs are constructed. Preoperational thought is anything but a convenient waiting period for concrete operational thought, although the label *preoperational* emphasizes that the child at this stage does not yet think in an operational way.

FIGURE 7.3

The three mountains task. View 1 shows the child's perspective from where he or she is sitting. View 2 is an example of the photograph the child would be shown mixed in with others from different perspectives. To correctly identify this view, the child has to take the perspective of a person sitting at spot (b). Invariably, a preschool child who thinks in a preoperational way cannot perform this task. When asked what a view of the mountains looks like from position (b), the child selects a photograph taken from location (a), the child's view at the time.

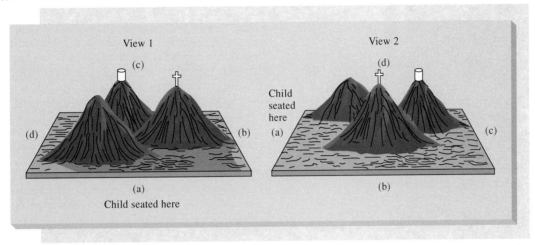

What are operations? **Operations** *are internalized sets of actions that allow the child to do mentally what before was done physically.* Operations are highly organized and conform to certain rules and principles of logic. The operations appear in one form in concrete operational thought and in another form in formal operational thought. Thought in the preoperational stage is still flawed and not well organized. Preoperational thought is the beginning of the ability to reconstruct at the level of thought what has been established in behavior. Preoperational thought also involves a transition from primitive to more sophisticated use of symbols.

The Substages of Preoperational Thought

Preoperational thought can be subdivided into two substages: the symbolic function substage and the intuitive thought substage.

Symbolic Function Substage

The **symbolic function substage** *is the first substage of preoperational thought, occurring roughly between the ages of 2 and 4. In this substage, the young child gains the ability to mentally represent an object that is not present.* The ability to engage in such symbolic thought is called symbolic function, and it vastly expands the child's mental world. Young children use scribbled designs to represent people, houses, cars, clouds, and so on. More on young children's scribbles and art appears in Explorations in Child Development 7.2). Other examples of symbolism in early childhood are the prevalence of pretend play (to be discussed in chapter 16) and language (to be discussed in chapter 10). In sum, the ability to think symbolically and represent the world mentally predominates in this early substage of preoperational thought. However, although young children make distinct progress during this substage, their thought still has several important limitations, two of which are egocentrism and animism.

Egocentrism *is a salient feature of preoperational thought. It is the inability to distinguish between one's own perspective and someone else's perspective.* The following telephone conversation between 4-year-old Mary, who is at home, and her father, who is at work, typifies Mary's egocentric thought:

Father: Mary, is Mommy there?

Mary: (Silently nods)

Father: Mary, may I speak to Mommy?

Mary: (Nods again silently)

Mary's response is egocentric in that she fails to consider her father's perspective before replying. A nonegocentric thinker would have responded verbally.

Piaget and Barbel Inhelder (1969) initially studied young children's egocentrism by devising the three mountains task (see figure 7.3). The child walks around the model of the mountains and becomes familiar with what the mountains look like from different perspectives and can see that there are different objects on the mountains. The child is then seated on one side of the table on which the mountains are placed. The experimenter moves a doll to different locations around the table, at each location asking the child to select, from a series of photos, the one photo that most accurately reflects the view the doll is seeing. Children in the preoperational stage often pick their view from where they are sitting rather than the doll's view.

EXPLORATIONS IN CHILD DEVELOPMENT 7.2

Where Pelicans Kiss Seals, Cars Float on Clouds, and Humans Are Tadpoles

At about 3 years of age and sometimes even 2, children's spontaneous scribbles begin to resemble pictures. One 3½-year-old child looked at the scribble he had just drawn and said it was a pelican kissing a seal (figure 7.A). At about 3 to 4 years of age, children begin to create symbols of humans. Invariably the first symbols look curiously like tadpoles.

These observations of children's drawings were made by Densie Wolf, Carol Fucigna, and Howard Gardner at Harvard University. They point out that many people think young children draw a person in this rather odd way because it is the best they can do. Piaget said children intend their drawings to be realistic; they draw what they know rather than what they see. So the tadpole with its strange exemptions of trunk and arms might reflect a child's lack of knowledge of the human body and how its parts fit together. However, children know more about the human body than they are capable of drawing. One 3-year-old child drew a tadpole but described it in complete detail, pointing out where the feet, chin, and neck were. When 3-and 4-year-old children are asked to draw someone playing ball, they produce symbols of humans that include arms, since the task implicitly requires arms.

Possibly because preschool children are not very concerned about reality, their drawings are fanciful and inventive. Suns are blue, skies are yellow, trees are purple, and cars float on clouds in the preschool child's symbolic world. The symbolism is simple but strong, not unlike the abstractions found in some contemporary art. In the elementary school years, the child's symbols become more realistic, neat, and precise. Suns are yellow, skies are blue, trees are green, and cars are placed on roads (figure 7.B).

A child's ability to symbolically represent the world on paper is related to the development of perceptual motor skills. But once such skills are developed, some artists revert to the style of young children's drawings. As Picasso once commented, "I used to draw like Raphael but it has taken me a whole lifetime to lean to draw like children" (Winner, 1986).

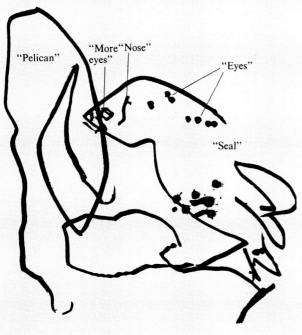

FIGURE 7.A

A 3½-year-old's symbolic drawing. Halfway into this drawing, the 3½-year-old artist said it was "a pelican kissing a seal."

FIGURE 7.B

An 11-year-old's drawing. An 11-year-old's drawing is neater and more realistic but also less inventive.

"Mrs. Hammond! I'd know you anywhere from little Billy's portrait of you."
Drawing by Frascino; © 1988 The New Yorker Magazine, Inc.

Perspective-taking does not seem to develop uniformly in preschool children, who frequently show perspective skills on some tasks but not others (Shantz, 1983).

> *False would be a picture which insisted on the brutal egocentrism of the child, and ignored the physical beauty which softens it.*
>
> —A. A. Milne

Animism, *another facet of preoperational thought, is the belief that inanimate objects have "lifelike" qualities and are capable of action.* A young child might show animism by saying, "That tree pushed the leaf off, and it fell down," or "The sidewalk made me mad; it made me fall down." A young child who uses animism fails to distinguish the appropriate occasions for using human and nonhuman perspectives. Some developmentalists, though, believe that animism represents incomplete knowledge and understanding, not a general conception of the world (Dolgin & Behrend, 1984).

Intuitive Thought Substage

Tommy is 4 years old. Although he is starting to develop his own ideas about the world he lives in, they are still simple and he is not very good at thinking things out. He has difficulty understanding events he knows are taking place but cannot see. He has little control over reality, to which his fantasized thoughts bear little resemblance. He cannot yet reliably answer the question "What if?" For example, he has only a vague idea of what would happen if a car were to hit him. He also has difficulty negotiating traffic because he cannot do the mental calculations necessary to estimate whether an approaching car will hit him when he crosses the road (Goodman, 1979).

The **intuitive thought substage** *is the second substage of preoperational thought, occurring approximately between 4 and 7 years of age. In this substage, children begin to use primitive reasoning and want to know the answers to all sorts of questions.* Piaget called this time period *intuitive* because, on one hand, young children seem sure about their knowledge and understanding yet are unaware of how they know what they know. That is, they say they know something but know it without the use of rational thinking.

An example of young children's reasoning ability is the difficulty they have putting things into their correct classes. Faced with a random collection of objects that can be grouped

together on the basis of two or more properties, a preoperational child is seldom capable of using these properties consistently to sort the objects into appropriate categories. Look at the collection of objects in figure 7.4a. You would respond to the direction "Put the things together that you believe belong together" by sorting them by size and shape. Your sorting might look something like that shown in figure 7.4b. In the social realm, a 4-year-old girl might be given the task of dividing her peers into groups according to whether they are friends and whether they are boys or girls. She would be unlikely to arrive at the following classification: friendly boys, friendly girls, unfriendly boys, unfriendly girls. Another example of classification shortcomings involves the preoperational child's understanding of religious concepts (Elkind, 1976). When asked "Can you be a Protestant and an American at the same time?" 6- and 7-year-olds usually say no; 9-year-olds are likely to say yes, understanding that objects can be cross-classified simultaneously.

Many of these examples show a characteristic of preoperational thought called **centration,** *the focusing, or centering, of attention on one characteristic to the exclusion of all others.* Centration is most clearly evidenced in young children's lack of **conservation,** *the idea that an amount stays the same regardless of how its container changes.* To adults, it is obvious that a certain amount of liquid stays the same regardless of a container's shape, but this is not obvious at all to young children; instead, they are struck by the height of the liquid in the container. In the conservation task—Piaget's most famous—a child is presented with two identical beakers, each filled to the same level with liquid (see figure 7.5). The child is asked if the beakers have the same amount of liquid, and she usually says yes. Then the liquid from one beaker is poured into a third beaker, which is taller and thinner than the first two. The child is then asked if the amount of liquid in the tall, thin beaker is equal to that which remains in one of the original beakers. If the child is younger than 7 or 8 years old, she usually says no and justifies her answer in terms of the differing height or width of the beakers. Older children usually answer yes and justify their answers appropriately ("If you poured the milk back, the amount would still be the same"). The older child can mentally reverse actions; the preoperational child cannot.

In Piaget's theory, failing the conservation of liquid task is a sign that children are at the preoperational stage of cognitive development, whereas passing this test is a sign that they are at the concrete operational stage. In Piaget's view, preoperational children not only fail to show conservation of liquid but also of number, matter, length, volume, and area (see figure 7.6).

Some developmentalists do not believe Piaget was entirely correct in his estimate of when children's conservation skills emerge. For example, Rochel Gelman (1969; Gelman & Baillargeon, 1983) has shown that, when an experimenter instructs a child to attend to relevant aspects of the conservation task, the child is more likely to conserve. Gelman has also demonstrated that attentional training on one type of task, such as numbers, improves the preschool child's performance on another type of task, such as mass. Thus, Gelman believes

FIGURE 7.4A
A random array of objects.

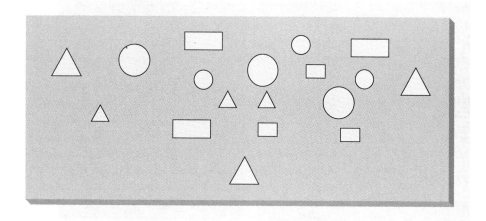

FIGURE 7.4B

An ordered array of objects.

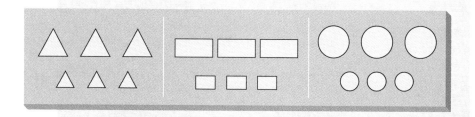

FIGURE 7.5

Piaget's conservation task. The beaker test is a well-known Piagetian test to determine whether a child can think operationally—that is, can mentally reverse actions and show conservation of the substance. (*a*) Two identical beakers are presented to the child. Then, the experimenter pours the liquid from B into C, which is taller and thinner than A or B. (*b*) The child is asked if these beakers (A and C) have the same amount of liquid. The preoperational child says no. When asked to point to the beaker that has more liquid, the preoperational child points to the tall, thin beaker.

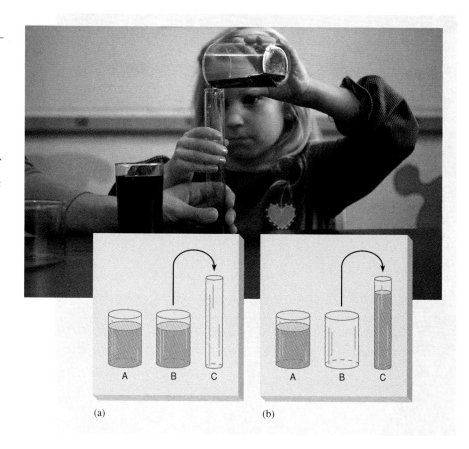

(a)   (b)

FIGURE 7.6

Some dimensions of conservation: number, matter, length, volume, and area.

Type of conservation	Initial presentation	Manipulation	Preoperational child's answer
Number	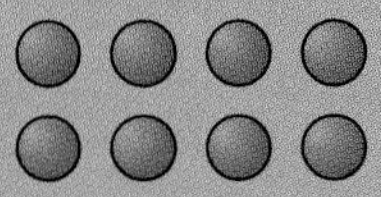 Two identical rows of objects are shown to the child, who agrees they have the same number.	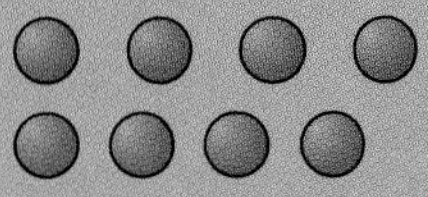 One row is lengthened and the child is asked whether one row now has more objects.	Yes, the longer row.
Matter	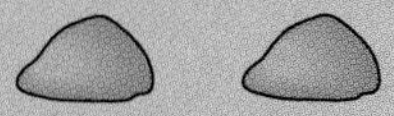 Two identical balls of clay are shown to the child. The child agrees that they are equal.	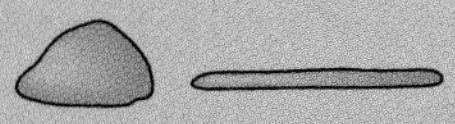 The experimenter changes the shape of one of the balls and asks the child whether they still contain equal amounts of clay.	No, the longer one has more.
Length	 Two sticks are aligned in front of the child. The child agrees that they are the same length.	 The experimenter moves one stick to the right, then asks the child if they are equal in length.	No, the one on the top is longer.
Volume	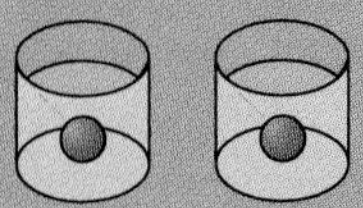 Two balls are placed in two identical glasses with an equal amount of water. The child sees the balls displace equal amounts of water.	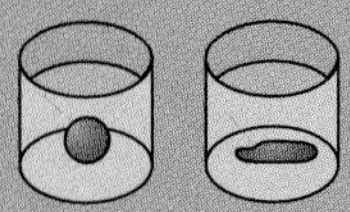 The experimenter changes the shape of one of the balls and asks the child if it still will displace the same amount of water.	No, the longer one on the right displaces more.
Area	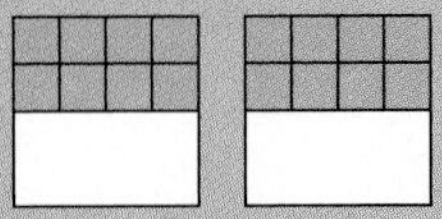 Two identical sheets of cardboard have wooden blocks placed on them in identical positions. The child agrees that the same amount of space is left on each piece of cardboard.	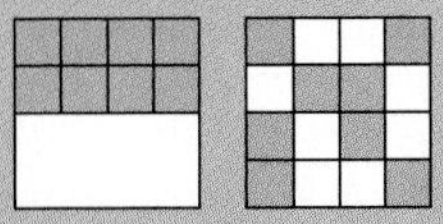 The experimenter scatters the blocks on one piece of cardboard and then asks the child if one of the cardboard pieces has more space covered.	Yes, the one on the right has more space covered up.

that conservation appears earlier than Piaget thought and that the process of attention is especially important in explaining conservation.

Critical Thinking

Is preoperational thought something that develops through maturation, or is it something that can be taught? Explain your answer.

Yet another characteristic of preoperational children is that they ask a barrage of questions. Children's earliest questions appear around the age of 3 and, by the age of 5, they have just about exhausted the adults around them with "why" questions. Their questions yield clues about their mental development and reflect intellectual curiosity. These questions signal the emergence of children's interest in reasoning and figuring out why things are the way they are. Some samples of the questions children ask during the questioning period of 4 to 6 years of age are the following (Elkind, 1976):

CONCEPT TABLE 7.1

Piaget's Place in Developmental Psychology, Cognitive Developmental Theory,
Cognitive Processes, Sensorimotor Development, and Preoperational Development

Concept	Processes/Related Ideas	Characteristics/Description
Piaget's place in developmental psychology and cognitive developmental theory	Piaget's giant stature	Piaget's contribution to developmental psychology may be as important as Freud's contribution to personality and abnormal psychology. We owe him the present field of cognitive development.
	Cognitive developmental theory	The developing child's rational thinking and stages of thought are emphasized. Thoughts are the central focus of development, the primary determinants of children's action.
Cognitive processes in Piaget's theory	Adaptation	Piaget developed this concept of the child's effective interaction with the environment. The interaction is a cognitive one that involves assimilation and accommodation.
	Assimilation and accommodation	Assimilation occurs when children incorporate new information into their existing knowledge. Accommodation occurs when children adjust to new information.
	Organization	Organization is Piaget's concept of grouping isolated behaviors into a higher-order, more smoothly functioning cognitive system. Every level of thought is organized.
	Equilibration	Equilibration is a mechanism in Piaget's theory involved to explain how children shift from one stage of thought to the next. The shift occurs as the child experiences cognitive conflict or a disequilibrium in trying to understand the world. Eventually, the child resolves the conflict and reaches a balance, or equilibrium, of thought. Piaget believed there is considerable movement between states of cognitive equilibrium and disequilibrium as assimilation and accommodation work in concert to produce cognitive change.
Sensorimotor thought	Basic features	The infant is able to organize and coordinate sensations with physical movements. The stage lasts from birth to about 2 years of age and is nonsymbolic through most of its duration.

"What makes you grow up?"

"What makes you stop growing?"

"Why does a lady have to be married to have a baby?"

"Who was the mother when everybody was a baby?"

"Why do leaves fall?"

"Why does the sun shine?"

At this point, we have discussed a number of preoperational thought's characteristics. To help you remember these characteristics, turn to figure 7.7. We also have discussed a number of ideas about Piaget and his place in child psychology, cognitive developmental theory, cognitive processes, sensorimotor thought, and preoperational thought. A summary of these ideas is presented in Concept Table 7.1.

CONCRETE OPERATIONAL THOUGHT

Remember that, according to Piaget, concrete operational thought is made up of operations—mental actions or representations that are reversible. In the well-known test of reversibility of thought involving conservation of matter, a child is presented with two identical balls of clay. An experimenter rolls one ball into a long, thin shape; the other remains in its original ball shape. The child is then asked if there is more clay in the ball or in the long, thin piece of clay. By the time children reach the age of 7 or 8, most answer that the amount of clay is the same. To answer this problem correctly, children have to imagine that the clay ball is rolled out into a long, thin strip and then returned to its original round shape—imagination that involves a reversible mental action. Thus, a concrete

Concept	Processes/Related Ideas	Characteristics/Description
	Substages of sensorimotor thought	Sensorimotor thought has six substages: simple reflexes; first habits and primary circular reactions; secondary circular reactions; coordination of secondary circular reactions; tertiary circular reactions, novelty, and curiosity; and internalization of schemes.
	Object permanence	Object permanence refers to the ability to understand that objects and events continue to exist even though the infant no longer is in contact with them. Piaget believed that this ability develops over the course of the six substages of sensorimotor thought.
	A new perspective on cognitive development in infancy	In the past decade, a new understanding of infants' cognitive development has been occurring. Piaget's theory has been attacked from two sources. First, extensive research in perceptual development suggests that a stable and differentiated perceptual world is established much earlier than Piaget envisioned. Second, researchers recently have found that memory and other forms of symbolic activity occur by at least the second half of the first year.
Preoperational thought	Its nature	It is the beginning of the ability to reconstruct at the level of thought what has been established in behavior, and a transition from primitive to more sophisticated use of symbols. The child does not yet think in an operational way.
	Symbolic function substage	This substage occurs roughly between 2 and 4 years of age and is characterized by symbolic thought, egocentrism, and animism.
	Intuitive thought substage	This substage stretches from approximately 4 to 7 years of age and is called intuitive because children seem sure about their knowledge, yet they are unaware of how they know what they know. The preoperational child lacks conservation and asks a barrage of questions.

operation is a reversible mental action on real, concrete objects. Concrete operations allow children to coordinate several characteristics rather than focus on a single property of an object. In the clay example, a preoperational child is likely to focus on height or width; a concrete operational child coordinates information about both dimensions. We can get a better understanding of concrete operational thought by considering further ideas about conservation and the nature of classification.

Conservation

We already have highlighted some of Piaget's basic ideas on conservation in our discussion of preoperational children's failure to answer questions correctly about such circumstances as the beaker task. Remember that conservation involves the recognition that the length, number, mass, quantity, area, weight, and volume of objects and substances do not change by transformations that alter their appearance. An important point that needs to be made about conservation is that children do not conserve all quantities or on all tasks simultaneously. The order of their mastery is number, length, liquid quantity, mass, weight, and volume. **Horizontal décalage** *is Piaget's concept that describes how similar abilities do not appear at the same time within a stage of development.* As we have just seen, during the concrete operational stage, conservation of number usually appears first and conservation of volume last. Also, an 8-year-old child may know that a long stick of clay can be rolled back into a ball but not understand that the ball and the stick weigh the same. At about 9 years of age, the child recognizes that they weigh the same and, eventually, at about 11 to 12 years of age, the child understands that the clay's volume is unchanged by rearranging it. Children initially master tasks in which the dimensions are more salient and visible, only later mastering those not as visually apparent, such as volume.

FIGURE 7.7

Preoperational thought's characteristics.

More symbolic than sensorimotor thought

Inability to engage in operations; can't mentally reverse actions: lacks conservation skills

Egocentric (inability to distinguish between own perspective and someone else's)

Intuitive rather than logical

Do children in all cultures acquire conservation skills at about the same age? To learn the answer to this question, turn to Sociocultural Worlds of Children 7.1.

Classification

Many of the concrete operations identified by Piaget focus on the way children reason about the properties of objects. One important skill that characterizes concrete operational children is the ability to classify or divide things into sets or subsets and to consider their interrelationships. An example of concrete operational classification skills involves a family tree of four generations (Furth & Wachs, 1975) (see figure 7.8). This family tree suggests that the grandfather (A) has three children (B, C, and D), each of whom has two children (E through J), and that one of these children (J) has three children (K, L, and M). A child who comprehends this classification system can move up and down a level (vertically), across a level (horizontally), and up and down and across (obliquely) within the system. The concrete operational child understands that person J can, at the same time, be father, brother, and grandson, for example.

Although concrete operational thought is more advanced than preoperational thought, it has its limitations. Logical reasoning replaces intuitive thought as long as the principles can be applied to specific or *concrete* examples. For example, a concrete operational child cannot imagine the steps necessary to complete an algebraic equation, which is too abstract for thinking at this stage of cognitive development. A summary of the characteristics of concrete operational thought is shown in figure 7.9.

Application of Piaget's Ideas to Education

Piaget was not an educator, but he did provide a sound conceptual framework from which to view educational problems. What are some of the principles in Piaget's theory of cognitive development that can be applied to children's education? David Elkind (1976) describes three. First, the foremost issue in education is *communication*. In Piaget's theory, a child's mind is not a blank slate; to the contrary, the child has a host of ideas about the physical and natural world, but these ideas differ from those of adults. Adults must learn to comprehend what children are saying and to respond in the same mode of discourse that

FIGURE 7.8

Classification: an important ability in concrete operational thought. A family tree of four generations (I to IV): the preoperational child has trouble classifying the members of the four generations; the concrete operational child can classify the members vertically, horizontally, and obliquely (up and down and across).

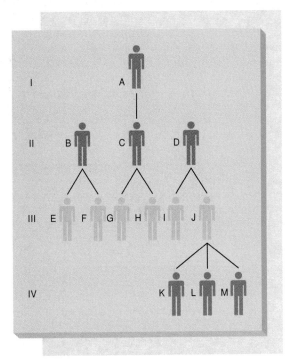

FIGURE 7.9

Characteristics of concrete operational thought.

children use. Second, the child is always unlearning and relearning in addition to acquiring knowledge. Children come to school with their own ideas about space, time, causality, quantity, and number. Third, the child is a knowing creature, motivated to acquire knowledge. The best way to nurture this motivation for knowledge is to allow the child to interact spontaneously with the environment; education needs to ensure that it does not dull the child's eagerness to know by providing an overly rigid curriculum that disrupts the child's rhythm and pace of learning.

FORMAL OPERATIONAL THOUGHT

Adolescents' developing power of thought opens up new cognitive and social horizons. Their thought becomes more abstract, logical, and idealistic; more capable of examining one's own thoughts, others' thoughts, and what others are thinking about one's self; and more likely to interpret and monitor the social world.

Characteristics of Formal Operational Thought

Piaget believed that formal operational thought comes into play between the ages of 11 and 15. Formal operational thought is more *abstract* than a child's thinking. Adolescents are no longer limited to actual concrete experience as the anchor of thought. Instead, they may conjure up make-believe situations, hypothetical possibilities, or purely abstract propositions and reason about them. Adolescents increasingly think about thought itself. One adolescent pondered, "I began thinking about why I was thinking what I was. Then I began thinking about why I

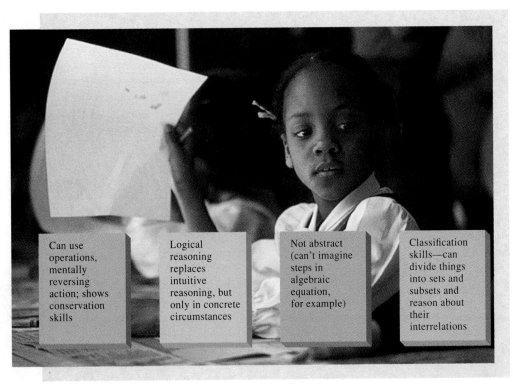

Can use operations, mentally reversing action; shows conservation skills

Logical reasoning replaces intuitive reasoning, but only in concrete circumstances

Not abstract (can't imagine steps in algebraic equation, for example)

Classification skills—can divide things into sets and subsets and reason about their interrelations

SOCIOCULTURAL WORLDS OF CHILDREN 7.1

Conservation Skills Around the World

Psychologist Patricia Greenfield (1966) conducted a series of studies among Wolof children in the West African nation of Senegal to see if Piaget's theory of concrete operational thought is universal. Using Piaget's beaker tasks, she found that only 50 percent of the 10-to-13-year-olds understood the principle of conservation. Comparable studies among cultures in central Australia, New Guinea (an island north of Australia), the Amazon jungle region of Brazil, and rural Sardinia (an island off the coast of Italy) yielded strongly similar results (Dasen, 1977). These findings suggested that adults in some cultures do not reach the stage of concrete operational thought.

However, if this were so, such adults would be severely handicapped in everyday life. Like preschool children, they would be unable to think through the implications of their actions and would be unable to coordinate various kinds of information about objects. They also would be incapable of going beyond an egocentric perspective to understand another person's point of view.

Some researchers believe that the failure to find concrete operational thought in various cultures is due to inadequate communication between the experimenter and the children. For example, in one study of two cultural groups from Cape Breton, NovaScotia—one English-speaking European, the other Micmac Indian—no difference in conservation abilities appeared between the groups of 10- to-11-year-olds when they were interviewed in their native languages (Nyiti, 1982). The Micmac children all spoke their ancestral tongue at home but had also spoken English since the first grade. However, when the Micmac children were interviewed in English, they understood the concept of conservation only half as well as the English-speaking children of European descent. This study illustrates the importance of communication between the experimenter and the research participants in cross-cultural studies.

Researchers have also investigated whether or not a child's ability to use the concept of conservation can improve if the child comes from a culture in which conservation is not widely practiced. In one study, rural aboriginal Australian children performed some exercises similar to Piaget's beaker task (Dasen, Ngini, & Lavaleé, 1979). This "training" improved their performance on the beaker task. Even so, their grasp of the conservation concept lagged behind children from the Australian city of Canberra by approximately 3 years. These

---

was thinking about why I was thinking about what I was." If this sounds abstract, it is, and it characterizes adolescents' increased interest on thought itself and the abstractness of thought.

Accompanying the abstract nature of adolescent thought is the quality of idealism. Adolescents begin to think about ideal characteristics for themselves and others and to compare themselves and others to these ideal standards. In contrast, children think more in terms of what is real and what is limited. During adolescence, thoughts often take fantasy flights into the future. It is not unusual for adolescents to become impatient with these newfound ideal standards and to be perplexed about which of many ideal standards to adopt.

At the same time adolescents think more abstractly and idealistically, they also think more logically. Adolescents begin to think more as a scientist thinks, devising plans to solve problems and systematically testing solutions. This type of problem solving has an imposing name. **Hypothetical-deductive reasoning** *is Piaget's formal operational concept that adolescents have the cognitive ability to develop hypotheses, or best guesses, about ways to solve problems, such as an algebraic equation. They then systematically deduce or conclude, which is the best path to fol-*

low in solving the problem. By contrast, children are more likely to solve problems in a trial-and-error fashion. An example of a hypothetical-deductive reasoning problem is presented in table 7.2 and a summary of the main features of formal operational thought is shown in figure 7.10.

> *The error of youth is to believe that intelligence is a substitute for experience, while the error of age is to believe that experience is a substitute for intelligence.*
>
> —Slyman Bryson

Adolescent Egocentrism

Another characteristic of adolescent thought is adolescent egocentrism. David Elkind (1978) believes that **adolescent egocentrism** *has two parts: an imaginary audience and a personal fable.* An **imaginary audience** *is an adolescent's belief that others are as preoccupied with her as she is.* Attention-getting behavior, common in adolescence, reflects egocentrism and the desire to be on-stage, noticed, and visible. Imagine an eighth-grade boy who thinks he is an actor and all others the audience as he stares

The age at which individuals acquire conversation skills is related to the extent to which the culture provides practice relevant to the concept of conservation. The children shown here live in Nepal, and they have extensive experience as potters. They gain an understanding of the concept of conservation of quantity earlier than children the same age who do not have experience manipulating a material like clay.

findings suggest that the aboriginal culture does not provide practice that is relevant to the conservation concept.

In sum, the age at which individuals acquire conservation skills is associated with the degree to which their culture provides relevant practice. However, such cross-cultural differences tend to disappear when the studies are conducted by experimenters who are familiar with the language of the people being studied or when the participants receive special training (Cole, 1992 a, b; Cole & Cole, 1989).

at the small spot on his trousers. Imagine the seventh-grade girl who thinks that all eyes are riveted on her complexion because of the tiny blemish she has. Current controversy about the nature of egocentrism focuses on whether it emerges because of formal operational thought (Elkind, 1985) or because of perspective-taking and interpersonal understanding (Lapsley, 1989a; Lapsley & Murphy, 1985).

Jennifer talks with her best friend, Anne, about something she has just heard. "Anne, did you hear about Barbara? You know she fools around a lot. Well, the word is that she is pregnant. Can you believe it? That would never happen to me." Later in the conversation, Anne tells Jennifer, "I really like Bob, but sometimes he's a jerk. He just can't understand me. He has no clue about what my personal feelings are." **Personal fable** *refers to adolescents' sense of personal uniqueness and indestructibility.* In their efforts to maintain a sense of uniqueness and indestructibility, adolescents sometimes create fictitious stories, or fables. Imagine a girl who is having difficulty getting a date. She may develop fictitious account of a handsome young man living in another part of the country who is madly in love with her.

". . . and give me good abstract-reasoning ability, interpersonal skills, cultural perspective, linguistic comprehension, and a high sociodynamic potential."
Drawing by Ed Fisher; © 1981 The New Yorker Magazine, Inc.

TABLE 7.2

An Example of Hypothetical-Deductive Reasoning

A common task for all of us is to determine what can be inferred logically from a statement made by someone else. Young children are often told by teachers that, if they work hard, they will receive good grades. Regardless of the empirical truth of the claim, the children may believe that good grades are the result of hard work and that, if they do not get good grades, they did not work hard enough. (Establishing the direction of the relationship between variables is an important issue.)

Children in the late concrete operational stage, too, are concerned with understanding the relations between their behavior and their teachers' grading practices. However, they are beginning to question the "truths" of their childhood. First, they now know that there are four possible combinations if two variables are dichotomized (work hard-not work hard; good grades-not good grades):

Behavior	Consequences
1 Work hard	Good grades
2 Work hard	Not good grades
3 Not work hard	Good grades
4 Not work hard	Not good grades

Two combinations are consistent with the hypothesis that hard work is necessarily related to good grades: (1) students work hard and get good grades and (4) they do not work hard and do not get good grades. When the presumed "cause" is present, the effect is present; when the cause is absent, the effect is absent. There are also two combinations that do not fit the hypothesis of a direct relation between hard work and good grades: (2) students work hard and do not get good grades and (3) they get good grades without working hard.

An adolescent's notion of possibility allows him or her to take this analysis of combinations one important step further. Each of the four basic combinations of binary variables may be true or it may not. If 1, 2, 3, or 4 is true alone or is true in combination, there are 16 possible patterns of truth values:

1 or 2 or 3 or 4 is true	4 patterns
1-2 or 1-3 or 1-4 or 2-3 or 2-4 or 3-4 are true	6 patterns
1-2-3 or 1-2-4 or 1-3-4 or 2-3-4 are true	4 patterns
All (1-2-3-4) are true	1 pattern
All are false	1 pattern
Total	16 patterns

The list is critically important because each pattern leads to a different conclusion about the possible relation between two variables.

Excerpt from *PIAGET: WITH FEELING* by Phillip Cowan, copyright © 1978 by Holt, Rinehart and Winston, Inc., reprinted by permission of the publisher.

Early and Late Formal Operational Thought

Formal operational thought has been conceptualized as occurring in two phases. In the first phase, the increased ability to think hypothetically produces unconstrained thoughts with unlimited possibilities. This early formal operational thought submerges reality (Broughton, 1983). Reality is overwhelmed. Idealism and possibility dominate. During the middle years of adolescence, an intellectual balance is restored; adolescents test the products of their reasoning against experience and develop a consolidation of formal operational thought.

Piaget's (1952) early writings seemed to indicate that the onset and consolidation of formal operational thought is completed during early adolescence, from about 12 to 15 years of age. Later, Piaget (1972) concluded that formal operational thought is not achieved until later in adolescence, between approximately 15 and 20 years of age.

Piaget's concepts of assimilation and accommodation help us understand the two phases of formal operational thought. Remember that *assimilation* occurs when adolescents incorporate new information into their existing knowledge; *accommodation* occurs when adolescents adjust to new information. During early adolescence, there is an excess of assimilation as the world is perceived too subjectively and idealistically. In the middle years of adolescence, an intellectual balance is restored, as the individual accommodates to the cognitive upheaval that has taken place. In this view, the assimilation of formal operational thought marks the transition to adolescence; accommodation marks a later consolidation of thought (Lapsley, 1989b).

Variations in Adolescent Cognition

Piaget's theory emphasizes universal and consistent patterns of formal operational thought; his theory does not adequately account for the unique differences that characterize the cognitive development of adolescents. These individual variations in adolescents' cognitive development have been documented in a number of investigations (Bart, 1971; Kaufmann & Flaitz, 1987; Neimark, 1982).

Some individuals in early adolescence are formal operational thinkers; others are not. A review of formal operational thought investigations revealed that only about one of every three eighth-grade students is a formal operational thinker (Strahan, 1983). Some investigators have found that formal operational thought increases with age in adolescence (Martorano, 1977); others have not (Strahan, 1987). Many college students and adults do not think in formal operational ways, either. For example, investigators have found that from 17 percent to 67 percent of all college students think in formal operational ways (Elkind, 1961; Tomlinson-Keasey, 1972).

Figure 7.10

Characteristics of formal operational thought. Adolescents begin to think more as scientists think, devising plans to solve problems and systematically testing solutions. Piaget gave this type of thinking the imposing name of hypothetical-deductive reasoning.

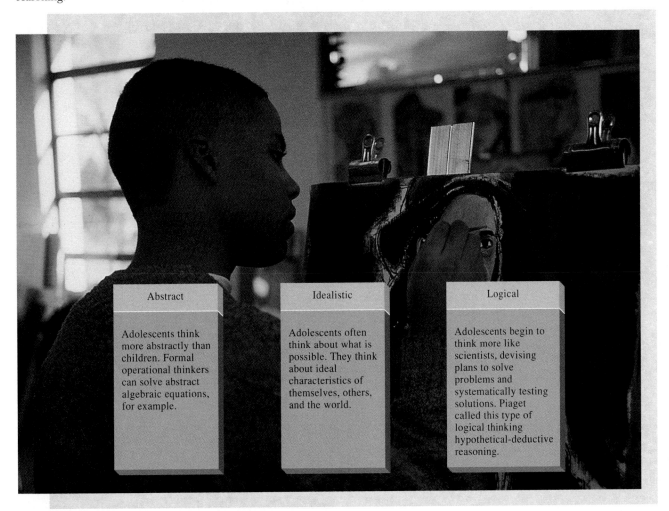

Abstract

Adolescents think more abstractly than children. Formal operational thinkers can solve abstract algebraic equations, for example.

Idealistic

Adolescents often think about what is possible. They think about ideal characteristics of themselves, others, and the world.

Logical

Adolescents begin to think more like scientists, devising plans to solve problems and systematically testing solutions. Piaget called this type of logical thinking hypothetical-deductive reasoning.

Many young adolescents are at the point of consolidating their concrete operational thought, using it more consistently than in childhood. At the same time, many young adolescents are just beginning to think in a formal operational manner. By late adolescence, many adolescents have begun to consolidate their formal operational thought, using it more consistently, and there often is variation across the content areas of formal operational thought, just as there is in concrete operational thought in childhood. A 14-year-old may reason at the formal operational level when it comes to analyzing algebraic equations but not do so with verbal problem solving or when reasoning about interpersonal relations.

Formal operational thought is more likely to be used in areas in which adolescents have the most experience and knowledge (Carey, 1988; Flavell, Miller, & Miller, 1993). Children and adolescents gradually build up elaborate knowledge through extensive experience and practice in various sports, games, hobbies, and school subjects such as math, English, and science. The development of expertise in different domains of life may make possible high-level, developmentally mature-looking thought. In some instances, the sophisticated reasoning of formal operational thought may be responsible. In other instances, however, the thought may be largely due to the accumulation of knowledge that allows more automatic, memory-based processes to function. Some developmentalists wonder if the acquisition of knowledge accounts for all cognitive growth. Most, however, argue that *both* cognitive changes in such areas as concrete and formal operational thought *and* the development of expertise through experience are at work in understanding the adolescent's cognitive world. More about knowledge's role in the adolescent's thinking appears in the next chapter.

Beyond Formal Operational Thought

Some critics of Piaget's theory argue that specialized thinking about a specific skill represents a higher stage of thought than formal operational thought. Piaget did not believe that this was so. For him, the change to reasoning about a special skill (such as the kind of thinking engaged in by a nuclear physicist or a medical researcher) is no more than window dressing. According to Piaget, a nuclear physicist may think in ways that an adolescent cannot think, but the adolescent and the nuclear physicist differ only in their familiarity with an academic field of inquiry. They differ in the content of their thought, not in the operations they bring to bear on the content (Piaget, 1970).

Some developmentalists believe that the absolute nature of adolescent logic and buoyant optimism diminish in early adulthood. According to Gisela Labouvie-Vief (1982, 1986), a new integration of thought takes place in early adulthood. She thinks that the adult years produce pragmatic constraints that require an adaptive strategy of less reliance on logical analysis in solving problems. Commitment, specialization, and channeling energy into finding one's niche in complex social and work systems replace the youth's fascination with idealized logic. If we assume that logical thought and buoyant optimism represent the criteria for cognitive maturity, we would have to admit that the cognitive activity of adults is too concrete and pragmatic. But from Labouvie-Vief's view, the adult's understanding of reality's constraints reflects maturity, not immaturity.

Even Piaget (1967) detected that formal operational thought may have its hazards:

> With the advent of formal intelligence, thinking takes wings and it is not surprising that at first this unexpected power is both used and abused. . . . Each new mental ability starts off by incorporating the world in a process of egocentric assimilation. Adolescent egocentricity is manifested by a belief in the omnipotence of reflection, as though the world should submit itself to idealistic schemes rather than to systems of reality. (pp. 63–64)

Our cognitive abilities are very strong in early adulthood, and they do show adaptation to life's pragmatic concerns. Less clear is whether our logical skills actually decline. Competence as a young adult probably requires doses of both logical thinking skills and pragmatic adaptation to reality. For example, when architects design a building, they logically analyze and plan the structure but understand the cost constraints, environmental concerns, and the time it will take to get the job done effectively.

William Perry (1981) also has charted some important changes in the way young adults think differently than adolescents. He believes that adolescents often view the world in a basic dualistic fashion of polarities—right/wrong, black/white, we/they, or good/bad, for example. As youth mature and move into the adulthood years, they gradually become aware of the diversity of opinion and the multiple perspectives that others hold, which shakes their dualistic perceptions. Their *dualistic*

(a)

(b)

(c)

(a) *Adolescents' thoughts are more abstract and idealistic than children's thoughts.* (b) *Young adults' thoughts are more pragmatic, specialized, and multiple (less dualistic) than adolescents' thoughts.* (c) *Older adults may not be as quick with their thoughts as younger adults, but they may have more general knowledge and wisdom. This elderly woman shares the wisdom of her experiences with a classroom of children.*

thinking gives way to *multiple thinking*, as they come to understand that authorities may not have all of the answers. They begin to carve out their own territory of individualistic thinking, often believing that everyone is entitled to their own opinion and that one's personal opinion is as good as anyone else's. As these personal opinions become challenged by others, multiple thinking yields to *relative subordinate thinking*, in which an analytical, evaluative approach to knowledge is consciously and actively pursued. Only in the shift to *full relativism* does the adult completely comprehend that truth is relative, that the meaning of an event is related to the context in which that event occurs and on the framework that the knower uses to understand that event. In full relativism, the adult recognizes that relativism pervades all aspects of life, not just the academic world. And in full relativism, the adult understands that knowledge is constructed, not given; contextual, not absolute. Perry's ideas, which are oriented toward well-educated, bright individuals (Rybash, Roodin, & Santrock, 1991), have been widely used by educators and counselors in working with young adults in academic settings.

Another candidate for thought that is more advanced than formal operational thought is wisdom, which like good wine, may get better with age. What is this thing we call wisdom? **Wisdom** *is expert knowledge about the practical aspects of life* (Baltes & Baltes, in press; Baltes & others, 1990). This practical knowledge involves exceptional insight into human development and life matters, good judgment, and an understanding of how to cope with difficult life problems. Thus, wisdom, more than standard conceptions of intelligence, focuses on life's pragmatic concerns and human conditions. This practical knowledge system takes many years to acquire, accumulating through intentional, planned experiences and through incidental experiences. Of course, not all older adults solve practical problems in wise ways. In one recent investigation, only 5 percent of adults' responses to life-planning problems were considered wise, and these wise responses were equally distributed across the early, middle, and late adulthood years (Smith & Baltes, in press).

What does the possibility that older adults are as wise or wiser than younger adults mean in terms of the basic issue of intellectual decline in adulthood? Remember that intelligence comes in different forms. In many instances, older adults are not as intelligent as younger adults when speed of processing is involved, and this probably harms their performance on many traditional school-related tasks and standardized intelligence tests. But consideration of general knowledge and something we call wisdom may result in an entirely different interpretation.

Now that we have considered many different ideas about Piaget's theory of adolescent cognition, including the issue of whether there are forms of thought more advanced than formal operational thinking, we turn our attention to evaluating Piagetian contributions and criticisms.

PIAGETIAN CONTRIBUTIONS AND CRITICISMS

We have spent considerable time outlining Piaget's theory of cognitive development. Let's briefly summarize some of Piaget's main contributions, and then enumerate criticisms of his theory.

Contributions

To restate what we said at the beginning of the chapter, we owe Piaget the present field of cognitive development. We owe him

Piaget, shown sitting on a bench, was a genius at observing children. By carefully observing and interviewing children, Piaget constructed his comprehensive theory of children's cognitive development.

a long list of masterful concepts of enduring power and fascination, such as object permanence, conservation, assimilation, and accommodation. We also owe Piaget the currently accepted vision of children as active, constructive thinkers who, through their commerce with the environment, make them manufacturers of their own development (Flavell, 1992).

Piaget was a genius when it came to observing children; his astute observations showed us inventive ways to discover how children, and even infants, act on and adapt to their world. Piaget showed us some important things to look for in children's cognitive development, including the shift from preoperational to concrete operational thought. He also showed us how we must make experiences fit our cognitive framework yet simultaneously adapt out cognitive orientation to experience. Piaget also revealed how cognitive change is likely to occur if the situation is structured to allow gradual movement to the next higher level (Beilin, 1992).

Criticisms

Piaget's theory has not gone unchallenged, however. Questions are raised about the following areas: estimates of the child's competence at different developmental levels; stages; training of children to reason at higher levels; and culture and education.

Estimates of Children's Competence. Some cognitive abilities emerge earlier than Piaget thought, and their subsequent development is more prolonged than he believed. As we saw earlier in the chapter, some aspects of object permanence emerge much earlier in infancy than Piaget believed. Even 2-year-olds are nonegocentric in some contexts—when they realize that another person will not see an object they see if the person is blindfolded or is looking in a different direction (Lempers, Flavell, & Flavell, 1977). Conservation of number has been demonstrated in children as young as 3 years of age, although Piaget did not think it came about until 7 years of age. Young children are not as "pre" this and "pre" that (precausal, preoperational) as Piaget thought (Flavell, 1992). Some aspects of formal operational thinking that involve abstract reasoning do not consistently emerge in early adolescence as Piaget envisioned. And adults often reason in far more irrational ways than Piaget believed (Siegler, 1991). In sum, recent trends highlight the cognitive competencies of infants and young children and the cognitive shortcomings of adolescents and adults (Flavell, 1992).

Stages. Piaget conceived of stages as unitary structures of thought, so his theory assumes synchrony in development. That is, various aspects of a stage should emerge at about the same time. However, several concrete operational concepts do not appear in synchrony. For example, children do not learn to conserve at the same time they learn to cross-classify.

Most contemporary developmentalists agree that children's cognitive development is not a grand stage-like as Piaget thought. **Neo-Piagetians** *are developmentalists who have elaborated on Piaget's theory, believing children's cognitive development is more specific in many respects than he thought* (Case, 1987, 1992, 1993; Pascual-Leone, 1987). Neo-Piagetians don't believe all of Piaget's ideas should be junked. However, they argue that a more accurate vision of the child's cognitive development involves fewer references to grand stages and more emphasis on the roles of strategies, skills, how fast and automatically children can process information, the task-specific nature of children's cognition, and the importance of dividing cognitive problems into smaller, more precise steps.

Neo-Piagetians still believe that children's cognitive development contains some general properties (Flavell, 1992). They stress that there is a regular, maturation-based increase with age in some aspects of the child's information-processing capacity, such as how fast or efficient the child processes information (Case, 1987, 1992; Demetriou & Efkides, in press; Fischer & Farrar, 1987; Halford, in press; Pascual-Leone, 1987; Sternberg, 1987). As the child's information-processing capacity increases with increasing age, new and more complex forms of cognition in all content domains are possible because the child can now hold in mind and think about more things at once. For example, Canadian developmentalist Robbie Case (1985) argues that adolescents have increasingly more available cognitive resources than they did as children because they can process information more automatically, they have more information-processing capacity, and they are more familiar

An outstanding teacher and education in the logic of science and mathematics are important cultural experiences that promote the development of formal operational thought. Schooling and education likely play more important roles in the development of formal operational thought than Piaget envisioned.

with a range of content knowledge. We will discuss the nature of children's information processing in much greater detail in the next chapter.

Training Children to Reason at a Higher Level. Children who are at one cognitive stage—such as preoperational thought—can be trained to reason at a higher cognitive stage—such as concrete operational thought. This poses a problem for Piaget, who argued that such training works only on a superficial level and is ineffective unless the child is at a transitional point from one stage to the next.

Culture and Education. Culture and education exert stronger influences on children's development than Piaget believed. Earlier in the chapter, we studied how the age at which individuals acquire conservation skills is associated to some extent with the degree to which their culture provides relevant practice. And in many developing countries, formal operational thought is a rare occurrence. And as you will learn shortly, there has been a wave of interest in how children's cognitive development progresses through interaction with skilled adults and peers, and how the children's embeddedness in a culture influences their cognitive growth. Such views stand in stark contrast to Piaget's view of the child as a solitary little scientist.

VYGOTSKY'S THEORY OF COGNITIVE DEVELOPMENT

Children's cognitive development does not occur in a social vacuum. Lev Vygotsky (1896–1934), a Russian psychologist, recognized this important point about children's minds more than half a century ago. Vygotsky's theory is increasingly receiving attention as we move toward the close of the twentieth century (Belmont, 1989; Butterworth, 1993; Glick, 1991; Light & Butterworth, 1993; Moll, 1991; Rogoff, in press; Rogoff &

Morelli, 1989; Wertsch & Tulviste, 1992). Before we turn to Vygotsky's ideas on language and thought and culture and society, let's examine his important concept called the zone of proximal development.

Zone of Proximal Development

The **zone of proximal development (ZPD)** *is Vygotsky's term for the range of tasks too difficult for children to master alone but that can be mastered with the guidance and assistance of adults or more highly skilled children.* Thus, the lower limit of the ZPD is the level of problem solving reached by a child working independently. The upper limit is the level of additional responsibility the child can accept with the assistance of an able instructor (see figure 7.11). Vygotsky's emphasis on ZPD underscored his belief in the importance of social influences on cognitive development and the role of instruction in children's development. As children experience verbal instruction or demonstration, they organize information into their existing mental structures so they can eventually perform the skill or task without assistance (Vygotsky, 1962).

The zone of proximal development is conceptualized as a measure of learning potential. IQ, or intelligence quotient, also is a measure of learning potential. However, IQ emphasizes that intelligence is a property of the child, whereas ZPD emphasizes that learning is interpersonal, a dynamic social event that depends on a minimum of two minds, one better informed or more drilled than the other. It is inappropriate to say that the child *has* a ZPD; rather, a child *shares* a ZPD with an instructor.

The practical teaching involved in ZPD begins toward the zone's upper limit, where the child is able to reach a goal only through close collaboration with an instructor. With adequate continuing instruction and practice, the child organizes and masters the behavioral sequences necessary to perform the target skill. As the instruction continues, the performance transfers from the instructor to the child as the teacher gradually reduces the explanations, hints, and demonstrations until the child is able to perform adequately alone. Once the goal is achieved, it may become the foundation for the development of a new ZPD.

Learning by toddlers provides an example of how the zone of proximal development works. Toddlers have to be motivated and must be involved in activities that involve skill at a reasonably high level of difficulty—that is, toward the zone's upper end. The teacher must have the know-how to exercise the target skill at any level required by the activity, and the teacher must be able to locate and stay in the zone. The teacher and the child also must adapt to each other's requirements. The reciprocal relationship between the toddler and the teacher adjusts dynamically as the division of labor is negotiated and aimed at increasing the weaker partner's share of the goal attainment. Vygotsky's concept of the zone of proximal development is also being effectively applied to teaching children math and how to read (Cox, 1993; Lightfoot, 1993).

FIGURE 7.11

Vygotsky's zone of proximal development. Vygotsky's zone of proximal development has a lower limit and an upper limit. Tasks in the ZPD are too difficult for the child to perform alone. They require assistance from an adult or a skilled child. As children experience the verbal instruction or demonstration, they organize the information in their existing mental structures so they can eventually perform the skill or task alone.

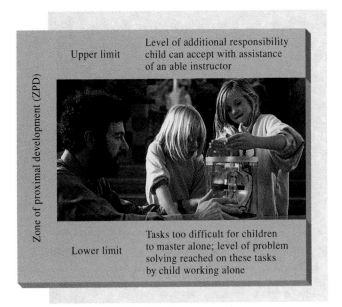

Language and Thought

In Vygotsky's view, a child's mental or cognitive structures are made of relations between mental functions. The relation between language and thought is believed to be especially important in this regard (Vygotsky, 1962). Vygotsky said that language and thought initially develop independently of each other but eventually merge.

Two principles govern the merging of thought and language. First, all mental functions have external or social origins. Children must use language and communicate with others before they focus inward to their own mental processes. Second, children must communicate externally and use language for a long period of time before the transition from external to internal speech takes place. This transition period occurs between 3 and 7 years of age and involves talking to oneself. After a while, the self-talk becomes second nature to children and they can act without verbalizing. When this occurs, children have internalized their egocentric speech in the form of inner speech, which becomes their thoughts. Vygotsky believed that children who engage in a large amount of private speech are more socially competent than those who do not use it extensively. He argued that private speech represents an early transition in becoming more socially communicative.

Vygotsky's theory challenges Piaget's ideas on language and thought. Vygotsky argued that language, even in its earliest forms, is socially based, whereas Piaget emphasized young children's egocentric and nonsocially oriented speech. According to Vygotsky, young children talk to themselves to govern their behavior and to guide themselves (Duncan, 1991). By contrast, Piaget stressed that young children's egocentric speech reflects social and cognitive immaturity.

Culture and Society

Many developmentalists who work in the field of culture and development are comfortable with Vygotsky's theory, which focuses on the sociocultural context of development (Pellegrini & others, 1990; Rogoff & Morelli, 1989). Vygotsky's theory offers a portrayal of human development that is inseparable from social and cultural activities. Vygotsky emphasized how the development of higher mental processes, such as memory, attention, and reasoning, involve learning to use the inventions of society such as language, mathematical systems, and memory devices. He also emphasized how children are aided in development by the guidance of individuals who are already skilled in these tools. Vygotsky's emphasis on the role of culture in cognitive development and society contrasts with Piaget's description of the solitary little scientist.

Vygotsky stressed both the institutional and the interpersonal levels of social contexts. At the institutional level, cultural history provides organizations and tools useful to cognitive activity through such institutions as schools and such inventions as the computer and literacy. Institutional interaction gives children broad behavioral and societal norms to guide their lives. The interpersonal level has a more direct influence on a child's mental functioning. According to Vygotsky (1962), skills in mental functioning develop through immediate social interaction. Information about cognitive tools, skills, and interpersonal relations are transmitted through direct interaction with people. Through the organization of these social interactional experiences embedded in a cultural backdrop, children's mental development matures.

Critical Thinking

How are Vygotsky's and Piaget's theories different? Are their implications for education different? Explain.

At this point, we have discussed a number of ideas about concrete operational thought, formal operational thought, the contributions and criticisms of Piaget's theory, and Vygotsky's theory of cognitive development. A summary of these ideas is presented in Concept Table 7.2. In the next chapter, we will turn our attention to two other important views of children's development—learning and information processing.

PERSPECTIVES ON PARENTING AND EDUCATION

Apprenticeship Training

According to American developmental psychologist Barbara Rogoff (1990a, b), children's cognitive development is an apprenticeship that occurs through participation in social activity, guided by companions who stretch and support children's understanding of and skill in using the "tools" of the culture. Some of the technologies that are important tools for handling information in a culture are (1) language systems that organize categories of reality and structure ways of approaching situations, (2) literate practices to record information and transform it through written exercises, (3) mathematical systems that handle numerical and spatial problems, and (4) memory strategies to preserve information in memory over time. Some of these technologies have material supports such as pencil and paper, word-processing programs, alphabets, calculators, abacus and slide rule, notches on sticks, and knots on ropes. These tools provide a mechanism for transmitting information from one generation to the next.

In presenting her ideas on apprenticeship in thinking, Rogoff draws heavily on Vygotsky's theory. Rogoff argues that guided participation is widely used around the world, but with important variations in activities for and communication with children in different cultures. The most salient differences focus on the goals of development—what lessons are to be learned—and the means available for children either to observe and participate in culturally important activities or to receive instruction

CONCEPT TABLE 7.2

Concrete Operational Thought, Formal Operational Thought, Piagetian Contributions and Criticisms, and Vygotsky's Theory of Cognitive Development

Concept	Processes/Related Ideas	Characteristics/Description
Concrete operational thought	Its nature	It is made up of operations, mental actions that are reversible. The concrete operational child shows conservation and classification skills. Conservation involves a horizontal décalage. Concrete operational thought is limited by the inability to reason about abstract matters. Piaget's ideas have been widely applied to children's education. Emphasis is on communication and the belief that the child has many ideas about the world, that the child is by nature a knowing creature.
Formal operational thought	Its nature	Piaget believed that formal operational thought comes into play between 11 and 15 years of age. Formal operational thought is more abstract, idealistic, and logical than concrete operational thought. Piaget believed that adolescents become capable of using hypothetical-deductive reasoning.
	Adolescent egocentrism	Adolescents develop a special type of egocentrism that involves an imaginary audience and a personal fable about being unique and indestructible.
	Early and late formal operational thought and individual variation	Formal operational thought has two phases—an assimilation phase in which reality is overwhelmed (early adolescence) and an accommodation phase in which intellectual balance is restored through a consolidation of formal operational thought (middle years of adolescence). Individual variation in formal operational thought is extensive. Piaget did not give adequate consideration to individual variation. Many young adolescents are not formal operational thinkers but, rather, are consolidating their concrete operational thought.
	Beyond formal operational thought	Many life-span developmentalists believe that Piaget was incorrect in assuming that formal operational thought is the highest form of cognition. They argue that more pragmatic, specialized, and multiple (less dualistic) thought takes place in early adulthood and that wisdom may increase throughout the adult years.
Piagetian contributions and criticisms	Contributions	Piaget was a genius at observing children. He showed us some important things to look for and mapped out some general cognitive changes.
	Criticisms	Criticisms focus on such matters as estimates of children's competence, stages (neo-Piagetians offer more precise views and information-processing explanations), training children to reason at a higher level, and culture and education.
Vygotsky's theory of cognitive development	Zone of proximal development	ZPD is Vygotsky's term for tasks too difficult for children to master alone but can be mastered with the guidance and assistance of adults or more highly skilled children.
	Language and thought	Language and thought develop independently and then merge. The merging of language and thought takes place between 3 and 7 years of age and involves talking to oneself.
	Culture and society	Vygotsky's theory stresses how the child's mind develops in the context of the sociocultural world. Cognitive skills develop through social interaction embedded in a cultural backdrop.

At about 7 years of age, Mayan girls in Guatemala are assisted in beginning to learn to weave a simple belt, with the loom already set up for them. The young girl shown here is American developmental psychologist Barbara Rogoff's daughter, being taught to weave by a Mayan woman.

outside the context of skilled activity (Morelli, Rogoff, & Angelillo, 1992).

The general processes of guided participation appear around the world. Caregivers and children arrange children's activities and revise children's responsibilities as they gain skill and knowledge. With guidance, children participate in cultural activities that socialize them into skilled activities. For example, Mayan mothers in Guatemala help their daughters learn to weave in a process of guided participation. In the United States and in many other nations, the development of prominent and creative thinkers is promoted through interaction with a knowledgeable person rather than by studying books or by attending classes and exhibits (John-Steiner, 1985).

Children begin to practice the skills for using cultural tools, such as literacy, even before the children have contact with the technology. For example, most middle-class American parents involve their children in extensive conversation long before they go to kindergarten or elementary school, and they provide their young children with picture books and read stories to them at bedtime as part of their daily routine. Most middle-class American parents embed their children in a way of life in which reading and writing are integral parts of communication, recreation, and livelihood (Rogoff, 1990).

By contrast, consider the practices of two communities whose children have trouble reading (Heath, 1989). Parents in an Appalachian mill town taught their children respect for the written word but did not involve book characters or information in the children's everyday lives. Their children did well in the first several years of learning to read but had difficulty when required to *use* these literate skills to express themselves or interpret text. Children of rural origin in another mill town learned the skillful and creative use of language but were not taught about books or the style of communication and language used in school. These children had difficulty learning to read, which kept them from using their creative skills with language in the school setting. Early childhood in both of these communities did not include school-style reading and writing in the context of daily life and, not surprisingly, the children experienced difficulties with literacy in school.

In sum, Rogoff argues that guided participation—the participation of children in skilled cultural activities with other people of varying levels of skill and status—is an important aspect of children's cognitive development. Guided participation may be universal, although communities vary in their goals of socialization and in their means of communication. ■

CONCLUSIONS

The child is a thinking child and this thinking translates into adaptation. As children's thinking develops, they construct all sorts of ideas about what is happening in their world. With cognitive growth children refine their thinking and move through a number of cognitive milestones.

In this chapter, we began by observing the faults of the Doman "better baby institute" and quickly turned our attention to the ideas of the giant in developmental psychology, Jean Piaget. We studied some basic ideas about Piaget's stages and cognitive process and then explored each of his four stages—sensorimotor, preoperational, concrete operational, and formal operational—in depth. His contributions and criticisms of his work were noted. Vygotsky's theory, which is receiving increased attention, was outlined and the nature of apprenticeship training was discussed. You can obtain a much more detailed summary of the entire chapter by again reading the two concept tables on pages 212 and 225.

One criticism of cognitive developmental theory is that it pays little attention to individual variations. In the next chapter, we turn our attention to the study of children's learning and information processing. The approaches discussed in the next chapter place a premium on individual differences in children's cognition.

KEY TERMS

assimilation   Piagetian concept of the incorporation of new information into existing knowledge. (200)

accommodation   Piagetian concept of adjustment to new information. (200)

organization   Piaget's concept of grouping isolated behaviors into a higher-order, more smoothly functioning cognitive system. (200)

equilibration   A mechanism in Piaget's theory invoked to explain how children shift from one stage to the next. The shift occurs as children experience cognitive conflict or a disequilibrium in trying to understand the world. Eventually, they resolve the conflict and reach equilibrium of thought. (200)

scheme   The basic unit of an organized pattern of sensorimotor functioning. (201)

simple reflexes   Piaget's first sensorimotor substage, which corresponds to the first month after birth. The basic means of coordinating sensation and action is through reflexive behaviors, such as rooting and sucking, which infants have at birth. (201)

first habits and primary circular reactions   Piaget's second sensorimotor substage, which develops between 1 and 4 months of age. Infants learn to coordinate sensation and types of schemes or structures—that is, habits and primary circular reactions. (201)

primary circular reactions   Schemes based on the infant's attempt to reproduce an interesting or pleasurable event that initially occurred by chance. (201)

secondary circular reactions   Piaget's third sensorimotor substage, which develops between 4 and 8 months of age. Infants become more object oriented or focused on the world, moving beyond preoccupation with the self in sensorimotor interactions. (201)

coordination of secondary circular reactions   Piaget's fourth sensorimotor substage, which develops between 8 and 12 months of age. In this substage, several significant changes take place involving the coordination of schemes and intentionality. (201)

tertiary circular reactions, novelty, and curiosity   Piaget's fifth sensorimotor substage, which develops between 12 and 18 months of age. Infants become intrigued by the variety of properties that objects possess and by the multiplicity of things they can make happen to objects. (201)

tertiary circular reactions   Schemes in which the infant purposely explores new possibilities with objects, continually changing what is done to them and exploring the results. (201)

internalization of schemes   Piaget's sixth sensorimotor substage, which develops between 18 and 24 months of age. In this substage, infants' mental functioning shifts from a purely sensorimotor plane to a symbolic plane, and they develop the ability to use primitive symbols. (202)

object permanence   The Piagetian term for one of an infant's most important accomplishments: understanding that objects and events continue to exist even when they cannot directly be seen, heard, or touched. (202)

A$\overline{\text{B}}$ error   The Piagetian object permanence concept in which an infant progressing into Substage 4 makes frequent mistakes, selecting the familiar hiding place (A) rather than the new hiding place (B). (202)

operations   Internalized sets of actions that allow children to do mentally what before was done physically. (207)

symbolic function substage   The first substage of preoperational thought, occurring roughly between the ages of 2 and 4. In this substage, the young child gains the ability to represent mentally an object that is not present. (207)

egocentrism   A salient feature of preoperational thought, the inability to distinguish between one's own and someone else's perspective. (207)

animism   A facet of preoperational thought, the belief that inanimate objects have "lifelike" qualitites and are capable of action. (209)

intuitive thought substage   The second substage of preoperational thought, occurring approximately between 4 and 7 years of age. Children begin to use primitive reasoning and want to know the answers to all sorts of questions. (209)

centration   The focusing of attention on one characteristic to the exclusion of all others. (209)

conservation   The idea that an amount stays the same regardless of how its container changes. (209)

horizontal décalage   Piaget's concept that describes how similar abilities do not appear at the same time within a stage of development. (213)

hypothetical-deductive reasoning   Piaget's formal operational concept that adolescents have the cognitive ability to develop hypotheses about ways to solve problems. They then systematically deduce which is the best path to follow in solving the problem. (216)

adolescent egocentrism   A characteristic of adolescence composed of an imaginary audience and a personal fable. (216)

imaginary audience   An adolescent's belief that others are as preoccupied with her as she is. (216)

personal fable   An adolescent's sense of personal uniqueness and indestructibility. (217)

wisdom   Expert knowledge about the practical aspects of life. (221)

neo-Piagetians   Developmentalists who have elaborated on Piaget's theory, believing children's cognitive development is more specific in many respects than he thought. (222)

zone of proximal development (ZPD)   Vygotsky's term for the range of tasks too difficult for children to master alone but that can be mastered with the guidance and assistance of adults or more highly skilled children. (223)

SUGGESTED READINGS

Flavell, J. H., Miller, P. A., & Miller, S. A., (1993). *Cognitive development* (2nd ed.). Englewood Cliffs, NJ: Prentice-Hall. This is an excellent statement of contemporary thinking about children's cognitive development by leading scholars in the field. Although inspired by Piaget's work, the authors go well beyond it, offering new insights, critical evaluations, and reflections about their own research.

Ginsburg, H., & Opper, S. (1988). *Piaget's theory of intellectual development* (3rd ed.). Englewood Cliffs, NJ: Prentice-Hall. This text is one of the best explanations and descriptions of Piaget's theory of development.

Rogoff, B. (1990). *Apprenticeship in thinking: Cognitive development in social context.* New York: Oxford University Press. One of the leading scholars in research on the cultural contexts of cognitive development, Barbara Rogoff describes the important roles that social and cultural interaction play in cognitive development.

Wilson, L. C. (1990). *Infants and toddlers: Curriculum and teaching.* Albany, NY: Delmar. This excellent book is intended for individuals who provide care for infants and toddlers; it includes information to help caregivers select and use a curriculum appropriately individualized for each infant and toddler in their care.

The Piano Lesson, 1983,
Romare Bearden (Detail)

Learning and
Information Processing

Chapter Outline

PERSPECTIVES ON PARENTING AND EDUCATION

*Observing and Imitating Parents, Teachers,
and Peers 261*

Chapter Boxes

To learn is a natural pleasure
—Aristotle

Knowledge is power.

—Francis Bacon

IMAGES OF CHILDREN

Observational Learning and *Sesame Street*

Much of what we do results from what we have *learned*. If you had grown up in another part of the world, you would speak a different language, would like different foods and clothing, and would behave in ways characteristic of that culture. Why? Because your *learning* experiences in that culture would have been different.

One way we learn is by watching what other people do and say. This kind of learning is called *observational learning*. Observational learning has changed drastically in the twentieth century because of the introduction and pervasive use of television, which has touched virtually every American's life. Television has been called a lot of names, not all of them good—the one-eyed monster and the boob tube, for example. Television has also been accused of interfering with children's learning; critics say television lures children from schoolwork and books and makes them passive learners. Rarely does television require active responses from its audience.

Television can contribute to children's learning, however. For example, television can introduce children to worlds that are different from the one in which they live. *Sesame Street* was designed to improve children's cognitive and social skills. Almost half of America's

2-to-5-year-olds watch it regularly (Liebert & Sprafkin, 1988). Highly successful at teaching children, *Sesame Street* uses fast-paced action, sound effects, music, and humorous characters to grab the attention of its young audience. With their eyes glued to the screen, young children learn basic academic skills, such as letter and number recognition. Studies have shown that regular *Sesame Street* viewers from low-income families, when they enter first grade, are rated by their teachers as better prepared for school than their light-viewing counterparts (Bogatz & Ball, 1972).

When *Sesame Street* first appeared in 1969, the creators of the show had no idea that this "street" would lead to locations as distant as Kuwait, Israel, Latin America, and the Philippines. Since *Sesame Street* first aired in the United States, the show has been televised in 84 countries. Thirteen foreign-language versions of the show have been produced. *Plaza Sesamo* is shown in 17 South and Central American countries, as well as Puerto Rico. Learning about the diver-

Don Pimpon of Spain's Barrio Sesamo is a shaggy old codger who has traveled extensively and entertains with stories of his adventures. Barrio Sesamo helps young children in Spain learn social and cognitive skills.

sity of cultures and life-styles in South America is emphasized. *Rechov Sumsum* is shown in Israel; it especially encourages children to learn how people from different ethnic and religious backgrounds can live in harmony. *Sesamstraat* is shown in the Netherlands; children learn about the concept of school, and a 7-foot-tall blue bird named Pino is always eager to learn. Let's now explore the concept of learning in more detail.

PREVIEW

In this chapter we explore the type of learning involved when young children watch *Sesame Street* —observational learning. We also examine other ways children learn, how children process information, and compare the information processing approach to Piaget's approach and to the learning approach.

THE NATURE OF LEARNING

The term *learning* is used extensively in our everyday conversation. As a result, most of us have fairly rich ideas about what it means to learn and we can call to mind a number of concrete experiences to illustrate actual cases of learning. We might associate learning with what takes place in school, with the conscious efforts of a parent to "teach" a child something, with the outcome of a child exploring a new place or a new object, with the practice of a physical or athletic skill, and so forth. Although many of these examples may involve learning, psychologists try to be more formal and precise about the definition of learning: Learning occurs only when certain features of situations are evident.

One feature that shows evidence of learning is *change*. When a parent shows a child how to hold a spoon, when a teacher shows a child how to use a computer keyboard, or when a child attempts to head a soccer ball, the child probably does not perform these feats appropriately at first—for example, holding the spoon backwards, stroking the keys of the keyboard randomly, or missing the soccer ball or striking it with the face. Later however, the child does complete these behaviors appropriately—in effect, changing from not being able to respond correctly to being able to do so.

A second feature that shows evidence of learning is the *relative permanence* of the change in responding. Consider the examples given. We can presume that most children will continue to hold spoons, stroke keyboards, and head soccer balls correctly for a considerable time to come, once they have mastered these feats. These actions have become relatively permanent in the children's repertoire of behavior and skills.

A third feature of learning is the central role of *experience*. Roughly speaking, experience is the opportunity to practice or repeatedly observe events and actions. The infant may repeatedly try to grasp the spoon, the child may practice at the keyboard, and the soccer novice will repeatedly try to head the ball accurately. The practice may be combined with time spent observing skilled adults doing these things.

> *Experience is the only teacher.*
> —Ralph Waldo Emerson

To summarize, then, **learning** *is defined as a relatively permanent change in behavior that occurs through experience.* This definition helps us distinguish between behaviors that the child acquires through learning and behaviors that originate primarily in another way. For example, if a child is physically ill, drugged, or injured, she may talk and act in unusual and distinct ways that never occurred before and never occur in normal states. Ordinarily, we would not say that the child has learned new behaviors as a result of the illness, drug state, or injury. However, we might waive this disclaimer for a child whose "distressed" condition lasts for a long time, because, then, the behaviors may be practiced to the extent that they become relatively permanent. Another example is that many behaviors develop in children through maturational processes primarily and only secondarily through learning processes. For example, children learn to walk and talk, and adolescents experience intense interest in members of the opposite sex. These behaviors are heavily influenced by biological processes. A child learns to walk and talk as part of the natural process of maturation, although practice helps shape these behaviors. An adolescent's interest in members of the opposite sex is largely caused by the physical and hormonal changes occurring at the same time.

What are the major ways in which children learn? In this section, we will discuss the major, traditional forms of learning that psychologists have used to describe a wide range of changes. These include classical conditioning, operant conditioning, habituation, imitation, and cognitive learning. There are other forms of learning, some of which are described in the chapters on cognitive development, and Piaget's Theory (chapter 7) and language (chapter 10). Our discussion of information processing later in the chapter will also highlight recent ideas on the role of information processing in children's learning. The forms of learning we describe in the first half of this chapter are especially useful when the change in question involves an easily observed behavior that is shaped by experiences and is relatively easy to define (for example, smiling, crying, hitting). Other behaviors, which involve a considerable amount of cognitive activity and organization (such as talking) and biological supports, are best described by other forms of learning.

CLASSICAL CONDITIONING

It is a nice spring day. A father takes his baby out for a walk. The baby reaches over to touch a pink flower and is badly stung by a bumblebee sitting on the petals. The next day, the baby's mother brings home some pink flowers. She removes a flower from the arrangement and takes it to her baby to smell. The baby cries loudly as soon as she sees the pink flower. The baby's panic at the sight of the pink flower illustrates the learning process of **classical conditioning,** *in which a neutral stimulus acquires the ability to produce a response originally produced by another stimulus.*

How Classical Conditioning Works

In the early 1900s, Russian physiologist Ivan Pavlov investigated the way the body digests food. As part of his experimentation on digestion, he routinely placed meat powder in a dog's mouth, causing the dog to salivate. Pavlov began to notice that the meat powder was not the only stimulus that caused the dog to salivate. The dog salivated in response to a number of stimuli associated with the food, such as the sight of the food dish, the sight of the individual who brought the food into the room, and the sound of the door closing when the food arrived. Pavlov recognized that the dog's association of these sights and sounds with the food was an important type of learning that came to be called classical conditioning.

Pavlov set aside his work on digestion and extensively studied the association of various stimuli with food. He wanted to know *why* the dog salivated to various sights and sounds before eating the meat powder. Pavlov observed that the dog's behavior included both learned and unlearned components. The "unlearned" part of classical conditioning is based on the fact that some stimuli automatically produced certain responses apart from any prior learning; in other words, they are inborn, or innate. **Reflexes** *are automatic stimulus-response connections.* They

If a bee stings this young girl while she is holding a pink flower, how would classical conditioning explain her panic at the sight of pink flowers in the future?

include salivation in response to food, nausea in response to bad food, shivering in response to low temperature, coughing in response to the throat being clogged, pupil constriction in response to light, and withdrawal in response to blows or burns. An **unconditioned stimulus (UCS)** *is a stimulus that produces a response without prior learning;* food was the UCS in Pavlov's experiments. An **unconditioned response (UCR)** *is an unlearned response that is automatically associated with the UCS.* In Pavlov's experiments, the saliva that flowed from the dog's mouth in response to the food was the UCR. In the case of the baby and the flower, the baby's learning and experience did not cause her to cry when the bee stung her. Her crying was unlearned and occurred automatically. The bee's sting was the UCS and the crying was the UCR.

In classical conditioning, the **conditioned stimulus (CS)** *is a previously neutral stimulus that eventually elicits the conditioned response after being paired with the unconditioned stimulus.* The **conditioned response (CR)** *is the learned response to the conditioned stimulus that occurs after CS-UCS pairing* (Pavlov, 1927). In studying a dog's response to various stimuli associated with meat powder, Pavlov rang a bell before giving the meat powder

Cartoon by John Chase.

FIGURE 8.1

Classical conditioning procedure. At the start of conditioning, the UCS will evoke the UCR, but the CS does not have this capacity. During conditioning, the CS and UCS are paired so that the CS comes to elicit the response. The key learning ingredient is the association of the UCS and CS.

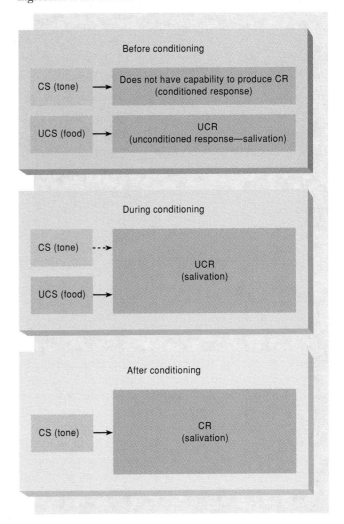

to the dog. Until then, ringing the bell did not have a particular effect on the dog, except perhaps to wake it from a nap; the bell was a neutral stimulus. However, the dog began to associate the sound of the bell with the food and salivated when the bell was sounded. The bell had become a conditioned (learned) stimulus (CS) and the salivation a conditioned response (CR). Before conditioning (or learning), the bell and the food were not related. After their association, however, the conditioned stimulus (the bell) produced a conditioned response (salivation). A summary of how classical conditioning works is shown in figure 8.1.

Classical Conditioning with Children

Since Pavlov's experiments, children have been conditioned to respond to the sound of a buzzer, a glimpse of light, or the touch of a hand. Classical conditioning has a great deal of survival value for children. Because of classical conditioning, children jerk their hands away before they are burned by fire and they move out of the way of a rapidly approaching truck before it hits them. Classical conditioning is at work in words that serve as important signals. A boy walks into an abandoned house with a friend and yells, "Snake!" His friend bolts out the door. An adolescent imagines a peaceful, tranquil scene—an abandoned beach with waves lapping onto the sand—and relaxes as if she were actually lying on the beach.

Phobias *are irrational fears.* Classical conditioning provides an explanation of these and other fears. Behaviorist John Watson conducted an investigation to demonstrate classical conditioning's role in phobias. A little boy named Albert was shown a white laboratory rat to see if he was afraid of it. He was not. As Albert played with the rat, a loud noise was sounded behind his head. As you might imagine, the noise caused little Albert to cry. After only seven pairings of the loud noise with the white rat, Albert began to fear the rat even when the noise was not sounded. Albert's fear was generalized to a rabbit, a dog, and sealskin coat (see figure 8.2). Today, we could not ethically conduct such an experiment. Especially noteworthy is the fact that Watson did not remove Albert's fear of rats, so presumably, this phobia remained with him after the experiment. Many of our fears—fear of the dentist from a painful experience, fear of driving from being in an automobile accident, fear of heights from falling off a high chair when we were infants, and fear of dogs from being bitten, for example—can be learned through classical conditioning.

If we can produce fears by classical conditioning, we should be able to eliminate them. **Counterconditioning** *is a classical conditioning procedure for weakening a CR by associating the stimuli with a new response incompatible with the CR.* Though Watson did not eliminate little Albert's fear of white rats, an associate of Watson's, Mary Cover Jones (1924), did eliminate the fears of a 3-year-old boy named Peter. Peter had many of

FIGURE 8.2

Little Albert's generalized fear. In 1920, 9-month-old little Albert was conditioned to fear a white rat by pairing the rat with a loud noise. When little Albert was subsequently placed with other stimuli similar to the white rat, such as the rabbit shown here with little Albert, he was afraid of them too. This illustrates the principle of stimulus generalization in classical conditioning.

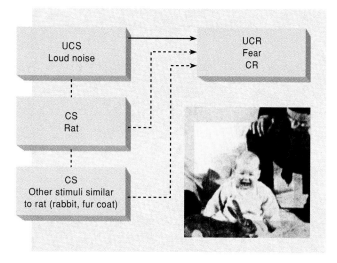

the same fears as Albert; however, Peter's fears were not produced by Jones. Among Peter's fears were white rats, fur coats, frogs, fish, and mechanical toys. To eliminate these fears, a rabbit was brought into Peter's view but kept far enough away that it would not upset him. At the same time the rabbit was brought into view, Peter was fed crackers and milk. On each successive day, the rabbit was moved closer to Peter as he ate crackers and milk. Eventually, Peter reached the point at which he could eat the food with one hand and pet the rabbit with the other.

Some of the behaviors we associate with health problems or mental disturbances can involve classical conditioning. Certain physical complaints—asthma, headaches, ulcers, and high blood pressure, for example—may partly be the products of classical conditioning. We usually say that such health problems are caused by stress, but often what has happened is that certain stimuli, such as a teacher's critical attitude or fighting by parents, are conditioned stimuli for children's physiological responses. Over time, the frequent presence of the physiological responses may produce health disorders.

Evaluating Classical Conditioning

Pavlov described all learning in terms of classical conditioning. In reality, children learn in many ways. Still, classical conditioning helps children learn about their environment and has been successful in eliminating children's fears. However, a view that describes children as *responding* to the environment fails to capture the *active* nature of children and their influence on the environment.

OPERANT CONDITIONING

Classical conditioning excels at explaining how neutral stimuli become associated with unlearned, involuntary responses, but it does not do as well in explaining voluntary behaviors, such as studying hard for a test, learning to play Ping-Pong, or memorizing a song. Operant conditioning is usually better than classical conditioning at explaining *voluntary* behavior.

What Is Operant Conditioning?

The concept of operant conditioning was developed by American psychologist B. F. Skinner (1938). **Operant conditioning** *(or instrumental conditioning) is a form of learning in which the consequences of behavior produce changes in the probability of the behavior's occurrence.* In operant conditioning, an organism acts, or operates, on the environment to produce a change in the probability of the behavior's occurrence; Skinner chose the term operants to describe the responses that are actively emitted because of the consequences for the organism. The consequences are *contingent,* or dependent, on the organism's behavior. For example, a simple operant might be the pressing of a lever that leads to the delivery of food (the consequence); the delivery of food is contingent on pressing the lever.

We have mentioned one main difference between classical and operant conditioning—that classical conditioning is better at explaining involuntary responses, whereas operant conditioning is better at explaining voluntary responses. A second difference is that the stimuli which govern behavior in classical conditioning precede the behavior; the stimuli that govern behavior in operant conditioning *follow* the behavior. For example, if we teach a dog a trick, such as learning to roll over and "play dead," in classical conditioning we would present the conditioned stimulus (such as the sound of a bell paired with meat [UCS]) before the dog performed the trick. In operant conditioning, we would present the rewarding stimulus (meat or a pat on the head, for example) *after* the dog performed the trick.

Earlier we indicated that Skinner described operant conditioning as a form of learning in which the consequences of behavior lead to changes in the probability of that behavior's occurrence. The consequences—rewards or punishments—are contingent on the organism's behavior. **Reinforcement** *(or reward) is a consequence that increases the probability a behavior will occur.* By contrast, **punishment** *is a consequence that decreases the probability a behavior will occur.* For example, if an adult smiles at a child, and the adult and child continue talking for some time, the smile reinforced the child's talking. However, if an adult meets a child and frowns at the child, and the child quickly leaves the situation, then the frown punished the child's talking with the adult.

Reinforcement can be complex. Usually we think of reinforcement as positive, but it can also be negative. In **positive reinforcement,** *the frequency of a response increases because it is followed by a pleasant stimulus, as in the example of the smile increasing talking.* By contrast, in **negative reinforcement,** *the frequency of a response increases because the response either removes an unpleasant stimulus or lets the child avoid the stimulus.* For example, a boy's mother nags at him to clean his room. She keeps nagging. Finally, the son gets tired of the nagging and cleans his room. The child's response (cleaning his room) removed the unpleasant stimulus (nagging). Taking an aspirin works the

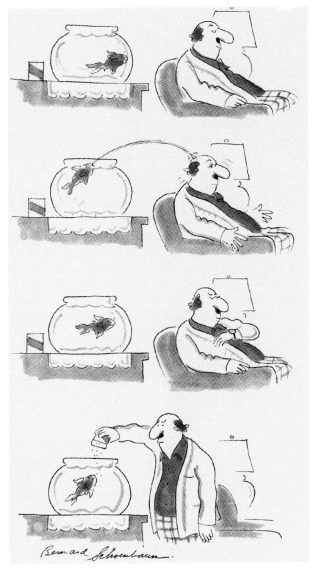

Drawing by Bernard Schoenbaum; © 1987 The New Yorker Magazine, Inc.

TABLE 8.1

Positive Reinforcement, Negative Reinforcement, and Punishment

Process	Type of Stimulus	Effect on Response
Positive reinforcement	Pleasant	Increases
Negative reinforcement	Aversive	Increases
Punishment	Aversive	Decreases

Punishment

The use of punishment is pervasive in our world. Consider Mark, who asks Valerie for a date and hears, "Are you kidding? Me go out with you?!" Mark does not ask Valerie out again. Also consider a 1-year-old whose mother spanks him for playing with an electrical socket. After the spanking, the infant does not go near the socket again. For ethical reasons, psychologists do not spank infants to see whether such a stimulus decreases behavior. However, a number of laboratory experiments on punishment have been conducted with animals, and some modified versions of punishment experiments with animals have been conducted with humans.

> *It is not the whip that makes men, but the lure of things that are worthy to be loved.*
>
> —Woodrow Wilson

Psychologists have made recommendations on the effective use of punishment and on decisions about when it might be called for in human behavior. First, punishment may lead to escape or avoidance. Second, when a response is successfully reduced or eliminated by punishment and no appropriate alternative behavior is strengthened, other undesirable behaviors may take the place of the punished behavior. Third, a person who administers punishment is serving as an aggressive model, possibly inadvertently modeling how to behave in an aggressive, punishing manner. Fourth, desirable behaviors may be eliminated along with undesirable ones. For example, a child may stop interacting with other children altogether when he is slapped for biting another child. Because punishment has so many side effects, are there circumstances when it is called for? There may be some circumstances when punishment is beneficial. For example, when positive reinforcement has not been found to work, punishment can be considered, and, when the behavior that is being punished is considered more destructive than the punishment itself, the process may be justified. For example, some children engage in behavior that is very dangerous to their well-being, such as head banging. In such cases, the use of punishment, even electric shock, may reduce the injurious behavior. Nonetheless, as punishment is reduced, it is always wise to reinforce an alternative behavior so that undesirable behavior does not replace the punished response.

same way: Taking aspirin is reinforced when this behavior is followed by a reduction in pain.

Another way to remember the distinction between positive and negative reinforcement is that, in positive reinforcement, something is *added*, or obtained. In negative reinforcement, something is *subtracted*, avoided, or escaped. For example, if a child receives a sweater from her parents for getting a good grade in a class, something has been added to increase the child's achievement behavior. Consider the situation, however, in which a child's parents criticize him for not studying hard enough. As the child studies harder, they stop criticizing him—their criticism has been subtracted.

Negative reinforcement and punishment are easily confused because they both involve aversive or unpleasant stimuli, such as a slap in the face. To keep them straight, remember that negative reinforcement *increases* the probability a response will occur, whereas punishment *decreases* the probability a response will occur. An overview of the distinctions between positive reinforcement, negative reinforcement, and punishment is presented in table 8.1.

Most childrearing experts in the United States today do not advocate the physical punishment of children, but the United States does not have a law that prohibits parents from spanking their children. However, in 1979, a law was passed in Sweden that specifically forbids parents from using physical punishment, including spanking and slapping, when disciplining their children (Ziegert, 1983). The physical punishment of children is treated as an offense, just like any other attack on a person. Sweden is the only industrial country in the world to pass such a law, which is especially designed to curb child abuse. Could the United States pass this type of law? Probably not at this point in time, because fewer Americans would probably be in favor of the law than Swedes were in 1979. Many Americans would also probably view such a law as totalitarian, and the law would likely stimulate protest from civil libertarians and others. An important factor in Sweden's ability to pass the "anti-spanking" law is its attitude toward laws. The United States enforces laws through punishment. However, Sweden takes a softer approach to its laws, encouraging respect for laws through education designed to change attitudes and behavior.

When people, often teachers or doctors, suspect that a parent has spanked a child, they frequently report the incident because they know that the state will try to provide the parent with emotional and educational support rather than assessing a fine or sending the parent to jail. Accompanying the anti-spanking law in Sweden was a parenting guide—*Can One Manage to Raise Children Without Spanking or Slapping?*—that was widely available at day-care centers, preschool programs, physicians' offices, and other similar locations. The publication includes advice about why physical punishment is not a good strategy for disciplining children, along with specific information about better ways to handle children's problems.

> ### Critical Thinking
>
> Are there circumstances when children need to be spanked, or should parents never spank their children? Explain your answer.

Applications of Operant Conditioning

A preschool child repeatedly throws down his glasses and breaks them. A young girl feels depressed. An adolescent mother lacks appropriate parenting skills. Operant conditioning has helped individuals such as these adapt more effectively and cope with their problems.

Behavior modification *is the application of operant conditioning principles to changing human behavior; its main goal is to replace unacceptable responses with acceptable, adaptive ones.* Consequences for behavior are established to ensure that acceptable responses are reinforced and unacceptable ones are not. Advocates of behavior modification believe that many emotional and behavioral problems are caused by inadequate (or inappropriate) response consequences.

The child who throws down his glasses and breaks them may be receiving too much attention from his teacher and peers for his behavior; thus, an unacceptable behavior is unwittingly reinforced. In this instance, the parents and teachers would be instructed to remove their attention from the destructive behavior and transfer it to more constructive behavior such as working quietly and playing cooperatively with peers (Harris, Wolf, & Baer, 1964).

Consider another circumstance. Barbara and her parents were on a collision course. Things got so bad that her parents decided to see a clinical psychologist. The psychologist, who had a behavioral orientation, talked with each family member, trying to get them to pinpoint the problem. The psychologist got the family to sign a behavioral contract that spelled out what everyone needed to do to reduce the conflict. Barbara agreed to: (1) be home before 11 P.M. on weeknights, (2) look for a part-time job so she could begin to pay for some of her activities; and (3) refrain from calling her parents insulting names. Her parents agreed to: (1) talk to Barbara in a low tone of voice if they were angry, rather than yell, (2) refrain from criticizing teenagers, especially Barbara's friends, and (3) give Barbara a small sum of money each week for gas, makeup, and socializing, but only until she obtained a job.

Behavior modification is not only effective in therapy, but it has also been applied to the world of computers to promote better instruction. Some years ago, Skinner developed a machine to assist teachers with their instruction of students. The teaching machine engaged students in a learning activity, paced the material at the students' own rate, tested the students' knowledge of the material, and provided immediate feedback about correct and incorrect answers. Skinner hoped that the machine would revolutionize learning in schools, but the revolution never took place.

Today, the idea behind Skinner's teaching machine has been applied to computers, which assist teachers in the instruction of students. Research comparisons of computer-assisted instruction with traditional teacher-based instruction suggest that, in some areas, such as drill and practice on math problems, computer-assisted instruction produces superior results (Mandell & Mandell, 1989).

HABITUATION

If a stimulus—a sight or sound—is presented to an infant several times in a row, the infant usually pays less attention to it each time, suggesting that the infant has become bored with the stimulus. This is the process of **habituation,** *the repeated presentation of a stimulus, which causes reduced attention to the stimulus.* **Dishabituation** *is an infant's renewed interest in a stimulus.* Among the measures researchers use to study whether habituation is occurring are sucking behavior (sucking behavior stops when a young infant attends to a novel object), heart and respiration rates, and the length of time the infant looks at an object. Newborn infants can habituate to repetitive stimulation in virtually every stimulus modality—vision, audition, touch,

FIGURE 8.3

Bandura's experiment on imitation and aggression. In the frames on the top, an adult model aggressively attacks a Bobo doll. In the frames on the bottom, the preschool-aged girl who has observed the adult model's aggressive actions follows suit.

and so on (Rovee-Collier, 1987). However, habituation becomes more acute during the first 3 months of life. The extensive assessment of habituation in recent years has resulted in its use as a measure of an infant's maturity and well-being. Infants who have brain damage or have suffered birth traumas, such as lack of oxygen, do not habituate well and later may have developmental and learning problems.

A knowledge of habituation and dishabituation can benefit parent-infant interaction. Infants respond to changes in stimulation. If a parent repeats a stimulation often, the infant's response will decrease to the point that the infant no longer responds to the parent. In parent-infant interaction, it is important for parents to do novel things and to repeat them often until the infant stops responding. The wise parent senses when the infant shows an interest and realizes that many repetitions of the stimulus may be necessary for the infant to process the information. The parent stops or changes behaviors when the infant redirects her attention (Rosenblith, 1992).

IMITATION AND COGNITIVE LEARNING

When children learn, they often cognitively represent or transform their experiences. In Skinner's operant view and Pavlov's classical conditioning view, no room is given to the possibility that cognitive factors, such as memory, thinking, planning, and expectations, might be important in learning. Skinnerians point out that they do not deny the existence of thinking, but, since they cannot observe thinking, they do not believe it is an important factor in the scientific study of learning. Many contemporary learning experts, though, advocate the importance of cognitive factors in learning. Albert Bandura has been a pioneer in promoting the role of cognition in learning. First we will describe his important thoughts and research on imitation and

then turn to the fascinating issue of whether infants can imitate an adult's behavior. Finally, we will describe Bandura's recently developed cognitive social learning model.

Bandura's Concept of Imitation

Would it make sense to teach a 15-year-old boy how to drive by either classical conditioning or operant conditioning procedures? Driving a car is a voluntary behavior, so classical conditioning doesn't really apply. In terms of operant conditioning, we would ask him to drive down the road and then reward his positive behaviors. Not many of us would want to be on the road, though, when some of his disastrous mistakes occur. Albert Bandura (1971, 1986, 1989) believes that, if we learned only in such a trial-and-error fashion, it would be exceedingly tedious and, at times, hazardous. Instead, many of our complex behaviors are due to our exposure to competent models who display appropriate behavior in solving problems and in coping with their world.

Recall from our description earlier in the chapter that *imitation*, or modeling, occurs when children learn new behaviors by watching someone else perform the behaviors. The capacity to learn behavior patterns by observation eliminates tedious trial-and-error learning. In many instances, imitation takes less time than operant conditioning.

The following experiment by Bandura (1965) illustrates how observational learning can occur by watching a model who is neither reinforced nor punished. The only requirement for learning is that the individual be connected with the model in time and space. The experiment also illustrates an important distinction between learning and performance. An equal number of boys and girls of nursery school age watched one of three films in which an individual beat up an adult-sized plastic Bobo doll (see figure 8.3). In the first film, the aggressor was rewarded with candy, soft drinks, and praise for aggressive behavior; in the second film, the aggressor was criticized and spanked for the aggressive behavior; and, in the third film, there were no consequences to the aggressor for the behavior. Subsequently, each child was left alone in a room filled with toys, including a Bobo doll. The child's behavior was observed through a one-way mirror. Children who watched the aggressor be reinforced or suffer no consequences for aggressive behavior imitated the aggressive behavior more than the children who watched the aggressor be punished. As might be expected, boys were more aggressive than girls. The important point about these results is that observational learning occurred just as extensively when modeled aggressive behavior was not reinforced as when it was reinforced.

A second important point focuses on the distinction between learning and performance. Just because an organism does not *perform* a response does not mean it did not *learn* the response. When the children in Bandura's study were offered rewards (in the form of stickers or fruit juice) for imitating the model, the differences in the children's imitative behavior in the three conditions were eliminated. In this experiment, all of the children *learned* about the model's behavior, but some children did not *perform* the behavior until presented with reinforcement. Bandura believes that, when an individual observes behavior but makes no observable response, the individual still may have acquired the modeled response in cognitive form.

Since his early experiments, Bandura (1986, 1989) has focused on some of the specific processes that influence an observer's behavior following exposure to a model. One of these is *attention*. Before individuals can reproduce a model's actions, they must attend to what the model is doing or saying. You may not hear what a friend says if the stereo is blaring or you might miss your teacher's analysis of a problem if you are admiring someone sitting in the next row. Attention to a model is influenced by a host of characteristics. For example, warm, powerful, atypical individuals command more attention than do cold, weak, typical individuals.

The next consideration is the individual's *retention*. To reproduce a model's actions, you must code the information and keep it in memory so that it can be retrieved. A simple verbal description or a vivid image of what the model did assists retention.

Another process involved in observational learning is *motor reproduction*. Individuals may attend to a model and code in memory what they have seen, but, because of limitations in motor development, they may not be able to reproduce the model's action. A 13-year-old may see Chris Evert hit a great two-handed backhand or Michael Jordan do a reverse two-handed dunk but be unable to reproduce the pro's actions.

FIGURE 8.4

Bandura's model of the processes involved in imitation. Bandura argues that observational learning consists of four main processes: attention, retention, motor reproduction, and reinforcement or incentive conditions. Consider a circumstance involving a child learning to ski. The child needs to attend to the instructor's words and demonstrations. The child also must remember what the instructor did and the instructor's tips for avoiding disaster. The child also needs the abilities to reproduce what the instructor has demonstrated. Praise from the instructor after the child has completed a few moves on the slopes should improve the child's motivation to continue skiing.

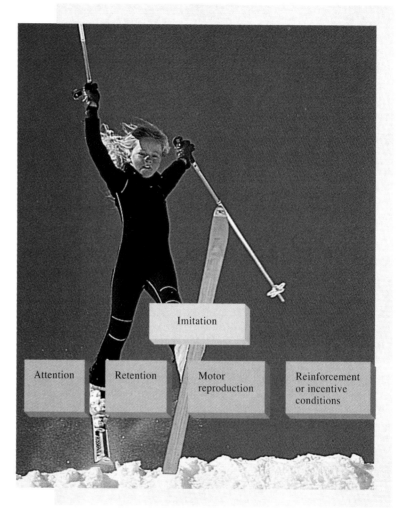

A final process in Bandura's conception of observational learning involves *reinforcement* or *incentive conditions*. On many occasions, we may attend to what a model says or does, retain the information in memory, and possess the motor capabilities to perform the action but we may fail to repeat the behavior because adequate reinforcement is not present. This was demonstrated in Bandura's study (1965) when the children who had seen a model punished for aggression reproduced the model's aggression only when they were offered an incentive to do so. A summary of Bandura's model of observational learning is shown in figure 8.4.

At the beginning of this chapter, we discussed the powerful role of television in children's lives and how observational

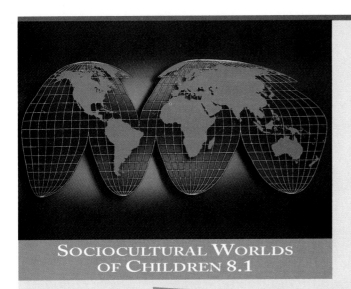

SOCIOCULTURAL WORLDS OF CHILDREN 8.1

Ethnicity, Observational Learning, Television, and Mentoring

Ethnic minorities have historically been underrepresented and misrepresented on television (Pouissant, 1972). Blacks, Asians, Hispanics, and Native Americans have been presented as less positive and less dignified than White characters (Condry, 1989). One study looked at portrayals of ethnic minorities during children's heavy viewing hours (weekdays 4–6P.M. and 7–11P.M.) (Williams & Condry, 1989). The percentage of White characters far exceeded the actual percentage of White in the United States; the percentage of Black, Asian, and Hispanic characters fell short of their true representations. Hispanic characters were especially underrepresented—only .6 percent of the characters were Hispanic, although the Hispanic population was actually 6.4 percent of the total U.S. population in 1989. When portrayed on television, ethnic minorities tended to hold lower-status jobs and were more likely than Whites to be cast as criminals or victims.

It is important for children from ethnic minority groups to be exposed to competent role models with whom they can identify and from whom they can learn, not just on television but in school and other realms of society as well. A number of educators believe that the exposure of children and adolescents to competent role models is one way to reduce the high school dropout problem. One way this is being accomplished is

through mentoring, which occurs when an older, more experienced person helps a younger person in a one-to-one relationship that goes beyond the formal obligations of a teaching or supervisory role. Mentors, who are competent and caring, offer young people important role models. As such, mentors provide young people with a concrete image of who a younger person can become and lend guidance and support to enable the younger person to become whoever he or she chooses to be.

In the Each One/Reach One Program in Milwaukee, Wisconsin, Black professional women are recruited and trained to serve as role models. Paired with an adolescent, they spend a minimum of 10 hours a month together, visiting each other's homes and attending cultural events. The adolescent may also visit the professional at work. Because the program hopes to expose not only the girl but her whole family to an alternative life-style, the mother and siblings of the adolescent are included whenever possible. One study of mentoring, an adopt-a-student program in Atlanta, Georgia, paired 200 underachieving juniors and seniors with mentors from the business community, who helped students plan their futures and counseled them about achieving goals. The participating students were much more likely to be employed or to continue their education than similar students who did not take part (Anson, 1988; William T. Grant Foundation Commission, 1988).

A special concern is that children and adolescents from ethnic minority groups be exposed to competent role models with whom they can identify and from whom they can learn. One way this is being accomplished is through mentoring.

learning is the basic way people learn information from television. To find out about the types of models children observe on television and in schools, turn to Sociocultural Worlds of Children 8.1.

Infant Imitation

Bandura views imitation as an information-processing activity. As a child observes, information about the world is transformed into cognitive representations that serve as guides to action. An interesting question is whether young infants can engage in im-

itation. Can a young infant imitate someone else's emotional expressions? If adults smile, will the baby follow with a smile? If adults protrude their lower lips, wrinkle their foreheads, and frown, will the baby show a saddened look? If adults open their mouths, widen their eyes, and raise their eyebrows as though startled, will the baby follow suit? Can infants only 1 day old do these things?

Children need models more than they need critics.

—Joseph Joubert

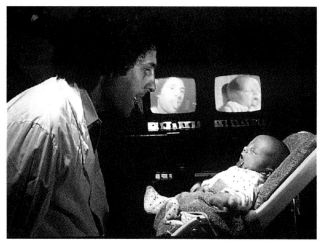

Shown here is infant development researcher Andrew Meltzoff displaying tongue protrusion, prompting an infant to imitate his behavior. Researchers have demonstrated that infants can imitate adults' behavior far earlier than traditionally believed.

FIGURE 8.5

Bandura's model of reciprocal influences of behavior—B, personal and cognitive factors—P(C), and environment—E. The arrows reflect how relations between these factors are reciprocal rather than unidirectional. Examples of personal factors include intelligence, skills, and self-control.

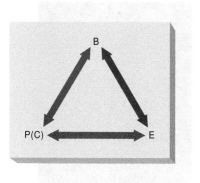

Infancy researcher Tiffany Field and her colleagues (1982) explored these questions with newborns only 36 hours after their birth. The model held the newborns' heads upright, with the model's and the newborns' faces separated by 10 inches. The newborns' facial expressions were recorded by an observer who stood behind the model. The observer could not see which facial expressions the model was showing. The model expressed one of the three emotions: happiness, sadness, or surprise. Infants were most likely to imitate the model's display of surprise by widely opening their mouths. When the infants observed a happy mood, they frequently widened their lips. When the model expressed sadness, the infants followed with lips that reflected pouting. Other research supports the belief that young infants can imitate an adult's emotional expressions.

Infant development researcher Andrew Meltzoff (1988, 1990) has conducted numerous studies of infants' imitative abilities. He believes that infants' imitative abilities are biologically based because infants can imitate a facial expression within the first few days after birth, before they have had the opportunity to observe social agents in their environment engage in tongue protrusion and other behaviors. He also believes that infants' imitative abilities are not like the ethologists' concept of a hardwired, reflexive, innate releasing mechanism, but rather these abilities involve flexibility, adaptability, and intermodal perception. In Meltzoff's observations of infants in the first 72 hours of life, the infants gradually displayed a full imitative response of an adult's facial expressions, such as tongue protrusion or wide opening of the mouth. Initially, a young infant may only get its tongue to the edge of its lips, but, after a number of attempts and observations of adult behavior, the infant displays a more full-blown response.

Meltzoff also has studied *deferred imitation,* which is the imitation that occurs after a time delay of hours or days. In one recent investigation, Meltzoff (1988) demonstrated that 9-month-old infants can imitate actions they saw performed 24 hours earlier. Each action consisted of an unusual gesture—for example, pushing a recessed button in a box (which produced a beeping sound). Piaget believed that deferred imitation does not occur until about 18 months of age; Meltzoff's research suggests that it occurs much earlier in infant development.

> *We are in truth, more than half what we are by imitation.*
> —Lord Chesterfield

Behavior, Person (Cognition), and Environment

Bandura's (1986, 1989) most recent model of social learning involves behavior, the person (cognition), and the environment. As shown in figure 8.5, behavior, environment, and personal or cognitive factors operate interactively. Behavior can influence cognition and vice versa, the child's cognitive activities can influence the environment, environmental influences can change the child's thought processes, and so on.

Let's consider how Bandura's model might work in the case of students' behavior. As students diligently study and get good grades, their behavior produces positive thoughts about their abilities. As part of their effort to make good grades, they plan a number of strategies to make studying more efficient. In these ways, their behavior has influenced their thoughts, and their thoughts have influenced their behavior. At the beginning of the school year, their counselor made a special effort to involve them in a study-skills program. Their success has stimulated the school to expand the program. In these ways, the environment influenced the behavior, and the behavior influenced the environment. The expectations of the school's counselor and principal that the program would work made it possible in the first place. The program's success has spurred expectations that this type of program could work in other schools. In these ways, cognition changed the environment, and the environment changed cognition. Expectations are important in Bandura's model.

BIOLOGICAL AND CULTURAL INFLUENCES ON LEARNING

Albert Einstein had many talents. He combined enormous creativity with great analytic ability to develop some of this century's most important insights about the nature of matter and the universe. Genes obviously provided Einstein extraordinary intellectual skills to think and reason on a very high plane, but cultural factors also contributed to Einstein's genius. Einstein received an excellent, rigorous European education, and later in the United States he experienced the freedom and support believed to be important in creative exploration. It is unlikely that Einstein would have been able to fully develop his intellectual skills and make such brilliant insights if he had grown up in the more primitive cultures of his time or even in a Third World country today. Both biological *and* cultural factors contribute to learning.

We can't breathe under water, fish can't play Ping-Pong, and cows can't solve math problems. The structure of an organism's body permits certain kinds of learning and inhibits others. For example, chimpanzees cannot learn to speak English because they lack the necessary vocal equipment. Some of us cannot solve difficult calculus problems; others of us can; and the differences do not all seem to be the result of experiences.

In traditional views of learning, such concepts as culture and ethnicity have been given little or no attention. The behavioral orientation that dominate American psychology for much of the twentieth century focuses on the contexts of learning, but the organisms in those contexts have often been animals. When humans have been the subjects, there has been no interest in the cultural context. Esteemed psychologist Robert Guthrie (1976) once wrote a book entitled *Even the Rat Was White* —a comment on psychology's heavy reliance on animal research and the failure to consider cultural and ethnic factors in behavioral research.

How does culture influence learning? Most psychologists agree that the principles of classical conditioning, operant conditioning, and observational learning are universal and are powerful learning process in every culture. However, culture can influence the degree to which these learning processes are used, and it often determines the content of learning. For example, punishment is a universal learning process, but as we learned in the discussion of punishment, its use and type show considerable sociocultural variation.

The content of learning is also influenced by culture (Cushner, 1990). Children cannot learn about something they cannot experience. A 4-year-old who grows up among the Bushmen of the Kalahari desert is unlikely to learn about taking baths or pouring water from one glass into another. Similarly, a child growing up in Chicago is unlikely to be skilled at tracking animals or finding water-bearing roots in the desert. Learning usually requires practice, and certain behaviors are practiced much more often in some cultures than in others. In Bali, many children are skilled dancers by the age of 6, whereas Norwegian children are much more likely to be good skiers and skaters by that age. Children growing up in a Mexican village famous for its pottery may work with clay day after day, whereas

children in a nearby village famous for its woven rugs and sweaters rarely become expert clay pot makers (Price-Williams, Gordon, & Ramirez, 1969). More about a culture's role in learning is presented in Sociocultural Worlds of Children 8.2, where you will read about cultural influences on the learning of mathematics.

In the last decade, the poor performance of American children in math and science has become well publicized. For example, in one recent cross-national comparison of the math and science achievement of 9- to 13-year-old students, the United States finished 13th (out of 15) in science and 15th (out of 16) in math achievement (Educational Testing Service, 1992). In this study, Korean and Taiwanese students placed first and second, respectively.

Harold Stevenson and his colleagues (1992; Stevenson, Chen, & Lee, 1993; Stevenson & others, 1990) have conducted a series of cross-national studies of children's learning and achievement in various Asian countries and the United States over a period of about 15 years. Rather than just describe the deficiencies of the American children's achievement in comparison to children from other nations, Stevenson has sought to answer the all important question of "why?" He has found that contrary to popular stereotypes, Asian children's high level of achievement does not result from rote learning and repeated drilling in tension-filled schools. Rather, children are motivated to learn and teaching is innovative and interesting in many Asian schools. Knowledge is not force-fed to children, but rather children are encouraged to construct their own ways of representing the knowledge. Long school days in Asia are punctuated by extended recess periods. Asian schools embrace many of the ideals Americans have for their own schools, but are more successful in implementing them in interesting and productive ways that make learning more enjoyable for children.

These conclusions were reached by Stevenson and his colleagues following five different cross-national studies of children in the United States, China, Taiwan, and Japan. In these studies, Asian children consistently outperformed U.S. children in math. And the longer the children were in school, the wider the gap between the Asian and American children's math scores became, with the lowest differential in the first grade, the biggest in the eleventh grade.

To learn more about the reasons for these large cross-cultural differences in achievement, the researchers spent hundreds of hours observing classrooms; interviewing teachers, children, and mothers; and giving questionnaires to the fathers. They found that parental satisfaction with American children's achievement and education is high but their standards are low in comparison with their Asian counterparts. And while American parents emphasize that their children's math achievement is primarily determined by innate ability, Asian parents believe their children's math achievement is mainly the result of effort and training.

In 1990, former President Bush and the nation's governors adopted a well-publicized goal: to change American education in ways that will help students to lead the world in math achievement by the year 2000. Stevenson (1992; Stevenson,

SOCIOCULTURAL WORLDS OF CHILDREN 8.2

Learning Math in New Guinea and Brazil

Children's math learning depends not only on their innate ability to handle abstractions and adult efforts to teach math concepts, but also on the adults' own knowledge about numbers, which in turn depends on culture's heritage (Cole & Cole,

1989). Children growing up among the Oksapmin of New Guinea seem to have the same ability to grasp basic number concepts as children growing up in Tokyo or Los Angeles. However, the counting system used in the Oksapmin culture—counting by body parts—does not support the more sophisticated development of algebraic thinking (Saxe, 1981). The Oksapmin use 29 body parts in their system of counting (see figure 8.A). In America it is not unusual for children to use their fingers to keep track of numbers early in their math learning, but because of American schooling they go far beyond Oksapmin children in learning math.

Although schooling often helps with learning math, in some cultures children who do not attend school learn math as part of their everyday experience. For example, whereas most Brazilian children attend school, Brazilian market children do not, yet they learn remarkable math skills in the context of everyday buying and selling. However, when presented with the same math problems in a schoollike format, they have difficulty (Carraher & Carraher, 1981). In another example, many high school students in the United States can solve certain physics problems, which they consider elementary, that baffled the brilliant Greek philosopher Aristotle in ancient times. In each of these instances, culture has shaped the course of learning.

FIGURE 8.A

The counting system of the Oksapmin of New Guinea. The arithmetic counting of the Oksapmin of New Guinea is based on 29 numbers that correspond to a sequence of body parts.

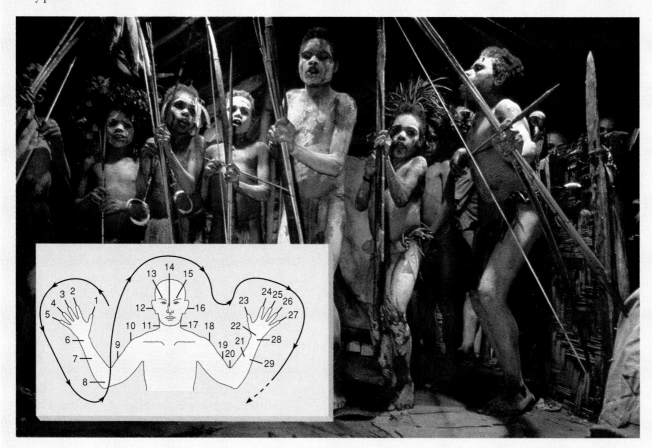

Asian grade schools intersperse studying with frequent periods of activities. This approach helps children maintain their attention and likely makes learning more enjoyable. Shown here are Japanese fourth graders making wearable masks.

Chen, & Lee, 1993) says that is unlikely to happen because American standards and expectations for children's math achievement are too low by international standards.

While Asian students are doing so well in math achievement, might there be a dark underside of too much stress and tension in the students and their schools? Stevenson and his colleagues (1993) have not found that to be the case. They asked 11th-grade students in Japan and the United States how often in the past month they had experienced feelings of stress, depression, aggression, and other problems, such as not being able to sleep well. They also asked the students about how often they felt nervous when they took tests. On all of these characteristics, the Japanese students expressed less distress and fewer problems than the American students. Such findings do not support the Western stereotype that Asian students are tense, wired individuals driven by relentless pressures for academic excellence.

Critics of cross-national studies say that such comparisons are flawed because the percentage of children who go to school and the curricula vary widely within each country. Even in the face of such criticisms, there is a growing consensus based on information collected by different research teams that American children's achievement is very low, that American educators' and parents' expectations for children's math achievement are too low, and that American schools are long overdue for an extensive overhaul.

At this point we have discussed a number of ideas about the nature of learning, classical conditioning, operant conditioning, habituation, imitation and cognitive learning, and biological and cultural factors in learning. A summary of these ideas is presented in Concept Table 8.1.

Bandura's theory gives cognition a more important role in learning than the traditional views of learning, such as classical and operant conditioning. Next, we will see that the information-processing approach places a very high premium on children's cognitive activities.

INFORMATION PROCESSING

Information processing is at once a framework for thinking about children's development and a facet of that development. As a framework, information processing includes certain ideas about how people's minds work and the best methods for studying this. As a facet of development, we can think of the different aspects of information processing that change as children mature. For example, changes in children's attention and memory capabilities are, in effect, changes in information-processing capabilities. In the discussion that follows, we will turn our attention first to how the information-processing approach differs from the Piagetian and learning approaches.

Our life is what our thoughts make it.

—Marcus Aurelius

Comparing the Information-Processing, Piagetian, and Learning Approaches

For many experts, the **information-processing approach** *is a framework for understanding how children learn and think* (Siegler, 1983, 1986). *It assumes that, to understand children's learning and thinking, we need to analyze the way children take in information (sights, sounds, smells, and so on), how they store the information, and how they evaluate it for some clearly defined purposes and goals.* Concepts of learning, if you remember from earlier in the chapter, focus on behaviors and the events in the environment that change these behaviors. Traditional principles of learning do little to explain what is going on in a child's mind, however. Piagetian theory, on the other hand, has quite a lot to say about the child's mind. For example, Piaget described the ways in which a child structures thought at different ages; these are the stage descriptions of sensorimotor, preoperational, concrete, and formal operational thought. The Piagetian description is general; it doesn't tell us much about how the child reads, solves mathematical problems, learns new scientific facts, or composes an essay. It leaves out a lot of important details about how the mind actually works on specific kinds of tasks such as reading, writing, doing arithmetic, and solving a variety of

CONCEPT TABLE 8.1

Learning

Concept	Processes/Related Ideas	Characteristics/Description
The nature of learning	Key features	Learning is a relatively permanent change in behavior that occurs through experience.
Classical conditioning	How classical conditioning works	Pavlov discovered that organisms learn the association between an unconditioned stimulus (UCS) and a conditioned stimulus (CS). The UCS automatically produces the unconditioned response (UCR). After conditioning (CS-UCS pairing), the CS elicits the conditioned response (CR) by itself.
	Classical conditioning with children	Classical conditioning has survival value for children, for example, when they develop a fear of hazardous conditions. Irrational fears are explained by classical conditioning. Counterconditioning has been used to eliminate children's fears.
	Evaluating classical conditioning	Classical conditioning is important in explaining how some learning occurs, but it is not the predominant way children learn because it misses the active nature of the child.
Operant conditioning	What is operant conditioning?	Operant conditioning is a form of learning (also called instrumental conditioning) in which the consequences of behavior produce changes in the probability of the behavior's occurrence. Operant conditioning focuses on what happens after a response is made, classical conditioning on what occurs before a response is made. The key connection in classical conditioning is between two stimuli, in operant conditioning between the organism's response and its consequences. Operant conditioning mainly involves voluntary behavior, classical conditioning involuntary behavior. Distinctions in operant conditioning are made between positive reinforcement, negative reinforcement, and punishment.
	Punishment	Reasoning is often more effective than high-intensity punishment. Experts recommend that alternatives to punishment be explored before punishment is used.

problems. The information-processing approach attempts to correct the shortcomings of traditional learning theory and Piagetian ideas about development. It describes mental processes and offers specific details about how these processes work in concrete situations. Where possible, these descriptions include analyses of all the steps needed to complete a task, the specific mental processes needed to complete these steps, and precise mathematical estimates of how "hard" or how "long" the mind has to work to execute these steps. Often, information-processing psychologists try to write computer programs to represent the steps needed to solve problems. Computer "models" of how something is done force scientists to be precise. Computers are basically "dumb" machines. They do only what one tells them to do. If a dumb machine can be made to complete a task, so goes the reasoning, we will have an exhaustive understanding of everything that a person might possible need to complete the task. In practice, it is not possible to list every step for such complex activities as reading and writing, but we can study particular features of these activities and try to understand them in great detail. To summarize the information-

processing approach is a framework for studying children's development that attempts to be detailed about the mental processes underlying learning and thinking in very specific situations and, where possible, to model the specific steps needed to complete a task using computer programs and mathematical estimates of mental activities.

Man is but a reed, the weakest in nature; but he is a thinking reed.

—Pascal

Let's consider an example of how the information-processing approach differs from the learning and Piagetian approaches. Suppose we observe a third-grade student attempting to perform some subtraction problems—for example, 176 minus 47, 395 minus 46, and 272 minus 34, written out in the usual form:

$$
\begin{array}{ccc}
176 & 395 & 272 \\
-47 & -46 & -34 \\
\end{array}
$$

Concept	Processes/Related Ideas	Characteristics/Description
	Applications of operant conditioning	Behavior modification is the application of operant conditioning principles to changing human behavior; its main goal is to replace unacceptable responses with acceptable, adaptive ones.
Habituation	Its nature	Habituation is the repeated presentation of a stimulus, causing reduced attention to the stimulus. If a different stimulus is presented and the infant pays attention to it, dishabituation is occurring. Newborn infants can habituate, although habituation becomes more acute over the first 3 months of infancy.
Imitation and cognitive learning	Bandura's concept of imitation	Imitation, also called modeling, occurs when children learn new behaviors by watching someone else perform the behaviors. Bandura believes imitation involves attention, retention, motor reproduction, and reinforcement or incentive conditions.
	Infant imitation	Infants can imitate facial expressions in the first few days of life. Meltzoff has demonstrated that deferred imitation occurs at about 9 months of age, much earlier than Piaget believed.
	Cognitive learning	Many psychologists recognize the importance of studying how cognitive factors mediate environment-behavior connections. Bandura's contemporary model emphasizes reciprocal connections between behavior, person (cognition), and environment.
Biological and cultural influences on learning	Their nature	Biological factors restrict what an organism can learn from experience. Many learning processes, such as classical conditioning, operant conditioning, and imitation, are universal. However, cultural influences the degree these learning processes are used and the content of the learning

The student calculates the answers to be 21, 241, and 132, respectively. It will help you to write out these problems on a piece of paper, calculate the correct answers, and then note the incorrect answers provided by our hypothetical third-grader. Can you figure out the student's errors? Why were these errors made?

Learning theory might explain these mistakes by arguing that the child has not yet learned the correct "behavior" of "borrowing" numbers. There has been insufficient practice, modeling, and/or reinforcement for the child. Piagetian theory would have little to say about these problems. Information-processing theory, on the other hand, would give a detailed description of all the steps needed to solve these arithmetic problems (Brown & Burton, 1978) and predict precisely when a child would and would not have difficulty, based on an explanation of the child's flaws. What are the steps? A partial list includes: (1) recognizing that each is a subtraction problem, (2) understanding which number is to be subtracted from which other number, (3) beginning to subtract the right-most digit

on the bottom from the corresponding top digit, (4) realizing that step 3 cannot be done immediately, (5) borrowing 10 from the 10's column, (6) marking the new value of the 10's column, (7) marking 1 to represent the borrowed 10 near the top of the digit's column, (8) performing the new subtraction, (9) repeating the process for the 10's column, and so on.

What are the flaws present in this child's subtraction? These seem to be two "bugs," as they sometimes have been called (Brown & Burton, 1978). First, even though the child may borrow from the 10's column, he still performs the first (digit's column) subtraction incorrectly—ignoring the borrowed number and choosing to subtract the smaller digit's value number on top from the larger one on the bottom. The 10's column subtraction is performed correctly, because the higher and lower numbers are in the locations that the child would expect (top and bottom, respectively). The second "bug" occurs when we move to the 100's column. The child has incorrectly continued to borrow and has reduced the value of the 100's digit, when no borrowing was necessary.

The value of this information-processing analysis, even though it becomes tedious when it is spelled out in such great detail, is that it forces us to consider exactly what the child may be doing and exactly what his procedural "bugs" are. If you know precisely how children think about this task, you have a good beginning point for trying to change and improve their thinking.

Developmental Change

In general, then what aspects of information processing change as children mature? How can these changes be described? There are two equally good answers. One is of the "life just is not simple" variety; that is, there are no compelling general changes. The nature of information processing is such that, to understand how younger children differ from older children, we have to examine specific processes (such as attention and memory) and tasks (such as reading, writing, and communicating), observing how children differ on each of them. Much of the remainder of this chapter details this answer, process by process.

You might have anticipated the second answer. It is exactly the opposite of the first. Information processing is complicated, but there are some general features of it that readily distinguish the ways children at different ages perform a variety of mental processes and tasks. It is possible, then, to offer a modest and general description of developmental changes in information processing without getting bogged down in details. What are these general features? Three important ones are processing speed, processing capacity, and automaticity, each of which we will consider in turn.

Processing Speed

Many things children do are constrained by how much time is available (Geary & Brown, 1991). A child is told to finish writing a letter in 5 minutes so the family can leave. A phone message must be written down before it is forgotten. The teacher gives children 5 minutes to finish a series of arithmetic problems. There is abundant evidence that the speed with which such tasks are completed improves dramatically across the childhood years (Kail, 1993; Stigler, Nusbaum, & Chalip, 1988). In fact, it is difficult to find any cognitive tasks for which there is *not* some striking developmental change. The causes of the change are not always clear, however. Is a 7-year-old slower to write down a phone message than a 13-year-old because of limitations in the physical act of writing or because of other, more mental limitations such as the time needed to think of how to spell words correctly or to summarize a message briefly? Are such differences readily overcome by concentrated practice or will such age differences persist despite practice, suggesting some maturational, central nervous system differences in maturity?

In one recent study, evidence that processing speed continues to improve in early adolescence was found (Hale, 1990). Ten-year-olds were approximately 1.8 times slower in processing information than young adults on such tasks as reaction time, letter matching, mental rotation, and abstract matching.

Twelve-year-olds were approximately 1.5 times slower than young adults, but 15-year-olds processed information on the tasks as fast as the young adults.

Processing Capacity

Information-processing capacity can be viewed as a type of mental energy needed to perform mental work (Halford, 1993). Our difficulty in dividing attention between two things at once is attributed to our limits on capacity. So also is the trouble we have performing complex tasks (such as mentally working complicated arithmetic problems). Although capacity is believed to be limited at all ages, there is no generally accepted measure of a child's capacity; thus, the findings are ambiguous. For example, it is possible that capacity does not change with age but that young children must spend more capacity on lower-level processes (such as identifying stimuli), leaving less capacity for higher-level processes (such as dividing attention or performing complex computations).

Automaticity

Automaticity *is the ability to process information with little or no effort.* Consider a bright 4-year-old, who picks up some crayons and quickly labels them—yellow, green, brown, blue, and red. An able 10-year-old zips through a practice list of single-digit addition problems (for instance, 5 + 8) with little conscious effort. An adult picks up a newspaper and quickly reads a lead paragraph that reveals the results of an important basketball game held the previous evening. Each of these examples illustrates relatively automatic information processing. By comparison, imagine a 4-year-old trying to sound out the words in a primer, a 10-year-old doing long division with three-to-five-digit numbers, or an adult trying to decipher the meaning of a lead news paragraph in a foreign language studied years ago in high school. These activities require considerable mental processing and effort. Although automatic processing can probably be performed at the same time the individual is completing another (parallel) activity, effortful tasks such as these demand single-minded direction and focus. For any given task, such as calculating, reading, or writing, children's automaticity—the ability to perform automatically with little or no effort—improves dramatically as children get older (Brown & others, 1983; Keating, 1990; Siegler, 1986). Automaticity is linked to speed and processing capacity; as an activity is completed faster, it requires less processing capacity. As processing capacity increases, it becomes easier to complete tasks that were previously considered to be difficult.

ELEMENTARY COGNITIVE PROCESSES

What are the elementary processes necessary for children to process information about their world? They are attention and memory, each of which we will consider in turn.

Attention

"Pay attention" is a phrase children hear all of the time. Just what is attention? **Attention** *is the concentration and focusing of mental effort. Attention also is both selective and shifting.* For example, when children take a test, they must attend to it. This implies that they have the ability to focus their mental effort on certain stimuli (the test questions) while excluding other stimuli, an important aspect of attention called *selectivity.* When selective attention fails children, they have difficulty ignoring information that is irrelevant to their interests or goals (Posner & Rothbart, 1989). For example, if a television set or stereo is blaring while a child is studying, the child may have difficulty concentrating.

Not only is attention selective, but it is also *shiftable.* If a teacher asks students to pay attention to a certain question and they do so, their behavior indicates they can shift the focus of their mental effort from one stimulus to another. If the telephone rings while an adolescent is studying, the adolescent may shift attention from studying to the telephone. An external stimulus is not necessary to elicit an attention shift. At any moment children may be able to shift their attention from one topic to another virtually at will. They might think about the last time they played basketball, then think about the last time they played soccer, then think about the upcoming baseball game, and so on.

How does attention develop in children? Remember from earlier in the chapter that attention was discussed in the context of habituation, which is something like being bored in the sense that infants become disinterested in a stimulus and no longer attend to it. Researchers have found that both a decrease and recovery of attention—when measured in the first 6 months of life—are associated with higher intelligence toward the end of the preschool years (Bornstein & Sigman, 1986). Although the infant's attention has important implications for cognitive development in the preschool years, significant changes in a child's ability to pay attention take place during this time (Pillow, 1988; Ruff & Lawson, 1990). The toddler wanders around, shifting attention from one activity to another, usually seeming to spend little time focused on any one object or event. By comparison, the preschool child might be observed watching television for a half hour.

The changes in ability to pay attention continue beyond the preschool years into the elementary school years. In the classroom, children are able to observe the teacher for extended periods of time, and they can pore over their books in long hours of independent study. These demands on attention exceed what was required of the preschooler, who is generally free to move about in various play activities. These apparent changes in attention have a dramatic influence on children's learning (Stevenson, 1972).

One deficit in attention during the preschool years concerns the dimensions that stand out, or are *salient,* compared with those that are relevant to solving a problem or performing well on a task. For example, a problem might have a flashy, attractive clown that presents the directions for solving the problem. Preschool children are influenced strongly by the features of the task that stand out—such as the flashy, attractive clown. After the age of 6 or 7, children attend more efficiently to the dimensions of the task that are relevant—such as the directions for solving a problem. Developmentalists believe that this change reflects a shift to cognitive control of attention so that children act less precipitously and reflect more (Paris & Lindauer, 1982).

Memory

There are few moments when children's lives are not steeped in memory. Memory is at work with each step children take, each thought they think, and each word they utter. **Memory** *is the retention of information over time. It is central to mental life and to information processing.* To successfully learn and reason, children need to hold on to information and to retrieve the information they have tucked away. Two important memory systems are short-term memory and long-term memory. **Short-term memory** *is a limited-capacity memory system in which information is retained for as long as 30 seconds, unless the information is rehearsed, in which case it can be retained longer.* **Long-term memory** *is a relatively permanent memory system, which holds huge amounts of information for a long period of time.*

> *I come into the fields and spacious palaces of my memory, where are treasures of countless images of things in every manner.*
>
> —St. Augustine

Short-Term Memory

As a child listens to instructions from her mother, to directions from a teacher, or to a story on television, the information she encounters lasts for a short while in her memory. For this information to last longer, it has to be elaborated or transformed in order to move into long-term memory, which may last for years. A child's short-term memory is severely limited, as is the short-term memory of an adult. Only a handful of "bits" of information can be handled. Many years ago, cognitive scientist George Miller (1956) suggested that memory's limit is seven plus or minus two bits of information. If too much information is encountered, some of the information circulating in short-term memory is displaced and may be lost forever.

One way to illustrate this is to present a list of items to children to remember, perhaps the most common method for studying short-term memory is psychology (Case, 1985). A task that has been used in this manner is the memory span task. If you have taken an IQ test, you probably were exposed to one of these tasks. A short list of stimuli—usually digits—are presented at a rapid pace (for example, one per second). Then you are asked to repeat the digits. Research with the memory span task suggests that short-term memory increases during early childhood. For example, in one investigation, memory span increased from about two digits in 2- to 3-year-old children to about five digits in 7-year-old children; however, between 7 and 13 years of age, memory span increased only by one and one half digits (Dempster, 1981). Keep in mind, though, that memory is affected by individual differences, which is why IQ and various aptitude tests are used.

Why are there age differences in memory span? Rehearsal of information seems important—older children rehearse the digits more than younger children do. Also important are the speed and efficiency of information processing, especially the speed with which memory items can be identified. For example, in one investigation, children were tested on their speed of repeating auditorially presented words (Case, Kurland, & Goldberg, 1982). Speed of repetition strongly predicted memory span using these same words. When speed of repetition was controlled, the 6-year-olds' memory spans were equal to those of young adults.

Long-Term Memory

Remember that long-term memory retains information indefinitely—it can be used over and over again. Is the same pattern of developmental change found for short-term memory also found for long-term memory? Long-term memory shows a different developmental pattern: Long-term memory increases with age during middle and late childhood; long-term memory depends on the activities individuals engage in when learning and remembering information (Siegler & Campbell, 1989).

Strategies *are cognitive processes that do not occur automatically but require work and effort. They are under the learner's conscious control and can be used to improve memory.* Four important strategies that improve children's memory are rehearsal, organization, elaboration, and imagery.

My thoughts are my company; I can bring them together, select them, detain them, dismiss them.

—Walter Savage Landor

Rehearsal *is extended repetition of material after it has been presented.* If someone tells a child to remember a phone number, how might the child remember it more effectively? A classic study by John Flavell and his colleagues (Flavell, Beach, & Chinsky, 1966) illustrates the importance of rehearsal and developmental changes in its use. Children from 5 to 10 years old were given the task of remembering the names of a set of two to five pictures for 15 seconds. The novel feature of the experiment was that the experimenter was a trained lip-reader. Some of the children made lip movements showing rehearsal of names and pictures. The percentage of children making lip movements increased with age—10 percent of the 5-year-olds, 60 percent of the 7-year-olds, and 85 percent of the 10-year-olds. In a later study of 6-year-olds, the research team found that children who rehearsed showed better recall than those who did not. When nonrehearsers were taught to rehearse, their performance rivaled that of the spontaneous rehearsers (Keeney, Cannizzo, & Flavell, 1967). More recent investigations make the interesting point that rudimentary, rehearsal-like processes begin to appear at very young ages (DeLoache, Cassidy, & Brown, 1985; Wellman, Ritter, & Flavell, 1985). In one study, 3- and 4-year-old children watched a toy dog

being hidden under one of three cups. Instructed to remember where the dog was hidden, the children looked at, pointed to, and touched the appropriate cup (Wellman, Ritter, & Flavell, 1985).

Organization *is the grouping or arranging of items into categories.* The use of organization improves long-term memory. Children show increased organization in middle and late childhood. In one investigation, children were presented with a circular array of pictures from four categories: clothing, furniture, animals, and vehicles (Moely & others, 1969). The children were told to study the pictures so that later they could say their names back to the experimenter. They also were told they could move the pictures around to remember them better. The 10- and 11-year-olds performed such groupings; the younger children did not. When younger children were put through a brief training procedure that encouraged grouping, they were able to follow this strategy, and their memory for the pictures improved.

Elaboration *is the use of more extensive processing of information, often in the form of association.* For example, children's understanding of the concept of travel will be enhanced if they can come up with examples of different ways they have traveled—such as by car, by boat, or by plane—rather than simply memorizing the definition of the word *travel.* Thinking of examples of a concept is a good way to understand it. Self-reference is another effective way to elaborate information. For example, if the word *win* is on a list of words to remember, children might think of the last time they won a bicycle race with a friend, or, if the word *cook* appears, they might imagine the last time their father cooked dinner. In general, elaboration is an excellent way to remember (Schacter & McGlynn, 1989).

One reason that elaboration enhances memory is that it adds to the *distinctiveness* of the memory code (Ellis, 1987). To remember a piece of information, such as a name, an experience, or a fact about geography, a child needs to search for the code that contains this information among the mass of codes in the child's long-term memory. The search process is easier if the code is somehow unique. The situation is like a child searching for a friend in a crowded park. If the child's friend has a highly distinctive appearance, the child will more easily find the friend in the park. Similarly, highly distinctive memory codes are more easily differentiated from other memory codes.

Developmental psychologists have found that, as children get older, they are more likely to use elaborative strategies (without being instructed to do so). There are especially impressive increases in the use of elaboration from late childhood to late adolescence (Schneider & Pressley, 1989). However, elementary-school-aged children benefit considerably from instruction on using elaboration in remembering information.

Imagine walking up the sidewalk to your house, opening the door, and going inside. What do you see when you are standing inside the door? Now mentally walk through the house to a room in the back and form a picture of what this room is like. Now picture your bedroom in the house. Where is your bed in relation to the door? Imagining these things is reasonably easy for most adults and children. **Imagery** *refers to sensations without the presence of an external stimulus* (Paivio,

FIGURE 8.6

The keyword method. To help children remember the state capitals, the keyword method was used. A special component of the keyword method is the use of mental imagery, which was stimulated by presenting the children with a vivid visual image, such as two apples being married. The strategy is to help the children associate *apple* with Annapolis and *marry* with Maryland.

1986). Imagery is another strategy that enables children to improve their memory (Johnson & others, 1993). The **keyword method** *is a powerful imagery strategy that uses vivid imagery of important words, or keywords, to improve memory.* This method has been used to practical advantage by teaching children how to master new information rapidly such as foreign vocabulary words, the states and capitals of the United States, and the names of presidents of the United States. For example, in teaching children that Annapolis is the capital of Maryland, instructors taught the children the keywords for the states, such that when a state was given (*Maryland*), the children could supply the keyword (*marry*) (Levin, 1980). Then, children were given the reverse type of keyword practice with the capitals. That is, they had to respond with the capital (*Annapolis*) when given a keyword (*apple*). Finally, an illustration was provided (see figure 8.6). The keyword strategy's use of vivid mental imagery, such as the image in figure 8.6 was effective in increasing children's memory of state capitals. Developmentalists today encourage the use of imagery in our nation's schools, believing it helps increase children's memory (McDaniel & Pressley, 1987).

HIGHER-ORDER COGNITIVE PROCESSES

The use of attention and memory may occur rather quickly as children examine information or attempt to complete a task. Children may devote little effort and complete the new activity quickly. By contrast, a variety of activities usually occur over an extended period of time and require the mobilization of considerable cognitive resources on the part of children. When children read or write, for example, the activity usually extends over a period of time, and, when children encounter a difficulty

or lapse of attention, they must overcome the temporary impasse and get back on track. Three themes in children's information processing illuminate the ability to guide and take control of activity: problem solving, cognitive monitoring, and critical thinking.

Problem Solving

Problem solving *is an attempt to find an appropriate way of attaining a goal when the goal is not readily available.* We face many problems in our everyday lives—trying to figure out why our car won't start, planning how to get enough money to buy a stereo, or estimating our chances of winning the lottery. Children also face many problems in their everyday lives—working a jigsaw puzzle, doing math homework, or getting some money that is out of reach, for example.

With children, a common research tactic has been to formulate a problem that requires them to apply some newly learned academic skills in a practical context. Word problems in mathematics have been a popular topic of study (Carpenter, Moser, & Romberg, 1982; Hiebert & Wearne, 1988). For example, consider the following word problems.

1. Marie has 9 fish. Her sister Jill has 14 fish. How many more fish does Jill have than Marie?
2. Fred has 8 pieces of candy. How many more pieces does he have to put with them so he has 13 altogether?
3. There are 5 jars of paint. Three jars are red and the rest are blue. How many blue jars of paint are there?

Try to solve the following problem. If a human being has an inoperable stomach tumor, how can the tumor be removed by rays that destroy organic tissue (at sufficient intensity) without destroying the healthy tissue surrounding the tumor (Duncker, 1945)? The question has been posed to many generations of college students to study how they proceed to think through alternative solutions (the answer to the tumor problem appears at the end of the chapter).

How do children and adults solve these and other problems? What accounts for change in problem-solving ability as children mature? There seem to be at least four important parts involved—problem finding and goal setting, planning the approach, monitoring progress, and checking solutions.

First, we have to figure out precisely what the problem is and set one or more goals. This has sometimes been referred to as *problem finding and goal setting.* The examples of problems given earlier are reasonably well defined. The creators of these problems have taken pains to set up the context and to tell us what they want us to find. In everyday problem solving, however, we often have to find out what the problem is and what we have to do to solve it. For example, if a child is asked to clean her room, she must first figure out what must be done. What must the room look like when she is finished and what currently is out of order?

Once the problem and goal have been defined, a second step is to *plan the approach* to solving the problem. Planning may involve isolating the correct pieces to the puzzle and working out the general pattern to solve the problem with these pieces. For example, in Duncker's tumor-removal problem, the student would have to isolate these crucial elements: A tumor is to be destroyed with an intense ray, the tumor is in the stomach, and no tissue around the tumor can be destroyed. The plan then becomes to devise ways to focus the ray intensely on the tumor but not anywhere else. By brainstorming and calling on popular knowledge about technology and physics, a number of ideas may be tried and discarded as impractical, until a single elegant solution suggests itself. With arithmetic word problems, a similar phenomenon of planning may occur for younger children. In the third word problem, for example, the child must recognize that there are five jars of paint, three of a certain color and the remaining ones of a different color. The plan is to figure out how many remaining ones there are.

A third step is to *monitor the progress* of the problem-solving activity. Basically, this involves taking stock of how the solution process is faring, which is a kind of self-assessment in midstream. As ideas for solving the tumor problem come forth, for example, the student may stop to ponder whether a given idea is an improvement over the preceding one and whether he is still keeping the correct problem elements and goal in mind. As another example, younger children working out the arithmetic problems may wonder if they are proceeding smoothly. There are several common approaches taken by first and second graders to solve these problems. Some count on their fingers, some rely on number facts in their heads, and some use counting props made available by the experimenter. The monitoring activity, then, may consist of children's self-assessments of the viability of the counting technique they have chosen.

The fourth step is to *check solutions*. Whereas monitoring focuses on the progress of problem-solving efforts, this final step occurs when individuals feel they have completed their tasks. In the tumor problem, the student may compare the final solution offered against the initial criteria that had to be met, against the solutions that other classmates have thought up, or against published accounts of its ideal solution. Children solving the arithmetic problems may recheck their adding and subtracting or check the internal consistency of answers (for example, by seeing in the third problem if the number of jars of blue paint computed yields five when added to the three jars of red paint). Children writing essays usually need to revise their writing. In one study, 12-year-olds were much better than 10-year-olds at skillfully revising problematic texts (Beal, 1990).

Cognitive Monitoring

Cognitive monitoring *is the process of taking stock of what you are currently doing, what you will do next, and how effectively the mental activity is unfolding.* When children engage in an activity like reading, writing, or solving a math problem, they are repeatedly called on to take stock of what they are doing and what they plan to do next (Baker & Brown, 1984; Beal & Bonitabitus, 1991; Brown, 1993; Brown & Palincsar, 1989; Lawton, Turner, & Paris, 1991). For example, when children begin to solve a math problem—especially one that might take a while to finish—they must figure out what kind of problem they are working on and what would be a good approach to solving it.

Once they undertake a problem solution, it is helpful to check on whether the solution seems to be working or whether another approach would be better.

The source of much cognitive monitoring for young children is other people—especially parents and teachers. Adults provide a lot of guidance and direction for children's activities, and they tell children what specific strategies to use to complete various cognitive tasks (Wertsch, 1985; Yussen, 1985). They suggest when children should start an activity, they intervene at points when they think children might encounter difficulty (to explain difficult words, how to get started writing on a topic, how to look at math problems, or how to study), and they check children's progress and understanding (giving oral spelling quizzes, asking for explanations, or holding discussions). An important aspect of children's progress in cognitive monitoring as they mature, then, is their abilities to take control of their own cognitive activities and to develop the knowledge base to permit significant, strategic performances.

Instructional programs in reading comprehension (Brown & others in press; Brown & Palincsar, 1984, 1989), writing (Scardamalia, Bereiter, & Steinbach, 1984), and mathematics (Schoenfeld, 1985) have been designed to foster the development of cognitive monitoring (Collins, Brown, & Newman, 1989; Glaser, 1989). Developmental psychologists Ann Brown and Annemarie Palincsar's program for reading comprehension is an excellent example of a cognitive monitoring instructional program. Students in the program acquire specific knowledge and also learn strategies for monitoring their understanding. **Reciprocal teaching** *is an instructional procedure used by Brown and Palincsar to develop cognitive monitoring; it requires that students take turns in leading a study group in the use of strategies for comprehending and remembering text content.* The instruction involves a small group of students, often working with an adult leader, actively discussing a short text, with the goal of *summarizing* it, asking *questions to* promote understanding, offering *clarifying* statements for difficult or confusing words and ideas, and *predicting* what will come next. The procedure actively involves children, it teaches them some techniques to reflect about their own understanding, and the group interaction is highly motivating and engaging. A flurry of recent research has documented the power of peer collaboration in learning and problem solving (Ayman-Nolley & Church, 1993; Grannott, 1993; Saxe & Guberman, 1993; Tudge & Winterhoff, 1993).

Critical Thinking

Much of the knowledge children are exposed to in the course of their education passes through their minds like grains of sand washed through a sieve. Children need to do more than just memorize or passively absorb new information. They must learn how to think critically. Currently, a number of psychologists and educators are studying children's critical thinking skills (Ennis, 1991; Jones, Idol, & Brandt, 1991), although it is not a new idea. Educator John Dewey (1933) was working with a similar concept when he contrasted "reflective thinking" with "nonreflective thinking" in the use of formulas or rules to achieve goals. So was Gestalt psychologist Max Wertheimer (1945) when he distinguished between "productive thinking" and "blind induction." Although today's definitions vary, they all have in common the notion that **critical thinking** *involves grasping the deeper meaning of problems, keeping an open mind about different approaches and perspectives, and thinking reflectively rather than accepting statements and carrying out procedures without significant understanding and evaluation.* Another, often implicit assumption is that critical thinking is an important aspect of everyday reasoning (Galotti, 1989). Critical thinking can and should be used not just in the classroom, but outside it as well.

How can we cultivate the ability to think critically and clearly in children? According to a leading cognitive psychologist, Robert J. Sternberg (1987), we need to teach children to use the right thinking processes, to develop problem-solving strategies, to improve their mental representation, to expand their knowledge base, and to become motivated to use their newly learned thinking skills.

To think critically—or to solve any problem or learn any new knowledge—children need to take an active role in learning. This means that children need to call on a variety of active thinking processes, such as:

- Listening carefully

- Identifying or formulating questions

- Organizing their thoughts

- Noting similarities and differences

- Deducing (reasoning from the general to the specific)

- Distinguishing between logically valid and invalid inferences

Children also need to learn how to ask questions of clarification, such as "What is the main point?" "What do you mean by that?" and "Why?"

Good thinkers use more than just the right thinking processes. They also know how to combine them into workable strategies for solving problems. Rarely can a problem be solved by a single type of thought process used in isolation. Children need to learn how to combine thinking processes to master a new task. Critical thinking involves combining thought processes in a way that makes sense, not just by jumbling them together.

Children need to learn to see things from multiple points of view. Unless children can interpret information from more than one point of view, they may rely on an inadequate set of information. If children are not encouraged to seek alternative explanations and interpretations of problems and issues, their conclusions may be based solely on their own expectations, prejudices, stereotypes, and personal experiences, which may lead to erroneous conclusions.

It is important to keep in mind that thinking does not occur in the absence of knowledge. Children need *something* to think *about.* It is a mistake, however, to concentrate only on information to the exclusion of thinking skills, because children simply would become individuals who have a lot of knowledge but are unable to evaluate and apply it. It is equally a mistake to concentrate only on thinking skills, because children would become individuals who know how to think but have nothing to think about.

Finally, all of the thinking skills children could possibly master would be irrelevant if they were not actually put to use. Critical thinking is both a matter for academic study *and* a part of living. Children need to be motivated to put their critical thinking skills to practical use.

So far, we have learned a great deal about how children process information about their world. We have studied how children attend to information, how they perceive it and retain it over time, how they solve problems, how they engage in cognitive monitoring, and how they develop critical thinking skills. In our discussion of critical thinking skills, we examined some ways in which critical thinking could be encouraged in schools. To read further about how information processing might be applied to children's education, turn to Explorations in Child Development 8.1.

Critical Thinking

Imagine that you have been asked to develop an information-processing-based curriculum for first-grade students. What would the curriculum be like?

KNOWLEDGE AND EXPERTISE

As we study changes in children's information-processing skills, it does not take long to realize that specific processes, such as memory, depend on what children already know. It seems obvious that most of what children try to remember and understand in everyday activities depends on the children's knowledge about people, places, and things (Albro, 1993; Neisser, 1982; Wilkening & Anderson, 1991). If a child makes a trip to a toy store, her ability to recount what she saw is largely governed by what the child knows about toy stores and the things found there, for example. With little knowledge about what is usually found in a toy store, the child would have a much harder time recounting what was there. Although prior knowledge proves helpful in this way, it can also be distorting. For example, in an investigation by Ann Brown and her colleagues (1977), third-, fifth-, and seventh-grade children heard the following story with either George or Galen as the main character.

The Fugitive

Galen (George) was alone. He knew they would soon be here. They were not far behind him when he left the village, hungry and cold. He dared not stop for food or shelter for fear of falling into the hands of his pursuers. There were many of them; they were strong and he was weak. Galen (George) could hear the noise as the uniformed band beat its

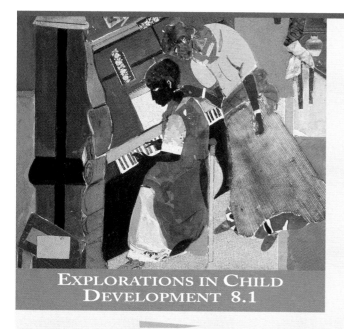

EXPLORATIONS IN CHILD DEVELOPMENT 8.1

Information Processing, the Information Age, and Children's Education

When you were in elementary school, did any teacher at any time work with you on improving your memory strategies? Did any of your teachers work with you on your reading skills after the first and second grade? Did any of your teachers discuss with you ways in which imagery could be used to enhance your processing of information? If you are like most individuals, you spent little or no time in elementary school on improving these important processes involved in our everyday encounters with the world.

Why is it important to have an educational goal of improving the information-processing skills of children? Think for a moment about yourself and the skills necessary for you to be successful in adapting to your environment and for improving your chances of getting a good job and having a successful career. To an extent, knowledge itself is important; more precisely, content knowledge in certain areas is important. For example, if you plan to become a chemical engineer, a knowledge of chemistry is required. Our schools have done a much better job of imparting knowledge than in instructing students how to process information.

Another important situation in your life where instruction in information processing would have helped you tremendously was when you took the SAT or ACT test. SAT cram courses are popping up all over the United States, in part because schools have not done a good job of developing information-processing skills. For example, is speed of processing information important on the SAT? Most of you probably felt you did not have as much time as you would have liked to handle difficult questions. Are memory strategies important on the SAT? You had to read paragraphs and hold a considerable amount of information in your mind to answer some of the questions. You certainly had to remember how to solve a number of math problems. Didn't you also have to remember the definitions of a large number of vocabulary words, and what about problem solving, inferencing, and understanding? Remember the difficult verbal problems you had to answer and the inferences you had to make when reasoning was required?

The story of information processing is one of attention, perception, memory (especially the control processes in memory), and thinking. These information-processing skills become even more crucial in education when we consider that we are now in the midst of a transition from an industrial to a postindustrial information society, with approximately 65 to 70 percent of all workers involved in service industries. The information revolution in our society has placed strains on workers who are called on daily to process huge amounts of information rapidly, to have efficient memories, to attend to relevant details, to reason logically about difficult issues, and to make inferences about information that may be unclear. Students graduate from high school, college, or postgraduate work and move into jobs requiring information-processing skills, yet they have had little or no instruction in improving these skills.

At this time, there is no specified curriculum of information processing that can be taught in a stepwise, developmental fashion to our nation's children. We also do not have the trained personnel for this instruction. Further, some information-processing experts believe that such processes as attention and memory cannot be trained in a general way. Rather, they argue that information processing is domain, or content, specific; for example, we should work on improving information-processing skills that are specific to math or to history. They do believe, though, that an infusion of the information-processing approach into all parts of the curriculum would greatly benefit children (Dillon & Sternberg, 1988; McPeck, 1990; Stankov, 1991).

Researchers are beginning to study the importance of information-processing skills for school learning. Ellen Gagne (1985) provided a menu of information-processing skills that need to be given attention when instructing children in specific content areas—reading, writing, math, and science, for example. Her review concludes that successful students—those who get better grades and higher achievement test scores—are better at such information-processing skills as focusing attention, elaborating and organizing information, and monitoring their study strategies. As yet, though, we do not know the extent to which these information-processing skills can be taught. Nonetheless, in one investigation, Gagne and her colleagues (1984) demonstrated that children can be taught effective ways to elaborate information so that it can be remembered more efficiently. Elaboration refers to more extensive processing. Getting children to think of examples of a concept is a good way to improve their memory of the concept; so is getting them to think about how the concept relates to themselves. Other experts in cognitive psychology also believe that information-processing skills can be taught. For example, Joan Baron and R.J. Sternberg (1987) believe we need to teach children to think in less irrational ways; children need to be more critical of the first ideas that pop into their minds. They should be taught to think longer about problems and to search in more organized ways for evidence to support their views.

Drawing by Koren; © 1986 The New Yorker Magazine, Inc.

Simple stories have structure; after reading or hearing about enough stories, children develop a strong expectation about what kind of information will be contained in a story. That expectation is a story schema.

way through the trees not far behind him. The sense of their presence was everywhere. His spine tingled with fear. Eagerly he awaited darkness. In darkness he would find safety.

Children who heard the story about Galen immediately assumed that the vignette was about a popular character in the television show "Planet of the Apes." In recalling the story later, they inferred that the character was an ape, that the pursuers were apes, that his "fur" tingled, and that the pursuers made their way using trees rather than walking among them. Those who read about George had no such " intrusions" in their memories.

As we evaluate the contribution of knowledge to children's information processing in succeeding sections, we will explore the different kinds of knowledge children acquire, how the knowledge is put to use, and how experts differ from novices in the kind of knowledge they have and the way they use it.

Knowledge

Among the most important aspects of understanding how knowledge is involved in the child's cognitive activities are concepts, semantic networks, schemas, and metacognitive knowledge, each of which we will consider in turn.

Concepts

In everyday learning and thinking, children use many simple concepts to understand the world. Words for ordinary objects, people, and places—such as *house, man,* and *street* —stand for simple ideas and concepts that are the building blocks for children's thoughts. A **concept** *is a category used to group objects, events, and characteristics on the basis of common properties.* Why are concepts important? Concepts allow children to relate experiences and objects. For example, New York, California, and Texas are states. Without the concept of "state," children would be unable to compare these states. Without concepts, each object in a child's world would be unique. Generalization would be impossible.

Semantic Networks

Semantic networks *are the organized stores of general information in memory.* Simple concepts are often organized into rich patterns in memory. These semantic networks gradually grow in size and complexity as children develop. As children become older, the increased size and complexity of semantic networks help them connect many ideas quickly and have all of these ideas in hand to accomplish whatever task is necessary. A good example of a semantic network is provided by an investigation of a 4-year-old dinosaur "expert" (Chi & Koeske, 1983). Like many children his age, this young boy enjoyed hearing stories about dinosaurs and examining picture books of dinosaurs. Unlike most children his, however, he was able to name at least 46 dinosaurs and could identify at least one, and often many, features of each (for example, whether it ate plants or flew). The researchers carefully mapped out what the child knew about each dinosaur and how directly each dinosaur name was linked in the child's mind to other dinosaur names. Figure 8.7 shows a complete mapping of the boy's semantic dinosaur network. It represents visually how the dinosaurs were linked and the particular features associated with each dinosaur in the child's mind. Although the figure is complicated, some simple points can be learned from it. Each line represents a link, each circled letter represents a dinosaur attribute, and the individual dinosaur names/concepts are included in the boxes. Notice, first, that some dinosaurs are not linked to many others. This is true of Dimetrodon and Pterodactyl. We would not expect these dinosaurs to be as easily remembered or used compared with others. Notice, second, that, among the dinosaurs that are linked, some have more links (for example, Styracosaur has more links than Ornitholestes). Notice, third, that some dinosaurs are more centrally located in a network than those surrounding them. We would expect dinosaur names with more links and a more central location in the network to be more salient in the child's mind when he thinks about dinosaurs.

FIGURE 8.7

A 4-year-old expert's semantic network of dinosaurs.

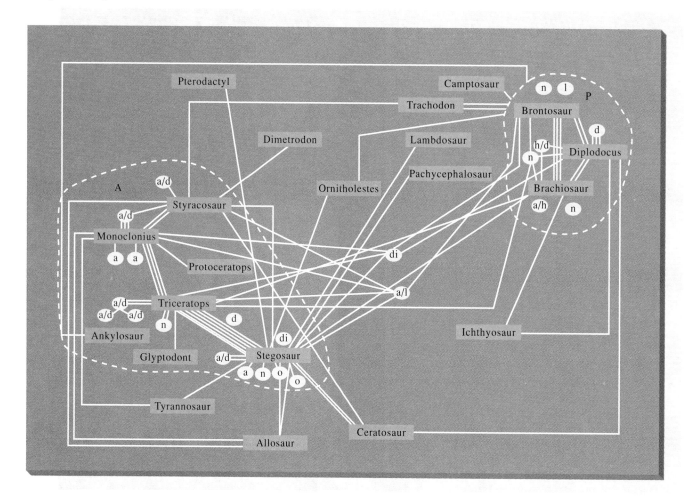

You may be somewhat intimidated by this young child's knowledge. You can get a good personal understanding of semantic networks by creating your own mapping of a domain of concepts familiar to you. Perhaps try one of these domains: "foods I like to eat," "games I know," or "places I visit."

Schema

Long-term memory has been compared to a library. A library stores books, just as children's long-term memory stores information. Children retrieve the information as they do when they locate and check out a book. The process of retrieving information is not as precise as the library analogy suggests, however. When children search through their long-term memory store, they don't always find *exactly* the "book" they want, or they might find the book they want but discover that only several pages of the book are intact. Children have to reconstruct the rest. When children reconstruct information, they often fit it into information that already exists in their mind. A **schema** *is information—concepts, events, and knowledge—that already exists in an individual's mind. A schema influences how a child interprets new information.* Schemas come from prior encounters with the environment and influence the way children encode, make in-

ferences about, and retrieve information. Children have schemas for stories, scenes, spatial layouts (a bathroom or a park, for example), and common events (such as going to a restaurant, playing with toys, or practicing the piano), and sociocultural dimensions such as gender and race (Levy & Katz, 1993).

Children frequently hear and tell stories, and, as they develop the ability to read, they are exposed to many kinds of stories in print. Simple stories have a structure; after hearing enough stories, children develop a strong expectation about what kind of information will be contained in a story. This expectation is a *story schema*. For example, a story tells about what happens in a particular place and circumstance. This context is called the setting. A story also has at least one main character, the protagonist, who attempts to achieve a purposeful goal for a clear reason. The protagonist's actions are usually captured in one or more episodes of a story, which can be further broken down, depicting a fairly simple, one-episode story (see figure 8.8).

A decade of research has shown that children at a very young age are able to use structures like these to fill in missing information, remember better, and tell relatively coherent stories (Ackerman, 1988; Buss & others, 1983; Rahman & Bisanz,

FIGURE 8.8

"Albert, the Fish," a representative story.

Setting	1	Once there was a big gray fish named Albert.
	2	He lived in a pond near the edge of a forest.
Initiating event	3	One day Albert was swimming around the pond.
	4	Then he spotted a big juicy worm on top of the water.
Internal response	5	Albert knew how delicious worms tasted.
	6	He wanted to eat that one for his dinner.
Attempt	7	So he swam very close to the worm.
	8	Then he bit into him.
Consequence	9	Suddenly, Albert was pulled through the water into a boat.
	10	He had been caught by a fisherman.
Reaction	11	Albert felt sad.
	12	He wished he had been more careful.

Cognitive developmentalist John Flavell has been a pioneer in providing insights into the ways in which children think.

Although in some ways children are universal novices, some children have high levels of skill in chess.

1986; Stein & Glenn, 1979; Yussen & others, 1988). Changes occur throughout the childhood years, however, in children's abilities to identify salient events in stories, to unscramble mixed-up stories, and to keep multiple plot lines straight in their minds when facing more complex stories involving several episodes and more than one major character.

A **script** *is a schema for an event* (Schank & Abelson, 1977). Children's first scripts appear very early in development, perhaps as early as the first year of life. Children clearly have scripts by the time they enter school (Firush & Cobb, 1989; Flannagan & Tate, 1989; Furman & Walden, 1989, 1990; Gomez & Thompson, 1993). As children develop, their scripts become less crude and more sophisticated. For example, a 4-year-old's script for a restaurant might include information only about sitting down and eating food. By middle and late childhood, the child adds information to the restaurant script about the types of people who serve food, about paying the cashier, and so on.

Metacognitive Knowledge and the Child's Theory of Mind

Metacognitive knowledge *is the segment of acquired world knowledge that involves cognitive matters.* It is the knowledge children have accumulated through experience and stored in long-term memory that concern the human mind and its workings. There has been a flurry of recent interest in the young child's theory of mind, that is, how the human mind exists (Bartsch & Wellman, 1993; Delcielo & others, 1993;

DeLoache, 1993; Gopik & Wellman, 1993; Kuebli & Fivushl, 1993; Olson, 1993; Sheffield, Sosa, & Hudson, 1993; Zelazo & Frye, 1993).

Young children are curious about the human mind. By the age of 3, they turn some of their thoughts inward and understand that they and others have internal mental states (Flavell, Miller, & Miller, 1993). Beginning at about 3 years of age, children also show an understanding that the internal beliefs and desires of a person can be connected to that person's actions (Wellman, 1990; Wellman & Gelman, 1992). Young children also know that they cannot physically touch thoughts, believe that a person has to see an object to know about it, and grasp that their mental image of an object represents something that exists in the world (Wellman, 1990).

Expertise

What is an expert? An **expert** *is someone who has a great deal of knowledge about a domain of human interest and a great deal of experience performing tasks typical of that domain.* These individuals are recognized by others in their field as having reached the highest levels of knowledge and performance. Examples of experts are easy to offer. Any list would include, but not be limited to, exceptional athletes, talented musicians, acclaimed artists, highly esteemed professionals in medicine and law, highly skilled manual tradespeople, and chess masters. Experts are often contrasted with novices, who are just beginning to learn in the domain (Harnishfeger & Cassel, 1991; Metz, 1991). A great deal of research has been done in the past two decades to characterize the differences between experts and others. Most of this work is with adults, a result of the limited time children have had to become expert at anything. Our survey of the topic considers why an understanding of expertise is important in the study of children's information processing, some of the differences between experts and others, and implications for learning and instruction.

Developmental Implications of Expertise

In some ways, young children are universal novices. They perform almost any cognitive task with very little of the knowledge and experience of adults. Adults are not always experts, but neither are they rank novices, at reading, writing, solving mathematics problems, following travel directions, and so on. However, young children are almost always novices at these tasks. There are exceptions, of course; we can find children with high levels of skill in chess, handling an abacus, and dinosaur identification, for example, but our interest in these forms of childhood expertise is partly a result of the novelty and rarity with which it occurs. If we were to study such forms of childhood expertise carefully, we would probably conclude that the children are not really experts at all. Our 4-year-old dinosaur "expert" is certainly a wonder, but he hardly has the knowledge of paleontologists—among whom the real dinosaur experts would be found.

It is wise, then, not to make children experts. This is not a feat we're likely to manage with any great success. The attraction, instead, is to understand what an expert does, how the expert got to that level of functioning, and the stages or landmarks that led to the high level of functioning. With this knowledge in hand, we can have realistic goals about fostering high levels of competence in children and of cultivating expertise in children who seem to have interest and potential in particular fields.

Differences between Experts and Novices

How do experts and novices differ in the way they approach tasks in a particular domain? One difference concerns initial *planning time* (Berg & Sansone, 1991; Friedman, 1991; Trabasso, 1991). Present a problem to an expert and the expert spends more time, relative to the total time needed to complete the task, than a novice or less experienced person would in thinking about how to solve the problem or complete the task. Expert writers spend a great deal of time thinking about what they want to communicate, how to communicate it, and what the parts or units of their written product will look like. Expert computer programmers spend a considerable amount of time describing to themselves what their finished program will accomplish and the form their program will take. Expert athletes

spend a great deal of effort planning their approach to conditioning, polishing skills, and choosing competition. Novices, on the other hand, leap right in. They may not have the skill to plan effectively or they may not realize the value of initial planning. The experts' emphasis on planning often surprises people, because a common stereotype of experts is that they know how to do everything in their domain of expertise with relatively little effort.

In fact, if a task is straightforward and not a "problem" to solve, experts are extremely fast. Their performances seem *automatic* and *effortless*. Having planned an essay, an expert writer may dash off pages of print in just several hours. Having planned a computer program, a programmer writes code at a speed that dazzles beginners. Having prepared physically and mentally for a match, an expert tennis player serves, volleys, and returns ground strokes with speed and grace. The contrasting performance of a novice is one of sluggish fits and starts, conscious thought about what to do, and great effort.

Another feature of expert performance is the tendency to see what might be called the *underlying structure* of the task and to ignore surface details. Faced with creating a political speech, an expert writer will set aside the fact that the speech must be 10 pages long and must cover certain current issues. These are less important than to communicate the message, the perspective, and the leadership qualities that the candidate wants to project to a particular audience. These goals define the underlying structure of the writing task. A novice is more likely to focus on the length and topics to be covered; these will be sufficiently challenging, although ultimately not what writing a speech is principally about.

A final characteristic is the tendency of an expert to use **heuristics,** *strategies or rules of thumb that suggest a solution to a problem but do not guarantee it will work,* and intuition to complete tasks rather than formal rules and principles (Yaniv & Shatz, 1990). In school, we are taught to do things according to formal rules and guidelines. To write a good essay, we need a central thesis and supporting arguments. To do well on an exam, we should review all the material likely to be on a test and distribute our study time over a reasonable period of days and hours. To perform well in an athletic contest, we must remember the fundamentals of the game and concentrate on doing things simply and cleanly. Rules such as these serve most of us, who are not experts, quite well most of the time. Novices also need rules to perform tasks with a degree of proficiency. However, experts often throw rules and principles out the window when they are functioning at their highest form. They rely, instead, on their own informal rules and intuition. Have you ever read a political essay by Mike Royko? His form is usually meandering, with a tone of outrage and disbelief, in the form of a story. Have you every watched a chess match among masters? What is the player thinking while waiting to make a move? The chess master isn't computing all possible moves, as is commonly thought. Usually he comes up with one or two likely moves very quickly and intuitively (based on experience and a fantastic memory of similar game situations faced before) and spends the rest of the time making sure these are not going to cause trouble later (in other words, backtracking).

Expertise, Learning, and Instruction

Experts are made, not born. It takes a long time and a lot of practice to reach high levels of expertise in most fields of human endeavor. Cognitive scientist Herbert Simon has estimated that world-class athletes, for example, are the product of 10 or more years of continuous training for the equivalent of about 8 hours a day. Experts in academic and creative walks of life may likely require much more time than this.

There are no shortcuts. One simply cannot emulate the characteristics of experts (spending more time planning, looking for underlying structure, and functioning intuitively) and expect to mimic their levels of performance. If an area of human endeavor holds some appeal to a child, the best advice to the child is to learn patiently, to acquire more knowledge and experience, and to practice the skills of the discipline.

Experts must be sought out as teachers, because they have insight into what was required to reach high levels of accomplishment. Although instruction in school is a good starting point to build toward an expert level in a domain, school is limited. Usually, expert levels are achieved at a later point in a person's life. If we take Simon's estimate to heart, we see, for example, that, in 12 years of public school, there is simply not sufficient time for most children to focus on a single area of endeavor for the number of hours necessary to reach a true expert level. The exceptions to this, of course, are some areas of athletics (swimming and gymnastics), in which learning and practice begin very early; relative "youth" is a necessity for speed, strength, and agility; and students manage to cram in 3 to 5 hours of practice per day.

INDIVIDUAL DIFFERENCES IN INFORMATION PROCESSING

Virtually all teachers are aware that the children in their classrooms vary in their ability to process information—some may attend efficiently to the teacher's instructions, others may rarely listen to what the teacher says; some students may be able to remember efficiently, others not so well; some students seem to process information rapidly, others more slowly; some students are impulsive in solving problems, others are more reflective; and some students focus on the details or elements of information, others on the gist or the overall picture of the information. Researchers who have studied individual differences in information processing have primarily focused on **cognitive styles,** *the general, usually consistent ways individuals process information. Cognitive style is determined not only by an individual's attention to a task, organizational skills, and cognitive strategies, but by the person's personality and motivation as well.* The type of cognitive style that has received the most attention is impulsivity versus reflection.

According to our discussion of the differences between novices and experts, how might this gymnastics expert differ from novices in gymnastics?

Impulsivity *is a cognitive style in which individuals act before they think, usually making rapid scans of information and, if fine discriminations of information are required, making errors.* **Reflection** *is cognitive style in which individuals think before they act, usually scanning information carefully and slowly and, if fine discriminations of information are required, making few errors* (Entwistle, 1981). Impulsive students usually finish objective tests quickly, whereas reflective students are still contemplating their answers when the exam period is almost over. The test most often used to measure individual differences in impulsivity/reflection is the Matching Familiar Figures Test (Kagan, 1965) (see figure 8.9). On this test, children are presented a series of pictures in which they must select the one picture of the six at the bottom that exactly matches the picture at the top. Impulsive children scan the six options quickly, making a choice that often is inaccurate. By contrast, reflective children carefully examine the six pictures, slowly making a choice that often is correct.

Much learning that takes place in classrooms requires reflection rather than impulsivity. To do well on school tasks, children must carefully examine the details of information, reflect on what the best answer is, and evaluate their errors after they have failed at a task (Pascual-Leone & Shafrir, 1991; Shafrir, 1991; Siegel, 1991). Researchers have trained impulsive children to become more reflective by improving their scanning strategies, teaching them to take more time, and instructing them to talk to themselves to control their behavior (Egeland, 1974; Meichenbaum & Goodman, 1971). Even with reflection training, though, impulsive children rarely attain a competence level of careful examination of information that

Critical Thinking

What is your cognitive style of information processing? Are there ways that you could improve your style of processing information?

FIGURE 8.9

Two sample items from the matching familiar figures test. The child is asked to find the object in the six items at the bottom of each card that is identical to the object at the top of the card.

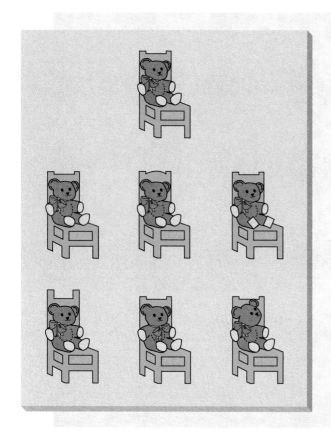

characterizes their reflective counterparts, and no long-term benefits of reflection training have been demonstrated. Also, it is important to keep in mind that not all cognitive tasks require extensive examination of the fine details of information. Sometimes a quick scan of information is all that is needed to discover the information one needs. If a child wakes up in the morning, looks out the window, and sees it is raining, she does not have to reflect at length when she looks in her closet to determine what type of coat she will wear to school. She only has to quickly pick out her raincoat.

The ability to process information rapidly is often an important ability in our society. We usually do not have unlimited amounts of time to perform what is requested of us, either in school or at work. Consider the exams that children and college students take in classes, as well as standardized national tests of achievement and ability. Most tests have time limits. Consider also the jobs that employees are given to do. A supervisor may want an information-processing task finished in 15 minutes, not 1 or 2 hours. In one investigation, the speed of decoding information significantly differentiated college students who did extremely well on the verbal portion of the SAT, college students who did not do well on the verbal portion of the SAT, young adults not in a university, 10-year-old children, and mildly retarded school children (Hunt, 1978). The high-verbal SAT college students were the most rapid processors of information, the mildly retarded school children the slowest. Apparently, some individuals, such as the talented college students who did well

on the verbal part of the SAT, do not fit neatly into the impulsive or the reflective category. These individuals may work rapidly *and* accurately. By contrast, other individuals may work slowly *and* inaccurately.

Most information-processing psychologists have not been interested in individual differences. Rather, they are interested in capturing the *typical* way people process information rather than the *variations* in how they process information (Siegler & Campbell, 1989). Also, most information-processing psychologists view the concept of cognitive style as too global and general, believing that more precise cognitive processes, such as specific attentional, memory, and thinking strategies, are the keys to understanding children's cognition (Ackerman, Sternberg, & Glaser, 1989). In one recent investigation that combined an emphasis on individual differences and specificity of cognitive processes, Robert Siegler (in press) found that, in math classes, "not so good" students, who would normally be called "impulsive," had a memory system in which they set very low standards for retrieving information (answers to a math problem), whereas "perfectionist" students, who would normally be called "reflective," had a memory system with high standards for retrieving answers to math problems.

At this point, we have discussed a number of ideas about information processing. A summary of these ideas is presented in Concept Table 8.2. In the next chapter, we will turn our attention to another important area of children's cognition: intelligence.

PERSPECTIVES ON PARENTING AND EDUCATION

Observing and Imitating Parents, Teachers, and Peers

Think for a moment about the thousands of hours most children spend observing their parents' behavior. Often on a daily basis, children watch and listen to their parents comment about their work and careers, observe whether they drink too much or not at all, experience their model of marital relationships and whether their mother and father argue a lot or very little, see and hear if they solve problems calmly or with great discharge of anger, view whether they are generous toward others or are more selfish, and see how male and female adults act.

Why are children motivated to imitate their parents' behaviors? Children can gain and maintain their parents' affection and avoid punishment by behaving in ways similar to their parents. Children also acquire a sense of mastery over their environment by imitating the behavior of warm, competent, and powerful parents.

One issue in observational learning is whether parents can get by with telling their children, "Do what I say, not what I do," and not harm their children's development. Such parents often hope that by rewarding their children's positive behavior and/or punishing their negative behaviors, they still can engage in their own maladaptive, selfish, and inappropriate ways without jeopardizing their children's development. Imitation often occurs without parents knowingly trying to influence their children, but when parents verbalize standards and try to get children to abide by them, they are usually consciously shaping their children's behavior.

Child developmentalists believe a "do as I say, but not as I do" approach by parents is not a wise parenting strategy. Children who see their parents attend church regularly and hear them talk

Observational learning is a primary way children learn from their parents.

about how moral they are, but then observe them cheat on their income tax, never give money to charity, turn down requests to help others in need, and treat others with little respect, will often imitate their parents' *actions* rather than their *words*. In the case of children's imitation of parents, then, a familiar saying often holds true: Actions speak louder than words.

How much children learn by observing parents also is influenced by what children see are the consequences of that behavior for the parent. If parental models are rewarded for their behavior, children are more likely to imitate their behavior than if parents receive no reward or are punished for their behavior. The consequences to the model can be either external (someone else says or does something positive to the parents after the parent engages in a particular action) or internal (the parent engages in self-reinforcement by showing pleasure after performing a behavior). For example, a father may give to a charity and subsequently smile and say how good it made him feel. The father's children ob-

serve these consequences and then may imitate the father's kind, generous behavior as long as it makes the children feel good. Parents may find it ineffective to exhort their children to share their toys because children will not feel good letting others share what they want themselves. However, if children see their parents derive pleasure from sharing, the self-sacrificing behavior probably will bring more joy to the children. Thus, imitation is an important part of the process in getting children to behave in kind ways toward others (Jensen & Kingston, 1986).

Children not only learn by observing and imitating their parents, but also by observing and imitating their teachers and peers at school. Teachers who are effective models are well-organized, achievement-oriented people. They value achievement, work, and effort, and they are self-disciplined. Students pick up on such characteristics of models very quickly. Researchers have found that it is especially important for teachers to set an achievement-oriented tone early in the semester, as well as establishing a climate of warmth and respect.

The most imitated person in many classrooms however, is not the teacher, but the most popular student(s). If the most popular students are not very achievement-oriented, this may encourage other students to follow suit. In such circumstances, teachers need to determine early on in the school year which students are the most popular and seek to get them to be more achievement-oriented.

In sum, parents (as well as siblings), teachers, and peers serve as important models for children to observe and imitate. Through memories and continued observation of these important models in children's lives, children learn extensively. ■

CONCEPT TABLE 8.2

Information Processing

Concept	Processes/Related Ideas	Characteristics/Description
The nature of information processing	Framework	The information-processing approach attempts to be very detailed about the mental processes underlying learning and thinking in specific situations and, where possible, to model the specific steps needed to complete a task using computer programs and mathematical estimates of mental activities.
	Development	The information-processing approach emphasizes that, with age, children's processing speed, processing capacity, and automaticity increase.
Elementary cognitive processes necessary to process information	Attention	Attention is the concentration and focusing of mental effort. Attention is both selective and shifting. In infancy, attention is often studied through habituation experiments. Children's attention increases dramatically in the preschool years and becomes even more efficient in the elementary school years. During the elementary school years, scanning of visual patterns and attention to relevant dimensions of problems increase.
	Memory	Memory is the retention of information over time. Two important memory systems are short-term memory and long-term memory. Short-term memory is a limited-capacity memory system in which information is retained for as long as 30 seconds, unless the information is rehearsed, in which case it can be retained longer. Long-term memory is a relatively permanent memory system, which holds huge amounts of information for a long period of time. There is evidence that short-term memory improves the most during the preschool years, long-term memory the most during the elementary school years.
	Memory strategies	Memory strategies are cognitive processes that do not occur automatically but require work and effort. They are under the learner's control and can be used to improve memory. Four important strategies are rehearsal, organization, elaboration, and imagery. As children get older, they become more likely to use these strategies without being instructed to do so, but instructions to children to use the strategies usually improve their memory.
Higher-order cognitive processes	Problem solving	Problem solving is an attempt to find an appropriate way of attaining a goal when the goal is not readily available. The components of problem solving include: problem finding and goal setting, planning the approach to the problem, monitoring the progress on the problem, and checking solutions.
	Cognitive monitoring	Cognitive monitoring is the process of taking stock of what one is currently doing, what will be done next, and how effectively the mental activity is unfolding. The source of much cognitive monitoring in young children is other people. With development through the elementary school years, greater independence in cognitive

Concept	Processes/Related Ideas	Characteristics/Description
		monitoring is usually achieved. Instructional programs in reading comprehension, writing, and mathematics have been designed to foster the development of cognitive monitoring in children. Reciprocal teaching is an instructional procedure used by Brown and Palincsar to develop children's cognitive monitoring.
	Critical thinking	Critical thinking refers to grasping the deeper meaning of problems, keeping an open mind about different approaches and perspectives, and thinking reflectively rather than accepting statements and carrying out procedures without significant understanding and evaluation. To cultivate critical thinking in children, we need to teach them to use the right thinking processes, to develop problem-solving strategies, to improve their mental representation, to expand their knowledge base, and to become motivated to use their newly developed thinking skills.
Knowledge and expertise	Knowledge	Among the most important aspects of understanding how knowledge is involved in the child's cognitive activities are concepts (categories used to group objects, events, and characteristics on the basis of common properties), semantic networks (organized stores of general information in memory), a schema (information that already exists in an individual's mind that influences how the individual interprets new information), and metacognitive knowledge (the segment of acquired knowledge that involves cognitive matters, especially the way the human mind works). There has been a flurry of recent interest in the young child's theory of mind.
	Expertise	Expertise is a highly developed knowledge base coupled with a considerable amount of experience in a domain, which permits individuals to perform at a very effective levels. Experts are the best at what they do. They differ from novices in several ways: they plan more, their performances are often automatic and effortless, they search for underlying structure in cognitive tasks, and they use heuristics and intuition.
Individual differences in information processing	Their nature	Researchers who have studied individual differences in information processing have primarily focused on cognitive styles—the general, usually consistent ways individuals process information. Cognitive styles are not only determined by individuals' attention to the task, organizational skills, and cognitive strategies, but by personality and motivation as well. The type of cognitive style that has received the most attention is impulsivity versus reflection. Most information-processing psychologists have been interested in the typical way people process information rather than in variations in the way they process information. Many information-processing psychologists also believe that the concept of cognitive style is too global.

CONCLUSIONS

As children move through their lives they learn and process information. And they do this in many different ways.

We began the chapter by exploring the type of learning involved when children watch *Sesame Street*—observational learning. Then, we studied the nature of children's learning, classical conditioning, operant conditioning, habituation, observational learning/imitation, and cognitive learning. In the second half of the chapter, we read about children's information processing. We compared the information processing perspectives with the Piagetian and learning perspectives, discussed the nature of children's information processing, studied their elementary—attention and memory—and higher order cognitive processes—problem solving, cognitive monitoring, and critical thinking. We also read about knowledge and expertise, as well as individual differences in information processing. To conclude the chapter, the powerful role of parents, teachers, and peers as models was discussed. Don't forget to again read the concept tables on pages 246 and 262 to obtain an overall summary of the chapter.

So far in this section of the book we have studied the nature of cognitive development and Piaget's theory, learning, and information processing. In the next chapter, we turn our attention to yet another approach to children's cognition, that of individual differences and intelligence tests.

KEY TERMS

learning   A relatively permanent change in behavior that occurs through experience. (233)

classical conditioning   A neutral stimulus acquires the ability to produce a response originally produced by another stimulus. (234)

reflexes   Automatic stimulus-response connections. (234)

unconditioned stimulus (UCS)   A stimulus that produces a response without prior learning. (234)

unconditioned response (UCR)   An unlearned response automatically associated with the UCS. (234)

conditioned stimulus (CS)   A previously neutral stimulus that eventually elicits the conditioned response after being paired with the unconditioned stimulus. (234)

conditioned response (CR)   The learned response to the conditioned stimulus that occurs after CS-UCS pairing. (234)

phobias   Irrational fears. (235)

counterconditioning   A classical conditioning procedure for weakening a CR by associating the stimuli with a new response incompatible with the CR. (235)

operant conditioning   A form of learning in which the consequences of behavior lead to changes in the probability of that behavior's occurrence. (236)

reinforcement   A consequence or reward that increases the probability a behavior will occur. (236)

punishment   A consequence that decreases the probability a behavior will occur. (236)

positive reinforcement   The frequency of a response increases because it is followed by a pleasant stimulus. (236)

negative reinforcement   The frequency of a response increases because the response either removes an unpleasant stimulus or allows one to avoid the stimulus. (236)

behavior modification   The application of operant conditioning principles to changing human behavior; its main goal is to replace unacceptable responses with acceptable, adaptive ones. (238)

habituation   The repeated presentation of a stimulus, which causes reduced attention to the stimulus. (238)

dishabituation   An infant's renewed interest in a stimulus. (238)

information-processing approach   A framework for understanding how children learn and think that considers how information is taken in; how it is stored and transformed; and how it is evaluated and used to perform complex thinking activities, such as problem solving, in order to meet clearly defined purposes and goals. (245)

automaticity   The ability to process information with little or no effort. (248)

attention   The concentration and focusing of mental effort. (249)

memory   The retention of information over time. It is central to mental life and to information processing. (249)

short-term memory   A limited-capacity memory system in which information is retained for as long as 30 seconds, unless the information is rehearsed, in which case it can be retained longer. (249)

long-term memory   A relatively permanent memory system, which holds huge amounts of information for a long time. (249)

strategies   Cognitive processes that do not occur automatically but require work and effort. They are under a learner's conscious control and can be used to improve memory. (250)

rehearsal   The extended repetition of material after it has been presented. (250)

organization   The arranging of items into categories, improving long-term memory. (250)

elaboration   The extensive processing of information, often in the form of association. (250)

imagery   Sensations without the presence of an external stimulus. (250)

keyword method   A powerful strategy that uses vivid imagery of important words, or keywords, to improve memory. (251)

problem solving   Attempting to find a way of attaining a goal when the goal is not readily available. (251)

cognitive monitoring   The process of taking stock of what you are currently doing, what you will do next, and how effectively the mental activity is unfolding. (252)

reciprocal teaching   An instructional procedure used by Brown and Palincsar to develop cognitive monitoring: it requires that students take turns leading a study group in the use of strategies for comprehending and remembering text content. (252)

critical thinking   Grasping the deeper meaning of problems, keeping an open mind about different approaches and perspectives, and thinking reflectively rather than accepting statements and carrying out procedures without significant understanding and evaluations. (253)

concept   A category used to group objects, events, and characteristics on the basis of common properties. (255)

semantic networks   Organized stores of general information in memory. (255)

schema   Information—concepts, events, and knowledge—that already exists in an individual's mind. (256)

script   A schema for events. (257)

metacognitive knowledge   The segment of acquired knowledge that involves cognitive matters. (257)

expert   Someone who has a great deal of knowledge about a domain of human interest and a great deal of experience performing tasks typical of that domain. (257)

heuristics   Strategies that suggest a solution to a problem but do not guarantee it will work. (258)

cognitive styles   The general, usually consistent, ways individuals process information. Cognitive style is determined not only by an individual's attention to a task, organizational skills, and cognitive strategies, but by the person's personality and motivation as well. (259)

impulsivity   A cognitive style in which individuals act before they think, usually making rapid scans of information and, if fine discriminations of information are required, making errors. (259)

reflection   A cognitive style in which individuals think before they act, usually scanning information carefully and slowly and, if fine discriminations of information are required, making few errors. (259)

SUGGESTED READINGS

Axelrod, S., & Apsche, J. (Eds.). (1983). *The effects of punishment on human behavior.* New York: Academic Press. This authoritative volume tells how punishment can be used effectively to control behavior. Considerable detail about reducing the negative side effects of punishment and a full consideration of the ethical issues involved in the use of punishment are included.

Baron, J. B., & Sternberg, R. J. (Eds.). (1987). *Teaching thinking skills: Theory and practice.* New York: W.H. Freeman. Ten eminent psychologists, educators, and philosophers describe ways to improve critical thinking skills and offer various strategies and exercises for children and adults.

Becker, W. C. (1986). *Applied psychology for teachers.* Chicago: SRA. This behaviorally oriented book includes detailed information about the use of behavior modification in classrooms.

Brown, A. L., & Palincsar, A. M. (1989). Guided, cooperative learning and individual knowledge acquisition. In L. B. Resnick (Ed.), *Knowing and learning: Essays in honor of Robert Glaser.* Hillsdale, NJ: Erlbaum. This is a detailed presentation of Brown and Palincsar's provocative ideas about teaching cognitive monitoring skills to children.

Schneider, W., & Pressley, M. (1989). *Memory development between 2 and 20.* New York: Springer-Verlag. Two leading researchers provide up-to-date, detailed analyses and insightful information about the nature and development of children's memory.

Skinner, B. F. (1960). *Walden two.* New York: Macmillan. Skinner once entertained the possibility of a career as a writer. In this interesting and provocative book, he outlines his ideas on how a more complete understanding of the principles of instrumental conditioning can lead to a happier life. Critics argue that his approach is far too manipulative.

PROBLEM SOLUTION

Duncker's problem: the inoperable stomach tumor.

The solution is to isolate the tumor tissue and focus several rays (such as a laser beam) on it through an optical arrangement that guarantees that the rays are intensely focused only on the one spot, and too diffuse to harm any surrounding tissue.

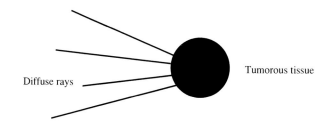

Delfina Flores, Diego Rivera (Detail)

Intelligence

*The thirst to know and understand . . .
these are the goods in life's rich hand.*
—Sir William Watson, 1905

> *Children are remarkable for their intelligence and ardor, for their curiosity,*
> *their intolerance of shams, the clarity of their vision.*
>
> —Aldous Huxley

IMAGES OF CHILDREN

Impassioned Debate about Children's Intelligence

Information about children's intelligence and intelligence tests frequently makes the news. The following two stories appeared in the *Los Angeles Times:*

> IQ testing that leads to the placement of an unusually large number of black children in so-called mentally retarded classes has been ruled unconstitutional by a federal judge. On behalf of five black children, Chief District Court Judge Robert Peckham said the use of standardized IQ tests to place children in educable mentally retarded (EMR) classes violated recently enacted federal laws and the state and federal constitutions. . . . Peckham said the history of IQ testing and special education in California "revealed an

unlawful discriminatory intent . . . not necessarily to hurt black children, but it was an intent to assign a grossly disproportionate number of black children to the special, inferior and dead-end EMR classes." (October 18, 1979)

> A controversial Escondido sperm bank for superbrains has produced its first baby—a healthy, nine-pound girl born to a woman identified only as a small-town resident in "a sparsely populated state.". . . Founded by inventor Robert K. Graham of Escondido in 1979, the facility contains sperm donated by at least three Nobel Prize winners, plus other prominent researchers. . . . The sperm bank was founded to breed

children of higher intelligence. The goal has been denounced by many critics, who say that a child's intelligence is not determined so much by his genes as by his upbringing and environment. (May 25, 1982)

As you might expect, these stories sparked impassioned debate (Kail & Pellegrino, 1985). Some arguments focus on the ethical and moral implications of selective breeding of bright children and selective placement of children in special classes. Other arguments concern the statistical basis of conclusions of intelligence tests, such as whether the tests are really biased if the data are analyzed properly. What you hear *less* often but should hear *more* often is a discussion of the construct of intelligence itself (Sternberg, 1990). That is, what is intelligence? How should it be conceptualized?

PREVIEW

Children's intelligence includes a number of controversies, such as the use of intelligence tests to place children in EMR classes and the Escondido sperm bank. In this chapter we will also explore other controversies in children's intelligence, examine how to measure their intelligence, describe the extremes of intelligence—mental retardation and giftedness—and discuss children's creativity. But to begin, we need to determine just what intelligence is.

WHAT IS INTELLIGENCE?

Intelligence is a possession most of us value highly, yet it is an abstract concept with few agreed-upon referents. We all would agree on referents for such characteristics as children's height, weight, and age, but there is less certainty about the referents for a child's size. Size is more *abstract* than height or weight. Also, size is more difficult to measure directly. We can only estimate size from a set of empirical measures of height and weight. Measuring intelligence is much the same as measuring size, though intelligence is *much more* abstract. That is, we believe children's intelligence exists, but we do not measure their intelligence directly. We cannot peel back a child's scalp and observe her intellectual processes in action. We can only study those intellectual processes *indirectly,* by evaluating the intelligent acts that children generate. For the most part, psychologists have relied on intelligence tests to provide an estimate of children's intellectual processes.

While many psychologists and laypeople equate intelligence with verbal ability and problem-solving skills, others prefer to define it as the individual's ability to learn from and adapt to the experiences of everyday life. If we were to settle on a definition of intelligence based on these criteria, it would be that **intelligence** *is verbal ability, problem-solving skills, and the ability to learn from and adapt to the experiences of everyday life* (see figure 9.1)

> *What a piece of work is a man! How noble in reason! how infinite in faculty! in form, in moving, how express and admirable! in action how like an angel! in apprehension how like a god!*
>
> —William Shakespeare

Although we have just defined general intelligence, keep in mind that the way intelligence is expressed in behavior may vary from culture to culture (Lonner, 1990). For example, in most Western cultures, people are considered intelligent if they are both smart (have considerable knowledge and can solve verbal problems) and fast (can process information quickly). On the other hand, in the Buganda culture in Uganda, people who are wise, slow in thought, and say the socially correct thing are considered intelligent (Wober, 1974).

The components of intelligence are very close to the information processing skills we discussed in chapter 8. The difference between how we discussed information processing skills and how we will discuss intelligence lies in the concepts of individual differences and assessment. **Individual differences** *are the stable, consistent ways in which children are different from each other.* The history of the study of intelligence has focused extensively on individual differences. We can talk about individual differences in personality or in any other domain of development, but it is in the area of intelligence that the most attention is given to individual differences. For example, an intelligence test tells us whether a child can reason better than most others who have taken the test. **Psychometrics** *is the field that involves the assessment of indi-*

> *As many men, as many minds; everyone his own way.*
>
> —Terence

vidual differences. We will examine several of the most widely used tests to assess children's intelligence, but first we need to know something very important in psychometrics—how tests are constructed and evaluated.

HOW TESTS ARE CONSTRUCTED AND EVALUATED

The first evidence of formal tests comes from China. In 2200 B.C. the emperor Ta Yu conducted a series of three oral "competency tests" for government officials; based on the results, they were either promoted or fired (Sax, 1989). Numerous variations on those early exams have been causing anxiety for employees and students ever since. Any good test must meet three criteria—it must be reliable, it must be valid, and it must be standardized. With a reliable test, scores should not fluctuate significantly as a result of chance factors, such as how much sleep the test taker got the night before, who the examiner is, or the temperature in the testing room. **Reliability** *is how consistently a person performs on a test.* One method of assessing reliability is **test-retest reliability,** *which involves giving the same person the same test on two different occasions.* For example, a reliable test would be one on which the same students who score high one day also score high 6 months later. One drawback of test-retest reliability is that people sometimes do better the second time they take the test because they are familiar with it.

Another way that consistency can be deceptive is that a test may or may not measure the attribute we seek. For example, let's say we want to measure intelligence but the test design is flawed and we actually measure something else, such as anxiety. The test might consistently measure how anxious the subjects are and, thus, have high reliability but fail to measure intelligence. **Validity** *is the extent to which a test measures what it is intended to measure.* Two important forms of validity are content and criterion validity.

Content validity *refers to a test's ability to give a broad picture of what is to be measured.* For example, if your instructor for this class plans a comprehensive final exam, it will probably cover topics from each of the chapters rather than just two or three chapters. If an intelligence test purports to measure both verbal ability and problem-solving ability, the test should include a liberal sampling of each. The test would not have high content validity if it asked you to define several vocabulary items (one measure of verbal ability) and did not require you to use reason in solving a number of problems.

Criterion validity *refers to a test's ability to predict other measures, or criteria, of an attribute.* For example, rather than relying solely on the results of one intelligence test to assess a person's intelligence, a psychologist might also ask that person's employer how he or she performs at work. The employer's perceptions would be another criterion for assessing intelligence. Using more than one measure—such as administering a different

FIGURE 9.1

Defining intelligence. Intelligence is an abstract concept that has been defined in various ways. The three most commonly agreed-upon aspects of intelligence are the following: (*a*) verbal ability, as reflected in the verbal skills of these students searching for library books; (*b*) problem-solving skills, as reflected in the ability of this girl to solve the design problem presented her; and (*c*) ability to learn from and adapt to experiences of everyday life, as reflected in this handicapped child's adaptation to her inability to walk.

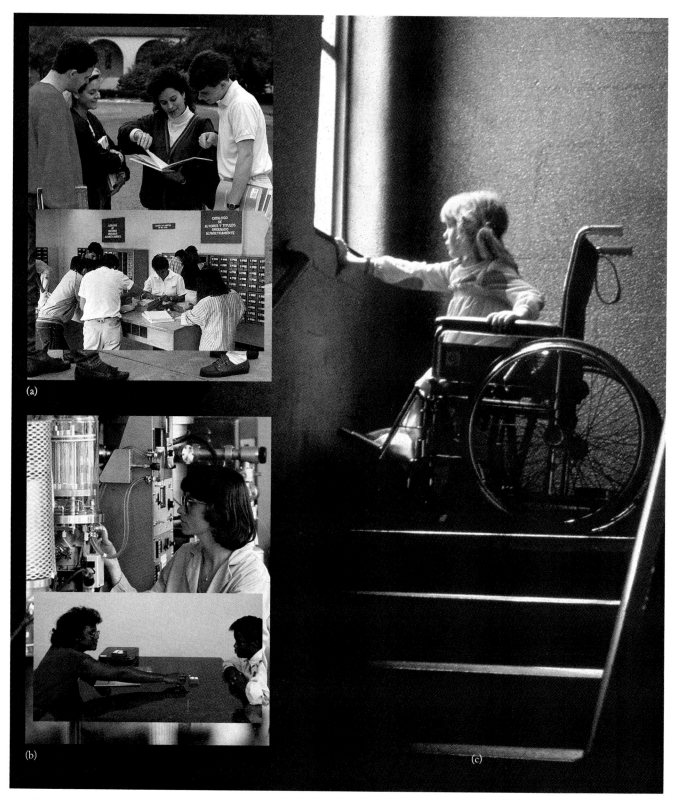

(a)

(b)

(c)

intelligence test, soliciting an employer's perception of intelligence, and observing a person's problem-solving ability—is a good strategy for establishing criterion validity.

Good tests are not only reliable and valid, but they also are standardized. **Standardization** *involves developing uniform procedures for administering and scoring a test, and it also involves developing norms for the test.* Uniform testing procedures require that the testing environment be as similar as possible for everyone who takes the test. For example, the test directions and the amount of time allowed to complete the test should be uniform. **Norms** *are established standards of performance for a test. This is accomplished by giving the test to a large group of people who represent the target population. This allows the researcher to determine the distribution of test scores. Norms inform us which scores are considered high, low, or average.* For example, a score of 120 on an intelligence test has little meaning alone. The score takes on meaning when we compare it with other scores. If only 20 percent of the standardized group scores above 120, then we can interpret that score as high, rather than average or low. Many tests of intelligence are designed for people from diverse groups. So that the tests will be applicable to such different groups, many tests have norms—that is, established standards of performance for people of different ages.

> *No man is smart, except by comparison with others who know less.*
>
> —Edgar Watson Howe

Although there has been some effort to standardize intelligence tests for Blacks and Hispanics, little has been done to standardize tests for people from other ethnic minorities. Psychologists need to ensure that the tests are standardized for a person's particular ethnic group and to put the test results in an appropriate cultural context (Sue, 1990). Otherwise they must use caution interpreting the test's results.

THE MEASUREMENT AND NATURE OF CHILDREN'S INTELLIGENCE

Robert J. Sternberg recalls being terrified of taking IQ tests as a child. He literally froze, he says, when the time came to take such tests. Even as an adult, Sternberg stings with humiliation when he recalls being in sixth grade and taking an IQ test with the fifth graders. Sternberg finally overcame his anxieties about IQ tests and not only performed much better on them, but at age 13 he even devised his own IQ test and began assessing his classmates—until the school psychologist found out and scolded him. In fact, Sternberg became so fascinated with the topic that he's made it a lifelong pursuit. Sternberg's theory of intelligence, which we will discuss later in the chapter, has received considerable attention recently. We will begin at the beginning, with the first intelligence test, in our discussion of measuring intelligence and its nature.

The Binet Tests

In 1904 the French Ministry of Education asked psychologist Alfred Binet to devise a method of identifying children who were unable to learn in school. School officials wanted to reduce crowding by placing those who did not benefit from regular classroom teaching into special schools. Binet and his student Theophile Simon developed an intelligence test to meet this request. The test is referred to as the 1905 Scale and consisted of 30 questions ranging from the ability to touch one's nose or ear when asked to the ability to draw designs from memory and define abstract concepts.

Binet developed the concept of **mental age (MA),** *which is an individual's level of mental development relative to others.* Binet reasoned that a mentally retarded child would perform like a normal child of a younger age. He developed averages for intelligence by testing 50 normal children from 3 to 11 years of age. Children who were thought to be mentally retarded also were tested. Their scores were then compared with the scores of normal children the same chronological age. Average mental-age scores (MA) correspond to chronological age (CA), which is age from birth. A bright child has an MA above CA; a dull child has an MA below CA.

The term **intelligence quotient (IQ)** *was devised in 1912 by William Stern. IQ consists of a person's mental age divided by chronological age, multiplied by 100:*

$$IQ = MA/CA \times 100$$

If mental age is the same as chronological age, then the person's IQ is 100; if mental age is above chronological age, then IQ is more than 100; if mental age is below chronological age, then IQ is less than 100. Scores noticeably above 100 are considered above average, and scores noticeably below 100 are considered below average. For example, a 6-year-old child with a mental age of 8 would have an IQ of 133, whereas a 6-year-old child with a mental age of 5 would have an IQ of 83.

The Binet test has been revised many times to incorporate advances in the understanding of intelligence and intelligence testing. These revisions are called the Stanford-Binet tests (Stanford University is where the revisions were done). Many of the revisions were carried out by Lewis Terman, who applied Stern's IQ concept to the test, developed extensive norms, and provided detailed, clear instructions for each problem on the test.

In an extensive effort to standardize the Stanford-Binet test, it has been given to thousands of children and adults of different ages, selected at random from various parts of the United States. By administering the test to large numbers of people and recording the results, researchers have found that intelligence measured by the Stanford-Binet approximates a normal distribution (see figure 9.2). A **normal distribution** *is symmetrical, with a majority of cases falling in the middle of the possible range of scores and few scores appearing toward the extremes of the range.*

FIGURE 9.2

The normal curve and Stanford-Binet IQ scores. The distribution of IQ scores approximates a normal curve. Most of the population falls in the middle range of scores. Notice that extremely high and extremely low scores are very rare. Slightly more than two-thirds of the scores fall between 84 and 116. Only about 1 in 50 individuals has an IQ of more than 132 and only about 1 in 50 individuals has an IQ of less than 68.

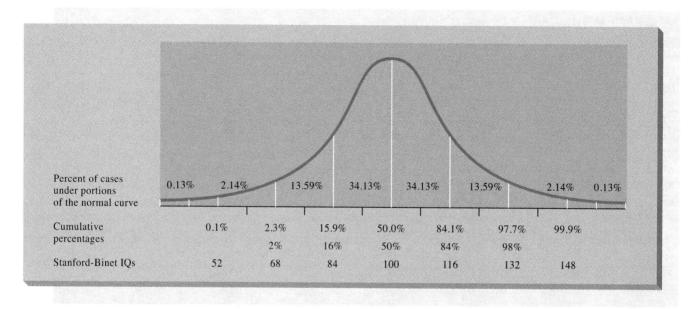

The current Stanford-Binet is given to individuals from the age of 2 through adulthood. It includes a wide variety of items, some requiring verbal responses, others nonverbal responses. For example, items that characterize a 6-year-old's performance on the test include the verbal ability to define at least six words, such as *orange* and *envelope,* and the nonverbal ability to trace a path through a maze. Items that reflect an average adult's intelligence include defining such words as *disproportionate* and *regard,* explaining a proverb, and comparing idleness and laziness.

The fourth edition of the Stanford-Binet was published in 1985 (Thorndike, Hagan, & Sattler, 1985). One important addition to this version is the analysis of the individuals' responses in terms of four content areas: verbal reasoning, quantitative reasoning, abstract/visual reasoning, and short-term memory. A general composite score also is obtained to reflect overall intelligence. The Stanford-Binet continues to be one of the most widely used individual tests of intelligence.

The Wechsler Scales

Besides the Stanford-Binet, the other widely used intelligence tests are the Wechsler scales, developed by David Wechsler. They include the Wechsler Adult Intelligence Scale-Revised (WAIS-R); the Wechsler Intelligence Scale for Children-Revised (WISC-R), to test children between the ages of 6 and 16; and the Wechsler Preschool and Primary Scale of Intelligence (WPPSI), to test children from the ages of 4 to 6½ (Wechsler, 1949, 1955, 1967, 1974, 1981).

Not only do the Wechsler scales provide an overall IQ score, but the items are grouped according to 11 subscales, 6 of which are verbal and 5 nonverbal. This allows an examiner to obtain separate verbal and nonverbal IQ scores and to see quickly the areas of mental performance in which a tested individual is below average, average, or above average. The inclusion of a number of nonverbal subscales makes the Wechsler test more representative of verbal and nonverbal intelligence; the Stanford-Binet test includes some nonverbal items but not as many as the Wechsler scales. Several of the Wechsler subscales are shown in figure 9.3.

Does Intelligence Have a Single Nature?

Is it more appropriate to think of a child's intelligence as a general ability or as a number of specific abilities? Psychologists were debating the nature of the components of intelligence long before David Wechsler analyzed intelligence in terms of general and specific abilities (giving a child an overall IQ but also providing information about specific subcomponents of intelligence).

Early Factor Approaches

Charles Spearman (1927) proposed that intelligence has two factors. **Two-factor theory** *is Spearman's theory that children have both general intelligence, which he called* g, *and a number of specific types of intelligence, which he called* s. Spearman believed that these two factors account for a child's performance on an intelligence test.

FIGURE 9.3

Sample subtests of the Wechsler Intelligence Scale for Children, revised.

Simulated items similar to those in the Wechsler Intelligence Scales for Adults and Children. Copyright © 1949, 1955, 1974, 1981, 1991 by The Psychological Corporation. Reproduced by permission. All rights reserved.

Verbal subtests

Similarities

An individual must think logically and abstractly to answer a number of questions about how things might be similar.

For example, "In what ways are boats and trains the same?"

Comprehension

This subtest is designed to measure an individual's judgment and common sense.

For example, "Why do individuals buy automobile insurance?"

Performance subtests

Picture arrangement

A series of pictures out of sequence is shown to an individual, who is asked to place them in their proper order to tell an appropriate story. This subtest evaluates how individuals integrate information to make it logical and meaningful.

For example, "The pictures below need to be placed in an appropriate order to tell a story."

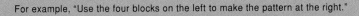

Block design

An individual must assemble a set of multicolored blocks to match designs that the examiner shows. Visual-motor coordination, perceptual organization, and the ability to visualize spatially are assessed.

For example, "Use the four blocks on the left to make the pattern at the right."

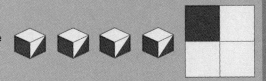

Remember that the Wechsler includes 11 subscales, 6 verbal and 5 nonverbal. Four of the subscales are shown here.

However, some factor approaches abandoned the idea of general intelligence and searched for specific factors only. **Multiple-factor theory** *is L. L. Thurstone's (1938) theory that intelligence consists of seven primary abilities: verbal comprehension, number ability, word fluency, spatial visualization, associative memory, reasoning, and perceptual speed.*

Gardner's Seven Frames of Mind

A more recent attempt to classify intelligence, developed by Howard Gardner (1983, 1989), includes seven components, which he calls *frames of mind,* although they are not the same as Thurstone's seven factors. For example, the talents of Larry Bird and Ludwig von Beethoven reflect the diversity of Gardner's concept of intelligence. Bird and Beethoven are two different types of individuals, with different types of abilities. Bird, the 6'9" former superstar of the Boston Celtics, springs into motion. Grabbing a rebound off the defensive board, he quickly moves across two-thirds of the 94-foot basketball court, all the while processing the whereabouts of his five opponents and four teammates. As the crowd screams, Bird calmly looks left, finesses his way past a defender, and whirls a behind-the-back pass to a fast-breaking teammate, who dunks the ball for two points. Is there specific intelligence in Bird's movement and perception of the basketball court's spatial layout? Now we turn the clock back 200 years. A tiny boy just 4 years old is standing on a footstool in front of a piano keyboard, practicing. At the age of 6, the boy is given the honor of playing concertos and trios at a concert. Beethoven's musical genius was evident at a young age. Did Beethoven have a specific type of intelligence, one we might call musical intelligence?

Gardner argues that Bird's talent reflects his movement intelligence and his ability to analyze the world spatially, and that Beethoven's talent reflects his musical intelligence. Beyond these three forms of intelligence, Gardner believes there are four other main forms of intelligence: verbal intelligence, mathematical intelligence, insightful skills for analyzing ourselves, and insightful skills for analyzing others.

Gardner believes that each of the seven intelligences can be destroyed by brain damage, that each involves unique cognitive skills, and that each shows up in exaggerated fashion in both the gifted and *idiots savants* (individuals who are mentally retarded but who have unbelievable skill in a particular domain, such as drawing, music, or computing).

Gardner is especially interested in musical intelligence, particularly when it is exhibited at an early age. He points out that musically inclined preschool children not only have the remarkable ability to learn musical patterns easily, but that they rarely forget them. He recounts a story about Stravinsky, who, as an adult, could still remember the musical patterns of the tuba, drums, and piccolos of the fife-and-drum band that marched outside his window when he was a young child.

To measure musical intelligence in young children, Gardner might ask a child to listen to a melody and then ask the child to recreate the tune on some bells he provides. He believes that such evaluations can be used to develop a profile of a child's intelligence. He also believes that it is during this early

Howard Gardner, here working with a young child, developed the view that intelligence comes in seven different forms: verbal, mathematical, ability to spatially analyze the world, movement skills, insightful skills for analyzing ourselves, insightful skills for analyzing others, and musical skills.

time in life that parents can make an important difference in how a child's intelligence develops.

Critics of Gardner's approach point out that there are geniuses in many domains other than music. There are outstanding chess players, prize-fighters, writers, politicians, physicians, lawyers, preachers, and poets, for example, yet we do not refer to chess intelligence, prize-fighter intelligence, and so on.

Sternberg's Triarchic Theory of Intelligence

Robert J. Sternberg (1986, 1989, 1990) developed a theory which states that intelligence has three factors. **Triarchic theory** *is Sternberg's theory that intelligence consists of componential intelligence, experiential intelligence, and contextual intelligence.* Consider, Ann, who scores high on traditional intelligence tests, such as the Stanford-Binet, and is a star analytical thinker. Consider Todd, who does not have the best test scores but has an insightful and creative mind. Consider Art, a street-smart child who has learned to deal in practical ways with his world, although his scores on traditional IQ tests are low.

Sternberg calls Ann's analytical thinking and abstract reasoning *componential intelligence;* it is the closest to what we call intelligence in this chapter and what is commonly measured by intelligence tests. Sternberg calls Todd's insightful and creative thinking *experiential intelligence,* and Art's street smarts and practical know-how *contextual intelligence.*

In Sternberg's view, the basic unit of intelligence is a *component,* simply defined as a basic unit of information processing. Sternberg believes that such components include the ability to acquire or store information, to retain or retrieve information, to transfer information, to plan, to make decisions, to solve problems, and to translate thought into performance.

The second part of Sternberg's model focuses on experience. According to Sternberg, intellectual individuals have the ability to solve new problems quickly, but they also learn how to solve familiar problems in an automatic, rote way so that their minds are free to handle other problems that require insight and creativity.

The third part of Sternberg's model involves practical intelligence—such as how to get out of trouble, how to replace a fuse, and how to get along with people. Sternberg describes this practical, or contextual, intelligence as all of the important information about getting along in the real word that you are not taught in school. He believes that contextual intelligence is sometimes more important than the "book knowledge" that is taught in school.

Why Are There So Many Different Theories of the Components of Intelligence?

As we discussed different approaches to intelligence, you probably noticed that theorists often disagree about the definition of intelligence. Two reasons explain this disagreement (Kail & Pellegrino, 1985). First, the same data can be analyzed in many ways. Different apparent solutions, which produce different psychological interpretations, can be obtained from the same data. Second, the data obtained in separate studies differ. The critical data for interpretations of whether intelligence is a general ability or a cluster of specific abilities involves correlations (recall our discussion of this in chapter 2). The pattern of correlations depends on the group tested (school children, armed service recruits, or criminals, for example), the total number of tests administered, and the specific tests that are included in the battery (Meehl, 1990). The outcome of such studies is that the abilities thought to make up the core of intelligence may vary across investigations. Despite these inconsistencies, evidence suggests that intelligence is *both* a general ability and a number of specific abilities.

Critical Thinking

We have examined a number of the components of intelligence. What do you believe are the basic components of intelligence? How would you find out empirically if your theory is accurate?

"You're wise, but you lack tree smarts."
Drawing by D. Reilly; © 1988 The New Yorker Magazine, Inc.

INFANT INTELLIGENCE AND THE STABILITY OF INTELLIGENCE

Many standardized intelligence tests do not assess infant intelligence. Intelligence tests that have been created for infants are often called *developmental scales.* What are these tests like? Can we predict a child's or an adolescent's intelligence from the individual's scores on an infant intelligence test? How much do intelligence test scores change as children grow and develop?

Infant Intelligence Tests

In chapter 4, we discussed the Brazelton Neonatal Behavioral Assessment Scale, which is widely used to evaluate newborns. Developmentalists want to know how development proceeds during the course of infancy as well. If an infant advances at an especially slow rate, then enrichment may be necessary. If an infant develops at an advanced pace, parents may be advised to provide toys that stimulate cognitive growth in slightly older infants.

The infant testing movement grew out of the tradition of IQ testing with older children. However, the measures that assess infants are necessarily less verbal than IQ tests that assess the intelligence of older children. The infant developmental scales contain far more items related to perceptual motor development. They also include measures of social interaction.

The most important early contributor to the developmental testing of infants was Arnold Gesell (1934). He developed a measure that served as a clinical tool to help sort out potentially normal babies from abnormal ones. This was especially useful to adoption agencies, which had large numbers of babies awaiting placement. Gesell's examination was used widely for many years and still is frequently employed by pediatricians in their assessment of normal and abnormal infants. The current version of the Gesell test has four categories of behavior: motor, language, adaptive, and personal-social. The **developmental**

quotient (DQ) *is an overall developmental score that combines subscores in the motor, language, adaptive, and personal-social domains in the Gesell assessment of infants.* Overall scores on such tests as the Gesell do not correlate highly with IQ scores obtained later in childhood. This is not surprising, since the nature of the items on the developmental scales are considerably less verbal than the items on intelligence tests given to older children.

The **Bayley Scales of Infant Development,** *developed by Nancy Bayley (1969), are widely used in the assessment of infant development. The current version has three components: a Mental scale, a Motor scale, and an Infant Behavior Profile.* Unlike Gesell, whose scales were clinically motivated, Bayley wanted to develop scales that could document infant behavior and predict later development. The early version of the Bayley scales covered only the first year of development; in the 1950s, the scales were extended to assess older infants.

According to the Bayley scales, at approximately 6 months of age an average baby should be able to:

1. Accept a second cube—the baby holds the first cube, while the examiner places the second cube within easy reach of the infant
2. Grasp the edge of a piece of paper when it is presented
3. Vocalize pleasure and displeasure
4. Persistently reach for objects placed just out of immediate reach
5. Turn his or her head after a spoon the experimenter suddenly drops on the floor
6. Approach a mirror when the examiner places it in front of the infant

At approximately 12 months of age, an average baby should be able to:

1. Inhibit behavior when commanded to do so—for example, when the infant puts a block in his or her mouth and the examiner says, "No, no," the infant should cease the activity
2. Repeat an action if he or she is laughed at
3. Imitate words the experimenter says, such as *mama* and *dada*
4. Imitate the experimenter's actions—for example, if the experimenter rattles a spoon in a cup, the infant should imitate this action
5. Respond to simple requests, such as "take a drink"

The Stability of Intelligence

In one study conducted by Nancy Bayley, no relation was found between the Bayley scales and intelligence as measured by the Stanford-Binet at the ages of 6 and 7 (Bayley, 1943). Another investigation found correlations of only .01 between intelligence measured at 3 months and at 5 years of age and .05 between measurements at 1 year and at 5 years (Anderson, 1939). These findings indicate virtually no relationship between in-

fant development scales and intelligence at 5 years of age. Again, it should be remembered that one of the reasons for this finding is that the components of intelligence tested in infancy are not the same as the components of intelligence tested at the age of 5.

There is a strong relation between IQ scores obtained at the ages of 6, 8, and 9 and IQ scores obtained at the age of 10. For example, in one study, the correlation between IQ at the age of 8 and IQ at the age of 10 was .88. The correlation between IQ at the age of 9 and IQ at the age of 10 was .90. These figures show a very high relation between IQ scores obtained in these years. The correlation of IQ in the preadolescent years and IQ at the age of 18 is slightly less but still statistically significant. For example, the correlation between IQ at the age of 10 and IQ at the age of 18 was .70 in one study (Honzik, MacFarlane, & Allen, 1948).

What has been said so far about the stability of intelligence has been based on measures of groups of individuals. The stability of intelligence also can be evaluated through studies of individuals. As we will see next, there can be considerable variability in an individual's scores on IQ tests.

Let's look at an example of the absence of a relation between intelligence in infancy and intelligence in later years for two children in the same family. The first child learned to speak at a very early age. She displayed the characteristics of an extravert, and her advanced motor coordination was indicated by her ability to walk at a very early age. The second child learned speech very late, saying very few words until she was 2½ years old. Both children were given standardized tests of intelligence during infancy and then later, during the elementary school years. In the earlier test, the first child's scores were higher than her sister's. In the later test, their scores were reversed. What are some of the possible reasons for the reversal in the IQ scores of the two girls? When the second child did begin to speak, she did so prolifically, and the complexity of her language increased rapidly, undoubtedly as a result of her biological readiness to talk. Her sensorimotor coordination had never been as competent as the first child's, perhaps also accounting in part for her lower scores on the infant intelligence tests. The parents recognized that they had initially given the first child extensive amounts of their time. They were not able to give the second child as much of their time, but, when the second child was about 3 years old, they made every opportunity to involve her in physical and academic activities. They put her in a Montessori preschool program, gave her dancing and swimming lessons, and frequently invited other children of her age in to play with her. There may have been other reasons as well for the changes in scores, but these demonstrate that infant intelligence tests may not be good predictors of intelligence in later years.

Can you predict what a child's IQ will be when she is 10 or 18 years old from her scores on an IQ test administered when she is 2, 3, and 4 years old? IQ tests still do not provide very reliable predictions of this sort. Based on statistical techniques, IQ scores obtained at 2 and 3 years of age are related to the IQ scores of the same individuals even at 10 and 18 years, although they are not very strongly related. IQ scores obtained at the age of 4 are much better at predicting IQ at the age of 10 than at the age of 18 (Honzik, MacFarlane, & Allen, 1948).

Robert McCall and his associates (1973) studied 140 children between the ages of 2½ and 17. They found that the average range of IQ scores was more than 28 points. The scores of one out of three children changed by as much as 30 points and one out of seven by as much as 40 points. These data suggest that intelligence test scores can fluctuate dramatically across the childhood years and that intelligence is not as stable as the original intelligence theorists envisioned.

Use of Information-Processing Tasks in Infancy to Predict Intelligence

The explosion of interest in infant development has produced many new measures, especially tasks that evaluate the way infants process information (Ensher & Meller, 1989; Fagan & Knevel, 1989; Gottfried & Bathurst, 1989; Rose, 1989; Rose, Feldman, & Wallace, 1992). Evidence is accumulating that measures of habituation and dishabituation predict intelligence in childhood (Bornstein, 1989; Bornstein & Sigman, 1986; Sigman & others, 1989). Quicker decays or less cumulative looking in the habituation situation and greater amounts of looking in the dishabituation situation reflect more efficient information processing. Both types of attention—decrement and recovery—when measured in the first 6 months of infancy, are related to higher IQ scores on standardized intelligence tests given at various times between infancy and adolescence. In sum, more precise assessment of infant cognition with information-processing tasks involving attention has led to the conclusion that continuity between infant and childhood intelligence is greater than was previously believed (Bornstein & Krasnegor,1989).

What can we conclude about the nature of stability and change in childhood intelligence? Children are adaptive beings. They have the capacity for intellectual changes but they do not become entirely new intelligent beings. In a sense, children's intelligence changes but has connections to earlier points in development—amid intellectual changes is some underlying coherence and continuity.

At this point, we have discussed many ideas about the nature of intelligence, test construction, and intelligence tests. A summary of these ideas is presented in Concept Table 9.1. Now we will turn our attention to some controversies and issues in intelligence.

CONTROVERSIES AND ISSUES IN INTELLIGENCE

Intelligence has been one of psychology's concepts that seems to attract controversy. Among the most controversial issues of intelligence are those related to hereditary-environmental determination, cultural and ethnic differences, and the use and misuse of intelligence tests.

The Heredity-Environment Controversy

Arthur Jensen (1969) sparked lively and at times hostile debate when he stated his theory that intelligence is primarily inherited and that environment and culture play only a minimal role in intelligence. In one of his most provocative statements, Jensen claimed that genetics account for clear-cut differences in the average intelligence among races, nationalities, and social classes. When Jensen published an article in the *Harvard Educational Review* stating that lower intelligence probably is the reason that Blacks do not perform as well in school as Whites, he was called naive and racist. He received hate mail by the bushel and police had to escort him to his classes at the University of California at Berkeley.

Jensen reviewed the research on intelligence, much of which involved comparisons of identical and fraternal twins. Remember that identical twins have exactly the same genetic makeup. If intelligence is genetically determined, Jensen reasoned, identical twins' IQs should be similar. Fraternal twins and ordinary siblings are less similar genetically, so their IQs should be less similar. Jensen found support for his argument. The studies on intelligence in identical twins that Jensen examined showed an average correlation between IQs of .82, a very high positive association. Investigations of fraternal twins, however, produced an average correlation of .50, a moderately high positive correlation. Note the substantial difference of .32. To show that genetic factors are more important than environmental factors, Jensen compared the intelligence of identical twins reared together with that of those reared apart. The correlation for those reared together was .89 and for those reared apart it was .78, a difference of .11. Jensen argued that, if environmental factors are more important than genetic factors, siblings reared apart, who experience different environments, should have IQs that differ more than .11. Jensen places heredity's influence on intelligence at about 80 percent.

Today most researchers agree that genetics do not determine intelligence to the extent Jensen envisioned. Their estimates fall more in the 50/50 range—50 percent genetic makeup, 50 percent environmental factors (Plomin, 1989; Plomin, DeFries, & McClearn, in press). For most people, this means that modifying their environment can change their IQ scores considerably (Weinberg, 1989). It also means that programs designed to enrich a person's environment can have a considerable impact, improving school achievement and the acquisition of skills needed for employability. Although genetic endowment may always influence a person's intellectual ability, the environmental influences and opportunities we provide children and adults make a difference (Brody, 1992).

CONCEPT TABLE 9.1

Intelligence, Test Construction, and Intelligence Tests

Concept	Processes/Related Ideas	Characteristics/Description
What is intelligence?	Its nature	Intelligence is an abstract concept that is measured indirectly. Psychologists rely on intelligence tests to estimate intellectual processes. Verbal ability and problem-solving skills are included in a definition of intelligence. Some psychologists believe intelligence includes an ability to learn from and adapt to everyday life. Extensive effort is given to assessing individual differences in intelligence. This is called psychometrics.
How tests are constructed and evaluated	Reliability	Reliability is the consistency with which a test measures performance. One form of reliability is test-retest.
	Validity	Validity is the extent to which a test measures what it is intended to measure. Two methods of assessing validity are by determining content validity and criterion validity.
	Standardization	Standardization involves uniform procedures for administering and scoring a test; it also involves norms.
The measurement and nature of intelligence	Alfred Binet and the Binet tests	Alfred Binet developed the first intelligence test, known as the 1905 Scale. He developed the concept of mental age, whereas William Stern developed the concept of IQ. The Binet has been standardized and revised a number of times. The many revisions are called the Stanford-Binet tests. The test approximates a normal distribution. The current test is given to individuals from the age of 2 through adulthood.
	The Wechsler scales	Besides the Binet, the Wechsler scales are the most widely used intelligence tests. They include the WAIS-R, the WISC-R, and the WPPSI. These tests produce an overall IQ, verbal and performance IQ, and information about subtests.
	Does intelligence have a single nature?	Psychologists debate whether intelligence is a general ability or a number of specific abilities. Spearman's two-factor theory and Thurstone's multiple-factor theory state that a number of specific factors are involved. Current thinking suggests that Spearman's conceptualization of intelligence as both a set of specific abilities and a general ability was right. Gardner's seven frames of mind and Sternberg's triarchic theory—componential, experiential, and contextual intelligence—are contemporary efforts to determine the components of intelligence.
Infant intelligence and the stability of intelligence	Infant intelligence tests	Many standardized intelligence tests do not assess infant intelligence. Intelligence tests designed to assess infant intelligence are often referred to as developmental scales, the most widely used being the Bayley scales. Gesell was an important early contributor to the developmental testing of infants. The developmental quotient (DQ) is an overall score in the Gesell assessment of infants.
	Stability of intelligence	Although intelligence is more stable across the childhood years than are many attributes, many children's scores on intelligence tests fluctuate considerably.
	Use of information-processing tasks in infancy to predict intelligence	Recently, developmentalists have found that information-processing tasks that involve attention—especially habituation and dishabituation—are related to scores on standardized tests in childhood.

Keep in mind, though, that environmental influences are complex. Growing up with "all the advantages," for example, does not necessarily guarantee success. Children from wealthy families may have easy access to excellent schools, books, travel, and tutoring, but they may take such opportunities for granted and fail to develop the motivation to learn and achieve. In the same way, being "poor" or "disadvantaged" does not automatically equal "doomed."

Some years ago, I (your author) knocked on the door of a house in a low-income area of a large city. The father came to the door and invited the author into the living room. Even though it was getting dark outside, no lights were on inside the house. The father excused himself, then returned with a light bulb, which he screwed into a lamp socket. He said he could barely pay his monthly mortgage and the electric company had threatened to turn off the electricity, so he was carefully monitoring how much electricity his family used. There were seven children in the family, ranging in age from 2 to 16 years old. Neither parent had completed high school. The father worked as a bricklayer when he could find a job, and the mother ironed clothes in a laundry. The parents wanted their children to pursue education and to have more opportunities in life than they had had. The children from the inner-city family were exposed to both positive and negative influences. On the one hand, they were growing up in an intact family in which education was encouraged, and their parents provided a model of the work ethic. On the other hand, they were being shortchanged by society and had few opportunities to develop their intellectual abilities.

Researchers increasingly are interested in manipulating the early environment of children who are at risk for impoverished intelligence. The emphasis is on prevention rather than remediation (Garwood & others, 1989; Heinicke, Beckwith, & Thompson, 1988). Many low-income parents have difficulty providing an intellectually stimulating environment for their children. Programs that educate parents to be more sensitive caregivers and that train them to be better teachers, as well as support services such as Head Start, can make a difference in a child's intellectual development (Ramey, 1989).

Culture and Ethnicity

Are there cultural and ethic differences in intelligence? How does adaptation affect the role culture plays in understanding intelligence? Are standard intelligence tests biased? If so, can we develop tests that are fair?

Cultural and Ethnic Comparisons

In the United States, children from Black and Hispanic families score below children from White families on standardized intelligence tests. On the average, Black American school children score 10 to 15 points lower on standardized intelligence tests than White American school children (Anastasi, 1988). We are talking about average scores, though. Estimates also indicate that 15 to 25 percent of all Black school children score

higher than half of all White school children, and many Whites score lower than most Blacks. This is because the distributions of the scores for Blacks and Whites overlap.

Although the greatest interest has been in Black-White comparisons, studies on intelligence suggest some differences among Jewish, Chinese, Black, and Puerto Rican children (Lesser, Fifer, & Clark, 1965). Jewish children score higher on verbal abilities, lower on numerical and spatial abilities; Chinese children score higher on numerical and spatial abilities, lower on verbal abilities; Black children score higher on verbal abilities, lower on reasoning and numerical abilities; Puerto Rican children score higher on spatial and reasoning abilities, lower on verbal abilities.

How extensively are ethnic differences in intelligence influenced by heredity and environment? There is no evidence to support a genetic interpretation. For example, as Black Americans have gained social, economic, and educational opportunities, the gap between Black and White children on standardized intelligence tests has begun to narrow, and when children from disadvantaged Black families are adopted into more advantaged middle-class families their scores on intelligence tests more closely resemble national averages for middle-class than for lower-class children (Scarr, 1989; Scarr & Weinberg, 1976).

Culture, Intelligence, and Adaptation

People adapt to their environment, and what's appropriate in one environment may not be appropriate in another. As mentioned earlier in the chapter, intelligence is expressed differently in different cultures (Berry & Bennett, 1992; Berry & others, 1992). In one study, the researcher asked members of the Kpelle in Liberia (located on the western coast of Africa) to sort 20 objects (Glick, 1975). Rather than sort the objects into the "appropriate" categories the researcher had predicted, the Kpelle sorted the objects into functional groups—such as a knife with an apple and a potato with a hoe. Surprised by the answers, the researcher asked the Kpelle to explain their reasoning. The Kpelle responded that that was the way a wise person would group things. When the researcher asked how a fool would classify the objects, the Kpelle answered that four neat piles of food in one category, four tools in another category, and so on was the fool's way. The Kpelle were not lacking in intelligence; the researcher lacked an understanding of the Kpelle culture. The Kpelle sorted the items in ways that were adaptive for their culture.

Another example of human adaptability involves spatial ability. One study showed that people who live in hunter-gatherer societies score higher on spatial ability tests than do people from industrialized societies (Berry, 1971). People who must hunt to eat depend on their spatial skills for survival.

Few of us will ever have first-hand experience with hunter-gatherer societies, but many of us know people who are adaptable, savvy, and successful yet do not score correspondingly high

FIGURE 9.4

(*a*) Berry's model of the contexts of intelligence. In this model of intelligence, there is much more to consider than the actual context in which a test is being administered (the experimental context). In addition, it is also important to consider three other contextual levels—the performance context, experiential context, and ecological context. (*b*) Canadian cross-cultural psychologist John Berry has been an important pioneer in developing theoretical ideas pertaining to how various dimensions of culture influence intelligence.

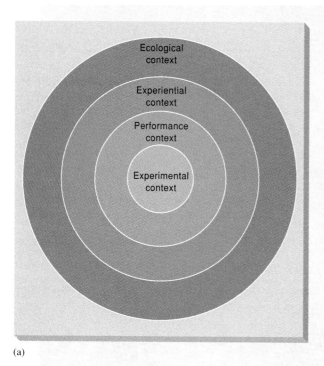

(a)

(b)

on intelligence tests. Canadian cross-cultural psychologist John Berry (1983) has an explanation for this gap between intelligence exhibited in one's own culture and intelligence displayed in a formal testing situation. He describes people as being embedded in four levels of environmental contexts. Level one, the ecological context, is an individual's natural habitat. Level two, the experiential context, is the pattern of recurring experiences from which the individual regularly learns. Level three, the performance context, is the limited set of circumstances in which the individual's natural behavior is observed. Level four, the experimental context, is the set of environmental circumstances under which test scores are actually generated (Berry's model is presented in figure 9.4).

When the experimental context differs considerably from the ecological or experiential context, Berry says, the individuals being tested are at a disadvantage. Presumably, the greater the difference, the greater the disadvantage. However, relations among contexts change. If an individual has been given the same test previously, some of the gap between the experiential and experimental contexts closes, resulting in higher test scores.

Cultural Biases and Culture–Fair Tests

Many of the early intelligence tests were culturally biased, favoring people from urban rather than rural environments, middle-class rather than lower-class people, and Whites rather than Blacks (Miller-Jones, 1989). For example, a question on an early test asked what should be done if you find a 3-year-old child in the street. The correct answer was "call the police"; however, children from inner-city families who perceive the police as adversaries are unlikely to choose this answer. Similarly, children from rural areas might not choose this answer if there is no police force nearby. Such questions clearly do not measure the knowledge necessary to adapt to one's environment or to be "intelligent" in an inner-city neighborhood or in rural America (Scarr, 1984). Also, members of minority groups often do not speak English or may speak nonstandard English. Consequently, they may be at a disadvantage in trying to understand verbal questions framed in standard English, even if the content of the test is appropriate (Gibbs & Huang, 1989).

Cultures also vary in the way they define intelligence (Rogoff, 1990). Most European Americans, for example, think

FIGURE 9.5

Iatmul and Caroline Islander intelligence. (*a*) The intelligence of the Iatmul people of
Papua, New Guinea, involves the ability to remember the names of many clans.
(*b*) The Caroline Islands number 680 in the Pacific Ocean east of the Philippines.
The intelligence of their inhabitants includes the ability to navigate by the stars.

(a)   (b)

of intelligence in terms of technical skills, but people in Kenya
consider responsible participation in family and social life an
integral part of intelligence. Similarly, an intelligent person in
Uganda is someone who knows what to do and then follows
through with appropriate action. Intelligence to the Iatmul people of Papua, New Guinea, involves the ability to remember
the names of 10,000 to 20,000 clans, and the islanders in the
widely dispersed Caroline Islands incorporate the talent of nav-
igating by the stars into the their definition of intelligence (see
figure 9.5).

Cultural bias is dramatically underscored by such tests as
the one shown in table 9.1. This test was developed to reduce
the cultural disadvantage Black children face. More information about cultural bias in intelligence testing appears in
Sociocultural Worlds of Children 9.1, where you will read
about a widely publicized case in which a 6-year-old Black boy
was classified as mentally retarded.

Another example of possible cultural bias in intelligence
tests can be seen in the life of Gregory Ochoa. When Gregory

was a high school student, he and his classmates took an IQ
test. When Gregory looked at the test questions, he understood
only a few words, since he did not speak English very well and
spoke Spanish at home. Several weeks later, Gregory was placed
in a special class for mentally retarded students. Many of the
students in the class, it turns out, had last names such as
Ramirez and Gonzales. Gregory lost interest in school, dropped
out, and eventually joined the Navy. In the Navy, Gregory took
high school courses and earned enough credits to attend college
later. He graduated from San Jose City College as an honor
student, continued his education, and became a professor of social work at the University of Washington in Seattle.

As a result of such cases, researchers have tried to develop
tests that accurately reflect a person's intelligence. **Culture-fair
tests** *are intelligence tests that attempt to reduce cultural bias.* Two
types of culture-fair tests have been devised. The first includes
questions that are familiar to people from all socioeconomic and
ethnic backgrounds. For example, a child might be asked how a
bird and a dog are different, on the assumption that virtually all

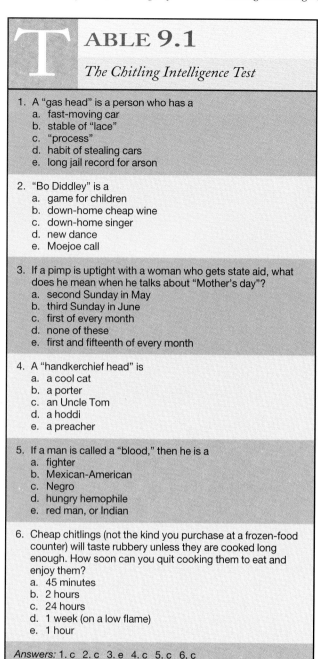

TABLE 9.1

The Chitling Intelligence Test

1. A "gas head" is a person who has a
   a. fast-moving car
   b. stable of "lace"
   c. "process"
   d. habit of stealing cars
   e. long jail record for arson

2. "Bo Diddley" is a
   a. game for children
   b. down-home cheap wine
   c. down-home singer
   d. new dance
   e. Moejoe call

3. If a pimp is uptight with a woman who gets state aid, what does he mean when he talks about "Mother's day"?
   a. second Sunday in May
   b. third Sunday in June
   c. first of every month
   d. none of these
   e. first and fifteenth of every month

4. A "handkerchief head" is
   a. a cool cat
   b. a porter
   c. an Uncle Tom
   d. a hoddi
   e. a preacher

5. If a man is called a "blood," then he is a
   a. fighter
   b. Mexican-American
   c. Negro
   d. hungry hemophile
   e. red man, or Indian

6. Cheap chitlings (not the kind you purchase at a frozen-food counter) will taste rubbery unless they are cooked long enough. How soon can you quit cooking them to eat and enjoy them?
   a. 45 minutes
   b. 2 hours
   c. 24 hours
   d. 1 week (on a low flame)
   e. 1 hour

Answers: 1. c 2. c 3. e 4. c 5. c 6. c

Source: Adrian Dove, 1968.

children are familiar with birds and dogs. The second type of culture-fair test removes all verbal questions. Figure 9.6 shows a sample question from the Raven Progressive Matrices Test. Even though such tests as the Raven Progressive Matrices are designed to be culture-fair, people with more education still score higher than those with less education.

One test that takes into account the socioeconomic background of children is the SOMPA, which stands for System of Multicultural Pluralistic Assessment (Mercer & Lewis, 1978). This test can be given to children from 5 to 11 years of age and was especially designed for children from low-income families. Instead of relying on a single test, SOMPA is based on information from four areas of a child's life: (1) verbal and nonver-

FIGURE 9.6

Sample item from the Raven Progressive Matrices Test. Individuals are presented with a matrix arrangement of symbols, such as the one at the top of this figure and must then complete the matrix by selecting the appropriate missing symbol from a group of symbols.

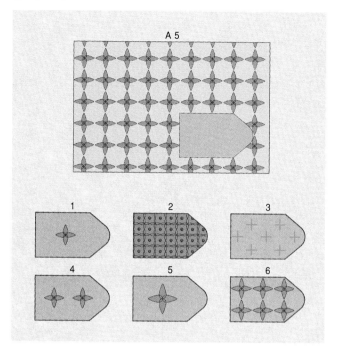

bal intelligence, assessed by the WISC-R; (2) social and economic background, obtained through a 1-hour parent interview; (3) social adjustment to school, determined through a questionnaire that parents complete; and (4) physical health, assessed by a medical examination.

The Kaufman Assessment Battery for Children (K-ABC) has been trumpeted as an improvement over other culture-fair tests (Kaufman & Kaufman, 1983). The test is based on a more representative sample, which includes a greater number of minority and handicapped children. The intelligence portion focuses less on language than the Stanford-Binet does, and the K-ABC includes an achievement section, with subtests for arithmetic and reading. However, the K-ABC, like other culture-fair tests, has its detractors. Based on the three main criteria for evaluating tests, the K-ABC fares well on reliability and standardization, but not as well on validity (Sax, 1989).

Most researchers agree that traditional intelligence tests are probably culturally biased. However, efforts to develop culture-fair tests so far have yielded unsatisfactory results.

The Use and Misuse of Intelligence Tests

Psychological tests are tools. Like all tools, their effectiveness depends on the knowledge, skill, and integrity of the user. A hammer can be used to build a beautiful kitchen cabinet or it can be used as a weapon of assault. Like a hammer, psychological tests can be used for positive purposes or they can be badly

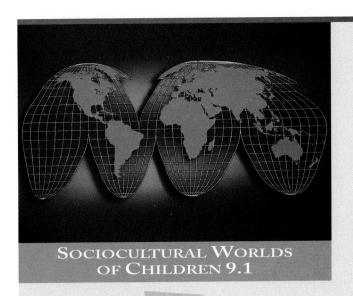

SOCIOCULTURAL WORLDS OF CHILDREN 9.1

Larry P., Intelligent but Not on Intelligence Tests

Larry P. is Black and poor. When he was 6 years old, he was placed in a class for the "educable mentally retarded" (EMR), which to school psychologists means that Larry learns much more slowly than average children. The primary reason Larry was placed in the EMR class was his very low score of 64 on an intelligence test.

Is there a possibility that the intelligence test Larry was given is culturally biased? Psychologists still debate this issue. The controversy has been the target of a major class action suit challenging the use of standardized IQ tests to place Black elementary school students in EMR classes. The initial lawsuit, filed on behalf of Larry P., claimed that the IQ test he took underestimated his true learning ability. The lawyers for Larry P. argued that IQ tests place too much emphasis on verbal skills

and fail to account for the background of Black children. Therefore, it was argued, Larry was incorrectly labeled mentally retarded and may forever be saddled with that stigma.

As part of the lengthy court battle involving Larry P., six Black EMR students were independently retested by members of the Bay Association of Black Psychologists in California. The psychologists made sure they established good rapport with the students and made special efforts to overcome the students' defeatism and distraction. For example, items were reworded in terms more consistent with the children's social background, and recognition was given to nonstandard answers that showed a logical, intelligent approach to problems. This testing approach produced scores of 79 to 104—17 to 38 points higher than the scores the students received when initially tested by school psychologists. In every case, the retest scores were above the ceiling for placement in an EMR class.

In Larry's case, the judge ruled that IQ tests are biased and that their use discriminates against Blacks and other ethnic minorities. IQ tests cannot be used now in California to place children in EMR classes. During the Larry P. trial, it was revealed that 66 percent of the elementary school students in EMR classes in San Francisco were Black, whereas Blacks make up only 28.5 percent of the San Francisco school population.

What was the state's argument for using intelligence tests as one criterion for placing children in EMR classes? At one point, the state suggested that, because Blacks tend to be poor and poor pregnant women tend to suffer from inadequate nutrition, it is possible that the brain development of many Black children has been retarded by their mothers' poor prenatal diet. The state also argued that Blacks are genetically inferior to Whites in intelligence.

The decision in favor of Larry P. was upheld by a three-judge appeals panel in 1984. However, in another court case, *Pase v. Hannon* in Illinois, a judge was unconvinced by the same arguments and ruled that IQ tests are not culturally biased.

abused. It is important for both the test constructor and the test examiner to be familiar with the current state of scientific knowledge about intelligence and intelligence tests (Anastasi, 1988; Reynolds & Kamphaus, 1990).

Even though they have limitations, tests of intelligence are among psychology's most widely used tools. To be effective, though, intelligence tests must be viewed realistically. They should not be thought of as unchanging indicators of intelligence. They should be used in conjunction with other information about an individual, not relied on as the sole indicator of intelligence. For example, an intelligence test should not solely determine whether a child is placed in a special education or gifted class. The child's developmental history, medical background, performance in school, social competencies, and family experiences should be taken into account too.

The single number provided by many IQ tests can easily lead to stereotypes and expectations about an individual (Mensh & Mensh, 1991). Many people do not know how to interpret the results of intelligence tests, and sweeping generalizations are too often made on the basis of an IQ score. For example,

imagine that you are a teacher in the teacher's lounge the day after school has started in the fall. You mention a student—Johnny Jones—and a fellow teacher remarks that she had Johnny in class last year; she comments that he was a real dunce and points out that his IQ is 78. You cannot help but remember this information, and it may lead to thoughts that Johnny Jones is not very bright so it is useless to spend much time teaching him. In this way, IQ scores are misused and stereotypes are formed (Rosenthal & Jacobsen, 1968).

Ability tests can help a teacher divide children into homogeneous groups who function at roughly the same level in math or reading so they can be taught the same concepts together. However, when children are placed in tracks, such as "advanced," "intermediate," and "low," extreme caution needs to be taken. Periodic assessment of the groups is needed, especially with the "low" group. Ability tests measure *current* performance, and maturational changes or enriched environmental experiences may advance a child's intelligence, requiring that she be moved to a higher group.

TABLE 9.2

Comparison of Approaches to Children's Learning, Cognitive Development, and Intelligence

	Piagetian/ Cognitive Development	Vygotsky's Theory	Learning	Cognitive Social Learning
Maturation/ environment	Strong maturational view, but maturation does interact with environmental experiences	Interactionist, but much stronger role for culture than in Piaget's view; interaction with skilled people	Strong emphasis on environment; little contribution by heredity/maturation	Strong environmental emphasis
Stages	Strong emphasis; cognitive stages are core of this approach	No stages emphasized	No stages	No stages
Individual differences	No emphasis	No emphasis	No emphasis	No emphasis
Cognitive processes/ mechanisms	Assimilation, accommodation, equilibration, organization, conservation, and hypothetical-deductive reasoning skills	Discussion and reasoning through social interaction with skilled others	None	Attention, memory, plans, expectancies, problem-solving skills; self-efficacy; imitation
Model of child	Active, cognitive constructivist, solitary little scientist	Active, interactive, sociocultural constructivist	Passive, environmental determinist; empty vessicle	Interactive, reciprocal determinist

Despite their limitations, when used judiciously by a competent examiner, intelligence tests provide valuable information about individuals. There are not many alternatives to these tests. Subjective judgments about individuals simply reintroduce the bias the tests were designed to eliminate.

COMPARISON OF APPROACHES TO CHILDREN'S LEARNING, COGNITIVE DEVELOPMENT, AND INTELLIGENCE

In chapters 7, 8, and so far in this chapter, we have studied a number of different approaches to children's learning, cognitive development, and intelligence. This is a good time to review some of the basic ideas of these approaches to get a feel for how they conceptualize children's development. So far we have examined six different approaches to children's learning, cognitive development, and intelligence: Piaget's cognitive developmental theory, Vygotsky's theory, learning, social learning theory, information processing, and psychometric. Let's explore how these approaches view some important aspects of children's development: maturation/environmental influences, stages, individual differences, cognitive processes/mechanisms, and model of the child.

With regard to maturation/environmental influences, Piaget's theory is the strongest maturational approach;

Vygotsky's theory also emphasizes maturation but to a lesser degree. Both Piaget's and Vygotsky's theories are interactionist in the sense that they emphasize maturation/environment interaction. The psychometric approach doesn't deal with this issue extensively, but its age-related emphasis implies a maturational underpinning. The information-processing approach also does not focus on this issue to any degree, but is also best conceptualized as interactionist. The learning and cognitive social learning views are primarily environmental.

With regard to stages, only the Piagetian cognitive view has a strong stage emphasis. Indeed, stages of cognitive development—sensorimotor, preoperational, concrete operational, and formal operational—are at the heart of Piaget's theory. The neo-Piagetians, who combine some of Piaget's ideas with an emphasis on more precise aspects of information processing, place some emphasis on age-changes in cognition. The Vygotskian, learning, social learning, and psychometric approaches do not emphasize stages at all.

With regard to individual differences, only the psychometric approach emphasizes them strongly. Recently, some information-processing researchers have begun to study individual differences in information processing, but the information-processing approach does not give individual differences a high priority. The Piagetian, Vygotskian, learning, and social learning approaches do not emphasize individual differences at all.

With regard to cognitive processes/mechanisms, Piaget's cognitive developmental approach stresses the importance of

Information Processing	Psychometric
Interactionist, but little attention given to this, except by Neo-Piagetians who emphasize age-related changes	Little attention to this issue, although age-related emphasis implies maturational emphasis
No stages	No stages
No emphasis, although recently some information-processing researchers have started to investigate	Strong emphasis; at core of the approach
Processing speed, capacity, and automaticity; attention; memory; problem solving; cognitive monitoring; critical thinking; knowledge and expertise	General intelligence and a number of specific forms of intelligence that vary with the theory
Cognitive constructivist	Individual difference

assimilation, accommodation, equilibration, organization, conservation, and hypothetical-deductive reasoning. Vygotsky's theory stresses the importance of discussion and reasoning through interaction with skilled others. The learning approach does not emphasize cognitive processes/mechanisms at all, but rather the environmental processes of reinforcement, punishment, and classical conditioning. The cognitive social learning approach places importance on the cognitive processes of attention, memory, plans, expectancies, problem-solving skills, and self-efficacy. The information-processing approach emphasizes a large number of cognitive processes/mechanisms, among them: processing speed, capacity, and automaticity; attention; memory; problem solving; cognitive monitoring; critical thinking; knowledge and expertise. The psychometric approach focuses on general intelligence and/or a number of specific forms of intelligence, such as Sternberg's three forms—componential, experiential, and contextual.

With regard to conceptualization of the basic nature of the child or a model of how the child develops, Piagetian theory emphasizes a model of the child as active, cognitive constructivist, and a solitary little scientist. Vygotsky's theory describes the child as active, interactive, and sociocultural constructivist. The learning approach focuses on the child as passive, environmentally determined, and as an empty vessicle. Cognitive social learning portrays the child as interactive and reciprocal determinist (behavior, cognition, and environment reciprocally

interact). The information-processing approach conceptualizes the child as cognitive constructist, and the psychometric approach in terms of individual differences.

A summary of how the six different approaches we have discussed in the last three chapters portray children's development is presented in table 9.2. So far in this chapter we have focused mainly on the psychometric approach that emphasizes individual differences and the assessment of intelligence through intelligence tests. Next, we continue our discussion of intelligence and its related dimensions by examining the extremes of intelligence.

THE EXTREMES OF INTELLIGENCE: MENTAL RETARDATION AND GIFTEDNESS

Intelligence tests have been used to discover indications of mental retardation or intellectual giftedness, the extremes of intelligence. At times intelligence tests have been misused for this purpose. Keep in mind the theme that an intelligence test should not be used as the sole indicator of mental retardation or giftedness as we explore the nature of these intellectual extremes.

Mental Retardation

The most distinctive feature of mental retardation is inadequate intellectual functioning. Long before formal tests were developed to assess intelligence, the mentally retarded were identified by a lack of age-appropriate skills in learning and caring for themselves. Once intelligence tests were developed, numbers were assigned to indicate degree of mental retardation. It is not unusual to find two retarded people with the same low IQ, one of whom is married, employed, and involved in the community and the other requiring constant supervision in an institution. These differences in social competence led psychologists to include deficits in adaptive behavior in their definition of mental retardation. **Mental retardation** *is a condition of limited mental ability in which an individual has a low IQ, usually below 70 on a traditional intelligence test, and has difficulty adapting to everyday life.* About 5 million Americans fit this definition of mental retardation.

There are several classifications of mental retardation. About 89 percent of the mentally retarded fall into the mild category, with IQs of 55 to 70. About 6 percent are classified as moderately retarded, with IQs of 40 to 54; these people can attain a second-grade level of skills and may be able to support themselves as adults through some type of labor. About 3.5 percent of the mentally retarded are in the severe category, with IQs of 25 to 39; these individuals learn to talk and engage in very simple tasks but require extensive supervision. Less than 1 percent have IQs below 25; they fall into the profoundly mentally retarded classification and are in constant need of supervision.

Mental retardation can have an organic cause, or it can be social and cultural in origin. **Organic retardation** *is mental retardation caused by a genetic disorder or by brain damage;* organic

FIGURE 9.7

A Down syndrome child. What causes a child to develop Down syndrome? In what major classification of mental retardation does the condition fall?

refers to the tissues or organs of the body, so there is some physical damage in organic retardation. Down syndrome, one form of mental retardation, occurs when an extra chromosome is present in an individual's genetic makeup (see figure 9.7). It is not known why the extra chromosome is present, but it may involve the health or age of the female ovum or male sperm. Most people who suffer from organic retardation have IQs that range between 0 and 50.

Cultural-familial retardation *is a mental deficit in which no evidence of organic brain damage can be found; individuals' IQs range from 50 to 70. Psychologists suspect that such mental deficits result from the normal variation that distributes people along the*

range of intelligence scores above 50, combined with growing up in a below-average intellectual environment. (Hodapp, Burack, & Zigler, in press). As children those who are familially retarded can be detected in schools, where they often fail, need tangible rewards (candy rather than praise), and are highly sensitive to what others—both peers and adults—want from them. However, as adults the familially retarded are usually invisible, perhaps because adult settings don't tax their cognitive skills as sorely. It may also be that the familially retarded increase their intelligence as they move toward adulthood (Sattler, 1988).

Giftedness

There have always been people whose abilities and accomplishments outshine others'—the whiz kid in class, the star athlete, the natural musician. People who are **gifted** *have above-average intelligence (an IQ of 120 or higher) and/or superior talent for something.* When it comes to programs for the gifted, most school systems select children who have intellectual superiority and academic aptitude. Children who are talented in the visual and performing arts (arts, drama, dance), athletics, or other special aptitudes tend to be overlooked.

> *Never to be cast away are the gifts of the gods, magnificent.*
> —Homer, *The Iliad*, 9th Century, B.C.

Until recently giftedness and emotional distress were thought to go hand in hand. English novelist Virginia Woolf suffered from severe depression, for example, and eventually committed suicide. Sir Isaac Newton, Vincent van Gogh, Ann Sexton, Socrates, and Sylvia Plath all had emotional problems. However, these are the exception rather than the rule; in general, no relation between giftedness and mental disorder has been found. A number of recent studies support the conclusion that gifted people tend to be more mature, have fewer emotional problems than others, and grow up in a positive family climate (Draper & others, 1993; Janos & Robinson, 1985).

Lewis Terman (1925) has followed the lives of approximately 1,500 children whose Stanford-Binet IQs averaged 150 into adulthood; the study will not be complete until the year 2010. Terman has found that this remarkable group is an accomplished lot: of the 800 males, 78 have obtained doctorates (they include two past presidents of the American Psychological Association), 48 have earned M.D.s, and 85 have been granted law degrees. Most of these figures are 10 to 30 times greater than those found among the 800 men of the same age chosen randomly as a comparison group. These findings challenge the commonly held belief that the intellectually gifted are emotionally disturbed or socially maladjusted.

Critical Thinking

What should be the criteria for placing a child in a gifted program?

There is a special concern about gifted disadvantaged children. When gifted disadvantaged children learn to adapt their behavior to the values and demands of school, they begin to accomplish required tasks successfully, their achievements start to attract teachers' attention, and more opportunities are made available to them (Hale, Seitz, & Zigler, in press). This "snowball effect" has crucial implications for the child's personal and motivational development (Arroyo & Sternberg, 1993).

Parents in low-income families can help their children develop the self-management skills required to function well in a school setting, but in many instances they do not. For gifted disadvantaged children, teachers and other influential persons within the school can compensate for the lack of appropriate direction these children have received at home. Alternative socialization agents can expose gifted disadvantaged children to wide-ranging experiences that influence their emerging view of themselves and their future.

Especially important in the case of gifted disadvantaged children is the development of measures to identify who they are. Traditionally, giftedness has been assessed in one dimension—intellectual exceptionality. However, to adequately identify gifted disadvantaged children, it is necessary to widen the assessment procedure to include not only intellectual abilities but also behavior, motivation, and personality attributes. Researchers have found that high-achieving disadvantaged children are self-confident, industrious, tough-minded, individualistic, and raceless (Allen, 1985; Comer, 1988; Fordham & Ogbu, 1986). These same characteristics often appear in children high in creativity that come from advantaged backgrounds.

The behaviors of the gifted disadvantaged are often motivated by the desire to transform their social and economic conditions. Because this goal requires long-range planning and self-management, giftedness among disadvantaged children needs to be assessed over time (Arroyo & Sternberg, 1993).

CREATIVITY

Most of us would like to be both gifted and creative. Why was Thomas Edison able to invent so many things? Was he simply more intelligent than most people? Did he spend long hours toiling away in private? Surprisingly, when Edison was a young boy, his teacher told him he was too dumb to learn anything. Other famous people whose creative genius went unnoticed when they were young include Walt Disney, who was fired from a newspaper job because he did not have any good ideas; Enrico Caruso, whose music teacher told him that his voice was terrible; and Winston Churchill, who failed 1 year of secondary school.

Disney, Edison, Caruso, and Churchill were intelligent and creative men; however, experts on creativity believe that intelligence is not the same as creativity. One common distinction is between **convergent thinking,** *which produces one correct answer and is characteristic of the kind of thinking on standardized intelligence tests* and **divergent thinking,** *which produces many answers to the same question and is more characteristic of creativity* (Guilford, 1967). For example, the following is a typical problem on an intelligence test that requires convergent thinking: "How many quarters will you get in return for 60 dimes?" The following question, though, has many possible answers: "What image comes to mind when you hear the phrase `sitting alone in a dark room'?" (Barron, 1989). Such responses as "the sound of a violin with no strings" and "patience" are considered creative answers. Conversely, common answers, such as "a person in a crowd" or "insomnia" are not very creative.

Creativity *is the ability to think about something in novel and unusual ways and to come up with unique solutions to problems.* When creative people, such as artists and scientists, are asked what enables them to solve problems in novel ways, they say that the ability to find affinities between seemingly unrelated elements plays a key role. They also say they have the time and independence in an enjoyable setting to entertain a wide range of possible solutions to a problem. How strongly is creativity related to intelligence? Although most creative people are quite intelligent, the reverse is not necessarily true. Many highly intelligent people (as measured by IQ tests) are not very creative.

Some experts remain skeptical that we will ever fully understand the creative process. Others believe that a psychology of creativity is in reach. Most experts agree, however, that the concept of creativity as spontaneously bubbling up from a magical well is a myth. Momentary flashes of insight, accompanied by images, make up only a small part of the creative process. At the heart of the creative process are ability and experience that shape an individual's intentional and sustained effort, often over the course of a lifetime (Baer, 1993). Based on his research on creativity and analysis of the literature, Daniel Perkins (1984; Perkins & Gardner, 1989) has developed a model that takes into account the complexity of the creative process. An overview of Perkins' model and its application to children's education is presented in Explorations in Child Development 9.1. As we learn more about creativity, we come to understand how important it is as a human resource and as truly one of life's wondrous gifts.

> *The artist finds a greater pleasure in painting than in having completed the picture.*
>
> —Seneca

At this point, we have discussed a number of ideas about controversies and issues in intelligence, different approaches to children's learning, cognitive development, and intelligence, and about the extremes of intelligence. A summary of these ideas is presented in Concept Table 9.2.

EXPLORATIONS IN CHILD DEVELOPMENT 9.1

The Snowflake Model of Creativity and Its Application to Education

Daniel Perkins (1984) describes his view as the *snowflake model of creativity*. Like the six sides of a snowflake, each with its own complex structure, Perkins' model consists of six characteristics common to highly creative individuals (figure 9.A). Children and adults who are creative may not have all six characteristics, but the more they have, the more creative they tend to be, says Perkins.

First, creative thinking involves aesthetics as much as practical standards. Aesthetics involves beauty. Outside of literature and the arts, conventional schooling pays little attention to the aesthetics of human inquiry. For example, the beauty of scientific theories, mathematical systems, and historical syntheses is rarely addressed by teachers, and how often do teachers comment on the aesthetics of students' work in math and science?

Second, creative thinking involves an ability to excel in finding problems. Creative individuals spend an unusual amount of time thinking about problems. They also explore a number of options in solving a particular problem before choosing a solution to pursue. Creative individuals value good questions because they can produce discoveries and creative answers. A student once asked Nobel laureate Linus Pauling how he came up with good ideas. Pauling said he developed a lot of ideas and threw away the bad ones. Most assignments in school are so narrow that students have little opportunity to generate or even select among different ideas, according to Perkins.

Third, creative thinking involves mental mobility, which allows individuals to find new perspectives and approaches to problems. One example of mental mobility is being able to think in terms of opposites and contraries while seeking a new solution. According to Perkins, most problems students work on in school are convergent, not divergent. For the most part, the learning problems students face in school lack the elbow room for exercising mental mobility.

Fourth, creative thinking involves the willingness to take risks. Accompanying risk is the acceptance of failure as part of the creative quest and the ability to learn from failures. Creative geniuses don't always produce masterpieces. For example, Picasso produced more than 20,000 works of art, but much of it was mediocre. The more children produce, the better is their

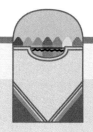

PERSPECTIVES ON PARENTING AND EDUCATION

Parenting, Schools, and Gifted Children

While the parents of gifted children are blessed in many ways, they must deal with a number of issues related to their children's giftedness or talent (Keirouz, 1990). Parents often feel ambivalent about having their child labeled "gifted," proud that their child is talented but worried about how it will affect the child and whether the child will have a normal life. Parents of gifted children express concern over how to find the proper level of encouragement, fearing that they will overstimulate or understimulate the child. Parents want their gifted children to be able to reach their full potential. Some parents overindulge their gifted child, which often increases the child's

FIGURE 9.A

Snowflake model of creativity. Like a snowflake, Perkin's model of creativity has six parts: commitment to a personal aesthetic, excellence in finding problems, mental mobility, willingness to take risks, objectivity, and inner motivation.

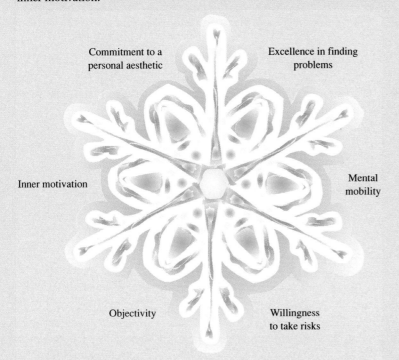

Commitment to a
personal aesthetic

Excellence in finding
problems

Inner motivation

Mental
mobility

Objectivity

Willingness
to take risks

chance of creating something unique. According to Perkins, most schools do not challenge students to take the risk necessary to think creatively and to produce creative work.

Fifth, creative thinking involves objectivity. The popular image of creative individuals usually highlights their subjective, personal insights and commitments; however, without some objectivity and feedback from others, they would create a private world that is distant from reality and could not be shared or appreciated by others. Creative individuals not only criticize their own work but they also seek criticism from others. Schools typically do highlight objectivity, although usually not in the arts.

Sixth, creative thinking involves inner motivation. Creative individuals are motivated to produce something for its own sake, not for school grades or for money. Their catalyst is the challenge, enjoyment, and satisfaction of the work itself. Researchers have found that individuals ranging from preschool children through adults are more creative when they are internally rather than externally motivated. Work evaluation, competition for prizes, and supervision tend to undermine internal motivation and diminish creativity (Amabile & Hennessey, 1988).

self-confidence, but unfortunately carries with it the potential for having a spoiled and egocentric child. Heaping too much attention on a gifted child also has negative repercussions for nongifted siblings.

Researchers have found that nongifted siblings often do suffer from negative social comparison with the gifted sibling, have lower self-esteem than the gifted sibling, and show poorer emotional adjustment than the gifted sibling (Cornell & Grossberg, 1986). Friction between siblings is the greatest when the gifted child is the oldest (Bridges, 1973).

In addition to concerns about sibling issues, parents of gifted children also may worry about the education of their gifted child. Parents of gifted children may become critical of the school's efforts, or lack of efforts, to provide a positive, stimulating education for the gifted child. No matter how competent the efforts of the school or the teacher, some parents still criticize the education their gifted child is receiving.

Another important issue for parents to consider is that the gifted child's social and emotional growth may lag behind his or her intellectual growth and that the gifted child often does not have the same abilities in different domains of development. Parents should not expect the gifted child to be perfect; even in the domain of their gifted talent, gifted children have "bad days" when they don't perform at their gifted level. Not recognizing these variations in gifted children can lead parents to place unrealistic expectations on their gifted children and harm their development. ■

CONCEPT TABLE 9.2

Controversies and Issues in Intelligence, Different Approaches, the Extremes of Intelligence, and Creativity

Concept	Processes/Related Ideas	Characteristics/Description
Controversies and issues	The heredity-environment controversy	In the late 1960s, Jensen argued that intelligence is approximately 80 percent hereditary and that genetic differences exist in the average intelligence of ethnic groups and social classes. Intelligence is influenced by heredity, but not as strongly as Jensen believed. The environments we provide children do make a difference.
	Culture and ethnicity	The environments we provide children and adults make a difference. There are cultural and ethnic differences on intelligence tests, but the evidence suggests they are not genetically based. In recent decades, the gap between Blacks and Whites on intelligence test scores has diminished as Blacks have experienced more socioeconomic opportunities. To understand intelligence within a given culture, the adaptive requirements of the culture must be known. Early intelligence tests favored White, middle-class, urban individuals. Current tests try to reduce this bias. Culture-fair tests are an alternative to traditional tests; most psychologists believe they cannot completely replace the traditional tests.
	The use and misuse of intelligence tests	Despite limitations, when used by a judicious examiner, tests are valuable tools for determining individual differences in children's intelligence. The tests should be used with other information about children. IQ scores can produce unfortunate stereotypes and expectations. Ability tests can help divide children into homogeneous groups. However, periodic testing should be done. Intelligence or a high IQ is not necessarily the ultimate human value.
Different approaches to children's learning, cognitive development, and intelligence	Nature of differences	We compared six different approaches to children's learning, cognitive development, and intelligence in the following areas: maturation/environment, stages, individual differences, cognitive processes/mechanisms, and model of the child. The approaches we evaluated were Piaget's (chapter 7), Vygotsky's (chapter 7), learning (chapter 8), cognitive social learning (chapter 8), information processing (chapter 8), and psychometric (this chapter). For example, only Piaget's approach is a strong maturational approach and a strong stage theory, while the psychometric approach is the only one that underscores the importance of individual differences.
The extremes of intelligence	Mental retardation	A mentally retarded child has a low IQ, usually below 70 on a traditional IQ test, and has difficulty adapting to everyday life. Classifications of mental retardation have been made. The two main types of retardation are organic and cultural-familial.
	Giftedness	A gifted child has above-average intelligence (an IQ of 120 or more) and/or superior talent for something. There is a special concern for gifted disadvantaged children.
Creativity	Its nature	Creativity is the ability to think about something in a novel or unusual way and to come up with unique solutions to problems.

CONCLUSIONS

The study of children's intelligence has historically focused on the assessment of children's intelligence through intelligence tests and the nature of individual differences. There also has been a special interest in what intelligence is, including debate about its components.

In this chapter, we began by briefly discussing several issues that often incite inflammatory debate—the use of IQ tests to place children in special classes and sperm banks designed to genetically engineer children's intelligence. Then, we evaluated what intelligence is and how it is measured, infant intelligence and the stability of intelligence, and controversies and issues in intelligence. Among the issues and controversies are the degree intelligence is due to heredity or to environment, cultural and ethnic influences on intelligence, cultural biases and culture-fair tests, and the use and misuse of intelligence tests. We also reviewed and compared different approaches to children's learning, cognitive development, and intelligence, and studied the extremes of intelligence—mental retardation and giftedness—and creativity. You also read about parenting, schools, and gifted children. Remember that you can obtain a summary of the chapter by again reading the two concept tables on pages 280 and 292.

In the next chapter, we evaluate another very important part of children's development—language.

KEY TERMS

intelligence   Verbal ability, problem-solving skills, and the ability to learn from and adapt to the experiences of everyday life. (271)

individual differences   The stable, consistent ways in which children are different from each other. (271)

psychometrics   The field that involves the assessment of individual differences. (271)

reliability   The extent to which a test yields a consistent, reproducible measure of performance. (271)

test-retest reliability   A form of reliability in which a child is given the same test on two different occasions. (271)

validity   The extent to which a test measures what it is intended to measure. (271)

content validity   A form of validity; a test's ability to give a broad picture of what is to be measured. (271)

criterion validity   A form of validity; a test's ability to predict other measures, or criteria, of an attribute. (271)

standardization   The development of uniform procedures for administering and scoring a test. It also involves the development of norms for the test. (273)

norms   Established standards of performance for a test. (273)

mental age (MA)   A child's level of mental development relative to others. (273)

intelligence quotient (IQ)   Devised in 1912 by William Stern, IQ consists of mental age divided by chronological age, multiplied by 100. (273)

normal distribution   A symmetrical configuration of scores, with a majority of cases falling in the middle of the possible range of scores and few scores appearing toward the extremes of the range. (273)

two-factor theory   Spearman's theory that children have both general intelligence, called *g*, and a number of specific types of intelligence, called *s*. (274)

multiple-factor theory   Thurstone's theory that intelligence consists of seven primary abilities: verbal comprehension, number ability, word fluency, spatial visualization, associative memory, reasoning, and perceptual speed. (276)

triarchic theory   Sternberg's theory that intelligence consists of componential intelligence, experiential intelligence, and contextual intelligence. (276)

developmental quotient (DQ)   An overall developmental score that combines subscores in the motor, language, adaptive, and personal-social domains in the Gesell assessment of infants. (277)

Bayley Scales of Infant Development   An instrument, developed by Nancy Bayley, to be used in the assessment of infant development. The current version has three components: a mental scale, a motor scale, and an infant behavior profile. (278)

culture-fair tests   Intelligence tests that attempt to reduce cultural bias. (283)

mental retardation   A condition of limited mental ability in which individuals have a low IQ, usually below 70 on a traditional test of intelligence, and have difficulty adapting to everyday life. (287)

organic retardation   Mental retardation caused by a genetic disorder or brain damage; "organic" refers to the tissue or organs of the body, so there is some physical damage in organic retardation. (287)

cultural-familial retardation   Mental retardation in which there is no evidence of organic brain damage; individuals' IQs range from 50 to 70. (288)

gifted   Having above average intelligence (an IQ of 120 or higher), a superior talent for something, or both. (288)

convergent thinking   Thinking that produces one correct answer and is characteristic of the kind of thinking required on standardized intelligence tests. (289)

divergent thinking   Thinking that produces many answers to a question and is characteristic of creativity. (289)

creativity   The ability to think about something in a novel and unusual way and to come up with unique solutions to problems. (289)

SUGGESTED READINGS

Anastasi, A. (1988). *Psychological testing* (6th ed.). New York: Macmillan. This widely used text on psychological testing provides extensive information about test construction, test evaluation, and the nature of intelligence testing.

Gardner, H., & Perkins, D. (Eds.). (1989). *Art, mind, and education.* Ithaca, NY: The University of Illinois Press. Extensive, valuable information is provided about enhancing the creative thinking of children.

McCullough, V. E. (1992). *Testing & Your Child.* New York: Penguin. This extensive reference guide provides essential information on more than 150 tests for children, including a number of intelligence tests. Full description and evaluation of tests are given.

Sattler, J. M. (1982). *Assessment of children's intelligence and special abilities.* Boston: Allyn & Bacon. Extensive information is provided about the measurement of children's intelligence, both for normal children and for those from special populations, such as the mentally retarded.

Reading, Theodore Butler,
1876-1937 (Detail)

C H A P T E R

10

Language Development

Chapter Outline

PERSPECTIVES ON PARENTING AND EDUCATION

Live, Concrete Parent Talk to Infants 317

Chapter Boxes

*Words not only affect us temporarily;
they change us, they socialize us and they
unsocialize us.*

—David Riesman

Children pick up words as pigeons pick up peas.

—John Ray

IMAGES OF CHILDREN

Chimps and Language

You are an intelligent young female who has been captured by a group of some rather bizarre creatures, members of a highly advanced species who interact with all sorts of complex devices, drape unusual garments all over themselves, frequently emit long sequences of sound, and in general behave in complex and mysterious ways. You have no idea where these creatures came from or what they want with you. On the bright side, they appear to be friendly, even affectionate, and give you plenty of good food, including lots of chocolate, which you love. However, they won't let you go, and they insist that you play a weird game they have invented.

They started the game one day at your snack time. You expected some fruit, and one of your captors came with a banana. However, instead of giving the banana to you, he placed it where you could see it but could not get to it. Then he gave you a small, plastic, pink square and a small board. Not knowing what else to do, you took the pink square and placed it on the board. It stuck in place.

Your captor then made some very strange excited sounds and gave you the banana.

Your captors repeated this game again and again. After a time, they started using other fruits as well as bananas. It soon became obvious that, for you to get different fruits, you had to put certain pieces of plastic on the board. For example, to get an apple, you had to put a blue triangle on the board. If you put the pink square on the board, your captors made some of their very strange sounds, but the apple stayed where it was—out of reach.

Various chips for different foods was only the start of the complexity that followed. Before long, getting some food depended not only on you sticking the corresponding chip on the board; in addition, you had to put a special chip above it. This chip was a funny-looking, six-sided thing. Order was important. If you put the six-sided shape below the chip instead of above it, you did not get your food.

After a while, the captors taught you a plastic "name" for yourself, as well as a

name for each of them and for each of your fellow prisoners. If you wanted one of your captors to give you an apple, you had to put his plastic name at the top of the board, put the six-sided chip below it, put the blue-triangle chip (for apple) below that, and, finally, put your own plastic name at the bottom. So much work, just for an apple?

Later, your captors taught you ways of asking and answering questions and of making strange deals. For example, one of your captors wrote to you on the board, "If you pick up the apple, you will get some chocolate; if you pick up the banana, you will get no chocolate." You picked up the apple, and sure enough, they gave you chocolate.

What could this game be about? Who are these creatures and why are they interested in you? These creatures are psychologists who are studying language. You are one of their nonhuman subjects, a chimpanzee named Sarah. They are interested in you because they want to find out if nonhuman species can learn simple languages.

PREVIEW

In this chapter, we will tell the elegant story of children's language development. Among the questions we will explore are the following: What is language? What are language's rule systems? What is language's biological heritage (including the question of whether chimpanzees can learn language)? What is language's environmental heritage? What is cognition's role in language? What is the course of children's language development? How should reading be taught to children? What issues are involved in bilingualism?

WHAT IS LANGUAGE?

Every human society has language. There are thousands of human languages, and they differ so dramatically that many individuals despair of ever mastering more than one. However, all human languages have some things in common. What are the characteristics that all human languages share?

Language has been defined by one expert as a sequence of words (Miller, 1981). This definition describes language as having two characteristics—the presence of words and sequencing. It might seem obvious that all languages have *words*, but think for a minute about what words are. We produce and perceive words every day—yet words have an almost magical property: They stand for, or symbolize, things. We use words to refer to objects, people, actions, events, and even abstract ideas. What a word refers to is arbitrary in the sense that it is based on convention; a word symbolizes something commonly agreed on by a group of language users. To understand this point, consider the fact that different languages have different names for the same thing. What we call a *house* is called *casa* in Spanish and *maison* in French. Since different languages have different words, we are forced to conclude that words are linked arbitrarily and by convention to their referents.

Although words are important in language, the mere presence of words is not enough to make a language. Sequencing of the words also is required. Can you imagine a language with only one-word utterances? A 13-month-old infant may use one-word utterances, but, as we will see later in the chapter, experts argue that the infant has whole sentences in mind when uttering a single word.

Why is sequencing important for language? The answer leads us to a third characteristic of language—**infinite generativity,** *an individual's ability to generate an infinite number of meaningful sentences using a finite set of words and rules, which makes language a highly creative enterprise.* It is possible for us to say things never said before by anyone else.

Yet another characteristic of language is **displacement,** *the use of language to communicate information about another place and time,* although we also use language to describe what is currently happening in our immediate environment. Anyone hooked on reading light fiction can attest to the power of displacement in language. However, reading light fiction is just one example of how language gives secondhand experience. Consider the everyday experience of being told what happened elsewhere or what someone else said. Language not only contributes to the transmission of knowledge from one individual to another but also from one generation to the next (Brown, 1986).

> *The maker of a sentence launches out into the infinite and builds a road into chaos and old night, and is followed by those who hear him with something of wild, creative delight.*
>
> —Ralph Waldo Emerson

A final, very important aspect of language is that it is characterized by rule systems. Thus, we can define **language** *as a system of symbols and sequence of words, used to communicate with others, that involves infinite generativity, displacement, and rule systems.* Let's now examine these important rule systems.

LANGUAGE'S RULE SYSTEMS

When nineteenth-century American writer Ralph Waldo Emerson said, "The world was built in order and the atoms march in tune," he must have had language in mind. The truly elegant system of language is highly ordered and organized. What is this order and organization like? The order and organization of language involve five rule systems: phonology, morphology, syntax, semantics, and pragmatics (see figure 10.1).

Phonology

Language is made up of basic sounds, or *phonemes.* In the English language, there are approximately 36 phonemes. **Phonology** *is the study of a language's sound system.* Phonological rules ensure that certain sound sequences occur (for example, *sp, ba,* or *ar*) and others do not (for example, *zx* or *qp*). A good example of a phoneme in the English language is /k/, the sound represented by the letter *k* in the word *ski* and the letter *c* in the word *cat.* Although the /k/ sound is slightly different in these two words, the variation is not distinguished and the /k/ sound is described as a single phoneme. In some languages, such as Arabic, this kind of variation is represented by separate phonemes.

Imagine what language would be like if there were no phonology. Each word in the language would have to be represented by a signal—a sound, for example—that differed from the signals of all other words. The obvious consequence is that the number of words could be no larger than the number of different signals that an individual could efficiently produce and perceive. We do not know precisely what that number is, but we do know that it is very small, especially in the case of speech, in contrast to the tens or even hundreds of thousands of words that commonly constitute a language.

What phonology does is to provide a basis for constructing a large and expandable set of words—all that are or ever will be—out of two to three dozen signal elements. We do not need five hundred thousand. All we need is two to three dozen.

Morphology

Morphology *refers to the rules for combining morphemes; a morpheme is the smallest string of sounds that gives meaning to what we say and hear.* Every word in the English language is made up of one or more morphemes. Some words consist of a single morpheme (for example, *help*), whereas others are made up of more than one morpheme (for example, *helper*, which has two morphemes, *help + er*, with the morpheme *er* meaning "one who"—in this case "one who helps"). However, not all morphemes are words (for example, *pre-, -tion,* and *-ing*). Just as the rules that govern phonemes ensure that certain sound sequences

FIGURE 10.1

Language's rule systems.

occur, the rules that govern morphemes ensure that certain strings of sounds occur in meaningful sequences. For example, we would not reorder *helper* to *erhelp*.

Syntax

Syntax *involves the way words are combined to form acceptable phrases and sentences.* Because you and I share the same syntactic understanding of sentence structure, if I say to you, "Bob slugged Tom" and "Bob was slugged by Tom," you know who did the slugging and who was slugged in each case. You also understand that the sentence "You didn't stay, did you?" is a grammatical sentence but that "You didn't stay, didn't you?" is unacceptable and ambiguous.

A concept closely related to syntax is **grammar,** *the formal description of syntactical rules.* In elementary school and high school, most of us learned rules about sentence structure. Linguists devise rules of grammar that are similar to those you learned in school but are much more complex and powerful. Many contemporary linguists distinguish between the "surface" and "deep" structure of a sentence. **Surface structure** *is the actual order of words in a sentence.* **Deep structure** *is the syntactic relation of the words in a sentence.* By applying syntactic rules in different ways, one sentence can have two very different deep structures. For example, consider this sentence: "Mrs. Smith found drunk on her lawn." Was Mrs. Smith drunk or did she find a drunk on the lawn? Either interpretation fits the sentence, depending on the deep structure applied.

> *The adjective is the banana peel of the parts of speech.*
> —Clifton Fadiman

"If you don't mind my asking, how much does a sentence diagrammer pull down a year?"
© Bob Thaves.

Semantics

Semantics *refers to the meaning of words and sentences.* Every word has a set of semantic features. Girl and woman, for example, share the same semantic features as the words female and human but differ in regard to age. Words have semantic restrictions on how they can be used in sentences. The sentence "The bicycle talked the boy into buying a candy bar" is syntactically correct but semantically incorrect. The sentence violates our semantic knowledge—bicycles do not talk.

> *A person gets from a symbol the meaning he puts into it, and what is one man's comfort and inspiration is another's jest and scorn.*
>
> —Justice Robert Jackson

Pragmatics

A final set of language rules involves **pragmatics,** *the use of appropriate conversation.* The domain of pragmatics is broad, covering such circumstances as: (a) taking turns in discussions instead of everyone talking at once; (b) using questions to convey commands ("Why is it so noisy in here?" "What is this, Grand Central Station?"); (c) using words like *the* and *a* in a way that enhances understanding ("I read *a* book last night. *The* plot was boring."); (d) using polite language in appropriate situations (for example, when talking to one's teacher); and (e) telling stories that are interesting, jokes that are funny, and lies that convince.

Pragmatic rules can be complex and differ from one culture to another. If you were to study the Japanese language, you would come face to face with countless pragmatic rules about conversing with individuals of various social levels and with various relationships to you. Some of these pragmatic rules concern the ways of saying thank you. Indeed, the pragmatics of saying thank you are complex even in our own culture. Preschoolers' use of this term varies with sex, socioeconomic status, and the age of the individual they are addressing. Through pragmatics, children learn to convey meaning with words, phrases, and sentences. Pragmatics helps children communicate more smoothly with others (Anderson, 1989; Didow, 1993; Gleason, 1988; Gleason, Hay, & Cain, 1989; Pan, Rollins, & Snow, 1991).

Is this ability to generate rule systems for language and then use them to create an almost infinite number of words the product of biology and evolution, or is it learned?

LANGUAGE'S BIOLOGICAL AND SOCIOCULTURAL/ ENVIRONMENTAL HERITAGES

In 1882, 2-year-old Helen Keller was left deaf, blind, and mute by a severe illness. By the time she was 7 years old, she had learned to fear the world she could not see or hear. Alexander Graham Bell suggested to her parents that they hire a tutor named Anne Sullivan to help Helen overcome her fears.

By using sign language, Anne was able to teach Helen a great deal about language. Helen Keller became an honors graduate of Radcliffe College and had this to say: "Whatever the process, the result is wonderful. Gradually from naming an object we advance step by step until we have traversed the vast distance between our first stammered syllable and the sweep of thought in a line of Shakespeare."

What is the process of learning language? Helen Keller had the benefit of a marvelous teacher, which suggests that experience is important in learning language. However, might there have been biological explanations for her language capabilities?

Biological Influences

How strongly is language influenced by biological evolution? Are children biologically prewired to learn language? What is the brain's role in language? Do animals have language? Is there a critical period for learning language? We will consider each of these questions in turn.

Biological Evolution

A number of experts on language stress its biological basis (Chomsky, 1957; Howe, 1993; Maratsos, 1989; Miller, 1981; Studdert-Kennedy, 1991). They believe that human infants are not unlike newborn birds, who come into the world biologically prepared to sing the song of their species. These language experts believe that biological evolution shaped humans into linguistic creatures. In terms of biological evolution, the brain, nervous system, and vocal system changed over hundreds of thousands of years. Prior to *Homo sapiens,* the physical equipment to produce language did not exist; *Homo sapiens* went beyond the groans and shrieks of their predecessors to develop abstract speech. Estimates vary as to how long ago humans acquired language—from about 20,000 to 70,000 years ago. In evolutionary time, then, language is a very recent acquisition.

Biological Prewiring—LAD

Linguist Noam Chomsky (1957) believes that humans are biologically prewired to learn language at a certain time and in a certain way. He also has said that children are born into the world with a **Language Acquisition Device (LAD),** *a biological prewiring that enables children to detect certain language categories, such as phonology, syntax, and semantics. LAD is an innate grammatical ability that underlies all human languages.*

The Brain's Role in Language

Another aspect of biology's role in language involves the accumulating evidence that language processing is controlled in the brain's left hemisphere (Gazzaniga, 1986; Sperry, 1974). Studies of language in brain-damaged individuals have pinpointed two areas of the left hemisphere that are especially critical. In 1861, a patient of Paul Broca, a French surgeon and anthropologist, received an injury to the left side of his brain. The patient became known as Tan, because that was the only word he could speak after his brain injury. Tan suffered from **aphasia,** *a language disorder, resulting from brain damage, that involves a loss of the ability to articulate ideas in any form.* Tan died several days after Broca evaluated him, and an autopsy revealed the location of the injury. Today, we refer to the part of the brain in which Broca's patient was injured as **Broca's area,** *an area of the left frontal lobe of the brain that directs the muscle movements involved in speech production.* Another place in the brain where an injury can seriously impair language is **Wernicke's area,** *an area of the brain's left hemisphere involved in language comprehension.* Individuals with damage to Wernicke's area often babble words in a meaningless way (Geschwind, 1979). The locations of Broca's area and Wernicke's area are shown in figure 10.2.

Although the brain's left hemisphere is especially important in language, keep in mind that, in most activities, there is an interplay between the brain's two hemispheres (Efron, in press; Heller, 1990; Hellige, 1990). For example, in reading, the left hemisphere comprehends syntax and grammar, which the right hemisphere does not. However, the right hemisphere is better at understanding a story's intonation and emotion.

Do Animals Have Language?

Many animal species have complex and ingenious ways to signal danger and to communicate about basic needs, such as food and sex. For example, in one species of firefly, the females have learned to imitate the flashing signal of another species to lure the aliens into their territory. Then they eat the aliens. However, is this language in the human sense? What about higher animals, such as apes? Is ape language similar to human language? Can we teach language to them?

Some researchers believe that apes can learn language. One simian celebrity in this field is a chimp named Washoe, who was adopted when she was about 10 months old (Gardner & Gardner, 1971). Since apes do not have the vocal apparatus to speak, the researchers tried to teach Washoe American Sign Language, which is one of the sign languages of the deaf. Washoe used sign language during everyday activities, such as

FIGURE 10.2

Broca's area and Wernicke's area. Damage to Broca's area causes problems in speech production, whereas damage to Wernicke's area causes problems in language comprehension. These areas are in the left hemisphere of the brain.

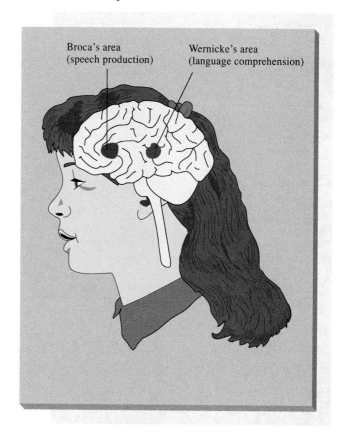

meals, play, and car rides. In 2 years, Washoe learned 38 signs and, by the age of 5, she had a vocabulary of 160 signs. Washoe learned how to put signs together in novel ways, such as "you drink" and "you me tickle." A number of other efforts to teach language to chimps have had similar results (Premack, 1986).

The debate about chimpanzees' ability to use language focuses on two key issues. Can apes understand the meaning of symbols—that is, can they comprehend that one thing stands for another—and can apes learn syntax—that is, can they learn the mechanics and rules that give human language its creative productivity? The first of these issues may have been settled recently by Duane Rumbaugh and Sue Savage-Rumbaugh (1990). The researchers found strong evidence that two chimps named Sherman and Austin can understand symbols (see figure 10.3). For example, if Sherman or Austin is sitting in a room and a symbol for an object is displayed on a screen, the chimp goes into another room, finds the object, and brings it back. If the object is not there, the chimp comes back empty-handed (Cowley, 1988). Austin can play a game in which one chimp points to a symbol for food (candy), the other chimp selects the food from a tray, then they both eat it. These observations are clear evidence that chimps can understand symbols (Rumbaugh & others, 1991; Savage-Rumbaugh, 1991).

FIGURE 10.3

Sue Savage-Rumbaugh with a chimp in front of a board with languagelike symbols. The Rumbaughs (Sue and Duane) of the Yerkes Primate Center and Georgia State University have studied the basic question of whether chimps understand symbols. Their research evidence suggests chimps can understand symbols.

Letter from Lonso . . . and he sounds pretty lonely."

THE FAR SIDE © 1989 FarWorks, Inc. Dist. UNIVERSAL PRESS SYNDICATE. Reprinted with permission. All rights reserved.

Although there still is no strong evidence that chimps can learn syntax, perhaps other animals can. Ron Schusterman has worked with a sea lion named Rocky, teaching him to follow such commands as "ball fetch" and "disc ball fetch." The first command means that Rocky should take a disc to a ball in his tank. The second command means that Rocky should take the ball to the disc. Although Rocky and other sea lions make some errors in decoding these complex commands, they perform much better than chance, indicating they have learned rules that link the ordering of symbols to abstract meanings. Such rules are either syntax or something close to it.

The debate over whether or not animals can use language to express thoughts is far from resolved. Researchers agree that animals can communicate with each other and that some can be trained to manipulate languagelike symbols. However, although such accomplishments may be remarkable, they fall far short of human language, with its infinite number of novel phrases to convey the richness and subtleties of meaning that are the foundation of human relationships.

Is There a Critical Period for Learning Language?

Former Secretary of State Henry Kissinger's heavy German accent illustrates the theory that there is a critical period for learning language. According to this theory, people who emigrate after the age of 12 will probably speak the new country's language with a foreign accent the rest of their lives, but, if people emigrate as young children, the accent goes away as the new language is learned (Asher & Garcia, 1969). Acquiring an accent is less related to how long you have lived somewhere than to the age at which you moved there. For example, if you move to a certain part of New York City before you turn 12 you'll probably "tawk" like a native. Apparently, puberty marks the close of a critical period for acquiring the phonological rules of various languages and dialects.

The stunted language development of a modern "wild child" also supports the idea of a critical period for language acquisition. In 1970 a California social worker made a routine visit to the home of a partially blind woman who had applied for public assistance. The social worker discovered that the woman and her husband had kept their 13-year-old daughter Genie locked away from the world. Kept in almost total isolation during childhood, Genie could not speak or stand erect. During the day, she was left to sit naked on a child's potty seat, restrained by a harness her father had made—she could move only her hands and feet. At night she was placed in a kind of straitjacket and caged in a crib with wire mesh sides and a cover. Whenever Genie made a noise, her father beat her. He never communicated with her in words but growled and barked at her instead.

Genie spent a number of years in extensive rehabilitation programs, such as speech and physical therapy (Curtiss, 1977). She eventually learned to walk with a jerky motion and to use the toilet. Genie also learned to recognize many words and to speak in rudimentary sentences. At first she spoke in one-word utterances. Later she was able to string together two-word combinations, such as "big teeth," "little marble," and "two hand." Consistent with the language development of most children, three-word combinations followed—for example, "small two cup." Unlike normal children, however, Genie did not learn how to ask questions and she doesn't understand grammar. Genie is not able to distinguish between pronouns or passive and active verbs. Four years after she began stringing words together, her speech still sounded like a garbled telegram. As an adult she speaks in short, mangled sentences, such as "father hit leg," "big wood," and "Genie hurt."

Children who are abandoned, abused, and not exposed to language for years, such as Genie, rarely learn to speak normally. Such tragic evidence supports the critical period hypothesis in language development.

Sociocultural and Environmental Influences

In 1799, a nude boy was observed running through the woods of France. The boy was captured when he was approximately 11 years old. It was believed he had lived in the wild for at least 6 years. He was called the Wild Boy of Aveyron (Lane, 1976). When the boy was found, he made no effort to communicate. Even after a number of years, he could not communicate effectively. His social isolation likely contributed to his language inadequacies, just as Genie's social isolation did. We do not learn language in a social vacuum. Most of us are bathed in language from a very early age. We need this early exposure to language to acquire competent language skills (Rogoff, 1990; Schegloff, 1989; Snow, 1989).

Cultural Change and the Sociocultural Context of Language

In our discussion of biological evolution, we indicated that, prior to *Homo sapiens*, the physical equipment to produce speech did not exist. Anthropologists speculate about the social conditions that led to the development of language. Social forces may have pushed humans to develop abstract reasoning and to create an economical system for communicating with others (Crick, 1977). For example, humans probably developed complex plans and strategies for obtaining food and finding shelter, and they may have been motivated to develop language to reach a higher level of competence.

The sociocultural context continues to play an important role in children's language today. In chapter 7, we discussed Vygotsky's theory, which emphasizes the important role of adults or more highly skilled children in a child's development. Middle-class parents impart the skills for the use of cultural tools, such as literacy, to their children very early in life (Rogoff, 1990). In one recent study, middle-class mothers talked more with their 21-month-old infants and sustained longer sequences of verbal

interaction with them than did mothers from low-income backgrounds (Hoff-Ginsberg, 1991). The low-income mothers limited their utterances to directions and corrections rather than acknowledging their children's actions or trying to engage them in conversation. The middle-class mothers also exposed their children to a richer vocabulary with longer sentences. In Sociocultural Worlds of Children 10.1 (p. 306), you can read about how children who grow up in the slum areas of large cities are not usually exposed to the guided participation in language that middle-class children are. You will also read about how the rich language tradition of Black Americans is being shut down in such poverty infested areas.

American psychologist Jerome Bruner (1983, 1989) also believes that the sociocultural context is extremely important in understanding children's language development. Like Vygotsky, Bruner stresses the role of parents and teachers in constructing a child's communication environment. **Language Acquisition Support System (LASS)** *is Bruner's concept that describes the behaviors of a language-skilled individual, especially a parent, in structuring and supporting the child's development of language.* Bruner's concept has much in common with Vygotsky's zone of proximal development, which was discussed in chapter 7. Thus, language development requires social involvement as well as a child's natural propensity to learn language (Furrow & Moore, 1991; Hoff-Ginsberg, 1991; Lock, 1991; Rogoff, 1990). In this view, the Language Acquisition Device (LAD), developed by Chomsky (1957) to account for the complexity and speed of young children's understanding of grammar, interacts with the Language Acquisition Support System (LASS) to make the language system function (see figure 10.4).

Social Supports for Language

What are some of the social supports that provide infants and children with a rich language learning environment? They include the parental simplification and framing of language through motherese, recasting, echoing, expanding, labeling, modeling, and corrective feedback.

One intriguing element of the environment in a young child's language acquisition is called **motherese,** *the way mothers and other adults often talk to babies in a higher-than-normal frequency and greater-than-normal pitch and with simple words and sentences.* It is hard to talk in motherese when not in the presence of a baby, but, as soon as you start talking to a baby, you immediately shift into motherese. Much of this is automatic and something most parents are not aware that they are doing. Motherese has the important functions of capturing the infant's attention and maintaining communication (Snow, 1989). When parents are asked why they use motherese, they point out that it is designed to teach their baby to talk. Older peers also talk motherese to infants (Dunn & Kendrick, 1982).

Other than motherese, are there other strategies adults use to enhance the child's acquisition of language? Four candidates are recasting, echoing, expanding, and labeling. **Recasting** *is phrasing the same or a similar meaning of a sentence in a different way, perhaps turning it into a question.* For example, if a child says, "The dog was barking," the adult can respond by asking,

FIGURE 10.4

An interactionist view of language: Chomsky's LAD and Bruner's LASS. In the interactionist view, language acquisition involves the child's natural propensity to learn language (described by Chomsky as the Language Acquisition Device [LAD]) and social involvement (described by Bruner as the Language Acquisition Support System [LASS]).

"When was the dog barking?" The effects of recasting fit with suggestions that "following in order to lead" helps a child learn language. That is, letting a child initially indicate an interest and then proceeding to elaborate that interest—commenting, demonstrating, and explaining—may enhance communication and help language acquisition. In contrast, an overly active, directive approach to communicating with the child may be harmful (Rice, 1989). **Echoing** *is repeating what the child says to you, especially if it is an incomplete phrase or sentence.* **Expanding** *is restating what the child has said in a linguistically sophisticated form.* **Labeling** *is identifying the names of objects.* Young children are forever being asked to identify the names of objects. Roger Brown (1986) identified this as the great word game and claimed that much of the early vocabulary acquired by children is motivated by this adult pressure to identify the words associated with objects. Information about picture books, first words, and labeling is presented in Explorations In Child Development 10.1.

Parents and teachers also contribute to children's language development through their roles as language models and through corrective feedback to children (Bohannon, MacWhinney, & Snow, 1990). Children who are slow in developing language skills can be helped if parents use carefully selected lists of words and grammatical constructions of speech to the children (Whitehurst & Valdez-Menchaca, 1988). Parents also shape children's grammatical utterances by correcting their grammatical errors (Bohannon & Stanowicz, 1988; Penner, 1987). Nonetheless, a number of experts on language believe that imitation and reinforcement facilitate language but are not absolutely necessary for its acquisition (de Villiers, 1988; de Villiers & de Villiers, 1978).

Critical Thinking

What should be the nature of parents' responses to children's grammatical mistakes in conversation? Should parents allow the mistakes to continue and assume that their young children will grow out of them, or should they closely monitor their children's grammar and correct mistakes whenever they hear them? Explain your answer.

SOCIOCULTURAL WORLDS OF CHILDREN 10.1

Language Traditions in Black Americans and Urban Poverty

Shirley Heath (1989) recently examined the language traditions of Black Americans from low-income backgrounds. She traced some aspects of Black English to the time of slavery. Heath also examined how those speech patterns have carried over into Black English today. She found that agricultural areas in the southern United States have an especially rich oral tradition.

Specifically she found that adults do not simplify or edit their talk for children, in essence challenging the children to be highly active listeners. Also, adults ask only "real questions" of children—that is, questions for which the adult does not already know the answer. Adults also engage in a type of teasing with children, encouraging them to use their wits in communication. For example, a grandmother might pretend that she wants to take a child's hat and then starts a lively exchange in which the child must understand many subtleties of argument, mood, and humor—does Grandma really want my hat? Is she mad at me? Is she making a joke? Can I persuade her to give it back to me? Finally, there is an appreciation of wit and flexibility in how language is used, as well as an acknowledgment of individual differences—one person might be respected for recounting stories, another for negotiating and peace-making skills.

Heath argues that the language tradition she describes is richly varied, cognitively demanding, and well suited to many real-life situations. She says that the oral and literary traditions among poor Blacks in the cities are well suited for many job situations. Years ago many inner-city jobs required only that a person follow directions in order to perform repetitious tasks. Today many positions require continuous interactions involving considerable flexibility in language, such as the ability to persuade co-workers or to express dissatisfaction, in a subtle way, for example.

Despite its utility in many job situations, the rich language tradition possessed by low-income Black Americans does not meet with the educational priorities of our nation's schools. Too

Children who grow up in low-income, poverty-ridden neighborhoods of large cities often experience a lack of family and community support, which can seriously undermine the development of their language skills.

often schools stress rote memorization, minimizing group interaction and discouraging individual variations in communicative style. Also, the language tradition of Black culture is rapidly dying in the face of current life among poor Blacks, where the structure of low-income, frequently single-parent families often provides little verbal stimulation for children.

One mother agreed to let researcher Shirley Heath (in press) tape-record her interactions with her children over a 2-year period and to write notes about her activities with them. Within 500 hours of tape and more than 1,000 lines of notes, the mother initiated talk with her three preschool children on only 18 occasions (other than giving them a brief directive or asking a quick question). Few of the mother's conversations involved either planning or executing actions with or for her children.

Heath (1989) points out that the lack of family and community supports is widespread in urban housing projects, especially among Black Americans. The deteriorating, impoverished conditions of these inner-city areas severely impede the ability of young children to develop the cognitive and social skills they need to function competently.

EXPLORATIONS IN CHILD DEVELOPMENT 10.1

Picture Books, First Words, and Labeling

Anat Ninio and Jerome Bruner (1978) took a close look at the subtle interplay between a mother and her infant son as the two performed the great word game in its quintessential setting—reading picture books and playing with objects. The mother and child were part of a longitudinal study that covered the period of 8 to 18 months in the child's life. The child was firstborn, and his parents were White, English, and middle class. Labeling was part of the filmed play activity captured in the videotape records, made every 2 to 3 weeks in the infant's home.

The investigators uncovered some remarkable findings. Chief among these was the ritualized nature of mother-child labeling activity. The labeling of pictures was a highly structured activity that obeyed clear rules and had the texture of a dialogue. A number of scholars have described such conversations as having fairly tight patterns in ascribing roles, turn taking, imitating, and responding (Bruner, 1983; Snow, 1989). So did the labeling activity. Each time the mother and child interacted over a picture name, for example, they took about the same number of turns, which lasted about the same length of time. The linguistic forms of the mother's utterances in book reading were very limited. She made repeated use of four key types of statements: (1) "Look!" (to get the child's attention);

(2) "What's that?"; (3) "It's an X!" (labeling the picture for the child); and (4) "Yes!" (giving the child feedback on his utterance). These types of statements accounted for virtually all of the language the mother directed toward the child while reading books during the entire period of the study, and they obeyed some simple rules of occurrence. For example, the attention getter "Look!" always preceded the query "What's that?" or the labeling phrase "It's an X!" Similarly, the query always preceded the labeling phrase.

At the outset of the study, of course, few of the child's verbal responses to the mother's queries were distinguishable words. At best, the child produced consistent babble. By the end of the period, however, words were present. Associated with this change, the mother dropped the question "What's that?" from the ritual, since the child now could produce a word for the picture.

The "dialogue reading" concept, which encourages children to talk about picture books and gives them models and feedback for progressively more sophisticated language use, was recently used in a day-care setting with 20 Mexican 2-year-olds from low-income backgrounds (Valdez-Menchaca & Whitehurst, 1992). Children in the intervention group were read to individually using the dialogue reading strategy. The control group children were given individual arts and crafts instruction by the same teacher. The dialogue reading strategy was effective in increasing the Mexican 2-year-olds' language production, including their spontaneous use of language.

Mothers and children often play the great word game involving mother-child labeling. In this game, mother and child take about the same number of turns, lasting about the same length of time.

The Behavioral View

Behaviorists view language as just another behavior, like sitting, walking, or running. They argue that children's language is acquired through the learning processes of reinforcement (Skinner, 1957) and imitation (Bandura, 1977). However, many of the sentences children produce are novel in the sense that they have not previously heard them. For example, children might hear the sentence "The plate fell on the floor" and then say, "My mirror fell on the blanket," after they drop the mirror on the blanket. The behavioral mechanisms of reinforcement

(smiles, hugs, pats on the back, corrective feedback) and imitation (modeling of words and syntax) cannot completely explain this utterance.

While spending long hours observing parents and their young children, American pioneer in language research Roger Brown (1973) searched for evidence that parents reinforce their children for speaking grammatically. He found that parents sometimes smiled and praised their children for sentences they liked, but that they also reinforced sentences that were ungrammatical. Brown concluded that no evidence exists to document that reinforcement is responsible for language's rule systems. However, recently, some researchers have found evidence that many parents provide more corrective feedback for children's ungrammatical utterances than Brown originally thought (Penner, 1987).

Famous American linguist Noam Chomsky (1957, 1986) believes that the behavioral view of language is wrong. Chomsky says that children do learn the language of their sociocultural world, but the speed at which they acquire words and grammar cannot be explained by learning principles such as reinforcement and imitation. Remember that Chomsky says that children come into the world equipped with a biologically prewired Language Acquisition Device, which is much like a biological machine with switches. According to Chomsky, all that is needed to turn on the switches of the biological machine is for the child to hear a particular language spoken.

As can be seen, the question of how children acquire language has met with spirited debate. Basically, the debate is another version of the pervasive nature-nurture controversy, which was first introduced in chapter 1 and which we have frequently visited throughout this book. How do children acquire language? Their biological foundations prepare them to learn language as they and their caregivers interact socially. As in other areas of children's development, once again we find biology and experience interacting and working together.

At this point, we have discussed a number of ideas about what language is, language's rule systems, and the biological and sociocultural environmental heritages of language. A summary of these ideas is presented in Concept Table 10.1.

THE ROLE OF COGNITION IN LANGUAGE

Noam Chomsky's idea of the young language learner as richly endowed with prewired equipment is widely accepted today, but there is a question about the type of equipment the child possesses. Is the equipment specifically linguistic, like Chomsky's Language Acquisition Device, or is it more cognitive, being derived from humans' generally high level of intelligence (Maratsos, 1983)? The basic claim of the cognitive theorists is that a child's growing intelligence and desire to express meanings, together with language input from parents, "drive" the acquisition of language (Markman, 1989; Waxman & Kosowski, 1990). Thus, the cognitive view's focus is on the semantic and pragmatic levels of language rather than on the syntactic, morphological, and phonological levels.

Language is the dress of thought.

—Samuel Johnson

One type of evidence for the cognitive view is that children's early utterances seem to indicate knowledge of semantic categories, such as agent and action, rather than linguistic categories such as noun and verb (Bowerman, 1989). In support of this view, children can tell that semantically deviant sentences are wrong before they can tell syntactically deviant sentences are wrong (Washburn & Hakes, 1985). This implies that a 5-year-old might detect the unacceptability of the sentence "The bicycle talked to the boy" (semantically deviant), yet fail to reject the sentences "The boy ride the bicycle" and "What you are doing today?" (syntactically deviant).

Evidence that cognition is important for language comes from studies of deaf children. On a variety of thinking and problem-solving skills, deaf children perform at the same level as children of the same age who have no hearing problems. Some of the deaf children in these studies do not even have command of written or sign language (Furth, 1973).

Another argument for a cognitive theory of language concerns what we know about how language evolved. Since a spoken language leaves no physical trace, the age of human language is difficult to determine. According to some estimates, however, language evolved as recently as 10,000 to 100,000 years ago (Swadesh, 1971)—quite recent in evolutionary time—perhaps too recent for a large amount of purely linguistic machinery to have evolved in the brain. From an evolutionary perspective, cognition is much older than human language. For example, tool-making activity—a clear sign of high intellectual functioning—is at least 2 million years old (Miller, 1981). Considerations such as these favor the view that language is at least partly a product of cognition, not being solely determined by specific linguistic abilities.

HOW LANGUAGE DEVELOPS

In the thirteenth century, the Holy Roman Emperor Frederick II had a cruel idea. He wanted to know what language children would speak if no one talked to them. He selected several newborns and threatened their caregivers with death if they ever talked to the infants. Frederick never found out what language the children spoke because they all died. As we move toward the twenty-first century, we are still curious about infants' development of language, although our experiments and observations are, to say the least, far more humane than the evil Frederick's.

Language Development in Infancy

When does an infant utter her first word? The event usually occurs at about 10 to 13 months of age, though some infants wait longer. Many parents view the onset of language development as coincident with this first word, but some significant accomplishments are attained earlier. Before babies say words, they babble, emitting such vocalizations as "goo-goo" and "ga-ga." Babbling starts at about 3 to 6 months of age. The start is determined by biological maturation, not reinforcement or the ability to hear (Locke & others, 1991). Even deaf babies babble for a time (Lenneberg, Rebelsky, & Nichols, 1965). Babbling exercises the baby's vocal apparatus and facilitates the development of articulation skills that are useful in later speech (Clark & Clark, 1977). The purpose of a baby's earliest communication, however, is to attract attention from parents and

CONCEPT TABLE 10.1

What Is Language, Language's Rule Systems, and Language's Biological and Sociocultural/Environmental Heritages

Concept	Processes/Related Ideas	Characteristics/Description
What is language?	Its nature	Language is a system of symbols and sequence of words, used to communicate with others, that involves infinite generativity, displacement, and rule systems.
Language's rule systems	Phonology	Phonology governs the sequencing of phonemes (basic sounds that differ in their distinctive features).
	Morphology	Morphology governs the sequencing of morphemes (the smallest units of language that carry meaning).
	Syntax	Syntax governs the ordering of words within sentences or phrases. These rules apply to deep and surface structures.
	Semantics	Semantics places restrictions on how words must be used to make meaningful sentences.
	Pragmatics	Pragmatics facilitates good communication and good social relations among language users.
Biological influences	Biological evolution	The fact that biological evolution shaped humans into linguistic creatures is undeniable.
	Biological prewiring—LAD	Linguist Noam Chomsky believes that humans are prewired to learn language. He said children are born with a Language Acquisition Device (LAD), a biological prewiring that enables a child to detect certain language categories. LAD is an innate grammatical ability.
	The brain's role in language	The brain's left hemisphere plays an important role in language. Damage to Broca's area affects speech production, whereas damage to Wernicke's area affects language comprehension. Although the left hemisphere has a powerful influence on language, keep in mind that, in most activities, there is an interplay between the brain's two hemispheres.
	Do animals have language?	Animals can communicate and chimpanzees can be taught to use symbols. Whether animals have all of the properties of human language is debated.
	Is there a critical period for learning language?	The experiences of Genie and other children suggest that the early years of childhood are a critical time for learning language. If exposure to language does not occur before puberty, lifelong deficits in grammar occur.
Cultural, environmental, and behavioral influences	Cultural change and the sociocultural context of language	Sociocultural conditions may have pushed humans to develop abstract reasoning and to create an economical system for communicating with others. Bruner believes that the Language Acquisition Support System (LASS) plays an important role in structuring and supporting children's language. Among the social supports that contribute to children's language are parental simplification and framing of language through motherese, recasting, echoing, expanding, labeling, modeling, and corrective feedback.
	The behavioral view	Behaviorists view language as just another behavior, like sitting, walking, or running. They argue that children's language is acquired through reinforcement and imitation. Chomsky believes that the behavioral view is wrong. An interactionist view emphasizes the contributions of both biology and experience in language—that is, children are biologically prepared to learn language as they and their caregivers interact.

others in the environment. Infants engage the attention of others by making or breaking eye contact, by vocalizing sounds, and by performing manual actions such as pointing. All of those behaviors involve pragmatics.

A child's first words include those that name important people (*dada*), familiar animals (*kitty*), vehicles (*car*), toys (*ball*), food (*milk*), body parts (*eye*), clothes (*hat*), household items (*clock*), or greeting terms (*bye*). These were the first words of babies 50 years ago and they are the first words of babies today (Clark, 1983). At times, it is hard to tell what these one-word utterances mean. One possibility is that they stand for an entire sentence in the infant's mind. Because of limited cognitive or linguistic skills, possibly only one word comes out instead of the whole sentence. The **holophrase hypothesis** *is the theory that a single word is used to imply a complete sentence; it is characteristic of an infant's first words.*

Children sometimes overextend or underextend the meanings of the words they use. **Overextension** *is the tendency of children to misuse words by extending one word's meaning to include objects that are not related to or are inappropriate for the word's meaning.* For example, when children learn to say the word *dada* for "father," they often apply the word beyond the individual it was intended to represent, using it for other men, strangers, or boys. With time, such overextensions decrease and eventually disappear. **Underextension** *occurs when children fail to use a noun to name a relevant event or object.* For example, children may learn to use the word *boy* to describe a 5-year-old neighbor but not apply the word to a male infant or a 9-year-old male.

By the time children are 18 to 24 months of age, they usually have begun to utter two-word statements. During this two-word stage, they quickly grasp the importance of expressing concepts and the role that language plays in communicating with others. To convey meaning with two-word utterances, the child relies heavily on gesture, tone, and context. The wealth of meaning children can communicate with a two-word utterance includes:

Identification: See doggie.

Location: Book there.

Repetition: More milk.

Nonexistence: Allgone thing.

Negation: Not wolf.

Possession: My candy.

Attribution: Big car.

Agent-action: Mama walk.

Action-direct-object: Hit you.

Action-indirect-object: Give papa.

Action-instrument: Cut knife.

Question: Where ball? (Slobin, 1972)

One of the most striking aspects of this list is that it is used by children all over the world. The examples are taken from utterances in English, German, Russian, Finnish, Turkish, Samoan, and Luo.

Telegraphic speech *is the use of short, precise words to communicate; it is characteristic of young children's two-word utterances.* When we write telegrams, we try to be terse, excluding any unnecessary words. As indicated in the examples of telegraphic speech from children from around the world, articles, auxiliary verbs, and other connectives usually are omitted. Of course, telegraphic speech is not limited to two-word utterances. "Mommy give ice cream" and "Mommy give Tommy ice cream" also are examples of telegraphic speech.

In expanding this concept of classifying children's language development in terms of number of utterances, Roger Brown (1973) has proposed that **mean length of utterance (MLU),** *an index of language development based on the number of words per sentence a child produces in a sample of about 50 to 100 sentences,* is a good index of language maturity. Brown identified five stages based on MLU:

Stage	MLU
1	1 + to 2.0
2	2.5
3	3.0
4	3.5
5	4.0

The first stage begins when a child generates sentences consisting of more than one word, such as the examples of two-word utterances mentioned earlier. The 1 + designation suggests that the average number of words in each utterance is greater than one but not yet two, because some of the child's utterances are still holophrases. This stage continues until the child averages two words per utterance. Subsequent stages are marked by increments of .5 in mean length of utterance. Brown's stages are shown in figure 10.5.

Around the world, young children learn to speak in two-word utterances, in most cases at about 18 to 24 months of age.

FIGURE 10.5

Brown's stages of language development.

Stage	Age Range (months)	Mean Length of Utterance (average number of words per sentence)	Characteristics	Typical Sentences
1	12–26	1.00–2.00	Vocabulary consists mainly of nouns and verbs with a few adjectives and adverbs; word order is preserved	Baby bath.
2	27–30	2.00–2.50	Correct use of plurals; use of past tense, use of *be*, definite and nondefinite articles, some prepositions	Cars go fast.
3	31–34	2.50–3.00	Use of yes-no questions, *wh*-questions (who, what, where); use of negatives and imperatives	Put the baby down.
4	35–40	3.00–3.75	Embedding one sentence within another	That's the truck mommy buyed me.
5	41–46	3.75–4.50	Coordination of simple sentences and propositional relations	Jenny and Cindy are sisters.

Brown's stages are important for several reasons. First, children who vary in chronological age as much as one half to three fourths of a year still have similar speech patterns. Second, children with similar mean lengths of utterance seem to have similar rule systems that characterize their language. In some ways, then, MLU is a better indicator of language development than is chronological age. Figure 10.6 shows the individual variation in chronological age that characterizes children's MLU.

Language Development in Early Childhood

Young children's understanding sometimes gets way ahead of their speech. One 3-year-old, laughing with delight as an abrupt summer breeze stirred his hair and tickled his skin, commented, "It did winding me!" Adults would be understandably perplexed if a young child ventured, "Anything is not to break, only plates and glasses," when she meant, "Nothing is breaking except plates and glasses." Many of the oddities of young children's language sound like mistakes to adult listeners. From the children's point of view, however, they are not mistakes; they represent the way young children perceive and understand their world at that point in their development. Among the important issues in language during the early childhood years are those involving developmental changes in language's rule systems and the role of early childhood education in literacy.

Changes in Rule Systems

What kinds of changes occur in language development during early childhood? Language continues to obey certain principles, following the rules of phonology, morphology, syntax, semantics, and pragmatics.

Regarding phonology, some preschool children have difficulty speaking in consonant clusters (for example, *str* as in *string*). Pronouncing some of the more difficult phonemes—*r*, for example—is still problematic and can continue to be a problem in the elementary school years. Also, some of the phonological rules for pronouncing word endings (in the past tense, for example) are not mastered until children are 6 to 8 years of age.

Regarding morphology, as children move beyond two-word utterances, there is clear evidence that they know morphological rules. Children begin using the plural and possessive

FIGURE 10.6

Roger Brown and his examination of MLU in three children. The graph shows the average length of utterances generated by three children ranging in age from 1½ to just over 4 years. The photograph shows Roger Brown talking with a young girl. Brown has been a pioneer in providing rich insights about children's language development. Among his contributions is the concept of MLU, or mean length of utterance, which has been documented as a good index of a child's language maturity.

forms of nouns (*dogs* and *dog's*); putting appropriate endings on verbs (*s* when the subject is third-person singular, *ed* for the past tense, and *ing* for the present progressive tense); and using prepositions (*in* and *on*), articles (*a* and *the*), and various forms of the verb *to be* ("I was going to the store"). Some of the best evidence for morphological rules appears in the form of *overgeneralizations* of these rules. Have you ever heard a preschool child say "foots" instead of "feet" or "goed" instead of "went"? If you do not remember having heard such things, talk to some parents who have young children or to the young children themselves. You will hear some interesting errors in the use of morphological rule endings.

In a classic experiment, children's language researcher Jean Berko (1958) presented preschool and first-grade children with cards such as the one shown in figure 10.7. Children were asked to look at the card while the experimenter read the words on it aloud. Then the children were asked to supply the missing word. This might sound easy, but Berko was interested not just in the children's ability to recall the right word but their ability to say it "correctly" (with the ending that was dictated by morphological rules). *Wugs* would be the correct response for the card in figure 10.7. Although the children were not perfectly accurate, they were much better than chance would dictate. Moreover, they demonstrated their knowledge of morphological rules not only with the plural forms of nouns ("There are two wugs") but also with possessive forms of nouns and with the third-person singular and past-tense forms of verbs. What makes Berko's study impressive is that most of the words were fictional; they were

FIGURE 10.7

Stimuli in Berko's study of young children's understanding of morphological rules. In Jean Berko's (1958) study, young children were presented cards such as this one with a "wug" on it. Then the children were asked to supply the missing word and say it correctly. "Wugs" is the correct response here.

This is a wug.

Now there is another one.
There are two of them.
There are two _____.

"No, Timmy, not 'I sawed the chair.' It's 'I saw the chair' or 'I have seen the chair.'"
© BERNHARDT.

created especially for the experiment. Thus, the children could not base their responses on remembering past instances of hearing the words. It seems, instead, that they were forced to rely on *rules*. Their performance suggested that they did so successfully.

Similar evidence that children learn and actively apply rules can be found at the level of syntax (Budwig, 1993). After advancing beyond two-word utterances, the child speaks word sequences that show a growing mastery of complex rules for how words should be ordered. Consider the case of *wh*-questions: "Where is Daddy going?" and "What is that boy doing?" for example. To ask these questions properly, the child has to know two important differences between *wh*-questions and simple affirmative statements (for instance, "Daddy is going to work" and "That boy is waiting on the school bus"). First, a *wh*- word must be added at the beginning of the sentence. Second, the auxiliary verb must be "inverted"—that is, exchanged with the subject of the sentence. Young children learn quite early where to put the *wh*- word, but they take much longer to learn the auxiliary-inversion rule. Thus, it is common to hear preschool children asking such questions as "Where daddy is going?" and "What that boy is doing?"

As children move into the elementary school years, they become skilled at using syntactical rules to construct lengthy and complex sentences. Sentences such as "The man who fixed the house went home" and "I don't want you to use my bike" are impressive demonstrations of how the child can use syntax to combine ideas into a single sentence. Just how a young child achieves the mastery of such complex rules, while at the same time she may be struggling with relatively simple arithmetic rules, is a mystery we have yet to solve.

Regarding semantics, as children move beyond the two-word stage, their knowledge of meanings also rapidly advances. The speaking vocabulary of a 6-year-old child ranges from 8,000 to 14,000 words (Carey, 1977). Assuming that word learning began when the child was 12 months old, this translates into a rate for new word meanings of five to eight words a day between the ages of 1 and 6. After 5 years of word learning, the 6-year-old child does not slow down. According to some estimates, the average child of this age is moving along at the awe-inspiring rate of 22 words a day (Miller, 1981). How would you fare if you were given the task of learning 22 new words every day? It is truly miraculous how quickly children learn language.

Although there are many differences between a 2-year-old's language and a 6-year-old's language, none are more important than those pertaining to pragmatics—that is, rules of conversation. A 6-year-old is simply a much better conversationalist than a 2-year-old. What are some of the improvements in pragmatics that are made in the preschool years? At about 3 years of age, children improve in their ability to talk about things that are not physically present; that is, they improve their command of the characteristic of language known as *displacement*. One way displacement is revealed is in games of pretend. Although a 2-year-old might know the word *table*, he is unlikely to use this word to refer to an imaginary table that he pretends is standing in front of him. A child over 3 years of age probably has this ability, though, even if she does not always use it. There are large individual differences in preschoolers' talk about imaginary people and things.

Somewhat later in the preschool years—at about 4 years of age—children develop a remarkable sensitivity to the needs of others in conversation (Gleason, 1988). One way in which they show such sensitivity is their use of the articles *the* and *an* (or *a*). When adults tell a story or describe an event, they generally use *an* (or *a*) when they first refer to an animal or an object, and then use *the* when referring to it later (for example, "Two boys were walking through the jungle when *a* fierce lion appeared. *The* lion lunged at one boy while the other ran for cover"). Even

As children develop, they become much better conversationalists. At about 4 years of age, children become more sensitive to the needs of others in conversation.

3-year-olds follow part of this rule (they consistently use the word *the* when referring to previously mentioned things). However, using the word *a* when something is initially mentioned develops more slowly. Although 5-year-old children follow this rule on some occasions, they fail to follow it on others.

Another pragmatic ability that appears around 4 to 5 years of age involves speech style. As adults, we have the ability to change our speech style in accordance with social situations and persons with whom we are speaking. An obvious example is that adults speak in a simpler way to a 2-year-old child than to an older child or to an adult. Interestingly, even 4-year-old children speak differently to a 2-year-old than to a same-aged peer (they "talk down" to the 2-year-old using shorter utterance lengths). They also speak differently to an adult than to a same-aged peer, using more polite and formal language with the adult (Shatz & Gelman, 1973).

Literacy and Early Childhood Education

The concern about our nation's **literacy,** *the ability to read and write,* has led to a careful examination of preschool and kindergarten children's experiences, with the hope that children will develop a positive orientation toward reading and writing early in life (Dickinson & Moreton, 1991; Early Childhood and Literacy Development Committee, 1986; Liberg, 1990; Linden & Whimbey, 1990). Literacy begins in infancy. Reading and writing skills in young children should build on their existing understanding of oral and written language. Learning should occur in a supportive environment, one in which children can generate a positive perception of themselves and develop a positive attitude toward reading and writing (Beals & De Temple, 1991; Bloome, 1989; Garton & Pratt, 1989).

Critical Thinking

Assume that you have been hired as a consultant to an early childhood education program. Many of the parents want their children to learn to read early and want reading to be a main focus of the program. How would you handle the pushy parents?

Unfortunately, in the push to develop a nation of literate people by emphasizing the early development of reading and writing skills, some dangers have emerged (Early Childhood and Literacy Development Committee, 1986). Too many preschool children are being subjected to rigid, formal prereading programs with expectations and experiences that are too advanced for children of their levels of development. Too little attention is being given to the individual development of young children's learning styles and skills. Too little attention is given to reading for pleasure, which may keep children from associating reading with enjoyment. The pressure to achieve high scores on standardized tests, which often are inappropriate for preschool children, has resulted in a curriculum that is too advanced and too intense. Such programs frequently restrict curiosity, critical thinking, and creative expression.

What should a literacy program for preschool children be like? Instruction should be built on what children already know about oral language, reading, and writing. All young children should experience feelings of success and pride in their early reading and writing exercises. Teachers need to help them perceive themselves as people who can enjoy exploring oral and written language. Reading should be integrated into the broad communication process, which includes speaking, listening, and writing, as well as other communication systems such as art, math, and music. Children's early writing attempts should be encouraged without concern for the proper formation of letters or correct conventional spelling. Children should be encouraged to take risks in reading and writing, and errors should be viewed as a natural part of the child's growth. Teachers and parents should regularly take time to read to children from a wide variety of poetry, fiction, and nonfiction. Teachers and parents should present models for young children to emulate by using language appropriately, listening and responding to children's talk, and engaging in their own reading and writing (Benson, 1993; DeBarshye, 1993; Scarborough, 1993; Snow, 1993). Children also should be encouraged to be active participants in the learning process rather than passive recipients of knowledge. This can be accomplished by using activities that stimulate their experimentation with talking, listening, writing, and reading.

In a real sense, the writer writes to teach himself, to understand himself, to satisfy himself.

—Alfred Kazin

Language Development in Middle and Late Childhood

As children develop during middle and late childhood, changes in their vocabulary and grammar take place. Reading assumes a prominent role in their language world. An increasingly important consideration is bilingualism. We will consider each of these aspects of children's language development in turn.

Vocabulary and Grammar

During middle and late childhood, a change occurs in the way children think about words. They become less tied to the actions and perceptual dimensions associated with words, and they become more analytical in their approach to words. For example, when asked to say the first thing that comes to mind when they hear a word, such as *dog*, preschool children often respond with a word related to the immediate context of a dog. A child might associate *dog* with a word that indicates its appearance (*black*, *big*) or to an action associated with it (*bark*, *sit*). Older children more frequently respond to *dog* by associating it with an appropriate category (*animal*) or to information that intelligently expands the context (*cat*, *veterinarian*) (Holzman, 1983). The increasing ability of elementary school children to analyze words helps them understand words that have no direct relation to their personal experiences. This allows children to add more abstract words to their vocabulary. For example, *precious stones* can be understood by understanding the common characteristics of *diamonds* and *emeralds*. Also, children's increasing analytic abilities allow them to distinguish between such similar words as *cousin* and *nephew* or *city*, *village*, and *suburb*.

Children make similar advances in grammar. The elementary school child's improvement in logical reasoning and analytical skills helps in the understanding of such constructions as the appropriate use of comparatives (*shorter*, *deeper*) and subjectives ("If you were president, . . ."). By the end of the elementary school years, children can usually apply many of the appropriate rules of grammar (de Villiers & de Villiers, 1978).

Reading

Reading becomes a special skill during the elementary school years. Not being a competent reader places children at a substantial disadvantage in relation to their peers.

In the history of learning-to-read techniques, three approaches have dominated: the ABC method, the whole-word method, and the phonics method. The **ABC method** *is a learning-to-read technique that emphasizes memorizing the names and letters of the alphabet.* The **whole-word method** *is a learning-to-read technique that emphasizes learning direct associations between whole words and their meanings.* The **phonics method** *is a learning-to-read technique that emphasizes the sounds that letters make when in words (such sounds can differ from the names of these letters, as when the sound of the letter* C *is not found in* cat). The ABC method is in ill repute today. Because of the imperfect relationship between the names of letters and their sounds in words, the technique is regarded as ineffective, if not harmful, in teaching children to read. Despite its poor reputation, the ABC method was the technique that taught many children in past generations to read successfully. Disputes in recent years have centered on the merits of the whole-word and phonics methods (Goswami & Bryant, 1990). Although some research has been done comparing these two techniques, the findings have not been conclusive (Carbo, 1987). However, there is evidence that drill practice with the sounds made by letters in words (part of some phonics methods) improves reading ability (Williams, 1979). Many current techniques of reading instruction incorporate components of both whole-word and phonics (Karlin & Karlin, 1987).

Reading is more than the sum of whole-word and phonics methods. Information-processing skills are also involved in successful reading (Bowers & Wolf, 1993; Carr & Alejanu, 1993; Cerro & Baker, 1993; Evans & Baraball, 1993; Hall, 1989; Rieben & Perfetti, 1991). When children read, they process information and interpret it, so reading serves as a practical example to illustrate the approach of information processing we have talked about at various other times in this book. Remember that information processing is concerned with how children analyze the many different sources of information available to them in the environment and how they make sense of those experiences. When children read, for example, a rich and complex set of visual symbols is available to their senses. The symbols are associated with sounds, the sounds are combined to form words, and the words and large units that contain them (phrases, sentences, paragraphs) have conventional meanings. To read effectively, children must perceive and attend to words and sentences. They must also hold information in memory while processing new information (Berninger, 1993). A number of information-processing skills, then, are involved in children's ability to read effectively.

Bilingualism

Octavio's Mexican parents moved to the United States one year before Octavio was born. They do not speak English fluently and have always spoken to Octavio in Spanish. At 6 years of age, Octavio has just entered the first grade at an elementary school in San Antonio, Texas, and he speaks no English. What is the best way to teach Octavio? How much easier would elementary school be for Octavio if his parents had been able to speak to him in Spanish *and* English when he was an infant?

Well over 6 million children in the United States come from homes in which English is not the primary language. Often, like Octavio, they live in a community in which non-English language is the main means of communication. These children face a more difficult task than most of us: They must master the native tongue of their family to communicate effectively at home and they must also master English to make their way in the larger society. The number of bilingual children is expanding at such a rapid rate in our country (some experts predict a tripling of their number early in the twenty-first century) that they constitute an important subgroup of language learners that society must deal with. Although the education of such children in the public schools has a long history, only recently has a national policy evolved to guarantee a high-quality language experience for them.

Bilingual education *refers to programs for students with limited proficiency in English that instruct students in their own language part of the time while they learn English.* The rationale for bilingual education was provided by the United States Commission on Civil Rights (1975): Lack of English proficiency is the main reason language minority students do poorly in school; bilingual education should keep students from falling far behind in a subject while they are learning English. Bilingual

Reading is more than the sum of whole-word and phonics methods. Information-processing skills are involved in successful reading. When children read, they process information and interpret it.

What are the arguments for and against bilingual education?

programs vary extensively in content and quality. At a minimum, they include English instruction as a second language for students with limited English proficiency. Bilingual programs often include some instruction in Spanish as well. The largest number of bilingual programs in the United States are in Spanish, so our examples refer to Spanish, although the principles also apply to bilingual programs in other languages. Bilingual programs differ in the extent to which the Hispanic culture is taught to all students, and some bilingual programs teach Spanish to all students, regardless of whether their primary language is Spanish.

Most bilingual education programs are simply transitional programs developed to support students in Spanish until they can understand English well enough to function in the regular classroom, which is taught in English. A typical bilingual program begins teaching students with limited English proficiency in their primary language in kindergarten and then changes to English-only classes at the end of the first or second grade (Slavin, 1988).

Research evaluation of bilingualism has led to the conclusion that bilingualism does not interfere with performance in either language (Hakuta & Garcia, 1989). There is no evidence that the native language should be eliminated as early as possible because it might interfere with learning a second language. Instead, higher degrees of bilingualism are associated with cognitive flexibility and improved concept formation (Diaz, 1983). These findings are based primarily on research in additive bilingual settings—that is, in settings where the second language is added as an enrichment to the native language and not at its expense. Causal relations between bilingualism and cognitive or language competence are difficult to establish, but, in general, positive outcomes are often noted in communities where bilingualism is not socially stigmatized.

Increasingly, researchers are recognizing the complexity of bilingualism's effects (Brislin, 1993; Fillmore, 1989). For example, as indicated earlier, the nature of bilingualism programs varies enormously—some are of excellent quality; others are of poor quality. Some teachers in bilingual education programs are completely bilingual; others are not. Some programs begin in kindergarten, others in elementary school. Some programs end in the first or second grade; others continue through the fifth or sixth grade. Some include instruction in the Hispanic culture; others focus only on language instruction. Some researchers select outcome measures that include only proficiency in English; others focus on cognitive variables such as cognitive flexibility and concept formation; and still others include more social variables such as integration into the school, self-esteem, and attitude toward school. In sum, there is more to understanding the effects of bilingual education than simple language proficiency (Hakuta & Garcia, 1989).

One final point about bilingualism deserves attention. The United States is one of the few countries in the world in which most students graduate from high school knowing only their own language. For example, in the Soviet Union, schools have 10 grades, called forms, which correspond roughly to the 12 grades in American schools. Children begin school at age 7. In the third form, Russian students begin learning English. Because of the emphasis on teaching English in their schools, most Russian citizens today under the age of 35 speak at least some English (Cameron, 1988).

Critical Thinking

Assume that you have taken a position as a director of bilingual education in a large school system in a major U.S. city. What social policy on bilingual education would you urge the school board to adopt? Explain your answer.

At this point, we have discussed a number of ideas about the role of cognition in language and the development of language. A summary of these ideas is presented in Concept Table 10.2.

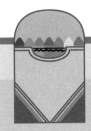

PERSPECTIVES ON PARENTING AND EDUCATION

Live, Concrete Parent Talk to Infants

An interest of most parents is how to talk to babies, especially what to say to them at different points in infant development. Infancy expert Burton White (1990) recently described appropriate ways for caregivers to interact with infants to promote their language development. An overview of White's ideas follows.

Some parents do not talk to their baby in the first several months or even the entire first year, waiting until the baby speaks its first word before beginning to do much talking to the infant. However, it is unquestionably a good idea for parents to begin talking to their babies right from the start. The best language teaching occurs when the talking is begun earlier than the first intelligible speech from an infant.

To assure good early language learning, it is important to talk in particular ways to babies. This particular method involves identifying, as well as the parent is able, what the baby is attending to at the moment. For the first two years of life, infants mainly orient to the here-and-now. They are simply incapable of understanding references to nonpresent objects. Talking about a trip that will be taken in a week is much less likely to register with the infant than comments about the parent's own face or the baby's hand, if that is what the baby is looking

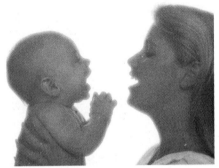

It is unquestionably a good idea for parents to begin talking to their babies right at the start. The best language teaching occurs when the talking is begun before the infant becomes capable of its first intelligible speech.

at. Diaper-changing, bath, and play times lend themselves nicely to identifying what the baby is attending to at the moment and then talking directly to the baby about the situation in simple, normal language. For example, the parent can talk about the sock she is putting on the infant, the toy she is holding before the baby, or some feature of the baby's fingers.

Another important consideration for parents interested in promoting their infant's language development involves looking and listening to language. A typical example in the second year of life is the toddler who sees and hears the mother and older sibling talking at a level

that is within the toddler's capacity to understand. A distinction can be made between *live language*—spoken language the infant may overhear or spoken language directed toward the infant by another person—and *mechanical language*—spoken language delivered by a television set, a radio, or a record or tape player. White argues that the more live language directed at toddlers—especially about what they seem to be attending to at the moment—the better for their language development.

It is also important for parents to act like they understand the toddler's words even when they don't. Correcting the toddler or trying to make the toddler say a word again "properly" only bores the toddler (Leach, 1990). As we have seen, toddlers are primarily developing language rather than imitating it, so parents' corrections will not have much effect anyway. The toddler's own words will develop into something more correct in time, but not under the caregiver's direct commands. Toddlers' own words are the best they have to offer at that point in development. Remember also that it is pleasure, affection, and excitement that motivate early talk. Refusing to hand the infant her bottle until she says "milk" instead of "bah-boo" will make her frustrated and cross. You are more likely to get tears than words. ■

CONCEPT TABLE 10.2

The Role of Cognition in Language and How Language Develops

Concept	Processes/Related Ideas	Characteristics/Description
The role of cognition	Its nature	Although children have prewired machinery for language, the cognitive view emphasizes that at least some of it is cognitive rather than strictly linguistic.
Language development in infancy and early childhood	Infancy	Vocalization begins with babbling at about 3 to 6 months of age. A baby's earliest communication skills are pragmatic. One-word utterances occur at about 10 to 13 months; the holophrase hypothesis has been applied to this. By 18 to 24 months, most infants have begun to use two-word utterances. Language at this point is referred to as telegraphic. Brown developed the idea of mean length of utterance (MLU). Five stages of MLU have been identified, providing a valuable indicator of language maturity.
	Early childhood	Advances in phonology, morphology, syntax, semantics, and pragmatics continue in early childhood. There has been increased interest in teaching young children reading and writing skills. Unfortunately, this has led to some dangers, with too many preschool children subjected to rigid, intense programs too advanced for their development. Young children need to develop positive feelings about their reading and writing skills through a supportive environment. Children should be active participants and be immersed in a wide range of interesting and enjoyable listening, talking, writing, and reading experiences.
Language development in middle and late childhood	Vocabulary and grammar	In middle and late childhood, children become more analytical and logical in their approach to words and grammar.
	Reading	In the history of learning to read, three techniques dominate: ABC, whole-word, and phonics. Current strategies often focus on a combination of the whole-word and phonics methods. However, reading is much more than the sum of these approaches. Understanding how reading works requires consideration of information processing.
	Bilingualism	This has become a major issue in our nation's schools, with debate raging over the best way to conduct bilingual education. No negative effects of bilingualism have been found, and bilingual education is often associated with positive outcomes, although causal relations are difficult to establish. Increasingly, researchers are recognizing the complexity of bilingual education.

CONCLUSIONS

Children's language development has some magnificent moments and milestones—from first babbles and words to the development of a sophisticated vocabulary and utterance of complex sentences. Language is a wonderful tool that helps children in their adaptation to the world.

In this chapter, we began by briefly considering how scientists study chimpanzees to determine if they have language, and then we discussed what language is and language's important rule systems—phonology, morphology, syntax, semantics, and pragmatics. Then, we explored language's biological and sociocultural/environmental heritages, the role of cognition in language development, and how language develops in infancy, early childhood, and middle and late childhood. We concluded the chapter by underscoring the importance of live, concrete talk to infants. Don't forget that to obtain a summary of the chapter, again read the two concept tables on pages 309 and 318.

This chapter—language development—concludes our study of Section Three in the book. In Section Four we turn our attention to the nature of children's socioemotional development and the self, beginning with chapter 11, Attachment, Temperament, and Emotional Development.

KEY TERMS

infinite generativity An individual's ability to generate an infinite number of meaningful sentences using a finite set of words and rules, which makes language a highly creative enterprise. (299)

displacement The use of language to communicate information about another place and time. (299)

language A system of symbols and sequence of words, used to communicate with others, that involves infinite generativity, displacement, and rule systems. (299)

phonology The study of a language's sound system. (299)

morphology The rules for combining morphemes; a morpheme is the smallest string of sounds that gives meaning to what we say and hear. (299)

syntax The way words are combined to form acceptable phrases and sentences. (300)

grammar The formal description of syntactical rules. (300)

surface structure The order of words in a sentence. (300)

deep structure The syntactic relation among words in a sentence. (300)

semantics The meaning of words and sentences. (301)

pragmatics The use of appropriate conversation. (301)

Language Acquisition Device (LAD) A biological prewiring that enables children to detect certain language categories, such as phonology, syntax, and semantics. LAD is an innate grammatical ability that underlies all human languages. (302)

aphasia A language disorder, resulting from brain damage, that involves a loss of the ability to articulate ideas in any form. (302)

Broca's area The area of the left frontal lobe of the brain that directs the muscle movement involved in speech production. (302)

Wernicke's area An area of the brain's left hemisphere involved in language comprehension. (302)

Language Acquisition Support System (LASS) Bruner's concept that describes the behaviors of a language-skilled individual in structuring and supporting a child's development of language. (304)

motherese The way mothers and other adults often talk to babies at a higher-than-normal frequency and greater-than-normal pitch and with simple words and sentences. (304)

recasting Phrasing the same or a similar meaning of a sentence in a different way, perhaps turning it into a question. (304)

echoing Repeating what someone says, especially if it is an incomplete phrase or sentence. (305)

expanding Restating what someone has said in a linguistically sophisticated form. (305)

labeling Identifying the names of objects. (305)

holophrase hypothesis The theory that a single word is used to imply a complete sentence; it is characteristic of an infant's first words. (310)

overextension Children's tendency to misuse words by extending one word's meaning to include objects that are not related to or are

inappropriate for the word's meaning. (310)

underextension Children's tendency to fail to use a noun to name a relevant event or object. (310)

telegraphic speech The use of short, precise words to communicate; it is characteristic of young children's two-word utterances. (310)

mean length of utterance (MLU) An index of language development based on the number of words per sentence a child produces in a sample of about 50 to 100 sentences. (310)

literacy The ability to read and write. (314)

ABC method A learning-to-read technique that emphasizes

memorizing the names and letters of the alphabet. (315)

whole-word method A learning-to-read technique that emphasizes learning direct associations between whole words and their meanings. (315)

phonics method A learning-to-read technique that emphasizes the sounds that letters make when in words (such sounds can differ from the names of the letters, as when the sound of the letter *c* is not found in *cat*). (315)

bilingual education Programs for students with limited proficiency in English that instruct students in their own language part of the time while they learn English. (315)

SUGGESTED READINGS

Bloome, D. (Ed.). (1989). *Classrooms and literacy.* Norwood, NJ: Ablex. This book includes extensive discussion of how education should be improved to increase the literacy of children. A number of experts discuss programs to improve children's reading and writing skills.

Bruner, J. (1983). *Child talk.* New York: W. W. Norton. This is a fascinating view of children's language development by one of the leading cognitive theorists.

Curtiss, S. (1977). *Genie.* New York: Academic Press. Susan Curtiss tells the remarkable story of Genie, a

modern-day wild child and her ordeal of trying to acquire language.

Hakuta, K., & Garcia, E. E. (1989). Bilingualism and education. *American Psychologist, 44,* 374–379. An up-to-date review of research and policy on bilingual education is provided.

Socioemotional Development and the Self

The thoughts of youth are I thoughts.
—Henry Wadsworth

As children develop, they need the meeting eyes of love. They split the universe into two halves: "me" and "not me." They juggle the need to curb their own will with becoming what they can will freely. They also want to fly but discover that first they have to learn to stand and walk and climb and dance. As they become adolescents, they try on one face after another trying to find a face of their own. In Section Four you will read four chapters: Attachment, Temperament, and Emotional Development (11), The Self and Identity (12), Gender (13), and Moral Development (14).

Mother and Child, Diego Rivera (Detail)

Attachment, Temperament, and Emotional Development

*Blossoms are scattered by the wind
And the wind cares nothing, but
The blossoms of the heart
No wind can touch.*

—Youshida Kenko

The beast and the bird their common charge attend the mothers nurse it, and the sires defend; the young dismissed, to wander earth or air, their stops the instinct, and there the care. A longer care man's helpless kind demands, that longer care contracts more lasting bonds.

—Alexander Pope

IMAGES OF CHILDREN

The Newborn Opossum, Wildebeest, and Human

The newborns of some species function independently in the world; other species are not so independent. At birth, the opossum is still considered fetal and is capable of finding its way around only in its mother's pouch, where it attaches itself to her nipple and continues to develop. This protective environment is similar to the uterus. By contrast, the newborn wildebeest must run with the herd moments after birth. The behavior often is far more adult than the opossum's, although the wildebeest does have to obtain food through suckling. The maturation of the human infant lies somewhere between these two extremes; much learning and development must take place before the infant can sustain itself (Maccoby, 1980).

Variations in the dependency of newborns of different species. (a) The newborn opossum is fetal, capable of finding its way around only in its mother's pouch, where it attaches itself to her nipple and continues to develop. (b) By contrast, the wildebeest runs with the herd moments after birth. (c) The human newborn's maturation lies somewhere in between that of the opossum and that of the wildebeest.

PREVIEW

Because it cannot sustain itself, the human infant requires extensive care. What kind of care is needed and how does the infant start down the road to social maturity? Much of the interest in infant care focuses on attachment and parent-infant interaction, although the roles of day care and temperament in infant development also are important considerations. Recently, child developmentalists have also shown increased interest in children's emotional development.

ATTACHMENT

A small curly-haired girl named Danielle, age 11 months, begins to whimper. After a few seconds, she begins to wail. The psychologist observing Danielle is conducting a research study on the nature of attachment between infants and their mothers. Subsequently, the mother reenters the room, and Danielle's crying ceases. Quickly, Danielle crawls over to where her mother is seated and reaches out to be held. This scenario is one of the main ways that psychologists study the nature of attachment during infancy.

What Is Attachment?

In everyday language, attachment refers to a relationship between two individuals who feel strongly about each other and do a number of things to continue the relationship. Many pairs of people are attached: relatives, lovers, a teacher and a student. In the language of developmental psychology, though, attachment is often restricted to a relationship between particular social figures and a particular phenomenon that is thought to reflect unique characteristics of the relationship. In this case, the developmental period is infancy, the social figures are the infant and one or more adult caregivers, and the phenomenon is a bond (Bowlby, 1969, 1989). To summarize, **attachment** *is a close emotional bond between the infant and the caregiver.*

There is no shortage of theories about infant attachment. Freud believed that infants become attached to the person or object that provides oral satisfaction; for most infants, this is the mother, since she is most likely to feed the infant.

However, is feeding as important as Freud thought? A classic study by Harry Harlow and Robert Zimmerman (1959) suggests that the answer is no. These researchers evaluated whether feeding or contact comfort was more important to infant attachment. Infant monkeys were removed from their mothers at birth and reared for 6 months by surrogate (substitute) "mothers." As shown in figure 11.1, one of the mothers was made of wire, the other of cloth. Half of the infant monkeys were fed by the wire mother, half by the cloth mother. Periodically, the amount of time the infant monkeys spent with either the wire or the cloth monkey was computed. Regardless of whether they were fed by the wire or the cloth mother, the infant monkeys spent far more time with the cloth

FIGURE 11.1

Harlow's classic "Contact Comfort" study. Regardless of whether they were fed by a wire mother or by a cloth mother, the infant monkeys overwhelmingly preferred to be in contact with the cloth mother, demonstrating the importance of contact comfort in attachment.

mother. This study clearly demonstrated that feeding is not the crucial element in the attachment process and that contact comfort is important.

Most toddlers develop a strong attachment to a favorite soft toy or a particular blanket. Toddlers may carry the toy or blanket with them everywhere they go, just as Linus does in the "Peanuts" cartoon strip, or they may run for the toy or blanket only in moments of crisis, such as after an argument or a fall. By the time they have outgrown the security object, all that may be left is a small fragment of the blanket, or an animal that is hardly recognizable, having had a couple of new faces and all its seams resewn half a dozen times. If parents try to replace the security object with something newer, the toddler will resist. There is nothing abnormal about a toddler carrying around a security blanket. Children know that the blanket or teddy bear is not their mother, and yet they react affectively to these objects and derive comfort from them as if they were their mother. Eventually, they abandon the security object as they grow up and become more sure of themselves.

Might familiarity breed attachment? The famous study by ethologist Konrad Lorenz (1965) suggests that the answer is yes. Remember from our description of this study in chapter 2 that newborn goslings became attached to "father" Lorenz rather than to their mother because he was the first moving object they saw. The time period during which familiarity is important for goslings is the first 36 hours after birth; for human beings, it is more on the order of the first year of life.

Erik Erikson (1968) believes that the first year of life is the key time frame for the development of attachment. Recall his proposal—also discussed in chapter 2—that the first year of life represents the stage of trust versus mistrust. A sense of trust requires a feeling of physical comfort and a minimal amount of fear and apprehension about the future. Trust in infancy sets the stage for a lifelong expectation that the world will be a good and pleasant place to be. Erikson also believes that responsive, sensitive parenting contributes to an infant's sense of trust.

The ethological perspective of British psychiatrist John Bowlby (1969, 1989) also stresses the importance of attachment in the first year of life and the responsiveness of the caregiver. Bowlby believes that an infant and its mother instinctively form an attachment. He argues that the newborn is biologically equipped to elicit the mother's attachment behavior. The baby cries, clings, coos, and smiles. Later, the infant crawls, walks, and follows the mother. The infant's goal is to keep the mother nearby. Research on attachment supports Bowlby's view that, at about 6 to 7 months of age, the infant's attachment to the caregiver intensifies (Sroufe, 1985).

Individual Differences

Although attachment to a caregiver intensifies midway through the first year, isn't it likely that some babies have a more positive attachment experience than others? Mary Ainsworth (1979) thinks so and says that, in **secure attachment,** *infants use the caregiver, usually the mother, as a secure base from which to explore the environment. Ainsworth believes that secure attachment in the first year of life provides an important foundation for psychological development later in life.* The caregiver's sensitivity to the infant's signals increases secure attachment. The securely attached infant moves freely away from the mother but processes her location through periodic glances. The securely attached infant responds positively to being picked up by others and, when put back down, freely moves away to play. An insecurely attached infant, by contrast, avoids the mother or is ambivalent toward her, fears strangers, and is upset by minor, everyday separations.

A child forsaken, waking suddenly,
Whose gaze affeard on all things round doth rove,
And seeth only that it cannot see
The meeting eyes of love.

—George Eliot

Ainsworth believes that insecurely attached infants can be classified as either anxious-avoidant or anxious-resistant, making three main attachment categories: secure (type B), anxious-avoidant (type A), and anxious-resistant (type C). **Type B babies** *use the caregiver as a secure base from which to explore the environment.* **Type A babies** *exhibit insecurity by avoiding the mother (for example, ignoring her, averting her gaze, and failing to seek proximity).* **Type C babies** *exhibit insecurity by resisting the mother (for example, clinging to her but at the same time fighting against the closeness, perhaps by kicking and pushing away).*

Why are some infants securely attached and others insecurely attached? Following Bowlby's lead, Ainsworth believes that attachment security depends on how sensitive and responsive a caregiver is to an infant's signals. For example, infants who are securely attached are more likely to have mothers who are more sensitive, accepting, and expressive of affection toward them than those who are insecurely attached (Pederson & others, 1989).

If early attachment to a caregiver is important, it should relate to a child's social behavior later in development. Research by Alan Sroufe (1985; Hiester, Carlson, & Sroufe, 1993) documents this connection. In one investigation, infants who were securely attached to their mothers early in infancy were less frustrated and happier at 2 years of age than their insecurely attached counterparts (Matas, Arend, & Sroufe, 1978). In another longitudinal investigation, securely attached infants were more socially competent and had better grades in the third grade (Egeland, 1989). Linkages between secure attachment and many other aspects of children's competence have been found (Gruys, 1993).

Attachment, Temperament, and the Wider Social World

Not all developmentalists believe that a secure attachment in infancy is the only path to competence in life. Indeed, some developmentalists believe that too much emphasis is placed on the importance of the attachment bond in infancy. Jerome Kagan (1987, 1989), for example, believes that infants are highly resilient and adaptive; he argues that they are evolutionarily equipped to stay on a positive developmental course even in the face of wide variations in parenting. Kagan and others stress that genetic and temperament characteristics play more important roles in a child's social competence than the attachment theorists, such as Bowlby, Ainsworth, and Sroufe, are willing to acknowledge (Calkins & Fox, 1992; DiBiase, 1993; Fish, 1989; Fox & others, 1989). For example, infants may have inherited a low tolerance for stress; this, rather than an insecure attachment bond, may be responsible for their inability to get along with peers.

Another criticism of attachment theory is that it ignores the diversity of socializing agents and contexts that exist in an infant's world (Thompson, 1991). In some cultures, infants show attachments to many people. In the Hausa culture in Nigeria, both grandmothers and siblings provide a significant amount of care to infants (Super, 1980). Infants in agricultural societies tend to form attachments to older siblings who are assigned a

(a)

(b)

The attachment theorists argue that early experience plays an important role in the child's social behavior later in development. (a) Secure attachment to the mother in infancy was related to (b) the preschool child's social competence as reflected in more happy feelings and less frustration in one investigation.

major responsibility for younger siblings' care. The attachments formed by infants in group care in Israeli kibbutzim provide another challenge to the singular attachment thesis.

Researchers recognize the importance of competent, nurturant caregivers in an infant's development—at issue, though, is whether or not secure attachment, especially to a single caregiver, is critical.

Fathers as Caregivers of Infants

Can fathers take care of infants as competently as mothers can? Observations of fathers and their infants suggest that fathers have the ability to act sensitively and responsively with their infants (Parke & Sawin, 1980). Probably the strongest evidence of the plasticity of male caregiving abilities is derived from information about male primates who are notoriously low in their interest in offspring but are forced to live with infants whose female caregivers are absent. Under these circumstances, the adult male competently rears the infants. Remember, however, that, although fathers can be active, nurturant, involved caregivers with their infants, most of the time they choose not to follow this pattern.

Do fathers behave differently toward infants than mothers do? Whereas maternal interactions usually center around child-care activities—feeding, changing diapers, bathing—paternal interactions are more likely to include play. Fathers engage in more rough-and-tumble play, bouncing the infant, throwing him up in the air, tickling him, and so on (Lamb, 1986). Mothers do play with infants, but their play is less physical and arousing than that of fathers.

In stressful circumstances, do infants prefer their mother or father? In one investigation, twenty 12-month-olds were observed interacting with their parents (Lamb, 1977). With both parents present, the infants preferred neither their mother nor their father. The same was true when the infants were alone with the mother or the father. However, the entrance of a stranger, combined with boredom and fatigue, produced a shift in the infants' social behavior toward the mother. In stressful circumstances, then, infants show a stronger attachment to the mother.

In the Hausa culture, older siblings provide a significant amount of caregiving to their younger siblings. In such cultures, younger siblings often form strong attachments to older siblings.

Might the nature of parent-infant interaction be different in families that adopt nontraditional gender roles? This question was investigated by Michael Lamb and his colleagues (1982). They studied Swedish families in which the fathers were the primary caregivers of their firstborn, 8-month-old infants. The mothers were working full time. In all observations,

SOCIOCULTURAL WORLDS OF CHILDREN 11.1

Child–Care Policy Around the World

Sheila Kamerman (1989) recently surveyed the nature of child-care policies around the world with special attention given to European countries. Maternity and paternity policies for working parents include paid, job-protected leaves, which are sometimes supplemented by additional unpaid, job-protected leaves. Child-care policy packages also often include full health insurance. An effective child-care policy is designed to get an infant off to a competent start in life and to protect maternal health while maintaining income. More than a hundred countries around the world have such child-care policies, including all of Europe, Canada, Israel, and many developing countries (Kamerman & Kahn, 1988). Infants are assured of at least 2 to 3 months of maternal/paternal care, and in most European countries 5 to 6 months.

The maternity policy as now implemented in several countries involves a paid maternity leave that begins 2 to 6 weeks prior to expected childbirth and lasts from 8 to 20 or even 24 weeks after birth. This traditional maternal policy stems from an effort to protect the health of pregnant working women, new mothers, and their infants. Only since the 1960s has the maternity policy's link with employment become strong. A second child-care policy emphasizes the importance of parenting and recognizes the potential of fathers as well as mothers to care for their infants. In Sweden a parent insurance benefit provides protection to the new mother before birth and for 6 to 12 weeks after birth but then allows the father to participate in the postchildbirth leave. Approximately one-fourth of Swedish fathers take at least part of the postchildbirth leave, in addition to the two weeks of paid leave all fathers are entitled to at the time of childbirth. In a typical pattern in Sweden, the working mother might take off 3 months, after which she and her husband might share child care between them, each working half-time for 6 months. In addition, Swedish parents have the option of taking an unpaid but fully protected job leave until their child is 18 months old and working a 6-hour day (without a reduction in pay) from the end of the parental leave until their child is 8 years old. Table 11.A outlines the paid maternity/paternity leave provisions in various Western countries.

In sum, almost all the industrialized countries have recognized the importance of developing maternity/paternity policies that allow working parents some time off after childbirth to physically recover, to adapt to parenting, and to improve the well-being of the infant. These policies are designed to let parents take maternity/paternity leave without losing employment or income.

---

the mothers were more likely to discipline, hold, soothe, kiss, and talk to the infants than were the fathers. These mothers and fathers dealt with their infants differently, along the lines of American fathers and mothers following traditional gender roles. Having fathers assume the primary caregiving role did not seem to alter substantially the way they interacted with their infants. This may be because of biological reasons or because of deeply ingrained socialization patterns in cultures.

In Sweden, mothers or fathers are given paid maternity or paternity leave for up to 9 months. Sweden and many other European countries have well-developed child-care policies. To learn about these policies, turn to Sociocultural Worlds of Children 11.1. In Sweden, day care for infants under 1 year of age is usually not a major concern because one parent is on paid leave for child care. As we will see, since the United States does not have a policy of paid leave for child care, day care in the United States has become a major national concern.

Day Care

Each weekday at 8:00 A.M., Ellen Smith takes her 1-year-old daughter Tanya to the day-care center at Brookhaven College in Dallas. Then Mrs. Smith goes to work and returns in the afternoon to take Tanya home. After 3 years, Mrs. Smith reports that her daughter is adventuresome and interacts confidently with peers and adults. Mrs. Smith believes that day care has been a wonderful way to raise Tanya.

In Los Angeles, however, day care has been a series of horror stories for Barbara Jones. After 2 years of unpleasant experiences with sitters, day-care centers, and day-care homes, Mrs. Jones has quit her job as a successful real estate agent to stay home and take care of her 2½-year-old daughter, Gretchen. "I didn't want to sacrifice my baby for my job," said Mrs. Jones, who was unable to find good substitute care in day-care homes. When she put Gretchen into a day-care center, she said that she felt her daughter was being treated like a piece of merchandise—dropped off and picked up.

TABLE 11.A

Paid Maternity/Paternity Leave Provisions in Various Western Countries

Country	Date	Duration of Paid Leave	Available to Fathers (Y = Yes)	Supplementary Unpaid or Paid Parental Leave
Benefit Level at 100% of Earnings[a]				
Norway	1984	4 months	Y	Y
Austria	1987	16 weeks		10 more months, at lower level[b]
Portugal	1984	3 months		Y
Netherlands	1984	12 weeks[c]		
Benefit Level at 90% of Earnings				
Sweden	1987	9 months plus 3 months at flat rate	Y	Up to 18 months; 6-hour work day; up to 8 years
Denmark	1987	24 weeks	Y	Y
France	1987	16 weeks[c]		Up to 2 years
United Kingdom	1987	6 weeks + 12 weeks at flat rate		Maternity leave
Benefit Level at 80% of Earnings				
Finland	1987	11 months	Y	Y
Italy	1984	5 months[d]		Y
Belgium	1984	14 weeks		
Ireland	1982	14 weeks		
Benefit Level at 75% of Earnings				
Spain	1982	14 weeks		
Israel	1984	12 weeks		
Canada	1984	17 weeks, 15 paid		
Benefit Level at 50% of Earnings				
Greece	1982	12 weeks		

[a]Up to maximum covered under Social Security.

[b]Plus 2 years for low-income single mothers if they cannot find child care.

[c]6 weeks must be taken before expected birth; in other countries this time is voluntary.

[d]100% paid for first 4 weeks; 2 months' leave before birth mandated.

From S. B. Kamerman, "Child Care, Women, Work, and the Family: An International Overview of Child Care Services and Related Policies" in J. S. Lande, et al., *Caring for Children: Challenge to America.* Copyright © 1989 Lawrence Erlbaum Associates, Hillsdale, NJ.

Many parents worry whether day care will adversely affect their children. They fear that day care will reduce their infants' emotional attachment to them, retard the infants' cognitive development, fail to teach them how to control anger, and allow them to be unduly influenced by their peers. How extensive is day care? Are the worries of these parents justified?

In the 1990s, far more young children are in day care than at any other time in history; about 2 million children currently receive formal, licensed day care, and more than 5 million children attend kindergarten. Also, uncounted millions of children are cared for by unlicensed baby-sitters. Day care clearly has become a basic need of the American family (Caldwell, 1991; Phillips, 1992).

The type of day care that young children receive varies extensively. Many day-care centers house large groups of children and have elaborate facilities. Some are commercial operations, others are nonprofit centers run by churches, civic groups, and employers. Child care is frequently provided in private homes, at times by child-care professionals, at others by mothers who want to earn extra money.

The quality of care children experience in day care varies extensively. Some caregivers have no training, others extensive training; some day-care centers have a low caregiver-child ratio, others have a high caregiver-child ratio. Some experts have recently argued that the quality of day care most children receive in the United States is poor. Infant researcher Jay Belsky (1989, 1992) not only believes that the quality of day care children experience is generally poor, but he also believes this translates into negative developmental outcomes for children. Belsky concludes that extensive day-care experience during the first 12 months of life—as typically experienced in the United States—is associated with insecure attachment as well as increased aggression, noncompliance, and possibly social withdrawal during the preschool and early elementary school years.

Provision of day care in most developing countries has improved, but this often has been in a form that denies access to the poorest children. In some locations in India, mobile day-care centers have provided intensive integrated child services to young children in slum settlements within large cities and rural villages.

One study supports Belsky's beliefs (Vandell & Corasinti, 1988). Extensive day care in the first year of life was associated with long-term negative outcomes. In contrast to children who began full-time day care later, children who began full-time day care (defined as more than 30 hours per week) as infants were rated by parents and teachers as being less compliant and as having poorer peer relations. In the first grade, they received lower grades and had poor work habits by comparison.

Belsky's conclusions about day care are controversial. Other respected researchers have arrived at a different conclusion; their review of the day-care research suggests no ill effects of day care (Anderson, 1992; Broberg, Hwang, & Chase, 1993; Clarke-Stewart, 1989, 1992; Field, in press; Scarr, 1984, 1992; Scarr, Lande, & McCartney, 1989).

What can we conclude? Does day care have adverse effects on children's development? Trying to combine the results into an overall conclusion about day-care effects is a problem because of the different types of day care children experience and the different measures used to assess outcome (Park & Honing, 1991). Belsky's analysis does suggest that parents should be very careful about the quality of day care they select for their infants, especially those 1 year of age or less. Even Belsky agrees, though, that day care itself is not the culprit; rather it is the quality of day care that is problematic in this country. Belsky acknowledges that no evidence exists to show that children in high-quality day care are at risk in any way (Belsky, 1992; Doll, 1988).

What constitutes a high-quality day-care program for infants? The demonstration program developed by Jerome Kagan and his colleagues (1978) at Harvard University is exemplary. The day-care center included a pediatrician, a nonteaching director, and an infant-teacher ratio of 3 to 1. Teachers' aides assisted at the center. The teachers and aides were trained to smile frequently, to talk with the infants, and to provide them with a safe environment that included many stimulating toys. No adverse effects of day care were observed in this project. More information about what to look for in a quality day-care center is presented in Explorations in Child Development 11.1. Using such criteria, Carolee Howes (1988) discovered that children who entered low-quality child care as infants were least likely to be socially competent in early childhood (less compliant, less self-controlled, less task-oriented, more hostile, and having more problems in peer interaction).

Critical Thinking

If your own children were attending day care, which of the criteria listed in Explorations in Child Development 11.1 would you feel were most important? Are there criteria not listed that you believe should be considered?

Edward Zigler (1987) proposed a solution to the day-care needs of families. Zigler says that we should not think of school as an institution, but rather as a building, one that is owned by tax-paying parents who need day care for their children. Part of the school building would be for teaching and part would be for child care and supervision. This system could provide parents with competent developmental child-care services. Zigler believes it should be available to every child over the age of 3. He does not think children should start formal schooling at age 3; they would be in the schools only for day care. At the age of 5, children would start kindergarten, but only for half days. If the child has a parent at home, the child would spend the remainder of the day at home. If the parents are working, the child would spend the second half of the day in the day-care part of the school. For children aged 6 to 12, after-school and vacation care would be available to those who need it.

Zigler does not believe that teachers should provide day care; they are trained as educators and are too expensive. What we need, he says, is a child development associate, someone who is trained to work with children, someone we can afford to pay. This is a large vision, one that involves a structural change in society and a new face for our school system. As Zigler remembers, between the fall of 1964 and the summer of 1965, we managed to put 560,000 children into Head Start programs, an educational program for impoverished children. He believes we can do the same thing with day care (Trotter, 1987). Despite the efforts of Zigler and others, the child-care bills currently being introduced in Congress do not adequately address the quality of child care and the low pay of child-care workers (DeAngelis, 1990).

EXPLORATIONS IN CHILD DEVELOPMENT 11.1

What Is Quality Day Care?

What constitutes quality child care? The following recommendations were made by the National Association for the Education of Young Children (1986). They are based on a consensus arrived at by experts in early childhood education and child development. It is especially important to meet the adults who will care for their child. They are responsible for every aspect of the program's operation.

1. The adult caregivers.
   - The adults should enjoy and understand how infants and young children grow.
   - There should be enough adults to work with a group and to care for the individual needs of children. More specifically, there should be no more than four infants for each adult caregiver, no more than eight 2- to 3-year-old children for each caregiver, and no more than ten 4- to 5-year-old children for each adult caregiver.
   - Caregivers should observe and record each child's progress and development.
2. The program activities and equipment.
   - The environment should foster the growth and development of young children working and playing together.
   - A good center should provide appropriate and sufficient equipment and play materials and make them readily available.
   - Infants and children should be helped to increase their language skills and to expand their understanding of the world.
3. The relation of staff to families and the community.
   - A good program should consider and support the needs of the entire family. Parents should be

Quality day care includes having adult caregivers who enjoy being with infants and young children. The adult caregivers also should be knowledgeable about how infants and young children grow.

welcome to observe, discuss policies, make suggestions, and work in the activities of the center.
   - The staff in a good center should be aware of and contribute to community resources. The staff should share information about community recreational and learning opportunities with families.
4. The facility and the program should be designed to meet the varied demands of infants and young children, their families, and the staff.
   - The health of children, staff, and parents should be protected and promoted. The staff should be alert to the health of each child.
   - The facility should be safe for children and adults.
   - The environment should be spacious enough to accommodate a variety of activities and equipment. More specifically, there should be a minimum of 35 square feet of usable playroom floor space indoors per child and 75 square feet of play space outdoors per child.

We have all the knowledge necessary to provide absolutely first-rate child care in the United States. What is missing is the commitment and the will.

—Edward Zigler, *1987*

In our discussion of attachment, we learned that some developmentalists believe temperament plays a more important role in infant development than many attachment enthusiasts. Next, we take a closer look at temperament's effects on children's development.

TEMPERAMENT

Temperament *is an individual's behavioral style and characteristic way of responding.* Developmentalists are especially interested in the temperament of infants (Parker & Barrett, 1992). Some infants are extremely active, moving their arms, legs, and mouths incessantly. Others are tranquil. Some children explore their environment eagerly for great lengths of time. Others do not. Some infants respond warmly to people. Others fuss and fret. All of these behavioral styles represent a person's temperament (Carson & Bittner, 1993; Goldsmith & others, 1991; Gottfried & Lussier, 1993; Mehegany, 1992; Rothbart & Ahadi, 1993).

A widely debated issue in temperament research is just what the key dimensions of temperament are. Psychiatrists Alexander Chess and Stella Thomas (Chess & Thomas, 1977; Thomas & Chess, 1987, 1991) believe there are three basic types, or clusters, of temperament—easy, difficult, and slow-to-warm-up.

1. An **easy child** *is generally in a positive mood, quickly establishes regular routines in infancy, and adapts easily to new experiences.*
2. A **difficult child** *tends to react negatively and cry frequently, engages in irregular daily routines, and is slow to accept new experiences.*
3. A **slow-to-warm-up child** *has a low activity level, is somewhat negative, shows low adaptability, and displays a low intensity of mood.*

Critical Thinking

Consider your own temperament. Does it fit into one of the clusters described by Chess and Thomas? How stable has your temperament been in the course of your development? What factors contributed to this stability or lack of stability?

Different dimensions make up these three basic clusters of temperament. The three basic clusters and their dimensions are shown in table 11.1. In their longitudinal investigation, Chess and Thomas found that 40 percent of the children they studied could be classified as "easy," 10 percent as "difficult," and 15 percent as "slow-to-warm-up." Researchers have found that these three basic clusters of temperament are moderately stable across the childhood years.

Other researchers suggest that temperament is composed of different basic components. Personality psychologist Arnold Buss and behavior geneticist Robert Plomin (1984, 1987) believe that infants' temperament falls into three basic categories: emotionality, sociability, and activity level.

1. **Emotionality** *is the tendency to be distressed.* It reflects the arousal of a person's sympathetic nervous system. During infancy, distress develops into two separate emotional responses: fear and anger. Fearful infants try to escape something that is unpleasant; angry ones protest it. Buss and Plomin argue that children are labeled "easy" or "difficult" on the basis of their emotionality.
2. **Sociability** *is the tendency to prefer the company of others to being alone.* It matches a tendency to respond warmly to others.
3. **Activity level** *involves tempo and vigor of movement.* Some children walk fast, are attracted to high-energy games, and jump or bounce around a lot; others are more placid.

Some experts on temperament believe there should be even further differentiation of certain domains of temperament (Eisenberg, 1992). As an example, in the general domain of social withdrawal, researchers are beginning to distinguish between shyness (inhibited and awkward behavior with strangers or acquaintances, accompanied by feelings of tension and a desire to escape), introversion (a nonfearful preference for not affiliating with others), sociability (a preference for affiliating with others), and extroversion (the tendency to seek social interaction as a source of stimulation rather than true social interest in others).

A number of scholars, including Chess and Thomas, conceive of temperament as a stable characteristic of newborns that comes to be shaped and modified by the child's later experiences (Thomas & Chess, 1987; Goldsmith, 1988). This raises the question of heredity's role in temperament. Twin and adoption studies have been conducted to answer this question (Braungart & others, 1992; Emde & others, 1992; Plomin, 1989; Matheny, Dolan, & Wilson, 1976; Robinson & others, 1992). The researchers find a heritability index in the range of .50 to .60, suggesting a moderate influence of heredity on temperament. However, the strength of the association usually declines as infants become older (Goldsmith & Gottesman, 1981). This finding supports the belief that temperament becomes more malleable with experience. Alternatively, it may be that, as a child becomes older, behavior indicators of temperament are more difficult to spot. To read about ethnic differences in temperament that are likely to be biologically based, turn to Sociocultural Worlds of Children 11.2.

The consistency of temperament depends, in part, on the "match" or "fit" between the child's nature and the parent's nature (Nitz & Lerner, 1991; Plomin & Thompson, 1987; Rothbart, 1988). Imagine a high-strung parent with a child who is difficult and sometimes slow to respond to the parent's affection. The parent may begin to feel angry or rejected. A father who does not need much face-to-face social interaction

TABLE 11.1

Chess and Thomas' Dimensions and the Basic Clusters of Temperament

Temperament Dimension	Description	Temperament Cluster		
		Easy Child	Difficult Child	Slow-to-Warm-Up Child
Rhythmicity	Regularity of eating, sleeping, toileting	Regular	Irregular	
Activity level	Degree of energy movement		High	Low
Approach-withdrawal	Ease of approaching new people and situations	Positive	Negative	Negative
Adaptability	Ease of tolerating change in routine plans	Positive	Negative	Negative
Sensory threshold	Amount of stimulation required for responding			
Predominant quality of mood	Degree of positive or negative affect	Positive	Negative	
Intensity of mood expression	Degree of affect when pleased, displeased, happy, sad	Low to moderate	High	Low
Distractibility/attention span/persistence	Ease of being distracted			

This table identifies those dimensions that were critical in spotting a basic cluster of temperament and the level of responsiveness for each critical feature. A blank space indicates that the dimension was not strongly related to a basic cluster of temperament.

will find it easy to manage a similarly introverted baby, but he may not be able to provide an extraverted baby with sufficient stimulation. Parents influence infants, but infants also influence parents. Parents may withdraw from difficult children, or they may become critical and punish them; these responses may make the difficult child even more difficult. A more easygoing parent may have a calming effect on a difficult child or may continue to show affection even when the child withdraws or is hostile, eventually encouraging more competent behavior.

In sum, heredity does seem to influence temperament. However, the degree of influence depends on parents' responsiveness to their children and on other environmental childhood experiences.

At this point we have discussed a number of ideas about attachment, fathers as caregivers of infants, day care, and temperament. A summary of these ideas is presented in Concept Table 11.1. Next, we turn our attention to the study of children's emotional development.

EMOTIONAL DEVELOPMENT

Children's worlds are filled with emotions and emotional experiences. What is the nature of children's emotions? How do

emotions develop in infancy? Why do some children become depressed, and how are children affected when their parents are depressed? What causes children's stress, and how can they cope more effectively with such stress?

The Nature of Children's Emotions

What is an emotion? What are the functions of emotion in children? What is the role of emotion in parent-infant relationships?

Defining Emotion

Defining emotion is difficult because it is not easy to tell when a child or an adult is in an emotional state. Are children in an emotional state when their hearts beat fast, their palms sweat, and their stomachs churn? Or are they in an emotional state when they smile or grimace? The body and face play important roles in understanding children's emotion, although psychologists debate how important each is in determining whether a child is in an emotional state (Harris, 1989; Izard, 1993). For our purposes, we will define **emotion** as *feeling or affect that involves a mixture of physiological arousal (fast heart beat, for example) and overt behavior (smile or grimace, for example).*

**SOCIOCULTURAL WORLDS
OF CHILDREN 11.2**

Imperturbability in European American, Chinese American, and Navaho Indian Newborns

Do newborns from different cultures have different biological predispositions of temperament? In one investigation, researchers observed 24 Chinese American and 24 European American 2-day-old babies (Freedman & Freedman, 1969). The Chinese American infants had a less rapid buildup to an excited state of arousal, showed less facial and body reddening, and showed fewer state changes. When placed in the prone po-

sition, the Chinese Americans tended to remain inactive, face flat against the bed. By contrast, the European Americans were more likely to lift their head or turn their face to one side. The Chinese American babies were easier to control when crying and were able to stop by themselves without being consoled. The researchers suggested that these behaviors reflect the temperament of "imperturbability," which affects the way adults care for infants. Recent observations of 4-month-old Chinese infants born in Beijing confirm the earlier findings that Chinese infants are less aroused than white infants (Kagan & others, 1992). Further comparison of this temperament indicated that newborn Navaho Indians are more perturbable than newborn Chinese Americans (Freedman, 1971).

Researchers have found that Chinese American newborns are calmer than European American and Navaho Indian newborns.

When we think about children's emotions, a few dramatic feelings, such as rage, fear, and glorious joy, usually spring to mind. But emotions can be subtle as well—the feeling a mother has when she holds her baby, the mild irritation of boredom, and the uneasiness of being in a new situation.

While psychologists have classified emotions in many different ways, one characteristic of most all classifications is whether an emotion is positive or negative (Pennebaker, 1992). **Positive affectivity (PA)** *refers to the range of positive emotions from high energy, enthusiasm, and excitement, to calm, quiet, and withdrawn. Joy, happiness, and laughter involve positive affectivity.* **Negative affectivity (NA)** *refers to emotions that are negatively toned, such as anxiety, anger, guilt, and sadness.* PA and NA are independent dimensions in that a child can be high along both dimensions at the same time (for example, in a high energy state and enthusiastic yet angry).

Functions of Emotions in Children's Development

The three main functions of emotions are: adaptation and survival, regulation, and communication (Bretherton & others, 1986).

With regard to adaptation and survival, various fears—such as fear of the dark and fear of sudden changes in the environment—are adaptive because there are clear links between such events and possible dangers. With regard to regulation, emotions influence the information children select from the perceptual world and the behaviors they display. For example, children who are feeling happy are more likely to attend to what they are studying and learning than children who are feeling sad. With regard to communication, children use emotions to inform others about their feelings and needs. Children who smile are likely telling others that they are feeling pleasant; children who cry are often communicating that something is unpleasant for them.

CONCEPT TABLE 11.1

Attachment, Fathers, Day Care, and Temperament

Concept	Processes/Related Ideas	Characteristics/Description
Attachment	What is attachment?	Attachment is a relationship between two people in which each person feels strongly about the other and does a number of things to ensure the relationship's continuation. In infancy, attachment refers to the bond between caregiver and infant. Feeding is not the critical element in attachment, although contact comfort, familiarity, and trust are important. Bowlby's ethological theory stresses that the mother and infant instinctively trigger attachment. Attachment to the caregiver intensifies at about 6 to 7 months.
	Individual differences	Ainsworth believes that individual differences in attachment can be classified into secure, avoidant, and resistant categories. Ainsworth believes that securely attached babies have sensitive and responsive caregivers. In some investigations, secure attachment is related to social competence later in childhood.
	Attachment, temperament, and the wider social world	Some developmentalists believe that too much emphasis is placed on the role of attachment; they believe that genetics and temperament, on the one hand, and the diversity of social agents and contexts, on the other, deserve more credit.
Fathers as caregivers of infants	Nature of father-infant interaction	Fathers have increased their interaction with their children, but they still lag far behind mothers, even when mothers are employed. Fathers can act sensitively to the infant's signals, but most of the time they do not. The mother's role in the infant's development is primarily caregiving. That of the father involves playful interaction. Infants generally prefer their mother under stressful circumstances. Even in nontraditional families, as when the father is the main caregiver, the behaviors of mothers and fathers follow traditional gender lines.
Day care	Its nature	Day care has become a basic need of the American family; more children are in day care today than at any other time in history.
	Quality of care and effects on development	The quality of day care is uneven. Belsky concluded that most day care is inadequate and that extensive day care in the first 12 months of an infant's life has negative developmental outcomes. Other experts disagree with Belsky. Day care remains a controversial topic. Quality day care can be achieved and it seems to have few adverse effects on children.
Temperament	Its nature	Temperament refers to behavioral style; temperament has been studied extensively. Chess and Thomas described three temperamental clusters—"easy," "difficult," and "slow-to-warm-up." Temperament is influenced strongly by biological factors in early infancy but becomes more malleable with experience. An important consideration is the fit of the infant's temperament with the parents' temperament.

Affect in Parent–Child Relationships

Emotions are the first language that parents and infants communicate with before the infant acquires speech (Maccoby, 1992). Infants react to their parents' facial expressions and tones of voice. In return, parents "read" what the infants are trying to communicate, responding appropriately when their infants are either distressed or happy.

The initial aspects of infant attachment to parents is based on affectively toned interchanges, as when an infant cries and the caregiver sensitively responds to the infant (Berlin, 1993; Hommerding & Kriger, 1993). By the end of the first year, a mother's facial expression—either smiley or fearful—influences whether an infant will explore an unfamiliar environment. And when children hear their parents quarreling, children often react with distressed facial expressions and inhibited play (Cummings, 1987). Exceptionally well-functioning families often include humor in their interactions, sometimes making each other laugh and developing light, pleasant mood states to defuse conflicts. And when a positive mood has been induced in the child, the child is more likely to comply with a parent's directions (Lay, Waters, and Park, 1989).

Infant and adult affective communicative capacities make possible coordinated infant-adult interactions (Holt & Fogel, 1993; Tronick, 1989). The face-to-face interactions of even 3-month-old infants and adults are bidirectional (mutually regulated). That is, infants modify their affective displays and behaviors on the basis of their appreciation of their parents' affective displays and behaviors. This coordination has led to characterizations of the mother-infant interaction as reciprocal or synchronous. These terms are attempts to capture the quality of interaction when it is going well.

Emotional Development in Infancy

Infants express some emotions earlier than others. Let's examine the developmental timetable for the expression of emotions, and then explore two important emotionally expressive behaviors in detail—crying and smiling.

Developmental Timetable of Emotions

To determine whether infants are actually expressing a particular emotion, we have to have some system for measuring emotions. Carroll Izard (1982) developed such a system. The **Maximally Discriminative Facial Movement Coding System,** *called MAX for short, is Izard's system of coding infants' facial expressions related to emotion. Using MAX, coders watch slow-motion and stop-action videotapes of infants' facial reactions to stimuli.* Among the stimulus conditions are: giving an infant an ice cube, having tape put on the backs of their hands, handing the infant a favorite toy and then taking it away, separating the infant from the mother and then reuniting them, having a stranger approach the infant, restraining the infant's head, placing a ticking clock next to the infant's ear, popping a balloon in front of the infant's face, and giving the infant camphor to sniff, and lemon rind and orange juice to taste. To give just one example of how an emotion is coded, anger is indicated when the

FIGURE 11.2

The developmental course of facial expressions of emotions.

Emotional expression	Approximate time of emergence
Interest, neonatal smile (a sort of half smile that appears spontaneously for no apparent reason),* startled response,* distress,* disgust	Present at birth
Social smile	4 to 6 weeks
Anger, surprise, sadness	3 to 4 months
Fear	5 to 7 months
Shame/shyness	6 to 8 months
Contempt, guilt	2 years

* These expressions are precursors of the social smile and the emotions of surprise and sadness, which appear later. No evidence exists to suggest that they are related to inner feelings when they are observed in the first few weeks of life.

infant's brows are sharply lowered and drawn together, eyes are narrowed or squinted, and mouth is open in an angular, square shape. Based on Izard's classification system, interest, distress, and disgust are present at birth; a social smile appears at about 4 to 6 weeks; anger, surprise, and sadness emerge at about 3 to 4 months; fear is displayed at about 5 to 7 months; shame and shyness are displayed at about 6 to 8 months; and contempt and guilt don't appear until 2 years of age. A summary of the approximate timetable for the emergence of facial expressions of emotions is shown in figure 11.2.

Crying

Crying is the most important mechanism newborns have for communicating with their world (Gustafson, Green, & Kalinowski, 1993; Rosenblith, 1992). This is true for the first cry, which tells the mother and doctor the baby's lungs have filled with air. Cries also may tell physicians or researchers something about the central nervous system.

Babies don't just have one type of cry. They have at least three (Wasz-Hockert & others, 1968; Wolff, 1969). The **basic cry** *is a rhythmic pattern that usually consists of a cry, followed by a briefer silence, then a shorter inspiratory whistle that is somewhat higher pitch than the main cry, then another brief rest before the next cry.* Some infancy experts believe that hunger is one of the conditions that incites the basic cry. The **anger cry** *is a variation of the basic cry. However, in the anger cry more excess air is forced through the vocal cords. The anger cry gets its name from mothers who infer exasperation or rage from it.* The **pain cry,** *which is stimulated by high-intensity stimuli, differs from other types of cries in that there is a sudden appearance of loud crying without preliminary moaning and a long initial cry followed by an extended period of breath holding.*

Most parents, and adults in general, can determine whether an infant's cries signify anger or pain (Barr, Desilets,

& Rortman, 1991; Zeskind, Klein, & Marshall, 1992). Parents also can distinguish the cries of their own baby better than those of a strange baby (Wiesenfeld & others, 1981). There is little consistent evidence to support the idea that mothers or females, but not fathers or males, are innately programmed to respond nurturantly to an infant's crying (Rosenblith, 1992).

To soothe or not to soothe? Should a crying baby be given attention and soothed, or does this spoil the infant? Many years ago the famous behaviorist John Watson (1928) argued that parents spend too much time responding to infant crying. As a consequence, he said, parents are actually rewarding infant crying and increasing its incidence. By contrast, more recently ethnologically oriented infant experts Mary Ainsworth (1979) and John Bowlby (1989) stress that you can't respond too much to infant crying in the first year of life. They believe that the caregiver's quick, comforting response to the infant's cries is an important ingredient in the development of secure attachment. In one of Ainsworth's studies, mothers who responded quickly to their infants when they cried at 3 months of age had infants who cried less later in the first year of life (Bell & Ainsworth, 1972). By contrast, behaviorist Jacob Gewirtz (1977) found that a caregiver's quick, soothing response to crying increased subsequent crying.

Controversy, then, still swirls about the issue of whether parents should respond to an infant's cries. However, many developmentalists increasingly argue that an infant cannot be spoiled in the first year of life, which suggests that parents should quickly soothe a crying infant rather than be unresponsive. In this manner, infants are likely to develop a sense of trust and secure attachment to the caregiver in the first year of life.

Smiling

Smiling is another important communicative affective behavior of the infant. Two types of smiling can be distinguished in infants—one reflexive, the other social. A **reflexive smile** *does not occur in response to external stimuli. It appears during the first month after birth, usually during irregular patterns of sleep, not when the infant is in an alert state.* By contrast, a **social smile** *occurs in response to an external stimulus, which early in development typically is in response to a face.* Social smiling does not occur until 2 to 3 months of age (Emde, Gaensbauer, & Harmon, 1976), although some researchers believe that infants grin in response to voices as early as 3 weeks of age (Sroufe & Waters, 1976). The power of the infant's smiles was appropriately captured by British attachment theorist John Bowlby (1969): "Can we doubt that the more and better an infant smiles the better he is loved and cared for? It is fortunate for their survival that babies are so designed by nature that they beguile and enslave mothers."

> He who binds himself to joy
> Does the winged life destroy;
> But he who kisses the joy as it
> Flies lives in eternity's sun rise.
> —William Blake

Children's Depression and Depressed Parents

A special concern is children who become depressed. We will evaluate some ideas about what causes children to become depressed and then study the growing interest in the effects of depressed parents on children's development.

Children's Depression

Depression is a mood disorder in which the individual is unhappy, demoralized, self-derogatory, and bored. The individual does not feel well, loses stamina easily, often has a poor appetite, is listless, and unmotivated. In childhood, the features of depression are often mixed with a broader array of behaviors than in adulthood. During childhood, aggression, school failure, anxiety, antisocial behavior, and poor peer relations are frequently associated with depression, which makes its diagnosis more difficult (Weiner, 1980). Depression is more likely to occur during adolescence than childhood and is a more pervasive problem for females than males (Lewinsohn & others, 1993; Peterson, Leffert, & Miller, 1993).

Why does depression occur in childhood? Biogenetic, cognitive, and environmental causes have been proposed. Among the views currently being given special attention are: Bowlby's developmental, Beck's cognitive, and Seligman's learned helplessness.

John Bowlby (1969, 1989) believes that insecure attachment, a lack of love and affection in childrearing, or the actual loss of a parent in childhood leads to a negative cognitive schema. The schema that is built up during early experiences causes children to interpret later losses as yet other failures in producing enduring and close positive relationships. From Bowlby's view, early experiences, especially those involving loss, create cognitive schema that are carried forward to influence the way later experiences are interpreted. When these new experiences involve further loss, the loss precipitates depression.

In Aaron Beck's (1973) cognitive view, individuals become depressed because early in their development they acquire cognitive schema that are characterized by self-devaluation and lack of confidence about the future. These habitual negative thoughts magnify and expand a depressed person's negative experiences. Depressed children blame themselves far more than is warranted in Beck's view. Expanding on Beck's cognitive view, developmentalist Nancy Quiggle and her colleagues (1992) presented a social information processing view of children's depression. They argue that depressed children attend to negative cues in their environment and identify the source of negative outcomes as being within themselves.

Yet another theory of depression is **learned helplessness,** *Martin Seligman's view that when individuals are exposed to negative experiences, such as prolonged stress or pain, over which they have no control, they are likely to become depressed* (Seligman, 1975). In a reformulation of the learned helplessness view, depression follows the experience of a negative event when the individual explains the event with negative, self-blaming attributions (Abramson, Metalsky, & Alloy, 1989). This explanatory style results in the expectation that no action will control the outcome of similar events in the future, resulting in helplessness, hopelessness, passivity, and depression.

Depressed Parents

While depression has traditionally been perceived as a problem of the individual, today we believe that this view is limited. Researchers have found an interdependence between depressed persons and their social contexts—this is especially true in the case of parents' depression and children's adjustment (Campbell & others, 1993; Downey & Coyne, 1990; Goodman & others, 1993; Kulcsar, Harbaugh, & Gelfand, 1993; Sameroff & others, 1993). Depression is a highly prevalent disorder—so prevalent it has been called the common cold of mental disorders. It occurs often in the lives of women of child-bearing age—about 8%, a figure that rises to 12% for women who have recently given birth (O'Hara, 1986). As a result, large numbers of children are exposed to depressed parents.

Research on the children of depressed parents clearly documents that depression in parents is associated with problems of adjustment and disorders, especially depression, in their children (Downey & Coyne, 1990; Radke-Yarrow & others, 1992). Depressed mothers show lower rates of behavior and show constricted affect, adopt less-effortful control strategies with their children, and sometimes act hostile and negative toward them as well. In considering the effects of parental depression on children it is important to evaluate the social context of the family (Hammen, 1993). For example, marital discord and stress may precede, precipitate, or co-occur with maternal depression. In such instances, it may be marital turmoil that is the key factor that contributes to children's adjustment problems, not parental depression per se (Gelfand, Teti, & Fox, 1992).

Stress

Stress is a sign of the times. No one really knows whether today's children experience more stress than their predecessors, but it does seem that their stressors have increased. Among the stress-related questions we examine are: What is stress? How do cognitive factors influence stress? What roles do life events and daily hassles play in children's stress? And, how do sociocultural factors influence the stress children experience?

What Is Stress?

Stress is not an easy term to define. Initially the term *stress* was loosely borrowed from physics. Humans, it was thought, are in some ways similar to physical objects such as metals that resist moderate outside forces but lose their resiliency at some point of greater pressure. But unlike metal, children can think and reason; they experience a myriad of social circumstances that make defining stress more complex in psychology than in physics (Hobfoll, 1989). Is stress the threats and challenges that the environment places on us (as when we say, "Sally's world is so stressful, it is overwhelming her")? Is stress our response to such threats and challenges (as when we say, "Bob is not coping well with the problems in his life; he is experiencing a lot of stress and his body is falling apart")? While there is continuing debate on whether stress is the threatening event or the response to those demands, we will define it broadly. **Stress** *is the response of individuals to the circumstances and events (called stressors) that threaten them and tax their coping abilities.*

Cognitive Factors

Most of us think of stress as environmental events that place demands on an individual's life, events such as an approaching test, being in a car wreck, or losing a friend. While there are some common ways children and adults experience stress, not everyone perceives the same events as stressful. For example, one child may perceive an approaching test as threatening, another child may perceive it as challenging. To some degree, then, what is stressful for children depends on how they cognitively appraise and interpret events. This view has been presented most clearly by stress researcher Richard Lazarus (1966, 1990). **Cognitive appraisal** *is Lazarus' term that describes children's interpretations of events in their lives as harmful, threatening, or challenging, and their determination of whether they have the resources to effectively cope with the event.*

In Lazarus' view, events are appraised in two steps: primary appraisal and secondary appraisal. In **primary appraisal,** *children interpret whether an event involves harm or loss that has already occurred, a threat to some future danger, or a challenge to be overcome. Harm* is the child's appraisal of the damage the event has already inflicted. For example, if a child failed a test in school yesterday the harm has already been done. *Threat* is the child's appraisal of potential future damage an event may bring. For example, failing the test may lower the teacher's opinion of the child and increase the probability the child will get a low grade at the end of the year. *Challenge* is the child's appraisal of the potential to overcome the adverse circumstances of an event and ultimately profit from the event. In the case of the child failing a test in school, the child may develop a commitment to never get into that situation again and become a better student.

After children cognitively appraise an event for its harm, threat, or challenge, Lazarus says they subsequently engage in secondary appraisal. In **secondary appraisal,** *children evaluate their resources and determine how effectively they can cope with the event.* This appraisal is called *secondary* because it comes after primary appraisal and depends on the degree to which the event has been appraised as harmful, threatening, or challenging. Coping involves a wide range of potential strategies, skills, and abilities for effectively managing stressful events. In the example of failing the exam, if the child learns that his or her parents will get a tutor to help him or her, then the child likely will be more confident in coping with the stress than if the parents provide no support.

Lazarus believes a child's experience of stress is a balance of primary and secondary appraisal. When harm and threat are high, and challenge and resources are low, stress is likely to be high; when harm and threat are low, and challenge and resources are high, stress is more likely to be moderate or low.

To help buffer the stress in their lives, many ethnic minority groups have developed their own social structures, which include the African American church, Mexican American kin systems, Chinese American family associations, and Native American tribal associations.

Life Events and Daily Hassles

Children can experience a spectrum of stresses, ranging from ordinary to severe. At the ordinary end are experiences that occur in most children's lives and for which there are reasonably well-defined coping patterns. For example, most parents are aware that siblings are jealous of each other and that when one sibling does well at something the other sibling(s) will be jealous. They know how jealousy works and know ways to help children cope with it. More severe stress occurs when children become separated from their parents. Healthy coping patterns for this stressful experience are not as well spelled out. Some children are well cared for; others are ignored when there is a separation caused by divorce, death, illness, or foster placement. Even more severe are the experiences of children who have lived for years in situations of neglect or abuse. Victims of incest also experience severe stress, with few coping guidelines.

> *It's not the large things that send a man to the madhouse. . . . No, it's the continuing series of small tragedies that send a man to the madhouse. . . . Not the death of his love but a shoelace that snaps with no time left.*
>
> —Charles Bukowski

Recently, psychologists have emphasized that life's daily experiences as well as life's major events may be the culprits in stress. Enduring a tense family life and living in poverty do not show up on scales of major life events in children's development, yet the everyday pounding children take from these living conditions can add up to a highly stressful life and eventually psychological disturbance or illness (Compas, 1989; Creasy & others, 1993; Folkman & Lazarus, 1991).

Sociocultural Factors

Among the sociocultural factors involved in stress are acculturative stress and socioeconomic stress, each of which we consider in turn.

Acculturative Stress **Acculturation** *refers to cultural change that results from continuous, first-hand contact between two distinctive cultural groups. Acculturative stress is the negative consequence of acculturation.* Members of ethnic minority groups have historically encountered hostility, prejudice, and lack of effective support during crises, which contributes to alienation, social isolation, and heightened stress (Huang & Gibbs, 1989). As upwardly mobile ethnic minority families have attempted to penetrate all-White neighborhoods, interracial tensions often

Poverty is related to threatening and uncontrollable events in children's lives. Poverty also undermines sources of social support that play a role in buffering the effects of stress.

Social scientist Deborah Belle, shown here interviewing a young girl, has documented how poverty imposes considerable stress on children. Chronic living conditions, such as inadequate housing, dangerous neighborhoods, burdensome responsibilities, and economic uncertainties are potent stressors in the lives of the poor.

mount. Similarly, racial tensions and hostility often emerge among the various ethnic minorities as they each struggle for limited housing and employment opportunities, seeking a fair share of a limited market. Clashes become inevitable as Hispanic family markets spring up in Black urban neighborhoods; as Vietnamese extended families displace Puerto Rican apartment dwellers; as the increasing enrollment of Asian students on college campuses is perceived as a threat to affirmative action policies by other non-White ethnic minority students. While race relations in the United States have historically been conceptualized as Black/White, this is no longer the only combination producing ethnic animosity.

As the number of Hispanics and Asians have increased dramatically, and as Native Americans have crossed the boundaries of their reservations, the visibility of these groups has brought them in contact not only with the mainstream White society, but with one another as well. Depending on the circumstances, this contact has sometimes been harmonious, sometimes antagonistic.

Although the dominant White society has tried on many occasions to enslave or dispossess entire populations, these ethnic minority groups have survived and flourished. In the face of severe stress and oppression, these ethnic minority groups have shown remarkable resilience and adaptation (Phinney, Chavira, & Williamson, 1992; Rick & Foward, 1992; Root, 1992). Confronted with overt or covert attempts at segregation, they have developed their own communities and social structures, which include Black churches, Vietnamese mutual assistance associations, Chinese American family associations, Japanese-language schools, Indian "bands" and tribal associations, and Mexican American kin systems; at the same time they have learned to negotiate with the dominant White culture in America. They essentially have mastered two cultures and have developed impressive competencies and coping strategies for adapting to life in America. The resilience and adaptation

shown by ethnic minority groups can teach us much about coping and survival in the face of overwhelming adversity (Ceballo & Olson, 1993; Jackson, 1992; Kavanaugh & Kennedy, 1992).

Socioeconomic Status   Poverty imposes considerable stress on children and their families (Aber, 1993; Belle, 1990; McLoyd, 1993; Strawn, 1992). Chronic life conditions such as inadequate housing, dangerous neighborhoods, burdensome responsibilities, and economic uncertainties are potent stressors in the lives of the poor. The incidence of poverty is especially pronounced among ethnic minority children and their families (Braham, Rattansi, & Skellington, 1992). For example, Black women heading families face a risk of poverty that is more than 10 times that of White men heading families. Puerto Rican female family heads face a poverty rate that is almost 15 times that found among White male family heads (National Advisory Council on Economic Opportunity, 1980). Many individuals who become poor during their lives remain poor for one or two years. However, Blacks and female family heads are at risk for experiencing persistent poverty. The average poor Black child experiences poverty that will last almost 20 years (Wilson & Neckerman, 1986).

Poverty is related to threatening and uncontrollable events in children's lives (Belle, 1990; Russo, 1990). For example, poor females are more likely to experience crime and violence than middle-class females. Poverty also undermines sources of social support that play a role in buffering the effects of stress. Sometimes just one person can make a difference in children's lives in low-income neighborhoods. To read about one such person—Madeline Cartwright—turn to Sociocultural Worlds of Children 11.3.

At this point we have discussed a number of ideas about emotional development. A summary of these ideas is presented in Concept Table 11.2.

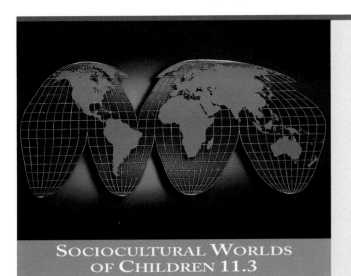

Making a Difference in North Philadelphia: Madeline Cartwright

Madeline Cartwright was formerly the principal of the James G. Blaine public school in a neighborhood enshrouded in poverty and rocked by violence. Cartwright became the principal of Blaine school in 1979. She grew up in Pittsburgh's poor Hill District, and she was determined to make a difference in North Philadelphia, one of America's most drug-ridden, devastated inner-city areas.

One of the first things Cartwright did when she became principal was to install a washer and dryer in the school's kitchen, where each morning she and her staff personally washed much of the children's clothing. A Philadelphia chemical company provided her with free soap powder. Cartwright said this is the only way many of the children in her school will know what it is like to have clean clothes. She is proud that the kids in her school "looked good and had clean clothes," and she knows it made them feel better about themselves.

The most important thing Cartwright did when she became the principal was to, as she said, "browbeat" parents into getting involved in the school. She told them that she came from the same circumstances they did and that, here at Blaine school, the children were going to get a better education and have a better life than most children who attended her elementary school when she was growing up. But she told the parents that this was only going to happen if they worked with her and became partners with the school in educating and socializing the children.

When she came to Blaine school, she told the parents, "This place is dirty! How can your kids go to school in a place like this!" One of the parents commented, "You must think you are in the suburbs." The parent expected the neighborhood and the school to be dirty. Cartwright told the parent, "The dirt in the suburbs is the same as the dirt in North Philadelphia—if you don't *move* it. And the same detergents work here."

Cartwright rounded up 18 parents and scrubbed the building until it was clean.

Blaine school's auditorium overflowed with parents when parent meetings were scheduled. Cartwright made children bring their parents to the meetings. She told the children, "Your parents need to know what we are doing in school." She gave the children a doughnut or a pretzel the next day if one of their parents came. She told the parents they could come to her if they had problems—that she could direct them to places and people who would help them solve their problems. Because of Cartwright's efforts, parents now feel comfortable at Blaine school.

Cartwright believes that a very important aspect of intervening in children's lives who come from low-income families is increasing the positive role models they see and with whom they can interact. She wants the state of Pennsylvania to set up "mentor houses," into which salvageable families can be moved. These vacant houses are located in better neighborhoods and a family with positive values is appointed or paid to be a mentor or role model for the family. Says Cartwright, "I would like to be a mentor."

Some people would say that Cartwright's dreams are naive, but maybe not. One safe and clean school, one set of clean clothes, one clean toilet, one safe house—and then another safe school, and another, and another. Concludes Cartwright, "I'm telling you; there are things you can do!" (Louv, 1990).

Madeline Cartwright (above) is an elementary school principal who has made a powerful difference in many impoverished children's lives. Especially important was Cartwright's persistence and persuasiveness in getting parents more involved in their children's education.

CONCEPT TABLE 11.2

Emotional Development

Concept	Processes/Related Ideas	Characteristics/Description
The nature of children's emotion	What is emotion?	Emotion is feeling or affect that involves a mixture of physiological arousal and overt behavior. Emotions can be classified in terms of positive affectivity and negative affectivity.
	Functions of emotions in children's development	The three main functions are adaption and survival, regulation, and communication.
	Affect in parent-child relationships	Emotions are the first language that parents and infants communicate with before the infant acquires speech. Infant and adult affective communicative capacities make possible coordinated infant-adult interaction.
Emotional development in infancy	Developmental timetable of emotions	Izard developed the Maximally Discriminative Facial Coding System (called MAX) for coding infants' expression of emotions. Based on this coding system, interest, distress, and disgust are present at birth; a social smile appears at about 4–6 weeks; anger, surprise, and sadness emerge at about 3–4 months; fear is displayed at about 5–7 months; shame and shyness emerge at about 6–8 months; and contempt and guilt appear at about 2 years of age.
	Crying	Crying is the most important mechanism newborns have for communicating with their world. Babies have at least three types of cries—basic, anger, and pain. Most parents, and adults in general, can tell whether an infant's cries signify anger or pain. Controversy still swirls about whether babies should be soothed when they cry. An increasing number of developmentalists support Ainsworth and Bowlby's idea that infant crying should be responded to immediately in the first year of life.
	Smiling	Smiling is an important communicative affective behavior of the infant. Two types of smiling can be distinguished in infants: reflexive and social.
Children's depression and depressed parents	Children's depression	Depression is a mood disorder in which the individual is unhappy, demoralized, self-derogatory, and bored. In childhood, the features of depression are often mixed with a broader array of behaviors than in adulthood. Depression is more likely to occur in adolescence than in childhood, and is more frequent among females than

Concept	Processes/Related Ideas	Characteristics/Description
		males. Bowlby's developmental view, Beck's cognitive view, and Seligman's learned helplessness view are three perspectives on children's depression.
	Depressed parents	Depression is especially prominent in women of child-bearing age. Depression in parents is associated with problems of adjustment and disorders, especially depression, in their children. In considering the role of depressed parents in children's problems it is important to evaluate the social context of the family, especially marital discord.
Stress	What is stress?	Stress is the response of individuals to the circumstances and events, called stressors, that threaten them and tax their coping abilities.
	Cognitive factors in stress	Lazarus believes that children's stress depends on how they cognitively appraise and interpret events. Cognitive appraisal is the term Lazarus uses to describe individuals' interpretation of events in their lives as harmful, threatening, or challenging (primary appraisal), and their determination of whether they have the resources to effectively cope with the event (secondary appraisal).
	Life events and daily hassles	Both life events—such as divorce, incest, death of a parent—and daily hassles—such as living in an impoverished world—can cause stress.
	Sociocultural influences	Acculturation refers to cultural change that results from continuous, first-hand contact between two distinctive cultural groups. Acculturative stress refers to the negative consequences of acculturation. Members of ethnic minority groups have historically encountered hostility, prejudice, and lack of effective support during crises, which contribute to alienation, social isolation, and heightened stress. Poverty also imposes considerable stress on children and their families. Chronic life conditions such as inadequate housing, dangerous neighborhoods, burdensome responsibilities, and economic uncertainties are potent stresses in the lives of the poor. The incidence of poverty is especially pronounced among ethnic minority children and their families.

PERSPECTIVES ON PARENTING AND EDUCATION

Personal Characteristics of Competent Caregivers

Some caregivers are more competent than others. What makes a competent caregiver? That question was addressed by child-care expert LaVisa Wilson (1990). She believes the following personal characteristics define a competent caregiver:

Competent caregivers are physically healthy. Good health is necessary to provide the high level of energy required for competent caregiving. In day care, good health is required to resist the variety of illnesses to which caregivers are exposed.

Competent caregivers are mentally healthy. In daily interactions with infants, caregivers need to provide physical closeness and nurturance for an extended period of time, to give emotionally more than they often receive, and to be patient longer than they would

like. Emotionally stable caregivers who have learned how to cope with a variety of emotional demands in their daily experiences often are able to encourage mental health in others.

Competent caregivers have a positive self-image. Feelings of self-confidence and positive self-worth show that caregivers believe in themselves. Caregivers who have positive self-images are people who infants and toddlers want to approach rather than avoid.

Competent caregivers are flexible. Competent caregivers do not get upset if they have to change the daily schedule, daily plans, or responsibilities.

Competent caregivers are patient. Infants and toddlers are very demanding and require considerable attention and monitoring, which can stretch the caregiver's patience. However, competent

caregivers show patience as they respond to the infants' and toddlers' needs.

Competent caregivers are positive models for infants. Caregivers' behaviors are observed and imitated by infants and toddlers. Competent caregivers monitor their own behavior, knowing it is a model for infants and toddlers.

Competent caregivers are open to learning. Competent caregivers seek to develop additional skills and are open to new insights, understanding, and skills.

Competent caregivers enjoy caregiving. Competent caregivers gain considerable enjoyment and satisfaction in providing effective, high-quality care for infants and toddlers. Competent caregivers reflect these positive feelings as they interact with infants and toddlers. ■

CONCLUSIONS

Babies are wrapped in a socioemotional world with their caregivers from birth. Babies and their caregivers communicate with each other through their emotions, their senses, and their words. Through interaction with their caregivers, infants learn to adapt to their world.

We began this chapter by briefly examining how the human infant cannot sustain itself, and therefore requires extensive care. Much of the interest in the infant's social world has focused on attachment. We considered what attachment is, individual differences in

attachment (secure and insecure), and attachment, temperament, and the wider social world. We evaluated fathers as caregivers of infants and the role of day care in children's lives and how it affects their development. We learned that temperament is an important aspect of the infant's development, and we studied many different facets of children's emotional development, including the nature of children's emotion, emotional development in infancy, children's depression and depressed parents, and stress. The chapter concluded with a discussion of

the personal characteristics of competent caregivers. Don't forget to again read the two concept tables on pages 337 and 344 that together will provide you with a summary of the chapter.

In the next chapter, we turn our attention to the self and identity development. Some theorists, especially Ainsworth and Bowlby, believe that secure attachment provides an important foundation for the development of a positive sense of self.

KEY TERMS

attachment   A close emotional bond between an infant and a caregiver. (327)

secure attachment   The infant uses a caregiver as a secure base from which to explore the environment. Ainsworth believes that secure attachment in the first year of life provides an important foundation for psychological development later in life. (328)

type B babies   Infants who use a caregiver as a secure base from which to explore the environment. (328)

type A babies   Infants who exhibit insecurity by avoiding a caregiver—for example, by failing to seek proximity. (328)

type C babies   Infants who exhibit insecurity by resisting a caregiver—for example, clinging but at the same time fighting against closeness. (328)

temperament   An individual's behavioral style and characteristic way of responding. (334)

easy child   A child who is generally in a positive mood, who quickly establishes regular routines in infancy, and who adapts easily to new experiences. (334)

difficult child   A child who tends to react negatively and cry frequently, who engages in irregular daily routines, and who is slow to accept new experiences. (334)

slow-to-warm-up child   A child who has a low activity level, is somewhat negative, shows low adaptability, and displays a low intensity mood. (334)

emotionality   The tendency to be distressed. (334)

sociability   The tendency to prefer the company of others to being alone. (334)

activity level   The tempo and vigor of movement. (334)

emotion   The feeling or affect that involves a mixture of physiological arousal (fast heart beat, for example) and overt behavior (smile or grimace, for example). (335)

positive affectivity (PA)   The range of positive emotions from high energy, enthusiasm, and excitement, to calm, quiet, and withdrawn. Joy, happiness, and laughter may involve PA. (336)

negative affectivity (NA)   Emotions that are negatively toned, such as anxiety, guilt, and sadness. (336)

Maximally Discriminative Facial Movement Coding System (MAX)   Izard's system of coding infants' facial expressions related to emotions. Using MAX, coders watch slow-motion and stop-action videotapes of infants' facial reactions to stimuli. (338)

basic cry   A rhythmic pattern that usually consists of a cry, followed by a briefer silence, then a shorter inspiratory whistle that is somewhat higher pitch than the main cry, then a brief rest before the next cry. (338)

anger cry   A variation of the basic cry in which more excess air is forced through the vocal cords. (338)

pain cry   A sudden appearance of loud crying without preliminary moaning and a long initial cry

followed by an extended period of breath holding. (338)

reflexive smile   A smile that does not occur in response to external stimuli. It happens during the first month after birth, usually during irregular patterns of sleep, not when the infant is in an alert state. (339)

social smile   A smile in response to an external stimulus, which, early in development, typically is in response to a face. (339)

learned helplessness   Seligman's view that when individuals are exposed to negative situations over which they have no control they are likely to become depressed. (339)

stress   This is the response of individuals to the circumstances and events, called stressors, that threaten them and tax their coping abilities. (340)

cognitive appraisal   Lazarus' term describes individuals' interpretation of events in their lives as harmful, threatening, or challenging, and their determination of whether they have the resources to cope effectively with the event. (340)

primary appraisal   Children's interpretation whether an event involves harm or loss that has already occurred, a threat to some future danger, or a challenge to be overcome. (340)

secondary appraisal   Children evaluate their resources and determine how effectively they can cope with the event. (340)

acculturation   This term refers to cultural change that results from continuous, first-hand contact between two distinctive cultural groups. (341)

SUGGESTED READINGS

Brenner, A. (1984). *Helping children cope with stress.* Lexington, MA: D. C. Heath. An excellent, insightful portrayal of children's stress and effective ways to cope with the stress.

Lande, J. S., Scarr, S., & Gunzenhauser, N. (Eds.). (1989). *Caring for children: Challenge to America.* Hillsdale, NJ: Erlbaum. This up-to-date treatment of child care includes chapters on child care in European countries, child care in Black families, licensing of child-care facilities, and future directions of child care in the United States.

Sroufe, L. A., & Fleeson, J. (1986). Attachment and the construction of relationships. In W. Hartup and Z. Rubin (Eds.), *Relationships and development.* Hillsdale, NJ: Erlbaum. Gives insight into the importance of attachment in our development of relationships.

White, B. L. (1990). *The first three years of life.* New York: Prentice-Hall. Infant expert Burton White provides an excellent overview of how parents can interact with their infants and toddlers to produce competent, happy individuals.

Camille Roulin, Vincent van Gogh
(Detail)

12

The Self and Identity

*Explore thyself. Herein are demanded
the eye and the nerve.*

—Henry David Thoreau

When I say "I," I mean something absolutely unique not to be confused with any other.

Ugo Betti, *The Inquiry*, 1941

IMAGES OF CHILDREN

A 15-Year-Old Girl's Self-description

How do adolescents describe themselves? How would you have described yourself when you were 15 years old? What features would you have emphasized? The following is a self-portrait of one 15-year-old girl:

What am I like as a person? Complicated! I'm sensitive, friendly, outgoing, popular, and tolerant, though I can also be shy, self-conscious, and even obnoxious. Obnoxious! I'd *like* to be friendly and tolerant all of the time. That's the kind of person I *want* to be, and I'm disappointed when I'm not. I'm responsible, even studious now and then, but on the other hand, I'm a goof-off, too, because if you're too studious, you won't be popular. I don't usually do that well at school. I'm a pretty cheerful person, especially with my friends, where I can even get rowdy. At home I'm more likely to be anxious around my parents. They expect me to get all A's. It's not fair! I worry about

how I probably *should* get better grades. But I'd be mortified in the eyes of my friends. So I'm usually pretty stressed-out at home, or sarcastic, since my parents are always on my case. But I really don't understand how I can switch so fast. I mean, how can I be cheerful one minute, anxious the next, and then be sarcastic? Which one is the *real* me? Sometimes, I feel phony, especially around boys. Say I think some guy might be interested in asking me out. I try to act different, like Madonna. I'll be flirtatious and fun-loving. And then everybody, I mean *everybody* else is looking at me like they think I'm totally weird. Then I get self-conscious and embarrassed and become radically introverted, and I don't know who I really am! Am I just trying to impress them or what? But I don't really care what they think anyway. I don't *want* to care, that is. I just want to know

what my close friends think. I can be my true self with my close friends. I can't be my real self with my parents. They don't understand me. What do *they* know about what it's like to be a teenager? They still treat me like I'm still a kid. At least at school people treat you more like you're an adult. That gets confusing, though. I mean, which am I, a kid or an adult? It's scary, too, because I don't have any idea what I want to be when I grow up. I mean, I have lots of *ideas*. My friend Sheryl and I talk about whether we'll be stewardesses, or teachers, or nurses, veterinarians, maybe mothers, or actresses. I know I *don't* want to be a waitress or a secretary. But how do you decide all of this? I really don't know. I mean, I think about it a lot, but I can't resolve it. There are days when I wish I could just become immune to myself (Harter, 1990b, pp. 352–353).

PREVIEW

The 15-year-old girl's self-description that you just read about exemplifies the increased introspective nature of self-portrayal in adolescence and the adolescent's complex search for identity. This chapter is about the self in infancy, childhood, and adolescence, and about the search for identity in adolescence.

THE SELF

In recent years, developmentalists have given special attention to two aspects of the self and self-conceptions: self-understanding and self-esteem.

Self-understanding

What is self-understanding? When do children initially develop a self-understanding? How does self-understanding develop during the childhood and adolescent years? What is the role of perspective taking in self-understanding? We will examine each of these questions.

What Is Self-understanding?

Self-understanding *is a child's cognitive representation of the self, the substance and content of the child's self-conceptions* (Damon & Hart, 1988). For example, an 11-year-old boy understands that he is a student, a boy, a football player, a family member, a video game lover, and a rock music fan. A 13-year-old girl understands that she is a middle school student, in the midst of puberty, a girl, a cheerleader, a student council member, and a movie fan. A child's self-understanding is based, in part, on the various roles and membership categories that define who children are (Harter, 1990a,b). Though not the whole of personal identity, self-understanding provides its rational underpinnings (Damon & Hart, 1988).

> *Know thyself, for once we know ourselves, we may learn how to care for ourselves, but otherwise we never shall.*
> —Socrates

Infancy—The Development of Self-recognition

Infants cannot verbally express their views on the nature of the self. They also cannot understand the complex instructions required to engage in a child developmentalist's tasks. Given these restrictions, how can researchers study infants' self-understanding? They test infants' *visual self-recognition* by presenting them with images of themselves in mirrors, pictures, and other visual media. For example, let's examine how the mirror technique works. An infant's mother puts a dot of rouge on the infant's nose. An observer watches to see how often the infant touches its nose. Next, the infant is placed in front of a mirror, and observers detect whether nose touching increases. In two separate investigations, in the second half of the second year of life, infants recognized their own images in the mirror and coordinated the images they saw with the actions of touching their own bodies (Amsterdam, 1968; Lewis & Brooks-Gunn, 1979) (see figure 12.1). In sum, human infants initially develop a sense of rudimentary self-understanding called self-recognition at approximately 18 months of age (Lewis & others, 1989).

Early Childhood

Because children can verbally communicate their ideas, research on self-understanding in childhood is not limited to visual self-recognition, as it is during infancy. Mainly through interviews, researchers have probed children's conceptions of many aspects of self-understanding, including mind and body, self in relation to others, and pride and shame in self. In early childhood, children usually conceive of the self in physical terms. Most young children conceive of the self as part of the body, which usually means the head. Young children generally confuse self, mind, and body (Broughton, 1978). Because the self is a body part, it can be described along many material dimensions, such as size, shape, and color. Young children distinguish themselves from others through many different physical and material attributes. Says 4-year-old Sandra, "I'm different from Jennifer because I have brown hair and she has blonde hair." Says 4-year-old Ralph, "I am different from Hank because I am taller and I am different from my sister because I have a bicycle."

Researchers also believe that the *active dimension* is a central component of the self in early childhood (Keller, Ford, & Meacham, 1978). If we define the category "physical" broadly enough, we can include physical actions as well as body image and material possessions. For example, preschool children often describe themselves in terms of activities such as play. In sum, in early childhood, children often describe themselves in terms of a physical self or an active self.

Middle and Late Childhood

In middle and late childhood, self-understanding increasingly shifts from defining oneself through external characteristics to defining oneself through internal characteristics. Also, elementary-school-aged children are more likely to define themselves in terms of social characteristics and social comparison.

In middle and late childhood, children not only recognize differences between inner and outer states, but they are also more likely to include subjective inner states in their definition of self. For example, in one investigation, second-grade children were much more likely than younger children to name psychological characteristics (such as preferences or personality traits) in their self-definition and less likely to name physical characteristics (such as eye color or possessions) (Aboud & Skerry, 1983). For example, 8-year-old Todd includes in his self-description, "I am smart and I am popular." Ten-year-old Tina says about herself, "I am pretty good about not worrying most of the time. I used to lose my temper but I'm better about that now. I also feel proud when I do well in school."

In addition to the increase of psychological characteristics in self-definition during the elementary school years, the *social aspects* of the self also increase at this point in development. In one investigation, elementary school children included references to social groups in their self-description (Livesly & Bromley, 1973). For example, some children referred to themselves as Girl Scouts, as Catholics, or as someone who has two close friends.

Children's self-understanding in the elementary school years also includes increasing reference to *social comparison*. At this point in development, children are more likely to distinguish themselves from others in comparative rather than in absolute terms. That is, elementary-school-aged children are no longer as likely to think about what I do or do not do, but are more likely to think about what I can do *in comparison with others.* This developmental shift provides an increased tendency of

FIGURE 12.1

Development of self-recognition in infancy. The graph gives the findings of two studies in which infants of different ages showed recognition of rouge by touching, wiping, or verbally referring to it. Notice that self-recognition did not occur extensively until the second half of the second year of life.

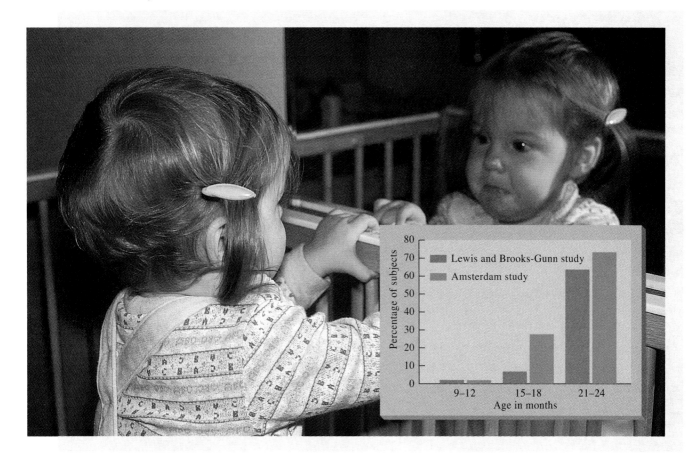

establishing one's differences as an individual apart from others. In a series of studies, Diane Ruble (1983) investigated children's use of social comparison in their self-evaluations. Children were given a difficult task and then offered feedback on their performance, as well as information about the performances of other children their age. The children were then asked for self-evaluations. Children younger than 7 made virtually no reference to the information about other children's performances. However, many children older than 7 included socially comparative information in their self-descriptions.

Adolescence

The development of self-understanding in adolescence is complex and involves a number of aspects of the self. Let's examine how the adolescent's self-understanding differs from the child's.

Abstract and Idealistic. Remember from our discussion of Piaget's theory of cognitive development in chapters 2 and 7 that many adolescents begin to think in more *abstract* and *idealistic* ways. When asked to describe themselves, adolescents are more likely than children to use abstract and idealistic labels. Consider 14-year-old Laurie's abstract description of herself: "I am a human being. I am indecisive. I don't know who I am."

Also consider her idealistic description of herself: "I am a naturally sensitive person who really cares about people's feelings. I think I'm pretty good-looking." Not all adolescents describe themselves in idealistic ways, but most adolescents distinguish between the real self and the ideal self, as we see next.

Real and Ideal, True and False Selves. The adolescent's emerging ability to construct ideal selves in addition to actual ones can be perplexing to the adolescent. The capacity to recognize a discrepancy between *real* and *ideal* selves represents a cognitive advance, but humanistic theorist Carl Rogers (1961) believed that, when the real and ideal selves are too discrepant, it is a sign of maladjustment.

Researchers have found that the discrepancy between the real self and the ideal self is greater in middle adolescence than in early or late adolescence (Strachen & Jones, 1982). While, as just mentioned, some theorists consider a strong discrepancy between the ideal and real selves as maladaptive, others argue that this is not always true, especially in adolescence. For example, in one view, an important aspect of the ideal or imagined self is the **possible self,** *what individuals might become, what they would like to become, and what they are afraid of becoming* (Markus & Nurius, 1986). Thus, adolescents' possible selves include both what adolescents hope to be as well as what they dread they will become. In this view, the presence of both hoped-for as well as dreaded selves is psychologically healthy, providing a balance between positive, expected selves and negative, feared selves. The attributes of future positive selves (getting into a good college, being admired, having a successful career) can direct future positive states, while attributes of future negative selves (being unemployed, being lonely, not getting into a good college) can identify what is to be avoided in the future.

Can adolescents distinguish between their *true* and *false* selves? In one research study, they could (Harter & Lee, 1989). Adolescents are most likely to show their false self in romantic or dating situations, and with classmates; they are least likely to show their false self with close friends. Adolescents display a false self to impress others, to try out new behaviors or roles, because others force them to behave in false ways, and because others do not understand their true self (Harter, 1990b). Some adolescents report that they do not like their false-self behavior, but others say that it does not bother them.

Differentiated. Adolescents' self-understanding becomes increasingly *differentiated*. Adolescents are more likely than children to describe the self with contextual or situational variations. For example, 15-year-old Amy describes herself with one set of characteristics in her relationship with her family and another set of characteristics in her relationship with peers and friends. Yet another set of characteristics appears in her description of her romantic relationship. In sum, adolescents are more likely than children to understand that one possesses different selves, depending on one's role or particular context (Harter, 1990a,b).

Contradictions within the Self. Self-understanding in adolescence also involves more *contradictions* within the self. In one investigation, Susan Harter and Ann Monsour (1992) asked seventh-, ninth-, and eleventh-graders to describe themselves. They found a dramatic increase between the seventh and ninth grades in the number of contradictory terms used to describe oneself (moody *and* understanding, ugly *and* attractive, bored *and* inquisitive, caring *and* uncaring, introverted *and* fun-loving, and so on). The contradictory self-descriptions declined in the eleventh grade, but were still higher than in the seventh grade. Adolescents develop the cognitive ability to detect these inconsistencies in the self as they strive to construct a general theory of the self or of one's personality (Damon, 1991).

Self-conscious. Adolescents are more likely than children to be *self-conscious* about and *preoccupied* with their self-understanding. As part of their self-conscious and preoccupied self-exploration, adolescents become more introspective. However, the introspection is not always done in social isolation. Sometimes, adolescents turn to their friends for support and self-clarification, obtaining their friends' opinions of an emerging self-definition. As one researcher on self-development commented, adolescents' friends are often the main source of reflected self-appraisals, becoming the social mirror into which adolescents anxiously stare (Rosenberg, 1979). This self-consciousness and self-preoccupation reflect the concept of adolescent egocentrism, which we discussed in chapter 7.

Self-protective. Adolescents' self-understanding includes more mechanisms to *protect the self* (Harter 1990a,b). Although adolescents often display a sense of confusion and conflict stimulated by introspective efforts to understand the self, they also call on mechanisms to protect and enhance the self. In protecting the self, adolescents are prone to denying their negative characteristics. For example, in Harter's investigation of self-understanding, positive self-descriptions, such as attractive, fun-loving, sensitive, affectionate, and inquisitive, were more likely to be placed at the core of the self, indicating more importance, whereas negative self-descriptions, such as ugly, mediocre, depressed, selfish, and nervous, were more likely to be placed at the periphery of the self, indicating less importance. Adolescents' tendency to protect themselves fits with the earlier description of adolescents' tendency to describe themselves in idealistic ways.

Unconscious. Adolescents' self-understanding involves greater recognition that the self includes *unconscious*, as well as conscious, components, a recognition not likely to occur until late adolescence (Selman, 1980). That is, older adolescents are more likely than younger adolescents to believe that certain aspects of their mental experience are beyond their awareness or control.

Social Comparison. Some developmentalists believe that adolescents are more likely than children to use *social comparison* to evaluate themselves (Ruble & others, 1980). However, adolescents' willingness to *admit* that they engage in social comparison to evaluate themselves declines in adolescence because they view social comparison as socially undesirable. They think that acknowledging their social comparison motives will endanger their popularity (Harter, 1990a). Relying on social comparison information in adolescence may be confusing because of the large number of reference groups. For example, should adolescents compare themselves to classmates in general? To friends? To their own gender? To popular adolescents? To good-looking adolescents? To athletic adolescents? Simultaneously considering all of these social comparison groups can get perplexing for adolescents.

The Fluctuating Self. Given the numerous selves of adolescents, especially their contradictory ones and the tension between true and false selves, it is not surprising that adolescents' selves often *fluctuate* across situations and over time (Harter, 1990a). The 15-year-old girl quoted at the beginning of the chapter in the "Images of Children" section remarked that she could not understand how she could switch so fast—from being cheerful one moment, to anxious the next, and then sarcastic a short time later. One researcher described the fluctuating nature of the adolescent's self with the metaphor of "the barometric self" (Rosenberg, 1986). The adolescent's self continues to be characterized by instability until a more unified theory of self is constructed, usually not until late adolescence or even early adulthood.

Self-integration Adolescents' self-understanding becomes more *integrative*, with the disparate parts of the self more systematically pieced together, especially in late adolescence. Older adolescents are more likely to detect inconsistencies in their earlier self-descriptions as they attempt to construct a general theory of self, an integrated sense of identity (Harter, 1990b; Selman, 1980).

Because the adolescent creates multiple self-concepts in adolescence, the task of integrating these varying self-conceptions becomes problematic. At the same time that adolescents are faced with pressures to differentiate the self into multiple roles, the emergence of formal operational thought presses for *integration* and the development of a consistent, coherent theory of self (Harter, 1990b). These budding formal operational skills initially present a liability because they first allow adolescents to *detect* inconsistencies in the self across varying roles, only later providing the cognitive capacity to *integrate* such apparent contradictions. In the "Images of Children" narrative that opened the chapter, the 15-year-old girl could not understand how she could be cheerful yet depressed and sarcastic, wondering "which is the real me." Researchers have found that 14- to 15-year-olds not only detect inconsistencies across their various roles (with parents, friends, and romantic partners, for example) but that they are much more troubled by these contradictions than younger (11- to 12-year-old) and older (17- to 18-year-old) adolescents (Damon & Hart, 1988; Harter, 1986).

Critical Thinking

Think about your development of self-understanding when you were an adolescent. Can you think of other aspects of the development of self-understanding in adolescence than those we have discussed?

At this point, we have discussed a number of characteristics of adolescents' self-understanding. A summary of these characteristics is presented in figure 12.2.

Further Developmental Considerations in Self-understanding

In the developmental sequence of self-understanding just outlined, we presented the emergence of various self-dimensions. It is important to keep in mind that just because a particular dimension of the self is listed in a particular period that the dimension does not occur exclusively in that period. For example, early childhood is described as the time period for the emergence of a physical and active self; however, many elementary school children also describe themselves in terms of physical characteristics and various activities. We described middle and late childhood as the time period when the internal self, social self, and social comparative self become more prominent. These characteristics of the self also are very important in adolescent self-understanding and, in many cases, are more prevalent in adolescent self-description than in children's self-description. However, these characteristics were placed in the middle and late childhood period because that is the time when many developmentalists believe they emerge to become important self-dimensions.

The Role of Perspective Taking in Self-understanding

Many child developmentalists believe that perspective taking plays an important role in self-understanding. As you learned

earlier, perspective taking is the ability to assume another person's perspective and understand his or her thoughts and feelings. Robert Selman (1980) has proposed a developmental theory of perspective taking that has been given considerable attention. He believes that perspective taking involves a series of five stages, ranging from 3 years of age through adolescence (see table 12.1). These stages begin with the egocentric viewpoint in early childhood and end with in-depth perspective taking in adolescence.

To study children's perspective taking, Selman interviews individual children, asking them to comment on such dilemmas as the following:

> Holly is an 8-year-old girl who likes to climb trees. She is the best tree climber in the neighborhood. One day while climbing down from a tall tree, she falls, . . . but does not hurt herself. Her father sees her fall. He is upset and asks her to promise not to climb trees anymore. Holly promises.
>
> Later that day, Holly and her friends meet Shawn. Shawn's kitten is caught in a tree and can't get down. Something has to be done right away or the kitten may fall. Holly is the only one who climbs trees well enough to reach the kitten and get it down but she remembers her promise to her father. (Selman, 1976, p. 302)

Subsequently, Selman asks each child a series of questions about the dilemma, such as:

- Does Holly know how Shawn feels about the kitten?
- How will Holly's father feel if he finds out she climbed the tree?
- What does Holly think her father will do if he finds out she climbed the tree?
- What would you do in this situation?

By analyzing children's responses to these dilemmas, Selman (1980) concluded that children's perspective taking follows the developmental sequence described in table 12.1.

Children's perspective taking not only can increase their self-understanding, but it can also improve their peer group status and the quality of their friendships. For example, one investigation found that the most popular children in the third and eighth grades had competent perspective-taking skills (Kurdek & Krile, 1982). Children who are competent at perspective taking are better at understanding the needs of their companions, so they likely can communicate more effectively with them (Hudson, Forman, & Brion-Meisels, 1982).

At this point, we have studied a number of developmental changes in self-understanding. Remember from our introduction to the self that self-conception not only involves self-understanding but also self-esteem.

Self-esteem

Among the questions we will explore regarding children's self-esteem are the following: What is self-esteem? How is self-esteem measured? How do parent-child relationships contribute to children's self-esteem? How is group identity involved in

FIGURE 12.2

Characteristics of adolescents' self-understanding.

| Abstract and idealistic |
| Construction of ideal and real, true and false selves |
| Differentiated |
| Contradictions within the self |
| Self-conscious |
| Self-protective |
| Recognition that the self includes an unconscious dimension |
| Social comparison |
| Fluctuating |
| Integrative |

children's self-esteem? How can children's self-esteem be enhanced? We will consider each of these questions in turn.

What Is Self-esteem?

Self-esteem *is the evaluative and affective dimension of self-concept. Self-esteem also is referred to as self-worth or self-image.* That is, a child may perceive that she is not merely a student, but a *good* student. Another child may perceive that he is not merely a basketball player, but a *good* basketball player. These self-evaluations often stimulate an emotional reaction. The good student feels proud that she just received an *A* on an exam;

the good basketball player feels elated that he scored the winning basket in last night's game. Of course, not all self-evaluations are positive. A child may feel sad that she is not a good student. Another child may feel ashamed that he is a poor reader. These are all evaluative judgments regarding the child's self-esteem.

It is difficult to make people miserable when they feel worthy of themselves.

—Abraham Lincoln

TABLE 12.1

Selman's Stages of Perspective Taking

Stage	Perspective-Taking Stage	Ages	Description
0	Egocentric viewpoint	3–6	Child has a sense of differentiation of self and other but fails to distinguish between the social perspective (thoughts, feelings) of other and self. Child can label other's overt feelings but does not see the cause-and-effect relation of reasons to social actions.
1	Social-informational perspective taking	6–8	Child is aware that other has a social perspective based on other's own reasoning, which may or may not be similar to child's. However, child tends to focus on one perspective rather than coordinating viewpoints.
2	Self-reflective perspective taking	8–10	Child is conscious that each individual is aware of the other's perspective and that this awareness influences self and other's view of each other. Putting self in other's place is a way of judging other's intentions, purposes, and actions. Child can form a coordinated chain of perspectives but cannot yet abstract from this process to the level of simultaneous mutuality.
3	Mutual perspective taking	10–12	Adolescent realizes that both self and other can view each other mutually and simultaneously as subjects. Adolescent can step outside the two-person dyad and view the interaction from a third-person perspective.
4	Social and conventional system perspective taking	12–15	Adolescent realizes mutual perspective taking does not always lead to complete understanding. Social conventions are seen as necessary because they are understood by all members of the group (the generalized other), regardless of their position, role, or experience.

From R. L. Selman, "Social-Cognitive Understanding" in T. Lickona (ed.), *Moral Development and Behavior,* 1976. Reprinted by permission of Thomas Lickona.

Susan Harter has greatly advanced our knowledge of self-understanding and self-esteem in children and adolescents. She has constructed excellent measures of perceived competence in different domains, provided insightful analyses of adolescents' self-understanding, and contributed to awareness of what causes low self-esteem.

Until recently, theorists and researchers conceptualized self-esteem as a general, global judgment about the self. However, children make evaluative judgments about many different aspects of their lives. For example, they perceive that they are good or bad in physical skills, good or bad in cognitive skills, and good or bad in social skills. As we will see next, interest in the domain-specific aspects of self-esteem has led to the development of new measures of self-esteem.

Measuring Self-esteem

Psychologists have had a difficult time trying to measure self-worth or self-esteem (Harter, 1990a; Wylie, 1979; Yardley, 1987). One frequently used method is the Piers-Harris Scale, which consists of 80 items designed to measure overall self-esteem. By responding "yes" or "no" to such items as "I have good ideas," children reveal whether they have high or low self-esteem.

However, as indicated earlier, self-esteem may vary according to different skill domains or areas of competence. The scales developed by Susan Harter have been welcome additions to the assessment of self-esteem or self-worth. The Self-Perception Profile for Children is a revision of the original instrument, the Perceived Competence Scale for Children (Harter, 1982). The Self-Perception Profile for Children taps five specific domains—scholastic competence, athletic competence, social acceptance, physical appearance, and behavioral conduct—plus general self-worth (Harter, 1985). Harter's scale does an excellent job of separating children's self-evaluations in different skill areas, and when general self-worth is assessed, questions focus on overall perceptions of self-esteem rather than specific skill domains. Many developmentalists believe that the differentiated assessment of self-concept in various skill domains, as well as the independent assessment of general self-worth, provides a richer picture than those measures that yield only a single self-worth score.

FIGURE 12.3

Behavioral indicators of self-esteem.

Source: Savin-Williams, R. C., & Demo, D. H. Conceiving or misconceiving the self: Issues in adolescent self-esteem. *Journal of Early Adolescence*, 3, 121–140. Reprinted with permission of H.E.L.P. Books, Inc.

Behavioral Indicators of Self-Esteem	
Positive Indicators	**Negative Indicators**
1. Gives others directives or commands	1. Puts down others by teasing, name-calling, or gossiping
2. Uses voice quality appropriate for situation	2. Uses gestures that are dramatic or out of context
3. Expresses opinions	3. Engages in inappropriate touching or avoids physical contact
4. Sits with others during social activities	4. Gives excuses for failures
5. Works cooperatively in a group	5. Glances around to monitor others
6. Faces others when speaking or being spoken to	6. Brags excessively about achievements, skills, appearance
7. Maintains eye contact during conversation	7. Verbally puts self down; self-depreciation
8. Initiates friendly contact with others	8. Speaks too loudly, abruptly, or in a dogmatic tone
9. Maintains comfortable space between self and others	9. Does not express views or opinions, especially when asked
10. Little hesitation in speech, speaks fluently	10. Assumes a submissive stance

The Self-Perception Profile for Children is designed to be used with third-grade through sixth-grade children. Harter also has developed a separate scale for adolescents, recognizing important developmental changes in self-perceptions. The Self-Perception Profile for Adolescents (Harter, 1989) taps eight domains—scholastic competence, athletic competence, social acceptance, physical appearance, behavioral conduct, close friendship, romantic appeal, and job competence—plus global self-worth. Thus the adolescent version has three skill domains not present in the children's version—job competence, romantic appeal, and close friendship.

Some assessment experts believe that a combination of several methods should be used to measure children's self-esteem. In addition to self-report scales, ratings of a child's self-esteem by others and observations of the child's behavior in various settings may provide a more comprehensive portrait of self-esteem. Children's facial expressions and the extent to which they congratulate or condemn themselves are also good indicators of self-esteem. For example, children who rarely smile or act happy reveal something about their self-esteem. By turning to figure 12.3, you can examine the behavioral categories that were used to measure self-esteem in one investigation (Savin-Williams & Demo, 1983).

Parent–Child Relationships and Self–esteem

In the most extensive investigation of parent-child relationships and self-esteem, a measure of self-esteem was given to elementary school boys, and the boys and their mothers were interviewed about their family relationships (Coopersmith, 1967). Based on these assessments, the following parenting attributes were associated with boys' high self-esteem:

- Expression of affection
- Concern about the child's problems
- Harmony in the home
- Participation in joint family activities

- Availability to give competent, organized help to the boys when they need it
- Setting clear and fair rules
- Abiding by these rules
- Allowing the children freedom within well-prescribed limits

Remember that these findings are correlational, and so, we cannot say that these parenting attributes *cause* children's high self-esteem. Such factors as parental acceptance and allowing children freedom within well-prescribed limits probably are important determinants of children's self-esteem, but we still must say that they *are related to* rather than *they cause* children's self-esteem, based on the available research data.

Group Identity and Self–esteem

Children's group identity is also related to their self-esteem. **Social identity theory** *is social psychologist Henry Tajfel's (1978) theory that, when individuals are assigned to a group, they invariably think of that group as an in-group for them. This occurs because individuals want to have a positive self-image.* According to Tajfel, self-image consists of both a personal identity and many different social identities. Tajfel argues that individuals can improve their self-image by enhancing either their personal or their social identity. Tajfel believes that social identity is especially important. When children or adults compare the social identity of their group with the social identity of another group, they often maximize the distinctions between the two groups. For example, think of an adolescent's identity with the school's football or basketball team. When the school's teams win, students' self-images are enhanced, regardless of whether they play on the teams or not. Why? Because they have a social identity with the school and the school's teams.

As children and adults strive to promote their social identities, it is not long before proud, self-congratulatory remarks are interspersed with nasty comments about the opposing

SOCIOCULTURAL WORLDS OF CHILDREN 12.1

Ethnicity, Self, and Self-esteem

Many of the early attempts to assess the nature of self-esteem in various ethnic groups compared Black and White individuals (Clark & Clark, 1939; Coopersmith, 1967; Deutsch, 1967). The early reports indicated that Black individuals, especially Black children, have less self-esteem than White individuals. However, more recent research suggests that Black American, Mexican American, and Puerto Rican American children and adults report equal if not higher self-esteem than children and adults from other ethnic groups, such as Anglo American children and adults (Allen & Majidi-Ahi, 1989; Powell & Fuller, 1972).

A generation of ethnic awareness and pride appears to have advanced the self-esteem of ethnic minority groups (Garbarino, 1985). Ethnic pride based on success within a subgroup has both costs and benefits for individuals. An obvious benefit is that their cultural roles are more clearly defined by the subgroup (such as Black American, Mexican American, or Native American) and that they know what they must do to become competent people in the subculture. In these usually tight-knit neighborhoods, there is a feeling of closeness and support among neighbors. Thus, individuals from the ethnic group can obtain help and learn strategies for coping with problems, which makes developing a positive sense of self somewhat easier. An ethnic-group individual gains a sense of rootedness and acceptance.

However, there is no indication that the distribution of self-acceptance in a group is related to the social prestige of the group in American society at large (Rosenberg, 1965). Thus, there may be a negative reality in the social environment beyond the ethnic-group neighborhood with which individuals must eventually come to terms if they are to succeed in the larger society. The ethnic-group neighborhood's beliefs, values, morals, and behaviors may not be accepted by the society as a whole, which can impede the development of social competence in the mainstream of society.

A discussion of ethnicity and self-esteem raises the fundamental question of "What kind of people does the world need?" (Garbarino, 1980, 1985). There is a growing recognition of the need for individuals to develop more harmonious, cooperative relationships if the quality of life on this planet is to be enhanced. Such a society needs persons to define themselves in new ways that deemphasize competition, achievement, and materialism in favor of cooperation, connectedness with others, empathy, and spiritual development. We need to ask whether we are socializing children to develop the kind of self that is needed to create a competent, caring, sustainable society.

group(s). In a capsule, the theme becomes, "My group is good and I am good. Your group is bad and you are bad." So it goes with the sexes, ethnic groups, teams, social classes, religions, and countless other groups, all seeking to improve their respective self-images through social identity with the group and comparison of the group with other groups. These comparisons can easily lead to competition, conflict, and even a perception that discrimination against other groups is legitimate.

Tajfel showed that it does not take much to get children or adults to think in terms of "we" and "they," or in-group and out-group. He assigned children to two groups based on a trivial task. For example, one individual was assigned to one group because she overestimated the number of dots on a screen and another individual was assigned to another group because he underestimated the number. Once assigned to the two groups, the members were asked to award amounts of money to pairs of other subjects. Those eligible to receive the money were anonymous except for their membership in one of the two groups Tajfel created. Invariably, the children acted favorably toward (awarded money to) members of their own group. It is no wonder, then, that, if we favor our own group based on such trivial criteria, we will show intense in-group favoritism when differences are not as trivial.

Closely related to group identity and self-esteem is **ethnocentrism,** *the tendency to favor one's own group over other groups.* Ethnocentrism's positive side appears in the sense of in-group pride that fulfills our strong urge to attain and maintain a positive self-image. In-group pride has mushroomed as we approach the end of the twentieth century. Children observe and listen to their parents speak about Black pride, Hispanic pride, Native American pride, Irish pride, Italian pride, and so on. Unfortunately, sometimes prejudice develops. **Prejudice** *is an unjustified negative attitude toward an individual because of that person's membership in a group.* People can be prejudiced against groups of people made up of a particular ethnic group, sex, age, religion, or other detectable difference.

Also related to group identity and self-esteem is the self-esteem of various ethnic minority groups. To learn more about self-esteem in ethnic-minority-group children, turn to Sociocultural Worlds of Children 12.1.

FIGURE 12.4

Four key aspects of improving self-esteem.

Identifying the
causes of low
self-esteem and
which domains of
competence are
important to
the self

Emotional
support and
social approval

Achievement

Coping

Increasing Children's Self-esteem

Four ways children's self-esteem can be improved are: (1) identifying the causes of low self-esteem and the domains of competence important to the self, (2) through emotional support and social approval, (3) through achievement, and (4) through coping (see figure 12.4).

Identifying children's sources of self-esteem—that is, competence in domains important to the self—is critical to improving self-esteem. Self-esteem theorist and researcher Susan Harter (1990b) points out that the self-esteem enhancement programs of the 1960s, in which self-esteem itself was the target and individuals were encouraged to simply feel good about

CONCEPT TABLE 12.1

The Self

Concept	Processes/Related Ideas	Characteristics/Description
Self-understanding	What is it?	It is a child's cognitive representation of self, the substance and content of the child's self-conceptions. Self-understanding provides the rational underpinnings of personal identity.
	Infancy—the development of self-recognition	Infants initially develop a rudimentary form of self-understanding—self-recognition—at approximately 18 months of age.
	Early childhood	The physical and active self becomes a part of self-understanding as young children often describe themselves in physical or active terms.
	Middle and late childhood	The internal self, the social self, and the socially comparative self become more prominent in self-understanding. Elementary-school-aged children increasingly describe themselves with internal, psychological characteristics. They also are more likely to define themselves in terms of social characteristics and social comparison.
	Adolescence	Dimensions of adolescents' self-understanding include: abstract and idealistic; construction of ideal and real, true and false selves; differentiated; contradictions within the self; self-conscious; self-protective; recognition that the self includes an unconscious dimension; social comparison; fluctuating and integrative.
	Further developmental considerations	Once the characteristics emerge as a part of self-understanding, they continue to be part of self-understanding, although they may wax and wane in varying degrees as development proceeds. For example, although the internal self is described as becoming more prominent in middle and late childhood, the internal self continues to be an integral part of self-understanding in adolescence. The physical self continues to be a part of self-description in adolescence, but it is often less central in self-description than in early childhood.
	Perspective taking	It is the ability to assume another person's perspective and understand his or her thoughts and feelings. Selman proposed a developmental theory of perspective taking with five stages, ranging from 3 years of age through adolescence, beginning with the egocentric viewpoint in early childhood and ending with the in-depth perspective taking of adolescence.

themselves, were ineffective. Rather, Harter believes that intervention must occur at the level of the *causes* of self-esteem if the individual's self-esteem is to improve significantly.

Children have the highest self-esteem when they perform competently in domains important to the self. Therefore, children should be encouraged to identify and value areas of competence. Emotional support and social approval in the form of confirmation from others also powerfully influence children's self-esteem (Harter, 1990b). Some children with low self-esteem come from conflicted families or conditions in which they experience abuse or neglect—situations in which support is unavailable. In some cases, alternative sources of support can be implemented, either informally through the encouragement of a teacher, a coach, or other significant adult, or more formally, through programs such as Big Brothers and Big Sisters. While peer approval becomes increasingly important during adolescence, both adult and peer support are important influences on the adolescent's self-esteem.

Achievement also can improve children's self-esteem (Bednar, Wells, & Peterson, 1989). For example, the straightforward teaching of real skills to children often results in increased achievement and, thus, in enhanced self-esteem. Children develop higher self-esteem because they know the important tasks to achieve goals, and they have experienced performing them or similar behaviors. The emphasis on the importance of achievement in improving self-esteem has much in common with Bandura's cognitive social learning concept of *self-efficacy,* which refers to individuals' beliefs that they can master a situation and produce positive outcomes.

Concept	Processes/Related Ideas	Characteristics/Description
Self-esteem	What is it?	It is the evaluative and affective dimension of self-concept. Self-esteem is also referred to as self-worth or self-image. Until recently, self-esteem was described in global terms. Today, domain-specific aspects of self-esteem are also considered.
	Measuring self-esteem	Measuring self-esteem is a difficult task. Harter's measures have been appealing to many developmentalists because they provide a differentiated assessment of self-esteem in various skill domains, as well as an independent assessment of general self-worth. Some assessment experts believe several methods should be used to measure self-esteem, including observations of a child's behavior.
	Parent-child relationships and self-esteem	In Coopersmith's study, children's self-esteem was associated with such parenting attributes as parental acceptance and allowing children freedom within well-prescribed limits. It is important to remember that these associations are correlational.
	Group identity and self-esteem	Social identity theory is Tajfel's theory that, when individuals are assigned to a group, they invariably think of the group as an in-group for them. This occurs because they want to have a positive self-image. Tajfel believes self-image consists of a personal *and* many different social identities related to group membership and identity. Group identity often leads to competitiveness, and sometimes conflict, between groups. Closely related to group identity and self-esteem is ethnocentrism, the tendency to favor one's own group over other groups. The positive side of ethnocentrism is the sense of in-group pride, but sometimes a negative side—prejudice—develops. A special concern is the self-esteem of ethnic minority children.
	Improving children's self-esteem	Four ways to increase children's self-esteem involve: (1) identifying the causes of adolescents' low self-esteem and which domains of competence are important to the self, (2) emotional support and social approval, (3) achievement, and (4) coping.

Self-esteem also is often increased when children face a problem and try to cope with it rather than avoid it (Bednar, Wells, & Peterson, 1989). If coping rather than avoidance prevails, children often face problems realistically, honestly, and nondefensively. This produces favorable self-evaluative thoughts, which lead to the self-generated approval that raises self-esteem. The converse is true of low self-esteem. Unfavorable self-evaluations trigger denial, deception, and avoidance in an attempt to disavow that which has already been glimpsed as true. This process leads to self-generated disapproval as a form of feedback to the self about personal adequacy.

At this point, we have discussed a number of ideas about the self in adolescence, including information about self-understanding and self-esteem. A summary of these ideas is presented in Concept Table 12.1. Next, we turn our attention to an important concept related to the self—identity.

IDENTITY

By far the most comprehensive and provocative theory of identity development has been told by Erik Erikson. Some experts on adolescence consider Erikson's ideas to be the single most influential theory of adolescent development. Erikson's theory was introduced in chapter 2. Here that introduction is expanded, beginning with reanalysis of his ideas on identity. Then we examine some contemporary thoughts on identity, the four

EXPLORATIONS IN CHILD DEVELOPMENT 12.1

Hitler, Luther, and Gandhi— The Development of Their Identities

Erik Erikson is a master at analyzing famous individuals' lives and discovering historical clues about their identity formation. Erikson also developed ideas for his view of identity development by analyzing the developmental history of clients in his clinical practice. Erikson (1968) believes that an individual's developmental history must be carefully scrutinized and analyzed to obtain clues about identity. He also believes that the best clues to understanding the world's history appear in the composite of individual life cycles. In the excerpts that follow,

Erikson analyzes the lives of Adolf Hitler, Martin Luther, and Mahatma Gandhi.

About Hitler, Erikson (1962) commented:

I will not go into the symbolism of Hitler's urge to build except to say that his shiftless and brutal father had consistently denied the mother a steady residence: one must read how Adolf took care of his mother when she wasted away from breast cancer to get an inkling of this young man's desperate urge to cure. But it would take a very extensive analysis, indeed, to indicate in what way a single boy can daydream his way into history and emerge a sinister genius, and how a whole nation becomes ready to accept the emotive power of that genius as a hope of fulfillment for its national aspirations and as a warrant for national criminality. . . .

The memoirs of young Hitler's friend indicate an almost pitiful fear on the part of the future dictator that he might be nothing. He had to challenge this possibility by being deliberately and totally anonymous; and only out of this self-chosen nothingness could he become everything. (pp. 108–109)

Although the identity crisis of Adolf Hitler led him to politics in a pathological effort to create a world order, the identity crisis of Martin Luther in a different era lead him to theology in an attempt to deal systematically with human nothingness, or lack of identity:

In confession, for example, he was so meticulous in the attempt to be truthful that he spelled out

statuses of identity, developmental changes, identity and gender, family influences on identity, cultural and ethnic aspects of identity, and identity and intimacy.

Erikson's Ideas on Identity

Who am I? What am I all about? What am I going to do with my life? What is different about me? How can I make it on my own? Not usually considered during childhood, these questions surface as common, virtually universal, concerns during adolescence. Adolescents clamor for solutions to these questions that revolve around the concept of identity, and it was Erik Erikson who first understood how central such questions are to understanding adolescent development. That today identity is believed to be a key concept in adolescent development is a result of Erikson's masterful thinking and analysis (Adams, 1992).

Revisiting Erikson's Views on Identity and the Human Life Cycle

Identity versus identity confusion *is Erikson's fifth developmental stage, which individuals experience during the adolescent years. At this time, adolescents face finding out who they are, what*

they are all about, and where they are going in life. Adolescents are confronted with many new roles, such as vocational and romantic, for example. A **psychological moratorium** *is Erikson's term for the gap between childhood security and adult autonomy that adolescents experience as part of their identity exploration.* As adolescents explore and search their culture's identity files, they often experiment with different roles. Youths who successfully cope with these conflicting identities emerge with a new sense of self that is both refreshing and acceptable. Adolescents who do not successfully resolve this identity crisis suffer what Erikson calls identity confusion. The confusion takes one of two courses: Individuals withdraw, isolating themselves from peers and family, or they immerse themselves in the world of peers and lose their identity in the crowd.

Erikson's ideas about adolescent identity development reveal rich insights into adolescents' thoughts and feelings, and reading one or more of his original writings is worthwhile. A good starting point is *Identity: Youth and Crisis* (1968). Other works that portray identity development are *Young Man Luther* (1962) and *Gandhi's Truth* (1969)—the latter won a Pulitzer Prize. A sampling of Erikson's writings from these books is presented in Explorations in Child Development 12.1.

every intention as well as every deed; he splintered relatively acceptable purities into smaller and smaller impurities; he reported temptations in historical sequence, starting back in childhood; and after having confessed for hours, would ask for special appointments in order to correct previous statements. In doing this, he was obviously both exceedingly compulsive and, at least unconsciously, rebellious. . . .

At this point, we must note a characteristic of great young rebels: their inner split between the temptation to surrender and the need to dominate. A great young rebel is torn between, on the one hand, tendencies to give in and fantasies of defeat (Luther used to resign himself to an early death at times of impending success), and the absolute need, on the other hand, to take the lead, not only over himself but over all the forces and people who impinge on him. (Erikson, 1968, p. 155–157)

And in his Pulitzer-Prize-winning novel on Mahatma Gandhi's life, Erikson describes the personality formation of Gandhi during his youth:

Straight and yet not stiff; shy and yet not withdrawn; intelligent and yet not bookish; willful and yet not stubborn; sensual and yet not soft. . . . We must try to reflect on the relation of such a youth to his father because the Mahatma places service to the father and the crushing guilt of failing in such service in the center of his adolescent turbulence. Some historians and political scientists seem to find it easy to interpret this account in

psychoanalytic terms; I do not. For the question is not how a particular version of the Oedipal complex "causes" a man to be both great and neurotic in a particular way, but rather how such a young person . . . manages the complexes which constrict other men. (Erikson, 1969, p. 113).

In these passages, the workings of an insightful, sensitive mind is shown looking for a historical perspective on personality development. Through analysis of the lives of such famous individuals as Hitler, Luther and Gandhi, and through the thousands of youth he has talked with in person, Erikson has pieced together a descriptive picture of identity development.

Mahatma Gandhi was the spiritual leader of India in the middle of the twentieth century. What factors does Erikson believe contributed to Gandhi's identity development?

"Who are you?" said the caterpillar. Alice replied rather shyly, "I—I hardly know; sir, just at present—at least I know who I was when I got up this morning, but I must have changed several times since then."
—Lewis Carroll
Alice in Wonderland, 1865

Personality and Role Experimentation

Two core ingredients in Erikson's theory of identity development are personality and role experimentation. As indicated earlier, Erikson believes that adolescents face an overwhelming number of choices and at some point during youth enter a period of psychological moratorium. During this moratorium, they try out different roles and personalities before they reach a stable sense of self. They may be argumentative one moment, cooperative the next. They may dress neatly one day, sloppily the next day. They may like a particular friend one week, despise the friend the next week. This personality experimentation is a deliberate effort on the part of adolescents to find out where they fit in the world.

"Do you have any idea who I am?"
Drawing by Koren; © 1988 The New Yorker Magazine, Inc.

As they gradually come to realize that they will be responsible for themselves and their own lives, adolescents search for what those lives are going to be. Many parents and other adults, accustomed to having children go along with what they say, may be bewildered or incensed by the wisecracks, the rebelliousness, and the rapid mood changes that accompany adolescence. It is important for adults to give adolescents the time and opportunities to explore roles and personalities. In turn, most adolescents eventually discard undesirable roles.

There are literally hundreds of roles for adolescents to try out, and probably just as many ways to pursue each role. Erikson believes that, by late adolescence, vocational roles are central to identity's development, especially in a highly technological society such as the United States. Youths who have been well trained to enter a workforce that offers the potential of reasonably high self-esteem will experience the least stress during the development of identity. Some youths have rejected jobs offering good pay and traditionally high social status, choosing instead to work in situations that allow them to be more genuinely helpful to their fellow humans, such as in the Peace Corps, in mental health clinics, or in schools for children from low-income backgrounds. Some youths prefer unemployment to the prospect of working at a job they feel they would be unable to perform well or at which they would feel useless. To Erikson, this attitude reflects the desire to achieve a meaningful identity through being true to oneself, rather than burying one's identity in that of the larger society. More information about Erikson's ideas on identity development appears in Explorations in Child Development 12.1, where you can read about his analysis of the identity development of some famous individuals.

"*While we're at supper, Billy, you'd make Daddy and Mommy very happy if you'd remove your hat, your sunglasses, and your earring.*"
Drawing by Ziegler; © 1985 The New Yorker Magazine, Inc.

Critical Thinking

Is identity development more difficult for adolescents today than it was 50 years ago? Explain your answer.

Some Contemporary Thoughts about Identity

Contemporary views of identity development suggest several important considerations. First, identity development is a lengthy process; in many instances it is a more gradual, less cataclysmic transition than Erikson's term *crisis* implies. Second, identity development is extraordinarily complex (Marcia, 1980, 1987). Identity formation neither begins nor ends with adolescence. It begins with the appearance of attachment, the development of a sense of self, and the emergence of independence in infancy, and reaches its final phase with a life review and integration in old age. What is important about identity in adolescence, especially late adolescence, is that for the first time physical development, cognitive development, and social development advance to the point at which the individual can sort through and synthesize childhood identities and identifications to construct a viable pathway toward adult maturity. Resolution of the identity issue at adolescence does not mean identity will be stable through the remainder of one's life. A person who develops a healthy identity is flexible, adaptive, and open to changes in society, in relationships, and in careers. This openness assures numerous reorganizations of identity features throughout the life of the person who has achieved identity.

Identity formation does not happen neatly, and it usually does not happen cataclysmically. At the bare minimum, it involves commitment to a vocational direction, an ideological stance, and a sexual orientation. Synthesizing the identity components can be a long, drawn-out process with many negations and affirmations of various roles and faces. Identities are developed in bits and pieces. Decisions are not made once and for all, but have to be made again and again. And the decisions may seem trivial at the time: whom to date, whether or not to break up, whether or not to have intercourse, whether or not to take drugs, whether to go to college after high school or get a job, which major to choose, whether to study or whether to play, whether or not to be politically active, and so on. Over the years of adolescence, the decisions begin to form a core of what the individual is all about as a person—what is called identity (Archer, 1989).

The Four Statuses of Identity

Eriksonian researcher James Marcia (1966, 1980, 1989, 1991) believes that Erikson's theory of identity development contains four statuses of identity, or ways of resolving the identity crisis: identity diffusion, identity foreclosure, identity moratorium, and identity achievement. The extent of an adolescent's crisis and commitment is used to classify the individual according to one of the four identity statuses. **Crisis** *is defined as a period of identity development during which the adolescent is choosing among meaningful alternatives.* Most researchers use the term *exploration* rather than *crisis,* although, in the spirit of Marcia's formulation, the term *crisis* is used here. **Commitment** *is a part of identity development in which adolescents show a personal investment in what they are going to do.*

Identity diffusion *is the term Marcia uses to describe adolescents who have not yet experienced a crisis (that is, they have not yet explored meaningful alternatives) or made any commitments.* Not only are they undecided about occupational and ideological choices, they are also likely to show little interest in such matters. **Identity foreclosure** *is the term Marcia uses to describe*

FIGURE 12.5

Marcia's four statuses of identity.

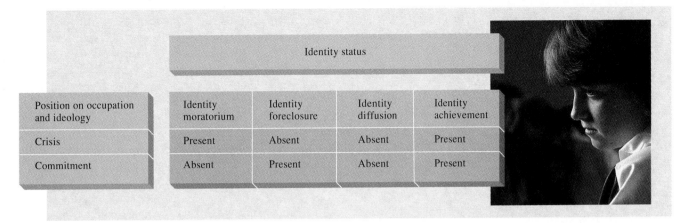

Identity status				
Position on occupation and ideology	Identity moratorium	Identity foreclosure	Identity diffusion	Identity achievement
Crisis	Present	Absent	Absent	Present
Commitment	Absent	Present	Absent	Present

adolescents who have made a commitment but have not experienced a crisis. This occurs most often when parents hand down commitments to their adolescents, usually in an authoritarian way. In these circumstances, adolescents have not had adequate opportunities to explore different approaches, ideologies, and vocations on their own. **Identity moratorium** *is the term Marcia uses to describe adolescents who are in the midst of a crisis, but whose commitments either are absent or are only vaguely defined.* **Identity achievement** *is Marcia's term for adolescents who have undergone a crisis and have made a commitment.* Marcia's four statuses of identity development are summarized in figure 12.5.

The identity status approach has been sharply criticized by some researchers and theoreticians (Blasi, 1988; Cote & Levine, 1988a,b; Lapsley & Power, 1988). They believe that the identity status approach distorts and trivializes Erikson's notions of crisis and commitment. For example, concerning crisis, Erikson emphasized youths' questioning the perceptions and expectations of one's culture and developing an autonomous position with regard to one's society. In the identity status approach, these complex questions are dealt with by simply evaluating whether a youth has thought about certain issues and has considered alternatives. Erikson's idea of commitment loses the meaning of investing one's self in certain lifelong projects and is interpreted simply as having made a firm decision or not. Others still believe that the identity status approach is a valuable contribution to understanding identity (Archer, 1989; Marcia, 1991; Waterman, 1989).

Developmental Changes

Young adolescents are primarily in Marcia's identity diffusion or moratorium statuses. At least three aspects of the young adolescent's development are important in identity formation (Marcia, 1987): Young adolescents must establish confidence in parental support, develop a sense of industry, and gain a self-reflective perspective on their future.

Some researchers believe the most important identity changes take place in youth rather than earlier in adolescence (Kroger, 1992). For example, Alan Waterman (1985, 1989, 1992) has found that from the years preceding high school

through the last few years of college, an increase in the number of individuals who are identity achieved occurs, along with a decrease in those who are identity diffused. College upperclassmen are more likely to be identity achieved than college freshmen or high school students. Many young adolescents are identity diffused. These developmental changes are especially true for vocational choice. For religious beliefs and political ideology, fewer college students have reached the identity achieved status, with a substantial number characterized by foreclosure and diffusion. Thus, the timing of identity may depend on the particular role involved, and many college students are still wrestling with ideological commitments (Arehart & Smith, 1990; Harter, 1990a,b).

> *The thoughts of youth are long, long thoughts.*
> —Henry Wadsworth Longfellow, 1858

Many identity status researchers believe that a common pattern of individuals who develop positive identities is to follow what are called "MAMA" cycles of *m*oratorium-*a*chievement-*m*oratorium-*a*chievement (Archer, 1989). These cycles may be repeated throughout life (Francis, Fraser, & Marcia, 1989). Personal, family, and societal changes are inevitable, and as they occur, the flexibility and skill required to explore new alternatives and develop new commitments are likely to facilitate an individual's coping skills.

Family Influences on Identity

Parents are important figures in the adolescent's development of identity. In studies that relate identity development to parenting styles, democratic parents, who encourage adolescents to participate in family decision making, foster identity achievement. Autocratic parents, who control the adolescent's behavior without giving the adolescent an opportunity to express opinions, encourage identity foreclosure. Permissive parents, who provide little guidance to adolescents and allow them to make their own decisions, promote identity diffusion (Bernard, 1981; Enright & others, 1980; Marcia, 1980).

Margaret Beale Spencer, shown here talking with adolescents, believes that adolescence is often a critical juncture in the identity development of ethnic minority individuals. Most ethnic minority individuals consciously confront their ethnicity for the first time in adolescence.

In addition to studies on parenting styles, researchers have also examined the role of individuality and connectedness in the development of identity. Developmentalist Catherine Cooper and her colleagues (Carlson, Cooper, & Hsu, 1990; Cooper & Grotevant, 1989; Grotevant & Cooper, 1985) believe that the presence of a family atmosphere that promotes both individuality and connectedness are important in the adolescent's identity development. **Individuality** *consists of two dimensions: self-assertion, the ability to have and communicate a point of view; and separateness, the use of communication patterns to express how one is different from others.* **Connectedness** *also consists of two dimensions: mutuality, sensitivity to and respect for others' views; and permeability, openness to others' views.* In general, Cooper's research findings reveal identity formation is enhanced by family relationships that are both individuated, which encourages adolescents to develop their own point of view, and connected, which provides a secure base from which to explore the widening social worlds of adolescence.

Stuart Hauser and his colleagues (Hauser & Bowlds, 1990; Hauser & others, 1984) have also illuminated family processes that promote the adolescent's identity development. They have found that parents who use *enabling* behaviors (such as explaining, accepting, and giving empathy) facilitate the adolescent's identity development more than parents who use *constraining* behaviors (such as judging and devaluing). In sum, family interaction styles that give the adolescent the right to question and to be different, within a context of support and mutuality, foster healthy patterns of identity development (Harter, 1990b).

Cultural and Ethnic Aspects of Identity

Erikson is especially sensitive to the role of culture in identity development. He points out that, throughout the world, ethnic minority groups have struggled to maintain their cultural identities while blending into the dominant culture (Erikson, 1968). Erikson says that this struggle for an inclusive identity,

or identity within the larger culture, has been the driving force in the founding of churches, empires, and revolutions throughout history.

For ethnic minority individuals, adolescence is often a special juncture in their development (Phinney, Espinoza, & Onwughalu, 1992; Phinney & Rosenthal, 1992; Spencer & Dornbusch, 1990; Spencer & Markstrom-Adams, 1990). Although children are aware of some ethnic and cultural differences, most ethnic minority individuals consciously confront their ethnicity for the first time in adolescence. In contrast to children, adolescents have the ability to interpret ethnic and cultural information, to reflect on the past, and to speculate about the future (Harter, 1990a,b). As they cognitively mature, ethnic minority adolescents become acutely aware of the evaluations of their ethnic group by the majority White culture (Comer, 1980; Ogbu, 1989). As one researcher commented, the young Black American child may learn that Black is beautiful, but conclude as an adolescent that White is powerful (Semaj, 1985).

Ethnic minority youths' awareness of negative appraisals, conflicting values, and restricted occupational opportunities can influence life choices and plans for the future (Spencer & Dornbusch, 1990). As one ethnic minority youth stated, "The future seems shut off, closed. Why dream? You can't reach your dreams. Why set goals? At least if you don't set any goals, you don't fail."

For many ethnic minority youth, a lack of successful ethnic minority role models with whom to identify is a special concern (Blash & Unger, 1992). The problem is especially acute for inner-city ethnic minority youth. Because of the lack of adult ethnic minority role models, some ethnic minority youth may conform to middle-class White values and identify with successful White role models. However, for many adolescents, their ethnicity and skin color constrain their acceptance by the White culture. Thus, many ethnic minority adolescents have a difficult task: negotiating two value systems—that of their own ethnic group and that of the White society. Some adolescents reject the mainstream, foregoing the rewards controlled by White Americans; others adopt the values and standards of the majority White culture; and yet others take the difficult path of biculturality (Hiraga & others, 1993).

In one investigation, ethnic identity exploration was higher among ethnic minority than among White American college students (Phinney & Alipura, 1990). In this same investigation, ethnic minority college students who had thought about and resolved issues involving their ethnicity had higher self-esteem than their ethnic minority counterparts who had not. In another investigation, the ethnic identity development of Asian American, Black American, Hispanic American, and White American tenth-grade students in Los Angeles was studied (Phinney, 1989). Adolescents from each of the three ethnic minority groups faced a similar need to deal with their ethnic-group identification in a predominately White American culture. In some instances, the adolescents from the three ethnic minority groups perceived different issues to be important in their resolution of ethnic identity. For Asian American adolescents, pressures to achieve academically and concerns about quotas that make it difficult to get into good colleges were

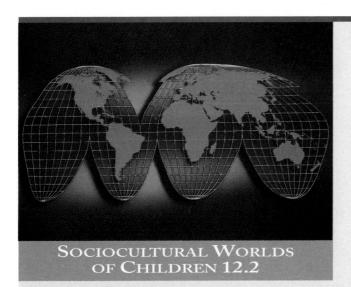

SOCIOCULTURAL WORLDS OF CHILDREN 12.2

The Development of Identity in Native American Children and Youth

Substandard living conditions, poverty, and chronic unemployment place many Native American youths at risk for school failure and poor health, which can contribute to problems in developing a positive identity (LaFromboise & Low, 1989). A special concern is the negative image of Native Americans that has been perpetuated for centuries in the majority White American culture. To consider further the development of identity in Native American youth, we will examine the experiences of a 12-year-old Hopi Indian boy.

The Hopi Indians are a quiet, thoughtful people who go to great lengths not to offend anyone. In a pueblo north of Albuquerque, a 12-year-old boy speaks: "I've been living in Albuquerque for a year. The Anglos I've met, they're different. I don't know why. In school, I drew a picture of my father's horse. One of the other kids wouldn't believe that it was ours. He said, 'You don't really own that horse.' I said, 'It's a horse my father rides, and I feed it every morning.' He said, 'How come?' I said, 'My uncle and my father are good riders, and I'm pretty good.' He said, 'I can ride a horse better than you, and I'd rather be a pilot.' I told him I never thought of being a pilot."

The Hopi boy continues, "Anglo kids, they won't let you get away with anything. Tell them something, and fast as lightning and loud as thunder, they'll say, 'I'm better than you, so there!' My father says it's always been like that."

The Indian adolescent is not really angry or envious of the White adolescent. Maybe he is in awe of his future power, maybe he fears it, and the White adolescent can't keep from wondering somehow that he has missed out on something and may end up "losing" (Coles, 1986).

The following words of another American Indian vividly capture some important ingredients of a Hopi adolescent's interest in a peaceful identity:

Rivers flow.	A small pebble
The sea sings.	On a giant shore;
Oceans roar.	Who am I
Tides rise.	To ask who I am?
Who am I?	Isn't it enough to be?

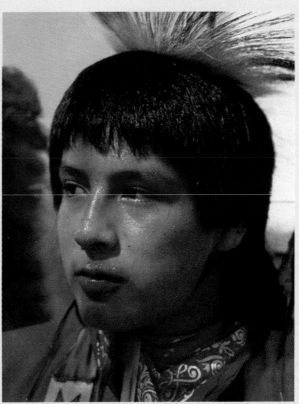

The Native American adolescent's quest for identity involves a cultural meshing of tribal customs and the technological, educational demands of modern society.

salient issues. Many Black American adolescent females discussed their realization that White American standards of beauty (especially hair and skin color) did not apply to them; Black American adolescent males were concerned with possible job discrimination and the need to distinguish themselves from a negative societal image of Black male adolescents. For Hispanic American adolescents, prejudice was a recurrent theme, as was conflicting values between their Hispanic culture heritage and the majority culture. To read further about identity development in ethnic minority youth, turn to Sociocultural Worlds of Children 12.2.

Gender and Identity Development

In Erikson's (1968) classic presentation of identity development, the division of labor between the sexes was reflected in his assertion that males' aspirations were mainly oriented toward career and ideological commitments, while females' were centered around marriage and childbearing. In the 1960s and 1970s researchers found support for Erikson's assertion about gender differences in identity. For example, vocational concerns were more central to the identity of males, and affiliative concerns were more important in the identity of females (La Voie,

1976). However, in the last decade, as females have developed stronger vocational interests, gender differences are turning into gender similarities (Waterman, 1985).

Some investigators believe the order of stages proposed by Erikson are different for females and males. One view is that for males, identity formation precedes the stage of intimacy, while for females, intimacy precedes identity (Douvan & Adelson, 1966). These ideas are consistent with the belief that relationships and emotional bonds are more important concerns of females, while autonomy and achievement are more important concerns of males (Gilligan, 1990). In one study, the development of a clear sense of self by adolescent girls was related to their concerns about care and response in relationships (Rogers, 1987). In another investigation, a strong sense of self in college women was associated with their ability to solve problems of care in relationships while staying connected with both self and others (Skoe & Marcia, 1988). Indeed, conceptualization and measurement of identity development in females should include interpersonal content (Patterson, Sochting, & Marcia, 1992).

The task of identity exploration may be more complex for females than males in that females may try to establish identities in more domains than males. In today's world, the options for females have increased, and thus may at times be confusing and conflicting, especially for females who hope to successfully integrate family and career roles (Archer, 1989, 1992; Gilligan, 1990).

At this point we have discussed many different ideas about culture and identity in adolescence. A summary of these ideas is presented in Concept Table 12.2.

PERSPECTIVES ON PARENTING AND EDUCATION

Explorations in Education, Work, and Identity Development

Susan Harter (1990a,b) addressed the importance of developing programs for youth that promote the *active* and *realistic* exploration of broad identity goals, such as educational and occupational choices. Such programs may take the form of on-the-job experiences, as occurs in the Boston Compact Youth Incentive Program, which provides students with good-paying summer jobs if they maintain a good record of school attendance and performance. Another program strengthens the link between high school activities and the world of work and provides opportunities for exploring alternatives (Lang & Rivera, 1987). This program emphasizes adolescents' choice of areas in which they are both interested and competent, letting them choose educational opportunities that further their development in these domains. This strategy is consistent with Harter's conclusion that the highest levels of self-esteem are found in individuals who are performing competently in domains that are important to the self.

One strategy is to encourage society to recognize the positive benefits of competence in many different domains, not just academic competence. Another strategy is to acknowledge that education

Shown here is a scene from the movie Stand and Deliver, *in which Hispanic high school teacher, Jaime Escalante (in the center with a cap), spent many evenings and weekends tutoring Hispanic students in math in addition to effectively teaching the students math in the classroom. Escalante's commitment and motivation was transferred to the students, many of whom obtained college scholarships and passed advanced placement tests in calculus.*

is the primary means for achieving success, and to provide individuals with poor academic skills and low self-esteem better support and more individualized attention. The inspiration of Hispanic high school teacher Jaime Escalante, documented in the movie *Stand and Deliver,* reflects this latter strategy. Escalante was a California high school teacher who spent many evenings and weekends tutoring Hispanic students in math, in addition to effectively teaching the students math in the classroom. Escalante's commitment and motivation were transferred to the Hispanic high school students, many of whom obtained college scholarships and

CONCEPT TABLE 12.2

Identity

Concept	Processes/Related Ideas	Characteristics/Description
Erikson's ideas on identity	Their nature	Erikson argues that identity versus identity confusion is the fifth stage in the human life cycle, occurring at about the time of adolescence, a time when individuals enter a psychological moratorium between the security of childhood and the autonomy of adulthood. Personality exploration and the exploration of roles are two important ingredients of identity development. In technological societies, such as the United States, the vocational role is especially important.
	Some contemporary thoughts about identity	Identity development is a lengthy process, in many cases more gradual than Erikson implied. Identity development is extraordinarily complex. Identity development is done in bits and pieces. For the first time in development, individuals during adolescence are physically, cognitively, and socially mature enough to synthesize their lives and pursue a viable path toward adult maturity.
	The four statuses of identity	Marcia proposed four identity statuses—identity diffusion, identity foreclosure, identity moratorium, and identity achievement—that are based on crisis (exploration) and commitment. Some experts believe that the identity status approach oversimplifies Erikson's ideas.
	Developmental changes	Some experts believe that the main identity changes take place in youth rather than earlier in adolescence. College juniors and seniors are more likely to be identity achieved than freshmen or high school students, although many college students are still wrestling with the ideological commitments. Individuals often follow "moratorium-achievement-moratorium-achievement" cycles throughout life.
Family influences, cultural and ethnic aspects, and gender	Family influences	Parents are important figures in adolescents' identity development. Democratic parenting facilities identity development in adolescence; autocratic and permissive parenting do not. Cooper and her colleagues have shown that both individuality and connectedness in family relations are important contributors to adolescent identity development. Hauser has shown that enabling behaviors promote identity development more than constraining behaviors.
	Cultural and ethnic aspects of identity	Erikson is especially sensitive to the role of culture in identity development, underscoring how, throughout the world, ethnic minority groups have struggled to maintain their cultural identities while blending into dominant cultures. Adolescence is often a special juncture in the identity development of ethnic minority individuals because for the first time they consciously confront their ethnic identity. Although children are aware of some ethnic and cultural differences, most individuals first consciously confront their ethnicity in adolescence. A problem for many ethnic minority youths is the lack of successful ethnic minority role models with whom to identify.
	Identity and gender	Erikson's classical theory argued that gender differences in identity development exist, with adolescent males having a stronger interest in vocational roles, adolescent females a stronger interest in marriage and family roles. More recent studies have revealed that, as females have developed stronger vocational interests, gender differences in identity have turned into similarities. However, others argue that relationships and emotional bonds are more central to the identity development of females than of males and that female identity development is more complex than male identity development.

passed advanced placement tests in calculus. Insisting that high school and college athletes maintain a respectable grade point average is a policy that endorses the importance of academic achievement and competence in other domains, as is the requirement that students maintain respectable grades to participate in jobs programs.

One program in Washington, D.C., has helped many ethnic minority adolescents do better in school. In 1983, Dr. Henry Gaskins began an after-school tutorial program for ethnic minority students. For four hours every weeknight and all day Saturday, 80 students receive one-on-one assistance from Gaskins and his wife, two adult volunteers, and academically talented peers. Those who can afford it contribute five dollars to cover the cost of school supplies. In addition to tutoring in specific subjects, Gaskin's home-based academy helps students set personal goals and commit to a desire to succeed. Many of his students come from families in which the parents are high school dropouts and either can't or are not motivated to help their adolescent sons and daughters achieve in school. In addition, the academy prepares students

Dr. Henry Gaskins, here talking with three high school students, began an after-school tutorial program for ethnic minority students in 1983 in Washington, D.C. Volunteers like Dr. Gaskins can be especially helpful in developing a stronger sense of the importance of education in ethnic minority adolescents.

to qualify for scholarships and college entrance exams. Gaskins recently received the President's Volunteer Action Award at the White House. ▪

CONCLUSIONS

This chapter on the self and identity has been about how children perceive themselves, evaluate themselves, feel about themselves, and explore who they are.

We began by examining a 15-year-old girl's complex self-description and then studied two very important aspects of the self—self-understanding and self-esteem. In reading about self-understanding, we learned what self-understanding is, its developmental course, and the role of perspective taking in self-understanding.

In reading about self-esteem, we learned what it is, how it can be measured, the role of parenting in children's self-esteem, how group identity is related to self-esteem, and how children's self-esteem can be improved. Our exploration of identity focused on Erikson's ideas about identity, some contemporary thoughts about identity, the four statuses of identity, family influences on identity, cultural and ethnic aspects of identity, and the relation of gender to identity development. We also identified how education and work are linked to identity development. By again reading the two in-chapter reviews on pages 362 and 371 you can obtain a summary of the chapter.

While in this chapter we only briefly studied gender development—exploring gender's role in identity development—in the next chapter we extensively examine the role of gender in children's development.

KEY TERMS

self-understanding   This is the child's cognitive representation of the self, the substance and content of the child's self-concept. (353)

possible self   What individuals might become, what they would like to become, and what they are afraid of becoming. (354)

self-esteem   The evaluative and affective dimension of self-concept. (357)

social identity theory   Social psychologist Henry Tajfel's theory that, when individuals are assigned to a group, they invariably think of that group as an in-group for them, because individuals want to have a positive self-image. (359)

ethnocentrism   The tendency to favor one's own group over other groups. (360)

prejudice   An unjustified negative attitude toward an individual because of that person's membership in a group. (360)

identity versus identity confusion   Erikson's fifth stage of development during which adolescents face finding out who they are, what they are all about, and where they are going in life. (364)

psychological moratorium   The long gap between childhood security and adult autonomy that adolescents experience as part of their identity exploration. (364)

crisis   A period of identity development during which the adolescent is choosing among meaningful alternatives. (366)

commitment   The part of identity development in which adolescents show a personal investment in what they are going to do. (366)

identity diffusion   Marcia uses this term to describe adolescents who have not yet experienced a crisis or made any commitments. (366)

identity foreclosure   This is Marcia's term to describe adolescents who have made a commitment, but have not experienced a crisis. (366)

identity moratorium   Adolescents who are in the midst of a crisis, but whose commitments either are absent or are only vaguely defined. (367)

identity achievement   Marcia's term for adolescents who have undergone a crisis and have made a commitment. (367)

individuality   An important element in adolescent identity development. It consists of two dimensions: self-assertion (the ability to have and communicate a point of view) and separateness (the use of communication patterns to express how one is different from others). (368)

connectedness   An important element in adolescent identity development. It consists of two dimensions: mutuality (sensitivity to and respect for other's views) and permeability (openness to other's views). (368)

SUGGESTED READINGS

Comer, J. P., & Poussaint, A. F. (1992). *Raising Black children.* New York: Plume. The well-respected authors provide answers to nearly 1,000 questions on the problems involved in raising Black children; special attention is given to Black children's self-esteem and identity.

Damon, W., & Hart, D. (1988). *Self-understanding in childhood and adolescence.* New York: Cambridge University Press. An extensive description of the development of self-understanding is provided, including Damon and Hart's integrative, developmental model of self-understanding.

Erikson, E. H. (1969). *Gandhi's truth.* New York: W. W. Norton. In this Pulitzer Prize-winning novel, Erikson weaves an insightful picture of Gandhi's development of identity.

Harter, S. (1990). Self and identity development. In S. S. Feldman & G. R. Elliott (Eds.), *At the threshold: The developing adolescent.* Cambridge, MA: Harvard University Press. This is an excellent overview of contemporary theory and research on the nature of self and identity development in adolescence by one of the leading researchers in the area of self-understanding.

Selman, R. L. (1980). *The growth of interpersonal understanding.* New York: Academic Press. Considerable detail about Selman's developmental theory of perspective taking and self-development is provided. The book includes information about clinical implications for helping children with problems.

Girl Leaning on a Window Sill,
Rembrandt, 1601–1669 (Detail)

13

Gender

Chapter Outline

Chapter Boxes

It is fatal to be man or woman pure and simple; one must be woman-manly or man-womanly.

—Virginia Woolf

> *What are little boys made of?*
> *Frogs and snails,*
> *And puppy dogs' tails.*
> *What are little girls made of?*
> *Sugar and spice*
> *And all that's nice.*
>
> —J. O. Halliwell,
> —*Nursery Rhymes of England,* 1844

IMAGES OF CHILDREN

Tomorrow's Gender Worlds of Today's Children

Controversial currents swirl around today's females and males. Females increasingly struggle to gain influence and change the worlds of business, politics, and relationships with males. The changes are far from complete, but social reformers hope that, a generation from now, the struggles of the last decades of the twentieth century will have generated more freedom, influence, and flexibility for females. Possibly a decade or two from now today's children will live in a world in which equal pay, child care, abortion, rape, and domestic violence will no longer be discussed as "women's issues" but rather as economic issues, family issues, and ethical issues—reflecting equal concern of females and males. Possibly a 10-year-old girl today will head a major corporation in 30 years and the circumstance will not make headlines by virtue of her gender. Half the presidential candidates may be women and nobody will notice.

What would it take to get from here to there? The choices are not simple ones. When Barbara Bush went to Wellesley College to celebrate motherhood and wifely virtues, she stimulated a national debate on what it means to be a successful woman. The debate was further fueled by TV anchorwoman Connie Chung's announcement that she would abandon the fast track at CBS in a final drive to become a mother at 44. At the same time, children's male role models are also in a state of flux. Wall street star Peter Lynch, the head of Fidelity Investment's leading mutual fund, resigned to have more time with his family and pursue humanitarian projects (Gibbs, 1990).

When asked to sketch their futures, many of today's college students say they want good careers, good marriages, and two or three children, but they don't want their children to be raised by strangers (Spade & Reese, 1991). Idealistic? Maybe. Some of you will reach these goals, while others of you will make other choices. Some women will choose to remain single as they pursue their career goals, others will become married but not have children, and yet others will balance the demands of family and work. In a word, not all females have the same goals; neither do all males. What is important for us is to develop a society free of barriers and discrimination, one that allows today's children—whether female or male—to choose freely, to meet their expectations, and to realize their potential.

PREVIEW

The famous quotation at the beginning of this chapter describes the behavior of boys and girls as being very different—boys are made of frogs and snails and puppy dogs' tails, girls of sugar and spice and all that's nice. In this chapter we will tackle the question of how different or similar boys and girls really are. We also will discuss biological, cognitive, and social influences on gender, how gender roles can be classified, the feminist perspective on gender, and the relation between gender and ethnicity. But to begin, we first need to define gender.

What Is Gender?

What exactly is meant by gender? **Gender** *refers to the sociocultural dimension of being female or male.* Two aspects of gender bear special mention: gender identity and gender role. **Gender identity** *is the sense of being female or male, which most children acquire by the time they are 3 years old.* A **gender role** *is a set of expectations that prescribe how females and males should think, act, and feel.*

Biological, Social, and Cognitive Influences on Gender

How strong is biology's influence on gender? How extensively do children's social experiences shape their gender development? How do cognitive factors influence gender development?

Biological Influences

It was not until the 1920s that researchers confirmed the existence of human sex chromosomes, the genetic material that determines our sex. In chapter 3, you learned that humans normally have 46 chormosomes arranged in pairs. The 23rd pair may have two X-shaped chromosomes to produce a female, or it may have an X-shaped and a Y-shaped chromosome to produce a male.

In the first few weeks of gestation, female and male embryos look alike. Male sex organs start to differ from female sex organs when XY chromosomes in the male embryo trigger the secretion of **androgen,** *the main class of male sex hormones.* Low levels of androgen in a female embryo allow the normal development of female sex organs.

Although rare, an imbalance in this system of hormone secretion can occur during fetal development. If there is insufficient androgen in a male embryo or an excess of androgen in a female embryo, the result is an individual with both male and female sex organs, a hermaphrodite. When genetically female (XX chromosomes) infants are born with masculine-looking genitals, surgery at birth can achieve a genital/genetic match. **Estrogen** *is the main class of female sex hormones.* At puberty, the production of estrogen begins to influence both physical development and behavior, but before then these females often behave in a "tomboyish" manner, acting more aggressively than most girls. They also dress and play in ways that are more characteristic of boys than girls (Ehrhardt, 1987; Money, 1987).

Is the behavior of these surgically corrected girls due to their prenatal hormones, or is it the result of their social experiences? Experiments with various animal species reveal that, when male hormones are injected into female embryos, the females develop masculine physical traits and behave more aggressively (Hines, 1982). However, in humans, hormones exert less control over behavior. Perhaps, because these girls look more masculine, they are treated more like boys and so adopt their boyish ways.

Although prenatal hormones may or may not influence gender behavior, psychoanalytic theorists, such as Sigmund Freud and Erik Erikson, have argued that an individual's genitals do play a pivotal role. Freud argued that human behavior and history are directly influenced by sexual drives and suggested that gender and sexual behavior are essentially unlearned and instinctual. Erikson went even further: he argued that, because of genital structure, males are more intrusive and aggressive, females more inclusive and passive. Erikson's critics contend that he has not given enough credit to experience and they argue that women and men are more free to choose their behavior than Erikson allowed. In response, Erikson has clarified his view, pointing out that he never said that biology is the sole determinant of differences between the sexes. Biology, he said, interacts with both cultural and psychological factors to produce behavior.

No one argues about the presence of genetic, biochemical, and anatomical differences between the sexes. Even child developmentalists with a strong environmental orientation acknowledge that boys and girls are treated differently because of their physical differences and their different roles in reproduction. The importance of biological factors is not at issue. What is at issue is the directness or indirectness of their effects on social behavior (Huston, 1983). For example, if a high androgen level directly influences the central nervous system, which, in turn, increases activity level, then the biological effect on behavior is direct. By contrast, if a child's high level of androgen produces strong muscle development, which, in turn, causes others to expect the child to be a good athlete and, in turn, leads the child to participate in sports, then the biological effect on behavior is indirect.

Although virtually everyone thinks that children's behavior as males or females is due to an interaction of biological and environmental factors, an interactionist position means different things to different people (Bancroft & Reinisch, 1990; Hinde, 1992; Maccoby, 1987b; Money, 1987). For some, it suggests that certain environmental conditions are required before preprogrammed dispositions appear. For others, it suggests that a particular environment will have different effects depending on the child's predispositions. For still others, it means that children shape their environments, including their interpersonal environment, and vice versa. The processes of influence and counterinfluence unfold over time. Throughout development, males and females actively construct their own versions of acceptable masculine and feminine behavior patterns.

Social Influences

In our culture, adults discriminate between the sexes shortly after the infant's birth. The "pink and blue" treatment may be applied to boys and girls before they leave the hospital. Soon afterward, differences in hair styles, clothes, and toys become obvious. Adults and peers reward these differences throughout development. And boys and girls learn gender roles through imitation or observational learning by watching what other people say and do. In recent years, the idea that parents are the critical socializing agents in gender role development has come under fire (Huston, 1983). Parents are only one of many sources through which the individual learns gender roles. Culture, schools, peers, the media, and other family members are others.

FIGURE 13.1

Parents influence their children's gender development by action and example.

Theory	Processes	Outcome
Freud's identification theory	Sexual attraction to opposite-sex parent at 3–5 years of age; anxiety about sexual attraction and subsequent identification with same-sex parent at 5–6 years of age	Gender behavior similar to same-sex parent
Social learning theory	Rewards and punishments of gender-appropriate and inappropriate behavior by adults and peers; observation and imitation of models' masculine and feminine behavior	Gender behavior

Yet it is important to guard against swinging too far in this direction because—especially in the early years of development—parents are important influences on gender development.

Identification and Social Learning Theories

Two prominent theories address the way children acquire masculine and feminine attitudes and behaviors from their parents. **Identification theory** *stems from Freud's view that the preschool child develops a sexual attraction to the opposite-sex parent, then by approximately 5 or 6 years of age, renounces this attraction because of anxious feelings, and subsequently identifies with the same-sex parent, unconsciously adopting the same-sex parent's characteristics.* However, today many child developmentalists do not believe gender development proceeds on the basis of identification, at least in terms of Freud's emphasis on childhood sexual attraction. Children become gender-typed much earlier than 5 or 6 years of age, and they become masculine or feminine even when the same-sex parent is not present in the family.

Children need models rather than critics.
                              —Joseph Joubert

The **social learning theory of gender** *emphasizes that children's gender development occurs through observation and imitation of gender behavior, and through the rewards and punishments children experience for gender appropriate and inappropriate behavior.* Unlike identification theory, social learning theory argues that sexual attraction to parents is not involved in gender development. (A comparison of identification and social learning views is presented in figure 13.1.) Parents often use rewards and punishments to teach their daughters to be feminine ("Karen, you are being a good girl when you play gently with your doll") and masculine ("Keith, a boy as big as you is not supposed to cry"). Peers also extensively reward and punish gender behavior. And by observing adults and peers at home, at school, in the neighborhood, and on television, children are widely exposed to a myriad of models who display masculine and feminine behavior. Critics of the social learning view argue that gender development is not as passively acquired as it indicates. Later we will discuss the cognitive views of gender development, which stress that children actively construct their gender world.

Parental Influences

Parents, by action and example, influence their children's gender development. Both mothers and fathers are psychologically important in children's gender development. Mothers are more consistently given responsibility for nurturance and physical care; fathers are more likely to engage in playful interaction and be given responsibility for ensuring that boys and girls conform to existing cultural norms. And whether or not they have more influence on them, fathers are more involved in socializing their sons than their daughters (Lamb, 1986). Fathers seem to play an especially important part in gender role development—they

As reflected in this tug-of-war battle between boys and girls, the playground in elementary school is like going to "gender school." Elementary school children show a clear preference for being with and liking same-sex peers.

are more likely to act differently toward sons and daughters than mothers, and thus contribute more to distinctions between the genders (Huston, 1983).

Many parents encourage boys and girls to engage in different types of play and activities (Fagot, Leinbach, & O'Boyle, 1992; Fisher-Thompson & others, 1993). Girls are more likely to be given dolls to play with during childhood and, when old enough, are more likely to be assigned baby-sitting duties. Girls are encouraged to be more nurturant and emotional than boys, and their fathers are more likely to engage in aggressive play with their sons than their daughters. As adolescents increase in age, parents permit boys more freedom than girls, allowing them to be away from home and stay out later without supervision. When parents place severe restrictions on their adolescent sons, it has been found to be especially disruptive to the sons' development (Baumrind, 1989).

Peer Influences

Parents provide the earliest discrimination of gender roles in development, but before long, peers join the societal process of responding to and modeling masculine and feminine behavior. Children who play in sex-appropriate activities tend to be rewarded for doing so by their peers. Those who play in cross-sexed activities tend to be criticized by their peers or left to play alone. Children show a clear preference for being with and liking same-sex peers (Buhrmester, 1993; Maccoby, 1989, 1993), and this tendency usually becomes stronger during the middle and late childhood years (Hayden-Thomson, Rubin, & Hymel,

1987). After extensive observations of elementary school playgrounds, two researchers characterized the play settings as "gender school," pointing out that boys teach one another the required masculine behavior and enforce it strictly (Luria & Herzog, 1985). Girls also pass on the female culture and mainly congregate with one another. Individual "tomboy" girls can join boys' activities without losing their status in the girls' groups, but the reverse is not true for boys, reflecting our society's greater sex-typing pressure for boys.

Peer demands for conformity to gender role become especially intense during adolescence. While there is greater social mixing of males and females during early adolescence, in both formal groups and in dating, peer pressure is strong for the adolescent boy to be the very best male possible and for the adolescent girl to be the very best female possible.

School and Teacher Influences

In a recent Gallup poll, 80 percent of the respondents agreed that the federal government should promote educational programs intended to reduce such social problems as poverty and unequal educational opportunities for minorities and females (Gallup & Clark, 1987). Discriminatory treatment on the basis of gender can be found across all ability groups, but in many cases the stereotypically lower-valued group (in this case, females) is treated as though they are a lower-ability group. For example, girls with strong math abilities are frequently given fewer quality instructional interactions from teachers than their male counterparts (Eccles, MacIver, & Lange, 1986). And, minority females are given fewer teacher interactions than other females, who are given fewer than Black males, who are given fewer than White males (Sadker, Sadker, & Klein, 1986).

In one study, researchers were trained in an observation system to collect data in more than a hundred fourth-, sixth-, and eighth-grade classrooms (Sadker & Sadker, 1986). At all three grade levels, male students were involved in more interactions than female students, and male students were given more attention from teachers. Male students were also given more remediation, more criticism, and more praise than female students.

Historically, education in the United States has been male defined rather than gender balanced. In many instances, traditional male activities, especially White male activities, have been the educational norm. Although females mature earlier, are ready for verbal and math training at a younger age, and have control of small-motor skills earlier than males, educational curricula have been constructed mainly to mirror the development of males. Decisions about the grade in which students should read *Huckleberry Finn,* do long division, or begin to write essays are based primarily on male developmental patterns. Some experts believe that this state of educational affairs means that some girls may become bored or give up, with most girls learning simply to hold back, be quiet, and smile (Shakeshaft, 1986).

Three trends in sex equity education research have been identified (Klein, 1988). First, there is a trend toward greater investigation of subtle discrimination and stereotyping. Much of the gender equity research and initial gender equity policies in the 1970s focused on identifying and putting an end to overt discrimination and stereotyping. By 1981, it was noted that while some progress had been made toward equity in areas of overt sex discrimination such as athletics and college admissions, many subtle types of sex discrimination and stereotyping, such as sex bias in classroom interactions, still remained. Gender equity researchers are now calling attention to sex discrimination and stereotyping in less visible problem areas such as home economics, foreign language, visual arts, and sex education (Spencer, 1986).

A second trend in gender equity education research is a shift toward male- and female-valued educational outcome goals. In addition to assisting females in achieving parity with males, researchers and policymakers are focusing more on the development of skills associated with females (Belenky & others, 1986). For example, placing more value on skills such as writing and human relations, areas in which females excel, can change the content covered in many standardized academic achievement tests. This type of change could improve females' achievement test scores, self-esteem, and job prospects.

A third trend in gender equity education research is an increased emphasis on gender equity outcomes. Much of the initial gender equity education research focused on identifying inequities or problems. Once researchers understand how far we are from attaining gender equity goals, they can emphasize the effectiveness of various gender equity solutions in reaching these goals. For example, researchers have found that girls' participa-

tion and achievement in mathematics becomes more equal to that of boys through the use of multiple strategies that include anxiety reduction, "hands-on" math instructional experiences, career awareness activities, "girl-friendly" classrooms, and role models (Eccles, MacIver, & Lange, 1986; Stage & others, 1985).

Media Influences

As we have described, children encounter masculine and feminine roles in their everyday interactions with parents, peers, and teachers. The messages carried by the media about what is appropriate or inappropriate for males and for females are important influences on gender development as well.

A special concern is the way females are pictured on television. In the 1970s, it became apparent that television was portraying females as less competent than males. For example, about 70 percent of the prime-time characters were males, men were more likely to be shown in the workforce, women were more likely to be shown as housewives and in romantic roles, men were more likely to appear in higher status jobs and in a greater diversity of occupations, and men were presented as more aggressive and constructive (Sternglanz & Serbin, 1974).

In the 1980s, television networks became more sensitive to how males and females were portrayed on television shows. Consequently, many programs now focus on divorced families, cohabitation, and women in high-status roles. Even with the onset of this type of programming researchers continue to find that television portrays males as more competent than females (Durkin, 1985). In one investigation, young adolescent girls indicated that television occupations are more extremely stereotyped than real-life occupations (Wroblewski & Huston, 1987).

Gender role stereotyping also appears in the print media. In magazine advertising, females are shown more often in advertisements for beauty products, cleaning products, and home appliances, while males are shown more often in advertisements for cars, liquor, and travel. As with television programs, females are being portrayed as more competent in advertisements than in the past, but advertisers have not yet given them equal status with males.

So far in our discussion of gender, we have seen that both biological and social factors play important roles in children's gender development. Recently, many child developmentalists have also recognized the important role that cognitive factors play.

Cognitive Influences

What is the cognitive developmental view of gender? What is the gender schema theory of gender development? What role does language play in gender development? We consider each of these questions in turn.

Cognitive Developmental Theory

In the **cognitive developmental theory of gender,** *children's gender typing occurs after they have developed a concept of gender. Once they consistently conceive of themselves as male or female, children often organize their world on the basis of gender.* Initially developed by psychologist Lawrence Kohlberg (1966), this theory argues that gender development proceeds in the following way: a child realizes, "I am a girl; I want to do girl things; therefore, the opportunity to do girl things is rewarding." Having acquired the ability to categorize, children then strive toward consistency in the use of categories and behavior. Kohlberg based his ideas on Piaget's cognitive developmental theory. As children's cognitive development matures, so does their understanding of gender. Although 2-year-olds can apply the labels of *boy* and *girl* correctly to themselves and others, their concept of gender is simple and concrete. Preschool children rely on physical features, such as dress and hairstyle, to decide who falls into which category. Girls are people with long hair, they think, whereas boys are people who never wear dresses. Many preschool children believe that people can change their own gender at will by getting a haircut or a new outfit. They do not yet have the cognitive machinery to think of gender as adults do. According to Kohlberg, all the reinforcement in the world won't modify that fact. However, by the concrete operational stage (the third stage in Piaget's theory, entered at about 6 or 7 years of age), children understand gender constancy—that a male is still a male regardless of whether he wears pants or a skirt, or his hair is short or long (Tavris & Wade, 1984). When their concept of gender constancy is clearly established, children are then motivated to become a competent, or "proper," girl or boy. Consequently, she or he finds female or male activities rewarding and imitates the behavior of same-sex models.

> *Childhood decides.*
> —Jean-Paul Sartre

Gender Schema Theory

A **schema** *is a cognitive structure, a network of associations that organizes and guides an individual's perceptions.* A **gender schema** *organizes the world in terms of female and male.* **Gender schema theory** *states that an individual's attention and behavior are guided by an internal motivation to conform to gender-based sociocultural standards and stereotypes* (Bem, 1981; Levy, 1991; Levy & Carter, 1989; Liben & Signorella, 1987, 1993; Martin, 1989, 1993; Martin & Halverson, 1987; Martin & Rose, 1991; Rose & Martin, 1993). Gender schema theory suggests that "gender typing" occurs when individuals are ready to encode and organize information along the lines of what is considered appropriate or typical for males and females in a society. Whereas Kohlberg's cognitive developmental theory argues that a particular cognitive prerequisite—gender constancy—is necessary for gender typing, gender schema theory states that a general readiness to respond to and categorize information on the basis of culturally defined gender roles fuels children's gender-typing activities. A comparison of the cognitive developmental and gender schema theories is presented in figure 13.2.

While researchers have shown that the appearance of gender constancy in children is related to their level of cognitive development, especially the acquisition of conservation skills (which supports the cognitive developmental theory of gender)

FIGURE 13.2

A comparison of cognitive developmental and gender schema theories of gender development.

Theory	Processes	Outcome
Cognitive developmental theory	Development of gender constancy, especially around 6–7 years of age, when conservation skills develop; after children develop ability to consistently conceive of themselves as male or female, children often organize their world on the basis of gender, such as selecting same-sex models to imitate	Gender-typed behavior
Gender schema theory	Sociocultural emphasis on gender-based standards and stereotypes; children's attention and behavior are guided by an internal motivation to conform to these gender-based standards and stereotypes, allowing children to interpret the world through a network of gender-organized thoughts	Gender-typed behavior

(Emmerich & others, 1977; Serbin & Sprafkin, 1986), they have also shown that young children who are pre-gender constant have more gender role knowledge than the cognitive developmental theory of gender predicts (which supports gender schema theory) (Carter & Levy, 1988; Carter & Taylor, in press). Today, gender schema theorists acknowledge that gender constancy is one important aspect of gender role development, but stress that other cognitive factors—such as gender schema—are also very important (Levy & Carter, 1989).

Critical Thinking

How do cognitive theories of gender differ from the social learning and identification theories of gender discussed earlier?

Two main theories about the structure of gender schema have been proposed. Janet Spence (1984, 1985) believes that monolithic concepts such as gender schema or sex-role identification are not very useful. Rather, she argues that gender-related phenomena are multidimensional in nature, with the different factors being somewhat independent of each other. From this perspective, consistency in stereotyping across domains and people would not be expected. Spence also stresses that gender schema may be monolithic in their origin (that is, when they first appear in young children's minds), but that they become more differentiated across the lifespan (Bigler, Liben, & Yekel, 1992). The second main theory about the structure of gender schema was proposed by Sandra Bem (1979, 1981), who argued that there is considerable consistency in stereotyping across domains and people. Which theory is correct? Data have been offered in support of both theories, and the issue of consistency and independence across the domains of gender has not yet been settled.

The Role of Language in Gender Development

Gender is present in the language children use and encounter (Hort & Leinbach, 1993; Quay, Minore, & Fraizer, 1993). The nature of the language children hear most of the time is sexist. That is, the English language contains gender bias, especially through the use of "he" and "man" to refer to everyone (O'Donnel, 1989). For example, in one investigation, mothers and their 1- to 3-year-old children looked at popular children's books, such as "The Three Bears" together (DeLoache, Cassidy, & Carpenter, 1987). The three bears were almost always referred to as boys: 95 percent of all characters of indeterminate gender were referred to by mothers as males. More about children's experiences with sexist language appears in Explorations in Child Development 13.1.

At this point, we have discussed a number of ideas about what gender is and about the biological, social, and cognitive influences on gender. A summary of these ideas is presented in Concept Table 13.1. Now we will turn our attention to gender stereotyping and the similarities and differences between boys and girls.

GENDER STEREOTYPES, SIMILARITIES, AND DIFFERENCES

How pervasive is gender role stereotyping? What are the real differences between boys and girls?

Gender Role Stereotyping

Gender role stereotypes *are broad categories that reflect our impressions and beliefs about females and males.* All stereotypes, whether they are based on gender, ethnicity, or other groupings, refer to an image of what the typical member of a particular social category is like. The world is extremely complex. Every day we are confronted with thousands of different stimuli. The use of stereotypes is one way we simplify this complexity. If we simply assign a label (such as the quality of softness) to someone, we then have much less to consider when we think about the individual. However, once labels are assigned they are remarkably difficult to abandon, even in the face of contradictory evidence.

Many stereotypes are so general they are very ambiguous. Consider the stereotypes for "masculine" and "feminine." Diverse behaviors can be called on to support each stereotype, such as scoring a touchdown or growing facial hair for "masculine" and playing with dolls or wearing lipstick for "feminine." The stereotype may be modified in the face of cultural change. At one point in history, muscular development may be thought of as masculine; at another point, it may be a more lithe, slender physique. The behaviors popularly agreed upon as reflecting a stereotype may also fluctuate according to socioeconomic circumstances. For example, lower socioeconomic groups might be more likely than higher socioeconomic groups to include "rough and tough" as part of a masculine stereotype.

If you are going to generalize about women, you will find yourself up to here in exceptions.

—Dolores Hitchens, *In a House Unknown* (1973)

Even though the behaviors that are supposed to fit the stereotype often do not, the label itself can have significant consequences for the individual. Labeling a male "feminine" and a female "masculine" can produce significant social reactions to the individuals in terms of status and acceptance in groups, for example (Mischel, 1970).

How widespread is feminine and masculine stereotyping? According to a far-ranging study of college students in 30 countries, stereotyping of females and males is pervasive (Williams & Best, 1982). Males were widely believed to be dominant, independent, aggressive, achievement oriented, and enduring, while females were widely believed to be nurturant, affiliative, less esteemed, and more helpful in times of distress.

In a more recent investigation, women and men who lived in more highly developed countries perceived themselves as more similar than women and men who lived in less-developed countries (Williams & Best, 1989). In the more

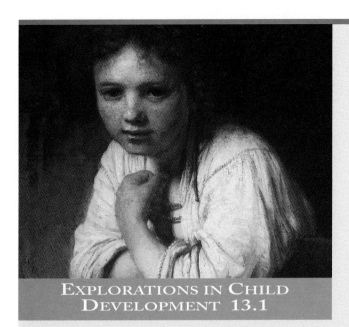

EXPLORATIONS IN CHILD DEVELOPMENT 13.1

How Good Are Girls at Wudgemaking If the Wudgemaker Is He?

In one investigation, the following description of a fictitious gender-neutral occupation—wudgemaker—was read to third- and fifth-grade children, with repeated references to *he, they, he or she,* or *she* (Hyde, 1984):

> Few people have heard of a job in factories, being a wudgemaker. Wudges are made of oddly shaped plastic and are an important part of video games. The wudgemaker works from a plan or pattern posted at eye level as *he or she* puts together the pieces at a table while *he or she* is sitting down. Eleven plastic pieces must be snapped together. Some of the pieces are tiny, so that *he or she* must have good coordination in *his or her* fingers. Once all eleven pieces are put together, *he or she* must test out the wudge to make sure that all of the moving pieces move properly. The wudgemaker is well paid, and must be a high school graduate, but

FIGURE 13.A

Children's mean ratings of women and men as wudgemakers. Elementary school children's ratings of women's competence were lowest when the pronoun *he* was used, intermediate when *they* or *he or she* was used, and highest when *she* was used.

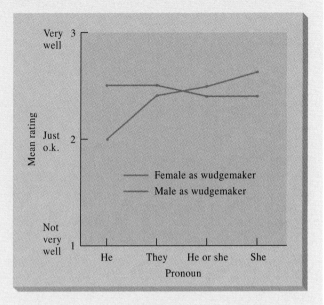

he or she does not have to have gone to college to get the job. (Hyde, 1984, p. 702)

One fourth of the children were read the story with *he* as the pronoun, one fourth with *they,* one fourth with *he or she* (as shown), and one fourth with *she.* The children were asked to rate how well women could do the job of wudgemaking and also how well they thought men could perform the job. As shown in figure 13.A, ratings of how well women could make wudges were influenced by the pronoun used; women's competence was rated lowest when *he* was used, intermediate when *they* and *he or she* were used, and highest when *she* was used. This suggests that the use of *he,* compared with other pronouns, influences children's conceptions of how competent males and females are in our society.

highly developed countries, women were more likely to attend college and be gainfully employed. Thus, as sexual equality increases, male and female stereotypes, as well as actual behavioral differences, may diminish. In this investigation, women were more likely to perceive similarity between the sexes than men were (Williams & Best, 1989). And the sexes were perceived more similarly in Christian than in Muslim societies.

Gender-role stereotyping also changes developmentally. Stereotypic gender beliefs increase during the preschool years, peak in the early elementary school years, and then decrease in the middle and late elementary school years (Bigler, Liben, &

Yekel, 1992). In one recent study, age-related decreases in gender stereotyping were related to the acquisition of cognitive skills (Bigler & Liben, in press). Next, we go beyond stereotyping and examine the similarities and differences between the sexes.

Gender Similarities and Differences

There is a growing consensus in gender research that differences between the sexes have often been exaggerated (Hyde, 1981; Hyde, in press). Remember our discussion of reducing sexist research in psychology in chapter 2. It is not unusual to

CONCEPT TABLE 13.1

The Nature of Gender and Biological, Cognitive, and Social Influences on Gender

Concept	Processes/Related Ideas	Characteristics/Description
What is gender?	Gender, gender identity, and gender roles	Whereas sex refers to the biological dimension of being male or female, *gender* refers to the social dimension of being male or female. Gender identity is the sense of being male or female, which most children acquire by 3 years of age. A gender role is a set of expectations that prescribes how females or males should think, act, and feel.
Biological influences	Their nature	Freud's and Erikson's theories promote the idea that anatomy is destiny. Hormones influence gender development, although not as pervasively as in animals. Hermaphrodites are individuals whose genitals become intermediate between male and female because of a hormonal imbalance. Today's child developmentalists are all interactionists when biological and environmental influences on gender are considered. However, interaction means different things to different people.
Social influences	Identification and social learning theories	Identification theory stems from Freud's view that a preschool child develops a sexual attraction to the opposite-sex parent, then, by 5 to 6 years of age, renounces this attraction because of anxious feelings, subsequently identifying with the same-sex parent and unconsciously adopting that parent's characteristics. This theory is not widely accepted by child developmentalists today. The social learning view states that gender development occurs through observation and imitation of gender behavior, and through rewards and punishments for gender-appropriate and gender-inappropriate behavior.
	Parents	Parents, by action and example, influence gender role development. Mothers and fathers often play different roles—mothers more nurturant and responsible for physical care, fathers more playful and demanding. Fathers are more likely than mothers to act differently toward sons and daughters.
	Peer influences	Peers are especially adept at rewarding gender-appropriate behavior. Strong same-sex preference is shown in elementary school; in adolescence, more cross-sex mixing occurs, as sexuality and dating become more prominent interests. Peer demands for conforming to gender become intense during early adolescence.
	School and teacher influences	Historically, in the United States, education has been male defined rather than gender balanced. Males receive more attention and teacher interaction in schools.

find statements such as the following: "While only 32 percent of the females were found to . . . fully 37 percent of the males were. . . ." This difference of 5 percent likely is a very small difference, and may or may not even be statistically significant or capable of being replicated in a separate study (Denmark & Paludi, in press). And when statements are made about female-male comparisons, such as "males outperform females in math," this does not mean all females versus all males. Rather, it usually means the average math achievement scores for males at certain ages are higher than the average math achievement scores for females. The math achievement scores of females and males overlap considerably, so that while an *average* difference may favor males, many females have higher math achievement than many males. Further, there is a tendency to think of differences between females and males as biologically based. Remember that when differences occur they may be socioculturally based.

There is more difference within the sexes than between them.

—Ivy Compton-Burnett

Concept	Processes/Related Ideas	Characteristics/Description
		Current trends focus on the investigation of subtle sex discrimination and stereotyping, male- and female-valued educational goals, and increased emphasis on gender equity outcomes. A special concern is that most middle and junior high schools are better suited to the learning styles of males than females because they are more impersonal and encourage independence more than elementary schools.
	The media	Despite improvements, television and advertising still portray males as more competent than females. Early adolescence may be a period of heightened sensitivity to television messages about gender roles, especially gender-appropriate behavior in heterosexual relationships.
Cognitive influences	Cognitive developmental theory	Children's gender-typing occurs after they have developed a concept of gender. Once children consistently think of themselves as male or female, they organize their world on the basis of gender, such as selecting same-sex models to imitate. Kohlberg initially developed this theory of gender, believing that gender constancy is achieved in concert with the development of conservation skills at about 6 to 7 years of age.
	Gender schema theory	Gender schema theory states that children's attention and behavior are guided by an internal motivation to conform to gender-based, sociocultural standards, and stereotypes. Rather than emphasizing gender constancy as the sole prerequisite for gender-typing, as cognitive developmental theory does, gender schema theory stresses the child's general readiness to respond to and categorize information on the basis of culturally defined gender roles as the key ingredient that fuels children's gender-typing activities. Researchers have found that conservation skills and the child's cognitive developmental level are related to gender-typed behavior (which supports cognitive developmental theory), but that pre-gender-constant young children have more gender role knowledge than cognitive developmental theory would predict (which supports gender schema theory). Two main theories about the structure of gender schema have been proposed—Spence's belief that independence characterizes the domains of gender and Bem's belief that there is consistency across the domains.
	The role of language	Gender is present in the language children use and encounter. The language children hear most of the time is sexist.

Let's now examine some of the differences between the sexes, keeping in mind that: (a) the differences are averages—not all females versus all males; (b) even when differences are reported, there is considerable overlap between the sexes; and (c) the differences may be due primarily to biological factors, sociocultural factors, or both. First, we examine physical and biological differences, and then we turn to cognitive and social differences.

From conception on, females are less likely than males to die, and females are less likely than males to develop physical or mental disorders. Estrogen strengthens the immune system, making females more resistant to infection, for example. Female hormones also signal the liver to produce more "good" cholesterol, which makes their blood vessels more elastic than males. Testosterone triggers the production of low-density lipoprotein, which clogs blood vessels. Males have twice the risk of coronary disease as females. Higher levels of stress hormones cause faster clotting in males, but also higher blood pressure than in females. Adult females have about twice the body fat of their male counterparts, most concentrated around breasts and hips. In males, fat is more likely to go to the abdomen. On the average, males grow to be 10 percent taller than females. Male

"So according to the stereotype, you can put two and two together, but I can read the handwriting on the wall."
© 1993 Joel Pett, Phi Delta Kappan.

FIGURE 13.3

Visuospatial ability of males and females. Notice that, although an average male's visuospatial ability is higher than an average female's, the overlap between the sexes is substantial. Not all males have better visuospatial ability than all females—the substantial overlap indicates that, although the average score of males is higher, many females outperform many males on such tasks.

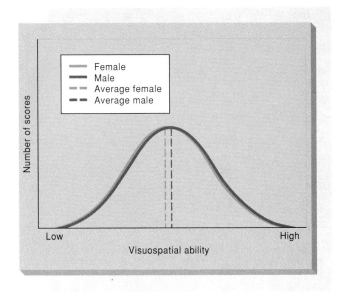

hormones promote the growth of long bones; female hormones stop such growth at puberty. In sum, there are many physical differences between females and males. But are there as many cognitive differences?

According to a classic review of gender differences in 1974, Eleanor Maccoby and Carol Jacklin (1974) concluded that males have better math skills and better visuospatial ability (the kind of skills an architect would need to design a building's angles and dimensions), while females have better verbal abilities. More recently, Maccoby (1987a) revised her conclusion about several gender dimensions. She commented that the accumulation of research evidence now indicates that the verbal differences in males and females have virtually disappeared, but that the math and visuospatial differences are still present.

A number of researchers in the gender area point out that there are more cognitive similarities than differences between females and males. They also believe that the differences that do exist, such as the math and visuospatial differences, have been exaggerated. Males do outperform females in math, but only within a certain portion of the population—the gifted (Hyde, in press). Further, males do not always outperform females on all visuospatial tasks—consistent differences occur only in the ability to rotate objects mentally (Linn & Petersen, 1986). And keep in mind our earlier comment about the considerable overlap that exists between females and males, even when differences are reported. Figure 13.3 shows the small average difference on visuospatial tasks that favors males, but also clearly reveals the substantial overlap in the visuospatial abilities of females and males. Combined with the recent information about convergence in the verbal abilities of males and females (females used to have higher scores on the verbal section of the SAT, but now there are no differences, for example), we can conclude that cognitive differences between females and males do not exist in many areas, are disappearing in other areas, and are small when they do exist.

Most males are more active and aggressive than most females (Maccoby, 1987a; Maccoby & Jacklin, 1974). The consistent difference in aggression often appears in children's development as early as 2 years of age. With regard to helping behavior, Alice Eagly and Maureen Crowley (1986) argue that

the female gender role fosters helping that is nurturant and caring, whereas the male gender role promotes helping that is chivalrous. They found that males are more likely to help in situations in which there is a perceived danger and in which males feel most competent to help. For example, males are more likely than females to help when a person is standing by the roadside with a flat tire, a situation involving some danger and a circumstance in which many males feel a sense of competence—automobile problems. In contrast, if the situation involves volunteering time to help a disturbed child, most researchers have found more helping by females, because there is little danger present for the helper and because females feel more competent in nurturing (Hyde, 1990). As early as elementary school, girls show more caregiving behavior (Zahn-Waxler, 1990). However, in cultures where boys and girls both care for younger siblings, boys and girls are more similar in their nurturant behavior (Whiting, 1989). In one recent study, Judith Blakemore (1993) found that preschool girls spent more time with and nurtured babies more than preschool boys did.

Achievement

For some areas of achievement, gender differences are so large they can best be described as nonoverlapping. For example, no major league baseball players are female, and 96 percent of all registered nurses are female. In contrast, many measures of achievement-related behaviors do not reveal gender differences. For example, girls show just as much persistence at tasks. The

Some of the brightest and most gifted girls do not have achievement and career aspirations that match their talents. Gender researchers hope that gender role stereotypes that prevent girls from developing a more positive orientation toward math and science can be eliminated.

question of whether males and females differ in their expectations for success at various achievement tasks is not yet settled (Eccles, 1987).

Because females are often stereotyped as less competent than males, incorporation of gender-role stereotypes into a child's self-concept could cause girls to have less confidence than boys in their general intellectual abilities. This could lead girls to have lower expectations for success at difficult academic and vocational activities. It could also lead girls to expect to have to work harder to achieve success at these activities than boys expect to have to work. Evidence supports these predictions (Eccles, Harold-Goldsmith, & Miller, 1989). Either of these beliefs could keep girls from selecting demanding educational or vocational options, especially if these options are not perceived as important or interesting.

A special concern is that some of the brightest and most gifted girls do not have achievement and career aspirations that match their talents. In one investigation, high-achieving girls

had much lower expectations for success than high-achieving boys (Stipek & Hoffman, 1980). In the gifted research program at Johns Hopkins University, many mathematically precocious girls did select scientific and medical careers, although only 46 percent aspired to a full-time career, compared with 98 percent of the boys (Fox, Brody, & Tobin, 1979).

To help talented girls redirect their paths, some high schools are using programs developed by colleges and universities. Project CHOICE (Creating Her Options In Career Education) was designed by Case Western University to detect barriers in reaching one's potential. Gifted eleventh-grade females receive individualized counseling that includes interviews with female role models, referral to appropriate occupational groups, and information about career workshops. A program at the University of Nebraska (Kerr, 1983) was successful in encouraging talented female high school students to pursue more prestigious careers. This was accomplished by individualized counseling and participation in a "Perfect Future

Day," in which girls shared career fantasies and discussed barriers that might impede their fantasies. Internal and external constraints were evaluated, gender-role stereotypes were discouraged, and high aspirations were applauded. Although these programs have shown short-term success in redirecting the career paths of high-ability females, in some instances, the benefits fade over time—6 months or more, for example. It is important to be concerned about improving the awareness of career alternatives for all girls, however, and not just those of high ability.

> *The test for whether or not you can hold a job should not be the arrangement of your chromosomes.*
>
> —Bella Abzug, *Bella!* (1972)

Emotion

Unless you've been isolated on a mountaintop away from people, television, magazines, and newspapers, you probably know the master stereotype about gender and emotion: She is emotional, he is not. This stereotype is a powerful and pervasive image in our culture (Shields, 1991a).

Is this stereotype borne out when researchers study the nature of emotional experiences in females and males? Researchers have found that females and males are often more alike in the way they experience emotion than the master stereotype would lead us to believe. Females and males often use the same facial expressions, adopt the same language, and describe their emotional experiences similarly when they keep diaries about their life experiences. Thus, the master stereotype about females being emotional and males not is simply that—a stereotype. Given the complexity and vast territory of emotion, we should not be surprised that this stereotype is not supported when actual emotional experiences are examined. Thus, for many emotional experiences, researchers do not find differences between females and males—both sexes are equally likely to experience love, jealousy, anxiety in new social situations, be angry when they are insulted, grieve when close relationships end, and be embarrassed when they make mistakes in public (Tavris & Wade, 1984).

When we go beyond the master stereotype and consider some specific emotional experiences, the context in which emotion is displayed, and certain beliefs about emotion, gender does matter in understanding emotion (Shields, 1991 a,b). Consider anger. Males are more likely to show anger toward strangers, especially other males, when they feel they have been challenged, and males are more likely to turn their anger into aggressive action than females are (Tavris, 1989).

Female-male differences in emotion are more likely to occur in contexts that highlight social roles and relationships (Brown & others, 1993). For example, females are more likely than males to give accounts of emotion that include interpersonal relationships (Saarni, 1988). And females are more likely to express fear and sadness than males, especially when communicating with their friends and family.

FEIFFER®

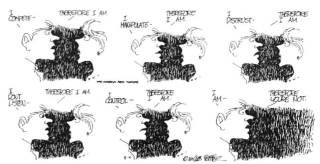

FEIFFER © 1991 Jules Feiffer. Reprinted with permission of UNIVERSAL PRESS SYNDICATE. All rights reserved.

Beliefs about emotion play an important role in understanding how gender and emotion work in our culture. We often use beliefs about emotion to define the difference between what is masculine and feminine, male and female (Shields, 1991a). For example, in one study, males were more likely to agree with the belief that men should conceal their feelings, but when reporting their own behavior, females, more than males, reported greater inhibition of emotional expression. Sex differences in self-reports tend to be consistent with emotion stereotypes, as if individuals compare themselves to a cultural standard when generating a response—"I must be emotional, after all I'm a female," or "I must be inexpressive, after all I'm a male." (Shields, 1991b).

Talk

Might the way females and males are socialized as they grow up produce differences in the way they talk with each other? Sociolinguist Deborah Tannen (1990) thinks so. She analyzed the talk of women and men, and found that a common complaint that wives have about their husbands is, "He doesn't listen anymore." Another is, "He doesn't talk to me anymore." Lack of communication, while high on women's list of reasons for divorce, is much less often mentioned by men.

Tannen distinguishes between rapport talk and report talk. **Rapport talk** *is the language of conversation and a way of establishing connections and negotiating relationships.* **Report talk** *is public speaking and talk designed to impart information.* Men hold center stage through such verbal performances as story telling, joking, and lecturing with information. By contrast, women enjoy private speaking more and conversation that is relationship-oriented.

How did women and men get this way? Tannen believes that women and men have different conversational styles because as girls and boys they were brought up in two virtually distinct cultures. Even when they grow up in the same neighborhood, on the same block, or in the same house, girls and boys grow up in a different world of words. Parents, siblings, peers, teachers, and other adults talk to girls and boys differently. And the differences in the way they are talked to begins early in their development. What is this different talk like? It is the words of rapport talk and report talk. Boys play in large groups that are hierarchically structured, and their groups often

Female–male differences in emotion are most likely to occur in contexts that highlight social roles and relationships. Females are more likely to engage in rapport talk, males in report talk.

have a leader who tells others what to do and how to do it. Another way boys achieve status is to take center stage by telling stories and jokes. Boys' games have winners and losers that are often the subject of arguments. And boys are frequently heard to boast of their skill and argue about who is best at what.

By contrast, girls are more likely to play in small groups or in pairs, and the center of a girl's social world is often a best friend. In girls' friendships and peer groups, intimacy is pervasive. In one recent study, preschool girls showed a stronger preference for dyadic interaction than their male counterparts (Benerson, in press). In some girls' favorite games, like hopscotch and jump rope, everyone gets a turn. Many of their activities, such as playing house, don't have winners and losers. Girls are expected to boast about their skills less than boys are. Girls also are less likely to give orders than boys, expressing their preferences as suggestions. Boys are more likely to say "Gimme that!" or "Get outta here!" However, girls are more likely to say "Let's do this" or "How about doing that." Girls are less likely to grab center stage and don't challenge others as directly as boys do. And much of the time, girls simply sit together and talk, being more concerned about being liked by others than jockeying for status in some obvious way.

GENDER ROLE CLASSIFICATION

How were gender roles classified in the past? What is androgyny? Is a strong masculine orientation related to problem behaviors in adolescent males? What is gender role transcendence?

The Past

At a point not too long ago, it was accepted that boys should grow up to be masculine and that girls should grow up to be feminine, that boys are made of frogs and snails and puppy dogs' tails, and that girls are made of sugar and spice and all that's nice. Today, diversity characterizes gender roles and the feedback individuals receive from their culture. A girl's mother might promote femininity, the girl might be close friends with a tomboy, and the girl's teachers at school might encourage her assertiveness.

In the past, the well-adjusted male was expected to be independent, aggressive, and power oriented. The well-adjusted female was expected to be dependent, nurturant, and uninterested in power. Further, masculine characteristics were considered to be healthy and good by society; female characteristics were considered to be undesirable. A classic study in the early 1970s summarized the traits and behaviors that college students believed were characteristic of males and those they believed were characteristic of females (Broverman & others, 1972). The traits clustered into two groups that were labeled "instrumental" and "expressive." The instrumental traits paralleled the male's purposeful, competent entry into the outside world to gain goods for his family; the expressive traits paralleled the female's responsibility to be warm and emotional in the home. Such stereotypes are more harmful to females than to males because the characteristics assigned to males are more valued than those assigned to females. The beliefs and stereotypes have led to the negative treatment of females because of their sex, or what is called *sexism*. Females receive less attention in schools, are less visible in leading roles on television, are rarely depicted as competent, dominant characters in children's books, are paid less than males even when they have more education, and are underrepresented in decision-making roles throughout our society, from corporate executive suites to Congress.

TABLE 13.1

The Bem Sex-Role Inventory: Are You Androgynous?

The following items are from the Bem Sex-Role Inventory. To find out whether you score as androgynous, first rate yourself on each item, on a scale from 1 (never or almost never true) to 7 (always or almost always true).

1. self-reliant	16. strong personality	31. makes decisions easily	46. aggressive
2. yielding	17. loyal	32. compassionate	47. gullible
3. helpful	18. unpredictable	33. sincere	48. inefficient
4. defends own beliefs	19. forceful	34. self-sufficient	49. acts as a leader
5. cheerful	20. feminine	35. eager to soothe hurt feelings	50. childlike
6. moody	21. reliable	36. conceited	51. adaptable
7. independent	22. analytical	37. dominant	52. individualistic
8. shy	23. sympathetic	38. soft-spoken	53. does not use harsh language
9. conscientious	24. jealous	39. likable	54. unsystematic
10. athletic	25. has leadership abilities	40. masculine	55. competitive
11. affectionate	26. sensitive to the needs of others	41. warm	56. loves children
12. theatrical	27. truthful	42. solemn	57. tactful
13. assertive	28. willing to take risks	43. willing to take a stand	58. ambitious
14. flatterable	29. understanding	44. tender	59. gentle
15. happy	30. secretive	45. friendly	60. conventional

SCORING

(a) Add up your ratings for items 1, 4, 7, 10, 13, 16, 19, 22, 25, 28, 31, 34, 37, 40, 43, 46, 49, 55, and 58. Divide the total by 20. That is your masculinity score.

(b) Add up your ratings for items 2, 5, 8, 11, 14, 17, 20, 23, 26, 29, 32, 35, 38, 41, 44, 47, 50, 53, 56, and 59. Divide the total by 20. That is your femininity score.

(c) If your masculinity score is above 4.9 (the approximate median for the masculinity scale) and your femininity score is above 4.9 (the approximate femininity median) then you would be classified as androgynous on Bem's scale.

From Janet S. Hyde, *Half the Human Experience: The Psychology of Women,* 3d ed. Copyright © 1985 D. C. Heath and Company, Lexington, MA.

Androgyny

In the 1970s, as both males and females became dissatisfied with the burdens imposed by their strictly stereotyped roles, alternatives to "masculinity" and "femininity" were explored. Instead of thinking of masculinity and femininity as a continuum, with more of one meaning less of the other, it was proposed that individuals could show both expressive *and* instrumental traits. This thinking led to the development of the concept of **androgyny,** *the presence of desirable masculine and feminine characteristics in the same individual* (Bem, 1977; Spence & Helmreich, 1978). The androgynous individual might be a male who is assertive (masculine) and nurturant (feminine), or a female who is dominant (masculine) and sensitive to others' feelings (feminine).

Measures have been developed to assess androgyny. One of the most widely used gender measures, the Bem sex-role inventory, was constructed by a leading early proponent of androgyny, Sandra Bem. To see what the items on Bem's measure are like, see table 13.1. Based on their responses to the items in the Bem sex-role inventory, individuals are classified as having one of four gender role orientations: masculine, feminine, androgynous, or undifferentiated (see figure 13.4). The androgynous individual is simply a female or a male who has a high degree of both feminine (expressive) and masculine (instrumental) traits. No new characteristics are used to describe the androgynous individual. A feminine individual is high on feminine (expressive) traits and low on masculine (instrumental) traits; a masculine individual shows the reverse of these traits. An undifferentiated person is not high on feminine or masculine traits.

Androgynous individuals are described as more flexible and more mentally healthy than either masculine or feminine individuals. Individuals who are undifferentiated are the least

FIGURE 13.4

Gender role classification.

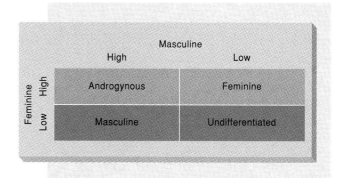

competent. To some degree, though, the context influences which gender role is most adaptive. In close relationships, a feminine or androgynous gender role may be more desirable because of the expressive nature of close relationships. However, a masculine or androgynous gender role may be more desirable in academic and work settings because of the instrumental nature of these settings. And the culture in which individuals live also plays an important role in determining what is adaptive. On the one hand, increasing numbers of children in the United States and other modernized countries such as Sweden are being raised to behave in androgynous ways. On the other hand, traditional gender roles continue to dominate the cultures of many countries around the world. To read about traditional gender-role practices in Egypt, as well as the nature of gender roles in China, turn to Sociocultural Worlds of Children 13.1.

SOCIOCULTURAL WORLDS OF CHILDREN 13.1

Gender Roles in Egypt and China

In recent decades, roles assumed by males and females in the United States have become increasingly similar—that is, androgynous. In many countries, though, gender roles have remained more gender specific. For example, in Egypt, the division of labor between Egyptian males and females is dramatic: Egyptian males are socialized to work in the public sphere, females in the private world of home and child rearing. The Islamic religion dictates that the man's duty is to provide for his family, the woman's duty to care for her family and household (Dickersheid & others, 1988). Any deviations from this traditional gender role orientation are severely disapproved of.

Egypt is not the only country in which males and females are socialized to behave, think, and feel in strongly genderspecific ways. Kenya and Nepal are two other cultures in which children are brought up under very strict gender-specific guidelines (Munroe, Himmin, & Munroe, 1984). In the People's Republic of China, the female's status has historically been lower than the male's. The teachings of the fifth century B.C. Chinese philosopher Confucius were used to reinforce the concept of the female as an inferior being. Beginning with the 1949 revolution in China, women began to achieve more economic freedom and more equal status in marital relationships. However, even with the sanctions of a socialist government, the old patriarchal traditions of male supremacy in China have not been completely uprooted. Chinese women still make considerably less money than Chinese men in comparable positions, and in rural China, a tradition of male supremacy still governs women's lives.

Thus, while in China, females have made considerable strides, complete equality remains a distant objective. And in many cultures, such as Egypt and other countries where the Muslim religion predominates, gender-specific behavior is pronounced, and females are not given access to high-status positions.

In Egypt near the Aswan Dam, women are returning from the Nile River, where they have filled their water jugs. How might gender role socialization for girls in Egypt compare to that in the United States?

In China, females and males are usually socialized to behave, feel, and think differently. The old patriarchal traditions of male supremacy have not been completely uprooted. Chinese women still make considerably less money than Chinese men, and, in rural China (such as here in the Lixian village of Sichuan), male supremacy still governs many women's lives.

Critical Thinking

How extensively are parents rearing their children to become androgynous? Are parents rearing their daughters to be more androgynous than they are their sons? Are middle-class parents more likely to rear their children to be androgynous than parents from low-income backgrounds? Explain.

Traditional Masculinity and Problem Behaviors in Adolescent Males

In our discussion of masculinity so far, we have discussed how the masculine role has been accorded a prominent status in the United States, as well as in most other cultures. However, might there be a negative side to traditional masculinity, especially in adolescence? An increasing number of gender theorists and researchers believe there is.

Joseph Pleck and his colleagues (Pleck, 1983; Pleck, Sonnenstein, & Ku, in press) believe that what defines traditional masculinity in many Western societies includes engaging in certain behaviors that, although officially socially disapproved, validate masculinity. That is, in the male adolescent culture, male adolescents perceive that they are more masculine, and that others will perceive them as more masculine, if they engage in premarital sex, drink alcohol and take drugs, and participate in delinquent activities.

In one recent investigation, the gender role orientation and problem behaviors of 1,680 15- to 19-year-old males were assessed (Pleck, Sonnenstein, & Ku, in press). In this study—referred to as the National Survey of Adolescent Males—there was strong evidence that problem behaviors in adolescent males are associated with their attitudes toward masculinity. The adolescent males who reported traditional beliefs about masculinity (for example, endorsing such items as "A young man should be tough, even if he's not big," "It is essential for a guy to get respect from others," and "Men are always ready for sex") also were likely to say that they had school difficulties, engaged in alcohol and drug use, participated in delinquent activities, and were sexually active.

The idea that male problem behaviors have something to do with "masculinity" has recently gotten the attention of policy makers. Former U.S. Department of Health and Human Services Secretary Louis Sullivan (1991) called for action to address a generation whose manhood is measured by the caliber of gun he carries or the number of children he fathers. In a similar vein, Virginia Governor Douglas Wilder (1991) urged policy makers to get across the message that, contrary to what many of today's youths think, making babies is no act of manhood. Addressing and challenging traditional beliefs about masculinity in adolescent males may have the positive outcome of helping reduce their problem behaviors.

Gender Role Transcendence

Although the concept of androgyny was an improvement over exclusive notions of femininity and masculinity, it has turned out to be less of a panacea than many of its early proponents envisioned (Doyle & Paludi, 1991). Some theorists, such as Pleck (1981), believe that the idea of androgyny should be replaced with **gender role transcendence,** *the belief that, when an individual's competence is at issue, it should not be conceptualized on the basis of masculinity, femininity, or androgyny, but rather on a personal basis.* Thus, rather than merging gender roles or stereotyping people as "masculine" or "feminine," Pleck believes we should begin to think about people as people. However, both the concepts of androgyny and gender role transcendence draw attention away from women's unique needs and the power imbalance between women and men in most cultures (Hare-Muston & Maracek, 1988). As we will see next, a major focus of the feminist agenda is to reduce that imbalance of power.

To be meek, patient, tactful, modest, honorable, brave, is not to be either manly or womanly; it is to be humane.

—Jane Harrison

THE FEMINIST PERSPECTIVE ON GENDER

Many feminist scholars believe that, historically, psychology has portrayed human behavior with a "male dominant theme" (DeFour & Paludi, in press; Denmark & Paludi, in press; Paludi, 1992). They also believe that sexism is still rampant in society. As leading feminist scholar Jean Baker Miller (1986) wrote in *Toward a New Psychology of Women,*

> In the last decade it has become clearer that if women are trying to define and create a full personhood, we are engaged in a huge undertaking. We see that this attempt means building a new way of living which encompasses all realms of life, from global economic, social and political levels to the most intimate personal relationships. (p. xi)

Feminist scholars are putting greater emphasis on women's life experiences and development, including girls and women as authorities about their own experiences, or as Harvard psychologist Carol Gilligan (1990, 1992) advocates, listening to women's voices; on women's ways of knowing (Belenky & others, 1986); on women's career and family roles (Baruch, Biener, & Barnett, 1987); on the abuse of women and rape (McBride, 1990; Russo, 1990); and women's experiences of connectedness and self-determination (Brown & Gilligan, 1990; Chodorow, 1978; Gilligan, Brown, & Rogers, 1990; Josselson, 1987; Lerner, 1989; Miller, 1986).

We need every human gift and cannot afford to neglect any gift because of artificial barriers of sex or race or class or national origin.

—Margaret Mead, *Male and Female* (1949)

Miller (1976, 1986) has been an important voice in stimulating the examination of psychological issues from a female perspective. She believes that the study of women's psychological development opens up paths to a better understanding of all psychological development, male or female. She also concludes that, when researchers examine what women have been doing in life, they find that a large part of it is active participation in the development of others. In Miller's view, women often try to interact with others in ways that foster the others' development along many dimensions—emotionally, intellectually, and socially.

Many feminist thinkers believe that it is important for women not only to maintain their competency in relationships but to be self-motivated too. Miller believes that, through increased self-determination and already developed relationship skills, many women will gain greater power in the American culture. As feminist scholar Harriet Lerner (1989) concludes in her book *The Dance of Intimacy,* it is important for women to bring to their relationships nothing less than a strong, assertive, independent, and authentic self. She believes that competent relationships are those in which the separate "I-ness" of both persons can be appreciated and enhanced while staying emotionally connected to each other.

Not only is a distinct female voice an important dimension of the feminist perspective on gender, but so is the effort to reduce and eventually end prejudice and discrimination against women (Paludi, 1992; Yentsch & Sindermann, 1992). Although women have broken through many male bastions in the past several decades, feminists argue that much work is left to be done. Feminists today believe that too many people passively accept traditional gender roles and believe that discrimination no longer exists in politics, work, the family, and education. They encourage individuals to question these assumptions, and especially strive to get females to evaluate the gender circumstances of their lives. For example, if you are a female, you may remember situations in which you were discriminated against because of your sex. If derogatory comments are made to you because you are a female, you may ask yourself why you have allowed these comments to go unchallenged or why they made you so angry. Feminists hope that, if you are a male, you will become more conscious of gender issues, of female and male roles, and of fairness and sensitivity in female-male interactions and relationships.

ETHNICITY AND GENDER

Are gender-related attitudes and behavior similar across different ethnic groups? All ethnic minority females are females and all ethnic minority males are males, so there are many similarities in the gender-related attitudes of females across different ethnic minority groups and of males across different ethnic minority groups. Nevertheless, the different ethnic and cultural experiences of Black American, Hispanic American, Asian American, and Native American females and males need to be considered in understanding their gender-related attitudes and behavior, because in some instances even small differences can be important. For example, the socialization of males and females in other cultures who subsequently migrate to America often reflects a stronger gap between the status of males and females than is experienced in America. Keeping in mind that there are many similarities between females in all ethnic minority groups and between males in all ethnic minority groups, we examine, first, information about females from specific ethnic minority groups, followed by a discussion of males from specific ethnic minority groups.

Ethnic Minority Females

Let's now consider the behavior and psychological orientations of females from specific ethnic minority groups, beginning with Black females, and then in turn, study Asian American females, Hispanic American females, and Native American females.

> *In the end, antiblack, antifemale, and all forms of discrimination are equivalent to the same thing—antihumanism.*
> —Shirley Chisholm, *Unbought and Unbossed* (1970)

Researchers in psychology have only begun to focus on the behavior of Black females. For too long, Black females only served as a comparison group for White females on selected psychological dimensions, or they served as the subjects in studies in which the primary research interest related to poverty, unwed motherhood, and so on (Hall, Evans, & Selice, 1989). This narrow research approach could be viewed as attributing no personal characteristics to Black females beyond the labels given to them by society.

The nature and focus of psychological research on Black females has begun to change—to some extent paralleling societal changes (Hall, Evans, & Selice, 1989). In the last decade, more individualized, positive dimensions of Black females are being studied, such as self-esteem, achievement, motivation, and self-control. In the 1980s, psychological studies of Black females began to shift away from studies focused only on the problems of Black females and toward research on the positive aspects of Black females in a pluralistic society.

Black females, as well as other ethnic minority females, have experienced the double jeopardy of racism and sexism. The ingenuity and perseverance shown by ethnic minority females as they have survived and grown against the odds is remarkable. For example, 499 Black women earned doctoral degrees in 1986. This represents only 2 percent of the Ph.D.'s awarded (compared to the 6.4 percent of the general population represented by Black females). However, the positive side of these figures is that the Ph.D.'s earned by Black women in 1986 represented an almost 16 percent increase over the number earned in 1977. Despite such gains, our society needs to make a strong commitment to providing Black, and other ethnic minority, females with the opportunities they deserve (Wilson & Stith, 1993; Young, 1993).

Asian females are often expected to carry on domestic duties, to marry, to become obedient helpers of their mothers-in-law, and to bear children, especially males (Nishio & Bilmes, 1993; Sue, 1989). In China, the mother's responsibility for the emotional nurturance and well-being of the family, and for raising children, derives from Confucian ethics (Huang & Ying, 1989). However, as China has become modernized, these roles have become less rigid. Similarly, in acculturated Chinese families in the United States, only derivatives of these rigidly defined roles remain. For example, Chinese American females are not entirely relegated to subservient roles.

Traditionally in Mexican families, women assume the expressive role of homemaker and caretaker of children. This continues to be the norm, although less so than in the past (Comas-Diaz, 1993; Domino, 1992; Ramirez, 1989). Historically, the Mexican female's role has been one of self-denial and her needs were considered to be subordinate to those of other family members. Joint decision making and greater equality of males' and females' roles are becoming more characteristic of Mexican American families (Ramirez & Arce, 1981). Of special significance is the increased frequency of Mexican American women's employment outside the home, which in many instances has enhanced a wife's status in the family and in decision making (Baca Zinn, 1980; Espin, 1993; Knouse, 1992).

For Native Americans, the amount of social and governing control exhibited by women or men depends on the tribe (LaFromboise, 1993; LaFromboise & Low, 1989; LaFromboise, Trimble, & Mohatt, 1993). For example, in the traditional matriarchal Navajo family, an older woman might live with her husband, her unmarried children, her married daughter, and the daughter's husband and children (Ryan, 1980). In patriarchal tribes, women function as the central "core" of the family, maintaining primary responsibility for the welfare of children. Grandmothers and aunts often provide child care. As with other ethnic minority females, Native American females who have moved to urban areas experience the cultural conflict of traditional ethnic values and the values of the American society.

Ethnic Minority Males

Just as ethnic minority females have experienced considerable discrimination and have had to develop coping strategies in the face of adversity, so have ethnic minority males. As with ethnic minority females, our order of discussion will be Black males, Asian American males, Hispanic American males, and Native American males.

Some statistics provide a portrayal of the difficulties many Black males have faced (Parham & McDavis, 1993). Black American males of all ages are three times as likely as White males to live below the poverty line. Black males aged 20 to 44 are twice as likely to die as White males. Black male heads of household earn 70 percent of the income of their White male counterparts. Although they make up only 6.3 percent of the U.S. population, Black males comprise 42 percent of jail inmates and more than 50 percent of men executed for any reason in the last fifty years! Murder by gun is the leading cause of death among Black males aged 15–19 and it is getting worse. From 1979 to 1989, the death rate by guns among this age group of Black males increased 71 percent. In one recent study, the problem of inadequate male role models in Black American boys' development surfaced (Browne & others, 1993).

Statistics sometimes do not tell the complete story (Evans & Whitfield, 1988). The sociocultural aspects of historical discrimination against an ethnic minority group must be taken into account to understand these statistics. Just as with Black females, researchers are beginning to focus on some of the more positive dimensions of Black males. For example, researchers are finding that Black males are especially efficient at the use of body language in communication, decoding nonverbal cues, multilingual/multicultural expression, and improvised problem solving.

Asian cultural values are reflected in traditional patriarchal Chinese and Japanese families (Sue, 1989; Sue & Sue, 1993). The father's behavior in relation to other family members is generally dignified, authoritative, remote, and aloof. Sons are generally valued over daughters. Firstborn sons have an especially high status. As with Asian American females, the acculturation experienced by Asian American males has eroded some of the rigid gender roles that characterized Asian families in the past. Fathers still are often the figurative heads of families, especially when dealing with the public, but in private, they have relinquished some of their decision-making powers to their wives (Huang & Ying, 1989; Root, 1993).

In Mexican families, men traditionally assume the instrumental role of provider and protector of the family (Ramirez, 1989). The concept of machismo—being a macho man—continues to influence the role of the male and the patriarchal orientation of Mexican families, though less so than in the past. Traditionally, this orientation required men to be forceful and strong, and also to withhold affectionate emotions. Ideally, it involved a strong sense of personal honor, family, loyalty, and care for children. However, it also has involved exaggerated masculinity and aggression (Trankina, 1983). The concepts of machismo and absolute patriarchy are currently diminishing in influence. Adolescent males are still given much more freedom than adolescent females in Mexican American families.

Some Native American tribes are also patriarchal, with the male being the head of the family and primary decision maker. In some tribes, though, child care is shared by men. For example, Mescalero Apache men take responsibility for children when not working away from the family (Ryan, 1980). Autonomy is highly valued among the male children in many Native American tribes, with the males operating semi-independently at an early age (LaFromboise & Low, 1989). As with Native American females, increased movement to urban areas has led to modifications in the values and traditions of some Native American males.

At this point, we have discussed a number of ideas about gender stereotypes, similarities and differences, emotion, and achievement; gender role classification; the feminist perspective on gender; and ethnicity and gender. A summary of these ideas is presented in Concept Table 13.2. In the next chapter, we will turn our attention to another important facet of children's development—their moral development. As part of our discussion of moral development, we will examine Carol Gilligan's ideas on connectedness and relationships in greater detail.

PERSPECTIVES ON PARENTING AND EDUCATION

Parenting, Gender, Achievement, and Careers

How much influence do parents have on their daughters' and sons' achievement and career orientation? Developmental psychologist Jacqueline Eccles and her colleagues (Eccles, 1993; Eccles & Harold, 1991; Harold & Eccles, 1990) believe the influence is substantial. In one recent study, 1,500 mothers and their daughters and sons were studied to determine the role of maternal expectations, advice, and provision of opportunities in their sons' and daughters' occupational aspirations. Mothers were more likely to encourage their sons to consider the military, to expect their sons to go into the military right after high school, and to discuss with their sons the education needed for and likely income of various jobs. Expecting marriage right after high school and discussing the problems of combining work and family were more common to daughters. Also, mothers were more worried that their daughters would not have a happy marriage, and they were more likely to want their sons to have a job that would support a family. Further, mothers worked more with

their sons on computers, and also more often provided them with computers, software, and programs. The mothers also bought more math or science books and games for the boys and more often enrolled them in computer classes. The sons were provided more sports opportunities, while girls were given more opportunities in music, art, and dance. The mothers said their sons had more talent in math and were better suited for careers in math, although they believed their daughters had more talent in English and were better suited for English-related careers.

The maternal advice, provision of opportunities, expectations, and ability assessments were associated with adolescents' occupational aspirations in the previous study. More often, these mothers tended to provide math or science books to daughters who aspired to male-typed occupations (nontraditional girls) than to daughters who aspired to female-typed jobs (traditional girls). The mothers talked more about the importance of looking good to their daughters who aspired to more female-typed occupations

than to their daughters who aspired to male-typed jobs. They also expected their daughters who aspired to more female-typed occupations to be more likely to get married right after high school than their nontraditional counterparts. Further, several of the mothers' and adolescent daughters' family/work role values were related. For example, the mothers' belief that it was better for a man to be a breadwinner and a woman to take care of the family was related to the adolescents' belief. The mothers' belief that working mothers can establish just as warm and secure a relationship with their children as nonworking mothers was related to their adolescents' belief that it is all right for mothers to have full-time careers. The nontraditional girls were more likely to endorse the belief that women are better wives and mothers if they have paid jobs. In sum, this research study documented that parental socialization practices in the form of provision of opportunities, expectations, and beliefs are important sources of daughters' and sons' occupational aspirations (Eccles, 1993; Harold & Eccles, 1990). ■

CONCLUSIONS

This chapter has been about gender, our social worlds as females and males. Nowhere in children's social development have there been more sweeping changes and more controversial issues than in gender. Few aspects of life are more central to children's identity and social relationships than gender.

We began by contemplating tomorrow's gender worlds of today's children, and then defined what gender is. We studied biological, cognitive, and social influences on gender and charted the na-

ture of gender stereotypes, as well as gender similarities and differences. We gave special attention to three areas of gender similarities/differences: achievement, emotion, and talk. Our examination of gender-role classification focused on the past, androgyny, traditional masculinity and problem behaviors in adolescent males, and gender role transcendence. We also explored the feminist perspective on gender and the relation of ethnicity to gender. And we read about the roles of parenting and gender in chil-

dren's achievement and career interests. Don't forget to again read the concept tables on pages 384 and 396 that provide a summary of the chapter.

In the next chapter, we will turn our attention to another important facet of children's development—their moral development. In our discussion of moral development, we will study Carol Gilligan's ideas on connectedness and relationships in greater detail.

CONCEPT TABLE 13.2

Gender Role Stereotypes, Similarities, Differences, and Classification;
the Feminist Perspective; and Gender and Ethnicity

Concept	Processes/Related Ideas	Characteristics/Description
Gender stereotypes, similarities, and differences	Stereotypes	Gender role stereotypes are broad categories that reflect our impressions and beliefs about males and females. These stereotypes are widespread around the world, especially emphasizing the male's power and the female's nurturance. However, in more highly developed countries, females and males are more likely to be perceived as more similar.
	Similarities and differences	Many gender researchers believe that a number of differences between females and males have been exaggerated. In considering differences, it is important to recognize that the differences are averages; there is considerable overlap between the sexes; and the differences may be due primarily to biological factors, sociocultural factors, or both. There are a number of physical differences between the sexes, but cognitive differences are either small or nonexistent. At the level of the gifted, the average male outperforms the average female in math achievement. In terms of social behavior, males are more aggressive and active than females. Overall, though, there are more similarities than differences between females and males. The social context plays an important role in gender differences and similarities.
	Achievement	Although the answer to the question of whether males and females differ in their expectations for success is not yet settled, some of the brightest and most gifted girls do not have achievement and career aspirations that match their talents.
	Emotion	The master stereotype of gender and emotion is: females are emotional, males are not. This is a stereotype; understanding emotion and gender is far more complex. When we go beyond the master stereotype and consider some of the specific dimensions of emotion, the context in which emotion is displayed, and certain beliefs about emotion, gender does matter in understanding emotion. Female-male differences in emotion are more likely to occur in contexts that highlight social roles and relationships.
	Talk	Tannen argues that girls and boys grow up in two very different social worlds of talk—the female world of rapport talk, the male world of report talk.
How can gender roles be classified?	The past	In the past, a well-adjusted male was supposed to show instrumental traits, a well-adjusted female expressive traits. Masculine traits were more valued by society. Sexism was widespread.
	Androgyny	In the 1970s, alternatives to traditional masculinity and femininity were explored. It was proposed that individuals could show both expressive and instrumental traits. This thinking led to the development of the concept of androgyny, the presence of desirable

Concept	Processes/Related Ideas	Characteristics/Description
		masculine and feminine traits in one individual. Gender role measures often categorize individuals as masculine, feminine, androgynous, or undifferentiated. Androgynous individuals are often flexible and mentally healthy, although the particular context and the individual's culture also determine the adaptiveness of a gender role orientation.
	Traditional masculinity and problem behaviors in adolescent males	What defines traditional masculinity in many Western societies includes engaging in certain behaviors, that, while officially disapproved of, validate masculinity. Researchers have found that problem behaviors in adolescent males—school problems, drug use, and delinquency—are associated with their traditional beliefs in masculinity.
	Gender role transcendence	One alternative to androgyny is gender role transcendence, but like androgyny, it draws attention away from the imbalance of power between males and females.
The feminist perspective on gender	Its nature	Feminist scholars are developing new perspectives that focus on girls' and women's experiences and development. Girls' and women's strengths have been especially important in relationships and connections with others. A special emphasis is, that, while staying emotionally connected to significant others, females can enhance their psychological well-being by developing stronger self-determination. The feminist perspective emphasizes the importance of reducing and eventually ending prejudice and discrimination against females.
Ethnicity and gender	Similarities and differences	There are many similarities among the females in various ethnic minority groups and among the males in different ethnic minority groups, but even small differences can sometimes be important.
	Ethnic minority females	Researchers in psychology have only begun to focus on female behavior in specific ethnic groups in a positive way. Many ethnic minority females have experienced the double jeopardy of racism and sexism. In many instances, Asian American, Hispanic American, and Native American females have lived in patriarchal, male-dominated families, although gender roles have become less rigid in these ethnic groups in recent years.
	Ethnic minority males	Just as ethnic minority females have experienced considerable discrimination and have had to develop coping strategies in the face of adversity, so have ethnic minority males. Just as with Black American females, researchers are beginning to focus more on the positive dimensions of Black American males. A patriarchal, male-dominant orientation has characterized many ethnic minority groups, such as Asian American, Hispanic American, and Native American, although females are gaining greater decision-making power in these cultures, especially those who develop careers and work outside of the home.

KEY TERMS

gender   The social dimension of being male or female. (377)

gender identity   The sense of being male or female, which most children acquire by the time they are 3 years old. (377)

gender role   A set of expectations that prescribes how females or males should think, act, or feel. (377)

androgen   The main class of male sex hormones. (377)

estrogen   The main class of female sex hormones. (377)

identification theory   A theory that stems from Freud's view that preschool children develop a sexual attraction to the opposite-sex parent, then, at 5 to 6 years of age, renounce the attraction because of anxious feelings, subsequently identifying with the same-sex parent and unconsciously adopting the same-sex parent's characteristics. (378)

social learning theory of gender   The idea that children's gender development occurs through observation and imitation of gender behavior, as well as through the rewards and punishments children experience for gender-appropriate and gender-inappropriate behaviors. (378)

cognitive developmental theory of gender   In this view, children's gender-typing occurs after they have developed a concept of gender. Once they begin to consistently conceive themselves as male or female, children often organize their world on the basis of gender. (380)

schema   A cognitive structure, a network of associations that organizes and guides an individual's perception. (381)

gender schema   A cognitive structure that organizes the world in terms of female and male. (381)

gender schema theory   The theory that children's attention and behavior are guided by an internal motivation to conform to gender-based, sociocultural standards and stereotypes. (381)

gender role stereotypes   Broad categories that reflect our impressions and beliefs about females and males. (382)

rapport talk   This involves communication that is oriented toward connectedness with others. It is used more by females than by males. (388)

report talk   This involves communication designed to give or receive information. It is used more often by males than females. (388)

androgyny   The presence of desirable masculine and feminine characteristics in one individual. (390)

gender role transcendence   This is the belief that, when an individual's competence is at issue, it should not be conceptualized on the basis of masculinity, femininity, or androgyny but, rather, on a personal basis. (392)

SUGGESTED READINGS

Gilligan, D., Lyons, N., & Hanmer, T. J. (Eds.). (1990). *Making connections: The relational worlds of adolescent girls at the Emma Willard School.* Cambridge, MA: Harvard University Press. Gilligan's ideas about adolescence as a critical juncture in the development of females are presented, with many excerpts from adolescent interviews.

Huston, A. C. (1983). Sex-typing. In P. H. Mussen (Ed.), *Handbook of child psychology* (4th ed., Vol. 4). New York: Wiley. This is a lengthy, comprehensive review of what is known about gender role development.

Jacklin, C. N. (1989). Female and male: Issues of gender. *American Psychologist, 44,* 127–133. Gender expert Carol Nagy Jacklin describes a number of contemporary issues involving gender, including gender differences and public policy considerations.

Sex Roles. This journal is devoted solely to articles about gender. Go to a library and leaf through the issues of the past several years to discover the concerns that researchers are currently studying.

Tavris, C. (1992). *The mismeasure of woman.* New York: Touchstone. Tavris highlights how females are too often judged by male standards and criteria. This is a very up-to-date account of gender that is original, provocative, and entertaining.

Women: The Road Ahead (1990, Fall). *Time* (Special Issue). A number of articles on gender issues are included. Special attention is given to such topics as the road to equality and changing gender roles in the family.

Girl With Watering Can
1876, Renoir (Detail)

14

Moral Development

Chapter Outline

Chapter Boxes

*It is one of the beautiful
compensations of this life that no
one can sincerely try to help
another without helping himself.*
—Charles Dudley Warner, 1873

> *There is nothing so bad it can masquerade as moral.*
>
> —Walter Lippman

IMAGES OF CHILDREN

Children's Perceptions of Morals on the Make-Believe Planet of Pax

Can children understand such concepts as discrimination, economic inequality, affirmative action, and comparable worth? Probably not if we use these terms, but might we be able to construct circumstances involving these terms that they are able to understand? Phyllis Katz (1987) asked elementary-school-aged children to pretend that they had taken a long ride on a spaceship to a make-believe planet called Pax. She asked for their opinions about various situations in which they found themselves. The situations involved conflict, socioeconomic inequality, and civil-political rights. For example, included in the conflict items was the question of what a teacher should do when two students were tied for a prize or when they have been fighting. The economic equality dilemmas included a proposed field trip that not all students could afford, a comparable worth situation in which janitors were paid more than teachers, and an employment situation that discriminated against those with dots on their noses instead of stripes. The rights items dealt with minority rights and freedom of the press.

The elementary school children did indeed recognize injustice and often came up with interesting solutions to problems. For example, all but two children believed that teachers should earn as much as janitors—the holdouts said teachers should make less because they stay in one room or because cleaning toilets is more disgusting and, therefore, deserves higher wages. Children were especially responsive to the economic inequality items. All but one thought that not giving a job to a qualified applicant who had different physical characteristics (a striped rather than a dotted nose) was unfair. The majority recommended an affirmative action solution—giving the job to the one from the discriminated minority. None of the children verbalized the concept of freedom of the press or seemed to understand that a newspaper has the right to criticize a mayor in print without being punished. What are our schools teaching children about democracy? Some of the courses of action suggested were intriguing. Several argued that the reporters should be jailed. One child said that, if she were the mayor

being criticized, she would worry, make speeches, and say, "I didn't do anything wrong," not unlike what American presidents have done in recent years. Another said that the mayor should not put the newspaper people out of work because that might make them print more bad things. "Make them write comics instead," he said. The children believed that poverty exists on Earth but mainly in Africa, big cities, or Vietnam. War was mentioned as the biggest problem on Earth, although children were not certain where it is presently occurring. Other problems mentioned were crime, hatred, school, smog, meanness, and Delta Air Lines (the questions were asked in the summer of 1986, just after a Delta Air Lines crash killed hundreds of passengers). Overall, the types of rules the children believed a society should abide by were quite sensible—almost all included the need for equitable sharing of resources and work and prohibitions against aggression.

PREVIEW

In this chapter we will explore such matters as equitable sharing, helping, rules and regulations, moral dilemmas, values, and self-control. Among the questions we will attempt to answer are: What is moral development? What is the nature of children's moral thoughts, moral behavior, moral feelings, and altruism? Should children be morally educated, and if so, what should that education be like? And, what is the nature of juvenile delinquency?

WHAT IS MORAL DEVELOPMENT?

Moral development is one of the oldest topics of interest to those who are curious about human nature. In prescientific periods, philosophers and theologians heatedly debated children's moral status at birth, which they felt had important implications for how children should be reared. Today, people are hardly neutral about moral development; most have very strong opinions about acceptable and unacceptable behavior, ethical and unethical conduct, and the ways in which acceptable and ethical behaviors are to be fostered in children.

Moral development *concerns rules and conventions about what people* should *do in their interactions with other people.* In studying these rules, developmentalists examine three domains. First, how do children *reason* or *think* about rules for ethical conduct? For example, consider cheating. A child can be presented with a story in which someone has a conflict about whether or not to cheat in a particular situation, such as when taking a test in school. The child is asked to decide what is appropriate for the character to do and why. The focus is placed on the reasoning children use to justify their moral decisions.

Second, how do children actually *behave* in moral circumstances? In our example of cheating, emphasis is on observing the child's cheating and the environmental circumstances that produced and maintain the cheating. Children might be presented with some toys and asked to select which one they believe is the most attractive. Then, the experimenter tells the young child that the particular toy selected is someone else's and is not to be played with. Observations of different conditions under which the child deviates from the prohibition or resists temptation are conducted.

Third, how does the child *feel* about the moral matters? In the example of cheating, does the child feel enough guilt to resist temptation? If children cheat, do feelings of guilt after the transgression keep them from cheating the next time they face temptation?

MORAL THOUGHTS

How do children think about the standards of right and wrong? Piaget had some thoughts about this question and so did Lawrence Kohlberg.

Piaget's Ideas about Moral Development

Interest in how children think about moral issues was stimulated by Piaget (1932), who extensively observed and interviewed children from the ages of 4 to 12. Piaget watched children play marbles to learn how they used and thought about the game's rules. He also asked children questions about ethical issues—theft, lies, punishment, and justice, for example. Piaget concluded that children think in two distinct ways about morality, depending on their developmental maturity. **Heteronomous morality** *is the first stage of moral development in Piaget's theory, occurring from 4 to 7 years of age. Justice and rules* are conceived of as unchangeable properties of the world, removed from the control of people. **Autonomous morality** *is the second stage of moral development in Piaget's theory, displayed by older children (about 10 years of age and older). The child becomes aware that rules and laws are created by people and that, in judging an action, one should consider the actor's intentions as well as the consequences.* Children 7 to 10 years of age are in a transition between the two stages, evidencing some features of both.

Let's consider Piaget's two stages of moral development further. A heteronomous thinker judges the rightness or goodness of behavior by considering the consequences of the behavior, not the intentions of the actor. For example, the heteronomous thinker says that breaking 12 cups accidentally is worse than breaking 1 cup intentionally while trying to steal a cookie. For the moral autonomist, the reverse is true. The actor's intentions assume paramount importance. The heteronomous thinker also believes that rules are unchangeable and are handed down by all-powerful authorities. When Piaget suggested to a group of young children that new rules be introduced into the game of marbles, they resisted. They insisted that the rules had always been the same and could not be altered. By contrast, older children—who are moral autonomists—accept change and recognize that rules are merely convenient, socially agreed-upon conventions, subject to change by consensus.

The heteronomous thinker also believes in **immanent justice,** *Piaget's concept that, if a rule is broken, punishment will be meted out immediately.* The young child somehow believes that the violation is connected automatically to the punishment. Thus, young children often look around worriedly after committing a transgression, expecting inevitable punishment. Older children, who are moral autonomists, recognize that punishment is socially mediated and occurs only if a relevant person witnesses the wrongdoing and that, even then, punishment is not inevitable.

Piaget argued that, as children develop, they become more sophisticated in thinking about social matters, especially about the possibilities and conditions of cooperation. Piaget believed that this social understanding comes about through the mutual give-and-take of peer relations. In the peer group, where others have power and status similar to the individual, plans are negotiated and coordinated, and disagreements are reasoned about and eventually settled. Parent-child relations, in which parents have the power and children do not, are less likely to advance moral reasoning because rules are often handed down in an authoritarian way.

Remember that Piaget believed that adolescents usually become formal operational thinkers. Thus, they are no longer tied to immediate and concrete phenomena but are more logical, abstract, and deductive reasoners. Formal operational thinkers frequently compare the real to the ideal; create contrary-to-fact propositions; are cognitively capable of relating the distant past to the present; understand their roles in society, in history, and in the universe; and can conceptualize their own thoughts and think about their mental constructs as objects. For example, it usually is not until about the age of 11 or 12 that boys and girls spontaneously introduce concepts of belief, intelligence, and faith into their definitions of their religious identities.

Kohlberg's Ideas about Moral Development

The most provocative view of moral development in recent years was crafted by Lawrence Kohlberg (Kohlberg, 1958, 1976, 1986). Kohlberg believed that moral development is based primarily on moral reasoning and unfolds in a series of stages. He arrived at his view after about 20 years of using a unique interview with children. In the interview, children are presented with a series of stories in which characters face moral dilemmas. The following is the most popular of the Kohlberg dilemmas:

> In Europe a woman was near death from a special kind of cancer. There was one drug that the doctors thought might save her. It was a form of radium that a druggist in the same town had recently discovered. The drug was expensive to make, but the druggist was charging ten times what the drug cost him to make. He paid $200 for the radium and charged $2,000 for a small dose of the drug. The sick woman's husband, Heinz, went to everyone he knew to borrow the money, but he could only get together $1,000, which is half of what it cost. He told the druggist that his wife was dying and asked him to sell it cheaper or let him pay later. But the druggist said, "No, I discovered the drug, and I am going to make money from it." So Heinz got desperate and broke into the man's store to steal the drug for his wife. (Kohlberg, 1969, p. 379)

This story is one of 11 Kohlberg devised to investigate the nature of moral thought. After reading the story, interviewees answer a series of questions about the moral dilemma. Should Heinz have stolen the drug? Was stealing it right or wrong? Why? Is it a husband's duty to steal the drug for his wife if he can get it no other way? Would a good husband steal? Did the druggist have the right to charge that much when there was no law setting a limit on the price? Why?

Based on the answers interviewees gave for this and other moral dilemmas, Kohlberg believed that three levels of moral development exist, each of which is characterized by two stages. A key concept in understanding moral development, especially Kohlberg's theory, is **internalization,** *the developmental change from behavior that is externally controlled to behavior that is controlled by internal, self-generated standards and principles.* As children develop, their moral thoughts become more internalized. Let's look further at Kohlberg's three levels of development.

1. Kohlberg's Level 1: preconventional reasoning. **Preconventional reasoning** *is the lowest level in Kohlberg's theory of moral development. At this level, the child shows no internalization of moral values—moral reasoning is controlled by external rewards and punishments.*

- Stage 1. **Punishment and obedience orientation** *is the first stage in Kohlberg's theory of moral development. At this stage, moral thinking is based on punishment.* Children obey because adults tell them to obey.
- Stage 2. **Individualism and purpose** *is the second stage in Kohlberg's theory of moral development. At this stage, moral thinking is based on rewards and self-interest.* Children obey when they want to obey and when it is in their best interest to obey. What is right is what feels good and what is rewarding.

2. Kohlberg's Level 2: conventional reasoning. **Conventional reasoning** *is the second, or intermediate, level in Kohlberg's theory of moral development. At this level, children's internalization is intermediate. The child abides by certain standards (internal), but they are the standards of others (external), such as parents or the laws of society.*

- Stage 3. **Interpersonal norms** *is the third stage in Kohlberg's theory of moral development. At this stage, children value trust, caring, and loyalty to others as the basis of moral judgments.* Children often adopt their parents' moral standards at this stage, seeking to be thought of by their parents as a "good girl" or a "good boy."
- Stage 4. **Social system morality** *is the fourth stage in Kohlberg's theory of moral development. At this stage, moral judgments are based on understanding the social order, law, justice, duty.* For example, an individual might say that it is always wrong to steal because laws that have been developed are for the good of society.

3. Kohlberg's Level 3: postconventional reasoning. **Postconventional reasoning** *is the highest level in Kohlberg's theory of moral development. At this level, morality is completely internalized and not based on others' standards.* The person recognizes alternative moral courses, explores the options, and then decides on a personal moral code.

- Stage 5. **Community rights versus individual rights** *is the fifth stage in Kohlberg's theory of moral development. At this stage, the person understands that values and laws are relative and that standards may vary from one person to another.* The person recognizes that laws are important for society but knows that laws can be changed. The person believes that some values, such as liberty, are more important than the law.
- Stage 6. **Universal ethical principles** *is the sixth and highest stage in Kohlberg's theory of moral development. At this stage, one has developed a moral standard based on universal human rights.* When faced with a conflict between law and conscience, the person will follow conscience, even though the decision might involve personal risk.

TABLE 14.1

Moral Reasoning at Kohlberg's Stages in Response to the "Heinz and the Druggist" Story

Stage description	Examples of moral reasoning that support Heinz's theft of the drug	Examples of moral reasoning that indicate Heinz should not steal the drug
Preconventional reasoning		
Stage 1: Avoid punishment	Heinz should not let his wife die; if he does, he will be in big trouble.	Heinz might get caught and sent to jail.
Stage 2: Seek rewards	If Heinz gets caught, he could give the drug back and maybe they would not give him a long jail sentence.	The druggist is a businessman and needs to make money.
Conventional reasoning		
Stage 3: Gain approval/avoid disapproval especially with family	Heinz was only doing something that a good husband would do; it shows how much he loves his wife.	If his wife dies, he can't be blamed for it; it is the druggist's fault. He is the selfish one.
Stage 4: Conformity to society's rules	If you did nothing, you would be letting your wife die; it is your responsibility if she dies. You have to steal it with the idea of paying the druggist later.	It is always wrong to steal; Heinz will always feel guilty if he steals the drug.
Postconventional reasoning		
Stage 5: Principles accepted by the community	The law was not set up for these circumstances; taking the drug is not really right, but Heinz is justified in doing it.	You can't really blame someone for stealing, but extreme circumstances don't really justify taking the law into your own hands. You might lose respect for yourself if you let your emotions take over; you have to think about the long term.
Stage 6: Individualized conscience	By stealing the drug, you would have lived up to society's rules, but you would have let down your conscience.	Heinz is faced with the decision of whether to consider other people who need the drug as badly as his wife. He needs to act by considering the value of all the lives involved.

Some of the responses to the dilemma of Heinz and the druggist are given in table 14.1, which should provide you with a better understanding of the reasoning that occurs at the six stages in Kohlberg's theory. Notice that whether Heinz steals the drug is not the important issue in Kohlberg's cognitive developmental theory. What is crucial is how the person reasons about the moral dilemma.

Kohlberg believed that these levels and stages occur in a sequence and are age related: Before age 9, most children reason about moral dilemmas in a preconventional way; by early adolescence, they reason in more conventional ways; and, by early adulthood, a small number of people reason in postconventional ways. In a 20-year longitudinal investigation, the uses of Stages 1 and 2 decreased. Stage 4, which did not appear at all in the moral reasoning of the 10-year-olds, was reflected in 62 percent of the moral thinking of the 36-year-olds. Stage 5 did not appear until the age of 20 to 22 and never characterized more than 10 percent of the individuals. Thus, the moral stages appeared somewhat later than Kohlberg initially envisioned, and the higher stages, especially Stage 6, were extremely elusive (Colby & others, 1983). Recently, Stage 6 was removed from the Kohlberg scoring manual but is still considered to be theoretically important in the Kohlberg scheme of moral development.

Influences on the Kohlberg Stages

Kohlberg believed that children's moral orientation unfolds as a consequence of their cognitive development. Children construct their moral thoughts as they pass from one stage to the next rather than passively accepting a cultural norm of morality. Investigators have sought to understand the factors that influence children's movement through the moral stages, among them modeling, cognitive conflict, peer relations, and perspective-taking opportunities.

Several investigators have attempted to advance individuals' levels of moral development by having a model present arguments that reflect moral thinking one stage above the individuals' established levels. These studies are based on the cognitive developmental concepts of equilibrium and conflict (Walker & Taylor, 1991b). By presenting moral information slightly beyond the children's cognitive level, a disequilibrium is created that motivates them to restructure their moral

Both Piaget and Kohlberg believed that peer relations are a critical part of the social stimulation that challenges children to advance their moral reasoning. The mutual give-and-take of peer relations provides children with role-taking opportunities that give children a sense that rules are generated democratically.

thought. The resolution of the disequilibrium and conflict should be toward increased competence, but the data are mixed. In one of the pioneer studies on this topic, Eliot Turiel (1966) discovered that children prefer a moral judgment stage one stage above their current stage over two stages above it. However, in the study, they chose one stage below their stage more often than one stage above it. Apparently, the children were motivated more by security needs than by the need to reorganize their thought to a higher level. Other studies indicate children prefer a more advanced stage over a less advanced stage (Rest, Turiel, & Kohlberg, 1969).

Since the early studies of stage modeling, a number of investigations have attempted to determine more precisely the effectiveness of various forms of stage modeling and argument (Lapsley & Quintana, 1985). The upshot of these studies is that virtually any plus-stage discussion format, for any length of time, seems to promote more advanced moral reasoning. For example, in one investigation (Walker, 1982), exposure to plus-two stage reasoning (arguments two stages above the child's current stage of moral thought) was just as effective in advancing moral thought as plus-one stage reasoning. Exposure to plus-two stage reasoning did not produce more plus-two stage reasoning but rather, like exposure to plus-one stage reasoning, increased reasoning at one stage above the current stage. Other research has found that exposure to reasoning only one third of a stage higher than the individual's current level of moral thought advances that person's moral thought (Berkowitz & Gibbs, 1983). In sum, current research on modeling and cognitive conflict reveals that moral thought can be moved to a higher level through exposure to models or discussion that is more advanced than the child's level.

Kohlberg believed that peer interaction is a critical part of the social stimulation that challenges children to change their moral orientation. Whereas adults characteristically impose rules and regulations on children, the mutual give-and-take in peer interaction provides children with an opportunity to take the perspective of another person and to generate rules democratically. Kohlberg stressed that perspective-taking opportunities can, in principle, be engendered by any peer group encounter. Although Kohlberg believed that such perspective-taking opportunities are ideal for moral development, he also believed that certain types of parent-child experiences can induce the child to think at more advanced levels of moral thinking. In particular, parents who allow or encourage conversation about value-laden issues promote more advanced moral thought in their children; however, many parents do not systematically provide their children with such perspective-taking opportunities. Nonetheless, in one recent study, children's moral development was related to their parents' discussion style, which involved questioning and supportive interaction (Walker & Taylor, 1991a).

Critical Thinking

Are parents more important in children's moral development than Kohlberg envisioned? Explain your answer.

Kohlberg's Critics

Kohlberg's provocative theory of moral development has not gone unchallenged (Kurtines & Gewirtz, 1991; Lapsley, 1992; Puka, 1991). The criticisms involve the link between moral thought and moral behavior, the quality of the research, inadequate consideration of culture's role in moral development, and underestimation of the care perspective.

Moral Thought and Moral Behavior

Kohlberg's theory has been criticized for placing too much emphasis on moral thought and not enough emphasis on moral behavior. Moral reasons can sometimes be a shelter for immoral behavior. Bank embezzlers and presidents endorse the loftiest of moral virtues when commenting about moral dilemmas, but their own behavior may be immoral. No one wants a nation of cheaters and thieves who can reason at the postconventional level. The cheaters and thieves may know what is right, yet still do what is wrong.

Assessment of Moral Reasoning

Some developmentalists fault the quality of Kohlberg's research and believe that more attention should be paid to the way moral development is assessed (Boyes, Giordano, & Galperyn, 1993). For example, James Rest (1976, 1983, 1986) argued that alternative methods should be used to collect information about moral thinking instead of relying on a single method that requires individuals to reason about hypothetical moral dilemmas. Rest also said that Kohlberg's stories are extremely difficult to score. To help remedy this problem, Rest developed his own measure of moral development, called the Defining Issues Test (DIT).

The DIT attempts to determine which moral issues individuals feel are more crucial in a given situation by presenting them with a series of dilemmas and a list of definitions of the major issues involved (Kohlberg's procedure does not make use

FIGURE 14.1

Actual moral dilemmas generated by adolescents.

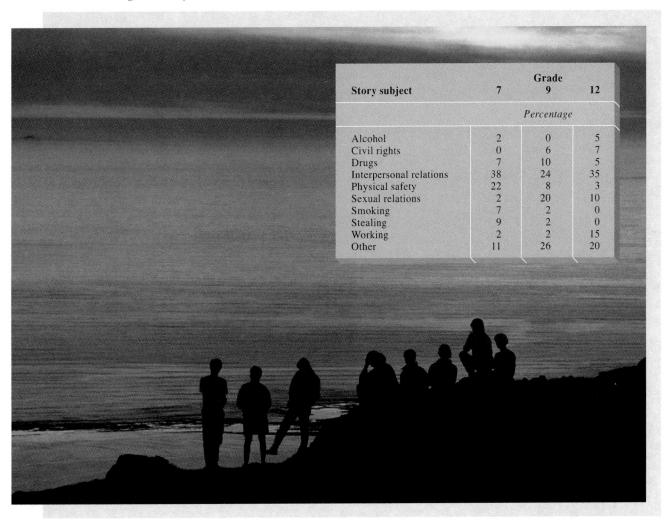

Story subject	Grade		
	7	9	12
	Percentage		
Alcohol	2	0	5
Civil rights	0	6	7
Drugs	7	10	5
Interpersonal relations	38	24	35
Physical safety	22	8	3
Sexual relations	2	20	10
Smoking	7	2	0
Stealing	9	2	0
Working	2	2	15
Other	11	26	20

of such a list). In the dilemma of Heinz and the druggist, individuals might be asked whether a community's laws should be upheld or whether Heinz should be willing to risk being injured or caught as a burglar. They might also be asked to list the most important values that govern human interaction. They are given six stories and asked to rate the importance of each issue involved in deciding what ought to be done. Then they are asked to list what they believe are the four most important issues. Rest argued that this method provides a more valid and reliable way to assess moral thinking than Kohlberg's method.

Researchers also have found that the hypothetical moral dilemmas posed in Kohlberg's stories do not match the moral dilemmas many children and adults face in their everyday lives (Walker, de Vries, & Trevethan, 1987; Yussen, 1977). Most of Kohlberg's stories focus on the family and authority. However, when one researcher invited adolescents to write stories about their own moral dilemmas, the adolescents generated dilemmas that were broader in scope, focusing on friends, acquaintances, and other issues, as well as family and authority (Yussen, 1977). The adolescents' moral dilemmas also were analyzed in

terms of their content. As shown in figure 14.1, the moral issue that concerned adolescents more than any other was interpersonal relationships.

Culture and Moral Development

Yet another criticism of Kohlberg's view is that it is culturally biased (Banks, 1993; Bronstein & Quina, 1988; Miller, 1991; Miller & Bersoff, in press). A review of research on moral development in 27 countries concluded that moral reasoning is more culture specific than Kohlberg envisioned and that Kohlberg's scoring system does not recognize higher-level moral reasoning in certain cultural groups (Snarey, 1987). Examples of higher-level moral reasoning that would not be scored as such by Kohlberg's system are values related to communal equity and collective happiness in Israel, the unity and sacredness of all life-forms in India, and the relation of the individual to the community in New Guinea. These examples of moral reasoning would not be scored at the highest level in Kohlberg's system because they do not emphasize the individual's rights and abstract principles of justice. One recent study

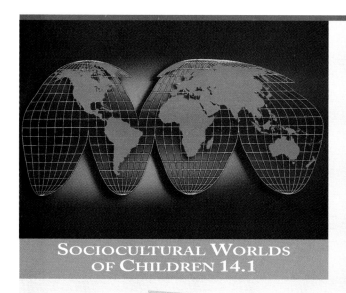

SOCIOCULTURAL WORLDS OF CHILDREN 14.1

Agreement/Disagreement between American and Indian Hindu Brahman Children about Right and Wrong

Cultural meaning systems vary around the world, and these systems shape children's morality (Damon, 1988; Miller, 1991; Miller & Bersoff, 1993). Consider a comparison of American and Indian Hindu Brahman children (Shweder, Mahapatra, & Miller, 1987). Like people in many other non-Western societies, Indians view moral rules as part of the natural world order. This means that Indians do not distinguish between physical, moral, and social regulation, as Americans do. For example, in India, violations of food taboos and marital restrictions can be just as serious as acts intended to cause harm to others. In India, social rules are seen as inevitable, much like the law of gravity.

As shown in figure 14.A, there is some, but not much, overlap in the moral concerns of children in Indian and American cultures. For Americans accustomed to viewing morality as a freely chosen social contract, Indian beliefs pose a different world view, one that is not easy to reconcile with such treasured ideas as the autonomy of an individualized conscience. The interviews conducted by Richard Shweder and his colleagues (1987) with Indian and American children revealed sharp cultural differences in what people judge to be right and

In one recent study of 20 adolescent Buddhist monks in Nepal, their main concerns were not the issue of justice (as Kohlberg's theory argues) but, rather, the prevention of suffering and the importance of compassion.

wrong. For example, Indian and American children disagree about eating beef. On the other hand, there are areas of overlap between the two cultures. For example, both think that breaking promises and ignoring beggars is wrong.

According to moral development theorist and researcher William Damon (1988), where culturally specific practices take on profound moral and religious significance, as in India, the moral development of children focuses extensively on their adherence to custom and convention. In contrast, Western moral doctrine tends to elevate abstract principles, such as justice and welfare, to a higher moral status than customs or conventions. As in India, socialization practices in many Third-World countries actively instill in children a great respect for their culture's traditional codes and practices (Edwards, 1987).

Another recent research investigation by Joan Miller and David Bersoff (in press) documented how the majority of Asian Indian children, adolescents, and adults give priority to interpersonal needs in moral conflict situations, whereas the majority of Americans give priority to an individual's justice. Americans were more likely than Indians to downplay the importance of caring in conflict situations, which is likely an outgrowth of the stronger emphasis on an individual's rights in America.

---

assessed the moral development of 20 adolescent male Buddhist monks in Nepal (Huebner, Garrod, & Snarey, 1990). The issue of justice, a basic theme in Kohlberg's theory, was not of paramount importance in the monks' moral views, and their concerns about prevention of suffering and the role of compassion are not captured by Kohlberg's theory. More about cultural variations in adolescents' moral thought appears in Sociocultural Worlds of Children 14.1. In sum, moral reasoning is shaped more by the values and beliefs of a culture than Kohlberg acknowledged.

Gender and the Care Perspective

In chapter 13, we discussed Carol Gilligan's view that relationships and connections to others are critical aspects of female development. Gilligan (1982, 1990, 1991, 1992) also has

criticized Kohlberg's theory of moral development. She believes that his theory does not adequately reflect relationships and concern for others. The **justice perspective** *is a moral perspective that focuses on the rights of the individual; individuals stand alone and independently make moral decisions. Kohlberg's theory is a justice perspective.* By contrast, the **care perspective** *is a moral perspective that views people in terms of their connectedness with others and emphasizes interpersonal communication, relationships with others, and concern for others. Gilligan's theory is a care perspective.* According to Gilligan, Kohlberg greatly underplayed the care perspective in moral development. She believes that this may have happened because he was a male, because most of his research was with males rather than females, and because he used male responses as a model for his theory.

FIGURE 14.A

Agreements/disagreements between American and Indian Hindu Brahman children about right and wrong.

Source: After Damon, 1988.

**Disagreement: Brahman children think it is right;
American children think it is wrong.**

—Hitting an errant child with a cane
—Eating with one's hands
—Father opening a son's letter

**Disagreement: Brahman children think it is wrong;
American children think it is right.**

—Addressing one's father by his first name
—Eating beef
—Cutting one's hair and eating chicken after father's death

Agreement: Brahman and American children think it is wrong.

—Ignoring a beggar
—Destroying another's picture
—Kicking a harmless animal
—Stealing flowers

Agreement: Brahman and American children think it is right.

—Men holding hands

Critical Thinking

Can you think of some ways that children's moral development might vary across cultures, other than those variations described in this text?

In extensive interviews with girls from 6 to 18 years of age, Gilligan and her colleagues found that girls consistently interpret moral dilemmas in terms of human relationships and base these interpretations on listening and watching other people (Gilligan, 1990, 1992; Gilligan, Brown, & Rogers, 1990). According to Gilligan, girls have the ability to sensitively pick up different rhythms in relationships and often are able to follow the pathways of feelings. Gilligan believes that girls reach a critical juncture in their development when they reach adolescence. Usually around 11 to 12 years of age, girls become aware that their intense interest in intimacy is not prized by the male-dominated culture, even though society values women as caring and altruistic. The dilemma is that girls are presented with a choice that makes them look either selfish or selfless. Gilligan believes that, as adolescent girls experience this dilemma, they increasingly silence their "distinctive voice."

Researchers have found support for Gilligan's claim that females' and males' moral reasoning often centers around different concerns and issues (Bussey & Maughan, 1982; Galotti, Kozberg, & Appleman, in press; Galotti, Kozberg, & Farmer, 1990; Hanson & Mullis, 1985; Lyons, 1983; Scheidel & Marcia, 1985; Yussen, 1977). However, one of Gilligan's initial claims—that traditional Kohlbergian measures of moral development are biased against females—has been extensively

Carol Gilligan is shown with some of the students she has interviewed about the importance of relationships in a female's development. According to Gilligan, the sense of relationships and connectedness is at the heart of female development.

disputed. For example, most research studies using the Kohlberg stories and scoring system do not find sex differences (Walker, 1984, 1991a, b). Thus, the strongest support for Gilligan's claims comes from studies that focus on items and scoring systems pertaining to close relationships, pathways of feelings, sensitive listening, and the rhythm of interpersonal behavior (Galotti, Kozberg, & Farmer, 1990).

While females often articulate a care perspective and males a justice perspective, the gender difference is not absolute, and the two orientations are not mutually exclusive (Gilligan & Attanucci, 1988; Lyons, 1990; Rothbart, Hanley, & Albert, 1986). For example, in one study, 53 of 80 females and males showed either a care or a justice perspective, but 27 subjects used both orientations, with neither predominating (Gilligan & Attanucci, 1988). Explorations in Child Development 14.1 presents more information about adolescent girls' care considerations, justice considerations, and mixed considerations of care and justice.

MORAL BEHAVIOR

What are the basic processes that behaviorists believe are responsible for children's moral behavior? What is the nature of

resistance to temptation and self-control? How do cognitive social learning theorists view children's moral development? We will explore each of these questions in turn.

Reinforcement, Punishment, Imitation, and Situational Variations

The study of moral behavior has been influenced primarily by social learning theory. The familiar processes of reinforcement, punishment, and imitation have been invoked to explain how and why children learn certain responses and why their responses differ from one another; the general conclusions to be drawn are the same as elsewhere. When children are reinforced for behavior that is consistent with laws and social conventions, they are likely to repeat that behavior. When provided with models who behave "morally," children are likely to adopt their actions. Finally, when children are punished for "immoral" or unacceptable behaviors, those behaviors can be eliminated, but at the expense of sanctioning punishment by its very use and of causing emotional side effects for the child.

To these general conclusions are added some qualifiers. The effectiveness of reward and punishment depends on the consistency with which they are administered and the schedule (for example, continuous, partial) that is adopted. The effectiveness of modeling depends on the characteristics of the model (esteem, power) and the presence of symbolic codes to enhance retention of the modeled behavior.

What kind of adult moral models are children being exposed to in our society? Do such models usually do what they say? There is evidence that the adult models children are exposed to often display a double standard, with their moral thinking not always corresponding to their actions. A poll of 24,000 Americans sampled their views on a wide variety of moral issues. Eight detailed scenarios of everyday moral problems were developed to test moral decision making. A summary of the responses to these moral dilemmas is shown in table 14.2. Consider the example of whether the person queried would knowingly buy a stolen color television set. More than 20 percent of the respondents said they would, even though 87 percent said that such an act is probably morally wrong. Further, approximately 31 percent of the adults said that, if they knew they would not get caught, they would be more likely to buy the stolen television. Although moral thought is a very important dimension of moral development, these data glaringly point out that what people believe about right and wrong does not always predict how they will act in moral situations.

In addition to emphasizing the role of reinforcement, punishment, and imitation in determining moral behavior, behaviorists make a strong claim that moral behavior is situationally dependent. That is, from the behavioral perspective, children do not consistently display moral behavior in different situations. In a classic investigation of moral behavior, one of the most extensive ever conducted, Hugh Hartshorne and Mark May (1928–1930) observed the moral responses of 11,000 children who were given the opportunity to lie, cheat, and steal in a variety of circumstances—at home, at school, at social events, and in athletics. A completely honest or a completely dishonest

EXPLORATIONS IN CHILD DEVELOPMENT 14.1

Adolescent Girls—Their Care, Justice, and Mixed Care/Justice Considerations

According to Nona Lyons (1990), an associate of Carol Gilligan, in interpreting moral dilemmas, adolescents may show care considerations, justice considerations, or mixed care/justice considerations. The following comments of adolescent girls from the Emma Willard School in Troy, New York, illustrate these three moral considerations (Lyons, 1990, pp. 38–39):

1. *Justice Considerations.* Justice considerations involve a self-focus that includes respecting and upholding rights, as well as a contract or fairness emphasis in relationships.
   - I didn't get my math homework done. . . . We had to hand in the computer tapes, and my friend had an extra computer tape, and I knew the teacher was going to absolutely freak out and scream at me, and I would get into trouble if I didn't hand in a tape. And my friend had an extra one she was offering me, but I couldn't do it. I couldn't take it. . . . I couldn't hand it in when I didn't do it. It would have been like cheating.
   - I don't go to chapel anymore because I find that offensive, and I guess that's moral. We have required chapel once a week, and I don't like the idea of being required to go, of being forced into

   religion. I go to church on my own sometimes. I think that's enough for me, and I don't feel that I need to go to these required services. It was a big decision.

2. *Care Considerations.* Care considerations involve creating and maintaining interdependence and response in relationships.
   - I lied to my parents about my grades. I told them that my biology grade was going to be marvelous, and it is not going to be marvelous. . . . Suddenly, my sister, who has always been National Honor Society and all those wonderful things, has gotten horrible grades this past month, and (my parents) called me up and told me this and then wanted to know how mine were. And it was the difference between, knowing my parents, they would go to the ends of the earth if they knew both their children were doing horribly in school—my parents are educational fanatics—and so I've told them that my grades are fine, and there was almost a sigh of relief from my father. And I think that outweighed the idea that I was lying to them. . . . I couldn't bring myself on the phone to say, "Well, Dad, you are looking at two academic failures for the term." And I think that's a moral dilemma.
   - My roommate and I were in the same class, and I lost my book, and she lost her book. And then I lost my book and she found hers, and I borrowed her book one night to do my homework. And I noticed my name in it, and I realized that she had taken my book and erased my name and wrote hers over it. And I had to decide whether I should save embarrassing her by confronting her with the problem and just go out and get another book, or whether I should say, "Hey, did you take my book? I know this is my book; give it back."

3. *Mixed Care/Justice Considerations.* Mixed care/justice considerations involve responses to moral dilemmas that include both care and justice components.
   - Last year, some friends and I went out, and we were having a little celebration. . . . One girl met a friend of hers, and she wanted to stay longer and talk. . . . The next morning we realized that our friend had gotten busted. . . . I didn't know if I should turn myself in or what. In the end, I really had a hard time deciding what to do because I felt it was really unfair . . . she had gotten busted and we hadn't. And the problem was, if I turned myself in, I would have been responsible for four other people.

child was difficult to find. Situation-specific behavior was the rule. Children were more likely to cheat when their friends put pressure on them to do so and when the chance of being caught was slim. Other analyses of the consistency of moral behavior suggest that, although moral behavior is influenced by situational determinants, some children are more likely to cheat, lie, and steal than others (Burton, 1984).

Resistance to Temptation and Self-control

A key ingredient of moral development from the social learning perspective is a child's ability to resist temptation and to develop self-control (Bandura, 1986; Mischel, 1987). When pressures mount for children to cheat, lie, or steal, it is important to ask whether they have developed the ability to control themselves and to resist such temptations.

TABLE 14.2

The Hypocrisy of Adult Moral Models

Would You:	Percent Who Said Yes, or Probably:	Percent Who Said It Is, or Probably Is, Unethical:	Percent Who Would, or Probably Would, Be More Likely to If Sure They Would Not Get Caught:
Drive away after scratching a car without telling the owner?	44%	89%	52%
Cover for a friend's secret affair?	41	66	33
Cheat on your spouse?	37	68	42
Keep $10 extra change at a local supermarket?	26	85	33
Knowingly buy a stolen color television set?	22	87	31
Try to keep your neighborhood segregated?	13	81	8
Drive while drunk?	11	90	24
Accept praise for another's work?	4	96	8

REPRINTED WITH PERMISSION FROM *PSYCHOLOGY TODAY MAGAZINE.* Copyright © 1981 American Psychological Association.

Developmentalists have invented a number of ways to investigate such temptations. In one procedure, children are shown attractive toys and told that the toys belong to someone else, who has requested that they not be touched. Children then experience social influence, perhaps in the form of a discussion of virtues about respecting other people's property or in the form of a model resisting or giving in to the temptation to play with prohibited objects. Children are left alone in the room to amuse themselves when the experimenter departs (under a pretext), announcing that he or she will return in 10 to 15 minutes. The experimenter then watches through a one-way mirror to see whether children resist or give in to the temptation to play with the toys.

There has been considerable interest in examining the effects of punishment on children's ability to resist temptation (Parke, 1972, 1977). For the most part, offering children cognitive rationales enhances most forms of punishment, such as reasons a child should not play with a forbidden toy. Cognitive rationales have been more effective in getting children to resist temptation over a period of time than have strategies that do not use reasoning, such as when parents place children in their rooms without explaining the consequences for others of the children's deviant behavior.

The ability to resist temptation is closely tied to delay of gratification. Self-control is involved in both the ability to resist temptation and the ability to delay gratification. In the case of resisting temptation, children must overcome their impulses to get something that is desired but is known to be prohibitive. Similarly, children must show a sense of patience and self-control in delaying gratification for a desirable future reward rather than succumbing to the immediate pressure of pursuing a smaller reward.

Considerable research has been conducted on children's self-control. Walter Mischel (1974, 1987) believes that self-control is strongly influenced by cognitive factors. Researchers have shown that children can instruct themselves to be more patient and, in the process, show more self-control. In one investigation, preschool children were asked to perform a very dull task (Mischel & Patterson, 1976). Close by was a very enticing talking mechanical clown that tried to persuade the children to play with it. The children who had been trained to say to themselves, "I'm not going to look at Mr. Clown when Mr. Clown says to look at him" were more likely to control their behavior and continue working on the dull task than children who were not given the self-instructional strategy.

Interest in the cognitive factors in resistance to temptation, delay of gratification, and self-control reflects the increasing interest among social learning theorists in the ways in which such cognitions mediate the link between environmental experiences and moral behavior. Next, we will examine a view that captures this cognitive trend.

Cognitive Social Learning Theory

The **cognitive social learning theory of morality** *emphasizes a distinction between a child's* moral competence—*the ability to produce moral behaviors*—and moral performance—*those behaviors in specific situations* (Mischel & Mischel, 1975). Moral competence, or acquisition of moral knowledge, depends primarily on cognitive-sensory processes; it is the outgrowth of these processes. Competencies include what children are capable of doing, what they know, their skills, their awareness of moral rules and regulations, and their cognitive ability to construct behaviors. Children's moral performance, or behavior, however, is determined by their motivation and the rewards and incentives to act in a specific moral way. Albert Bandura (1991) also believes that moral development is best understood by considering a combination of social and cognitive factors, especially those involving self-control.

In general, social learning theorists have been critical of Kohlberg's theory of moral development. Among other reasons, they believe he placed too little emphasis on moral behavior and the situational determinants of morality. However, although Kohlberg argued that moral judgment is an important determinant of moral behavior, he, like the Mischels, stressed that an individual's interpretation of both the moral and factual aspects of a situation leads to a moral decision (Kohlberg & Candee, 1979). For example, Kohlberg mentioned that "extra-moral" factors, such as the desire to avoid embarrassment, may cause children to avoid doing what they believe to be morally right. In sum, according to both the Mischels and Kohlberg, moral action is influenced by a complex of factors. Overall, the findings are mixed with regard to the association of moral thought and behavior (Arnold, 1989), although in one investigation with college students, individuals with both high-principled moral reasoning and high ego strength were less likely to cheat in a resistance-to-temptation situation than were their low-principled and low-ego-strength counterparts (Hess, Lonky, & Roodin, 1985).

At this point, we have discussed a number of ideas about what moral development is, moral thoughts, and moral behavior. A summary of these ideas is presented in Concept Table 14.1. In the next section, we will turn our attention to moral feelings.

MORAL FEELINGS

Among the ideas formulated about the development of children's moral feelings have been the concepts developed by psychoanalytic theorists, the role of childrearing techniques, the nature of empathy, and the role of emotions in moral development.

Psychoanalytic Theory

In chapter 2, we discussed Sigmund Freud's psychoanalytic theory, which describes the *superego* as one of the three main structures of personality (the id and ego are the other two). In Freud's classical psychoanalytic theory, a child's superego—the moral branch of personality—develops as the child resolves the Oedipal conflict and identifies with the same-sex parent in the early childhood years. One reason children resolve the Oedipal conflict is to alleviate the fears of losing their parents' love and of being punished for their unacceptable sexual wishes toward the opposite-sex parent. To reduce anxiety, avoid punishment, and maintain parental affection, children form a superego by identifying with the same-sex parent. Through this identification, children internalize the parent's standards of right and wrong that reflect societal prohibitions. Also, the child turns inward the hostility that was previously aimed externally at the same-sex parent. This inwardly directed hostility is then experienced self-punitively (and unconsciously) as guilt. In the psychoanalytic account of moral development, self-punitiveness of guilt keeps children from committing transgressions. That is, children conform to societal standards to avoid guilt.

> *What is moral is what you feel good after and what is immoral is what you feel bad after.*
>
> —Ernest Hemingway

In Freud's view, the superego consists of two main components, ego-ideal and conscience, which promote children's development of moral feelings. The **ego-ideal** *is the component of the superego that involves ideal standards approved of by parents,* whereas **conscience** *is the component of the superego that involves prohibitions disapproved of by parents.* A child's ego-ideal rewards the child by conveying a sense of pride and personal value when the child acts according to moral standards. The conscience punishes the child for acting immorally by making the child feel guilty and worthless. In this way, self-control replaces parental control.

Critical Thinking

How would you assess children's feelings of guilt? Describe the kind of measure(s) you would use.

Childrearing Techniques and Moral Development

In Freud's psychoanalytic theory, the aspects of childrearing that encourage moral development are practices that instill the fears of punishment and of losing parental love. Child developmentalists who have studied childrearing techniques and moral development have focused on parents' discipline. These discipline techniques include love withdrawal, power assertion, and induction (Hoffman, 1970). Love withdrawal comes closest to the psychoanalytic emphasis on fear of punishment and of losing parental love. **Love withdrawal** *is a discipline technique in which a parent removes attention or love from the child,* as when the parent refuses to talk to the child or states a dislike for the child. For example, the parent might say, "I'm going to leave you if you do that again," or "I don't like you when you do that." **Power assertion** *is a discipline technique in which a parent attempts to gain control over the child or the child's resources.* Examples include spanking, threatening, or removing privileges. **Induction** *is the discipline technique in which a parent uses*

CONCEPT TABLE 14.1

The Nature of Moral Development, Moral Thought, and Moral Behavior

Concept	Processes/Related Ideas	Characteristics/Description
What is moral development?	Its nature	Moral development concerns rules and regulations about what people should do in their interactions with others. Developmentalists study how children think, behave, and feel about such rules and regulations.
Moral thought	Piaget's theory	It distinguishes between the heteronomous morality of younger children and the autonomous morality of older children. Piaget's ideas on formal operational thought have implications for understanding adolescents' moral development.
	Kohlberg's theory	Kohlberg developed a provocative view of the development of moral reasoning. He argued that moral development consists of three levels—preconventional, conventional, and postconventional—and six stages (two at each level). Increased internalization characterizes movement to Levels 2 and 3. Kohlberg's longitudinal data show a relation of the stages to age, although the highest two stages, especially Stage 6, rarely appear.
	Influences on the Kohlberg stages	Influences include cognitive development, imitation and cognitive conflict, peer relations, and perspective taking.
	Kohlberg's critics	Criticisms involve an overemphasis on cognitive and underemphasis on behavior, the quality of the research, inadequate consideration of the care perspective, and an underestimation of the role of culture. Carol Gilligan advocates a stronger care perspective (which views people in terms of their connectedness to others and interpersonal communication). Gilligan also believes that early adolescence is a critical juncture in the development of a moral voice for females. Researchers have found support for Gilligan's claim that females' and males' moral reasoning often center on different concerns, although gender differences in Kohlberg's stages have not been found consistently. Studies that focus more extensively on the items pertaining to close relationships, and use of scoring systems that emphasize connectedness, support Gilligan's claims.
Moral behavior	Reinforcement, punishment, imitation, and situational variations	Behaviorists argue that children's moral behavior is determined by the processes of reinforcement, punishment, and imitation. Situational variability in morality is stressed.
	Resistance to temptation and self-control	Behaviorists who study children's moral behavior often examine resistance to temptation and the development of self-control. The use of cognitive rationales has improved children's ability to resist temptation. Children's self-control is also influenced by cognitive factors, such as self-instruction.
	Cognitive social learning theory	It emphasizes a distinction between moral competence—the ability to produce moral behaviors—and moral performance—those behaviors in specific situations. In general, social learning theorists have been critical of Kohlberg's theory, believing he placed too little emphasis on moral behavior and its situational variability.

reason and explanation of the consequences for others of the child's actions. Examples of induction include, "Don't hit him. He was only trying to help," and "Why are you yelling at her? She didn't mean to trip you."

Moral development theorist and researcher Martin Hoffman (1970) believes that any discipline produces arousal on the child's part. Love withdrawal and power assertion are likely to evoke a very high level of arousal, with love withdrawal generating considerable anxiety and power assertion considerable hostility. Induction is more likely to produce a moderate level of arousal in children, a level that permits them to attend to the cognitive rationales parents offer. When a parent uses power assertion and love withdrawal, the child may be so aroused that, even if the parent gives accompanying explanations about the consequences for others of the child's actions, the child may not attend to them. Power assertion presents parents as weak models of self-control—as individuals who cannot control their feelings. Accordingly, children may imitate this model of poor self-control when they face stressful circumstances. The use of induction, however, focuses the child's attention on the action's consequences for others, not on the child's own shortcomings. For these reasons, Hoffman (1988) believes that parents should use induction to encourage children's moral development. In research on parenting techniques, induction is more positively related to moral development than is love withdrawal or power assertion, although the findings vary according to children's developmental level and socioeconomic status. Induction works better with elementary-school-aged children than with preschool children (Brody & Shaffer, 1982) and better with middle-class than lower-class children (Hoffman, 1970). Older children are probably better able to understand the reasons given to them and are better at perspective taking. Some theorists believe that the internalization of society's moral standards is more likely among middle-class than lower-class individuals because internalization is more rewarding in the middle-class culture (Kohn, 1977).

In sum, a number of child developmentalists believe that family processes play a more important role in children's moral development than Kohlberg did. They believe that inductive discipline contributes to moral motivation and that parental values influence children's developing moral thoughts (Costanzo & Dunsmore, 1993; Gibbs, 1993; Jagers & Bingham, 1993; Kelley & Berndt, 1993; Walker, 1993).

Empathy

Positive feelings, such as empathy, contribute to the child's moral development. Feeling **empathy** *means reacting to another's feelings with an emotional response that is similar to the other's response* (Damon, 1988). Although empathy is experienced as an emotional state, it often has a cognitive component—the ability to discern another's inner psychological states, or what we have previously called *perspective taking* (Eisenberg & others, 1991). Infants have the capacity for some purely empathic responses, but, for effective moral action, children need to learn to identify a wide range of emotional states in others and to anticipate what kinds of action will improve another person's emotional state.

What are the main milestones in children's development of empathy? According to a recent analysis by child developmentalist William Damon (1988), changes in empathy take place in early infancy, at 1 to 2 years in age, in early childhood, and at 10 to 12 years of age. **Global empathy** *is the young infant's empathic response in which clear boundaries between the feelings and needs of the self and those of another have not yet been established* (Hoffman, 1983). For example, one 11-month-old infant fought off her own tears, sucked her thumb, and buried her head in her mother's lap after she had seen another child fall and hurt himself. Not all infants cry every time someone else is hurt, though. Many times, an infant will stare at another's pain with curiosity. Although global empathy is observed in some infants, it does not consistently characterize all infants' behavior.

Between 1 and 2 years of age, the infant's undifferentiated feelings of discomfort at another's distress grow into more genuine feelings of concern. The infant realizes that others are independent persons in their own right, with their own unhappy feelings. The infant may sense that these unhappy feelings in others need attention and relief, but the infant cannot translate this realization into effective behavior. For example, toddlers may offer a beloved blanket or doll for comfort to an unhappy-looking adult.

In the early childhood years, children become aware that every person's perspective is unique and that someone else may have a reaction to a situation that is different from their own. Such awareness permits the child to respond more appropriately to another's distress. For example, at the age of 6, a child may realize that, in some instances, an unhappy person may best be left alone rather than helped, or the child may learn to wait for just the right time to give comfort. In sum, at this point, children make more objective assessments of others' distress and needs.

Toward the end of the elementary school years, at about 10 to 12 years of age, children develop empathy for people who live in unfortunate circumstances. Children's concerns are no longer limited to the feelings of particular persons in situations the child observes directly. Instead, children expand their concerns to the general problems of people in unfortunate situations—the poor, the handicapped, and the socially outcast, for example. This newfound sensitivity may lead to altruistic behavior by the older elementary school child and later, in adolescence, give a humanitarian flavor to the adolescent's development of ideological and political views. A summary of Damon's description of empathy development is shown in figure 14.2.

Although everyone may be capable of responding with empathy, not all individuals do. There is considerable variation in individual empathic behavior. For example, in older children and adolescents, emphathic dysfunctions can contribute to antisocial behavior. Some delinquents convicted of violent crimes show a lack of feeling for their victims' distress. A 13-year-old boy convicted of violently mugging a number of elderly people, when asked about the pain he had caused for one blind woman, said, "What do I care? I'm not her" (Damon, 1988).

FIGURE 14.2

Damon's description of developmental changes in empathy.

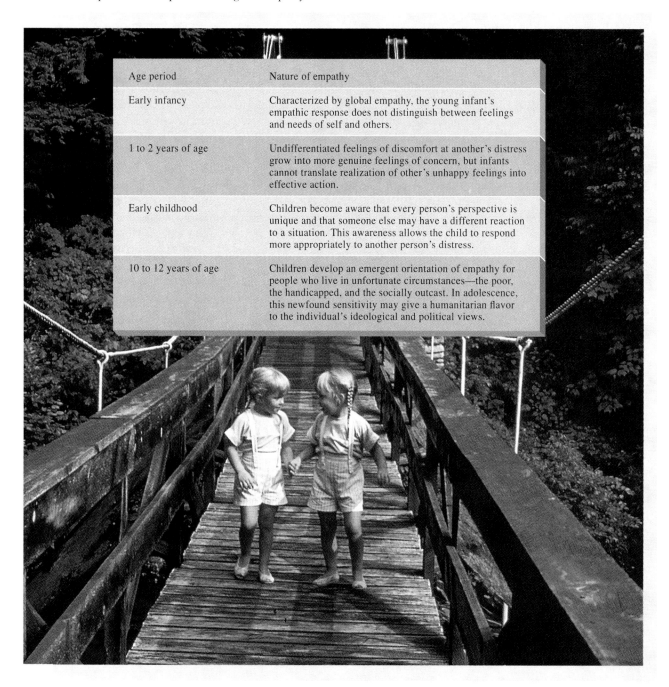

Age period	Nature of empathy
Early infancy	Characterized by global empathy, the young infant's empathic response does not distinguish between feelings and needs of self and others.
1 to 2 years of age	Undifferentiated feelings of discomfort at another's distress grow into more genuine feelings of concern, but infants cannot translate realization of other's unhappy feelings into effective action.
Early childhood	Children become aware that every person's perspective is unique and that someone else may have a different reaction to a situation. This awareness allows the child to respond more appropriately to another person's distress.
10 to 12 years of age	Children develop an emergent orientation of empathy for people who live in unfortunate circumstances—the poor, the handicapped, and the socially outcast. In adolescence, this newfound sensitivity may give a humanitarian flavor to the individual's ideological and political views.

Not only is there individual variation in adolescents' empathy and concern about the welfare of others, but sociohistorical influences also may be involved. Over the past two decades, adolescents have shown an increased concern for personal well-being and a decreased concern for the welfare of others, especially for the disadvantaged (Astin, Green, & Korn, 1987; Conger, 1981, 1988). As shown in figure 14.3, today's college freshmen are more strongly motivated to be well-off financially and less motivated to develop a meaningful philosophy of life than were their counterparts 20 or even 10 years ago. Among high school seniors, increasing numbers are motivated by the opportunity to make a considerable amount of money (Bachman, Johnston, & O'Malley, 1987).

However, two values that increased during the 1960s continue to characterize today's youth: self-fulfillment and self-expression (Conger, 1981, 1988). As part of their motivation for self-fulfillment, many adolescents show great interest in their physical health and well-being. Greater self-fulfillment and self-expression can be laudable goals, but, if they become the only goals, self-destruction, loneliness, or alienation may result. Young people also need to develop a corresponding sense of commitment to others' welfare. Encouraging adolescents to

FIGURE 14.3

Changing freshman life goals, 1968–1990. The percentages indicated are in response to the question of identifying a life goal as "essential" or "very important." There has been a significant reversal in freshman life goals in the last two decades, with a far greater percentage of today's college freshmen stating that a "very important" life goal is to be well-off financially, and far fewer stating that developing a meaningful philosophy of life is a "very important" life goal.

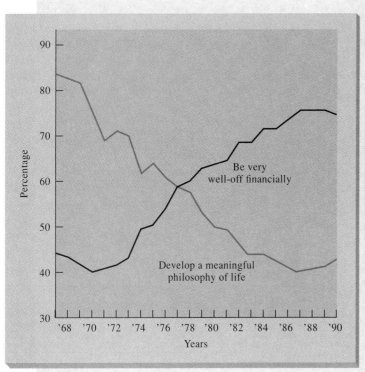

have a strong commitment to others, in concert with an interest in self-fulfillment, is a major task for our nation at the close of the twentieth century.

The Contemporary Perspective on the Role of Emotions in Moral Development

We have seen that classical psychoanalytic theory emphasizes the power of unconscious guilt in moral development but that other theorists, such as Hoffman and Damon, emphasize the role of empathy. Today, many child developmentalists believe that both positive feelings, such as empathy, sympathy, admiration, and self-esteem, and negative feelings, such as anger, outrage, shame, and guilt, contribute to children's moral development (Damon, 1988). When strongly experienced, these emotions influence children to act in accord with standards of right and wrong. Such emotions as empathy, shame, guilt, and anxiety over other people's violations of standards are present early in development and undergo developmental change throughout childhood and beyond (Damon, 1988). These emotions provide a natural base for children's acquisition of moral values, both orienting children toward moral events and motivating them to pay close attention to such events.

However, moral emotions do not operate in a vacuum to build a child's moral awareness, and they are not sufficient in themselves to generate moral responsivity. They do not give the "substance" of moral regulation—the rules, values, and standards of behavior that children need to understand and act on. Moral emotions are inextricably interwoven with the cognitive and social aspects of children's development. The web of feeling, cognition, and social behavior is also experienced in altruism—the aspect of children's moral development we will discuss next.

ALTRUISM

Altruism *is an unselfish interest in helping someone.* Human acts of altruism are plentiful—the hardworking laborer who places $5 in a Salvation Army kettle; rock concerts to feed the hungry, help farmers, and fund AIDS research; and the child who takes in a wounded cat and cares for it. How do psychologists account for such acts of altruism?

> *But you cannot give to people what they are incapable of receiving.*
>
> —Agatha Christie, *Funerals Are Fatal* (1953)

Reciprocity and exchange are involved in altruism. Reciprocity is found throughout the human world. Not only is it the highest moral principle in Christianity but it is also present in every widely practiced religion in the world—Judaism, Hinduism, Buddhism, and Islam. Reciprocity encourages children to do unto others as they would have others do unto them. Human sentiments are wrapped up in this reciprocity. Trust is probably the most important principle over the long run in altruism. Guilt surfaces if the child does not reciprocate, and anger may result if someone else does not reciprocate. Not all altruism is motivated by reciprocity and exchange, but self-other interactions and relationships help us understand altruism's nature. The circumstances most likely to involve altruism are empathic emotion for an individual in need or a close relationship between benefactor and recipient (Batson, 1989).

In addition to presenting a developmental sequence of children's empathy, which we discussed earlier, Damon (1988) has also described a developmental sequence of children' altruism, especially of sharing. Most sharing during the first 3 years of life is done for nonempathic reasons, such as for the fun of the social play ritual or out of mere imitation. Then, at about 4 years of age, a combination of empathic awareness and adult encouragement produces a sense of obligation on the part of the child to share with others. This obligation forces the child to share, even though the child may not perceive this as the best way to have fun. Most 4-year-olds are not selfless saints, however. Children believe they have an obligation to share but do not necessarily think they should be as generous to others as they are to themselves. Neither do their actions always support their beliefs, especially when the object of contention is a coveted one. What is important developmentally is that the child has developed an internal belief that sharing is an obligatory part of a social relationship and that this involves a question of right and wrong. However, a preschool child's sense of reciprocity does not constitute a moral duty but, rather, a pragmatic means of getting one's way. Despite their shortcomings, these ideas about justice formed in early childhood set the stage for giant strides that children make in the years that follow.

Every man takes care that his neighbor shall not cheat him. But a day comes when he begins to care that he does not cheat his neighbor. Then all goes well.

—Ralph Waldo Emerson

By the start of the elementary school years, children genuinely begin to express more objective ideas about fairness. These notions about fairness have been used throughout history to distribute goods and to resolve conflicts. They involve the principles of equality, merit, and benevolence. *Equality* means that everyone is treated the same. *Merit* means giving extra rewards for hard work, a talented performance, or other laudatory behavior. *Benevolence* means giving special consideration to individuals in a disadvantaged condition. Equality is the first of these principles used regularly by elementary school children. It is common to hear 6-year-old children use the word "fair" as synonymous with "equal" or "same." By the mid- to late-elementary-school years, children also believe that equity means special treatment for those who deserve it—the principles of merit and benevolence.

Missing from the factors that guide children's altruism is one that many adults might expect to be the most influential of all: the motivation to obey adult authority figures. Surprisingly, a number of studies have shown that adult authority has only a small influence on children's sharing. For example, when child developmentalist Nancy Eisenberg (1982) asked children to explain their own altruistic acts, they mainly gave empathic and pragmatic reasons for their spontaneous acts of sharing. Not one of the children referred to the demands of adult authority. Parental advice and prodding certainly foster standards of sharing, but the give-and-take of peer requests and arguments provide the most immediate stimulation of sharing. Parents may set examples that children carry into peer interaction and communication, but parents are not present during all of their children's peer exchanges. The day-to-day construction of fairness standards is done by children in collaboration and negotiation with each other. Over the course of many years and thousands of encounters, children's understanding of altruism deepens. With this conceptual elaboration that involves such notions as equality, merit, benevolence, and compromise come a greater consistency and generosity in children's sharing behavior (Damon, 1988).

Without civic morality communities perish; without personal morality their survival has no value.

—Bertrand Russell

Moral Education

The moral education of children has become a widely discussed topic. Many parents worry that their children are growing up without traditional values. Teachers complain that many of their students are unethical. Among the questions about moral education we will examine are the following: What is the hidden curriculum? What is the nature of direct moral education versus indirect moral education? What is values clarification? What is cognitive moral education?

The Hidden Curriculum

The **hidden curriculum** *is the pervasive moral atmosphere that characterizes schools. This atmosphere includes school and classroom rules, attitudes toward academics and extracurricular activities, the moral orientation of teachers and school administrators, and text materials.* More than half a century ago, educator John Dewey (1933) recognized that, whether or not they offer specific programs in moral education, schools provide moral education through the hidden curriculum. Schools, like families, are settings for moral development. Teachers serve as models of ethical or unethical behavior. Classroom rules and peer relations at school transmit attitudes about cheating, lying, stealing, and consideration of others, and the school administration, through its rules and regulations, represents a value system to children.

Direct and Indirect Moral Education

The approaches to moral education can be classified as either direct or indirect (Benninga, 1988). **Direct moral education** *involves either emphasizing values or character traits during specified time slots or integrating those values or traits throughout the curriculum.* **Indirect moral education** *involves encouraging children to define their own and others' values and helping them define the moral perspectives that support those values.*

In the direct moral education approach, instruction in specified moral concepts can assume the form of example and definition, class discussions and role playing, or rewarding students for proper behavior (Jensen & Knight, 1981). The use of McGuffey Readers during the early part of the twentieth century exemplifies the direct approach. The stories and poems in the readers taught moral behavior and character in addition to academics. A number of contemporary educators advocate a direct approach to moral education. Former U.S. Secretary of Education William Bennett (1986) wrote:

> If a college is really interested in teaching its students a clear lesson in moral responsibility, it should tell the truth about drugs in a straightforward way. This summer our college presidents should send every student a letter saying they will not tolerate drugs on campus—period. The letter should then spell out precisely what the college's policy will be toward students who use drugs. Being simple and straightforward about moral responsibility is not the same as being simplistic and unsophisticated.

Bennett also believes that every elementary and secondary school should have a discipline code, making clear to adolescents and parents what the school expects of them. Then the school should enforce the code.

The most widely adopted indirect approaches to moral education are values clarification and cognitive moral education. We will consider each of these in turn.

Values Clarification

Values clarification *is an indirect moral education approach that focuses on helping students clarify what their lives are for and what is worth working for.* In values clarification, students are asked questions or presented with dilemmas and expected to respond, either individually or in small groups. The intent is to help students define their own values and to become aware of others' values (Nucci & Weber, 1991).

In the following example of values clarification, students are asked to select from among 10 people the 6 who will be admitted to a fallout shelter during World War III:

> Suppose you are a government decision maker in Washington, D.C., when World War III breaks out. A fallout shelter under your administration in a remote Montana highland contains only enough space, air, food, and water for 6 people for 3 months, but 10 people wish to be admitted. The 10 have agreed by radio contact that, for the survival of the human race, you must decide which 6 of them

shall be saved. You have exactly 30 minutes to make up your mind before Washington goes up in smoke. These are your choices:

1. A 16-year-old girl of questionable IQ, who is a high school dropout and pregnant
2. A policeman with a gun (which cannot be taken from him), thrown off the force recently for brutality
3. A clergyman, 75
4. A woman physician, 36, known to be a confirmed racist
5. A male violinist, 46, who served 7 years for pushing narcotics
6. A 20-year-old Black militant with no special skills
7. A former prostitute, female, 39
8. An architect who is a male homosexual
9. A 26-year-old law student
10. The law student's 25-year-old wife, who spent the past 9 months in a mental hospital and is still heavily sedated; they refuse to be separated

In this exercise, no answers are considered right or wrong. The clarification of values is left up to individual students. Advocates of the values clarification approach argue that it is value free, but critics argue that, because of its controversial content, it offends community standards (Eger, 1981). Critics also say that, because of its relativistic nature, values clarification undermines accepted values and fails to stress truth and right behavior (Oser, 1986).

Cognitive Moral Education

Like values clarification, cognitive moral education also challenges direct moral instruction. **Cognitive moral education** *is an indirect moral education approach that emphasizes that children adopt such values as democracy and justice as their moral reasoning is developed.* In this approach, students' moral standards are allowed to develop through their attention to environmental settings and exercises that encourage more advanced moral thinking. Thus, in contrast to values clarification, cognitive moral education is not value free. Such values as democracy and justice are emphasized. The advocates of cognitive moral education argue that when moral standards are imposed—as in the direct instruction approach—children can never completely integrate and fully understand moral principles. Only through participation and discussion can children learn to apply the rules and principles of cooperation, trust, community, and self-reliance.

Lawrence Kohlberg's theory of moral development has extensively influenced the cognitive moral education approach. Contrary to what some critics say, Kohlberg's theory is not completely relativistic and it is not completely morally neutral. It treats higher-level moral thinking as better than lower-level moral thinking, and it stresses that higher-level thinking can be stimulated through focused discussion of moral dilemmas (Higgins, 1991; Power, 1991). Also, in the 1980s, Kohlberg (1981, 1986) revised his views on moral education by placing more emphasis on the school's moral atmosphere, as John Dewey did many years ago.

JUVENILE DELINQUENCY

What is a juvenile delinquent? What are the antecedents of delinquency? What types of interventions have been used to prevent or reduce delinquency?

What Is Juvenile Delinquency?

The term **juvenile delinquency** *refers to a broad range of behaviors, from socially unacceptable behavior (such as acting out in school) to status offenses (such as running away) to criminal acts (such as burglary)* (Quay, 1987). For legal purposes, a distinction is made between index offenses and status offenses. **Index offenses** *are criminal acts, whether they are committed by juveniles or adults. They include such acts as robbery, aggravated assault, rape, and homicide.* **Status offenses,** *such as running away, truancy, drinking under age, sexual promiscuity, and uncontrollability, are less serious acts. They are performed by youth under a specified age, which classifies them as juvenile offenses* (Dryfoos, 1990). States often differ in the age used to classify an individual as a juvenile or an adult. Approximately three-fourths of the states have established age 18 as a maximum for defining juveniles. Two states use age 19 as the cutoff, seven states use age 17, and four states use age 16. Thus, running away from home at age 17 may be an offense in some states but not others.

In addition to the legal classifications of index offenses and status offenses, many of the behaviors considered delinquent are included in widely used classifications of abnormal behavior. **Conduct disorder** *is the psychiatric diagnostic category used when multiple behaviors occur over a six-month period. These behaviors include truancy, running away, fire setting, cruelty to animals, breaking and entering, excessive fighting, and others. When three or more of these behaviors co-occur before the age of 15 and the child or adolescent is considered unmanageable or out of control, the clinical diagnosis is conduct disorder.*

In sum, most children or adolescents at one time or another act out or do things that are destructive or troublesome for themselves or others. If these behaviors occur often in childhood or early adolescence, psychiatrists diagnose them as conduct disorders (Myers & Burket, 1992). If these behaviors result in illegal acts by juveniles, society labels them as *delinquents.*

How many juvenile delinquents or children and adolescents with conduct disorder are there? Figures are somewhat sketchy and depend on the criteria used. The most concrete figures are legally defined, but many adolescents who engage in delinquent behavior are never arrested. About 3 percent of 10- to 14-year-olds and 11 percent of 15- to 17-year-olds were arrested in 1986 for an offense. Based on self-reported patterns of behavior, a large number of adolescents—as many as 20 percent—are at risk for committing offenses that could result in arrests. Overall, the prevalence of delinquency has probably not changed much in the last decade (Dryfoos, 1990).

What Are the Antecedents of Delinquency?

Predictors of delinquency include: identity (negative identity), self-control (low degree), age (early initiation), sex (males), expectations for education (low expectations, little commitment), school grades (low achievement in early grades), peer influence (heavy influence, low resistance), socioeconomic status (low), parental role (lack of monitoring, low support, and ineffective discipline), and neighborhood quality (urban, high crime, high mobility). A summary of these antecedents of delinquency is presented in figure 14.4. We now examine several of these antecedents in greater detail: identity, family processes, and social class/community.

Identity

According to Erik Erikson's (1968) theory of development, adolescence is the stage when the crisis of identity versus identity diffusion should be resolved. Not surprisingly, Erikson's ideas about delinquency are linked to adolescent's ability to positively resolve this crisis. Erikson believes that the biological changes of puberty initiate concomitant changes in the social expectations placed on adolescents by family, peers, and schools. These biological and social changes allow for two kinds of integration to occur in adolescents' personality: (1) the establishment of a sense of consistency in life, and (2) the resolution of role identity, a sort of joining of adolescents' motivation, values, abilities, and styles with the role demands placed on adolescents.

Erikson believes that delinquency is characterized more by a failure of adolescents to achieve the second kind of integration, involving the role aspects of identity. He comments that adolescents whose infant, childhood, or adolescent experiences have somehow restricted them from acceptable social roles or made them feel that they cannot measure up to the demands placed on them may choose a negative course of identity development. Some of these adolescents may take on the role of delinquent, enmeshing themselves in the most negative currents of the youth culture available to them. Thus, for Erikson, delinquency is an attempt to establish an identity, although it is a negative one.

Family Processes

While there has been a long history of interest in defining the family factors that contribute to delinquency, the most recent focus has been on the nature of family support and family management practices. Disruptions or omissions in the parents' applications of family support and management practices are consistently linked with antisocial behavior by children and adolescents (Novy & others, 1992; Rosenbaum, 1989). These family support and management practices include monitoring adolescents' whereabouts, using effective discipline for antisocial behavior, calling on effective problem-solving skills, and supporting the development of prosocial skills (Offord & Boyle, 1988).

FIGURE 14.4

The antecedents of juvenile delinquency.

Antecedent	Association with delinquency	Description
Identity	Negative identity	Erikson believes delinquency occurs because the adolescent fails to resolve a role identity.
Self-control	Low degree	Some children and adolescents fail to acquire the essential controls that others have acquired during the process of growing up.
Age	Early initiation	Early appearance of antisocial behavior is associated with serious offenses later in adolescence. However, not every child who acts out becomes a delinquent.
Sex	Males	Boys engage in more antisocial behavior than girls do, although girls are more likely to run away. Boys engage in more violent acts.
Expectations for education and school grades	Low expectations and low grades	Adolescents who become delinquents often have low educational expectations and low grades. Their verbal abilities are often weak.
Parental influences	Monitoring (low), support (low), discipline (ineffective)	Delinquents often come from families in which parents rarely monitor their adolescents, provide them with little support, and ineffectively discipline them.
Peer influences	Heavy influence, low resistance	Having delinquent peers greatly increases the risk of becoming delinquent.
Socioeconomic status	Low	Serious offenses are committed more frequently by lower-class males.
Neighborhood quality	Urban, high crime, high mobility	Communities often breed crime. Living in a high-crime area, which also is characterized by poverty and dense living conditions, increases the probability that a child will become a delinquent. These communities often have grossly inadequate schools.

The parents of delinquents are less skilled in discouraging antisocial behavior than the parents of nondelinquents. Parental monitoring of adolescents is especially important in whether adolescents become delinquents. In one investigation, parental monitoring of adolescents' whereabouts was the most important family factor in predicting delinquency (Patterson & Stouthamer-Loeber, 1984). "It's 10 P.M., do you know where your children are?" seems to be an important question for parents to answer affirmatively. Family discord and inconsistent and inappropriate discipline also are associated with delinquency.

An important question is whether family experiences cause delinquency, are the consequences of delinquency, or are merely associated or correlated with delinquency (Rutter & Garmezy, 1983). The associations may simply reflect some third factor, such as genetic influences; may be the result of the disturbing effect of the child's behavior on the family; or may indicate that family stress may produce delinquency through some environmental effect. In a review of research on the family-delinquency link, Michael Rutter and Norman Garmezy (1983) concluded that family influences do have some kind of environmental influence on delinquency. The research by Gerald Patterson and his colleagues (Patterson, DeBaryshe, & Ramsey, 1989) documents that inadequate parental supervision, involving poor monitoring of adolescents, and inconsistent, inappropriate discipline are key family factors in determining delinquency.

A recent, special concern in low-income areas is escalating gang violence.

Social Class/Community

Although juvenile delinquency is less exclusively a lower-class problem than it was in the past, some characteristics of the lower-class culture are likely to promote delinquency (Jenkins & Bell, 1992; Kennedy, 1991; Mednick, Baker, & Carothers, 1990). The norms of many lower-class peer groups and gangs are antisocial or counterproductive to the goals and norms of society at large (McCord, 1990). Getting into and staying out of trouble in some instances becomes a prominent feature of the lives of some adolescents from lower-class backgrounds (Miller, 1958). Status in the peer group may be gauged by how often the adolescent can engage in antisocial conduct, yet manage to stay out of jail. Since lower-class adolescents have less opportunity to develop skills that are socially desirable, they may sense that they can gain attention and status by performing antisocial actions. Being "tough" and "masculine" are high-status traits for lower-class boys, and these traits are often gauged by adolescents' success in performing delinquent acts and getting away with them.

The nature of a community may contribute to delinquency (Chesney-Lind, 1989). A community with a high crime rate allows adolescents to observe many models who engage in criminal activities and may be rewarded for their criminal accomplishments. Such communities often are characterized by poverty, unemployment, and feelings of alienation from the middle class. The quality of schools, funding for education, and organized neighborhood activities are other community factors that may be related to delinquency. Are there caring adults in the schools and neighborhood who can convince adolescents with delinquent tendencies that education is the best route to success? When family support becomes inadequate, then such community supports take on added importance in preventing delinquency.

Even if adolescents grow up in high-crime communities, their peer relations may influence whether or not they become delinquents. In one investigation of 500 delinquents and 500 nondelinquents in Boston, Massachusetts, a much higher percentage of the delinquents had regular associations with delinquent peers (Glueck & Glueck, 1950).

A recent, special concern in low-income areas is escalating gang violence, which is being waged on a level more lethal than ever before. Knives and clubs have been replaced by grenades and automatic weapons, frequently purchased with money made from selling drugs. The lure of gang membership is powerful, especially for children and adolescents who are disconnected from family, school, work, and the community. Children as young as 9 to 10 years of age cling to the fringes of neighborhood gangs, eager to prove themselves worthy of membership by the age of 12. Once children are members of a gang, it is difficult to get them to leave. Recommendations for preventing gang violence include identifying disconnected children in elementary schools and initiating counseling with the children and their families (Calhoun, 1988; Huff, 1990). More about life in gangs and an effort in Detroit, Michigan, that has made a difference in reducing gang participation appears in Sociocultural Worlds of Children 14.2.

Prevention and Intervention

Brief descriptions of the varied attempts to reduce delinquency would fill a large book. These attempts include forms of individual and group psychotherapy, family therapy, behavior modification, recreation, vocational training, alternative schools, survival camping and wilderness canoeing, incarceration and probation, "Big Brothers" and "Big Sisters," community organizations, and Bible reading (Gold & Petronio, 1980). However, surprisingly little is known about what actually does help to reduce delinquency, and in many instances, prevention and intervention have not been successful (Leitenberg, 1986; Lundman, 1984; Rabkin, 1987).

While few successful models of delinquency prevention and intervention have been identified, many experts on delinquency agree that the following points deserve closer examination as prevention and intervention possibilities (Dryfoos, 1990):

1. Programs should be broader than just focusing on delinquency (McMahon & Bierman, 1993; O'Donnell, Manos, & Chesney-Lind, 1987). For example, it is virtually impossible to improve delinquency prevention without considering the quality of education available to high-risk youth.
2. Programs should have multiple components because no one component has been found to be the "magic bullet" that decreases delinquency.
3. Programs should begin early in the child's development to prevent learning and conduct problems (Berrueta-Clement & others, 1986).
4. Schools play an important role. Schools with strong governance, fair discipline policies, student participation in decision making, and high investment in school outcomes by both students and staff have a better chance of curbing delinquency (Hawkins & Lam, 1986; Hawkins & Lishner, 1987).
5. Efforts should often be directed at institutional rather than individual change. Especially important is upgrading the quality of education for disadvantaged children.

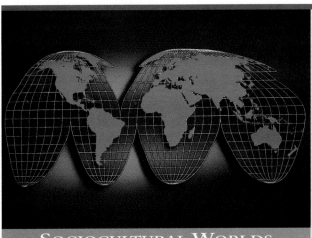

SOCIOCULTURAL WORLDS OF CHILDREN 14.2

Frog and Dolores

He goes by the name of Frog. He is the cocky prince of the barrio in East Los Angeles. He has street-smarts. Frog happily smiles as he talks about raking in $200 a week or, in some cases, even a day, selling crack cocaine. He proudly details his newly acquired membership in a violent street gang, the Crips. Frog brags about using his drug money to rent a convertible on weekends, even though at less than 5 feet in height, he can barely see over the dashboard. Frog is 13 years old.

With the advent of crack, juvenile arrests in New York City tripled from 1983 to 1987 and almost quadrupled in the same time frame in Washington, D.C. Adults who founded the crack trade recognized early on that young adolescents do not run the risk of mandatory jail sentences that courts hand out to adults. Being a lookout is the entry-level position for 9- and 10-year-olds. They can make as much as $100 a day warning dealers that police are in the area. The next step up the ladder is as a runner, a job that can pay as much as $300 a day. A runner transports drugs to the dealers on the street from makeshift factories where cocaine powder is cooked into rock-hard crack. And, at the next level, older adolescents can reach the status of dealer. In a hot market like New York City, they can make over $1,000 a day.

The escalating drug-related gang violence is difficult to contain or reduce. Police crackdowns across the country seem to have had a minimal impact. In a recent weekend-long raid of drug-dealing gangs in Los Angeles, police arrested 1,453 individuals, including 315 adolescents. Half had to be released for lack of evidence. The Los Angeles County juvenile facilities are designed to house 1,317. Today more than 2,000 adolescents are overflowing their facilities.

Counselors, school officials, and community workers report that turning around the lives of children and adolescents involved in drug-related gang violence is extremely difficult. When impoverished children can make $100 a day, it is hard to wean them away from gangs. Federal budgets for training and employment programs, which provide crucial assistance to disadvantaged youth, have been reduced dramatically.

However, in Detroit, Michigan, Dolores Bennett has made a difference. For 25 years, she has worked long hours trying to find things to keep children from low-income families busy. Her activities have led to the creation of neighborhood sports teams, regular fairs and picnics, and an informal job-referral service for the children and youth in the neighborhood. She also holds many casual get-togethers for the youth in her small, tidy, yellow frame house. The youth talk openly and freely about their problems and their hopes, knowing that Dolores will listen. Dolores says that she has found being a volunteer to be priceless. On the mantel in her living room are hundreds of pictures of children and adolescents with whom she has worked. She points out that most of them did not have someone in their homes who would listen to them and give them love. America needs more Dolores Bennetts.

Dolores Bennett, volunteer in a low-income area of Detroit, Michigan, talks with and listens to one of her "children."

6. While point 5 is accurate, researchers have found that intensive individual attention and personalized planning also are important factors in working with children at high risk for becoming delinquent.

7. Program benefits often "wash out" after the program stops. Thus, maintenance programs and continued effort are usually necessary.

In her recent review of delinquency prevention, Joy Dryfoos (1990) has outlined what has *not* worked in preventing delinquency. Ineffective attempts include preventive casework, group counseling, pharmacological interventions (except for extremely violent behavior), work experience, vocational education, "scaring straight" efforts, and the juvenile justice system. Current school practices that are ineffective in reducing delinquency include suspension, detention, expulsion, security guards, and corporal punishment.

At this point, we have discussed a number of ideas about moral feelings, altruism, moral education, and delinquency. A summary of these ideas is presented in Concept Table 14.2.

CONCEPT TABLE 14.2

Moral Feelings, Altruism, Moral Education, and Juvenile Delinquency

Concept	Processes/Related Ideas	Characteristics/Description
Moral feelings	Psychoanalytic theory	The superego is one of the three main structures of personality. The child's superego—the moral branch of personality—develops as the child resolves the Oedipal conflict and identifies with the same-sex parent in the early childhood years. Through identification, children internalize a parent's standards of right and wrong. Children conform to societal standards to avoid guilt. The superego consists of two main components: ego-ideal and conscience.
	Childrearing techniques and moral development	The focus is on parents' discipline, which involves love withdrawal, power assertion, and induction. Love withdrawal and power assertion have been ineffective in promoting children's moral growth, but induction has been effective, especially with older, middle-class children.
	Empathy	Feeling empathy means reacting to another's feelings with an emotional response that is similar to the other's response. Empathy often has a cognitive component—perspective taking. Developmental changes in empathy include: global empathy in early infancy, more genuine feelings of concern at 1 to 2 years of age, awareness of each person's uniqueness and more appropriate empathy in early childhood, and empathy for people who live in unfortunate circumstances in late childhood. Individual variation and sociohistorical changes are involved in empathy.
	The contemporary perspective on the role of emotions in moral development	Both positive feelings—such as empathy, sympathy, admiration, and self-esteem—and negative feelings—such as anger, outrage, shame, and guilt—contribute to children's moral development. When strongly experienced, these emotions influence children to act in accord with moral standards. Moral emotions do not operate in a vacuum—they are interwoven with the cognitive and social aspects of moral development.
Altruism	Its nature	Altruism is an unselfish interest in helping someone. Reciprocity and exchange are involved in altruism. Damon described a developmental sequence of altruism, especially sharing: At 0 to 3 years, sharing is done for nonempathic reasons; at about 4 years of age, the combination of empathic awareness and adult encouragement produces a sense of obligation to share; in the early elementary years, children genuinely begin to show more objective ideas about fairness, at which time the principle of equality is understood; in the middle to late elementary years, the principles of merit and benevolence are understood.

Concept	Processes/Related Ideas	Characteristics/Description
Moral education	Hidden curriculum	The hidden curriculum is the pervasive moral atmosphere that characterizes any school, regardless of whether there is a specific moral curriculum.
	Direct and indirect moral education	Direct moral education involves either emphasizing values or character traits during specified time slots or integrating them throughout the curriculum. Indirect moral education involves encouraging children to define their own and others' values and helping them define the moral perspectives that support those values. The two main indirect moral education approaches are values clarification and cognitive moral education. Values clarification is a moral education approach that focuses on helping students clarify what their lives are for and what is worth looking for. Cognitive moral education emphasizes that such values as democracy and justice will be adopted through the development of students' moral reasoning. Kohlberg's theory has extensively influenced the cognitive moral education approach.
Juvenile delinquency	What is juvenile delinquency?	Juvenile delinquency refers to a broad range of behaviors, from socially unacceptable behavior to status offenses to criminal acts. For legal purposes, a distinction is made between index offenses (criminal acts, whether they are committed by juveniles or adults) and status offenses (performed by youth under a certain age). Conduct disorder is the psychiatric diagnosis category used when multiple behaviors—such as truancy, running away, and breaking and entering—occur before the age of 15, and the child or adolescent is considered unmanageable. Figures on the number of juvenile delinquents are sketchy, although 3 percent of 10- to 14-year-olds and 11 percent of 15- to 17-year-olds were arrested for an offense in one recent year. Self-reported patterns suggest that approximately 20 percent of adolescents engage in delinquent behavior.
	What are the antecedents of delinquency?	Predictors of delinquency include a negative identity, a low degree of self-control, early initiation of delinquency, being a male, low expectations for education and little commitment to education, heavy peer influence and low resistance to peer pressure, failure of parents to adequately monitor their adolescents, ineffective discipline by parents, and living in an urban, high-crime, mobile neighborhood.
	Prevention and intervention	Successful programs do not focus on delinquency alone (rather, they include other components, such as education), have multiple components (but no one component is a "magic bullet"), begin early in the child's development, often involve schools, focus on institutions while also giving individualized attention to delinquents, and include maintenance.

PERSPECTIVES ON PARENTING AND EDUCATION

A Comprehensive Approach to Moral Education

William Damon (1988) believes that moral education should follow from what we know about the nature of children's moral development. Based on scientific studies and observations of children's moral development, Damon believes that the following six principles should serve as a foundation for the development of moral education programs:

1. Children experience classic moral issues facing humans everywhere simply by participating in social relationships: issues of fairness, honesty, responsibility, kindness, and obedience, for example. Thus, children's moral awareness develops within their normal social experiences. Their moral awareness may need to be guided, informed, and enhanced, but it does not need to be imposed directly in a punitive, authoritarian manner.

2. Children's moral awareness is shaped and supported by natural emotional reactions to observations and events, which begin as early as infancy. Such emotional reactions as empathy support moral compassion and altruism. Such reactions as shame, guilt, and fear support obedience and rule adoption. Children's love and attachment feelings for parents provide an affective foundation for children's developing respect for authority.

3. Interactions with parents, teachers, and other adults introduce children to important social standards and rules. These interactions produce knowledge and respect for the social order, including its principles of organization and legitimate authority. Authoritative adult-child (for example, parent-child or teacher-child) relationships, in which extensive verbal give-and-take and nonpunitive adult control that justifies demands are present, yield the most positive results for children's moral judgment and behavior.

4. Peer relations introduce children to the norms of direct reciprocity and to the standards for sharing, cooperation, and fairness. Through peer relations, children learn about mutuality, equality, and perspective taking, which promote the development of altruism.

5. Broad variations in social experiences can produce broad differences in moral orientation among children. One such variation is the different roles and expectations that girls and boys experience, especially in traditional social environments. As we learned earlier in our discussion of Carol Gilligan's ideas, the moral development of girls is oriented more toward relationships and care, whereas the moral development of boys is oriented more toward the individual and justice. There is reason to believe that such orientations can be socially transformed as cultures change. According to Damon, there should be an increased emphasis on learning the principles of care *and* justice by both boys and girls.

6. Moral development in schools is determined by the same cognitive and social processes that apply to moral development in other settings. This means that children acquire moral values by actively participating in adult-child and peer relationships that support, enhance, and guide their natural moral tendencies. According to Damon, children's morality is not enhanced by lessons or lectures in which children are passive recipients of information or, even worse, are captive and recalcitrant audiences. Further, the quality of social interaction in a school setting communicates a moral message that is more enduring than direct, declarative statements and lectures by teachers. To receive a competent moral education in a democratic society, children need to experience egalitarian interactions that reflect democratic values—among them, equality, fairness, and responsibility.

Damon (1988) argues that, for teachers and parents to contribute positively to a child's moral development, they need to practice *respectful engagement* with the child. Children need adult guidance, but, for the guidance to register, children need to be productively engaged and their own initiatives and reactions must be respected.

Damon recognizes that parents alone, or schools alone, are not completely responsible for children's moral development. Children's moral education occurs both in and out of school through their interactions with parents, peers, and teachers, and through their experiences with society's standards. These interactions are not value free, and, although there is some disagreement about exactly what should be communicated to children in the course of moral education, there also is more agreement than is commonly acknowledged. There are some fundamental values that are shared widely enough for them to be transmitted without hesitation to children; no one wants children to follow a path of dishonesty, drug abuse, or cruel antisocial behavior. All of us want children to endorse justice, abide by legitimate authority, consider the needs of others, and be responsible citizens in a democratic society.

Damon's approach stands in contrast to the permissive approach, which assumes children's moral growth is enhanced when they are left alone. It also stands in contrast to the indoctrinational approach of direct moral education that

children can learn moral values by passively listening to the demands of authority figures. Damon's ideas have much in common with cognitive moral education, but they go beyond the traditional views of cognitive moral education, which focus almost exclusively on the role of schools, peers, and cognition in moral development. Damon's view is more

comprehensive than the traditional cognitive moral education views because it recognizes the importance of emotions, parent-child relations, and culture in moral development, integrating them with the influence of schools, peers, and cognition in a meaningful way. ■

CONCLUSIONS

One of childhood's most important tasks is learning right from wrong. To accomplish this task, children need to *think* and *feel* morally, and *behave* accordingly.

We began this chapter by examining children's perceptions of what morals should be like on the make-believe planet of Pax. Then we explored what moral development is, followed by extensive coverage of the cognitive dimensions of moral development. We studied Piaget's and Kohlberg's theories and devoted attention to influences on Kohlberg's

stages and Kohlberg's critics, especially Carol Gilligan and her care perspective. Our study of moral behavior focused on reinforcement, punishment, imitation, and situational variations, resistance to temptation and self-control, and cognitive social learning theory. Then we read about moral feelings, including psychoanalytic theory, childrearing techniques, empathy, and the contemporary perspective on the role of emotion in moral development. We also explored the nature of altruism, moral education, and juve-

nile delinquency. We concluded with examination of Damon's comprehensive approach to moral education. Remember that you can obtain a summary of the entire chapter by again reading the two concept tables on pages 414 and 424.

This chapter—Moral Development—is the final chapter in Section Four—Socioemotional Development and the Self—in the book. Next, we turn our attention to Section Five—Social Contexts of Development, beginning with chapter 15, Families.

KEY TERMS

moral development Rules and conventions about what people should do in their interactions with other people. (403)

heteronomous morality The first stage of moral development in Piaget's theory, occurring from 4 to 7 years of age. Justice and rules are conceived of as unchangeable properties of the world, removed from the control of people. (403)

autonomous morality The second stage of moral development in Piaget's theory, displayed by older children (about 10 years of age and older). The child becomes aware that rules and laws are created by people and that, in judging an action, one should consider the actor's intentions as well as the consequences. (403)

immanent justice Piaget's concept that, if a rule is broken, punishment will be meted out immediately. (403)

internalization The developmental change from behavior that is externally controlled to behavior that is controlled by internal, self-generated standards and principles. (404)

preconventional reasoning The lowest level in Kohlberg's theory of moral development. The child shows no internalization of moral values—moral reasoning is controlled by external rewards and punishment. (404)

punishment and obedience orientation The first stage in Kohlberg's theory of moral development. Moral thinking is based on punishment. (404)

individualism and purpose The second stage in Kohlberg's theory of moral development. Moral thinking is based on rewards and self-interest. (404)

conventional reasoning The second, or intermediate, level in Kohlberg's

theory of moral development. Children's internalization is intermediate. They abide by certain standards (internal), but they are the standards of others (external), such as parents or the laws of society. (404)

interpersonal norms The third stage in Kohlberg's theory of moral development. Children value trust, caring, and loyalty to others as the basis of moral judgment. (404)

social system morality The fourth stage in Kohlberg's theory of moral development. Moral judgments are based on understanding the social order, law, justice, and duty. (404)

postconventional reasoning The highest level in Kohlberg's theory of moral development. Morality is completely internalized. (404)

community rights versus individual rights The fifth stage in Kohlberg's theory of moral development. Children understand that values and laws are relative and that standards vary from one person to another. (404)

universal ethical principles   The sixth and highest stage in Kohlberg's theory of moral development. Individuals develop a moral standard based on universal human rights. (404)

justice perspective   A moral perspective that focuses on the rights of the individual; individuals independently make moral decisions. (408)

care perspective   The moral perspective of Carol Gilligan, that views people in terms of their connectedness to others and focuses on interpersonal communication, relationships with others, and concern for others. (408)

cognitive social learning theory of morality   The theory that distinguishes between a child's moral competence—the ability to produce moral behavior—and moral performance—those behaviors in specific situations. (413)

ego-ideal   The component of the superego that involves ideal standards approved of by parents. (413)

conscience   The component of the superego that involves behaviors disapproved of by parents. (413)

love withdrawal   A discipline technique in which a parent removes attention or love from a child. (413)

power assertion   A discipline technique in which a parent attempts to gain control over a child or a child's resources. (413)

induction   A discipline technique in which a parent uses reason and explanation of the consequences for others of a child's actions. (413)

empathy   Reacting to another's feelings with an emotional response that is similar to the other's response. (415)

global empathy   A young infant's empathic response in which clear boundaries between the feelings and needs of the self and those of another have not yet been established. (415)

altruism   An unselfish interest in helping someone. (417)

hidden curriculum   The pervasive moral atmosphere that characterizes schools. This atmosphere includes school and classroom rules, attitudes toward academics and extracurricular activities, the moral orientation of teachers and school administrators, and the text materials. (418)

direct moral education   An educational approach that involves either emphasizing values or character traits during specified time slots or integrating those values or traits throughout the curriculum. (419)

indirect moral education   An educational approach that involves encouraging children to define their own and others' values and helping define the moral perspectives that support those values. (419)

values clarification   An indirect moral education approach that focuses on helping students clarify what their lives are for and what is worth working for. (419)

cognitive moral education   An indirect moral education approach that emphasizes that children adopt such values as democracy and justice as their moral reasoning is developed. (419)

juvenile delinquency   Refers to a broad range of behaviors, from socially unacceptable behavior to status offenses to criminal acts. (420)

index offenses   Criminal acts, whether they are committed by juveniles or adults, such as robbery, aggravated assault, rape, and homicide. (420)

status offenses   Committed by youths under a specified age, these acts classify children as juvenile delinquents and include such acts as running away, truancy, drinking under age, and sexual promiscuity. (420)

conduct disorder   The psychiatric diagnostic category used when multiple behaviors such as running away, setting fires, cruelty to animals, or truancy occur over a six-month period. (420)

Suggested Readings

Damon, W. (1988). *The moral child.* New York: Free Press. Damon presents his intelligent views on the nature of children's moral development, including some excellent ideas about moral education.

Gilligan, C. (1982). *In a different voice.* Cambridge, MA: Harvard University Press. This book advances Gilligan's provocative view that a care perspective is underrepresented in Kohlberg's theory and research.

Modgil, S., & Modgil, C. (Eds.). (1986). *Lawrence Kohlberg.* Philadelphia: Falmer. A number of experts evaluate Kohlberg's theory of moral development. The book includes a concluding chapter by Kohlberg.

Quay, H. C. (Ed.). (1987). *Handbook of juvenile delinquency.* New York: Wiley. This collection of articles by leading experts explores the many dimensions of delinquency.

Social Contexts of Development

It is not enough for parents to understand children. They must also accord children the privilege of understanding them.

—Milton Saperstein

Parents cradle children's lives, but children's growth is also shaped by successive choirs of siblings, peers, friends, and teachers. Children's small worlds widen as they discover new refuges and new people. In the end there are but two lasting bequests that parents can leave children: one being roots, the other wings. In this section, we will study three chapters: Families (15), Peers, Play, and the Media (16), and Schools (17).

Poppyfield, 1873,
Claude Monet (Detail)

15

Families

Chapter Outline

PERSPECTIVES ON PARENTING AND EDUCATION

The Goals of Caregiving 461

Chapter Boxes

*There's no vocabulary for love within a
family, love that's lived in but not looked
at, love within the light of which all else
is seen, the love within which all other
love finds speech. This love is silent.*

—T. S. Eliot

We never know the love of our parents until we have become parents.

—Henry Ward Beecher, 1887

IMAGES OF CHILDREN

The Diversity of Families and Parenting

Children grow up in a diversity of families. Some children live in families that have never experienced divorce, some live virtually their entire childhood in single-parent families, and yet others live in stepfamilies. Some children live in poverty, others in economically advantaged families. Some children's mothers work full time and place them in day care, while some mothers stay home with their children. Some children grow up in an Anglo American culture, others in ethnic minority cultures. Some children have siblings, others don't. Some children's parents treat them harshly and abuse them, other children have parents who nurture and support them.

In thinking about the diversity of families and parenting, consider the following two circumstances and predict how they might influence the child's development:

A young-looking mother is holding an infant in her arms and is trying to keep track of two boys walking behind her (Dash, 1986). The younger boy, who is about 3, clutches an umbrella but seems to be having trouble with it. He drags its curved handle along the ground and that irritates his mother. She tells him to carry the umbrella right or she will knock the (expletive) out of him. "Carry it right, I said," she says, and then she slaps him in the face, knocking him off balance. She rarely nurtures her son and has beaten him so hard that at times he has bruises that don't go away for days. The mother lives in the poverty of an inner city and she is unemployed. She is unaware of how her own life stress affects her parenting behavior.

Now consider another child who is growing up in a very different family environment:

A 28-year-old mother is walking along the street with her 4-year-old daughter. They are having a conversation about her daughter's preschool. As the conversation continues, they smile back and forth several times as the daughter describes some activities she did. As they reach home, the mother tells her daughter that she loves her and gives her a big hug. The mother lives in an economically advantaged suburb and the preschool her daughter attends has high ratings. The mother reports that she sincerely enjoys being with her daughter and loves to plan enjoyable things for her to do.

PREVIEW

The first young boy's mother was experiencing the strains of poverty and it was affecting her ability to effectively rear him. In the second situation, the mother and daughter had a warm, enjoyable relationship. In this chapter, we will explore the many and diverse worlds of families. We will examine the family life cycle, the parenting role and parenting styles, sibling relationships and birth order, family processes in adolescence, effects of divorce, stepfamilies, working parents, culture and ethnicity, and gender. But to begin, we will study some basic ideas about the nature of family processes.

FIGURE 15.1

Interaction between children and their parents: direct and indirect effects.

THE NATURE OF FAMILY PROCESSES

Among the important considerations in studying children and their families are reciprocal socialization, synchrony, and the family system; how children construct relationships and how such relationships influence the development of social maturity; adapting parenting to developmental changes in the child; and social and historical influences on the family.

Reciprocal Socialization and the Family as a System

For many years, socialization between parents and children was viewed as a one-way process: Children were considered to be the products of their parents' socialization techniques. Today, however, we view parent-child interaction as reciprocal. **Reciprocal socialization** *is the view that socialization is bidirectional; children socialize parents just as parents socialize children.* For example, the interaction of mothers and their infants is symbolized as a dance or dialogue in which successive actions of the partners are closely coordinated. This coordinated dance or dialogue can assume the form of mutual synchrony (each person's behavior depends on the partner's previous behavior), or it can be reciprocal in a more precise sense; the actions of the partners can be matched, as when one partner imitates the other or when there is mutual smiling (Cohn & Tronick, 1988).

When reciprocal socialization has been investigated in infancy, mutual gaze or eye contact has been found to play an important role in early social interaction (Fogel, Toda, & Kawai, 1988). In one investigation, the mother and infant engaged in a variety of behaviors while they looked at each other; by contrast, when they looked away from each other, the rate of such behaviors dropped considerably (Stern & others, 1977). In sum,

the behaviors of mothers and infants involve substantial interconnection and synchronization. And in one recent investigation, synchrony in parent-child relationships was positively related to children's social competence (Harrist, 1993).

Scaffolding *is a term used to describe an important caregiver's role in early parent-child interaction. Through their attention and choice of behaviors, caregivers provide a framework around which they and their infants interact. One function of scaffolding is to introduce infants to social rules, especially turn taking.* (Bruner, 1989; Lyons, 1991; Stringer & Neal, 1993). For example, in the game peek-a-boo, mothers initially cover their babies, then remove the covering, and finally register "surprise" at the reappearance. As infants become more skilled at peek-a-boo, they do the covering and uncovering. Infant researcher Tiffany Field (1987) observed that, in addition to peek-a-boo, pat-a-cake and "so big," there are other caregiver-infant games that involve scaffolding and its turn-taking sequences. In one investigation, infants who had more extensive scaffolding experiences with their parents, especially in the form of turn taking, were more likely to engage in turn taking as they interacted with their peers (Vandell & Wilson, 1988).

As a social system, the family can be thought of as a constellation of subsystems defined in terms of generation, gender, and role. Divisions of labor among family members define particular subunits, and attachments define others. Each family member is a participant in several subsystems—some dyadic (involving two people), some polyadic (involving more than two people). The father and child represent one dyadic subsystem, the mother and father another; the mother-father-child represent one polyadic subsystem, the mother and two siblings another (Belsky, Rovine, & Fish, 1989).

An organizational scheme that highlights the reciprocal influences of family members and family subsystems is shown in figure 15.1 (Belsky, 1981). As the arrows in the figure show, marital relations, parenting, and infant/child behavior can have both direct and indirect effects on each other. An example of a direct effect is the influence of the parent's behavior on the child; an example of an indirect effect is how the relationship between the spouses mediates the way a parent acts toward the child. For example, marital conflict might reduce the efficiency of parenting, in which case marital conflict would be an indirect effect on the child's behavior.

The Developmental Construction of Relationships

Developmentalists have shown an increased interest in understanding how we construct relationships as we grow up (Costanzo, 1993; Putallaz & others, 1993; Shaver, 1993). Psychoanalytic theorists have always been interested in how this process works in families. However, the current explanations of how relationships are constructed is virtually stripped of Freud's psychosexual stage terminology and also is not always confined to the first five years of life, as has been the case in classical psychoanalytic theory. Today's **developmental construction view** *share the belief that as individuals grow up they acquire modes of relating to others. There are two main variations within this view, one of which emphasizes continuity and stability in relationships through the life span and one of which emphasizes discontinuity and change in relationships through the life span.*

The Continuity View

In the **continuity view,** *emphasis is on the role that early parent-child relationships play in constructing a basic way of relating to people throughout the life span.* These early parent-child relationships are carried forward to later points in development to influence all subsequent relationships (with peers, with friends, with teachers, and with romantic partners, for example) (Ainsworth, 1979; Bowlby, 1969, 1989; Sroufe, 1985, in press; Urban & others, 1992). In its extreme form, this view states that the basic components of social relationships are laid down and shaped by the security or insecurity of parent-infant attachment relationships in the first year or two of the infant's life (remember our discussion of attachment in chapter 11).

Close relationships with parents also are important in the child's development because these relationships function as models or templates that are carried forward over time to influence the construction of new relationships. Clearly, close relationships do not repeat themselves in an endless fashion over the course of the child's development. And the quality of any relationship depends to some degree on the specific individual with whom the relationship is formed. However, the nature of earlier relationships that are developed over many years often can be detected in later relationships, both with those same individuals and in the formation of relationships with others at a later point in time (Gjerde, Block, & Block, 1991). Thus, the nature of parent-adolescent relationships does not depend only on what happens in the relationship during adolescence. Relationships with parents over the long course of childhood

are carried forward to influence, at least to some degree, the nature of parent-adolescent relationships. And the long course of parent-child relationships also could be expected to influence, again at least to some degree, the fabric of the adolescent's peer relationships, friendships, and dating relationships.

The Discontinuity View

In the **discontinuity view,** *emphasis is on change and growth in relationships over time.* As people grow up, they develop many different types of relationships (with parents, with peers, with teachers, and with romantic partners, for example). Each of these relationships is structurally different. With each new type of relationship, individuals encounter new modes of relating (Buhrmester & Furman, 1987; Furman & Wehner, 1993; Piaget, 1932; Sullivan, 1953; Youniss, 1980). For example, Piaget (1932) argued that parent-child relationships are strikingly different from children's peer relationships. Parent-child relationships, he said, are more likely to consist of parents having unilateral authority over children. By contrast, peer relationships are more likely to consist of participants who relate to each other on a much more equal basis. In parent-child relationships, since parents have greater knowledge and authority, their children often must learn how to conform to rules and regulations laid down by parents. In this view, we use the parental-child mode when relating to authority figures (such as with teachers and experts) and when we act as authority figures (when we become parents, teachers, and experts).

By contrast, relationships with peers have a different structure and require a different mode of relating to others. This more egalitarian mode is later called upon in relationships with romantic partners, friends, and coworkers. Because two peers possess relatively equal knowledge and authority (their relationship is reciprocal and symmetrical), children learn a democratic mode of relating that is based on mutual influence. With peers, children learn to formulate and assert their own opinions, appreciate the perspective of peers, cooperatively negotiate solutions to disagreements, and evolve standards for conduct that are mutually acceptable. Because peer relationships are voluntary (rather than obligatory, as in the family), children and adolescents who fail to become skillful in the symmetrical, mutual, egalitarian, reciprocal mode of relating have difficulty being accepted by peers.

While the change, growth variation of the developmental construction view does not deny that prior close relationships (such as with parents) are carried forward to influence later relationships, it does stress that each new type of relationship that children and adolescents encounter (such as with peers, with friends, and with romantic partners) requires the construction of different and ever more sophisticated modes of relating to others. Further, in the change, growth version, each period of development uniquely contributes to the construction of relationship knowledge; development across the life span is not solely determined by a sensitive or critical period during infancy.

Adapting Parenting to Developmental Changes in the Child

Children change as they grow from infancy to early childhood and on through middle and late childhood and adolescence. Being a competent parent involves adapting to the child's developmental changes. Parents should not treat a 5-year-old the same as a 2-year-old. The 5-year-old and 2-year-old have different needs and abilities. In the first year, parent-child interaction moves from a heavy focus on routine caretaking—feeding, changing diapers, bathing, and soothing—to later include more noncaretaking activities, such as play and visual-vocal exchanges. During the child's second and third years, parents often handle disciplinary matters by physical manipulation: They carry the child away from a mischievous activity to the place they want the child to go; they put fragile and dangerous objects out of reach; they sometimes spank. As the child grows older, however, parents increasingly turn to reasoning, moral exhortation, and giving or withholding special privileges. As children move toward the elementary school years, parents show them less physical affection (Maccoby, 1984).

Parent-child interactions during early childhood focus on such matters as modesty, bedtime regularities, control of temper, fighting with siblings and peers, eating behavior and manners, autonomy in dressing, and attention seeking. Although some of these issues—fighting and reaction to discipline, for example—are carried forward into the elementary school years, many new issues appear by the age of 7 (Maccoby, 1984). These include whether children should be made to perform chores and, if so, whether they should be paid for them, how to help children learn to entertain themselves rather than relying on parents for everything, and how to monitor children's lives outside the family in school and peer settings.

As children move into the middle and late childhood years, parents spend considerably less time with them. In one investigation, parents spent less than half as much time with their children aged 5 to 12 in caregiving, instruction, reading, talking, and playing as when the children were young (Hill & Stafford, 1980). This drop in parent-child interaction may be even more extensive in families with little parental education. Although parents spend less time with their children in middle and late childhood than in early childhood, parents continue to be extremely important socializing agents in their children's lives. Children also must learn to relate to adults outside the family on a regular basis—adults who interact with the child much differently than parents. During middle and late childhood, interactions with adults outside the family involve more formal control and achievement orientation.

Discipline during middle and late childhood is often easier for parents than it was during early childhood; it may also be easier than during adolescence. In middle and late childhood, children's cognitive development has matured to the point where it is possible for parents to reason with them about resisting deviation and controlling their behavior. By adolescence, children's reasoning has become more sophisticated and they may be less likely to accept parental discipline. Adolescents also push more strongly for independence, which contributes to parenting difficulties. Parents of elementary school children use less physical discipline than do parents of preschool children. By contrast, parent's of elementary school children are more likely to use deprivation of privileges, appeals directed at the child's self-esteem, comments designed to increase the child's sense of guilt, and statements indicating to the child that she is responsible for her actions.

During middle and late childhood, some control is transferred from parent to child, although the process is gradual and involves *coregulation* rather than control by either the child or the parent alone (Maccoby, 1984). The major shift to autonomy does not occur until about the age of 12 or later. During middle and late childhood, parents continue to exercise general supervision and exert control while children are allowed to engage in moment-to-moment self-regulation. This coregulation process is a transition period between the strong parental control of early childhood and the increased relinquishment of general supervision of adolescence.

During this coregulation, parents should:

- Monitor, guide, and support children at a distance
- Effectively use the times when they have direct contact with the child
- Strengthen in their children the ability to monitor their own behavior, to adopt appropriate standards of conduct, to avoid hazardous risks, and to sense when parental support and contact are appropriate

To be a competent parent, further adaptation is required as children become adolescents, which will be discussed later in the chapter. As we will see next, however, other important aspects of understanding parenting are cultural, social class, and ethnic variations in families.

Sociocultural, Historical Changes

Family development does not occur in a social vacuum. Important sociocultural and historical influences affect family processes (Bornstein, 1993; Parke, 1993). Family changes may be due to great upheavals in a nation, such as war, famine, or mass immigration. Or they may be due more to subtle transitions in ways of life. The Great Depression in the early 1930s had some negative effects on families. During its height, the Depression produced economic deprivation, adult discontent, depression about living conditions, marital conflict, inconsistent child rearing, and unhealthy life-styles—heavy drinking, demoralized attitudes, and health disabilities—especially in the father (Elder, 1980). Subtle changes in a culture that have significant influences on the family were described by the famous anthropologist Margaret Mead (1978). The changes focus on the longevity of the elderly and the role of the elderly in the family, the urban and suburban orientation of families and their mobility, television, and a general dissatisfaction and restlessness.

Fifty years ago, the older people who survived were usually hearty and still closely linked to the family, often helping to maintain the family's existence. Today, older people live longer, which means that their middle-aged children are often pressed into a caretaking role for their parents or the elderly parents may be placed in a nursing home. Elderly parents may have lost some of their socializing role in the family during the twentieth century as many of their children moved great distances away.

Many of these family moves are away from farms and small towns to urban and suburban settings. In the small towns and farms, individuals were surrounded by lifelong neighbors, relatives, and friends. Today, neighborhood and extended-family support systems are not nearly as prevalent. Families now move all over the country, often uprooting the child from a school and peer group he or she has known for a considerable length of time. And for many families, this type of move occurs every year or two, as one or both parents are transferred from job to job.

Television also plays a major role in the changing family. Many children who watch television find that parents are too busy working to share this experience with them. Children increasingly experience a world their parents are not a part of. Instead of participating in neighborhood peer groups, children come home after school and plop down in front of the television set. And television allows children and their families to see new ways of life. Lower-class families can look into the family lives of the middle class by simply pushing a button.

Another subtle change in families has been an increase in general dissatisfaction and restlessness. Women have become increasingly dissatisfied with their way of life, placing great strain on marriages. With fewer elders and long-term friends close by to help and advise young people during the initial difficult years of marriage and childbearing, marriages begin to fracture at the first signs of disagreement. Divorce has become epidemic in our culture. As women move into the labor market, men simultaneously become restless and look for stimulation outside of family life. The result of such restlessness and the tendency to divorce and remarry has been a hodgepodge of family structures, with far greater numbers of single-parent and stepparent families than ever before in history. Later in the chapter, we discuss such aspects of the changing social world of the child and the family in greater detail.

THE FAMILY LIFE CYCLE

As we go through life, we are at different points in the family life cycle. The stages of the family cycle include: leaving home and becoming a single adult, the joining of couples through marriage—the new couple, becoming parents and families with children, families with adolescents, families at midlife, and the

family in later life. A summary of these stages in the family life cycle are shown in figure 15.2, along with key aspects of emotional processes involved in the transition from one stage to the next, and changes in family status required for developmental change to take place (Carter & McGoldrick, 1989).

Leaving Home and Becoming a Single Adult

Leaving home and becoming a single adult *is the first stage in the family life cycle and involves the concept of launching.* **Launching** *is the process in which the youth moves into adulthood and exits his or her family of origin.* Adequate completion of launching requires that the young adult separate from the family of origin without cutting off ties completely or fleeing in a reactive way to find some form of substitute emotional refuge (Alymer, 1989). The launching period is a time for the youth and young adult to formulate personal life goals, to develop an identity, and to become more independent before joining with another person to form a new family. This is a time for young people to sort out emotionally what they will take along from the family of origin, what they will leave behind, and what they will create themselves.

Complete cut-offs from parents rarely or never resolve emotional problems (Bowen, 1978; Carter & McGoldrick, 1989). The shift to adult-to-adult status between parents and children requires a mutually respectful and personal form of relating, in which young adults can appreciate parents as they are, needing neither to make them into what they are not nor to blame them for what they could not be. Neither do young adults need to comply with parental expectations and wishes at their own expense.

The Joining of Families Through Marriage: The New Couple

The new couple *is the second stage in the family life cycle in which two individuals from separate families of origin unite to form a new family system.* This stage not only involves the development of a new marital system, but also a realignment with extended families and friends to include the spouse. Women's changing roles, the increasingly frequent marriage of partners from divergent cultural backgrounds, and the increasing physical distances between family members are placing a much stronger burden on couples to define their relationship for themselves than was true in the past (McGoldrick, 1989). Marriage is usually described as the union of two individuals, but in reality it is the union of two entire family systems and the development of a new, third system. Some experts on marriage and the family believe that marriage represents such a different phenomenon for women and men that we need to speak of "her" marriage and "his" marriage (Bernard, 1972). In American society, women have anticipated marriage with greater enthusiasm and more positive expectations than men have, although statistically it has not been a very healthy system for them.

Becoming Parents and Families with Children

Becoming parents and families with children *is the third stage in the family life cycle. Entering this stage requires that adults now move up a generation and become caregivers to the younger generation.* Moving through the lengthy stage successfully requires a commitment of time as a parent, understanding the roles of parents, and adapting to developmental changes in children (Santrock, 1993). Problems that emerge when a couple first assumes the parental role are struggles with each other about taking responsibility, as well as refusal or inability to function as competent parents to children.

When people become parents through pregnancy, adoption, or stepparenting, they face disequilibrium and must adapt. Parents want to develop a strong attachment to their infant, but they still want to maintain strong attachments to their spouse and friends, and possibly continue their careers. Parents ask themselves how this new being will change their lives. A baby places new restrictions on partners; no longer will they be able to rush out to a movie on a moment's notice, and money will not be readily available for vacations and other luxuries. Dual-career parents ask, "Will it harm the baby to place her in day care? Will we be able to find responsible baby-sitters?"

The excitement and joy that accompany the birth of a healthy baby are often followed by "postpartum blues" in mothers—a depressed state that lasts as long as nine months into the infant's first year (Fleming & others, 1988; Osofsky, 1989). The early months of the baby's physical demands may bring not only the joy of intimacy but also the sorrow of exhaustion. Pregnancy and childbirth are demanding physical events that require recovery time for the mother.

Many fathers are not sensitive to these extreme demands placed on the mother. Busy trying to make enough money to pay the bills, fathers may not be at home much of the time. A father's ability to sense and adapt to the stress placed on his wife during the first year of the infant's life has important implications for the success of the marriage and the family.

Becoming a father is both wonderful *and* stressful. In a longitudinal investigation of couples from late pregnancy until three and one-half years after the baby was born, Carolyn and Phillip Cowan (Cowan, 1988, 1991; Cowan & others, 1991) found that the couples enjoyed more positive marital relations before the baby was born than after. Still, almost one-third showed an increase in marital satisfaction. Some couples said that the baby had brought them closer together *and* moved them further apart. They commented that being parents enhanced their sense of themselves and gave them a new, more stable identity as a couple. Babies opened men up to a concern with intimate relationships, and the demands of juggling work and family roles stimulated women to manage family tasks more efficiently and pay attention to their personal growth.

At some point during the early years of the child's life, parents do face the difficult task of juggling their roles as parents and as self-actualizing adults. Until recently in our culture, nurturing our children and having a career were thought to be incompatible. Fortunately, we have come to recognize that the balance between caring and achieving, nurturing and working—although difficult to manage—can be accomplished.

The Family with Adolescents

The **family with adolescents** *represents the fourth stage of the family life cycle. Adolescence is a period of development in which individuals push for autonomy and seek to develop their own identity.* The development of mature autonomy and identity is a lengthy process, transpiring over at least 10 to 15 years. Compliant children become noncompliant adolescents. Parents tend to adopt one of two strategies to handle noncompliance—clamp down and put more pressure on the adolescent to conform to parental values or become more permissive and let the adolescent have extensive freedom. Neither is a wise overall strategy; rather a more flexible, adaptive approach is best. Later in the chapter we will explore the family worlds of adolescents and their parents in greater detail.

Midlife Families

Family at midlife *is the fifth stage in family cycle. It is a time of launching children, playing an important role in linking generations, and adapting to midlife changes in development.* Until about a generation ago, most families were involved in raising their children for much of their adult lives until old age. Because of the lower birth rate and the longer life of most adults, parents now launch their children about 20 years before retirement, which frees many midlife parents to pursue other activities.

> *The generations of living things pass in a short time, and like runners hand on the torch of life.*
>
> Lucretius, 1st Century B.C.

For the most part, family members maintain considerable contact across generations (Sprey, 1991). Parent-child similarity is most noticeable in religious and political areas, least in gender roles, life-style, and work orientation. Gender differences also characterize intergenerational relationships (Nydegger & Mitteness, 1991; Troll, 1989). In one investigation, mothers and their daughters had much closer relationships during their adult years than mothers and sons, fathers and daughters, and fathers and son (Rossi, 1989). Also, in this same investigation, married men were more involved with their wives' kin than their own. These findings underscore the significance of the woman's role as mother in monitoring access to and feelings toward kin (Barnett & others, 1991; Fischer, 1991).

The Family in Later Life

The **family in later life** *is the sixth and final stage in the family life cycle. Retirement alters a couple's lifestyle, requiring adaptation. Grandparenting also characterizes many families in this period.* The greatest changes occur in the traditional family, in which the husband works and the wife is a homemaker. The husband may not know what to do with his time, and the wife may feel uneasy

FIGURE 15.2

The stages of the family life cycle.

Family Life Cycle Stage	Emotional Process of Transition: Key Principles	Changes in Family Status Required to Proceed Developmentally
1. Leaving home: Single young adults	Accepting emotional and financial responsibility for self	a. Differentiation of self in relation to family of origin b. Development of intimate peer relationships c. Establishment of self in relation to work and financial independence
2. The joining of families through marriage: The new couple	Commitment to new system	a. Formation of marital system b. Realignment of relationships with extended families and friends to include spouse
3. Becoming parents and families with children	Accepting new members into the system	a. Adjusting marital system to make space for child(ren) b. Joining in childrearing, financial, and household tasks c. Realignment of relationships with extended family to include parenting and grandparenting roles

having him around the house all of the time. In traditional families, both partners may need to move toward more expressive roles. The husband must adjust from being the good provider to being a helper around the house; the wife must change from being only a good homemaker to being even more loving and understanding. Marital happiness as an older adult is also affected by each partner's ability to deal with personal conflicts, including aging, illness, and eventual death (Duvall & Miller, 1985).

Grow old with me!
The best is yet to be,
The last of life,
For which the first was made.

—Browning

Family Life Cycle Stage	Emotional Process of Transition: Key Principles	Changes in Family Status Required to Proceed Developmentally	
4. Families with adolescents	Increasing flexibility of family boundaries to include children's independence and grandparents' frailties	a. Shifting of parent-child relationships to permit adolescent to move in and out of system b. Refocus on mid-life marital and career issues c. Beginning shift toward joint caring for older generation	
5. Mid-life families	Accepting a multitude of exits from and entries into the family system	a. Renegotiation of marital system as a dyad b. Development of adult to adult relationships between grown children and their parents c. Realignment of relationships to include in-laws and grandchildren d. Dealing with disabilities and death of parents (grandparents)	
6. Families in later life	Accepting the shifting of generational roles	a. Maintaining own and/or couple functioning and interests in face of physiological decline; exploration of new familial and social role options b. Support for a more central role of middle generation c. Making room in the system for the wisdom and experience of the elderly, supporting the older generation without overfunctioning for them d. Dealing with loss of spouse, siblings, and other peers and preparation for own death. Life review and integration	

Individuals who are married in late adulthood are usually happier than those who are single (Lee, 1978). Marital satisfaction is greater for women than for men, possibly because women place more emphasis on attaining satisfaction through marriage than men do. However, as more women develop careers, this gender difference may not continue.

About three of every four adults over the age of 65 has at least one living grandchild, and most grandparents have some regular contact with their grandchildren (Bahr, 1989). About 80 percent of grandparents say they are happy in their rela-

tionships with their grandchildren, and a majority of grandparents say that grandparenting is easier than parenthood and enjoy it more than parenthood (Brubaker, 1985). In one investigation, grandfathers were less satisfied with grandparenthood than grandmothers, and middle-aged grandparents (aged 45–60) were more willing to give advice and to assume responsibility for watching and disciplining grandchildren than older grandparents (aged 60 and older) (Thomas, 1986). Also, maternal grandparents often interact more with their grandchildren than paternal grandparents (Bahr, 1989).

CHEEVERWOOD

by Michael Fry

CHEEVERWOOD © 1986 Michael Fry.

THE PARENTAL ROLE AND PARENTING STYLES

What is the nature of the parental role? What parenting techniques and styles do parents use with children?

The Parental Role

For many adults, the parental role is well planned and coordinated with other roles in life and is developed with the individual's economic situation in mind. For others, the discovery that they are about to become parents is a startling surprise. In either event, the prospective parents may have mixed emotions and romantic illusions about having a child. Parenting consists of a number of interpersonal skills and emotional demands, yet there is little in the way of formal education for this task. Most parents learn parenting practices from their own parents—some they accept, some they discard. Husbands and wives may bring different viewpoints of parenting practices to the marriage. Unfortunately, when methods of parents are passed on from one generation to the next, both desirable and undesirable practices are perpetuated.

> *For years we have given scientific attention to the care and rearing of plants and animals, but we have allowed babies to be raised chiefly by tradition.*
> —Edith Belle Lowry, *False Modesty* (1912)

The needs and expectations of parents have stimulated many myths about parenting (Okun & Rappaport, 1980):

- The birth of a child will save a failing marriage
- As a possession or extension of the parent, the child will think, feel, and behave like the parents did in their childhood
- Children will take care of parents in old age
- Parents can expect respect and get obedience from their children
- Having a child means that the parents will always have someone who loves them and is their best friend
- Having a child gives the parents a "second chance" to achieve what they should have achieved
- If parents learn the right techniques, they can mold their children into what they want
- It's the parents fault when children fail
- Mothers are naturally better parents than fathers
- Parenting is an instinct and requires no training

Parenting Styles

Parents want their children to grow into socially mature individuals, and they may feel frustrated in trying to discover the best way to accomplish this. Developmentalists have long searched for the ingredients of parenting that promote competent social development in children. For example, in the 1930s, John Watson argued that parents were too affectionate with their children. In the 1950s, a distinction was made between physical and psychological discipline, with psychological discipline, especially reasoning, emphasized as the best way to rear a child. In the 1970s and beyond, the dimensions of competent parenting have become more precise.

Especially widespread is the view of Diana Baumrind (1971), who believes parents should be neither punitive nor aloof, but should instead develop rules for their children and be affectionate with them. She emphasizes three types of parenting that are associated with different aspects of the child's social behavior: authoritarian, authoritative, and laissez-faire (permissive). More recently, developmentalists have argued that permissive parenting comes in two different forms: permissive-indulgent and permissive-indifferent. What are these forms of parenting like?

> *I looked on child rearing not only as a work of love and duty but as a profession that was fully as interesting and challenging as any honorable profession in the world and one that demanded the best that I could bring to it.*
> —Rose Kennedy

Authoritarian parenting *is a restrictive, punitive style that exhorts the child to follow the parent's directions and to respect work and effort. The authoritarian parent places firm limits and controls on the child with little verbal exchange allowed. Authoritarian parenting is associated with children's social incompetence.* For example, an authoritarian parent might say, "You do it my way or else. There will be no discussion!" Children of authoritarian parents are often anxious about social comparison, fail to initiate activity, and have poor communication skills. And in one recent study, early harsh discipline was associated with child aggression (Weiss & others, 1992).

Authoritative parenting *encourages children to be independent but still places limits and controls on their actions. Extensive verbal give-and-take is allowed and parents are warm and nurturant toward the child. Authoritative parenting is associated with children's social competence.* An authoritative parent might put his arm around the child in a comforting way and say, "You know you should not have done that; let's talk about how you can handle the situation better next time." Children whose parents are authoritative are socially competent, self-reliant, and socially responsible.

Permissive parenting comes in two forms: permissive-indifferent and permissive-indulgent (Maccoby & Martin, 1983). **Permissive-indifferent parenting** *is a style in which the parent is very uninvolved in the child's life; it is associated with children's social incompetence, especially a lack of self-control.* This parent cannot answer the question, "It is 10 P.M. Do you know where your child is?" Children have a strong need for their parents to care about them; children whose parents are permissive-indifferent develop the sense that other aspects of the parents' lives are more important than they are. Children whose parents are permissive-indifferent are socially incompetent—they show poor self-control and do not handle independence well.

Permissive-indulgent parenting *is a style of parenting in which parents are highly involved with their children but place few demands or controls on them. Permissive-indulgent parenting is associated with children's social incompetence, especially a lack of self-control.* They let their children do what they want, and the result is the children never learn to control their own behavior and always expect to get their way. Some parents deliberately rear their children in this way because they believe the combination of warm involvement with few restraints will produce a creative, confident child. One boy I knew whose parents deliberately reared him in a permissive-indulgent manner moved his parents out of their bedroom suite and took it over for himself. He is now 18 years old and has not learned to control his behavior; when he can't get something he wants, he still throws temper tantrums. As you might expect, he is not very popular with his peers. Children whose parents are permissive-indulgent rarely learn respect for others and have difficulty controlling their behavior.

> *Parenting is a very important profession, but no test of fitness for it is ever imposed in the interest of children.*
>
> —George Bernard Shaw,
> *Everybody's Political about What*, 1944.

The four classifications of parenting just discussed involve combinations of acceptance and responsiveness on the one hand, and demand and control on the other. How these dimensions combine to produce authoritarian, authoritative, permissive-indifferent, and permissive-indulgent parenting is shown in figure 15.3.

Child Abuse

Unfortunately, parental hostility toward children in some families escalates to the point where one or both parents abuse the children. Child abuse is an increasing problem in the United States. Estimates of its incidence vary, but some authorities say that as many as 500,000 children are physically abused every year. Laws in many states now require doctors and teachers to report suspected cases of child abuse, yet many cases go unreported, especially those of battered infants.

Child abuse is such a disturbing circumstance that many people have difficulty understanding or sympathizing with parents who abuse or neglect their children (Crittenden, 1988a, b; Martin, 1992). Our response is often outrage and anger directed at the parent. This outrage focuses our attention on parents as bad, sick, monstrous, sadistic individuals who cause their children to suffer. Experts on child abuse believe that this view is too simple and deflects attention away from the social context of the abuse and parents' coping skills. It is especially important to recognize that child abuse is a diverse condition, that it is usually mild to moderate in severity, and that it is only partially caused by individual personality characteristics of parents (Emery, 1989).

The Multifaceted Nature of Child Maltreatment

Whereas the public and many professionals use the term *child abuse* to refer to both abuse and neglect, developmentalists increasingly are using the term *child maltreatment* (Toth, Manly, & Cicchetti, in press). This term reduces the emotional impact of the term *abuse* and acknowledges that maltreatment includes several different conditions. Among the different types of maltreatment are physical and sexual abuse; fostering delinquency; lack of supervision; medical, educational, and nutritional neglect; and drug or alcohol abuse (Barrett & McGee, 1993). In one large survey, approximately 20 percent of the reported cases involved abuse alone, 46 percent neglect alone, 23 percent both abuse and neglect, and 11 percent sexual abuse (American Association for Protecting Children, 1986). Researchers have recently documented that maltreated children are more likely to have lower performance in school, more discipline problems, poorer peer relations, and more internalized and externalized disorders than nonmaltreated children (Eckenrode, Laird, & Doris, 1993; Salzinger & others, 1993; Toth, 1993).

Severity of Abuse

The concern about child abuse began with the identification of the "battered child syndrome" and has retained the characteristic of severe, brutal injury for several reasons. First, the media tend to underscore the most bizarre and vicious incidents.

FIGURE 15.3

Classification of parenting styles. The four types of parenting styles (authoritative, authoritarian, permissive-indulgent, and permissive-indifferent) involve the dimensions of acceptance and responsiveness on the one hand, and demand control on the other.

Second, much of the funding for child-abuse prevention, identification, and treatment depends on the public's perception of the horror of child abuse and the medical profession's lobby for funds to investigate and treat abused children and their parents. The emphasis is often on the worst cases. These horrific cases do exist, and are indeed terrible, but they make up only a small minority of abused children. Less than 1 percent of abused children die, and another 11 percent suffer life-threatening, disabling injuries (American Association for Protecting Children, 1986). By contrast, almost 90 percent suf-

fer temporary physical injuries. These milder injuries, though, are likely to be experienced repeatedly in the context of daily hostile family exchanges. Similarly, neglected children, who suffer no physical injuries, often experience extensive, long-term psychological harm (Paget & Abramczyk, 1993).

The Cultural Context of Maltreatment

The extensive violence that takes place in the American culture is reflected in the occurrence of violence in the family (Gelles & Conte, 1990). A regular diet of violence appears on television screens, and parents often resort to power assertion as a disciplinary technique. In China, where physical punishment is rarely used to discipline children, the incidence of child abuse is reported to be very low. In the United States, many abusing parents report that they do not have sufficient resources or help from others. This may be a realistic evaluation of the situation experienced by many low-income families, who do not have adequate preventive and supportive services (Rodriguez-Haynes & Crittenden, 1988).

Community support systems are especially important in alleviating stressful family situations, thereby preventing child abuse. An investigation of the support systems in 58 counties in New York State revealed a relation between the incidence of child abuse and the absence of support systems available to the family (Garbarino, 1976). Both family resources—relatives and friends, for example—and such formal community support systems as crisis centers and child abuse counseling were associated with a reduction in child abuse.

Family Influences

To understand abuse in the family, the interaction of all family members needs to be considered, regardless of who actually performs the violent acts against the child (Daro, 1988). For example, even though the father may be the one who physically abuses the child, contributions by the mother, the child, and siblings also should be evaluated. Many parents who abuse their children come from families in which physical punishment was used. These parents view physical punishment as a legitimate way of controlling the child's behavior and physical punishment may be a part of this sanctioning. Children themselves may unwittingly contribute to child abuse: An unattractive child may receive more physical punishment than an attractive child, and a child from an unwanted pregnancy may be especially vulnerable to abuse (Harter, Alexander, & Neimeyer, 1988). Husband-wife violence and financial problems may result in displaced aggression toward a defenseless child. Displaced aggression is commonly involved in child abuse.

A Model of Intervention

Dante Cicchetti and his colleagues (Cicchetti, 1991; Cicchetti & Lynch, in press; Cicchetti & Toth, in press; Cicchetti, Toth, & Lynch, in press) have developed a model of intervention with maltreated children that is receiving increased attention. The model is used at the Mount Hope Family Center of the University of Rochester. Intervention with maltreating families is difficult because of the multiple risk factors involved and the difficulty in getting such families to deal with the chaos in their lives. Poverty, intellectual and educational limitations, social isolation, and mental disorders are but a few of the factors that make it difficult to involve these families in effective treatment. A multidisciplinary approach uses the expertise of social workers, special educators, speech therapists, and psychologists to address the complexities associated with child maltreatment. Therapeutic preschool services are provided for children 3 to 5 years of age, individual and group psychotherapy are offered to

Dante Cicchetti has significantly advanced our knowledge of maltreated children. He and his colleagues at Mount Hope Family Center in Rochester, New York, have developed a model of intervention with maltreated children that is receiving increased attention.

children and parents, and families also participate in a home-based component. Therapists assist families in modifying their caregiving style, provide support in times of crisis, and encourage them to develop supportive social networks.

Both afterschool and summer camps are available at Mount Hope Family Center. One of the main goals of the afterschool program is to provide maltreated children with some positive relationships. Because many of the relationship histories of the children are characterized by inconsistency, unavailability, and lack of warmth, the program attempts to provide the children with stable supportive relationships with counselors and peers. Much of the relationship-building occurs in the context of recreational games and activities. Parenting groups also part of the afterschool program. Because many of the families involved are on welfare and do not have the means to send their children to a summer camp, the camp is free of charge. Children are invited to attend the camp annually to encourage reliability and consistency in relationships.

SIBLING RELATIONSHIPS AND BIRTH ORDER

Sandra describes to her mother what happened in a conflict with her sister:

> We had just come home from the ball game. I sat down on the sofa next to the light so I could read. Sally (the sister) said, "Get up, I was sitting there first. I just got up for a second to get a drink." I told her I was not going to get up and that I didn't see her name on the chair. I got mad and started pushing her. Her drink spilled all over her. Then she got really mad; she shoved me against the wall, hitting and clawing at me. I managed to grab a handful of hair.

At this point, Sally comes into the room and begins to tell her side of the story. Sandra interrupts, "Mother, you always take her side." Sound familiar? Any of you who have grown up with siblings probably have a rich memory of aggressive, hostile interchanges; but sibling relationships have many pleasant, caring moments as well. Children's sibling relationships include helping, sharing, teaching, fighting, and playing. Children can act as emotional supports, rivals, and communication partners (Conger, 1992; Eisenberg, Wolfe, and Mick, 1993; Vandell, 1987). More than 80 percent of American children have one or more siblings (brothers or sisters). Because there are so many possible sibling combinations, it is difficult to generalize about sibling influences. Among the factors to be considered are the number of siblings, age of siblings, birth order, age spacing, sex of siblings, and whether sibling relationships are different from parent-child relationships.

Critical Thinking

Sibling rivalry is a common occurrence in families. What aspects of family life are likely to increase sibling rivalry? What techniques could be used to reduce sibling conflict?

Is sibling interaction different than parent-child interaction? There is some evidence that it is. Observations indicate that children interact more positively and in more varied ways with their parents than with their siblings (Baskett & Johnson, 1982). Children also follow their parents' dictates more than those of their siblings, and they behave more negatively and punitively with their siblings than with their parents.

In some instances, siblings may be stronger socializing influences on the child than parents are (Cicirelli, 1977). Someone close in age to the child—such as a sibling—may be able to understand the child's problems and be able to communicate more effectively than parents can. In dealing with peers, coping with difficult teachers, and discussing taboo subjects such as sex, siblings may be more influential in the socialization process than parents.

Birth order is a special interest of sibling researchers. When differences in birth order are found, they usually are explained by variations in interactions with parents and siblings associated with the unique experiences of being in a particular position in the family. This is especially true in the case of the firstborn child (Murphy, 1993; Teti & others, 1993). The oldest child is the only one who does not have to share parental love and affection with other siblings—until another sibling comes along. An infant requires more attention than an older child; this means that the firstborn sibling now gets less attention than before the newborn arrived. Does this result in conflict between parents and the firstborn? In one research study, mothers became more negative, coercive, restraining, and played less with the firstborn following the birth of a second child (Dunn & Kendrick, 1982). Even though a new infant requires more attention from parents than does an older child, an especially intense relationship is often maintained between parents and

The one-child family is becoming much more common in China because of the strong motivation to limit population growth in the People's Republic of China. The policy is still new, and its effects on children have not been fully examined.

firstborns throughout the life cycle. Parents have higher expectations for, put more pressure for achievement and responsibility on, and interfere more with the activities of firstborn than later-born children (Rothbart, 1971).

Birth order is also associated with variations in sibling relationships. The oldest sibling is expected to exercise self-control and show responsibility in interacting with younger siblings. When the oldest sibling is jealous or hostile, parents often protect the younger sibling. The oldest sibling is more dominant, competent, and powerful than the younger siblings; the oldest sibling is also expected to assist and teach younger siblings. Indeed, researchers have shown that older siblings are both more antagonistic—hitting, kicking, and biting—and more nurturant toward their younger siblings than vice versa (Abramovitch & others, 1986). There is also something unique about same-sex sibling relationships. Aggression and dominance occur more in same-sex relationships than in opposite-sex sibling relationships (Minnett, Vandell, & Santrock, 1983).

Given the differences in family dynamics involved in birth order, it is not surprising that firstborns and later-borns have different characteristics. Firstborn children are more adult oriented, helpful, conforming, anxious, self-controlled, and less aggressive than their siblings. Parents give more attention to firstborns and this is related to firstborns' nurturant behavior (Stanhope & Corter, 1993). Parental demands and high standards established for firstborns result in these children excelling in academic and professional endeavors. Firstborns are overrepresented in *Who's Who* and Rhodes scholars, for example. However, some of the same pressures placed on firstborns for high achievement may be the reason they also have more guilt, anxiety, difficulty in coping with stressful situations, and higher admission to child guidance clinics.

What is the only child like? The popular conception of the only child is a "spoiled brat" with such undesirable characteristics as dependency, lack of self-control, and self-centered behavior. But researchers present a more positive portrayal of the only child, who often is achievement oriented and displays a desirable personality, especially in comparison to later-borns and children from large families (Falbo & Polit, 1986; Falbo & Poston, 1993; Thomas, Coffman, & Kipp, 1993).

So far our consideration of birth-order effects suggests that birth order might be a strong predictor of behavior. However, an increasing number of family researchers believe that birth order has been overdramatized and overemphasized. The critics argue that, when all of the factors that influence behavior are considered, birth order itself shows limited ability to predict behavior. Consider just sibling relationships alone. They not only vary in birth order, but also in number of siblings, age of siblings, age spacing of siblings, and sex of siblings.

Consider also the temperament of siblings. Researchers have found that siblings' temperamental traits (such as "easy" and "difficult," for example), as well as differential treatment of siblings by parents, influence how siblings get along (Stocker & Dunn, 1991). Siblings with "easy" temperaments who are treated in relatively equal ways by parents tend to get along with each other the best, whereas siblings with "difficult" temperaments, or when parents gave one sibling preferential treatment, get along the worst.

Beyond temperament and differential treatment of siblings by parents, think about some of the other important factors in children's lives that influence their behavior beyond birth order. They include heredity, models of competency or incompetency that parents present to children on a daily basis, peer influences, school influences, socioeconomic factors, sociohistorical factors, cultural variations, and so on. When someone says firstborns are always like this, but lastborns are always like that, you now know that they are making overly simplistic statements that do not adequately take into account the complexity of influences on a child's behavior. Keep in mind, though, that, while birth order itself may not be a good predictor of adolescent behavior, sibling relationships and interaction are important dimensions of family processes.

FAMILY PROCESSES IN ADOLESCENCE

What are some of the most important issues and questions that need to be raised about family relationships in adolescence? They include: What is the nature of autonomy and attachment in adolescence? How extensive is parent-adolescent conflict and how does it influence the adolescent's development?

When I was a boy of 14, my father was so ignorant I could hardly stand to have the man around. But when I got to be 21, I was astonished at how much he had learnt in 7 years.

—Mark Twain

Autonomy and Attachment

The adolescent's push for autonomy and a sense of responsibility puzzles and angers many parents. Parents see their teenager slipping from their grasp. They may have an urge to take stronger control as the adolescent seeks autonomy and responsibility. Heated emotional exchanges may ensue, with either side calling names, making threats, and doing whatever seems necessary to gain control. Parents may seem frustrated because they *expect* their teenager to heed their advice, to want to spend time with the family, and to grow up to do what is right (Collins & Luebker, 1993). Most parents anticipate that their teenager will have some difficulty adjusting to the changes that adolescence brings, but few parents can imagine and predict just how strong an adolescent's desires will be to spend time with peers or how much adolescents will want to show that it is they—not their parents—who are responsible for their successes and failures.

The ability to attain autonomy and gain control over one's behavior in adolescence is acquired through appropriate adult reactions to the adolescent's desire for control. At the onset of adolescence, the average individual does not have the knowledge to make appropriate or mature decisions in all areas of life. As the adolescent pushes for autonomy, the wise adult relinquishes control in those areas where the adolescent can make reasonable decisions but continues to guide the adolescent to make reasonable decisions in areas where the adolescent's knowledge is more limited. Gradually, adolescents acquire the ability to make mature decisions on their own.

But adolescents do not simply move away from parental influence into a decision-making process all their own. There is continued connectedness to parents as adolescents move toward and gain autonomy. In the last decade, developmentalists have begun to explore the role of secure attachment, and related concepts such as connectedness to parents, in adolescent development. They believe that attachment to parents in adolescence may facilitate the adolescent's social competence and well-being, as reflected in such characteristics as self-esteem, emotional adjustment, and physical health (Kobak, 1992; Kobak & Cole, in press; Kobak & others, 1992; Kobak & others, 1993). For example, adolescents who have secure relationships with their parents have higher self-esteem and better emotional well-being (Armsden & Greenberg, 1987). In contrast, emotional detachment from parents is associated with greater feelings of parental rejection and a lower sense of one's own social and romantic attractiveness (Ryan & Lynch, 1989).

Thus, attachment to parents during adolescence may serve the adaptive function of providing a secure base from which adolescents can explore and master new environments and a widening social world in a psychologically healthy manner. Secure attachment to parents may buffer adolescents from the anxiety and potential feelings of depression or emotional distress associated with the transition from childhood to adulthood. In one recent study, when young adolescents had a secure attachment to their parents, they perceived their family as cohesive and reported little social anxiety or feelings of depression (Papini, Roggman, & Anderson, 1990).

Secure attachment or connectedness to parents promotes competent peer relations and positive close relationships outside of the family. In one investigation, attachment to parents and peers was assessed (Armsden & Greenberg, 1984). Adolescents who were securely attached to parents were also securely attached to peers; those who were insecurely attached to parents were also more likely to be insecurely attached to peers. In another investigation, college students who were securely attached to their parents as young children were more likely to have securely attached relationships with friends, dates, and spouses than their insecurely attached counterparts (Hazen & Shaver, 1987). And in yet another investigation, older adolescents who had an ambivalent attachment history with their parents reported greater jealousy, conflict, and dependency along with less satisfaction in their relationship with their best friend than their securely attached counterparts (Fisher, 1990). There are times when adolescents reject closeness, connection, and attachment to their parents as they assert their ability to make decisions and to develop an identity. But for the most part, the worlds of parents and peers are coordinated and connected, not uncoordinated and disconnected (Haynie & McLellan, 1992).

Parent-Adolescent Conflict

While attachment and connectedness to parents remains strong during adolescence, the attachment and connectedness is not always smooth. Early adolescence is a time when conflict with parents escalates beyond childhood levels (Steinberg, 1991). This increase may be due to a number of factors: the biological changes of puberty, cognitive changes involving increased idealism and logical reasoning, social changes focused on independence and identity, maturational changes in parents, and violated expectations on the part of parents and adolescents. The adolescent compares her parents to an ideal standard and then criticizes the flaws. A 13-year-old girl tells her mother, "That is the tackiest-looking dress I have ever seen. Nobody would be caught dead wearing that." The adolescent demands logical explanations for comments and discipline. A 14-year-old boy tells his mother, "What do you mean I have to be home at 10 P.M. because it's the way we do things around here? Why do we do things around here that way? It doesn't make sense to me."

Adolescence is like cactus.
Anaïs Nin, *A Spy in the House of Love* (1959)

Many parents see their adolescent changing from a compliant child to someone who is noncompliant, oppositional, and resistant to parental standards. When this happens, parents tend to clamp down and put more pressure on the adolescent to conform to parental standards (Collins, 1990). Parents often expect their adolescents to become mature adults overnight instead of understanding that the journey takes 10 to 15 years. Parents who recognize that this transition takes time handle their youth more competently and calmly than those who demand immediate conformity to adult standards. The opposite tactic—letting adolescents do as they please without supervision—is also unwise.

While conflict with parents does increase in early adolescence, it does not reach the tumultuous proportions G. Stanley Hall envisioned at the beginning of the twentieth century (Kupersmidt & others, 1992). Rather, much of the conflict involves the everyday events of family life such as keeping a bedroom clean, dressing neatly, getting home by a certain time, not talking forever on the phone, and so on. The conflicts rarely involve major dilemmas like drugs and delinquency.

It is not unusual to talk to parents of young adolescents and hear them ask, "Is it ever going to get better?" Things usually do get better as adolescents move from early to late adolescence. Conflict between parents often escalates during early adolescence, remains somewhat stable during the high school years, and then lessens as the adolescent reaches 17 to 20 years of age. Parent-adolescent relationships become more positive if adolescents go away to college than if they stay at home and go to college (Sullivan & Sullivan, 1980).

The everyday conflicts that characterize parent-adolescent relationships may actually serve a positive developmental function (Blos, 1989; Hill, 1983). These minor disputes and negotiations facilitate the adolescent's transition from being dependent on parents to becoming an autonomous individual. For example, in one investigation, adolescents who expressed disagreement with parents explored identity development more actively than adolescents who did not express disagreement with their parents (Cooper & others, 1982).

As suggested earlier, one way for parents to cope with the adolescent's push for independence and identity is to recognize that adolescence is a 10- to 15-year transitional period in the journey to adulthood rather than an overnight accomplishment. Recognizing that conflict and negotiation can serve a positive developmental function can tone down parental hostility, too. Understanding parent-adolescent conflict, though, is not simple.

In sum, the old model of parent-adolescent relationships suggested that as adolescents mature they detach themselves from parents and move into a world of autonomy apart from parents. The old model also suggested that parent-adolescent conflict is intense and stressful throughout adolescence. The new model emphasizes that parents can serve as important attachment figures and support systems, a circumstance that helps adolescents explore a wider, more complex social world. The new model also emphasizes that in the majority of families, parent-adolescent conflict is moderate rather than severe, and that the everyday negotiations and minor disputes are normal and can

FIGURE 15.4

Old and new models of parent-adolescent relationships.

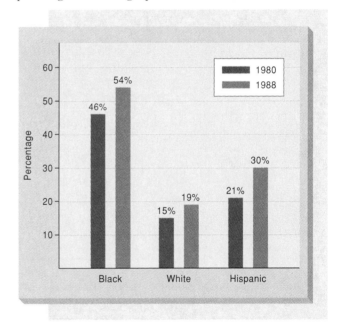

Old model	
Autonomy, detachment from parents; parent and peer worlds are isolated	Intense, stressful conflict throughout adolescence; parent-adolescent relationships are filled with storm and stress on virtually a daily basis

New model	
Attachment and autonomy; parents are important support systems and attachment figures; adolescent-parent and adolescent-peer worlds have some important connections	Moderate parent-adolescent conflict common and can serve a positive developmental function; conflict greater in early adolescence, especially during the apex of puberty

serve the positive developmental function of helping the adolescent make the transition from childhood dependency to adult independence (see figure 15.4).

Still, a high degree of conflict characterizes some parent-adolescent relationships. One estimate of the percentage of parents and adolescents who engage in prolonged, intense, repeated, unhealthy conflict is about one in five families (Montemayor, 1982). While this figure represents a minority of adolescents, it indicates that 4 to 5 million American families encounter serious, highly stressful parent-adolescent conflict. And, this prolonged, intense conflict is associated with a number of adolescent problems—moving away from home, juvenile delinquency, school dropout rates, pregnancy and early marriage, joining religious cults, and drug abuse (Barber & others, 1992; Brook & others, 1990; Ullman, 1982).

At this point we have studied a number of ideas about the nature of family processes, the family life cycle, the parental role and parenting styles, sibling relationships and birth order, and family processes in adolescence. A summary of these ideas is presented in Concept Table 15.1.

EFFECTS OF DIVORCE ON CHILDREN

The increasing number of children growing up in single-parent families is staggering. As shown in figure 15.5, a substantial increase in the number of children under the age of 18 who lived in a single-parent family occurred between 1980 and 1988. Also note that a much higher percentage of Black families than White or Hispanic families are single-parent families. If current trends continue, by the year 2000 one in every four children will also have lived a portion of their lives in a step-parent family. And, as we saw earlier, fathers perform more childrearing duties than in the past.

Models of Divorce Effects

Two main models have been proposed to explain how divorce affects children's and children's development: the father-absence model and the multiple-factor model. The **father-absence model** *states that, when adolescents from father-absent*

FIGURE 15.5

Percentage of children under 18 living with one parent in 1980 and 1988. The percentage of children under 18 living with one parent increased from 20 percent in 1980 to 24 percent in 1988. This figure reveals the breakdown of single parents in Black, White, and Hispanic families. Note the substantially higher percentage of Black single-parent families.

and father-present families are compared, any differences that occur are attributed to the family structure variations, such as the father being absent in one set of the families. However, family structure (such as father-present versus father-absent) is only one of many factors that influence the child's development and adjustment in single-parent families. Even when researchers compare the development of children in more precise family structures (such as divorced versus widowed), there are many factors other than family structure that need to be examined to explain the child's development. As we see next, a second model of the effects of divorce on children's development goes beyond the overly simplistic family structure father-absence model.

CONCEPT TABLE 15.1

The Nature of Family Processes, the Family Life Cycle, the Parental Role and Parenting Styles,
Sibling Relationships and Birth Order, and Family Processes in Adolescence

Concept	Processes/Related Ideas	Characteristics/Description
The nature of family processes	Reciprocal socialization and the family as a system	Children socialize parents just as parents socialize children. Scaffolding, synchronization, and mutual regulation are important dimensions of reciprocal socialization. The family is a system of interacting individuals with different subsystems, some dyadic, others polyadic. Belsky's model describes direct and indirect effects.
	The developmental construction of relationships	The developmental construction views share the belief that as individuals grow up they acquire modes of relating to others. There are two main variations within this view, one that emphasizes continuity and stability in relationships through the life span (called the continuity view) and one that emphasizes discontinuity and change in relationships through the life span (called the discontinuity view).
	Adapting parenting to developmental changes in the child	Parents need to adapt their interaction strategies as the child grows older, using less physical manipulation and more reasoning in the process. Parents spend less time with children during middle and late childhood, including less time in caregiving, instruction, reading, talking, and playing. Nonetheless, parents still are powerful and important socializing agents in this period. New parent-child issues emerge, and discipline changes. Control becomes more coregulatory.
	Sociocultural and historical changes	Sociocultural and historical changes in families may be due to great upheavals, such as war, or more subtle changes, such as television and the mobility of families.
The family life cycle	Its nature	As we go through life, we are at different points in the family life cycle. The stages of the family life cycle include: leaving home and becoming a single adult, the joining of couples through marriage—the new couple, becoming parents and families with children, families with adolescents, families at midlife, and the family in later life.
The parental role and parenting styles	The parental role	For some, the parental role is well planned and coordinated. For others, there is surprise and sometimes chaos. There are many myths about parenting, including the myth that the birth of a child will save a failing marriage.

The **multiple-factor model of divorce effects** *takes into account the complexity of the divorce context and examines a number of influences on the child's development, including not only family structure, but also the strengths and weaknesses of the child prior to the divorce, the nature of the events surrounding the divorce itself, the type of custody involved and visitation patterns, socioeconomic status, and post-divorce family functioning.* Researchers are finding that the availability of and use of support systems (relatives, friends, housekeepers), an ongoing positive relationship between the custodial parent and the ex-spouse, authoritative parenting, financial resources, and the child's competencies at the time of the divorce are important factors in how successfully the child adapts to the divorce of parents (Barber & Eccles,

1992; Barber & others, 1992; Block, Block, & Gjerde, 1986; Ceballo & Olson, 1993; Hetherington, Anderson, & Hagan, 1991; Hetherington & Clingempeel, 1992; Miller, Kliewer, & Burkeman, 1993; Santrock & Warshak, 1986; Wallerstein, 1989; Wallerstein & Kelly, 1980). Thus, just as the family structure factor of birth order by itself is not a good predictor of children's development, neither is the family structure factor of father absence. In both circumstances—birth order and father absence—there are many other factors that always have to be taken into consideration when explaining the child's development is at issue. Let's further examine what some of those complex factors are in the case of children who experience the divorce of their parents.

Concept	Processes/Related Ideas	Characteristics/Description
	Parenting styles	Authoritarian, authoritative, permissive-indulgent, and permissive-indifferent are four main categories of parenting. Authoritative parenting is associated with children's social competence more than the other styles.
	Child abuse	Child abuse is an increasing problem in the United States. Child abuse is a multifaceted problem. Increasingly, developmentalists use the term *maltreatment* rather than *abuse* or *neglect.* Understanding child maltreatment requires information about the cultural context and family influences. Cicchetti's intervention model at the Mount Hope Family Center is receiving increased attention.
Sibling relationships and birth order	Sibling relationships	More than 80 percent of American children have one or more siblings. Siblings interact with each other in more negative, less positive, and less varied ways than parents and children interact. In some cases, siblings are stronger socializing influences than parents.
	Birth order	The relationship of the firstborn child and parents seems to be especially close and demanding, which may account for the greater achievement orientation and anxiety in firstborn children. Some critics argue that birth order is not a good predictor of behavior.
Family processes in adolescence	Attachment and autonomy	The old model of parent-adolescent relationships emphasized autonomy and detachment from parents. The new model emphasizes both attachment and autonomy, with parents acting as important support systems and attachment figures for adolescents.
	Parent-adolescent conflict	The old model emphasized intense, stressful conflict between parents and adolescents. The new model emphasizes that moderate, rather than severe, conflict is common and that it can serve a positive developmental function. Conflict with parents is greater during early adolescence, especially during the apex of puberty, than in late adolescence.

Age and Developmental Changes

The age of the child at the time of the divorce needs to be considered. Young children's responses to divorce are mediated by their limited cognitive and social competencies, their dependency on parents, and possibly inferior day care (Hetherington, Hagan, & Anderson, 1989). The cognitive immaturity that creates considerable anxiety for children who are young at the time of their parents' divorce may benefit the children over time. Ten years after the divorce of their parents, adolescents had few memories of their own earlier fears and suffering or their parents' conflict (Wallerstein, Corbin, & Lewis, 1988). Nonetheless, approximately one-third of these children continued to express anger about not being able to grow up in an intact, never-divorced family. Those who were adolescents at the time of their parents' divorce were more likely to remember the conflict and stress surrounding the divorce some 10 years later, in their early adult years. They, too, expressed disappointment at not being able to grow up in an intact family and wondered if their life would not have been better if they had been able to do so. And in one recent study, adolescents who experienced the divorce of their parents during adolescence were more likely to have drug problems than adolescents whose parents were divorced when the adolescents were children or than adolescents living in continuously married families (Needle, Su, & Doherty, 1990).

Evaluations of children and adolescents six years after the divorce of their parents by developmental psychologist E. Mavis Hetherington and her colleagues (1989) found that living in a nonremarried mother-custody home had long-term negative effects on boys, with deleterious outcomes appearing consistently from kindergarten to adolescence. No negative effects on preadolescent girls were found. However, at the onset of adolescence, early-maturing girls from divorced families engaged in frequent conflict with their mothers, behaved in noncompliant ways, had lower self-esteem, and experienced more problems in heterosexual relationships.

Conflict

Many separations and divorces are highly emotional affairs that immerse the child in conflict. Conflict is a critical aspect of family functioning that often outweighs the influence of family structure on the child's development. For example, children in divorced families low in conflict function better than children in intact, never-divorced families high in conflict (Bishop & Ingersoll, 1989; Black & Pedro-Carroll, 1993; Rutter, 1983; Wallerstein, 1989). Although the escape from conflict that divorce provides may be a positive benefit for children, in the year immediately following the divorce, the conflict does not decline but increases. At this time, children—especially boys—in divorced families show more adjustment problems than children in intact families with both parents present. During the first year after the divorce, the quality of parenting the child experiences is often poor; parents seem to be preoccupied with their own needs and adjustment—experiencing anger, depression, confusion, and emotional instability—which inhibits their ability to respond sensitively to the child's needs. During the second year after the divorce, parents are more effective in their childrearing duties, especially with daughters (Hetherington, 1993; Hetherington & Clingempeel, 1992; Hetherington, Cox, & Cox, 1982; Hetherington, Anderson, & Hagan, 1991; Hetherington, Hagan, & Anderson, 1989).

Sex of the Child and the Nature of Custody

The sex of the child and the sex of the custodial parent are important considerations in evaluating the effects of divorce on children.

One research study directly compared 6- to 11-year-old children living in father-custody and mother-custody families (Santrock & Warshak, 1979, 1986). On a number of measures, including videotaped observations of parent-child interaction, children living with the same-sex parent were more socially competent—happier, more independent, higher self-esteem, and more mature—than children living with the opposite-sex parent. Some researchers have recently found support for the same-sex parent-child custodial arrangement (Camara & Resnick, 1988; Furstenberg, 1988), while others have found

that, regardless of their sex, adolescents are better adjusted in mother-custody or joint-custody families than in father-custody families (Buchanan, Maccoby, & Dornbusch, 1992; Buchanan & Maccoby, 1990; Maccoby & Mnookin, 1993).

In a recent investigation by Christy Buchanan and her colleagues (Buchanan & Maccoby, 1990; Buchanan, Maccoby, & Dornbusch, 1992) 522 adolescents from 10 to 18 years of age were interviewed by telephone approximately 4½ years after their parents had separated. The adolescents were living in mother-custody, father-custody, or joint-custody families. They were asked about their depression/anxiety, deviant behavior, and grades and effort in school, as well as about various aspects of their family life. The adolescents in father custody reported higher levels of problem behaviors than adolescents in mother- or joint-custody families. Adolescents in joint custody reported the fewest problem behaviors, although other researchers have found no advantage for joint-custody over single-custody arrangements (Kline & others, 1989). It is important to note that in Buchanan and Maccoby's study, adolescents who had been shifted to the father over time were having more problems 4½ years after separation than adolescents who had been with the father all along or adolescents who had never lived with the father. Also, "shifters" (regardless of which type of family they were shifted to) had more problems than adolescents who remained in the same custody across time, and there was a higher proportion of shifters in father custody than other arrangements. In this study, the best predictors of positive adolescent outcomes were the closeness of the adolescent to the custodial parent and the custodial parent's monitoring of the adolescent.

Critical Thinking

Imagine you are a judge in a custodial dispute. What are some of the key factors you would consider in awarding custody?

Conclusions

In sum, large numbers of children are growing up in divorced families. Most children initially experience considerable stress when their parents divorce, and they are at risk for developing problem behaviors. However, divorce can also remove children from conflicted marriages. Many children emerge from divorce as competent individuals. In recent years, developmentalists have moved away from the view that single-parent families are atypical or pathological, focusing more on the diversity of children's responses to divorce and the factors that facilitate or disrupt the development and adjustment of children (Hetherington, Hagan, & Anderson, 1989). To read about parenting recommendations for communicating more effectively with children about divorce, turn to Explorations in Child Development 15.1.

EXPLORATIONS IN CHILD
DEVELOPMENT 15.1

Parenting Recommendations: Communicating with Children about Divorce

Ellen Galinsky and Judy David (1988) developed a number of guidelines for communicating with young children about divorce.

Explaining the Separation

As soon as the daily activities in the home make it obvious that one parent is leaving, tell the children. If possible, both parents should be present when the children are made aware of the separation to come. The reasons for the separation are very difficult for young children to understand. No matter what parents tell children, children can find reasons to argue against the separation. A child may say something like, "If you don't love each other anymore, you need to start trying harder." One set of parents told their 4-year-old, "We both love you. We will both always love you and take care of you, but we aren't going to live in the same house anymore. Daddy is moving to an apartment near the stores where we shop." It is extremely important for parents to tell the children who will take care of them and to describe the specific arrangements for seeing the other parent.

Explaining That the Separation Is Not the Child's Fault

Young children often believe their parents' separation or divorce is their own fault. Therefore, it is important to tell children that they are not the cause of the separation. Parents need to repeat this a number of times.

Explaining That It May Take Time to Feel Better

It is helpful to tell young children that it's normal to not feel good about what is happening, and that lots of other children feel this way when their parents become separated. It is also okay for divorced parents to share some of their emotions with children, by saying something like, "I'm having a hard time since the separation, just like you, but I know it's going to get better after awhile." Such statements are best kept brief, and should not criticize the other parent.

Keeping the Door Open for Further Discussion

Tell your children that anytime they want to talk about the separation to come to you. It is healthy for children to get their pent-up emotions out in the open in discussions with their parents, and to learn that the parents are willing to listen to their feelings and fears.

Providing As Much Continuity As Possible

The less children's worlds are disrupted by the separation, the easier their transition to a single-parent family will be. This means maintaining as much as possible the rules already in place. Children need parents who care enough to not only give them warmth and nurturance, but also set reasonable limits. If the custodial parent has to move to a new home, it is important to preserve as much of what is familiar to the child as possible. In one family, the child helped to arrange her new room exactly as it had been prior to the divorce. If children must leave friends behind, it is important for parents to help the children stay in touch by phone or by letter. Keeping the children busy and involved in the new setting can also keep their mind off of the stressful thoughts about the separation.

Providing Support for Your Children and Yourself

After a divorce or separation, parents are as important to children as before the divorce or separation. Divorced parents need to provide children with as much support as possible. Parents function best when other people are available to give them support as adults and as parents. Divorced parents can find people who provide practical help and with whom they can talk about their problems. Too often divorced parents criticize themselves and say they feel that they don't deserve help. One divorced parent commented, "I've made a mess of my life. I don't deserve anybody's help." However, seeking out others for support and feedback about problems can make the transition to a single-parent family more bearable.

STEPFAMILIES

The number of remarriages involving children has grown steadily in recent years, although both the rate of increase in divorce and stepfamilies slowed in the 1980s. Stepfather families, in which a woman has custody of children from a previous marriage, make up 70 percent of stepfamilies. Stepmother families make up almost 20 percent of stepfamilies, and a small minority are blended with both partners bringing children from a previous marriage. A substantial percentage of stepfamilies produce children of their own.

Like divorce, remarriage has also become commonplace in American society. The United States has the highest remarriage rate in the world, and Americans tend to remarry soon after divorce. Younger women remarry more quickly than older women, and childless women, divorced prior to the age of 25, have higher remarriage rates than women with children. The more money a divorced male has, the more likely he is to remarry, but for women the opposite is true. Remarriage satisfaction, similar to satisfaction in first marriages, appears to decrease over time (Guisinger & others, 1989). In fact, few differences have been found between the factors that predict marital satisfaction in first marriages and remarriage (Coleman & Ganong, 1990).

Just as couples who are first married, remarried individuals often have unrealistic expectations about their stepfamily. Thus, an important adjustment for remarried persons is to develop realistic expectations. Money and the complexities of family structure in the remarried family often contribute to marital conflict.

Many variations in remarriage have the potential for what is called **boundary ambiguity**—*the uncertainty in stepfamilies of who is in or out of the family and who is performing or responsible for certain tasks in the family system.* The uncertainty of boundaries likely increases stress for the family system and the probability of behavior problems in children.

Research on stepfamilies has lagged behind research on divorced families, but a number of investigators have turned their attention to this increasingly common family structure (Anderson, 1992; Hetherington, 1993; Hetherington & Clingempeel, 1992; Hetherington, Hagan, & Anderson, 1989; Lindner, 1992; Lyons & Barber, 1992; O'Conner, 1992; Santrock & Sitterle, 1987; Santrock, Sitterle, & Warshak, 1988). Following remarriage of their parents, children of all ages show a resurgence of behavior problems (Freeman, 1993). Younger children seem to eventually form an attachment to a stepparent and accept the stepparenting role. However, the developmental tasks facing adolescents make them especially vulnerable to the entrance of a stepparent. At the time they are searching for an identity and exploring sexual and other close relationships outside the family, a nonbiological parent may increase the stress associated with these important tasks. In one recent study, entrance of a stepfather when children were 9 years or older was associated with more problems than when the stepfather family was formed earlier (Hetherington, 1993).

Following the remarriage of the custodial parent, an emotional upheaval usually occurs in girls, and problems in boys often intensify. Over time, preadolescent boys seem to improve more than girls in stepfather families. Sons who frequently are involved in conflicted or coercive relations with their custodial mothers probably have much to gain from living with a warm, supportive stepfather. In contrast, daughters who have a close relationship with their custodial mothers and considerable independence frequently find a stepfather both disruptive and constraining.

Children's relationships with their biological parents are more positive than with their stepparents, regardless of whether a stepmother or stepfather family is involved. However, stepfathers are often distant and disengaged from their stepchildren. As a rule, the more complex the stepfamily, the more difficult the child's adjustment. Families in which both parents bring children from a previous marriage have the highest level of behavioral problems.

Critical Thinking

What might parents do to improve the adjustment of children in stepfamilies?

In the recent investigation by E. Mavis Hetherington (1993), both parenting techniques and the school environment were associated with whether children coped effectively both with living in divorced family and a stepfamily. From the first grade on, an authoritative environment (an organized predictable environment with clearly defined standards, and a responsive, nurturant environment) was linked with greater achievement and fewer problems in children than three other environments—authoritarian (coercive, power assertive, punitive, more criticism than praise, little responsiveness to individual children's needs, and low nurturance), permissive (low structure, disorganized, and high warmth), and chaotic/neglecting (disorganized, ineffective, erratic though usually harsh control, unstructured, low expectations, and hostile relationships). In divorced families, when only one parent was authoritative, or when neither parent was authoritative, an authoritative school improved the child's adjustment. A chaotic/neglecting school environment had the most adverse effects on children, which were most marked when there was no authoritative parent in the home.

WORKING PARENTS

Interest in the effects of parental work on children has increased in recent years. Our examination of parental work focuses on the following issues: the role of working mothers, the adjustment of latchkey children, the effects of relocation, and the influence of unemployment.

What issues do women face as they combine a career and family? What are the effects of working mothers on children's development?

Working Mothers

Because household operations have become more efficient and family size has decreased in America, it is not certain that children with mothers working outside the home actually receive less attention than children in the past whose mothers were not employed. Outside employment—at least for mothers with school-aged children—may simply be filling time previously taken up by added household burdens and more children. It also cannot be assumed that, if the mother did not go to work, the child would benefit from the time freed by streamlined household operations and smaller families. Mothering does not always have a positive effect on the child. The educated, nonworking mother may overinvest her energies in her children, fostering an excess of worry and discouraging the child's independence. In such situations, the mother may inject more parenting than the child can profitably handle.

As Lois Hoffman (1989) comments, maternal employment is a part of modern life. It is not an aberrant aspect of it, but a response to other social changes that meets the needs that cannot be met by the previous family ideal of a full-time mother and homemaker. Not only does it meet the parent's needs, but in many ways, it may be a pattern better suited to socializing children for the adult roles they will occupy. This is especially true for daughters, but it is also true for sons. The broader range of emotions and skills that each parent presents is more consistent with this adult role. Just as his father shares the breadwinning role and the childrearing role with his mother, so the son, too, will be more likely to share these roles. The rigid gender role stereotyping perpetuated by the divisions of labor in the traditional family is not appropriate for the demands children of either sex will have made on them as adults. The needs of the growing child require the mother to loosen her hold on the child, and this task may be easier for the working woman whose job is an additional source of identity and self-esteem. Overall, researchers have found no detrimental effects of maternal employment on children's development (Gottfried, 1993). Working and nonworking mothers have similar attitudes toward parenting (O'Brien 1993).

A common experience of working mothers (and working fathers) is feeling guilty about being away from their children. The guilt may be triggered by parents missing their child, worrying that their child is missing them, being concerned about the implications of working (such as whether the child is receiving good child care), and worrying about the long-term effects of working (such as having anxiety about jeopardizing the child's future). To reduce guilt, the guilt needs to be acknowledged. Pediatrician T. Berry Brazelton (1983) believes that parents respond to guilt either by admitting it and working through it or by denying it and rationalizing it away. The latter tendency is not recommended. Working parents' guilt can also be reduced if they begin paying closer attention to how their children are doing. If there is work/family interference, how can working parents solve the problem? To read about some working parent solutions, turn to Explorations in Child Development 15.2.

Latchkey Children

While the mother's working is not associated with negative outcomes for children, a certain set of children from working-mother families bears further scrutiny—those called latchkey children. Latchkey children typically do not see their parents from the time they leave for school in the morning until about 6:00 or 7:00 P.M. They are called latchkey children because they often are given the key to their home, take the key to school, and let themselves into the home while their parents are still at work. Many latchkey children are largely unsupervised for two to four hours a day during each school week, or for entire days, five days a week, during the summer months.

Thomas and Lynette Long (1983) interviewed more than 1,500 latchkey children. They concluded that a slight majority of these children had negative latchkey experiences. Some latchkey children may grow up too fast, hurried by the responsibility placed on them (Elkind, 1981). How do latchkey children handle the lack of limits and structure during the latchkey hours? Without limits and parental supervision, it become easier for latchkey children to find their way into trouble—possibly abusing a sibling, stealing, or vandalizing. The Longs found that 90 percent of the adjudicated juvenile delinquents in Montgomery County, Maryland, were from latchkey families. In another investigation of more than 4,900 eighth-graders in Los Angeles and San Diego, those who cared for themselves 11 hours a week or more were twice as likely to have abused alcohol and other drugs than their counterparts who did not care for themselves at all before or after school (Richardson & others, 1989). Adolescent expert Joan Lipsitz (1983), testifying before the Select Committee on Children, Youth, and Families, called the lack of adult supervision of children and adolescents in the afterschool hours one of the nation's major problems. Lipsitz

**EXPLORATIONS IN CHILD
DEVELOPMENT 15.2**

Some Working Parent Solutions When Work/Family Interference Occurs

Ellen Galinsky is the co-president of the new Families and Work Institute in New York City and was recently elected president of the National Association for the Education of Young Children. Judy David is a researcher on the Work and Family Life Studies Project at the Bank Street College of Education in New York. Galinsky and David (1988) offered these working parent solutions when work/family interference occurs.

Making a List of the Problems

The first step in handling work/family interference is to understand it. Making a list of its stressful dimensions helps because they become less confusing. A parent who is a teacher might have the following list:

Teaching problems at work:

- Administration—lack of understanding
- Budget—not enough money
- Demands from parents
- Needs of children
- Lack of classroom help

    Problems at home:

- Finding time for everything

- Finding time for myself
- Coping with stress

Understanding Expectations and Determining If They Are Realistic

When the list of problems is completed, the next step is to understand the role of expectations in each situation—what are the "shoulds" and are they realistic? Some of this parent's stress involves her anger that things are not like they *should* be. A school administrator *should* manage the budget and resources better so she can teach more effectively; her pupils *should* be prepared better for school; her husband and children *should* know to help her; her home *should* be clean all of the time; she *should* do it all! Once she becomes aware of these expectations, the parent can begin understanding them better and start examining ways to cope with them more effectively.

Solving One Problem at a Time

The third step for the working parent is to decide how to go about solving one problem at a time. Too often working parents try to tackle everything at once. Selecting one problem to work on increases the working parent's likelihood of success.

Escaping

At times, each of us needs to escape from the routines of everyday life. So do working parents. For one employed parent, it might mean reading mystery novels for half an hour a day, even if the dishes are waiting to be done. For another, it might mean watching television while exercising on a stationary bicycle. For still another, it might mean a regular dinner with college friends.

Exercising

Exercise is a great stress reducer. Working parents can get up earlier and jog before breakfast, or possibly jog or work out during the lunch hour. Some join team sports or participate in an aerobics class.

Finding Social Support

Social support is important in helping working parents cope with stress. Working parents may need a variety of people to form networks of support—friends at work to talk with about office politics, as well as friends for talking about family issues, for example. Parents also can provide important support for each other. Compliments and thanks for helping out can be very satisfying when they are given by one spouse to another.

called it the "3:00 to 6:00 P.M. problem" because it was during this time frame that the Center for Early Adolescence in North Carolina, where she was director, experienced a peak of adolescent referrals for clinical help.

But while latchkey children may be vulnerable to problems, keep in mind that the experiences of latchkey vary enormously, just as do the experiences of all children with working mothers (Belle & Burr, 1992). Parents need to give special attention to the ways their latchkey children's lives can be monitored effectively. Variations in latchkey experiences suggest that parental monitoring and authoritative parenting help the children to cope more effectively with latchkey experiences, especially in resisting peer pressure (Galambos & Maggs, 1989; Steinberg, 1986). The degree to which latchkey are at developmental risk remains unsettled. A positive sign is that researchers are beginning to conduct more precise analysis of latchkey experiences in an effort to determine which aspects of latchkey circumstances are the most detrimental and which aspects foster better adaptation (Rodman, Pratto, & Nelson, 1988; Steinberg, 1988).

Relocation

Geographical moves or relocations are a fact of life for many American families. The U.S. Census Bureau estimates that 17 percent of the population changes residences on a yearly basis (U.S. Bureau of the Census, 1986). This figure does not include multiple moves within the same year, so it may even underestimate the mobility of the U.S. population. The majority of these moves are made because of job demands (Cook & others, 1992). Moving can be especially stressful for children, disrupting friendship ties and activities (Brown & Orthner, 1990). The sources of support to which children and their parents turn, such as extended-family members and friends, are often unavailable to recently moved families.

While relocations are often stressful for all individuals involved, they may be especially stressful for adolescents because of their developing sense of identity and the importance of peer relations in their lives. In one study, geographical relocation was detrimental to the well-being of 12- to 14-year-old females but not their male counterparts (Brown & Orthner, 1990). The adolescent girls' life satisfaction was negatively related to both recent moves and to a high number of moves in their history, and a history of frequent moves was also associated with the girls' depression. However, the immediate negative effects on the girls disappeared over time. The researchers concluded that female adolescents may require more time to adapt to family relocations. Male adolescents may use sports and other activities in their new locale to ease the effects of relocation.

Unemployment

Unemployment rates and economic distress in the last decade reached levels unknown since the Great Depression. Plant closings, layoffs, and demotions are facts of life for many contemporary parents. What effects do they have on families and children's development? During the Great Depression, unemployment dramatically increased parental stress and undermined the school achievement and health of children (Angell, 1936; Elder, 1974).

In one recent investigation, the effects of changes in parental work status on young adolescents' school adjustment were explored (Flanagan & Eccles, 1993). Four groups were compared. *Deprived* families reported a layoff or demotion at time 1 but no recovery two years later. *Declining* families experienced a layoff or demotion between times 1 and 2. *Recovery* families reported similar losses at time 1 but reemployment two years later. *Stable* families reported no layoffs or demotion between times 1 and 2. Adolescents in deprived and declining families showed less competent peer interaction, and adolescents in deprived families were the most disruptive in school. The transition to adolescence was especially difficult for children whose parents were coping with changes in their work status.

CULTURE AND ETHNICITY

Cultures vary on a number of issues involving families, such as what the father's role in the family should be, the extent to which support systems are available to families, and how children should be disciplined. Although there are cross-cultural variations in parenting (Whiting & Edwards, 1988), in one study of parenting behavior in 186 cultures around the world, the most common pattern was a warm and controlling style, one that was neither permissive nor restrictive (Rohner & Rohner, 1981). The investigators commented that the majority of cultures have discovered, over many centuries, a "truth" that only recently emerged in the Western world—namely, that children's and adolescents' healthy social development is most effectively promoted by love and at least some moderate parental control.

Ethnic minority families differ from White American families in their size, structure and composition, reliance on kinship networks, and level of income and education (MacPhee, Fritz, & Miller-Heyl, 1993; Spencer & Dornbusch, 1990; Voight & Hans, 1993). Large and extended families are more common among ethnic minority groups than White Americans (Wilson, 1989). For example, more than 30 percent of Hispanic American families consists of five or more individuals (Keefe & Padilla, 1987). Black American and

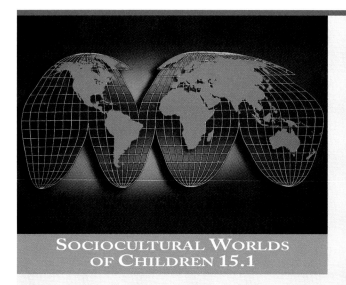

SOCIOCULTURAL WORLDS OF CHILDREN 15.1

Black and Hispanic Family Orientations

In the 1985 Children's Defense Fund Study, "Black and White Children in America: Key Facts" (Edelman, 1987), Black children were three times as likely as White children to:

- Be poor.
- Live with a parent who was separated from a spouse.
- Die of child abuse.

They are five times as likely to:

- Be dependent on welfare.

And they are 12 times as likely to:

- Live with a parent who never married.

Nonetheless, it is important to keep in mind that millions of Black American families are not on welfare, have children who stay in school and out of trouble, and find ways to cope with and overcome problems they experience during difficult times. In

A fourteen-year-old adolescent, his 6-year-old sister, and their grandmother. The Black cultural tradition of an extended family household has helped many Black parents cope with adverse social conditions.

1967, Martin Luther King reflected on the Black American family and gave the following caution: "As public awareness of the predicament of the Black family increases, there will be danger and opportunity. The opportunity will be to deal fully rather than haphazardly with the problem as a whole, as a social catastrophe brought on by many years of oppression. The danger is that the problems will be attributed to innate Black

Hispanic American children interact more with grandparents, aunts, uncles, cousins, and more distant relatives than do White American children.

Single-parent families are more common among Black Americans and Hispanic Americans than among White Americans. In comparison with two-parent households, single parents often have more limited resources of time, money, and energy. This shortage of resources may prompt them to encourage early autonomy among their children (Spencer & Dornbusch, 1990). Also, ethnic minority parents are less well educated and engage in less joint decision making than White American parents. And ethnic minority children are more likely to come from low-income families than White American children (Committee for Economic Development, 1987; McLoyd, in press). Although impoverished families often raise compe-

tent youth, poor parents may have a diminished capacity for supportive and involved parenting (McLoyd, in press).

Some aspects of home life can help to protect ethnic minority children from social patterns of injustice (Spencer & Dornbusch, 1990). The community and family can filter out destructive racist messages, parents can provide alternate frames of reference than those presented by the majority, and parents can also provide competent role models and encouragement (Bowman & Howard, 1985; Jones, 1990). And the extended family system in many ethnic minority families provides an important buffer to stress (Munsch, Wampler, & Dawson, 1992). To read further about the extended family system in Black American and Hispanic American families turn to Sociocultural Worlds of Children 15.1.

The Hispanic family reunion of the Limon family in Austin, Texas. Hispanic American children often grow up in families with a network of relatives that runs into scores of individuals.

weaknesses and used to justify further neglect and to rationalize continued oppression." In today's world, Dr. King's words still ring true. (McLoyd, in press; Ogbu, 1989; Spencer & Dornbusch, 1990).

The Black cultural tradition of an extended family household—in which one or several grandparents, uncles, aunts, siblings, or cousins, either live together or provide support—has helped many Black parents cope with adverse social conditions such as economic impoverishment (McAdoo, 1988). The Black extended family can be traced to the African heritage of many Black Americans, where in many cultures a newly married couple does not move away from relatives. Instead, the extended family assists its members with basic family functions. Researchers have found that the extended Black family helps to reduce the stress of poverty and single parenting through emotional support, sharing income and economic responsibility,

and surrogate parenting (McAdoo, 1988; Taylor & others, 1990). The presence of grandmothers in the households of many Black adolescents and their infants has been an important support system for both the teenage mother and the infant (Stevens, 1984). Active and involved extended family support systems also help a parent or parents from other ethnic minority groups cope with poverty and its related stress.

A basic value in Mexico is represented by the saying "As long as our family stays together, we are strong." Mexican children are brought up to stay close to their family, often playing with siblings rather than with schoolmates or neighborhood children, as American children usually do. Unlike the father in many American families, the Mexican father is the undisputed authority on all family matters and is usually obeyed without question. The mother is revered as the primary source of affection and care. This emphasis on family attachment leads the Mexican to say, "I will achieve mainly because of my family, and for my family, rather than myself." By contrast, the self-reliant American would say, "I will achieve mainly because of my ability and initiative and for myself rather than for my family." Unlike most Americans, families in Mexico tend to stretch out in a network of relatives that often runs to scores of individuals (Vega, 1990).

Both cultures—Mexican and American—have undergone considerable change in recent decades. Whether Mexican children will gradually take on the characteristics of American children, or whether American children will shift closer to Mexican children, is difficult to predict. The cultures of both countries will probably move to a new order more in keeping with future demands, retaining some common features of the old while establishing new priorities and values (Holtzmann, 1982).

GENDER AND PARENTING

What is the mother's role in the family? The father's role? How can mothers and fathers become cooperative, effective partners in parenting?

The Mother's Role

What do you think of when you hear the word *motherhood*? If you are like most people, you associate motherhood with a number of positive images, such as warm, selfless, dutiful, and tolerant (Matlin, 1993). And while most women expect that motherhood will be happy and fulfilling, the reality is that motherhood has been accorded relatively low prestige in our society (Hoffnung, 1984). When stacked up against money, power, and achievement, motherhood unfortunately doesn't fare too well and mothers rarely receive the appreciation they warrant. When children don't succeed or develop problems, our society has had

a tendency to attribute the lack of success or the development of problems to a single source—mothers. One of psychology's most important lessons is that behavior is multiply determined. So it is with children's development—when development goes awry, mothers are not the single cause of the problems even though our society stereotypes them in this way.

The reality of motherhood in the 1990s is that while fathers have increased their child-rearing responsibilities somewhat, the main responsibility for children still falls on the mother's shoulders (Matlin, 1993; Paludi, 1992). Mothers do far more family work than fathers do—two to three times more (Thompson & Walker, 1989). A few "exceptional" men do as much family work as their wives; in one study the figure was 10 percent of the men (Berk, 1985). Not only do women do more family work than men, the family work most women do is unrelenting, repetitive, and routine, often involving cleaning, cooking, child care, shopping, laundry, and straightening up.

Children can significantly benefit from interaction with a caring, accessible, and dependable father who fosters a sense of trust and confidence.

The family work most men do is infrequent, irregular, and non-routine, often involving household repairs, taking out the garbage, and yard work. Women report that they often have to do several tasks at once, which helps to explain why they find domestic work less relaxing and more stressful than men do (Shaw, 1988).

Because family work is intertwined with love and embedded in family relations, it has complex and contradictory meanings (DeVault, 1987). Most women feel that family tasks are mindless but essential. They usually enjoy tending to the needs of their loves ones and keeping the family going, even if they do not find the activities themselves enjoyable and fulfilling. Family work is both positive and negative for women. They are unsupervised and rarely criticized, they plan and control their own work, and they have only their own standards to meet. However, women's family work is often worrisome, tiresome, menial, repetitive, isolating, unfinished, inescapable, and often unappreciated. It is not surprising that men report that they are more satisfied with their marriage than women do.

In sum, the role of the mother brings with it benefits as well as limitations. Although motherhood is not enough to fill most women's entire lives, for most mothers, it is one of the most meaningful experiences in their lives (Hoffnung, 1984).

The Father's Role

The father's role has undergone major changes (Biller, 1993; Bronstein, 1988; Davis, DeLuccie, & Chebra, 1993; Lamb, 1986). During the colonial period in America, fathers were primarily responsible for moral teaching. Fathers provided guidance and values, especially through religion. With the Industrial Revolution, the father's role changed; he gained the responsibility as the breadwinner, a role that continued through the Great Depression. By the end of World War II, another role for fathers emerged, that of a gender role model. Although being a breadwinner and moral guardian continued to be important father roles, attention shifted to his role as a male, especially for sons. Then, in the 1970s, the current interest in the father as an active, nurturant, caregiving parent emerged. Rather than being responsible only for the discipline and control of older children and for providing the family's economic base, the father now is being evaluated in terms of his active, nurturant involvement with his children (McBride, 1991).

How actively involved are today's fathers with their children? Fathers in two-parent families typically spend about one-fourth to one-third as much time with young children as do mothers, although in the past decade fathers have slightly increased their participation (Biller, 1993). Having a father at home is no guarantee of meaningful paternal involvement with the child. While some fathers are exceptionally committed parents, other fathers are virtual strangers to their children even though they reside in the same household.

Children's social development can significantly benefit from interaction with a caring, accessible, and dependable father who fosters a sense of trust and confidence (Bretherton, Golby, & Page, 1993). The father's positive family involvement assumes special importance in developing children's social competence because he is often the only male the child encounters on a regular day-to-day basis.

In one recent investigation, Frank Furstenberg and Kathleen Harris (1992) documented how nurturant fathering can overcome children's difficult life circumstances. In low-income Black American families, children who reported close attachments and feelings of identification with their fathers during adolescence were twice as likely as young adults to have found a stable job or to have entered college, and were 75 percent less likely to have become unwed parents, 80 percent less likely to have been in jail, and 50 percent less likely to have developed depression. Unfortunately, however, only 10 percent of the economically disadvantaged children they studied experienced a stable, close relationship with their father during childhood and adolescence. In two other studies, college females and males reported better personal and social adjustment when they had grown up in a home with a nurturant, involved father rather than a negligent or rejecting father (Fish & Biller, 1973; Reuter & Biller, 1973).

Partners in Parenting

Father-mother cooperation and mutual respect helps the child to develop positive attitudes toward both males and females (Biller, 1993). It is much easier for working parents to cope with changing family circumstances and day care issues when the father and mother equitably share child-rearing responsibilities. Mothers feel less stress and have more positive attitudes toward their husbands when they are supportive partners.

At this point we have discussed a number of ideas about the effects of divorce on children, stepfamilies, working parents, culture and ethnicity, and gender and parenting. A summary of these ideas is presented in Concept Table 15.2.

The father's role in China has been slow to change, but it is changing. Traditionally in China, the father has been expected to be strict, the mother kind. The father is characterized as a stern disciplinarian; the child is expected to fear the father. The notion of the strict father has ancient roots. The Chinese character for father (fu) evolved from a primitive character representing a hand holding a cane, which symbolizes authority. However, the twentieth century has witnessed a decline in the father's authority. Younger fathers are more inclined to allow children to express their opinions and be more independent. Influenced to a degree by the increased employment of mothers, Chinese fathers are becoming more involved in caring for their children. In some instances, intergenerational tension has developed between fathers and sons, as younger generations behave in less traditional ways (Ho, 1987).

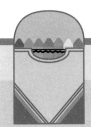

PERSPECTIVES ON PARENTING AND EDUCATION

The Goals of Caregiving

Are there some overarching goals that caregivers should set in their effort to take responsibility for the development of infants? Infant researcher and parent educator Burton White (1990) believes there are three basic general goals that caregivers should pursue:

- To give the infant a sense of being loved and cared for
- To help the infant to develop specific skills
- To encourage the infant's interest in the outside world

Giving the Infant a Sense of Being Loved and Cared For

In the first two years of life, all infants and toddlers have a strong need to establish an attachment to one or more older humans. In the process of developing this attachment they begin their long road to being socialized and socializing others. As we have seen, Erikson (1968) believes the central goal of the first year of life is the development of a sense of trust rather than mistrust on the part of the infant. This is in keeping with White's perspective as well as of this text. The frequency and degree of discomfort and distress babies feel depends in large part on the kind of treatment they experience. There is no way to prevent a fair amount of unhappiness from such factors as hunger, indigestion, teething, and a cold diaper. However, such unhappiness can be prolonged and allowed to escalate if the avoidable discomfort and distress are not responded to promptly.

CONCEPT TABLE 15.2

The Effects of Divorce on Children, Stepfamilies, Working Parents, Culture and Ethnicity, and Gender and Parenting

Concept	Processes/Related Ideas	Characteristics/Description
The effects of divorce on children	Their nature	Two main models of divorce effects have been proposed: the father-absence model and the multiple-factor model. The father-absence model that emphasizes only family structure effects is overly simplistic. The contemporary multiple-factor model takes into account the complexity of the divorce context, including conflict and post-divorce family functioning. Among the important factors in understanding the effects of divorce on children are age and developmental changes, conflict, sex of the child, and the nature of custody. In recent years, developmentalists have moved away from the model of single parents as atypical or pathological, focusing more on the diversity of children's responses to divorce and the factors that facilitate or disrupt the adjustment of children in these family circumstances.
Stepfamilies	Their effects	Just as divorce produces disequilibrium and stress for adolescents, so does remarriage. Over time, preadolescent boys seem to improve more than girls in stepfather families. Adolescence is an especially difficult time for adjustment to the entrance of a stepparent. Children's relationships with biological parents are consistently better than with stepparents, and children's adjustment is adversely affected the more complex the stepfamily becomes. An authoritative environment at home and at school help children adjust to living in a divorced or stepparent family.
Working parents	Nature of their effects on children	Overall, the mother working outside the home does not have an adverse effect on the child's development. Latchkey experiences do not have a uniformly negative influence on children's development. Parental monitoring and participation in structured activities with competent supervision are important influences on

Caregivers who respond to infants with loving care and attention make strong contributions to the development of competence in the infant. As White indicates, no requirement of good caregiving is more natural or more rewarding than tending to the baby in a loving and attentive way.

Helping the Infant to Develop Specific Skills

Over the course of the first two years of life, an infant develops from a creature who cannot think, use language, socialize with a human being, run, walk, or even deliberately move around, to a socialized individual who has accumulated a number of specific skills. Good childrearing in the first two years of an infant's life includes knowing what the normal pattern of emerging skills is and facilitating their emergence and development. Most of these skills evolve unaided under average rearing circumstances, but good parenting ensures the optimal development of these skills. Throughout the three chapters on infant development, we have specified the normal patterns of development of physical, cognitive, and social skills during the infant years and how caregivers can interact with infants in developmentally appropriate ways to enhance these skills. Facilitating the development of the infant's specific skills is tied to White's third general goal of caregiving competence.

Encouraging the Infant's Interest in the Outside World

Whether an infant first learns to reach for objects at 3 months or at 5 months is probably of less consequence than seeing that the babies are regularly involved in activities that interest them. Instead of trying to push infants to develop skills beyond their current level (and become a "superbaby"), it is more important for parents to interact with the infant in ways that keep the infant interested, cheerful, and alert. After the first several months, infants should be actively enjoying themselves at least some of the time. ■

Concept	Processes/Related Ideas	Characteristics/Description
		latchkey children's adjustment. Relocation may have a more adverse effect on adolescents than children, but research on this issue is sparse. Unemployment of parents has a detrimental effect on children's development.
Culture and ethnicity	Nature of their effects	Authoritative parenting is the most common child-rearing pattern around the world. Ethnic minority families differ from White American families in their size, structure, and composition; their reliance on kinship networks; and their levels of income and education.
Gender and parenting	The mother's role	Most people associate motherhood with a number of positive images, but the reality is that motherhood is accorded a relatively low status in our society. Unfortunately, when children's development goes awry, mothers are often labeled as the single cause of the problem. Mothers do far more family work than fathers do. Despite its stressful aspects, for most mothers, motherhood is one of the most meaningful experiences in their lives.
	The father's role	Over time, the father's role in the child's development has evolved from moral teacher to breadwinner to gender role model to nurturant caregiver. Fathers are much less involved in childrearing than mothers are. Children's social development can significantly benefit from interaction with a caring, accessible, and dependable father who fosters trust and confidence.
	Partners in parenting	Father-mother cooperation and mutual respect help the child to develop positive attitudes toward both males and females. Mothers feel less stress and have more positive attitudes toward their husband when he is a supportive partner.

CONCLUSIONS

Parents cradle children's lives. For most children, parents are the critical caregivers.

We began this chapter by describing the diversity of families and parenting. Then, we examined the nature of some important family processes—reciprocal socialization and the family as a system, the developmental construction of relationships, adapting parenting to developmental changes in the child, and sociocultural, historical changes. We studied the family life cycle and its six stages: leaving home and becoming an adult, the new couple, becoming parents and families with children, the family with adolescents, midlife families, and the family in later life. We read about the parental role and parenting styles, sibling relationships and birth order, and family processes in adolescence. We also explored the effects of divorce on children, stepfamilies, working parents, culture and ethnicity, and gender and parenting, especially focusing on the mother's role, the father's role, and the importance of being partners in parenting. At the end of the chapter we considered the goals of caregiving. Remember that to obtain a summary of the chapter again read the two concept tables on pages 450 and 462.

In the next chapter, we turn our attention to the roles of peers, play, and the media in children's development. You will discover that the worlds of families and peers are more connected than once was believed.

KEY TERMS

reciprocal socialization The view that socialization is bidirectional: children socialize parents just as parents socialize them. (435)

scaffolding An important caregiver's role in early parent-child interaction. Through their attention and choice of behaviors, caregivers provide a framework around which they interact with infants. (435)

developmental construction view The belief that as individuals grow up they acquire modes of relating to others. (436)

continuity view In this view, the emphasis is on the role that early parent-child relationships play in constructing a basic way of relating to others throughout the lifespan. (436)

discontinuity view In this view, the emphasis is on change and variety of interaction partner in relationships over time as those influence formation modes of relating to others. (436)

leaving home and becoming a single adult In this first stage in the family life cycle, the young adult separates from the family of origin without cutting off ties completely or fleeing in a reactive way to find some form of substitute emotional refugee. (438)

launching The process in which the youth moves into adulthood and exits his/her family of origin. (438)

the new couple In this second stage in the family life cycle, two individuals from separate families of origin unite to form a new family system. (438)

becoming parents and families with children The third stage in the family life cycle requires that adults now move up a generation and become caregivers to the younger generation. (439)

family with adolescents During this fourth stage in the family life cycle, parents cope with the adolescent who is seeking autonomy and his or her own identity. In this stage, parents often either clamp down and put pressure on the adolescent to conform, or they may become more permissive, giving the adolescent extensive freedom. Developing a flexible, adaptive approach to parenting is best in this stage. (439)

family at midlife The fifth stage in the family life cycle is a time of launching children, playing an important role in linking generations, and adapting to midlife changes in development. (439)

family in later life In this sixth and final stage in the family life cycle, retirement alters a couple's lifestyle. Grandparenting also characterizes many families in later life. (439)

authoritarian parenting A restrictive, punitive style that exhorts a child to follow the parent's directions and to respect work and effort. Firm limits and controls are placed on a child, and little verbal exchange is allowed. This style is associated with children's social incompetence. (443)

authoritative parenting A parenting style that encourages children to be independent but still places limits and controls on their actions.

Extensive verbal give-and-take is allowed, and parents are warm and nurturant toward the child. This style is associated with children's social competence. (443)

permissive-indifferent parenting A parenting style in which the parent is very uninvolved in the child's life. It is associated with children's social incompetence, especially lack of self-control. (443)

permissive-indulgent parenting A parenting style in which parents are highly involved with their children but place few demands or controls on them. This is associated with children's social incompetence, especially lack of self-control. (443)

father-absence model States that, when adolescents from father-absent and father-present families are compared, any differences that occur are attributed to the family structure variations. (449)

multiple-factor model of divorce effects Takes into account the complexity of the divorce context and examines a number of influences on the child's development, including not only family structure, but also the strengths and weaknesses of the child prior to the divorce, the nature of the events surrounding the divorce itself, the type of custody involved, and visitation patterns. (450)

boundary ambiguity The uncertainty in stepfamilies of who is in or out of the family and who is performing or responsible for certain tasks in the family system. (454)

SUGGESTED READINGS

Brazelton, T. B. (1984). *To listen to a child.* Reading, MA: Addison-Wesley. This book is written for parents and addresses parenting issues throughout the childhood years. It especially focuses on problematic events that arise in children's lives and how parents can effectively handle them.

Dreikurs, R. (1964). *Children: The challenge.* New York: Hawthorn Books. Dreikurs tells parents how to discipline their children more effectively by understanding them and meeting their needs. He especially advocates democratic "family counsel" sessions.

Ginott, H. (1969). *Between parent and teenager.* New York: Avon. Despite the fact that this book is well past adolescence in its own years (it was published in 1969), it continues to be one of the best books for parents who want to communicate more effectively with their teenagers.

Kalter, N. (1990). *Growing up with divorce.* New York: The Free Press. This book is written for divorced parents and provides them with guidelines for helping their children avoid emotional problems. It is especially designed to counteract the long-term effects of divorce on children.

Visher, E., & Visher, J. (1988). *Old loyalties, new ties.* New York: Brunner/Mazel. This book covers a number of strategies that will help stepfamilies cope more effectively with problems they face. The authors also provide insights about different types of therapy with stepfamilies.

West Church, Boston 1900,
Maurice Brazil Prendergast
(Detail)

16

Peers, Play, and the Media

The little ones leaped, and shouted, and
Laugh'd and all the hills echoed.

—William Blake

> *You are troubled at seeing him spend his early years in doing nothing. What!*
> *Is it nothing to be happy? Is it nothing to skip, to play, to run about all day*
> *long? Never in his life will he be so busy as now.*
>
> —Jean-Jacques Rousseau

IMAGES OF CHILDREN

The Importance of Friends

Think back over your childhood and adolescent years for a moment. Who were your best friends? Why were they important to you? Consider the important role that friendship plays in this 13–year-old girl's life:

> My best friend is nice. She is honest, and I can trust her. I can tell her my innermost secrets and know that nobody else will find out about them. I have other friends, too, but she is my best friend. We consider each other's feelings and don't want to hurt each other. We help each other when we have problems. We have most of our classes together at school and we often do our homework together. We make up funny names for people and laugh ourselves silly. We make lists of which boys are the sexiest and which are the ugliest. My best friend means a lot to me. I don't know what I would do without her.

Researchers have found that friendships play an important role in children's development. One aspect of children's development that friendship influences is school behavior. In one study, children with many friends at the time they entered kindergarten developed more positive perceptions of school than children with fewer friends (Ladd, 1990). And children who maintained these friend-ships also liked school better as the school year progressed. Making new friends in the classroom also predicted gains in school performance over the year while being disliked by other children forecast unfavorable school attitudes and performance.

Friendships also can help ease the stressful transition from elementary school to middle or junior high school. In one study, as children moved from an elementary school through the first year of junior high school, those who reported more contact with their friends and higher quality friendships had more positive perceptions of themselves and of their junior high school than their low-friendship counterparts (Berndt, Hawkins, & Hoyle, 1986).

PREVIEW

Children's growth is shaped by successive waves of peers and friends and play is their work. This chapter focuses on three important dimensions of children's lives: Peers, play, and the media.

PEERS

As children grow older, peer relations consume increasing amounts of their time. What is the function of a child's peer group? Although children spend increasingly more time with peers as they become older, are there ways in which family and peer relations are coordinated? What is the developmental course of peer relations in childhood? Why are some children popular, rejected, or neglected? What is the role of cognition in peer relations? What is the nature of friendship and of peer relations in adolescence?

Peer Group Functions

Peers *are children of about the same age or maturity level.* Same-age peer interaction fills a unique role in our culture (Hartup, 1976). Age grading would occur even if schools were not age graded and children were left alone to determine the composition of their own societies. One of the most important functions of the peer group is to provide a source of information and comparison about the world outside the family. Children receive feedback about their abilities from their peer group. Children evaluate what they do in terms of whether it is better than, as good as, or worse than what other children do. It is hard to do this at home because siblings are usually older or younger.

Are peers necessary for development? When peer monkeys who have been reared together are separated, they become depressed and less advanced socially (Suomi, Harlow, & Domek, 1970). The human development literature contains a classic example of the importance of peers in social development. Anna Freud (Freud & Dann, 1951) studied six children from different families who banded together after their parents were killed in World War II. Intensive peer attachment was observed; the children formed a tightly knit group, dependent on one another and aloof with outsiders. Even though deprived of parental care, they became neither delinquent nor psychotic.

Thus, good peer relations may be necessary for normal social development. Social isolation, or the inability to "plug in" to a social network, is linked with many problems and disturbances ranging from delinquency and problem drinking to depression (Kupersmidt & Coie, 1990; Simons, Conger, & Wu, 1992). In one investigation, poor peer relations in childhood was associated with a tendency to drop out of school and delinquent behavior in adolescence (Roff, Sells, & Golden, 1972). In another investigation, harmonious peer relations in adolescence were related to positive mental health at midlife (Hightower, 1990).

As you might have detected from our discussion of peer relations thus far, peer influences can be both positive and negative. Both Jean Piaget (1932) and Harry Stack Sullivan (1953) were influential theorists who stressed that it is through peer interaction that children and adolescents learn the symmetrical reciprocity mode of relationships discussed in chapter 15. Children explore the principles of fairness and justice by working through disagreements with peers. They also learn to be keen observers of peers' interests and perspectives in order to smoothly integrate themselves into ongoing peer activities. In addition, Sullivan argued that adolescents learn to be skilled and sensitive partners in intimate relationships by forging close friendships with selected peers. These intimacy skills are carried forward to help form the foundation of later dating and marital relationships, according to Sullivan (Buhrmester, 1993).

By contrast, some theorists have emphasized the negative influences of peers on children's and adolescents' development. Being rejected or overlooked by peers leads some adolescents to feel lonely or hostile. Further, such rejection and neglect by peers are related to an individual's subsequent mental health and criminal problems. Some theorists have also described the adolescent peer culture as a corrupt influence that undermines parental values and control. Further, peers can introduce adolescents to alcohol, drugs, delinquency, and other forms of behavior that adults view as maladaptive.

The Distinct but Coordinated Worlds of Parent-Child and Peer Relations

What are some of the similarities and differences between peer and parent-child relationships? Children touch, smile, frown, and vocalize when they interact with both parents and peers. However, rough-and-tumble play occurs mainly with other children, not with adults, and, in times of stress, children often move toward their parents rather than toward their peers.

In addition to evaluating whether children engage in similar or dissimilar behaviors when interacting with parents and peers, it is also important to examine whether children's peer relations develop independently of parent-child relationships or are wedded to them. Recall our discussion of the developmental construction of relationships in chapter 15, which consists of two different views. In the continuity view, early parent-child relationships strongly influence children's subsequent peer relations and friendships. By contrast, in the discontinuity view, peer relations and friendship have a more independent developmental path.

A number of theorists and researchers argue that parent-child relationships serve as emotional bases for exploring and enjoying peer relations (Cassidy & others, 1992; Hart, Ladd, & Burelson, 1990; Hartup, 1989; Leonoff, 1993; Lollis, 1993; McFadyen-Ketchum, 1993; Mize & others, 1993; Park, 1993; Crockenberg & Lourie, 1993; Pettit, Dodge, & Brown, 1988; Profilet & Ladd, 1993; Youngblade & Belsky, 1992). In one study, the relationship history of each peer helped to predict the nature of peer interaction (Olweus, 1980) (see figure 16.1). Some boys were highly aggressive ("bullies") and other boys were the recipients of aggression ("whipping boys") throughout their preschool years. The bullies and the whipping boys had distinctive relationship histories. The bullies' parents frequently rejected them, were authoritarian, were permissive about their sons' aggression, and the bullies' families were characterized by discord. By contrast, the whipping boys' parents were anxious and overprotective, taking special care to have their sons avoid aggression. The well-adjusted boys in the study were much less likely to be involved in aggressive peer interchanges than the bullies and whipping boys. Their parents did not sanction aggression, and their responsive involvement with their sons promoted the development of self-assertion rather than aggression or wimpish behavior.

Parents also may model or coach their children in the ways of relating to peers. In one investigation, parents indicated they recommended specific strategies to their children regarding peer relations (Rubin & Sloman, 1984). For example, parents told their children how to mediate disputes or how to become less shy with others. They also encouraged them to be tolerant and to resist peer pressure. In another study, parents who frequently indicated peer contacts for their preschool children had children who were more accepted by their peers and higher levels of prosocial behavior (Ladd & Hart, 1992).

A key aspect of peer relations can be traced to basic lifestyle decisions by parents (Cooper & Ayers-Lopez, 1985). Parents' choices of neighborhoods, churches, schools, and their own friends influence the pool from which their children might select possible friends. For example, the chosen schools can lead to specific grouping policies, as well as particular academic and extracurricular activities. In turn, such facts affect which students their children meet, their purpose in interacting, and eventually who become friends. For example, classrooms in

FIGURE 16.1

Peer aggression: The influence of the relationship histories of each peer.

which teachers encourage more cooperative peer interchanges have fewer isolates.

In sum, parent-child and peer worlds are coordinated. But they also are distinct. Earlier we indicated that rough-and-tumble play occurs mainly with other children, not in parent-child interaction. And, in times of stress, children often turn to parents, not peers, for support. Peer relations also are more likely to consist of interaction on a much more equal basis than parent-child relations. In parent-child relations, since parents have greater knowledge and authority, their children must often learn how to conform to rules and regulations laid down by parents. With peers, children learn to formulate and assert their own opinions, appreciate the perspective of peers, cooperatively negotiate solutions to disagreements, and evolve standards of conduct that are mutually acceptable.

The Developmental Course of Peer Relations in Childhood

Although we generally think of peer relations as assuming an important role in early childhood, some researchers believe that the quality of peer interaction in infancy provides valuable information about social development (Hay, 1985; Mueller, 1985; Vandell, 1985). For example, in one investigation, positive affect in infant peer relations was related to easy access to peer play groups and to peer popularity in early childhood

(Howes, 1985). As increasing numbers of children attend day care, peer interaction in infancy takes on a more important developmental role.

The frequency of peer interaction, both positive and negative, picks up considerably during early childhood (Hartup, 1983). Although aggressive interaction and rough-and-tumble play increase, the *proportion* of aggressive exchanges to friendly exchanges decreases. Children tend to abandon their immature and inefficient social exchanges with age and acquire more mature ways of relating to peers.

Children spend an increasing amount of time in peer interaction during middle and late childhood and adolescence. In one investigation, children interacted with peers 10 percent of their day at age 2, 20 percent at age 4, and more than 40 percent between the ages of 7 and 11. In a typical school day, episodes with peers totaled 299 times per day (Barker & Wright, 1951).

Peer Popularity, Rejection, and Neglect

Children often think, "What can I do to get all of the kids at school to like me?" or "What's wrong with me? Something must be wrong or I would be more popular." What makes a child popular with peers? Children who give out the most reinforcements are often popular. So is a child who listens carefully to other children and maintains open lines of communication. Being themselves, being happy, showing enthusiasm and concern for others, and being self-confident but not conceited are characteristics that serve children well in their quest for peer popularity (Hartup, 1983). In one study, popular children were more likely to communicate clearly with their peers, to elicit their peers' attention, and to maintain conversation with peers more than were unpopular children (Kennedy, 1990).

Recently, developmentalists have distinguished between two types of children who often have low acceptance with their peers: those who are neglected and those who are rejected (Coie, 1993; Coie & Koeppl, 1990; East, 1991; Parker & Asher, 1987). **Neglected children** *often receive little attention from their peers and have few, if any, friends, but they are not necessarily disliked.* **Rejected children** *are disliked by their peers. They are more likely to be disruptive and aggressive than their neglected counterparts.* Rejected children often have more serious adjustment problems than those who are neglected (Kupersmidt & Patterson, 1993; Parker & Asher, 1987). For example, in one recent study, 112 fifth-grade boys were evaluated over a period of seven years until the end of high school (Kupersmidt & Coie, 1990). The key factor in predicting whether rejected children would engage in delinquent behavior or drop out of school later during adolescence was their aggression toward peers in elementary school.

Not all rejected children are aggressive (Bierman, Smoot, & Aumillel, 1993). While aggression and its related characteristics of impulsiveness and disruptiveness underlie rejection about half the time, approximately 10 to 20 percent of rejected children are shy (Cillessen & others, 1992).

An important question to ask is: How can neglected children and rejected children be trained to interact more effectively with their peers? The goal of training programs with neglected children is often to help them attract attention from their peers in positive ways and to hold their attention by asking questions, by listening in a warm and friendly way, and by saying things about themselves that relate to the peers' interests. They also are taught to enter groups more effectively (Duck, 1988).

The goal of training programs with rejected children is often to help them listen to peers and "hear what they say" instead of trying to dominate peer interactions. Rejected children are trained to join peers without trying to change what is taking place in the peer group.

Children may need to be persuaded or motivated that these strategies work effectively and are satisfying. In some programs, children are shown videotapes of appropriate peer interaction; then they are asked to comment on them and to draw lessons from what they have seen. In other training programs, popular children are taught to be more accepting of neglected or rejected peers.

One issue that has recently been raised about improving the peer relations of rejected children is whether the focus should be on improving their prosocial skills (better empathy, careful listening, improved communication skills, and so on) or on reducing their aggressive, disruptive behavior and improving their self-control (Coie & Koeppl, 1990). Improving the prosocial skills of rejected children does not automatically

eliminate their aggressive or disruptive behavior. Aggression often leads to reinforcement because peers give in to aggressive children's demands. Thus, in addition to teaching better prosocial skills to rejected children, direct steps must also be taken to eliminate their aggressive actions. Further, acquiring positive status with peers may take time to achieve because it is hard for peers to change their opinions if children frequently engage in aggressive conduct. Next, we turn our attention to the role of social cognition in understanding peer relations. Part of this discussion further considers ideas about reducing the aggression of children in their peer encounters.

Social Cognition

How might children's thoughts contribute to their peer relations? Three possibilities are through their perspective-taking ability, social information-processing skills, and social knowledge.

Perspective taking *involves the ability to take another's point of view.* As children enter the elementary school years, both their peer interaction and perspective-taking ability increase. Reciprocity is especially important in peer interchanges at this point in development—playing games, functioning in groups, and cultivating friendships, for example. One of the important skills that helps elementary school children improve their peer relations is communication effectiveness. In one investigation, the communication exchanges among peers at kindergarten, first-, third-, and fifth-grade levels were evaluated (Krauss & Glucksberg, 1969). Children were asked to tell a peer about a new set of block designs. The peer sat behind a screen with blocks similar to those the subject communicated to her (see figure 16.2). The kindergarten children made numerous errors in telling the peer how to duplicate the novel block stack. The older children were much more efficient in communicating to a peer how to construct the novel block stack, especially the fifth-graders. They were sensitive to the communication demands of the task and were far superior at perspective taking and figuring out how they had to talk for the peer to understand them. During elementary school, children also become more efficient at understanding complex messages, so the listening skills of the peer in this experiment probably helped the communicating peer as well. Other researchers have documented the link between perspective-taking skills and the quality of peer relations, especially in the elementary school years (LeMare & Rubin, 1987).

Of special interest is how children process information about peer relations (Dodge, 1993; Quiggle & others, 1992). For example, a boy accidentally trips and knocks a peer's soft drink out of his hand. The peer misinterprets the encounter as hostile, which leads him to retaliate aggressively against the boy. Through repeated encounters of this kind, other peers come to perceive the aggressive boys as habitually acting inappropriately. Peer relations researcher Kenneth Dodge (1983) argues that children go through five steps in processing information about their social world: decoding social cues, interpreting, searching for a response, selecting an optimal response, and enacting. Dodge has found that aggressive boys are more likely to perceive another child's actions as hostile when the

FIGURE 16.2

Experimental arrangement of speaker and listener in the investigation of the development of communication skills.

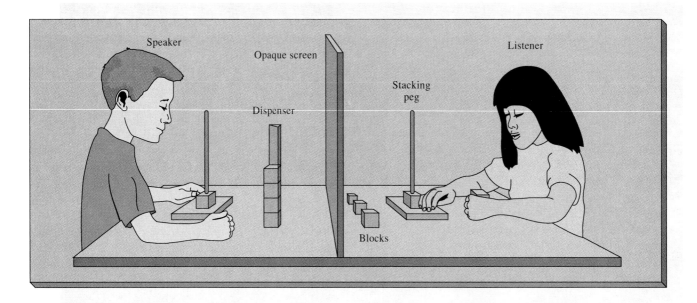

child's intention is ambiguous, and when aggressive boys search for clues to determine a peer's intention, they respond more rapidly, less efficiently, and less reflectively than nonaggressive children. These are among the social cognitive factors believed to be involved in the nature of children's conflicts (Dodge & Feldman, 1990; Schantz, 1988).

Social knowledge also is involved in children's ability to get along with peers. An important part of children's social life involves choosing which goals to pursue in poorly defined or ambiguous situations. Social relationship goals are also important, such as how to initiate and maintain a social bond. Children need to know what scripts to follow to get children to be their friends. For example, as part of the script for getting friends, it helps to know that saying nice things, regardless of what the peer does or says, will make the peer like the child more.

From a social cognitive perspective, children who are maladjusted do not have adequate social cognitive skills to interact skillfully with others (Kelly & de Armas, 1989; Rabiner & others, 1991; Weissberg, Caplan, & Sivo, 1989). One investigation explored the possibility that maladjusted children do not have the social cognitive skills necessary for positive social interaction (Asarnow & Callan, 1985). Boys with and without peer adjustment difficulties were identified, and their social cognitive skills were assessed. Boys without peer adjustment problems generated more alternative solutions to problems, proposed more assertive and mature solutions, gave less intense aggressive solutions, showed more adaptive planning, and evaluated physically aggressive responses less positively than did the boys with peer adjustment problems.

The world of peers is one of varying acquaintances; children interact with some children they barely know and with others they know well for hours every day. It is to the latter type—friends—that we now turn.

Friendships

At the beginning of the chapter, we learned that friendships play an important role in helping children adapt to school. Let's now explore the world of children's friendships in more detail, examining the importance of friendships, Sullivan's ideas on friendships, and intimacy and similarity in friendships.

The Importance of Friendship

Friendships serve six functions (Gottman & Parker, 1987) (see figure 16.3):

1. Companionship. Friendship provides children with a familiar partner, someone who is willing to spend time with them and join in collaborative activities.
2. Stimulation. Friendship provides adolescents with interesting information, excitement, and amusement.
3. Physical support. Friendship provides time, resources, and assistance.
4. Ego support. Friendship provides the expectation of support, encouragement, and feedback that helps children to maintain an impression of themselves as competent, attractive, and worthwhile individuals.
5. Social comparison. Friendship provides information about where children stand vis-à-vis others and whether children are doing okay.
6. Intimacy/affection. Friendship provides children with a warm, close, trusting relationship with another individual, a relationship that involves self-disclosure.

FIGURE 16.3

The functions of friendships.

Companionship

Stimulation

Physical support

Ego support

Social comparison

Intimacy/affection

Each friend represents a world in us, a world possibly not born until they arrive, and it is only by this meeting that a new world is born.

—Anaïs Nin

Sullivan's Ideas on Friendship

Harry Stack Sullivan (1953) was the most influential theorist to discuss the importance of friendships. He argued that there is a dramatic increase in the psychological importance and intimacy of close friends during early adolescence. In contrast to other psychoanalytic theorists' narrow emphasis on the importance of parent-child relationships, Sullivan contended that friends also play important roles in shaping children's and adolescents' well-being and development. In terms of well-being, he argued that all people have a number of basic social needs, including the need for tenderness (secure attachment), playful companionship, social acceptance, intimacy, and sexual relations. Whether or not these needs are fulfilled largely determines our emotional well-being. For example, if the need for playful companionship goes unmet, then we become bored and depressed; if the need for social acceptance is not met, we suf-

fer a lowered sense of self-worth. Developmentally, friends become increasingly depended upon to satisfy these needs during adolescence, and thus the ups-and-downs of experiences with friends increasingly shape adolescents' state of well-being. In particular, Sullivan believed that the need for intimacy intensifies during early adolescence, motivating teenagers to seek out close friends. He felt that, if adolescents failed to forge such close friendships, they would experience painful feelings of loneliness coupled with a reduced sense of self-worth.

Research findings support many of Sullivan's ideas. For example, adolescents report more often disclosing intimate and personal information to their friends than do younger children (Buhrmester & Furman, 1987). Adolescents also say they depend more on friends than parents to satisfy needs for companionship, reassurance of worth, and intimacy (Furman & Buhrmester, in press). In one recent study, daily interviews with 13- to 16-year-old adolescents over a five-day period were conducted to find out how much time they spent engaged in meaningful interactions with friends and parents (Carbery & Buhrmester, 1993). Adolescents spent an average of 103 minutes per day in meaningful interactions with friends compared to just 28 minutes per day with parents. In addition, the quality of friendship is more strongly linked to feelings of well-being during adolescence than during childhood. Teenagers with superficial friendships, or no close friendships at all, report feeling lonelier and more depressed and anxious, and they have a lower sense of self-esteem that teenagers with intimate friendships (Buhrmester, 1990).

A man's growth is seen in the successive choirs of his friends.

—Ralph Waldo Emerson

The increased closeness and importance of friendship challenges adolescents to master evermore sophisticated social competencies. Viewed from the developmental constructionist perspective described in chapter 15, adolescent friendship represents a new mode of relating to others that is best described as a *symmetrical intimate mode.* During childhood, being a good friend involves being a good playmate: Children must know how to play cooperatively and must be skilled at smoothly entering ongoing games on the playground (Putallaz, 1983; Taylor & Machida, 1993). By contrast, the greater intimacy of adolescent friendships demand that teenagers learn a number of close relationship competencies, including knowing how to self-disclose appropriately, being able to provide emotional support to friends, and managing disagreements in ways that do not undermine the intimacy of the friendship (Buhrmester, 1990; Paul & White, 1990). These competencies require more sophisticated skills in perspective taking, empathy, and social problem solving than were involved in childhood playmate competencies (Buhrmester & others, 1988; Selman, 1980).

In addition to the role they play in the socialization of social competence, friendship relationships are often important sources of support. Sullivan described how friends support one another's sense of personal worth. When close friends disclose their mutual insecurities and fears about themselves, they discover that they are not "abnormal" and that they have nothing to be ashamed of. Friends also act as important confidants that help children and adolescents work through upsetting problems (such as difficulties with parents or the breakup of romance) by providing both emotional support and informational advice (Savin-Williams & Berndt, 1990). In addition, friends can become active partners in building a sense of identity. During countless hours of conversation, friends act as sounding boards as teenagers explore issues ranging from future plans to stances on religious and moral issues.

Intimacy and Similarity in Friendship

In the context of friendship, *intimacy* has been defined in different ways. For example, it has been defined broadly to include everything in a relationship that makes the relationship seem close or intense. In most research studies, though, **intimacy in friendship** *is defined narrowly as self-disclosure or sharing of private thoughts.* Private or personal knowledge about a friend also has been used as an index of intimacy (Selman, 1980; Sullivan, 1953).

The most consistent finding in the last two decades of research on friendships is that intimacy is an important feature of friendship (Berndt & Perry, 1990; Rotenberg, 1993). When individuals are asked what they want from a friend or how they can tell someone is their best friend, they frequently say that a best friend will share problems with them, understand them, and listen when they talk about their own thoughts or feelings. When young children talk about their friendships, comments about intimate self-disclosure or mutual understanding are rare. In one investigation, friendship intimacy was more prominent in 13- to 16-year-olds than in 10- to 13-year-olds (Buhrmester, 1989).

Are the friendships of girls more intimate than the friendships of boys? When asked to describe their best friends, girls refer to intimate conversations and faithfulness more than boys do. For example, girls are more likely to describe their best friend as "sensitive just like me," or "trustworthy just like me" (Duck, 1975). The assumption behind this gender difference is that girls are more oriented toward interpersonal relationships. Boys may discourage one another from openly disclosing their problems as part of their masculine, competitive nature (Maccoby, 1991). Boys make themselves vulnerable to being called "wimps" if they can't handle their own problems and insecurities.

Adolescents also regard loyalty or faithfulness as more critical in friendships than children do (Berndt & Perry, 1990). When talking about their best friend, adolescents frequently refer to the friend's willingness to stand up for them when around other people. Typical comments are: "Bob will stick up for me in a fight," "Sally won't talk about me behind my back," or "Jennifer wouldn't leave me for somebody else." In these descriptions, adolescents underscore the obligations of a friend in the larger peer group.

Another predominant characteristic of friendship is that, throughout the childhood and adolescent years, friends are generally similar—in terms of age, sex, ethnicity, and many other factors (Hartup, 1991; Lempers & Clark-Lempers, 1993; Rawlins, 1992). Friends often have similar attitudes toward school, similar educational aspirations, and closely aligned

Without question, one of the most important dimensions of friendships is intimacy. Children want to be able to share problems with a friend, have their friend understand them, and listen when they talk about their own thoughts and feelings. Girls are more likely to describe their best friend with greater intimacy than boys are.

achievement orientations. Friends like the same music, wear the same kind of clothes, and prefer the same leisure activities (Berndt, 1982). If friends have different attitudes about schools, one of them may want to play basketball or go shopping rather than do homework. If one friend insists on completing homework while the other insists on playing basketball, the conflict may weaken the friendship, and the two may drift apart.

Peer Relations in Adolescence

Imagine you are back in junior or senior high school, especially during one of your good times. Peers, friends, cliques, dates, parties, and clubs probably come to mind. Adolescents spend huge chunks of time with peers, more than in middle and late childhood. Among the important issues and questions to be asked about peer relations in adolescents are the following: What is the nature of peer pressure and conformity? How important are cliques in adolescence? How do children and adolescent groups differ? What is the nature of dating in adolescence?

Peer Pressure and Conformity

Consider the following statement made by an adolescent girl:

> Peer pressure is extremely influential in my life. I have never had very many friends, and I spend quite a bit of time alone. The friends I have are older. . . . The closest friend I have had is a lot like me in that we are both sad and depressed a lot. I began to act even more depressed than before when I was with her. I would call her up and try to act even more depressed than I was because that is what I thought she liked. In that relationship, I felt pressure to be like her. . . .

Conformity to peer pressure in adolescence can be positive or negative (Camarena, 1991; Foster-Clark & Blyth, 1991; Pearl, Bryan, & Herzog, 1990; Wall, 1993). Teenagers engage in all sorts of negative conformity behavior—use seedy language, steal, vandalize, and make fun of parents and teachers. However, a great deal of peer conformity is not negative and consists of the desire to be involved in the peer world, such as dressing like friends and wanting to spend huge chunks of time with members of a clique. Such circumstances may involve prosocial activities as well, as when clubs raise money for worthy causes.

> *Each of you, individually, walkest with the tread of a fox, but collectively ye are geese.*
>
> —Solon, Ancient Greece

During adolescence, especially early adolescence, we conformed more to peer standards than we did in childhood. Investigators have found that, around the standards than we did in childhood. Investigators have found that, around the eighth and ninth grades, conformity to peers—especially to their antisocial standards—peaks (Berndt, 1979; Berndt & Perry, 1990). At this point in development, an adolescent is most likely to go along with a peer to steal hubcaps off a car, draw graffiti on a wall, or steal cosmetics from a store counter.

Cliques and Crowds

Most peer group relationships in adolescence can be categorized in one of three ways: the crowd, the clique, or individual friendships. the **crowd** *is the largest and least personal of adolescent groups.* Members of the crowd meet because of their mutual interest in activities, not because they are mutually attracted to each other. **Cliques** *are smaller, involve greater intimacy among members, and have more group cohesion than crowds.*

Allegiance to cliques, clubs, organizations, and teams exerts powerful control over the lives of many adolescents (McLellan, Haynie, & Strouse, 1993). Group identity often overrides personal identity. The leader of a group may place a member in a position of considerable moral conflict by asking, in effect, "What's more important, out code or your parents'?" or "Are you looking out for yourself, or the members of the group?" Such labels as "brother" and "sister" sometimes are adopted and used in the members' conversations with each other. These labels symbolize the bond between the members and suggest the high status of group membership.

One of the most widely cited studies of adolescent cliques and crowds is that of James Coleman (1961). Students from 10 high schools were asked to identify the leading crowds in their schools. They also were asked to identify the students who were the most outstanding in athletics, popularity, and various school activities. Regardless of the school sampled, the leading crowds were composed of athletes and popular girls. Much less power in the leading crowd was attributed to bright students.

Think about your high school years. What were the cliques, and which one were you in? Although the names of cliques change, we could go to almost any high school in the United States and find three to six well-defined cliques or

Peer conformity becomes especially strong during the early adolescent years, as reflected in the uniform dress and behavior of these young adolescent "Madonnas."

crowds. In one recent investigation, six peer group structures emerged: populars, unpopulars, jocks, brains, druggies, and average students (Brown & Mounts, 1989). The proportion of students placed in these cliques was much lower in multiethnic schools because of the additional existence of ethnically based crowds.

In one study, clique membership was associated with the adolescent's self-esteem (Brown & Lohr, 1987). Cliques included jocks (athletically oriented), populars (well-known students who lead social activities), normals (middle-of-the-road students who make up the masses), druggies or toughs (known for illicit drug use or other delinquent activities), and nobodies (low in social skills or intellectual abilities). The self-esteem of the jocks and the populars was highest, whereas that of the nobodies was lowest. One group of adolescents not in a clique had self-esteem equivalent to that of the jocks and the populars; this group was the independents, who indicated that clique membership was not important to them. Keep in mind that these data are correlational; self-esteem could increase an adolescent's probability of becoming a clique member, just as clique membership could increase the adolescent's self-esteem.

Adolescent Groups Versus Children Groups

Children groups differ from adolescent groups in several important ways. The members of children groups often are friends or neighborhood acquaintances, and their groups usually are not as formalized as many adolescent groups. During the adolescent years, groups tend to include a broader array of members. In other words, adolescents other than friends or neighborhood acquaintances often are members of adolescent groups. Try to recall the student council, honor society, or football team at your junior high school. If you were a member of any of these organizations, you probably remember that they

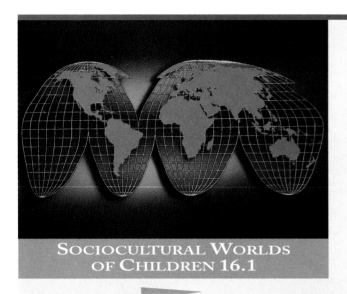

SOCIOCULTURAL WORLDS OF CHILDREN 16.1

Ethnic Minority Adolescents' Peer Relations

As ethnic minority children move into adolescence and enter schools with more heterogeneous school populations, they become more aware of their ethnic minority status (Phinney & Cobb, 1993). Ethnic minority adolescents may have difficulty joining peer groups and clubs in predominantly White schools. Similarly, White adolescents may have peer relations difficulties in predominately ethnic minority schools. However, schools are only one setting in which peer relations take place; they also occur in the neighborhood and in the community.

Ethnic minority adolescents often have two sets of peer relationships, one at school, the other in the community. Community peers are more likely to be from their own ethnic group in their immediate neighborhood. Sometimes, they go to the same church and participate in activities together, such as Black History Week, Chinese New Year's, or Cinco de Mayo Festival. Because ethnic group adolescents usually have two sets of peers and friends, when researchers ask about their peers and friends, questions should focus on both relationships at school and in the neighborhood and community. Ethnic minority group adolescents who are social isolates at school may be sociometric stars in their segregated neighborhood. Also, because adolescents are more mobile than children, inquiries should be made about the scope of their social networks (Gibbs & Huang, 1989; Mounts, 1992).

In one investigation the school and neighborhood friendship patterns of 292 Black and White adolescents who attended an integrated junior high school were studied (DuBois & Hirsch, 1990). Most students reported having an other-ethnic school friend, but only 28 percent of the students saw such a friend frequently outside of school. Reports of an interethnic school friendship that extended to nonschool settings were more common among Black adolescents than White adolescents and among adolescents who lived in an integrated rather than a segregated neighborhood. Black adolescents were more likely than White adolescents to have extensive neighborhood friendship networks, but Black adolescents said they talked with fewer friends during the school day.

Of special interest to investigators is the degree of peer support for an ethnic minority adolescent's achievement orientation. Some researchers argue that peers often dissuade Black adolescents from doing well in school (Fordham & Ogbu, 1986; Fuller, 1984). However, in one recent investigation, peer support of achievement was relatively high among Asian American adolescents, moderate among Black American and Hispanic American adolescents, and relatively low among Anglo American adolescents (Brown & others, 1990). The low peer support of achievement among Anglo American adolescents possibly is due to their strong individual, competitive, and social comparison orientation.

Adolescent peer relations take place in a number of settings—at school, in the neighborhood, and in the community, for example. Ethnic minority adolescents often have two sets of peer relationships—one at school, the other in the community. A special interest is the degree to which peers support an ethnic minority adolescent's achievement orientation.

were made up of many people you had not met before and that they were a more heterogeneous group than your childhood peer groups. For example, peer groups in adolescence are more likely to have a mixture of individuals from different ethnic groups than are peer groups in childhood. To read further about ethnic minority adolescents' peer groups, turn to Sociocultural Worlds of Children 16.1. Also, in adolescent peer groups, rules and regulations are usually defined more precisely than in children's peer groups. For example, captains or leaders are often formally elected or appointed in adolescent peer groups.

A well-known observational study by Dexter Dunphy (1963) supports the notion that opposite-sex participation in

groups increases during adolescence. In late childhood, boys and girls participate in small, same-sex cliques. As they move into the early adolescent years, the same-sex cliques begin to interact with each other. Gradually, the leaders and high-status members form further cliques based on heterosexual relationships. Eventually, the newly created heterosexual cliques replace the same-sex cliques. The heterosexual cliques interact with each other in large crowd activities, too—at dances and athletic events, for example. In late adolescence, the crowd begins to dissolve as couples develop more serious relationships and make long-range plans that may include engagement and marriage (see figure 16.4).

FIGURE 16.4

Dunphy's progression of peer group relations in adolescence.

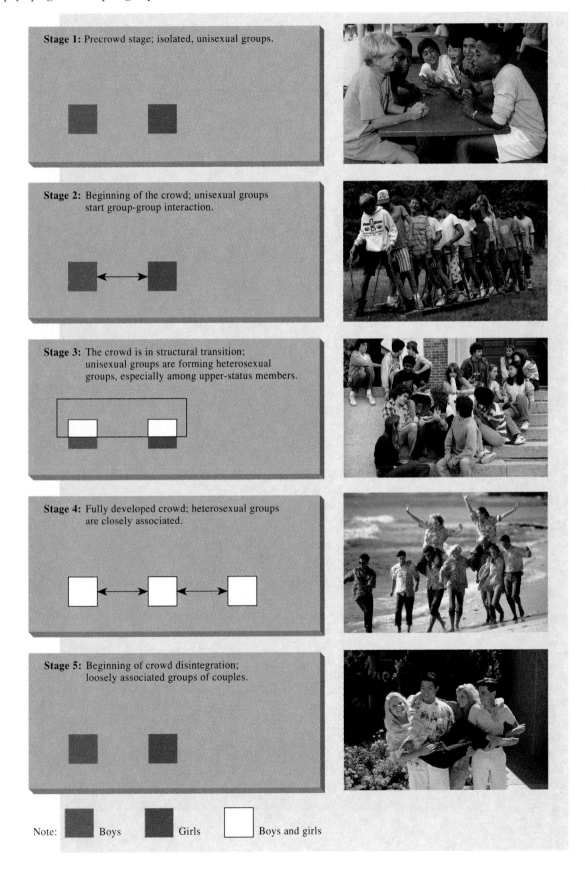

Stage 1: Precrowd stage; isolated, unisexual groups.

Stage 2: Beginning of the crowd; unisexual groups start group-group interaction.

Stage 3: The crowd is in structural transition; unisexual groups are forming heterosexual groups, especially among upper-status members.

Stage 4: Fully developed crowd; heterosexual groups are closely associated.

Stage 5: Beginning of crowd disintegration; loosely associated groups of couples.

Note: Boys   Girls   Boys and girls

CONCEPT TABLE 16.1

Peers

Concept	Processes/Related Ideas	Characteristics/Description
Peer group functions	Their nature	Peers are individuals who are about the same age or maturity level. Peers provide a means of social comparison and a source of information about the world outside the family. Good peer relations may be necessary for normal social development. The inability to "plug in" to a social network in childhood is associated with a number of problems. Thus, peer influences can be both positive and negative. Both Piaget and Sullivan stressed that peer relations provide the context for learning the symmetrical reciprocity mode of relationships.
The distinct but coordinated worlds of parent-child and peer relations	Coordination	Children touch, smile, and vocalize when they interact with parents and peers. Healthy family relations usually promote healthy peer relations. Parents also may model or coach their children in ways of relating to peers, and parents' choices of neighborhoods, churches, schools, and their own friends influence the pool from which their children might select possible friends.
	Distinctness	Rough-and-tumble play occurs mainly with peers, and in time of stress, children usually turn to parents rather than peers. Peer relations occur on a more equal basis than parent-child relations.
The developmental course of peer relations in childhood	Infancy	Some researchers believe that the quality of social interaction with peers in infancy provides valuable information about social development. As increasing numbers of children attend day care, infant peer interaction has increased.
	Childhood	The frequency of peer interaction, both positive and negative, increases during the preschool years, and children spend even more time with peers in the elementary and secondary school years.
Peer popularity, rejection, and neglect	Their nature	Listening skills and effective communication, being yourself, being happy, showing enthusiasm and concern for others, and indicating self-confidence by not conceit are predictors of peer popularity. Rejected children are at risk for adjustment problems; the risk status of neglected children is less clear. Of special interest is the improvement of the peer relations of neglected and rejected children. One issue involving

Dating

Dating takes on added importance during adolescence (Connolly & Johnson, 1993; Dowdy & Howard, 1993). As Dick Cavett (1974) remembers, the thought of an upcoming dance or sock hop was absolute agony: "I knew I'd never get a date. There seemed to be only this limited set of girls I could and should be seen with, and they were all taken by the jocks." Adolescents spend considerable time either dating or thinking about dating, which has gone far beyond its original courtship function to a form of recreation, a source of status and achieve-

ment, and a setting for learning about close relationships. One function of dating, though, continues to be mate selection.

Most girls in the United States begin dating at the age of 14, whereas most boys begin sometime between the ages of 14 and 15 (Douvan & Adelson, 1966). The majority of adolescents have their first date between the ages of 12 and 16. Fewer than 10 percent have a first date before the age of 10, and by the age of 16, more than 90 percent have had at least one date. More than 50 percent of high school students average one or more dates per week (Dickinson, 1975). About 15

Concept	Processes/Related Ideas	Characteristics/Description
		rejected children is whether to initially train their prosocial skills or to reduce their aggressive behavior and improve their self-control. It is important to remember that rejected children reflect a heterogenous group.
Social cognition	Its nature	Perspective taking, information-processing skills, and social knowledge are important dimensions of social cognition in peer relations.
Friendships	Functions and characteristics	Children's friendships serve six functions: companionship, stimulation, physical support, ego support, social comparison, and intimacy/affection.
	Sullivan's ideas on friendship	Harry Stack Sullivan was the most influential theorist to discuss the importance of friendships. He argued that there is a dramatic increase in the psychological importance and intimacy of close friends during early adolescence. Research findings support many of Sullivan's ideas.
	Intimacy and similarity	These are two of the most common characteristics of friendships. Intimacy in friendship is defined narrowly as self-disclosure or sharing of private thoughts. Similarity—in terms of age, sex, ethnicity, and many other factors—is also important to a friendship.
Peer relations in adolescence	Peer pressure and conformity	The pressure to conform to peers is strong during adolescence, especially during the eighth and ninth grades.
	Cliques and crowds	There usually are three to six well-defined cliques in every secondary school. Membership in certain cliques—especially jocks and populars—is associated with increased self-esteem. Independents also show high self-esteem.
	Adolescent groups versus children groups	Children groups are less formal, less heterogeneous, and less heterosexual than adolescent groups.
	Dating	Dating can be a form of mate selection, a type of recreation, a source of status, and achievement, and a setting for learning about close relationships. Most adolescents are involved in dating. Adolescent females appear to be more interested in intimacy and personality exploration than adolescent males are.

percent date less than once per month, and about three or every four students have gone steady at least once by the end of high school.

Female adolescents bring a stronger desire for intimacy and personality exploration to dating than do male adolescents (Duck, 1975; Feiring, 1992). Adolescent dating is a context in which gender-related role expectations intensify. Males feel pressured to perform in "masculine" ways and females feel pressured to perform in "feminine" ways. Especially in early adolescence, when pubertal changes are occurring, the adolescent male wants to show that he is the very best male possible, and the adolescent female wants to show that she is the very best female possible.

At this point, we have discussed a number of ideas about peer relations. A summary of these ideas is presented in Concept Table 16.1. Now we will turn our attention to the world of children's play.

Critical Thinking

Earlier in this chapter, we discussed the distinct but coordinated worlds of parent-child and peer relations. How might adolescent dating be distinct but coordinated with parent-adolescent relations?

PLAY

An extensive amount of peer interaction during childhood involves play; however, social play is but one type. **Play** *is a pleasurable activity that is engaged in for its own sake.* Our coverage of play includes its functions, Parten's classic study of play, the types of play, and the sociocultural contexts of play.

> *And that park grew up with me; that small world widened as I learned its secret boundaries, as I discovered new refuges in the woods and jungles: hidden homes and lairs for the multitudes of imagination, for cowboys and devon-facing seashore, hoping for gold watches or the skull of a sheep or a message in a bottle to be washed up by the tide.*
>
> —Dylan Thomas

Play's Functions

Play is essential to a young child's health. As today's children move into the twenty-first century and continue to experience pressure in their lives, play becomes even more crucial. Play increases affiliation with peers, releases tension, advances cognitive development, increases exploration, and provides a safe haven in which to engage in potentially dangerous behavior. Play increases the probability that children will converse and interact with each other. During this interaction, children practice the roles they will assume later in life.

According to Freud and Erickson, play is an especially useful form of human adjustment, helping the child master anxieties and conflicts. Because tensions are relieved in play, the child can cope with life's problems. Play permits the child to work off excess physical energy and to release pent-up tensions. **Play therapy** *allows children to work off frustrations and is a medium through which therapists can analyze children's conflicts and ways of coping with them. Children may feel less threatened and be more likely to express their true feelings in the context of play.*

Piaget (1962) saw play as a medium that advances children's cognitive development. At the same time, he said that children's cognitive development constrains the way they play. Play permits children to practice their competencies and acquired skills in a relaxed, pleasurable way. Piaget believed that cognitive structures need to be exercised, and play provides the perfect setting for this exercise. For example, children who have just learned to add or multiply begin to play with numbers in different ways as they perfect these operations, laughing as they do so.

Vygotsky (1962), whose developmental theory was discussed in chapter 7, also believed that play is an excellent setting for cognitive development. He was especially interested in the symbolic and make-believe aspects of play, as when a child substitutes a stick for a horse and rides the stick as if it were a horse. For young children, the imaginary situation is real. Parents should encourage such imaginary play because it advances the child's cognitive development, especially creative thought.

Daniel Berlyne (1960) described play as exciting and pleasurable in itself because it satisfies the exploratory drive each of us possesses. This drive involves curiosity and a desire for information about something new or unusual. Play is a means whereby children can safely explore and seek out new information—something they might not otherwise do. Play encourages this exploratory behavior by offering children the possibilities of novelty, complexity, uncertainty, surprise, and incongruity.

Parten's Classic Study of Play

Many years ago, Mildred Parten (1932) developed one of the most elaborate attempts to categorize children's play. Based on observations of children in free play at nursery school, Parten arrived at the following play categories:

1. **Unoccupied play** *occurs when the child is not engaging in play as it is commonly understood and may stand in one spot, look around the room, or perform random movements that do not seem to have a goal.* In most nursery schools, unoccupied play is less frequent than other forms.
2. **Solitary play** *occurs when the child plays alone.* In this type of play, children seem engrossed in what they are doing and do not care much about what others are doing. Two- and three-year-olds engage more frequently in solitary play than older preschoolers do.
3. **Onlooker play** *occurs when the child watches other children play.* The child may talk with other children and ask questions but does not enter into their play behavior. The child's active interest in other children's play distinguishes onlooker play from unoccupied play.
4. **Parallel play** *occurs when the child plays separately from others, but with toys like those the others are using or in a manner that mimics their play.* Young preschool children engage in this type of play more often than do older preschool children, but even older preschool children engage in parallel play quite often.
5. **Associative play** *occurs when play involves social interaction with little or no organization.* In this type of play, children seem to be more interested in each other than in the tasks they are performing. Borrowing or lending toys and following or leading one another in line are examples of associative play.
6. **Cooperative play** *involves social interaction in a group with a sense of group identity and organized activity.* Children's formal games, completion aimed at winning, and groups formed by the teacher for doing things together are examples of cooperative play. Cooperative play is the prototype for the games of middle childhood. Little cooperative play is seen in the preschool years.

Types of Play

Parten's categories represent one way of thinking about the different types of play. However, today researchers and practitioners who are involved with children's play believe other types of play are important in children's development. Whereas

FIGURE 16.5

Five important types of children's play are : (*a*) sensorimotor/practice play; (*b*) pretense/symbolic play; (*c*) social play; (*d*) constructive play; and (*e*) games. What type of play is represented in the large background photograph?

(a)   (b)   (c)   (d)   (e)

Parten's categories emphasize the role of play in the child's social world, the contemporary perspective on play emphasizes both the cognitive and social aspects of play. Among the most widely studied types of children's play today are: sensorimotor/practice play, pretense/symbolic play, social play, constructive play, and games (see figure 16.5).

Sensorimotor/Practice Play

Sensorimotor play *is behavior engaged in by infants to derive pleasure from exercising their existing sensorimotor schemas.* The development of sensorimotor play follows Piaget's description of sensorimotor thought, which we discussed in chapter 7. Infants initially engage in exploratory and playful visual and motor transactions in the second quarter of the first year of life. By 9 months of age, infants begin to select novel objects for exploration and play, especially those that are responsive, such as toys that make noise or bounce. By 12 months of age, infants

enjoy making things work and exploring cause and effect. At this point in development, children like toys that perform when they act on them.

In the second year, infants begin to understand the social meaning of objects and their play reflects this awareness. And 2-year-olds may distinguish between exploratory play that is interesting but not humorous and "playful" play, which has incongruous and humorous dimensions (McGhee, 1984). For example, a 2-year-old might "drink" from a shoe or call a dog a "cow." When 2-year-olds find these deliberate incongruities funny, they are beginning to show evidence of symbolic play and the ability to play with ideas.

Practice play *involves the repetition of behavior when new skills are being learned or when physical or mental mastery and coordination of skills is required for games or sports. Sensorimotor play, which often involves practice play, is primarily confined to infancy, while practice play can be engaged in throughout life.* During the preschool years, children often engage in play that involves

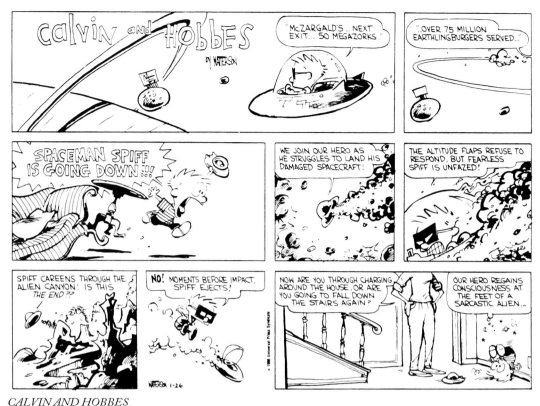

CALVIN AND HOBBES
© 1988 Watterson. Reprinted with permission of UNIVERSAL PRESS SYNDICATE. All rights reserved.

practicing various skills. Estimates indicate that practice play constitutes about one-third of the preschool child's play activities, but less than one-sixth of the elementary school child's play activities (Rubin, Fein, & Vandenberg, 1983). Practice play contributes to the development of coordinated motor skills needed for later game playing. While practice play declines in the elementary school years, practice play activities such as running, jumping, sliding, twirling, and throwing balls or other objects are frequently observed on the playgrounds at elementary schools. While these activities appear similar to the earlier practice play of the preschool years, practice play in the elementary school years differs from earlier practice play because much of it is ends rather than means related. That is, elementary school children often engage in practice play for the purpose of improving motor skills needed to compete in games or sports.

Pretense/Symbolic Play

Pretense/symbolic play *occurs when the child transforms the physical environment into a symbol* (Doyle & others, 1992; Fein, 1986; Rogers & Sawyers, 1988). Between 9 and 30 months of age, children increase their use of objects in symbolic play. They learn to transform objects, that is, substituting them for other objects and acting toward them as if they were these other objects. For example, a preschool child treats a table as if it is a car and says, "I'm fixing the car" as he grabs a leg of the table.

Many experts on play consider the preschool years the "golden age" of pretense/symbolic play that is dramatic or so-

ciodramatic in nature (Bergin, 1988; Singer & Singer, 1988). This type of make-believe play often appears at about 18 months of age and reaches a peak at 4 to 5 years of age, then gradually declines. In the early elementary school years, children's interests often shift to games.

I imagine, therefore I am free.

—Lawrence Durrell

Catherine Garvey (1977) has spent many years observing young children's play. She indicates that three elements are found in almost all of the pretend play she has observed: props, plot, and roles. Children use objects as *props* in their pretend play. Children can pretend to drink from a real cup or from a seashell. They can even create a make-believe cup from thin air, if nothing else is available. Most pretend play also has a story line, though the *plot* may be quite simple. Pretend play themes often reflect what children see going on in their lives, as when they play family, school, or doctor. Fantasy play can also take its theme from a story children have heard or a show they have seen. In pretend play, children try out many different *roles*. Some roles, like mother or teacher, are derived from reality. Other roles, like cowgirls or superman, come from fantasy. More about superhero play appears in Explorations in Child Development 16.1.

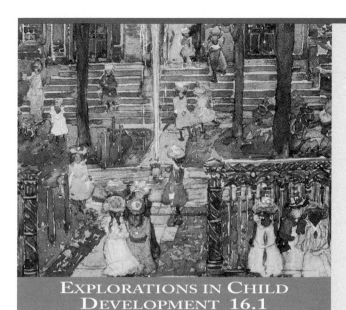

EXPLORATIONS IN CHILD DEVELOPMENT 16.1

Superhero Play

Jonathan runs into the classroom, charges over to the block cabinet, and selects a long, thin board. He shoves it under his sweater, takes a fighting stance, and announces, "I have the power." He laughingly advances toward his playmates, who run from him, leaping, shouting, and giggling.

Another day of superhero play has begun. Superhero play is a common occurrence in young children's lives and there is little doubt that they find it exhilarating. Marilyn Kostelnik, Alice Whiren, and Laura Stein (1988) recently described why children find superhero play attractive and how it relates to their development.

Superhero characters have been endowed with powers and qualities that embody the best of human nature. Consider Superman, Wonder Woman, Princess Leia, and He-Man. These superheroes and superheroines

- Are unquestionably good, being wise, fearless, clever, and strong
- Possess powers children wished they had themselves; superheroes have amazing speed, strength, or endurance and can fly, swim under water for miles, or change the shape of their bodies
- Solve every problem and overcome all obstacles and their solutions are always accepted
- Are in control—no one tells them what to do
- Know what is right—they rarely, if ever, make a mistake
- Receive praise and recognition from powerful adults; everyone wants to be their friend

Children have little power in the world because it is dominated by adults, yet, through their play, children can take on powerful roles that allow them to dominate villains or experience circumstances that entail no real risk. Feelings of fear and vulnerability can be overcome and transformed through playful shows of courage, strength, and wisdom. Superhero play also provides children the opportunity to pretend to be someone they admire and would like to resemble. Because superheroes are all good and antiheroes are all bad, children have clear, precise models for imitation. Finally, as with all other forms of dramatic play, through superhero play, children improve their language skills, problem-solving abilities, and cooperation.

How can teachers and parents help children make superhero play a constructive experience? They can

- Help children recognize the humane characteristics of superheros they admire—for example, a teacher might say, "Barbara, your must have felt as helpful as Wonder Woman when you carried the chairs over to the table"
- Discuss real heroes and heroines with children; introduce children to such people as Martin Luther King, Jr., and Helen Keller
- Help children understand what happens when play goes awry; children often are surprised when one of them is injured or frightened during play—the teacher might say, "Jane did not know you were playing," or "That was a real hit, not a pretend hit"
- Make it clear that aggression is unacceptable; children's aggressive acts need to be stopped, and adults need to make it clear that aggression will not be tolerated

In summary, superhero play is a specialized form of dramatic pretense play that is considerably appealing to young children. Although superhero play should not be actively promoted, when carefully monitored and directed, superhero play can have positive benefits.

A preschool "superhero" at play.

Social Play

Social play *is play that involves social interaction with peers.* Parten's categories, which we described earlier, are oriented toward social play. Social play with peers increases dramatically during the preschool years. In addition to general social play with peers and group pretense or sociodramatic play, another form of social play is rough-and-tumble play. The movement patterns of rough-and-tumble play are often similar to those of hostile behavior (running, chasing, wrestling, jumping, falling, hitting), but in rough-and-tumble play these behaviors are accompanied by signals such as laughter, exaggerated movement, and open rather than closed hands, which indicates this is play (Bateson, 1956).

Constructive Play

Constructive play *combines sensorimotor/practice repetitive activity with symbolic representation of ideas. Constructive play occurs when children engage in self-regulated creation or construction of a product or a problem solution.* Constructive play increase in the preschool years as symbolic play increases and sensorimotor play decreases. In the preschool years, some practice play is replaced by constructive play. For example, instead of moving their fingers around and around in finger paint (practice play), children are more likely to draw the outline of a house or a person in the paint (constructive play). Some researchers have found that constructive play is the most common type of play during the preschool years (Hetherington, Cox, & Cox, 1979; Rubin, Maioni, & Hornung, 1976). Constructive play is also a frequent form of play in the elementary school years, both in and out of the classroom. Constructive play is one of the few playlike activities allowed in work-centered classrooms. For example, having children create a play about a social studies topic involves constructive play. Whether such activities are considered play by children usually depends on whether they get to choose whether to do it (it is play) or whether the teacher imposes (it is not play), and also whether it is enjoyable (it is play) or not (it is not play) (King, 1982).

Critical Thinking

Are elementary schools too work centered? Should constructive play be used more extensively in the education of elementary school children? Explain your answer.

Constructive play can also be used in the elementary school years to foster academic skill learning, thinking skills, and problem solving. Many educators plan classroom activities that include humor, encourage playing with ideas, and promote creativity (Bergin, 1988). Educators also often support the performance of plays, the writing of imaginative stories, the expression of artistic abilities, and the playful exploration of computers and other technological equipment. However, distinctions between work and play frequently become blurred in the elementary school classroom.

Games

Games *are activities engaged in for pleasure that include rules and often competition with one or more individuals.* Preschool children may begin to participate in social game play that involves simple rules of reciprocity and turn-taking, but games take on a much more salient role in the lives of elementary school children. In one investigation, the highest incidence of game playing occurred between 10 and 12 years of age (Eiferman, 1971). After age 12, games decline in popularity, often being replaced by practice play, conversations, and organized sports (Bergin, 1988).

In the elementary years, games feature the meaningfulness of a challenge (Eiferman, 1971). This challenge is present if two or more children have the skills required to play and understand the rules of the game. Among the types of games children engage in are steady or constant games, such as tag, which are played consistently; recurrent or cyclical games, such as marbles or hopscotch, which seem to follow cycles of popularity and decline; sporadic games which are rarely played; and one-time games, such as hula hoop contests, which rise to popularity once and then disappear.

In sum, play is a multidimensional, complex concept. It ranges from an infant's simple exercise of a newfound sensorimotor talent to a preschool child's riding a tricycle to an older child's participation in organized games.

The Sociocultural Contexts of Play

American children's freewheeling play once took place in rural fields and city streets, using equipment largely made by children themselves. Today, play is becoming confined to back yards, basements, playrooms, and bedrooms and derives much of its content from video games, television dramas, and Saturday morning cartoons (Sutton-Smith, 1985). Modern children spend a large part of their lives alone with their toys, which was inconceivable several centuries earlier. Childhood was once part of collective village life. Children did not play separately but joined adults in seasonal festivals that intruded on the work world with regularity and boisterousness.

One of the most widely debated issues in the sociocultural contexts of play is whether children from low socioeconomic groups and traditional, non-Western societies have underdeveloped skills in the imaginative and sociodramatic aspects of pretense play (Johnson, Christie, & Yawkey, 1987). Some researchers believe there are developmental deficiencies in the imaginative and sociodramatic play of children from low socioeconomic groups and traditional, non-Western societies, whereas others believe that many methodological shortcomings in this research cloud the results. For example, many of these studies do not adequately measure socioeconomic status, do not systematically measure classroom and school variables, and in some cases do not use statistical analysis (McLoyd, 1982).

(a)

(b)

(a) *Is the play of today's children different from the play of children in collective village life, as shown in Children's Games by Pieter Breughel?* (b) *American children's play once took place in the rural fields and city streets. Today play is often confined to backyards, basements, playrooms, and bedrooms. The content of children's play today is often derived from video games, television dramas, and Saturday morning cartoons.*

The form and content of children's play are influenced by cultural and socioeconomic factors. The typical daycare or preschool environment is designed for middle-class children. Play experts recommend that children from low-income backgrounds be given considerable time to adapt to these new surroundings, and they also recommend that educators be ready to modify the environment to accommodate the diverse backgrounds of children. The need for adaptation was underscored in an observation of a group of young Navajo children (Curry, 1971). These children were familiar with the props available for dramatic play in the housekeeping corner of their middle-class-oriented preschool center. Teachers reported that the Navajo children would not engage in dramatic play. Many of the Navajo children came from homes with no running water and the cooking was performed over an open fire. The Navajo children did not use the domestic corner because it was set up for free play. One day—not by teacher design—the toys were left against the wall after cleaning, which prompted the Navajo children to engage vigorously in sociodramatic play. Why? Because the props were in the position they were familiar with in their circular homes.

We have seen that play is diverse and complex and that it is essential to the child's healthy development. We have also seen that the child's sociocultural world influences the nature of play. One of the main changes in children's sociocultural worlds in the twentieth century has been the introduction of television, which influences play, because it both competes for the child's time and stimulates or implants ideas for play themes and content. Next, we will study not only television's influence on children's development, but also the influence of other media, especially computers.

Some children may be capable of high-level imaginative play but require adult prompting and encouragement to overcome their initial shyness (Johnson, Christie, & Yawkey, 1987). Before expecting high-level play from children, teachers should determine if the children have had adequate time to become familiar with the materials and routines in their day-care center or preschool classroom. This familiarity is especially important for children whose main language is not English or for any child who comes from a home environment that is in marked contrast with the school environment.

MEDIA INFLUENCES

In the twentieth century, media influences on children's development have increased. Media are forms of mass communication, such as television, newspapers, magazines, movies, and computers. In this section, we will consider two powerful media in children's lives today—television and computers.

Television

Few developments in society in the second half of the twentieth century have had a greater impact on children than television has. Many children spend more time in front of the television set than they do with their parents. Although it is only one mass medium that affects children's behavior, television is the most influential. The persuasive capabilities of television are staggering; the 20,000 hours of television watched by the time the average American adolescent graduates from high school are greater than the number of hours spent in the classroom.

Television's Many Roles

Television can have a negative influence on children's development by taking them away from homework, making them passive learners, teaching them stereotypes, providing them with violent models of aggression, and presenting them with unrealistic views of the world. However, television can also have a positive influence on children's development by presenting motivating educational programs, increasing children's information about the world beyond their immediate environment, and providing models of prosocial behavior (Esty & Fisch, 1991).

> *Television is a medium of entertainment which permits millions of people to listen to the same joke at the same time, and yet remain lonesome.*
>
> —T. S. Eliot

Television has been called many things, not all of them good. Depending on one's point of view, it may be a "window on the world," the "one-eyed monster," or the "boob tube." Television has been attacked as one of the reasons that scores on national achievement tests in reading and mathematics are lower now than in the past. Television, it is claimed, attracts children away from books and schoolwork. In one study, children who read printed materials, such as books, watched television less than those who did not read (Huston, Seigle, & Bremer, 1983). Furthermore, critics argue that television trains children to become passive learners; rarely, if ever, does television require active responses from the observer.

Television also is said to deceive; that is, it teaches children that problems are resolved easily and that everything always comes out right in the end. For example, TV detectives usually take only 30 to 60 minutes to sort through a complex array of clues to reveal a killer—and they *always* find the killer. Violence is a way of life on many shows. It is all right for police to use violence and to break moral codes in their fight against evildoers. The lasting results of violence are rarely brought home to the viewer. A person who is injured on TV suffers for only a few seconds; in real life, the person might need months or years to recover, or might not recover at all. One out of every two first-grade children says that the adults on television are like adults in real life (Lyle & Hoffman, 1972).

Sesame Street demonstrates that education and entertainment can work well together. Through *Sesame Street*, children experience a world of learning that is both exciting and enter-

taining. *Sesame Street* also follows the principle that teaching can be accomplished both directly and indirectly. Using the direct way, a teacher might tell children exactly what they are going to be taught and then teach them. However, in real life, social skills are often communicated in direct ways. Rather than merely telling children, "You should cooperate with others," TV can show children so that they can figure out what it means to be cooperative and what the advantages are.

Amount of Television Children Watch

Just how much television do young children watch? They watch a lot, and they seem to be watching more all the time. In the 1950s, 3-year-old children watched television for less than 1 hour a day; 5-year-olds watched just over 2 hours a day. In the 1970s, however, preschool children watched television for an average of 4 hours a day; elementary school children watched for as long as 6 hours a day (Friedrich & Stein, 1973). In the 1980s, children averaged 11 to 28 hours of television per week (Huston, Watkins, & Kunkel, 1989), which is more than for any other activity except sleep. Of special concern is the extent to which children are exposed to violence and aggression on television. Up to 80 percent of the prime time shows include violent acts, including beatings, shootings, and stabbings. The frequency of violence increases on the Saturday morning cartoon shows, which average more than 25 violent acts per hour.

Effects of Television on Aggression and Prosocial Behavior

What are the effects of television violence on children's aggression? Does television merely stimulate a child to go out and buy a Star Wars ray gun, or can it trigger an attack on a playmate? When the child grows up, can television violence increase the likelihood he will violently attack someone?

"Mrs. Horton, could you stop by school today?"
©1981 Martha F. Campbell.

In one longitudinal investigation, the amount of violence viewed on television at age 8 was significantly related to the seriousness of criminal acts performed as an adult (Huesmann, 1986). In another investigation, long-term exposure to television violence was significantly related to the likelihood of aggression in 1,565 12-to-17-year-old boys (Belson, 1978). Boys who watched the most aggression on television were the most likely to commit a violent crime, swear, be aggressive in sports, threaten violence toward another boy, write slogans on walls, or break windows. These investigations are *correlational,* so we cannot conclude from them that television violence causes children to be more aggressive, only that watching television violence is *associated with* aggressive behavior. In one experiment, children were randomly assigned to one of two groups: One watched television shows taken directly from violent Saturday morning cartoon offerings on 11 different days; the second group watch television cartoon shows with all of the violence removed (Steur, Applefield & Smith, 1971). The children were then observed during play at their preschool. The preschool children who saw the TV cartoon shows with violence kicked, choked, and pushed their playmates more than the preschool children who watched nonviolent TV cartoon shows did. Because children were randomly assigned to the two conditions (TV cartoons with violence versus no violence), we can conclude that exposure to TV violence *caused* the increased aggression in children in this investigation.

Whereas some critics have argued that the effects of television violence do not warrant the conclusion that TV violence causes aggression (Freedman, 1984), others have concluded that TV violence can induce aggressive or antisocial behavior in children (Condry, 1989; Huston, Watkins, & Kunkel, 1989; Liebert & Spratkin, 1988). Of course, television is not the *only* cause of aggression. There is no *one,* single cause of any social behavior. Aggression, like all other social behaviors, is multiply determined.

Children need to be taught critical viewing skills to counter the adverse effects of television violence. In one investigation, elementary school children were randomly assigned to either an experimental or a control group (Huesmann & others, 1983). In the experimental group, children assisted in making a film to help children who had been fooled or harmed by television. The children also composed essays that focused on how television is not like real life and why it is bad to imitate TV violence or watch too much television. In the control group, children received no training in critical viewing skills. The children who were trained in critical viewing skills developed more negative attitudes about TV violence and reduced their aggressive behavior.

Television can also teach children that it is better to behave in positive, prosocial ways than in negative, antisocial ways. Television research Aimee Leifer (1973) demonstrated that television is associated with prosocial behavior in young children; she selected a number of *Sesame Street* episodes that reflected positive social interchanges. She was especially interested in situations that taught children how to use their social skills. For example, in one interchange, two men were fighting over the amount of space available to them; they gradually began to cooperate and to share the space. Children who watched these episodes copied these behaviors and, in later social situations, they applied the prosocial lessons they had learned.

Parent's Role in Children's Television Viewing

How much do parents take an active role in discussing television with their children? For the most part, parents do not discuss the content of television shows with their children (Leiffer, Gordon, & Graves, 1974). Parents need to be especially sensitive to young children's viewing habits because the age period of 2½ to 6 is when long-term television-viewing habits begin to be established (Murphy, Talley, & Huston, 1991). Children from lower socioeconomic status families watch television more than children from higher socioeconomic status families (Huston, Seigle, & Bremer, 1983). Also, children who live in families involved in high conflict watch more television than children who live in families low in conflict (Price & Feshbach, 1982). In one investigation (Tangney, 1988), the children of parents who showed more empathy and sensitivity toward them preferred less fantasy fare on television. In dysfunctional families, children may use the lower developmental level of fantasy-oriented children's programs to escape from the taxing, stressful circumstances of their home environment.

Parents can make television a more positive influence in children's lives. The following guidelines developed by Dorothy and Jerome Singer (1987) can go a long way in reducing television's negative effects and improving its role as a positive influence in children's development:

1. Develop good viewing habits early in the child's life.
2. Encourage planned viewing of specific programs rather than random viewing. Be active with young children between planned programs.
3. Look for children's programs that feature children in the child's age group.
4. Make sure that television is not used as a substitute for participating in other activities.
5. Develop discussions about sensitive television themes with children. Give them the opportunity to ask questions about the programs.
6. Balance reading and television activities. Children can "follow up" interesting television programs by checking out the library books for which some programs are adapted and by pursuing additional stories by the authors of those books.
7. Help children develop a balanced viewing schedule of education, action, comedy, fine arts, fantasy, sports, and so on.
8. Point out positive examples that show how various ethnic and cultural groups contribute to making a better society.
9. Point out positive examples of females performing competently both in professions and at home.

Computers and Children

At mid-twentieth century, commercial television had barely made its debut and IBM had yet to bring its first computer to market. Now as we move toward the close of the twentieth century, both television *and* computers are important influences in children's lives. For some, the computer is a positive tool with the power to transform our schools and revolutionize children's learning. For others, the computer is a menacing force, more likely to undermine than to improve children's education. Let's examine some of the possible positive and negative influences of computers in children's lives.

Positive Influences of Computers on Children

Among the potential positive influences of computers on children's development are those involving the computer as a personal tutor, as a medium for experiential learning, and as a multipurpose tool, as well as motivational and social effects (Lepper & Gurtner, 1989).

Computer-assisted instruction *is a method of education that uses the computer as a tutor to individualize instruction. The concept behind computer-assisted instruction is to use the computer to present information, give students practice, assess their level of understanding, and provide additional instruction if needed.* Computer-assisted instruction requires the active participation of the student; it is patient and nonjudgmental in giving immediate feedback to students. Over the past two decades, more than 200 research studies involving computer-assisted instruction have been conducted. In general, the effects of computer-assisted instruction are positive (Steinberg, 1990). More precisely, the effects are more positive with programs involving tutorials rather than drill and practice, with younger rather than older students, and with children of lower ability than with average or general populations (Lepper & Gurtner, 1989).

A second important influence of the computer in children's lives is its role in experiential learning. Some experts view the computer as an excellent medium for open-ended, exploratory, and experiential learning. The most widely studied activity has been the use of the Logo computing language, especially its simplified "turtle graphics" programming environment, as a way to improve children's planning and problem-solving abilities (Papert, 1980). Logo involves children in active experimentation with "turtle graphics." The research on the effects of Logo are mixed. The early studies of Logo essentially found no benefits for children's learning: however, more recent studies have been supportive of Logo. In recent studies, more favorable adult-child ratios are present, prepared support materials and explicit tasks requirements are included, younger children are studied, and a wider array of dependent variable measures are used (such as creativity, cognitive monitoring, and solution checking) (Lehrer & Littlefield, 1991).

A third important influence of the computer in children's lives is its function as a multipurpose tool in helping children achieve academic goals and become more creative. The computer is especially helpful in improving children's writing and communication skills (Lehrer, 1992; Lehrer & others, in press). Word-processing programs diminish the drudgery of writing, increasing the probability that children will edit and revise their work. Programs that assist students in outlining a paper may help them organize their thoughts before they write.

Several other themes appear in the discussion of the computer's positive influence on children's development. For one, computer adherents argue that the computer makes learning more intrinsically motivating (Lepper, 1985). Computer enthusiasts also argue that the computer can make learning more fun, and lessons can often be embedded in instructional "games" or puzzles that encourage children's curiosity and sense of challenge. Some computer adherents also argue that increase computer use in schools will lead to increased cooperation and collaboration on the part of students, as well as increased intellectual discussion among students. If the computer does increase student's interest, it may free teachers to spend more time working with students individually. Finally, computer adherents hope that the computer can increase the equality of educational opportunity (Becker & Sterling, 1987). Since the computer allows students to work at their own pace, it may help students who do not normally succeed in school. The computer's fairness and impartiality should minimize any adverse influences of teacher prejudice and stereotyping.

Negative Influences of Computers on Children

Among the potential negative influences of computers on children's development are the regimentation and dehumanization of the classroom, unwarranted "shaping" of the curriculum, and the generalization and limitations of computer-based teaching (Lepper & Gurtner, 1989).

Skeptics worry that, rather than increased individualization of instruction, computers will bring a much greater regimentation and homogenization of classroom learning experiences. Whereas some students may prefer to work autonomously and may learn most effectively when they are allowed to progress on their own, other students may rely on social interaction with and guidance by the teacher for effective learning. Some computer skeptics also worry that the computer will ultimately increase inequality, rather than equality, in educational outcomes (Malcom, 1988). School funding in middle-class neighborhoods is usually better than in low-income areas, and the homes of children in middle-class neighborhoods are more likely to have computers than are those in low-income neighborhoods. Thus, an increasing emphasis on computer literacy may be inequitable for children from low-income backgrounds because they have likely had fewer opportunities to use computers. Some critics also worry about the dehumanization of the classroom. They argue that school is a social world as well as a cognitive, learning world. From this perspective, children plugged into a computer all day long have little opportunity to engage in social interaction.

The influence of computer use on children's learning, motivation, and social behavior continues to be a source of debate and controversy.

erature. Consequently, there is concern that the computer may eventually shape the curriculum exclusively in the direction of science and math because these areas are more easily computerized.

Yet another issue is the transfer of learning and motivation to domains outside the computer. If the instructional effectiveness and motivational appeal of computer-based education depends on the use of impressive technical devices, such as color, animation, and sound effects, how effectively will student learning or motivation transfer to other contexts without these technical supports? Will children provided with the editorial assistance of the computer still learn the basic skills needed to progress to more complex forms of creative writing later in their careers? Will children using computers in math gain the proficiency to deal with more complicated math in the future or will their ability to solve complex conceptual problems without the computer have atrophied? Presently, we do not know the answers to these important questions about the computer's role in children's development.

Critical Thinking

In our discussion of television, we mentioned ways that parents could effectively monitor children's television viewing. What roles can parents play in their children's use of computers?

At this point, we have discussed a number of ideas about play and about media influences on children's development. A summary of these ideas is presented in Concept Table 16.2.

A further concern is that computers may inadvertently and inappropriately shape the curriculum. Some subjects, such as mathematics and science, seem to be more easily and successfully adapted to computers than are such subjects as art and lit-

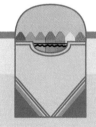

PERSPECTIVES ON PARENTING AND EDUCATION

Improving Children's Peer Relations at School

"You jerk, what are you trying to do to me?" Jess yelled at his teacher. "I got no use for this school and people like you. Leave me alone and quit hassling me."

Jess is 10 years old and has already had more than his share of confrontations with society. He has been arrested three times for stealing and has been suspended from school twice. He also has a great deal of difficulty getting along with people in social circumstances. He especially has difficulty with authority figures. No longer able to cope with his outbursts in class, his teacher recommends that he

be suspended from school once again; however, the principal knows of a different kind of school she thinks might help Jess.

Jess is transferred to the Manville School, a clinic in the Judge Baker Guidance Center in Boston for learning disabled and emotionally disturbed children 7 to 15 years of age. Like many other students at the Manville School, Jess has shown considerable difficulty in interpersonal relationships. Peer relationships become a crucial aspect of development during the elementary school

years, so Robert Selman designed a peer therapy program at the Manville School to help students like Jess improve their peer relations in classroom settings, group activities, and sports (Selman, Newberger, & Jacquette, 1977). The staff at the Manville School was trained to help peers support and encourage one another in such group settings.

Structured programs at the Manville School are designed to help the children assist each other in such areas as cooperation, trust, leadership, and conformity. Four school activities were developed to

CONCEPT TABLE 16.2

Play and Media Influences

Concept	Processes/Related Ideas	Characteristics/Description
Play	Play's functions	They include affiliation with peers, tension release, advances in cognitive development, exploration, and provision of a safe haven in which to engage in potentially dangerous activities.
	Parten's classic study of play	Parten examined the categories of unoccupied, solitary, onlooker, parallel, associative, and cooperative play. Three-year-old children engage in more solitary play and parallel play than 5-year-old children, whereas 5-year-old children engage in cooperative and associative play more than other types of play.
	Types of play	The contemporary perspective emphasizes both the cognitive and social aspects of play. Among the most widely studied aspects of children's play today are sensorimotor and practice play, pretense/symbolic play, social play, constructive play, and games.
	The sociocultural contexts of play	Modern children spend a large part of their lives with toys, and play is increasingly confined to back yard, basements, playrooms, and bedrooms rather than occurring in rural fields and city streets. A widely debated issue is whether children from low socioeconomic and traditional, non-Western societies have underdeveloped skills in the imaginative and sociodramatic aspects of pretense play. The form and content of children's play are influenced by cultural and socioeconomic factors.
Media influences	Television	Although television can have a negative influence on children's development by taking them away from homework, making them passive learners, teaching them stereotypes, providing them with violent models of aggression, and presenting them with unrealistic views of the world, television can also have a positive influence by presenting motivating educational programs, increasing children's information about the world beyond their immediate environment, and providing models of prosocial behavior. Children watch huge amounts of television, with preschool children watching an average of 4 hours a day. Up to 80 percent of the prime time shows have violent episodes. Television violence is not the only cause of children's aggression, but most experts conclude that it can induce aggression and antisocial behavior in children. Prosocial behavior on television is associated with increased positive behavior by children. Parents rarely discuss television's contents with their children. Television-viewing habits are often formed in the early childhood years.
	Computers and children	Among the potential positive effects of computers on children's development are those involving the computer as a personal tutor (computer-assisted instruction), as a medium for experiential learning, and as a multipurpose tool, as well as the motivational and social aspects of computers. Among the potential negative effects of computers on children's development are the regimentation and dehumanization of the classroom, unwarranted "shaping" of the curriculum, and the generalization and limitations of computer-based teaching.

improve students' social reasoning skills in these areas. First, there is a weekly peer problem-solving session in the classroom, in which the peers work cooperatively to plan activities and relate problems. At the end of each week, the peers evaluate their effectiveness in making improvements in such areas as cooperation and conflict resolution. Second, class members, numbering from six to eight students, plan a series of weekly field trips—for example, going to the movies or visiting historical sites.

Although the counselor provides some assistance, peer decision making dominates. When each activity is completed, the students discuss how things went and what might have been done to improve social relations with each other on the outings. Third, Selman recognizes that there are times when students have to get away from settings where intense frustration occurs. When students find themselves in a highly frustrating situation (for example, angry enough to strike out at a classmate), they are allowed to

leave the room and go to a private "time-out" area of the school to regain composure. In time-out, students also are given the opportunity to discuss the problems with a counselor who has been trained to help children or adolescents improve their social reasoning skills. Fourth, during social studies and current events discussion sessions, the students evaluate a number of moral and societal issues that incorporate the thinking of such theorists as Lawrence Kohlberg. ∎

CONCLUSIONS

Good peer relations, friendships, and opportunities for play provide developmental advantages for children.

We began this chapter by discussing the importance of friendship and how it can positively influence children's school behavior. We spent considerable time exploring children's peer worlds, learning about peer group functions, the distinct but coordinated worlds of parent-child and peer relations, the developmental

course of peer relations, peer popularity, rejection, and neglect, social cognition, friendships, and peer relations in adolescence. Our coverage of play focused on play's functions, Parten's classic study of play, types of play, and the sociocultural contexts of play. We also studied media influences—television and computers—on children's development. And we learned some strategies for improving children's peer relations at school. Don't

forget to again read the two concept tables on pages 478 and 490, which together will give you a summary of the chapter.

In this chapter we briefly touched on several aspects of schools in children's lives—the role of friendships in school behavior, how to improve children's peer relations at school, and the role of computers in children's education and development. In the next chapter, we turn our attention exclusively to schools.

KEY TERMS

peers Children of about the same age or maturity level. (468)

neglected children Children who receive little attention from their peers, but who are not necessarily disliked. (471)

rejected children Children who are disliked by their peers. They are more likely to be disruptive and aggressive than are neglected children. (471)

perspective taking Taking another's point of view. (471)

intimacy in friendship Self-disclosure and the sharing of private thoughts. (474)

crowd The largest and least personal adolescent group. (475)

cliques Small adolescent groups that involve greater intimacy among members and more group cohesion than crowds. (475)

play Pleasurable activity engaged in for its own sake. (480)

play therapy Therapy that allows children to work off frustration and a medium through which therapists can analyze children's conflicts and ways of coping with them. Children may feel less threatened and be more likely to express their true feelings in the context of play. (480)

unoccupied play Play that occurs when a child is not engaging in play as it is commonly understood; the child may stand in one spot, look around the room, or perform

random movements that do not seem to have a goal. (480)

solitary play Play when a child is alone. (480)

onlooker play Play that occurs when a child watches other children play. (480)

parallel play Play that occurs separately from other children, but with toys like those the others are using or in a manner that mimics their play. (480)

associative play Play that involves social interaction, with little or no organization. (480)

cooperative play Play that involves social interaction in a group, with a sense of group identity and organized activity. (480)

sensorimotor play   Behavior engaged in by infants to derive pleasure from exercising their sensorimotor schemas. (481)

practice play   Play that involves the repetition of behavior when new skills are being learned or when physical or mental mastery and coordination are required for sports. (481)

pretense/symbolic play   Play that occurs when a child transforms the physical environment into a symbol. (482)

social play   Play that involves social interaction with peers. (484)

constructive play   Play that combines sensorimotor and practice repetitive activity with the symbolic representation of ideas. Constructive play occurs when children engage in self-regulated creation or construction of a product or problem solution. (484)

games   Activities engaged in for pleasure that include rules and often competition. (484)

computer-assisted instruction   A method of education that uses the computer as a tutor to individualize instruction: to present information, give students practice, and provide additional instruction if needed. (488)

SUGGESTED READINGS

Hartup, W. W. (1983). The peer system. In P. H. Mussen (Ed.), *Handbook of child psychology* (4th ed., Vol. 4). New York: Wiley. This is a detailed look at the development of peer relations by one of the leading experts in the field.

Lepper, M. R., & Gurtner, J. (1989). Children and computers: Approaching the twenty-first century. *American Psychologist, 44,* 170–178. This article provides an excellent, well-balanced treatment of the computer's role in children's development.

Liebert, R. M., & Spratkin, J. N. (1988). *The early window: Effects of television on children and youth* (3rd ed.). Elmsford, NY: Pergamon. This updated account of theory and research addresses the effect of television on children's development.

Rogers, C. R., & Sawyers, J. K. (1988). *Play in the lives of children.* Washington, DC: National Association for the Education of Young Children. This book includes a wealth of material on various types of play. Especially valuable are the examples of play in the lives of children.

Claude Drawing, Pablo Picasso,
1881–1973 (Detail)

17

Schools

Chapter Outline

PERSPECTIVES ON PARENTING AND EDUCATION

The Role of Parenting in Young Children's Learning and Education 517

Chapter Boxes

The world rests on the breath of the children in the schoolhouse.

—The *Talmud*

*Children have to be educated, but they also
have to be left to educate themselves.*

—Ernest Dimnet

IMAGES OF CHILDREN

From No More "What If" Questions to Authors' Week

Some schools are ineffective, others effective, as revealed in the following excerpts (Lipsitz, 1984):

A teacher in a social studies class squelches several imaginative questions, exclaiming, "You're always asking 'what if' questions. Stop asking 'what if.'" When a visitor asks who will become president if the president-elect dies before the electoral college meets, the teacher explodes, "You're as bad as they are! That's another 'what if' question!"

A teacher drills students for a seemingly endless amount of time on prime numbers. After the lesson, not one student can say why it is important to learn prime numbers.

A visitor asks a teacher if hers is an eighth-grade class. "It's called eighth grade," the teacher answers archly, "but we know it's really kindergarten, right class?"

In a predominantly Hispanic school, only the one adult hired as a bilingual teacher speaks Spanish.

In a biracial school, the principal and the guidance counselor cite test scores with pride. They are asked if the difference between the test scores of black and white students is narrowing: "Oh, that's an interesting question!" says the guidance counselor with surprise. The principal agrees. It has never been asked by or of them before.

The preceding vignettes are from schools where life seems to be difficult and unhappy for students. By contrast, consider the following circumstances in effective schools (Lipsitz, 1984):

Everything is peaceful. There are open cubbies instead of locked lockers. There is no theft. Students walk quietly in the corridors. "Why?" they are asked. "So as not to disturb the media center," they answer, which is self-evident to them, but not the visitor, who is left wondering. . . . When asked, "Do you like this school?" (They) answer, "No, we don't like it. We love it!"

When asked how the school feels, one student answered, "It feels smart. We're smart. Look at our test scores." Comments from one of the parents of a student at the school are revealing: "My child would have been a dropout. In elementary school, his teacher said to me, 'That child isn't going to give you anything but heartaches.' He had perfect attendance here. He didn't want to miss a day. Summer vacation was too long and boring. Now he's majoring in communications at the University of Texas. He got here and all of a sudden, someone cared for him. I had been getting notes about Roger every other day, with threats about exclusion. Here, the first note said, 'It's just a joy to have him in the classroom.'"

The humane environment that encourages teachers'

growth . . . is translated by the teachers . . . into a humane environment that encourages students' growth. The school feels cold when one first enters. It has the institutional feeling of any large school building with metal lockers and impersonal halls. Then one opens the door to a team area, and it is filled with energy, movement, productivity, doing. There is a lot of informal relating among students and between students and teachers. Visible from one vantage point are students working on written projects, putting the last touches on posters, watching a film, and working independently from reading kits. . . . Most know what they are doing, can say why it is important, and go back to work immediately after being interrupted.

Authors' Week is a special activity built into the school's curriculum that entices students to consider themselves in relation to the rich variety of making and doing in peoples' lives. Based on student interest, availability, and diversity, authors are invited . . . to discuss their craft. Students sign up to meet with individual authors. They must have read one individual book by the author. . . . Students prepare questions for their sessions with the authors. . . . Sometimes, an author stays several days to work with a group of students on his or her manuscript.

PREVIEW

In school children spend many years as members of a small society that exerts tremendous influence on who they will become. In addition to teaching children to write and read, schools help children develop the fundamental aspects of their personality, such as identity and standards of right and wrong. Schools also help children understand how social systems outside the family function. Our coverage of schools explores the following questions: What is the nature of children's schooling? What is early childhood education like? How do children experience the transition to elementary school? How do various characteristics of classrooms and teachers influence children's development? What roles do social class and ethnicity play in schooling? What are schools for adolescents like? How should children with special needs be educated?

THE NATURE OF CHILDREN'S SCHOOLING

Two important issues that pertain to the nature of children's schooling are: What is the function of schools? What is the nature of changing social developmental contexts in schools?

Functions of Children's Schools

What should the functions of school be? In the 1980s, the back-to-basics movement gained momentum. The **back-to-basics movement** *stresses that the function of schools should be the rigorous training of intellectual skills through such subjects as English, math, and science.* Advocates of the back-to-basics movement point to the excessive fluff in elementary and secondary school curricula, with too many alternative subjects that do not give students a basic education in intellectual subjects. Back-to-basics advocates also believe that schools should be in the business of imparting knowledge to children and should not be as concerned about their social and emotional lives. Critics of the fluff in schools also sometimes argue that the school day should be longer and that the school year should be extended into the summer months.

The back-to-basics advocates want students to have more homework, more tests, and more discipline. They usually believe that children should be behind their desks and not roaming around the room. Teachers should be at the head of the classroom, drilling knowledge into children's minds. Much of the current back-to-basics emphasis is a reaction against the trend toward open education in the 1970s. Based on the British educational system, the open education approach allowed children to learn and develop at their own pace within a highly structured classroom. However, too many school systems that implemented open education in the United States thought that it meant tearing down classroom walls and letting children do whatever they wanted. Because open education was incorrectly applied in American schools, there was a strong backlash against it (Kantrowitz & Wingert, 1989).

In the first place God made idiots. This was for practice. Then he made school boards.

—Mark Twain

At the same time, parents, too, were demanding more from their elementary schools. By the mid-1980s, the majority of 3- and 4-year-old children were attending preschool, and their parents expected these classroom veterans to be reading by the second semester of kindergarten. However, the truth is that many 5-year-old children are not ready for reading—or most of the other demanding academic tasks that are more easily learned by older children—no matter how many years of school they have completed (Elkind, 1988). Thus, as we approach the end of the twentieth century, preschool and kindergarten programs are becoming downward extensions of traditional elementary school education. Many educators and psychologists also worry that, in the push for back-to-basics, more discipline, more homework, and more tests, elementary and secondary schools are becoming pressure cookers for students (Beane, 1990; Duke & Canady, 1991).

The back-to-basics movement became very popular in children's education in the 1980s. The back-to-basics approach is still the dominant form of education, although a number of educators and child developmentalists believe that a more comprehensive approach that takes into consideration both social and cognitive development should characterize children's education.

Today, a number of experts on education and child development advocate a more comprehensive education than back-to-basics that includes social as well as cognitive development. They also believe that the back-to-basics movement, which emphasizes discipline, extensive homework, and considerable testing, has increased the stress in children's lives. The experts believe that the back-to-basics movement does not give adequate attention to individual variation in children's development.

What does education often do? It makes a straight-cut ditch of a free, meandering brook.

—Henry David Thoreau

The debate about the function of schools produces shifts of emphasis much like a swinging pendulum, moving toward basic skills and intellectual development at one point in time and toward options and comprehensive training for life in intellectual and social development at another, and so on back and forth (Cross, 1984). In the 1980s, the pendulum swung strongly in the direction of back-to-basics, but today a number of experts on education and child development are trying to push the pendulum toward a more comprehensive education

that includes social as well as cognitive development. These experts also believe that the back-to-basics movement has increased the stress in children's lives and does not give adequate attention to individual variations among children.

Schools' Changing Social Developmental Contexts

Social contexts differ at the preschool, elementary, and secondary levels. The preschool setting is a protected environment, whose boundary is the classroom. In this limited social setting, preschool children interact with one or two teachers, usually female, who are powerful figures in the young child's life. The preschool child also interacts with peers in a dyadic relationship or in small groups. Preschool children have little concept of the classroom as an organized social system, although they are learning how to make and maintain social contacts and communicate their needs. The preschool serves to modify some patterns of behavior developed through family experiences. Greater self-control may be required in the preschool than earlier in development.

The classroom is still the major context for the elementary school child, although it is more likely to be experienced as a social unit than is the preschool classroom. The network of social expression also is more complex. Teachers and peers have a prominent influence on children during the elementary school years. The teacher symbolizes authority, which establishes the climate of the classroom, the conditions of social interaction, and the nature of group functioning. Peer groups become more salient, with increased interest in friendship, belonging, and status. Peer groups also become learning communities in which social roles and standards related to work and achievement are formed.

As children move into middle or junior high schools, the school environment increases in scope and complexity. The social field is the school as a whole rather than the classroom. Adolescents interact socially with many different teachers and peers from a range of social and ethnic backgrounds. Students are often exposed to a greater mix of male and female teachers, and their social behavior is heavily weighted toward peers, extracurricular activities, clubs, and the community. The student in secondary school is usually aware of the school as a social system and may be motivated to conform and adapt to the system or challenge it (Minuchin & Shapiro, 1983).

EARLY CHILDHOOD EDUCATION

With increased understanding of how young children develop and learn has come greater emphasis on the education of young children. We explore the following questions about early childhood education: What is child-centered kindergarten? What are developmentally appropriate and inappropriate practices in programs for young children? Does it really matter if children attend preschool before kindergarten? What are the effects of early childhood education? What is the nature of education for disadvantaged young children? What constitutes school readiness?

Child-Centered Kindergarten

Kindergarten programs vary a great deal. Some approaches place more emphasis on young children's social development, others on their cognitive development. Some experts on early childhood education believe that the curriculum of many of today's kindergarten and preschool programs places too much emphasis on achievement and success, putting pressure on young children too early in their development (Bredekamp & Shepard, 1989; Charlesworth, 1989; Elkind, 1987). Placing such heavy emphasis on success is not what kindergartens were originally intended to do. In the 1840s, Friedrich Froebel's concern for quality education for young children led to the founding of the kindergarten, literally "a garden for children." The founder of the kindergarten understood that, like growing plants, children require careful nurturing. Unfortunately, too many of today's kindergartens have forgotten the importance of careful nurturing for our nation's young children.

In the **child-centered kindergarten,** *education involves the whole child and includes concern for the child's physical, cognitive, and social development. Instruction is organized around the child's needs, interests, and learning styles. The process of learning, rather than what is learned, is emphasized.* Each child follows a unique developmental pattern, and young children learn best through firsthand experiences with people and materials. Play is extremely important in the child's total development. *Experimenting, exploring, discovering, trying out, restructuring, speaking,* and *listening* are all words that describe excellent kindergarten programs. Such programs are closely attuned to the developmental status of 4- and 5-year-old children. They are based on a state of being, not on a state of becoming (Ballenger, 1983).

Critical Thinking

Most of you went to a preschool or kindergarten. Can you remember what it was like? In what ways could the kindergarten you attended have been improved? How can we make our nation's preschool education programs better?

Developmentally Appropriate and Inappropriate Practices

It is time for number games in a kindergarten class at the Greenbrook School in South Brunswick, New Jersey. With little prodding from the teacher, twenty-three 5- and 6-year-old children pick up geometric puzzles, playing cards, and counting equipment from the shelves lining the room. At one round table, some young children fit together brightly colored shapes. One girl forms a hexagon out of triangles. Other children gather around her to count up how many parts were needed to make the whole. After about half an hour the children prepare for story time. They put away their counting equipment and sit in a circle around one young girl. She holds up a giant book about a character named Mrs. Wishywashy, who insists on giving the farm animals a bath. The children recite the whimsical lines, clearly enjoying one of their favorite stories. The hallway outside the kindergarten is lined with drawings depicting the chil-

dren's own interpretation of the book. After the first reading, volunteers act out various parts of the book. There is not one bored face in the room (Kantrowitz & Wingert, 1989).

This is not reading, writing, and arithmetic the way most individuals remember it. A growing number of educators and psychologists believe that preschool and young elementary school children learn best through active, hands-on teaching methods like games and dramatic play. They know that children develop at varying rates and that schools need to allow for these individual differences. They also believe that schools should focus on improving children's social development as well as their cognitive development. Educators refer to this type of schooling as **developmentally appropriate practice,** *which is based upon knowledge of the typical development of children within an age span (age appropriateness) as well as the uniqueness of the child (individual appropriateness). Developmentally appropriate practice contrasts with developmentally inappropriate practice, which ignores the concrete, hands-on approach to learning. Direct teaching largely through abstract, paper-and-pencil activities presented to large groups of young children is believed to be developmentally inappropriate.*

One of the most comprehensive documents addressing the issue of developmentally appropriate practice in early childhood programs is the position statement by the NAEYC (National Association for the Education of Young Children) in 1986 (Bredekamp, 1987). This document represents the expertise of many of the foremost experts in the field of early childhood education. By turning to figure 17.1, you can examine some of the NAEYC recommendations for developmentally appropriate practice. In one recent study, children who attended developmentally appropriate kindergartens displayed more appropriate classroom behavior, had better conduct records, and better work-study habits in the first grade than children who attended developmentally inappropriate kindergartens (Hart & others, 1993).

A special worry of early childhood educators is that the back-to-basics movement that has recently characterized educational reform is filtering down to kindergarten. Another worry is that many parents want their children to go to school earlier than kindergarten for the purpose of getting a "head start" in achievement.

Does It Really Matter If Children Attend Preschool before Kindergarten?

According to child developmentalist David Elkind (1987), parents who are exceptionally competent and dedicated and who have both the time and the energy can provide the basic ingredients of early childhood education in their home. If parents have the competence and resources to provide young children with a variety of learning experiences and exposure to other children and adults (possibly through neighborhood play groups), along with opportunities for extensive play, then home schooling may sufficiently educate young children. However, if parents do not have the commitment, the time, the energy, and the resources to provide young children with an environment

FIGURE 17.1

Developmentally appropriate and inappropriate practice in early childhood education:
NAEYC recommendations.

Component	Appropriate practice	Inappropriate practice
Curriculum goals 	Experiences are provided in all developmental areas—physical, cognitive, social, and emotional.	Experiences are narrowly focused on cognitive development without recognition that all areas of the child's development are interrelated.
	Individual differences are expected, accepted, and used to design appropriate activities.	Children are only evaluated against group norms and all are expected to perform the same tasks and achieve the same narrowly defined skills.
	Interactions and activities are designed to develop children's self-esteem and positive feelings toward learning.	Children's worth is measured by how well they conform to rigid expectations and perform on standardized tests.
Teaching strategies 	Teachers prepare the environment for children to learn through active exploration and interaction with adults, other children, and materials.	Teachers use highly structured, teacher-directed lessons almost exclusively.
	Children select many of their own activities from among a variety the teacher prepares.	The teacher directs all activity, deciding what children will do and when.
	Children are expected to be mentally and physically active.	Children are expected to sit down, be quiet, and listen, or do paper-and-pencil tasks for long periods of time. A major portion of time is spent passively sitting, watching, and listening.
Guidance of socioemotional development 	Teachers enhance children's self-control by using positive guidance techniques such as modeling and encouraging expected behavior, redirecting children to a more acceptable activity, and setting clear limits.	Teachers spend considerable time enforcing rules, punishing unacceptable behavior, demeaning children who misbehave, making children sit and be quiet, or refereeing disagreements.
	Children are provided many opportunities to develop social skills such as cooperating, helping, negotiating, and talking with the person involved to solve interpersonal problems.	Children work individually at desks and tables most of the time and listen to the teacher's directions to the total group.

that approximates a good early childhood program, then it *does* matter whether a child attends preschool. In this case, the issue is not whether preschool is important, but whether home schooling can closely duplicate what a competent preschool program can offer (Beardslee & Richmond, 1992).

We should always keep in mind that the view of early childhood education as an early start to ensure that participants will finish early or on top in an educational race is an unfortunate one. Elkind (1988) points out that perhaps the choice of the phrase "head start" for the education of disadvantaged children was a mistake. "Head start" does not imply a race. Not surprisingly, when middle-class parents heard that low-income

children were getting a "head start," they wanted a "head start" for their own young children. In some instances, starting children in formal academic training too early can produce more harm than good. In Denmark, where reading instruction follows a language experience approach and formal instruction is delayed until the age of 7, illiteracy is virtually nonexistent. By contrast, in France, where state-mandated formal instruction in reading begins at age 5, 30 percent of the children have reading problems. Education should not be stressful for young children. Early childhood education should not be solely an academic prep school.

Component	Appropriate practice	Inappropriate practice
Language development, literacy, and cognitive development	Children are provided many opportunities to see how reading and writing are useful before they are instructed in letter names, sounds, and word identification. Basic skills develop when they are meaningful to children. An abundance of these activities is provided to develop language and literacy: listening to and reading stories and poems, taking field trips, dictating stories, participating in dramatic play; talking informally with other children and adults; and experimenting with writing.	Reading and writing instruction stresses isolated skill development, such as recognizing single letters, reading the alphabet, singing the alphabet song, coloring within predefined lines, or being instructed in correct formation of letters on a printed line.
	Children develop an understanding of concepts about themselves, others, and the world around them through observation, interacting with people and real objects, and seeking solutions to concrete problems. Learning about math, science, social studies, health, and other content areas is integrated through meaningful activities.	Instruction stresses isolated skill development through memorization. Children's cognitive development is seen as fragmented in content areas such as math or science, and times are set aside for each of these.
Physical development	Children have daily opportunities to use large muscles, including running, jumping, and balancing. Outdoor activity is planned daily so children can freely express themselves.	Opportunity for large muscle activity is limited. Outdoor time is limited because it is viewed as interfering with instructional time, rather than as an integral part of the children's learning environment.
	Children have daily opportunities to develop small muscle skills through play activities, such as puzzles, painting, cutting, and similar activities.	Small motor activity is limited to writing with pencils, coloring predrawn forms, or engaging in similar structured lessons.
Aesthetic development and motivation	Children have daily opportunities for aesthetic expression and appreciation through art and music. A variety of art media is available.	Art and music are given limited attention. Art consists of coloring predrawn forms or following adult-prescribed directions.
	Children's natural curiosity and desire to make sense of their world are used to motivate them to become involved in learning.	Children are required to participate in all activities to obtain the teacher's approval, to obtain extrinsic rewards like stickers or privileges, or to avoid punishment.

Preschool is rapidly becoming a norm in early childhood education. Twenty-three states already have legislation pending to provide schooling for 4-year-old children, and there are already many private preschool programs. The increase in public preschools underscores the growing belief that early childhood education should be a legitimate component of public education. There are dangers, though. According to David Elkind (1988), early childhood education is often not well understood at higher levels of education. The danger is that public preschool education for 4-year-old children will become little more than a downward extension of traditional elementary ed-

ucation. This is already occurring in preschool programs in which testing, workbooks, and group drill are imposed on 4- and 5-year-old children.

Elkind believes that early childhood education should become a part of public education but on its own terms. Early childhood should have its own curriculum, its own methods of evaluation and classroom management, and its own teacher-training programs. Although there may be some overlap with the curriculum, evaluation, classroom management, and teacher training at the upper levels of schooling, they certainly should not be identical.

502 Social Contexts of Development

Researchers are already beginning to document some of the stress that increased academic pressure can bring to young children (Greenberg, 1992). In one recent investigation, Diane Burts and her colleagues (1989) compared the frequencies of stress-related behaviors observed in young children in classrooms with developmentally appropriate and developmentally inappropriate instructional practices. They found that children in the developmentally inappropriate classrooms exhibited more stress-related behaviors than children in the developmentally appropriate classrooms. In another recent investigation, children in a high academically oriented early childhood education program were compared with children in a low academically oriented early childhood education program (Hirsch-Pasek & others, 1989). No benefits appeared for children in the high academically oriented early childhood education program, but some possible harmful effects were noted. Higher test anxiety, less creativity, and a less positive attitude toward school characterized the children who attended the high academic program more than the low academic program.

One of the concerns of Americans is that our school children fare poorly when their achievement test scores in math and science are compared with the test scores of school children from many other industrialized nations, especially such Asian nations as Japan and China (McKnight & others, 1987). Many Americans attribute the differences in achievement scores to a rigid system that sets young children in a lock-step march from cradle to college. In fact, the early years of Japanese schooling are anything but a boot camp. To read further about the nature of early childhood education in Japan, turn to Sociocultural Worlds of Children 17.1.

Are most American parents too concerned and pushy about their young children's preschool education? Are we putting too much pressure on young children in our nation's preschools?

The Effects of Early Childhood Education

Because kindergarten and preschool programs are so diverse, it is difficult to make overall conclusions about their effects on children's development. Nonetheless, in one review of early childhood education's influence (Clarke-Stewart & Fein, 1983), it was concluded that children who attend preschool or kindergarten:

- Interact more with peers, both positively and negatively
- Are less cooperative with and responsive to adults than home-reared children
- Are more socially competent and mature in that they are more confident, extraverted, assertive, self-sufficient, independent, verbally expressive, knowledgeable about the social world, comfortable in social and stressful circumstances, and better adjusted when they go to school (exhibiting more task persistence, leadership, and goal direction, for example)

- Are less socially competent in that they are less polite, less compliant to teacher demands, louder, and more aggressive and bossy, especially if the school or family supports such behavior

In sum, early childhood education generally has a positive effect on children's development, since the behaviors just mentioned—while at times negative—seem to be in the direction of developmental maturity in that they increase as the child ages through the preschool years.

Education for Disadvantaged Children

For many years, children from low-income families did not receive any education before they entered the first grade. In the 1960s, an effort was made to try to break the cycle of poverty and poor education for young children in the United States through compensatory education. **Project Head Start** *is a compensatory education program designed to provide children from low-income families the opportunity to acquire the skills and experiences important for success in school.* Project Head Start began in the summer of 1965, funded by the Economic Opportunity Act, and it continues to serve disadvantaged children today. In 1990, the Head Start program was reauthorized at its highest funding level ever with the hope that it would serve all eligible 3- to 5-year-olds through 1994 (National Association for the Education of Young Children, 1991; Report on Preschool Programs, 1992).

Initially, Project Head Start consisted of many different types of preschool programs in different parts of the country. Little effort was made to find out whether some programs worked better than others, but it became apparent that some programs did work better than others. **Project Follow Through** *was implemented in 1967 as an adjunct to Project Head Start. In Project Follow Through, different types of educational programs were devised to determine which programs were the most effective. In the Follow Through programs, the enriched programs were carried through the first few years of elementary school.*

These preschool children are attending a Head Start program, a national effort to provide children from low-income families the opportunity to experience an enriched environment.

SOCIOCULTURAL WORLDS
OF CHILDREN 17.1

Early Childhood Education in Japan

In the midst of low academic achievement by children in the United States, many Americans are turning to Japan, a country of high academic achievement and economic success, for possible answers. However, the answers provided by Japanese preschools are not the ones Americans expected to find. In most Japanese preschools, surprisingly little emphasis is put on academic instruction. In one recent investigation, 300 Japanese and 210 American preschool teachers, child development specialists, and parents were asked about various aspects of early childhood education (Tobin, Wu, & Davidson, 1989). Only 2 percent of the Japanese respondents listed "to give children a good start academically" as one of their top three reasons for a society to have preschools. In contrast, over half the American respondents chose this as one of their top three choices. To pre-

pare children for successful careers in first grade and beyond, Japanese schools do not teach reading, writing, and mathematics but rather skills, such as persistence, concentration, and the ability to function as a member of a group. The vast majority of young Japanese children are taught to read at home by their parents.

In the recent comparison of Japanese and American preschool education, 91 percent of Japanese respondents chose providing children with a group experience as one of their top three reasons for a society to have preschools (Tobin, Wu, & Davidson, 1989). Sixty-two percent of the most individually oriented Americans listed group experience as one of their top three choices. An emphasis on the importance of the group seen in Japanese early childhood education continues into elementary school education.

Lessons in living and working together grow naturally out of the Japanese culture. In many Japanese kindergartens, children wear the same uniforms, including caps, which are of different colors to indicate the classrooms to which they belong. They have identical sets of equipment, kept in identical drawers and shelves. This is not intended to turn the young children into robots, as some Americans have observed, but to impress on them that other people, just like themselves, have needs and desires that are equally important (Hendry, 1986).

Like in America, there is diversity in Japanese early childhood education. Some Japanese kindergartens have specific aims, such as early musical training or the practice of Montessori aims (Hendry, 1986). In large cities, some kindergartens are attached to universities that have elementary and secondary schools. Some Japanese parents believe that, if their young children attend a university-based program, it will increase the children's chances of eventually being admitted to top-rated schools and universities. Several more progressive programs have introduced free play as an antidote for the heavy intellectualizing in some Japanese kindergartens.

In Japan, learning how to cooperate and participating in group experiences are viewed as extremely important reasons for the existence of early childhood education.

Were some Follow Through programs more effective than others? Many of the different variations were able to produce the desired effects on children. For example, children in academically oriented, direct-instruction learning environments did better on achievement tests and were more persistent on tasks than were children in the other approaches. Children in affective education approaches were absent from school less often and showed more independence than children taught under other approaches. Thus, Project Follow Through was important in demonstrating that variations in early childhood education does have significant effects in a wide range of social and cognitive areas (Stallings, 1975).

The effects of early childhood compensatory education continue to be studied, and recent evaluations support the positive influence on both the cognitive and social worlds of disadvantaged young children (Haskins, 1989; Kagan, 1988; Lee, Brooks-Gunn, & Schnur, 1988). Of special interest are the long-term effects such intervention might produce. Model preschool programs lead to lower rates of placement in special education, dropping out of school, grade retention, delinquency, and use of welfare programs. Such programs might also lead to higher rates of high school graduation and employment. For every dollar invested in high-quality, model preschool programs, taxpayers receive about $1.50 in return by the time the participants reach the age of 20 (Haskins, 1989). The benefits include savings on public school education (such as special education services), tax payments on additional earnings, reduced welfare payments, and savings in juvenile justice system costs. Predicted benefits over a lifetime are much greater to the taxpayer, a return of $5.73 on every dollar invested.

One long-term investigation of early childhood education was conducted by Irving Lazar, Richard Darlington, and their colleagues (1982). They pooled their resources into what they called a consortium for longitudinal studies, developed to share information about the long-term effects of preschool programs so that better designs and methods could be created. At the time the data from the 11 different early education studies were analyzed together, the children ranged in age from 9 to 19 years. The early education models varied substantially, but all were carefully planned and executed by experts in early childhood education. Outcome measures included indicators of school competence (such as special education and grade retention), abilities (as measured by standardized intelligence and achievement tests), attitudes and values, and impact on the family. The results indicated substantial benefits of competent preschool education with low-income children on all four dimensions investigated. In sum, ample evidence indicates that well-designed and well-implemented early childhood education programs with low-income children are successful (Haskins, 1989; Kagan, 1988).

While educational intervention in impoverished young children's lives is important, not all Head Start programs are created equal. Edward Zigler and Susan Muenchow (1992) concluded that 40 percent of the 1,400 Head Start programs are of questionable quality. More attention needs to be given to developing consistently high-quality Head Start programs. One high-quality early childhood education program is the Perry Preschool program in Ypsilanti, Michigan, that was designed by David Weikart (1982, 1993). The Perry Preschool program is a two-year preschool program that includes weekly home visits from program personnel. In a recent analysis of the long-term effects of the program, as young adults the Perry Preschool children had higher high school graduation rates, more are in the workforce, fewer need welfare, crime rates are lower among them, and there are fewer teen pregnancies than a control group from the same background who did not get the enriched early childhood education experience (Weikart, 1993).

School Readiness

Educational reform has prompted considerable concern about children's readiness to enter kindergarten and first grade. The issue gained national attention when the president and the nation's governors adopted school readiness as a national educational goal, vowing that by the year 2000 all children will start to school ready to learn. The concept of school readiness is based on the assumption that all children need to possess a predetermined set of capabilities before they enter school. Thus, any discussions of school readiness should consider three important factors:

- The diversity and inequity of children's early life experiences
- The wide range of variation in young children's development and learning
- The degree to which school expectations for children entering kindergarten are reasonable, appropriate, and supportive of individual differences in children

The National Association for the Education of Young Children (1990; Willer & Bredekamp, 1990) stresses that government officials and educators who promote universal school readiness should commit to the following:

- Addressing the inequities in early life experiences so that all children have access to the opportunities that promote success in school
- Recognizing and supporting individual differences in children
- Establishing reasonable and appropriate expectations for children's capabilities upon school entry

The National Association for the Education of Young Children believes that every child, except in the most severe instances of abuse, neglect, or disability, enters school ready to learn. However, all children do not succeed in school. Inadequate health care and economic difficulties place many children at risk for academic failure before they enter school. Families who lack emotional resources and support also are not always capable of preparing their children to meet school expectations.

Therefore, according to the NAEYC, it is important to provide families with access to the services and support necessary to prepare children to succeed in school. Such services include basic health care, economic support, basic nutrition, adequate housing, family support services, and high-quality early childhood education programs.

Expectations for young children's skills and abilities need to be based on knowledge of child development and how children learn. A basic principle of child development is that *there is tremendous normal variability both among children of the same chronological age and within an individual child.* Children's social skills, physical skills, cognitive skills, and emotional adjustment are equally important areas of development, and each contributes to how well children do in school. Within any group of children, one child may possess advanced language and cognitive skills, but show poor social skills and emotional adjustment; another child may have advanced social skills, be well adjusted emotionally, and have good physical skills, but have poor language skills, and so on. Readiness expectations should not be based on a narrow checklist focusing on only one or two dimensions of development. Such a narrow focus—only considering language or cognitive skills, for example—ignores the complexity and multidimensionality of children's development.

Wide variability also occurs in the rate of children's development. The precise time at which children will achieve a certain level of development or acquire specific skills is difficult to predict. Learning and development often do not occur in rigid, uniform ways. Thus, raising the legal entry age for school or holding a child out of school for a year may not be wise, but could be misdirected efforts that only serve to impose a rigid schedule on the child's development despite their normal differences from other children (Spitzer & Dicker, 1993).

At this point, we have discussed a number of ideas about children's education and early childhood education. A summary of these ideas is presented in Concept Table 17.1. Next, we will turn our attention to the transition to elementary school.

THE TRANSITION TO ELEMENTARY SCHOOL

For most children, entering the first grade signals a change from being a "homechild" to being a "schoolchild" in which new roles and obligations are experienced. Children take up a new role (being a student), interact and develop relationships with new significant others, adopt new reference groups, and develop new standards by which to judge themselves. School provides children with a rich source of new ideas to shape their sense of self (Stipek, 1992).

> *Knowledge which is acquired under compulsion obtains no hold on the mind.*
>
> —Plato

A special concern about children's early school experiences is emerging. Evidence is mounting that early schooling proceeds mainly on the basis of negative feedback. For example, children's self-esteem in the latter part of elementary school is lower than it is in the earlier part, and older children rate themselves as less smart, less good, and less hard-working than do younger ones (Blumenfeld & others, 1981). In one investigation, the first year of school was identified as a period of con-

siderable importance in shaping achievement, especially for ethnic minority children (Alexander & Entwisle, 1988). Black and White children began school with similar achievement test scores but, by the end of the first year, Black children's performance lagged noticeably behind that of the White children, and the gap widened over the second year of schooling. The grades teachers gave to Black children in the first two grades of school also were lower than those they gave to White children.

Critical Thinking

Why does early elementary school involve so much negative feedback? What aspects of our culture and the nature of education are responsible?

In school, as well as out of school, children's learning, like children's development, is *integrated* (NAEYC, 1988). One of the main pressures on elementary teachers has been the need to "cover the curriculum." Frequently, teachers have tried to do so by tightly scheduling discrete time segments for each subject. This approach ignores the fact that children often do not need to distinguish learning by subject area. For example, they advance their knowledge of reading and writing when they work on social studies projects; they learn mathematical concepts through music and physical education (Katz & Chard, 1989; Van Deusen-Henkel & Argondizza, 1987). A curriculum can be facilitated by providing learning areas in which children plan and select their activities. For example, the classroom may include a fully equipped publishing center, complete with materials for writing, illustrating, typing, and binding student-made books; a science area with animals and plants for observation and books to study; and other similar areas (Van Deusen-Henkel & Argondizza, 1987). In this type of classroom, children learn reading as they discover information about science; they learn writing as they work together on interesting projects. Such classrooms also provide opportunities for spontaneous play, recognizing that elementary schoolchildren continue to learn in all areas through unstructured play, either alone or with other children.

Education experts Lillian Katz and Sylvia Chard (1989) recently described two elementary school classrooms. In one, children spent an entire morning making identical pictures of traffic lights. The teacher made no attempt to get the children to relate the pictures to anything else the class was doing. In the other class, children were investigating a school bus. They wrote to the district's school superintendent and asked if they could have a bus parked at their school for a few days. They studied the bus, discovered the functions of its parts, and discussed traffic rules. Then, in the classroom, they built their own bus out of cardboard. The children had fun, but they also practiced writing, problem solving, and even some arithmetic. When the class had their parents' night, the teacher was ready with reports on how each child was doing. However, all the parents wanted to see was the bus because their children had been coming home and talking about it for weeks. Many contemporary education experts believe that this is the kind of education all children deserve. That is, they believe that children should be taught through concrete, hands-on experience.

CONCEPT TABLE 17.1

The Nature of Children's Schooling and Early Childhood Education

Concept	Processes/Related Ideas	Characteristics/Description
The nature of children's schooling	Functions of children's schools	In the 1980s, the back-to-basics movement gained momentum. The back-to-basics movement emphasizes rigorous academic training. This movement especially opposed the misapplied open education orientation that became popular in the 1970s. A special worry is that early childhood education is becoming a downward extension of back-to-basics elementary and secondary education. Many experts on education and child development believe the back-to-basics movement has increased the stress in children's lives and does not adequately address individual variation in children. They also believe education should be more comprehensive, focusing on social as well as cognitive development.
	Schools' changing social developmental contexts	Social contexts differ at the preschool, elementary, and secondary levels, becoming much more expansive for adolescents.
Early childhood education	Child-centered kindergarten	It involves education of the whole child, with emphasis on individual variation, the process of learning, and the importance of play in development.
	Developmentally appropriate and inappropriate practices in the education of young children	Developmentally appropriate practice is based on knowledge of the typical development of children within an age span (age appropriateness) as well as the uniqueness of the child (individual appropriateness). Developmentally appropriate practice contrasts with developmentally inappropriate practice, which ignores the concrete, hands-on approach to learning. Direct teaching largely through abstract, paper-and-pencil activities presented to large groups of young children is believed to be developmentally inappropriate. The National Association for the Education of Young Children has been a strong proponent of developmentally appropriate practice and has developed extensive recommendations for its implementation.

SCHOOLS, CLASSROOMS, AND TEACHERS

Schools, classrooms, and teachers vary on many dimensions, among them school size and classroom size, classroom structure and climate, and teacher traits. We will consider each of these in turn.

School Size and Classroom Size

A number of factors led to the increased size of schools in the United States: increasing urban enrollments, decreasing budgets, and an educational rationale of increased academic stimulation in consolidated institutions (Conant, 1959; Minuchin & Shapiro, 1983). However, is bigger really better? No systematic relation between school size and academic achievement has been found, but more prosocial and possibly less antisocial behavior take place in small schools (Rutter & others, 1979). For secondary schools, the upper limit has been set at various levels between 500 and 1,000 students (Garbarino, 1980b). Large schools may not provide a personalized climate that al-

lows for an effective system of social control. Students may feel alienated and not take responsibility for their conduct. This may be especially true for unsuccessful students who do not identify with their school and who become members of oppositional peer groups. The responsiveness of the school may mediate the impact of school size on adolescent behavior. For example, in one investigation, low-responsive schools (that is, schools that offer few rewards for desirable behavior) had higher crime rates than did high-responsive schools (McPartland & McDill, 1976). Even though school responsiveness may mediate conduct, small schools may be more flexible and responsive than larger schools.

Besides the belief that smaller schools provide children and adolescents with a better education, there also is a belief that smaller classes are better than larger classes. Traditional schools in the United States have about 30 to 35 students. An analysis of a large number of investigations revealed that, as class size increases, achievement decreases (Glass & Smith, 1978). The researchers concluded that a pupil who would score at about the 63rd percentile on a national test when taught individually

Concept	Processes/Related Ideas	Characteristics/Description
	Does it matter if children attend preschool before kindergarten?	Parents can educate their young children just as effectively as schools can. However, many parents do not have the commitment, time, energy, and resources needed to provide young children with an environment that approaches a competent early childhood education program. Too often, parents see education as a race and preschool as a chance to get ahead in the race. However, education is not a race and it should not be stressful for young children. Public preschools are appearing in many states. A concern is that they should not become merely simple versions of elementary school. Early childhood education has some issues that overlap with upper levels of schooling, but in many ways the agenda of early childhood education is different.
	How does early childhood education influence children's development?	It is difficult to evaluate, but the effects overall seem to be positive. However, outcome measures reveal areas in which social competence is more positive, others in which it is less competent.
	Education for disadvantaged young children	Compensatory education has tried to break through the poverty cycle with such programs as Head Start and Follow Through. Long-term studies reveal that model preschool programs have positive effects on development.
	School readiness	Educational reform has prompted considerable concern about children's readiness to enter kindergarten and first grade. The National Association for the Education of Young Children believes that the proposed guidelines for school readiness often do not adequately take into account the diversity and inequity of children's early life experiences and the opportunities needed to succeed in school, do not recognize and support individual differences in children, and do not establish reasonable and appropriate expectations of children's capabilities upon school entry.

would score at about the 37th percentile when taught in a class of 40 students. They also concluded that being taught in a class of 20 students rather than in a class of 40 students is an advantage of about 10 percentile points on national achievement tests. These researchers also found that the greatest gains in achievement occurred among students who were taught in classes of 15 or fewer students. In classes of 20 to 40 students, class size had a less dramatic influence on students' achievement. Although this research has been criticized on methodological grounds, other researchers have reanalyzed the data using different techniques and have arrived at the same conclusions (Hedges & Stock, 1983).

Unfortunately, to maximize each child's learning potential, classes must be so small that few schools can afford to staff and house them (Klein, 1985; Slavin, 1989a). Although a class size of 15 or fewer students is not feasible for all subjects, one alternative is to allocate a larger portion of resources to the grade levels or subjects that seem the most critical. For example, some schools are beginning to reduce class size in core academic subjects, such as math, English, and science, while increasing class size in elective subjects.

Classroom Structure and Climate

The most widely debated issue in classroom structure and climate in recent years has focused on open versus traditional classrooms. The open versus traditional classroom concept is multidimensional. Open classrooms, or open schools, have such characteristics as the following:

- Free choice by students of activities they will participate in
- Space flexibility
- Varied, enriched learning materials
- Emphasis on individual and small-group instruction
- The teacher is more a facilitator than a director of learning

- Students learn to assume responsibility for their learning
- Multi-age grouping of children
- Team teaching
- Classrooms without walls in which the physical nature of the school is more open

Overall, researchers have found that open classrooms are associated with lower language achievement but improved attitudes toward school (Giaconia & Hedges, 1982).

Beyond the overall effects of open versus traditional classrooms, it is important to evaluate how specific dimensions of open classrooms are related to specific dimensions of a child's development. In this regard, researchers have found that individualized instruction (adjusting rate, methods, materials, small-group methods) and the role of the child (the degree of activity in learning) are associated with positive effects on the child's self-concept (Giaconia & Hedges, 1982).

The characteristics of the child also need to be considered when evaluating the effects of classroom structure and climate (Linney & Seidman, 1989). For example, some children may benefit from structure more than others. **Aptitude-treatment interaction (ATI)** *stresses the importance of both children's aptitudes or characteristics and the treatments or experiences they are given in classrooms. Aptitude refers to such characteristics as the academic potential and personality characteristics on which students differ; treatment refers to educational techniques, such as structured versus flexible classrooms* (Cronbach & Snow, 1977). Researchers have found that children's achievement level (aptitude) interacts with classroom structure (treatment) to produce the best learning (Peterson, 1977). For example, students who are highly achievement-oriented usually do well in a flexible classroom and enjoy it; low-achievement-oriented students usually fare worse and dislike such flexibility. The reverse often appears in structured classrooms.

Teachers

Almost everyone's life is affected in one way or another by teachers. You were probably influenced by teachers as you grew up; you may become a teacher yourself or work with teachers through counseling or psychological services; and you may one day have children whose education will be guided by many teachers through the years. You can probably remember several of your teachers vividly. Perhaps one never smiled, another required you to memorize everything in sight, and yet another always appeared happy and vibrant and encouraged verbal interaction. Psychologists and educators have tried to create a profile of a good teacher's personality traits, but the complexity of personality, education, learning, and individual differences makes the task difficult (Sadker & Sadker, 1991). Nonetheless, some teacher traits are associated with positive student outcomes more than others; enthusiasm, ability to plan, poise, adaptability, warmth, flexibility, and awareness of individual differences are a few (Gage, 1965). In one recent study, teacher support had a strong influence on students' achievement (Goodenow, 1993).

> *The whole art of teaching is only the art of awakening the natural curiosity of young minds.*
> —Anatole France

Erik Erikson (1968) believes that good teachers should be able to produce a sense of industry, rather than inferiority, in their students. Good teachers are trusted and respected by the community and know how to alternate work and play, study and games, says Erikson. They know how to recognize special efforts and to encourage special abilities. They also know how to create a setting in which children feel good about themselves and how to handle children to whom school is not important. In Erikson's (1968) words, children should be "mildly but firmly coerced into the adventure of finding out that one can learn to accomplish things which one would never have thought of by oneself" (p. 127).

SOCIAL CLASS AND ETHNICITY IN SCHOOLS

Sometimes it seems as though the major function of schools has been to train children to contribute to a middle-class society. Politicians who vote on school funding have been from middle-class or elite backgrounds, school board members have often been from middle-class backgrounds, and principals and teachers also have had middle-class upbringing. Critics argue that schools have not done a good job of educating lower-class and ethnic minority children to overcome the barriers that block the enhancement of their position (Glasser, 1990; Holtzman, 1992; Huang & Gibbs, 1989).

Social Class

In *Dark Ghetto,* Kenneth Clark (1965) described the ways in which lower- and middle-class children are treated differently in school. According to Clark's observations, teachers in middle-class schools spend more time teaching students and evaluate students' work more than twice as much as teachers in low-income schools. He observed that teachers in low-income schools made three times as many negative comments to students as teachers did in middle-class schools, who made more positive than negative comments to students. The following observations vividly describe a school in a large urban slum area:

> It is 2 P.M., beginning of the sixth-period class, and Warren Benson, a young teacher, looks around the room. Eight students are present out of thirty. "Where is everybody?" he demands. "They don't like your class," a girl volunteers. Three girls saunter in. Cora, who is playing a cassette recorder, bumps over to her desk in time with the music. She lowers the volume. "Don't mark us down late," she shouts. "We was right here."
> . . . Here you find students from poverty homes, students who can't read, students with drug problems, students wanting to drop out. . . .

Teachers' expectations for children from low-income families are lower than for children from middle-income families (Entwistle, 1990). A teacher who knows that a child comes from a lower-class background may spend less time trying to help the child solve a problem and may anticipate that the child will get into trouble. The teacher may believe that the parents in low-income families are not interested in helping the children, so she may make fewer efforts to communicate with the children. However, there is evidence that teachers of lower-class origin may have different attitudes toward lower-class students than teachers of middle-class origin (Gottlieb, 1966). Perhaps because they have experienced many inequities themselves, teachers of lower-class origin may be more empathetic to the problems that lower-class children encounter. When asked to list the most outstanding characteristics of their lower-class students, middle-class teachers checked lazy, rebellious, and fun-loving; lower-class teachers checked happy, cooperative, energetic, and ambitious. The teachers with lower-class backgrounds perceived the lower-class children's behaviors as adaptive; the middle-class teachers viewed the same behaviors as falling short of middle-class standards.

Ethnicity

Children from lower-class backgrounds are not the only students who have difficulties in school; so do children from various ethnic backgrounds (Fenzel & Magaletta, 1993; Tharp, 1989). In his famous speech "I Have a Dream," Martin Luther King, Jr. said, "I have a dream that my four little children will one day live in a nation where they will not be judged by the color of their skin but by the content of their character." In most American schools, Blacks, Mexicans, Puerto Ricans, Native Americans, Japanese, and Asian Indians are minorities, and many teachers have been ignorant of the different cultural meanings non-Anglo children have learned in their community (Huang & Gibbs, 1989). The social and academic development of children from minority groups depends on teacher expectations; the teacher's experience in working with children from different backgrounds; the curriculum; the presence of role models in the schools for minority students; the quality of relations between school personnel and parents from different ethnic, economic, and educational backgrounds; and the relations between the school and the community (Minuchin & Shapiro, 1983).

Do teachers have lower academic expectations for minority-group children? The evidence indicates that teachers look for and reward achievement-oriented behavior in White students more often than in Black students (Scott-Jones & Clark, 1986). When teachers praise Black students for their academic performance, the praise is often qualified: "This is a good paper. It is better than yesterday's." Also, teachers have been found to criticize gifted Black students more than gifted White students, possibly because they do not expect intellectual competence in Black students (Baron, Tom, & Cooper, 1985).

One of the largest efforts to study ethnicity in schools has focused on desegregation through busing (Bell, 1980). Desegregation attempts to make the proportions of minority-

Some critics argue that one of the main functions of schools has been to train children to contribute to a middle-class, White society. These critics argue that schools have not done a competent job of educating low-income, ethnic minority children.

group and White student populations in schools more equal. Efforts to improve this ratio have often involved busing students, usually minority-group students, from their home neighborhoods to more distant schools. The underlying belief is that bringing different groups together will reduce stereotyped attitudes and improve intergroup relations. However, busing tells us nothing about what goes on inside the school once students get there. Minority-group children bused to a predominantly White school are often resegregated in the classroom through seating patterns, ability grouping, and tracking systems. Overall, the findings pertaining to desegregation through busing have shown dismal results (Minuchin & Shapiro, 1983).

My country is the world; My countrymen are mankind.
—William Lloyd Garrison, 1803

Improvements in interracial relations among children in schools depend on what happens after students arrive at the school. In one comprehensive national investigation of factors that contribute to positive interracial relations, more than 5,000 fifth-grade students and more than 400 tenth-grade students were evaluated (Forehand, Ragosta, & Rock, 1976). Multiethnic curricula, projects focused on ethnic issues, mixed work groups, and supportive teachers and principals led to improved interethnic relations.

When the schools of Austin, Texas, were desegregated through extensive busing, the outcome was increased ethnic tension among Blacks, Mexican Americans, and Whites, producing violence in the schools. The superintendent consulted with Eliot Aronson, a prominent social psychologist who was at the University of Texas at Austin at the time. Aronson thought it was more important to prevent ethnic hostility than to control it. This led him to observe a number of elementary school classrooms in Austin. What he saw was fierce competition between persons of unequal status. To learn how Aronson proposed to reduce the tension and fierce competition, turn to Explorations in Child Development 17.1

EXPLORATIONS IN CHILD
DEVELOPMENT 17.1

The Jigsaw Classroom

Aronson stressed that the reward structure of elementary school classrooms needed to be changed from a setting of unequal competition to one of cooperation among equals, without making any curriculum changes. To accomplish this, he put together the *jigsaw classroom.* How might this work? Consider a class of 30 students, some White, some Black, some Hispanic. The lesson to be learned in the class focuses on the life of Joseph Pulitzer. The class might be broken up into five groups of six students each, with the groups being as equal as possible in terms of ethnic composition and academic achievement level. The lesson about Pulitzer's life could be divided into six parts, with one part given to each member of each six-person group. The parts might be paragraphs from Pulitzer's

biography, such as how the Pulitzer family came to the United States, Pulitzer's childhood, his early work, and so on. The components are like parts of a jigsaw puzzle. They have to be put together to form the complete puzzle.

All students in each group are given an allotted time to study their parts. Then the groups meet and each member tries to teach a part to her group. After an hour or so, each member is tested on the entire life of Pulitzer, with each member receiving an individual rather than a group score. Each student, therefore, must learn the entire lesson; learning depends on the cooperation and effort of the other members. Aronson (1986) believes that this type of learning increases the students' interdependence through cooperatively reaching the same goal.

The strategy of emphasizing cooperation rather than competition and the jigsaw classroom have been widely used in classrooms in the United States. A number of research studies reveal that this type of cooperative learning is associated with increased self-esteem, better academic performance, friendships among classmates, and improved interethnic perceptions (Aronson, 1986; Slavin, 1987, 1989).

Although the cooperative classroom strategy has many merits, it may have a built-in difficulty that restricts its effectiveness. Academic achievement is as much an individual as a team "sport" (Brown, 1986). It is individuals, not groups, who enter college, take jobs, and follow careers. Parents with advantaged children in the jigsaw classroom might react with increased ethnic hostility when their children bring home lower grades than they had been used to getting before the jigsaw classroom was introduced. A child may tell his father, "The teacher is getting us to teach each other. In my group, we have a kid named Carlos, who can barely speak English." Although the jigsaw classroom can be an important strategy for reducing ethnic hostility, caution needs to be exercised in its use because of the unequal status of the participants and the individual nature of achievement.

American anthropologist John Ogbu (1974, 1986, 1989) proposed a controversial view that ethnic minority children are placed in a position of subordination and exploitation in the American educational system. He believes that ethnic minority children, especially Black and Hispanic Americans, have inferior educational opportunities, are exposed to teachers and administrators who have low academic expectations for them, and encounter negative stereotypes about ethnic minority groups. Ogbu states that ethnic minority opposition to the middle-class White educational system stems from a lack of trust because of years of discrimination and oppression. Says Ogbu, it makes little sense to do well academically if occupational opportunities are often closed to ethnic minority youth.

Completing high school, or even college, does not always bring the same job opportunities for many ethnic minority youth as for White youth (Entwistle, 1990). In terms of earnings and employment rates, Black American high school graduates do not do as well as their White counterparts. Giving up in school because of a perceived lack of reward with regard to future job opportunities characterizes many Hispanic American youth as well.

According to American educational psychologist Margaret Beale Spencer and sociologist Sanford Dornbusch (1990), a form of institutional racism prevails in many American schools. That is, well-meaning teachers, acting out of misguided liberalism, often fail to challenge ethnic minority students. Knowing the handicaps these children face, some teachers accept a low level of performance from them, substituting warmth and affection for academic challenge and high standards of performance. Ethnic minority students, like their White counterparts, learn best when teachers combine warmth with challenging standards.

One person who is trying to do something about the poor quality of education for inner-city children is Black American psychiatrist James Comer (1988). He has devised an intervention model that is based on a simple principle: Everyone with a stake in a school should have a say in how it's run. Comer's model calls for forming a school-governance team, made up of the principal, psychologists, and even cafeteria workers. The team develops a comprehensive plan for operating the school, including a calendar of academic and social events that encourage parents to come to school as often as possible. Comer

James Comer (left) is shown with some of the inner-city Black American children who attend a school that became a better learning environment because of Comer's intervention. Comer is convinced that a strong, familylike atmosphere is a key to improving the quality of inner-city schools.

is convinced that a strong family orientation is a key to educational success, so he tries to create a familylike environment in schools and also makes parents feel comfortable in coming to their children's school. Among the reasons for Comer's concern about the lack of parental involvement in Black American and Hispanic American children's education is the high rate of single-parent families in these ethnic minority groups. A special concern is that 70 percent of the Black American and Hispanic American single-parent families headed by mothers are in poverty (McLoyd, in press). Poor school performance among many ethnic minority children is related to this pattern of single-parenting and poverty (Dornbusch & others, 1985; Spencer & Dornbusch, 1990).

THE NATURE OF ADOLESCENTS' SCHOOLING

Among the special concerns about adolescents' schooling are the transition to middle or junior high school, what makes an effective school for young adolescents, and high school dropouts.

The Transition to Middle or Junior High School

The emergence of junior high schools in the 1920s and 1930s was justified on the basis of physical, cognitive, and social changes that characterize early adolescence, as well as the need

for more schools for the growing student population. Old high schools became junior high schools and new regional high schools were built. In most systems, the ninth grade remained a part of the high school in content, although physically separated from it in a 6-3-3 system. Gradually, the ninth grade has been restored to the high school as many school systems have developed middle schools that include the seventh and eighth grades, or sixth, seventh, and eighth grades. The creation of middle schools has been influenced by the earlier onset of puberty in recent decades.

> *In youth we learn, in age we understand.*
> —Marie Ebner von Eschenbach

One worry of educators and psychologists is that junior high and middle schools have simply become watered-down versions of high schools, mimicking their curricular and extracurricular schedules (Hill, 1980). The critics argue that unique curricular and extracurricular activities reflecting a wide range of individual differences in biological and psychological development in early adolescence should be incorporated into our junior high and middle schools. The critics also stress that many high schools foster passivity rather than autonomy, and that schools should create a variety of pathways for students to achieve an identity.

The transition to middle school or junior high school from elementary school interests developmentalists because, even though it is a normative experience for virtually all children, the transition can be stressful. Why? Because the transition takes place at a time when many changes—in the individual, in the family, and in school—are taking place simultaneously (Eccles & Midgely, 1990; Hawkins & Berndt, 1985; Hirsch, 1989; Simmons & Blyth, 1987). These changes include puberty and related concerns about body image; the emergence of at least some aspects of formal operational thought, including accompanying changes in social cognition; increased responsibility and independence in association with decreased dependency on parents; change from a small, contained classroom structure to a larger, more impersonal school structure; change from one teacher to many teachers and a small, homogeneous set of peers to a larger, more heterogeneous set of peers; and increased focus on achievement and performance, and their assessment. This list includes a number of negative, stressful features, but there can be positive aspects to the transition. Students are more likely to feel grown up, have more subjects from which to select, have more opportunities to spend time with peers and to locate compatible friends, enjoy increased independence from direct parental monitoring, and may be more challenged intellectually by academic work.

When students make the transition from elementary school to middle or junior high school, they experience the **top-dog phenomenon,** *the circumstance of moving from the top position (in elementary school, the oldest, biggest, and most powerful students in the school) to the lowest position (in middle or junior high school, the youngest, smallest, and least powerful students in school).* Researchers who have charted the transition from elementary to

The transition from elementary to middle or junior high school occurs at the same time a number of other changes take place in development. Biological, cognitive, and social changes converge with this schooling transition to make it a time of considerable adaptation.

middle or junior high school find that the first year of middle or junior high school can be difficult for many students (Eccles & Midgely, 1990; Hawkins & Berndt, 1985; Simmons & Blyth, 1987). For example, in one investigation of the transition from sixth grade in an elementary school to the seventh grade in a junior high school, adolescents' perceptions of the quality of their school life plunged in the seventh grade (Hirsch & Rapkin, 1987). In the seventh grade, the students were less satisfied with school, were less committed to school, and liked their teachers less. The drop in school satisfaction occurred regardless of how academically successful the students were.

Effective Schools for Young Adolescents

What makes a successful middle school? Joan Lipsitz (1984) and her colleagues searched the nation for the best middle schools. Extensive contacts and observations were made. Based on the recommendations of education experts and observations in schools in different parts of the United States, four middle schools were chosen for their outstanding ability to educate young adolescents. What were these middle schools like? The most striking feature was their willingness and ability to adapt all school practices to the individual differences in physical, cognitive, and social development of their students. The schools

took seriously the knowledge we have developed about young adolescents. This seriousness was reflected in the decisions about different aspects of school life. For example, one middle school fought to keep its schedule of minicourses on Friday so that every student could be with friends and pursue personal interests. Two other middle schools expended considerable energy on a complex school organization so that small groups of students worked with small groups of teachers who could vary the tone and pace of the school day, depending on the students' needs. Another middle school developed an advisory scheme so that each student had daily contact with an adult who was willing to listen, explain, comfort, and prod the adolescent. Such school policies reflect thoughtfulness and personal concern about individuals who have compelling developmental needs.

Another aspect of the effective middle schools was that early in their existence—the first year in three of the schools and the second year in the fourth school—they emphasized the importance of creating an environment that was positive for the adolescent's social and emotional development. This goal was established not only because such environments contribute to academic excellence, but also because social and emotional development are valued as intrinsically important in adolescents' schooling.

Critical Thinking

Analyze your own middle school or junior high school. How did it measure up to Lipsitz's criteria for effective schools for young adolescents?

Recognizing that the vast majority of middle schools do not approach the excellent schools described by Joan Lipsitz (1984), in 1989 the Carnegie Corporation issued an extremely negative evaluation of our nation's middle schools. In the report, "Turning Points: Preparing American Youth for the 21st Century," the conclusion was put forth that most young adolescents attend massive, impersonal schools, learn from seemingly irrelevant curricula, trust few adults in school, and lack access to health care and counseling. The Carnegie report (1989) recommended the following:

- Develop smaller "communities" or "houses" to lessen the impersonal nature of large middle schools

- Lower student-to-counselor ratios from several hundred-to-1 to 10-to-1

- Involve parents and community leaders in schools

- Develop curricula that produce students who are literate, understand the sciences, and have a sense of health, ethics, and citizenship

- Have teachers team teach in more flexibly designed curriculum blocks that integrate several disciplines instead of presenting students with disconnected, rigidly separated 50-minute segments

- Boost students' health and fitness with more in-school programs and help students who need public health care to get it

Joan Lipsitz (shown here talking with young adolescents) has been an important spokesperson for the needs of adolescents. Former director of the Center for Early Adolescence at the University of North Carolina, she wrote the widely acclaimed book, Successful Schools for Young Adolescents.

Many of these same recommendations were echoed in a report from the National Governor's Association (America in Transition, 1989), which stated that the very structure of middle school education in America neglects the basic developmental needs of young adolescents. Many educators and psychologists strongly support these recommendations (Entwisle, 1990; MacIver & others, 1992). The Edna McConnell Clark Foundation's Program for Disadvantaged Youth is an example of a multiyear, multisite effort designed to implement many of the proposals for middle school improvement. The Foundation has engaged the Center for Early Adolescence at the University of North Carolina to guide five urban school districts in their middle school reform (Scales, 1990). In sum, middle schools throughout the nation need a major redesign if they are to be effective in educating adolescents for becoming competent adults in the twenty-first century.

High School Dropouts

For many decades, dropping out of high school has been viewed as a serious educational and societal problem. By leaving high school before graduating, many dropouts take with them educational deficiencies that severely curtail their economic and social well-being throughout their adult lives (Rumberger, 1987). We will study the scope of the problem, the causes of dropping out, and ways to reduce dropout rates. While dropping out of high school often has negative consequences for youth, the picture is not entirely bleak (William T. Grant Foundation Commission on Work, Family, and Citizenship, 1988). Over the last forty years, the proportion of adolescents who have not finished high school has decreased considerably. In 1940, more than 60 percent of all individuals 25 to 29 years of age had not completed high school. By 1986, this proportion had dropped to less than 14 percent. From 1973 to 1983, the annual dropout rate nationwide fell by almost 20 percent, from 6.3 to 5.2 percent.

Despite the decline in overall high school dropout rates, a major concern is the higher dropout rate of minority group and low-income students, especially in large cities. While the student dropout rates of most minority groups have been declining, they remain substantially above those of White adolescents. The proportion of Hispanic American youth who finish high school is not keeping pace with the gains by Black American and other minority groups. High school completion rates for Hispanic American youth dropped from 63 percent in 1985 to 56 percent in 1989; the completion rate was 52 percent in 1972. In contrast to the pattern among Hispanic American youth, the high school graduation rate for Black American youth increased from 67 percent in 1972 to 76 percent in 1989. The comparable rates for White youth remained the same—82 percent in both 1972 and 1989.

Dropout rates are also high for Native Americans (fewer than 10 percent graduate from high school (LaFromboise & Low, 1989). In some inner-city areas the dropout rate for ethnic minority students is especially high, reaching more than 50 percent in Chicago, for example (Hahn, 1987).

Students drop out of schools for many reasons. In one investigation, almost 50 percent of the dropouts cited school-related reasons for leaving school, such as not liking school or being expelled or suspended (Rumberger, 1983). Twenty percent of the dropouts (but 40 percent of the Hispanic students) cited economic reasons for leaving school. One-third of the female students dropped out for personal reasons, such as pregnancy or marriage.

To help reduce the dropout rate, community institutions, especially schools, need to break down the barriers between work and school. Many youth step off the education ladder long before reaching the level needed for a professional career, often with nowhere to step next, and left to their own devices to search for work. These youth need more assistance than they are now receiving. Among the approaches worth considering are (William T. Grant Foundation on Work, Family, and Citizenship, 1988):

- Monitored work experiences, such as through cooperative education, apprenticeships, internships, pre-employment training, and youth-operated enterprises

- Community and neighborhood services, including voluntary and youth-guided services

- Redirected vocational education, the principal thrust of which should not be preparation for specific jobs but acquisition of basic skills needed for a wide range of jobs

- Guarantees of continuing education, employment, or training, especially in conjunction with mentor programs

- Career information and counseling to expose youth to job opportunities and career options as well as to successful role models

- School volunteer programs, not only for tutoring but also for providing access to adult friends and mentors

The juku, or "cramming school," is available to Japanese children and adolescents in the summertime and after school. It provides coaching to help them improve their grades and their entrance exam scores for high schools and universities. The Japanese practice of requiring an entrance exam for high school is a rarity among the nations of the world.

Cross-Cultural Comparisons of Secondary Schools

Secondary schools in different countries share a number of features, but differ on others (Cameron & others, 1983; George, 1987; Thomas, 1988). Let's explore the similarities and differences in secondary schools in six countries: Australia, Brazil, Germany, Japan, Russia, and the United States.

Most countries mandate that children begin school at 6 to 7 years of age and stay in school until they are 14 to 17 years of age. Brazil only requires students to go to school until they are 14 years of age, while Russia mandates that students stay in school until they are 17. Germany, Japan, Australia, and the United States require school attendance until ages 15 to 16.

Most secondary schools around the world are divided into two or more levels, such as middle school (or junior high school) and high school. However, Germany's schools are divided according to three educational ability tracks: (1) The *main school* provides a basic level of education, (2) the *middle school* gives students a more advanced education, and (3) the *academic school* prepares students for entrance to a university. German schools, like most European schools, offer a classical education, which includes courses in Latin and Greek.

Japanese secondary schools have an entrance exam, but secondary schools in the other five countries do not. Only Australia and Germany have comprehensive exit exams.

The United States is the only country in the world in which sports are an integral part of the public school system. Only a few private schools in other countries have their own sports teams, sports facilities, and highly organized sports events.

The nature of the curriculum is often similar in secondary schools in different countries, although there are some differences in content and philosophy. For example, at least until recently, the secondary schools in Russia have emphasized the preparation of students for work. The "labor education program," which is part of the secondary school curriculum, includes vocational training and on-the-job experience. The idea is to instill in youth a love for manual work and a positive atti-

tude about industrial and work organizations. Russian students who are especially gifted—academically, artistically, or athletically—attend special schools where the students are encouraged to develop their talents and are trained to be the very best in their vocation. With the breakup of the Soviet Union, it will be interesting to follow what changes in education take place in Russia.

In Brazil, students are required to take Portuguese (the native language) and four foreign languages (Latin, French, English, and Spanish). Brazil requires these languages because of the country's international character and emphasis on trade and commerce. Seventh-grade students in Australia take courses in sheep husbandry and weaving, two areas of economic and cultural interest in the country. In Japan, students take a number of Western courses in addition to their basic Japanese courses; these courses include Western literature and languages (in addition to Japanese literature and language), Western physical education (in addition to Japanese martial arts classes), and Western sculpture and handicrafts (in addition to Japanese calligraphy). The Japanese school year is also much longer than that of other countries (225 days versus 180 days in the United States, for example).

EDUCATING CHILDREN WITH SPECIAL NEEDS

A final consideration in our discussion of schools is the education of children with special needs. First, we will examine the scope and education of handicapped children; second, children with a learning disability; and, third, children with attention-deficit hyperactivity disorder.

Handicapped Children

The elementary school years are a time when handicapped children become more sensitive about their differentness and how it is perceived by others. One 6-year-old girl came home from school and asked, "Am I disabled or handicapped?" Another articulate 6-year-old girl described in detail how her premature birth was the cause of her cerebral palsy: "I was a teensy-weensy baby. They put me in an incubator and I almost died." Later, when asked about being teased by her classmates because she could not walk, she replied, "I hate their guts, but if I said anything the teacher would get mad at me." A 7-year-old handicapped boy commented about how he had successfully completed a rocket-making course during the summer; he was the youngest and the most knowledgeable child in the class: "For the first time, some kids really liked me" (Howard, 1982). Life is not always fair, especially for handicapped children. As evidenced by the comments of the handicapped children just mentioned, adjusting to the world of peers and school often is painful and difficult.

An estimated 10 to 15 percent of the United States population of children between the ages of 5 and 18 are handicapped (see table 17.1). The estimates range from the 0.1 percent who are visually impaired to the 3 to 4 percent who have speech handicaps. Estimates vary because of problems in classification

TABLE 17.1

Estimates of the Percentage and Number of Handicapped Children in the United States

Handicap	% of Population	Number of Children, Ages 5 to 18
Visual impairment (includes blindness)	0.1	55,000
Hearing impairment (includes deafness)	0.5–0.7	275,000–385,000
Speech handicap	3.0–4.0	1,650,000–2,200,000
Orthopedic and health impairments	0.5	275,000
Emotional disturbance	2.0–3.0	1,100,000–1,650,000
Mental retardation (both educable and trainable)	2.0–3.0	1,100,000–1,650,000
Learning disabilities	2.0–3.0	1,100,000–1,650,000
Multiple handicaps	0.5–0.7	275,000–385,000
Total	10.6–15.0	5,830,000–8,250,000

Reprinted with the permission of Merrill, an imprint of Macmillan Publishing Company, from *The Exceptional Student in the Regular Classroom,* Fourth Edition by Bill R. Gearheart, Mel W. Weishahn, and Carol J. Gearheart. Copyright © 1988 by Merrill Publishing Company.

and testing. Experts sometimes differ in how they define the various categories of handicapped children, and different tests may be used by different school systems or psychologists to assess whether a child is handicapped.

Public Law 94-142 *(PL 94-142) is the federal government's mandate to all states to provide a free, appropriate education for all children.* This law, also called the Education for All Handicapped Children Act, was passed by Congress in 1975. A key provision of the bill was the development of an individualized education program for each identified handicapped child. Another provision of Public Law 94-142 is to provide the *least restrictive environment* for the education of handicapped children. Each state must ensure that all handicapped students are educated with students who are not handicapped. Special education classes, separate schooling, or other removal of handicapped children from the regular education environment should occur only when the nature or severity of the handicap is such that an education in regular classes with the use of supplementary aids and services cannot be satisfactorily achieved (Gaylord-Ross, 1989; Lipsky & Gartner, 1989).

Mainstreaming *occurs when handicapped children attend regular school classes with nonhandicapped children.* In this way, handicapped children enter the "mainstream" of education in the school and are not separated from nonhandicapped students. However, even under PL 94-142, which emphasizes mainstreaming, certain types of handicapped children, such as those with hearing impairments, usually spend part of each day in separate classes taught by specially trained teachers. The results of mainstreaming have met with mixed results. In some schools, teachers assign children to environments that are not the best contexts for learning. Some people believe that mainstreaming means there will be a number of profoundly retarded, drugged children sitting in classrooms in dazed, unresponsive states. Others believe that including handicapped children in regular classrooms will detract from the quality of the education given to nonhandicapped children. The picture is not as bleak

Public Law 94–142 mandates free, appropriate education for all children. A key provision of the bill was the development of an individualized education program for each identified handicapped child. Among the important issues involved in the education of handicapped children are mainstreaming and labeling.

as some of these criticisms suggest. Virtually all profoundly retarded children are institutionalized and will never be schooled in public classrooms. Only the mildly retarded are mainstreamed. Mainstreaming makes children and teachers become more aware of the special needs of handicapped people.

In practice, mainstreaming has not been the simple solution its architects hoped for. Many handicapped children require extensive and expensive services to help them become effective learners in regular classrooms. As school systems have become increasingly strapped financially, many services for handicapped children have been cut back. Some teachers, already burdened with heavy course loads and time demands, have felt overwhelmed by the added requirement of developing special teaching arrangements for handicapped children, and the social interaction of handicapped and nonhandicapped children has not always gone smoothly in mainstreamed classrooms (Gallagher, Trohanis, & Clifford, 1989).

The hope that mainstreaming would be a positive solution for all handicapped children needs to be balanced with the reality of each handicapped child's life and special needs. The specially tailored education program should meet with the acceptance of parents and counselors, educational authorities, and, when feasible, the children themselves (Hallahan & others, 1988).

Is there a disadvantage to referring to these children as handicapped or disabled? Children who are labeled as handicapped or disabled may feel permanently stigmatized and rejected, and they may be denied opportunities for full development. Children labeled as handicapped or disabled may be assigned to inferior educational programs or placed in institutions without the legal protection given to "normal" individuals. Paradoxically, however, if handicapped or disabled children are not labeled, they may not be able to take advantage of the special programs designed to help them (Hobbs, 1975; Horne, 1988).

There are no quick fixes for the education of handicapped children. Although progress has been made in recent years to provide supportive instruction for handicapped children, increasing effort needs to be devoted to developing the skills of handicapped children (Hynd & Obrzut, 1986). Handicapped children have a strong will to survive, to grow, and to learn. They deserve our very best educational efforts (Wood, 1988).

Learning Disabilities

Paula doesn't like kindergarten and can't seem to remember the names of her teacher or classmates. Bobby's third-grade teacher complains that his spelling is awful and that he is always reversing letters. Ten-year-old Tim hates to read. He says it is too hard for him and the words just don't make any sense to him. Each of these children is learning disabled. Children with

learning disabilities *(1) are of normal intelligence or above, (2) have difficulties in several academic areas but usually do not show deficits in others, and (3) are not suffering from some other conditions or disorders that could explain their learning problems* (Reid, 1988). The breadth of definitions of learning disabilities has generated controversy about just what learning disabilities are (Chalfant, 1989; Gerber, 1992).

Within the global concept of learning disabilities fall problems in listening, thinking, memory, reading, writing, spelling, and math. (Andrews & Conte, 1993; Jackson, Breitmeyer, & Fletcher, 1993; Olson & Forsberg, 1993). Attention deficits involving an inability to sit still, pay attention, and concentrate are also classified under learning disabilities. Estimates of the number of learning-disabled children in the United States are as broad as the definition, ranging from 1 to 30 percent (Lerner, 1988). The U.S. Department of Education puts the number of identified learning-disabled children between the ages of 3 and 21 at approximately 2 million.

Improving the lives of learning-disabled children will come from (1) recognizing the complex, multifaceted nature of learning disabilities (biological, cognitive, and social aspects of learning disabilities need to be considered) and (2) becoming more precise in our analysis of the learning environments in which learning-disabled children participate (Drew & Luftig, 1993; Vaughn, 1993; Wenz-Gross & Siperstein, 1993). The following discussion of one subtype of learning disability, attention-deficit hyperactivity disorder, exemplifies this complexity and preciseness.

Attention-Deficit Hyperactivity Disorder

Matthew failed the first grade. His handwriting was messy. He did not know the alphabet and never attended very well to the lessons the teacher taught. Matthew is almost always in motion. He can't sit still for more than a few minutes at a time. His mother describes him as very fidgety. Matthew has **attention-deficit hyperactivity disorder,** *the technical term for what is commonly called hyperactivity. This disorder is characterized by a short attention span, distractibility, and high levels of physical activity* (Barkeley, 1989; Berman, 1992; O'Connor, Crowell, & Sprafin, 1993). In short, these children do not pay attention and have difficulty concentrating on what they are doing. Estimates of the number of children with attention-deficit hyperactivity disorder vary from less than 1 percent to 5 percent. While young children or even infants show characteristics of this disorder, the vast majority of hyperactive children are identified in the first three grades of elementary school when teachers recognize that they have great difficulty paying attention, sitting still, and concentrating on their schoolwork.

What makes Jimmy so impulsive, Sandy so distractible, and Harvey so excitable? Possible causes include heredity, prenatal damage, diet, family dynamics, and the physical environment. As we saw in chapter 3, the influence of heredity on temperament is increasingly considered, with activity level being one aspect of temperament that differentiates one child from another very early in development. Approximately four times as many boys as girls are hyperactive. This sex difference may be due to differences in the brains of boys and girls determined by genes on the Y chromosome. The prenatal hazards we discussed in chapter 4 may also produce hyperactive behavior. Excessive drinking by women during pregnancy is associated with poor attention and concentration by their offspring at 4 years of age, for example (Streissguth & others, 1984). With regard to diet, severe vitamin deficiencies can lead to attentional problems. Vitamin B deficiencies are of special concern. Caffeine and sugar may also contribute to attentional problems.

A wide range of psychotherapies and drug therapy has been used to improve the lives of hyperactive children. For unknown reasons, some drugs that stimulate the brains and behaviors of adults have a quieting effect on the brains and behaviors of children. The drugs most widely prescribed for hyperactive children are amphetamines, especially Ritalin. Amphetamines work effectively for some hyperactive children, but not all. As many as 20 percent of hyperactive children treated with Ritalin do not respond to it. Even when Ritalin works, it is also important to consider the social world of the hyperactive child. The teacher is especially important in this social world, helping to monitor the child's academic and social behavior to determine whether the drug works and whether the prescribed dosage is correct.

At this point, we have discussed a number of ideas about the transition to elementary school; schools, classrooms, and teachers; social class and ethnicity in schools; the nature of adolescents' schooling; and the education of children with special needs. A summary of these ideas is presented in Concept Table 17.2.

PERSPECTIVES ON PARENTING AND EDUCATION

The Role of Parenting in Young Children's Learning and Education

Mothers and fathers play important roles in the development of young children's positive attitudes toward learning and education (Cowan, Hemming, & Shuck, 1993). In one investigation, mothers and their preschool children were evaluated and then the children's academic competence was assessed when they were in sixth grade (Hess & others, 1984). Maternal behavior in the preschool years was related to the children's academic competence in sixth grade. The best predictors of academic competence in sixth grade were the following maternal behaviors shown during the preschool years: effective communication with the child, a warm relationship with the child, positive expectations for achievement, use of rule-based rather than authority-based discipline, and not believing that success in school was based on luck.

The father's involvement with the child can also help to build positive attitudes toward school and learning. Competent fathers of preschool children set aside regular time to be with the child, listen to the child and respond to questions, become involved in the child's play, and show an interest in the child's preschool and kindergarten activities. Fathers can help with the young child's schooling in the following ways (Swick & Manning, 1983):

• Supporting their children's efforts in school and their children's unique characteristics

• Helping children with their problems when the children seek advice

• Communicating regularly with teachers

• Participating in school functions

The relationship between the school and the parents of children is an important aspect of education (Helling, 1993; Innocenti & Huh, 1993; Marcon, 1993; McAdoo, Luster, & Perkins, 1993). Schools and parents can cooperate to provide young children with the best possible educational experience, and a positive orientation toward learning. In one investigation, the most important factor in contributing to the success of the preschool program was the positive involvement of the parents in their young children's learning and education (Lally, Mangione, & Honig, 1987). ■

CONCEPT TABLE 17.2

The Transition to Elementary School; Schools, Classrooms, and Teachers; Social Class and Ethnicity in Schools; the Nature of Adolescents' Schooling; and the Education of Children with Special Needs

Concept	Processes/Related Ideas	Characteristics/Description
The transition to elementary school	Its nature	A special concern is that early elementary school education proceeds mainly on the basis of negative feedback to children. The curriculum in elementary schools should be integrated. Many educators and psychologists believe that children should be taught through concrete, hands-on experience in the early elementary school years.
Schools, classrooms, and teachers	School size and classroom size	Smaller is usually better when school size and classroom size are at issue. Recommended maximum secondary school size ranges from 500 to 1,000 children. Most class sizes are 30 to 35 students, but a class size of 15 or fewer benefits student learning.
	Classroom structure and climate	The open classroom concept is multidimensional. Specific dimensions of open and traditional classrooms need to be considered, as well as specific outcomes. Overall, open classrooms are associated with lower language achievement but improved school attitudes. Individualized instruction and the role of the child are associated with positive self-concept. Aptitude-treatment interaction also needs to be considered.
	Teachers	Teacher characteristics involve many different dimensions, and coming up with a profile of a competent teacher of children is difficult. Erikson believes that a good teacher creates a sense of industry rather than inferiority.
Social class and ethnicity in schools	Social class	Schools have a strong middle-class orientation. Teachers have lower expectations for children from low-income backgrounds, although teachers from these backgrounds perceive these students' behavior as more adaptive than do teachers from other backgrounds.
	Ethnicity	Many teachers have been ignorant of the different cultural meanings non-Anglo children have learned in their communities. John Ogbu proposed a controversial view that ethnic minority children are placed in a position of subordination and exploitation in the American educational system. Some experts believe that a form of institutional racism exists in some schools because teachers fail to academically challenge ethnic minority children. Teachers have lower expectations for ethnic minority children. Desegregation through busing has shown virtually no benefits in reducing racial tension. What is important to study is what goes on at school after children arrive. Multiethnic curricula, supportive teachers and administrators, and cooperative learning benefit students from ethnic minority backgrounds.
The nature of adolescents' schooling	Transition to middle or junior high school	The emergence of junior highs in the 1920s and 1930s was justified on the basis of physical, cognitive, and social changes in early adolescence and the need for more schools in response to a growing student population. Middle schools have become more popular in recent years and coincide with puberty's earlier arrival. The transition to middle or junior high school coincides with many social, familial, and individual changes in the

Concept	Processes/Related Ideas	Characteristics/Description
		adolescent's life. The transition involves moving from the top-dog to the lowest position. Successful schools for young adolescents take individual differences in development seriously, show a deep concern for what is known about early adolescence, and emphasize social and emotional development as much as intellectual development. In 1989, the Carnegie Corporation recommended a major redesign of middle schools.
	High school dropouts	Dropping out has been a serious problem for decades. Many dropouts have educational deficiencies that curtail their economic and social well-being for much of their adult life. Some progress has been made in that dropout rates for most ethnic minority groups have declined in recent decades, although dropout rates for inner-city, low-income minorities, Hispanic Americans, and Native Americans are still precariously high. Dropping out of school is associated with demographic, family-related, peer-related, school-related, economic, and individual factors. Reducing the dropout rate and improving the lives of noncollege youth could be accomplished by strengthening schools and bridging the gap between school and work.
	Cross-cultural comparisons of secondary schools	There are a number of similarities and differences in secondary schools around the world. We compared secondary schools in six countries: Australia, Brazil, Germany, Japan, Russia, and the United States. Japanese schools were the only ones to require an entrance exam; U.S. schools the only ones to emphasize sports so strongly.
Educating children with special needs	Handicapped children	Approximately 10 to 15 percent of children in the United States are estimated to be handicapped. Public Law 94-142 ordered a free, appropriate education for every handicapped child. The law emphasizes an individually tailored education program for every child and the provision of a least restrictive environment, which has led to extensive mainstreaming of handicapped children into the regular classroom. Mainstreaming has been a controversial topic. Another issue is the labeling of handicapped children and its benefits and drawbacks.
	Learning disabilities	Such children have normal or above-normal intelligence, have difficulties in some areas but not others, and do not suffer from any other disorder that could explain their learning problems. Learning disabilities are complex and multifaceted and require precise analysis.
	Attention-deficit hyperactivity disorder	The technical term of hyperactivity, this disorder is characterized by a short attention span, distractibility, and high levels of physical activity. Possible causes include heredity, prenatal damage, diet, family dynamics, and the physical environment. Amphetamines have been used with some success in treatment, but they do hot work for all hyperactive children.

CONCLUSIONS

Children spend many years in school where there are tasks to be accomplished, people to socialize and be socialized by, and competencies to be developed.

We began the chapter by exploring several effective schools and several ineffective schools, as well the nature of children's schooling. Our coverage of early childhood education examined child-centered kindergarten, developmentally appropriate and inappropriate education, whether it matters if children attend preschool before kindergarten, the effects of early childhood education, education for disadvantaged children, and school readiness. We also studied the transition to elementary school, schools, classrooms, and teachers, and social class and ethnicity in schools. Our focus on the nature of adolescents' schooling involved the transition to middle or junior high school, effective schools for young adolescents, high school dropouts, and secondary schools around the world. We also read about educating children with special needs—handicapped children, learning disabilities, and attention-deficit hyperactivity disorder. Toward the end of the chapter we studied the role of parenting in young children's learning and education. Remember that, to obtain a summary of the chapter, you can again read the two concept tables on pages 506 and 518.

This chapter—schools—is the last chapter in the book. However, there is a final part to the book—an epilogue—that summarizes some of the main themes of children's development we have discussed, helps you to think critically about sociocultural issues in children's lives, and portrays the importance of children in our society.

KEY TERMS

back-to-basics movement The idea that the function of school should be rigorous training of intellectual skills through such subjects as English, math, and science. (497)

child-centered kindergarten The education of the whole child, including concern for the child's physical, cognitive, and social development. Instruction is organized around the child's needs, interests, and learning style. The process of learning, rather than the finished product, is emphasized. (499)

developmentally appropriate practice Education based on knowledge of the typical development of children within an age span (age appropriateness) and the uniqueness of each child (individual appropriateness). (499)

Project Head Start A compensatory education program designed to give children from low-income families the opportunity to acquire the skills and experiences important for success in school. (502)

Project Follow Through A program implemented in 1967 as an adjunct to Project Head Start. In the Follow Through programs, the enriched planned variation was carried through the first few years of elementary school. (502)

aptitude-treatment interaction (ATI) ATI stresses the importance of both children's aptitudes or characteristics and the treatments or experiences they are given in the classroom. "Aptitude" refers to such characteristics as the academic potential and personality characteristics on which students differ, "treatment" refers to educational techniques, such as structured versus flexible classrooms. (508)

top-dog phenomenon The circumstance of moving from the top position (in elementary school, the oldest, biggest, and most powerful students in the school) to the lowest position (in middle or junior high school, the youngest, smallest, and least powerful students in the school). (511)

Public Law 94-142 The federal government's mandate to all states to provide a free, appropriate education for all children. (515)

mainstreaming Integrating handicapped children into regular school classes with nonhandicapped children. (515)

learning disabilities Children with learning disabilities are of normal or higher intelligence, have difficulties in several academic areas but usually do not show deficits in others, and are not suffering from other conditions or disorders that could explain their learning problems. (516)

attention-deficit hyperactivity disorder Hyperactivity, characterized by a short attention span, high distractibility, and high levels of physical activity. (516)

SUGGESTED READINGS

Fiske, E. B. (1992). *Smart schools, smart kids.* New York: Touchstone. This book describes dozens of pioneering school programs that are successful.

Ingersoll, B. (1988). *Your hyperactive child: A parent's guide to coping with attention deficit disorder.* New York: Doubleday. This book describes a number of strategies for effectively rearing hyperactive children. A number of myths about these children are debunked as well.

Lipsitz, J. (1984). *Successful schools for young adolescents.* New Brunswick, NJ: Transaction. This is important reading for anyone interested in better schools for young adolescents; it is filled with rich examples of adolescents in schools.

Phi Delta Kappan. Leaf through the 1990s issues of this leading educational journal to get a feel for the controversial, widely debated ideas in secondary education.

William T. Grant Foundation Commission on Work, Family, and Citizenship (1988). *The forgotten half: Non-college-bound youth in America.* New York: William T. Grant Foundation. This excellent report on the status of non-college-bound youth in America calls attention to ways our society can help these individuals make the school-to-work transition more effectively.

Young Children, published by the National Association for the Education of Young Children, Washington, DC. This journal includes a variety of articles about young children's physical, cognitive, and social development. Special attention is given to how various aspects of development can be fostered in our nation's preschool and kindergarten programs. Look through the issues of the past 5 years to get a feel for the important concerns in this area.

Children: The Future of Society

As the twenty-first century approaches, the well-being of children is one of our most important concerns. We all cherish the future of our children for they are the future of any society. Children who do not reach their full potential, who are destined to make fewer contributions to society than society needs, and who do not take their place as productive adults diminish the power of that society's future. In this epilogue, we will summarize some of the most important concepts and issues that have been discussed in the book and present a montage of thoughts that convey the power, beauty, and complexity of children's development.

Our journey through childhood has been long and complex, and you have read about many different facets of children's lives. This is a good time to stand back and ask yourself what you have learned. What theories, studies, and ideas struck you as more important than others? What did you learn about your own development as an infant, child, and adolescent? Did anything you learn stimulate you to rethink how children develop? How you developed into the person you are today?

In the end the power behind development is life.

—Erik Erikson

THEMES IN CHILDREN'S DEVELOPMENT

As we look back across the chapters of *Child Development*, some common themes emerge. Let's explore some of these main themes.

Knowledge about Children's Development Has Benefitted from a Diversity of Theories and an Extensive Research Enterprise

A number of theories have made important contributions to our understanding of children's development. From the biological theory of ethology to the cognitive theories of Piaget and Vygotsky to the social theories of Erikson and Bronfenbrenner, each has contributed an important piece of the developmental puzzle. However, no single theory is capable of predicting, explaining, and organizing the rich, complex, multifaceted landscape of the child's developmental journey. The inability of a single theory to explain all of children's development should not be viewed as a shortcoming of a theory. Any theory that attempts to explain all of children's development is too general. The field of child development has been moved forward by theories that are precise and zero in on key aspects of one or two dimensions of children's lives rather than by theories that try to do everything.

Knowledge about children's development has also benefitted from a research effort that has greatly expanded over the last several decades. The science of child development has become a highly sophisticated field in which collecting evidence about children is based on well-defined rules, exemplary practices, mathematical procedures for handling the evidence, and drawing inferences from what has been found.

Children Benefit from Both Basic Research and Applied Research

Across the 17 chapters of *Child Development*, we have discussed both basic research and applied research. Basic research, sometimes called pure research, is the study of issues to obtain knowledge for its own sake rather than practical application. By contrast, applied research is the study of issues that have direct practical significance, often with the intent of changing human behavior. Social policy research is applied research rather than basic research.

A developmentalist who conducts basic research might ask: How is the cognitive development of children different from adolescents? By contrast, a developmentalist who conducts applied research might ask: How can knowledge about children's and adolescents' cognitive development be used to educate them more effectively or to help them cope more effectively with stress? A basic researcher might also ask: Can a nonhuman primate, such as a chimpanzee, learn to use sign language? An applied researcher might ask: Can strategies used to teach language to chimpanzees be applied to improve the language abilities of retarded children who do not speak?

Most developmentalists believe that both basic and applied research contribute to improving children's lives. Although basic research sometimes produces information that can be applied to improve the welfare of children, it does not guarantee this application. By contrast, insisting that research always be relevant is like trying to grow flowers by focusing only on the blossoms and not tending to the roots (Walker, 1970). Basic research is root research. Without the discovery of basic principles, we would have little information to apply (Wade & Tavris, 1993).

Children's Development Is Influenced by an Interaction of Heredity and Environment

Both heredity and environment are necessary even for children to exist. Heredity and environment operate together—or cooperate—to produce a child's height and weight, ability to shoot a basketball, intelligence, reading skills, temperament, and all other dimensions of the child's development.

In chapter 1, we discussed the nature-nurture controversy, the debate about whether development is primarily influenced by heredity and maturation (nature) or by environment and experience (nurture). The debate shows no signs of subsiding, but for now, virtually all developmentalists are interactionists, accepting that children's development is determined by both heredity and environment. Behavior geneticists continue to specify more precisely the nature of heredity-environment interaction through such concepts as passive, evocative, and active genotype/environment interactions, as well as shared and nonshared environmental influences.

Children's Development Involves Both Continuity and Discontinuity

Some developmentalists emphasize the continuity of development, the view that development involves gradual, cumulative change from conception to death. Others stress the discontinuity of development, the view that development consists of distinct stages in the life span.

Development involves both continuity and discontinuity. For example, while Piaget's stages reflect discontinuity in the sense that when children change from being preoperational to concrete operational thinkers, researchers recently have found that young children's intelligence shows more continuity than was once believed. Who is right? Probably both. As Piaget envisioned, most preschool children are egocentric and center on the obvious physical characteristics of stimuli. Most concrete operational children do not think hypothetically and don't solve problems in a scientific manner. In these ways, children's development is stage-like, as Piaget proposed. However, as information processing oriented researchers believe, children's thinking is not as stage-like as Piaget thought.

Children's Development Is Determined by Both Early and Later Experiences

While children's development is influenced by both early and later experiences, developmentalists still debate how strong the contributions of each type of experience are. The early experience advocates argue that early experiences, especially in infancy, are more important than later experiences. They believe, for example, that warm, nurturant, sensitive caregiving in the first year of life is necessary for optimal later development. Later experiences are not as important in shaping the child's developmental path, they say.

By contrast, other developmentalists stress that later experiences are just as important as early experiences in children's development. That is, warm, nurturant, sensitive parenting is just as important in the elementary school years in shaping children's development as it is in infancy. People in Western cultures are stronger advocates of early experience, those in Eastern cultures of later experiences. The debate goes on.

Children's Development Is Determined by an Interaction of Biological, Cognitive, and Social Processes

Biological processes involve changes in a child's physical nature, such as genes inherited from parents, development of the brain, prenatal and pubertal hormonal changes, and the development of motor skills. Cognitive processes involve changes in the child's thought, intelligence, and language, such as developing symbols for objects, memorizing a poem, solving a math problem, and putting together a sentence. Socioemotional processes involve changes in the child's relationships with other people, emotions, and personality, such as infant's smile in response to her mother's touch, the intimate conversation of two friends, and a girl's development of assertiveness.

In many parts of the book, you read about how biological, cognitive, and socioemotional processes are intricately interwoven. For example, biology plays an important role in children's temperament, especially influencing how shy or gregarious children are. Inadequate parenting early in children's development can seriously undermine their intelligence. Cognitive changes substantially alter how children think about their parents and peers. Both theory and research involving chil-

dren's development are becoming more integrated and less compartmentalized as links across different domains of development are sought.

Children's Development Involves Both Communalities with Other Children and Individual Variation

Every child develops in certain ways like all other children. Every child, unless afflicted by a serious handicap, walks by the age of 1 to 1½ years, talks by the age of 2 or 2½ years, engages in fantasy play in early childhood, is reared by adult caregivers who have more power and control than the child does, engages in mutual give-and-take in peer relations, goes to school, and becomes more independent and searches for an identity as an adolescent.

But children are not just like collections of geese; they are also unique, each child writing an individual history. One child may grow up in the well-coiffured lawns of suburbia, another in the ghetto confines of an inner city. One child may be short, another tall. One child may be a genius, another mentally retarded. One child may be abused, another lavished with love. And one child may be highly motivated to learn, another couldn't care less.

Children's Behavior Is Multiply Determined

An important aspect of thinking about the behavior of any child is that the child's behavior is multiply determined. When we think about what causes a child's behavior, we often lean toward explaining it in terms of a single cause. Consider a 7-year-old boy named Bobby. His teacher says that he is having trouble in school because he is from a father-absent home. The implication is that not having a father present in the home causes Bobby's poor academic performance. Not having a father may be one factor in Bobby's poor performance in school, but many others also influence his behavior. These factors include his genetic heritage and a host of environmental and sociocultural experiences, both in the past and the present. On closer inspection of Bobby's circumstances, we learn that not only has he been father-absent all of his life, never knowing his father, but that his extended family support system has also been weak. We also learn that he lives in a low-income area with little community support for recreation, libraries, and child services. The school system Bobby is enrolled in has a poor record of helping low-achieving children and has little interest in developing programs for children from disadvantaged circumstances. We could find other reasons that help explain Bobby's poor school achievement, but these examples illustrate the importance of going beyond accepting a single cause as *the* reason for a child's behavior. As with each of us, Bobby's behavior is multiply determined.

Children's Development Is Determined by Internal/External and Self/Other Influences

Controversy still surrounds whether children are architects of their own development (internal, self-determined) or whether their development is primarily orchestrated by the external forces of others. However, most experts on children recognize that development is not entirely internal and self-generated and, likewise, not entirely external and other-determined. Trying to tease apart internal/external and self/other influences is extraordinarily difficult because the child is always embedded in a social context with others. To be certain, children are not buffeted about helplessly by their environment. Children bring developmental capacities to any situation and act on the situation. At the same time, however, they interact with others who offer their own version of the world, one which children sometimes learn from and adopt for themselves. At times, children are solitary little scientists, crafting their own book of dreams and reality, as Piaget envisioned; at others, they are socially intertwined with skilled teachers and peers, as Vygotsky conceived.

America, especially male America, has had a history of underscoring the importance of self-determination and individualism. Recently, however, females have challenged the status of self-determination as a more important human value than being connected to others and competent at relationships. And, as psychologists have become more interested in cultures around the world, they have begun to recognize that many cultures, especially Eastern cultures, promote values that emphasize concern for others, interdependence, and harmonious relationships. It is important for us to raise a nation of children who not only value a separate "I" ness, uniqueness, and self-determination, but who also value connectedness with others, concern for others, and harmony in relationships.

We Need to Dramatically Reduce the Number of Children at Risk of Not Reaching Their Full Potential

Far too many children in America are not reaching their full potential because they are not being adequately reared by caregivers, not being adequately instructed in school, and not being adequately supported by society. Children who do reach their full potential and grow up to make competent contributions to their world invariably have been given considerable individual attention and support as they were growing up. Children need parents who are extensively involved with them, are sensitive to their needs, and have a sound understanding of their own and their children's development.

We also need schools that place a greater emphasis on a curriculum that is developmentally appropriate. This needs to be accomplished at all levels of education, especially in early childhood education, elementary school education, and middle school education. And we need to give more attention to our nation's social policy, especially in terms of ways to break through the poverty cycle that enshrouds more than 25 percent of the children in the United States. Our nation's political values need to reflect greater concern for the inadequate conditions in which far too many children live. And, to reduce the number of children at risk for not reaching their potential, we should focus our attention on the prevention of problems or early intervention in the problems.

Children Will Benefit from an Interdisciplinary Approach to Their Development

Some of you taking this class in child development are being taught by a child psychologist, others by someone who specializes in human development or family relationships, others by an educational psychologist or professor in an education department, others by a nurse or pediatrician, and yet others by professors from different disciplines. The field of child development has become more interdisciplinary. Our knowledge about children, and how to improve children's lives, has benefitted, and will continue to benefit, from the contributions of scholars and professionals from a number of different disciplines, including developmental psychology, education and educational psychology, pediatrics and nursing, child clinical psychology and child psychiatry, sociology, anthropology, and law. The collaboration between child developmentalists and pediatricians/nurses is one example of this interdisciplinary cooperation, with the emerging area of how development influences children's health reflecting this cross-disciplinary trend. Another example is the interest in children's eyewitness testimony that links the fields of child development and law.

Children's Development Is Embedded in Sociocultural, Historical Circumstances

Throughout this book we have emphasized the importance of considering the contexts in which the child develops. Context refers to the setting in which development occurs, a setting that is influenced by historical, economic, social, and cultural factors. These contexts or settings include homes, schools, peer groups, churches, cities, neighborhoods, communities, university laboratories, the United States, Russia, France, Japan, Egypt, and many others—each with meaningful historical, economic, social, and cultural legacies.

In the twentieth century alone in the United States, successive waves of children have witnessed dramatic historical changes, including two world wars and their violence, the Great Depression and its economic woes, the advent of television and computers, increased levels of education, and altered gender roles. And as new generations of babies have been born, they have increasingly been babies with an ethnic minority heritage.

THE JOURNEY OF CHILDHOOD

I hope you can look back and say that you learned a lot about children, not only other children, but yourself as a child and how your childhood contributed to who you are today. The insightful words of philosopher Soren Kierkegaard capture the importance of looking back to understand ourselves: "Life is lived forward but understood backwards." I also hope that those of you who become the parents of children or who work with children in some capacity—whether as teacher, counselor, or community leader—feel that you have a better grasp of what children's development is all about.

Future generations depend on our ability to face our children. At some point in our adult lives, each one of us needs to examine the shape of our life and ask whether we have met the responsibility of competently and caringly carving out a better world for our children. Twenty-one centuries ago, Roman poet and philosopher Lucretius described one of adult life's richest meanings: Grasping that the generations of living things pass in a short while and, like runners, pass on the torch of life. More than twenty centuries later, American writer James Agee captured yet another of life's richest meanings: In every child who is born the potentiality of the human race is born again.

As we come to the end of this book, I leave you with the following montage of thoughts and images that convey the beauty and complexity of children's development.

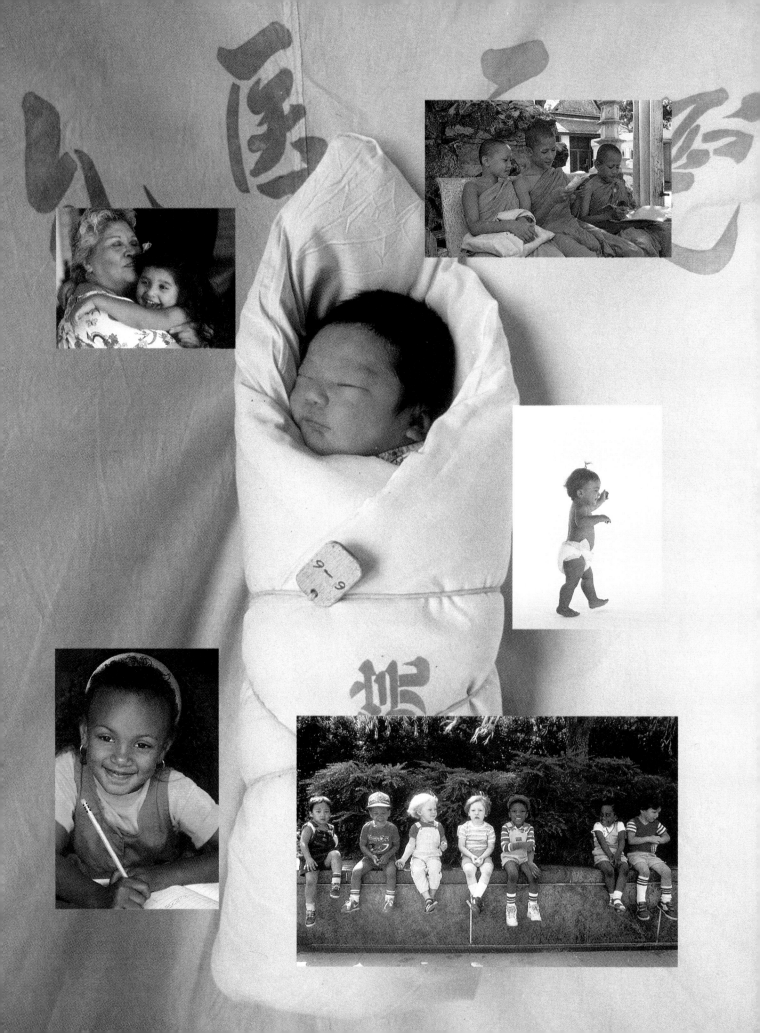

The rhythm and meaning of human development involve beginnings, when questions of whence and whither, when and how are asked. How from so simple a beginning do endless forms develop and grow and mature? What was this organism, what is it now, and what will it become? Birth's fragile moment arrives, when the newborn is on a threshold between two worlds.

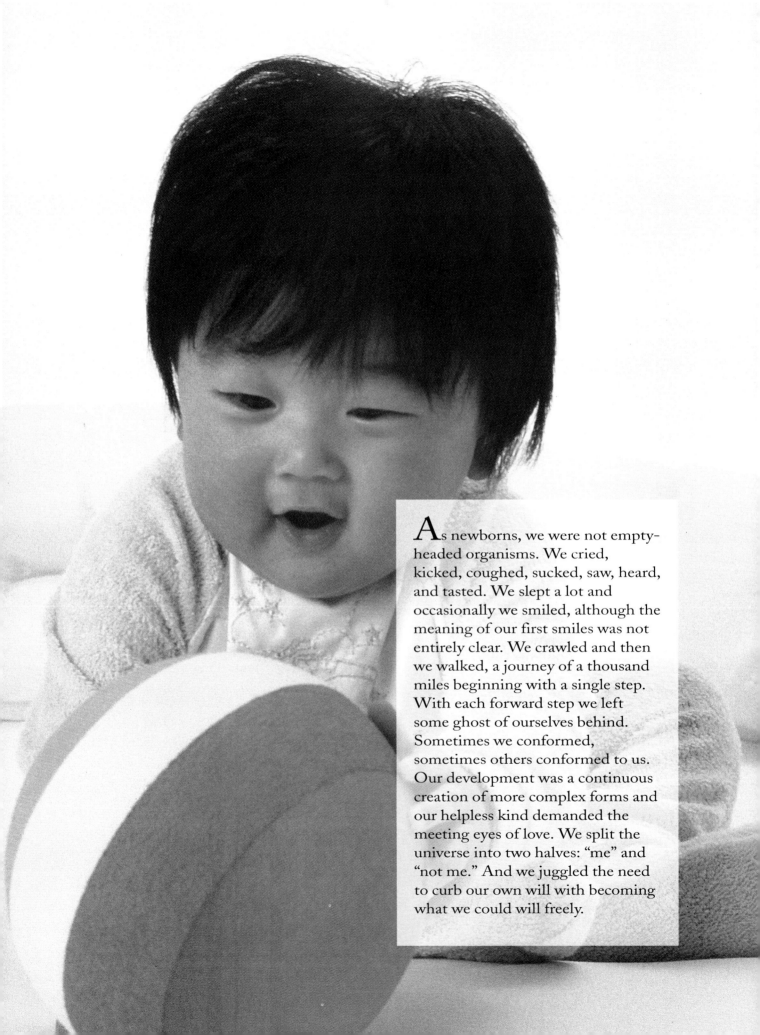

As newborns, we were not empty-headed organisms. We cried, kicked, coughed, sucked, saw, heard, and tasted. We slept a lot and occasionally we smiled, although the meaning of our first smiles was not entirely clear. We crawled and then we walked, a journey of a thousand miles beginning with a single step. With each forward step we left some ghost of ourselves behind. Sometimes we conformed, sometimes others conformed to us. Our development was a continuous creation of more complex forms and our helpless kind demanded the meeting eyes of love. We split the universe into two halves: "me" and "not me." And we juggled the need to curb our own will with becoming what we could will freely.

In early childhood, our greatest untold poem was being only four years old. We skipped, played, and ran all the day long, never in our lives so busy, busy becoming something we had not quite grasped yet. Who knew our thoughts, which we worked up into small mythologies all our own. While our thoughts and feelings took wings, the blossoms of our heart no wind could touch. Our small world widened as we discovered new refuges and new people. When we said "I" we meant something totally unique, not to be confused with any other.

In middle and late childhood, we were on a different plane, belonging to a generation and feeling properly our own. It is the wisdom of human development that at no other time are we more ready to learn than at the end of early childhood's expansive imagination. Our thirst was to know and to understand. Our parents continued to cradle our lives but our growth was also being shaped by successive choirs of friends. We did not think much about the future or the past, but enjoyed the present.

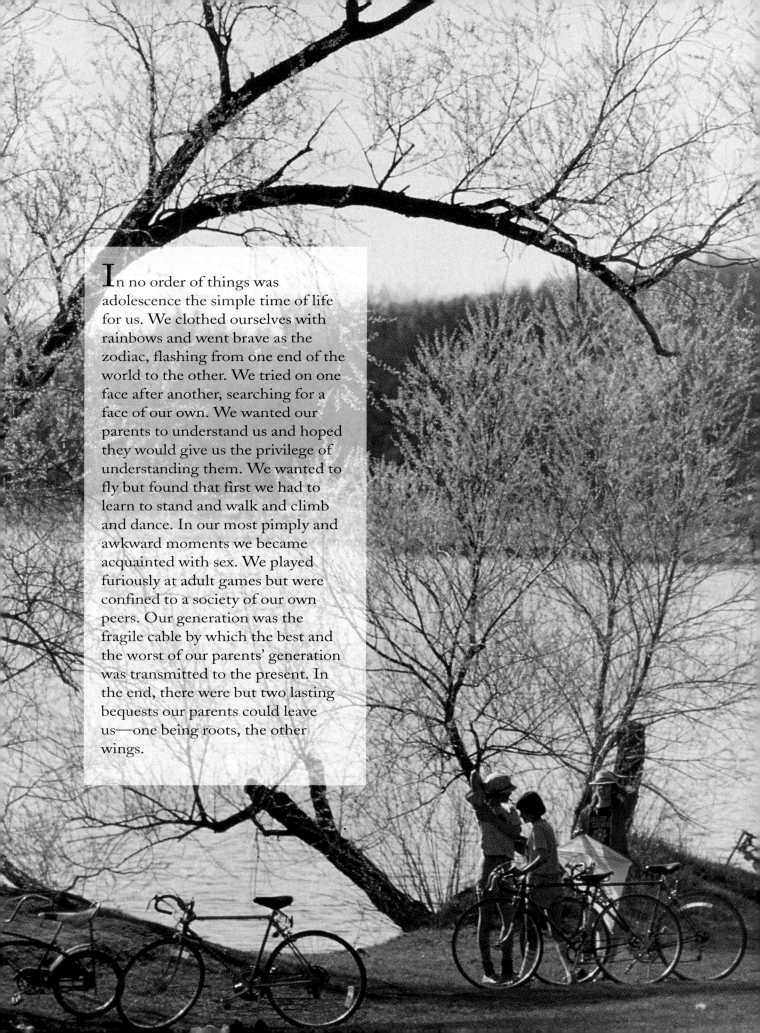

In no order of things was adolescence the simple time of life for us. We clothed ourselves with rainbows and went brave as the zodiac, flashing from one end of the world to the other. We tried on one face after another, searching for a face of our own. We wanted our parents to understand us and hoped they would give us the privilege of understanding them. We wanted to fly but found that first we had to learn to stand and walk and climb and dance. In our most pimply and awkward moments we became acquainted with sex. We played furiously at adult games but were confined to a society of our own peers. Our generation was the fragile cable by which the best and the worst of our parents' generation was transmitted to the present. In the end, there were but two lasting bequests our parents could leave us—one being roots, the other wings.

GLOSSARY

A

ABC method A learning-to-read technique that emphasizes memorizing the names and letters of the alphabet. (315)

A$\bar{B}$ error The Piagetian object permanence concept in which an infant progressing into Substage 4 makes frequent mistakes, selecting the familiar hiding place (A) rather than the new hiding place (B). (202)

accommodation Piagetian concept of adjustment to new information. (200)

acculturation This term refers to cultural change that results from continuous, first-hand contact between two distinctive cultural groups. (341)

active (niche-picking) genotype/environment interactions The type of interactions that occur when children seek out environments they find companionable and stimulating. (92)

activity level The tempo and vigor of movement. (334)

adolescence The developmental period of transition from childhood to early adulthood, entered at approximately 10 to 12 years of age and ending at 18 to 22 years of age. (19)

adolescent egocentrism A characteristic of adolescence composed of an imaginary audience and a personal fable. (216)

adoption study A study in which investigators seek to discover whether the behavior and psychological characteristics of adopted children are more like their adoptive parents, who provide a home environment, or their biological parents, who contributed their heredity. (89)

afterbirth The third birth stage, when the placenta, umbilical cord, and other membranes are detached and expelled. (112)

AIDS (acquired immune deficiency syndrome) A virus that destroys the body's immune system. Consequently, germs that usually do not harm someone with a normal immune system produce devastating results and death. (181)

altruism An unselfish interest in helping someone. (417)

amniocentesis A prenatal medical procedure in which a sample of amniotic fluid is withdrawn by syringe and tested to discover if the fetus is suffering from any chromosomal or metabolic disorders. It is performed in the 12th to 16th week of pregnancy. (84)

amnion A bag or envelope that contains a clear fluid in which the developing embryo floats. The amnion is an important life-support system. It provides an environment that is temperature and humidity controlled, as well as shockproof. (102)

anal stage The second Freudian stage of development, occurring between 1½ and 3 years of age, in which the child's greatest pleasure involves the anus or the eliminative functions associated with it. (38)

androgen The main class of male sex hormones. (377)

androgyny The presence of desirable masculine and feminine characteristics in one individual. (390)

anger cry A variation of the basic cry in which more excess air is forced through the vocal cords. (338)

animism A facet of preoperational thought, the belief that inanimate objects have "lifelike" qualities and are capable of action. (209)

anorexia nervosa An eating disorder that involves the relentless pursuit of thinness through starvation. (186)

anoxia The insufficient availability of oxygen to the infant. (112)

Apgar scale A widely used method to assess the health of newborns at 1 to 5 minutes after birth. The Apgar scale evaluates infants' heart rate, respiratory effort, muscle tone, body color, and reflex irritability. (120)

aphasia A language disorder, resulting from brain damage, that involves a loss of the ability to articulate ideas in any form. (302)

aptitude-treatment interaction (ATI) ATI stresses the importance of both children's aptitudes or characteristics and the treatments or experiences they are given in the classroom. "Aptitude" refers to such characteristics as the academic potential and personality characteristics on which students differ, "treatment" refers to educational techniques, such as structured versus flexible classrooms. (508)

assimilation Piagetian concept of the incorporation of new information into existing knowledge. (200)

associative play Play that involves social interaction, with little or no organization. (480)

attachment A close emotional bond between an infant and a caregiver. (327)

attention The concentration and focusing of mental effort. (249)

attention-deficit hyperactivity disorder Hyperactivity, characterized by a short attention span, high distractibility, and high levels of physical activity. (516)

authoritarian parenting A restrictive, punitive style that exhorts a child to follow the parent's directions and to respect work and effort. Firm limits and controls are placed on a child, and little verbal exchange is allowed. This style is associated with children's social incompetence. (443)

authoritative parenting A parenting style that encourages children to be independent but still places limits and controls on their actions. Extensive verbal give-and-take is allowed, and parents are warm and nurturant toward the child. This style is associated with children's social competence. (443)

automaticity The ability to process information with little or no effort. (248)

autonomous morality The second stage of moral development in Piaget's theory, displayed by older children (about 10 years of age and older). The child becomes aware that rules and laws are created by people and that, in judging an action, one should consider the actor's intentions as well as the consequences. (403)

autonomy versus shame and doubt
Erikson's second stage of development, occurring in late infancy and toddlerhood (1–3 years). (39)

B

back-to-basics movement The idea that the function of school should be rigorous training of intellectual skills through such subjects as English, math, and science. (497)

basic cry A rhythmic pattern that usually consists of a cry, followed by a briefer silence, then a shorter inspiratory whistle that is somewhat higher pitch than the main cry, then a brief rest before the next cry. (338)

Bayley Scales of Infant Development An instrument, developed by Nancy Bayley, to be used in the assessment of infant development. The current version has three components: a mental scale, a motor scale, and an infant behavior profile. (278)

becoming parents and families with children The third stage in the family life cycle requires that adults now move up a generation and become caregivers to the younger generation. (439)

behavior genetics The degree and nature of behavior's hereditary basis. (89)

behaviorism The theory that emphasizes the scientific study of observable behavioral responses and their environmental determinants. (44)

behavior modification The application of operant conditioning principles to changing human behavior; its main goal is to replace unacceptable responses with acceptable, adaptive ones. (238)

bilingual education Programs for students with limited proficiency in English that instruct students in their own language part of the time while they learn English. (315)

biological processes Changes in an individual's physical nature. (17)

blastocyst The inner layer of cells that develops during the germinal period. These cells later develop into the embryo. (100)

bonding Close contact, especially physical, between parents and their newborn in the period shortly after birth. (124)

boundary ambiguity The uncertainty in stepfamilies of who is in or out of the family and who is performing or responsible for certain tasks in the family system. (454)

Brazelton Neonatal Behavioral Assessment Scale A test, given several days after birth, to assess newborns' neurological development, reflexes, and reactions to people. (120)

breech position The baby's position in the uterus that causes the buttocks to be the first part to emerge from the vagina. (112)

Broca's area The area of the left frontal lobe of the brain that directs the muscle movement involved in speech production. (302)

bulimia An eating disorder that involves a binge-and-purge sequence on a regular basis. (187)

C

canalization The process by which characteristics take a narrow path or developmental course. Apparently, preservative forces help protect a person from environmental extremes. (88)

care perspective The moral perspective of Carol Gilligan, that views people in terms of their connectedness to others and focuses on interpersonal communication, relationships with others, and concern for others. (408)

case study This is an in-depth look at an individual; it is used mainly by clinical psychologists when the unique aspects of a person's life cannot be duplicated, either for practical or ethical reasons. (54)

centration The focusing of attention on one characteristic to the exclusion of all others. (209)

cephalocaudal pattern The sequence in which the greatest growth occurs at the top—the head—with growth in size, weight, and feature differentiation gradually working from top to bottom. (135)

cesarean section The surgical removal of the baby from the uterus. (112)

child-centered kindergarten The education of the whole child, including concern for the child's physical, cognitive, and social development. Instruction is organized around the child's needs, interests, and learning style. The process of learning, rather than the finished product, is emphasized. (499)

chlamydia A sexually transmitted disease named for the bacteria that cause it. (180)

chorionic villus test A prenatal medical procedure in which a small sample of the placenta is removed at a certain point in the pregnancy from the 8th through the 11th week. (85)

chromosomes Threadlike structures that come in 23 pairs, one member of each pair coming from each parent. Chromosomes contain the genetic substance DNA. (79)

chronosystem This system involves the patterning of environmental events

and transitions over the life course and their sociohistorical contexts. (50)

classical conditioning A neutral stimulus acquires the ability to produce a response originally produced by another stimulus. (234)

cliques Small adolescent groups that involve greater intimacy among members and more group cohesion than crowds. (475)

cognitive appraisal Lazarus' term describes individuals' interpretation of events in their lives as harmful, threatening, or challenging, and their determination of whether they have the resources to cope effectively with the event. (340)

cognitive developmental theory of gender In this view, children's gender-typing occurs after they have developed a concept of gender. Once they begin to consistently conceive themselves as male or female, children often organize their world on the basis of gender. (380)

cognitive monitoring The process of taking stock of what you are currently doing, what you will do next, and how effectively the mental activity is unfolding. (252)

cognitive moral education An indirect moral education approach that emphasizes that children adopt such values as democracy and justice as their moral reasoning is developed. (419)

cognitive processes Changes in an individual's thoughts, intelligence, and language. (17)

cognitive social learning theory of morality The theory that distinguishes between a child's moral competence—the ability to produce moral behavior—and moral performance—those behaviors in specific situations. (413)

cognitive styles The general, usually consistent, ways individuals process information. Cognitive style is determined not only by an individual's attention to a task, organizational skills, and cognitive strategies, but by the person's personality and motivation as well. (259)

cohort effects Effects may occur due to an individual's time of birth or generation that have nothing to do with the individual's actual age. (59)

commitment The part of identity development in which adolescents show a personal investment in what they are going to do. (366)

community rights versus individual rights The fifth stage in Kohlberg's theory of moral development. Children understand that values and laws are relative and that standards vary from one person to another. (404)

computer-assisted instruction A method of education that uses the computer as a tutor to individualize instruction: to present information, give students practice, and provide additional instruction if needed. (488)

concept A category used to group objects, events, and characteristics on the basis of common properties. (255)

concrete operational stage Piaget's third developmental stage lasts from approximately 7 to 11 years of age. Children can perform operations, and logical reasoning replaces intuitive thought as long as the reasoning can be applied to specific concrete examples. (44)

conditioned response (CR) The learned response to the conditioned stimulus that occurs after CS-UCS pairing. (234)

conditioned stimulus (CS) A previously neutral stimulus that eventually elicits the conditioned response after being paired with the unconditioned stimulus. (234)

conduct disorder The psychiatric diagnostic category used when multiple behaviors such as running away, setting fires, cruelty to animals, or truancy occur over a six-month period. (420)

connectedness An important element in adolescent identity development. It consists of two dimensions: mutuality (sensitivity to and respect for other's views) and permeability (openness to other's views). (368)

conscience The component of the superego that involves behaviors disapproved of by parents. (413)

conservation The idea that an amount stays the same regardless of how its container changes. (209)

constructive play Play that combines sensorimotor and practice repetitive activity with the symbolic representation of ideas. Constructive play occurs when children engage in self-regulated creation or construction of a product or problem solution. (484)

constructivist view Piaget's view that the main perceptual abilities are completely uncoordinated at birth and that infants do not have intermodal perception. Infant perception involves a representation of the world that builds up as the infant constructs an image of experience. (151)

content validity A form of validity; a test's ability to give a broad picture of what is to be measured. (271)

context Development occurs in settings that are called contexts. These settings are influenced by historical, economic, social, and cultural factors. (9)

continuity of development The view that development involves gradual, cumulative change from conception to death. (20)

continuity view In this view, the emphasis is on the role that early parent-child relationships play in constructing a basic way of relating to others throughout the lifespan. (436)

conventional reasoning The second, or intermediate, level in Kohlberg's theory of moral development. Children's internalization is intermediate. They abide by certain standards (internal), but they are the standards of others (external), such as parents or the laws of society. (404)

convergent thinking Thinking that produces one correct answer and is characteristic of the kind of thinking required on standardized intelligence tests. (289)

cooperative play Play that involves social interaction in a group, with a sense of group identity and organized activity. (480)

coordination of secondary circular reactions Piaget's fourth sensorimotor substage, which develops between 8 and 12 months of age. In this substage, several significant changes take place involving the coordination of schemes and intentionality. (201)

correlational coefficient A number based on statistical analysis used to describe the degree of association between two variables. (57)

correlational strategy The goal in this strategy is to describe the strength of the relation between two or more events or characteristics. (56)

counterconditioning A classical conditioning procedure for weakening a CR by associating the stimuli with a new response incompatible with the CR. (235)

creativity The ability to think about something in a novel and unusual way and to come up with unique solutions to problems. (289)

crisis A period of identity development during which the adolescent is choosing among meaningful alternatives. (366)

criterion validity A form of validity; a test's ability to predict other measures, or criteria, of an attribute. (271)

critical period A fixed time period very early in development during which certain behaviors optimally emerge. (47)

critical thinking Grasping the deeper meaning of problems, keeping an open mind about different approaches and perspectives, and thinking reflectively rather than accepting statements and carrying out procedures without

significant understanding and evaluations. (253)

cross-cultural studies Studies of this type compare a culture with one or more other cultures. Such studies provide information about the degree to which children's development is similar, or universal, across cultures, or to the degree to which it is culture-specific. (9)

cross-sectional approach This is a research strategy in which individuals of different ages are compared all at one time. (58)

crowd The largest and least personal adolescent group. (475)

cultural-familial retardation Mental retardation in which there is no evidence of organic brain damage; individuals' IQs range from 50 to 70. (288)

culture The behavior patterns, beliefs, and all other products of a group that are passed from generation to generation. (9)

culture-fair tests Intelligence tests that attempt to reduce cultural bias. (283)

D

deep structure The syntactic relation among words in a sentence. (300)

defense mechanisms The psychoanalytic term for unconscious methods used by the ego to distort reality in order to protect itself from anxiety. (37)

dependent variable This is the factor that is measured in an experiment; it may change because of the manipulation of the independent variable. (57)

deprivation dwarfism A type of growth retardation caused by emotional deprivation; children are deprived of affection, which causes stress and alters the release of hormones by the pituitary gland. (161)

development The pattern of movement or change that begins at conception and continues through the life cycle. (17)

developmental construction view The belief that as individuals grow up they acquire modes of relating to others. (436)

developmentally appropriate practice Education based on knowledge of the typical development of children within an age span (age appropriateness) and the uniqueness of each child (individual appropriateness). (499)

developmental quotient (DQ) An overall developmental score that combines subscores in the motor, language, adaptive, and personal-social domains in the Gesell assessment of infants. (277)

difficult child A child who tends to react negatively and cry frequently, who engages in irregular daily routines, and who is slow to accept new experiences. (334)

direct moral education An educational approach that involves either emphasizing values or character traits during specified time slots or integrating those values or traits throughout the curriculum. (419)

direct perception view The view that infants are born with intermodal perception abilities that enable them to display intermodal perception early in infancy. Infants have to attend only to the appropriate sensory information; they do not have to build up an internal representation of the information through months of sensory experiences. (151)

discontinuity of development The view that development involves distinct stages in the life span. (20)

discontinuity view In this view, the emphasis is on change and variety of interaction partner in relationships over time as those influence formation modes of relating to others. (436)

dishabituation An infant's renewed interest in a stimulus. (238)

displacement The use of language to communicate information about another place and time. (299)

divergent thinking Thinking that produces many answers to a question and is characteristic of creativity. (289)

DNA A complex molecule that contains genetic information. (79)

dominant-recessive genes principle If one gene of a pair is dominant and one is recessive (goes back or recedes), the dominant gene exerts its effect, overriding the potential influence of the recessive gene. A recessive gene exerts its influence only if both genes in a pair are recessive. (86)

Down syndrome The most common genetically transmitted form of mental retardation, which is caused by the presence of an extra (47th) chromosome. (82)

E

early childhood The developmental period that extends from the end of infancy to about 5 or 6 years of age; sometimes called the preschool years. (19)

early-later experience issue This issue focuses on the degree to which early experiences (especially in infancy) or later experiences are the key determinants of the child's development. (21)

easy child A child who is generally in a positive mood, who quickly establishes regular routines in infancy, and who adapts easily to new experiences. (334)

echoing Repeating what someone says, especially if it is an incomplete phrase or sentence. (305)

eclectic theoretical orientation Uses whatever is considered the best in all theories. (51)

ecological theory Emphasis is given to the role of social contexts in development. (48)

ectoderm The outermost layer of cells, which becomes the nervous system, sensory receptors (ears, nose, and eyes, for example), and skin parts (hair and nails, for example). (101)

ego The Freudian structure of personality that deals with the demands of reality. (37)

egocentrism A salient feature of preoperational thought, the inability to distinguish between one's own and someone else's perspective. (207)

ego-ideal The component of the superego that involves ideal standards approved of by parents. (413)

elaboration The extensive processing of information, often in the form of association. (250)

embryonic period The period of prenatal development that occurs 2 to 8 weeks after conception. During the embryonic period, the rate of cell differentiation intensifies, support systems for the cells form, and organs appear. (101)

emic approach In this approach, the goal is to describe behavior in one culture or ethnic group in terms that are meaningful and important to the people in that group, without regard to other cultures or ethnic groups; culture-specific. (55)

emotion The feeling or affect that involves a mixture of physiological arousal (fast heart beat, for example) and overt behavior (smile or grimace, for example). (335)

emotionality The tendency to be distressed. (334)

empathy Reacting to another's feelings with an emotional response that is similar to the other's response. (415)

endoderm The inner layer of cells that develops into digestive and respiratory systems. (101)

equilibration A mechanism in Piaget's theory invoked to explain how children shift from one stage to the next. The shift occurs as children experience cognitive conflict or a disequilibrium in trying to understand the world. Eventually, they resolve the conflict and reach equilibrium of thought. (200)

erogenous zones Freud's concept of the parts of the body that have especially strong pleasure-giving qualities at each stage of development. (38)

estradiol A hormone associated with breast, uterine, and skeletal development in girls. (173)

estrogen The main class of female sex hormones. (377)

ethnic gloss Using an ethnic label, such as Black, Hispanic, Asian, or Native American, in a superficial way that makes an ethnic group seem more homogeneous than it actually is. (55)

ethnic identity An individual develops a sense of membership based upon the shared language, religion, customs, values, history, and race of an ethnic group. (9)

ethnicity A dimension of culture based on cultural heritage, nationality characteristics, race, religion, and language. (9)

ethnocentrism The tendency to favor one's own group over other groups. (360)

ethology The theory that behavior is strongly influenced by biology, is tied to evolution, and is characterized by critical or sensitive periods. (47)

etic approach The goal in this approach is to describe behaviors so that generalizations can be made across cultures; culture-universal. (55)

evocative genotype/environmental interactions The type of interactions that occur when the child's genotype elicits certain types of physical and social environments. (92)

exosystem This system is involved when experiences in another social setting—in which the individual does not have an active role—influence what the individual experiences in an immediate context. (48)

expanding Restating what someone has said in a linguistically sophisticated form. (305)

experimental strategy This strategy allows investigators to precisely determine behavior's causes by performing an experiment which is a precisely regulated setting in which one or more of the factors believed to influence the behavior being studied are manipulated and all others are held constant. (57)

expert Someone who has a great deal of knowledge about a domain of human interest and a great deal of experience performing tasks typical of that domain. (257)

F

family at midlife The fifth stage in the family life cycle is a time of launching children, playing an important role in linking generations, and adapting to midlife changes in development. (439)

family with adolescents During this fourth stage in the family life cycle, parents cope with the adolescent who is seeking autonomy and his or her own identity. In this stage, parents often either clamp down and put pressure on the adolescent to conform, or they may become more permissive, giving the adolescent extensive freedom. Developing a flexible, adaptive approach to parenting is best in this stage. (439)

family in later life In this sixth and final stage in the family life cycle, retirement alters a couple's lifestyle. Grandparenting also characterizes many families in later life. (439)

father-absence model of divorce effects States that, when adolescents from father-absent and father-present families are compared, any differences that occur are attributed to the family structure variations. (449)

fetal alcohol syndrome (FAS) A cluster of abnormalities that appears in the offspring of mothers who drink alcohol heavily during pregnancy. (109)

fetal period The prenatal period of development that begins 2 months after conception and lasts for 7 months on the average. (103)

fine motor skills Motor skills that involve more finely tuned movements, such as finger dexterity. (137)

first habits and primary circular reactions Piaget's second sensorimotor substage, which develops between 1 and 4 months of age. Infants learn to coordinate sensation and types of schemes or structures—that is habits and primary circular reactions. (201)

formal operational stage Piaget's fourth and final developmental stage appears between the ages of 11 and 15. Individuals move beyond the world of actual, concrete experiences and think in abstract and more logical ways. (44)

fraternal twins Twins who develop from separate eggs, making them genetically less similar than identical twins. (89)

G

games Activities engaged in for pleasure that include rules and often competition. (484)

gametes Human reproduction cells created in the testes of males and the ovaries of females. (79)

gender The sociocultural dimension of being male or female. (11, 377)

gender identity The sense of being male or female, which most children acquire by the time they are 3 years old. (377)

gender role A set of expectations that prescribes how females or males should think, act, or feel. (377)

gender role stereotypes Broad categories that reflect our impressions and beliefs about females and males. (382)

gender role transcendence This is the belief that, when an individual's competence is at issue, it should not be conceptualized on the basis of masculinity, femininity, or androgyny but, rather, on a personal basis. (392)

gender schema A cognitive structure that organizes the world in terms of female and male. (381)

gender schema theory The theory that children's attention and behavior are guided by an internal motivation to conform to gender-based, sociocultural standards and stereotypes. (381)

generativity versus stagnation Erikson's seventh developmental stage, which individuals experience in middle adulthood. (39)

genes Units of hereditary information on the DNA "staircase." Genes act like a blueprint for cells to reproduce themselves and manufacture the proteins that maintain life. (79)

genetic epistemology The study of how children's knowledge changes over the course of their development. (13)

genital stage The fifth and final Freudian stage of development, occurring from puberty on. This stage is one of sexual reawakening; the source of sexual pleasure now becomes someone outside of the family. (38)

genotype A person's genetic heritage; the actual genetic material. (87)

germinal period The period of prenatal development that takes place in the first two weeks after conception. It includes the creation of the zygote, continued cell division, and the attachment of the zygote to the uterine wall. (100)

gifted Having above average intelligence (an IQ of 120 or higher), a superior talent for something, or both. (288)

global empathy A young infant's empathic response in which clear boundaries between the feelings and needs of the self and those of another have not yet been established. (415)

grammar The formal description of syntactical rules. (300)

grasping reflex A neonatal reflex that occurs when something touches an infant's palm. The infant responds by grasping tightly. (135)

gross motor skills Motor skills that involve large muscle activities, such as walking. (137)

H

habituation The repeated presentation of a stimulus, which causes reduced attention to the stimulus. (238)

herpes simplex virus II A virus that causes a sexually transmitted disease whose symptoms include irregular cycles of sores and blisters in the genital area. (180)

heteronomous morality The first stage of moral development in Piaget's theory, occurring from 4 to 7 years of age. Justice and rules are conceived of as unchangeable properties of the world, removed from the control of people. (403)

heuristics Strategies that suggest a solution to a problem but do not guarantee it will work. (258)

hidden curriculum The pervasive moral atmosphere that characterizes schools. This atmosphere includes school and classroom rules, attitudes toward academics and extracurricular activities, the moral orientation of teachers and school administrators, and the text materials. (418)

holophrase hypothesis The theory that a single word is used to imply a complete sentence; it is characteristic of an infant's first words. (310)

horizontal décalage Piaget's concept that describes how similar abilities do not appear at the same time within a stage of development. (213)

hypotheses Assumptions that can be tested to determine their accuracy. (35)

hypothetical-deductive reasoning Piaget's formal operational concept that adolescents have the cognitive ability to develop hypotheses about ways to solve problems. They then systematically deduce which is the best path to follow in solving the problem. (216)

I

id The Freudian structure of personality that consists of instincts, which are an individual's reservoir of psychic energy. (37)

identical twins Twins who develop from a single fertilized egg, which splits into two genetically identical replicas, each of which becomes a person. (89)

identification theory A theory that stems from Freud's view that preschool children develop a sexual attraction to the opposite-sex parent, then, at 5 to 6 years of age, renounce the attraction because of anxious feelings, subsequently identifying with the same-sex parent and unconsciously adopting the same-sex parent's characteristics. (378)

identity achievement Marcia's term for adolescents who have undergone a crisis and have made a commitment. (367)

identity diffusion   Marcia uses this term to describe adolescents who have not yet experienced a crisis or made any commitments. (366)

identity foreclosure   This is Marcia's term to describe adolescents who have made a commitment, but have not experienced a crisis. (366)

identity moratorium   Adolescents who are in the midst of a crisis, but whose commitments either are absent or are only vaguely defined. (367)

identity versus identity confusion   Erikson's fifth developmental stage of development which individuals experience during the adolescent years. At this time, individuals are faced with finding out who they are, what they are all about, and where they are going in life. (39, 364)

idiographic needs   This refers to what is important to the individual, not the group. (62)

imagery   Sensations without the presence of an external stimulus. (250)

imaginary audience   An adolescent's belief that others are as preoccupied with her as she is. (216)

immanent justice   Piaget's concept that, if a rule is broken, punishment will be meted out immediately. (403)

implantation   The attachment of the zygote to the uterine wall, which takes place about 10 days after conception. (101)

imprinting   The ethological concept of rapid, innate learning within a limited critical period of time, which involves attachment to the first moving object seen. (47)

impulsivity   A cognitive style in which individuals act before they think, usually making rapid scans of information and, if fine discriminations of information are required, making errors. (259)

independent variable   This is the manipulated, influential, experimental factor in the experiment. (57)

index offenses   Criminal acts, whether they are committed by juveniles or adults, such as robbery, aggravated assault, rape, and homicide. (420)

indirect moral education   An educational approach that involves encouraging children to define their own and others' values and helping define the moral perspectives that support those values. (419)

individual differences   The stable, consistent ways in which children are different from each other. (271)

individualism and purpose   The second stage in Kohlberg's theory of moral development. Moral thinking is based on rewards and self-interest. (404)

individuality   An important element in adolescent identity development. It consists of two dimensions: self-assertion (the ability to have and communicate a point of view) and separateness (the use of communication patterns to express how one is different from others). (368)

induction   A discipline technique in which a parent uses reason and explanation of the consequences for others of a child's actions. (413)

industry versus inferiority   Erikson's fourth developmental stage, occurring approximately in the elementary school years. (39)

infancy   The developmental period that extends from birth to 18 to 24 months. (19)

infinite generativity   An individual's ability to generate an infinite number of meaningful sentences using a finite set of words and rules, which makes language a highly creative enterprise. (299)

information processing   A model of cognition concerned with how individuals process information about their world—how information enters the mind, how it is stored and transformed, and how it is retrieved to perform such complex activities as problem solving and reasoning. (44)

information-processing approach   A framework for understanding how children learn and think that considers how information is taken in; how it is stored and transformed; and how it is evaluated and used to perform complex thinking activities, such as problem solving, in order to meet clearly defined purposes and goals. (245)

initiative versus guilt   Erikson's third stage of development, occurring during the preschool years. (39)

innate goodness view   The idea, presented by Swiss-born philosopher Jean-Jacques Rousseau, that children are inherently good. (12)

integrity versus despair   Erikson's eighth and final development stage, which individuals experience during late adulthood. (40)

intelligence   Verbal ability, problem-solving skills, and the ability to learn from and adapt to the experiences of everyday life. (271)

intelligence quotient (IQ)   Devised in 1912 by William Stern, IQ consists of mental age divided by chronological age, multiplied by 100. (273)

intermodal perception   The ability to relate and integrate information about two or more sensory modalities, such as vision and hearing. (151)

internalization   The developmental change from behavior that is externally controlled to behavior that is controlled by internal, self-generated standards and principles. (404)

internalization of schemes   Piaget's sixth sensorimotor substage, which develops between 18 and 24 months of age. In this substage, infants' mental functioning shifts from a purely sensorimotor plane to a symbolic plane, and they develop the ability to use primitive symbols. (202)

interpersonal norms   The third stage in Kohlberg's theory of moral development. Children value trust, caring, and loyalty to others as the basis of moral judgment. (404)

intimacy in friendship   Self-disclosure and the sharing of private thoughts. (474)

intimacy versus isolation   Erikson's sixth developmental stage, which individuals experience during the early adulthood years. At this time, individuals face the developmental task of forming intimate relationships with others. (39)

intuitive thought substage   The second substage of preoperational thought, occurring approximately between 4 and 7 years of age. Children begin to use primitive reasoning and want to know the answers to all sorts of questions. (209)

in vitro fertilization   Conception outside the body. (80)

involution   The process by which the uterus returns to its prepregnant size 5 or 6 weeks after birth. (122)

J

justice perspective   A moral perspective that focuses on the rights of the individual; individuals independently make moral decisions. (408)

juvenile delinquency   Refers to a broad range of behaviors, from socially unacceptable behavior to status offenses to criminal acts. (420)

K

keyword method   A powerful strategy that uses vivid imagery of important words, or keywords, to improve memory. (251)

Klinefelter syndrome   A genetic disorder in which males have an extra X chromosome, making them XXY instead of just XY. (82)

L

labeling   Identifying the names of objects. (305)

laboratory   This is a controlled setting in which many of the complex factors of the "real world" are removed. (52)

Lamaze method A form of prepared childbirth developed by Fernand Lamaze, a pioneering French obstetrician. Widely accepted in the medical profession, it involves helping pregnant women cope actively with the pain of childbirth to avoid or reduce medication. (115)

language A system of symbols and sequence of words, used to communicate with others, that involves infinite generativity, displacement, and rule systems. (299)

Language Acquisition Device (LAD) A biological prewiring that enables children to detect certain language categories, such as phonology, syntax, and semantics. LAD is an innate grammatical ability that underlies all human languages. (302)

Language Acquisition Support System (LASS) Bruner's concept that describes the behaviors of a language-skilled individual in structuring and supporting a child's development of language. (304)

latency stage The fourth Freudian stage, which occurs between approximately 6 years of age and puberty; the child represses all interest in sexuality and develops social and intellectual skills. (38)

launching The process in which the youth moves into adulthood and exits his/her family of origin. (438)

learned helplessness Seligman's view that when individuals are exposed to negative situations over which they have no control they are likely to become depressed. (339)

learning A relatively permanent change in behavior that occurs through experience. (233)

learning disabilities Children with learning disabilities are of normal or higher intelligence, have difficulties in several academic areas but usually do not show deficits in others, and are not suffering from other conditions or disorders that could explain their learning problems. (516)

leaving home and becoming a single adult In this first stage in the family life cycle, the young adult separates from the family of origin without cutting off ties completely or fleeing in a reactive way to find some form of substitute emotional refugee. (438)

Leboyer method A birth process developed by French obstetrician, Fredrick Leboyer, that tends to make birth less stressful for infants. The procedure is referred to as "birth without violence." (114)

literacy The ability to read and write. (314)

longitudinal approach This is a research strategy in which the same individuals are studied over a period of time, usually several years or more. (58)

long-term memory A relatively permanent memory system, which holds huge amounts of information for a long time. (249)

love withdrawal A discipline technique in which a parent removes attention or love from a child. (413)

low-birthweight infants Infants born after a regular period of gestation (the length of time between conception and birth) of 38 to 42 weeks but who weigh less than 5½ pounds. (117)

M

macrosystem This system involves the culture in which individuals live. Culture refers to behavior patterns, beliefs, and all other products of a particular group of people that are passed on from generation to generation. (50)

mainstreaming Integrating handicapped children into regular school classes with nonhandicapped children. (515)

marasmus A wasting away of body tissues in an infant's first year, caused by a severe protein-calorie deficiency. (145)

maternal blood test A prenatal diagnostic technique that is used to assess blood alphaprotein level, which is associated with neural tube defects. This technique is also called alpha-fetoprotein test-AFP. (85)

maturation The orderly sequence of changes dictated by a genetic blueprint. (20)

Maximally Discriminative Facial Movement Coding System (MAX) Izard's system of coding infants' facial expressions related to emotions. Using MAX, coders watch slow-motion and stop-action videotapes of infants' facial reactions to stimuli. (338)

mean length of utterance (MLU) An index of language development based on the number of words per sentence a child produces in a sample of about 50 to 100 sentences. (310)

meiosis The process of cell division in which each pair of chromosomes in a cell separates, with one member of each pair going into each gamete. (79)

memory The retention of information over time. It is central to mental life and to information processing. (249)

menarche First menstruation. (172)

mental age (MA) A child's level of mental development relative to others. (273)

mental retardation A condition of limited mental ability in which individuals have a low IQ, usually below 70 on a traditional test of intelligence, and have difficulty adapting to everyday life. (287)

mesoderm The middle layer of cells, which becomes the circulatory system, bones, muscles, excretory system, and reproductive system. (101)

mesosystem This system involves relationships between microsystems or connections between contexts such as the family experience to the school experience. (48)

metacognitive knowledge The segment of acquired knowledge that involves cognitive matters. (257)

microsystem In Bronfenbrenner's ecology theory, this system is the setting or context in which an individual lives. This system includes the person's family, peers, school, and neighborhood. The most direct interactions with social agents occur in the microsystem. (48)

middle and late childhood The developmental period that extends from about 6 to 11 years of age, approximately corresponding to the elementary school years; sometimes called the elementary school years. (19)

moral development Rules and conventions about what people should do in their interactions with other people. (403)

Moro reflex A neonatal startle response that occurs in reaction to a sudden, intense noise or movement. When startled, the newborn arches its back, throws its head back, and flings out its arms and legs. Then the newborn rapidly closes its arms and legs to the center of its body. (135)

morphology The rules for combining morphemes; a morpheme is the smallest string of sounds that gives meaning to what we say and hear. (299)

motherese The way mothers and other adults often talk to babies at a higher-than-normal frequency and greater-than-normal pitch and with simple words and sentences. (304)

multiple-factor model of divorce effects Takes into account the complexity of the divorce context and examines a number of influences on the child's development, including not only family structure, but also the strengths and weaknesses of the child prior to the divorce, the nature of the events surrounding the divorce itself, the type of custody involved, and visitation patterns. (450)

multiple-factor theory Thurstone's theory that intelligence consists of seven primary abilities: verbal comprehension, number ability, word fluency, spatial visualization, associative memory, reasoning, and perceptual speed. (276)

myelination A process in which nerve cells are insulated with a layer of fat cells, which increases the speed at which information travels through the nervous system. (163)

N

naturalistic observation This is a method in which scientists observe behavior in real-world settings and make no effort to manipulate or control the situation. (54)

natural selection The evolutionary process that favors individuals within a species that are best adapted to survive and reproduce. (75)

nature-nurture controversy "Nature" refers to an organism's biological inheritance, "nurture" to environmental experiences. The "nature" proponents claim biological inheritance is the most important influence on development; the "nurture" proponents claim that environmental experiences are the most important. (20)

negative affectivity (NA) Emotions that are negatively toned, such as anxiety, guilt, and sadness. (336)

negative reinforcement The frequency of a response increases because the response either removes an unpleasant stimulus or allows one to avoid the stimulus. (236)

neglected children Children who receive little attention from their peers, but who are not necessarily disliked. (471)

neo-Piagetians Developmentalists who have elaborated on Piaget's theory, believing children's cognitive development is more specific in many respects than he thought. (222)

new couple, the In this second stage in the family life cycle, two individuals from separate families of origin unite to form a new family system. (438)

nomothetic research Research that is conducted at the group level in which individual variation is not a major focus. (62)

nonnutritive sucking Sucking behavior unrelated to the infant's feeding. (135)

nonshared environmental experiences The child's own unique experiences, both within a family and outside the family, that are not shared by another sibling. (92)

normal distribution A symmetrical configuration of scores, with a majority of cases falling in the middle of the possible range of scores and few scores appearing toward the extremes of the range. (273)

norms Established standards of performance for a test. (273)

O

obesity Weighing 20 percent or more above the ideal weight for a particular age; taking both age and sex into account. (168)

object permanence The Piagetian term for one of an infant's most important accomplishments: understanding that objects and events continue to exist even when they cannot directly be seen, heard, or touched. (202)

Oedipus complex The Freudian concept that young children develop an intense desire to replace the parent of the same sex and enjoy the affections of the opposite-sex parent. (38)

onlooker play Play that occurs when a child watches other children play. (480)

operant conditioning A form of learning in which the consequences of behavior lead to changes in the probability of that behavior's occurrence. (236)

operations Internalized sets of actions that allow children to do mentally what before was done physically. (207)

oral rehydration therapy (ORT) A treatment involving a range of techniques designed to prevent dehydration during episodes of diarrhea by giving children fluids by mouth. (168)

oral stage The first Freudian stage of development, occurring during the first 18 months of life, in which the infant's pleasure centers around the mouth. (38)

organic retardation Mental retardation caused by a genetic disorder or brain damage; "organic" refers to the tissue or organs of the body, so there is some physical damage in organic retardation. (287)

organization The arranging of items into categories, improving long-term memory. (250)

organization Piaget's concept of grouping isolated behaviors into a higher-order, more smoothly functioning cognitive system. (200)

organogenesis The process of organ formation that takes place during the first 2 months of prenatal development. (103)

original sin view The idea, especially advocated during the Middle Ages, that children are basically born bad and born into a world as evil beings. (11)

overextension Children's tendency to misuse words by extending one word's meaning to include objects that are not related to or are inappropriate for the word's meaning. (310)

oxytocin A hormone that stimulates and regulates the rhythmicity of uterine contractions. It has been widely used as a drug to speed delivery. Controversy surrounds its use. (114)

P

pain cry A sudden appearance of loud crying without preliminary moaning and a long initial cry followed by an extended period of breath holding. (338)

parallel play Play that occurs separately from other children, but with toys like those the others are using or in a manner that mimics their play. (480)

passive genotype/environment interactions The type of interactions that occur when the parents, who are genetically related to the child, provide the rearing environment for the child. (91)

perception The interpretation of what is sensed. (147)

peers Children of about the same age or maturity level. (468)

permissive-indifferent parenting A parenting style in which the parent is very uninvolved in the child's life. It is associated with children's social incompetence, especially lack of self-control. (443)

permissive-indulgent parenting A parenting style in which parents are highly involved with their children but place few demands or controls on them. This is associated with children's social incompetence, especially lack of control. (443)

personal fable An adolescent's sense of personal uniqueness and indestructibility. (217)

perspective taking Taking another's point of view. (471)

phallic stage The third Freudian stage of development, which occurs between the ages of 3 and 6; its name comes from the Latin word *phallus*, which means "penis." During this stage, the child's pleasure focuses on the genitals, and the child discovers that self-manipulation is enjoyable. (38)

phenotype The way an individual's genotype is expressed in observed and measurable characteristics. (87)

phenylketonuria (PKU) A genetic disorder in which an individual cannot properly metabolize protein. PKU is now easily detected but, if left untreated, results in mental retardation and hyperactivity. (82)

phobias Irrational fears. (235)

phonics method A learning-to-read technique that emphasizes the sounds that letters make when in words (such sounds can differ from the names of the letters, as when the sound of the letter *c* is not found in *cat*). (315)

phonology The study of a language's sound system. (299)

placenta A life-support system that consists of a disk-shaped group of tissues in which small blood vessels from the mother and offspring intertwine to join. (101)

play Pleasurable activity engaged in for its own sake. (480)

play therapy Therapy that allows children to work off frustration and a medium through which therapists can analyze children's conflicts and ways of coping with them. Children may feel less threatened and be more likely to express their true feelings in the context of play. (480)

polygenic inheritance A genetic principle that describes the interaction of many genes to produce a particular characteristic. (87)

positive affectivity (PA) The range of positive emotions from high energy, enthusiasm, and excitement, to calm, quiet, and withdrawn. Joy, happiness, and laughter may involve PA. (336)

positive reinforcement The frequency of a response increases because it is followed by a pleasant stimulus. (236)

possible self What individuals might become, what they would like to become, and what they are afraid of becoming. (354)

postconventional reasoning The highest level in Kohlberg's theory of moral development. Morality is completely internalized. (404)

postpartal period The period after childbirth or delivery. It is a time when the woman's body adjusts, both physically and psychologically, to the process of childbearing. It lasts for about 6 weeks or until the body has completed its adjustment and has returned to a near prepregnant state. (122)

power assertion A discipline technique in which a parent attempts to gain control over a child or a child's resources. (413)

practice play Play that involves the repetition of behavior when new skills are being learned or when physical or mental mastery and coordination are required for sports. (481)

pragmatics The use of appropriate conversation. (301)

precipitate A form of delivery that takes place too rapidly; the baby squeezes through the birth canal in less than 10 minutes. (112)

preconventional reasoning The lowest level in Kohlberg's theory of moral development. The child shows no internalization of moral values—moral reasoning is controlled by external rewards and punishment. (404)

prejudice An unjustified negative attitude toward an individual because of that person's membership in a group. (360)

prenatal period The time from conception to birth. (19)

preoperational stage The second Piagetian developmental stage, which lasts from about 2 to 7 years of age. Children begin to represent the world with words, images, and drawings. (44)

prepared, or natural, childbirth A childbirth strategy that includes being informed about what will happen during the procedure, knowing about comfort measures for childbirth, anticipating that little or no medication will be used, and if complications arise, expecting to participate in decisions made to resolve the problems. (115)

pretense/symbolic play Play that occurs when a child transforms the physical environment into a symbol. (482)

preterm infant An infant born prior to 38 weeks after conception. (117)

primary appraisal Children's interpretation whether an event involves harm or loss that has already occurred, a threat to some future danger, or a challenge to be overcome. (340)

primary circular reactions Schemes based on the infant's attempt to reproduce an interesting or pleasurable event that initially occurred by chance. (201)

problem solving Attempting to find a way of attaining a goal when the goal is not readily available. (251)

Project Follow Through A program implemented in 1967 as an adjunct to Project Head Start. In the Follow Through programs, the enriched planned variation was carried through the first few years of elementary school. (502)

Project Head Start A compensatory education program designed to give children from low-income families the opportunity to acquire the skills and experiences important for success in school. (502)

proximodistal pattern The sequence in which growth starts at the center of the body and moves toward the extremities. (135)

psychological moratorium The long gap between childhood security and adult autonomy that adolescents experience as part of their identity exploration. (364)

psychometrics The field that involves the assessment of individual differences. (271)

puberty A period of rapid skeletal and sexual maturation that occurs mainly in early adolescence. (173)

Public Law 94–142 The federal government's mandate to all states to provide a free, appropriate education for all children. (515)

punishment A consequence that decreases the probability a behavior will occur. (236)

punishment and obedience orientation The first stage in Kohlberg's theory of moral development. Moral thinking is based on punishment. (404)

Q

questionnaire This is similar to a highly structured interview except that respondents read the questions and mark their answers on paper, rather than responding verbally to an interviewer. (54)

R

race This term refers to a system for classifying plants and animals into subcategories according to specific physical and structural characteristics. (77)

random assignment This occurs when researchers assign subjects to experimental and control conditions by chance, thus reducing the likelihood that the results of the experiment will be due to preexisting differences in the two groups. (57)

rapport talk This involves communication that is oriented toward connectedness with others. It is used more by females than by males. (388)

reaction range The range of phenotypes for each genotype, suggesting the importance of the environment's restrictiveness or enrichment. (87)

recasting Phrasing the same or a similar meaning of a sentence in a different way, perhaps turning it into a question. (304)

reciprocal socialization The view that socialization is bidirectional: children socialize parents just as parents socialize them. (435)

reciprocal teaching An instructional procedure used by Brown and Palincsar to develop cognitive monitoring: it requires that students take turns leading a study group in the use of strategies for comprehending and remembering text content. (252)

reflection A cognitive style in which individuals think before they act, usually scanning information carefully and slowly and, if fine discriminations of information are required, making few errors. (259)

reflexes Automatic stimulus-response connections. (234)

reflexive smile A smile that does not occur in response to external stimuli. It happens during the first month after birth, usually during irregular patterns of sleep, not when the infant is in an alert state. (339)

rehearsal The extended repetition of material after it has been presented. (250)

reinforcement A consequence or reward that increases the probability a behavior will occur. (236)

rejected children Children who are disliked by their peers. They are more likely to be disruptive and aggressive than are neglected children. (471)

reliability The extent to which a test yields a consistent, reproducible measure of performance. (271)

REM (rapid eye movement) sleep A recurring sleep stage during which vivid dreams commonly occur among children and adults. (143)

report talk This involves communication designed to give or receive information. It is used more often by males than females. (388)

repression The most powerful and pervasive defense mechanism. It pushes unacceptable id impulses out of awareness and back into the unconscious mind. (38)

reproduction The process that occurs when a female gamete (ovum) is fertilized by a male gamete (sperm). (79)

rooting reflex A newborns' built-in reaction that occurs when the infant's cheek is stroked or the side of the mouth is touched. In response, the infant turns its head toward the side that was touched in an apparent effort to find something to suck. (135)

S

scaffolding An important caregiver's role in early parent-child interaction. Through their attention and choice of behaviors, caregivers provide a framework around which they interact with infants. (435)

schema Information that already exists in an individual's mind (256). A cognitive structure or network of associations that organizes and guides an individual's perceptions. (381)

scheme The basic unit of an organized pattern of sensorimotor functioning. (201)

scientific method An approach that can be used to discover accurate information about behavior and development and that includes the following steps: identify and analyze the problem, collect data, draw conclusions, and revise theories. (35)

script A schema for events. (257)

secondary appraisal Children evaluate their resources and determine how effectively they can cope with the event. (340)

secondary circular reactions Piaget's third sensorimotor substage, which develops between 4 and 8 months of age. Infants become more object oriented or focused on the world, moving beyond preoccupation with the self in sensorimotor interactions. (201)

secure attachment The infant uses a caregiver as a secure base from which to explore the environment. Ainsworth believes that secure attachment in the first year of life provides an important foundation for psychological development later in life. (328)

self-esteem The evaluative and affective dimension of self-concept. (357)

self-understanding This is the child's cognitive representation of the self, the substance and content of the child's self-concept. (353)

semantic networks Organized stores of general information in memory. (255)

semantics The meaning of words and sentences. (301)

sensation Information that contacts the sensory receptors (eyes, ears, tongue, nostrils, and skin). (147)

sensorimotor play Behavior engaged in by infants to derive pleasure from exercising their sensorimotor schemas. (481)

sensorimotor stage The first of Piaget's developmental stages, which lasts from birth to about 2 years of age. Infants construct an understanding of the world by coordinating sensory experiences (such as seeing and hearing) with motoric actions. (41)

set point This term refers to the weight maintained when no effort is made to gain or lose weight. (168)

sexual script A stereotyped pattern of role prescriptions for how individuals should behave sexually. (179)

shared environmental experiences Children's common environmental experiences that are shared with their siblings, such as their parents' personalities and intellectual orientation, the family's social class, and the neighborhood in which they live. (92)

short-term memory A limited-capacity memory system in which information is retained for as long as 30 seconds, unless the information is rehearsed, in which case it can be retained longer. (249)

sickle-cell anemia A genetic disorder that affects the red blood cells and occurs most often in Black individuals. (82)

simple reflexes Piaget's first sensorimotor substage, which corresponds to the first month after birth. The basic means of coordinating sensation and action is through reflexive behaviors, such as rooting and sucking, which infants have at birth. (201)

slow-to-warm-up child A child who has a low activity level, is somewhat negative, shows low adaptability, and displays a low intensity mood. (334)

sociability The tendency to prefer the company of others to being alone. (334)

social identity theory Social psychologist Henry Tajfel's theory that, when individuals are assigned to a group, they invariably think of that group as an in-group for them, because individuals want to have a positive self-image. (359)

social learning theory The view of psychologists who emphasize a combination of behavior, environment, and cognition as the key factors in development. (46)

social learning theory of gender The idea that children's gender development occurs through observation and imitation of gender behavior, as well as through the rewards and punishments children experience for gender-appropriate and gender-inappropriate behaviors. (378)

social play Play that involves social interaction with peers. (484)

social policy A national government's course of action designed to influence the welfare of its citizens. (14)

social smile A smile in response to an external stimulus, which, early in development, typically is in response to a face. (339)

social system morality The fourth stage in Kohlberg's theory of moral development. Moral judgments are based on understanding the social order, law, justice, and duty. (404)

sociobiology This is a contemporary evolutionary view in psychology that states that all behavior is motivated by the desire to contribute one's genetic heritage to the greatest number of descendants. (76)

socioemotional processes Changes in an individual's relationships with other people, emotions, and personality. (18)

solitary play Play when a child is alone. (480)

standardization The development of uniform procedures for administering and scoring a test. It also involves the development of norms for the test. (273)

standardized tests These require an individual to answer a series of written or oral questions. They have two distinct features. First, psychologists usually total an individual's score to yield a single score, or set of scores, that reflects something about the individual. Second, psychologists compare the individual's score with the scores of a large group of persons to determine how the individual responded relative to others. (54)

status offenses Committed by youths under a specified age, these acts classify children as juvenile delinquents and include such acts as running away, truancy, drinking under age, and sexual promiscuity. (420)

strategies Cognitive processes that do not occur automatically but require work and effort. They are under a learner's conscious control and can be used to improve memory. (250)

stress This is the response of individuals to the circumstances and events, called stressors, that threaten them and tax their coping abilities. (340)

sucking reflex Newborns' built-in reaction of automatically sucking an object placed in the mouth. The sucking reflex enables them to get nourishment before they have associated a nipple with food. (135)

sudden infant death syndrome (SIDS) A condition that occurs when an infant stops breathing, usually during the night, and suddenly dies without apparent cause. (143)

superego The Freudian structure of personality that is the moral branch. The branch that takes into account whether something is right or wrong. (37)

surface structure The order of words in a sentence. (300)

symbolic function substage The first substage of preoperational thought, occurring roughly between the ages of 2 and 4. In this substage, the young child gains the ability to represent mentally an object that is not present. (207)

syntax The way words are combined to form acceptable phrases and sentences. (300)

T

tabula rasa view The idea, proposed by John Locke, that children are not innately bad but instead are like a "blank tablet." (11)

telegraphic speech The use of short, precise words to communicate; it is characteristic of young children's two-word utterances. (310)

temperament An individual's behavioral style and characteristic way of responding. (334)

teratogen From the Greek word *tera*, meaning "monster," any agent that causes a birth defect. The field of study that investigates the causes of birth defects is called teratology. (106)

tertiary circular reactions Schemes in which the infant purposely explores new possibilities with objects, continually changing what is done to them and exploring the results. (201)

tertiary circular reactions, novelty, and curiosity Piaget's fifth sensorimotor substage, which develops between 12 and 18 months of age. Infants become intrigued by the variety of properties that objects possess and by the multiplicity of things they can make happen to objects. (201)

testosterone A hormone associated with the development of genitals, an increase in height, and a change in voice in boys. (173)

test-retest reliability A form of reliability in which a child is given the same test on two different occasions. (271)

theory A coherent set of ideas that helps explain data and make predictions. (35)

top-dog phenomenon The circumstance of moving from the top position (in elementary school, the oldest, biggest, and most powerful students in the school) to the lowest position (in middle or junior high school, the youngest, smallest, and least powerful students in the school). (511)

toxoplasmosis A mild infection that causes coldlike symptoms or no apparent illness in adults. However, toxoplasmosis can be a teratogen for the unborn baby, causing possible eye defects, brain defects, and premature birth. (111)

triarchic theory Sternberg's theory that intelligence consists of componential intelligence, experiential intelligence, and contextual intelligence. (276)

trophoblast The outer layer of cells that develops in the germinal period. These cells provide nutrition and support for the embryo. (101)

trust versus mistrust Erikson's first psychosocial stage, which is experienced in the first year of life. A sense of trust requires a feeling of physical comfort and a minimal amount of fear and apprehension about the future. (39)

Turner syndrome A genetic disorder in which females are missing an X chromosome, making them XO instead of XX. (82)

twin study A study in which the behavior of identical twins is compared to the behavior of fraternal twins. (89)

two-factor theory Spearman's theory that children have both general intelligence, called *g*, and a number of specific types of intelligence, called *s*. (274)

type A babies Infants who exhibit insecurity by avoiding a caregiver—for example, by failing to seek proximity. (328)

type B babies Infants who use a caregiver as a secure base from which to explore the environment. (328)

type C babies Infants who exhibit insecurity by resisting a caregiver—for example, clinging but at the same time fighting against closeness. (328)

U

ultrasound sonography A medical procedure in which high-frequency sound waves are directed into a woman's abdomen. (85)

umbilical cord A life-support system containing two arteries and one vein, that connects the baby to the placenta. (101)

unconditioned response (UCR) An unlearned response automatically associated with the UCS. (234)

unconditioned stimulus (UCS) A stimulus that produces a response without prior learning. (234)

underextension Children's tendency to fail to use a noun to name a relevant event or object. (310)

universal ethical principles The sixth and highest stage in Kohlberg's theory of moral development. Individuals develop a moral standard based on universal human rights. (404)

unoccupied play Play that occurs when a child is not engaging in play as it is commonly understood; the child may stand in one spot, look around the room, or perform random movements that do not seem to have a goal. (480)

V

validity The extent to which a test measures what it is intended to measure. (271)

values clarification An indirect moral education approach that focuses on helping students clarify what their lives are for and what is worth working for. (419)

W

Wernicke's area An area of the brain's left hemisphere involved in language comprehension. (302)

whole-word method A learning-to-read technique that emphasizes learning direct associations between whole words and their meanings. (315)

wisdom Expert knowledge about the practical aspects of life. (221)

X

XYY syndrome A genetic disorder in which males have an extra Y chromosome. (82)

Z

zone of proximal development (ZPD) Vygotsky's term for the range of tasks too difficult for children to master alone but that can be mastered with the guidance and assistance of adults or more highly skilled children. (223)

zygote A single cell formed through fertilization. (79)

REFERENCES

A

Aber, J. L. (1993, March). *Poverty and child development: The policy implications of understanding causal mechanisms.* Paper presented at the biennial meeting of the Society for Research in Child Development, New Orleans.

Aberman, S., & Kirchoff, K. T. (1985). Infant-feeding practices: Mothers' decision making. *Journal of Obstetrics and Gynecological Neonatal Nursing,* p. 394.

Aboud, F., & Skerry, S. (1983). Self and ethnic concepts in relation to ethnic constancy. *Canadian Journal of Behavioral Science, 15,* 3–34.

Abramovitch, R., Corter, C., Pepler, D. J., & Stanhope, L. (1986). Sibling and peer interaction: A final follow-up and comparison. *Child Development, 47,* 217–229.

Abramson, L. Y., Metalsky, G. I., & Alloy, L. B. (1989). Hopelessness depression: A theory-based subtype of depression. *Psychological Bulletin, 96,* 358–372.

Achenbach, T. M., Phares, V., Howell, V. A., & Nurcombe, B. (1990). Seven-year outcome of the Vermont Intervention Program for Low-Birthweight Infants. *Child Development, 61,* 1672–1681.

Ackerman, B. P. (1988). Thematic influences on children's judgments about story accuracy. *Child Development, 59,* 918–938.

Ackerman, P. L., Sternberg, R. J., & Glaser, R. (Eds.). (1989). *Learning and individual differences.* New York: W. H. Freeman.

Acredolo, L. P., & Hake, J. L. (1982). Infant perception. In B. B. Wolman (Ed.), *Handbook of developmental psychology.* Englewood Cliffs, NJ: Prentice-Hall.

Adams, G. R. (1991). Physical attractiveness and adolescent development. In R. M. Lerner, A. C. Petersen, & J. Brooks-Gunn (Eds.), *Encyclopedia of adolescence* (Vol. II). New York: Garland.

Adams, G. R. (1992). Introduction and overview. In G. R. Adams, T. P. Gullotta, & R. Montemayor (Eds.), *Adolescent identity formation.* Newbury Park, CA: Sage.

Adler, T. (1991, January). Seeing double? Controversial twins study is widely reported, debated. *APA Monitor, 22,* 1, 8.

Ahl, V. A. (1993, March). *Classification of infants prenatally exposed to cocaine.* Paper presented at the biennial meeting of the Society for Research in Child Development, New Orleans.

Ahlstrom, P. A., Richmond, D., Townsend, C., & D'Angelo, L. (1992, March). *The course of HIV infection in adolescence.* Paper presented at the meeting of the Society for Adolescent Medicine, Washington, DC.

Ainsworth, M. D. S. (1979). Infant-mother attachment. *American Psychologist, 34,* 932–937.

Alan Guttmacher Institute. (1981). *Teenage pregnancy: The problem that has not gone away.* New York: Alan Guttmacher Institute.

Alan Guttmacher Institute. (1990). *Adolescence sexuality.* New York: Alan Guttmacher Institute.

Albee, G. W., Bond, L. A., & Monsey, T. V. C. (1992). *Improving children's lives: Global perspectives on prevention.* Newbury Park, CA: Sage.

Albro, E. R. (1993, March). *The development of a story concept.* Paper presented at the biennial meeting of the Society for Research in Child Development, New Orleans.

Alexander, K. L., & Entwisle, D. R. (1988). Achievement in the first two years of school: Patterns and processes. *Monographs of the Society for Research in Child Development, 53,* (2, Serial No. 218).

Allen, L., & Majidi-Ahi, S. (1989). Black American children. In J. T. Gibbs & L. N. Huang (Eds.), *Children of color.* San Francisco: Jossey-Bass.

Allen, L., & Santrock, J. W. (1993). *Psychology: The contexts of behavior.* Dubuque, IA: Wm. C. Brown.

Allen, W. R. (1985). Black students, White campus: Structural, interpersonal, and psychological correlates of success. *Journal of Negro Education, 54*(2), 134–147.

Alymer, R. C. (1989). The launching of the single young adult. In B. Carter & M. McGoldrick (Eds.), *The changing family life cycle* (2nd ed.). Boston: Allyn & Bacon.

America in Transition. (1989). Washington, DC: National Governors' Association Task Force on Children.

American Association for Protecting Children. (1986). *Highlights of Official Child Neglect and Abuse Reporting: 1984.* American Humane Association, Denver.

American College Health Association. (1989, May). *Survey of AIDS on American college and university campuses.* Washington, DC: American College Health Association.

Amsterdam, B. K. (1968). *Mirror behavior in children under two years of age.* Unpublished doctoral dissertation, University of North Carolina, Chapel Hill.

Anastasi, A. (1988). *Psychological testing* (6th ed.). New York: Macmillan.

Anderson, E. R. (1992, March). *Consistency of parenting in stepfather families.* Paper presented at the meeting of the Society for Research on Adolescence, Washington, DC.

Anderson, K. M. (1993, March). *Children and poverty: Public policy perspectives.* Paper presented at the biennial meeting of the Society for Research in Child Development, New Orleans.

Anderson, L. D. (1939). The predictive value of infant tests in relation to intelligence at 5 years. *Child Development, 10,* 202–212.

Anderson, L. W. (1989, April). *The impact of sex and age on the resolutions of preschool children's conversational disagreements.* Paper presented at the Society for Research in Child Development meeting, Kansas City, MO.

Andersson, B. (1992). Effects of day care on cognitive and socioemotional competence of thirteen-year-old Swedish schoolchildren. *Child Development, 63,* 20–36.

Andrews, J., & Conte, R. (1993, March). *Enhancing the social cognition of learning disabled children through a cognitive strategies approach.* Paper presented at the biennial meeting of the Society for Research in Child Development, New Orleans.

Angell, R. C. (1936). *The family encounters the depression.* New York: Charles Scribner's Sons.

Anson, C. A. (1988). *Atlanta's adopt-a-student project.* William T. Grant Foundation Annual Report, New York.

Archer, S. L. (1989). The status of identity: Reflections on the need for intervention. *Journal of Adolescence, 12,* 345–359.

Archer, S. L. (1992). A feminist's approach to identity research. In G. R. Adams, T. P. Gullotta, & R. Montemayor (Eds.), *Adolescent identity formation.* Newbury Park, CA: Sage.

Arehart, D. M., & Smith, P. H. (1990). Identity in adolescence: Influences on dysfunction and psychosocial task issues. *Journal of Youth and Adolescence, 19,* 63–72.

Arendt, R., Singer, L., & Minnes, S. (1993, March). *Development of cocaine-exposed infants.* Paper presented at the biennial meeting of the Society for Research in Child Development, New Orleans.

Aries, P. (1962). *Centuries of childhood* (R. Baldrick, Trans.). New York: Knopf.

Armsden, G., & Greenberg, M. T. (1984). *The inventory of parent and peer attachment: Individual differences and their relationship to psychological well-being in adolescence.* Unpublished manuscript, University of Washington.

Armsden, G., & Greenberg, M. T. (1987). The inventory of parent and peer attachment: Individual differences and their relationship to psychological well-being in adolescence. *Journal of Youth and Adolescence, 16,* 427–454.

Arnold, M. L. (1989, April). *Moral cognition and conduct: A quantitative review of the literature.* Paper presented at the Society for Research in Child Development meeting, Kansas City, MO.

Aronson, E. (1986, August). *Teaching students things they think they already know about: The case of prejudice and desegregation.* Paper presented at the meeting of the American Psychological Association, Washington, DC.

Arroyo, C. G., & Sternberg, R. J. (1993). *Against all odds: A view of the gifted disadvantaged.* Department of Psychology, Yale University, New Haven, CT.

Asarnow, J. R., & Callan, J. W. (1985). Boys with peer adjustment problems: Social cognitive processes. *Journal of Consulting and Clinical Psychology, 53,* 80–87.

Asher, J., & Garcia, R. (1969). The optimal age to learn a foreign language. *Modern Language Journal, 53,* 334–341.

Astin, A. W., Green, K. C., & Korn, W. S. (1987). *The American freshman: Twenty year trends.* Los Angeles: UCLA Higher Education Research Institute.

Atkinson, D. R., Morten, G., & Sue, D. W. (1993). *Counseling American minorities: A cross-cultural perspective* (4th ed.). Dubuque, IA: Wm. C. Brown.

Ayman-Nolley, S., & Church, R. B. (1993, March). *Social and cognitive mechanisms of learning through interaction with peers.* Paper presented at the biennial meeting of the Society for Research in Child Development, New Orleans.

B

Baca Zinn, M. (1980). Employment and education of Mexican-American women: The interplay of modernity and ethnicity in eight families. *Harvard Educational Review, 50,* 47–62.

Bachman, J. G., Johnston, L. P., & O'Malley, P. M. (1987). *Monitoring the future.* Ann Arbor: University of Michigan, Institute of Social Research.

Baer, J. (1993). *Creativity and divergent thinking.* Hillsdale, NJ: Erlbaum.

Bahr, S. J. (1989). Prologue: A developmental overview of the aging family. In S. J. Bahr & E. T. Peterson (Eds.), *Aging and the family.* Lexington, MA: Lexington Books.

Bahrick, L. (1993, March). *Intermodal learning and transfer in three-month-old infants.* Paper presented at the biennial meeting of the Society for Research in Child Development, New Orleans.

Bahrick, L. E. (1988). Intermodal learning in infancy: Learning on the basis of two kinds of invariant relations in audible and visible events. *Child Development, 59,* 197–209.

Bahrick, L. E. (1992). Infants' perceptual differentiation of amodal and modality-specific audio-visual relations. *Journal of Experimental Child Psychology, 53,* 180–199.

Baillargeon, R. (1987). Object permanence in 3.5- and 4.5-month-old infants. *Developmental Psychology, 23,* 655–664.

Baillargeon, R. (1991, April). *Infants' reasoning about collision events.* Paper presented at the meeting of the Society for Research in Child Development, Seattle, WA.

Baillargeon, R. (in press). The object concept revisited: New directions in the investigation of infants' physical knowledge. In C. E. Granrud (Ed.), *Visual perception and cognition in infancy.* Hillsdale, NJ: Erlbaum.

Baillargeon, R., DeVos, J., & Graber, M. (1989). Location memory in 8-month-old infants in a nonsearch AB task: Further evidence. *Cognitive Development, 4,* 345–367.

Baillargeon, R., Spelke, E. S., & Wasserman, S. (1985). Object permanence in five-month-old infants. *Cognition, 20,* 191–208.

Bakeman, R., & Brown, J. V. (1980). Early interaction: Consequences for social and mental development at three years. *Child Development, 51,* 437–447.

Baker, L., & Brown, A. L. (1984). Metacognitive skills and reading. In P. D. Pearson (Ed.), *Handbook of reading research, Part 2.* New York: Longman.

Ballenger, M. (1983). Reading in the kindergarten: Comment. *Childhood Education, 59,* 187.

Baltes, P. B. (1987). Theoretical propositions of life-span developmental psychology: On the dynamics between growth and decline. *Developmental Psychology, 23,* 611–626.

Baltes, P. B., & Baltes, M. M. (Eds.), (in press). *Successful aging.* New York: Cambridge University Press.

Baltes, P. B., Smith, J., Staudinger, U. M., & Sowards, D. (1990). Wisdom: One facet of successful aging? In M. Perlmutter (Ed.), *Late-life potential.* Washington, DC: Gerontological Association of America.

Bancroft, J. (1990). The impact of sociocultural influences on adolescent development: Further considerations. In J. Bancroft & J. Reinisch (Eds.), *Adolescence and puberty.* New York: Plenum.

Bancroft, J., & Reinisch, J. M. (1990). *Adolescence and puberty.* New York: Oxford University Press.

Bandura, A. (1965). Influence of models' reinforcement contingencies on the acquisition of imitative responses. *Journal of Personality and Social Psychology, 1,* 589–595.

Bandura, A. (1971). *Social learning theory,* New York: General Learning Press.

Bandura, A. (1977). *Social learning theory,* Englewood Cliffs, NJ: Prentice-Hall.

Bandura, A. (1986). *Social foundations of thought and action: A social cognitive theory.* Englewood Cliffs, NJ: Prentice-Hall.

Bandura, A. (1989). Social cognitive theory. In R. Vasta (Ed.), *Six theories of child development.* Greenwich, CT: JAI.

Bandura, A. (1991). Self-efficacy: Impact of self-beliefs on adolescent life paths. In R. M. Lerner, A. C. Petersen, & J. Brooks-Gunn (Eds.), *Encyclopedia of adolescence* (Vol. II). New York: Garland.

Bandura, A. (1991). Social cognitive theory of moral thought and action. In W.M. Kurtines & J. Gewirtz (Eds.), *Moral behavior and development: Advances in theory, research, and application.* Hillsdale, NJ: Erlbaum.

Banks, E. C. (1993, March). *Moral education curriculum in a multicultural context: The Malaysian primary curriculum.* Paper presented at the biennial meeting of the Society for Research in Child Development, New Orleans.

Banks, M. S., & Salapatek, P. (1983). Infant visual perception. In P. H. Mussen (Ed.), *Handbook of child psychology* (4th ed., Vol. 2). New York: Wiley.

Barber, B. L., & Eccles, J. S. (1992). Long-term influence of divorce and single parenting on adolescent family- and work-related values, behaviors and aspirations. *Psychological Bulletin, 111,* 108–126.

Barber, B. L., Clark, J. J., Clossick, M. L., & Wamboldt, P. (1992, March). *The effects of parent-adolescent communication on adjustment: Variations across divorced and intact families.* Paper presented at the meeting of the Society for Research on Adolescence, Washington, DC.

Barkeley, R. (1989). Attention deficit disorders: History, definition, diagnosis. In M. Lewis & S. Miller (Eds.), *Handbook of developmental psychopathology.* New York: Plenum.

Barker, R., & Wright, H. F. (1951). *One boy's day.* New York: Harper & Row.

Barnes, G. M., Welte, J. W., & Dintcheff, B. (1992, March). *Trends and patterns of alcohol use among 5th–12th grade students in New York state.* Paper presented at the meeting of the Society for Research on Adolescence, Washington, DC.

Barness, L. A., & Gilbert-Barness, E. (1992). Cause of death: SIDS or something else? *Contemporary Pediatrics, 9,* 13–31.

Barnet, B., Joffe, A., Duggan, A., & Repke, J. (1992, March). *Depressive symptoms, stress, and social support in pregnant and postpartum adolescents.* Paper presented at the meeting of the Society for Adolescent Medicine, Washington, DC.

Barnett, D., & McGee, R. (1993, March). *Advances in the operationalization and quantification of child maltreatment: Implications for developmental theory, research, and social policy.* Paper presented at the biennial meeting of the Society for Research in Child Development, New Orleans.

Barnett, R. C., Kibria, N., Baruch, G. K., & Pleck, J. H. (1991). Adult daughter-parent relationships and their associations with daughters' subjective well-being and psychological distress. *Journal of Marriage and the Family, 53,* 29–42.

Baron, J. B., & Sternberg, R. J. (Eds.). (1987). *Teaching thinking skills.* New York: W. H. Freeman.

Baron, R., Tom, D., & Cooper, H. (1985). Social class, race, and teacher expectations. In J. Dusek & G. Joseph (Eds.), *Teacher expectancies.* Hillsdale, NJ: Erlbaum.

Barr, R. G., Desilets, J., & Rotman, A. (1991, April). *Parsing the normal crying curve: Is it really the evening fussing curve?* Paper presented at the biennial meeting of the Society for Research in Child Development, Seattle.

Barrett, D. E., Radke-Yarrow, M., & Klein, R. E. (1982). Chronic malnutrition and child behavior: Effects of calorie supplementation on social and emotional functioning at school age. *Developmental Psychology, 18,* 541–556.

Barron, F. (1989, April). The birth of a notion: Exercises to tap your creative potential. *Omni,* pp. 112–119.

Bart, W. M. (1971). The factor structure of formal operations. *The British Journal of Educational Psychology, 41,* 40–77.

Bartsch, K., & Wellman, H. (1993, March). *Before belief: Children's early psychological theory.* Paper presented at the biennial meeting of the Society for Research in Child Development, New Orleans.

Baruch, G. K., Biener, L., & Barnett, R. C. (1987). Women and gender in research on work and family. *American Psychologist, 42,* 130–136.

Baskett, L. M., & Johnson, S. M. (1982). The young child's interaction with parents versus siblings. *Child Development, 53,* 643–650.

Bassuk, E. L., Carman, R. W., & Weinreb, L. F. (Eds.). (1990). *Community care for homeless families: A program design manual.* Washington, DC: The Better Homes Foundation, Interagency Council on the Homeless.

Bateson, G. (1956). The message, "This is play." In B. Schaffner (Ed.), *Group processes.* New York: Josiah Macy Foundation.

Batson, C. D. (1989). Personal values, moral principles, and the three path model of prosocial motivation. In N. Eisenberg & J. Reykowski (Eds.), *Social and moral values.* Hillsdale, NJ: Erlbaum.

Baumrind, D. (1971). Current patterns of parental authority. *Developmental Psychology Monographs, 4* (1, Pt. 2).

Baumrind, D. (1989, April). *Sex-differentiated socialization effects in childhood and adolescence.* Paper presented at the biennial meeting of the Society for Research in Child Development, Kansas City, MO.

Bayley, N. (1943). Mental growth during the first three years. In R. G. Barker, J. S. Kounin, & H. F. Wright (Eds.), *Child behavior and development.* New York: McGraw-Hill.

Bayley, N. (1969). *Manual for the Bayley Scales of infant development.* New York: Psychological Corp.

Bayley, N. (1970). Development of mental abilities. In P. H. Mussen (Ed.), *Manual of child psychology* (3rd ed., Vol. 1). New York: Wiley.

Bazen, C., & Shaver, P. (1987). Romantic love conceptualized as an attachment process. *Journal of Personality and Social Psychology, 51,* 511–524.

Beal, C. R. (1990). The development of text evaluation and revision skills. *Child Development, 61,* 247–258.

Beal, C. R., & Bonitabitus, G. J. (1991, April). *Children's developing ability to identify alternative interpretations in narratives: The role of text structure.* Paper presented at the Society for Research in Child Development meeting, Seattle.

Beals, D. E., & De Temple, J. (1991, April). *Reading, reporting, and repast: Three R's for co-constructing language and literacy skills.* Paper presented at the Society for Research in Child Development meeting, Seattle.

Bean, C. R. (1990). *Methods of childbirth* (rev. ed.). New York: Quill.

Beane, J. A. (1990, May). Rethinking the middle school curriculum. *Middle School Journal, 21,* 1–5.

Beardslee, W. R., & Richmond, J. B. (1992). Day care and preschool programs. In R. A. Hoekelman, S. B. Friedman, N. M. Nelson, & S. H. Seidel (Eds.), *Primary pediatric care* (2nd ed.). St. Louis, MO: Mosby Yearbook.

Beck, A. T. (1973). *The diagnosis and management of depression.* Philadelphia, PA: University of Pennsylvania Press.

Becker, H. J., & Sterling, C. W. (1987). Equity in school computer use: National data and neglected considerations. *Journal of Educational Computing Research, 3,* 289–311.

Bednar, R. L., Wells, M. G., & Peterson, S. R. (1989). *Self-esteem.* Washington, DC: American Psychological Association.

Behnke, M., & Eyler, F. D. (1991, April). *Issues in perinatal cocaine abuse research: The interface between medicine and child development.* Paper presented at the biennial meeting of the Society for Research in Child Development, Seattle.

Beilin, H. (1992). Piaget's enduring contribution to developmental psychology. *Developmental Psychology, 28,* 191–204.

Belenky, M. F., Clinchy, B. M., Goldberger, N. R., & Tarule, J. M. (1986). *Women's ways of knowing: The development of self, voice, and mind.* New York: Basic Books.

Bell, A. P., Weinberg, M. S., & Mammersmith, S. K. (1981). *Sexual preference: Its development in men and women.* New York: Simon & Schuster.

Bell, D. (Ed.). (1980). *Shades of Brown: New perspectives on school desegregation.* New York: Teachers College Press.

Bell, S. M., & Ainsworth, M. D. S. (1972). Infant crying and maternal responsiveness. *Child Development, 43,* 1171–1190.

Belle, D. (1990). Poverty and women's mental health. *American Psychologist, 45,* 385–389.

Belle, D., & Burr, R. (1992, March). *The after-school experiences of young people: A contextual and longitudinal analysis.* Paper presented at the meeting of the Society for Research on Adolescence, Washington, DC.

Bellinger, D., Leviton, A., Waternaux, C., Needleman, H., & Rabinowitz, M. (1987). Longitudinal analysis of prenatal and postnatal lead exposure and early cognitive development. *New England Journal of Medicine, 316,* 1037–1043.

Belmont, J. M. (1989). Cognitive strategies and strategic learning: The socio-instructional approach. *American Psychologist, 44,* 142–148.

Belsky, J. (1981). Early human experience: A family perspective. *Developmental Psychology, 17,* 3–23.

Belsky, J. (1989). Infant-parent attachment and day care: In defense of the strange situation. In J. S. Lande, S. Scarr, & N. Gunzenhauser (Eds.), *Caring for children: Challenge to America.* Hillsdale, NJ: Erlbaum.

Belsky, J. (1992). Consequences of child care for children's development: A deconstructionist view. In A. Booth (Ed.), *Child care in the 1990s.* Hillsdale, NJ: Erlbaum.

Belsky, J., Rovine, M., & Fish, M. (1989). The developing family system. In M. R. Gunnar & E. Thelen (Eds.), *Systems and development: The Minnesota Symposia on Child Psychology Series* (Vol. 22). Hillsdale, NJ: Erlbaum.

Belson, W. (1978). *Television violence and the adolescent boy.* London: Saxon House.

Bem, S. L. (1977). On the utility of alternative procedures for assessing psychological androgyny. *Journal of Consulting and Clinical Psychology, 45,* 196–205.

Bem, S. L. (1979). Theory and measurement of androgyny: A reply to the Pedhazur-Tetenbaum and Locksley-Colten critiques. *Journal of Personality and Social Psychology, 37,* 1047–1054.

Bem, S. L. (1981). Gender schema theory: A cognitive account of sex typing. *Psychological Review, 88,* 354–364.

Benenson, F. F. (in press). Greater preference among females than males for dyadic interaction in early childhood. *Child Development.*

Bennett, W. I., & Gurin, J. (1982). *The dieter's dilemma: Eating less and weighing more.* New York: Basic Books.

Bennett, W. J. (1986). *First lessons: A report on elementary education in America.* Washington, DC: U.S. Government Printing Office.

Benninga, J. S. (1988, February). An emerging synthesis in moral education. *Phi Delta Kappan,* pp. 415–418.

Benson, M. S. (1993, March). *Promoting literacy: The storytelling skills of Head Start parents.* Paper presented at the biennial meeting of the Society for Research in Child Development, New Orleans.

Berardo, F. M. (1990). Trends and direction in family research in the 1980s. *Journal of Marriage and the Family, 52,* 809–817.

Berg, C. A., & Sansone, C. (1991, April). *To plan or not to plan?* Paper presented at the Society for Research in Child Development meeting, Seattle.

Berg, W. K., & Berg, K. M. (1987). Psychophysiological development in infancy: State, startle, & attention. In J. D. Osofsky (Ed.), *Handbook of infant development* (2nd ed.). New York: Wiley.

Bergen, D. (1988). Stages of play development. In D. Bergen (Ed.), *Play as a medium for learning and development.* Portsmouth, NH: Heinemann.

Berk, S. F. (1985). *The gender factory: The apportionment of work in American households.* New York: Plenum.

Berko, J. (1958). The child's learning of English morphology. *Word, 14,* 150–177.

Berkowitz, M., & Gibbs, J. (1983). Measuring the developmental features of moral discussion. *Merrill-Palmer Quarterly, 29,* 399–410.

Berlin, L. (1993, March). *Attachment and emotions in preschool children.* Paper presented at the biennial meeting of the Society for Research in Child Development, New Orleans.

Berlyne, D. E. (1960). *Conflict, arousal, and curiosity.* New York: McGraw-Hill.

Berman, B. D. (1992, June). *Attention deficit disorder: Early indicators and treatment strategies.* Paper presented at the conference on issues in early child development. San Diego, CA.

Bernard, H. S. (1981). Identity formation in late adolescence: A review of some empirical findings. *Adolescence, 16,* 349–358.

Bernard, J. (1972). *The future of marriage.* New York: Bantam.

Berndt, T. J. (1979). Developmental changes in conformity to peers and parents. *Developmental Psychology, 15,* 608–616.

Berndt, T. J. (1982). The features and effects of friendships in early adolescence. *Child Development, 53,* 1447–1460.

Berndt, T. J., & Perry, T. B. (1990). Distinctive features and effects of early adolescent friendships. In R. Montemayor (Ed.), *Advances in adolescent research.* Greenwich, CT: JAI.

Berndt, T. J., Hawkins, J. A., & Hoyle, S. G. (1986). Changes in friendship during a school year: Effects on children's and adolescents' impressions of friendship and sharing with friends. *Child Development, 57,* 1284–1297.

Bernhardt, B. A., & Pyeritz, R. E. (1992). The organizations and delivery of clinical genetic services. *Pediatric Clinics of North America, 39,* 1–12.

Berninger, V. W. (1993, March). *Independent contributions of orthographic, phonological, and working memory skills to component reading skills.* Paper presented at the biennial meeting of the Society for Research in Child Development, New Orleans.

Berrueta-Clement, J., Schweinhart, L., Barnett, W., & Weikart, D. (1986). The effects of early educational intervention on crime and delinquency in adolescence and early adulthood. In J. Burchard & S. Burchard (Eds.), *Prevention of delinquent behavior.* Newbury Park, CA: Sage.

Berry, J. W. (1971). Ecological and cultural factors in spatial perceptual development. *Canadian Journal of Behavioral Science, 3,* 324–336.

Berry, J. W. (1983). Textured contexts: Systems and situations in cross-cultural psychology. In S. H. Irvine & J. W. Berry (Eds.), *Human assessment and cultural factors.* New York: Plenum.

Berry, J. W., & Bennett, J. A. (1992). Conceptions of cognitive competence. *International Journal of Psychology, 27,* 73–88.

Berry, J. W., Poortinga, Y. H., Segall, M. H., & Dasen, P. R. (1992). *Cross-cultural psychology: Theory, method, and applications.* Cambridge, England: Cambridge University Press.

Bertenthal, B. (1993, March). *Emerging themes in perceptual development.* Paper presented at the biennial meeting of the Society for Research in Child Development, New Orleans.

Bidell, T. (1993, March). *The constructive web: Understanding cultural diversity in developmental pathways.* Paper presented at the biennial meeting of the Society for Research in Child Development, New Orleans.

Bierman, K. L., Smoot, D. L., & Aumiller, K. (1993). Characteristics of aggressive-rejected, aggressive (nonrejected), and rejected (nonaggressive) boys. *Child Development, 64,* 139–151.

Bigler, R. S., & Liben, L. S. (in press). Cognitive mechanisms in children's gender stereotyping: Theoretical and educational implications of a cognitive-based intervention. *Child Development.*

Bigler, R. S., Liben, L. S., & Yekel, C. A. (1992, August). *Developmental patterns of gender-related beliefs: Beyond unitary constructs and measures.* Paper presented at the meeting of the American Psychological Association, Washington, DC.

Biller, H. B. (1993). *Fathers and families: Paternal factors in child development.* Westport, CT: Auburn House.

Bishop, S. M., & Ingersoll, G. M. (1989). Effects of marital conflict and family structure on the self-concepts of pre- and early adolescents. *Journal of Youth and Adolescence, 18,* 25–38.

Black, A. E., & Pedro-Carroll, J. L. (1993, March). *The long-term effects of interpersonal conflict and parental divorce among late adolescents.* Paper presented at the biennial meeting of the Society for Research in Child Development, New Orleans.

Blakemore, J. E. O. (1993, March). *Preschool children's interest in babies: Observations in naturally occurring situations.* Paper presented at the biennial meeting of the Society for Research in Child Development, New Orleans.

Blash, R., & Unger, D. G. (1992, March). *Cultural factors and the self-esteem and aspirations of African-American adolescent males.* Paper presented at the meeting of the Society for Research on Adolescence, Washington, DC.

Blasi, A. (1988). Identity and the development of the self. In D. Lapsley & F. C. Power (Eds.), *Self, ego, and identity: Integrative approaches.* New York: Springer-Verlag.

Blau, G. M., & Gullotta, T. P. (1993). Sexual responsibility in adolescence. In T. P. Gullotta, G. R. Adams, & R. Montemayor (Eds.), *Adolescent sexuality.* Newbury Park, CA: Sage.

Bloch, M. (1992, August/September). Tobacco control advocacy: Winning the war on tobacco. *Zero to Three, 13,* 29–34.

Block, J. (1992, March). *Parental and personality antecedents of early menarche.* Paper presented at the meeting of the Society for Research in Adolescence, Washington, DC.

Block, J. H., Block, J., & Gjerde, P. (1986). The personality of children prior to divorce: A prospective study. *Child Development, 57,* 827–840.

Bloom, L. (1992, August). *Racism in developmental research.* Paper presented at the meeting of the American Psychological Association, Washington, DC.

Bloome, D. (Ed.). (1989). *Classrooms and literacy.* Norwood, NJ: Ablex.

Blos, P. (1989). The inner world of the adolescent. In A. H. Esman (Ed.), *International annals of adolescent psychiatry.* Chicago: University of Chicago Press.

Blumenfeld, P. C., Pintrich, P. R., Wessles, K., & Meece, J. (1981, April). *Age, and sex differences in the impact of classroom experiences on self-perceptions.* Paper presented at the biennial meeting of the Society for Research in Child Development, Boston.

Blyth, D. A., Bulcroft, R., & Simmons, R. G. (1981, August). *The impact of puberty on adolescents: A longitudinal study.* Paper presented at the meeting of the American Psychological Association, Los Angeles.

Bogatz, G., & Ball, S. (1972). *Reading with television: An evaluation of the Electric Company.* Princeton, NJ: Educational Testing Service.

Bohannon, J. N. III, & Stanowicz, L. (1988). The issue of negative evidence. Adult responses to children's language errors. *Developmental Psychology, 24,* 684–689.

Bohannon, J. N. III, MacWhinney, B., & Snow, C. (1990). No negative evidence revisited: Beyond learnability or who has to prove what to whom. *Developmental Psychology, 26,* 221–226.

Bonvillian, J. D., Orlansky, M. D., & Novack, L. L. (1983). Developmental milestones: Sign language and motor development. *Child Development, 54,* 1435–1445.

Boring, E. G. (1950). *A history of experimental psychology.* New York: Appleton-Century-Crofts.

Bornstein, M. H. (1989). Stability in early mental development. In M. H. Bornstein & N. A. Krasnegor (Eds.), *Stability and continuity in mental development.* Hillsdale, NJ: Erlbaum.

Bornstein, M. H. (1993, March). *Cross-cultural perspectives on parenting.* Paper presented at the biennial meeting of the Society for Research in Child Development, New Orleans.

Bornstein, M. H., & Krasnegor, N. A. (1989). *Stability and continuity in mental development.* Hillsdale, NJ: Erlbaum.

Bornstein, M. H., & Sigman, M. D. (1986). Continuity in mental development from infancy. *Child Development, 57,* 251–274.

Bouchard, T. J., Heston, L., Eckert, E., Keyes, M., & Resnick, S. (1981). The Minnesota Study of Twins Reared Apart: Project description and sample results in the developmental domain. *Twin Research, 3,* 227–233.

Bouchard, T. J., Lykken, D. T., McGue, M., Segal, N. L., & Tellegen, A. (1990). Source of human psychological differences: The Minnesota Study of Twins Reared Apart. *Science, 250,* 223–228.

Bowen, M. (1978). *Family therapy in clinical practice.* New York: Aronson.

Bower, B. (1985). The left hand of math and verbal talent. *Science News, 127,* 263.

Bower, T. G. R. (1977). *A primer of infant development.* New York: W. H. Freeman.

Bower, T. G. R. (1989). *The rational infant.* San Francisco: W. H. Freeman.

Bower, T. G. R. (1993, January). Personal communication. Program in psychology and human development, University of Texas at Dallas, Richardson, TX.

Bower, T. G. R. (1993, February). Personal communication. Program in psychology and human development, University of Texas at Dallas.

Bowerman, M. (1989). Learning a semantic system: What role do cognitive predispositions play? In M. L. Rice & R. L. Schiefelbusch (Eds.), *The teachability of language.* Baltimore: Paul Brooks.

Bowers, P. G., & Wolf, M. (1993, March). *A double-deficit hypothesis for developmental reading disorders.* Paper presented at the biennial meeting of the Society for Research in Child Development, New Orleans.

Bowlby, J. (1969). *Attachment and loss* (Vol. 1). London: Hogarth.

Bowlby, J. (1989). *Secure and insecure attachment.* New York: Basic Books.

Bowlby, J. (1989). *Secure attachment.* New York: Basic.

Bowman, P. J., & Howard, C. (1985). Race-related socialization, motivation, and academic achievement: A study of black youths in three-generation families. *Journal of the American Academy of Child Psychiatry, 24,* 134–141.

Boxer, A. M. (1988, August). *Developmental continuities of gay and lesbian youth.* Paper presented at the meeting of the American Psychological Association, Atlanta.

Boyer, C. B., & Hein, K. (1991). AIDS and HIV infection in adolescents: The role of education and antibody testing. In R. M. Lerner, A. C. Petersen, & J. Brooks-Gunn (Eds.), *Encyclopedia of adolescence* (Vol. I). New York: Garland.

Boyes, M. C., Giordano, R., & Galperyn, K. (1993, March). *Moral orientation and interpretive contexts of moral deliberation.* Paper presented at the biennial meeting of the Society for Research in Child Development, New Orleans.

Brackbill, Y. (1979). Obstetric medication and infant behavior. In J. D. Osofsky (Ed.), *Handbook of infant development.* New York: Wiley.

Bracken, M. B., Eskenazi, B., Sachse, K., McSharry, J., Hellenbrand, K., & Leo-Summers, L. (1990). Association of cocaine use with sperm concentration, motility, and morphology. *Fertility and Sterility, 53,* 315–322.

Braham, P., Rattansi, A., & Skellington, R. (Eds.). (1992). *Racism and anti-racism.* Newbury Park, CA: Sage.

Braithwaite, J. (1993, March). *Adolescent mothers and their infants: Determinants of caregiving competence in feeding interactions.* Paper presented at the biennial meeting of the Society for Research in Child Development, New Orleans.

Braungart, J. M., Plomin, R., DeFries, J. C., & Fulker, D. W. (1992). Genetic influence on tester-rated infant temperament as assessed by Bayley's Infant Behavior Record: Nonadoptive and adoptive siblings and twins. *Developmental Psychology, 28,* 40–47.

Brazelton, T. B. (1956). Sucking in infancy. *Pediatrics, 17,* 400–404.

Brazelton, T. B. (1973). *Neonatal Behavioral Assessment Scale.* London: Heinemann Medical Books.

Brazelton, T. B. (1983). *Infants and mothers: Differences in development.* New York, Delta.

Brazelton, T. B. (1990). Saving the bathwater. *Child Development, 61,* 1661–1671.

Brazelton, T. B., Nugent, J. K., & Lester, B. M. (1987). Neonatal Behavioral Assessment Scale. In J. D. Osofsky (Ed.), *Handbook of infant development* (2nd ed.). New York: Wiley.

Bredekamp, S. (1987). *Developmentally appropriate practice in early childhood programs serving children from birth through age 8.* Washington, DC: NAEYC.

Bredekamp, S., & Shepard, L. (1989). How to best protect children from inappropriate school expectations, practices, and policies. *Young Children, 44,* 14–24.

Brent, D. A. (1989). Suicide and suicidal behavior in children and adolescents. *Pediatrics in Review, 10,* 269–275.

Bretherton, I. (1993, August). *The dialogic self: Perspectives from attachment theory and psychoanalysis.* Paper presented at the meeting of the American Psychological Association, Toronto, CA.

Bretherton, I., Fritz, J., Zahn-Waxler, C., & Ridgeway, D. (1986). Learning to talk about emotions. *Child Development, 57,* 529–548.

Bretherton, I., Golby, B., & Page, T. (1993, March). *Fathers as caregivers: An interview study.* Paper presented at the biennial meeting of the Society for Research in Child Development, New Orleans.

Bridges, S. (1973). *IQ-150.* London: Priory Press.

Brislin, R. (1993). *Culture's influence on behavior.* Ft. Worth, TX: Harcourt Brace Jovanovich.

Brislin, R. (1993). *Understanding culture's influence on human behavior.* San Diego, CA: Harcourt Brace Jovanovich.

Brislin, R. W. (1987). Increasing awareness of class, ethnicity, culture, and race by expanding on students' own experiences. In *The G. Stanley Hall Lecture Series* (Vol. 8). Washington, DC: American Psychological Association.

Broberg, A. G., Hwang, C. P., & Chace, S. V. (1993, March). *Effects of day care on school performance and adjustment.* Paper presented at the biennial meeting of the Society for Research in Child Development, New Orleans.

Brody, G. H., & Shaffer, D. R. (1982). Contributions of parents and peers to children's moral socialization. *Developmental Review, 2,* 31–75.

Brody, N. (1992). *Intelligence* (2nd ed.). San Diego: Academic Press.

Brodzinsky, D. M., Schechter, D. E., Braff, A. M., & Singer, L. M. (1984). Psychological and academic adjustment in adopted children. *Journal of Consulting and Clinical Psychology, 52,* 582–590.

Bronfenbrenner, U. (1974). *Is early intervention effective?* DHEW Publication (OHD): 74-25.

Bronfenbrenner, U. (1979). Contexts of child rearing: Problems and prospects. *American Psychologist, 34,* 844–850.

Bronfenbrenner, U. (1986). Ecology of the family as a context for human development: Research perspectives. *Developmental Psychology, 22,* 723–742.

Bronfenbrenner, U. (1989, April). *The developing ecology of human development.* Paper presented at the biennial meeting of the Society for Research in Child Development, Kansas City, MO.

Bronfenbrenner, U. (1993). Ecological systems theory. In R. H. Wozniak (Ed.), *Development in context.* Hillsdale, NJ: Erlbaum.

Bronstein, P. (1988). Marital and parenting roles in transition. In P. Bronstein & C. P. Cowen (Eds.), *Contemporary fatherhood.* New York: Wiley.

Bronstein, P. A., & Quina, K. (Eds.). (1988). *Teaching a psychology of people.* Washington, DC: American Psychological Association.

Brook, D. W., & Brook, J. S. (in press). Family processes associated with alcohol and drug use and abuse. In E. Kaufman & P. Kaufman (Eds.), *Family therapy of drug and alcohol abuse: Ten years later.* New York: Gardner Press.

Brook, J. S., Brook, D. W., Gordon, A. S., Whiteman, M., & Cohen, P. (1990). The psychological etiology of adolescent drug use: A family interactional approach. *Genetic Psychology Monographs, 116,* no. 2.

Brooks-Gunn, J. (1991). Maturational timing variations in adolescent girls, antecedents of. In R. M. Lerner, A. C. Petersen, & J. Brooks-Gunn (Eds.), *Encyclopedia of adolescence* (Vol. II). New York: Garland.

Brooks-Gunn, J. (1993, March). *Adolescence.* Paper presented at the biennial meeting of the Society for Research in Child Development, New Orleans.

Brooks-Gunn, J., & Warren, M. P. (1989, April). *How important are pubertal and social events for different problem behaviors and contexts.* Paper presented at the biennial meeting of the Society for Research in Child Development, Kansas City, MO.

Brooks-Gunn, J., Klebanov, P. K., Liaw, F., & Spiker, D. (in press). Enhancing the development of low birth weight, premature infants: Changes in cognition and behavior over the first three years. *Child Development.*

Brooks-Gunn, J., McCarton, C., & Tonascia, J. (1992, May). *Enhancing the development of LBW, premature infants: Defining risk and targeting subgroups in the Infant Health and Development Program.* Paper presented at the International Conference on Infant Studies, Miami Beach, FL.

Brooks-Gunn, J., McCormick, M. C., Benasich, A. A., Shapiro, S., & Black, G. (1992). Secondary effects: Maternal education, maternal employment, and fertility. In R. T. Gross (Ed.), *Infant health and development program.* Stanford, CA: Stanford University Press.

Broughton, J. M. (1978). Development of concepts of self, mind, reality, and knowledge. In W. Damon (Ed.), *Social cognition.* San Francisco: Jossey-Bass.

Broughton, J. M. (1983). The cognitive developmental theory of self and identity. In B. Lee & G. Noam (Eds.), *Developmental approaches to self.* New York: Plenum.

Broverman, I., Vogel, S., Broverman, D., Clarkson, F., & Rosenkranz, P. (1972). Sex-role stereotypes: A current appraisal. *Journal of Social Issues, 28,* 59–78.

Brown, A. (1993, March). *Whither cognitive development in the 1990s?* Paper presented at the biennial meeting of the Society for Research in Child Development, New Orleans.

Brown, A. C., & Orthner, D. K. (1990). Relocation and personal well-being among early adolescents. *Journal of Early Adolescence, 10,* 366–381.

Brown, A. L., & Palincsar, A. M. (1984). Reciprocal teaching of comprehension-fostering and monitoring activities. *Cognition and Instruction, 1,* 175–177.

Brown, A. L., & Palincsar, A. M. (1989). Guided, cooperative learning and individual knowledge acquisition. In L. B. Resnick (Ed.), *Knowing and learning: Essays in honor of Robert Glaser.* Hillsdale, NJ: Erlbaum.

Brown, A. L., Bransford, J. D., Ferrara, R. A., & Campione, J. C. (1983). Learning, remembering, and understanding. In P. H. Mussen (Ed.), *Handbook of child psychology* (4th ed., Vol. 3). New York: Wiley.

Brown, A. L., Campione, J. C., Reeve, R. A., Ferrara, R. A., & Palincsar, A. S. (in press). Interactive learning, individual understanding: The case of reading and mathematics. In L. T. Landsmann (Ed.), *Culture, schooling, and psychological development.* Hillsdale, NJ: Erlbaum.

Brown, A. L., Smiley, S. S., Day, J. D., Townsend, M. A. R., & Lawton, S. C. (1977). Intrusion of a thematic idea in children's comprehension and retention of stories. *Child Development, 48,* 1454–1466.

Brown, B. B., & Lohr, M. J. (1987). Peer group affiliation and adolescent self-esteem: An integration of ego identity and symbolic interaction theories. *Journal of Personality and Social Psychology, 52,* 47–55.

Brown, B. B., & Mount, N. (1989, April). *Peer group structures in single versus multiethnic high schools.* Paper presented at the Society for Research in Child Development meeting, Kansas City, MO.

Brown, B. B., Steinberg, L., Mounts, N., & Philipp, M. (1990, March). *The comparative influence of peers and parents on high school achievement: Ethnic differences.* Paper presented at the meeting of the Society for Research on Adolescence, Atlanta.

Brown, E., James, L., & Schlosser, J. (1993, March). *Early social competence in children born to adolescent and adult mothers.* Paper presented at the biennial meeting of the Society for Research in Child Development, New Orleans.

Brown, J. L. (1964). States in newborn infants. *Merrill-Palmer Quarterly, 10,* 313–327.

Brown, J. L., & Pizer, H. F. (1987). *Living hungry in America.* New York: Macmillan.

Brown, J. S., & Burton, R. B. (1978). Diagnostic models for procedural bugs in basic mathematical skills. *Cognitive Science, 2,* 155–192.

Brown, L. M., & Gilligan, C. (1990, March). *The psychology of women and the development of girls.* Paper presented at the meeting of the Society for Research in Adolescence, Atlanta.

Brown, R. (1973). *A first language: The early stages.* Cambridge, MA: Harvard University Press.

Brown, R. (1986). *Social psychology* (2nd ed.). New York: Free Press.

Brown, S., Pippp, S., Waring, R., & Goetz, D. (1993, March). *The role of infant and parent gender in the development of infant-parent boundaries: The second year of life.* Paper presented at the biennial meeting of the Society for Research in Child Development, New Orleans.

Browne, C. R., Brown, J. V., Blumenthal, J., Anderson, L., & Johnson, P. (1993, March). *African-American fathering: The perception of mothers and sons.* Paper presented at the biennial meeting of the Society for Research in Child Development, New Orleans.

Brownell, K. D. (1990, August). *Dieting, weight, and body image: Where culture and physiology collide.* Paper presented at the meeting of the American Psychological Association, Boston, MA.

Brubaker, T. H. (1985). *Later life families.* Newbury Park, CA: Sage.

Bruner, J. S. (1983). *Child talk.* New York: W. W. Norton.

Bruner, J. S. (1989, April). *The state of developmental psychology.* Paper presented at the Society for Research in Child Development meeting, Kansas City, MO.

Bryant, D. M., & Ramey, C. T. (1987). An analysis of the effectiveness of early intervention programs for high-risk children. In M. Guralnick & C. Bennett (Eds.), *The effectiveness of early intervention for at-risk and handicapped children,* pp. 33–78. San Diego, CA: Academic Press.

Buchanan, C. M., Maccoby, E. E., & Dornbusch, S. M. (1992). Adolescents and their families after divorce: Three residential arrangements compared. *Journal of Research in Adolescence, 2*(3), 261–291.

Buchannon, C. M., & Maccoby, E. E. (1990, March). *Characteristics of adolescents and their families in three custodial arrangements.* Paper presented at the meeting of the Society for Research in Adolescence, Atlanta.

Buck, G. M., Cookfair, D. L., Michalek, A. M., Nasca, P. C., Standfast, S. J., Sever, L. E., & Kramer, A. A. (1989). Intrauterine growth retardation and risk of sudden infant death syndrome (SIDS). *American Journal of Epidemiology, 129,* 874–884.

Budwig, N. (1993). *A developmental functionalist approach to child language.* Hillsdale, NJ: Erlbaum.

Buhrmester, D. (1989). *Changes in friendship, interpersonal competence, and social adaptation during early adolescence.* Unpublished manuscript, Department of Psychology, UCLA, Los Angeles.

Buhrmester, D. (1990). Friendship, interpersonal competence, and adjustment in preadolescence and adolescence. *Child Development, 61,* 1101–1111.

Buhrmester, D. (1993, January). Personal Communication, Program in Psychology, University of Texas at Dallas, Richardson, TX.

Buhrmester, D. (1993, March). *Adolescent friendship and the socialization of gender differences in social interaction styles.* Paper presented at the biennial meeting of the Society for Research in Child Development, New Orleans.

Buhrmester, D., & Furman, W. (1987). The development of companionship and intimacy. *Child Development, 58,* 1101–1113.

Buhrmester, D., Furman, W., Wittenberg, M., & Reis, H. (1988). Five domains of interpersonal competence in peer relationships. *Journal of Personality and Social Psychology, 55,* 991–1008.

Burchinal, M. R. (1993, March). *Predictors of patterns of cognitive development among poverty: Early intervention and characteristics of the child and family.* Paper presented at the biennial meeting of the Society for Research in Child Development, New Orleans.

Burgess, R. L. (1993, March). *The family in a changing world: Winners and losers.* Paper presented at the biennial meeting of the Society for Research in Child Development, New Orleans.

Burton, R. V. (1984). A paradox in theories and research in moral development. In W. M. Kurtines & J. L. Gewirtz (Eds.), *Morality, moral behavior, and moral development.* New York: Wiley.

Burts, D. C., Hart, C. H., Charlesworth, R., Hernandez, S., Kirk, L., & Mosley, J. (1989, March). *A comparison of the frequencies of stress behaviors observed in kindergarten children in classrooms with developmentally appropriate vs. developmentally inappropriate instructional practices.* Paper presented at the annual meeting of the American Educational Research Association, San Francisco.

Buss, A. H., & Plomin, R. (1984). *A temperament theory of personality development.* New York: Wiley-Interscience.

Buss, A. H., & Plomin, R. (1987). Commentary. In H. H. Goldsmith, A. H. Buss, R. Plomin, M. K. Rothbart, A. Thomas, A. Chess, R. R. Hinde, & R. B. McCall (Eds.), Roundtable: What is temperament? Four approaches. *Child Development, 58,* 505–529.

Buss, R. R., Yussen, S. R., Mathews, S. R., Miller, G. E., & Rembold, K. L. (1983). Development of children's use of a story schema to retrieve information. *Developmental Psychology, 19,* 22–28.

Bussey, K., & Maughan, B. (1982). Gender differences in moral reasoning. *Journal of Personality and Social Psychology, 42,* 701–706.

Butterworth, G. (1993). Context and cognition in models of cognitive growth. In P. Light & G. Butterworth (Eds.), *Context and Cognition.* Hillsdale, NJ: Erlbaum.

Byer, C. O., & Shainberg, L. W. (1991). *Dimensions of human sexuality* (3rd ed.). Dubuque, IA: Wm. C. Brown.

C

Cairns, R. B. (1983). The emergence of developmental psychology. In P. H. Mussen (Ed.), *Handbook of child psychology* (4th ed., Vol. 1). New York: Wiley.

Cairns, R. B. (1991). Multiple metaphors for a singular idea. *Developmental Psychology, 27,* 23–236.

Cairns, R. B. (1992). The making of developmental science: The contributions and intellectual heritage of James Mark Baldwin. *Developmental Psychology, 28,* 17–24.

Caldwell, B. (1964). The effects of infant care. In M. Hoffman & L. Hoffman (Eds.), *Review of child development research* (Vol. 1). New York: Russell Sage.

Caldwell, B. (1991, October). *Impact on the child.* Paper presented at the symposium on day care for children, Arlington, VA.

Caldwell, M. B., & Rogers, M. F. (1992). Epidemiology of pediatric HIV infection. *Pediatric Clinics of North America, 38,* 1–16.

Calhoun, J. A. (1988, March). *Gang violence.* Testimony to the House Select Committee on Children, Youth, and Families, Washington, DC.

Calkins, S. D., & Fox, N. A. (1992). The relations among infant temperament, security of attachment, and behavioral inhibition at twenty-four months. *Child Development, 63,* 1456–1472.

Camara, K. A., & Resnick, G. (1988). Interparental conflict and cooperation: Factors moderating children's postdivorce adjustment. In E. M. Hetherington & J. D. Arasteh (Eds.), *Impact of divorce, single-parenting, and stepparenting on children.* Hillsdale, NJ: Erlbaum.

Camarena, P. M. (1991). Conformity in adolescence. In R. M. Lerner, A. C. Petersen, & J. Brooks-Gunn (Eds.), *Encyclopedia of adolescence* (Vol. 1). New York: Garland.

Cameron, D. (1988, February). Soviet schools. *NEA Today,* p. 15.

Cameron, J., Cowan, D., Holmes, B., Hurst, P., & McLean, M. (Eds.). (1983). *International handbook of educational systems.* New York: Wiley.

Campbell, F. A., & Ramey, C. T. (1993, March). *Mid-adolescent outcomes for high risk students: An examination of the continuing effects of early intervention.* Paper presented at the biennial meeting of the Society for Research in Child Development, New Orleans.

Campbell, S. B., Meyers, T., Ross, S., & Flanagan, C. (1993, March). *Chronicity of maternal depression and mother-infant interaction.* Paper presented at the biennial meeting of the Society for Research in Child Development, New Orleans.

Campos, J. J., Langer, A., & Krowitz, A. (1970). Cardiac responses on the visual cliff in prelocomotor human infants. *Science, 170,* 196–197.

Carbery, J., & Buhrmester, D. (1993, March). *The need-fulfilling roles of friendship during three young adults' phases.* Paper presented at the biennial meeting of the Society for Research in Child Development, New Orleans.

Carbo, M. (1987). Reading styles research: "What works" isn't always phonics. *Phi Delta Kappan,* pp. 431–435.

Carey, J. C. (1992). Health supervision and anticipatory guidance for children with genetic disorders. *Pediatric Clinics of North America, 39,* 35–54.

Carey, S. (1977). The child as word learner. In M. Halle, J. Bresnan, & G. A. Miller (Eds.), *Linguistic theory and psychological reality.* Cambridge, MA: MIT Press.

Carey, S. (1988). Are children fundamentally different kinds of thinkers and learners than adults? In K. Richardson & S. Sheldon (Eds.), *Cognitive development to adolescence.* Hillsdale, NJ: Erlbaum.

Carlson, C., Cooper, C., & Hsu, J. (1990, March). *Predicting school achievement in early adolescence: The role of family process.* Paper presented at the meeting of the Society for Research in Adolescence, Atlanta.

Carnegie Corporation. (1989). *Turning points: Preparing youth for the 21st century.* New York: Carnegie Corporation.

Carpenter, T. P., Moser, J. M., & Romberg, T. A. (Eds.). (1982). *Addition and subtraction: A cognitive perspective.* Hillsdale, NJ: Erlbaum.

Carr, T. H., & Alejano, A. R. (1993, March). *Levels of processing and benefit from practice during reading development.* Paper presented at the biennial meeting of the Society for Research in Child Development, New Orleans.

Carraher, T. H., & Carraher, D. W. (1981). Do Piagetian stages describe the reasoning of the unschooled adults? *Quarterly Newsletter of the Laboratory of Comparative Human Cognition, 3,* 61–68.

Carson, D., & Bittner, M. (1993, March). *Creative thinking and temperament as predictors of school-aged children's coping abilities and response to stress.* Paper presented at the biennial meeting of the Society for Research in Child Development, New Orleans.

Carter, B., & McGoldrick, M. (1989). Overview: The changing family life cycle— a framework for family therapy. In B. Carter & M. McGoldrick (Eds.), *The changing family life cycle* (2nd ed.). Boston: Allyn & Bacon.

Carter, D. B., & Levy, G. D. (1988). Cognitive aspects of children's early sex-role development: The influence of gender schemas on preschoolers' memories and preference for sex-typed toys and activities. *Child Development, 59,* 782–793.

Carter, D. B., & Taylor, R. D. (in press). The development of children's awareness and understanding of flexibility in sex-role stereotypes: Implications for preferences, attitude, and behavior. *Sex Roles.*

Case, R. (1985). *Intellectual development: A systematic reinterpretation.* New York: Academic Press.

Case, R. (1985). *Intellectual development: Birth to adulthood.* New York: Academic Press.

Case, R. (1987). Neo-Piagetian theory: Retrospect and prospect. *International Journal of Psychology, 22,* 773–791.

Case, R. (1993, March). *Central conceptual structures and their manifestation in specific task performance.* Paper presented at the biennial meeting of the Society for Research in Child Development, New Orleans.

Case, R. (Ed.) (1992). *The mind's staircase: Exploring the conceptual underpinnings of children's thought and knowledge.* Hillsdale, NJ: Erlbaum.

Case, R., Kurland, D. M., & Goldberg, J. (1982). Operational efficiency and the growth of short-term memory span. *Journal of Experimental Child Psychology, 33,* 386–404.

Cassell, C. (1984). *Swept away: Why women fear their own sexuality.* New York: Simon & Schuster.

Cassidy, J., Parke, R. D., Butkovsky, L., & Braungart, J. M. (1992). Family-peer connections: The role of emotional expressiveness within the family and children's understanding of emotions. *Child Development, 63,* 603–618.

Cavett, D. (1974). *Cavett.* San Diego: Harcourt Brace Jovanovich.

Ceballo, R., & Olson, S. L. (1993, March). *The role of alternative caregivers in the lives of children poor, single-parent families.* Paper presented at the biennial meeting of the Society for Research in Child Development, New Orleans.

Cerro, L., & Baker, L. (1993, March). "But I don't do anything when I read." *Developmental differences in self-reported strategy use.* Paper presented at the biennial meeting of the Society for Research in Child Development, New Orleans.

Chalfant, J. C. (1989). Learning disabilities: Policy issues and promising approaches. *American Psychologist, 44,* 392–398.

Chan, W. S. (1963). *A source book in Chinese philosophy.* Princeton, NJ: Princeton University Press.

Charlesworth, R. (1987). *Understanding child development* (2nd ed.). Albany, NY: Delmar.

Charlesworth, R. (1989). "Behind" before the start? *Young Children, 44,* 5–13.

Charlesworth, W. R. (1992). Commentary: Can biology explain human development? *Human Development, 35,* 9–11.

Chasnoff, I. J. (1991, April). *Cocaine versus tobacco: Impact on infant and child outcome.* Paper presented at the biennial meeting of the Society for Research in Child Development, Seattle.

Chasnoff, I. J., Griffith, D. R., Freier, C., & Murray, J. (1992). Cocaine/polydrug use in pregnancy: Two-year follow-up. *Pediatrics, 89,* 284–289.

Chasnoff, I. J., Griffith, D. R., MacGregor, S., Dirkes, K., & Burns, K. A. (1989). Temporal patterns of cocaine use in pregnancy. *Journal of the American Medical Association, 261,* 1741–1744.

Chesney-Lind, M. (1989). Girls' crime and woman's place: Toward a feminist model of female delinquency. *Crime and Delinquency, 35,* 5–30.

Chess, S., & Thomas, A. (1977). Temperamental individuality from childhood to adolescence. *Journal of Child Psychiatry, 16,* 218–226.

Chi, M. T. H., & Koeske, R. D. (1983). Network representation of a child's dinosaur knowledge. *Developmental Psychology, 19,* 29–39.

Children's Defense Fund. (1990). *Children 1990.* Washington, DC: Children's Defense Fund.

Children's Defense Fund. (1992). *The Health of America's Children.* Washington, DC. Childrens Defense Fund.

Chodorow, N. (1978). *The reproduction of mothering.* Berkeley: University of California Press.

Chodorow, N. (1989). *Feminism and psychoanalytic theory.* New Haven, CT: Yale University Press.

Chomsky, N. (1957). *Syntactic structures.* The Hague: Mouton.

Chomsky, N. (1986). *Knowledge of language.* New York: Praeger.

Cicchetti, D., & Lynch, M. (in press). Toward an ecological/transactional model of community violence and child maltreatment: Consequences for children's development. *Psychiatry.*

Cicchetti, D. (1991, April). *Developmental Theory: Lessons From the Study of Risk and Psychopathology.* Invited address at the biennial meeting of the Society for Research in Child Development, Seattle.

Cicchetti, D., & Toth, S. L. (Eds.). (in press). *Child Abuse, Child Development, and Social Policy.* Norwood, NJ: Ablex.

Cicchetti, D., Toth, S. L., & Lynch, M. (in press). The developmental sequelae of child maltreatment: Implications for war-related trauma. In L. A. Leavitt & N. A. Fox (Eds.), *Psychological effects of war and violence on children.* Hillsdale, NJ: Erlbaum.

Cicirelli, V. (1977). Family structure and interaction: Sibling effects on socialization. In M. McMillan & M. Sergio (Eds.), *Child psychiatry: Treatment and research.* New York: Brunner/Mazel.

Cillessen, A. H. N., Van Ijzendoorn, H. W., Van Lieshout, C. F. M., & Hartup, W. W. (1992). Heterogeneity among peer-rejected boys: Subtypes and stabilities. *Child Development, 63,* 893–905.

Clark, E. V. (1983). Meanings and concepts. In P. H. Mussen (Ed.), *Handbook of child psychology* (4th ed., Vol. 4). New York: Wiley.

Clark, H. H., & Clark, E. V. (1977). *Psychology and language.* New York: Harcourt Brace Jovanovich.

Clark, K. (1965). *Dark ghetto.* New York: Harper.

Clark, K. B., & Clark, M. K. (1939). The development of consciousness of self in the emergence of racial identification in Negro preschool children. *Journal of Social Psychology, 10,* 591–599.

Clark, S. D., Zabin, L. S., & Hardy, J. B. (1984). Sex, contraception, and parenthood: Experience and attitudes among urban black young men. *Family Planning Perspectives, 16,* 77–82.

Clarke-Stewart, A. (1992). Consequences of child care—one more time: A rejoinder. In A. Booth (Ed.), *Child care in the 1990s.* Hillsdale, NJ: Erlbaum.

Clarke-Stewart, K. (1989). Infant day care: Maligned or malignant? *American Psychologist, 44,* 266–273.

Clarke-Stewart, K. A., & Fein, G. G. (1983). Early childhood programs. In P. H. Mussen (Ed.), *Handbook of child psychology* (4th ed., Vol. 2). New York: Wiley.

Cohen, P., Brook, J. S., & Kandel, D. B. (1991). Drug use, predictors and correlates of. In R. M. Lerner, A. C. Petersen, & J. Brooks-Gunn (Eds.), *Encyclopedia of adolescence* (Vol. 1). New York: Garland.

Cohn, J. F., & Tronick, E. Z. (1988). Mother-infant face-to-face interaction. Influence is bidirectional and unrelated to periodic cycles in either partner's behavior. *Developmental Psychology, 24,* 396–397.

Coie, J. D. (1993, March). *The adolescence of peer relations.* Paper presented at the biennial meeting of the Society for Research in Child Development, New Orleans.

Colby, A., Kohlberg, L., Gibbs, J., & Lieberman, M. (1983). A longitudinal study of moral judgment. *Monographs of the Society for Research in Child Development* (Serial No. 201).

Cole, D. A. (1991). Suicide, adolescent. In R. M. Lerner, A. C. Petersen, & J. Brooks-Gunn (Eds.), *Encyclopedia of adolescence* (Vol. 2). New York: Garland.

Cole, J. D., & Koeppl, G. K. (1990). Adapting intervention to the problems of aggressive and disruptive rejected children. In S. R. Asher & J. D. Coie (Eds.), *Peer rejection in childhood.* New York: Cambridge University Press.

Cole, M. (1992a). Culture and cognitive development: From cross-cultural comparisons to model systems of cultural mediation. In A. F. Healy, S. M. Kosslyn, & E. M. Shiffrin (Eds.), *From learning processes to cognitive processes.* Hillsdale, NJ: Erlbaum.

Cole, M. (1992b). Culture in development. In M. H. Bornstein & M. E. Lamb (Eds.), *Developmental psychology: An advanced textbook* (3rd ed.). Hillsdale, NJ: Erlbaum.

Cole, M. (1993, March). *A cultural-historical goal for developmental research: Create sustainable model systems of diversity.* Paper presented at the biennial meeting of the Society for Research in Child Development, New Orleans, LA.

Cole, M., & Cole, S. R. (1989). *The development of children.* New York: Scientific American.

Cole, M., & Cole, S. R. (1989). *The development of children.* New York: W. H. Freeman.

Coleman, J. S. (1961). *The adolescent society.* New York: Free Press.

Coleman, L. L., & Coleman, A. D. (1991). *Pregnancy: The psychological experience* (rev. ed.). New York: Noonday Press.

Coleman, M., & Ganong, L. H. (1990). Remarriage and stepfamily research in the 1980s: Increased interest in an old form. *Journal of Marriage and the Family, 52,* 925–939.

Coles, C. D., Platzman, K. A., & Smith, I. E. (1991, April). *Substance abuse and neonates: Alcohol and cocaine effects.* Paper presented at the biennial meeting of the Society for Research in Child Development, Seattle.

Coles, R. (1970). *Erik H. Erikson: The growth of his work.* Boston: Little, Brown.

Coles, R. (1986). *The political life of children.* Boston: Little, Brown.

Collins, A., Brown, J. S., & Newman, S. E. (1989). Cognitive apprenticeship: Teaching the craft of reading, writing, and mathematics. In L. B. Resnick (Ed.), *Knowing and learning: Essays in honor of Robert Glaser.* Hillsdale, NJ: Erlbaum.

Collins, W. A. (1990). Parent-child relationships in the transition to adolescence: Continuity and change in interaction, affect, and cognition. In R. Montemayor, G. R. Adams, & T. P. Gulotta (Eds.), *From childhood to adolescence: A transitional period?* Newbury Park, CA: Sage.

Collins, W. A., & Luebker, C. (1993, March). *Parental behavior during adolescence: Individual and relational significance.* Paper presented at the biennial meeting of the Society for Research in Child Development, New Orleans.

Colombo, J., Moss, M., & Horowitz, F. D. (1989). Neonatal state profiles: Reliability and short-term prediction of neurobehavioral status. *Child Development, 60,* 1102–1110.

Colt, G. H. (1991, April). The birth of a family. *Life Magazine,* pp. 28–38.

Comas-Diaz, L. (1993). Hispanic/Latino communities: Psychological implications. In D. R. Atkinson, G. Morten, & D. W. Sue (Eds.), *Counseling American minorities.* Madison, WI: WCB Brown & Benchmark.

Comer, J. (1993, March). *African-American parents and child development: An agenda for school success.* Paper presented at the biennial meeting of the Society for Research in Child Development, New Orleans.

Comer, J. P. (1988). Educating poor minority children. *Scientific American, 259,* 42–48.

Committee for Economic Development (1987). *Children in need: Investment strategies for the educationally disadvantaged.* Washington, DC: Committee for Economic Development.

Compas, B. (1989, April). *Vulnerability and stress in childhood and adolescence.* Paper presented at the biennial meeting of the Society for Research in Child Development, Kansas City, MO.

Conant, J. B. (1959). *The American high school today.* New York: McGraw-Hill.

Condry, J. C. (1989). *The psychology of television.* Hillsdale, NJ: Erlbaum.

Conger, J. J. (1981). Freedom and commitment: Families, youth, and social change. *American Psychologist, 36,* 1475–1484.

Conger, J. J. (1988). Hostages to the future: Youth, values, and the public interest. *American Psychologist, 43,* 291–300.

Conger, K. J. (1992, March). *Sibling relationship quality as a mediator and moderator of the relationship between parental mood and behavior and adolescent self-esteem.* Paper presented at the meeting of the Society for Research on Adolescence, Washington, DC.

Conger, R. D., Conger, K. J., & Simons, R. L. (1992, March). *Family economic stress, parenting behavior, and adolescent drinking.* Paper presented at the meeting of the Society for Research on Adolescence, Washington, DC.

Connolly, J. A., & Johnson, A. M. (1993, March). *The psychosocial context of adolescent romantic relationships.* Paper presented at the biennial meeting of the Society for Research in Child Development, New Orleans.

Cook, T. D., Schleef, D. J., Miller, L. L., & Stockdill, B. C. (1992, March). *Moving as a strategy of family management.* Paper presented at the meeting of the Society for Research on Adolescence, Washington, DC.

Coons, S., & Guilleminault, C. (1984). Development of consolidated sleep and wakeful periods in relation to the day/night cycle of infancy. *Developmental Medicine and Child Neurology, 26,* 169–176.

Cooper, C. R., & Ayers-Lopez, S. (1985). Family and peer systems in early adolescence: New models of the role of relationships in development. *Journal of Early Adolescence, 5,* 9–22.

Cooper, C. R., & Grotevant, H. D. (1989, April). *Individuality and connectedness in the family and adolescents' self and relational competence.* Paper presented at the meeting of the Society for Research in Child Development, Kansas City, MO.

Cooper, C. R., Grotevant, H. D., Moore, M. S., & Condon, S. M. (1982, August). *Family support and conflict: Both foster adolescent identity and role taking.* Paper presented at the meeting of the American Psychological Association, Washington, DC.

Coopersmith, S. (1967). *The antecedents of self-esteem.* San Francisco: W. H. Freeman.

Cornell, D. G., & Grossberg, I. N. (1986). Siblings of children in gifted programs. *Journal for the Education of the Gifted, 9(4),* 253–264.

Corrigan, R. (1981). The effects of task and practice on search for invisibly displaced objects. *Developmental Review, 1,* 1–17.

Corwin, V. (1989, March). *Sesame Street* abroad. *Sesame Street Magazine Parent's Guide.* pp. 24, 26.

Costanzo, P. R. (1993, March). *Mental representations of relationships: Intergenerational and temporal continuity.* Paper presented at the biennial meeting of the Society for Research in Child Development, New Orleans.

Costanzo, P. R., & Dunsmore, J. (1993, March). *The impact of parental values on children's developing moral thought.* Paper presented at the biennial meeting of the Society for Research in Child Development, New Orleans.

Cote, J. E., & Levine, C. (1988a). A critical examination of the ego identity status paradigm. *Developmental Review, 8,* 147–184.

Cote, J. E., & Levine, C. (1988b). On critiquing the identity status paradigm: A rejoinder to Waterman. *Developmental Review, 8,* 209–218.

Cowan, C. P., Cowan, P. A., Heming, G., & Miller, N. (1991). Becoming a family: Marriage, parenting, and child development. In P. A. Cowan & E. M. Hetherington (Eds.), *Family transitions.* Hillsdale, NJ: Erlbaum.

Cowan, C. P., Heming, G. A., & Shuck, E. L. (1993, March). *The impact of interventions with parents of preschoolers on the children's adaptation to kindergarten.* Paper presented at the biennial meeting of the Society for Research in Child Development, New Orleans.

Cowan, P. A. (1988). Becoming a father: A time of change, an opportunity for development. In P. Bronstein & C. P. Cowan (Eds.), *Fatherhood today.* New York: Wiley.

Cowan, P. A. (1991). Individual and family life transitions: A proposal for a new definition. In P. A. Cowan & E. M. Hetherington (Eds.), *Family transitions.* Hillsdale, NJ: Erlbaum.

Cowley, G. (1988, May 23). The wisdom of animals. *Newsweek,* pp. 52–58.

Cox, B. D. (1993, March). *Internalization through the reinterpretation of spontaneous invention: The examples of mathematics instruction and metamemory.* Paper presented at the biennial meeting of the Society for Research in Child Development, New Orleans.

Craylord-Ross, R. (Ed.). (1989). *Integration strategies for students with handicaps.* Baltimore: Brooks.

Creasy, G. L., Mitts, N., Catanzaro, L. E., & Lustig, K. (1993, March). *Associations among daily hassles, coping, and behavior problems among kindergartners.* Paper presented at the biennial meeting of the Society for Research in Child Development, New Orleans.

Crick, M. (1977). *Explorations in language and meaning: Toward a scientific anthropology.* New York: Halstead.

Crisafi, M. A., & Driscoll, J. M. (1991, April). *Developmental outcome in very low birthweight infants at three years of age.* Paper presented at the biennial meeting of the Society for Research in Child Development, Seattle.

Crittenden, P. (1988a). Family and dyadic patterns of functioning in maltreating families. In K. Browne, C. Davies, & P. Stratton (Eds.), *Early prediction and prevention of child abuse.* New York: Wiley.

Crockenberg, S., & Lourie, A. (1993, March). *Conflict strategies: Parents with children and children with peers.* Paper presented at the biennial meeting of the Society for Research in Child Development, New Orleans.

Crockett, L. J., & Chopak, J. S. (1993). Pregnancy prevention in early adolescence. In R. M. Lerner (Ed.), *Early adolescence: Perspectives on research, policy, and intervention.* Hillsdale, NJ: Erlbaum.

Cronbach, L. J., & Snow, R. E. (1977). *Aptitudes and instructional methods.* New York: Irvington.

Cross, K. P. (1984, November). The rising tide of school reform reports. *Phi Delta Kappan,* pp. 167–172.

Cummings, E. M. (1987). Coping with background anger in early childhood. *Child Development, 58,* 976–984.

Curry, N. E. (1971). Consideration of current basic issues in play. In N. E. Curry & S. Arnaud (Eds.), *Play: The child strives toward self-regulation.* Washington, DC: NAEYC.

Curtiss, S. (1977). *Genie.* New York: Academic Press.

Cushner, K. (1990). Cross-cultural psychology and the formal classroom. In R. W. Brislin (Ed.), *Applied cross-cultural psychology.* Newbury Park: CA: Sage.

D

D'Angelo, D. A., & Adler, C. R. (1991). A catalyst for improving parent involvement. *Phi Delta Kappan,* pp. 350–354.

D'Augelli, A. R., & Bingham, C. R. (1993, March). Interventions to prevent HIV infections in young adolescents. In R. M. Lerner (Ed.), *Early adolescence: Perspectives on research, policy, and intervention.* Hillsdale, NJ: Erlbaum.

Damon, W. (1988). *The moral child.* New York: Free Press.

Damon, W. (1991). Self-concept, adolescent. In R. M. Lerner, A. C. Petersen, & J. Brooks-Gunn (Eds.), *Encyclopedia of adolescence* (Vol. 2). New York: Garland.

Damon, W., & Hart, D. (1988). *Self-understanding in childhood and adolescence.* New York: Cambridge University Press.

Darling, C. A., Kallen, D. J., & VanDusen, J. E. (1984). Sex in transition, 1900–1984. *Journal of Youth and Adolescence, 13,* 385–399.

Daro, D. (1988). *Confronting child abuse.* New York: Free Press.

Darwin, C. (1859). *On the origin of species.* London: John Murray.

Dasen, P. R. (1977). Are cognitive processes universal? A contribution to cross-cultural Piagetian psychology. In N. Warran (Ed.), *Studies in cross-cultural psychology* (Vol. 1). London: Academic Press.

Dasen, P. R., Ngini, L., & Lavalée, M. (1979). Cross-cultural training studies of concrete operations. In L. H. Eckenberger, W. J. Lonner, & Y. H. Poortinga (Eds.), *Cross-cultural contributions to psychology.* Boston: Allyn & Bacon.

Dash, L. (1986, January 26). Children's children: The crisis up close. *The Washington Post,* pp. A1, A12.

Davies, M. W. (1993, March). *Childcare, women, and work.* Paper presented at the biennial meeting of the Society for Research in Child Development, New Orleans.

Davis, A. J., DeLuccie, M. F., & Chebra, J. (1993, March). *The determinants of fathering: Developmental history and personal resources.* Paper presented at the biennial meeting of the Society for Research in Child Development, New Orleans.

Davis, J. M., & Mercier, C. E. (1992). The effects of drugs and other substances on the fetus. In R. A. Hoekelman, S. B. Friedman, N. M. Nelson, & H. M. Seidel (Eds.). *Primary pediatric care* (2nd ed.). St. Louis, MO: Mosby Yearbook.

Day, N. (1991, April). *Effects of alcohol and marijuana on growth and development.* Paper presented at the biennial meeting of the Society for Research in Child Development, Seattle.

de Villiers, J. (1988). Faith, doubt, and meaning. In F. S. Kessel (Ed.), *The development of language and language researchers.* Hillsdale, NJ: Erlbaum.

de Villiers, J., & de Villiers, P. A. (1978). *Language acquisition.* Cambridge, MA: Harvard University Press.

Dean, A. L. (1993, March). *Putting the pieces of the adolescent pregnancy puzzle together.* Paper presented at the biennial meeting of the Society for Research in Child Development, New Orleans.

DeAngelis, T. (1990, June). House child-care bill ignores quality issue. *APA Monitor,* p. 21.

DeBarshye, B. (1993, March). *Maternal reading-related beliefs regarding socialization practices in low-SES homes.* Paper presented at the biennial meeting of the Society for Research in Child Development, New Orleans.

DeCasper, A. J., & Spence, M. J. (1986). Prenatal maternal speech influences newborn's perception of speech sounds. *Infant Behavior and Development, 9,* 133–150.

Dedrick, C., Dedrick, R., Plunkett, J., Berlin, M., & Meisels, S. (1991, April). *Persistence of effects of prematurity in the second year of life: Maternal behavior and infant security.* Paper presented at the biennial meeting of the Society for Research in Child Development, Seattle.

DeFour, D. C., & Paludi, M. A. (in press). Integrating scholarship on ethnicity into the psychology of women course. *Teaching of psychology.*

DelCielo, D., Castaneda, M., Hui, J., & Frye, D. (1993, March). *Is theory of mind related to categorization?* Paper presented at the biennial meeting of the Society for Research in Child Development, New Orleans.

DeLoache, J. (1993, March). *What do young children understand about symbolic representations?* Paper presented at the biennial meeting of the Society for Research in Child Development, New Orleans.

DeLoache, J. S., Cassidy, D. J., & Brown, A. L. (1985). Precursors of mnemonic strategies in very young children's memory. *Child Development, 56,* 125–137.

DeLoache, J. S., Cassidy, D. J., & Carpenter, C. J. (1987). The Three Bears are all boys: Mothers' gender labeling of neutral picture book characters. *Sex roles, 17,* 163–178.

Demetriou, A., & Efklides, A. (in press). Experiential structuralism: A frame for unifying cognitive developmental theories. *Monographs of the Society for Research in Child Development.*

Dempster, F. N. (1981). Memory span: Sources of individual and developmental differences. *Psychological Bulletin, 89,* 63–100.

Denmark, F. L. (1993, August). *Women in psychology: Past, present, future.* Paper presented at the meeting of the American Psychological Association, Toronto, CA.

Denmark, F. L., & Paludi, M. A. (Eds.). (in press). *Handbook on the psychology of women.* Westport, CT: Greenwood.

Denmark, F. L., & Paludi, M. A. (Eds.). (in press). *Handbook on the psychology of women.* Westport, CT: Greenwood Press.

Denmark, F. L., Russo, N. F., Frieze, I. H., & Sechzur, J. (1988). Guidelines for avoiding sexism in psychological research: A report of the Ad Hoc Committee on Nonsexist Research. *American Psychologist, 43,* 582–585.

Deutsch, M. (Ed.). (1967). *The disadvantaged child: Selected papers of Martin Deutsch and his associates.* New York: Basic.

DeVault, M. L. (1987). Doing housework: Feeding and family life. In N. Ferstel & H. E. Gross (Eds.), *Families and work.* Philadelphia: Temple University Press.

Dewey, J. (1933). *How we think: A restatement of the relation of reflective thinking to the educative process.* Lexington, MA: D. C. Heath.

Diamond, A. (1985). Development of the ability to use recall to guide action, as indicated by infants' performance on AB. *Child Development, 56,* 868–883.

Diaz, R. M. (1983). Thought and two languages: The impact of bilingualism on cognitive development. *Review of Research in Education, 10,* 23–54.

DiBiase, R. (1993, March). *Attachment, temperament, and ego development in adolescence.* Paper presented at the biennial meeting of the Society for Research in Child Development, New Orleans.

Dickerscheid, J. D., Schwarz, P. M., Noir, S., & El-Taliawy, T. (1988). Gender concept development of preschool-aged children in the United States and Egypt. *Sex-Roles, 18,* 669–677.

Dickinson, D. K., & Moreton, J. (1991, April). *Predicting specific kindergarten literacy skills from three-year-olds'-preschool experiences.* Paper presented at the Society for Research in Child Development meeting, Seattle.

Dickinson, G. E. (1975). Dating behavior of black and white adolescents before and after desegregation. *Journal of Marriage and the Family, 37,* 602–608.

Didow, S. M. (1993, March). *Language and action: Toddlers' coordinated talk with a partner.* Paper presented at the biennial meeting of the Society for Research in Child Development, New Orleans.

Dillon, R. F., & Sternberg, R. J. (Eds.). (1988). *Cognition and instruction.* San Diego: Academic Press.

Dishion, T. J. (1992, March). *Parental factors in early adolescent substance use: Correlational and experimental evidence.* Paper presented at the meeting of the Society for Research on Adolescence, Washington, DC.

Dishion, T., Kavanagh, K., Andrews, D., Brown, G., & Patterson, G. R. (1992, April). *The effectiveness of social learning interventions with high risk young adolescents.* Paper presented at the meeting of the Society for Research on Adolescence, Washington, DC.

Dixon, S. D. (1991, April). *Infants exposed perinatally to cocaine or methamphetamine demonstrate behavioral and neurophysiologic changes.* Paper presented at the biennial meeting of the Society for Research in Child Development, Seattle.

Dodge, K. A. (1983). Behavioral antecedents of peer social status. *Child Development, 54,* 1386–1399.

Dodge, K. A. (1993, March). *Social information processing and peer rejection factors in the development of behavior problems in children.* Paper presented at the biennial meeting of the Society for Research in Child Development, New Orleans.

Dodge, K. A., & Feldman, E. (1990). Issues in social cognition and sociometric status. In S. R. Asher & J. D. Coie (Eds.), *Peer rejection in childhood.* New York: Cambridge University Press.

Dolgin, K. G., & Behrend, D. A. (1984). Children's knowledge about animates and inanimates. *Child Development, 55,* 1646–1650.

Doll, G. (1988, Spring). Day care. *Vanderbilt Magazine,* p. 29.

Domino, G. (1992). Acculturation of Hispanics. In S. B. Knouse, P. Rosenfeld, & A. Culbertson (Eds.), *Hispanics in the workplace.* Newbury Park, CA: Sage.

Dornbusch, S. M., Carlsmith, J. M., Bushwall, S. J., Ritter, P. I., Leidman, P. H., Hastorf, A. H., & Gross, R. T. (1985). Single parents, extended households, and the control of adolescents. *Child Development, 56,* 326–341.

Douvan, E., & Adelson, J. (1966). *The adolescent experience.* New York: Wiley.

Dowdy, B. B., & Howard, C. W. (1993, March). *The effects of dating and parent-adolescent consultant preferences during adolescence.* Paper presented at the biennial meeting of the Society for Research in Child Development, New Orleans.

Downey, G., & Coyne, J. C. (1990). Children of depressed parents: An integrative review. *Psychological Bulletin, 108,* 50–76.

Doyle, A. B., Doehring, P., Tessier, O., de Lorimier, S., & Shapiro, S. (1992). Transitions in children's play: A sequential analysis of states preceding and following social pretense. *Developmental Psychology, 28,* 137–144.

Doyle, J. A., & Paludi, M. A. (1991). *Sex and gender: The human experience* (2nd ed.). Dubuque, IA: Wm. C. Brown.

Draper, T. W., Larsen, J. M., Haupt, J. H., Robinson, C. C., & Hart, C. (1993, March). *Family emotional climate as a mediating variable between parent education and child social competence in an advantaged subculture.* Paper presented at the biennial meeting of the Society for Research in Child Development, New Orleans.

Drew, P. J., & Luftig, R. L. (1993, March). *Factors related to loneliness in students with and without learning disabilities at four developmental levels.* Paper presented at the biennial meeting of the Society for Research in Child Development, New Orleans.

Dreyer, P. H. (1982). Sexuality during adolescence. In B. B. Wolman (Ed.). *Handbook of developmental psychology.* Englewood Cliffs, NJ: Prentice-Hall.

Dryfoos, J. G. (1990). *Adolescents at risk: Prevalence and prevention.* New York: Oxford University Press.

Dryfoos, J. G. (1992, March). *Integrating services for adolescents: The community schools.* Paper presented at the meeting of the Society for Research on Adolescence. Washington, DC.

DuBois, D. L., & Hirsch, B. J. (1990). School and neighborhood friendship patterns of Blacks and Whites in early adolescence. *Child Development, 61,* 524–536.

Ducey, S. J. (1993, March). *Sex, pregnancy, and birth control information and activity across generations.* Paper presented at the biennial meeting of the Society for Research in Child Development, New Orleans.

Duck, S. W. (1975). Personality similarity and friendship choices by adolescents. *European Journal of Social Psychology, 5,* 351–365.

Duck, S. W. (1988). Child and adolescent friendships. In P. Marsh (Ed.), *Eye to eye: How people interact.* Topsfield, MA: Salem House.

Duke, D. L., & Canady, R. L. (1991). *School policy.* New York: McGraw-Hill.

Duncan, G. J. (1993, March). *Economic deprivation and child development.* Paper presented at the biennial meeting of the Society for Research in Child Development, New Orleans.

Duncan, R. M. (1991, April). *An examination of Vygotsky's theory of children's private speech.* Paper presented at the Society for Research in Child Development meeting, Seattle.

Duncker, K. (1945). On problem solving. *Psychological Monographs, 58* (Whole No. 270).

Dunn, J., & Kendrick, C. (1982). *Siblings.* Cambridge, MA: Harvard University Press.

Dunphy, D. C. (1963). The social structure of urban adolescent peer groups. *Society, 26,* 230–246.

Durkin, K. (1985). Television and sex-role acquisition: 1. Content. *British Journal of Social Psychology, 24,* 101–113.

Duvall, E. M., & Miller, B. C. (1985). *Marriage and family development* (6th ed.). New York: Harper & Row.

Dyk, P. K. (1993). Anatomy, physiology, and gender issues in adolescence. In T. P. Gullotta, G. R. Adams, & R. Montemayor (Eds.), *Adolescent sexuality.* Newbury Park, CA: Sage.

E

Eager, R. M. (1992). Child and adolescent sexuality: Perspectives and recommendations. In D. E. Greydanus & M. L. Wolraich (Eds.), *Behavioral pediatrics.* New York: Springer-Verlag.

Eagly, A. H., & Crowley, M. (1986). Gender and helping behavior: A meta-analytic review of the social psychological literature. *Psychological Bulletin, 100,* 283–308.

Early Childhood and Literacy Development Committee of the International Reading Association (1986). Literacy development and pre-first grade. *Young Children, 41,* 10–13.

East, P. L. (1991). Peer status groups. In R. M. Lerner, A. C. Petersen, & J. Brooks-Gunn (Eds.), *Encyclopedia of adolescence* (Vol. 2). New York: Garland.

Eccles, J., MacIver, D., & Lange, L. (1986). *Classroom practices and motivation to study math.* Paper presented at the annual meeting of the American Educational Research Association, San Francisco.

Eccles, J. S. (1987). Gender roles and achievement patterns: An expectancy value perspective. In J. M. Reinisch, L. A. Rosenblum, & S. A. Sanders (Eds.), *Masculinity/femininity: Basic perspectives.* New York: Oxford University Press.

Eccles, J. S. (1993, March). *Parents as gender-role socializers during middle childhood and adolescence.* Paper presented at the biennial meeting of the Society for Research in Child Development, New Orleans.

Eccles, J. S., & Buchanan, C. M. (1992, March). *Hormones and behavior at early adolescence: A theoretical overview.* Paper presented at the biennial meeting of the Society for Research in Adolescence, Washington, DC.

Eccles, J. S., & Harold, R. D. (1991, April). *Influences on, and consequences of, parents' beliefs regarding their children's abilities and interests.* Paper presented at the Society for Research in Child Development meeting, Seattle.

Eccles, J. S., & Midgley, C. (1990). Changes in academic motivation and self-perception during early adolescence. In R. Montemayor, G. R. Adams, & T. P. Gullotta (Eds.), *From childhood to adolescence: A transitional period?* Newbury Park, CA: Sage.

Eccles, J. S., Harold-Goldsmith, R., & Miller, C. R. (1989, April). *Parents' stereotyping beliefs about gender differences in adolescence.* Paper presented at the biennial meeting of the Society for Research in Child Development, Kansas City, MO.

Eckenrode, J., Laird, M., & Doris, J. (1993). School performance and disciplinary problems among abused and neglected children. *Developmental Psychology, 29,* 53–62.

Edelman, M. W. (1987). *Families in peril.* Cambridge, MA: Harvard University Press.

Edelman, M. W. (1992). *The state of America's children, 1992.* Washington, DC: Children's Defense Fund.

Educational Testing Service (1992). Cross-national comparison of children's learning and achievement. Unpublished data, Educational Testing Service, Princeton, NJ.

Edwards, C. P. (1987). Culture and the construction of moral values. In J. Kagan & S. Lamb (Eds.), *The emergence of morality in young children.* Chicago: University of Chicago Press.

Efron, R. (in press). *The decline and fall of hemispheric specialization.* Hillsdale, NJ: Erlbaum.

Egeland, B. (1974). Training impulsive children in the use of more efficient scanning techniques. *Child Development 45,* 165–171.

Egeland, B. (1989, January). *Secure attachment in infancy and competence in the third grade.* Paper presented at the meeting of the American Association for the Advancement of Science, San Francisco.

Eger, M. (1981). The conflict in moral education: An informal case study. *Public Interest, 63,* 62–80.

Ehrhardt, A. A. (1987). A transactional perspective on the development of gender differences. In J. M. Reinisch, L. A. Rosenblum, & S. A. Sanders (Eds.), *Masculinity/femininity: Basic perspectives.* New York: Oxford University Press.

Eiferman, R. R. (1971). Social play in childhood. In R. E. Herron & B. Sutton-Smith (Eds.), *Child's play.* New York: Wiley.

Eiger, M. S. (1992). The feeding of infants and children. In R. B. Hoekelman, S. B. Friedman, N. M. Nelson, & H. M. Seidel (Eds.), *Primary pediatric care* (2nd ed.). St. Louis, MO: Mosby Yearbook.

Eisenberg, A., Murkoff, H. E., & Hathaway, S. E. (1989). *What to expect in the first year.* New York: Workman.

Eisenberg, A. R., Wolfe, P., & Mick, M. (1993, March). *Who makes a good sibling?: Personality and the quality of sibling relationships.* Paper presented at the biennial meeting of the Society for Research in Child Development, New Orleans.

Eisenberg, N. (1992, Fall). Social development. Current trends and future possibilities. *SRCD Newsletter,* pp. 1, 10–11.

Eisenberg, N. (Ed.). (1982). *The development of prosocial behavior.* New York: Wiley.

Eisenberg, N., Shea, C. I., Carolo, G., & Knight, G. P. (1991). Empathy-related responding and cognition: A chicken and egg dilemma. In W. M. Kurtines & J. Gewirtz (Eds.), *Moral behavior and development* (Vol. 2). Hillsdale, NJ: Erlbaum.

Elder, G. H. (1974). *Children of the Great Depression.* Chicago: University of Chicago Press.

Elder, G. H. (1980). Adolescence in historical perspective. In J. Adelson (Ed.), *Handbook of adolescent psychology.* New York: Wiley.

Elkind, D. (1961). Quantity conceptions in junior and senior high school students. *Child Development, 32,* 551–560.

Elkind, D. (1976). *Child development and education.* New York: Oxford University Press.

Elkind, D. (1978). Understanding the young adolescent. *Adolescence, 13,* 127–134.

Elkind, D. (1981). *The hurried child.* Reading, MA: Addison-Wesley.

Elkind, D. (1985). Egocentrism redux. *Developmental Review, 5,* 218–226.

Elkind, D. (1987). *Miseducation: Preschoolers at risk.* New York: Knopf.

Elkind, D. (1988, January). Educating the very young: A call for clear thinking. *NEA Today,* pp. 22–27.

Ellis, H. C. (1987). Recent developments in human memory. In V. P. Makosky (Ed.), *The G. Stanley Hall Lecture Series.* Washington, DC: American Psychological Association.

Ellis, L., & Ames, M. A. (1987). Neurohormonal functioning and sexual orientation: A theory of homosexuality-heterosexuality. *Psychological Bulletin, 101,* 233–258.

Emde, R. N., Gaensbauer, T. G., & Harmon, R. J. (1976). Emotional expression in infancy: A biobehavioral study. *Psychological Issues: Monograph Series, 10* (37).

Emde, R. N., Plomin, R., Robinson, J., Corley, R., DeFries, J., Fulker, D. W., Reznick, J. S., Campos, J., Kagan, J., & Zahn-Waxler, C. (1992). Temperament, emotion, and cognition at fourteen months: The McArthur longitudinal twin study. *Child Development, 63,* 1437–1455.

Emery, R. E. (1989). Family violence. *American Psychologist, 44,* 321–328.

Emmerich, W., Goldman, K. S., Kirsch, B., & Sharabany, R. (1977). Evidence for a transitional phase in the development of gender constancy. *Child Development, 48,* 930–936.

Engle, P. L. (1991, April). *The effects of nutritional supplementation on cognitive functioning of preschoolers in Guatemala.* Paper presented at the biennial meeting of the Society for Research in Child Development, Seattle.

Enkin, M. W. (1989). Cesarian section: Why do the rates differ? *Birth, 16,* 207–208.

Ennis, R. H. (1991). Critical thinking: Literature review and needed research. In L. Idol & B. F. Jones (Eds.), *Educational values and cognitive instruction.* Hillsdale, NJ: Erlbaum.

Enright, R. D., Lapsley, D. K., Dricas, A. S., & Fehr, L. A. (1980). Parental influence on the development of adolescent autonomy and identity. *Journal of Youth and Adolescence, 9,* 529–546.

Ensher, G., & Miller, P. (1989, April). *The Syracuse Scales of Infant Development and Home Observation: A standardized measure for high risk and handicapped babies, birth to 12 months.* Paper presented at the Society for Research in Child Development meeting, Kansas City, MO.

Entwisle, D., & Alexander, K. (1992, March). *School organization and adolescent development.* Meet the scientist luncheon at the Society for Research on Adolescence, Washington, DC.

Entwisle, D. R. (1990). Schools and the adolescent. In S. S. Feldman & G. R. Elliott (Eds.), *At the threshold: The developing adolescent.* Cambridge: MA: Harvard University Press.

Entwistle, N. (1981). *Styles of learning and teaching.* New York: Wiley.

Epstein, J. (1990). School and family connections: Theory, research, and implications for integrating sociologies of education and family. In D. G. Unger & M. B. Sussman (Eds.), *Families in community settings.* New York: Haworth Press.

Epstein, J. L. (1992). School and family partnerships. *Encyclopedia of educational research* (6th ed.). New York: MacMillan.

Erikson, E. H. (1950). *Childhood and society.* New York: W. W. Norton.

Erikson, E. H. (1962). *Young man Luther.* New York: W. W. Norton.

Erikson, E. H. (1968). *Identity: Youth and crisis.* New York: W. W. Norton.

Erikson, E. H. (1969). *Gandhi's truth.* New York: W. W. Norton.

Espin, O. M. (1993). Psychological impact of migration on Latinos. In D. R. Atkinson, G. Morten, & D. W. Sue (Eds.), *Counseling American minorities.* Madison, WI: WCB Brown & Benchmark.

Esty, E. T., & Fisch, S. M. (1991, April). *SQUARE ONE TV: Using television to enhance children's problem solving.* Paper presented at the Society for Research in Child Development meeting, Seattle.

Etzel, R. (1988, October). *Children of smokers.* Paper presented at the American Academy of Pediatrics meeting, New Orleans.

Evans, B. J., & Whitfield, J. R. (Eds.). (1988). *Black males in the United States: An annotated bibliography from 1967 to 1987.* Washington, DC: American Psychological Association.

Evans, M. A., & Baraball, L. (1993, March). *Child-parent bookreading and parent-helping strategies.* Paper presented at the biennial meeting of the Society for Research in Child Development, New Orleans.

Eyler, F. D., Behnke, M. L., & Stewart, N. J. (1990). *Issues in identification and follow-up of cocaine-exposed neonates.* Unpublished manuscript, University of Florida, Gainesville, FL.

F

Fagan, J. F., & Knevel, C. R. (1989, April). *The prediction of above average intelligence from infancy.* Paper presented at the Society for Research in Child Development meeting, Kansas City, MO.

Fagot, B. I., Leinbach, M. D., & O'Boyle, C. (1992). Gender labeling, gender stereotyping, and parenting behaviors. *Developmental Psychology, 28,* 225–230.

Falbo, T., & Polit, D. F. (1986). A quantitative review of the only-child literature. Research evidence and theory development. *Psychological Bulletin, 100,* 176–189.

Falbo, T., & Poston, D. L. (1993). The academic, personality, and physical outcomes of only children in China. *Child Development, 64,* 18–35.

Fantz, R. L. (1963). Pattern vision in newborn infants. *Science, 140,* 296–297.

Farmer, J. E., Peterson, L., & Kashani, J. H. (1989, April). *Injury risk, parent and child psychopathology.* Paper presented at the biennial meeting of the Society for Research in Child Development, Kansas City, MO.

Fein, G. G. (1986). Pretend play. In D. Görlitz & J. F. Wohlwill (Eds.), *Curiosity, imagination, and play.* Hillsdale, NJ: Erlbaum.

Feiring, C. (1992, March). *Concepts of romance in mid-adolescence.* Paper presented at the meeting of the Society for Research on Adolescence, Washington, DC.

Fenzel, L. M., & Magaletta, P. R. (1993, March). *Predicting intrinsic motivation of Black early adolescents: The roles of school strain, academic competence, and self-esteem.* Paper presented at the biennial meeting of the Society for Research in Child Development, New Orleans.

Ferguson, D. M., Harwood, L. J., & Shannon, F. T. (1987). Breastfeeding and subsequent social adjustment in 6- to 8-year-old children. *Journal of Child Psychology and Psychiatry, 28,* 378–386.

Field, T. (1987, January). Interview. *Psychology Today,* p. 31.

Field, T. (1992, September). Stroking babies helps growth, reduces stress. *The Brown University Child and Adolescent Behavior Letter,* pp. 1, 6.

Field, T. (in press). Quality infant daycare and grade school behavior and performance. *Child Development.*

Field, T. M. (1979). Visual and cardiac responses to animate and inanimate faces by young term and preterm infants. *Child Development, 50,* 188–194.

Field, T. M. (1990). Alleviating stress in newborn infants in the intensive care unit. In B. M. Lester & E. Z. Tronick (Eds.), *Stimulation and the preterm infant: The limits of plasticity.* Philadelphia: W. B. Saunders.

Field, T. M., Woodson, R., Greenberg, R., & Cohen, D. (1982). Discrimination and imitation of facial expressions by neonates. *Science, 218,* 179–181.

Field, T., Scafidi, F., & Schanberg, S. (1987). Massage of preterm newborns to improve growth and development. *Pediatric Nursing, 13,* 385–387.

Fillmore, L. W. (1989). Teachability and second language acquisition. In M. L. Rice & R. L. Schiefelbusch (Eds.), *The teachability of language.* Baltimore: Paul Brooks.

Fineberg, H. V. (1988). Education to prevent AIDS: Prospects and obstacles. *Science, 239,* 592–596.

Firush, R., & Cobb, P. A. (1989, April). *Developing scripts.* Paper presented at the Society for Research in Child Development meeting, Kansas City, MO.

Fischer, K. W., & Farrar, M. J. (1987). Generalizations about generalization: How a theory of skill development explains both generality and specificity. *International Journal of Psychology, 22,* 643–677.

Fischer, L. R. (1991). Between mothers and daughters. *Marriage and Family Review, 16,* 237–248.

Fish, K. D., & Biller, H. B. (1973). Perceived childhood paternal relationships and college females' personal adjustment. *Adolescence, 8,* 415–420.

Fish, M. (1989, April). *Temperament and attachment of separation intolerance at three years.* Paper presented at the Society for Research in Child Development meeting, Kansas City, MO.

Fisher, C. B., & Brone, R. J. (1991). Eating disorders in adolescence. In R. M. Lerner, A. C. Petersen, & J. Brooks-Gunn (Eds.), *Encyclopedia of adolescence* (Vol. 1). New York: Garland.

Fisher, D. (1990, March). *Effects of attachment on adolescents' friendships.* Paper presented at the meeting of the Society for Research in Adolescence, Atlanta.

Fisher-Thompson, D., Polinski, L., Eaton, M., & Hefferman, K. (1993, March). *Sex-role orientation of children and their parents: Relationship to the sex-typing of Christmas toys.* Paper presented at the biennial meeting of the Society for Research in Child Development, New Orleans.

Flanagan, C. A., & Eccles, J. S. (1993). Changes in parents' work status and adolescents' adjustment at school. *Child Development, 64,* 246–257.

Flannagan, D. A., & Tate, C. S. (1989, April). *The effects of children's script knowledge on their communication and recall of scenes.* Paper presented at the Society for Research in Child Development meeting, Kansas City, MO.

Flavell, J. H. (1980, Fall). A tribute to Piaget. *Society for Research in Child Development Newsletter,* p. 1.

Flavell, J. H. (1992). Cognitive development: Past, present, and future. *Developmental Psychology, 28,* 998–1005.

Flavell, J. H., Beach, D. R., & Chinsky, J. M. (1966). Spontaneous verbal rehearsal in a memory task as a function of age. *Child Development, 37,* 283–299.

Flavell, J. H., Miller, P. A., & Miller, S. A. (1993). *Cognitive development* (3rd ed.). Englewood Cliffs, NJ: Prentice-Hall.

Fleming, A. S., Ruble, D. N., Flett, G. L., & Shoul, D. L. (1988). Postpartum adjustment in first-time mothers: Relations between mood, maternal attitudes, and mother-infant interactions. *Developmental Psychology, 24,* 71–81.

Fogel, A., Toda, S., & Kawai, M. (1988). Mother-infant face-to-face interaction in Japan and the United States: A laboratory comparison using 3-month-old infants. *Developmental Psychology, 24,* 398–406.

Folkman, S., & Lazarus, R. (1991). Coping and emotion. In N. Stein, B. L. Leventhal, & T. Trabasso (Eds.), *Psychological and biological approaches to emotion.* Hillsdale, NJ: Erlbaum.

Fordham, S., & Ogbu, J. U. (1986). Black students' school success: Coping with the burden of "acting white." *Urban Review, 18,* 176–206.

Forehand, G., Ragosta, J., & Rock, D. (1976). *Conditions and processes of effective school desegregation.* Princeton, NJ: Educational Testing Service.

Forrest, J. D. (1990). Cultural influences on adolescents' reproductive behavior. In J. Bancroft & J. M. Reinisch (Eds.), *Adolescence and puberty.* New York: Oxford University Press.

Forsyth, B. W. C., Leventhal, J. M., & McCarthy, P. L. (1985). Mothers' perceptions of feeding and crying behaviors. *American Journal of Diseases of Children, 139,* 269–272.

Foster-Clark, F. S., & Blyth, D. A. (1991). Peer relations and influences. In R. M. Lerner, A. C. Petersen, & J. Brooks-Gunn (Eds.), *Encyclopedia of adolescence* (Vol. 2). New York: Garland.

Fox, L. H., Brody, L., & Tobin, D. (1979). *Women and mathematics.* Baltimore, MD: Intellectually Gifted Study Group, Johns Hopkins University.

Fox, N. A., Sutton, B., Aaron, N., & Luebering, A. (1989, April). *Infant temperament and attachment: A new look at an old issue.* Paper presented at the Society for Research in Child Development meeting, Kansas City, MO.

Fraiberg, S. (1959). *The magic years.* New York: Charles Scribner's Sons.

Francis, J., Fraser, G., & Marcia, J. E. (1989). *Cognitive and experimental factors in Moratorium-Achievement (MAMA) cycles.* Unpublished manuscript. Department of Psychology, Simon Fraser University, Burnaby, British Columbia.

Freedman, D. G. (1971). Genetic influences on development of behavior. In G. B. A. Stoelinga & J. J. Van Der Werff Ten Bosch (Eds.), *Normal and abnormal development of behavior.* Leiden: Leiden University Press.

Freedman, D. G., & Freedman, N. (1969). Behavioral differences between Chinese-American and European-American newborns. *Nature, 224,* 1127.

Freedman, J. L. (1984). Effects of television violence on aggressiveness. *Psychological Bulletin, 96,* 227–246.

Freeman, H. S. (1993, March). *Parental control of adolescents through family transitions.* Paper presented at the biennial meeting of the Society for Research in Child Development, New Orleans.

Freud, A., & Dann, S. (1951). Instinctual anxiety during puberty. In A. Freud (Ed.), *The ego and its mechanisms of defense.* New York: International Universities Press.

Freud, S. (1917). *A general introduction to psychoanalysis.* New York: Washington Square Press.

Fried, P., & O'Connell, C. (1991, April). *Marijuana and tobacco as prenatal correlates of child behavior: Follow-up to school age.* Paper presented at the biennial meeting of the Society for Research in Child Development, Seattle.

Fried, P. A., & Watkinson, B. (1990). 36- and 48-month neurobehavioral follow-up of children prenatally exposed to marijuana, cigarettes, and alcohol. *Developmental and Behavioral Pediatrics, 11,* 49–58.

Fried, P. A., Watkinson, B., & Dillon, R. F. (1987). Neonatal neurological status in a low-risk population after prenatal exposure to cigarettes, marijuana, and alcohol. *Journal of Developmental and Behavioral Pediatrics, 8,* 318–326.

Friedman, H., & Caron, B. (1991, April). *Trends in outcome of very low birthweight (VLBW) children.* Paper presented at the biennial meeting of the Society for Research in Child Development, Seattle.

Friedman, S. L. (1991, April). *Development and change in planning skills: An overview.* Paper presented at the Society for Research in Child Development meeting, Seattle.

Friedrich, L. K., & Stein, A. H. (1973). Aggressive and prosocial TV programs and the natural behavior of preschool children. *Monographs of the Society for Research in Child Development, 38* (4, Serial No. 151).

Frost, J. L., & Wortham, S. C. (1988, July). The evolution of American playgrounds. *Young Children,* 19–28.

Fuller, M. (1984). Black girls in a London comprehensive school. In M. Hammersley & P. Woods (Eds.), *Life in school: The sociology of pop culture.* New York: Open University Press.

Furman, L. N., & Walden, T. A. (1989, April). *The effect of script knowledge on children's communicative interactions.* Paper presented at the Society for Research in Child Development meeting, Kansas City, MO.

Furman, L. N., & Walden, T. A. (1990). Effect of script knowledge on preschool children's communicative interactions. *Developmental Psychology, 26,* 227–233.

Furman, W., & Buhrmester, D. (in press). Age and sex differences in perceptions of networks of personal relationships. *Child Development.*

Furman, W., & Wehner, E. (1993, March). *Adolescent romantic relationships: A developmental perspective.* Paper presented at the biennial meeting of the Society for Research in Child Development, New Orleans.

Furrow, D., & Moore, C. (1991, April). *Mothers' feedback to children's utterances: The role of context.* Paper presented at the Society for Research in Child Development meeting, Seattle.

Furstenberg, F. F. (1988). Child care after divorce and remarriage. In E. M. Hetherington & J. D. Arasteh (Eds.), *Impact of divorce, single-parenting, and stepparenting on children.* Hillsdale, NJ: Erlbaum.

Furstenberg, F. F. (1991). Pregnancy and childbearing: Effects on teen mothers. In R. M. Lerner, A. C. Petersen, & J. Brooks-Gunn (Eds.), *Encyclopedia of adolescence* (Vol. 2). New York: Garland.

Furstenberg, F. F., Brooks-Gunn, J., & Chase-Lansdale, L. (1989). Teenage pregnancy and childbearing. *American Psychologist, 44,* 313–320.

Furstenberg, F. F., Jr., & Harris, K. T. (1992). When fathers matter/why fathers matter: The impact of paternal involvement on the offspring of adolescent mothers. In R. Lerman and T. Ooms (Eds.), *Young unwed fathers.* Philadelphia: Temple University Press.

Furth, H. G. (1973). *Deafness and learning: A psychosocial approach.* Belmont, CA: Wadsworth.

Furth, H. G., & Wachs, H. (1975). *Thinking goes to school.* New York: Oxford University Press.

G

Gage, N. L. (1965). Desirable behaviors of teachers. *Urban Education, 1,* 85–96.

Gagne, E. D. (1985). *The cognitive psychology of school learning.* Boston: Little, Brown.

Gagne, E. D., Weidemann, C., Bell, M. S., & Ander, T. D. (1984). Training thirteen-year-olds to elaborate while studying text. *Human Learning: Journal of Practical Research and Application, 3,* 281–294.

Galambos, N. L., & Maggs, J. L. (1989, April). *The after-school ecology of young adolescents and self-reported behavior.* Paper presented at the biennial meeting of the Society for Research in Child Development, Kansas City, MO.

Galinsky, E., & David, J. (1988). *The preschool years: Family strategies that work—from experts and parents.* New York: Ballentine.

Gallagher, J. J., Trohanis, P. L., & Clifford, R. M. (1989). *Policy implementation and PL 99–457.* Baltimore, MD: Brookes.

Gallup, A. M., & Clark, D. L. (1987). The 19th annual Gallup poll of the public's attitude toward the public schools. *Phi Delta Kappan, 69,* 17–30.

Gallup Report. (1987). Legalized gay relations. *Gallup Report,* No. 254, 25.

Galotti, K. M. (1989). Approaches to studying formal and everyday reasoning. *Psychological Bulletin, 105,* 331–351.

Galotti, K. M., Kozberg, S. F., & Appleman, D. (in press). Younger and older adolescents' thinking about commitments. *Journal of Experimental Child Psychology.*

Galotti, K. M., Kozberg, S. F., & Farmer, M. C. (1990, March). *Gender and developmental differences in adolescents' conceptions of moral reasoning.* Paper presented at the meeting of the Society for Research in Adolescence, Atlanta.

Garbarino, J. (1976). The ecological correlates of child abuse: The impact of socioeconomic stress on mothers. *Child Development, 47,* 178–185.

Garbarino, J. (1980). The issue is human quality: In praise of children. *Children and Youth Services Review, 1,* 353–377.

Garbarino, J. (1980b). Some thoughts on school size and its effects on adolescent development. *Journal of Youth and Adolescence, 9,* 19–31.

Garbarino, J. (1985). *Adolescent development: An ecological perspective.* Columbus, OH: Merrill.

Gardner, B. T., & Gardner, R. A. (1971). Two-way communication with an infant chimpanzee. In A. Schrier & F. Stollnitz (Eds.), *Behavior of nonhuman primates* (Vol. 4). New York: Academic Press.

Gardner, H. (1983). *Frames of mind.* New York: Basic.

Gardner, H. (1989). Beyond a modular view of mind. In W. Damon (Ed.), *Child development today and tomorrow.* San Francisco: Jossey-Bass.

Gardner, H. (1993, March). *A developmental approach to understanding developmental constraints and disciplinary opportunities.* Paper presented at the biennial meeting of the Society for Research in Child Development, New Orleans.

Gardner, L. I. (1972). Deprivation dwarfism. *Scientific American, 227,* 76–82.

Garelik, G. (1985, October). Are the progeny prodigies? *Discover, 6,* 45–47, 78–84.

Garton, A. F., & Pratt, C. (1989). *Learning to be literate.* New York: Basil Blackwell.

Garvey, C. (1977). *Play.* Cambridge: MA: Harvard University Press.

Garwood, S. G., Phillips, D., Hartman, A., & Zigler, E. F. (1989). As the pendulum swings: Federal agency programs for children. *American Psychologist, 44,* 434–440.

Gazzaniga, M. S. (1986). *The social brain.* New York: Plenum.

Geary, D. C., & Brown, S. C. (1991). Cognitive addition: Strategy choice and speed-of-processing differences in gifted, normal, and mathematically disabled children. *Developmental Psychology, 27,* 398–406.

Geballo, R., & Olson, S. L. (1993, March). *The role of alternative caregivers in the lives of poor, single-parent families.* Paper presented at the biennial meeting of the Society for Research in Child Development, New Orleans.

Gelfand, D. M., Teti, D. M., & Fox, C. E. R. (1992). Sources of parenting stress for depressed and nondepressed mothers of infants. *Journal of Clinical Child Psychology, 21,* 262–272.

Gelles, R. J., & Conte, J. R. (1990). Domestic violence and sexual abuse of children: A review of research in the eighties. *Journal of Marriage and the Family, 52,* 1045–1058.

Gelman, R. (1969). Conservation acquisition: A problem of learning to attend to relevant attributes. *Journal of Experimental Child Psychology, 7,* 67–87.

Gelman, R., & Baillargeon, R. (1983). A review of some Piagetian concepts. In P. H. Mussen (Ed.), *Handbook of child psychology* (4th ed., Vol. 3). New York: Wiley.

George, R. (1987). *Youth policies and programs in selected countries.* Washington, DC: The William T. Grant Foundation.

Gerber, A. (1992). *Language-related learning disabilities.* Baltimore, MD: Paul H. Brookes.

Geschwind, N. (1979, September). Specializations of the human brain. *Scientific American,* pp. 180–199.

Gesell, A. L. (1928). *Infancy and human growth.* New York: Macmillan.

Gesell, A. L. (1934). *An atlas of infant behavior.* New Haven, CT: Yale University Press.

Gewirtz, J. (1977). Maternal responding and the conditioning of infant crying: Directions of influence within the attachment-acquisition process. In B. C. Etzel, J. M. LeBlanc, & D. M. Baer (Eds.), *New developments in behavioral research.* Hillsdale, NJ: Erlbaum.

Giaconia, R. M., & Hedges, L. V. (1982). Identifying features of effective open education. *Review of Educational Research, 52,* 579–602.

Gibbs, J. C. (1993, March). *Inductive discipline's contribution to moral motivation.* Paper presented at the biennial meeting of the Society for Research in Child Development, New Orleans.

Gibbs, J. T., & Huang, L. N. (1989). A conceptual framework for assessing and treating minority youth. In J. T. Gibbs & L. N. Huang (Eds.), *Children of color.* San Francisco: Jossey-Bass.

Gibbs, N. (1990, Fall). The dreams of youth. *Time, Special Issue,* pp. 10–14.

Gibson, E. J. (1969). *The principles of perceptual learning and development.* New York: Appleton-Century-Crofts.

Gibson, E. J. (1989). Exploratory behavior in the development of perceiving, acting, and the acquiring of knowledge. *Annual Review of Psychology, 39.* Palo Alto, CA: Annual Reviews.

Gibson, E. J., & Spelke, E. S. (1983). The development of perception. In P. H. Mussen (Ed.), *Handbook of child psychology* (4th ed., Vol. 3). New York: Wiley.

Gibson, E. J., & Walk, R. D. (1960). The "visual cliff." *Scientific American, 202,* 64–71.

Gilligan, C. (1982). *In a different voice.* Cambridge, MA: Harvard University Press.

Gilligan, C. (1990). Teaching Shakespeare's sister. In C. Gilligan, N. Lyons, and T. Hanmer. (Eds.), *Making connections: The relational worlds of adolescent girls at Emma Willard School.* Cambridge: Harvard University Press.

Gilligan, C. (1991, April). *How should "we" talk about development?* Paper presented at the biennial meeting of the Society for Research in Child Development, Seattle.

Gilligan, C. (1992, May). *Joining the resistance: Girls' development in adolescence.* Paper presented at the symposium on development and vulnerability in close relationships, Montreal, Quebec.

Gilligan, C., & Attanucci, J. (1988). Two moral orientations. In C. Gilligan, J. V. Ward, J. M. Taylor, & B. Bardige (Eds.), *Mapping the moral domain.* Cambridge, MA: Harvard University Press.

Gilligan, C., Brown, L. M., & Rogers, A. G. (1990). Psyche embedded: A place for body, relationships, and culture in personality theory. In A. I. Rabin, R. A. Zuker, R. A. Emmons, & S. Frank (Eds.), *Studying persons and lives.* New York: Springer.

Gjerde, P. F., Block, J., & Block, J. H. (1991). The preschool family context of 18-year-olds with depressive symptoms: A prospective study. *Journal of Research on Adolescence, 1,* 63–92.

Glaser, R. (1989). The reemergence of learning theory within instructional research. *American Psychologist, 45,* 29–39.

Glass, G, V., & Smith, M. L. (1978, September). *Meta-analysis of research on the relationship of class size and achievement.* San Francisco: Far West Educational Laboratory.

Glasser, W. (1990). The quality school. *Phi Delta Kappan,* pp. 424–435.

Gleason, J. B. (1988). Language and socialization. In F. Kessel (Ed.), *The development of language and language researchers.* Hillsdale, NJ: Erlbaum.

Gleason, J. B., Hay, D., & Cain, L. (1989). Social and affective determinants of language acquisition. In M. L. Rice & R. L. Schiefelbusch (Eds.), *The teachability of language.* Baltimore: Paul Brooks.

Glick, J. (1975). Cognitive development in cross-cultural perspective. In F. Horowitz (Ed.), *Review of child development research* (Vol. 4). Chicago: University of Chicago Press.

Glick, J. (1991, April). *The uses and abuses of Vygotsky.* Paper presented at the Society for Research in Child Development meeting, Seattle.

Glueck, S., & Glueck, E. (1950). *Unraveling juvenile delinquency.* Cambridge, MA: Harvard University Press.

Gold, M., & Petronio, R. J. (1980). Delinquent behavior in adolescence. In J. Adelson (Ed.), *Handbook of adolescent psychology.* New York: Wiley.

Goldsmith, H. H, Rothbart, M. K., Crowley, J. M., Harmon-Losova, S. G., & Bowden, L. M. (1991, April). *Behavioral assessment of early temperament in the laboratory.* Paper presented at the biennial meeting of the Society for Research in Child Development, Seattle.

Goldsmith, H. H. (1988, August). *Does early temperament predict late development?* Paper presented at the meeting of the American Psychological Association, Atlanta.

Goldsmith, H. H., & Gottesman, I. I. (1981). Origins of variation in behavioral style: A longitudinal study of temperament in young twins. *Child Development, 52,* 91–103.

Goldstein, A. E., & Medora, N. (1993, March). *Are pregnant teens more romantic? A study of romanticism and self-esteem among pregnant adolescents and a control group.* Paper presented at the biennial meeting of the Society for Research in Child Development, New Orleans.

Golombok, S., & Fivush, R. (1994). *Gender development.* New York: Cambridge University Press.

Gomez, R., & Thompson, L. (1993, March). *How children organize their knowledge of everyday events: Exploring the generality of event representations.* Paper presented at the biennial meeting of the Society for Research in Child Development, New Orleans.

Goodchilds, J. D., & Zellman, G. L. (1984). Sexual signaling and sexual aggression in adolescent relationship. In N. M. Malamuth & E. D. Donnerstein (Eds.), *Pornography and sexual aggression.* New York: Academic Press.

Goodenow, C. (1993, March). *Friends, classmates, and teachers as influences on the academic motivation of early adolescent students.* Paper presented at the biennial meeting of the Society for Research in Child Development, New Orleans.

Goodman, G., Andrews, T., Jones, S., Weinstein, J., & Weissman, A. (1993, March). *Maternal depression and behavioral sensitivity, and children's attachment representations and behavioral outcomes.* Paper presented at the biennial meeting of the Society for Research in Child Development, New Orleans.

Goodman, R. A., Mercy, J. A., Loya, F., Rosenberg, M. L., Smith, J. C., Allen, N. H., Vargas, L., & Kolts, R. (1986). Alcohol use and interpersonal violence: Alcohol detected in homicide victims. *American Journal of Public Health, 76,* 144–149.

Goodman, S. (1979). *You and your child: From birth to adolescence.* Chicago: Rand McNally.

Gopnik, A., & Wellman, H. (1993, March). *The child's theory of mind.* Paper presented at the biennial meeting of the Society for Research in Child Development, New Orleans.

Gordon, I. (1978, June). *What does research say about the effects of parent involvement on schooling?* Paper presented at the meeting of the Association for Supervision and Curriculum Development, Washington, DC.

Gordon, S., & Gilgun, J. F. (1987). Adolescent sexuality. In V. B. Van Hasselt & M. Hersen (Eds.), *Handbook of adolescent psychology.* New York: Pergamon.

Goswami, U., & Bryant, P. (1990). *Phonological skills and learning to read.* Hillsdale, NJ: Erlbaum.

Gottfried, A. E. (1993, March). *Maternal employment and children's development: A longitudinal study from infancy through preadolescence.* Paper presented at the biennial meeting of the Society for Research in Child Development, New Orleans.

Gottfried, A. W., & Bathurst, K. (1989, April). *Infant predictors of IQ and achievement: A comparative analysis.* Paper presented at the Society for Research in Child Development meeting, Kansas City, MO.

Gottfried, A. W., & Lussier, C. M. (1993, March). *Continuity, stability, and change in temperament: A 10-year longitudinal investigation from infancy through adolescence.* Paper presented at the biennial meeting of the Society for Child Development, New Orleans.

Gottlieb, D. (1966). Teaching and students: The views of Negro and white teachers. *Sociology of Education, 37,* 345–353.

Gottlieb, G. (1991a). Epigenetic systems view of human development. *Developmental Psychology, 27,* 33–34.

Gottlieb, G. (1991b). Experiential canalization of behavioral development theory. *Developmental Psychology, 27,* 4–13.

Gottman, J. M., & Parker, J. G. (Eds.). (1987). *Conversations of friends.* New York: Cambridge University Press.

Gould, S. J. (1981). *The mismeasure of man.* New York: W. W. Norton.

Granott, N. (1993, March). *Co-construction of knowledge: Interaction model, types of interaction, and a suggested method of analysis.* Paper presented at the biennial meeting of the Society for Research in Child Development, New Orleans.

Grant, J. (1986). *The state of the world's children.* New York: UNICEF and Oxford University Press.

Grant, J. P. (1992). *The state of the world's children.* New York: UNICEF and Oxford University Press.

Greenberg, P. (1992). Why not academic preschool? Part 2. Autocracy or democracy in the early years. *Young Children, 47,* 54–64.

Greenfield, P. M. (1966). On culture and conservation. In J. S. Bruner, R. P. Oliver, & P. M. Greenfield (Eds.), *Studies in cognitive growth.* New York: Wiley.

Grotevant, H. D., & Cooper, C. R. (1985). Patterns of interaction in family relationships and the development of identity exploration in adolescence. *Child Development, 56,* 415–428.

Gruys, A. (1993, March). *Security of attachment and its relation to quantitative and qualitative aspects of friendship.* Paper presented at the biennial meeting of the Society for Research in Child Development, New Orleans.

Guilford, J. P. (1967). *The structure of intellect.* New York: McGraw-Hill.

Guisinger, S., Cowan, P., & Schuldberg, D. (1989). Changing parent and spouse relations in the first years of remarriage of divorced fathers. *Journal of Marriage and the Family, 51,* 445–456.

Gunnar, M. R., Malone, S., & Fisch, R. O. (1987). The psychobiology of stress and coping in the human neonate: Studies of the adrenocortical activity in response to stress in the first week of life. In T. Field, P. McCabe, & N. Scheiderman (Eds.), *Stress and coping.* Hillsdale, NJ: Erlbaum.

Gustafson, G. E., Green, J. A., & Kalinowski, L. L. (1993, March). *The development of communicative skills: Infants' cries and vocalizations in social context.* Paper presented at the biennial meeting of the Society for Research in Child Development, New Orleans.

Guthrie, R. (1976). *Even the rat was white: A historical view of psychology.* New York: Harper & Row.

H

Haffner, D. (1993, August). *Sex education: Trends and issues.* Paper presented at the meeting of the American Psychological Association, Toronto.

Hahn, A. (1987, December). Reaching out to America's dropouts: What to do? *Phi Delta Kappan,* pp. 256–263.

Haith, M. H. (1991, April). *Setting a path for the '90s: Some goals and challenges in infant sensory and perceptual development.* Paper presented at the Society for Research in Child Development, Seattle.

Hakuta, K., & Garcia, E. E. (1989). Bilingualism and education. *American Psychologist, 44,* 374–379.

Hale, B. A., Seitz, V., & Zigler, E. (in press). Health services and Head Start: A forgotten formula. *Journal of Applied Developmental Psychology.*

Hale, S. (1990). A global developmental trend in cognitive processing speed. *Child Development, 61,* 653–663.

Halford, G. S. (1993, March). *Experience and processing capacity in cognitive development: A PDP approach.* Paper presented at the biennial meeting of the Society for Child Development, New Orleans.

Halford, G. S. (in press). *Children's understanding: The development of mental models.* Hillsdale, NJ: Erlbaum.

Hall, C. C. I., Evans, B. J., & Selice, S. (Eds.). (1989). *Black females in the United States.* Washington, DC: American Psychological Association.

Hall, G. S. (1904). *Adolescence* (Vols. I & II). Englewood Cliffs, NJ: Prentice-Hall.

Hall, W. S. (1989). Reading comprehension. *American Psychologist, 44,* 157–161.

Hallahan, D. P., Kauffman, J. M., Lloyd, J. W., & McKinney, J. D. (1988). Questions about the regular education initiative. *Journal of Learning Disabilities, 21,* 3–5.

Halpern, C. T., Udry, J. R., Campbell, B., & Suchindran, C. (1992, March). *Hormonal influences on adolescent male sexual activity.* Paper presented at the meeting of the Society for Research in Adolescence, Washington, DC.

Hammen, C. (1993, March). *Risk and resilience in children and their depressed mothers.* Paper presented at the biennial meeting of the Society for Research in Child Development, New Orleans.

Hans, S. (1989, April). *Infant behavioral effects of prenatal exposure to methadone.* Paper presented at the biennial meeting of the Society for Research in Child Development, Kansas City, MO.

Hanson, R. A., & Mullis, R. L. (1985). Age and gender differences in empathy and moral reasoning among adolescents. *Child Study Journal, 15,* 181–188.

Hardyck, C., & Petrinovich, L. F. (1977). Left-handedness. *Psychological Bulletin, 84,* 385–404.

Hare-Muston, R., & Marecek, J. (1988). The meaning of difference: Gender theory, postmodernism, and psychology. *American Psychologist, 43,* 455–464.

Harkness, S. (1992). Cross-cultural research in child development: A sample of the State of the Art. *Developmental Psychology, 28,* 622–625.

Harlow, H. F., & Zimmerman, R. R. (1959). Affectional responses in the infant monkey. *Science, 130,* 421–432.

Harnishfeger, K. K., & Cassel, W. S. (1991, April). *Children's memory and knowledge base: When motivation is not an issue.* Paper presented at the Society for Research in Child Development meeting, Seattle.

Harold, R. D., & Eccles, J. S. (1990, March). *Maternal expectations, advice, and provision of opportunities: Their relationships to boys' and girls' occupational aspirations.* Paper presented at the meeting of the Society for Research in Adolescence, Atlanta.

Harris, P. L. (1989). *Children and emotion.* London, England: Basil Blackwell.

Harris, R. F., Wolf, N. M., & Baer, D. M. (1964). Effects of adult social reinforcement on child behavior. *Young Children, 20,* 8–17.

Harrist, A. W. (1993, March). *Family interaction styles as predictors of children's competence: The role of synchrony and nonsynchrony.* Paper presented at the biennial meeting of the Society for Research in Child Development, New Orleans.

Hart, C. H., Charlesworth, R., Burts, D. C., & DeWolf, M. (1993, March). *The relationship of attendance in developmentally appropriate or inappropriate kindergarten classrooms to first-grade behavior.* Paper presented at the biennial meeting of the Society for Research in Child Development, New Orleans.

Hart, G. H., Ladd, G. W., & Burleson, B. R. (1990). Children's expectations of the outcomes of social strategies: Relations with sociometric status and maternal disciplinary styles. *Child Development, 61,* 127–137.

Hart, P. D. (1987, June). *KidsPac poll on qualities for the next president.* Cambridge, MA: KidsPac.

Harter, S. (1982). The perceived competence scale for children. *Child Development, 53,* 87–97.

Harter, S. (1985). *Self-Perception Profile for Children.* Denver, CO: Department of Psychology, University of Denver.

Harter, S. (1989). *Self-Perception Profile for Adolescents.* Denver, CO: Department of Psychology, University of Denver.

Harter, S. (1990a). Processes underlying adolescent self-concept formation. In R. Montemayor, G. R. Adams, & T. P. Gulotta (Eds.), *From childhood to adolescence: A transitional period?* Newbury Park, CA: Sage.

Harter, S. (1990b). Self and identity development. In S. S. Feldman & G. R. Elliott (Eds.), *At the threshold: The developing adolescent.* Cambridge, MA: Harvard University Press.

Harter, S., & Lee, L. (1989). *Manifestations of true and false selves in adolescence.* Paper presented at the meeting of the Society for Research in Child Development, Kansas City, MO.

Harter, S., & Monsour, A. (1992). Developmental analysis of conflict caused by opposing attributes in the adolescent self-portrait. *Developmental Psychology, 28,* 251–260.

Harter, S., Alexander, P. C., & Neimeyer, R. A. (1988). Long-term effects of incestuous child abuse in college women. Social adjustment, social cognition, and family characteristics. *Journal of Consulting and Clinical Psychology, 56,* 5–8.

Hartshorne, H. & May, M. S. (1928–1930). *Moral studies in the nature of character: Studies in deceit* (Vol. 1); *Studies in self-control* (Vol. 2); *Studies in the organization of character* (Vol. 3). New York: Macmillan.

Hartup, W. W. (1976). Peer interaction and the development of the individual child. In E. Schopler & R. J. Reichler (Eds.), *Psychopathology and child development.* New York: Plenum.

Hartup, W. W. (1983). The peer system. In P. H. Mussen (Ed.), *Handbook of child psychology* (4th ed., Vol. 4). New York: Wiley.

Hartup, W. W. (1989). Social relationships and their developmental significance. *American Psychologist, 44,* 120–126.

Hartup, W. W. (1991). Friendships. In R. M. Lerner, A. C. Petersen, & J. Brooks-Gunn (Eds.), *Encyclopedia of adolescence* (Vol. 1). New York: Garland.

Haskins, R. (1989). Beyond metaphor: The efficacy of early childhood education. *American Psychologist, 44,* 274–282.

Hauser, S. T., & Bowlds, M. K. (1990). Stress, coping, and adaptation. In S. S. Feldman & G. R. Elliott (Eds.), *At the threshold: The developing adolescent.* Cambridge, MA: Harvard University Press.

Hauser, S. T., Powers, S. I., Noam, G. G., Jacobson, A. M., Weisse, B., & Follansbee, D. J. (1984). Familial contexts of adolescent ego development. *Child Development, 55,* 195–213.

Hawkins, D., & Lam, T. (1986). Teacher practices, social development, and delinquency. In J. Burchard & S. Burchard (Eds.), *Prevention of delinquent behavior.* Newbury Park, CA: Sage.

Hawkins, D., & Lishner, D. (1987). School and delinquency. In E. Johnson (Ed.), *Handbook on crime and delinquency prevention.* Westport, CT: Greenwood Press.

Hawkins, J. A., & Berndt, T. J. (1985, April). *Adjustment following the transition to junior high school.* Paper presented at the Society for Research in Child Development meeting, Toronto.

Hawley, T. L. (1993, March). *Maternal cocaine addiction: Correlates and consequences.* Paper presented at the biennial meeting of the Society for Research in Child Development, New Orleans.

Hay, D. F. (1985, April). *The search for general principles in social life: Some lessons from young peers.* Paper presented at the Society for Research in Child Development meeting, Toronto.

Hayden-Thomson, L., Rubin, K. M., & Hymel, S. (1987). Sex preferences in sociometric choices. *Developmental Psychology, 23,* 558–562.

Haynie, D., & McLellan, J. (1992, March). *Continuity in parent and peer relationships.* Paper presented at the meeting of the Society for Research on Adolescence, Washington, DC.

Hazen, C., & Shaver, P. (1987). Romantic love conceptualized as an attachment process. *Journal of Personality and Social Psychology, 51,* 511–524.

Heath, S. B. (1989). Oral and literate traditions among Black Americans living in poverty. *American Psychologist, 44,* 367–373.

Heath, S. B. (in press). The children of Trackton's children: Spoken and written language in social change. In J. Stigler, G. Herdt, & R. A. Schweder (Eds.), *Cultural psychology: The Chicago symposia.* New York: Cambridge University Press.

Heatherington, E. M. (1989). Coping with family transitions: Winners, losers, and survivors. *Child Development, 60,* 1–14.

Hedges, L. V., & Stock, W. (1983, Spring). The effects of class size: An examination of rival hypotheses. *American Education Research Journal,* 63–85.

Heinicke, C. M., Beckwith, L., & Thompson, A. (1988). Early intervention in the family system: A framework and review. *Infant Mental Health Journal, 9,* 2.

Heller, W. (1990, May/June). Of one mind: Second thoughts about the brain's dual nature. *The Sciences,* 38–44.

Hellige, J. B. (1990). Hemispheric asymmetry. *Annual Review of Psychology, 41.* Palo Alto, CA: Annual Reviews.

Helling, M. K. (1993, March). *Relations among information received from the school and parental behaviors.* Paper presented at the biennial meeting of the Society for Research in Child Development, New Orleans.

Helson, R. M. (1993, August). *Issues of change and stability in creative lives.* Paper presented at the meeting of the American Psychological Association, Toronto.

Hendry, J. (1986). *Becoming Japanese: The world of the preschool child.* Honolulu: University of Hawaii Press.

Herdt, G. H. (1988, August). *Coming out processes as an anthropological rite of passage.* Paper presented at the meeting of the American Psychological Association, Atlanta.

Hess, L., Lonky, E., & Roodin, P. A. (1985, April). *The relationship of moral reasoning and ego strength to cheating behavior.* Paper presented at the Society for Research in Child Development meeting, Toronto.

Hess, R. D., Holloway, S. D., Dickson, W. P., & Price, G. G. (1984). Maternal variables as predictors of children's school readiness and later achievement in vocabulary and mathematics in the sixth grade. *Child Development, 55,* 1902–1912.

Hetherington, E. M. (1989). Coping with family transitions: Winners, losers, and survivors. *Child Development, 60,* 1–14.

Hetherington, E. M. (1993, March). *An overview of the Virginia longitudinal study of divorce and remarriage with a focus on early adolescence.* Paper presented at the biennial meeting of the Society for Research in Child Development, New Orleans.

Hetherington, E. M., & Baltes, P. B. (1989). Child psychology and life-span development. In E. M. Hetherington, R. M. Lerner, & M. Perlmutter (Eds.), *Child development in a life-span perspective.* Hillsdale, NJ: Erlbaum.

Hetherington, E. M., & Clingempeel, W. G. (1992). Coping with marital transitions: A family systems perspective. *Society for Research in Child Development Monographs,* Serial No. 227.

Hetherington, E. M., Cox, M., & Cox, R. (1979). Play and social interaction in children following divorce. *Journal of Social Issues, 35,* 26–49.

Hetherington, E. M., Anderson, E. R., & Hagan, M. S. (1991). Divorce: Effects on adolescents. In R. M. Lerner, A. C. Petersen, & J. Brooks-Gunn (Eds.), *Encyclopedia of adolescence* (Vol. 1). New York: Garland.

Hetherington, E. M., Cox, M., & Cox, R. (1982). Effects of divorce on children and parents. In M. E. Lamb (Ed.), *Nontraditional families.* Hillsdale, NJ: Erlbaum.

Hetherington, E. M., Hagan, M. S., & Anderson, E. R. (1989). Marital transitions: A child's perspective. *American Psychologist, 44,* 303–312.

Hiebert, J., & Wearne, D. (1988). Instruction and cognitive change in mathematics. *Educational Psychologist, 23,* 105–118.

Hiester, M., Carlson, E., & Sroufe, L.A. (1993, March). *The evolution of friendships in preschool, middle childhood, and adolescence: Origins in attachment history.* Paper presented at the biennial meeting of the Society for Research in Child Development, New Orleans.

Higgins, A. (1991). Lawrence Kohlberg: The vocation of an educator, part II. In W. M. Kurtines & J. Gewirtz (Eds.), *Moral behavior and development* (Vol. 1). Hillsdale, NJ: Erlbaum.

Hightower, E. (1990). Adolescent interpersonal and familial precursors of positive mental health at midlife. *Journal of Youth and Adolescence, 19,* 257–275.

Hill, C. R., & Stafford, F. P (1980). Parental care of children: Time diary estimate of quantity, predictability, and variety. *Journal of Human Resources, 15,* 219–239.

Hill, J. P. (1980). The early adolescent and the family. In M. Johnson (Ed.), *The 79th yearbook of the National Society for the Study of Education.* Chicago: University of Chicago Press.

Hill, J. P. (1983, April). *Early adolescence: A research agenda.* Paper presented at the meeting of the Society for Research in Child Development, Detroit.

Hinde, R. A. (1984). Why do the sexes behave differently in close relationships? *Journal of Social and Personal Relationships, 1,* 471–501.

Hinde, R. A. (1992a). Commentary: Can biology explain human development? *Human Development, 35,* 34–39.

Hinde, R. A. (1992b). Developmental psychology in the context of other behavioral sciences. *Developmental Psychology, 28,* 1018–1029.

Hines, M. (1982). Prenatal gonadal hormones and sex differences in human behavior. *Psychological Bulletin, 92,* 56–80.

Hiraga, Y., Cauce, A. M., Mason, C., & Ordonez, N. (1993, March). *Ethnic identity and the social adjustment of biracial youth.* Paper presented at the biennial meeting of the Society for Research in Child Development, New Orleans.

Hirsch, B. J. (1989, April). *School transitions and psychological well-being in adolescence: Comparative longitudinal analyses.* Paper presented at the Society for Research in Child Development meeting, Kansas City, MO.

Hirsch, B. J., & Rapkin, B. D. (1987). The transition to junior high school: A longitudinal study of self-esteem, psychological symptomatology, school life, and social support. *Child Development, 58,* 1235–1243.

Hirsch-Pasek, K., Hyson, M., Rescorla, L., & Cone, J. (1989, April). *Hurrying children: How does it affect their academic, social, creative, and emotional development?* Paper presented at the Society for Research in Child Development meeting, Kansas City, MO.

Hirschhorn, K. (1992). Genetic counseling in chromosomal disorders. In R. E. Behrman (Ed.), *Nelson textbook of pediatrics* (14th ed.). Philadelphia, PA: W. B. Saunders.

Ho, D. Y. F. (1987). Fatherhood in Chinese culture. In M. E. Lamb (Ed.), *The father's role: Cross-cultural perspectives.* Hillsdale, NJ: Erlbaum.

Ho, M. K. (1992). *Minority children and adolescents in therapy.* Newbury Park, CA: Sage.

Hobbs, N. (Ed.). (1975). *Issues in the classification of children* (Vol. 1). San Francisco: Jossey-Bass.

Hobfoll, S. E. (1989). Conservation of resources: A new attempt at conceptualizing stress. *American Psychologist, 44,* 513–524.

Hodapp, R. M., Burack, J. A., & Zigler, E. (Eds.). (in press). *Issues in the developmental approach to mental retardation.* New York: Cambridge University Press.

Hodgman, C. H. (1992). Child and adolescent depression and suicide. In D. E. Greydanus & M. L. Wolraich (Eds.), *Behavioral pediatrics.* New York: Springer-Verlag.

Hoff-Ginsberg, E. (1991). *Mother-child conversation in different social classes and communicative settings.* Paper presented at the biennial meeting of the Society for Research in Child Development, Seattle.

Hofferth, S. L. (1990). Trends in adolescent sexual activity, contraception, and pregnancy in the United States. In J. Bancroft & J. M. Reinisch (Eds.), *Adolescence and puberty.* New York: Oxford University Press.

Hoffman, L. W. (1989). Effects of maternal employment in the two-parent family. *American Psychologist, 44,* 283–292.

Hoffman, M. L. (1970). Moral development. In P. H. Mussen (Ed.), *Manual of child psychology* (3rd ed., Vol. 2). New York: Wiley.

Hoffman, M. L. (1983). Empathy, guilt, and social cognition. In W. F. Overton (Ed.), *The relationship between social and cognitive development.* Hillsdale, NJ: Erlbaum.

Hoffman, M. L. (1988). Moral development. In M. H. Bornstein & M. E. Lamb (Eds.), *Developmental psychology: An advanced textbook* (2nd ed.). Hillsdale, NJ: Erlbaum.

Hoffnung, M. (1984). Motherhood: Contemporary conflict for women. In J. Freeman (Eds.), *Women: A feminist perspective* (3rd ed.). Palo Alto, CA: Mayfield.

Hofstede, G. (1980). *Culture's consequences: International differences in work-related values.* Newbury Park, CA: Sage.

Holmes, D. L., Reich, J. N., & Gyurke, J. S. (1989). The development of high-risk infants in low-risk families. In F. J. Morrison, C. Lord, & D. P. Keating (Eds.), *Psychological development in infancy.* San Diego: Academic Press.

Holmes, L. B. (1992). General clinical principles in genetic disorders. In R. E. Behrman (Ed.), *Nelson textbook of pediatrics* (14th ed.). Philadelphia, PA: W. B. Saunders.

Holt, S. A., & Fogel, A. (1993, March). *Emotions as components of dynamic systems.* Paper presented at the biennial meeting of the Society for Research in Child Development, New Orleans.

Holtzmann, W. H. (Ed.). (1992). *School of the future.* Austin, TX: American Psychological Association and Hogg Foundation for Mental Health.

Holtzmann, W. H. (Ed.). (1992). *School of the future.* Washington, DC: American Psychological Association and Hogg Foundation for Mental Health.

Holtzmann, W. H. (1982). Cross-cultural comparisons of personality development in Mexico and the United States. In D. A. Wagner & H. W. Stevenson (Eds.), *Cultural perspectives on child development.* New York: W. H. Freeman.

Holzman, M. (1983). *The language of children: Development in home and school.* Englewood Cliffs, NJ: Prentice-Hall.

Hommerding, K. D., & Kriger, M. (1993, March). *Stability and change in infant-mother attachment: A study of low-income families.* Paper presented at the biennial meeting of the Society for Research in Child Development, New Orleans.

Honzik, M. P., MacFarlane, J. W., & Allen, L. (1948). The stability of mental test performance between two and eighteen years. *Journal of Experimental Education, 17,* 309–324.

Hood, K. E. (1991). Menstrual cycle. In R. M. Lerner, A. C. Petersen, & J. Brooks-Gunn (Eds.), *Encyclopedia of adolescence* (Vol. 1). New York: Garland.

Horne, M. D. (1988). Handicapped, disabled, or exceptional: Terminological issues. *Psychology in the Schools, 25,* 419–421.

Horney, K. (1967). *Feminine psychology.* New York: W. W. Norton.

Horowitz, F. D., & O'Brien, M. (1989). In the interest of the nation: A reflective essay on the state of knowledge and the challenges before us. *American Psychologist, 44,* 441–445.

Hort, B. E., & Leinbach, M. D. (1993, March). *Children's use of metaphorical cues in gender-typing of objects.* Paper presented at the biennial meeting of the society for Research in Child Development, New Orleans.

Howard, J. (1982). Counseling: A developmental approach. In E. E. Bleck & D. A. Nagel (Eds.), *Physically handicapped children.* New York: Grune & Stratton.

Howe, C. J. (1993). *Language learning.* Hillsdale, NJ: Erlbaum.

Howes, C. (1985, April). *Predicting preschool sociometric status from toddler peer interaction.* Paper presented at the Society for Research in Child Development meeting, Toronto.

Howes, C. (1988, April). *Can the age of entry and the quality of infant child care predict behaviors in kindergarten?* Paper presented at the International Conference on Infant Studies, Washington, DC.

Huang, L. N., & Gibbs, J. T. (1989). Future directions: Implications for research training, and practice. In J. T. Gibbs & L. N. Huang (Eds.), *Children of color.* San Francisco: Jossey-Bass.

Huang, L. N., & Ying, Y. (1989). Japanese children and adolescents. In J. T. Gibbs & L. N. Huang (Eds.), *Children of color*. San Francisco: Jossey-Bass.

Hudson, L. M., Forman, E. R., & Brion-Meisels, S. (1982). Role-taking as a predictor of prosocial behavior in cross-age tutors. *Child Development, 53,* 1320–1329.

Huebner, A. M., Garrod, A. C., & Snarey, J. (1990, March). *Moral development in Tibetan Buddhist monks: A cross-cultural study of adolescents and young adults in Nepal.* Paper presented at the meeting of the Society for Research in Adolescence, Atlanta.

Huesmann, L. R. (1986). Psychological processes promoting the relation between exposure to media violence and aggressive behavior by the viewer. *Journal of Social Issues, 42,* 125–139.

Huesmann, L. R., Eron, L. D., Klein, R., Brice, P., & Fischer, P. (1983). Mitigating the imitation of aggressive behaviors by changing children's attitudes about media violence. *Journal of Personality and Social Psychology, 44,* 899–910.

Huff, C. R. (Ed.). (1990). *Gangs in America.* Newbury Park, CA: Sage.

Hughes, S. O., Power, T. G., & Francis, D. J. (1992, March). *Attachment, autonomy, and adolescent drinking: Differentiating abstainers, experimenters, and heavy users.* Paper presented at the meeting of the Society for Research on Adolescence. Washington, DC.

Hui, C. H., & Villareal, M. J. (1989). Individualism-collectivism and psychological needs. *Journal of Cross-Cultural Psychology, 20,* 310–323.

Hunt, E. (1978). Mechanics of verbal ability. *Psychological Review, 85,* 109–130.

Hunt, J. V., & Cooper, B. A. (1989). Determining the risk for high-risk preterm infants. In M. Bornstein & N. A. Krasnegor (Eds.), *Stability and continuity in mental development.* Hillsdale, NJ: Erlbaum.

Hunt, M. (1974). *Sexual behavior in the 1970s.* Chicago: Playboy Press.

Huston, A. C. (1983). Sex-typing. In P. H. Mussen (Ed.), *Handbook of child psychology* (4th ed., Vol. 4). New York: Wiley.

Huston, A. C. (Ed.). (1991). *Children in poverty.* New York: Cambridge University Press.

Huston, A. C., Seigle, J., & Bremer, M. (1983, April). *Family environment and television use by preschool children.* Paper presented at the Society for Research in Child Development meeting, Detroit.

Huston, A. C., Watkins, B. A., & Kunkel, D. (1989). Public policy and children's television. *American Psychologist, 44,* 424–433.

Hutchings, D. E., & Fifer, W. P. (1986). Neurobehavioral effects in human and animal offspring following prenatal exposure to methadone. In E. P. Riley & C. V. Vorhees (Eds.), *Handbook of behavioral teratology.* New York: Plenum.

Hyde, J. S. (1981). How large are cognitive gender differences? A meta-analysis using w^2 and *d. American Psychologist, 36,* 892–901.

Hyde, J. S. (1984). children's understanding of sexist language. *Developmental Psychology, 20,* 697–706.

Hyde, J. S. (1985). *Half the human experience.* (3rd ed.). Lexington, MA: D. C. Heath.

Hyde, J. S. (1990). Meta-analysis and the psychology of gender differences. *Signs: Journal of Women in Culture and Society, 16,* 55–69.

Hyde, J. S. (in press). Meta-analysis and the psychology of women. In F. L. Denmark & M. A. Paludi (Eds.), *Handbook on the psychology of women.* Dubuque, IA: Wm. C. Brown.

Hynd, G. W., & Obrzut, J. E. (1986). Exceptionality: Historical antecedents and present positions. In R. T. Brown & C. R. Reynolds (Eds.), *Psychological perspectives on childhood exceptionality: A handbook.* New York: Wiley.

I

Infant Health and Development Program Staff. (1990). Enhancing the outcomes of low birthweight, premature infants: A multisite randomized trial. *Journal of the American Medical Association, 263* (22), 3035–3042.

Innocenti, M., & Huh, K. (1993, March). *A comparative study of the child and family effects of adding parent involvement program to an existing early intervention program.* Paper presented at the biennial meeting of the Society for Research in Child Development, New Orleans.

Inoff-Germain, G., Arnold, G. S., Nottelmann, E. D., Susman, E. J., Cutler, G. B., & Chrousos, G. P. (1988). Relations between hormone levels and observational measures of aggressive behavior of young adolescents in family interactions. *Developmental Psychology, 24,* 129–139.

Irvin, F. S. (1988, August). *Clinical perspectives on resilience among gay and lesbian youth.* Paper presented at the annual meeting of the American Psychological Association, Atlanta.

Izard, C. E. (1982). *Measuring emotions in infants and young children.* New York: Cambridge University Press.

Izard, C. E. (1993, March). *Emotions in the development of personality and psychopathology.* Paper presented at the biennial meeting of the Society for Research in Child Development, New Orleans.

J

Jackson, I. I., Breitmeyer, B. G., & Fletcher, J. M. (1993). *Effects of color transparencies on reading in learning disability subgroups.* Paper presented at the biennial meeting of the Society for Research in Child Development, New Orleans.

Jackson, J. S. (Ed.). (1992). *Life in Black America.* Newbury Park, CA: Sage.

Jacobs, F. H., & Davies, M. W. (1991, Winter). Rhetoric or reality? Child and family policy in the United States. *Social Policy Report, Society for Research in Child Development,* pp. 1–25.

Jacobs, F. H., Little, P., & Almeida, C. (1993). *Supporting family life: A survey of homeless shelters.* Unpublished manuscript, Department of Child Study, Tufts University, Medford, MA.

Jacobson, J. L., Jacobson, S. W., Fein, G. G., Schwartz, P. M., & Dowler, J. K. (1984). Prenatal exposure to an environmental toxin: A test of the multiple-effects model. *Developmental Psychology, 20,* 523–532.

Jacobson, J. L., Jacobson, S. W., Padgett, R. J., Brumitt, G. A., & Billings, R. L. (1992). Effects of prenatal PCB exposure on cognitive processing efficiency and sustained attention. *Developmental Psychology, 28,* 297–306.

Jagers, R., & Bingham, K. (1993, March). *Parenting characteristics and moral judgment among inner-city African-American kindergartners.* Paper presented at the biennial meeting of the Society for Research in Child Development, New Orleans.

James, W. (1890/1950). *The principles of psychology.* New York: Dover.

Janos, P. M., & Robinson, N. N. (1985). Psychosocial development in intellectually gifted children. In F. D. Horowitz & M. O'Brien (Eds.), *The gifted and the talented.* Washington, DC: American Psychological Association.

Janzen, L., & Nanson, J. (1993, March). *Neuropsychological evaluation of preschoolers with fetal alcohol syndrome.* Paper presented at the biennial meeting of the Society for Research in Child Development, New Orleans.

Jeans, P. C., Smith, M. B., & Stearns, G. (1955). Incidence of prematurity in relation to maternal nutrition. *Journal of the American Dietary Association, 31,* 576–581.

Jenkins, E. J., & Bell, C. C. (1992). Adolescent violence: Can it be curbed? *Adolescent Medicine, 3,* 71–86.

Jensen, L. C., & Kingston, M. (1986). *Parenting.* Fort Worth, TX: Holt, Rinehart, & Winston.

Jensen, L. C., & Knight, R. S. (1981). *Moral education: Historical perspectives.* Washington, DC: University Press of America.

Jensen, R. A. (1969). How much can we boost IQ and scholastic achievement? *Harvard Educational Review, 39,* 1–123.

John-Steiner, V. (1985). *Notebooks of the mind: Explorations of thinking.* Albuquerque: University of New Mexico Press.

Johnson, D. D. L., Swank, P., Howie, V. M., Baldwin, C., & Owen, M. (1993, March). *Tobacco smoke in the home and child intelligence.* Paper presented at the biennial meeting of the Society for Research in Child Development, New Orleans.

Johnson, D. J., Jones, M. S., Guttentag, R., & Kee, D. W. (1993, March). *Knowledge access and recall benefits of imagery strategies.* Paper presented at the biennial meeting of the Society for Research in Child Development, New Orleans.

Johnson, D. L., & McGowan, R. J. (1984). Comparison of three intelligence tests as predictors of academic achievement and classroom behaviors of Mexican-American children. *Journal of Psychosexual Assessment, 2,* 345–352.

Johnson, J. E., Christie, J. F., & Yawkey, T. D. (1987). *Play and early childhood development.* Glenview, IL: Scott, Foresman.

Johnston, L. D., O'Malley, P. M., & Bachman, J. G. (1992, January 25; 1993). *Most forms of drug use decline among American high school and college students.* News release, Institute of Social Research, University of Michigan, Ann Arbor, MI.

Johnston, L., O'Malley, P., & Bachman, J. G. (1993, March). *Drug use rises among the nation's eighth-grade students.* Institute of Social Research, University of Michigan, Ann Arbor, MI.

Jones, B. F., Idol, L., & Brandt, R. S. (1991). Dimensions of thinking. In B. F. Jones & L. Idol (Eds.), *Dimensions of thinking and cognitive instruction.* Hillsdale, NJ: Erlbaum.

Jones, E. R., Forrest, J. D., Goldman, N., Henshaw, S. K., Lincoln, R., Rosoff, J. I., Westoff, C. G., & Wulf, D. (1985). Teenage pregnancy in developed countries: Determinants and policy implications. *Family Planning Perspectives, 17,* 53–63.

Jones, J. M. (1990, August). *Psychological approaches to race: What have they been and what should they be?* Paper presented at the meeting of the American Psychological Association, Boston.

Jones, J. M. (1993, August). *Racism and civil rights: Right problem, wrong solution.* Paper presented at the meeting of the American Psychological Association, Toronto, CA.

Jones, M. C. (1924). A laboratory study of fear: The case of Peter. *Journal of Genetic Psychology, 31,* 308–315.

Jones, M. C. (1965). Psychological correlates of somatic development. *Child Development, 36,* 899–911.

Jorgenson, S. R. (1993). Adolescent pregnancy and planning. In T. P. Gullotta, G. R. Adams, & R. Montemayor (Eds.), *Adolescent sexuality.* Newbury Park, CA: Sage.

Josselson, R. (1987). *Finding herself.* San Francisco: Jossey-Bass.

K

Kagan, J. (1965). Impulsive and reflective children: Significance of conceptual tempo. In J. D. Krumboltz (Ed.), *Learning and the educational process.* Chicago: Rand McNally.

Kagan, J. (1984). *The nature of the child.* New York: Basic Books.

Kagan, J. (1987). Perspectives on infancy. In J. D. Osofsky (Ed.), *Handbook on infant development* (2nd ed.). New York.

Kagan, J. (1989). *Unstable ideas: Temperament, cognition, and self.* Cambridge, MA: Harvard University Press.

Kagan, J. (1992). Yesterday's premises, tomorrow's promises. *Developmental Psychology, 28,* 990–997.

Kagan, J., & Snidman, N. (1991). Temperamental factors in human development. *American Psychologist, 46,* 856–862.

Kagan, J., Kearsley, R. B., & Zelazo, P. R. (1978). *Infancy.* Cambridge, MA: Harvard University Press.

Kagan, S. L. (1988, January). Current reforms in early childhood education. Are we addressing the issues? *Young Children, 43,* 27–38.

Kagitcibasi, C. (1988). Diversity of socialization and social change. In P. R. Dasen, J. W. Berry, & N. Sartorius (Eds.), *Health and cross-cultural psychology: Toward applications.* Newbury Park, CA: Sage.

Kagitcibasi, C., & Berry, J. W. (1989). Cross-cultural psychology: Current research and trends. *Annual Review of Psychology, 40,* Palo Alto, CA: Annual Reviews.

Kail, R. (1993, March). *The nature of global developmental change in processing time.* Paper presented at the biennial meeting of the Society for Research in Child Development, New Orleans.

Kail, R., & Pellegrino, J. W. (1985). *Human intelligence.* New York: W. H. Freeman.

Kamerman, S. B. (1989). Child care, women, work, and the family: An international overview of child care services and related policies. In J. S. Lande, S. Scarr, & N. Gunzenhauser (Eds.), *Caring for children: Challenge to America.* Hillsdale, NJ: Erlbaum.

Kamerman, S. B., & Kahn, A. J. (1988). Social policy and children in the United States and Europe. In J. L. Palmer, T. Smeeding, & B. B. Torrey (Eds.), *The vulnerable: America's young and old in the industrialized world.* Washington, DC: Urban Institute.

Kamerman, S. B., & Kahn, A. J. (Eds.). (1978). *Family policy: Government and families in fourteen countries.* New York: Columbia University Press.

Kandel, D. B. (1974). The role of parents and peers in marijuana use. *Journal of Social Issues, 30,* 107–135.

Kandel, D. B. (1991). Drug use, epidemiology and developmental stages of involvement. In R. M. Lerner, A. C. Petersen, & J. Brooks-Gunn (Eds.), *Encyclopedia of adolescence* (Vol. 1). New York: Garland.

Kantrowitz, B., & Wingert, P. (1989, April 17). How kids learn. *Newsweek,* pp. 4–10.

Karlin, R., & Karlin, A. R. (1987). *Teaching elementary reading.* San Diego: Harcourt Brace Jovanovich.

Katz, L., & Chard, S. (1989). *Engaging the minds of young children: The project approach.* Norwood, NJ: Ablex.

Katz, P. A. (1987, August). *Children and social issues.* Paper presented at the meeting of the American Psychological Association, New York.

Kaufman, A. S., & Kaufman, N. L. (1983). *Kaufman Assessment Battery for Children.* Circle Pines, MN: American Guidance Service.

Kaufmann, A. S., & Flaitz, J. (1987). Intellectual growth. In V. B. Van Hasselt & M. Hersen (Eds.), *Handbook of adolescent psychology.* New York: Pergamon.

Kavanaugh, K. H., & Kennedy, P. H. (1992). *Promoting cultural diversity.* Newbury Park, CA: Sage.

Kaye, K. (1993, March). *Cross-modal matching in human newborns.* Paper presented at the biennial meeting of the Society for Research in Child Development, New Orleans.

Keating, D. P. (1990). Structuralism, deconstruction, reconstruction: The limits of reasoning. In W. F. Overton (Ed.), *Reasoning, necessity, and logic: Developmental perspectives.* Hillsdale, NJ: Erlbaum.

Keefe, S. E., & Padilla, A. M. (1987). *Chicano ethnicity.* Albuquerque: University of New Mexico Press.

Keeney, T. J., Cannizzo, S. R., & Flavell, J. H. (1967). Spontaneous and induced verbal rehearsal in a recall task. *Child Development, 38,* 953–966.

Keirouz, K. S. (1990). Concerns of parents of gifted children: A research review. *Gifted Child Quarterly, 34,* 56–62.

Keller, A., Ford, L., & Meacham, J. (1978). Dimensions of self-concept in preschool children. *Developmental Psychology, 14,* 483–489.

Kelley, M. L., & Berndt, A. (1993, March). *Children's moral judgments: Relations with maternal childrearing variables.* Paper presented at the biennial meeting of the Society for Research in Child Development, New Orleans.

Kelly, J. A., & de Armas, A. (1989). Social relationships in adolescence: Skill development and training. In J. Worell & F. Danner (Eds.), *The adolescent as decision-maker.* San Diego: Academic Press.

Kennedy, J. H. (1990). Determinants of peer social status: Contributions of physical appearance, reputation, and behavior. *Journal of Youth and Adolescence, 19,* 233–244.

Kennedy, R. E. (1991). Delinquency. In R. M. Lerner, A. C. Petersen, & J. Brooks-Gunn (Eds.), *Encyclopedia of adolescence* (Vol. 2). New York: Garland.

Kerr, B. A. (1983). Raising the career aspirations of gifted girls. *Vocational Guidance Quarterly, 32,* 37–43.

Kessen, W., Haith, M. M., & Salapatek, P. (1970). Human infancy. In P. H. Mussen (Ed.), *Manual of child psychology* (3rd ed., Vol. 1). New York: Wiley.

Kilpatrick, A. C. (1992). *Long-range effects of childhood and adolescent sexual experiences: Myths, mores, and menaces.* Hillsdale, NJ: Erlbaum.

King, N. (1982). School uses of material traditionally associated with children's play. *Theory and research in social education, 10,* 17–27.

Kinsey, A. C., Pomeroy, W. B., & Martin, E. E. (1948). *Sexual behavior in the human male.* Philadelphia: W. B. Saunders.

Klaus, M., & Kennell, H. H. (1976). *Maternal-infant bonding.* St. Louis: Mosby.

Klein, K. (1985, April). The research on class size. *Phi Delta Kappan,* pp. 578–580.

Klein, S. S. (1988). Using sex equity research to improve education policies. *Theory into Practice, 27,* 152–160.

Kline, M., Tschann, J. M., Johnston, J. R., & Wallerstein, J. S. (1989). Children's adjustment in joint and sole physical custody families. *Developmental Psychology, 24,* 430–438.

Knouse, S. B. (1992). Hispanics and work: An overview. In S. B. Knouse, R. Rosenfeld, & A. Culbertson (Eds.), *Hispanics in the workplace.* Newbury Park, CA: Sage.

Kobak, R. (1992, March). *Autonomy as self-regulation: An attachment perspective.* Paper presented at the meeting of the Society for Research on Adolescence, Washington, DC.

Kobak, R., & Cole, H. (in press). Attachment and meta-monitoring: Implications for adolescent autonomy and psychopathology. In D. Cicchetti (Ed.), *Development and psychopathology* (Vol. 5). Rochester, NY: University of Rochester Press.

Kobak, R., Ferenz-Gillies, R., Everhart, E., & Seabrook, L. (1992, March). *Maternal attachment strategies and autonomy among adolescent offspring.* Paper presented at the meeting of the Society for Research on Adolescence, Washington, DC.

Kobak, R. R., Cole, H. E., Ferenz-Gillies, R., & Fleming, W. S. (1993). Attachment and emotional regulation during mother-teen problem-solving: A control theory analysis. *Child Development, 64,* 231–245.

Koff, E., & Riordan, J. (1991). Menarche and body image. In R. M. Lerner, A. C. Petersen, & J. Brooks-Gunn (Eds.), *Encyclopedia of adolescence* (Vol. II). New York: Garland.

Kohlberg, L. (1958). *The development of modes of moral thinking and choice in the years 10 to 16.* Unpublished doctoral dissertation. University of Chicago.

Kohlberg, L. (1966). A cognitive-developmental analysis of children's sex-role concepts and attitudes. In E. E. Maccoby (Ed.), *The development of sex differences.* Palo Alto, CA: Stanford University Press.

Kohlberg, L. (1969). Stage and sequence: The cognitive-developmental approach to socialization. In D. A. Goslin (Ed.), *Handbook of socialization theory and research.* Chicago: Rand McNally.

Kohlberg, L. (1976). Moral stages and moralization: The cognitive-developmental approach. In T. Lickona (Ed.), *Moral development and behavior.* New York: Holt, Rinehart & Winston.

Kohlberg, L. (1981). *The philosophy of moral development.* New York: Harper & Row.

Kohlberg, L. (1986). A current statement on some theoretical issues. In S. Modgil & C. Modgil (Eds.), *Lawrence Kohlberg.* Philadelphia: Falmer.

Kohlberg, L., & Candee, D. (1979). *Relationships between moral judgment and moral action.* Unpublished manuscript, Harvard University.

Kohn, M. L. (1977). *Class and conformity: A study in values* (2nd ed.). Chicago: University of Chicago Press.

Kontos, S., & Dunn, L. (1993, March). *Children's cognitive and social competence in center and family day care.* Paper presented at the biennial meeting of the Society for Research in Child Development, New Orleans.

Kopp, C. B. (1983). Risk factors in development. In P. H. Mussen (Ed.), *Handbook of child psychology* (4th ed., Vol. 2). New York: Wiley.

Kopp, C. B. (1992, October). *Trends and directions in studies of developmental risk.* Paper presented at the 27th Minnesota Symposium on Child Psychology, University of Minnesota, Minneapolis, MN.

Kopp, C. B., & Kaler, S. R. (1989). Risk in infancy: Origins and implications. *American Psychologist, 44,* 224–230.

Korner, A. F. (1971). Individual differences at birth: Implications for early experience and later development. *American Journal of Orthopsychiatry, 41,* 608–619.

Kostelnik, M. J., Whiren, A. P., & Stein, L. C. (1988). Living with He-Man: Managing superhero fantasy play. *Young Children, 41,* 3–9.

Krauss, R. A., & Glucksberg, S. (1969). The development of communication: Competence as a function of age. *Child Development, 40,* 255–266.

Kroger, J. (1992). Intrapsychic dimensions of identity during late adolescence. In G. R. Adams, T. P. Gullotta, & R. Montemayor (Eds.), *Adolescent identity formation.* Newbury Park, CA: Sage.

Kuebli, J., & Fivush, R. (1993, March). *Children's developing understanding of emotion and mind.* Paper presented at the biennial meeting of the Society for Research in Child Development, New Orleans.

Kuhn, D. (1991). Education for thinking: What can psychology contribute? In M. Schwebel, C. A. Maher, & N. S. Fagley (Eds.), *Promoting cognitive growth over the life span.* Hillsdale, NJ: Erlbaum.

Kuhn, D. (1993, March). *Missing links in the education equation.* Paper presented at the biennial meeting of the Society for Research in Child Development, New Orleans.

Kulcsar, E. N., Harbaugh, S. A., & Gelfand, D. M. (1993, March). *Maternal depression as a correlate of toddler interpersonal engagement.* Paper presented at the biennial meeting of the Society for Research in Child Development, New Orleans.

Kulin, H. E. (1991). Puberty, hypothalamic-pituitary changes of. In R. M. Lerner, A. C. Petersen, & J. Brooks-Gunn (Eds.), *Encyclopedia of adolescence* (Vol. II). New York: Garland.

Kupersmidt, J. B., & Cole, J. D. (1990). Preadolescent peer status, aggression, and school adjustment as predictors of externalizing problems in adolescence. *Child Development, 61,* 1350–1363.

Kupersmidt, J. B., & Patterson, C. (1993, March). *Developmental patterns of peer relations and aggression in the prediction of externalizing behavior problems.* Paper presented at the biennial meeting of the Society for Research in Child Development, New Orleans.

Kupersmidt, J. B., Burchinal, M. R., Leff, S. S. & Patterson, C. J. (1992, March). *A longitudinal study of perceived support and conflict with parents from middle childhood through early adolescence.* Paper presented at the meeting of the Society for Research on Adolescence, Washington, DC.

Kurdek, L. A., & Krile, D. (1982). A developmental analysis of the relation between peer acceptance and both interpersonal understanding and perceived social self-competence. *Child Development, 53,* 1485–1491.

Kurtines, W. M., & Gewirtz, J. (Eds.). (1991). *Moral behavior and development: Advances in theory, research, and application.* Hillsdale, NJ: Erlbaum.

L

Labouvie-Vief, G. (1982). Dynamic development and mature autonomy: A theoretical prologue. *Human Development, 25,* 161–191.

Labouvie-Vief, G. (1986, August). *Modes of knowing and life-span cognition.* Paper presented at the annual meeting of the American Psychological Association, Washington, DC.

Ladd, G., & Hart, C. H. (1992). Creating informal play opportunities: Are parents' and preschoolers' initiations related to children's competence with peers? *Developmental Psychology, 28,* 1179–1187.

Ladd, G. W. (1990). Having friends, keeping friends, making friends, and being liked by peers in the classroom: Predictors of children's early school adjustment. *Child Development, 61,* 1081–1100.

LaFromboise, T. D. (1993). American Indian mental health policy. In D. R. Atkinson, G. Morten, & D. W. Sue (Eds.), *Counseling American minorities.* Madison, WI: WCB Brown & Benchmark.

LaFromboise, T. D., & Low, K. G. (1989). American Indian children and adolescents. In J. T. Gibbs & L. N. Huang (Eds.), *Children of color.* San Francisco: Jossey-Bass.

LaFromboise, T. D., Trimble, J. E., & Mohatt, G. (1993). Counseling intervention and American Indian tradition: An integrative approach. In D. R. Atkinson, G. Morten, & D. W. Sue (Eds.), *Counseling American minorities.* Madison, WI: WCB Brown & Benchmark.

Lally, J. R., Mangione, P., & Honig, S. (1987). *The Syracuse University family development research program.* Unpublished manuscript, Syracuse University, Syracuse, NY.

Lamb, M. E. (1986). *The father's role: Applied perspectives.* New York: Wiley.

Lamb, M. E. (Ed.). (1986). *The father's role: Applied perspectives.* New York: Wiley.

Lamb, M. E. (1977). The development of mother-infant and father-infant attachments in the second year of life. *Developmental Psychology, 13,* 637–648.

Lamb, M. E., & Sternberg, K. J. (1992). Sociocultural perspectives on nonparental child care. In M. E. Lamb, K. J. Sternberg, C. Hwang, & A. G. Broberg (Eds.), *Child Care in Context.* Hillsdale, NJ: Erlbaum.

Lamb, M. E., Frodi, A. M., Hwang, C. P., Frodi, M., & Steinberg, J. (1982). Mother- and father-infant interaction involving play and holding in traditional and nontraditional Swedish families. *Developmental Psychology, 18,* 215–221.

Landesman-Dwyer, S., & Sackett, G. P. (1983, April). *Prenatal nicotine exposure and sleep-wake patterns in infancy.* Paper presented at the biennial meeting of the Society for Research in Child Development, Detroit.

Lane, H. (1976). *The wild boy of Aveyron.* Cambridge, MA: Harvard University Press.

Lang, E., & Rivera, J. (1987). In Harlem: Millionaire's promise still inspires. *New York Times,* June 20, 53.

Langlois, S. (1992). Genetic diagnosis based on molecular analysis. *Pediatric Clinics of North America, 39,* 91–110.

Lapsley, D. K. (1989a). The adolescent egocentrism theory and the "new look" at the imaginary audience and personal fable. In R. M. Lerner, A. C. Petersen, & J. Brooks-Gunn (Eds.), *The encyclopedia of adolescence*. New York: Garland.

Lapsley, D. K. (1989b). Continuity and discontinuity in adolescent social cognitive development. In R. Montemayor, G. Adams, & T. Gullota (Eds.), *Advances in adolescence research* (Vol. 2). Orlando, FL: Academic Press.

Lapsley, D. K. (1992, April). *Moral psychology after Kohlberg*. Paper presented at the meeting of the Midwestern Psychological Association, Chicago.

Lapsley, D. K., & Murphy, M. N. (1985). Another look at the theoretical assumptions of adolescent egocentrism. *Developmental Review, 5,* 201–217.

Lapsley, D. K., & Power, F. C. (Eds.). (1988). *Self, ego, and identity.* New York: Springer-Verlag.

Lapsley, D. K., & Quintana, S. M. (1985). Recent approaches in children's elementary moral and social education. *Elementary School Guidance and Counseling Journal, 19,* 246–251.

LaVoie, J. (1976). Ego identity formation in middle adolescence. *Journal of Youth and Adolescence, 5,* 371–385.

Lawton, T. A., Turner, J. C., & Paris, S. G. (1991, April). *Comprehension and metacognition of beginning readers*. Paper presented at the Society for Research in Child Development meeting, Seattle.

Lay, K., Waters, E., & Park, K. A. (1989). Maternal responsiveness and child compliance: The role of mood as a mediator. *Child Development, 60,* 1405–1411.

Lazar, I., & Darlington, R. (1982). Lasting effects of early education: A report from the consortium for longitudinal studies. *Monographs of the Society for Research in Child Development, 47* (2–3, Serial No. 195).

Lazar, L., Darlington, R., & Collaborators. (1982). Lasting effects of early education: A report from the consortium for longitudinal studies. *Monographs of the Society for Research in Child Development, 47.*

Lazarus, R. S. (1966). *Psychological stress and the coping process.* New York: McGraw-Hill.

Lazarus, R. S. (1990, August). *Progress on a cognitive-motivational-relational theory of emotion.* Paper presented at the meeting of the American Psychological Association, Boston, MA.

Leach, P. (1990). *Your baby and child* (2nd ed.). New York: Knopf.

Leboyer, F. (1975). *Birth without violence.* New York: Knopf.

Lee, G. R. (1978). Marriage and morale in late life. *Journal of Marriage and the Family, 40,* 131–139.

Lee, L. C. (1992, August). *The search for universals: Whatever happened to race?* Paper presented at the meeting of the American Psychological Association, Washington, DC.

Lee, V. E., Brooks-Gunn, J., & Schnur, E. (1988). Does Head Start Work? A 1-year follow-up comparison of disadvantaged children attending Head Start, no preschool and other preschool programs. *Developmental Psychology, 24,* 210–222.

Lehrer, R. (1992). Authors of knowledge: Patterns of hypermedia design. In S. Lajoie and S. Derry (Eds.), *Computers as cognitive tools.* Hillsdale, NJ: Erlbaum.

Lehrer, R., & Littlefield, J. (1991). Misconceptions and errors in LOGO: The role of instruction. *Journal of Educational Psychology, 83,* 124–133.

Lehrer, R., Erickson, J., Love, M., & Connell, T. (in press). Learning by designing hypermedia documents. *Computers in the schools, 9,* (2/3).

Leiffer, A. D. (1973). *Television and the development of social behavior.* Paper presented at the meeting of the International Society for the Study of Behavioral Development, Ann Arbor, MI.

Leiffer, A. D., Gordon, N. J., & Graves, S. B. (1974). Children's television: More than entertainment. *Harvard Educational Review, 44,* 213–245.

Leitenberg, H. (1986). Primary prevention in delinquency. In J. Burchard & S. Burchard (Eds.), *Prevention of delinquent behavior.* Newbury Park, CA: Sage.

LeMare, L. J., & Rubin, K. H. (1987). Perspective taking and peer interaction: Structural and developmental analyses. *Child Development, 58,* 306–315.

Lempers, J. D., & Clark-Lempers, D. S. (1993, March). *Adolescents' perceptions of their same-sex and opposite-sex friends: A longitudinal look.* Paper presented at the biennial meeting of the Society for Research in Child Development, New Orleans.

Lempers, J. D., Flavell, E. R., & Flavell, J. H. (1977). The development in very young children of tacit knowledge concerning visual perception. *Genetic Psychology Monographs, 95,* 3–53.

Lenneberg, E. H., Rebelsky, F. G., & Nichols, I. A. (1965). The vocalization of infants born to deaf and hearing parents. *Human Development, 8,* 23–37.

Leonoff, D. J. (1993, March). *Parental and peer factors in adolescent academic underachievement.* Paper presented at the biennial meeting of the Society for Research in Child Development, New Orleans.

Lepper, M. R. (1985). Microcomputers in education: Motivational and social issues. *American Psychologist, 40,* 1–18.

Lepper, M. R., & Gurtner, J. (1989). Children and computers: Approaching the twenty-first century. *American Psychologist, 44,* 170–178.

Lerner, H. G. (1989). *The dance of intimacy.* New York: Harper & Row.

Lerner, J. W. (1988). *Learning disabilities.* Boston, MA: Houghton Mifflin.

Lerner, R. M. (1991). Changing organism-context relations as the basic process of development: A developmental-contextual perspective. *Developmental Psychology, 27,* 27–32.

Lerner, R. M., & Karabenick, S. A. (1974). Physical attractiveness, body attitudes, and self-concept in late adolescence. *Journal of Youth and Adolescence, 3,* 307–316.

Lerner, R. M., Petersen, A. C., & Brooks-Gunn, J. (Eds.). (1991). *Encyclopedia of adolescence.* New York: Garland.

Lesser, G., Fifer, G., & Clark, D. (1965). Mental abilities of children from different social classes and cultural groups. *Monographs of the Society for Research in Child Development, 30* (4, Whole No. 102).

Lester, B. M. (1991, April). *Neurobehavioral syndromes in cocaine-exposed newborn infants.* Paper presented at the biennial meeting of the Society for Research in Child Development, Seattle.

Lester, B. M., & Tronick, E. Z. (1990a). Introduction. In B. M. Lester & E. Z. Tronick (Eds), *Stimulation and the preterm infant: The limits of plasticity.* Philadelphia: W. B. Saunders.

Lester, B. M., & Tronick, E. Z. (1990b). Preface. In B. M. Lester & E. Z. Tronick (Eds.), *Stimulation and the preterm infant: The limits of plasticity.* Philadelphia: W. B. Saunders.

Leukefeld, C. G., & Haverkos, H. W. (1993). Sexually transmitted diseases. In T. P. Gullotta, G. R. Adams, & R. Montemayor (Eds.), *Adolescent sexuality.* Newbury Park, CA: Sage.

Levin, J. (1980). *The mnemonic '80s: Keywords in the classroom.* Theoretical paper No. 86. Wisconsin Research and Development Center for Individualized Schooling, Madison.

Levy, A. B., Dixon, K. N., & Stern, S. L. (1989). How are depression and bulimia related? *American Journal of Psychiatry, 146,* 162–169.

Levy, G. D. (1991, April). *Effects of gender constancy, figure's sex and size on preschoolers' gender constancy: Sometimes big girls do cry.* Paper presented at the Society for Research in Child Development meeting, Seattle.

Levy, G. D., & Carter, D. B. (1989). Gender schema, gender constancy, and gender-role knowledge: The roles of cognitive factors in preschoolers' gender-role stereotype attributions. *Developmental Psychology, 25,* 444–449.

Levy, G. D., & Katz, P. A. (1993, March). *Differences in preschoolers' race schemas: Relations among schematization, race-based peer preferences, and memory for race-based stereotyped portrayals.* Paper presented at the biennial meeting of the Society for Research in Child Development, New Orleans.

Lewinsohn, P. M., Seeley, J. R., Rohde, P., Gotlib, I. H., & Hops, H. (1993). *Adolescent depression: II. Psychosocial risk factors.* Unpublished manuscript, Oregon Research Institute, University of Oregon, Eugene, OR.

Lewis, M., & Brooks-Gunn, J. (1979). *Social cognition and the acquisition of the self.* New York: Plenum.

Lewis, M., Sullivan, M. W., Sanger, C., & Weiss, M. (1989). Self-development and self-conscious emotions. *Child Development, 60,* 146–156.

Lewkowicz, D. J. (1988). Sensory dominance in infants: 1. Six-month-old infants' response to auditory-visual compounds. *Developmental Psychology, 24,* 155–171.

Lewkowicz, D. J. (1993, March). *The development of temporally based intersensory perception in human infants.* Paper presented at the biennial meeting of the Society for Research in Child Development, New Orleans.

Liaw, F. (1993, March). *Cumulative risks and early intervention in the context of poverty: The infant health and development program.* Paper presented at the biennial meeting of the Society for Research in Child Development, New Orleans.

Liaw, F., Meisels, S. J., & Brooks-Gunn, J. (1994). *Intervention with low birth weight, premature children: An examination of the experience of intervention.* Unpublished manuscript.

Liben, L. S., & Signorella, M. L. (1993). Gender-schematic processing in children: The role of initial presentation of stimuli. *Developmental Psychology, 29,* 141–149.

Liben, L. S., & Signorella, M. L. (Eds.). (1987). *Children's gender schemata: New directions in child development.* San Francisco: Jossey-Bass.

Liberg, C. (1990). "I am not guessing!": Children's achievement in early literacy. In G. Conti-Ramsden & C. E. Snow (Eds.), *Children's language* (Vol. 7). Hillsdale, NJ: Erlbaum.

Liebert, R. M., & Sprafkin, J. N. (1988). *The early window: Effects of television on children and youth* (3rd ed.). Elmsford, NY: Pergamon.

Lifshitz, F., Pugliese, M. T., Moses, N., & Weyman-Daum, M. (1987). Parental health beliefs as a cause of non-organic failure to thrive. *Pediatrics, 80,* 175–182.

Light, P., & Butterworth, G. (1993). (Eds.). *Context and cognition.* Hillsdale, NJ: Erlbaum.

Lightfoot, C. (1993, March). *Playing with desire.* Paper presented at the biennial meeting of the Society for Research in Child Development, New Orleans.

Linden, M. J., & Whimbey, A. (1990). *Why Johnny can't write: How to improve writing skills.* Hillsdale, NJ: Erlbaum.

Lindner, M. S. (1992, March). *When dad and mom and adolescent makes four: Adolescents' perceptions of relationships with three parents.* Paper presented at the meeting of the Society for Research on Adolescence, Washington, DC.

Linn, M. C., & Peterson, A. C. (1986). A meta-analysis of gender differences in spatial ability: Implications for mathematics and science achievement. In J. S. Hyde & M. C. Linn (Eds.), *The psychology of gender: Advances through meta-analysis.* Baltimore, MD: Johns Hopkins University Press.

Linney, J. A. (1993, March). *School transitions and youth at risk for substance abuse.* Paper presented at the biennial meeting of the Society for Research in Child Development, New Orleans.

Linney, J. A., & Seidman, E. (1989). The future of schooling. *American Psychologist, 44,* 336–340.

Lipsitt, L. P., Reilly, B. M., Butcher, M. J., & Greenwood, M. M. (1976). The stability and interrelations of newborn sucking and heart rate. *Developmental Psychology, 9,* 305–310.

Lipsitz, J. (1983, October). *Making it the hard way: Adolescents in the 1980s.* Testimony presented at the Crisis Intervention Task Force, House Select Committee on Children, Youth, and Families, Washington, DC.

Lipsitz, J. (1984). *Successful schools for young adolescents.* New Brunswick, NJ: Transaction.

Lipsky, D. K., & Gartner, A. (1989). *Beyond separate education.* Baltimore: Brooks.

Litt, I. F. (1991). Eating disorders, medical complications of. In R. M. Lerner, A. C. Petersen, & J. Brooks-Gunn (Eds.), *Encyclopedia of adolescence* (Vol. 1). New York: Garland.

Little, G. A. (1992). The fetus at risk. In R. A. Hoekelman, S. B. Friedman, N. M. Nelson, & H. M. Seidel (Eds.), *Primary pediatric care* (2nd ed.). St. Louis, MO: Mosby Yearbook.

Little, P. (in press). Homeless families in four cities: A multiple-site case study in policy formation. In F. H. Jacobs & M. Davies (Eds.), *Casebook in child and family policy.*

Lively, W., & Bromley, D. (1973). *Person perception in childhood and adolescence.* New York: Wiley.

Lock, A. (1991). The role of social interaction in early language development. In N. A. Krasnegor, D. M. Rumbaugh, M. Studdert-Kennedy, & R. L. Schiefelbusch (Eds.), *Biological and behavioral determinants of language development.* Hillsdale, NJ: Erlbaum.

Locke, J. L., Bekken, K. E., Wein, D., & Ruzecki, V. (1991, April). *Neuropsychology of babbling: Laterality effects in the production of rhythmic manual activity.* Paper presented at the Society for Research in Child Development meeting, Seattle.

Loehlin, J. C. (1992). *Genes and environment in personality development.* Newbury Park, CA: Sage.

Lollis, S. (1993, March). *The importance of context for mothers' interventions in children's peer interactions.* Paper presented at the biennial meeting of the Society for Research in Child Development, New Orleans.

Long, T., & Long, L. (1983). *Latchkey children.* New York: Penguin.

Longman, P. (1987). *Born to pay: The new politics of aging in America.* Boston: Houghton Mifflin.

Lonner, W. J. (1988). *The introductory psychology text and cross-cultural psychology. A survey of cross-cultural psychologists.* Bellingham, WA: Center for Cross-Cultural Research, Western Washington University.

Lonner, W. J. (1990). An overview of cross-cultural testing and assessment. In R. W. Brislin (Ed.), *Applied cross-cultural psychology.* Newbury Park, CA: Sage.

Lorenz, K. Z. (1965). *Evolution and the modification of behavior.* Chicago: University of Chicago Press.

Louv, R. (1990). *Childhood's future.* Boston, MA: Houghton Mifflin.

Lundman, R. (1984). *Prevention and control of juvenile delinquency.* New York: Oxford University Press.

Luria, A., & Herzog, E. (1985, April). *Gender segregation across and within settings.* Paper presented at the biennial meeting of the Society for Research in Child Development, Toronto.

Lyle, J., & Hoffman, H. R. (1972). Children's use of television and other media. In E. A. Rubenstein, G. A. Comstock, & J. P. Murray (Eds.), *Television and social behavior* (Vol. 4). Washington, DC: U.S. Government Printing Office.

Lynch, M. A., & Roberts, J. (1982). *The consequences of child abuse.* New York: Academic Press.

Lyons, J. M. (1991, April). *The influence of parental scaffolding on the development of coping skills in clinically distressed and nondistressed children.* Paper presented at the Society for Research in Child Development meeting, Seattle.

Lyons, J. M., & Barber, B. L. (1992, March). *Family environment effects on adolescent adjustment: Differences between intact and remarried families.* Paper presented at the meeting of the Society for Research on Adolescence, Washington, DC.

Lyons, N. P. (1983). Two perspectives: On self, relationships, and morality. *Harvard Educational Review, 53,* 125–145.

Lyons, N. P. (1990). Listening to voices we have not heard. In C. Gilligan, N. P. Lyons, & T. J. Hanmer (Eds.), *Making connections.* Cambridge, MA: Harvard University Press.

M

Mac Iver, D., Urdan, T., Beck, J., Midgley, C., Reuman, D., Tasko, A., Fenzel, L. M., Arhar, J., & Kramer, L. (1992, March). *Changing schools and classrooms in the middle grades: Research on new partnerships, processes, practices, and programs.* Paper presented at the meeting of the Society for Research on Adolescence, Washington, DC.

Maccoby, E. E. (1980). *Social development.* San Diego: Harcourt Brace Jovanovich.

Maccoby, E. E. (1984). Middle childhood in the context of the family. In *Development during middle childhood.* Washington, DC: National Academy Press.

Maccoby, E. E. (1987, November). (a) Interview with Elizabeth Hall: All in the family. *Psychology Today,* pp. 54–60.

Maccoby, E. E. (1987). The varied meanings of "masculine" and "feminine." In J. M. Reinisch, L. A. Rosenblum, & S. A. Sanders (Eds.), *Masculinity/femininity: Basic perspectives.* New York: Oxford University Press.

Maccoby, E. E. (1989, August). *Gender and relationships: A developmental account.* Paper presented at the meeting of the American Psychological Association, New Orleans.

Maccoby, E. E. (1991, April). Discussant, symposium on the development of gender and relationships. Symposium presented at the biennial meeting of the Society for Research in Child Development, Seattle.

Maccoby, E. E. (1992). The role of parents in the socialization of children: An historical overview. *Developmental Psychology, 28,* 1006–1018.

Maccoby, E. E. (1992). Trends in the study of socialization: Is there a Lewinian heritage? *Journal of Social Issues, 48,* 171–185.

Maccoby, E. E. (1993, March). *Trends and issues in the study of gender role development.* Paper presented at the biennial meeting of the Society for Research in Child Development, New Orleans.

Maccoby, E. E., & Jacklin, C. N. (1974). *The psychology of sex differences.* Palo Alto, CA: Stanford University Press.

Maccoby, E. E., & Martin, J. A. (1983). Socialization in the context of the family: Parent-child interaction. In P. H. Mussen (Ed.), *Handbook of child psychology* (4th ed., Vol. 4). New York: Wiley.

Maccoby, E. E., & Mnookin, R. H. (1993). *Dividing the child.* Cambridge, MA: Harvard University Press.

MacFarlane, J. A. (1975). Olfaction in the development of social preferences in the human neonate. In *Parent-infant interaction,* Ciba Foundation Symposium, 33. Amsterdam: Elsevier.

MacPhee, D., Fritz, J. J., & Miller-Heyl, J. (1993, March). *Ethnic variations in social support networks and child rearing.* Paper presented at the biennial meeting of the Society for Research in Child Development, New Orleans.

Maddux, J. E., Roberts, M. C., Sledden, E. A., & Wright, L. (1986). Developmental issues in child health psychology. *American Psychologist, 41,* 24–34.

Malcom, S. M. (1988). Technology in 2020: Educating a diverse population. In R. S. Nickerson & P. P. Zodhiates (Eds.), *Technology in education: Looking toward 2020.* Hillsdale, NJ: Erlbaum.

Malik, M. M. (1993, March). *Adolescent pregnancy in a rural Black community.* Paper presented at the biennial meeting of the Society for Research in Child Development, New Orleans.

Malina, R. M. (1991). Growth spurt, adolescent (II). In R. M. Lerner, A. C. Petersen, & J. Brooks-Gunn (Eds.), *Encyclopedia of adolescence* (Vol. I). New York: Garland.

Malinowski, B. (1927). *Sex and repression in savage society.* New York: Humanities Press.

Maltsberger, J. T. (1988). *Suicide risk.* New York: Human Services Press.

Mandell, C. J., & Mandell, S. L. (1989). *Computers in education today.* St. Paul, MN: West.

Mandler, J. M. (1990). A new perspective on cognitive development. *American Scientist, 78,* 236–243.

Mandler, J. M. (1992). The foundations of conceptual thought in infancy. *Cognitive Development, 7,* 273–285.

Mandler, J. M. (in press, a). How to build a baby II: Conceptual primitives. *Psychological Review.*

Mandler, J. M. (in press, b). The foundations of conceptual thought in infancy. *Cognitive Development.*

Mandler, J. M. (in press, b). The mind's eye or the hand's grasp? *Human Development.*

Maratsos, M. (1983). Some current issues in the study of the acquisition of grammar. In P. H. Mussen (Ed.), *Handbook of child psychology* (4th ed., Vol. 3). New York: Wiley.

Maratsos, M. P. (1989). Innateness and plasticity in language acquisition. In M. L. Rice & R. L. Schiefelbusch (Eds.), *The teachability of language.* Baltimore: Paul Brookes.

Marcia, J. E. (1966). Identity six years after: A follow-up study. *Journal of Youth and Adolescence, 5,* 145–160.

Marcia, J. E. (1980). Identity in adolescence. In J. Adelson (Ed.), *Handbook of adolescent psychology.* New York: Wiley.

Marcia, J. E. (1987). The identity status approach to the study of ego identity development. In T. Honess & K. Yardley (Eds.), *Self and identity: Perspectives across the lifespan.* London: Routledge & Kegan Paul.

Marcia, J. E. (1989). Identity and intervention. *Journal of Adolescence, 12,* 401–410.

Marcia, J. E. (1991). Identity and self-development. In R. M. Lerner, A. C. Petersen, & J. Brooks-Gunn (Eds.), *Encyclopedia of adolescence* (Vol. 1). New York: Garland.

Marcon, R. A. (1993, March). *Parental involvement and early school success following the 'class of 2000' at year five.* Paper presented at the biennial meeting of the Society for Research in Child Development, New Orleans.

Marieskind, H. I. (1989). Cesarean section in the United States: Has it changed since 1979? *Birth, 16,* 196–202.

Marín, G., & Marín, B. V. (1991). *Research with Hispanic populations.* Newbury Park, CA: Sage.

Markman, E. M. (1989). *Categorization and naming in children: Problems of induction.* Cambridge, MA: MIT Press.

Markus, H., & Nurius, P. (1986). Possible selves. *American Psychologist, 41,* 954–969.

Marquis, K. S., & Detweiler, R. A. (1985). Does adopted mean different? An attributional analysis. *Journal of Personality and Social Psychology, 48,* 1054–1066.

Martin, C. L. (1989, April). *Beyond knowledge-based conceptions of gender schematic processing.* Paper presented at the biennial meeting of the Society for Research in Child Development, Kansas City, MO.

Martin, C. L. (1993, March). *The influence of children's theories about groups on gender-based inferences.* Paper presented at the biennial meeting of the Society for Research in Child Development, New Orleans.

Martin, C. L., & Halverson, C. F. (1987). The role of cognition in sex role acquisition. In D. B. Carter (Ed.), *Current conceptions of sex roles and sex typing: Theory and research.* New York: Praeger.

Martin, C. L., & Rose, H. A. (1991, April). *Children's gender-based distinctive theories.* Paper presented at the Society for Research in Child Development, Seattle.

Martin, H. P. (1992). Child abuse and neglect. In R. A. Hoekleman, S. B. Friedman, N. M. Nelson, & H. M. Seidel (Eds.). *Primary pediatric care* (2nd ed.). St. Louis, Mosby Yearbook.

Martorano, S. (1977). A developmental analysis of performance on Piaget's formal operations tasks. *Developmental Psychology, 13,* 666–672.

Matas, L., Arend, R. A., & Sroufe, L. A. (1978). Continuity in adaptation: Quality of attachment and later competence. *Child Development, 49,* 547–556.

Matheny, A. P., Dolan, R. S., & Wilson, R. S. (1976). Relation between twins' similarity: Testing an assumption. *Behavior Genetics, 6,* 343–351.

Matlin, M. W. (1993). *The psychology of women* (2nd ed.). Fort Worth, TX: Harcourt Brace Jovanovich.

Mays, V. M. (1991, August). *Social policy implications of the definition of race.* Paper presented at the meeting of the American Psychological Association, San Francisco.

Mays, V. (1993, August). *Ethnic identification in the therapeutic process.* Paper presented at the meeting of the American Psychological Association, Toronto, CA.

McAdoo, H. P. (Ed.). (1988). *Black families.* Newbury Park, CA: Sage.

McAdoo, H. P. (Ed.) (1993). *Family ethnicity.* Newbury Park, CA: Sage.

McAdoo, H. P., Luster, T., & Perkins, D. (1993, March). *Family factors related to success among African-American adults: A secondary analysis of the Perry Preschool data.* Paper presented at the biennial meeting of the Society for Research in Child Development, New Orleans.

McBride, A. B. (1990). Mental health effects of women's multiple roles. *American Psychologist, 45,* 381–384.

McBride, B. A. (1991, April). *Variations in father involvement with preschool-aged children.* Paper presented at the biennial meeting of the Society for Research in Child Development, Seattle.

McCall, R. B., Applebaum, M. I., & Hogarty, P. S. (1973). Developmental changes in mental performance. *Monographs of the Society for Research in Child Development, 38* (Serial No. 150).

McCandless, B. R., & Trotter, R. J. (1977). *Children* (3rd ed.). New York: Holt, Rinehart & Winston.

McCartney, K., Rocheleau, Rosenthal, S., & Keefe, N. (1993, March). *Social development in the context of center-based child care and family factors.* Paper presented at the biennial meeting of the Society for Research in Child Development, New Orleans.

McCord, J. (1990). Problem behaviors. In S. S. Feldman & G. R. Elliott (Eds.), *At the threshold: The developing adolescent.* Cambridge, MA: Harvard University Press.

McDaniel, M. A., & Pressley, M. (1987). *Imagery and related mnemonic process.* New York: Springer-Verlag.

McFadyen-Ketchum, S. A. (1993, March). *Learning to interact competently with peers: The contribution of mother-child conversations at home.* Paper presented at the biennial meeting of the Society for Research in Child Development, New Orleans.

McGhee, P. E. (1984). Play, incongruity, and humor. In T. Yawkey & A. D. Pellegrini (Eds.), *Child's play: Developmental and applied.* Hillsdale, NJ: Erlbaum.

McGoldrick, M. (1989). The joining of families together through marriage. In B. Carter & M. McGoldrick (Eds.), *The changing family life cycle* (2nd ed.). Boston: Allyn & Bacon.

McKey, R. H., Condelli, L., Ganson, H., Barrett, B. J., McConkey, C., & Plantz, M. C. (1985). *The impact of Head Start on children, family, and communities: Head Start Synthesis Project.* DHHS Publication No. (ODHS) 85–31193. Washington, DC: U.S. Government Printing Office.

McKnight, C. C., Crosswhite, F. J., Dossey, J. A., Kifer, E., Swafford, J. O., Travers, K. J., & Cooney, T. J. (1987). *The underachieving curriculum: Assessing U.S. school mathematics from an international perspective.* Champaign, IL: Stipes.

McLellan, J. A., Haynie, D., & Strouse, D. (1993, March). *Membership in high school crowd clusters and relationships with family and friends.* Paper presented at the biennial meeting of the Society for Research in Child Development, New Orleans.

McLloyd, V. (1993, March). *Direct and indirect effects of economic hardship on socioemotional functioning in African-American adolescents.* Paper presented at the biennial meeting of the Society for Research in Child Development, New Orleans.

McLoyd, V. (in press). The declining fortunes of Black children: Psychological distress, parenting, and socioeconomic development in the context of economic hardship. *Child Development.*

McLoyd, V. C. (1982). Social class differences in sociodramatic play: A critical review. *Developmental Review, 2,* 1–30.

McLoyd, V. C. (1990). Minority children: An introduction to the special issue. *Child Development, 61,* 263–266.

McLoyd, V. C. (1993, March). *Sizing up the future: Economic stress, expectations, and adolescents' achievement motivation.* Paper presented at the biennial meeting of the Society for Research in Child Development, New Orleans.

McMahon, R. J., & Bierman, K. L. (1993, March). *The fast track clinical model for the prevention of conduct problems.* Paper presented at the biennial meeting of the Society for Research in Child Development, New Orleans.

McPartland, J. M., & McDill, E. L. (1976). *The unique role of schools in the causes of youthful crime.* Baltimore: Johns Hopkins University Press.

McPeck, J. E. (1990). Critical thinking and subject specificity: A reply to Ennis. *Educational Leadership, 19,* 10–12.

McWhirter, D. P., Reinisch, J. M., & Sanders, S. A. (1990). *Homosexuality/heterosexuality.* New York: Oxford University Press.

Mead, M. (1978, Dec. 30–Jan. 5). The American family: An endangered species. *TV Guide.*

Mednick, B. R., Baker, R. L., & Carothers, L. E. (1990). Patterns of family instability and crime: The association of timing of the family's disruption on subsequent adolescent and young adult criminality. *Journal of Youth and Adolescence, 19,* 201–219.

Meehl, P. (1990). Why summaries of research on a psychological theory are often uninterpretable. In R. E. Snow & D. E. Wiley (Eds.), *Improving inquiry in social science.* Hillsdale, NJ: Erlbaum.

Mehegany, D. V. (1992). The relation of temperament and behavior disorders in a preschool clinical sample. *Child Psychiatry and Human Development, 22,* 129–136.

Meichenbaum, D. H., & Goodman, J. (1971). Training impulsive children to talk to themselves: A means of developing self-control. *Journal of Abnormal Psychology, 77,* 115–126.

Meltzoff, A. N. (1988). Infant imitation and memory: Nine-month-old infants in immediate and deferred tests. *Child Development, 59,* 217–225.

Meltzoff, A. N. (1990, June). *Infant imitation.* Invited address at the University of Texas at Dallas.

Mensh, E., & Mensh, H. (1991). *The IQ mythology.* Carbondale, IL: Southern Illinois University Press.

Mercer, J. R., & Lewis, J. F. (1978). *System of multicultural pluralistic assessment.* New York: Psychological Corporation.

Meredith, H. V. (1978). Research between 1960 and 1970 on the standing height of young children in different parts of the world. In H. W. Reece & L. P. Lipsitt (Eds.), *Advances in child development and behavior* (Vol. 12). New York: Academic Press.

Metz, K. E. (1991, April). *Reflection on the methodology of microgenetic analysis: View from a study of novices learning physics.* Paper presented at the Society for Research in Child Development meeting, Seattle.

Michel, G. L. (1981). Right-handedness: A consequence of infant supine head-orientation preference? *Science, 212,* 685–687.

Miller, B. C., Christopherson, C. R., & King, P. K. (1993). Sexual behavior in adolescence. In T. P. Gullotta, G. R. Adams, & R. Montemayor (Eds.), *Adolescent sexuality.* Newbury Park, CA: Sage.

Miller, C. A. (1987). A review of maternity care programs in Western Europe. *Family Planning Perspectives, 19,* 207–211.

Miller, G. A. (1956). The magical number seven, plus or minus two: Some limits on our capacity for information processing. *Psychological Review, 63,* 81–97.

Miller, G. A. (1981). *Language and speech.* New York: W. H. Freeman.

Miller, J. B. (1976). *Toward a new psychology of women.* Boston: Beacon.

Miller, J. B. (1986). *Toward a new psychology of women* (2nd ed.). Boston: Beacon.

Miller, J. G. (1991). A cultural perspective on the morality of beneficience and interpersonal responsibility. In S. Ting-Toomey & F. Korzenny (Eds.), *International and intercultural communication annual, 15.* Newbury Park, CA: Sage.

Miller, J. G., & Bersoff, D. M. (1993, March). *Culture and affective closeness in the morality of caring.* Paper presented at the biennial meeting of the Society for Research in Child Development, New Orleans.

Miller, J. G., & Bersoff, D. M. (in press). Culture and moral judgment: How are conflicts between justice and interpersonal responsibilities resolved? *Journal of Personality and Social Psychology.*

Miller, M. E. (1992). Genetic disease. In R. A. Hoekelman (Ed.), *Primary pediatric care* (2nd ed.). St. Louis, MO: Mosby Yearbook.

Miller, P. A., Kliewer, W., & Burkeman, D. (1993, March). *Effects of maternal socialization on children's learning to cope with divorce.* Paper presented at the biennial meeting of the Society for Research in Child Development, New Orleans.

Miller, W. B. (1958). Lower-class culture as a generating milieu of gang delinquency. *Journal of Social Issues, 14,* 5–19.

Miller-Jones, D. (1989). Culture and testing. *American Psychologist, 44,* 360–366.

Minnett, A. M., Vandell, D. L., & Santrock, J. W. (1983). The effects of sibling status on sibling interaction: Influence of birth order, age spacing, sex of the child, and sex of the sibling. *Child Development, 54,* 1064–1072.

Minuchin, P. P., & Shapiro, E. K. (1983). The school as a context for social development. In P. H. Mussen (Ed.), *Handbook of child psychology* (4th ed., Vol. 4). New York: Wiley.

Mischel, W. (1970). Sex-typing and socialization. In P. H. Mussen (Ed.), *Manual of child psychology* (Vol. 2, 3rd ed.). New York: Wiley.

Mischel, W. (1973). Toward a cognitive social learning reconceptualization of personality. *Psychological Review, 80,* 252–283.

Mischel, W. (1974). Process in delay of gratification. In L. Berkowitz (Ed.), *Advances in experimental social psychology* (Vol. 7). New York: Academic Press.

Mischel, W. (1984). Convergences and challenges in the search for consistency. *American Psychologist, 39,* 351–364.

Mischel, W. (1987). *Personality* (4th ed.). New York: Holt, Rinehart & Winston.

Mischel, W. (1993, August). *Incorporating the psychological situation into theory and assessment of personality.* Paper presented at the meeting of the American Psychological Association, Toronto, CA.

Mischel, W., & Mischel, H. (1975, April). *A cognitive social-learning analysis of moral development.* Paper presented at the Society for Research in Child Development meeting, Denver.

Mischel, W., & Patterson, C. J. (1976). Substantive and structural elements of effective plans for self-control. *Journal of Social and Personality Psychology, 34,* 942–950.

Mize, J., Pettit, G. S., Laird, R. D., & Lindsey, E. (1993, March). *Mothers' coaching of social skills and children's peer competence: Independent contributions of content and style.* Paper presented at the biennial meeting of the Society for Research in Child Development, New Orleans.

Moely, B. E., Olson, F. A., Halwes, T. G., & Flavell, J. H. (1969). Production deficiency in young children's clustered recall. *Developmental Psychology, 1,* 26–34.

Moll, I. (1991, April). *The material and the social in Vygotsky's theory of cognitive development.* Paper presented at the Society for Research in Child Development meeting, Seattle.

Money, J. (1987). Sin, sickness, or status? Homosexual gender identity and psychoneuroendocrinology. *American Psychologist, 42,* 384–399.

Montemayor, R. (1982). The relationship between parent-adolescent conflict and the amount of time adolescents spend with parents, peers, and alone. *Child Development, 53,* 1512–1519.

Montemayor, R., Adams, G. R., & Gullotta, T. P. (Eds.). (1990). *From childhood to adolescence: A transitional period?* Newbury Park, CA: Sage.

Morelli, G. A., Rogoff, B., & Angelillo, C. (1992). *Cultural variation in young children's opportunities for involvement in adult activities.* Poster presented at the meeting of the American Anthropological Association, San Francisco.

Morrison, D. M. (1985). Adolescent contraceptive behavior: A review. *Psychological Bulletin, 98,* 538–568.

Morrongiello, B. A., Fenwick, K. D., & Chance, G. (1990). Sound localization acuity in very young infants: An observer-based testing procedure. *Developmental Psychology, 26,* 75–84.

Morrow, L. (1988, August 8). Through the eyes of children. *Time,* pp. 32–33.

Mortimer, E. A. (1992). Child health in the developing world. In R. E. Behrman, R. M. Kliegman, W. E. Nelson, & V. C. Vaughan (Eds.), *Nelson textbook of pediatrics* (14th ed.). Philadelphia, PA: W. B. Saunders.

Mott, F. L., & Marsiglio, W. (1985, September–October). Early childbearing and completion of high school. *Family Planning Perspectives,* p. 234.

Mounts, N. S. (1992, March). *An ecological analysis of peer influence on adolescent academic achievement and delinquency.* Paper presented at the meeting of the Society for Research on Adolescence, Washington, DC.

Muecke, L., Simons-Morton, B., Huang, I. W., & Parcel, G. (1992). Is childhood obesity associated with high-fat foods and low physical activity? *Journal of School Health, 62,* 19–23.

Mueller, E. (1985, April). *Early peer relations: Ten years of research.* Symposium presented at the Society for Research in Child Development meeting, Toronto.

Munroe, R. H., Himmin, H. S., & Munroe, R. L. (1984). Gender understanding and sex role preference in four cultures. *Developmental Psychology, 20,* 673–682.

Munroe, R. L., & Munroe, R. H. (1975). *Cross-cultural human development.* Monterey, CA: Brooks/Cole.

Munsch, J., Wampler, R. S., & Dawson, M. (1992, March). *Coping with school-related stress in multi-ethnic sample of early adolescents.* Paper presented at the meeting of the Society for Research on Adolescence, Washington, DC.

Murphy, K. C., Talley, J. A., & Huston, A. C. (1991, April). *Family ecology and young children's viewing of television designed for children.* Paper presented at the Society for Research in Child Development meeting, Seattle.

Murphy, S. O. (1993, March). *The family context and the transition to siblinghood: Strategies parents use to influence sibling-infant relationships.* Paper presented at the biennial meeting of the Society for Research in Child Development, New Orleans.

Myers, B. J., Olson, H. C., & Kaltenbach, K. (1992, August/September). Cocaine-exposed infants: Myths and misunderstandings. *Zero to Three, 13,* 1–5.

Myers, W. C., & Burket, R. C. (1992). Current perspectives on adolescent conduct disorder. *Adolescent Medicine, 3,* 61–70.

N

National Advisory Council on Economic Opportunity. (1980). *Critical choices for the 80s.* Washington, DC: U.S. Government Printing Office.

National Association for the Education of Young Children. (1986). *How to choose a good early childhood program.* Washington, DC: National Association for the Education of Young Children.

National Association for the Education of Young Children. (1988). NAEYC position statement on developmentally appropriate practices in the primary grades, serving 5- through 8-year-olds. *Young Children, 43,* 64–83.

National Association for the Education of Young Children. (1990). NAEYC position statement on school readiness. *Young Children, 46,* 21–28.

National Association for the Education of Young Children. (1991). Public policy report (101st Congress): The children's congress. *Young Children, 47,* 78–80.

National Research Council. (1987). *Risking the future: Adolescent sexuality, pregnancy, and childbearing.* Washington, DC: National Academy Press.

Needle, R. H., Su, S. S., & Doherty, W. J. (1990). Divorce, remarriage, and adolescent substance use: A prospective longitudinal study. *Journal of Marriage and the Family, 52,* 157–169.

Neimark, E. D. (1982). Adolescent thought: Transition to formal operations. In B. B. Wolman (Ed.), *Handbook of developmental psychology.* Englewood Cliffs, NJ: Prentice-Hall.

Neisser, U. (1982). *Memory observed.* New York: W. H. Freeman.

Nelson, N. M. (1992). Perinatal medicine. In R. B. Hoekelman, S. B. Friedman, N. M. Nelson, & H. M. Seidel (Eds.), *Primary pediatric care* (2nd ed.). St. Louis, MO: Mosby Yearbook.

Neugarten, B. L. (1988, August). *Policy issues for an aging society.* Paper presented at the meeting of the American Psychological Association, Atlanta.

Newcomb, M. D., & Bentler, P. M. (1988). Substance use and abuse among children and teenagers. *American Psychologist, 44,* 242–248.

Nickman, S. L. (1992). Adoption and foster care. In R. A. Hoekelman (Ed.), *Primary pediatric care* (2nd ed.). St. Louis, MO: Mosby Yearbook.

Ninio, A., & Bruner, J. (1978). The achievement and antecedent of labeling. *Journal of Child Language, 5,* 1–15.

Nishio, K., & Bilmes, M. (1993). Psychotherapy with Southeast Asian clients. In D. R. Atkinson, G. Morten, & D. W. Sue (Eds.), *Counseling American minorities.* Madison, WI: WCB Brown & Benchmark.

Nitz, V., & Lerner, J. V. (1991). Temperament during adolescence. In R. M. Lerner, A. C. Petersen, & J. Brooks-Gunn (Eds.), *Encyclopedia of adolescence* (Vol. 2). New York: Garland.

Nottelmann, E. D., Susman, E. J., Blue, J. H., Inoff-Germain, G., Dorn, L. D., Loriaux, D. L., Cutler, G. B., & Chrousos, G. P. (1987). Gonadal and adrenal hormone correlates of adjustment in early adolescence. In R. M. Lerner & T. T. Foch (Eds.), *Biological-psychological interactions in early adolescence.* Hillsdale, NJ: Erlbaum.

Novy, D. M., Gaa, J. P., Frankiewicz, R. G., Liberman, D., & Amerikaner, M. (1992). The association between patterns of family functioning and ego development of the juvenile offender. *Adolescence, 27,* 25–36.

Nucci, L., & Weber, E. K. (1991). The domain approach to values education: From theory to practice. In W. M. Kurtines & J. Gewirtz (Eds.), *Moral behavior and development* (Vol. 3). Hillsdale, NJ: Erlbaum.

Nydegger, C. N., & Mitteness, L. S. (1991). Fathers and their adult sons and daughters. *Marriage and Family Review, 16,* 249–266.

Nyiti, R. M. (1982). The validity of "cultural differences explanations" for cross-cultural variation in the rate of Piagetian cognitive development. In D. Wagner & H. Stevenson (Eds.), *Cultural perspectives on child development.* New York: W. H. Freeman.

O

O'Brien, M. (1993, March). *Are working mothers different? Attitudes toward parenthood in employed and nonemployed mothers of infants and toddlers.* Paper presented at the biennial meeting of the Society for Research in Child Development, New Orleans.

O'Conner, T. G. (1992, March). *Validating a closeness to stepfather scale.* Paper presented at the meeting of the Society for Research on Adolescence, Washington, DC.

O'Connor, E., Crowell, J. A., & Sprafkin, J. (1993, March). *Mother-child interaction in ADHD boys and its relation to secondary symptoms.* Paper presented at the biennial meeting of the Society for Research in Child Development, New Orleans.

O'Donnel, B. (1989, April). *Altering children's gender stereotypes about adult occupations with nonsexist books.* Paper presented at the biennial meeting of the Society for Research in Child Development, Kansas City, MO.

O'Donnell, C., Manos, M., & Chesney-Lind, M. (1987). Diversion and neighborhood delinquency programs in open settings. In E. Morris & C. Braukmann (Eds.), *Behavioral approaches to crime and delinquency.* New York: Plenum.

O'Hara, M. (1986). Social support, life events, and depression during pregnancy and the puererium. *Archives of General Psychiatry, 43,* 569–573.

Offord, D. R., & Boyle, M. H. (1988). The epidemiology of antisocial behavior in early adolescents, aged 12 to 14. In M. D. Levine & E. R. McAnarney (Eds.), *Early adolescent transitions.* Lexington, MA: Lexington Books.

Ogbu, J. U. (1974). *The next generation: An ethnography of education in an urban neighborhood.* New York: Academic Press.

Ogbu, J. U. (1986). The consequences of the American caste system. In U. Neisser (Ed.), *The school achievement of minority children: New perspectives.* Hillsdale, NJ: Erlbaum.

Ogbu, J. U. (1989, April). *Academic socialization of Black children: An inoculation against future failure?* Paper presented at the biennial meeting of the Society for Research in Child Development, Kansas City, MO.

Okun, B. F., & Rappaport, L. J. (1980). *Working with families.* North Scituate, MA: Duxbury Press.

Olds, S. B., London, M. L., & Ladewig, P. A. (1988). *Maternal newborn nursing: A family-centered approach.* Menlo Park, CA: Addison-Wesley.

Olson, D. R. (1993, March). *What are beliefs and why can a 4-year-old but not a 3-year-old understand them?* Paper presented at the biennial meeting of the Society for Research in Child Development, New Orleans.

Olson, H. C., Burgess, D. M., & Streissguth, A. P. (1992, August/September). Fetal alcohol syndrome (FAS) and fetal alcohol effects (FAE): A lifespan view, with implications for early intervention. *Zero to Three, 13,* 24–29.

Olson, R. K., & Forsberg, H. (1993, March). *Disabled and normal readers' eye movements: A reading level comparison.* Paper presented at the biennial meeting of the Society for Research in Child Development, New Orleans.

Olweus, D. (1980). Bullying among schoolboys. In R. Barnen (Ed.), *Children and violence.* Stockholm: Adaemic Litteratur.

Oppenheimer, M. (1982, October). What you should know about herpes. *Seventeen Magazine,* pp. 154–155, 170.

Oser, F. K. (1986). Moral education and values education: The discourse perspective. In M. C. Wittrock (Ed.), *Handbook of research on teaching.* New York: Macmillan.

Osofsky, J. D. (1989, April). *Affective relationships in adolescent mothers and their infants.* Paper presented at the biennial meeting of the Society for Research in Child Development, Kansas City, MO.

Osofsky, J. D. (1990, Winter). Risk and protective factors for teenage mothers and their infants. *SRCD Newsletter,* pp. 1–2.

Ottinger, D. R., & Simmons, J. E. (1964). Behavior of human neonates and prenatal maternal anxiety. *Psychological Reports, 14,* 391–394.

P

Padilla, A. (1993, March). *Growing up in two cultures.* Paper presented at the biennial meeting of the Society for Research in Child Development, New Orleans.

Paget, K. D., & Abramczyk, L. W. (1993, March). *Family functioning and child neglect: The contribution of maternal and child perceptions.* Paper presented at the biennial meeting of the Society for Research in Child Development, New Orleans.

Paikoff, R. L., Buchanan, C. M., & Brooks-Gunn, J. (1991). Hormone-behavior links at puberty, methodological links in the study of. In R. M. Lerner, A. C. Petersen, & J. Brooks-Gunn (Eds.), *Encyclopedia of adolescence* (Vol. I). New York: Garland.

Paivio, A. (1986). Mental representations: A dual coding approach. New York: Oxford University Press.

Paludi, M. (1992). *The psychology of women.* Dubuque, IA: Wm. C. Brown.

Pan, B. A., Rollins, P. R., & Snow, C. E. (1991, April). *Pragmatic development and its relationship to morphosyntactic indices.* Paper presented at the Society for Research in Child Development meeting, Seattle.

Papert, S. (1980). *Mindstorms: Children, computers, and powerful ideas.* New York: Basic.

Papini, D. R., Roggman, L. A., & Anderson, J. (1990). *Early adolescent perceptions of attachment to mother and father: A test of the emotional distancing hypothesis.* Paper presented at the meeting of the Society for Research in Adolescence, Atlanta.

Parcel, G. S., Simons-Morton, G. G., O'Hara, N. M., Baranowski, T., Kolbe, L. J., & Bee, D. E. (1987). School promotion of healthful diet and exercise behavior: An integration of organizational change and social learning theory interventions. *Journal of School Health, 57,* 150–156.

Parcel, G. S., Tiernan, K., Nadar, P. R., & Gottlob, D. (1979). Health education and kindergarten children. *Journal of School Health, 49,* 129–131.

Parham, T. A., & McDavis, R. J. (1993). Black men, an endangered species: Who's really pulling the trigger. In D. R. Atkinson, G. Morten, & D. W. Sue (Eds.), *Counseling American minorities.* Madison, WI: WCB Brown & Benchmark.

Paris, S. G., & Lindauer, B. K. (1982). The development of cognitive skills during childhood. In B. B. Wolman (Ed.), *Handbook of developmental psychology.* Englewood Cliffs, NJ: Prentice-Hall.

Park, K. A. (1993, March). *A longitudinal examination of links between mother-child attachment and children's friendships in early childhood.* Paper presented at the biennial meeting of the Society for Research in Child Development, New Orleans.

Park, K. J., & Honig, A. S. (1991, August). *Infant child care patterns and later ratings of preschool behaviors.* Paper presented at the meeting of the American Psychological Association, San Francisco.

Parke, R. D. (1972). Some effects of punishment on children's behavior. In W. W. Hartup (Ed.), *The young child* (Vol. 2). Washington, DC: NAEYC.

Parke, R. D. (1977). Some effects of punishment on children's behavior—Revisited. In E. M. Hetherington & R. D. Parke (Eds.), *Readings in contemporary child psychology.* New York: McGraw-Hill.

Parke, R. D. (1993, March). *Family research in the 1990s.* Paper presented at the biennial meeting of the Society for Research in Child Development, New Orleans.

Parke, R. D., & Sawin, D. B. (1980). The family in early infancy. In F. Pedersen (Ed.), *The father-infant relationship: Observational studies in family context.* New York: Praeger.

Parker, J. G., & Asher, S. R. (1987). Peer relations and later personal adjustment: Are low accepted children at risk? *Psychological Bulletin, 102,* 357–389.

Parker, S. J., & Barrett, D. E. (1992). Maternal type A behavior during pregnancy, neonatal crying, and infant temperament: Do type A women have type A babies? *Pediatrics, 89,* 474–479.

Parmalee, A. H. (1986). Children's illnesses: Their beneficial effects on behavioral development. *Child Development, 57,* 1–10.

Parmalee, A., Wenner, W., & Schulz, H. (1964). Infant sleep patterns from birth to 16 weeks of age. *Journal of Pediatrics, 65,* 572–576.

Parten, M. (1932). Social play among preschool children. *Journal of Abnormal and Social Psychology, 27,* 243–269.

Pascual-Leone, J. (1987). Organismic processes for Neo-Piagetian theories: A dialectical causal account of cognitive development. *International Journal of Psychology, 22,* 531–570.

Pascual-Leone, J., & Shafrir, U. (1991, April). *The development of post-failure reflectivity.* Paper presented at the Society for Child Development meeting, Seattle.

Patterson, C. J. (1992). Children of lesbian and gay parents. *Child Development, 63,* 1023–1042.

Patterson, G. R. (1991, April). *Which parenting skills are necessary for what?* Paper presented at the biennial meeting of the Society for Research in Child Development, Seattle.

Patterson, G. R., & Stouthamer-Loeber, M. (1984). The correlation of family management practices and delinquency. *Child Development, 55,* 1299–1307.

Patterson, G. R., Capaldi, D., & Bank, L. (1991). An early starter model for predicting delinquency. In D. Pepler & K. Rubin (Eds.), *The development and treatment of childhood aggression.* Hillsdale, NJ: Erlbaum.

Patterson, G. R., DeBaryshe, B. D., & Ramsey, E. (1989). A developmental perspective on antisocial behavior. *American Psychologist, 44,* 329–355.

Patterson, S. J., Sochting, I., & Marcia, J. E. (1992). The inner space and beyond: Women and identity. In G. R. Adams, T. P. Gullotta, & R. Montemayor (Eds.), *Adolescent identity formation.* Newbury Park, CA: Sage.

Paul, E. L., & White, K. M. (1990). The development of intimate relationships in late adolescence. *Adolescence, 25,* 375–400.

Pavlov, I. P. (1927). *Conditioned reflexes* (F. V. Anrep, Trans. and Ed.). New York: Dover.

Pearl, R., Bryan, T., & Herzog, A. (1990). Resisting or acquiescing to peer pressure to engage in misconduct: Adolescents' expectations of probable consequences. *Journal of Youth and Adolescence, 19,* 43–55.

Pederson, D. R., Moran, G., Sitko, C., Campbell, K., Ghesquire, K., & Acton, H. (1989, April). *Maternal sensitivity and the security of infant-mother attachment.* Paper presented at the Society for Research in Child Development meeting, Kansas City, MO.

Pellegrini, A. D., Perlmutter, J. C., Galda, L., & Brody, G. H. (1990). Joint reading between Black Head Start children and their mothers. *Child Development, 61,* 443–453.

Pennebaker, J. (1992). Commentary for *Psychology: The Science of Mind and Behavior* (4th ed.) by John W. Santrock.

Penner, S. G. (1987). Parental responses to grammatical and ungrammatical child utterances. *Child Development, 58,* 376–384.

Perkins, D. N. (1984, September). Creativity by design. *Educational Leadership,* 18–25.

Perkins, D. P., & Gardner, H. (1989). *Why "Zero"? A brief introduction to Project Zero.* In H. Gardner & D. P. Perkins (Eds.), *Art, mind, and education.* Ithaca, NY: The University of Illinois Press.

Perry, W. G. (1981). Cognitive and ethical growth. The making of meaning. In A. W. Chickering (Ed.), *The modern American college: Responding to the new realities of diverse students and a changing society.* San Francisco: Jossey-Bass.

Peskin, H. (1967). Pubertal onset and ego functioning. *Journal of Abnormal Psychology, 72,* 1–15.

Petersen, A. C. (1979, January). Can puberty come any faster? *Psychology Today,* pp. 45–56.

Petersen, A. C., Leffert, N., & Miller, K. (1993, March). *The role of interpersonal relationships in the development of depressed affect and depression in adolescence.* Paper presented at the biennial meeting of the Society for Research in Child Development, New Orleans.

Peterson, P. L. (1977). Interactive effects of student anxiety, achievement orientation, and teacher behavior on student achievement and attitude. *Journal of Educational Psychology, 69,* 779–792.

Pettit, G. S., Dodge, K. A., & Brown, M. M. (1988). Early family experience, social problem solving patterns, and children's social competence. *Child Development, 59,* 107–120.

Phillips, D. A. (1992). Child care and parental well-being: Bringing quality of care into the picture. In A. Booth (Ed.), *Child care in the 1990s.* Hillsdale, NJ: Erlbaum.

Phinney, J. S. (1989). Stages of ethnic identity development in minority group adolescents. *Journal of Early Adolescence, 9,* 34–49.

Phinney, J. S., & Alipuria, L. L. (1990). Ethnic identity in college students from four ethnic groups. *Journal of Adolescence, 13,* 171–183.

Phinney, J. S., & Cobb, N. J. (1993, March). *Adolescents' reasoning about discrimination: Ethnic and attitudinal predictors.* Paper presented at the biennial meeting of the Society for Research in Child Development, New Orleans.

Phinney, J. S., & Rosenthal, D. A. (1992). Ethnic identity in adolescence: Process, context, and outcome. In G. R. Adams, T. P. Gullotta, & R. Montemayor (Eds.), *Adolescent identity formation.* Newbury Park, CA: Sage.

Phinney, J. S., Chavira, V., & Williamson, L. (1992). Acculturation attitudes and self-esteem among high school and college students. *Youth and Society, 25,* 299–312.

Phinney, J. S., Espinoza, C., & Onwughalu, M. N. (1992, March). *Accommodation and conflict: The relationship of ethnic identity and American identity among Asian American, Black, and Hispanic adolescents.* Paper presented at the meeting of the Society for Research on Adolescence, Washington, DC.

Piaget, J. (1932). *The moral judgment of the child.* New York: Harcourt Brace Jovanovich.

Piaget, J. (1952). *The origins of intelligence in children* (M. Cook, Trans.). New York: International Universities Press.

Piaget, J. (1952a). Jean Piaget. In C. A. Murchison (Ed.), *A history of psychology in autobiography* (Vol. 4). Worcester, MA: Clark University Press.

Piaget, J. (1954). *The construction of reality in the child.* New York: Basic.

Piaget, J. (1962). *Play, dreams, and imitation in childhood.* New York: W. W. Norton.

Piaget, J. (1967). The mental development of the child. In D. Elkind (Ed.), *Six psychological studies by Piaget.* New York: Random House.

Piaget, J. (1970). Piaget's theory. In P. H. Mussen (Ed.), *Manual of child psychology* (3rd ed., Vol. 1). New York: Wiley.

Piaget, J. (1972). Intellectual evolution from adolescence to adulthood. *Human Development, 15,* 1–12.

Piaget, J., & Inhelder, B. (1969). *The child's conception of space* (F. J. Langdon & J. L. Lunzer, Trans.). New York: W. W. Norton. (Original work published 1948)

Pillow, B. H. (1988). Young children's understanding of attentional limits. *Child Development, 49,* 38–46.

Pipes, P. (1988). Nutrition in childhood. In S. R. Williams & B. S. Worthington-Roberts (Eds.), *Nutrition throughout the life cycle.* St. Louis: Times Mirror/Mosby.

Pleck, J. (1981). *Three conceptual issues in research on male roles.* Working paper no. 98, Wellesley College Center for Research on Women, Wellesley, MA.

Pleck, J. H. (1983). The theory of male sex role identity: Its rise and fall, 1936–present. In M. Levin (Ed.), *In the shadow of the past; Psychology portrays the sexes.* New York: Columbia University Press.

Pleck, J. H., Sonnenstein, F. L., & Ku, L. C. (in press). Problem behaviors and masculine ideology in adolescent males. In R. Ketterlinus & M. E. Lamb (Eds.), *Adolescent problem behaviors.* Hillsdale, NJ: Erlbaum.

Plomin, R. (1989). Environment and genes: Determinants of behavior. *American Psychologist, 44,* 105–111.

Plomin, R. (1991, April). *The nature of nurture: Genetic influence on "environmental" measures.* Paper presented at the biennial meeting of the Society for Research in Child Development, Seattle.

Plomin, R. (1993, March). *Human behavioral genetics and development: An overview and update.* Paper presented at the biennial meeting of the Society for Research in Child Development, New Orleans.

Plomin, R., & Daniels, D. (1987). Why are children in the same family so different from one another? *Behavioral and Brain Sciences, 10,* 1–60.

Plomin, R., & Thompson, L. (1987). Life-span developmental behavior genetics. In P. B. Baltes, D. L. Featherman, & R. M. Lerner (Eds.), *Life-span development and behavior* (Vol. 7). Hillsdale, NJ: Erlbaum.

Plomin, R., DeFries, J. C., & McClearn, G. E. (in press). *Behavioral genetics: A primer.* New York: W. H. Freeman.

Poest, C. A., Williams, J. R., Witt, D. D., & Atwood, M. E. (1990). Challenge me to move: Large muscle development in young children. *Young Children, 45,* 4–10.

Polivy, J., & Thomsen, L. (1987). Eating, dieting, and body image. In E. A. Blechman & K. D. Brownell (Eds.), *Handbook of behavioral medicine for women.* Elmsford, NY: Pergamon.

Porter, F. L., Porges, S. W., & Marshall, R. E. (1988). Newborn pain cries and vagal tone: Parallel changes in response to circumcision. *Child Development, 59,* 495–515.

Posner, M., & Rothbart, M. (1989, August). *Attention: Normal and pathological development.* Paper presented at the meeting of the American Psychological Association, New Orleans.

Potthof, S. J., (1992, March). *Modeling family planning expertise to predict oral contraceptive discontinuance in teenagers.* Paper presented at the meeting of the Society for Research on Adolescence, Washington, DC.

Pouissant, A. F. (1972, February). Blaxploitation movies—Cheap thrills that degrade Blacks. *Psychology Today,* pp. 22–33.

Powell, G. J., & Fuller, M. (1972). The variables for positive self-concept among young Southern Black adolescents. *Journal of the National Medical Association, 43,* 72–79.

Power, C. (1991). Lawrence Kohlberg: The vocation of an educator, part I. In W. M. Kurtines & J. Gewirtz (Eds.), *Moral behavior and development* (Vol. 1). Hillsdale, NJ: Erlbaum.

Premack, D. (1986). *Gavagai! The future history of the ape language controversy.* Cambridge, MA: MIT Press.

Price, J., & Feshbach, S. (1982, August). *Emotional adjustment correlates of television viewing in children.* Paper presented at the meeting of the American Psychological Association, Washington, DC.

Price-Williams, D., Gordon, W., & Ramirez, M. (1969). Skill and conservation: A study of pottery-making children. *Developmental Psychology, 1,* 796.

Pridham, K. F., & Van Riper, M. (1993, March). *Infant and maternal contributions to mothers' internal working model of infant feeding (IWMF).* Paper presented at the biennial meeting of the Society for Research in Child Development, New Orleans.

Profilet, S., & Ladd, G. W. (1993, March). *Preschoolers' peer relations: Mothers' perceptions, concerns, and management behaviors.* Paper presented at the biennial meeting of the Society for Research in Child Development, New Orleans.

Pryor, J. B., Reeder, G. D., Vinaco, R., & Kott, T. L. (1989). The instrumental and symbolic functions of attitudes toward persons with AIDS. *Journal of Applied Social Psychology, 19,* 377–404.

Puka, B. (1991). Toward the redevelopment of Kohlberg's theory: Preserving essential structure, removing controversial content. In W. M. Kurtines & J. Gewirtz (Eds.), *Moral behavior and development: Advances in theory, research, and application.* Hillsdale, NJ: Erlbaum.

Putallaz, M. (1983). Predicting children's sociometric status from their behavior. *Child Development, 54,* 1417–1426.

Putallaz, M., Klein, T. P., Costanzo, P. R., & Efron, L. A. (1993, March). *Continuities in peer relationships.* Paper presented at the biennial meeting of the Society for Research in Child Development, New Orleans.

Q

Quay, H. (Ed.). (1987). *Handbook of juvenile delinquency.* New York: Wiley.

Quay, L. C., Minore, D. A., & Fraizer, L. M. (1993, March). *Sex typing in stories and comprehension, recall, and sex-typed beliefs in young children.* Paper presented at the biennial meeting of the Society for Research in Child Development, New Orleans.

Quiggle, N. L., Garber, J., Panak, W. F., & Dodge, K. A. (1992). Social information processing in aggressive and depressed children. *Child Development, 63,* 1305–1320.

R

Rabin, D. S., & Chrousos, G. P. (1991). Androgens, gonadal. In R. M. Lerner, A. C. Petersen, & J. Brooks-Gunn (Eds.), *Encyclopedia of adolescence* (Vol. I). New York: Garland.

Rabiner, D. L., Gordon, L., Klumb, D., & Thompson, L. B. (1991, April). *Social problem solving deficiencies in rejected children: Motivational factors and skill deficits.* Paper presented at the Society for Research in Child Development meeting, Seattle.

Rabkin, J. (1987). *Epidemiology of adolescent violence: Risk factors, career patterns, and intervention programs.* Paper presented at the conference on adolescent violence. Stanford University, Stanford, CA.

Radke-Yarrow, M., Nottlemann, E., Martinez, P., Fox, M. B., & Belmont, B. (1992). Young children of affectively ill parents: A longitudinal study of psychosocial development. *Journal of the Academy of Child and Adolescent Psychiatry, 31,* 68–77.

Rahman, T., & Bisanz, G. L. (1986). Reading ability and use of a story schema in recalling and reconstructing information. *Journal of Educational Psychology, 5,* 323–333.

Ramey, C. T. (1989, April). *Parent-child intellectual similarities in natural and altered ecologies.* Paper presented at the Society for Research in Child Development meeting, Kansas City, MO.

Ramey, C. T., Bryant, D. M., Campbell, F. A., Sparling, J. J., & Wasik, B. H. (1988). Early intervention for high-risk children. The Carolina Early Intervention Program. In R. H. Price, E. L. Cowen, R. P. Lorion, & J. Ramos-McKay (Eds.), *14 ounces of prevention.* Washington, DC: American Psychological Association.

Ramirez, O. (1989). Mexican American children and adolescents. In J. T. Gibbs & L. N. Huang (Eds.), *Children of color.* San Francisco: Jossey-Bass.

Ramirez, O., & Arce, C. Y. (1981). The contemporary Chicago family: An empirically based review. In A. Baron (Ed.), *Explorations in Chicago psychology.* New York: Praeger.

Ramsay, D. S. (1980). Onset of unimanual handedness in infants. *Infant Behavior and Development, 3,* 377–385.

Rawlins, W. K. (1992). *Friendship matters.* Hawthorne, NY: Aldine.

Reilly, R. (1988, August 15). Here no one is spared. *Sports Illustrated,* pp. 70–77.

Report on Preschool Programs. (1992, February 26). Head Start, psychologists launch new mental health initiatives, page 42.

Resnick, L. (1993, March). *Developmental research and educational policy.* Paper presented at the biennial meeting of the Society for Research in Child Development, New Orleans.

Rest, J. R. (1976). New approaches in the assessment of moral judgment. In T. Lickona (Ed.), *Moral development and behavior.* New York: Holt, Rinehart & Winston.

Rest, J. R. (1983). Morality. In P. H. Mussen (Ed.), *Handbook of child psychology* (4th ed., Vol. 3). New York: Wiley.

Rest, J. R. (1986). *Moral development: Advances in theory and research.* New York: Praeger.

Rest, J. R., Turiel, E., & Kohlberg, L. (1969). Relations between level of moral judgment and preference and comprehension of the moral judgments of others. *Journal of Personality, 37,* 225–252.

Reuter, M. W., & Biller, H. B. (1973). Perceived paternal nurturance-availability and personality adjustment among college males. *Journal of Consulting and Clinical Psychology, 40,* 339–342.

Reynolds, C. R., & Kamphaus, R. W. (Eds.). (1990). *Handbook of psychological and educational assessment of children: Intelligence and achievement.* New York: Guilford.

Rice, M. L. (1989). Children's language acquisition. *American Psychologist, 44,* 149–156.

Rich, C. L., Young, D., & Fowler, R. C. (1986). San Diego suicide study. *Archives of General Psychiatry, 43,* 577–582.

Richardson, J. L., Dwyer, K., McGrugan, K., Hansen, W. B., Dent, C., Johnson, C. A., Sussman, S. Y., Brannon, B., & Glay, B. (1989). Substance use among eighth-grade students who take care of themselves after school. *Pediatrics, 84,* 556–566.

Rick, K., & Foward, J. (1992). Acculturation and perceived intergenerational differences among Hmong youth. *Journal of Cross-Cultural Psychology, 23,* 85–94.

Rieben, L., & Perfetti, C. A. (1991). *Learning to read: Basic research and its implications.* Hillsdale, NJ: Erlbaum.

Roberts, W. L. (1993, March). *Programs for the collection and analysis of observational data.* Paper presented at the biennial meeting of the Society for Research in Child Development, New Orleans.

Robinson, D. P., & Greene, J. W. (1988). The adolescent alcohol and drug problem: A practical approach. *Pediatric Nursing, 14,* 305–310.

Robinson, J. L., Kagan, J., Reznick, J. S., & Corley, R. (1992). The heritability of inhibited and uninhibited behavior: A twin study. *Developmental Psychology, 28,* 1030–1037.

Rode, S. S., Chang, P., Fisch, R. O., & Sroufe, L. A. (1981). Attachment patterns of infants separated at birth. *Developmental Psychology, 17,* 188–191.

Rodin, J. (1984, December). Interview: A sense of control. *Psychology Today,* pp. 38–45.

Rodin, J. (1992). *Body Traps.* New York: William Morrow.

Rodman, H., Pratto, D. J., & Nelson, R. S. (1988). Toward a definition of self-care children: A commentary on Steinberg (1986). *Developmental Psychology, 24,* 292–294.

Rodriguez-Haynes, M., & Crittenden, P. M. (1988). *Ethnic differences among abusing, neglecting, and non-maltreating families.* Paper presented at the Southeastern Conference on Human Development, Charleston, SC.

Roff, M., Sells, S. B., & Golden, M. W. (1972). *Social adjustment and personality development in children.* Minneapolis, MN: University of Minnesota Press.

Rogers, A. (1987). *Questions of gender differences: Ego development and moral voice in adolescence.* Unpublished manuscript, Department of Education, Harvard University.

Rogers, C. R. (1961). *On becoming a person.* Boston: Houghton Mifflin.

Rogers, C. S., & Sawyers, J. K. (1988). *Play in the lives of children.* Washington, DC: National Association for the Education of Young Children.

Rogoff, B. (1990). *Apprenticeship in thinking.* New York: Oxford University Press.

Rogoff, B. (1993, March, b). *Whither cognitive development in the 1990s?* Paper presented at the biennial meeting of the Society for Research in Child Development, New Orleans.

Rogoff, B. (1993a). Children's guided participation and participatory appropriation in sociocultural activity. In R. Wozniak & K. Fischer (Eds.), *Development in context: Acting and thinking in specific environments.* Hillsdale, NJ: Erlbaum.

Rogoff, B. (in press). Peer influences on cognitive development: Piagetian versus Vygotskian perspectives. In M. H. Bornstein & J. S. Bruner (Eds.), *Interaction in human development.* Hillsdale, NJ: Erlbaum.

Rogoff, B., & Morelli, G. (1989). Perspectives on children's development from cultural psychology. *American Psychologist, 44,* 343–348.

Rohner, K. Rohner, E. C. (1981). Parental acceptance-rejection and parental control: Cross-cultural codes. *Ethnology, 20,* 245–260.

Root, M. P. (1992). (Ed.). *Racially mixed people in America.* Newbury Park, CA: Sage.

Root, M. P. P. (1993). Guidelines for facilitating therapy with Asian-American clients. In D. R. Atkinson, G. Morten, & D. W. Sue (Eds.), *Counseling American minorities.* Madison, WI: WCB Brown & Benchmark.

Rose, H. A., & Martin, C. L. (1993, March). *Children's gender-based inferences about others' activities, emotions, and occupations.* Paper presented at the biennial meeting of the Society for Research in Child Development, New Orleans.

Rose, S. A. (1989). Measuring infant intelligence: New perspectives. In M. H. Bornstein & N. A. Krasnegor (Eds.), *Stability and continuity in mental development.* Hillsdale, NJ: Erlbaum.

Rose, S. A., & Ruff, H. A. (1987). Cross-modal abilities in human infants. In J. D. Osofsky (Ed.), *Handbook of infant development* (2nd ed.). New York: Wiley.

Rose, S. A., Feldman, J. F., McCarton, C. M., & Wolfson, J. (1988). Information processing in seven-month-old infants as a function of risk status. *Child Development, 59,* 489–603.

Rose, S.A., Feldman, J. F., & Wallace, I. F. (1992). Infant information processing in relation to six-year cognitive outcomes. *Child Development, 63,* 1126–1141.

Rosenbaum, J. L. (1989). Family dysfunction and female delinquency. *Crime and Delinquency, 35,* 31–44.

Rosenberg, M. (1965). *Society and the adolescent self-image.* Princeton, NJ: Princeton University Press.

Rosenberg, M. (1979). *Conceiving the self.* New York: Basic Books.

Rosenberg, M. (1986). Self-concept from middle childhood through adolescence. In J. Suls & A. G. Greenwald (Eds.), *Psychological perspective on the self* (Vol. 3). Hillsdale, NJ: Erlbaum.

Rosenblith, J. F. (1992). *In the beginning* (2nd ed.). Newbury Park, CA: Sage.

Rosenblith, J. F., & Sims-Knight, J. E. (1992). *In the beginning* (2nd ed.). Newbury Park, CA: Sage.

Rosenthal, R., & Jacobsen, L. (1968). *Pygmalion in the classroom.* New York: Holt, Rinehart & Winston.

Rossi, A. S. (1989). A life-course approach to gender, aging, and intergenerational relations. In K. W. Schaie & C. Schooler (Eds.), *Social structure and aging.* Hillsdale, NJ: Erlbaum.

Rosso, P. (1992). Maternal nutritional status and fetal growth. In R. Hoekleman, S. B. Friedman, N. M. Nelson, & H. M. Seidel (Eds.), *Primary pediatric care* (2nd ed.). St. Louis, MO: Mosby Yearbook.

Rotenberg, K. J. (1993, March). *Development of restrictive disclosure to friends.* Paper presented at the biennial meeting of the Society for Research in Child Development, New Orleans.

Rothbart, M. K. (1988). Temperament and the development of the inhibited approach. *Child Development, 59,* 1241–1250.

Rothbart, M. K., & Ahadi, S. A. (1993, March). *Temperament and socialization.* Paper presented at the biennial meeting of the Society for Research in Child Development, New Orleans.

Rothbart, M. K., Hanley, D., & Albert, M. (1986). Gender differences in moral reasoning. *Sex Roles, 15,* 645–653.

Rothbart, M. L. K. (1971). Birth order and mother-child interaction. *Dissertation Abstracts, 27,* 45–57.

Rovee-Collier, C. (1987). Learning and memory in children. In J. D. Osofsky (Ed.), *Handbook of infant development* (2nd ed.). New York: Wiley.

Rowe, D. C. (in press). As the twig is bent? The myth of child-rearing influences on personality development. *Journal of Counseling and Development.*

Rowlett, J. D., Patel, D., & Greydanus, D. E. (1992). Homosexuality. In D. E. Greydanus & M. L. Wolraich (Eds.), *Behavioral pediatrics.* New York: Springer-Verlag.

Rubenstein, J., Heeren, T., Houseman, D., Rubin, C., & Stechler, G. (1989). Suicidal behavior in "normal" adolescents: Risk and protective factors. *American Journal of Orthopsychiatry, 59,* 59–71.

Rubin, K. H., Maioni, T. L., & Hornung, M. (1976). Free play behaviors in middle and lower social class preschoolers: Parten and Piaget revisited. *Child Development, 47,* 414–419.

Rubin, K. N., Fein, G. G., & Vandenberg, B. (1983). Play. In P. H. Mussen (Ed.), *Handbook of child psychology* (4th ed., Vol. 4). New York: Wiley.

Rubin, Z., & Sloman, J. (1984). How parents influence their children's friendships. In M. Lewis (Ed.), *Beyond the dyad.* New York: Plenum.

Ruble, D. (1983). The development of social comparison processes and their role in achievement-related self-socialization. In E. Higgins, D. Ruble, & W. Hartup (Eds.), *Social cognitive development: A social-cultural perspective.* New York: Cambridge University Press.

Ruble, D. N., Boggiano, A. K., Feldman, N. S., & Loebl, J. H. (1980). Developmental analysis of the role of social comparison in self-evaluation. *Developmental Psychology, 16,* 105–115.

Ruff, H. A., & Lawson, K. R. (1990). Development of sustained, focused attention in young children during free play. *Developmental Psychology, 26,* 85–93.

Rumbaugh, D. M., & Rumbaugh, E. S. (1990, June). *Chimpanzees: Language, speech, counting and video tasks.* Paper presented at the meeting of the American Psychological Society, Dallas.

Rumbaugh, D. M., Hopkins, W. D., Washburn, D. A., & Savage-Rumbaugh, E. S. (1991). Comparative perspectives of brain, cognition, and language. In N. A. Krasnegor, D. M. Rumbaugh, M. Studdert-Kennedy, & R. L. Schiefelbusch (Eds.), *Biological and behavioral determinants of language development.* Hillsdale, NJ: Erlbaum.

Rumberger, R. W. (1983). Dropping out of high school: The influence of race, sex, and family background. *American Educational Research Journal, 20,* 199–220.

Rumberger, R. W. (1987). High school dropouts: A review of the issues and evidence. *Review of Educational Research, 57,* 101–121.

Rushton, J. P. (1985). Differential K theory: The sociobiology of individual and group differences. *Journal of Personality and Individual Differences, 9,* 1009–1024.

Rushton, J. P. (1988). Race differences in behavior: A review and evolutionary analysis. *Journal of Personality and Individual Differences, 9,* 1035–1040.

Russo, N. F. (1990). Overview: Forging research priorities for women's mental health. *American Psychologist, 45,* 368–374.

Rutter, M. (1983, April). *Influences from family and school.* Paper presented at the meeting of the Society for Research in Child Development, Detroit.

Rutter, M., & Garmezy, N. (1983). Developmental psychopathology. In P. H. Mussen (Ed.), *Handbook of child psychology* (4th ed., Vol. 4). New York: Wiley.

Rutter, M., Maughan, B., Mortimore, P., & Ouston, J. (1979). *Fifteen thousand hours: Secondary schools and their effects on children.* Cambridge, MA: Harvard University Press.

Ryan, R. A. (1980). *Strengths of the American Indian family: State of the art.* In F. Hoffman (Ed.), *The American Indian family: Strengths and stresses.* Isleta, NM: American Indian Social Research and Development Association.

Ryan, R. M., & Lynch, J. H. (1989). Emotional autonomy versus detachment: Revisiting the vicissitudes of adolescence and young adulthood. *Child Development, 60,* 340–356.

Rybash, J., Roodin, P., & Santrock, J. W. (1991). *Adult development and aging* (2nd ed.). Dubuque, IA: Wm. C. Brown.

S

Saarni, C. (1988). Children's understanding of the interpersonal consequences of dissemblance of nonverbal emotional-expressive behavior. *Journal of Nonverbal Behavior, 12,* 275–294.

Sadker, M., & Sadker, D. (1986, March). Sexism in the classroom: From grade school to graduate school. *Phi Delta Kappan,* pp. 512–515.

Sadker, M. P., & Sadker, D. M. (1991). *Teachers, schools, and society* (2nd ed.). New York: McGraw-Hill.

Sadker, M., Sadker, D., & Klein, S. S. (1986). Abolishing misperceptions about sex equity in education. *Theory into Practice, 25,* 219–226.

Sagan, C. (1977). *Dragons of Eden.* New York: Random House.

Sallade, J. B. (1973). A comparison of the psychological adjustment of obese versus non-obese children. *Journal of Psychosomatic Research, 17,* 89–96.

Salzinger, S., Feldman, R. S., Hammer, M., & Rosario, M. (1993). The effects of physical abuse on children's social relationships. *Child Development, 64,* 169–187.

Sameroff, A. J., Dickstein, S., Hayden, L. C., & Schiller, M. (1993, March). *Effects of family process and parental depression on children.* Paper presented at the biennial meeting of the Society for Child Development, New Orleans.

Santrock, J. W. (1993). *Children* (3rd ed.). Dubuque, IA: Wm. C. Brown.

Santrock, J. W. (1994). *Life-span development* (5th ed.). Dubuque, IA: Wm. C. Brown.

Santrock, J. W., & Sitterle, K. A. (1987). Parent-child relationships in stepmother families. In K. Pasley & M. Ihinger-Tallman (Eds.), *Remarriage and stepparenting.* New York: Guilford.

Santrock, J. W., & Warshak, R. A. (1979). Father custody and social development in boys and girls. *Journal of Social Issues, 35,* 112–125.

Santrock, J. W., & Warshak, R. A. (1986). Development, relationships, and legal/clinical considerations in father-custody families. In M. E. Lamb (Ed.), *The father's role: Applied perspectives.* New York: Wiley.

Santrock, J. W., Sitterle, K. A., & Warshak, R. A. (1988). Parent-child relationships in stepfather families. In P. Bronstein & C. P. Cowan (Eds.), *Fatherhood today.* New York: Wiley.

Sattler, J. (1988). *Assessment of children* (3rd ed.). San Diego: Jerome Sattler.

Savage-Rumbaugh, E. S. (1991). Language learning in the Bonobo: How and why they learn. In N. A. Krasnegor, D. M. Rumbaugh, M. Studdert-Kennedy, & R. L. Schiefelbusch (Eds.), *Biological and behavioral determinants of language development.* Hillsdale, NJ: Erlbaum.

Savin-Williams, R., & Rodriguez, R. G. (1993). A developmental clinical perspective on lesbian, gay male, and bisexual youths. In T. P. Gullotta, G. R. Adams, & R. Montemayor (Eds.), *Adolescent sexuality.* Newbury Park, CA: Sage.

Savin-Williams, R. C., & Berndt, T. J. (1990). Friendship and peer relations. In S. S. Feldman & G. R. Elliot (Eds.), *At the threshold: The developing adolescent.* Cambridge, MA: Harvard University Press.

Savin-Williams, R. C., & Demo, D. H. (1983). Conceiving or misconceiving the self: Issues in adolescent self-esteem. *Journal of Early Adolescence, 3,* 121–140.

Sax, G. (1989). *Principles of educational and psychological measurement* (3rd ed.). Belmont, CA: Wadsworth.

Saxe, G. B. (1981). Body parts as numerals: A developmental analysis of numeration among the Oksapmin in Papua, New Guinea. *Child Development, 52,* 306–316.

Saxe, G. B., & Guberman, S. R. (1993, March). *Peers' emergent arithmetical goals in a problem-solving game.* Paper presented at the biennial meeting of the Society for Research in Child Development, New Orleans.

Scafidi, F., & Wheeden, A. (1993, March). *Perinatal complications and Brazelton performance of cocaine-exposed preterm infants.* Paper presented at the biennial meeting of the Society for Research in Child Development, New Orleans.

Scales, P. (1990). Developing capable young people: An alternative strategy for prevention programs. *Journal of Early Adolescence, 10,* 420–438.

Scarborough, H. S. (1993, March). *Fostering literacy through shared parent-child reading: Past results and current directions.* Paper presented at the biennial meeting of the Society for Research in Child Development, New Orleans.

Scardamalia, M., Bereiter, C., & Steinbach, R. (1984). Teachability of reflective processes in written composition. *Cognitive Science, 8,* 173–190.

Scarr, S. (1984, May). Interview. *Psychology Today,* pp. 59–63.

Scarr, S. (1984). *Mother care/Other care.* New York: Basic Books.

Scarr, S. (1989, April). *Transracial adoption.* Discussion at the Society for Research in Child Development meeting, Kansas City, MO.

Scarr, S. (1992). Developmental theories for the 1990s: Development and individual differences. *Child Development, 63,* 1–19.

Scarr, S. (1992). Keep our eyes on the prize: Family and child care policy in the United States, as it should be. In A. Booth (Ed.), *Child care in the 1990s.* Hillsdale, NJ: Erlbaum.

Scarr, S., & Kidd, K. K. (1983). Developmental behavior genetics. In P. H. Mussen (Ed.), *Handbook of child psychology* (4th ed., Vol. 2). New York: Wiley.

Scarr, S., & McCarthney, K. (1983). How people make their own environments: A theory of genotype environment effects. *Child Development, 54,* 424–435.

Scarr, S., & Ricciuti, A. (in press). What effects do parents have on their children? In L. Okagaki & R. J. Sternberg (Eds.), *Directors of development: Influences on the development of children's thinking.* Hillsdale, NJ: Erlbaum.

Scarr, S., & Waldman, I. (1993, March). *IQ correlations among members of transracial adoptive families.* Paper presented at the biennial meeting of the Society for Research in Child Development, New Orleans.

Scarr, S., & Weinberg, R. A. (1976). IQ test performance of black children adopted by white families. *American Psychologist, 31,* 726–739.

Scarr, S., & Weinberg, R. A. (1980). Calling all camps! The war is over. *American Sociological Review, 45,* 859–865.

Scarr, S., & Weinberg, R. A. (1983). The Minnesota adoption studies: Genetic differences and malleability. *Child Development, 54,* 253–259.

Scarr, S., Lande, J., & McCartney, K. (1989). Child care and the family: Complements and interactions. In J. Lande, S. Scarr, & N. Gunzenhauser, (Eds.), *Caring for children: Challenge to America.* Hillsdale, NJ: Erlbaum.

Schacter, D. L., & McGlynn, S. M. (1989). Implicit memory: Effects of elaboration depend on unitization. *American Journal of Psychology, 102,* 151–181.

Schaff, E. A. (1992). Abortion. In R. A. Hoekleman, S. B. Friedman, N. M. Nelson, & H. M. Seidel (Eds.), *Primary pediatric care* (2nd ed.). St. Louis, MO: Mosby Yearbook.

Schank, R., & Abelson, R. (1977). *Scripts, plans, goals, and understanding.* Hillsdale, NJ: Erlbaum.

Schegloff, E. A. (1989). Reflections on language, development, and the interactional character of talk-in-interaction. In M. H. Bornstein & J. S. Bruner (Eds.), *Interaction in human development.* Hillsdale, NJ: Erlbaum.

Scheidel, D. G., & Marcia, J. E. (1985). Ego identity, intimacy, sex-role orientation, and gender. *Developmental Psychology, 21,* 149–160.

Schirmer, G. J. (Ed.). (1974). *Performance objectives for preschool children.* Sioux Falls, SD: Adapt Press.

Schneider, W., & Pressley, M. (1989). *Memory development between 2 and 20.* New York: Springer-Verlag.

Schnorr, T. M., & others (1991). Videodisplay terminals and the risk of spontaneous abortion. *New England Journal of Medicine, 324,* 727–733.

Schoendorf, K. C., & Kiely, J. L. (1992). Relationship of sudden infant death syndrome to maternal smoking during and after pregnancy. *Pediatrics, 90,* 905–908.

Schoenfeld, A. H. (1985). *Mathematical problem solving.* Orlando, FL: Academic Press.

Schorr, L. (1988). *Within our reach: Breaking the cycle of disadvantage.* New York: Anchor.

Schrag, S. G., & Dixon, R. L. (1985). Occupational exposure associated with male reproductive dysfunction. *Annual Review of Pharmacology and Toxicology, 25,* 467–592.

Schreiber, L. R. (1990). *The parent's guide to kids' sports.* Boston: Little, Brown.

Schwartz, D., & Mayaux, M. J. (1982). Female fecundity as a function of age: Results of artificial insemination in nulliparous women with azoospermic husbands. *New England Journal of Medicine, 306,* 304–406.

Scott-Jones, D., & Clark, M. L. (1986, March). The school experiences of black girls: The interaction of gender, race, and socioeconomic status. *Phi Delta Kappan,* pp. 520–526.

Scott-Jones, D., & White, A. B. (1990). Correlates of sexual activity in early adolescence. *Journal of Early Adolescence, 10,* 221–238.

Seidman, E., & Feinman, J. (1993, March). *Poor inner city youth and school transitions: Impact on self, system, and social context.* Paper presented at the biennial meeting of the Society for Research in Child Development, New Orleans.

Seligman, M. E. P. (1975). *Learned helplessness.* San Francisco: W. H. Freeman.

Selman, R. L. (1976). Social-cognitive understanding. In T. Lickona (Ed.), *Moral development and behavior.* New York: Holt, Rinehart & Winston.

Selman, R. L. (1980). *The growth of interpersonal understanding.* New York: Academic Press.

Selman, R. L., Newberger, C. M., & Jacquette, D. (1977, April). *Observing interpersonal reasoning in a clinic/educational setting: Toward the integration of developmental and clinical child psychology.* Paper presented at the Society for Research in Child Development meeting, New Orleans.

Semaj, L. T. (1985). Afrikanity, cognition, and extended self-identity. In M. B. Spencer, G. K. Brookins, & W. R. Allen (Eds.), *Beginnings: The social and affective development of black children.* Hillsdale, NJ: Erlbaum.

Senn, M. J. (1975). Insights on the child development movement in the United States. *Monographs of the Society for Research in Child Development, 40* (3–4, Serial No. 161).

Serbin, L. A., & Sprafkin, C. (1986). The salience of gender: The process of sex-typing in three- to seven-year-old children. *Child Development, 57,* 1188–1209.

Serdula, M., Williamson, D. F., Kendrick, J. S., Anda, R. F., & Byers, T. (1991). Trends in alcohol consumption by pregnant women: 1985 through 1988. *Journal of the American Medical Association, 265,* 876–879.

Sexton, M., & Hebel, J. R. (1984). A clinical trial of change in maternal smoking and its effects on birth weight. *Journal of the American Medical Association, 251,* 911–915.

Shafrir, U. (1991, April). *Diagnosing reflectivity.* Paper presented at the Society for Research in Child Development meeting, Seattle.

Shakeshaft, C. (1986, March). A gender at risk. *Phi Delta Kappan,* pp. 499–503.

Shantz, C. O. (1988). Conflicts between children. *Child Development, 59,* 283–305.

Shantz, C. U. (1983). The development of social cognition. In P. H. Mussen (Ed.), *Handbook of child psychology* (4th ed., Vol. 3). New York: Wiley.

Shatz, M., & Gelman, R. (1973). The development of communication skills: Modifications in the speech of young children as a function of the listener. *Monographs of the Society for Research in Child Development, 38* (Serial No. 152).

Shaver, P. R. (1993, March). *Where do adult romantic attachment patterns come from?* Paper presented at the biennial meeting of the Society for Research in Child Development, New Orleans.

Shaw, S. M. (1988). Gender differences in the definition and perception of household labor. *Family Relations, 37,* 333–337.

Sheffield, E. G., Sosa, B. B., & Hudson, J. A. (1993, March). *Narrative complexity and 2- and 3-year-olds' comprehension of false belief.* Paper presented at the biennial meeting of the Society for Research in Child Development, New Orleans.

Shields, S. A. (1991a, August). *Doing emotion/doing gender.* Paper presented at the meeting of the American Psychological Association, San Francisco.

Shields, S. A. (1991b). Gender in the psychology of emotion: A selective research review. In K. T. Strongman (Ed.), *International review of studies on emotion* (Vol. 1). New York: John Wiley.

Shneidman, E. S. (1971). Suicide among the gifted. *Suicide and life-threatening behavior, 1,* 23–45.

Shweder, R., Mahapatra, M., & Miller, J. (1987). Culture and moral development. In J. Kagan & S. Lamb (Eds.), *The emergence of morality in young children.* Chicago: University of Chicago Press.

Siegel, L. (1991, April). *Learning disabilities and post-failure reflectivity.* Paper presented at the Society for Research in Child Development meeting, Seattle.

Siegler, R. S. (1983). Information processing approaches to development. In P. H. Mussen (Ed.), *Handbook of child psychology* (4th ed., Vol. 1). New York: Wiley.

Siegler, R. S. (1986). *Children's thinking.* Englewood Cliffs, NJ: Prentice-Hall.

Siegler, R. S. (1991). *Children's thinking* (2nd ed.). Englewood Cliffs, NJ: Prentice-Hall.

Siegler, R. S. (1992). The other Alfred Binet. *Developmental Psychology, 28,* 179–190.

Siegler, R. S. (in press). Individual differences in strategy choices: Good students, not-so-good students, and perfectionists. *Child Development.*

Siegler, R. S., & Campbell, J. (1989). Individual differences in children's strategy choices. In P. L. Ackerman, R. J. Sternberg, & R. Glaser (Eds.), *Learning and individual differences.* New York: W. H. Freeman.

Sigman, G. S., & Flanery, R. C. (1992). Eating disorders. In D. E. Greydanus & M. L. Wolraich (Eds.), *Behavioral pediatrics.* New York: Springer-Verlag.

Sigman, M. D., Asarnow, R., Cohen, S., & Parmalee, A. H. (1989, April). *Infant attention as a measure of information processing.* Paper presented at the Society for Research in Child Development meeting, Kansas City, MO.

Simkin, P., Whalley, J., & Keppler, A. (1984). *Pregnancy, childbirth, and the newborn.* New York: Simon & Schuster.

Simmons, R. G., & Blyth, D. A. (1987). *Moving into adolescence.* Hawthorne, NY: Aldine.

Simons, R., Conger, R., & Wu, C. (1992, March). *Peer group as amplifier/moderator of the stability of adolescent antisocial behavior.* Paper presented at the meeting of the Society for Research on Adolescence, Washingotn, DC.

Simons, R. L., Whitbeck, L. B., Conger, R. B., & Chyi-In, W. (1991). Intergenerational transmission of harsh parenting. *Developmental Psychology, 27,* 159–171.

Singer, D. G., & Singer, J. L. (1987). Practical suggestions for controlling television. *Journal of Early Adolescence, 7,* 365–369.

Singer, J. L., & Singer, D. G. (1988). Imaginative play and human development: Schemas, scripts, and possibilities. In D. Bergen (Ed.), *Play as a medium for learning and development.* Portsmouth, NH: Heinemann.

Skinner, B. F. (1938). *The behavior of organisms: An experimental analysis.* New York: Appleton-Century-Crofts.

Skinner, B. F. (1957). *Verbal behavior.* New York: Appleton-Century-Crofts.

Skoe, E. E., & Marcia, J. E. (1988). *Ego identity and care-based moral reasoning in college women.* Unpublished manuscript, Acadia University.

Slavin, R. E. (1987). Developmental and motivational perspectives on cooperative learning: A reconciliation. *Child Development, 58,* 1161–1167.

Slavin, R. E. (1988). *Educational psychology* (2nd ed.). Englewood Cliffs, NJ: Prentice-Hall.

Slavin, R. E. (1989). Cooperative learning and student achievement. In R. E. Slavin (Ed.), *School and classroom organization.* Hillsdale, NJ: Erlbaum.

Slavin, R. E. (1989a). Achievement effects of substantial reductions in class size. In R. E. Slavin (Ed.), *School and classroom organization.* Hillsdale, NJ: Erlbaum.

Slobin, D. (1972, July). Children and language: They learn the same all around the world. *Psychology Today,* pp. 71–76.

Smith, B. A., Fillion, T. J., & Blass, E. M. (1990). Orally mediated sources of calming in 1- to 3-day-old human infants. *Developmental Psychology, 26,* 731–737.

Smith, J., & Baltes, P. B. (in press). A study of wisdom-related knowledge: Age-cohort differences in responses to life-planning problems. *Development Psychology*

Snarey, J. (1987, June). A question of morality. *Psychology Today,* pp. 6–8.

Snow, C. (1993, March). *Home influence on the development of language-related literacy skills.* Paper presented at the biennial meeting of the Society for Research in Child Development, New Orleans.

Snow, C. E. (1989). Understanding social interaction in language interaction: Sentences are not enough. In M. H. Bornstein & J. S. Bruner (Eds.), *Interaction in human development.* Hillsdale, NJ: Erlbaum.

Sophian, C. (1985). Perseveration and infants' search: A comparison of two- and three-location tasks. *Developmental Psychology, 21,* 187–194.

Spade, J. Z., & Reese, C. A. (1991). We've come a long way, maybe: College students' plans for work and family. *Sex Roles, 24,* 309–321.

Spearman, C. E. (1927). *The abilities of man.* New York: Macmillan.

Spelke, E. S. (1979). Perceiving bimodally specified events in infancy. *Developmental Psychology, 5,* 626–636.

Spelke, E. S. (1988). The origins of physical knowledge. In L. Weiskrantz (Ed.), *Thought without language.* New York: Oxford University Press.

Spelke, E. S. (1991). Physical knowledge in infancy: Reflections on Piaget's theory. In S. Carey & R. Gelman (Eds.), *The epigenesis of mind: Essays in biology and cognition.* Hillsdale, NJ: Erlbaum.

Spence, J. T. (1984). Masculinity, femininity, and gender-related traits: A conceptual analysis and critique of current research. In B. A. Maher & W. B. Maher (Eds.), *Progress in experimental personality research* (Vol. 13; pp. 1–97). Orlando, FL: Academic.

Spence, J. T. (1985). Gender identity and its implications for the concepts of masculinity and femininity. In T. B. Sonderegger (Ed.), *Psychology and gender: Nebraska Symposium on Motivation* (pp. 59–96). Lincoln: University of Nebraska Press.

Spence, J. T. (1992, August). *Gender identity: A multidimensional perspective.* Paper presented at the meeting of the American Psychological Association, Washington, DC.

Spence, J. T., & Helmreich, R. (1978). *Masculinity and femininity: Their psychological dimensions.* Austin: University of Texas Press.

Spencer, M. B., & Dornbusch, S. M. (1990). Challenges in studying minority youth. In S. S. Feldman & G. R. Elliott (Eds.), *At the threshold: The developing adolescent.* Cambridge, MA: Harvard University Press.

Spencer, M. B., & Markstrom-Adams, C. (1990). Identity processes among racial and ethnic minority children in America. *Child Development, 61,* 290–310.

Spencer, M. L. (1986). Sex equity in bilingual education. English as a second language, and foreign language instruction. *Theory into Practice, 25,* 257–266.

Sperry, R. W. (1974). Lateral specialization in surgically separated hemispheres. In F. O. Schmitt & F. G. Worden (Eds.), *The neurosciences: Third study program.* Cambridge, MA: MIT Press.

Spitzer, S., & Dicker, S. G. (1993, March). *School entrance age and social acceptance in kindergarten: Social policy implications.* Paper presented at the biennial meeting of the Society for Research in Child Development, New Orleans.

Sprey, J. (1991). Generational and intergenerational connections within the family and the community. *Marriage and Family Review, 16,* 221–236.

Sroufe, L. A. (1985). Attachment classification from the perspective of infant-caregiver relationships and infant temperament. *Child Development, 56,* 1–14.

Sroufe, L. A. (in press). Pathways to adaptation and maladaptation: Psychopathology as developmental deviation. In D. Cicchetti (Ed.), *Developmental psychopathology: Past, present, and future.* Hillsdale, NJ: Erlbaum.

Sroufe, L. A., & Waters, E. (1976). The ontogenesis of smiling and laughter: A perspective on the organization of development in infancy. *Psychological Review, 83,* 173–198.

Stage, E. K., Kreinberg, N., Eccles, J., & Becker, J. R. (1985). Increasing the participation and achievement of girls and women in mathematics, science, and engineering. In S. S. Klein (Ed.), *Handbook for achieving sex equity through education.* Baltimore, MD: Johns Hopkins University Press.

Stallings, J. (1975). Implementation and child effects of teaching practices in Follow Through classrooms. *Monographs of the Society for Research in Child Development, 40* (Serial No. 163).

Stanhope, L., & Corter, C. (1993, March). *The mother's role in the transition to siblinghood.* Paper presented at the biennial meeting of the Society for Research in Child Development, New Orleans.

Stankov, L. (1991). The effects of practice and training on human abilities. In H. A. H. Rowe (Eds.), *Intelligence: Reconceptualization and measurement.* Hillsdale, NJ: Erlbaum.

Stapp, J., Tucker, A. M., & VandenBos, G. R. (1985). Census of psychological personnel, 1983. *American Psychologist, 40,* 1317–1351.

Stein, N. L., & Glenn, C. G. (1979). An analysis of story comprehension in elementary school children. In R. O. Freedle (Ed.), *Discourse processing: Multidisciplinary perspectives* (pp. 53–120). Norwood, NJ: Ablex.

Steinberg, E. R. (1990a). *Computer-assisted instruction.* Hillsdale, NJ: Erlbaum.

Steinberg, L. (1991). Parent-adolescent relations. In R. M. Lerner, A. C. Petersen, & J. Brooks-Gunn (Eds.). *Encyclopedia of adolescence* (Vol. 2). New York: Garland.

Steinberg, L. D. (1986). Latchkey children and susceptibility to peer pressure: An ecological analysis. *Developmental Psychology, 22,* 433–439.

Steinberg, L. D. (1988). Reciprocal relation between parent-child distance and pubertal maturation. *Developmental Psychology, 24,* 122–128.

Steiner, J. E. (1979). Human facial expressions in response to taste and smell stimulation. In H. Reese & L. Lipsitt (Eds.), *Advances in child development and behavior* (Vol. 13). New York: Academic Press.

Stern, D. N., Beebe, B., Jaffe, J., & Bennett, S. L. (1977). The infant's stimulus world during social interaction: A study of caregiver behaviors with particular reference to repetition and timing. In H. R. Schaffer (Ed.), *Studies in mother-infant interaction.* London: Academic Press.

Sternberg, R. J. (1986). *Intelligence applied.* San Diego: Harcourt Brace Jovanovich.

Sternberg, R. J. (1987). A day at developmental downs: Sportscast for race #2—Neo-Piagetian theories of cognitive development. *International Journal of Psychology, 22,* 507–529.

Sternberg, R. J. (1987). Teaching intelligence: The application of cognitive psychology of intellectual skills. In J. B. Baron & R. J. Sternberg (Eds.), *Teaching thinking skills: Theory and practice.* New York: W. H. Freeman.

Sternberg, R. J. (1989). Introduction: In R. J. Sternberg (Ed.), *Advances in the psychology of human intelligence.* Hillsdale, NJ: Erlbaum.

Sternberg, R. J. (1990, April). *Academic and practical cognition as different aspects of intelligence.* Paper presented at the 12th West Virginia conference on life-span developmental psychology, Morgantown, WV.

Sternglanz, S. H., & Serbin, L. A. (1974). Sex-role stereotyping in children's television programming. *Developmental Psychology, 10,* 710–715.

Steur, F. B., Applefield, J. M., & Smith, R. (1971). Televised aggression and interpersonal aggression of preschool children. *Journal of Experimental Child Psychology, 11,* 442–447.

Stevens, J. H. (1984). Black grandmothers' and black adolescents mothers' knowledge about parenting. *Developmental Psychology, 20,* 1017–1025.

Stevens-Simon, C., & McAnarney, E. R. (1992). Adolescent pregnancy: Continuing challenges. In D. E. Greydanus & M. L. Wolraich (Eds.), *Behavioral pediatrics.* New York: Springer-Verlag.

Stevenson, H. W. (1972). *Children's Learning.* New York: Appleton-Century-Croft.

Stevenson, H. W. (1991, April). *Academic achievement and parental beliefs: A longitudinal study in Japan, Taiwan, and the United States.* Paper presented at the biennial meeting of the Society for Research in Child Development, Seattle.

Stevenson, H. W. (1992). Learning from Asian schools. *Scientific American,* December 1992, 267:6, 70–76.

Stevenson, H. W., Chen, C., & Lee, S. Y. (1993). Mathematics achievement of Chinese, Japanese & American children: ten years later. *Science, 259,* 53–58.

Stevenson, H. W., Lee, S., Chen, C., Stigler, J. W., Hsu, C., & Kitamura, S. (1990). Contexts of achievement. *Monograph of the Society for Research in Child Development, 55,* (Serial No. 221).

Stigler, J. W., Nusbaum, H. C., & Chalip, L. (1988). Developmental changes in speed of processing: Central limiting mechanism or skill transfer. *Child Development, 59,* 1144–1153.

Stipek, D. (1992). The child at school. In M. H. Bornstein & M. E. Lamb (Eds.), *Developmental psychology: An advanced textbook* (3rd ed.). Hillsdale, NJ: Erlbaum.

Stipek, D. J., & Hoffman, J. M. (1980). Children's achievement-related expectancies as a function of academic performance histories and sex. *Journal of Educational Psychology, 72,* 861–865.

Stocker, C., & Dunn, J. (1991). Sibling relationships in adolescence. In R. M. Lerner, A. C. Petersen, & J. Brooks-Gunn (Eds.), *Encyclopedia of adolescence* (Vol. 2). New York: Garland.

Strachen, A., & Jones, D. (1982). Changes in identification during adolescence: A personal construct theory approach. *Journal of Personality Assessment, 46,* 139–148.

Strahan, D. B. (1983). The emergence of formal operations in adolescence. *Transcendence, 11,* 7–14.

Strahan, D. B. (1987). A developmental analysis of formal reasoning in the middle grades. *Journal of Instructional Psychology, 14,* 67–73.

Strawn, J. (1992, Fall). *The states and the poor: Child poverty rises as the safety net shrinks.* Social Policy Report, Society for Research in Child Development, 1–19.

Streissguth, A. P., Carmichael-Olson, H., Sampston, P. D., & Barr, H. M. (1991, April). *Alcohol vs. tobacco as prenatal correlates of child behavior.* Paper presented at the biennial meeting of the Society for Research in Child Development, Seattle.

Streissguth, A. P., Martin, D. C., Barr, H. M., Sandman, B. M., Kirshner, G. L., & Darby, B. L. (1984). Intrauterine alcohol and nicotine exposure: Attention and reaction time in 4-year-old children. *Developmental Psychology, 20,* 533–541.

Stricker, G., Davis-Russell, E., Bourg, E., Duran, E., Hammond, W. R., McHolland, J., Polite, K., & Vaughn, B. E. (Eds.). (1990). *Toward ethnic diversification in psychology education and training.* Washington, DC: American Psychological Association.

Striegel-Moore, R., Pike, K., Rodin, J., Schreiber, G., & Wilfley, D. (1993, March). *Predictors and correlates of drive for thinness.* Paper presented at the biennial meeting of the Society for Research in Child Development, New Orleans.

Stringer, S., & Neal, C. (1993, March). *Scaffolding as a tool for assessing sensitive and contingent teaching: A comparison between high- and low-risk mothers.* Paper presented at the biennial meeting of the Society for Research in Child Development, New Orleans.

Studdert-Kennedy, M. (1991). Language development from an evolutionary perspective. In N. A. Krasnegor, D. M. Rumbaugh, M. Studdert-Kennedy, & R. L. Schiefelbusch (Eds.), *Biological and behavioral determinants of language development.* Hillsdale, NJ: Erlbaum.

Stunkard, A. J. (1987). The regulation of body weight and the treatment of obesity. In H. Weiner & A. Baum (Eds.), *Eating regulation and discontrol.* Hillsdale, NJ: Erlbaum.

Sue, D., & Sue, D. W. (1993). Ethnic identity: Cultural factors in the psychological development of Asians in America. In D. R. Atkinson, G. Morten, & D. W. Sue (Eds.), *Counseling American minorities.* Madison WI: WCB Brown & Benchmark.

Sue, D. W. (1989). Ethnic identity: The impact of two cultures on the psychological development of Asians in America. In D. R. Atkinson, G. Morten, & D. W. Sue (Eds.), *Counseling American minorities* (3rd ed.). Dubuque, IA: Wm. C. Brown.

Sue, S. (1990, August). *Ethnicity and culture in psychological research and practice.* Paper presented at the meeting of the American Psychological Association, Boston, MA.

Sue, S. (1992, August). *Asian American psychology: The untold story.* Paper presented at the meeting of the American Psychological Association, Washington, DC.

Sullivan, H. S. (1953). *The interpersonal theory of psychiatry.* New York: W. W. Norton.

Sullivan, K., & Sullivan, A. (1980). Adolescent-parent separation. *Developmental Psychology, 16,* 93–99.

Sullivan, L. (1991, May 25). US secretary urges TV to restrict "irresponsible sex and reckless violence." *Boston Globe,* p. A1.

Suomi, S. J., Harlow, H. F., & Domek, C. J. (1970). Effect of repetitive infant-infant separations of young monkeys. *Journal of Abnormal Psychology, 76,* 161–172.

Super, C. M. (1980). Cross-cultural research on infancy. In H. C. Triandis & A. Heron (Eds.), *Handbook of cross-cultural psychology, developmental psychology* (Vol. 4). Boston: Allyn & Bacon.

Super, C. M., Herrera, M. G., & Mora, J. O. (1990). Long-term effects of food supplementation and psychosocial intervention on the physical growth of Colombian infants at risk of malnutrition. *Child Development, 61,* 29–49.

Super, C. M., Herrera, M. G., & Mora, J. O. (1991, April). *Cognitive outcomes of early nutritional intervention in the Bogotá study.* Paper presented at the biennial meeting of the Society for Research in Child Development, Seattle.

Susman, E. J., & Dorn, L. (1991). Hormones and behavior in adolescence. In R. M. Lerner, A. C. Petersen, & J. Brooks-Gunn (Eds.), *Encyclopedia of adolescence* (Vol. I). New York: Garland.

Sutton-Smith, B. (1985, October). The child at play. *Psychology Today,* pp. 64–65.

Swadesh, M. (1971). *The origin and diversification of language.* Chicago: Aldine-Atherton.

Swick, K. J., & Manning, M. L. (1983). Father involvement in home and school settings. *Childhood Education, 60,* 128–134.

T

Tajfel, H. (1978). The achievement of group differentiation. In H. Tajfel (Ed.), *Differentiation between social groups: Studies in the social psychology of intergroup relations.* London: Academic Press.

Tangney, J. P. (1988). Aspects of the family and children's television viewing content preferences. *Child Development, 59,* 1070–1079.

Tannen, D. (1990). *You just don't understand: Women and men in conversation.* New York: Ballantine.

Tanner, J. M. (1978). *Fetus into man: Physical growth from conception into maturity.* Cambridge, MA: Harvard University Press.

Tanner, J. M. (1991). Growth spurt, adolescent (I). In R. M. Lerner, A. C. Petersen, & J. Brooks-Gunn, *Encyclopedia of adolescence* (Vol. I). New York: Garland.

Tavris, C. (1989). *Anger: The misunderstood emotion* (2nd ed.). New York: Touchstone.

Tavris, C., & Wade, C. (1984). *The longest war: Sex differences in perspective* (2nd ed.). San Diego, CA: Harcourt Brace Jovanovich.

Taylor, A., & Machida, S. (1993). *Effects of parent involvement and teacher support on school progress of Head Start children.* Paper presented at the biennial meeting of the Society for Research in Child Development, New Orleans.

Taylor, A. R., & Machida, S. (1993, March). *The contribution of peer relations to social competence in low-income children.* Paper presented at the biennial meeting of the Society for Research in Child Development, New Orleans.

Taylor, R. J., Chatters, L., Tucker, M. B., & Lewis, E. (1990). Developments in research on black families: A decade review. *Journal of Marriage and the Family, 52,* 993–1014.

Terman, L. (1925). *Genetic studies of genius:* Vol. 1. *Mental and physical traits of a thousand gifted children.* Stanford, CA: Stanford.

Teti, D. M., Sakin, J., Kucera, E., Caballeros, M., & Corns, K. M. (1993, March). *Transitions to siblinghood and security of firstborn attachment: Psychosocial and psychiatric correlates of changes over time.* Paper presented at the biennial meeting of the Society for Research in Child Development, New Orleans.

Tharp, R. G. (1989). Psychocultural variables and constants: Effects on teaching and learning in schools. *American Psychologist, 44,* 349–359.

Thoman, E. B. (1992, May). *Individualizing intervention for premature infants.* Paper presented at the International Conference on Infant Studies, Miami Beach, FL.

Thomas, A., & Chess, S. (1987). Commentary. In H. H. Goldsmith, A. H. Buss, R. Plomin, M. K. Rothbart, A. Thomas, A. Chess, R. R. Hinde, & R. B. McCall (Eds.), Roundtable: What is temperament? Four approaches. *Child Development, 58,* 505–529.

Thomas, A., & Chess, S. (1991). Temperament in adolescence and its functional significance. In R. M. Lerner, A. C. Petersen, & J. Brooks-Gunn (Eds.), *Encyclopedia of adolescence* (Vol. 2). New York: Garland.

Thomas, C. W., Coffman, J. K., & Kipp, K. L. (1993, March). *Are only children different from children with siblings? A longitudinal study of behavioral and social functioning.* Paper presented at the biennial meeting of the Society for Research in Child Development, New Orleans.

Thomas, G. (Ed.). (1988). *World education encyclopedia.* New York: Facts on File Publications.

Thomas, J. L. (1986). Age and sex differences in perceptions of grandparenting. *Journal of Gerontology, 41,* 417–423.

Thompson, E. T., & Hughes, E. C. (1958). *Race: Individual and collective behavior.* Glencoe, IL: Free Press.

Thompson, L., & Walker, A. J. (1989). Gender in families: Women and men in marriage, work, and parenthood. *Journal of Marriage and the Family, 51,* 845–871.

Thompson, R. A. (1991). Construction and reconstruction of early attachments: Taking perspective on attachment theory and research. In D. P. Keating & H. G. Rosen (Eds.), *Constructivist perspectives on atypical development.* Hillsdale, NJ: Erlbaum.

Thompson, R. J., & Oehler, J. M. (1991, April). *Very low birthweight (VLBW) infants: Maternal stress, coping, and psychological adjustment.* Paper presented at the biennial meeting of the Society for Research in Child Development, Seattle.

Thorndike, R. L., Hagan, E. P., & Sattler, J. M. (1985). *Stanford-Binet* (4th ed.). Chicago: Riverside.

Thurstone, L. L. (1938). *Primary mental abilities.* Chicago: University of Chicago Press.

Tinsley, B. (1992). Multiple influences on the acquisitions and socialization of children's health attitudes and behavior: An integrative review. *Child Development, 63,* 1043–1069.

Tishler, C. L. (1992). Adolescent suicide: Assessment of risk, prevention, and treatment. *Adolescent Medicine, 3,* 51–60.

Tobin, J. J., Wu, D. Y. H., & Davidson, D. H. (1989). Preschool in three cultures. New Haven, CT: Yale University Press.

Tomlinson-Keasey, C. (1972). Formal operations in females from 11 to 54 years of age. *Developmental Psychology, 6,* 364.

Tomlinson-Keasey, C., Warren, L. W., & Elliott, J. E. (1986). Suicide among gifted women: A prospective study. *Journal of Abnormal Psychology, 95,* 123–130.

Toth, A. (1991). *The fertility solution.* New York: Atlantic Monthly Press.

Toth, S. L. (1993, March). *The effect of child maltreatment on self development.* Paper presented at the biennial meeting of the Society for Research in Child Development, New Orleans.

Toth, S. L., Manly, J. T., & Cicchetti, D. (in press). Child maltreatment and vulnerability to depression. *Development and Psychopathology.*

Trabasso, T. (1991, April). *The development and use of planning knowledge in narrative production.* Paper presented at the Society for Research in Child Development meeting, Seattle.

Trankina, F. (1983). Clinical issues and techniques in working with Hispanic children and their families. In G. J. Powell, J. Yamamoto, A. Romero, & A. Morales (Eds.), *The psychosocial development of minority group children.* New York: Brunner/Mazel.

Trawick-Smith, J. (1993, March). *The ebb and flow of research on children's color: Trends since 1986.* Paper presented at the biennial meeting of the Society for Research in Child Development, New Orleans.

Treboux, D. A., & Busch-Rossnagel, N. A. (1991). Sexual behavior, sexual attitudes, and contraceptive use, age differences in adolescent. In R. M. Lerner, A. C. Petersen, & J. Brooks-Gunn (Eds.), *Encyclopedia of adolescence* (Vol. 2). New York: Garland.

Trehub, S. E., Schneider, B. A., Thorpe, L. A., & Judge, P. (1991). Observational measures of auditory sensitivity in early infancy. *Developmental Psychology, 27,* 40–49.

Triandis, H. (1985). Collectivism vs. individualism: A reconceptualization of a basic concept in cross-cultural social psychology. In C. Bagley & G. K. Verman (Eds), *Personality, cognition, and values.* London: Macmillan.

Trimble, J. E. (1989). *The enculturation of contemporary psychology.* Paper presented at the meeting of the American Psychological Association, New Orleans.

Troll, L. E. (1989). Myths of mid-life intergenerational relationships. In S. Hunter & M. Sundel (Eds.), *Mid-life myths.* Newbury Park, CA: Sage.

Tronick, E. Z. (1989). Emotions and emotional communication in infants. *American Psychologist, 44,* 112–119.

Trotter, R. J. (1987, December). Project Day-Care. *Psychology Today,* pp. 32–38.

Tucker, L. A. (1987). Television, teenagers, and health. *Journal of Youth and Adolescence, 16,* 415–425.

Tuckman, B. W., & Hinkle, J. S. (1988). An experimental study of the physical and psychological effects of aerobic exercise on school children. In B. G. Melamed, K. A. Matthews, D. K. Routh, B. Stabler, & N. Schneiderman (Eds.), *Child health psychology.* Hillsdale, NJ: Erlbaum.

Tudge, J., & Winterhoff, P. (1993, March). *The cognitive consequences of collaboration: Why ask how?* Paper presented at the biennial meeting of the Society for Research in Child Development, New Orleans.

Turiel, E. (1966). An experimental test of the sequentiality of developmental stages in the child's moral judgments. *Journal of Personality of Social Psychology, 3,* 611–618.

U

U.S. Bureau of the Census. (1986). *Geographical mobility: March 1980 to March 1985* (Current Population Reports Series P–20, No. 368). Washington, DC: U. S. Government Printing Office.

Ullman, C. (1982). Cognitive and emotional antecedents of religious conversion. *Journal of Personality and Social Psychology, 43,* 183–192.

Unger, R. K. (1993, August). *Social construction of biological sex.* Paper presented at the meeting of the American Psychological Association, Toronto, CA.

United States Commission on Civil Rights (1975). *A better chance to learn: Bilingual bicultural education.* Washington, DC: U. S. Government Printing Office.

Urban, J., Carlson, E., Egeland, B., & Sroufe, A. (1992, March). *Continuity in behavioral patterns across childhood.* Paper presented at the meeting of the Society for Research in Adolescence, Washington, DC.

V

Valdez-Menchaca, M. C., & Whitehurst, G. J. (1992). Accelerating language development through picture book reading: A systematic extension to Mexican day care. *Developmental Psychology, 28,* 1106–1114.

Van den Berghe, P. L. (1978). *Race and racism: A comparative perspective.* New York: John Wiley & Sons.

Van Deusen-Henkel, J., & Argondizza, M. (1987). Early elementary education: Curriculum planning for the primary grades. In *A framework for curriculum design.* Augusta, ME: Division of Curriculum, Maine Department of Educational and Cultural Services.

Vandell, D. L. (1987). Baby sister/Baby brother: Reactions to the birth of a sibling and patterns of early sibling relations. In F. F. Schachter & R. K. Stone (Eds.), *Practical concerns about siblings.* New York: The Haworth Press.

Vandell, D. L. (1985, April). *Relationship between infant-peer and infant-mother interactions: What we have learned.* Paper presented at the Society for Research in Child Development meeting, Toronto.

Vandell, D. L., & Corasaniti, M. A. (1988). Variations in early child care: Do they predict subsequent social, emotional, and cognitive differences? *Child Development, 59,* 176–186.

Vandell, D. L., & Wilson, K. S. (1988). Infants' interactions with mother, sibling, and peer: Contrasts and relations between interaction systems. *Child Development, 48,* 176–186.

Vaughn, S. (1993, March). *A prospective investigation of the social competence of youngsters with learning disabilities.* Paper presented at the biennial meeting of the Society for Research in Child Development, New Orleans.

Vega, W. A. (1990). Hispanic families in the 1980s: A decade of research. *Journal of Marriage and the Family, 52,* 1015–1024.

Vining, E. P. G. (1992). Down syndrome. In R. A. Hoekelman (Ed.), *Primary pediatric care* (2nd ed.). St. Louis, MO: Mosby Yearbook.

Voight, J., & Hans, S. (1993, March). *The mothers of adolescent mothers: Support and conflict in grandmothers' social networks.* Paper presented at the biennial meeting of the Society for Research in Child Development, New Orleans.

Vorhees, C. V., & Mollnow, E. (1987). Behavioral teratogenesis: Long-term influences in behavior from early exposure to environmental agents. In J. D. Osofsky (Ed.), *Handbook of infant development.* New York: Wiley.

Vygotsky, L. S. (1962). *Thought and language.* Cambridge, MA: MIT Press.

W

Waddington, C. H. (1957). *The strategy of the genes.* London: Allen & Son.

Wade, C., & Tavris, C. (1993). *Psychology* (3rd ed.). New York: Harper Collins.

Wagner, B. M., Cole, R. E., & Schwartzman, P. (1993, March). *Prediction of suicide attempts among junior and senior high school youth.* Paper presented at the biennial meeting of the Society for Research in Child Development, New Orleans.

Walker, E. L. (1970). Relevant psychology is a snark. *American Psychologist, 25,* 1081–1086.

Walker, L. (1982). The sequentiality of Kohlberg's stages of moral development. *Child Development, 53,* 1130–1136.

Walker, L. J. (1984). Sex differences in the development of moral reasoning. A critical review. *Child Development, 51,* 131–139.

Walker, L. J. (1991a). Sex differences in moral development. In W. M. Kurtines & J. Gewirtz (Eds.), *Moral behavior and development* (Vol. 2). Hillsdale, NJ: Erlbaum.

Walker, L. J. (1991b, April). *The validity of an ethic of care.* Paper presented at the Society for Research in Child Development meeting, Seattle.

Walker, L. J. (1993, March). *Is the family a sphere of moral growth for children?* Paper presented at the biennial meeting of the Society for Research in Child Development, New Orleans.

Walker, L. J., & Taylor, J. H. (1991a). Family interaction and the development of moral reasoning. *Child Development, 62,* 264–283.

Walker, L. J., & Taylor, J. H. (1991b). Stage transitions in moral reasoning: A longitudinal study of developmental processes. *Developmental Psychology, 27,* 330–337.

Walker, L. J., de Vries, B., & Trevethan, S. D. (1987). Moral stages and moral orientation in real-life and hypothetical dilemmas. *Child Development, 58,* 842–858.

Wall, J. A. (1993, March). *Susceptibility to antisocial peer pressure in Mexican-American adolescents and its relation to acculturation.* Paper presented at the biennial meeting of the Society for Research in Child Development, New Orleans.

Wallerstein, J. S. (1989). *Second chances.* New York: Ticknor & Fields.

Wallerstein, J. S., & Kelly, J. B. (1980). *Surviving the breakup: How children actually cope with divorce.* New York: Basic Books.

Wallerstein, J. S., Corbin, S. B., & Lewis, J. M. (1988). Children of divorce: A 10–year study. In E. M. Hetherington & J. D. Arasteh (Eds.), *Impact of divorce, single parenting, and stepparenting on children.* Hillsdale, NJ: Erlbaum.

Warshak, R. A. (1993, January 15). Personal communication, Department of Psychology, University of Texas at Dallas, Richardson, TX.

Washburn, K. J., & Hakes, D. T. (1985, April). *Changes in children's semantic and syntactic acceptability judgments.* Paper presented at the Society for Research in Child Development meeting, Toronto.

Wasz-Hockert, O., Lind, J., Vuorenkoski, V., Partanen, T., & Valanne, E. (1968). *The infant cry.* London, England: Spastics International Medical Publications.

Waterman, A. S. (1985). Identity in the context of adolescent psychology. In A. S. Waterman (Ed.), *Identity in adolescence: Processes and contents.* San Francisco: Jossey-Bass.

Waterman, A. S. (1989). Curricula interventions for identity change: Substantive and ethical considerations. *Journal of Adolescence, 12,* 389–400.

Waterman, A. S. (1992). Identity as an aspect of optimal psychological functioning. In G. R. Adams, T. P. Gullotta, & R. Montemayor (Eds.), *Adolescent identity formation.* Newbury Park, CA: Sage.

Watson, J. B. (1928). *Psychological care of infant and child.* New York: W. W. Norton.

Waxman, S. R., & Kosowski, T. D. (1990). Nouns mark category relations: Toddlers' and preschoolers' word-learning biases. *Child Development, 61,* 1461–1473.

Wechsler, D. (1949). *Wechsler Intelligence Scale for Children.* New York: Psychological Corp.

Wechsler, D. (1955). *Wechsler Adult Intelligence Scale manual.* New York: Psychological Corp.

Wechsler, D. (1967). *Wechsler Preschool and Primary Scale of Intelligence.* New York: Psychological Corp.

Wechsler, D. (1974). *Wechsler Intelligence Scale for Children—Revised.* New York: Psychological Corp.

Wechsler, D. (1981). *Wechsler Adult Intelligence Scale—Revised.* New York: Psychological Corp.

Weikart, D. P. (1982). Preschool education for disadvantaged children. In J. R. Travers & R. J. Light (Eds.), *Learning from experience: Evaluating early childhood demonstration programs.* Washington, DC: National Academy Press.

Weikert, D. P. (1993). *Long-term positive effects in the Perry Preschool Head Start program.* Unpublished data, The High Scope Foundation, Ypsilanti, MI.

Weinberg, R. A. (1989). Intelligence and IQ: Landmark issues and great debates. *American Psychologist, 44,* 98–104.

Weiner, I. B. (1980). Psychopathology in adolescence. In J. Adelson (Ed.), *Handbook of adolescent psychology.* New York: Wiley.

Weissberg, R. P., Caplan, M. Z., & Sivo, P. J. (1989). A new conceptual framework for establishing school-based social competence promotion programs. In L. A. Bond, B. E. Compas, & C. Swift (Eds.), *Prevention in the schools.* Menlo Park, CA: Sage.

Weizmann, F., Wiener, N. I., Wiesenthal, D. L., & Ziegler, M. (1990). Differential K theory and racial hierarchies. *Canadian Psychology, 31,* 1–13.

Wellman, H. M. (1990). *The child's theory of mind.* Cambridge, MA: M.I.T. Press.

Wellman, H. M., & Gelman, S. A. (1992). Cognitive development: Foundational theories of core domains. *Annual Review of Psychology, 43,* 337–375.

Wellman, H. M., Ritter, R., & Flavell, J. H. (1985). Deliberate memory behavior in the delayed reactions of very young children. *Developmental Psychology, 11,* 780–787.

Wender, P. H., Kety, S. S., Rosenthal, D., Schulsinger, F., Ortmann, J., & Lunde, I. (1986). Psychiatric disorders in the biological and adoptive families of adopted individuals with affective disorders. *Archives of General Psychiatry, 43,* 923–929.

Wenz-Gross, M., & Siperstein, G. (1993, March). *Social support and adjustment in children with special needs.* Paper presented at the biennial meeting of the Society for Research in Child Development, New Orleans.

Werner, E. E. (1979). *Cross-cultural child development: A view from planet earth.* Monterey, CA: Brooks/Cole.

Wertheimer, M. (1945). *Productive thinking.* New York: Harper.

Wertsch, J. V. (1985). Adult-child interaction as a source of self-regulation in children. In S. R. Yussen (Ed.), *The growth of reflection in children.* New York: Academic Press.

Wertsch, J. V., & Tulviste, P. (1992). L. S. Vygotsky and contemporary developmental psychology. *Developmental Psychology, 28,* 548–557.

Whaley, L. F., & Wong, D. L. (1988). *Essentials of pediatric nursing* (3rd ed.). St. Louis, MO: C. V. Mosby.

White, B. L. (1988). *Educating the infant and toddler.* Lexington, MA: Lexington Books.

White, B. L. (1990). *The first three years of life.* New York: Prentice-Hall.

White, B. L., & Held, R. (1966). Plasticity of sensorimotor development in human infants. In J. Rosenblith & W. Allinsmith (Eds.), *The causes of behavior.* Boston: Allyn & Bacon.

Whitehurst, G. J., & Valdez-Menchaca, M. C. (1988). What is the role of reinforcement in early language acquisition? *Child Development, 59,* 430–440.

Whiting, B. B. (1989, April). *Culture and interpersonal behavior.* Paper presented at the biennial meeting of the Society for Research in Child Development, Kansas City, MO.

Whiting, B. B., & Edwards, C. P. (1988). *Children of different worlds.* Cambridge, MA: Harvard University Press.

Whiting, B. B., & Whiting, J. W. M. (1975). *Children of six cultures.* Cambridge, MA: Harvard University Press.

Widmayer, S., & Field, T. (1980). Effects of Brazelton demonstrations on early patterns of preterm infants and their teenage mothers. *Infant Behavior and Development, 3,* 79–89.

Wiesenfeld, A. R., Malatesta, C. Z., & DeLoache, L. L. (1981). Differential parental response to familiar and unfamiliar infant distress signals. *Infant Behavior and Development, 4,* 281–295.

Wilder, D. (1991, March 28). To save the Black family, the young must abstain. *Wall Street Journal,* p. A14.

Wilkening, F., & Anderson, N. H. (1991). Representation and diagnosis of knowledge structures in developmental psychology. In N. H. Anderson (Ed.), *Contributions to information integration theory* (Vol. 3). Hillsdale, NJ: Erlbaum.

Willer, B., & Bredekamp, S. (1990). Redefining readiness: An essential requisite for educational reform. *Young Children, 45,* 22–26.

William T. Grant Foundation Commission on Work, Family, and Citizenship. (1988, February). *The forgotten half: Non-college bound youth in America.* Washington, DC: William T. Grant Foundation.

Williams, J. (1979). Reading instruction today. *American Psychologist, 34,* 917–922.

Williams, J. E., & Best, D. L. (1982). *Measuring sex stereotypes: A thirty-nation study.* Newbury Park, CA: Sage.

Williams, J. E., & Best, D. L. (1989). *Sex and psyche: Self-concept viewed cross-culturally.* Newbury Park, CA: Sage.

Williams, M. E., & Condry, J. (1989, April). *Minority portrayals and cross-racial interaction television.* Paper presented at the biennial meeting of the Society for Research in Child Development, Kansas City, MO.

Willis, S. L., & Schaie, K. W. (1986). Training the elderly on the ability factors of spatial orientation and inductive reasoning. *Psychology and Aging, 1,* 239–247.

Wilson, E. O. (1975). *Sociobiology: The new synthesis.* Cambridge, MA: Harvard University Press.

Wilson, L. C. (1990). *Infants and toddlers: Curriculum and teaching.* Albany, NY: Delmar.

Wilson, L. L., & Stith, S. M. (1993). Culturally sensitive therapy with Black clients. In D. R. Atkinson, G. Morten, & D. W. Sue (Eds.), *Counseling American minorities.* Madison, WI: WCB Brown & Benchmark.

Wilson, M. N. (1989). Child development in the context of the Black extended family. *American Psychologist, 44,* 380–383.

Wilson, W. J., & Neckerman, K. M. (1986). Poverty and family structure: The widening gap between evidence and public policy issues. In S. Danziger & D. Weinberg (Eds.), *Fighting poverty.* Cambridge, MA: Harvard University Press.

Windle, W. F. (1940). *Physiology of the human fetus.* Philadelphia: Saunders.

Winkelstein, W., Samuel, M., Padian, N. S., & Wiley, J. A. (1987). Selected sexual practices of San Francisco heterosexual men and risk of infection by human immunodeficiency virus. *Journal of the American Medical Association, 257,* 1470.

Winner, E. (1986, August). Where pelicans kiss seals. *Psychology Today,* pp. 24–35.

Witkin, H. A., Mednick, S. A., Schulsinger, R., Bakkestrom, E. Christiansen, K. O., Goodenbough, D. R., Hirchhorn, K., Lunsteen, C., Owen, D. R., Philip, J., Ruben, D. B., & Stocking, M. (1976). Criminality in XYY and XXY men. *Science, 193,* 547–555.

Wober, M. (1974). Towards an understanding of the Kiganda concept of intelligence. In J. W. Berry & P. R. Dasen (Eds.), *Culture and cognition.* London: Methuen.

Wolff, P. H. (1969). The natural history of crying and other vocalizations in early infancy. In B. M. Foss (Ed.), *Determinants of infant development* (Vol. 4). London, England: Methuen.

Wood, F. H. (1988). Learners at risk. *Teaching Exceptional Children, 20,* 4–9.

Woolsey, S. F. (1992). Sudden infant death syndrome. In R. B. Hoekleman, S. B. Friedman, N. M. Nelson, & H. M. Seidel (Eds.), *Primary pediatric care* (2nd ed.). St. Louis, MO: Mosby Yearbook.

Worobey, J., & Belsky, J. (1982). Employing the Brazelton Scale to influence mothering: An experimental comparison of three strategies. *Developmental Psychology, 18,* 736–743.

Worthington-Roberts, B. S. (1988). Lactation and human milk. In S. R. Williams & B. S. Worthington-Roberts (Eds.), *Nutrition throughout the life cycle.* St. Louis: Times Mirror/Mosby.

Wroblewski, R., & Huston, A. C. (1987). Televised occupational stereotypes and their effects on early adolescents: Are they changing? *Journal of Early Adolescence, 7,* 283–297.

Wylie, R. (1979). *The self concept.* Vol. 2.: *Theory and research on selected topics.* Lincoln: University of Nebraska Press.

Y

Yaniv, I., & Shatz, M. (1990). Heuristics of reasoning and analogy in children's visual perspective taking. *Child Development, 61,* 1491–1501.

Yardley, K. (1987). What do you mean "Who am I?": Exploring the implications of a self-concept measurement with subjects. In K. Yardley & T. Honess (Eds.), *Self and identity: Psychosocial perspectives.* New York: Wiley.

Yentsch, C. M., & Sindermann, C. J. (1992). *The woman scientist: Meeting the challenges for a successful career.* New York: Plenum.

Young, C. (1993). Psychodynamics of coping and survival of the African-American female in a changing world. In D. R. Atkinson, G. Morten, & D. W. Sue (Eds.), *Counseling American minorities.* Madison, WI: WCB Brown & Benchmark.

Young, K. T. (1990). American conceptions of infant development from 1955 to 1984: What the experts are telling parents. *Child Development, 61,* 17–28.

Youngblade, L., & Belsky, J. (1992). Parent-child antecedents of 5-year-olds' close friendships: A longitudinal analysis. *Developmental Psychology, 28,* 700–713.

Youniss, J. (1980). *Parents and peers in the social environment: A Sullivan Piaget perspective.* Chicago: University of Chicago Press.

Ysseldyke, J. E., Algozinne, B., & Thurlow, M. L. (1992). *Critical issues in special education* (2nd ed.). Boston, MA: Houghton Mifflin.

Yussen, S. R. (1977). Characteristics of moral dilemmas written by adolescents. *Developmental Psychology, 13,* 162–163.

Yussen, S. R. (1985). The role of metacognition in contemporary theories of cognitive development. In D. Forrest-Pressley and G. Waller (Eds.), *Contemporary research in cognition and metacogniton.* Orlando, FL: Academic Press.

Yussen, S. R., Mathews, S. R., Huang, S., & Evans, R. (1988). The robustness and temporal course of the story schema's influence on recall. *Journal of Experimental Psychology: Learning, Memory, and Cognition, 14,* 173–179.

Z

Zahn-Waxler, C. (1990, May 28). Commentary. *Newsweek,* p. 61.

Zelazo, P. D., & Frye, D. (1993, March). *Cognitive complexity and changes in children's theory of mind.* Paper presented at the biennial meeting of the Society for Research in Child Development, New Orleans.

Zeskind, P. S., Klein, L., & Marshall, T. R. (1992). Adults' perceptions of experimental modifications of durations and expiratory sounds in infant crying. *Developmental Psychology, 28,* 1153–1162.

Ziegert, K. A. (1983). The Swedish prohibition of corporal punishment: A preliminary report. *Journal of Marriage and the Family, 45,* 917–926.

Zigler, E. (1987, April). *Child care for parents who work outside the home: Problems and solutions.* Paper presented at the biennial meeting of the Society for Research in Child Development, Baltimore.

Zigler, E., & Muenchow, S. (1992). *The story of Head Start.* New York: Basic Books.

Zuckerman, M. (1979). *Sensation seeking: Beyond the optimal level of arousal.* Hilldsdale, NJ: Erlbaum.

CREDITS

PHOTOGRAPHS

Prologue

Opener: © Chiko

Section Openers

Section 1: © Francois Dardelet; **Section 2:** © Joe Devenney/The Image Bank; **Section 3:** © Lisl/The Image Bank; **Section 4:** © David Burnett/Contact Press Images; **Section 5:** © John P. Kelly/The Image Bank, Chicago

Chapter 1

Opener: National Gallery, London.; **1.1B:** © Courtesy of Nancy Agostini; **p. 11:** Courtesy of Rhoda Unger; **1.2A,B:** © Erich Lessing/Art Resource, NY; **p. 10 bottom:** © M. Richards/Photo Edit; **p. 10 top:** © Image Works; **p. 10 middle:** © Joseph Nettis/Photo Researchers; **1.3:** © Herbert Gehr, Life Magazine copyright 1947, Time Warner; **1.4:** © Mel DiGiacomo/Image Bank, Dallas; **p. 17:** © Kathy Tarantola Photography; **p. 19:** © Renato Rotola/Gamma Liason; **1.6 top:** © Mel Digiacomo/The Image Bank; **1.6 top middle:** © Maria Taglienti/The Image Bank; **1.6 middle:** © Suzanne Szasz/Photo Researchers, Inc.; **1.6 bottom:** © Landrum Shettles; **p. 22:** © Duka/Photo Network; **p. 26 left:** © Institute of Texan Cultures; **p. 26 right:** Courtesy of Kenneth Clark

Chapter 2

Opener: Hayward L. Oubre, Pensive Family; **p. 36:** Sharon Beals for "Insight Magazine"; **p. 37:** The Bettmann Archives; **p. 40:** © Robin Smith/Superstock; **p. 41 left:** The Bettmann Archives; **p. 41 right:** Courtesy of Nancy Chodorow, photo by Jean Margolis; **p. 39:** © Sarah Putnam/Picture Cube; **2.2 top:** © William Hopkins; **2.2 top middle:** © Suzanne Szasz/Photo Researchers, Inc.; **2.2 bottom middle:** © Suzanne Szasz/Photo Researchers, Inc.; **2.2 bottom:** © Melchior DiGiacomo/The Image Bank, Chicago; **2.2F:** © Sam Zarember/The Image Bank-Tx; **2.2G:** © Brett Froomer/The Image Bank-Tx; **2.2H:** © Alan Carey/The Image Works; **2.2I:** © Harold Sund/The Image Bank-Tx; **2.3:** © Paul Conklin; **p. 44:** © Yves DeBraine/Black Star; **p. 46 top:** © Ap/Wide World Photos; **p. 46 bottom:** Courtesy of Albert Bandura; **2.4:** Photo by Nina Leen/Time/Life Magazine, © Time Inc.; **2.5A:** © David Austen/Stock Boston; **p. 48:** Courtesy of Urie Bronfenbrenner; **p. 50:** © Fujifotos/Image Works; **p. 51:** © Ray Stott/Image Works; **p. 55:** © Anthro-Photo; **2.6B:** © Jeff Hunter/The Image Bank; **2.7B:** © Gary Chapman/The Image Bank-Tx; **2.A:** © Mel Digiacomo/The Image Bank; **p. 59:** Courtesy of Dr. Florence L. Denmark/Photo by Robert Wesner; **p. 64:** Courtesy of Charles Eickelberger

Chapter 3

Opener: Winslow Homer, Worcester Art Museum: **p. 72:** © Enrico Ferorelli; **3.1:** © John P. Kelly/The Image Bank; **3.1:** © Michael P. Gadomski/Photo Researchers, Inc.; **p. 76:** © Gabe Palmer/The Stock Market; **p. 78:** Courtesy of United Nations; **p. 78:** Courtesy of United Nations; **p. 78:** © Gio Barto/The Image Bank/Dallas; **p. 78:** © Elaine Sulle/The Image Bank; **p. 78:** © Image Bank; Janeart #214299; **p. 78:** © Harvey Lloyd/The Stock Market; **3.2:** Regents of the University of California; **3.3 top:** Superstock; **3.3 bottom:** © Elyse Lewin/The Image Bank, Dallas; **3.4:** © Sundstrom/Gamma Liason; **p. 80:** Drawing by Ziegler; copyright 1985 The New Yorker Magazine, Inc.; **3.5:** © Alexandra Tsiaras/Science Source/Photo Researchers, Inc.; **3.6:** © Will and Deni McIntyre/Photo Researchers Inc.; **3.7:** © J. Pavlousky/Sygma; **3.8:** © Grant A. Hall/Unicorn Stock Photos; **p. 89:** © Myrleen Ferguson/Photo Edit; **3.9 top:** © Tim Davis/Photo Researchers, Inc.; **3.9 bottom:** © Sandy Roessler/The Stock Market; **p. 91 top:** © Enrico Ferorelli; **p. 91 bottom:** © Enrico Ferorelli; **p. 91:** Courtesy of Sandra Scarr; **p. 94:** © Elizabeth Crews/Image Works

Chapter 4

Opener: Art Resource; **p. 103 all:** © Lennart Nilsson; **4.3 large:** © Petit Format Nestle Science Source; **4.3 top:** © Lennart Nilsson; **4.3 middle:** © Nestle/Photo Researchers, Inc.; **4.3 bottom:** © Nestle/Photo Researchers, Inc.; **4.5:** © Will, Deni McIntyre/Photo Researchers; **p. 109:** © Chas Cancellare/Picture Group; **p. 112:** © Erika Stone; **p. 117 left:** © Photo Edit; **p. 117 right:** © David Brownell/Image Bank; **p. 120:** © Charles Gupton/Stock Boston; **p. 119:** Courtesy of Dr. Tiffany Field; **4.6:** © Comstock/Comstock, Inc.; **p. 122:** © David Weintraub/Photo Researchers; **p. 128:** © Charles Gupton/Stock Boston; **p. 128:** Courtesy of Maternity Center Association

Chapter 5

Opener: John May Whitey Collection, National Gallery; **5.1 left:** © Elizabeth Crews/The Image Works; **5.1 middle:** © James G. White Photography; **5.1 right:** © Petit Format/Photo Researchers Inc.; **5.2:** © Mimi Cotter/Int'l Stock Photo; **5.3:** © Nancy Braun/The Image Bank; **p. 140:** © Bob Daemmrich/The Image Works; **5.5:** © Judith Canty/Stock Boston; **p. 144 top:** © Will McIntyre/Photo Researchers; **p. 144 bottom:** © Bruce McAllister/The Image Works; **p. 145:** © C. Vergara/Photo Researchers; **5.7:** © David Linton; **5.8:** © Enrico Ferorelli; **5.9:** © Michael Siluk; **5.9:** © Dr. Melanie Spencer, University of Texas; **5.10:** © Jean Guichard/SYGMA; **p. 153:** © George Goodwin/Monkmeyer

Chapter 6

Opener: © National Gallery of Art; **p. 160:** © Joe McNally/Sports Illustrated; **6.1:** © Walter Imber; **6.3 top:** Adapted from Schirmer, G. J. (Ed), 1974. *Performance Objectives for Preschool Children,* pp. 69–72, Adapt Press.; **p. 164 bottom:** © Marc Romanelli/The Image Bank; **6.4:** Adapted from Schirmer, G. J. (Ed), 1974. *Performance Objectives for Preschool Children,* pp. 74–75, Adapt Press.; **p. 167:** © Bob Daemmrich/The Image Works; **p. 169 left:** © Les Stone/Sygma; **p. 169 right:** © David Young Wolff/Photo Edit; **p. 171:** © Pat Lacroix/The Image Bank, Dallas; **6.6:** © Luis Villota/The Stock Market; **p. 170:** © Alan Carey/Image Works; **p. 172:** © Guiseppe Molteni/The Image Bank; **6.7B:** © Alan Carey/The Image Works; **p. 183:** © William Hopkins Photography; **p. 184:** © Superstock/Four By Five/Robert Llewellyn; **p. 185:** © Alan Carey/The Image Works; **p. 186:** © George Zimbel/Monkmeyer Press

Chapter 7

Opener: © Superstock; **p. 198:** © Jacques Chenet/Woodfin Camp and Assoc.; **p. 199:** © Yves DeBraine/Black Star; **7.1 top:** © D. Goodman/Monkmeyer Press; **7.1 bottom:** © D. Goodman/Monkmeyer Press; **p. 204 top:** © Laura Dwight/Peter Arnold; **p. 204 bottom:** © C & W Shields, Inc.; **p. 205 top:** © Gabor Demjen/Stock Boston; **p. 205 top middle:** © Sally & Richard Greenhill; **p. 205 bottom middle:** © Joel Gordon; **p. 205 bottom:** © Eric Wheater/The Image Bank; **7.2:** © Denise Marcotte/The Picture Cube; **7.5:** © Paul Fusco/Magnum Photos, Inc.; **7.7:** © Owen Franken/Stock Boston; **p. 217:** UNICEF/Photo by Sean Sprague; **7.9A:** © Richard Hutchings/Photo Researchers, Inc.; **7.10:** © Paul Conklin; **p. 220:** © Ellis Herwig/Stock Boston; **p. 220:** © Stacy Pick/Stock Boston; **p. 220:** © Elizabeth Crews/Image Works; **p. 221:** © Yves DeBraine/Black Star; **p. 222:** © M & E Bernheim/Woodfin Camp and Assoc.; **7.11:** © Alan Becker/The Image

Bank; **p. 226:** © 1990 Barbara Rogoff/ *Apprenticeship in Thinking* (Oxford University Press)

Chapter 8

Opener: © Romare Bearden; **p. 232:** © 1989 Children's Television Workshop (New York, New York); **p. 234:** © Whitney Lane/The Image Bank, Dallas; **8.2:** Photo courtesy of Prof. Benjamin Harris, University of Wisconsin; **8.3:** Courtesy of Albert Bandura; **8.4:** © David Brownell/The Image Bank; **p. 241:** Bruce Coleman; **p. 242:** © Enrico Ferorelli; **8.A:** David Gillison/Peter Arnold; **8.B:** © Eiji Miyazawa/ Black Star; **p. 255:** © Suzanne Szasz/Photo Researchers, Inc.; **p. 257 top:** Courtesy of John Flavell; **p. 257 bottom:** © E. C. Cohen/ Superstock, Inc.; **p. 259:** © Bob Daemmerich/ Stock Boston; **p. 261:** © Brian ViKander/West Light

Chapter 9

Opener: McNay Art Museum, San Antonio; **9.1 top:** Mark Antman/The Image Works; **9.1 top middle:** © Dr. Rose Gantner/Comstock; **9.1 large:** © Meike Mass/The Image Bank, Dallas; **9.1 bottom middle:** © M. Antman/The Image Works; **9.1 bottom:** © Dr. Rose Gantner/ Comstock; **p. 276:** © Rick Friedman/Black Star; **9.5:** © David Austen/Stock Boston; **9.5:** © Ben Simmons/The Stock Market; **9.7:** © Jill Cannefax/EKM Nepenthe

Chapter 10

Opener: Courtesy of Daniel B. Grossman Gallery; **10.1:** © H. Anders/The Image Bank; **10.3:** © Enrico Fervelli; **10.4:** © James L. Shaffer; **p. 306:** © Katrina Thomas/Photo Researchers; **p. 307:** © Margaret W. Peterson/ The Image Bank; **p. 310:** © Anthony Bannister/ Earth Scenes; **10.6:** Courtesy of Roger Brown; **p. 314:** © Brett Froomer/The Image Bank; **p. 316 left:** © Doug Menuez/Stock Boston; **p. 316 right:** © Lawrence Migdale/Photo Researchers, Inc.; **p. 317:** © John Carter/Photo Researchers

Chapter 11

Opener: © Mills College Art Gallery; **p. 326 top inset:** © Leonard Lee Rue/Photo Researchers, Inc.; **p. 326 bottom inset:** © Mitch Reardon/ Photo Researchers,Inc.; **p. 326:** © Anthony Boccaccio/The Image Bank; **11.1:** © Martin Rogers/Stock Boston; **p. 329 A:** © Chris Hackett/Image Bank,Texas; **p. 329 B:** © Kathleen Loewenberg; **p. 329:** AP/Wide World Photos; **p. 332:** © Cesar Lucas/The Image Bank; **p. 333:** © Elizabeth Crews/Image Works; **p. 336:** © Alan Oddie/Photo Edit; **p. 341 top inset:** © Bob Daemmerich/The Image Works; **p. 341:** © Luis Villota/Stock Market; **p. 341 middle inset:** © Catherine Gehm; **p. 341 bottom inset:** © Catherine Gehm; **p. 342 left:** © Olivier Rebbot/Woodfin Camp; **p. 342 right:** Courtesy of Deborah Belle; **p. 343:** Courtesy of Madeline Cartwright

Chapter 12

Opener: National Museum Vincent van Gogh; **12.1:** © Dennis Cox; **12.2:** © Michael Melford/ The Image Bank; **p. 358:** Courtesy of Susan Harter; **12.4:** © Eddie Adams/Time Picture; **p. 365:** © Paul Popper, Ltd.; **12.5:** © Jeff

Persons/Stock Boston; **p. 368:** /Courtesy of Margaret Beale Spencer; **p. 369:** © Bob Daemmrich/The Image Works; **p. 370:** © 1988 by Warner Bros. Inc., Photo by Tony Friedkin; **p. 372:** © Joan Marcus

Chapter 13

Opener: Collection Duluth College Picture Gallery London; **13.1:** © Larry Voight/Photo Researchers, Inc.; **p. 379:** © Suzanne Szasz/Photo Researchers, Inc.; **13.2:** © Ken Gaghan/ Jeroboam; **p. 387:** © Jeff Smith/The Image Bank, Texas; **p. 389:** © Sumo/The Image Bank; **p. 391 top:** © Bernard Pierre Wolff/Photo Researchers, Inc.; **p. 391 bottom:** © Catherine Gehm

Chapter 14

Opener: © Jerry Palubniak/Art Resources; **p. 406:** © Joan Bushno/Unicorn Stock Photos; **14.1:** © Janeart Ltd./The Image Bank; **p. 408:** © Margaret Finefrock/Unicorn Stock Photos; **14.A:** © David R. Frazier Photolibrary; **p. 410:** © Keith Carter Photography; **14.2:** © Barbara Feigles/Stock Boston; **14.3:** © D. W. Productions/The Image Bank; **p. 422:** © Edward Lettau/Photo Researchers, Inc; **p. 423:** © Andrew Sacks/Time Magazine

Chapter 15

Opener: Erich Lessing/Art Resource; **15.1:** © G&M David De Lossy/The Image Bank; **15.2B:** © Tony Freeman/Photo Edit; **15.2C:** © Alan Oddie/Photo Edit; **15.2D:** © John Carter/Photo Researchers; **15.2E:** © Llewellyn/ Superstock; **15.2F:** © K. Kasmauski/Woodfin Camp; **15.2G:** After: Carter, B., McGoldrick, M. *The Changing Family Life Cycle* 2/E, 1989 Allyn-Bacon, Boston p. 15; **15.3B:** © Eri Heller/The Picture Group; **p. 445:** Courtesy of Dr. Dante Cicchetti; **p. 446:** © Jim Richardson/ West Light; **15.4:** © Richard Hutchings/Photo Researchers, Inc.; **p. 455:** © Kenneth Jarecke/ Contact Press; **p. 458:** © Erika Stone/Peter Arnold, Inc; **p. 459:** © Bob Daemmrich/Image Works; **p. 460:** © Tim Bieber/Image Bank; **p. 461:** © Kathy Tarantola Photography

Chapter 16

Opener: Courtesy The Museum of Fine Arts Boston; **16.1:** © Erik Anderson/Stock Boston; **16.3:** © Gerald Brimacombe/The Image Bank; **p. 474:** © Erika Stone; **p. 476:** Nils Jorgensen/ Rex Features; **16.4 top:** © Mary Kate Denny/ PhotoEdit; **16.4 top middle:** © Jean Claude Lejeune; **16.4 middle:** © Peter Vandermark/ Stock Boston; **16.4 bottom middle:** © David De Lossy/The Image Bank; **16.4 bottom:** © Myrleen Ferguson/PhotoEdit; **16.5:** © Schuster/Photo Researchers, Inc.; **16.5A:** Superstock; **16.5B:** © Comstock; **16.5C:** © Stephen Marks/The Image Bank; **16.5D:** © Elizabeth Crews/Image Works; **16.5E:** © Patrick Watson/Image Works; **p. 476:** © Jan Doyle; **p. 483:** © Brian Peterson; **p. 485 top:** © Kunsthistorisches Museum; **p. 485 bottom:** © Bob Daemmrich/The Image Works; **p. 489:** © Bob Daemmrich/Stock Boston

Chapter 17

Opener: © Spadem/Art Resource; **p. 498 top:** © Don Klumpp/The Image Bank; **p. 498 bottom:** © John Ficara/Woodfin Camp and

Associates; **17.1 top:** © Elizabeth Crews/The Image Works; **17.1 middle:** © Jeffry W. Myers/The Stock Market; **17.1 bottom:** © Paul Conklin; **17.1 top:** © Elizabeth Crews/The Image Works; **17.1 middle:** © G. Hofstetter/ Photo Network; **17.1 bottom:** © Leo de Wys; **p. 502:** © Robert Wallis/SIPA Press, Newsweek, April 17, 1989, p. 8; **p. 503:** © R. Knowles/Black Star; **p. 509:** © Bob Daemmrich/The Image Works; **p. 511:** © John S. Abbott; **p. 512:** © Bob Daemmrich/The Image Works; **17.7:** Courtesy of Dr. Joan Lipsitz; **p. 514:** © H. Yamaguchi/ Gamma Liaison; **p. 515 top:** © Will McIntyre/Photo Researchers, Inc.; **p. 515 bottom:** © Richard Hutchings/Photo Researchers, Inc.

Epilogue

Opener: Comstock; **p. 528 middle left:** © Kelsh Marr Studios; **p. 528 top right:** © Cammermann Int'l; **p. 528 top left:** © Elyse Lewin/The Image Bank; **p. 528:** © Owen Franklin/Stock Boston; **p. 528 middle right:** © Elyse Lewin/The Image Bank; **p. 528 bottom right:** © Elyse Lewin/Image Bank; **p. 529:** © Lennart Nilsson; **p. 530:** © Niki Mareschal/Image Bank; **p. 531:** © Barbara Feigles/Stock Boston; **p. 532:** © Suma/The Image Bank, Texas; **p. 533:** © A. Upitis/The Image Bank

---

LINE ART
Prologue

poem, page 1: By Gwendolyn Brooks, © copyright 1991. Published by Third World Press, Chicago, 1991.

Chapter 1

figure 1.4 (text): Source: Data from the Children's Defense Fund, *Children 1990*, p. 4.

Chapter 2

figure 2.1: From *Psychology: A Scientific Study of Human Behavior* by L. S. Wrightsman, C. K. Sigelman, and F. H. Sanford. Copyright © 1961, 1965, 1975, 1979 by Wadsworth, Inc. Reprinted by permission of Brooks/Cole Publishing Company, Pacific Grove, California 93950. **figure 2.5 (art):** Figure 12.1 from Claire B. Kopp and Joanne B. Krakow, *The Child.* © 1982 Addison-Wesley Publishing Company. Reprinted by permission. **poem, page 38:** From *The Poetry of Robert Frost* edited by Edward Connery Lathem. Copyright 1936 by Robert Frost. Copyright © 1964 by Lesley Frost Ballantine. Copyright © 1969 by Henry Holt and Company, Inc. Reprinted by permission of Henry Holt and Company, Inc.

Chapter 3

figure 3.10 (graph): From I. Gottesman, "Genetic Aspects of Intellectual Behavior" in *Handbook of Mental Deficiency,* edited by Norman R. Ellis. Copyright © 1963 McGraw-Hill, Inc., New York, NY. Reprinted by permission of Norman R. Ellis. **poem, page 79:** From *Verses from 1929 On* by Ogden Nash. Copyright 1940 by Ogden Nash. By permission of Little, Brown and Company.

Chapter 4

figure 4.1: From Charles Carroll and Dean Miller, *Health: The Science of Human Adaptation,* 5th ed. Copyright © 1991 Wm. C. Brown Communications, Inc., Dubuque, Iowa. All Rights Reserved. Reprinted by permission. **figure 4.3 (text):** Copyright © 1979, 1984, 1991 by the Childbirth Education Association of Seattle. Reprinted from *Pregnancy, Childbirth and the Newborn: The Complete Guide,* by P. Simkin, R.P.T.; J. Whalley, R.N., B.S.N.; and A. Keppler, R.N., M.N., with permission of its publisher, Meadowbrook Press. **figure 4.4:** From K. L. Moore, *The Developing Human: Clinically Oriented,* 4th ed. Copyright © 1988 W.B. Saunders, Philadelphia, PA. Reprinted by permission. **figure 4.5 (graph):** The Marshall Cavendish Picture Library. **figure 4.6 (text):** From Virginia A. Apgar, "A Proposal for a New Method of Evaluation of a Newborn Infant" in *Anesthesia and Analgesia: Current Researches,* 32:260–267. Copyright © 1975 International Anesthesia Research Society. Reprinted by permission.

Chapter 5

figure 5.3 (charts): Source: National Center for Health Statistics, NCHS Growth Charts, *Monthly Vital Statistics Report.* **figure 5.4:** From W. K. Frankenburg and J. B. Dodds, "The Denver Development Screening Test" in *Journal of Pediatrics,* 71:181–192. Copyright © 1967 Mosby-Year Book, Inc., St. Louis, MO. Reprinted by permission. **figure 5.5:** Sources: Data from R. Charlesworth, *Understanding Child Development,* 2d ed., Delmar, Albany, NY, 1987; and G. J. Schirmer (ed.), *Performance Objectives for Preschool Children,* Adapt Press, Sioux Falls, SD, 1974. **figure 5.6:** J. L. Conel (1939–1963), *Postnatal Development of the Human Cerebral Cortex,* Vols. I–VI. Copyright © Harvard University Press, Cambridge, MA. Reprinted by permission. **excerpt, page 142:** Source: Janet L. Brown, "States in Newborn Infants" in *Merrill-Palmer Quarterly,* 10(4): 313–327, 1964.

Chapter 6

figure 6.1 (charts): Source: National Center for Health Statistics, NCHS Growth Charts, *Monthly Vital Statistics Report,* 25(3). **figure 6.2:** From Albert Damon, *Human Biology and Ecology.* Copyright © 1977 W.W. Norton & Company, Inc., New York, NY. Reprinted by permission. **figure 6.3 (text):** Source: Data from G. J. Schirmer (ed.), *Performance Objectives for Preschool Children,* Adapt Press, Sioux Falls, SD, 1974. **figure 6.4 (text):** Source: Data from G. J. Schirmer (ed.), *Performance Objectives for Preschool Children,* Adapt Press, Sioux Falls, SD, 1974. **figure 6.5:** From Clara Show Schuster and Shirley Smith Ashburn, *The Process of Human Development,* 2d ed. Copyright © 1986 Little, Brown and Company, Boston, MA. **figure 6.6: (graph)** © The Society for Research in Child Development, Inc. Reprinted by permission. **figure 6.7 (graph):** From J. M. Tanner, et al., "Standards from Birth to Maturity for Height, Weight, Height Velocity, and Weight Velocity: British Children, 1965" in *Archives of Diseases in Childhood,* 41. Copyright © 1966 British Medical Journal, London, England. Reprinted by permission. **figure 6.10:** From "The Impact of Puberty on Adolescence: A Longitudinal Study" in *Girls at Puberty* by Jeanne Brooks-Gunn. Copyright © Plenum Publishing Corporation, New York, NY. Reprinted by permission. **figure 6.11:** Source: Data from the Alan Guttmacher Institute, 1988.

Chapter 7

figure 7.A: Dennie Wolf/Josh Nove.
figure 7.B: Courtesy of Dr. Ellen Winner, Project Zero.

Chapter 8

figure 8.5: Albert Bandura, *Social Foundations of Thought and Action: A Social Cognitive Theory,* © 1986, p. 24. Adapted by permission of Prentice-Hall, Inc., Englewood Cliffs, NJ. **figure 8.A (art):** © The Society for Research in Child Development, Inc. **figure 8.6:** From Joel Levin, et al., "The Keyword Method in the Classroom" in *Elementary School Journal,* 80:4. Copyright © 1980 University of Chicago Press. Reprinted by permission. **figure 8.7:** From M. T. H. Chi and R. D. Koeske, "Network Representation of a Child's Dinosaur Knowledge" in *Developmental Psychology,* 19:29–39. Copyright 1983 by the American Psychological Association. Reprinted by permission. **figure 8.8:** From Steven R. Yussen, et al., "The Robustness and Temporal Cause of the Story Schemas Influence on Recall" in *Journal of Experimental Psychology, Learning, Memory, and Cognition,* 14:173–179. Copyright 1988 by the American Psychological Association. Reprinted by permission. **figure 8.9:** © The Society for Research in Child Development, Inc. Reprinted by permission.

Chapter 9

figure 9.4a: Reprinted by permission of John W. Berry. **figure 9.6:** Item A5 from the Raven *Standard Progressive Matrices,* reproduced by permission of J. C. Raven Limited.

Chapter 10

figure 10.5: From "Recognize Language Development and Delay in Early Childhood" by J. U. Dumtschin, March 1988, *Young Children,* 43, pp. 16–24. Copyright © 1988 by the National Association for the Education of Young Children. Reprinted by permission. **figure 10.6 (graph):** From Roger Brown, et al., *Minnesota Symposium on Child Psychology,* Vol. 2. Copyright © 1969 University of Minnesota Press, Minneapolis, MN. Reprinted by permission. **figure 10.7:** From J. Berko, *Word,* 14:361. Copyright © 1958 International Linguistic Association, New York, NY. Reprinted by permission.

Chapter 12

excerpt, page 352: Reprinted by permission of the publishers from *At the Threshold: The Developing Adolescent* by S. Shirley Feldman and Glen R. Elliott, Cambridge, Mass.: Harvard University Press, Copyright © 1990 by the President and Fellows of Harvard College. **figure 12.1 (graph):** From M. Lewis and J. G. Brooks-Gunn, *Social Cognition and the Acquisition of the Self.* Copyright © 1979 Plenum Publishing Corporation, New York, NY. Reprinted by permission. **figure 12.2:** Reprinted from the *Journal of Early Adolescence,* 3:121–140, 1983. By permission of the publisher, H.E.L.P. Books, Inc., Tucson, AZ.

Chapter 13

figure 13.A: From Janet S. Hyde, "Children's Understanding of Sexist Language" in *Developmental Psychology,* 20:703. Copyright 1984 by the American Psychological Association. Reprinted by permission. **figure 13.3:** From Janet S. Hyde, "Gender Differences in Mathematics Performance" in *Psychological Bulletin,* 107:139–155. Copyright 1990 by the American Psychological Association. Reprinted by permission.

Chapter 14

figure 14.1 (text): From Steven R. Yussen, "Characteristics of Moral Dilemmas Written by Adolescents" in *Developmental Psychology,* 13:162–163. Copyright 1977 by the American Psychological Association. Reprinted by permission. **figure 14.A (text):** From R. Shweder, et al., "Culture and Moral Development" in J. Kagan and S. Lamb (eds.), *The Emergence in Morality in Young Children.* Copyright © 1987 University of Chicago Press. Reprinted by permission. **figure 14.3a:** Source: Data from Dey, Astin, and Korn, *The American Freshman: Twenty-Five Year Trends,* Higher Education Research Institute, University of California—Los Angeles, 1987.

Chapter 15

figure 15.2: From Betty Carter and Monica McGoldrick, *The Changing Family Life Cycle: A Framework for Family Therapy,* Second Edition. Copyright © 1989 by Allyn and Bacon. Reprinted by permission.

Chapter 16

figure 16.2: © The Society for Research in Child Development, Inc. Reprinted by permission. **figure 16.4:** (left) Source: Data from Dexter C. Dunphy, "The Social Structure of Urban Adolescent Peer Groups" in *Sociometry,* Vol. 26, American Sociological Association, 1963.

Chapter 17

excerpt, page 496: From Joan Lipsitz, *Successful Schools for Young Adults.* Copyright © 1984 Transaction Publishers, Rutgers—The State University of New Jersey. Reprinted by permission. **figure 17.1 (text):** Copyright © 1986 by National Association for the Education of Young Children. Reprinted by permission from *Young Children,* 41, 1986, Washington, DC.

NAME INDEX

SUBJECT INDEX